Workshop Manual

Publication Part No. AKD 3259 (15th Edition)

With

ENGINE EMISSION CONTROL SUPPLEMENT

Publication Part No. AKD 4957 (5th Edition)

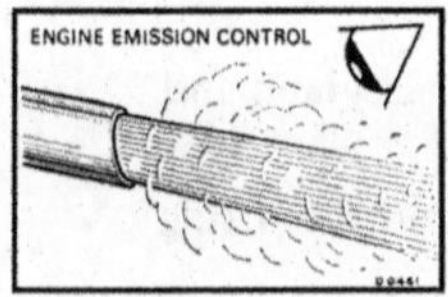

Leyland Cars - Service
Cowley, Oxford OX4 2PG, England

INTRODUCTION

DESCRIPTION

This manual is intended to assist the skilled mechanic in carrying out repairs and replacements in a minimum of time.

References to left- or right-hand side in this manual are made when viewing the car from the rear.

MANUAL ARRANGEMENT

The first part of the Manual includes the General Data, and Engine Tuning Data.

A Service Tools section and the Recommended Lubricants Chart are featured at the end of the Manual.

The remainder of the manual is divided into sections and each section carries a reference letter that identifies the section with an assembly or a major component. Each section is preceded by a contents page and is sub-divided numerically. The pages and illustrations are numbered consecutively within each section and the section title and letter are shown at the top of each page.

Maintenance items within the Sections should be carried out at the intervals specified in the Passport to Service or Drivers Handbook.

IMPORTANT 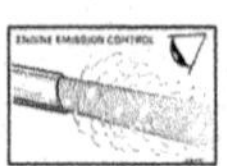 **Canada and U.S.A. only**

On cars fitted with vehicle emission control equipment service operations and adjustments showing this symbol must be followed by an exhaust emission check.

Servicing and adjusting vehicle emission control equipment must be carried out in accordance with the instructions given in **Workshop Manual Supplement AKD 4957.**

REPAIRS AND REPLACEMENTS

When replacements are required it is essential that only genuine **British Leyland** and **Unipart** parts are used.

Attention is particularly drawn to the following points concerning repairs and the fitting of replacement parts and accessories:

Safety features embodied in the car may be impaired if other than genuine parts are fitted. In certain territories, legislation prohibits the fitting of parts not to the vehicle manufacturers specification.

Torque wrench setting figures given in the Manual must be strictly adhered to.

Locking devices, where specified, must be fitted. If the efficiency of a locking device is impaired during removal it must be renewed.

Owners purchasing accessories while travelling abroad should ensure that the accessory and its fitted location on the car conform to mandatory requirements existing in their country of origin. **The terms of the Owner's Service Statement may be invalidated by the fitting of other than genuine British Leyland and Unipart parts.** All **British Leyland** parts and **Unipart** replacements have the full backing of the Owner's Service Statement.

Published by Brooklands Books Ltd., PO Box 146, Cobham,
Surrey KT11 1LG, England Phone: 01932 865051 Fax: 01932 868803
E-mail: sales@brooklands-books.com www.brooklands-books.com

Part Number: AKD 3259 (15th Edition) & AKD 4957 (5th Edition)

ISBN: 9781855201743 Ref: MG64WH 6T5/2494

CONTENTS

R.H.D. and L.H.D. EXCEPT NORTH AMERICA

SERVICE OPERATIONS–SUMMARY

After Sales Service = 1,000 miles (1 500 km)

A Every 6,000 miles (10 000 km) or 6 months

B Every 12,000 miles (20 000 km) or 12 months

Items included in the 3,000 miles (5 000 km) or 3 months interval Optional Inspection Check are indicated in **column C**

BRITISH LEYLAND **Leycare Service**

After Sales	A	B	C	ACTION OPERATION X
●	●	●	●	Fit seat cover
	X	X	X	Check condition and security of seats and seat belts
●	●	●	●	Drive on lift
X	X	X	X	Check function of lamps
X	X	X	X	Check function of horns
X	X	X	X	Check function of warning indicators
X	X	X	X	Check function of windscreen wipers
X	X	X	X	Check/adjust operation of windscreen washers
X	X	X	X	Check operation of hand brake; release fully
	X	X	X	Check rear view mirrors for cracks and crazing
X				Check operation of window controls
●	●	●	●	Open bonnet, fit wing covers. Raise lift to 18 in. and wheel free
	●	●		Mark stud to wheel relationship
	●	●		Remove road wheel
	X	X	X	Check tyre complies with manufacturer's specification
	X	X	X	Check tyre for tread depth
X	X	X	X	Check tyre visually for external cuts in fabric
X	X	X	X	Check tyre visually for external exposure of ply or cord
X	X	X	X	Check tyre visually for external lumps and bulges
X	X	X	X	Check/adjust tyre pressure
	X	X		Front: Inspect brake pads for wear and discs for condition
		X		Rear: Remove drum, brush out dirt, inspect brake shoes for wear and drum for condition, refit drum
X	X	X	X	Rear: Check/adjust brakes
X	X	X		Lubricate swivel pins and swivel lower links
	●	●		Refit: road wheel in original position
X	X	X	X	Check tightness of road wheel nuts
●	●	●	●	Raise lift to full height
X	X	X		Drain engine oil
X				Drain gearbox oil
		X		Drain gearbox oil, clean overdrive filters (every 24,000 miles)
X	X	X	X	Check visually brake pipes and unions for chafing, leaks, and corrosion
X	X	X	X	Check visually fuel and clutch pipes for chafing, leaks and corrosion
	X	X	X	Check exhaust system for leaks and security
X	X	X	X	Check for oil leaks from steering and fluid leaks from shock absorbers
X	X	X	X	Check condition and security of steering unit, joints and gaiters
X				Check security of suspension fixings
X				Check security of accessible engine mountings
	X	X		Lubricate hand brake mechanical linkage and cables
	X	X		Lubricate propeller shaft
X	X	X		Check/top up rear axle oil

Starting at the right-hand front wheel complete these operations at each wheel (applies to the operations from "Mark stud to wheel relationship" to "Check tightness of road wheel nuts")

R.H.D. and L.H.D. except North America–continued

After Sales	A	B	C	ACTION OPERATION X	
●	●	●		Refit engine drain plug	
●				Refit gearbox drain plug	
		●		Refit gearbox drain plug (every 24,000 miles)	
●	●	●		Paint timing marks (early models)	
●	●	●	●	Lower lift	
●	●	●		Fit exhaust extractor pipe	
	X	X		Renew engine oil filter	
	X	X		Check/top up gearbox oil	
X				Fill gearbox with oil	
		X		Fill gearbox with oil (every 24,000 miles)	
X				Check/adjust torque of cylinder head nuts	
X				Check/adjust torque of rocker shaft nuts	
X				Check/adjust torque of manifold nuts	
X		X		Check/adjust valve clearances	
X	X	X		Fill engine with oil	
			X	Check/top up engine oil	
		X		Lubricate water pump (early models only)	
	X	X		Lubricate dynamo bearing (early models only)	
X	X	X		Top up carburetter piston dampers	
X	X	X		Lubricate accelerator control, linkage and pedal pivot	
		X		Renew air cleaner elements	
X				Check security of accessible engine mountings	
X	X	X	X	Check driving belts, adjust or renew	
	X			Clean/adjust spark plugs	
		X		Renew spark plugs	
		X		Clean and test crankcase breather valve	
X	X	X	X	Check/top up clutch fluid reservoir	
X	X	X	X	Check/top up brake fluid reservoir	
X	X	X	X	Check/top up windscreen washer reservoir	
X	X	X	X	Check/top up cooling system	
		X		Renew fuel line filter	
		X		Clean brake servo filter	
X	X	X		Check cooling and heater systems for leaks	
	●	●		Run engine and check sealing of filter, stop engine	
X	X	X		Recheck/top up engine oil	
●	●	●		Connect instruments and check data	
X	X	X		Check/adjust distributor points, renew if necessary	
X	X	X		Check volt drop between coil CB and earth	Using electronic equipment
X	X	X		Lubricate distributor	
●	●	●		Run engine	
X	X	X		Disconnect vacuum pipe, check dwell angle, adjust points as necessary	
X	X	X		Check stroboscopic ignition timing	
X	X	X		Check distributor automatic advance	
X	X	X		Check advance increase as vacuum pipe is reconnected	
X	X	X		Check throttle operation, check/adjust carburetter idle speed and mixture settings	
X	X	X		Check/top up automatic gearbox fluid	
●	●	●		Stop engine	
●	●	●	●	Remove wing covers	

R.H.D. and L.H.D. except North America–continued

After Sales	A	B	C	ACTION / OPERATION X
X	X	X		Lubricate all locks and hinges (not steering lock)
	●	●		Fill in details and fix appropriate Unipart underbonnet stickers
●	●	●	●	Close bonnet
	X	X	X	Check and if necessary renew windscreen wiper blades
●	●	●		Remove exhaust extractor pipe
●	●	●	●	Remove spare wheel
	X	X	X	Check spare tyre complies with manufacturer's specification
	X	X	X	Check depth of tread
X	X	X	X	Check visually for external cuts in tyre fabric
X	X	X	X	Check visually for external exposure of ply or cord
X	X	X	X	Check visually for external lumps or bulges
X	X	X	X	Check/adjust tyre pressure
	X	X	X	Check fuel filler pipe connections
●	●	●	●	Refit spare wheel. Drive car off lift. Remove rear compartment floor covering and access panel
X	X	X	X	Check/top up battery electrolyte
	X	X		Clean and grease battery connections
●	●	●	●	Refit rear compartment floor covering and access panel
X	X	X	X	Check/adjust headlamp alignment
	X	X		Check/adjust front wheel alignment
X	X	X		Carry out road or roller test and check function of all instrumentation
	X	X	X	Report and additional work required
X	X	X	X	Ensure cleanliness of controls, door handles, steering wheel, etc

This Maintenance Summary was produced from Leycare Supplementary Job Sheet AKD 8469 (1st Edition). Job sheets used by British Leyland Distributors and Dealers operating Leycare Service are updated as modifications affecting routine maintenance are introduced and the content of this maintenance summary may differ from that currently used by Leycare Service operatives.

NORTH AMERICA

The following items should be checked weekly by the driver:

- Engine oil level
- Brake fluid level
- Battery electrolyte level
- Radiator coolant level
- Windshield washer reservoir level
- All tyre pressures
- All lights for operation
- Horn operation
- Windshield wipers operation

MAINTENANCE INTERVALS

†These items are emission related

Carry out the services indicated by **X** in column

The Lubrication Service at **3,000-mile or 3-month** intervals
A at **6,000-mile or 6-month** intervals
B at **12,000-mile or 12-month** intervals
***Specified otherwise**

	Lubrication Service	A	B
LUBRICATION			
Lubricate all points	X	X	X
Renew engine oil	X	X	X
Renew engine oil filter		X	X
Check level of all fluid reservoirs, brake, clutch, battery, rear axle, transmission, cooling system and windshield washer	X	X	X
ENGINE			
†Check all drive belts; adjust if necessary			X
†Check all hoses, vacuum, air and water for condition and tightness			X
†Renew all air filter cleaner elements (air pump and carburetter)			X
†Check restrictor in rocker cover purge line for obstruction			X
†Adjust valve rocker clearances		X	X
†Check gulp valve operation (renew if necessary)			X
FUEL SYSTEM			
†Renew fuel line filter			X
†Check condition of fuel filler cap seal			X
†Check fuel pipes and unions for chafing, corrosion and leaks			X
†Top up carburetter piston dampers		X	X
OSCILLOSCOPE AND COMBUSTION CHECK			
†Check distributor points, resistance and dwell		X	X
†Renew distributor points			X
†Check ignition timing and distributor advance or retard characteristics		X	X
†Check engine idle speed		X	X
†Check spark plugs (cruise and unload condition)		X	X
†Renew spark plugs			X
†Check distributor cap and wires		X	X
Check charging system output		X	X
†Power check, engine cylinder comparison			X
†Check choke and carburetter fast idle speed setting		X	X
†Check exhaust emission (CO HC) at idle		X	X

North America–continued

	A	B
SAFETY		
Check/adjust front wheel alignment		X
Check visually hydraulic pipes, unions for chafing, leaks and corrosion		X
Check/adjust handbrake operation	X	X
Inspect the brake pads for wear and discs for condition	X	
Inspect brake linings and pads for wear, drums and discs for condition		X
Check/adjust headlights	X	X
Check tyres visually, and report depth of tread, cuts in fabric, exposure of ply or cord structure, lumps or bulges	X	X
Check wiper blades for condition		X
Check condition, operation and security of seats, seat belts/interlock		X
Check operation of all door locks and window controls		X
ROAD TEST		
Ensure that operation of vehicle is satisfactory and report all items requiring attention	X	X

24,000-miles or 24-month intervals

*†Renew all drive belts
*†Check air pump (correct or renew if necessary)
*†Renew adsorption canister
*†Renew distributor cap and wires
* Clean overdrive filter

36,000-miles or 36-month intervals

*Renew all hydraulic brake seals

The maintenance summary on this and the preceding page is the minimum service required to maintain your vehicle under normal driving conditions. For other than normal driving conditions, and those caused by seasonal changes, we recommend that you consult your Dealer.

R.H.D. and L.H.D. EXCEPT NORTH AMERICA

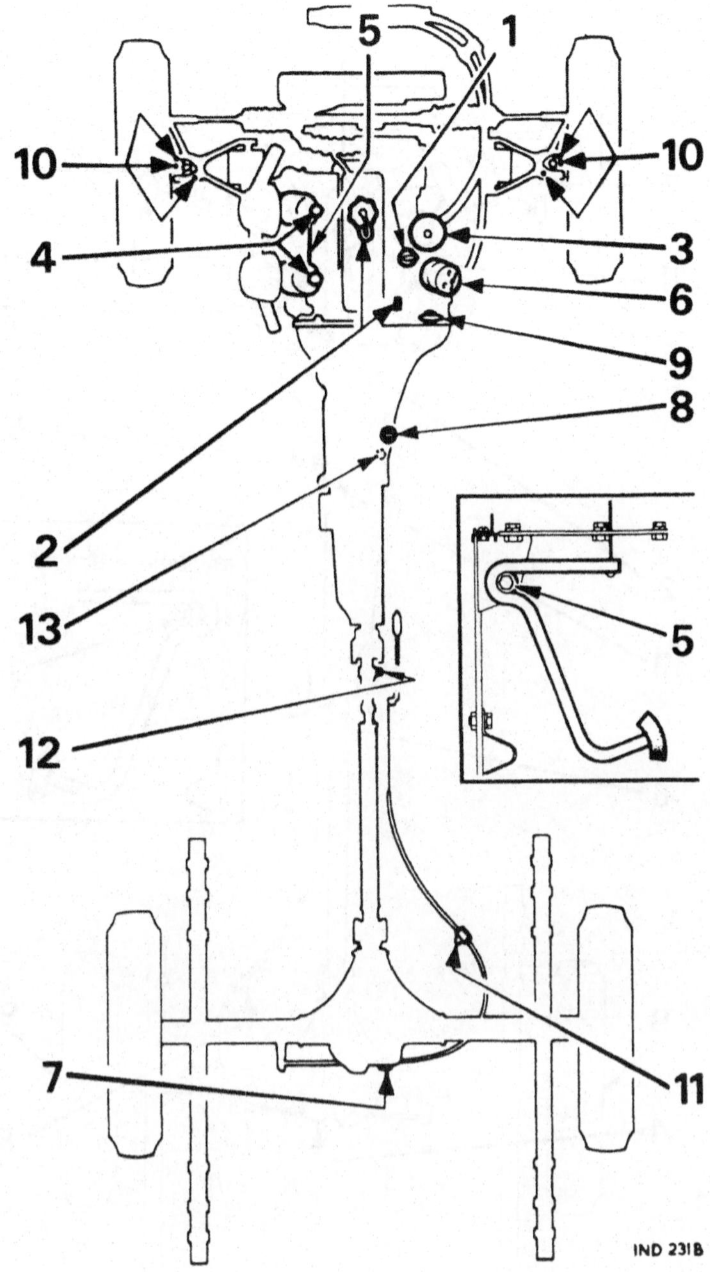

NOTE:—Ensure that the vehicle is standing on a level surface when checking the oil levels.

Weekly
(1) ENGINE. Check oil level, and top up if necessary.

Every 6,000 miles or 6 months
(2) ENGINE. Drain and refill with new oil.
(3) ENGINE OIL FILTER. Remove the disposable cartridge, fit new.
Early cars: Drain filter, wash filter bowl in fuel and fit new element.
(4) CARBURETTERS. Top up carburetter piston dampers.
(5) ACCELERATOR. Lubricate accelerator control linkage, cable and pedal fulcrum.
(6) DISTRIBUTOR. Lubricate all parts as necessary.
(7) REAR AXLE. Check oil level, and top up if necessary.
(8) GEARBOX AND OVERDRIVE. Check oil level, and top up if necessary.
(9) AUTOMATIC TRANSMISSION. Check fluid level, and top up if necessary.
(10) FRONT SUSPENSION (6 nipples)
(11) HAND BRAKE CABLE (1 nipple) AND MECHANICAL LINKAGE
(12) PROPELLER SHAFT (1 nipple)
] Give three or four strokes with a grease gun.
LOCKS AND HINGES. Lubricate the bonnet release safety catch and all locks and hinges.

Every 24,000 miles or 24 months
(13) GEARBOX WITH OVERDRIVE. Drain, clean overdrive filters and refill with new oil.

Optional lubrication at 3,000 miles or 3 months
(1) ENGINE. Check oil level and top up if necessary.

Recommended oils and greases are given at the end of the manual

NORTH AMERICA

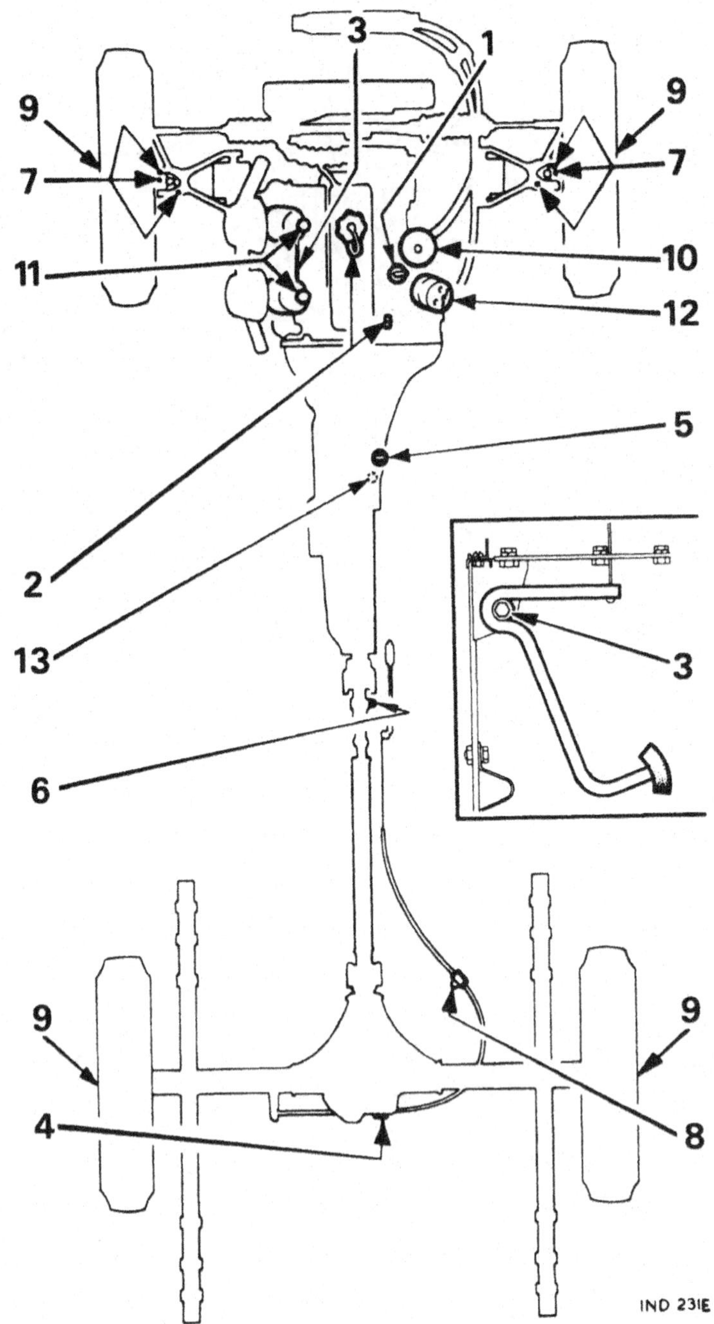

NOTE:—Ensure that the vehicle is standing on a level surface when checking the oil levels.

Weekly

(1) ENGINE. Check oil level, and top up if necessary.

Lubrication service every 3,000 miles or 3 months

(2) ENGINE. Drain and refill with new oil.
(3) THROTTLE AND CHOKE. Lubricate throttle and choke control linkages, cables, and accelerator pedal fulcrum.
(4) REAR AXLE. Check oil level, and top up if necessary.
(5) GEARBOX AND OVERDRIVE. Check oil level, and top up if necessary.
(6) PROPELLER SHAFT (1 nipple) } Give three or four strokes with a grease gun.
(7) FRONT SUSPENSION (6 nipples) } Give three or four strokes with a grease gun.
(8) HAND BRAKE CABLE (1 nipple) } Give three or four strokes with a grease gun.
(9) WHEELS AND HUBS. Lubricate wire wheel and hub splines.

LOCKS, HINGES AND LINKAGES. Lubricate all door, bonnet and boot locks and hinges; and the hand brake mechanical linkage.

FRICTION POINTS. Spray lubricant on all friction points.

'A' service every 6,000 miles or 6 months; AND 'B' service every 12,000 miles or 12 months

(10) ENGINE OIL FILTER. Remove disposable cartridge, fit new.
(11) CARBURETTERS. Top up carburetter piston dampers.
(12) DISTRIBUTOR. Lubricate all parts as necessary.

Every 24,000 miles or 24 months

(13) GEARBOX WITH OVERDRIVE. Drain, clean overdrive filter, refill with new oil.

Recommended oils and greases are given at the end of the manual

GENERAL DATA
(18G/18GA)

ENGINE

Type	18G, 18GA.
Number of cylinders	4.
Bore	3.16 in. (80.26 mm.).
Stroke	3.5 in. (89 mm.).
Capacity	1798 c.c. (109.8 cu. in.).
Combustion chamber volume (valves fitted)	42.5 to 43.5 c.c. (2.59 to 2.65 cu. in.).
Firing order	1, 3, 4, 2.
Valve operation	Overhead by push-rod.
Compression ratio: H.C.	8.8 : 1.
L.C.	8.0 : 1.
Compression pressure: H.C.	160 lb./sq. in. (11.25 kg./cm.^{2}).
L.C.	130 lb./sq. in. (9.15 kg./cm.^{2}).
Torque: H.C.	110 lb. ft. (15.2 kg.m.) at 3,000 r.p.m.
L.C.	105 lb. ft. (14.5 kg.m.) at 3,000 r.p.m.
Engine idle speed (approx.)	500 r.p.m.
Oversize bore: First	.010 in. (.254 mm.).
Max.	.040 in. (1.016 mm.).

Crankshaft

Main journal diameter	2.1262 to 2.127 in. (54.01 to 54.02 mm.).
Crankpin journal diameter	1.8759 to 1.8764 in. (47.648 to 47.661 mm.).
Crankshaft end-thrust	Taken on thrust washers at centre main bearing.
Crankshaft end-float	.004 to .005 in. (.10 to .13 mm.).

Main bearings

Number and type	Three thinwall.
Material	Steel-backed copper-lead.
Length	1⅛ in. (28.5 mm.).
Diametrical clearance	.001 to .0027 in. (.0254 to .068 mm.).
Undersizes	–.010, –.020, –.030 and –.040 in. (–.254, –.508, –.762 and –1.016 mm.).

Connecting rods

Type	Angular-split big-end, split clamp small-end.
Length between centres	6.5 in. (165.1 mm.).

Big-end bearings

Type	Shell.
Material	Steel-backed copper-lead.
Length	.995 to 1.005 in. (25.2 to 25.52 mm.).
Diametrical clearance	.001 to .0027 in. (.0254 to .068 mm.).
Undersizes	–.010, –.020, –.030 and –.040 in. (–.254, –.508, –.762 and –1.016 mm.).
End-float on crankpin (nominal)	.008 to .012 in. (.20 to .30 mm.).

Pistons

Type	Aluminium solid skirt.
Clearance in cylinder: Top	.0036 to .0045 in. (.091 to .121 mm.).
Bottom	.0018 to .0024 in. (.045 to .060 mm.).
Number of rings	4 (3 compression, 1 oil control).
Width of ring grooves: Top, Second, Third	.064 to .065 in. (1.625 to 1.651 mm.).
Oil control	.1578 to .1588 in. (4.008 to 4.033 mm.).
Gudgeon pin bore	.7501 to .7503 in. (19.052 to 19.057 mm.).

Piston rings

COMPRESSION	
Type: Top	Parallel } cast iron—molybdenum filled.
Second and third	Tapered } cast iron—molybdenum filled.
Width: Top / Second and third	.0615 to .0625 in. (1.562 to 1.587 mm.).
Fitted gap: Top / Second and third	.012 to .017 in. (.304 to .431 mm.).
Ring to groove clearance: Top / Second and third	.0015 to .0035 in. (.038 to .088 mm.).
OIL CONTROL	
Type	Slotted scraper.
Width	.1552 to .1562 in. (3.94 to 3.96 mm.).
Fitted gap	.012 to .017 in. (.304 to .431 mm.).
Ring to groove clearance	.0016 to .0036 in. (.04 to .09 mm.).

Gudgeon pin

Type	Semi-floating.
Fit in piston	Free-fit at 20°C. (68°F.).
Diameter (outer)	.7499 to .7501 in. (19.04 to 19.05 mm.).

Camshaft

Journal diameters: Front	1.78875 to 1.78925 in. (45.424 to 45.437 mm.).
Centre	1.72875 to 1.72925 in. (43.910 to 43.923 mm.).
Rear	1.62275 to 1.62325 in. (41.218 to 41.230 mm.).
Bearing liner inside diameter (reamed after fitting): Front	1.79025 to 1.79075 in. (45.472 to 45.485 mm.).
Centre	1.73025 to 1.73075 in. (43.948 to 43.961 mm.).
Rear	1.62425 to 1.62475 in. (41.256 to 41.269 mm.).
Diametrical clearance	.001 to .002 in. (.0254 to .0508 mm.).
End-thrust	Taken on locating plate.
End-float	.003 to .007 in. (.076 to .178 mm.).
Cam lift	.250 in. (6.35 mm.).
Drive	Chain and sprocket from crankshaft.
Timing chain	$\frac{3}{8}$ in. (9.52 mm.). pitch x 52 pitches.

Tappets

Type	Barrel with flat base.
Outside diameter	$\frac{13}{16}$ in. (20.64 mm.).
Length	2.293 to 2.303 in. (58.25 to 58.5 mm.).

Rocker gear

ROCKER SHAFT	
Length	$14\frac{1}{32}$ in. (.356 mm.).
Diameter	.624 to .625 in. (15.85 to 15.87 mm.).
ROCKER ARM	
Bore	.7485 to .7495 in. (19.01 to 19.26 mm.).
Rocker arm bush inside diameter	.6255 to .626 in. (15.8 to 15.9 mm.).
Ratio	1.4 : 1.

Valves

Seat angle: Inlet and exhaust	45½°.
Head diameter: Inlet	1.562 to 1.567 in. (38.67 to 38.80 mm.).
Exhaust	1.343 to 1.348 in. (34.11 to 34.23 mm.).
Stem diameter: Inlet	.3422 to .3427 in. (8.68 to 8.69 mm.).
Exhaust	.3417 to .3422 in. (8.660 to 8.661 mm.).
Stem to guide clearance: Inlet	.0015 to .0025 in. (.0381 to .0778 mm.).
Exhaust	.002 to .003 in. (.0508 to .0762 mm.).
Valve lift: Inlet and exhaust	.3645 in. (9.25 mm.).

Valve guides

Length: Inlet	$1\frac{5}{8}$ in. (41.275 mm.).
Exhaust	$2\frac{13}{64}$ in. (55.95 mm.).
Outside diameter: Inlet and exhaust	.5635 to .5640 in. (14.30 to 14.32 mm.).
Inside diameter: Inlet and exhaust	.3442 to .3447 in. (8.73 to 8.74 mm.).
Fitted height above head: Inlet and exhaust	$\frac{5}{8}$ in. (15.875 mm.).
Interference fit in head: Inlet and exhaust	.0005 to .00175 in. (.012 to .044 mm.).
(Later cars)	
Length: Inlet	$1\frac{7}{8}$ in. (47.63 mm.).
Fitting height above head: Inlet	¾ in. (19 mm.).

Valve springs

Free length: Inner	$1\frac{31}{32}$ in. (50.0 mm.).
Outer	$2\frac{9}{64}$ in. (54.4 mm.).
Fitted length: Inner	$1\frac{7}{16}$ in. (36.5 mm.).
Outer	$1\frac{9}{16}$ in. (39.7 mm.).
Load at fitted length: Inner	28 to 32 lb. (12.7 to 14.5 kg.).
Outer	72 lb. (32.7 kg.).
Load at top of lift: Inner	48 to 52 lb. (21.7 to 23.6 kg.).
Outer	117 lb. (53 kg.).
Valve crash speed	6,200 r.p.m.

Valve timing

Timing marks	Dimples on camshaft and crankshaft wheels.
Rocker clearance: Running	.015 in. (.38 mm.) cold.
Timing	.055 in. (1.4 mm.).
Inlet valve: Opens	16° B.T.D.C.
Closes	56° A.B.D.C.
Exhaust valve: Opens	51° B.B.D.C.
Closes	21° A.T.D.C.

ENGINE LUBRICATION

System	Wet sump, pressure fed.
System pressure: Running	Between 50 and 80 lb./sq. in. (3.51 and 5.6 kg./cm.^{2}).
Idling	Between 10 and 25 lb./sq. in. (.7 and 1.7 kg./cm.^{2}).
Oil pump	Hobourn-Eaton or eccentric rotor.
Capacity	3¼ gal./min. at 2,000 r.p.m.
Oil filter	Tecalemit full-flow felt element.
By-pass valve opens	13 to 17 lb./sq. in. (.9 to 1.1 kg./cm.^{2}).
Oil pressure relief valve	70 lb./sq. in. (4.9 kg./cm.^{2}).
Relief valve spring: Free length	3 in. (76.2 mm.).
Fitted length	$2\frac{5}{32}$ in. (54.7 mm.).
Load at fitted length	15.5 to 16.5 lb. (7.0 to 7.4 kg.).

FUEL SYSTEM

Carburetters	Twin S.U. type HS4.
Choke diameter	1½ in. (38.1 mm.).
Jet size	.090 in. (2.2 mm.).
Needles	No. 5 (Standard), No. 6 (Rich), No. 21 (Weak).
Piston spring	Red.
Air cleaners	Copper paper element.

Fuel pump

Type (Early cars)	S.U. electric HP.
Minimum flow	7 gal./hr. (31.8 litres/hr., 8.4 U.S. gal./hr.).

Suction head	2 ft. 6 in. (76.2 cm.).
Delivery head	4 ft. (122 cm.).
Minimum starting voltage	9.5 volts.
Type (Later cars)	S.U. electric AUF 300.
Minimum flow	15 gal./hr. (68.2 litre/hr. 18 U.S. gal./hr.).
Suction head	18 in. (457 mm.).

COOLING SYSTEM

Type	Pressurized. Pump-impeller- and fan-assisted.
Thermostat setting	
Standard	74°C. (165°F.).
Hot climate	74°C. (165°F.).
Cold climate	82°C. (180°F.).
Pressure cap	7 lb. (3.175 kg.).
Fan blades	3 at 24°.
Fan belt: Width	$\frac{3}{8}$ in. (9.5 mm.).
Outside length.	35½ in. (90.2 cm.).
Thickness	$\frac{5}{16}$ in. (7.9 mm.).
Tension	½ in. (12.8 mm.) movement.
Type of pump	Centrifugal.
Pump drive	Belt from crankshaft pulley.

IGNITION SYSTEM

Coil	HA.12 (oil-filled).	
Resistance at 20°C. (68°F.): Primary winding	3.1 to 3.5 ohms (cold).	
Consumption: Ignition switch on	3.9 amps.	
At 2,000 r.p.m.	1.4 amps.	
Distributor	25D4.	
Rotation of rotor	Anti-clockwise.	
Cam form	4-cylinder high-lift.	
Cam closed period	60°±3°.	
Cam opened period	30 ±3°.	
Automatic advance	Centrifugal and vacuum.	
	Serial Number 40897 (H.C.)	Serial Number 40916 (L.C.)
Automatic advance commences	400 r.p.m.	400 r.p.m.
Maximum advance (crankshaft degrees)	20° at 200 r.p.m.	24° at 4,400 r.p.m.
Vacuum advance (crankshaft degrees)	20° at 13 in. (33.3 cm.) Hg.	16° at 12 in. (30.5 cm.). Hg.
Decelerating check (crankshaft degrees, engine r.p.m.)	20° at 2,200 r.p.m.	24° at 4,400 r.p.m.
	15° at 1,600 r.p.m.	18° at 3,000 r.p.m.
	9° at 900 r.p.m.	9° at 1,000 r.p.m.
	6° at 700 r.p.m.	8° at 800 r.p.m.
	6° at 600 r.p.m.	6° at 600 r.p.m.
Contact point gap setting	.014 to .016 in. (.35 to .40 mm.).	
Breaker spring tension	18 to 24 oz. (510 to 680 gm.).	
Condenser capacity	.18 to .24 mF.	
Timing marks	Pointer on timing chain case and notch on crankshaft pulley.	
Static ignition timing: H.C.	10°B.T.D.C. (98/100-octane fuel).	
L.C.	8°B.T.D.C. (95/97-octane fuel).	
Stroboscopic ignition timing: H.C.	14°B.T.D.C. at 600 r.p.m.	
L.C.	12°B.T.D.C. at 600 r.p.m.	
Suppressors	Lucas W55 Type L.2. Fitted in plug leads.	
Sparking plugs	Champion N-9Y.	
Size	14 mm. ¾ in. (19.0 mm.) reach.	
Gap	.024 to .026 in. (.625 to .660 mm.).	

CLUTCH

Make and type	Borg & Beck 8 in. DS.G. diaphragm spring.
Diaphragm spring colour	Dark blue.
Clutch plate diameter	8 in. (20.32 cm.).
Facing material	Wound yarn.
Number of damper springs	6.
Damper spring load	110 to 120 lb. (49.8 to 54.3 kg.).
Damper spring colour	Black/light green.
Clutch release bearing	Graphite (MY3D).
Clutch fluid	Lockheed Disc Brake Fluid (Series II).

GEARBOX AND OVERDRIVE

Number of forward gears	4.	
Gearbox ratios: Reverse	4.76 : 1.	
First	3.64 : 1.	
Second	2.21 : 1.	
Third	1.37 : 1.	
Fourth	1.00 : 1.	
Overdrive ratio	.802 :1.	
Overall gear ratios: Reverse	18.588 : 1.	
First	14.214 : 1.	
Second	8.656 : 1.	Overdrive
Third	5.369 : 1.	4.306 : 1.
Fourth	3.909 : 1.	3.135 : 1.
Top gear speed per 1,000 r.p.m.: Standard	17.9 m.p.h. (27.3 km.p.h.).	
Overdrive	22.3 m.p.h. (35.5 km.p.h.).	
Speedometer gear ratio: Standard	9/28.	
Overdrive	5/16.	
Synchromesh hub springs: Free length	½ in. (12.7 mm.).	
Fitted length	$\frac{5}{16}$ in. (7.9 mm.).	
Load at fitted length	4 to 5 lb. (1.8 to 2.2 kg.).	
Shaft and reverse plunger detent springs: Free length	1$\frac{3}{16}$ in. (30.16 mm.).	
Fitted length	¾ in. (19.0 mm.).	
Load at fitted length	18 to 20 lb. (8.16 to 9.07 kg.).	
Reverse plunger springs: Free length	1 in. (25.4 mm.).	
Fitted length	$\frac{13}{16}$ in. (20.63 mm.).	
Load at fitted length	91½ to 92½ lb. (41.4 to 41.9 kg.).	
Mainshaft second and third gear end-float	.004 to.006 in. (.10 to .15 mm.).	
Laygear end-float	.002 to .003 in. (.05 to .08 mm.).	
Overdrive		
Pump spring: Free length	2.000 in. (50.8 mm.).	
Rate	11 lb. in. (12.7 kg.cm.).	
Clutch spring: Free length	1.510 in. (38.3 mm.).	
Rate	154 lb. in. (178 kg. cm.).	

PROPELLER SHAFT

Type	Open tubular, telescopic.
Universal joints	Hardy Spicer needle roller.
Angular movement	18° to 20°.
Overall length: Fully extended: Standard	30¾ in. (78.1 cm.).
Overdrive	31$\frac{7}{8}$ in. (81 cm.).
Fully compressed: Standard	29$\frac{1}{16}$ in. (74 cm.).
Overdrive	30$\frac{3}{16}$ in. (76.5 cm.).
Length of shaft assembly: Standard	25$\frac{11}{32}$ in. (64.3 cm.).
Overdrive	26$\frac{15}{32}$ in. (67 cm.).
Tube diameter	2 in. (50.8 mm.).

REAR AXLE

Type	Hypoid, three-quarter-floating.
Ratio	3.909 : 1 (11/43).
Differential bearing preload	.002 in. (.05 mm.) 'nip' per bearing.
Pinion bearing preload	7 to 9 lb. in. (.8 to 1.0 kg.m.).
Backlash adjustment: Crown wheel	Shims.
Pinion	Head washer.

STEERING

Type	Rack and pinion.
Steering-wheel diameter	16½ in. (419.10 mm.).
Turns—lock to lock	2.93.
Turning circle	32 ft. (9.75 m.).
Universal joint	Hardy Spicer KO518, GB166.
Pinion end-float	.002 to .005 in. (.05 to .12 mm.).
Damper end-float	.0005 to .003 in. (.012 to .076 mm.) (unladen).
Toe-in.	$\frac{1}{16}$ to $\frac{3}{32}$ in. (1.5 to 2.3 mm.) (unladen).
Angle of outer wheel with inner wheel at 20°	19°±1°.

FRONT SUSPENSION

Type	Independent. Coil spring and wishbone.
Spring: Coil diameter (mean)	3.238 in. (82.2 mm.).
Free height	9.9± $\frac{1}{16}$ in. (251.4±1.5 mm.).
Static length at 1,030 lb. (467.2 kg.) load	7± $\frac{1}{32}$ in. (178±.8 mm.).
Number of free coils	7.5.
Camber angle	Nominal 1° positive (+¼°, −1¼°) =1¼° positive, ¼° negative (unladen).
Castor angle	Nominal 7°(+¼°, −2°)=5° to 7¼° (unladen).
King pin inclination	Nominal 8°(+1°, −¾°)=7¼° to 9° (unladen).
Dampers	Armstrong piston type.
Arm centres	8 in. (203.2 mm.).
Wheel bearing end-float	.002 to .004 in. (.05 to .10 mm.).

REAR SUSPENSION

Type	Semi-elliptic leaf spring.
Number of spring leaves	5+ bottom plate. Interleaving 1/2, 2/3, 3/4.
Width of spring leaves	1¾ in. (44.4 mm.).
Gauge of leaves	
Early cars	$\frac{7}{32}$ in. (5.56 mm.).
Later cars	3 at $\frac{7}{32}$ in. (5.6 mm.), 3 at $\frac{3}{16}$ in. (4.8 mm.).
Working load (±15 lb. [7 kg.])	
Early cars	400 lb. (181.5 kg.).
Later cars	450 lb. (204.1 kg.).
Dampers	Armstrong piston type.
Arm centres	5¼ in. (133 mm.).

ELECTRICAL EQUIPMENT

System	12-volt, positive earth.
Charging system	Current/voltage control
Batteries—two 6-volt	Lucas SG9E or STGZ9E. Lucas BT9E or BTZ9E—later cars.
Capacity: 10-hour rate	51 amp.-hr.
20-hour rate	58 amp.-hr.
Plates per cell	9.
Electrolyte to fill one cell	1 pint (570 c.c.: 1.2 U.S. pints).

Regulator	RB.340.
Voltage setting at 3,000 r.p.m.: 10°C. (50°F.)	14.9 to 15.5 volts.
20°C. (68°F.)	14.7 to 15.3 volts.
30°C. (86°F.)	14.5 to 15.1 volts.
40°C. (104°F.)	14.3 to 14.9 volts.
Current setting at 4,000 r.p.m.	22 amps.
Cut-out relay: Cut-in voltage	12.7 to 13.3 volts.
Drop-off voltage	9.5 to 11.0 volts.
Reverse current	3.0 to 5.0 amps.
Current regulator	22±1 amp.
Dynamo	C40/1. 12-volt two-brush.
Maximum output	22 amps.
Cut-in speed	1,585 r.p.m. at 13.0 volts.
Field resistance	6.0 ohms.
Brush spring tension	22 to 25 oz. (623 to 708 gm.).
Drive	Belt from crankshaft.
Drive adjustment	Swinging link on dynamo.
Starter motor	M418G four-brush inertia type.
Lock torque	15 lb. ft. (2.1 kg. m.) at 425 amps.
Torque at 1,000 r.p.m.	8 lb. ft. (1.11 kg. m.) at 250 to 270 amps.
Brush spring tension	32 to 40 oz. (907 to 1133 gm.).
Starter gear ratio	13.3 : 1.
Wiper motor	DR.3A single speed.
Drive to wheelboxes	Rack and cable.
Armature end-float	.008 to .012 in. (.20 to .30 mm.).
Running current	2.7 to 3.4 amps.
Wiping speed	45 to 50 cycles per minute.
Horns	
Type	9H 12-volt.
Maximum current consumption	3½ amps.

BRAKES

Type	Lockheed hydraulic. Disc front, drum rear.
Brake fluid	Lockheed Disc Brake Fluid (Series II).
Front	
Disc diameter	10¾ in. (27.3 cm.).
Pad material	Don 55—FF.
Swept area	203.2 sq. in. (1311 cm.^{2}).
Rear	
Drum diameter	10 in. (25.4 cm.).
Lining material	Don 24—FE.
Swept area	106.8 sq. in. (683.9 cm.^{2}).
Lining dimensions	$9\frac{7}{16}$x1¾x $\frac{3}{16}$ in. (240x44.4x4.76 mm.).

WHEELS

Type	Ventilated disc, 4-stud fixing. Wire (optional).
Size: Disc	4Jx14.
Wire	4½Jx14.

TYRES

Standard:	Size	5.60–14 (tubed).
	Rolling radius	11.65 in. (29.5 cm.) at 30 m.p.h. (48 km.p.h.).
Optional:	Size	155–14.

TYRE PRESSURES

Condition	Standard tyres 5.60–14		Optional tyres 155–14	
	Front	Rear	Front	Rear
Normal car weight	18 lb./sq. in. (1.3 kg./cm.^{2})	18 lb./sq. in. (1.3 kg./cm.^{2})	21 lb./sq. in. (1.5 kg./cm.^{2})	24 lb./sq. in. (1.7 kg./cm.^{2})
Sustained speeds in excess of 90 m.p.h. (145 km.p.h.)	24 lb./sq. in. (1.7 kg./cm.^{2})	24 lb./sq. in. (1.7 kg./cm.^{2})	27 lb./sq. in. (1.9 kg./cm.^{2})	31 lb./sq. in. (2.2 kg./cm.^{2})

NOTE: Rear tyre pressures may be increased by 2 lb./sq. in. (.14 kg./cm.^{2}) with advantage when towing with a laden boot.

CAPACITIES

Fuel tank: Early cars	10 gallons (45.4 litres, 12 U.S. gallons).
Later cars	12 gallons (54 litres, 14 U.S. gallons).
Cooling system	9½ pints (5.4 litres, 11.4 U.S. pints).
Heater	½ pint (.28 litre, .6 U.S. pint).
Engine sump	7½ pints (4.26 litres, 9 U.S. pints).
Oil cooler	¾ pint (.42 litre, .9 U.S. pint).
Gearbox	4½ pints (2.56 litres, 5.6 U.S. pints).
Gearbox and overdrive	5⅓ pints (3.36 litres, 6 U.S. pints).
Rear axle	2¼ pints (1.28 litres, 2.75 U.S. pints).
Steering rack	⅓ pint (.19 litre, .39 U.S. pint).

DIMENSIONS

Overall length	12 ft. 8½ in. (3.874 m.).
Overall length (with over-riders)	12 ft. 9$\frac{3}{16}$ in. (3.897 m.).
Overall width	4 ft. 11$\frac{15}{16}$ in. (152.3 cm.).
Overall height (hood erected)	4 ft. 1$\frac{3}{8}$ in. (125.4 cm.).
Ground clearance (minimum)	5 in. (12.7 cm.).
Wheelbase	7 ft. 7 in. (231.1 cm.).
Track: Front (disc wheels)	4 ft. 1 in. (124.4 cm.).
Rear (disc wheels)	4 ft. 1¼ in. (125 cm.).
Front (wire wheels)	4 ft. 1¼ in. (125 cm.).
Rear (wire wheels)	4 ft. 1¼ in. (125 cm.).

WEIGHTS

Unladen weight	1,920 lb. (871 kg.).
Engine (dry, with clutch)	358 lb. (163.3 kg.) approx.
Gearbox	78 lb. (35.5 kg.) approx.
Rear axle: Disc wheels	117½ lb. (53.26 kg.) approx.
Wire wheels	123 lb. (55.79 kg.) approx.

TORQUE WRENCH SETTINGS

Engine

Main bearing nuts	70 lb. ft. (9.7 kg.m.).
Flywheel set screws	40 lb. ft. (5.5 kg.m.).
Gudgeon pin clamp bolt	25 lb. ft. (3.4 kg.m.).
Big-end bolts	35 to 40 lb. ft. (4.8 to 5.5 kg.m.).
Cylinder head nuts	45 to 50 lb. ft. (6.2 to 6.9 kg.m.).
Rocker bracket nuts	25 lb. ft. (3.4 kg.m.).
Oil pump to crankcase	14 lb. ft. (1.9 kg.m.).
Sump to crankcase	6 lb. ft. (.8 kg. m.).
Cylinder side cover screws	2 lb. ft. (.28 kg. m.).
Second type—deep pressed cover	5 lb. ft. (.7 kg. m.).
Timing cover—¼ in. screws	6 lb. ft. (.8 kg. m.).
Timing cover— $\frac{5}{16}$ in. screws	14 lb. ft. (1.9 kg. m.).
Rear plate— $\frac{5}{16}$ in. screws	20 lb. ft. (2.8 kg. m.).
Rear plate— $\frac{3}{8}$ in. screws	30 lb. ft. (4.1 kg. m.).
Water pump to crankcase	17 lb. ft. (2.4 kg. m.).
Water outlet elbow nuts	8 lb. ft. (1.1 kg. m.).
Rocker cover nuts	4 lb. ft. (.56 kg. m.).
Manifold nuts	15 lb. ft. (2.1 kg. m.).
Oil filter centre-bolt	15 lb. ft. (2.1 kg. m.).
Clutch to flywheel	25 to 30 lb. ft. (3.4 to 4.1 kg. m.).
Carburetter stud nuts	2 lb. ft. (.28 kg. m.).
Distributor clamp bolt (nut trapped)	4.16 lb. ft. (.57 kg. m.).
Distributor clamp nut (bolt trapped)	2.5 lb. ft. (.35 kg. m.).
Fan blade fixing screws	7.3 to 9.3 lb. ft. (1 to 1.3 kg. m.).

Rear axle

Crown wheel to differential carrier	55 to 60 lb. ft. (7.6 to 8.3 kg. m.).
Differential bearing cap	60 to 65 lb. ft. (8.3 to 8.9 kg. m.).
Pinion bearing nut	135 to 140 lb. ft. (18.6 to 19.3 kg. m.).
Rear brake adjuster securing nuts	5 to 7 lb. ft. (.69 to .97 kg. m.).
Bearing retaining nut	180 lb. ft. (24.8 kg. m.).

Rear suspension

Rear shock absorber bolts	55 to 60 lb. ft. (7.6 to 8.3 kg. m.).

Front suspension

Front shock absorber bolts	43 to 45 lb. ft. (5.9 to 6.2 kg. m.).
Brake disc to hub	40 to 45 lb. ft. (5.5 to 6.2 kg. m.).
Brake calliper mounting	40 to 45 lb. ft. (5.5 to 6.2 kg. m.).
Bearing retaining nut	40 to 70 lb. ft. (5.5 to 9.7 kg. m.).
Cross-member to body	54 to 56 lb. ft. (7.5 to 7.7 kg. m.).

Steering

Steering arm bolts	60 to 65 lb. ft. (8.3 to 8.9 kg. m.).
Steering wheel nut	41 to 43 lb. ft. (5.7 to 5.9 kg. m.).
Steering tie-rod lock nut	33.3 to 37.5 lb. ft. (4.6 to 5.2 kg. m.).
Steering lever ball joint nut	34 to 35 lb. ft. (4.7 to 4.8 kg. m.).
Steering universal joint bolt	20 to 22 lb. ft. (2.8 to 3.0 kg. m.).

Road wheels

Road wheel nuts	60 to 65 lb. ft. (8.3 to 9 kg. m.).

GENERAL DATA
(18GB)

The following information is applicable to the 18GB-engined cars and should be used in conjunction with the preceding specification for the 18G/18GA-engined car.

ENGINE	
Type	18GB.
Main bearings	
Number and type	5 thin-wall.
Length: Front, centre and rear	$1\frac{1}{8}$ in. (28.5 mm.).
Intermediate	$\frac{7}{8}$ in. (22.23 mm.).
Connecting rods	
Type	Angular-split big-end, bushed small-end.
Big-end bearings	
Length	.775 to .785 in. (19.68 to 19.94 mm.).
Pistons	
Gudgeon pin bore	.8126 to .8129 (20.610 to 20.167 mm.).
Clearance in cylinder skirt: Top	.0012 to .0006 in. (.030 to .015 mm.).
Bottom	.0033 to .0021 in. (.080 to .050 mm.).
Gudgeon pin	
Type	Fully floating.
Fit in piston	.0001 to .00035 in. (.0025 to .007 mm.).
Diameter (outer)	.8124 to .8127 (20.608 to 20.615 mm.).
FUEL SYSTEM	
Carburetter needles	FX (Standard); No. 6 (Rich); No. 21 (Weak).
REAR AXLE (GT)	
Type	Hypoid, semi-floating.
Ratio	3.909 : 1 (11.43).
Differential bearing preload	.002 in. (.05 mm.) nip per bearing.
Pinion bearing preload. New collapsible spacer only	14 to 18 lb. in. (.161 to .207 kg. m.).
Pinion bearing preload. Oil seal change spacer collapsed	Adjust to preload, refer Section Ha.4.
Backlash adjustment:	
Crown wheel	Shims.
Pinion	Head washer.
FRONT SUSPENSION (GT)	
Spring coil diameter (mean)	3.28 in. (83.3 mm.).
Free height	9.1±$\frac{1}{16}$ in. (231±1.6 mm.).
Number of free coils	7.2.
Static length at load of 1,193 lb. (541.5 kg.)±20 lb. (9.1 kg.) ..	6.6 in. (168 mm.).
REAR SUSPENSION (GT)	
Spring detail	
Working load (±15 lb. 7 kg.)	510 lb. (321.6 kg.).
WHEELS (GT)	
Size; Disc	5J x 14 in.

TYRES (GT)

Optional:	
Size and type—Early cars	165–14 SP41.
Later cars	165–14 SP68.
Standard tyres:	
Pressures (set cold):	
Front	20 lb./sq. in. (1.4 kg./cm.^{2}).
Rear	24 lb./sq. in. (1.7 kg./cm.^{2}).
Sustained speeds in excess of 90 m.p.h. (145 km.p.h.):	
Front	26 lb./sq. in. (1.8 kg./cm.^{2}).
Rear	30 lb./sq. in. (2.1 kg./cm.^{2}).
Optional tyres:	
Pressures (set cold):	
Front	21 lb./sq. in. (1.5 kg./cm.^{2}).
Rear	24 lb./sq. in. (1.7 kg./cm.^{2}).
Sustained speeds in excess of 90 m.p.h. (145 km.p.h.):	
Front	28 lb./sq. in. (2.0 kg./cm.^{2}).
Rear	31 lb./sq. in. (2.2 kg./cm.^{2}).

CAPACITIES

Rear axle (semi-floating type)	1½ pints (.85 litre, 2 U.S. pints).

DIMENSIONS

Overall height (GT)	4 ft. 1¾ in. (126.3 cm.).

WEIGHTS

Unladen weight (GT)	2,190 lb. (993 kg.).

TORQUE WRENCH SETTINGS

Rear Axle

Half-shaft nut (semi-floating axle)	150 lb. ft. (20.75 kg. m.).
Differential bearing cap bolts	50 to 55 lb. ft. (6.9 to 7.6 kg. m.).
Crown wheel bolts	60 to 65 lb. ft. (8.3 to 8.9 kg. m.).
Pinion nut, new spacer only	180 to 220 lb. ft. (28.89 to 30.42 kg. m.).
Pinion nut, oil seal change	Adjust to preload. See Section Ha.
Axle shaft nut	150 lb. ft. (20.6 kg. m.) and aligned to next split pin hole.

GENERAL DATA

(GHN4/GHD4 CARS, 18GD ENGINE–GHN5/GHD5 CARS, 18GG ENGINE)

The following information is applicable to the GHN4 and GHD4 series cars fitted with 18GD engines and GHN5/GHD5 cars fitted with 18GG engines and should be used in conjunction with the preceding specifications.

ENGINE

Type	18GD–18GG.

Pistons

Type	Aluminium solid skirt, three rings.
Clearance of skirt in cylinder: Top	.0021 to .0033 in. (.053 to .084 mm.).
Bottom	.006 to .0012 in. (.015 to .030 mm.).
Number of rings	Three; 2 compression. 1 oil control.
Width of ring grooves: Compression	.064 to .065 in. (1.625 to 1.651 mm.).
Oil control	.1578 to .1588 in. (4.01 to 4.033 mm.).

Piston rings

Type: Compression: Top	Plain, sintered alloy.
Second	Tapered, sintered alloy–marked 'TOP'.
Oil control	Two chrome-faced rings with expander, Apex.
Fitted gap: Compression	.012 to .022 in. (.305 to .600 mm.).
Oil control	.015 to .045 in. (.38 to 1.14 mm.).
Width: Compression	.0615 to .0625 in. (1.56 to 1.59 mm.).
Oil control	.152 to .158 in. (3.86 to 4.01 mm.).
Thickness: Compression: Top	.124 to .127 in. (3.14 to 3.22 mm.).
Second	.104 to .111 in. (2.64 to 2.81 mm.).

Gudgeon pin

Type	Press fit in connecting rod.
Diameter	.8125 to .8127 in. (20.63 to 20.64 mm.).
Fit in: Piston	Hand push fit at 16°C. (60°F.).
Small end	12 lb. ft. (1.7 kg. m.) minimum using 18G 1150 and adaptor type C.

Connecting rods

Type	Horizontal split big-end, solid small-end.
Length between centres	6.5 in. (165.1 mm.).
Locking method big-end	Multi-sided nut.

COOLING SYSTEM

Fan belt: Width	$\frac{15}{32}$ in. (11.9 mm.).
Length	35½ in. (90.2 cm.) at $\frac{3}{8}$ in. width equivalent.
Thickness	$\frac{27}{64}$ in. (10.7 mm.).
Tension	½ in. (12.8 mm.) movement at midway of longest run.

Thermostat:

Normal	82° C. (180° F.).
Hot climates	74° C. (165° F.).
Cold climates	88° C. (190° F.).

FUEL SYSTEM

Carburetter needles	FX (Standard), No. 6 (Rich), GZ (Weak).

CLUTCH

Fluid	Lockheed Disc Brake Fluid (Series 329).

GEARBOX AND OVERDRIVE

Number of forward gears	4.	
Synchromesh	All forward gears.	
Gearbox ratios: Reverse	3.095 : 1.	
First	3.44 : 1.	
Second	2.167 : 1.	
Third	1.382 : 1.	
Fourth	1.000 : 1.	
Overdrive: Type	Laycock L.H.	
Ratio	.82 : 1.	
Overall gear ratios: Reverse	12.098 : 1.	
First	13.45 : 1.	
Second	8.47 : 1.	OVERDRIVE
Third	5.4 : 1	4.43 : 1.
Fourth	3.909 : 1	3.2 : 1.
Top gear speed per 1,000 r.p.m.: Standard	18 m.p.h. (29 km.p.h).	
Overdrive	22 m.p.h. (35 km.p.h.).	
Speedometer gear ratio: Standard	10 : 26.	
Overdrive	8 : 21.	
Synchromesh hub springs: Free length	.72 in. (18.3 mm.).	
Fitted length	.385 in. (9.8 mm.).	
Load at fitted length	5.5 to 6 lb. (2.5 to 2.7 kg.).	
First and third speed gear end-float	.005 to .008 in. (.13 to .20 mm.).	
Second gear end-float	.005 to .008 in. (.13 to .20 mm.).	
Laygear end-float	.002 to .003 in. (.05 to .08 mm.).	

AUTOMATIC GEARBOX

Torque converter ratio	2.2 : 1 to 1 : 1.
Gearbox ratios: Reverse	2.09 : 1.
First	2.39 : 1.
Second	1.45 : 1.
Top	1.00 : 1.
Overall gear ratio (converter at 1 : 1): Reverse	8.17 : 1.
First	9.34 : 1.
Second	5.668 : 1.
Top	3.909 : 1.
Speedometer gear ratio	10 : 26.

REAR AXLE

Type	Hypoid; semi-floating.
Ratio	3.909 : 1 (11/43).
Differential bearing preload	.002 in. (.05 mm.) nip per bearing.
Pinion bearing preload	Refer to Section Ha.4.
Backlash adjustment: Crown wheel	Shims.
Pinion	Head washer.

(GHN4/GHD4 CARS, 18GD ENGINE—GHN5/GHD5 CARS, 18GG ENGINE)—*continued*

ELECTRICAL

System	12-volt, NEGATIVE earth.	

Batteries

		(Later cars)
Type (two 6-volt)	Lucas BT9E or BTZ9E	Lucas CA9E.
Capacity: 10-hour rate	51 amp.-hour	53 amp.-hour.
20-hour rate	58 amp.-hour	60 amp.-hour.
Plates per cell	9	9.
Electrolyte to fill one cell	1 pint (570 c.c., 1·2 U.S. pints).	

Control box

Type	4TR Electronic.
Voltage setting	14·3 to 14·7 volts at 5,000 r.p.m.

Alternator

	18GD engine	**18GG engine**
Type	Lucas 16AC	Lucas 16ACR
Output at 14 volts and 6,000 r.p.m.	34 amps.	*data as 16AC.*
Maximum permissible rotor speed	12,500 r.p.m.	
Pulley ratio—alternator/crankshaft	1·795 : 1.	
Stator phases	3.	
Rotor poles	12.	
Rotor winding resistance	4·33 ohms ±5% at 20° C. (68° F.).	
Brush length (new)	½ in. (12·6 mm.).	
Brush spring tension	7 to 10 oz. (198-283 gm.) with brush face flush with brush box.	

Starter

Type	Lucas M418G Pre-engaged.
Light running current	70 amp. at 5,800 to 6,500 r.p.m.
Lock torque	17 lb. ft. (2·35 kg. m.) at 465 amps.
Torque at 1,000 r.p.m.	7 lb. ft. (·97 kg. m.) at 260 amps.
Solenoid: Closing coil resistance	·13 to ·15 ohm.
Hold-on coil resistance	·63 to ·73 ohm.
Brush spring tension	36 oz. (1·02 kg.).

Starter motor relay

Type	Lucas Model 6RA-33243.
Winding resistance	76 ohms.
Bobbin core to underside of armature air gap:	
Contacts open	0·030±0·005 in. (0·76±0·13 mm.).
Contacts closed	0·010±0·003 in. (0·25±0·08 mm.).
Cut-in voltage	4·0 to 7·5 volts.
Drop-off voltage	5 volts (maximum).

Wiper motor

Type	Lucas, 14W (two-speed).
Armature end-float	·004 to ·008 in. (·1 to ·21 mm.).
Light running current: Normal speed	1·5 amp.
High speed	2·0 amp.
Light running speed: Normal speed	46 to 52 r.p.m.
High speed	60 to 70 r.p.m.

BRAKES

Brake fluid	Lockheed Disc Brake Fluid (Series 329).

CAPACITIES

Gearbox .. .. 5¼ pints (3 litres, 6 U.S. pints).
Gearbox and overdrive .. .. 6 pints (3·4 litres, 7 U.S. pints).
Automatic gearbox .. .. 10½ pints (6 litres, 12·7 U.S. pints).
Rear axle .. .. 1½ pints (·85 litres, 2 U.S. pints).

TYRE PRESSURES

Tourer	**5·60—14S Cross-ply tyres**		**155SR—14 Radial-ply tyres**	
	Front	*Rear*	*Front*	*Rear*
Normal car weight	19 lb./sq. in. (1·34 kg./cm.²)	22 lb./sq. in. (1·55 kg./cm.²)	21 lb./sq. in. (1·48 kg./cm.²)	24 lb./sq. in. (1·69 kg./cm.²)
Maximum weight	19 lb./sq. in. (1·34 kg./cm.²)	24 lb./sq. in. (1·69 kg./cm.²)	21 lb./sq. in. (1·48 kg./cm.²)	26 lb./sq. in. (1·83 kg./cm.²)
GT				
Normal car weight	20 lb./sq. in. (1·4 kg./cm.²)	24 lb./sq. in. (1·69 kg./cm.²)	**Tyre size 165SR—14 Pressures as Tourer**	
Maximum weight	20 lb./sq. in. (1·4 kg./cm.²)	26 lb./sq. in. (1·83 kg./cm.²)		

It is recommended that for sustained speeds at or near the maximum the above tyre pressures are increased by 6 lb./sq. in. (·42 kg./cm.²).

WEIGHTS

		Total weight		**Distribution**			
				Front		*Rear*	
		Tourer	*GT*	*Tourer*	*GT*	*Tourer*	*GT*
Kerbside	Including full fuel tank, all optional extras and accessories	2,303 lb. (1044 kg.)	2,401 lb. (1088 kg.)	1,127 lb. (512 kg.)	1,162 lb. (527 kg.)	1,176 lb. (534 kg.)	1,239 lb. (562 kg.)
Normal	Kerbside weight including driver, passenger and 50 lb. (22 kg.) luggage	2,653 lb. (1203 kg.)	2,751 lb. (1248 kg.)	1,235 lb. (560 kg.)	1,269 lb. (576 kg.)	1,418 lb. (643 kg.)	1,482 lb. (672 kg.)
Maximum	Normal weight including tow-bar hitch load	2,753 lb. (1249 kg.)	2,851 lb. (1293 kg.)	1,193 lb. (541 kg.)	1,231 lb. (558 kg.)	1,560 lb. (708 kg.)	1,620 lb. (735 kg.)
Maximum permissible towing weight		1,680 lb. (762 kg.)	1,680 lb. (762 kg.)				
Maximum towbar hitch load		100 lb. (45 kg.)	100 lb. (45 kg.)				

(GHN4/GHD4 CARS, 18GD ENGINE—GHN5/GHD5 CARS, 18GG ENGINE)—*continued*

WHEELS

Type: Pressed disc	4J × 14 (Tourer) 5J × 14 (GT)
Pressed spoked	5J F/H × 14
Wire (optional)	4½J × 14 (60-spoke)

TORQUE WRENCH SETTINGS

Automatic gearbox

Converter to drive plate bolts	25 to 30 lb. ft. (3·46 to 4·15 kg. m.).
Transmission case to converter housing bolts	8 to 13 lb. ft. (1·1 to 1·8 kg. m.).
Extension housing to transmission case bolts	8 to 13 lb. ft. (1·1 to 1·8 kg. m.).
Oil pan to gearbox bolts	8 to 13 lb. ft. (1·1 to 1·8 kg. m.).
Front servo bolts	8 to 13 lb. ft. (1·1 to 1·8 kg. m.).
Rear servo bolts	13 to 27 lb. ft. (1·8 to 3·73 kg. m.).
Pump adaptor to housing screw	2 to 3 lb. ft. (·28 to ·41 kg. m.).
Pump adaptor to housing bolts	17 to 32 lb. ft. (2·35 to 4·43 kg. m.).
Pump adaptor to transmission case bolts	8 to 18·5 lb. ft. (1·1 to 2·55 kg. m.).
Manual shaft locknut	7 to 9 lb. ft. (·97 to 1·24 kg. m.).
Pressure adaptor plug	4 to 5 lb. ft. (·55 to ·69 kg. m.).
Drain plug	8 to 10 lb. ft. (1·1 to 1·38 kg. m.).
Upper valve body to lower valve body screws	20 to 30 lb. in. (·23 to ·345 kg. m.).
Lower valve body to upper valve body screws	20 to 30 lb. in. (·23 to ·345 kg. m.).
Oil tube and end plate to valve bodies screws	20 to 30 lb. in. (·23 to ·345 kg. m.).
Valve bodies to transmission case bolts	4·5 to 9 lb. ft. (·61 to 1·24 kg. m.).
Cam bracket screws	20 to 40 lb. in. (·23 to ·46 kg. m.).
Governor to counter-weight screws	4 to 5 lb. ft. (·55 to ·69 kg. m.).
Governor cover-plate screws	20 to 48 lb. in. (·23 to ·552 kg. m.).
Front servo adjusting screw locknut	15 to 20 lb. ft. (2·07 to 2·77 kg. m.).
Rear servo adjusting screw locknut	25 to 30 lb. ft. (3·46 to 4·15 kg. m.).
Starter inhibitor switch locknut	4 to 6 lb. ft. (·55 to ·83 kg. m.)
Downshift cable adaptor bolts	8 to 9 lb. ft. (1·1 to 1·24 kg. m.).
Filler tube connector sleeve to transmission case	20 to 30 lb. ft. (2·76 to 4·15 kg. m.).
Filler tube to connector sleeve nut	17 to 18 lb. ft. (2·35 to 2·49 kg. m.).
Stone-guard screws	17 to 19 lb. in. (·196 to ·219 kg. m.).
Driving flange nut	55 to 60 lb. ft. (7·6 to 8·3 kg. m.).
Centre support bolts	10 to 18 lb. ft. (1·38 to 2·49 kg. m.).

General

Stiffnut to cross-member mounting bolt	44 to 46 lb. ft. (6·08 to 6·36 kg. m.).
Gearbox remote control cover to tunnel	7·5 to 9·5 lb. ft. (1·04 to 1·31 kg. m.).
Hydraulic brake pipe connection—⅜ in. UNF.	5 to 7 lb. ft. (·69 to ·96 kg. m.).
Hydraulic brake pipe connection—$\frac{7}{16}$ in. UNF.	7 to 10 lb. ft. (·96 to 1·38 kg. m.).
Steering-wheel nut—$\frac{9}{16}$ in. UNF.	27 to 29 lb. ft. (3·73 to 4·01 kg. m.).
Steering-wheel nut—$\frac{11}{16}$ in. UNF.	41 to 43 lb. ft. (5·66 to 5·94 kg. m.).

Electrical

Alternator shaft nut	25 to 30 lb. ft. (3·46 to 4·15 kg. m.).

GENERAL DATA

The information given in this section refers specifically to service operations on, or affected by, equipment fitted to the MGB (GHN5/GHN4 and GHD5/GHD4) in conformity with local and territorial requirements, and must be used in conjunction with the preceding DATA.

ENGINE

Type (1967–69)	18GF (EEC).
Type (1969–70)	18GH (EEC, Carburetter crankcase ventilation).
Type (1969–70)	18GJ (EEC, ELC, Carburetter crankcase ventilation).
Type (1970–1)	18GK (EEC, ELC).
Type (1971–2)	18V 584Z (EEC, ELC—Non overdrive).
Type (1971–2)	18V 585Z (EEC, ELC—Overdrive).
Type (1972–4)	18V 672Z (EEC, ELC—Non overdrive).
Type (1972–4)	18V 673Z (EEC, ELC—Overdrive).

Abbreviations: EEC, Exhaust Emission Control; ELC, Evaporative Loss Control.

Servicing, adjusting and tuning the above type engines and cars fitted with Vehicle Emission Control Equipment must be carried out in accordance with the instructions given in Workshop Manual Supplement AKD 4957.

FUEL SYSTEM

Fuel tank capacity (Engine types 18GJ and 18GK)	12 U.S. gallons (45·4 litres).
Carburetter needle: 18GF	FX.
18GH–18GJ	AAE.
18GK	AAL.
18V 584Z and 18V 585Z	AAU.
18V 672Z and 18V 673Z	ABD.

DISTRIBUTOR

Make/type	Lucas 25D4.
Serial number: 18GF	40897.
18GH–18GJ	41155.
18GK	41339.
18V 584Z and 18V 585Z	41370.
18V 672Z and 18V 673Z	41491.

TORQUE WRENCH SETTINGS

Interior mirror special screw	5 lb. in. (·058 kg. m.).
Steering-column top fixing bolts	12 to 17 lb. ft. (1·66 to 2·35 kg. m.).
Steering-column universal joint bolts	20 to 22 lb. ft. (2·8 to 3·04 kg. m.).
Steering-wheel nut	36 to 38 lb. ft. (4·98 to 5·26 kg. m.).
Steering-wheel nut—9/16 in. UNF.	27 to 29 lb. ft. (3·73 to 4·00 kg. m.).
Master cylinder port adaptors	33 lb. ft. (4·56 kg. m.).
Master cylinder reservoir fixing bolts	5 lb. ft. (·69 kg. m.).
Brake pressure failure switch (nylon)	15 lb. in. (·173 kg. m.).
Brake pressure failure switch assembly end plug	200 lb. in. (2·3 kg. m.).
Hydraulic brake pipe connection—3/8 in. UNF.	5 to 7 lb. ft. (·69 to ·96 kg. m.).
Hydraulic brake pipe connection—7/16 in. UNF.	7 to 10 lb. ft. (·96 to 1·38 kg. m.).

(GHN5/GHD5 CARS, 18V type ENGINE)

The following information is applicable to the GHN5 and GHD5 series cars from Car No. 258001 fitted with the 18V type engine, and should be used in conjunction with the preceding specifications.

ENGINE

Type: Synchromesh gearbox	18V 581F–18V 581Y–18V 779F–18V 846F
Synchromesh gearbox with overdrive	18V 582F–18V 582Y–18V 780F–18V 847F
Automatic transmission	18V 583F–18V 583Y.

Valves

Inlet valve: Seat angle	45½°.	
Head diameter	1.625 to 1.630 in. (41.27 to 41.40 mm.).	
Stem diameter	0.3429 to 0.3434 in. (8.70 to 8.72 mm.).	
Stem to guide clearance	0.0008 to 0.0018 in. (0.020 to 0.046 mm.).	
Later cars:	**INLET**	**EXHAUST**
Head diameter	1.562 to 1.567 in. (39.67 to 39.80 mm.).	1.343 to 1.348 in. (34.11 to 34.23 mm.).
Stem diameter	0.3429 to 0.3434 in. (8.70 to 8.72 mm.).	0.3423 to 0.3428 in. (8.69 to 8.70 mm.).
Stem to guide clearance	0.0007 to 0.0019 in. (0.020 to 0.045 mm.).	0.0013 to 0.0025 in. (0.03 to 0.06 mm.).

Valve spring

Free length	1.92 in. (48.77 mm.).
Fitted length	1.44 in. (36.58 mm.).
Load at fitted length	82 lb. (37.2 kg.).
Load at top of lift	142 lb. (64.4 kg.).

ELECTRICAL

Starter motor

Type	Lucas 2M100 Pre-engaged.
Brush spring tension	36 oz. (1.02 kg.).
Minimum brush length	⅜ in. (9.5 mm.).
Minimum commutator thickness	0.140 in. (3.5 mm.).
Lock torque	14.4 lb. ft. (2.02 kg. m.) with 463 amps.
Torque at 1,000 r.p.m.	7.3 lb. ft. (1.02 kg. m.) with 300 amps.
Light running current	40 amp. at 6,000 r.p.m. (approx.).
Maximum armature end-float	0.010 in. (0.25 mm.).
Solenoid: Closing (series) winding resistance	0.25 to 0.27 ohm.
Hold-on (shunt) winding resistance	0.76 to 0.80 ohm.

	Tourer	**Tourer**	**GT**
FRONT SUSPENSION–From Car No.	293446.	Later cars.	296196.
Free height	10.20±0.06 in. (259.08±1.5 mm.).	10.20 in. nominal. (259.08 mm.).	9.32±$\frac{1}{16}$ in. (236.73±1.6 mm.).
Static length at load of 1,030±20 lb. (467±9 kg.)	7.24 in (187.70 mm.).	7.44 in. (188.98 mm.).	––
Static length at load of 1,193±20 lb. (541±9 kg.)	––		6.84 in. (173.74 mm.).
No. of free coils	7.5.	9.	7.2.

REAR SUSPENSION

Number of spring leaves	6 interleaving between 1/2, 2/3.
Width of spring leaves	1.76 in. (44.7 mm.).
Gauge of leaves: 1st, 2nd, 3rd	0.2187 ± 0.006 in. (5.55 ± 0.152 mm.)
4th, 5th, 6th	0.1875 ± 0.006 in. (4.75 ± 0.152 mm.)
Working load	510 to 540 lbf. (231 to 245 kgf.)

(GHN5/GHD5 CARS, 18V type ENGINE)

TORQUE WRENCH SETTINGS

Engine

Big-end nuts (12 sided)	33 lbf. ft. (4.5 kgf. m.).
Crankshaft pulley nut	70 lbf. ft. (9.6 kgf. m.).
Camshaft nut	65 lbf. ft. (8.9 kgf. m.).
Carburetter–stud nuts	15 lbf. ft. (2.1 kgf. m.).
Spark plugs	18 lbf. ft. (2.5 kgf. m.).
Oil pipe banjo	37 lbf. ft. maximum (5.1 kgf. m.).
Oil release valve–dome nut	43 lbf. ft. (5.9 kgf. m.).
Front plate– 5/16 in. screws	20 lbf. ft. (2.8 kgf. m.).
Rear plate– 3/8 in. screws	30 lbf. ft. (4.1 kgf. m.).
Rear engine mounting bolt	38 lbf. ft. (5.22 kgf. m.).

WEIGHTS

Loading condition		Total weight		Distribution			
				Front		Rear	
		Tourer	*GT*	*Tourer*	*GT*	*Tourer*	*GT*
Kerbside	Including full fuel tank and all optional extras	2,394 lb (1088 kg)	2,446 lb (1110 kg)	1,216 lb (551 kg)	1,198 lb (543 kg)	1,178 lb (534 kg)	1,248 lb (566 kg)
Normal	Kerbside weight including driver and passenger	2,694 lb (1223 kg)	2,746 lb (1245 kg)	1,332 lb (604 kg)	1,314 lb (596 kg)	1,362 lb (618 kg)	1,432 lb (649 kg)
Gross	Maximum weight condition refer to note below	2,814 lb (1277 kg)	2,866 lb (1301 kg)	1,285 lb (583 kg)	1,267 lb (574 kg)	1,529 lb (693 kg)	1,599 lb (725 kg)
Maximum permissible towing weight		1,680 lb (762 kg)	1,680 lb (762 kg)				
Maximum towbar hitch load		100 lb (45 kg)	100 lb (45 kg)				
Maximum roof rack load			50 lb (23 kg)				

NOTE: Due consideration must be given to the overall weight when fully loading the car. Any loads carried on a luggage rack or downward load from a towing hitch must also be included in the maximum loading.

(GHN5/GHD5 CARS FROM CAR No. 410002)

CAPACITIES

Fuel tank	**12 gallons (54.5 litres, 14.4 U.S. gallons)**
Cooling system	**11½ pints (6.6 litres, 13.8 U.S. pints)**
Cooling system with Heater	**12 pints (6.8 litres, 14.4 U.S. pints)**

DIMENSIONS

Track:	Front	4 ft. 1½ in. (124.7 cm.)
	Rear	4 ft. 1¾ in. (126.4 cm.)

ENGINE TUNING DATA
18G, 18GA, AND 18GB ENGINES

ENGINE

Type	18G, 18GA, 18GB.
Displacement	109.8 cu. in. (1798 c.c.).
Firing order	1, 3, 4, 2.
Compression ratio: H.C.	8.8 : 1.
L.C.	8.0 : 1.
Compression pressure: H.C.	160 lb./sq. in. (11.25 kg./cm.²).
L.C.	130 lb./sq. in. (9.15 kg./cm.²).
Idle speed	500 r.p.m.
Valve rocker clearance	.015 in. (.38 mm.) set cold.
Static ignition timing: H.C.	10° B.T.D.C.
L.C.	8° B.T.D.C.
Stroboscopic ignition timing: H.C.	14° B.T.D.C. at 600 r.p.m.
L.C.	12° B.T.D.C. at 600 r.p.m.
Timing mark location	Pointer on timing case, notch on crankshaft pulley.

DISTRIBUTOR

Make/Type	Lucas/25D4.	
Contact breaker gap	.014 to .016 in. (.35 to .40 mm.).	
Contact spring tension	18 to 24 oz. (510 to 680 gm.).	
Rotation of rotor	Anti-clockwise.	
Dwell angle	60°±3°.	
Centrifugal advance	SERIAL NUMBER 40897 (H.C.)	SERIAL NUMBER 40916 (L.C.)
Crankshaft degrees/speed (vacuum pipe disconnected)	6° at 600 r.p.m.	6° at 600 r.p.m.
	6° at 700 r.p.m.	8° at 800 r.p.m.
	9° at 900 r.p.m.	9° at 1,000 r.p.m.
	15° at 1,600 r.p.m.	18° at 3,000 r.p.m.
	20° at 2,200 r.p.m.	24° at 4,400 r.p.m.
Vacuum advance		
Starts	5 in. Hg. (127 mm. Hg).	4 in. Hg (101.6 mm. Hg).
Finishes	13 in. Hg (330.2 mm. Hg).	12 in. Hg (304.8 mm. Hg).
Total crankshaft degrees	20°±2°.	16°±2°.

IGNITION COIL

Make/Type	Lucas/HA12.
Resistance: Primary	3.1 to 3.5 ohms at 20° C. (68° F.).

SPARKING PLUGS

Make/Type	Champion/N9Y.
Gap	.024 to .026 in. (.625 to .66 mm.).

CARBURETTERS

Make/Type	S.U./HS4.
Jet	.090 in. (2.2 mm.).
Needle: 18G and 18GA engines	No. 5 (Std.), No. 6 (Rich), No. 21 (Weak).
18GB engine	FX (Std.), No. 6 (Rich), No. 21 (Weak).
Piston spring	Red.

ELECTRICAL

Dynamo	Lucas C40/1.
Battery	Lucas BT9E or BTZ9E.
Volts/Polarity	12-volt/Positive earth.
Starter	Lucas M418G Inertia-type.
Control unit	Lucas RB.340.

ENGINE TUNING DATA

18GD AND 18GG ENGINES

ENGINE

Type	18GD–18GG.
Displacement	109.8 cu. in. (1798 c.c.).
Firing order	1, 3, 4, 2.
Compression ratio: H.C.	8.8 : 1.
L.C.	8.0 : 1.
Compression pressure: H.C.	160 lb./sq. in. (11.25 kg./cm.^{2}).
L.C.	130 lb./sq. in. (9.15 kg./cm.^{2}).
Idle speed	500 r.p.m.
Valve rocker clearance	.015 in. (.38 mm.) set cold.
Static ignition timing: H.C.	10° B.T.D.C.
L.C.	8° B.T.D.C.
Stroboscopic ignition timing: H.C.	14° B.T.D.C. at 600 r.p.m.
L.C.	12° B.T.D.C. at 600 r.p.m.
Timing mark location	Pointer on timing case, notch on crankshaft pulley.

DISTRIBUTOR

Make/Type	Lucas/25D4.	
Contact breaker gap	.014 to .016 in. (.35 to .40 mm.).	
Contact spring tension	18 to 24 oz. (510 to 680 gm.).	
Rotation of rotor	Anti-clockwise.	
Dwell angle	60°±3°.	
Centrifugal advance	SERIAL NUMBER 40897 (H.C.)	SERIAL NUMBER 40916 (L.C.)
Crankshaft degrees/Speed (vacuum pipe disconnected)	4° at 600 r.p.m.	6° at 600 r.p.m.
	6° at 700 r.p.m.	8° at 800 r.p.m.
	9° at 900 r.p.m.	9° at 1,000 r.p.m.
	15° at 1,600 r.p.m.	18° at 3,000 r.p.m.
	20° at 2,200 r.p.m.	24° at 4,400 r.p.m.
Vacuum advance		
Starts	5 in. Hg (127 mm. Hg).	4 in. Hg (101.6 mm. Hg).
Finishes	13 in. Hg (330.2 mm. Hg).	12 in. Hg (304.8 mm. Hg).
Total crankshaft degrees	20°±2°.	16°±2°.

IGNITION COIL

Make/Type	Lucas/HA12.
Resistance: Primary	3.1 to 3.5 ohms at 20° C. (68° F.).

SPARKING PLUGS

Make/Type	Champion/N9Y.
Gap	.024 to .026 (.625 to .66 mm.).

CARBURETTERS

Make/Type	SU/HS4.
Jet	.090 in. (2.2 mm.).
Needle	Standard, FX; Rich, No. 5; Weak, GZ.
Piston spring	Red.

ELECTRICAL

Alternator	18GD, Lucas 16AC, 18GG, Lucas 16ACR.
Battery	Lucas CA9E early cars, Lucas BT9E or BTZ9E.
Volts/Polarity	12-volt/NEGATIVE earth.
Starter	Lucas M418G Pre-engaged.
Regulator	Lucas 4TR (18GD only).

ENGINE TUNING DATA

18GF, 18GH, 18GK and 18V 584Z, 18V 585Z 18V 672Z
and 18V 673Z ENGINES

Servicing, adjusting and tuning the above type engines and cars fitted with Vehicle Emission Control Equipment must be carried out in accordance with the instructions given in Workshop Manual Supplement AKD 4957.

ENGINE TUNING DATA

18V 581F, 18V 582F and 18V 583F ENGINES

ENGINE

Type	18V.
Displacement	109.8 cu. in. (1798 c.c.).
Firing order	1, 3, 4, 2.
Compression ratio: H.C.	9.0 : 1.
L.C.	8.0 : 1.
Cranking pressure	Nominal 170 lbf./sq. in. (11.95 kgf./cm.^{2}) at 275 r.p.m.
Idle speed	750 to 800 r.p.m.
Valve rocker clearance: Set cold	.015 in. (.38 mm.).
Set hot	.013 in. (.33 mm.).
Static ignition timing: H.C.	10° B.T.D.C.
L.C.	10° B.T.D.C.
Stroboscopic ignition timing: H.C.	13° B.T.D.C. at 600 r.p.m.
L.C.	13° B.T.D.C. at 600 r.p.m.
Timing mark location	Pointer on timing case, notch on crankshaft pulley.

DISTRIBUTOR

Make/Type	Lucas/25D4.	
Contact breaker gap	.014 to .016 in. (.35 to .40 mm.).	
Contact spring tension	18 to 24 oz. (510 to 680 gm.).	
Rotation of rotor	Anti-clockwise.	
Dwell angle	60°±3°.	
Centrifugal advance	SERIAL NUMBER 41288 (H.C.)	SERIAL NUMBER 41290 (L.C.)
Crankshaft degrees/Speed (vacuum pipe disconnected)	0 to 6° at 600 r.p.m. 4 to 9° at 700 r.p.m. 7 to 11° at 900 r.p.m. 13 to 17° at 1,600 r.p.m. 18 to 22° at 2,200 r.p.m.	0 to 6° at 600 r.p.m. 6 to 10° at 800 r.p.m. 7 to 11° at 1,000 r.p.m. 16 to 20° at 3,000 r.p.m. 22 to 26° at 4,400 r.p.m.
Vacuum advance		
Starts	5 in. Hg (127 mm. Hg).	4 in. Hg (101.6 mm. Hg).
Finishes	13 in. Hg (330.2 mm. Hg).	12 in. Hg (304.8 mm. Hg).
Total crankshaft degrees	20°±2°.	16°±2°.

IGNITION COIL

Make/Type	Lucas/HA 12.
Resistance: Primary	3.1 to 3.5 ohms at 20° C. (68° F.).

SPARKING PLUGS

Make/Type	Champion/N9Y.
Gap	.024 to .026 in. (.625 to .66 mm.).

CARBURETTERS

Make/Type	SU/HS4.
Jet	.090 in. (2.2 mm.).
Needle	AAU.
Piston spring	Red.

ELECTRICAL

Alternator	Lucas 16ACR.
Battery	Lucas BT9E, BTZ9E, CA9E, SG9E or Exide 3XCK9L.
Volts/Polarity	12 volt/NEGATIVE earth.
Starter	Lucas 2M100 Pre-engaged.

18V ENGINES—To European emission control requirements (ECE 15)

ENGINE

Type	18V.
Displacement	109.8 cu. in. (1798 c.c.).
Firing order	1, 3, 4, 2.
Compression ratio	9.0 : 1.
Cranking pressure	Nominal 170 to 190 lbf./sq. in. (12 to 13.4 kgf./cm.^{2}).
Valve rocker clearance: set cold	.015 in. (.38 mm.).
Idle speed	750 r.p.m.
Fast idle speed	1,100 to 1,200 r.p.m.
Stroboscopic ignition timing	15° B.T.D.C. at 1,000 r.p.m.
Static ignition timing	5° B.T.D.C.
Timing mark location	Pointer on timing case, notch on crankshaft pulley.

DISTRIBUTOR

Make/Type	Lucas/25D4.
Contact breaker gap	.014 to .016 in. (.35 to .40 mm.).
Contact spring tension	18 to 24 oz. (510 to 680 gm.).
Rotation of rotor	Anti-clockwise.
Dwell angle	60°±3°.
Serial number	41032.

Centrifugal advance

Crankshaft degrees/Speed (vacuum pipe disconnected)	0 to 3° at 600 r.p.m.
	0 to 4° at 700 r.p.m.
	2 to 7° at 900 r.p.m.
	10 to 14° at 1,600 r.p.m.
	17 to 21° at 2,200 r.p.m.

Vacuum advance

Starts	3 in. Hg. (76 mm. Hg.).
Finishes	8 in. Hg. (203 mm. Hg.).
Total crankshaft degrees	14°±2°.

IGNITION COIL

Make/Type	Lucas/HA12.
Resistance: Primary	3.1 to 3.5 ohms at 20° C. (68° F.).

SPARKING PLUGS

Make/Type	Champion/N9Y.
Gap	.024 to .026 (.625 to .66 mm.).

CARBURETTERS

Make/Type	SU/HIF4.
Specification	AUD 434.
Jet	.090 in. (2.2 mm.).
Needle	AAU.
Piston spring	Red.

EXHAUST EMISSION

Exhaust gas analyser reading at engine idle speed	3 to 4.5% CO.

18V 779F and 18V 780F ENGINE–To European emission control requirements (ECE 15)

ENGINE

Type	18V.
Displacement	109.8 cu. in. (1798 c.c.).
Firing order	1, 3, 4, 2.
Compression ratio	9.0 : 1
Cranking pressure	Nominal 170 lbf/in² (11.95 kgf/cm²) at 275 r.p.m
Valve rocker clearance: set cold	0.015 in. (0.38 mm.).
Idle speed	850 r.p.m.
Fast idle speed	1,100 to 1,200 r.p.m.
Stroboscopic ignition timing	11° B.T.D.C. at 1,000 r.p.m.
Static ignition timing	6° B.T.D.C.
Timing mark location	Pointer on timing case, notch on crankshaft pulley

DISTRIBUTOR

Make/Type	Lucas/25D4.
Contact breaker gap	0.014 to 0.016 in. (0.35 to 0.40 mm.).
Contact spring tension	18 to 24 oz. (510 to 680 gm.).
Rotation of rotor	Anti-clockwise.
Dwell angle	60°±3°.
Serial number	41234 or 41391.

Centrifugal advance

Crankshaft degrees/Speed (vacuum pipe disconnected)	0 to 1° at 600 r.p.m.
	2 to 6° at 1,200 r.p.m.
	10 to 14° at 2,200 r.p.m.
	20 to 24° at 3,600 r.p.m.
	26 to 30° at 4,500 r p.m.
	28 to 32° at 6,000 r p.m.

Vacuum advance

Starts	4 in. Hg. (102 mm. Hg.).
Finishes	12 in. Hg. (305 mm. Hg.).
Total crankshaft degrees	16°±2°.

IGNITION COIL

Make/Type	Lucas/HA12.
Resistance: Primary	3.1 to 3.5 ohms at 20° C. (68°F.).
Consumption	3.4 to 4.0 amps.

SPARKING PLUGS

Make/Type	Champion/N9Y.
Gap	0.024 to 0.026 in. (0.625 to 0.66 mm.).

CARBURETTERS

Make/Type	SU/HIF4.
Specification	AUD 616.
Jet	0.090 in. (2.2 mm.).
Needle	AAU.
Piston spring	Red.

EXHAUST EMISSION

Exhaust gas analyser reading at engine idle speed	3 to 4.5% CO.

18V 846F and 18V 847F ENGINE—To European emission control requirements (ECE 15)

ENGINE	
Type	18V.
Displacement	109.8 cu. in. (1798 c.c.).
Firing order	1, 3, 4, 2.
Compression ratio	9.0 : 1.
Cranking pressure	Nominal 170 lbf/in² (11.95 kgf/cm²) at 275 r.p.m.
Valve rocker clearance	0.013 in. (0.33 mm.) cold, 0.015 in. (0.38 mm.) hot.
Idle speed	750 r.p.m.
Fast idle speed	1,300 r.p.m.
Stroboscopic ignition timing	10° B.T.D.C. at 1,000 r.p.m.
Static ignition timing	7° B.T.D.C.
Timing mark location	Pointer on timing case, notch on crankshaft pulley.
DISTRIBUTOR	
Make/type	Lucas/45D4.
Contact breaker gap	0.014 to 0.016 in. (0.35 to 0.40 mm.).
Contact spring tension	18 to 24 oz. (510 to 680 gm.).
Rotation of rotor	Anti-clockwise.
Dwell angle	51° ± 5°.
Serial number	41610.
Centrifugal advance	
Crankshaft degrees/Speed (vacuum pipe disconnected)	0 to 1° at 600 r.p.m. 1 to 5° at 1,600 r.p.m. 6 to 10° at 2,600 r.p.m. 10 to 14° at 3,400 r.p.m. 15 to 19° at 4,400 r.p.m. 20 to 24° at 5,400 r.p.m. 22 to 26° at 6,400 r.p.m.
Vacuum advance	
Starts	3 in. Hg. (76 mm. Hg.).
Finishes	11 in. Hg. (558 mm. Hg.).
Total crankshaft degrees	24° ± 2°.
IGNITION COIL	
Make/Type	Lucas/HA12.
Resistance: Primary	3.1 to 3.5 ohms at 20°C. (68°F.).
Consumption	3.4 to 4.0 amps.
SPARKING PLUGS	
Make/Type	Champion/N9Y.
Gap	0.035 in. (0.90 mm.).
CARBURETTERS	
Make/Type	SU/HIF4.
Specification	FZX 1001.
Jet	0.090 in. (2.2 mm.).
Needle	ACD.
Piston spring	Red.
EXHAUST EMISSION	
Exhaust gas analyser reading at engine idle speed	3% CO.

Year: 1976 on

To European emission control requirements (ECE 15)

ENGINE		
Type	18V 847F	
Capacity	109.8 in³	1798 cm³
Compression ratio	9.0 : 1	
Firing order	1, 3, 4, 2	
Compression pressure	170 to 195 lbf/in²	11.9 to 13.7 kgf/cm²
Idling speed	750 rev/min	
Fast idle speed	1300 rev/min	
Ignition timing:		
Stroboscopic	10° B.T.D.C. at 1,000 rev/min	
Advance check	19° to 23° at 3,400 rev/min	
Timing marks	Pointer on timing case, notch on crankshaft pulley	
Valve clearance: Inlet and exhaust (cold)	0.013 in	0.33 mm
SPARK PLUGS		
Make/type	Champion RN-9Y	
Gap	0.035 in	0.90 mm
IGNITION COIL		
Make/type	Lucas HA 12	
Primary resistance at 20°C (68°F)	3.1 to 3.5 ohms	
Consumption	3.9 A	
DISTRIBUTOR		
Make/type	Lucas 45D4	
Rotation of rotor	Anti-clockwise	
Dwell angle	51° ± 5°	
Contact breaker gap	0.014 to 0.016 in	0.35 to 0.40 mm
Condenser capacity	0.18 to 0.24 microfarad	
Serial No.	41610	
Centrifugal advance		
Decelerating check*†	20° to 24° at 5,400 rev/min 15° to 19° at 4,400 rev/min 10° to 14° at 3,400 rev/min 1° to 5° at 1,600 rev/min	
Vacuum advance	(3-11-12)	
Starts	3 inHg	76 mmHg
Maximum	11 inHg	558 mmHg
Total crankshaft degrees	24° ± 2°	
CARBURETTERS		
Make/type	Twin SU/HIF4	
Specification	FZX 1229	
Jet size	0.090 in	2.2 mm
Needle	ACD	
Piston sparing	Red	
EXHAUST EMISSION		
Exhaust gas analyser reading at engine idle speed	3.0% CO	

* Crankshaft degrees and rev/min † Vacuum pipe disconnected

SECTION A

THE ENGINE

† These operations must be followed by an exhaust emission check. 

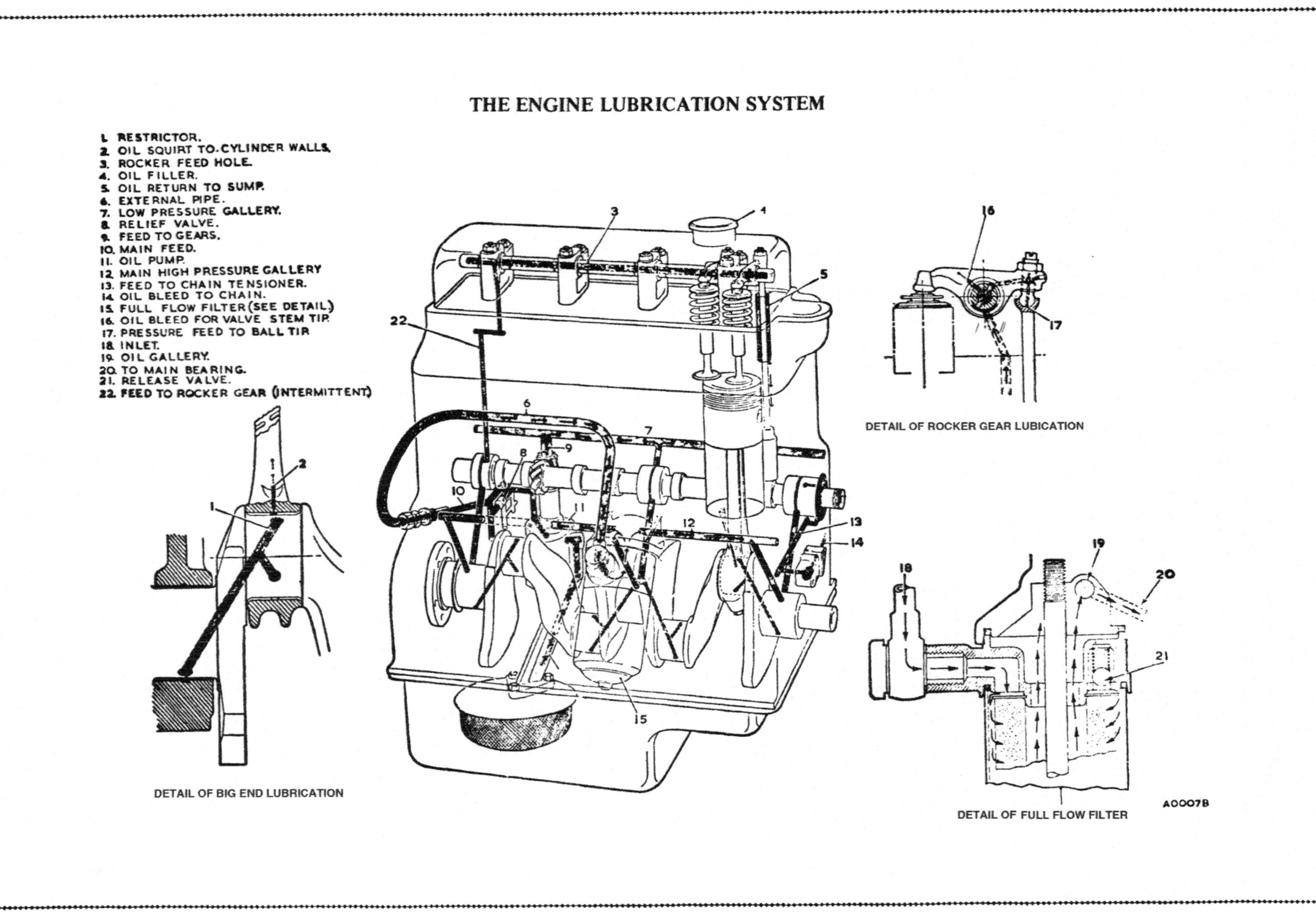
THE ENGINE LUBRICATION SYSTEM
1. RESTRICTOR.
2. OIL SQUIRT TO CYLINDER WALLS.
3. ROCKER FEED HOLE.
4. OIL FILLER.
5. OIL RETURN TO SUMP.
6. EXTERNAL PIPE.
7. LOW PRESSURE GALLERY.
8. RELIEF VALVE.
9. FEED TO GEARS.
10. MAIN FEED.
11. OIL PUMP.
12. MAIN HIGH PRESSURE GALLERY
13. FEED TO CHAIN TENSIONER.
14. OIL BLEED TO CHAIN.
15. FULL FLOW FILTER (SEE DETAIL)
16. OIL BLEED FOR VALVE STEM TIP.
17. PRESSURE FEED TO BALL TIR
18. INLET.
19. OIL GALLERY.
20. TO MAIN BEARING.
21. RELEASE VALVE.
22. FEED TO ROCKER GEAR (INTERMITTENT)
DETAIL OF BIG END LUBRICATION
DETAIL OF ROCKER GEAR LUBICATION
DETAIL OF FULL FLOW FILTER
A0007B

GENERAL DESCRIPTION

The overhead-valve engine is built in unit construction, with single-plate dry clutch. Cylinder bores are an integral part of the block and are water-jacketed their full length. The valves are set vertically in the detachable cylinder head and are operated through the medium of the rocker gear, push-rods, and tappets from the camshaft in the left-hand side of the cylinder block. Renewable, thinwall bearings support the counterbalanced crankshaft, while end-thrust is taken by the thrust washers fitted to the centre main bearing. The camshaft is driven by a duplex roller chain which is automatically adjusted by a spring-hydraulic-operated rubber slipper. The oil pump, distributor, and engine revolution indicator are driven from the camshaft; each component has its own drive shaft.

Section A.1

OIL PRESSURE

Under normal running conditions the oil pressure should not drop below 50 lb./sq. in. (3.5 kg./cm.^{2}) on the gauge at normal road speeds, whilst approximately 15 lb./sq. in. (1.05 kg./cm.^{2}) should be shown when the engine is idling. New engines with new oil will give considerably higher readings at low speeds.
Should there be a noticeable drop in pressure, the following points should be checked:

1. That there is a good supply of the correct grade of oil in the engine sump.
2. That the strainer in the sump is clean and not choked with sludge.
3. That the bearings, to which oil is fed under pressure, have the correct working clearances. Should the bearings be worn and the clearances excessive, the oil will escape more readily from the sides of the bearings, particularly when the oil is warm and becomes more fluid. This will cause a drop in pressure on the gauge as compared with that shown when the bearings are in good order.

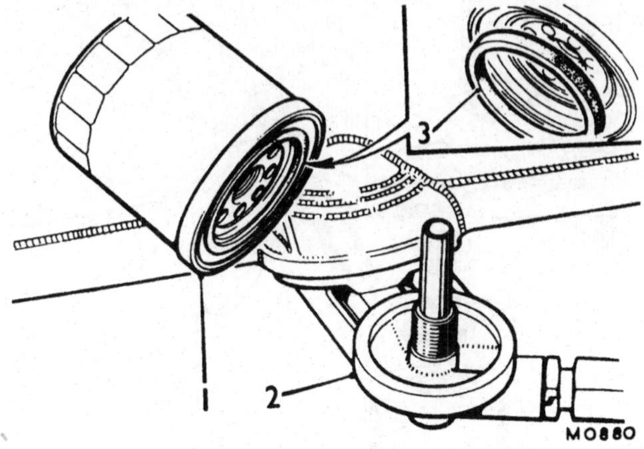

Later type filter (disposable cartridge)

1. Filter cartridge. 2. Filter head. 3. Seal.

Section A.2

LUBRICATION

Checking the engine oil level
Inspect the oil level in the engine and top up if necessary to the 'MAX' mark on the dipstick. The oil filler cap is on the top of the engine valve cover and is released by turning it anti-clockwise.

Changing the engine oil
Drain the oil from the engine by removing the drain plug on the right-hand side of the engine sump.
The oil will flow more readily if drained when the engine is hot; allow at least 10 minutes for draining before replacing the plug.
NOTE. Disconnect the battery cable from its terminal on the starter before starting work on the filter.

Engine oil filter
The external oil filter is of the disposable cartridge type and is located on the right-hand side of the engine. Early cars are fitted with the renewable element type of filter.

To change the filter cartridge. Unscrew the old filter cartridge from the filter head and discard. Smear the seal of the new filter cartridge with oil, locate on the filter head and tighten with the hands only. **DO NOT USE A SPANNER TO TIGHTEN. DO NOT OVERTIGHTEN.**

To renew the filter element, drain the filter by removing the plug; unscrew the filter body securing bolt and lift off the body. Wash out the casing with gasoline (fuel) and dry it before fitting a new element. Check that the sealing rings and the rubber washer are in a satisfactory condition.

Reassemble the filter, ensuring that the components are correctly positioned.

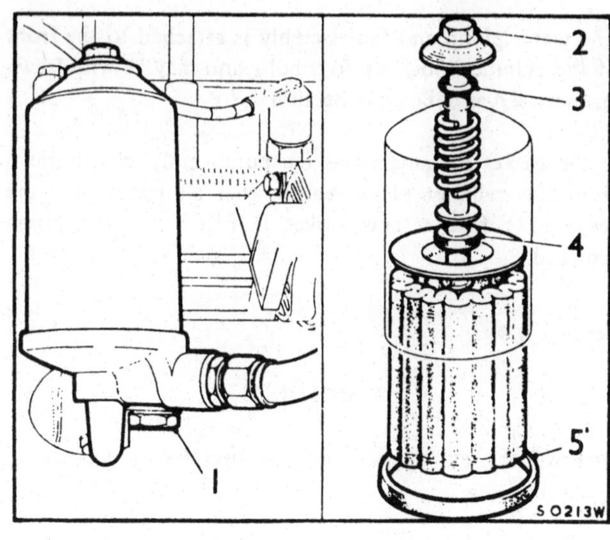

Early type filter (renewable element)

1. Drain plug. 2. Bolt. 3. Sealing ring. 4. Rubber washer. 5. Sealing ring.

Oil pressure relief valve

The automatic relief valve in the lubrication system deals with any excessive oil pressure when starting from cold. When hot, the pressure drops as the oil becomes more fluid.

Should the oil filter become blocked, two relief valves in the filter blow off to enable the oil to by-pass the filter and pass direct into the main gallery.

Continuous cold-running and unnecessary use of the mixture control are often the causes of serious oil dilution by fuel, with a consequent drop in pressure.

Particular attention is called to the recommended changes of oil.

The non-adjustable oil pressure relief valve is situated at the rear of the left-hand side of the cylinder block and is held in position by a domed hexagon nut sealed by two fibre washers or one copper washer. The relief valve spring maintains a valve cup against a seating machined in the block.

The valve should be examined to ensure that the cup is seating correctly and that the relief spring has not lost its tension. The latter can be checked by measuring the length of the spring to give the correct relief pressure (see 'GENERAL DATA'). Fit a new cup and spring if necessary.

Section A.3

WATER PUMP

The water pump is of the centrifugal impeller type and is mounted on a common spindle with the fan in a casting bolted to the front of the cylinder block.

The water pump and fan assembly is attached to the front of the cylinder block by four bolts and may be withdrawn and serviced as detailed in Section C.7.

If the gasket is damaged as the pump body is withdrawn from the cylinder block, ensure that all traces of it are removed before a new gasket is fitted and the pump replaced.

Section A.4

MANIFOLDS

Remove the air cleaners and carburetters as detailed in Section D.

Disconnect the distributor vacuum pipe and, on early cars, the heater pipe from the manifold.

Remove the six exhaust pipe to manifold clamp bolts and spring washers and release the pipe.

Six studs and nuts secure the manifolds to the cylinder head.

The four centre nuts have large washers, enabling them to secure both the inlet and exhaust manifolds. The two remaining nuts, one at each end of the manifolds, have small washers and secure the exhaust manifold only.

Replacements of the manifolds is a reversal of these instructions.

Use a new gasket.

Section A.5

ROCKER ASSEMBLY

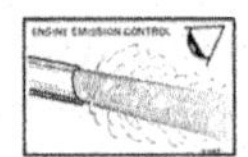

Drain the cooling system—Section C.4.

Disconnect the breather pipe from the rocker cover, on 18GD and 18GF engines, unscrew the nuts securing the heater pipe to the rocker studs and move the pipe clear of the rocker cover.

Release the breather pipe from the front of the rocker cover.

Withdraw the throttle cable from the lever and outer cable abutment. Unscrew the two nuts and lift off the rocker cover, taking care not to damage the cork gasket or lose the washers and rubber seals. Notice that under the right-hand rear rocker stud nut is a special locking plate. Unscrew the eight rocker shaft bracket fixing nuts gradually, a turn at a time, in the order shown in Fig. A.2 until all load has been released.

It is necessary to drain the radiator and slacken the seven external cylinder head securing nuts because four of the rocker shaft bracket fixing nuts also secure the cylinder head, and if the seven external cylinder head fixing nuts are not slackened distortion may result and water find its way from the cooling system into the cylinders and sump.

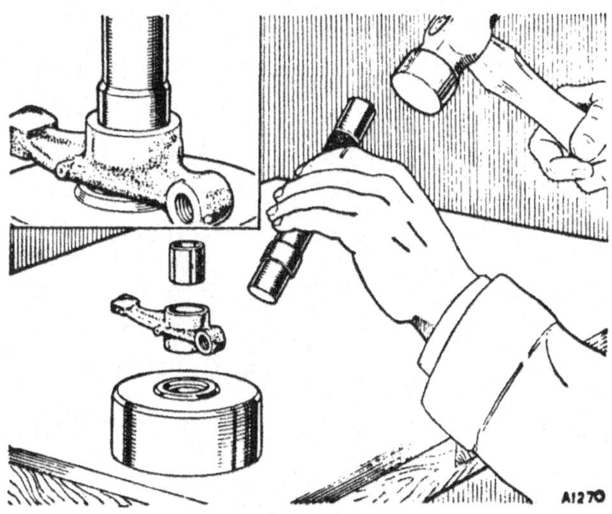

Fig. A.1
Fitting a valve rocker bush, using Service tool 18G 226

Completely unscrew the eight rocker shaft bracket nuts and remove the rocker assembly, complete with brackets and rockers. Withdraw the eight push-rods, storing them carefully so that they may be replaced in the same positions. To dismantle the rocker shaft assembly, first remove the grub screw which locates the rocker shaft in the rear rocker mounting bracket and remove the split pins, flat washers, and spring washers from each end of the shaft. Slide the rockers, brackets, and springs from the shaft.

Unscrew the plug from the front end of the shaft and clean out the oilways.

Reassembly and replacement is a reversal of the above procedure replacing the rockers and springs in their original positions on the shaft. Remember to replace the rocker shaft locating screw lock plate. Replace the rocker cover with the vent pipe to the front. Check that the two cap nut rubber bushes and the rocker cover cork gasket are undamaged; if they are found to be faulty, fit new ones or oil leaks may result.

Refitting rocker bushes

To remove and replace worn rocker bushes the use of Service tool 18G 226 is recommended; the bushes and the rockers can be very easily damaged by using improvised drifts. Place the rocker on the anvil and drive out the worn bush.

Place a new bush on the driver and position the bush with the butt joint at the top of the rocker bore and the oil groove in the bush at the bottom of the rocker bore, as shown in Fig. A.3

It will be necessary to drill the oil holes in the bush to coincide with the oilways in the rocker. The oil hole to the adjuster end can be drilled before the bush is fitted, extra care being taken to keep the holes of the bush and rocker in line during the pressing-in operation.

If the holes are drilled after fitting, the following procedure must be adopted. Remove the adjuster screw and use a .093 in. (2.36 mm.) drill to drill out the end plug and to continue the oilway through the bush. Replug the end after this operation with a rivet (Part No. 5C 2436) and weld the plug into position. The oil hole in the top of the rocker barrel must be continued through the bush with a No 47 drill, .0785 in. (1.98 mm.).

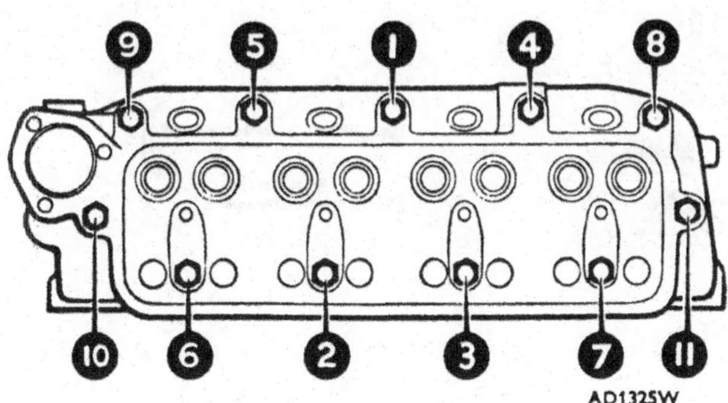

Fig. A.2
Cylinder head nut slackening and tightening sequence

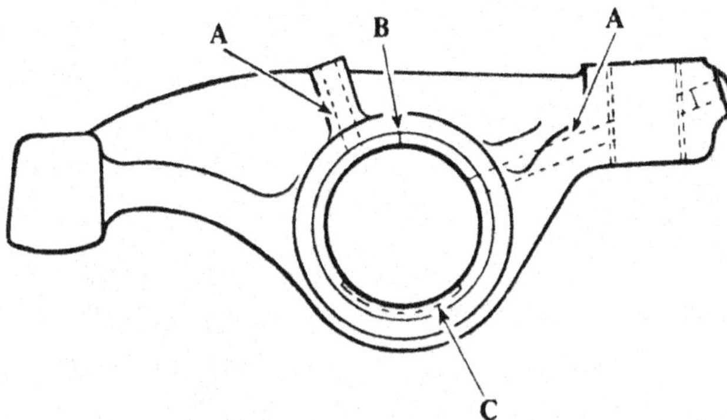

Fig. A.3
Showing the correct position for a valve rocker bush
A. Oilways. B. Joint in rocker bush C. Oil groove.

Finally, burnish-ream the bush to the dimensions given in the **'GENERAL DATA'** section.

Section A.6

CYLINDER HEAD ASSEMBLY

Drain the water from the cooling system. One drain tap is at the base of the radiator on the left-hand side and at the rear of the engine on the right-hand side. On later 18GD and 18GG engines the cylinder block drain tap is replaced by a removable plug and sealing washer. If anti-freeze mixture is being used it should be drained into a suitable clean container and carefully preserved for future use.

Remove the top water hose. Remove the three thermostat housing securing nuts and washers and remove the housing and thermostat.

Remove the air cleaners and carburetters as detailed in Section D.

Remove the inlet and exhaust manifolds as detailed in Section A.4.

Remove the rocker assembly as detailed in Section A.5 and remove the seven external cylinder head nuts at the same time. Withdraw the push-rods, keeping them in the order of their removal.

Disconnect the high-tension cables and remove the sparking plugs. Disconnect the heater hose and heater control cable from the water valve.

Unscrew the thermal transmitter from the front of the cylinder head and release the conductor from its supporting clip.

Slacken the clips and disconnect the hoses from the water pipe on the left-hand side of the cylinder head and remove the pipe. Release the ignition vacuum control pipe from the rear cylinder head stud and remove the cylinder head.

Break the cylinder head joint by levering at one end and withdraw the head evenly up the studs.

THE CYLINDER HEAD COMPONENTS

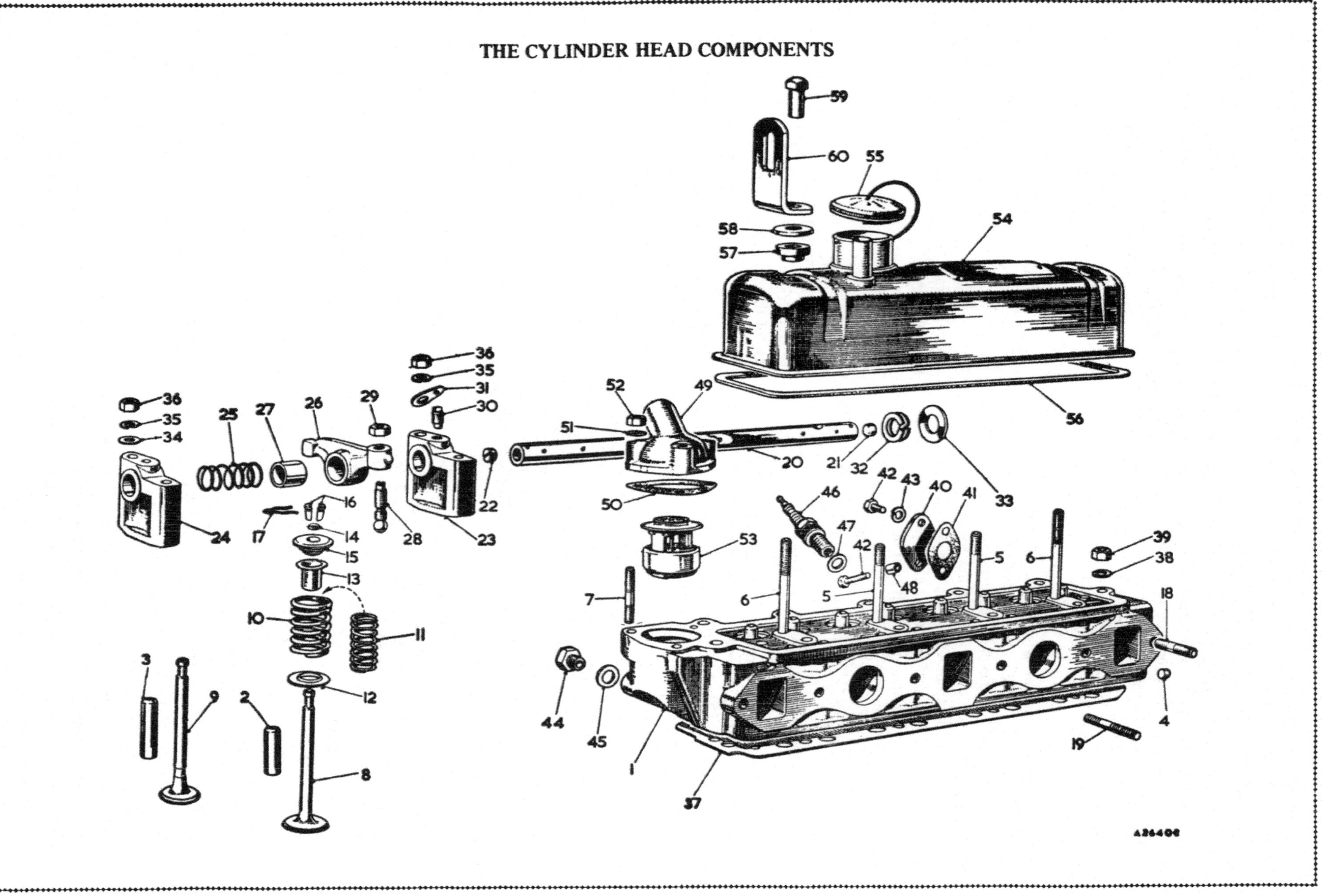

KEY TO THE CYLINDER HEAD COMPONENTS

No.	Description	No.	Description	No.	Description
1.	Cylinder head assembly–with guides.	21.	Plug–plain–valve rocker.	41.	Joint washer blanking plate.
2.	Guide–inlet valve.	22.	Plug–screwed–valve rocker.	42.	Screw–plate to cylinder head.
3.	Guide–exhaust valve.	23.	Bracket–tapped–rocker shaft.	43.	Washer–spring–screw.
4.	Plug–oil hole.	24.	Bracket–plain–rocker shaft.	44.	Plug–thermal transmitter boss.
5.	Stud–short–rocker–bracket.	25.	Spring–rocker spacing.	45.	Washer–plug.
6.	Stud–long–rocker–bracket.	26.	Rocker–valve–bushed.	46.	Plug–sparking.
7.	Stud–water outlet elbow to head.	27.	Bush–valve rocker.	47.	Gasket–steel–plug.
8.	Valve–inlet.	28.	Screw–adjusting–tappet.	48.	Distance piece–screw longer.
9.	Valve–exhaust.	29.	Nut–tappet adjusting screw.	49.	Elbow–outlet–water.
10.	Spring–outer–valve.	30.	Screw–locating–rocker shaft.	50.	Joint washer–elbow.
11.	Spring–inner–valve.	31.	Plate–lock–locating screw.	51.	Washer–plain–stud in cylinder head.
12.	Collar–valve spring.	32.	Washer–double-coil rocker shaft.	52.	Nut–stud.
13.	Shroud–valve guide (up to Engine No. H4385 and L2815).	33.	Washer–rocker shaft.	53.	Thermostat.
14.	Ring–valve packing.	34.	Washer–plain–rocker shaft stud.	54.	Cover–valve rocker.
15.	Cup–valve spring.	35.	Washer–spring–rocker shaft stud.	55.	Cap and cable–oil filler.
16.	Cotter–valve (halves).	36.	Nut–rocker bracket stud.	56.	Joint washer–valve rocker cover.
17.	Circlip–valve cotter.	37.	Joint washer–cylinder head.	57.	Bush–rubber–cover.
18.	Stud–exhaust manifold to head.	38.	Washer–cylinder head nut.	58.	Washer–cup.
19.	Stud–inlet and exhaust manifold to head.	39.	Nut–cylinder head stud.	59.	Nut–cap–rocker cover.
20.	Shaft–valve rocker–plugged.	40.	Plate–blanking–heater outlet elbow.	60.	Bracket–engine sling.

Refitting the cylinder head

Make sure that the surfaces of both the cylinder head and the cylinder block are clean. It will be noticed that the cylinder head gasket is marked 'FRONT' and 'TOP' to assist in replacing it correctly with the copper side uppermost. Having slipped the gasket over the studs, next lower the cylinder head into position. Replace the vacuum control pipe clip and fit the seven cylinder head external nuts finger tight.

Replace the push-rods in the positions from which they were taken. Replace the rocker assembly and securing nuts finger tight. Tighten the 11 cylinder head nuts, a turn at a time, in the order given in Fig. A.2. Finally, tighten the four rocker assembly nuts.

Reassembly continues in the reverse order to the dismantling procedure.

Switch on the ignition and check the fuel system for leaks. Start the engine and run it until the normal working temperature is reached. Remove the rocker cover and check the valve clearances (see Section A.7). Replace the rocker cover and connect the breather hose.

Section A.7

VALVE GEAR AND VALVES

Removing and replacing valves

Remove the cylinder head as in Section A.6.

Remove the valve circlip. Compress the double valve springs, using Service tool 18G45, and remove the two valve cotters. Release the valve springs and remove the compressor, valve spring cap, shroud (early engines only), inner and outer springs, and bottom collar.

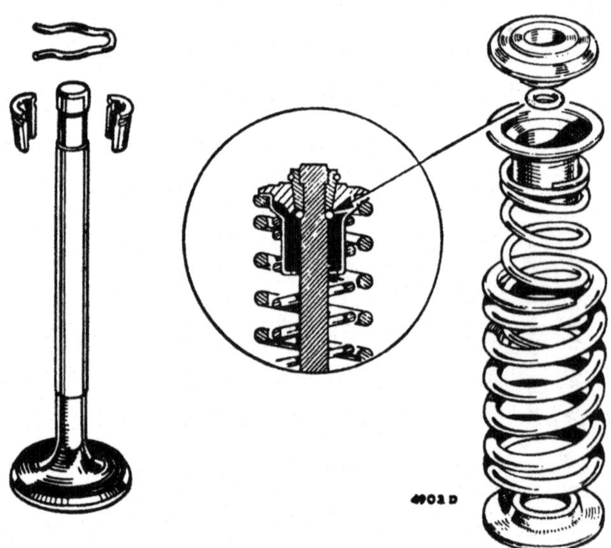

Fig. A.4
Parts of the valve assembly, showing the valve, cotters, circlip, bottom collar, double valve springs, shroud (early engines only), packing ring, and spring cap. The inset shows the valve packing ring fitted correctly at the bottom of the cotter groove below the cotters

Fig. A.5
Grinding in a valve, using Service tool 18G29. Occasionally lift the valve off its seat to spread the grinding paste evenly over the seat and valve face

Remove the valve packing ring from the cotter groove and withdraw the valve from the guide.

Keep the valves in their relative positions when removed from the head to ensure replacement in their original valve guides. The exhaust valve heads are concave and are smaller in diameter than the inlet valves.

To replace the valves place each valve into its guide and fit the bottom collars, inner and outer valve springs, shrouds (early engines only), and caps. Compress the valve springs and push a new synthetic rubber packing ring over the tip of the valve stem down to the bottom of the cotter groove (see Fig. A.4). Refit the two valve cotters and remove the compressor. Replace the valve circlip.

NOTE.—Do not fit old valve packing rings, or oil sealing may suffer. The rings are fitted more easily if they have been soaked in clean engine oil for a short period before use.

Removing and replacing valve guides

Rest the cylinder head with its machined face downwards on a clean surface and drive the valve guide downwards into the combustion space with a suitable-sized drift. This should take the form of a hardened steel punch $\frac{9}{16}$ in. (14 mm.) in diameter and not less than 4 in. (10 cm.) in length, with a locating spigot $\frac{5}{16}$ in. (7.9 mm.) diameter machined on one end for a length of 1 in. (2.5 cm.) to engage the bore of the guide.

When fitting new valve guides these should be driven in from the top of the cylinder head. The valve guides must be inserted with the end having the largest chamfer at the top. The valve guides should be driven into the combustion spaces until they are the required height above the machined surface of the valve spring seating (see Fig. A.6 and '**GENERAL DATA**').

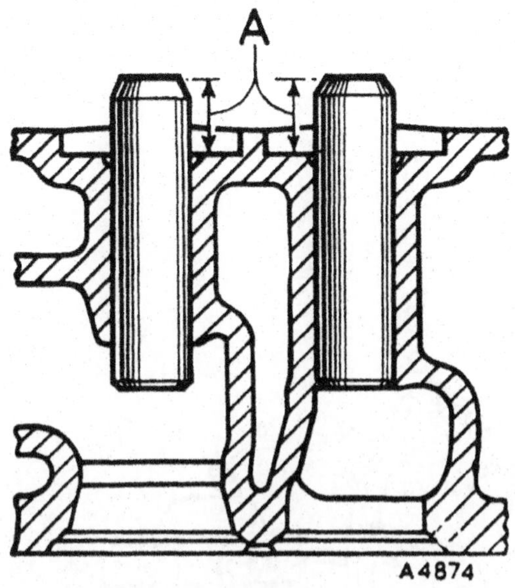

Fig. A.6
When fitting valve guides they must be driven in until they are the required height above the machined surface of the valve spring seating (A)

Grinding and testing valves and seatings

Each valve must be cleaned thoroughly and carefully examined for pitting. Valves in a pitted condition should be refaced with a suitable grinder or new valves should be fitted.

Pitted or uneven valve seats must be refaced using a grinder or cutter, care being taken that only the minimum quantity of metal necessary to restore the seat is removed. If the seats are very worn or damaged refer to Section A.28.

When grinding a valve onto its seating the valve face should be smeared lightly with fine- or medium-grade carborundum paste and then lapped in with a suction grinder (Service tool 18G 29). Avoid the use of excessive quantities of grinding paste and see that it remains in the region of the valve seating only.

Fig. A.7
Pitted valve seats should be re-faced, using Service tools, 18G 25, 18G 25 A, 18G 174 B, 18G 25 C, 18G 27, 18G 28, 18G 28 A, 18G 28 B, 18G 28 C, and 18G 174 D

A light coil spring placed under the valve head will assist considerably in the process of grinding. The valve should be ground to its seat with a semi-rotary motion and occasionally allowed to rise by the pressure of the light coil spring. This assists in spreading the paste evenly over the valve face and seat. It is necessary to carry out the grinding operation until a dull, even, mat surface, free from blemish, is produced on the valve seat and valve face.

On completion, the valve seat and ports should be cleaned thoroughly with a rag soaked in paraffin (kerosene), dried, and then thoroughly cleaned by compressed air. The valves should be washed in paraffin (kerosene) and all traces of grinding paste removed.

Fit a new valve packing ring when refitting the valves (see Fig. A.4).

Checking valve timing

Set No. 1 cylinder inlet valve to .055 in. (1.4 mm.) clearance with the engine cold, and then turn the engine until the valve is about to open.

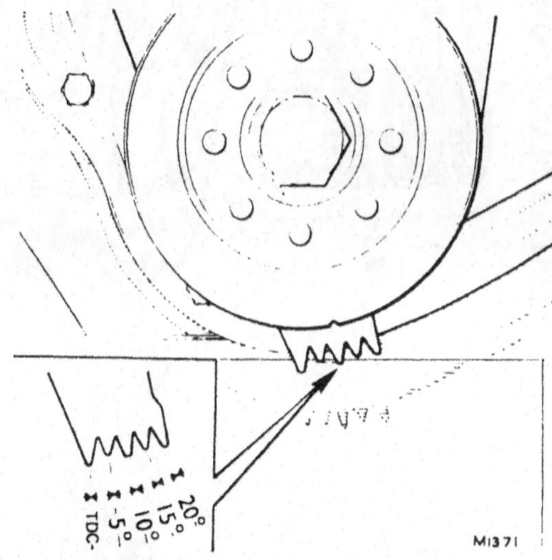

Fig. A.8
The notch in the pulley approaching the T.D.C. position for pistons 1 and 4. The inset shows the timing scale 5° marks

The indicating notch in the flange of the crankshaft pulley should then be opposite the longest of the three pointers on the timing cover, i.e. the valve should be about to open at T.D.C. and No. 4 piston will be at T.D.C. on its compression stroke.

Do not omit to reset the inlet valve clearance to the recommended clearance (see 'GENERAL DATA') when the timing check has been completed. The clearance of .055 in. (1.4 mm.) is necessary to bring the opening position of the valve to T D.C. It is not possible to check the valve timing accurately with the normal running valve clearance.

Adjusting valve rocker clearances

If the engine is to give its best performance and the valves are to retain their maximum useful life it is essential to

THE CYLINDER BLOCK COMPONENTS

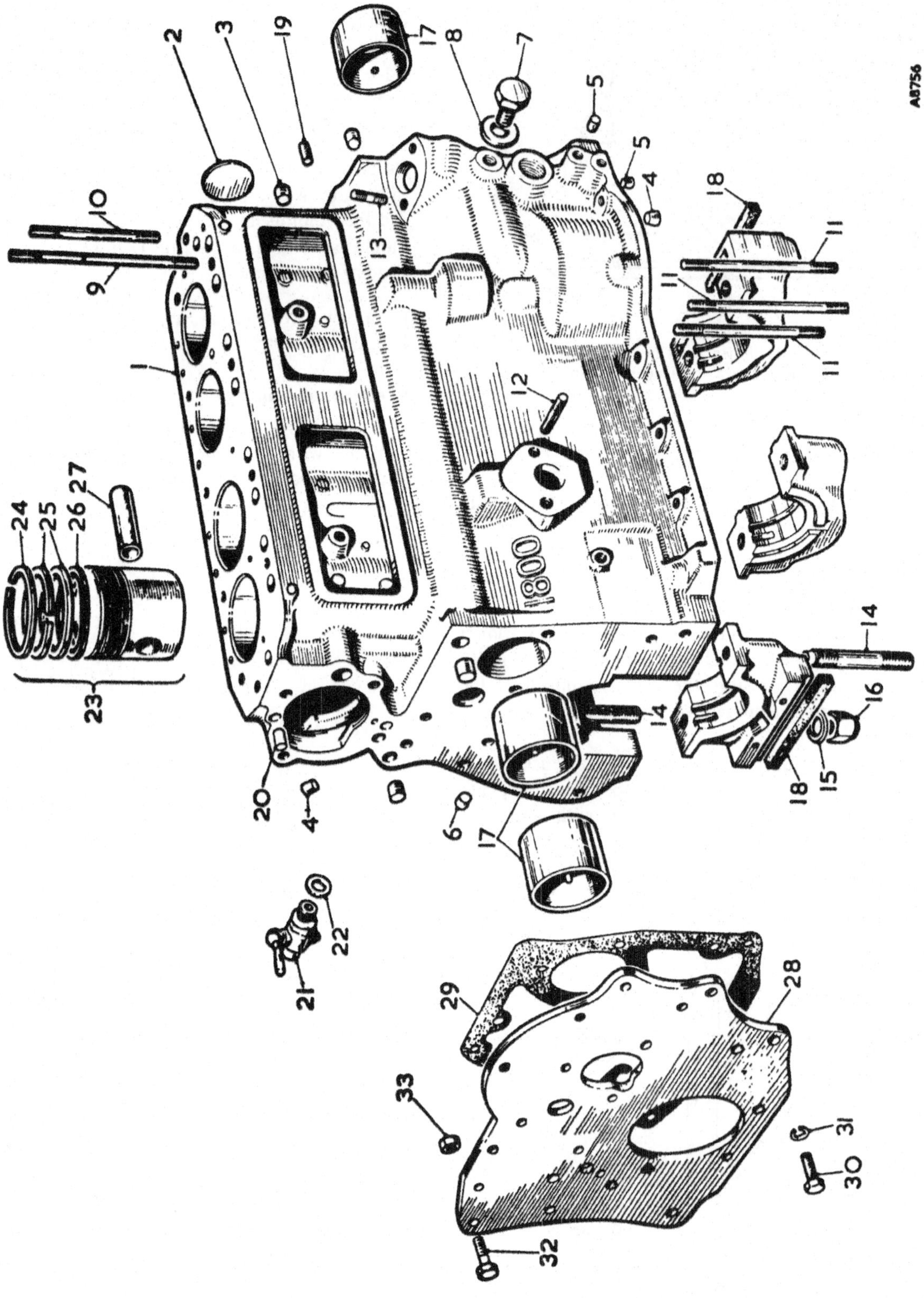

KEY TO THE CYLINDER BLOCK COMPONENTS

No.	Description	No.	Description	No.	Description
1.	Cylinder block assembly.	12.	Stud–crankcase vent pipe clip.	23.	Piston assembly–standard H.C.
2.	Plug–welch–large.	13.	Stud–tachometer spindle housing.	24.	Ring–compression–top–standard.
3.	Plug–crankcase oil gallery.	14.	Stud–main bearing cap.	25.	Rings–compression–2nd and 3rd–standard.
4.	Plug–taper–crankcase oil hole.	15.	Washer–plain–main bearing stud.	26.	Ring–scraper–standard.
5.	Plug–oil relief valve vent hole.	16.	Nut–main bearing stud.	27.	Pin–gudgeon.
6.	Plug–chain tensioner oil feed.	17.	Liner–camshaft bearing.	28.	Plate–engine mounting.
7.	Plug–oil hole–screwed.	18.	Joint–front and rear main bearing cap.	29.	Joint–washer–mounting plate.
8.	Washer–screwed plug.	19.	Dowel–gearbox mounting plate.	30.	Screw–mounting plate to crankcase.
9.	Stud–cylinder head–long.	20.	Dowel–water pump.	31.	Washer–spring–screw.
10.	Stud–cylinder head–short.	21.	Tap–drain–cylinder block.	32.	Bolt–engine mounting bracket to front plate. R.H. top.
11.	Stud–oil pump–short.	22.	Washer–drain tap.	33.	Nut–bolt.

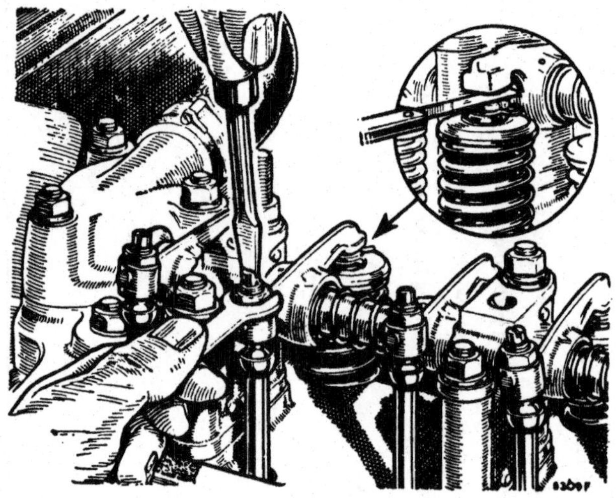

Fig. A.9
The method of adjusting the valve rocker clearance and the correct position for measuring it

maintain the correct valve clearance. Accordingly it is recommended that the clearance be checked at regular intervals and any necessary adjustments made.

For the correct valve rocker clearance refer to **'GENERAL DATA'**. The engine has been designed to operate with this clearance and no departure from it is permissible.

Provision for adjusting the valve clearance is made in the rocker arm by an adjustable screw and locknut.

The rocker adjusting screw is released by slackening the hexagon locknut with a spanner while holding the screw against rotation with a screwdriver. The valve clearance can then be set by carefully rotating the rocker screw while checking the clearance with a feeler gauge. This screw is then re-locked by tightening the hexagon locknut while again holding the screw against rotation.

It is important to note that while the clearance is being set the tappet of the valve being operated upon is on the back of its cam, i.e. opposite to the peak.

As this cannot be observed accurately, the rocker adjustment is more easily carried out in the following order, and this also avoids turning the engine over more than is necessary:

Adjust No. 1 rocker with No. 8 valve fully open.
,, No. 3 ,, ,, No. 6 ,, ,, ,,
,, No. 5 ,, ,, No. 4 ,, ,, ,,
,, No. 2 ,, ,, No. 7 ,, ,, ,,
,, No. 8 ,, ,, No. 1 ,, ,, ,,
,, No. 6 ,, ,, No. 3 ,, ,, ,,
,, No. 4 ,, ,, No. 5 ,, ,, ,,
,, No. 7 ,, ,, No. 2 ,, ,, ,,

Section A.8

TAPPETS

Remove the carburetters (see Section D) and the rocker cover.

Remove the manifolds (see Section A.4).

Disconnect the high-tension leads from the sparking plugs.

Remove the rocker assembly as in Section A.5 and withdraw the push-rods, keeping them in their relative positions to ensure their replacement onto the same tappets. Release the breather pipe, remove the tappet covers, and lift out the tappets, also keeping them in their relative positions.

New tappets should be fitted by selective assembly so that they just fall into their guides under their own weight when lubricated.

Assembly is a reversal of the above procedure, but care should be taken to see that the tappet cover joints are oil-tight and that the rockers are adjusted to give the correct valve clearance.

Section A.9

DECARBONIZING

Remove the cylinder head as described in Section A.6.

Withdraw the valves as described in Section A.7.

Remove the cylinder head gasket and plug the waterways with a clean rag.

If special equipment is not available for decarbonizing it will be necessary to scrape the carbon deposit from the piston crowns, cylinder block, and cylinder head, using a blunt scraper.

A ring of carbon should be left round the periphery of the piston crown, and the rim of carbon round the top of the cylinder bore should not be touched. To facilitate this an old piston ring can be sprung into the bore so that it rests on top of the piston.

The cylinder head is next given attention. The sparking plugs must be cleaned and adjusted. Clean off the carbon deposit from the valve stems, valve ports, and combustion spaces of the cylinder head. Remove all traces of carbon dust with compressed air or by the vigorous use of a tyre pump and then thoroughly clean with paraffin (kerosene) and dry off.

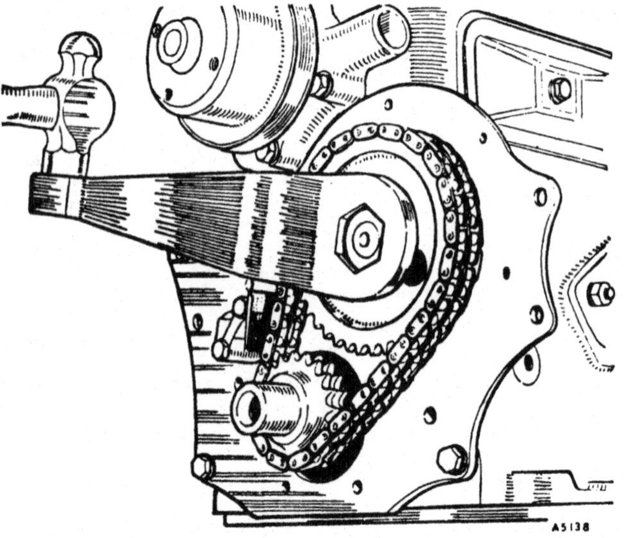

Fig. A.10
Unscrew the camshaft chain wheel securing nut with spanner 18G 98A

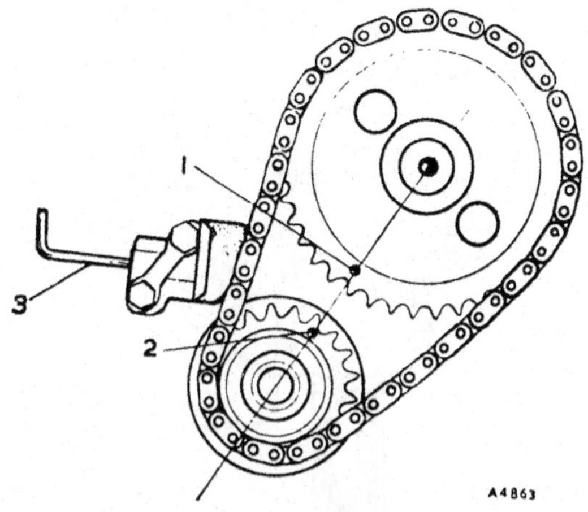

Fig. A.11
Crank the engine until the timing dimples (1) and (2) are opposite each other before removing the timing chain and chain wheels. The chain tensioner is retracted into the unloaded position by turning the Allen key (3) in a clockwise direction

Fit a new cylinder head gasket when replacing the head if the old has been damaged, noting that the gasket is marked to indicate the top face and the front end.

Section A.10

VALVE TIMING GEAR AND CHAIN TENSIONER

Timing cnain cover

Drain the cooling system and remove the radiator–Section C.7.

Slacken the dynamo or alternator securing bolts and remove the fan belt.

On 18GB and later engines, remove the bolts securing the steering-rack to the body and ease the rack assembly forward sufficiently to allow the crankshaft pulley to be withdrawn.

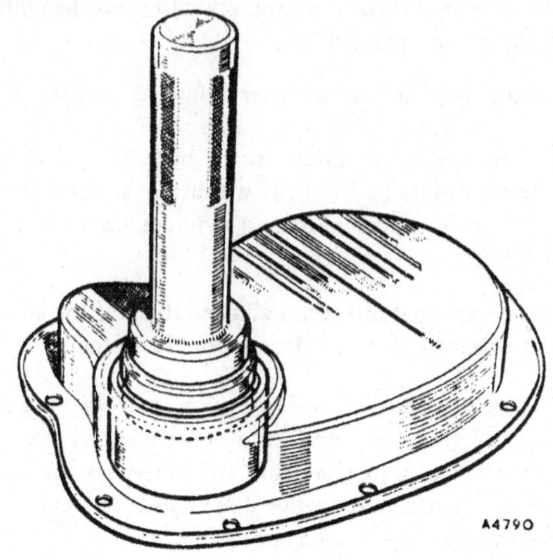

Fig. A.12
Replacing the oil seal in the crankcase front cover using Service tool 18G 134 and adaptor 18G 134 BD

Unlock the crankshaft pulley retaining bolt, unscrew the bolt using tool 18G 98 A and withdraw the pulley.

Unscrew the timing cover retaining bolts and remove the cover. Use a new gasket when refitting the timing cover.

The felt washer or oil seal (later cars) in the timing cover should also be renewed if necessary.

Ensure that the oil thrower behind the crankshaft pulley is fitted with the face marked 'F' away from the engine.

Replacement of the timing cover is a reversal of the above procedure.

When refitting the cover it is important to ensure that the seal, rubber or felt, is centralized on the crankshaft, and a Service tool (18G 1046) is available for the purpose.

NOTE.–The early type front cover and oil thrower mst be used together. When refitting, ensure that the oil thrower is fitted with its concave side facing away from the engine. Use Service tool 18G 3 to centralize the rubber seal on the crankshaft, or use the crankshaft pulley as follows:

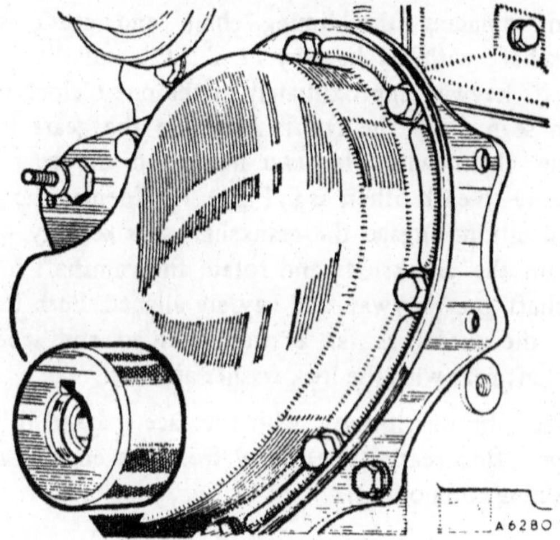

Fig. A.13
Install the securing screws finger tight and centralize the crankcase front cover with the crankshaft, using Service tool 18G 1046

If a rubber seal is fitted fill the annular groove between the lips with grease. Lubricate the hub of the pulley and push it into the seal, at the same time turning it to avoid damaging the felt or the lips of a rubber seal. Slide the pulley onto the shaft with the keyway in line with the key in the crankshaft. Turn the cover as necessary to align the set screw holes with those in the crankcase, taking care not to strain the cover against the flexibility of the seal.

Insert the set screws and tighten up.

Refit and tighten the pulley securing screw.

Timing chain

Remove the bottom plug from the chain tensioner, insert a ⅛ in. (3.18 mm.) Allen key in the cylinder, and turn the key clockwise until the rubber slipper head is fully retracted and locked behind the limit peg.

Unscrew and remove the two securing screws and then remove the tensioner and its backplate.

Unlock and remove the camshaft chain wheel nut and remove the nut and lock washer. Note that the locating tag on the lock washer fits into the keyway of the camshaft chain wheel.

The camshaft and crankshaft chain wheels may now be removed, together with the timing chain, by easing each wheel forward, a fraction at a time, with suitable smaller levers.

As the crankshaft gear wheel is withdrawn care must be taken not to lose the gear packing washers immediately behind it. When reassembling replace the same number of washers as was found when dismantling, unless new camshaft or crankshaft components have been fitted which will disturb the alignments of the two gear wheels. To determine the thickness of washers required place a straight edge across the sides of the camshaft wheel teeth and measure with a feeler gauge the gap between the straight-edge and the crankshaft gear. Subtract .005 in. (·13 mm.) from the feeler gauge reading and add the resultant thickness of crankshaft gear packing washers.

When replacing the timing chain and gears, set the crankshaft with its keyway at T.D.C., and the camshaft with its keyway approximately at the one o'clock position when seen from the front. Assemble the gears into the timing chain with the two marks on the gear wheels opposite to each other, as in Fig. A.11. Keeping the gears in this position, engage the crankshaft gear keyway with the key on the crankshaft and rotate the camshaft until the camshaft gear keyway and key are aligned. Push the gears onto the shafts as far as they will go and secure the camshaft gear with the lock washer and nut.

Replace the oil thrower, with the face marked 'F' or the concave side (early-type) away from the engine, and the remaining components.

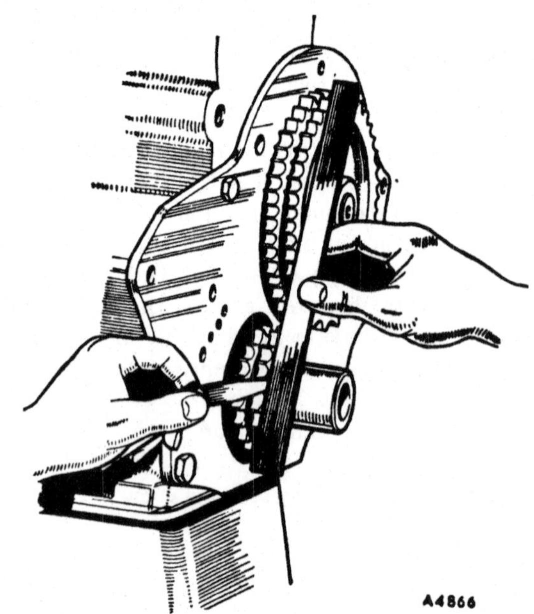

Fig. A.4
Checking the chain wheel alignment with a straight-edge and feeler gauge

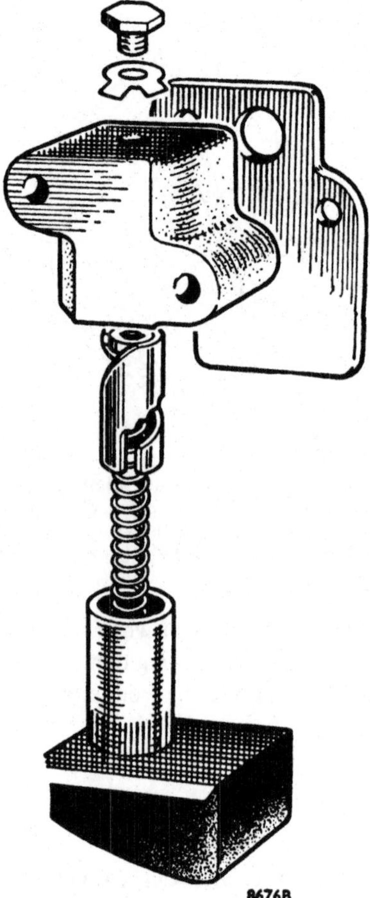

Fig. A.15
The chain tensioner components

Timing chain tensioner
Remove the tensioner assembly from the block as described above.

Withdraw the plunger and slipper assembly from the tensioner body and engage the lower end of the cylinder with the Allen key. Turn the key clockwise, holding the key and plunger securely until the cylinder and spring are released from inside the plunger.

Clean the components in petrol, and blow out the oil holes in the slipper and spigot.

Check the bore in the adjuster body for ovality. If the ovality is greater than .003 in. (.076 mm.) when measured on diameters near the mouth of the bore, then a complete new adjuster must be fitted. If within the acceptable limit, then fit a new slipper head and cylinder assembly in the existing body.

It is important that dirt is not allowed to enter the adjuster, so ensure that all parts are clean before reassembly.

When the tensioner is in operation and the engine is running, oil from the lubrication system enters the spigot on the back face under pressure and lubricates the bearing surface through a hole in the slipper pad. The pad is held against the chain by the coil spring.

Should the chain stretch with use, the slipper plunger rises and the limiting peg, bearing on the top of the helical slot, rotates the cylinder until the next recess in the lower edge of the slot comes into line with the limiting peg and prevents the plunger returning to its original position and allowing the timing chain to become slack again.

When reassembling, insert the spring in the plunger and place the cylinder on the other end of the spring.

Compress the spring until the cylinder enters the plunger bore, engaging the helical slot with the peg in the plunger. Hold the assembly compressed in this position and engage the Allen key. Turn the cylinder clockwise until the end of the cylinder is below the peg and the spring is held compressed. Withdraw the key and insert the plunger assembly in the body. Replace the backplate and secure the assembly to the cylinder block.

After refitting the tensioner, check the slipper head for freedom of movement and ensure that it does not bind on the backplate when it is moved in the body.

When the timing chain is in position the tensioner is released for operation by inserting the key and turning it clockwise until the slipper head moves forward under spring pressure against the chain.

Do not attempt to turn the key anti-clockwise or force the slipper head into the chain by external pressure.

Secure the bolts with the locking plate, replace the bottom plug, and lock with a tab washer.

Section A.11

SUMP AND STRAINER

Drain the radiator and disconnect the hoses, drain the sump, and then release the engine front mounting bolts. Sling the engine and lift it sufficiently to gain access to the front sump bolts.

Remove all the bolts and withdraw the sump from the crankcase.

To remove the oil strainer remove the two bolts securing it to the pump cover.

The strainer may be dismantled for cleaning by removing the centre-nut and bolt and the two delivery pipe flange bolts. Note that there is a locating tongue on the side of the cover which must be positioned correctly when replacing. Remember also to replace the distance tube.

Clean out the sump and strainer with paraffin (kerosene) and a stiff brush; never use rag.

When refitting the sump to the engine give particular attention to the sealing gaskets for the crankcase face and the two oil seal packings for the crankcase which fit into recesses in the crankcase.

If the gaskets are in good condition and have not been damaged during removal of the sump they may be used again, but it is always advisable to fit new ones. Before fitting new gaskets remove all traces of the old ones from the sump and crankcase faces. Smear the faces of the crankcase joint with grease and fit the two halves of the large gasket. Lift the sump into position on the crankcase, insert the 19 bolts, and tighten them evenly.

Refit the engine to its mountings and the hoses to the radiator. Refill the radiator and the sump with coolant and fresh oil respectively.

Section A.12

OIL PUMP

Two bolts secure the oil pump cover and three studs secure the pump to the crankcase. Unscrew the stud nuts and remove the pump and drive shaft.

When refitting the pump use a new joint washer.

Unscrew the two securing screws and carefully withdraw the cover, which is located on the base of the oil pump body by two dowels.

Withdraw the outer rotor, and the inner rotor complete with oil pump shaft, from the pump body.

Thoroughly clean all parts in paraffin (kerosene) and inspect them for wear. The rotor end-float and lobe clearances should be checked as follows:

1. Install the rotors in the pump body, place a straight-edge across the joint face of the pump body, and measure the clearance between the top face of the rotors and the under side of the straight-edge. The clearance should not exceed .005 in. (.127 mm.). In cases where the clearance is excessive this may be remedied by removing the two cover locating dowels and carefully lapping the joint face of the pump body.
2. Check the diametrical clearance between the outer rotor and the rotor pocket in the pump body. If this exceeds .010 in. (.254 mm.) and cannot be remedied by the renewal of either the pump body or the rotors, then the pump assembly should be renewed.
3. With the rotors installed in the pump body measure the clearance between the rotor lobes when they are in the positions shown in Fig. A.17. If the clearance is in excess of .006 in. (.152 mm.) the rotors must be renewed.

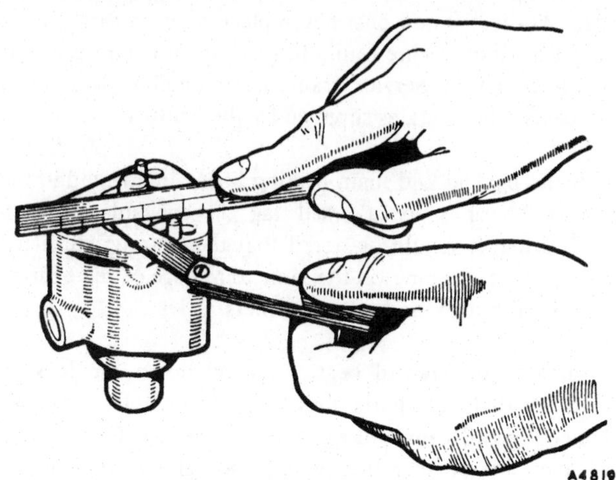

Fig. A.16
Checking the oil pump rotor end-float, which should not exceed .005 in. (.127 mm.)

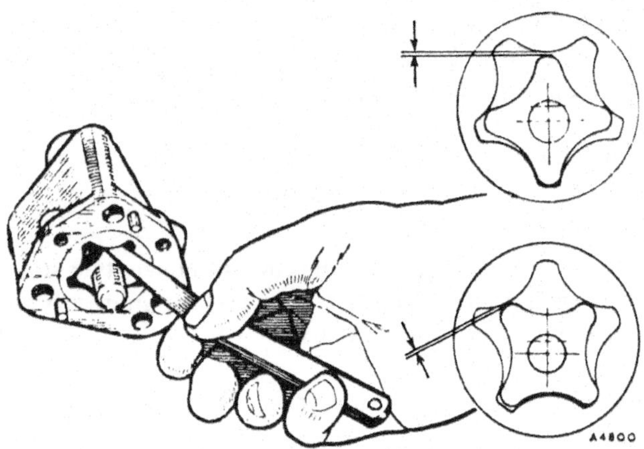

Fig. A.17
The lobe clearance should not exceed .006 in. (.152 mm.) when the oil pump rotors are in the positions illustrated

Reassembly is a reversal of the dismantling procedure noting the following points:

1. Lubricate all parts with clean engine oil.
2. Ensure that the outer rotor is installed in the pump body with its chamfered end at the driving end of the rotor pocket in the pump body.
3. After reassembling check the pump for freedom of action.

Section A.13

MAIN AND BIG-END BEARINGS

Unless the bearing journals are badly worn the big-end bearings may be renewed without removing the crankshaft. To renew the main bearings it is necessary to withdraw the crankshaft. Liners are used for both the main and the big-end bearings, which are of the shimless type and therefore non-adjustable.

Big-end bearings

Drain the engine oil and remove the sump as in Section A.11.

As the bearings are of the shimless type it is essential that no attempt should be made to adjust bearings which are worn. Always fit new bearings in place of worn parts. If the crankshaft journals are found to be in a worn condition it is advisable to fit a Service crankshaft, complete with main and big-end bearings, as supplied by the Factory.

Both the big-end and main bearing liners are located in the bearing housings by a small tag on one side of each half-bearing; it should be noted that the bearings are fitted so that the tags come on the same joint edge of the bearing housing, although on opposite corners.

To detach the big-end bearings, bend down the locking strips so that the bolts may be removed. Remove the connecting rod caps and extract the bearings. Care should be taken to see that the bearing journals are thoroughly cleaned before installing new bearings. No scraping is required, as the bearings are machined to give the correct diametrical clearance of .0016 in. (.04 mm.).

Main bearings

Remove the engine from the car and remove the flywheel and clutch, the timing chain (Section A.10), the sump and strainer (Section A.11) and the rear engine mounting plate.

Note that a thrust washer is fitted on each side of the centre main bearing to take the crankshaft end-thrust. These thrust washers each consist of two semi-circular halves, one having a lug which is located in a recess in the detachable half of the bearing and the other being plain.

Before refitting the crankshaft check the end-float (see '**GENERAL DATA**') and select and fit new upper and lower thrust washers as required. The washers are available in standard thickness and .003 in. (.076 mm.) oversize.

Remove the two bolts and locking plate securing the front main bearing cap to the engine front bearer plate.

Remove the main bearing cap retaining nuts and locking plates (early engines) or the self-locking nuts and plain washers (later engines).

When fitting new bearings no scraping is required as the bearings are machined to give the correct diametrical clearance of .001 to .0027 in. (.025 to .067 mm.).

In the case of a 'run' bearing it is always essential to clean out thoroughly all the oilways in the crankshaft and block, wash out the engine sump with paraffin (kerosene), and clean the oil pump and sump strainer to ensure that no particles of metal are left anywhere in the lubricating system. The rear main bearing cap horizontal joint surfaces should be thoroughly cleaned and lightly covered with Hylomar Jointing Compound before the cap is fitted to the cylinder block. This will ensure a perfect oil seal when the cap is bolted down to the block. Refit each main bearing and cap, refitting the thrust washers in their correct positions at the centre main bearing with the oil grooves away from the bearing.

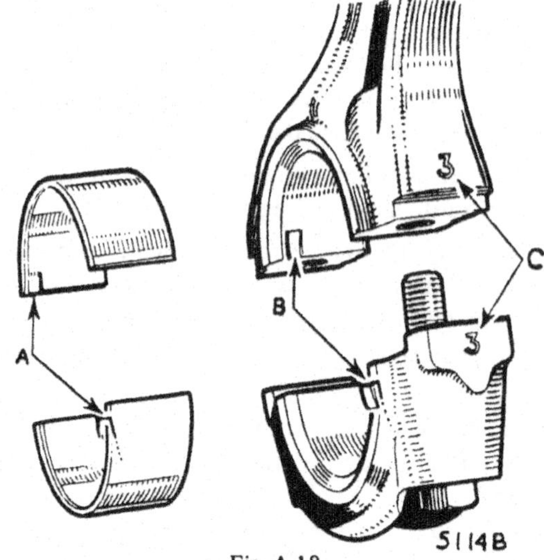

Fig. A.18
The connecting rod big-end bearing locating tags (A) and grooves (B). The figures (C) indicate the cylinder from which the rod and cap were removed

Lubricate the main bearing cap joint seal liberally with oil before refitting. When refitting the bearing caps on early engines use a new locking plate to lock the nuts; on later engines check that the self-locking nuts lock to the stud threads efficiently. Tighten the bearing cap nuts to the torque figure given in **'GENERAL DATA'**.

Section A.14

PISTONS AND CONNECTING RODS

Remove the cylinder head as in Section A.6. Drain and remove the sump and oil strainer as in Section A.11.

The pistons and connecting rods must be withdrawn from the top of the cylinder block.

Unlock and remove the big-end bolts and remove the bearing caps. Release the connecting rod from the crankshaft.

Withdraw the piston and connecting rod from the top of the cylinder block and refit the bearing cap. The big-end bearing caps are offset. When used parts are replaced after dismantling it is essential that they should be fitted in their original positions. In order to ensure this, mark the caps and connecting rods on their sides which are fitted together with the number of the cylinder from which each was taken.

Replacement of the piston and connecting rod is a direct reversal of the above, but the piston ring gaps should be set at 90° to each other.

It is essential that the connecting rod and piston assemblies should be replaced in their own bores and fitted the same way round, i.e. with the gudgeon pin clamp screw on the camshaft side of the engine. The piston crowns are marked 'FRONT' to assist correct assembly to the connecting rods.

Refit the big-end bearings in their original positions.

Pistons and gudgeon pins (18G/18GA)
The gudgeon pin is rigidly held in the split little-end of the connecting rod by a clamp bolt engaging the central groove of the gudgeon pin.

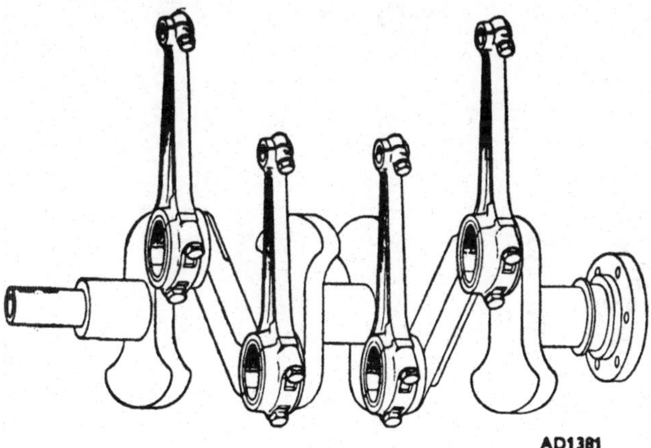

Fig. A.19
Assembly positions of the connecting rods, showing the offsets

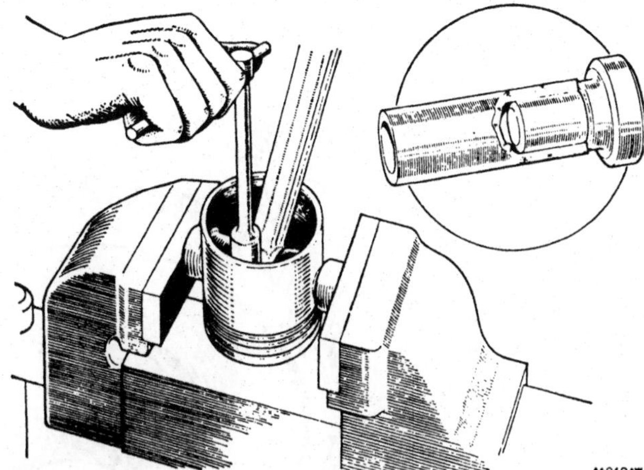

Fig. A.20
Method of loosening and tightening the gudgeon pin clamp bolts (18G/18GA)

Before the piston and gudgeon pin can be dismantled from the connecting rod it is necessary to remove the clamp screw. To enable the assembly to be held in a vice for this operation without damage holding plugs should be inserted in each end of the gudgeon pin.

Unscrew the gudgeon pin clamp and remove it completely.

Push out the gudgeon pin.

Reassembly is a reversal of the above.

IMPORTANT.–Attention must be given to the following points when assembling the piston to the connecting rod:

1. That the piston is fitted the correct way round on the connecting rod. The crown of the piston is marked 'FRONT' to assist this, and the connecting rod is fitted with the gudgeon pin clamp screw on the camshaft side.
2. That the gudgeon pin is positioned in the connecting rod so that its groove is in line with the clamp screw hole.
3. That the clamp screw spring washer has sufficient tension.
4. That the clamp screw will pass readily into its hole and screw freely into the threaded portion of the little-end, and also that it will hold firmly onto the spring washer.

A certain amount of selective assembly must be used when fitting new gudgeon pins. They must be a thumb-push fit for three-quarters of their travel, to be finally tapped in with a raw-hide mallet. This operation should be carried out with the piston and gudgeon pin cold.

Piston rings
If no special piston ring expander is available, use a piece of thin steel such as a smoothly ground hacksaw blade or a disused .020 in. (.50 mm.) feeler gauge.

Raise one end of the ring out of its groove. Insert the steel strip between the ring and the piston. Rotate the strip around the piston, applying slight upward pressure to the

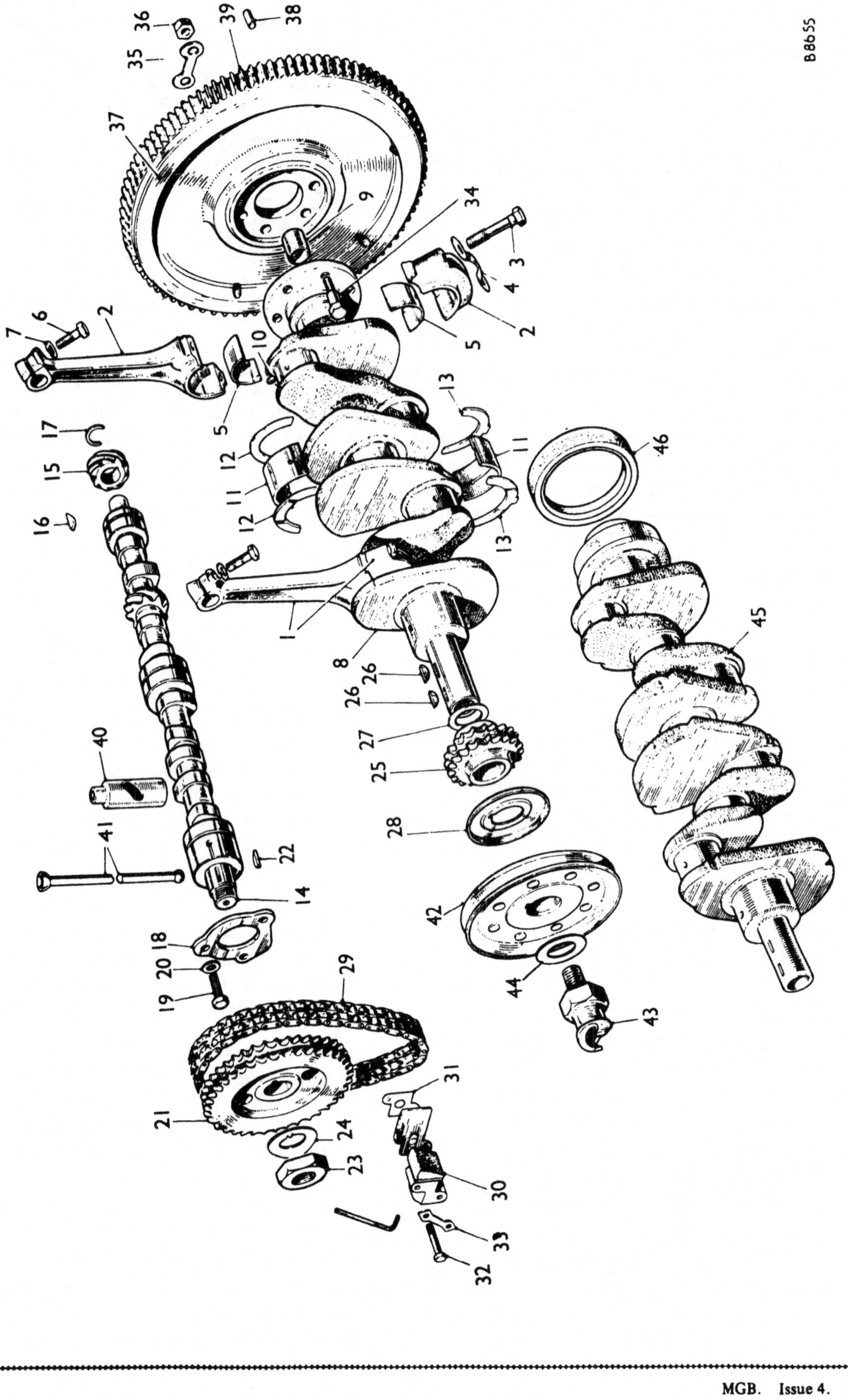

THE ENGINE INTERNAL COMPONENTS

B8655

KEY TO THE ENGINE INTERNAL COMPONENTS

No.	Description	No.	Description	No.	Description
1.	Connecting rod and cap–Nos. 1 and 3 cylinders.	17.	Ring–spring–tachometer gear.	32.	Screw–tensioner to crankcase.
2.	Connecting rod and cap–Nos. 2 and 4 cylinders.	18.	Plate–camshaft locating.	33.	Washer–lock–screw.
3.	Screw–cap.	19.	Screw–locating plate to crankcase.	34.	Bolt–flywheel to crankshaft.
4.	Washer–lock–screw.	20.	Washer–lock–screw.	35.	Washer–lock–bolt.
5.	Bearing–connecting rod–standard.	21.	Gear–camshaft.	36.	Nut–bolt.
6.	Screw–connecting rod clamping (18G/18GA).	22.	Key–camshaft gear.	37.	Flywheel.
7.	Washer–spring–screw (18G/18GA).	23.	Nut–camshaft gear.	38.	Dowel–clutch to flywheel.
8.	Crankshaft. (18G/18GA).	24.	Washer–lock-nut.	39.	Ring gear–starting.
9.	Bush–1st motion shaft.	25.	Gear–crankshaft.	40.	Tappet.
10.	Plug.	26.	Key–crankshaft gear and pulley.	41.	Push-rod.
11.	Bearing–main–standard.	27.	Washer–packing–crankshaft gear.	42.	Pulley–crankshaft.
12.	Washer–thrust–upper.	28.	Thrower–oil–front–crankshaft.	43.	Nut–starting.
13.	Washer–thrust–lower.	29.	Chain–timing.	44.	Washer–lock–starting nut.
14.	Camshaft.	30.	Tensioner–chain.	45.	Crankshaft (18GB).
15.	Gear–tachometer driving.	31.	Joint washer–tensioner.	46.	Oil seal (18GB).
16.	Key–tachometer gear.				

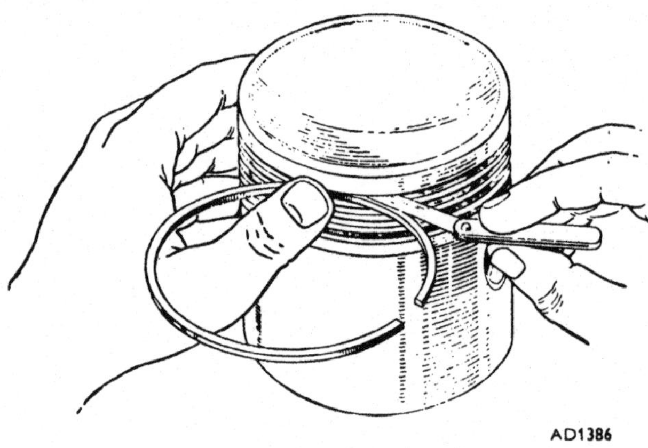

Fig. A.21
Checking the piston ring to groove clearance

raised portion of the ring until it rests on the land above the ring grooves. It can then be eased off the piston.

Do not remove or replace the rings over the piston skirt, but always over the top of the piston.

Before fitting new rings clean the grooves in the piston to remove any carbon deposit. Care must be taken not to remove any metal or sideplay between the ring and the groove will result, with consequent excessive oil consumption and loss of gas-tightness.

When refitting the rings note that the second and third compression rings are tapered and marked with the letter 'T' (top) for correct reassembly.

Examination

Thoroughly clean the bearing shells and the faces of the connecting rods and the bearing caps. Examine the shells for wear, pitting, or cracking, and renew them if necessary. New shells are finished with the correct diametrical clearances and do not require bedding in.

Blow the oil passages in the connecting rods with an air blast and ensure that they are free from obstruction.

Check the connecting rods for twist and bow as shown in Fig. A.22. Do not file the caps or rods.

Check the ring to groove clearance as shown in Fig. A.21.

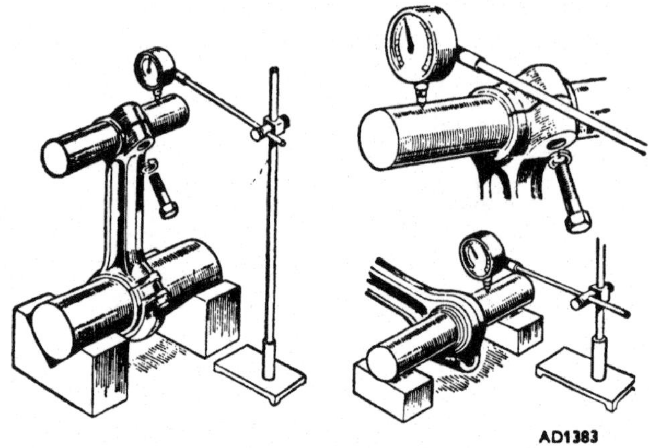

Fig. A.22
Checking the connecting rod alignment

New rings must be tested in the cylinder bore to ensure that the ends do not butt together. The best way to do this is to insert the piston approximately 1 in. (2.54 cm.) into the cylinder bore, push the ring down onto the top of the piston, and hold it there in order to keep it square with the bore. The correct ring gap is .008 to .013 in. (.20 to .33 mm.).

Section A.15

PISTON SIZES AND CYLINDER BORES

In addition to the standard pistons there is a range of oversize pistons available for service purposes.

Oversize pistons are marked with the actual oversize dimensions enclosed in an ellipse. A piston stamped .020 is only suitable for a bore .020 in. (.508 mm.) larger than the

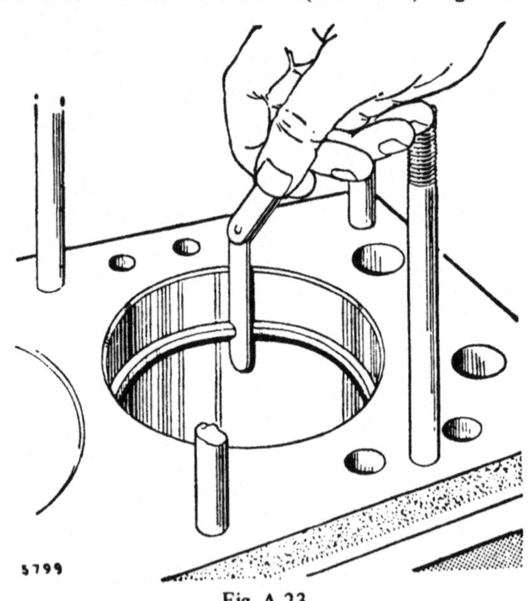

Fig. A.23
Checking a piston ring gap

standard bore; similarly, pistons with other markings are only suitable for the oversize bore indicated.

The piston markings indicate the actual bore size to which they must be fitted, the requisite running clearance being allowed for in the machining.

After reboring an engine, or whenever fitting pistons differing in size from those removed during dismantling, ensure that the size of the piston fitted is stamped clearly on the top of the cylinder block alongside the appropriate cylinder bore.

Section A.16

CAMSHAFT

Disconnect the battery.

Remove the inlet and exhaust manifold assembly (see Section A.4).

Remove the push-rods and take out the tappets (see Section A.8).

Remove the timing cover, timing chain, and gears (see Section A.7).

Disconnect the suction advance unit pipe from the distributor and take out the two bolts with flat washers securing the distributor to the housing. Do not slacken the clamping plate bolt or the ignition timing setting will be lost.

Remove the distributor assembly–Sections A.25 and A.26.

Remove the sump, oil pump, and oil pump drive shaft (see Section A.11).

If a drive-type tachometer is fitted, disconnect the drive, remove the securing nuts and washers and withdraw the drive gear.

Take out the three set screws and shakeproof washers which secure the camshaft locating plate to the cylinder block and withdraw the camshaft.

Before reassembly, which is a reversal of the dismantling procedure, assemble the camshaft retaining plate and the chain wheel to the camshaft, and check the camshaft end-float against the dimensions given in the '**GENERAL DATA**' section by measuring the clearance between the retaining plate and the thrust face of the camshaft front journal.

If the end-float is excessive the retaining plate should be renewed.

Section A.17

RENEWING THE CAMSHAFT BEARINGS

While the camshaft is removed it is advisable to check the bearing liners for damage and wear. If these are not in good condition they must be removed and new ones fitted.

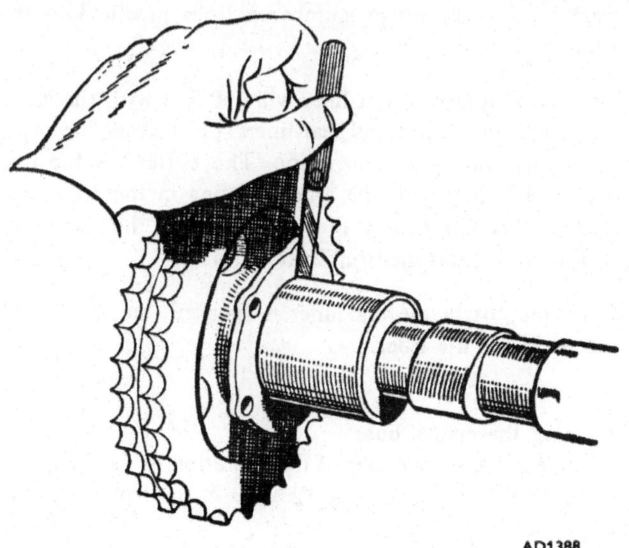

Fig. A.24
Checking the camshaft end-float

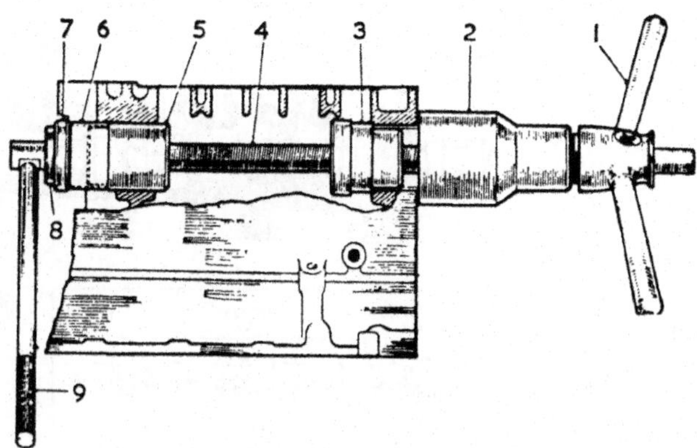

Fig. A.25
Replacing the camshaft centre bearing liner, using Service tool 18G 124 A with adaptors 18G 124 H and 18G 124 C

1. Wing nut.
2. Body.
3. Adaptor 18G 124 H.
4. Centre screw.
5. Adaptor 18G 124 C.
6. Bearing liner.
7. Large 'C' washer.
8. Slotted washer.
9. Tommy-bar.

The old bearings can be punched out. The new ones must be tapped into position. These bearings are easily damaged and the use of Service tool 18G 124 A is recommended.

This tool comprises a body with built-in thrust race, screw wing nut, stop plate, 'C' washer and handle, and must be used in conjunction with the following adaptors: 18G 124 B, 18G 124 C, 18G 124 F, 18G 124 H.

Removing the front and rear liners

Insert the small end of the adaptor 18G 124 F into the camshaft front liner from the inside of the cylinder block, thread the body of the tool onto the centre screw, and pass the screw through the adaptor from the front of the block. Place the slotted washer on the flat at the rear of the centre screw and insert the tommy-bar into the centre screw behind the slotted washer.

Tighten up the wing nut to withdraw the worn liner.

The rear liner is withdrawn by the same method, using the adaptor 18G 124 B and withdrawing the liner from the rear of the block.

Removing the centre liner

Insert the stepped pilot adaptor 18G 124 H into the camshaft liner front bore from the inside of the block and the adaptor 18G 124 C into the centre liner from the rear, small end first.

With the body of the tool positioned on the centre screw, pass the screw through the pilot adaptor and the adaptor in the centre liner.

Place the slotted washer on the flat at the rear of the centre screw and insert the tommy-bar into the screw behind the slotted washer.

Tighten up the wing nut to withdraw the liner.

Replacing the front and rear liners

Place the new liner on the smallest diameter of the adaptor 18G 124 F and insert the adaptor into the camshaft front

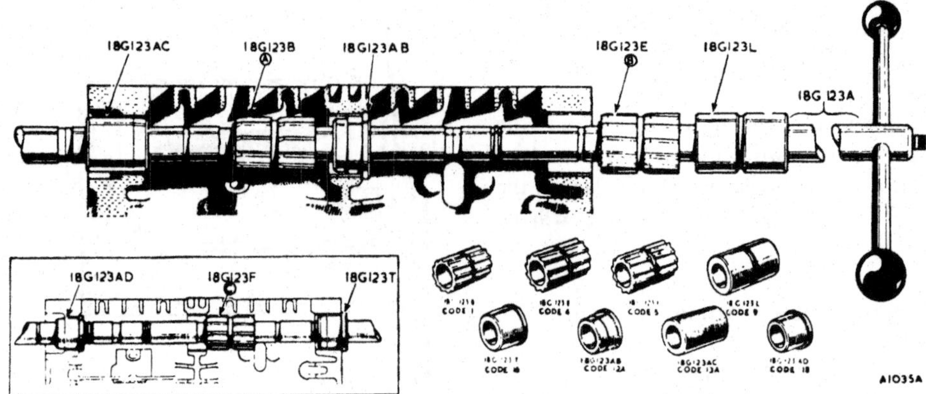

Fig. A.26

Showing the cutters and pilots positioned for reaming the front and rear liners. Inset are the pilots and cutter positioned for reaming the centre liner

A. Position No. 6 B. Position No. 10 C. Position No. 9

liner bore from the inside of the block, largest diameter first.

Line up the oil holes in the liner and the cylinder block and make certain that they remain correctly positioned during the whole operation.

Thread the body of the tool onto the centre screw and pass the screw through the adaptor located in the front liner from the front of the block.

Position the larger of the two 'C' washers on the centre screw with the cut-away portion turned away from the butt joint of the liner; this joint **must** be covered by the washer.

Place the slotted washer on the flat at the rear of the centre screw and insert the tommy-bar into the screw behind the slotted washer.

Tighten the wing nut to pull the liner squarely into position.

The rear liner is replaced by the same method, using the adaptor 18G 124 B and pulling the liner into position from the rear of the block.

Replacing the centre liner

Insert the stepped pilot adaptor into the camshaft front liner from the inside of the block.

Place a new centre liner on the small end of the adaptor 18G 124 C and position the adaptor in the centre liner bore from the rear, largest diameter first. Ensure that the oil holes in the liner and the cylinder block are lined up and remain so during the whole operation.

With the body of the tool positioned on the centre screw insert the screw through the pilot adaptor and the adaptor in the centre liner bore.

Position the larger of the two 'C' washers on the centre screw with the cut-away portion turned away from the butt joints of the liner; this joint **must** be covered by the washer.

Place the slotted washer and the tommy-bar in the centre screw and tighten up the wing nut to pull the liner into position.

Reaming the liners

Before the camshaft can be reassembled the liners must be reamed in line in order to obtain the correct clearance between the shaft journals and their bearings. For this purpose use tool 18G 123 A, which comprises an arbor with tommy-bar and Allen key, and must be used with the following adaptors: 18G 123 B, 18G 123 E, 18G 123 F, 18G 123 L, 18G 123 T, 18G 123 AB, 18G 123 AC, 18G 123 AD.

Reaming the front and rear liners

Insert the taper pilots 18G 123 AB and 18G 123 AC into the centre and rear liners respectively.

Place the plain pilot 18G 123 L on the arbor, followed by the cutter 18G 123 E.

Pass the arbor through the front liner and the pilot located in the centre liner.

Place the cutter 18G 123 B on the arbor and push the arbor through the taper on the rear liner.

Secure the cutters and pilots in their respective positions (see illustration), ensuring that the cutter locating pins are engaged in the correct numbered hole provided in the arbor.

The cutter for the front liner will cut first with the arbor piloting in the centre and rear liners. Clear away the swarf frequently during the operation. The cutter for the rear liner will follow with the arbor piloting in the front and centre liners. Clear away all the swarf before the plain pilot is allowed to enter the front liner.

When the cut in the rear liner is finished free the cutters and withdraw the arbor.

Reaming the centre liner

Set up for the second part of the operation by inserting the pilots 18G 123 T and 18G 123 AD in the front and rear liners.

Pass the arbor through the pilot in the front liner and place the cutter for the centre liner on the arbor. Push the arbor

through the centre liner and the pilot located in the rear liner.
Secure the cutter and pilots in position, ensuring that the locating pin of the cutter engages the correct numbered hole in the arbor.
Ream the centre liner, release the cutter, and withdraw the arbor.
IMPORTANT.–It is essential that the cutter flutes are kept clear of swarf at all times during the cutting operation, preferably with air-blast equipment. The cutter should be withdrawn from the liner half-way through the cut and the swarf removed from the cutter and the liner.
Feed the reamer very slowly, and keep the cutters dry.
The arbors should be lightly lubricated before assembling the cutters and pilots.

Section A.18

REMOVING AND REPLACING THE CRANKSHAFT (Engine Out of Car)

Take off the clutch and the flywheel (see Section A.19), the timing cover, the timing wheels and chain (see Section A.10), the sump and the oil pump strainer (see Section A.11), and the rear engine mounting plate.
Remove the big-end bearing cap and then take off the main bearing caps (see Section A.13).
Mark each big-end bearing cap and bearing to ensure that it is reassembled to the correct journal, taking care, in the case of the bearings, that they are not damaged or distorted when marking. Punches should not be used for this purpose.
Lift the crankshaft out of the bearings.
Replacement of the crankshaft is a reversal of the above operations.
Before replacing the crankshaft thoroughly clean out all oilways.
Check the condition of the rear engine mounting plate oil seal (18GB engines) and renew if necessary.
Note that each main bearing cap is stamped with a common number which is also stamped on the centre web of the crankcase near the main bearing.

Section A.19

REMOVING AND REPLACING THE FLYWHEEL (Engine Out of Car)

Remove the clutch by unscrewing the six bolts and spring washers securing it to the flywheel. Release the bolts a turn at a time to avoid distortion of the cover flange. Three dowels locate the clutch cover on the flywheel.
Unlock and remove the six nuts and three lock plates which secure the flywheel to the crankshaft and remove the flywheel.
When replacing the flywheel ensure that the 1 and 4 timing mark on the periphery of the flywheel is in line with and on the same side as the first and fourth throws of the crankshaft.

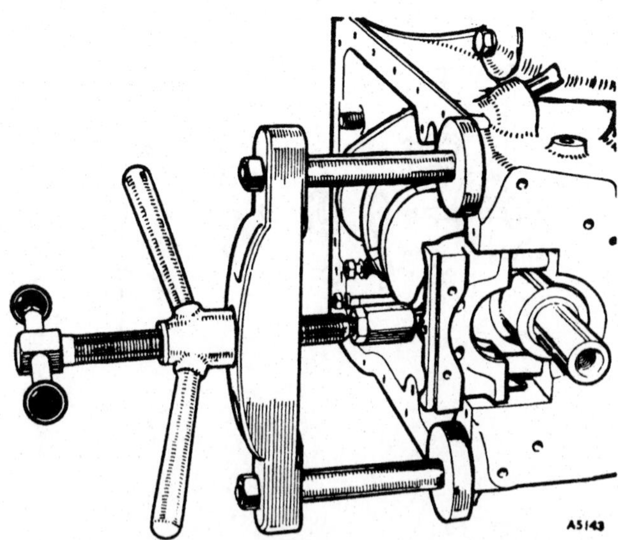

Fig. A.27
Withdrawing the front main bearing cap, using Service tool 18G 42 A and adaptor 18G 42 B

To assist correct location of the flywheel the depression in the crankshaft flange face is stamped with a similar timing mark which should be in line with the one on the flywheel periphery.
To release the special flywheel bolts the engine sump and rear main bearing cap must also be removed.

Section A.20

FITTING FLYWHEEL STARTER RINGS

To remove the old starter ring from the flywheel flange split the ring gear with a cold chisel, taking care not to damage the flywheel. Make certain that the bore of the new rings and its mating surface on the flywheel are free from burrs and are perfectly clean.
To fit the new ring it must be heated to a temperature of 300 to 400° C. (572 to 752° F.), indicated by a light-blue surface colour. If this temperature is exceeded the temper of the teeth will be affected. The use of a thermostatically controlled furnace is recommended. Place the heated ring on the flywheel with the lead of the ring teeth facing the flywheel register. The expansion will allow the ring to be fitted without force by pressing or tapping it lightly until the ring is hard against its register.
This operation should be followed by natural cooling, when the 'shrink fit' will be permanently established and no further treatment required.

Section A.21

REMOVING AND REFITTING THE ENGINE AND POWER UNIT

It is possible to remove the engine only from the car, but it is recommended that the engine and gearbox are removed together as a complete assembly thus avoiding possible damage to the clutch when separating and refitting the gearbox to the engine within the confines of the car.

THE ENGINE MOUNTINGS

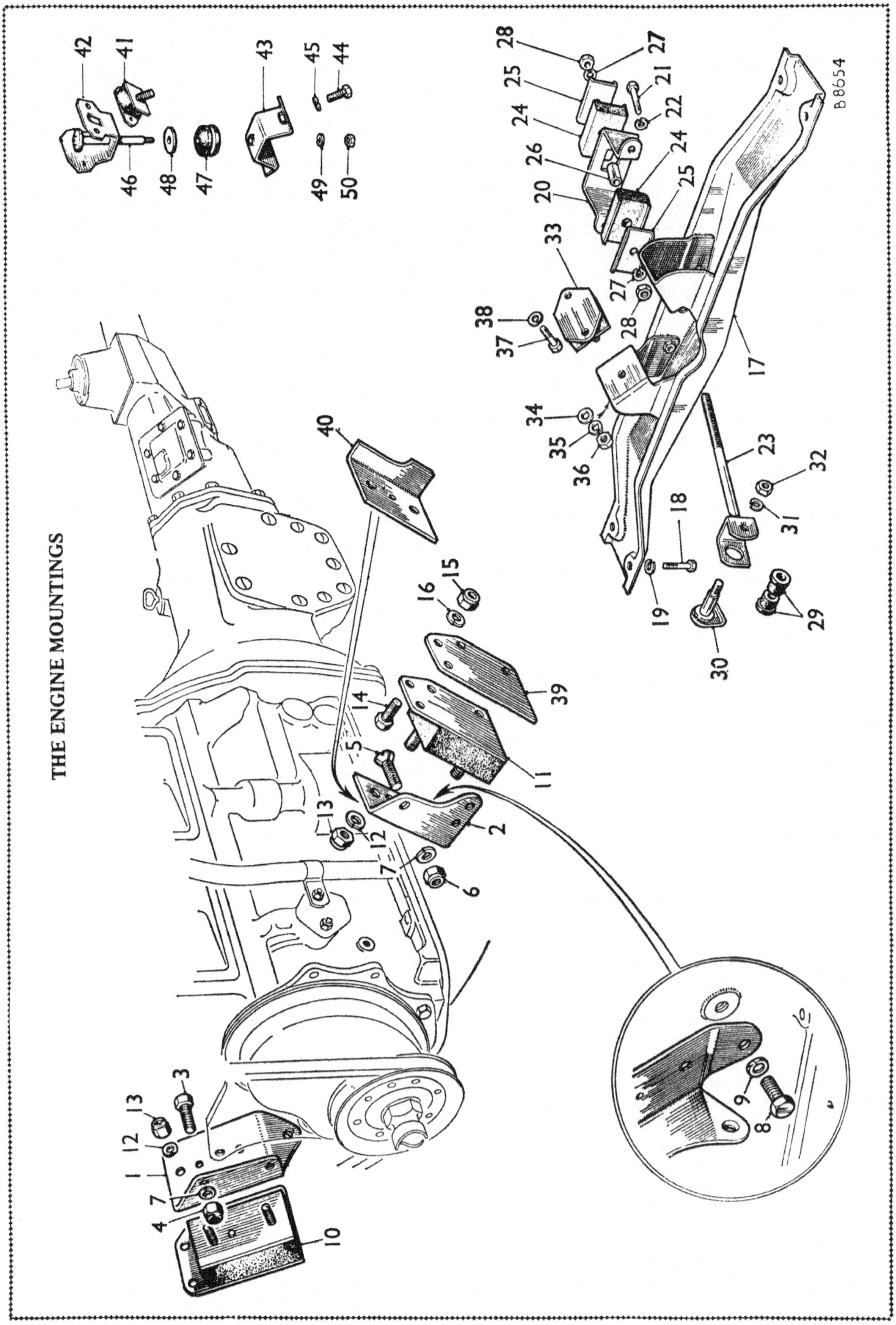

B8654

KEY TO THE ENGINE MOUNTINGS

No.	Description	
1.	Bracket–front engine mounting –R.H.	
2.	Bracket–front engine mounting –L.H.	
3.	Screw–bracket to mounting plate–R.H.	
4.	Nut for screw.	
5.	Screw–bracket to mounting plate–L.H.	
6.	Nut for screw.	
7.	Washer–spring.	
8.	Screw–bracket to block.	
9.	Washer–spring.	
10.	Rubber–front engine mounting–R.H.	
11.	Rubber–front engine mounting–L.H.	
12.	Washer–spring–mounting to bracket.	
13.	Nut–mounting to bracket.	
14.	Screw–mounting and coil bracket to frame bracket.	
15.	Nut for screw.	
16.	Washer–spring.	
17.	Cross-member assembly–rear mounting.	
18.	Screw–cross-member to frame.	
19.	Washer–spring.	
20.	Bracket–engine stay-rod.	
21.	Screw–bracket.	
22.	Washer–spring.	
23.	Stay-rod–engine.	
24.	Buffer–stay-rod.	
25.	Plate–buffer.	
26.	Distance tube for stay-rod.	
27.	Washer–spring–stay-rod.	
28.	Nut–stay-rod.	
29.	Bush–shouldered–gearbox rear extension.	
30.	Pin–stay-rod.	
31.	Washer–spring stay-rod pin.	
32.	Nut–stay-rod pin.	
33.	Mounting–engine–rear.	
34.	Washer–plain–rear mounting to cross-member.	
35.	Washer–spring–rear mounting to cross-member.	
36.	Nut–rear mounting to cross-member.	
37.	Screw–rear mounting to gearbox.	
38.	Washer–spring.	
39.	Plate–packing–L.H. rubber.	
40.	Control bracket–engine mounting	GT.
41.	Engine mounting–rear	GT.
42.	Bracket–rear engine mounting–upper	GT.
43.	Bracket–rear engine mounting–lower	GT.
44.	Screw–bracket to cross-member	GT.
45.	Washer–spring	GT.
46.	Pin–rear engine mounting	GT.
47.	Bush–pin.	GT.
48.	Washer–plain for pin	GT.
49.	Washer–spring for pin	GT.
50.	Nut for pin	GT.

Removing the power unit

ALL MODELS

1. Disconnect the batteries.
2. Remove the bonnet–Section R.9.
3. Drain the oil from the engine and gearbox.
4. Drain the coolant from the engine and radiator.
5. Disconnect the oil cooler and oil pressure gauge pipes from the engine.
6. Disconnect the top and bottom radiator hoses from the engine.
7. Remove the oil cooler securing bolts.
8. Remove the radiator and diaphragm assembly–Section C.6–complete with oil cooler and pipes.
9. Disconnect the wiring from the dynamo or alternator and the distributor.
10. Detach the leads from the sparking plugs and remove the distributor cap.
11. Disconnect the heater hoses and control cable.
12. Disconnect the thermometer thermal transmitter from the engine.
13. Disconnect the wiring from the starter.
14. Disconnect the petrol pipe and choke cable and remove the air cleaners from the carburetters.
15. Disconnect the tachometer (if drive type).

SYNCHROMESH GEARBOX AND OVERDRIVE

16. Remove the gear lever surround, raise the rubber boot, unscrew and remove the lever retaining bolts. Remove the gear lever.
17. Disconnect the wiring from the reverse light and overdrive isolation switches.
18. Detach the clutch slave cylinder from the gearbox casing and move it clear of the assembly.

AUTOMATIC GEARBOX

19. Disconnect the down-shift cable from the carburetters.
20. Disconnect the manual control lever from the gearbox shaft.
21. Disconnect the wiring from the inhibitor and reverse light switch.

ALL MODELS

22. Disconnect the speedometer cable from the gearbox.
23. Take the weight of the engine on a crane and support the gearbox.
24. Disconnect the exhaust pipe from the manifold and release the pipe clip from the gearbox.
25. Disconnect and remove the propeller shaft–Section G.2.
26. Remove the bolts securing the engine front mountings to the frame.

EARLY CARS

27. Remove the bolts securing the rear cross-member to the chassis frame and allow the gearbox to rest on the fixed cross-member.
28. Remove the stay rod from the gearbox.
29. Unscrew the bolts securing the rear mountings to the gearbox and remove the cross-member complete with stay-rod.

LATER CARS

30. Remove the four bolts securing the cross-member to the chassis frame.
31. Remove the two bolts securing the bottom tie bracket to the cross-member.
32. Lower the gearbox so that it rests on the fixed cross-member, remove the rear mounting securing nuts and remove the cross-member.

ALL MODELS

33. Ease the assembly forward until the gearbox is clear of the cross-member, tilt the assembly and lift from the car.
34. Remove the gearbox from the engine as described in Section F.1, Section Fb.1, or Section Fd.10.

Refitting the engine

35. Reverse the removing procedure, refill the engine and gearbox with a recommended lubricant, and refill the cooling system with coolant.

Section A.22

ENGINE CONTROLS

The engine controls comprise the accelerator pedal and the choke control. The accelerator pedal assembly pivots about a bush and distance piece that is supported by a bracket at the top of the pedal box. An accelerator pedal stop is bolted on the front of the pedal box and a pedal return stop on the pedal lever abuts a return stop screw in the top of the pedal box.

The upper end of the lever is slotted to accommodate a nipple on the inner end of the accelerator inner cable. The cable passes through a guide bolted to the bulkhead, through an outer cable, and then through a guide on the top of the heat shield. The outer end of the cable is clamped to a pin attached to the spindle and lever assembly that operates the throttles. The outer cable ends abut the bulkhead guide and the heat shield guide.

One end of an accelerator return spring is attached to the spindle and lever assembly and the other end to a clip at the bottom of the heat shield.

The choke control is mounted on the fascia adjacent to the ignition/starter switch and comprises a knob, inner cable, and outer cable assembly. The cables pass through a rubber grommet in the bulkhead.

The end of the inner cable is clamped to a choke control bracket secured to the front carburetter flange by the air cleaner securing bolts. The outer cable terminates in an abutment that is pinned to the carburetter choke operating lever. When the control is operated the inner cable length is reduced between the bulkhead guide and clamp pin. The outer cable therefore moves along the inner cable and operates the choke lever.

The upper ends of the choke return springs are fitted to the cam levers of the forward and rear carburetters and the lower ends to clips on the bottom of the heat shield.

To remove the accelerator control take off the air cleaners as detailed in Section D, release the inner cable from the spindle and lever assembly and withdraw the inner cable from the outer cable at the pedal end.

Release the accelerator cable clip in the engine compartment and remove the outer cable.

Unscrew the pedal assembly fulcrum bolt from the pedal bracket and remove the pedal, bush, and distance piece.

Replacement is a reversal of the removal sequence.

After replacement ensure that the control is adjusted correctly as detailed in Section D.

To remove the choke control release the inner cable from the pin on the choke control bracket and retain the cable abutment.

Free the grommet from the bulkhead.

From the rear of the fascia panel unscrew the securing nut and withdraw the assembly from the fascia.

Replacement is a reversal of the removal sequence.

After replacing the accelerator and choke controls ensure that they are correctly adjusted as detailed in Section D.

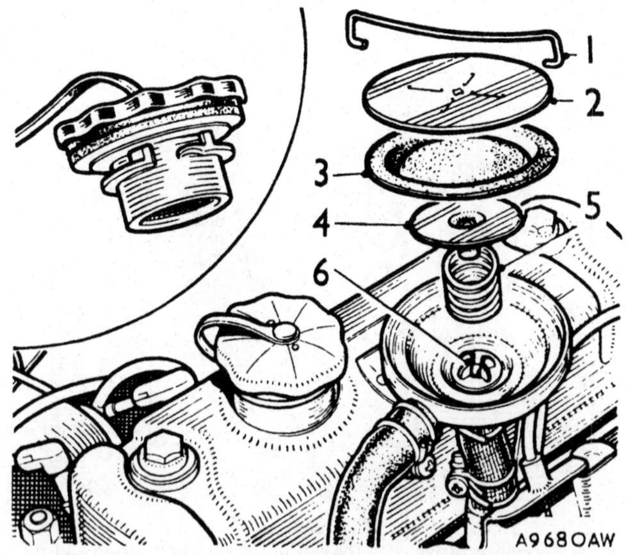

Fig. A.28
(2nd-type)

Closed-circuit breathing arrangement. (Inset) Oil filter cap with combined air filter and the breather control valve

1. Spring clip.
2. Cover.
3. Diaphragm.
4. Metering lever.
5. Spring.
6. Cruciform guides.

Section A.23

EXHAUST SYSTEM

The exhaust system is made up of a front pipe and junction assembly, a front intermediate pipe, a front silencer, a rear intermediate pipe, and a rear silencer and tail pipe. The assembly is welded together.

The front pipe and junction assembly mate with the exhaust manifold ports; joint washers are fitted to each pipe.

The front intermediate pipe is supported by a clip which is attached to a strap and bracket. The bracket is bolted to the lower flange of the gearbox.

A rubber mounting bolted to the rear frame member supports a bushed housing to which is attached the front silencer mounting bracket.

A second rubber mounting bolted to the rear frame embodies a split clamp that secures the tail pipe.

To remove the exhaust assembly remove the six nuts from the manifold port studs, allow the twin pipes to drop, and retain the joint washers.

Loosen the rear mounting tail pipe securing bolt, remove the front silencer support clip bolt, and draw the assembly forward and downward.

To refit the assembly reverse the removal sequence but leave the front silencer and tail pipe securing bolts slack until the twin down pipes and joint washers have been fitted and tightened. Tighten the silencer clip bolt and finally the split clamp bolt on the tail pipe.

Section A.24

CLOSED-CIRCUIT BREATHING SYSTEM

Oil filler cap

An air filter is incorporated in the oil filler cap and the two are renewed as an assembly, on engines other than types 18GH, 18GJ or 18GK.

Breather control valve (18GA, 18GB and 18GD engines only)

TESTING

Run the engine at idling speed at normal running temperature. Remove the oil filler cap and if the valve is functioning correctly the engine speed will be heard to rise by approximately 200 r.p.m. If no change in engine speed occurs the valve must be serviced or renewed.

SERVICING

Remove the spring clip and dismantle the valve.

Clean all metal parts with a solvent (trichlorethylene, fuel, etc.). Do not use an abrasive. If deposits are difficult to remove, immerse the parts in boiling water before applying the solvent.

Clean the diaphragm with detergent or methylated spirits.

Replace components showing signs of wear or damage.

Reassemble the valve, making sure the metering needle is in the cruciform guides and the diaphragm is seated correctly.

NOTE –The 1st-type valve assembly (without the cruciform guides) is serviced as an assembly.

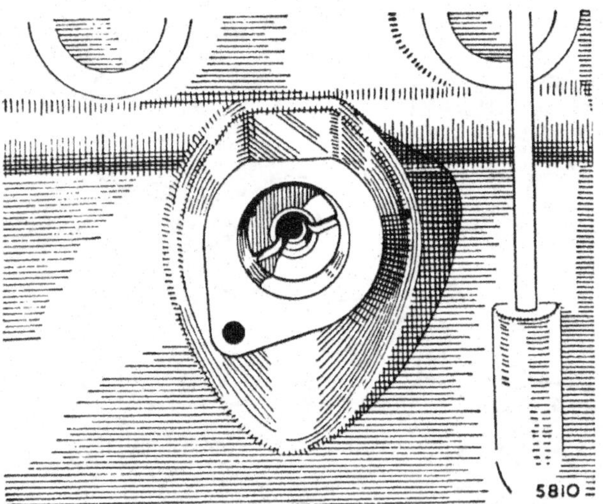

Fig. A.29
The distributor drive with the slot in the correct position and the large offset uppermost

Section A.25

DISTRIBUTOR DRIVING SPINDLE (18G/18GA)

Removing

Remove the distributor as detailed in Section B.

Take out the screw securing the distributor housing to the cylinder block and withdraw the housing.

Screw a $\frac{5}{16}$ in. UNF. bolt approximately 3½ in. (89 mm.) long into the threaded end of the distributor drive spindle and withdraw the spindle.

Refitting

Turn the crankshaft until No. 1 piston is at T.D.C. on its compression stroke. When the valves on No. 4 cylinder are 'rocking' (i.e. exhaust just closing and inlet just opening) No. 1 piston is at the top of its compression stroke. If the engine is set so that the groove in the crankshaft pulley is in line with the largest pointer on the timing chain cover, or the dimples in the crankshaft and camshaft gears are in line, the piston is exactly at T.D.C.

Screw the $\frac{5}{16}$ in. by 3½ in. UNF. bolt into the threaded end of the distributor drive gear and, holding the drive gear with the slot just below the horizontal and the large offset uppermost, enter the gear. As the gear engages with the camshaft the slot will turn in an anti-clockwise direction until it is approximately in the two o'clock position.

Remove the bolt from the gear, insert the distributor housing, and secure it with the special bolt and washer.

Ensure that the correct bolt is used and that the head does not protrude above the face of the housing.

Refit the distributor, referring to Section B.5 if the clamp plate has been released.

Section A.26

DISTRIBUTOR DRIVING SPINDLE (18GB)

Removing

Remove the distributor as detailed in Section B.

Take out the screw securing the distributoı housing to the cvlinder block and withdraw the housing.

Screw a $\frac{5}{16}$ in. UNF. bolt approximately 3½ in. (89 mm.) long into the threaded end of the distributor drive spindle and with the crankshaft at 90° or A.T.D.C. (pistons halfway up the bores) withdraw the spindle.

Refitting

Screw the $\frac{5}{16}$ in. UNF. bolt into the threaded end of the distributor drive spindle and with the crankshaft in the 90° B. or A.T.D.C. position, enter the spindle.

Turn the crankshaft until No. 1 piston is at T.D.C. on its compression stroke. When the valves on No. 4 cylinder are 'rocking' (i.e. exhaust just closing and inlet just opening) No. 1 piston is at the top of its compression stroke. If the

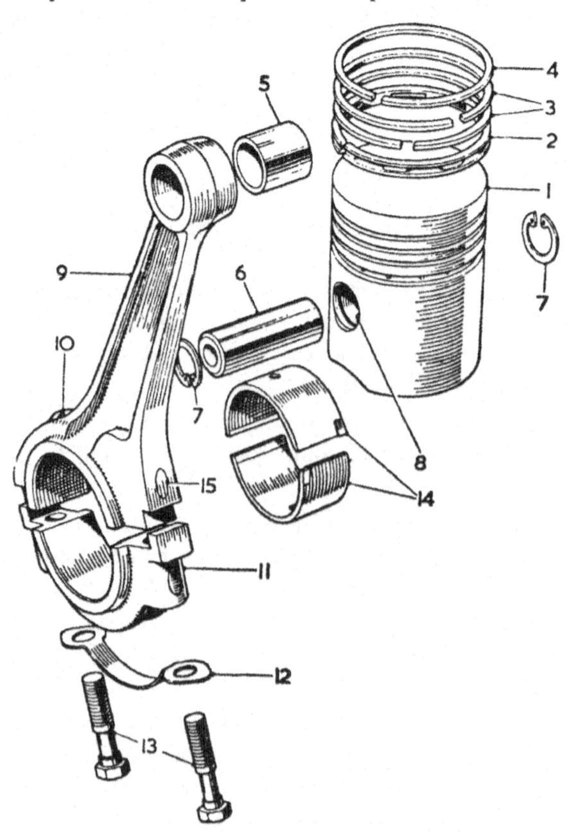

Fig. A.30
Piston and connecting rod

1. Piston.
2. Piston ring–scraper.
3. Piston rings–taper.
4. Piston ring–parallel.
5. Small-end bush.
6. Gudgeon pin.
7. Circlip.
8. Gudgeon pin lubricating hole.
9. Connecting rod.
10. Cylinder wall lubricating jet.
11. Connecting rod cap.
12. Lock washer.
13. Bolts.
14. Connecting rod bearings.
15. Connecting rod and cap marking.

engine is set so that the groove in the crankshaft pulley is in line with the largest pointer on the timing chain cover, or the dimples in the crankshaft and camshaft gears are in line, the piston is exactly at T.D C

Withdraw the spindle to clear the camshaft gear and holding the drive gear with the slot just below the horizontal and the large offset uppermost, re-enter the gear. As the gear engages with the camshaft the slot will turn in an anti-clockwise direction until it is approximately in the two o'clock position.

Remove the bolt from the gear, insert the distributor housing, and secure it with the special bolt and washer.

Ensure that the correct bolt is used and that the head does not protrude above the face of the housing.

Refit the distributor, referring to Section B if the clamp plate has been released.

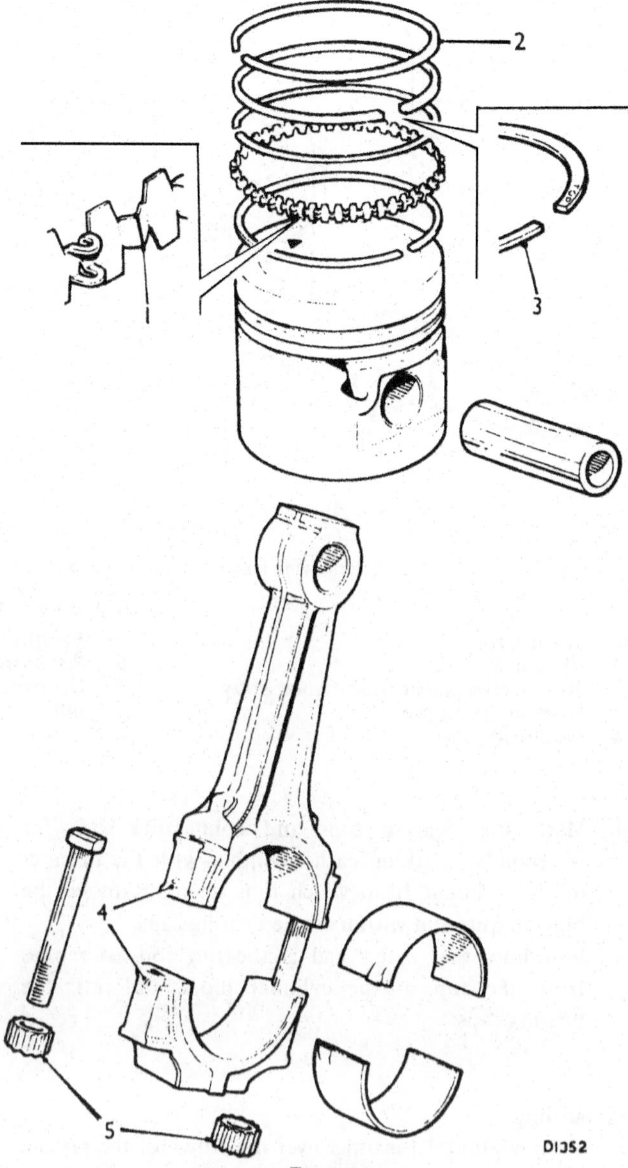

Fig. A.31
A piston and connecting rod assembly with a press fit gudgeon pin

1. Expander rail must butt.
2. Top compression ring.
3. Second compression ring.
4. Connecting rod and cap identification.
5. Multi-sided nut.

Section A.27

PISTONS AND CONNECTING RODS (18GB)

For removing and refitting pistons, piston rings and connecting rods see Section A.14.

Dismantling

The gudgeon pins are fully floating; remove the two circlips locating each pin and press the pins out. It is essential that the piston assemblies should be replaced in their own bores and fitted the same way round: they should be marked to facilitate this.

Reassembling

Assemble the pistons to the connecting rods with the gudgeon pin, which should be a hand push fit at a room temperature of 20° C. (68° F.). Secure each pin in its piston with two circlips, ensuring that they fit well into their grooves.

Section A.28

OIL COOLER

Removing

1. Disconnect the oil cooler pipes from the oil filter, cylinder block and oil cooler connections.
2. Remove the four oil cooler securing boits and remove the cooler.
3. Withdraw the pipes from the radiator diaphragm grommets.

Refitting

4. Reverse the removing procedure.

Section A 29

PISTONS AND CONNECTING RODS (Press fit gudgeon pin)

Pistons and connecting rod assemblies having a press fit gudgeon pin are fully interchangeable in complete sets with earlier assemblies having a fully floating gudgeon pin.

Removing

1. Remove the power unit (Section A.21).
2. Remove the engine sump.
3. Remove the cylinder head assembly (Section A.6).

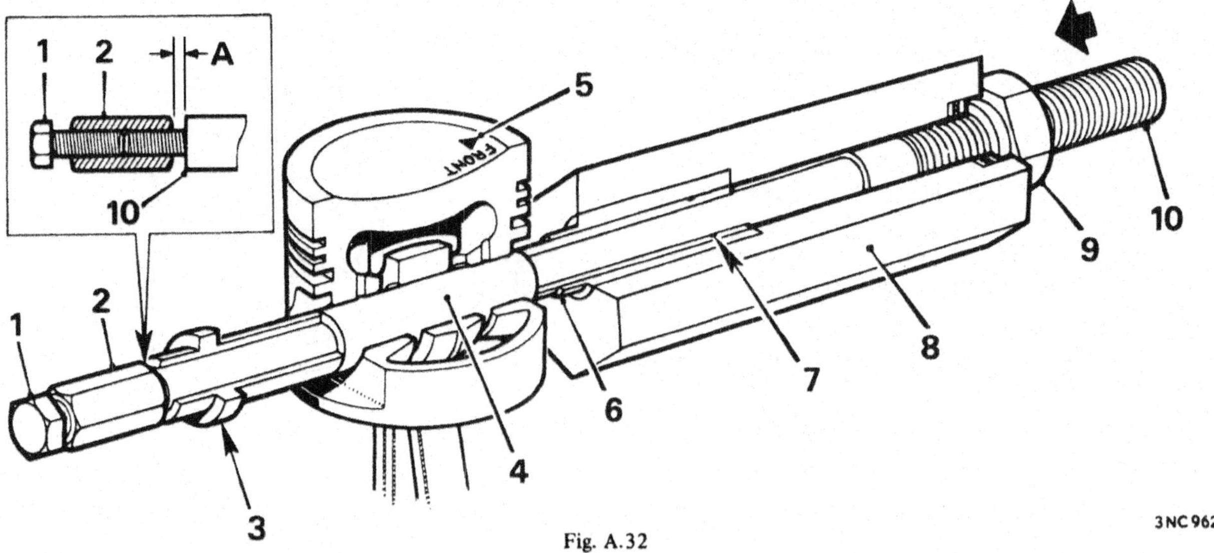

Fig. A.32

Removing a gudgeon pin, using Service tool 18G 1150 and adaptor set 18G 1150 D

'A' = 0.040 in. (1 mm.) end-float

1. Lock screw.
2. Stop nut.
3. Remover/replacer bush flange away from gudgeon pin.
4. Gudgeon pin.
5. Front of piston.
6. Piston adaptor.
7. Groove in sleeve away from gudgeon pin.
8. Hexagon body.
9. Large nut.
10. Centre screw.

4. Mark the bearing caps and connecting rods for reassembly, marking each assembly with the number of the cylinder from which it is taken. Remove the big-end nuts and withdraw the bearing caps.
5. Withdraw the piston and connecting rod assemblies from the top of the cylinder block and refit the bearing caps.

Dismantling

6. Remove the piston rings over the crown of the piston.
7. Hold the hexagon body of 18G 1150 in a vice.
8. Screw the large nut back until it is flush with the end of the centre screw, ensure the screw and large nut are well lubricated, and push the screw in until the nut contacts the thrust race.
9. Fit adaptor 18G 1150 D on to the centre screw with the piston ring cut-away uppermost.
10. Slide the parallel sleeve, groove end first, onto the centre screw.
11. Fit the piston, 'FRONT' or ▲ towards the adaptor, onto the centre screw. Fit the remover/replacer bush on the centre screw flange end away from the gudgeon pin.
    IMPORTANT. The gudgeon pin bore is offset and it is essential that the 'FRONT' or ▲ (marked on the piston crown) of the piston is fitted against the adaptor face.
12. Screw the stop nut onto the centre screw and adjust to the correct end-float ('A' Fig. A.32). Lock the stop nut securely with the lock screw.
13. Check that the remover/replacer bush and parallel sleeve are correctly positioned in the bore on both sides of the piston.
14. Screw the large nut up to the thrust race.
15. Hold the lock screw, and turn the large nut (use 18G 587) until the gudgeon pin is withdrawn from the piston.

Reassembling

GUDGEON PIN

16. Check the piston and connecting rod for alignment.
17. Remove the large nut of 18G 1150 and pull the centre screw out of the body a few inches. Ensure the nut and screw are well lubricated, and the piston support adaptor is in place.
18. Slide the parallel sleeve groove end last onto the centre screw and up to the shoulder.
19. Lubricate the gudgeon pin and bores of the connecting rod and piston with graphited oil (Acheson's Colloids 'Oildag'). Fit the connecting rod and piston 'FRONT' to the tool, with the connecting rod entered on the sleeve up to the groove.
20. Fit the gudgeon pin into the piston bore up to the connecting rod. Fit the remover/replacer bush flange end towards the gudgeon pin.
21. Screw the stop nut onto the centre screw and adjust to the correct end-float ('A' Fig. A.33). Lock the nut securely with the lock screw.
22. Screw the large nut up to the thrust race.
23. Set the torque wrench 18G 587 to 12 lb. ft. (1.64 kg. m.). This represents the **minimum load for an acceptable fit.**
    Using the torque wrench and 18G 587 on the large nut, and holding the lock screw, pull the gudgeon pin in until the flange of the remover/replacer bush is the correct distance from the piston skirt ('B' Fig. A.33).

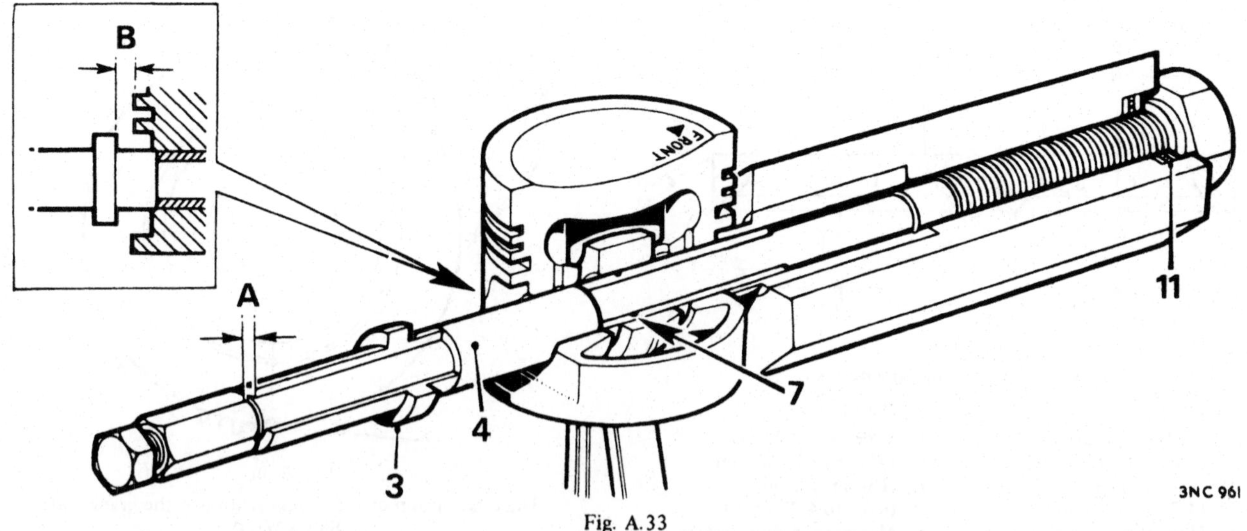

Fig. A.33

Fitting a gudgeon pin, using Service tool 18G 1150 and adaptor set 18G 1150 D

'A' = 0.040 in. (1 mm.) end-float. 'B' = 0.080 in. (2 mm.) from piston

3. Remover/replacer bush flange towards gudgeon pin.
4. Gudgeon pin.
7. Groove in sleeve towards gudgeon pin.
11. Lubricate thrust race and screw thread.

Under no circumstances must the flange be allowed to contact the piston.

NOTE.—If the torque wrench **has not broken** throughout the pull, the fit of the gudgeon pin to the connecting rod is not acceptable and necessitates the renewal of components. The large nut and centre screw of the tool must be kept well oiled.

24. Remove the Service tool.
25. Check that the piston pivots freely on the pin, and is free to slide sideways. If stiffness exists, wash the assembly in fuel or paraffin (kerosene), lubricate the gudgeon pin with graphited oil (Acheson's Colloids 'Oildag') and re-check. If stiffness persists dismantle and check for ingrained dirt or damage.

PISTON RINGS

26. Enter the piston rings squarely into the top of the cylinder bore and check the gaps (see **'GENERAL DATA'**). Check the ring to piston groove clearances.
27. Fit the bottom rail of the oil control ring to the piston and position it below the bottom groove.

    Fit the oil control expander into the bottom groove and move the bottom oil control ring rail up into the bottom groove. Fit the top oil control rail into the bottom groove.

    Check that the ends of the expander are butting but not overlapping (see Fig. A.31) and set the gaps of the rails and the expander at 90 degrees to each other.
28. Fit the thinner of the two compression rings into the second groove with the face marked 'TOP' uppermost.
29. Fit the top compression ring.
30. Position the ring gaps at 90 degrees to each other and away from the thrust side of the piston.

Refitting

31. Reverse the removal procedure noting the following points.
    (a) Lubricate the piston rings with graphited oil and stagger the compression ring gaps at 90° to each other.
    (b) Compress the piston rings using Service tool 18G 55 A.
    (c) Ensure that each connecting rod and piston is refitted into its original bore, the correct way round.
    (d) Check that the big-end bearings are correctly located in the connecting rods and caps. Use the special multi-sided locknuts and tighten to the torque figure given in **'GENERAL DATA'**.

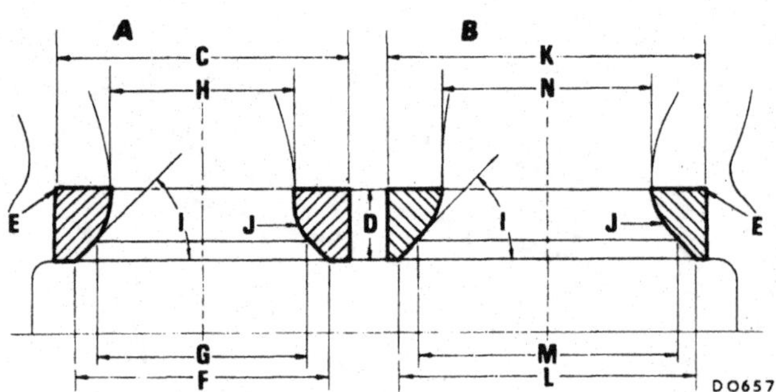

Fig. A.34
Valve seat machining dimensions

Exhaust (A)	Inlet (B)
C. 1.437 to 1.438 in. (36.50 to 36.53 mm.).	K. 1.592 to 1.593 in. (40.43 to 40.46 mm.).
D. .186 to..188 in. (4.72 to 4.77 mm.).	D. .186 to .188 in. (4.72 to 4.77 mm.).
E. Maximum radius .015 in. (.38 mm.)	E. Maximum radius .015 in. (.38 mm.).
F. 1.33 to 1.35 in. (33.78 to 34.29 mm.).	L. 1.552 to 1.572 in. (39.42 to 39.93 mm.).
G. 1.218 to 1.228 in. (30.94 to 31.19 mm.).	M. 1.427 to 1.447 in. (36.25 to 36.75 mm.).
H. Throat diameter 1.146 to 1.166 in. (29.11 to 29.62 mm.).	N. Throat diameter 1.302 to 1.322 in. (33.07 to 33.58 mm.).
I. 45°.	I. 45°.
J. Blend from seating to throat diameter.	J. Blend from seating to throat diameter.

Section A.30

VALVE SEAT INSERTS

Valve seats that cannot be restored to their original standard by normal cutting and refacing should have valve seat inserts fitted.

To fit an insert, machine the cylinder head to the dimensions given (see Fig. A.34). Press in the insert, which will be an interference fit of .0025 to .0045 in. (.06 to .11 mm.). Grind or machine the seats to the dimensions given. Normal valve 'grinding-in' may also be necessary to ensure efficient valve seating.

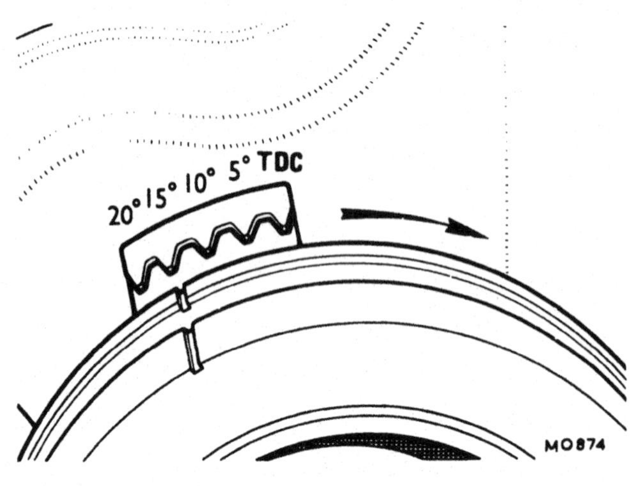

Fig. A.35
The timing indicator above the pulley. The groove is at 15°B.T.D.C. for pistons No. 1 and 4

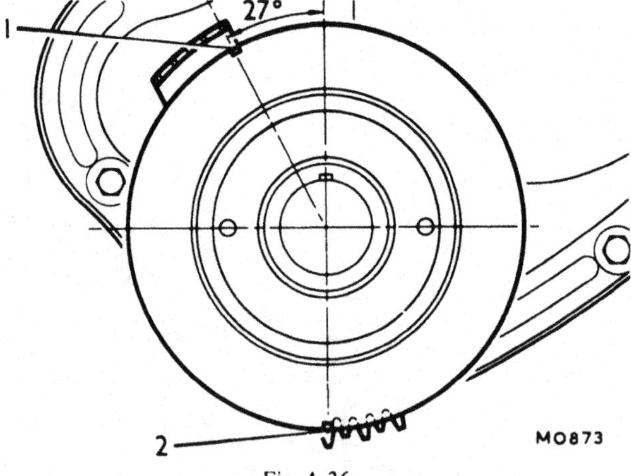

Fig. A.36
The relationship of the timing groove to the crankshaft pulley keyway

1. Position when indicator is above pulley.
2. Position when indicator is below pulley.

Section A.31

IGNITION TIMING INDICATOR

The ignition timing indicator is positioned above the crankshaft pulley on later engines (see Fig. A.35).
When changing a crankshaft pulley or front cover ensure that the timing groove on the new pulley is correct for the timing indicator position.
To modify a pulley, make a saw cut relative to the keyway and obliterate the old groove (see Fig. A.36).

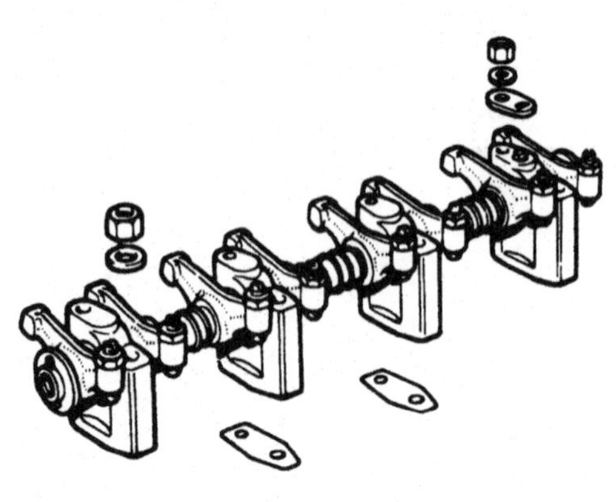

Fig. A.37
Rocker shaft assembly showing shims below the two centre brackets

Section A.32

ROCKER ASSEMBLY (Later engines)

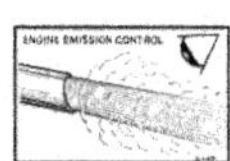

Remove and refit the rocker assembly as detailed in Section A.5, noting the following:

(a) Fit a 0.005 in.(0.13 mm.) shim under the two centre brackets. These shims should be fitted to early engines on reassembly.

(b) Later engines, identified by single valve springs, have bucket-type tappets, longer push-rods and a longer thread on the rocker adjusting screws which are interchangeable as a set with the first-type assembly.

Section A.33

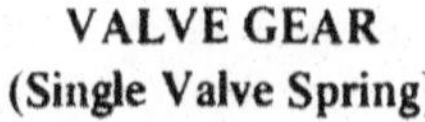

VALVE GEAR (Single Valve Spring)

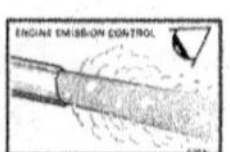

Removing

1. Remove the cylinder head - see Section A.6.
2. Compress the valve spring, using 18G 45, and remove the valve cotter.
3. Release the spring compressor and remove the valve collar, valve spring and valve spring cup.
4. Remove the packing ring and withdraw the valve from its guide.
5. Remove each valve assembly in turn and retain in their installed order.

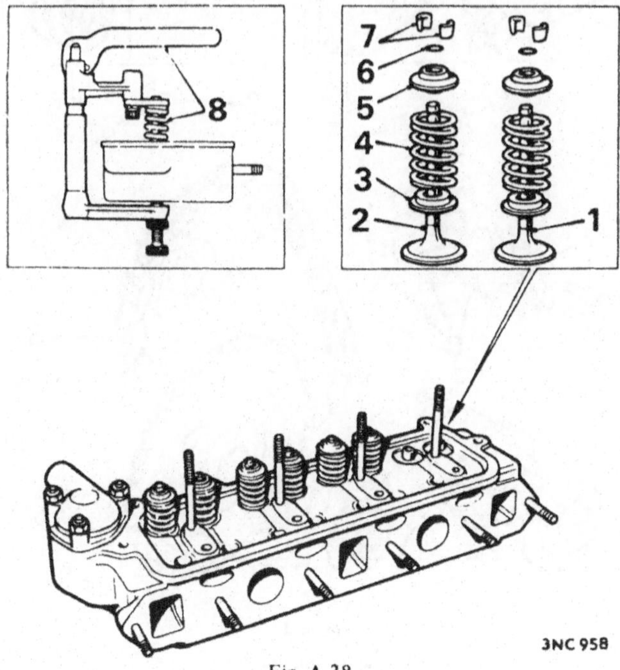

Fig. A.38
Valve Gear

1. Exhaust valve.
2. Inlet valve.
3. Valve spring cup.
4. Valve spring.
5. Valve spring collar.
6. Packing ring.
7. Valve cotter.
8. Compress valve spring using tool 18G 45.

Refitting

6. Insert each valve into its guide in turn and fit the valve spring cup, valve spring and valve collar. Compress the spring. Dip a **new** packing ring in oil and fit it over the valve stem to just below the cotter groove. Refit the valve cotter and release the spring compressor.

Refer to Section A.7 for:

Removing and replacing valve guides
Grinding and testing valves and seatings
Checking valve timing
Adjusting valve rocker clearances

Section A.34

FRONT COVER AND OIL SEAL (Later Engines)

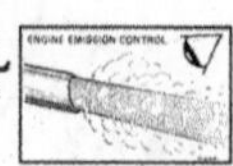

Removing

1. Drain the cooling system and remove the radiator –Section C.
2. Slacken the alternator mounting bolts and remove the drive belt.
3. Remove the cooling fan and pulley.
4. Release the locking washer and remove the crankshaft pulley retaining bolt–use tool 18G 98 A.
5. Pull the pulley from the crankshaft.
6. Remove the front cover and gasket; note the screw sizes.
7. Extract the oil seal from the front cover.

Refitting

8. Dip the new oil seal in engine oil and fit the seal into the cover, ensuring that the lips of the seal face inwards, using tool 18G 134 and 18G 134 BD.
9. Clean the front cover and front plate joint faces. Ensure the oil thrower is in position with the 'F' marking showing.
10. Smear the locating faces of tool 18G 1046 with oil and fit it into the oil seal.
11. Fit a new joint washer and position the front cover assembly on the crankshaft. Insert all the screws, ensure the seal is centralized and tighten up evenly. Remove tool 18G 1046.
12. Lubricate the hub of the crankshaft pulley, slide the pulley onto the shaft engaging the keyway.
13. Fit a new locking washer. Tighten and lock the retaining bolt.
14. Reverse the procedure in 1 to 3.

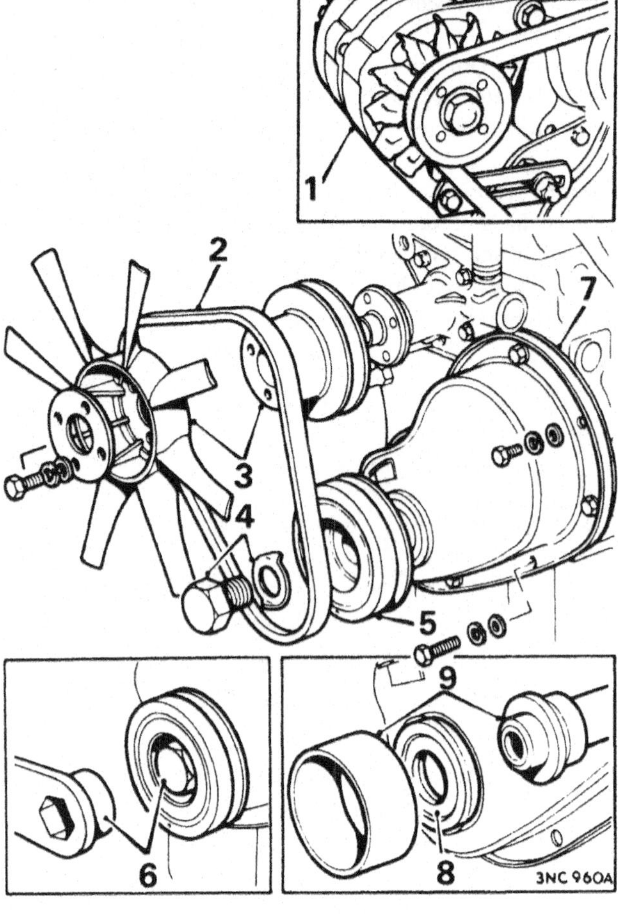

Fig. A.39

Front cover and oil seal

1. Alternator.
2. Drive belt–fan.
3. Fan and pulley.
4. Crankshaft nut and lock washer.
5. Crankshaft pulley.
6. Crankshaft pulley nut and tool 18G 98 A.
7. Front cover and gasket.
8. Oil seal.
9. Use tool 18G 134 BD to fit oil seal.

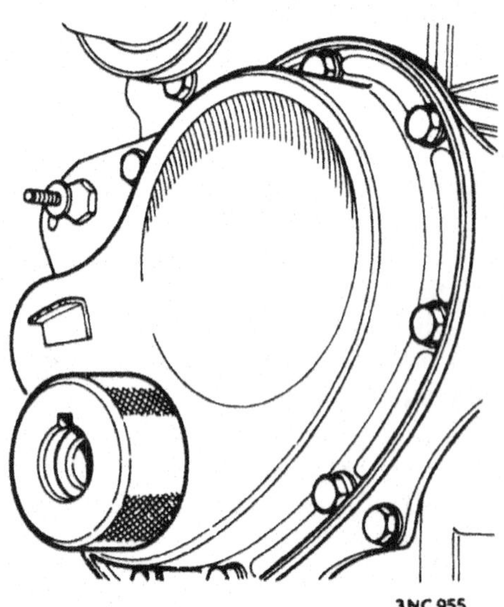

Fig. A.40

Centralize the oil seal on the crankshaft using tool 18G 1046 before tightening the front cover screws

Section A.35

TIMING CHAIN AND TENSIONER (single roller)

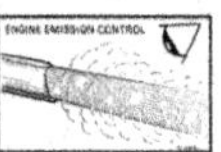

Removing

1. Remove the front cover, see Section A.34.
2. Unlock and remove the tensioner securing screws.
3. Prise the tensioner assembly out of its register in the front plate, taking care to retain the slipper head which is under spring tension, and remove the tensioner and its backplate. Remove the backplate and gasket.
4. Allow the spring tension against the slipper head to relax and withdraw the slipper head, spring and inner cylinder from the tensioner body.
5. Unlock and remove the camshaft nut, using tool 18G 98 A. Note that the lock washer tag fits into the groove of the camshaft wheel.
6. Withdraw the crankshaft and camshaft gears; use suitable levers and ease each gear forward a fraction at a time. Note the packing washers positioned behind the crankshaft gear.

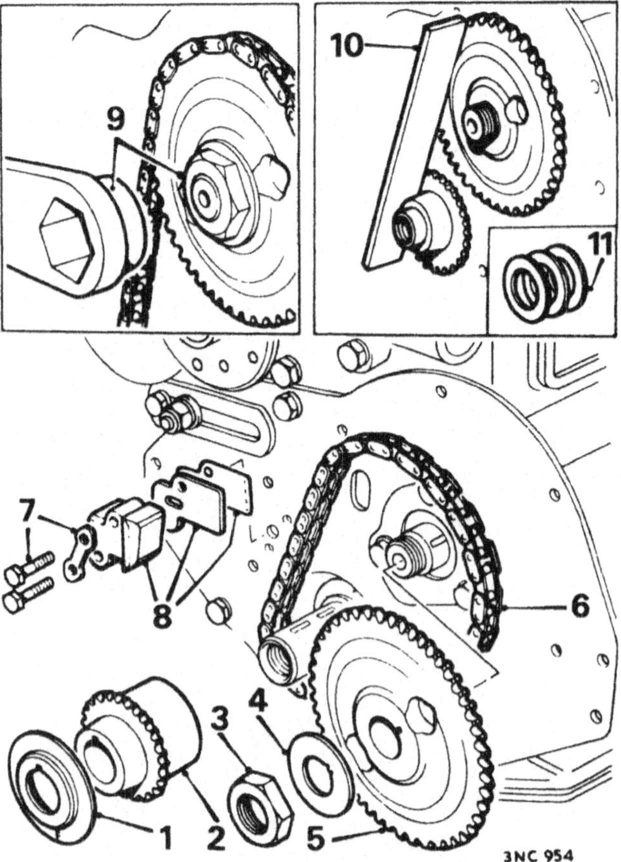

Fig. A.41

Timing chain and gears

1. Oil thrower–'F' marking.
2. Crankshaft gear.
3. Camshaft nut.
4. Lock washer.
5. Camshaft gear.
6. Timing chain–single.
7. Screws and lock washer.
8. Chain tensioner assembly and gasket.
9. Camshaft nut and tool 18G 98 A.
10. Check wheel alignment with a straight-edge.
11. Packing washers–crankshaft gear.

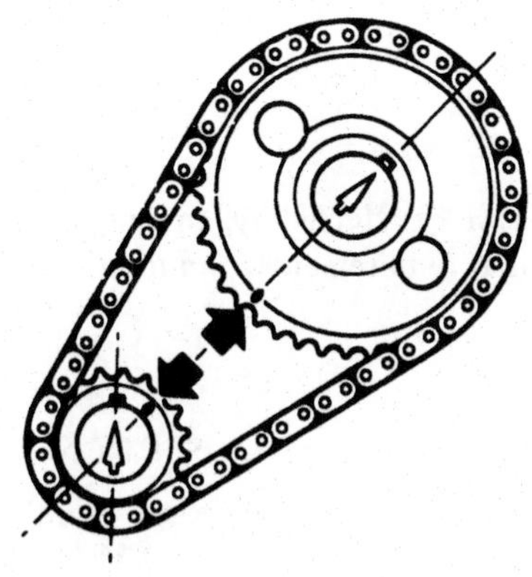

Fig. A.42
Crankshaft keyway at T.D.C. and the timing marks opposite to each other

Refitting

7. Crankshaft gear packing washers: Unless new crankshaft or camshaft components have been fitted use the same number of packing washers as original assembly.
   (i) Fit the crankshaft and camshaft gears hard against the shaft registers.
   (ii) Check the alignment of the gear teeth using a straight-edge. Measure the gap with a feeler gauge and subtract 0.005 in. (0.13 mm.).
   (iii) Remove the drive keys from the crankshaft and fit packing washers to the thickness calculated in (ii). Packing washers are supplied in a thickness of 0.006 in. (0.15 mm.). Refit the drive keys.
8. Rotate the crankshaft so that its keyways are at T.D.C. and camshaft with its keyway at two o'clock position.
9. Assemble the timing chain and gear wheels with the timing marks opposite each other, engage the crankshaft key and rotate the camshaft as necessary to engage the camshaft gear keyway.
10. Fit a new lock washer, tighten the nut and lock the camshaft nut.
11. Refit the chain tensioner:
    (i) Refit the inner cylinder and spring into the bore of the slipper head so that the serrated helical slot engages with the peg in the bore.
    (ii) Turn the inner cylinder clockwise against spring tension until the lower serration in the slot engages with the peg and retains the inner cylinder.
    (iii) Refit the slipper assembly into the tensioner body. Insert a 0.06 in. (1.6 mm.) spacer between the slipper head and body to prevent disengagement.
    (iv) Assemble the tensioner and its backplate to the engine.
    (v) Remove the spacer, press the slipper head into the body and release it to disengage the inner cylinder.
12. Position the oil thrower on the crankshaft with the 'F' marking showing.
13. Refit the front cover, see Section A.34.

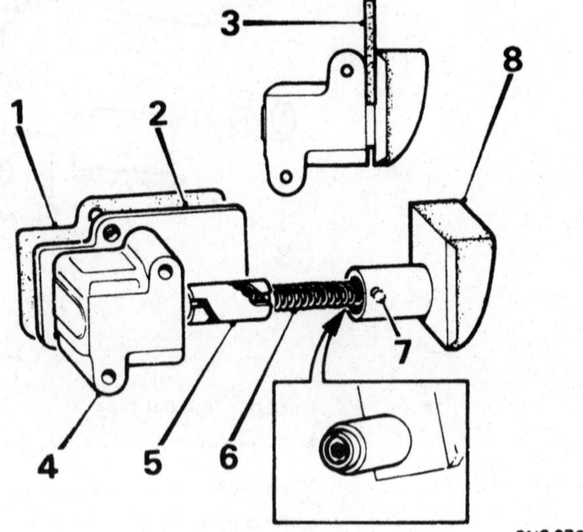

Fig. A.43
Timing chain tensioner assembly

1. Gasket.
2. Backplate.
3. Spacer to prevent disengagement.
4. Tensioner body.
5. Inner cylinder.
6. Spring.
7. Peg.
8. Slipper head.

Section Aa

The information given in this Section refers specifically to service operations on, or affected by, equipment fitted to the MGB (GHN5 and GHD5) in conformity with local and territorial requirements, and must be used in conjunction with Section A.

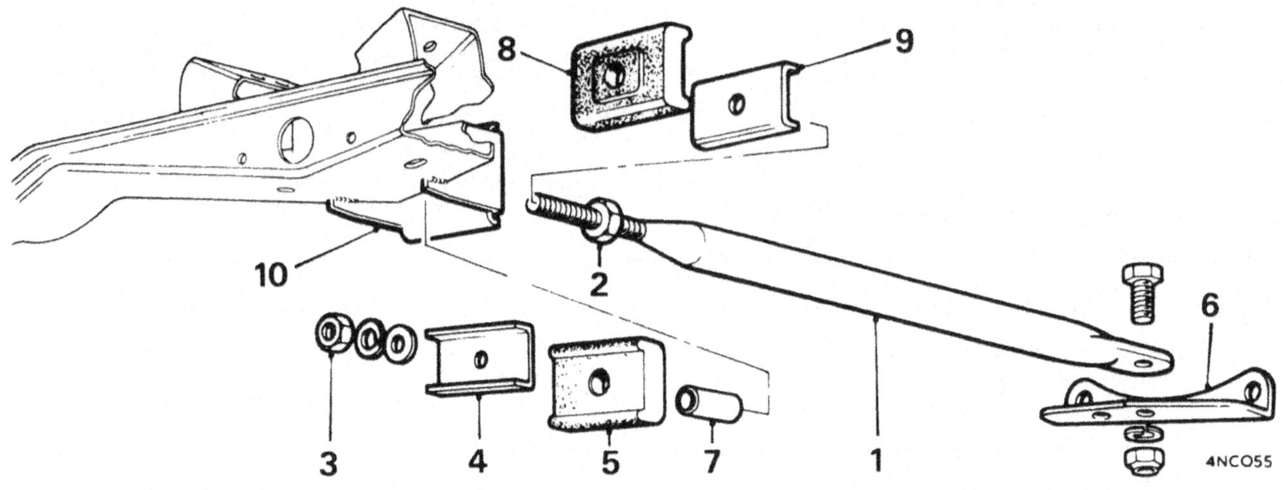

Fig. Aa.1
The engine restraint

1. Engine restraint tube.
2. Front nut.
3. Rear nut.
4. Rear plate.
5. Rear buffer.
6. Gearbox bracket.
7. Distance tube.
8. Front buffer.
9. Front plate.
10. Engine mounting rear cross-member bracket.

Section Aa.1

ENGINE RESTRAINT

(GHN5 and GHD5 Cars from Car No. 341295)

Removing

1. Slacken the restraint tube front nut.
2. Remove the restraint tube rear nut and withdraw the rear plate and buffer.
3. Remove the nut and bolt securing the restraint tube to the gearbox bracket and withdraw the restraint tube from the bracket on the rear engine mounting cross-member.
4. Remove the distance tube, front buffer and plate from the restraint tube.

Refitting

5. Reverse the procedure in 1 to 4, noting the following:
   a. Inspect the buffer for damage and deterioration, and renew if necessary.
   b. Tighten the restraint tube rear nut first, then tighten the front nut.

SECTION B

THE IGNITION SYSTEM

† These operations must be followed by an exhaust emission check. 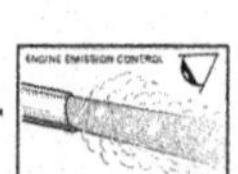

Section B.1

LUBRICATION

Distributor
CAM BEARING
Lift the rotor off the top of the spindle by pulling it squarely, and add a few drops of thin oil to the cam bearing. Do not remove the cam securing screw which is exposed: there is a clearance between the screw and the inner face of the spindle for the oil to pass.

Replace the rotor with its drive lug correctly engaging the spindle slot and push it onto the shaft as far as it will go.

CAM
Lightly smear the cam with a very small amount of grease or, if this is not available, clean engine oil may be used.

AUTOMATIC TIMING CONTROL
Add a few drops of thin oil through the hole in the contact breaker base through which the cam passes. Do not allow oil to get on or near the contacts. Do not over-oil.

Section B.2

IGNITION COIL

Removing
Disconnect the switch, contact breaker and H.T. cables, release the coil securing bolts and remove the coil.

Testing
An indication of the state of serviceability of the coil may be obtained by assessing the quality of spark produced by the coil under test conditions. The test circuit and equipment are illustrated in Fig. B.1.

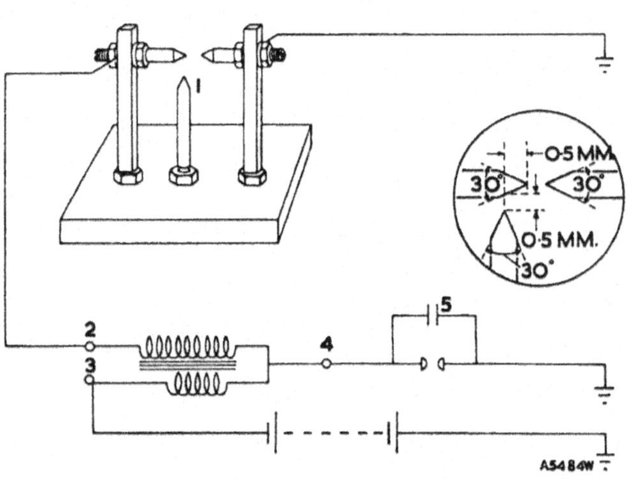

Fig. B.1
Test circuit and gap measurement

1. Auxiliary electrode.
2. H.T. contact.
3. S.W. contact.
4. C.B. contact.
5. Distributor.

The primary circuit make and break is obtained by using a six-lobe contact breaker cam and graduated scale and adjusting the contact breaker gap until a closed period of between 18 and 20° is obtained. The gap must be accurately set by using feeler gauges on each lobe of the cam in turn. The contact breaker lever spring tension must be between 18 and 20 oz. (510 and 566 gm.) measured at the contacts and the condenser capacity .18 to .25 mf.

The three-point test gap equipment is to be connected so that the auxiliary electrode is on the H.T. side of the circuit. This electrode causes the gap to break down at low voltage, a condition used during the setting of the gap for the high-speed performance test.

The coil must be mounted at an angle of 45° on the test rig with the C.B. terminal uppermost and the coil case earthed.

The mounting angle ensures that the primary winding take-off to the L.T. terminal is not covered with fluid and any internal tracking between the iron core and the primary lead will be shown up during test.

Earthing the coil case detects whether or not short circuits to earth are present.

High-speed performance test
Connect a peak voltmeter across the spark gap, run the distributor at any speed and then produce irregular sparking by tapping down the battery or by inserting a resistance in the primary circuit.

Adjust the gap until the peak reading on the voltmeter is 8 kV. Remove the voltmeter, and revert to 12 volts or remove the resistance from the circuit.

Run the distributor at 3,750 r.p.m. and check the spark. No missing should occur at this speed.

Low-speed performance test
Set the spark gap to .44 in. (11 mm.) and retain the auxiliary electrode in the circuit. The coil should be at 20° C. (68° F.).

Run the distributor at 100 r.p.m. and note the number of misses. These should not exceed 30 per minute.

Resistance test
Remove the coil and connect a Megger across the C.B. and H.T. contacts and note the reading and then across the S.W. and H.T. contacts and note the reading.

The readings must be within the limits given in the **'GENERAL DATA'**.

Section B.3

DISTRIBUTOR

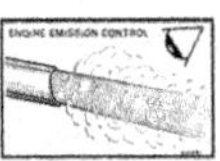

The Type 25D distributor incorporates a one-piece body-shank casting which houses the distributor drive shaft, automatic advance mechanism, contact breaker plate assembly, capacitor, cam, rotor arm and their associated electrical connections. The direction of rotation is stamped on the body.

The upper end of the body is closed by a bakelite cap which houses the plug lead segments and the H.T. lead brush and spring.

The automatic advance mechanism comprises a centrifugally operated rolling weight mechanism and a vacuum-operated mechanism which together advance the ignition point in proportion to the engine speed and load. The vacuum-operated mechanism has a vernier adjustment screw to enable small adjustments to be made to suit varying grades of fuel or to satisfy tuning requirements. A double-headed arrow marked 'A' and 'R' is stamped on the body adjacent to the vernier screw. A fuel trap is incorporated in the vacuum line from the induction manifold.

The contact breaker assembly is made up of a base plate secured to the distributor body, a moving contact breaker plate, a fixed contact breaker plate, the contact breaker points, and a capacitor.

The moving plate is supported on the base plate by two nylon pads, which minimizes friction when the automatic advance moves the plate. A 'C' spring anchored to a vacuum control spring post bears against the under side of the base plate and so pre-tilts the moving plate. The pressure of the cam on the heel of the contact breaker points supplements this action and so minimizes rocking of the moving plate at high cam speeds.

A stud fixed to the under side of the moving contact plate engages a slot in the base plate and so limits the horizontal movement of the moving plate; the stud also limits the angle of tilt of the moving plate.

The fixed contact breaker plate is secured by a screw which passes through a slot in the fixed plate. A notch cut in the free end of the plate permits the engagement of a screwdriver for adjustment purposes when setting the contact breaker points gap.

The distributor is secured to the engine by a split housing plate and clamp bolt. On some distributors the clamp bolt is trapped and the nut free and on others the nut is trapped and the bolt is free.

Section B.4

SERVICING THE DISTRIBUTOR

Contact breaker points

Examine the contact breaker points and if they are found to be burnt or blackened remove them as described in Section B.6 and clean them with a fine carborundum stone or emery-cloth.

After cleaning, remove all traces of dust and grease with a petrol-moistened cloth. Lightly smear the contact breaker pivot pin with molybdenized non-creep oil or a suitable grease and refit the points.

It is important that no oil or grease is allowed to contaminate the contact breaker points.

Reset the gap by rotating the crankshaft until the contacts are at their maximum open position, slacken the fixed plate securing screw, insert a screwdriver between the notches in the fixed plate and adjust the gap until it is between .014 and .016 in. (.36 and .40 mm.). Tighten the securing screw and re-check the gap setting.

Distributor cover

Thoroughly clean the moulded cover with a petrol-moistened cloth, paying particular attention to the spaces between the electrodes. Examine the cover for cracks and signs of tracking.

Inspect the carbon brush for serviceability and ensure that it moves freely in its holder.

Check the H.T leads for security and examine them for signs of deterioration. Cracked or perished leads must be renewed.

To fit new H T. leads, remove the old leads, fill the holes in the distributor cap with Silicone grease, and cut the new leads off to the required length. Push the ends of the leads fully home in the cap and secure them with the securing screws.

Remove the suppressors from the old leads and fit them to the new ones.

Vacuum advance

To check the vacuum advance, fit a modified cap having a window cut in the side. Start the engine, operate the throttle sharply, and observe the movement of the moving contact breaker plate.

Centrifugal advance

Remove the distributor cover, grasp the rotor firmly, and turn it in the direction of rotation. Release the rotor, when it should return to its original position without showing any tendency to stick.

Capacitor

If the capacitor is suspect it may be tested by substitution. Disconnect the suspect capacitor and connect a new one between the L.T terminal and earth.

Should a new capacitor be necessary, remove the old one and fit the new as described in Section B.

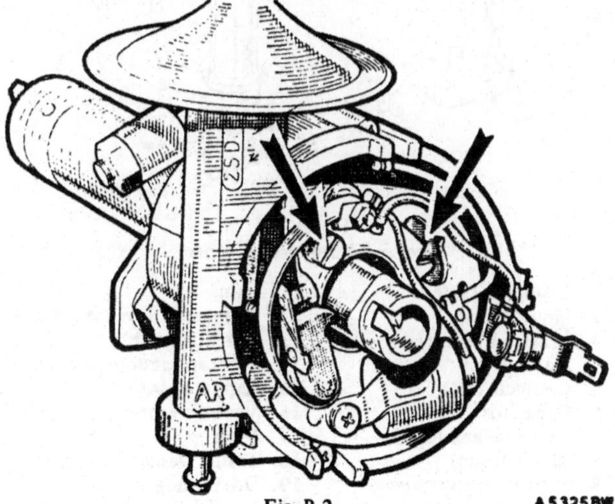

Fig. B.2 A5325BW

The distributor fixed plate securing screw and screwdriver notches

Section B.5

REMOVING AND REPLACING THE DISTRIBUTOR

To remove the distributor from the engine disconnect the suction advance pipe union from the distributor, the H.T. leads from the sparking plugs, and the L.T. lead from the distributor. Remove the two screws securing the split housing plate to the engine and lift the distributor from its housing.

Replacement is a reversal of these instructions, after which the ignition timing must be set or re-checked as described in Section B.9.

If it is desired to remove and replace the distributor without disturbing the timing proceed as follows:

1. Rotate the crankshaft until the rotor arm is pointing to the segment in the cover for No. 1 cylinder plug lead. This will provide a datum for replacement.
2. Remove the distributor cover, L.T. lead, and the suction advance pipe union from the distributor.
3. Remove the two screw securing the split housing plate to the distributor housing. **Do not remove or disturb the split housing plate clamp bolt.**
4. Withdraw the distributor from its housing.
5. Insert the distributor into its housing until the driving dogs on the distributor drive shaft rest on the distributor driving spindle.
6. Slowly rotate the rotor arm until the driving dogs engage the slots in the drive spindle. Both the dogs and the slots are offset to ensure correct replacement.
7. Turn the distributor body to align the holes in the housing plate with those in the housing and secure the plate with the two screws.
8. Provided the crankshaft has not been rotated the rotor arm will be opposite the segment for No. 1 plug lead.
9. Refit the cap, plug leads, L.T. lead, and vacuum pipe union.

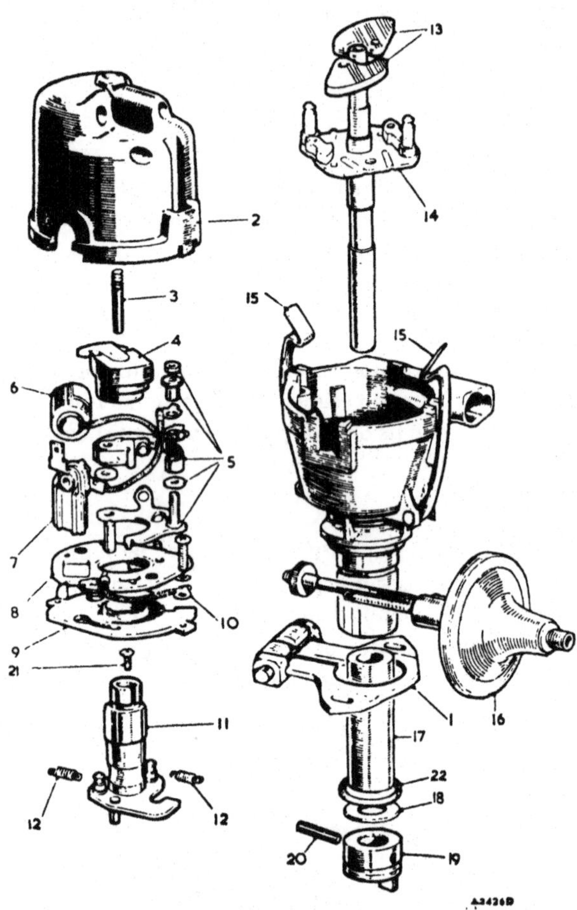

Fig. B.3
The distributor components

1. Clamping plate.
2. Moulded cap.
3. Brush and spring.
4. Rotor arm.
5. Contacts (set).
6. Capacitor.
7. Terminal and lead (low-tension)
8. Moving contact breaker plate.
9. Contact breaker base plate.
10. Earth lead.
11. Cam.
12. Automatic advance springs.
13. Weight assembly.
14. Shaft and action plate.
15. Cap retaining clips.
16. Vacuum unit.
17. Bush.
18. Thrust washer.
19. Driving dog.
20. Parallel pin.
21. Cam screw.
22. 'O' ring oil seal.

Section B.6

DISMANTLING THE DISTRIBUTOR

To dismantle the distributor for overhaul remove it from the engine as described in Section B.5 and then proceed as follows:

1. Remove the distributor cap and from it withdraw the carbon brush and its spring. Remove the rotor arm.
2. Lift the L.T. connector housing from the body, unscrew the two screws securing the contact breaker plates assembly, and disconnect the vacuum advance spring from its anchorage. Lift off the contact breaker plates assembly.
3. Unscrew the contact breaker spring anchorage nut and remove the nut, collar, L.T. lead and capacitor lead tags, moving contact breaker point, and the fibre washer.
4. Unscrew the fixed contact breaker plate securing screw and lift off the plate.
5. Remove the capacitor securing screw and the capacitor.
6. Rotate the removing plate and disengage the stud on it from the base plate. Disengage the base plate from the 'C' spring on the moving plate.
7. Remove the cam securing screw, the rolling weight springs, cam and action plate, and the weights.
8. Check the driving shaft end-float and clearance in the body bush.
9. Drive out the driving dog securing pin and remove the driving dog and thrust washer from the drive shaft. Withdraw the drive shaft from the body.

10. Remove the micro adjuster spring clip, unscrew the nut, and remove the spring and vacuum control from the body.

Section B.7

EXAMINING THE DISTRIBUTOR

In addition to carrying out the examination detailed in Section B.5 examine all parts for wear, deterioration, and thread damage, and the driving dog and rolling weights for indentation. Examine the 'O' ring oil seal (if fitted) on the shank for deterioration. Worn or unserviceable parts should be renewed.

If the clearance between the action plate shaft and the body bush is excessive the bush may be renewed as follows:

1. Soak the new bush in S.A.E. 30 or 40 oil for 24 hours. Alternatively, place the bush in oil and heat to 100°C. (212° F.) for 2 hours. Allow the oil to cool and remove bush.
2. Using a shouldered mandrel, press the old bush out from the inside of the body.
3. Insert the new bush into the shank end of the body smallest diameter of the bush leading. The bush will be a push fit until the large diameter contacts the body.
4. Use a mandrel, vice, press, or bush drawing tool to press the bush fully home with an applied steady pressure.
5. When pressed fully home the bush should be flush with the end of the body shank and should protrude slightly inside the body.
6. Using the shank drain hole as a guide, drill through the bush and then remove all fragments of metal.
7. Lubricate the action shaft with clean engine oil, ensure that no fraze exists around the hole in the shaft through which the driving dog pin passes, and then insert the shaft into the body shank.
8. If the shaft is a tight fit in the body repeat operation (7) until the shaft is free to rotate without binding. This is most important.
9. Run the shaft in the body with a lathe or test rig for 15 minutes, re-lubricate the shaft, and assemble the distributor.
10. Under no circumstances must the bush be over-bored since this will impair the porosity and thereby the effective lubricating qualities of the bush.

Section B.8

ASSEMBLING THE DISTRIBUTOR

Assembly is a reversal of the dismantling sequence, but attention must be given to the following points during assembly:

1. Lubricate the components.
2. Set the micro-adjuster to the mid-way position.

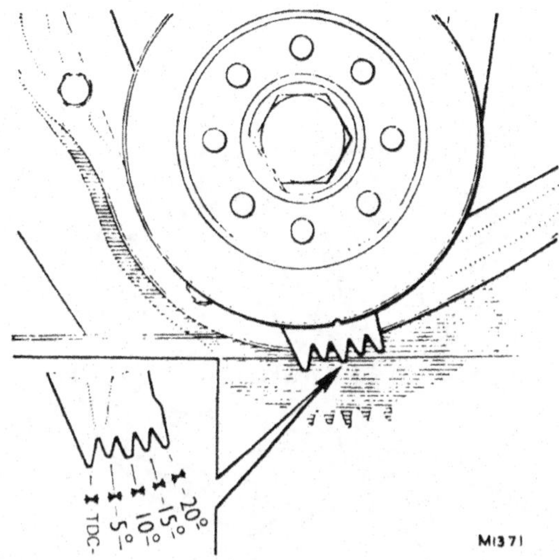

Fig. B.4
The notch in the pulley approaching the T.D.C. position for pistons 1 and 4. The inset shows the timing scale 5° marks

3. Adjust the contact breaker points to the correct gap.
4. Leave the clamp plate securing bolt slack.
5. After fitting the distributor to its housing rotate the rotor arm until the driving dog engages the recess in the distributor drive from the camshaft. The lugs on the dog are offset to ensure correct replacement.

Section B.9

STATIC IGNITION TIMING

To set the ignition timing proceed as follows:

1. Check the contact breaker gap setting.
2. Rotate the crankshaft until the valves of No. 4 cylinder are 'rocking' (i.e. exhaust valve just closing and inlet valve just opening). In this position No. 1 cylinder is approximately at T.D.C. compression stroke.
3. Refer to the **'GENERAL DATA'** for the correct ignition setting and rotate the crankshaft until the notch on the crankshaft pulley is opposite the correct pointer on the timing cover case for the required setting. The long pointer indicates T.D.C.
4. Rotate the distributor body anti-clockwise until the points are fully closed, then slowly rotate it in a clockwise direction until the points just commence to open.
   Alternatively, connect a 12-volt lamp in parallel with the contact breaker points (i.e. one lead to the L.T. terminal and the other to earth), switch on the ignition and turn the distributor as above until the lamp lights. This indicates that the points have just opened.
5. Slacken the clamp plate set bolts and secure the distributor body in this position by tightening the

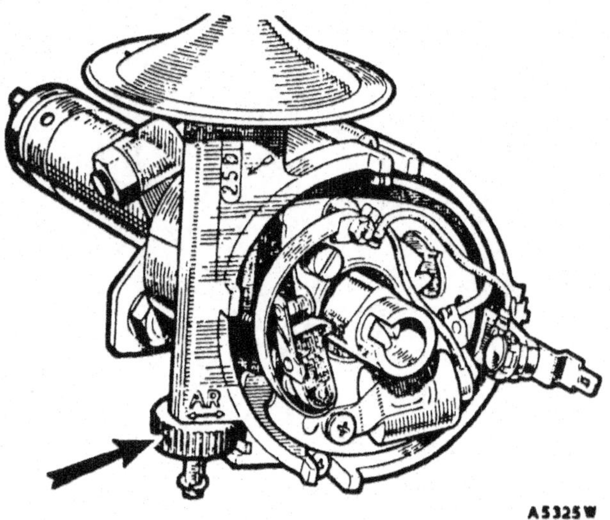

Fig. B.5
The vernier adjustment nut

clamp plate nut or bolt. The correct torque tightening figures are given in the '**GENERAL DATA**'. Tighten the clamp plate set bolts.

6. If the static ignition timing figures is between T.D.C. and 5° B.T.D.C., or between 5° B.T.D.C. and 10° B.T.D C., adjust the vacuum control adjusting screw to obtain the correct setting. Approximately 55 clicks of the screw will move the vacuum control barrel one graduation on the scale, and each graduation is equal to approximately 5° of movement on the moving plate.
7. Check that the rotor is opposite the correct electrode in the distributor cap for No. 1 cylinder.

Should a stroboscopic lamp be used for timing the ignition, care must be taken that with the engine running the speed is low enough to ensure that the centrifugal advance weights are not in operation. If the vacuum advance take-off is direct from the induction manifold the take-off must be disconnected before attempting the timing, otherwise the timing will be retarded.

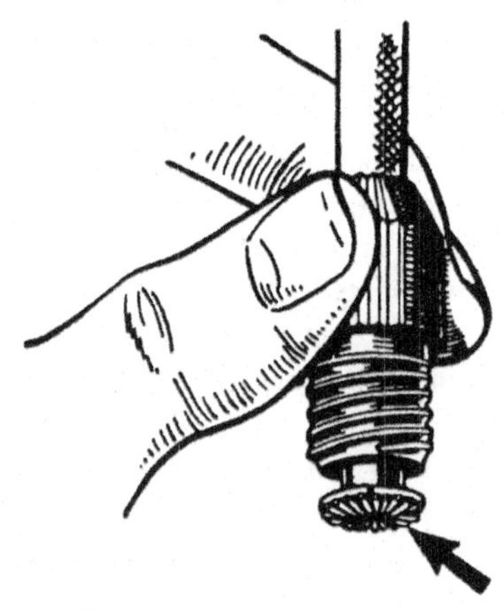

Fig. B.6
The correct method of fitting a high-tension cable to the ignition coil terminal nut

Section B.10

HIGH-TENSION CABLES

The high-tension cables must be examined carefully and any which have the insulation cracked, perished, or damaged in any way must be renewed.

To fit the cables to the terminal of the ignition coil thread the knurled moulded terminal nut over the lead, bare the end of the cable for about ¼ in. (6 mm.), thread the wire through the brass washer removed from the original cable, and bend back the strands over the washer. Finally, screw the terminal into the coil.

To make the connections to the terminals in the distributor moulded cap first remove the cap and slacken the screws on the inside of the moulding till they are clear of the cables.

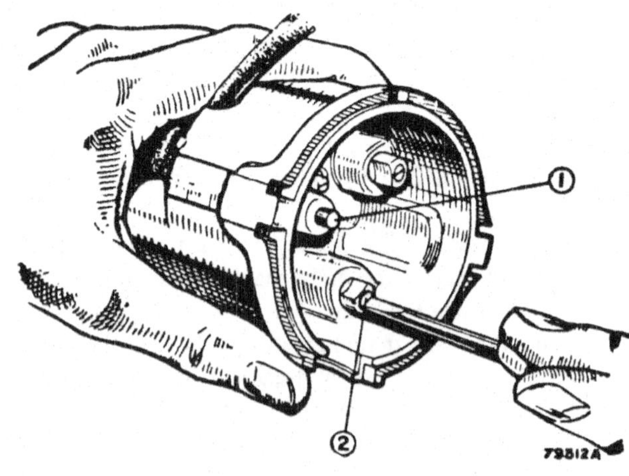

Fig. B.7
The correct method of connecting high-tension leads
1. Carbon brush. 2. Cable securing screw.

Remove the cables. Fill the holes in the distributor cap with Silicone grease, then cut the new cables off to the required length, push them completely home, and tighten the securing screws.

The cables from the distributor to the sparking plugs must be connected up in the correct firing order, which is 1, 3, 4, 2. Secure them firmly to the connectors.

Radio-frequency-suppressed high-tension cables are used on later cars. In this cable, a graphite-impregnated core replaces the metallic conductor of the earlier type of cable. Connectors used with the metal-cored cable are unsuitable for use with the later cable and new-type cable connectors have been introduced; these are a push-fit to the coil and distributor covers.

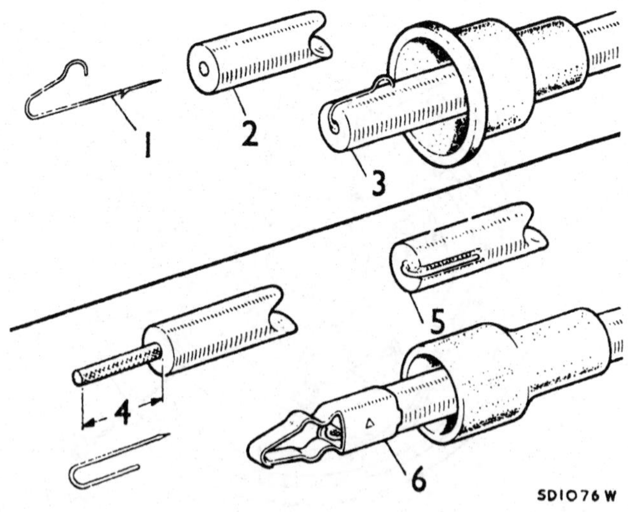

Fig. B.8
The correct assembly method for later-type suppressed high tension cables

Coil lead	*Plug leads*
1. Fish-hook connector.	4. Insulation removed for ½ in. (12.7 mm.).
2. Flush cable end.	5. Inner cord folded onto cable, staple pushed into the centre of the cord as far as possible.
3. Assembly of fish-hook and lead cover.	6. Cord and staple must make a good contact with body of connector.

Section B.11

SPARKING PLUGS

Inspect, clean, adjust and renew sparking plugs at the recommended mileage intervals.

Before replacing the plug in the engine, test it for correct functioning under air pressure in a plug tester, following out the instructions issued by the makers of the plug tester. Generally speaking, a plug may be considered satisfactory for further service if it sparks continuously under a pressure of 100 lb. per sq. in. (7 kg./cm.^{2}) with the gap between the points set at .022 in. (.56 mm.). It is essential that the plug points should be reset to the correct gap (see **'GENERAL DATA'**) before the plug is refitted to the engine.

When replacing a plug, always screw it down by hand as far as possible and use the spanner for final tightening only. Whenever possible use a box spanner to avoid possible fracture of the insulator. Where a torque spanner is available 14-mm. plugs should be tightened to between 27 and 30 lb. ft. (3.7 and 4.1 kg. m.).

Section B.12

LOCATING THE CAUSE OF UNEVEN FIRING

Start the engine and set it to run at a fairly fast idling speed.

Short-circuit each plug in turn by placing a hammer head or the blade of a screwdriver with a wooden or insulated handle between the terminal and the cylinder head. No difference in the engine performance will be noted when short-circuiting the plug in the defective cylinder. Shorting the other plugs will make uneven running more pronounced.

Having located the cylinder which is at fault, stop the engine and remove the cable from the terminal of the sparking plug. Restart the engine and hold the end of the cable about $\frac{3}{16}$ in. (4.8 mm.) from the cylinder head.

If the sparking is strong and regular, the fault probably lies in the sparking plug. Remove the plug, clean, and adjust the gap to the correct setting, or alternatively, fit a new plug (see Section B.11).

If there is no spark or if it is weak and irregular, examine the cable from the sparking plug to the distributor. After a long period of service, the insulation may be cracked or perished, in which case the cable should be renewed.

Finally, examine the distributor moulded cap, wipe the inside and outside with a clean dry cloth, see that the carbon brush moves freely in its holder and examine the moulding closely for signs of breakdown. After long service it may become tracked, that is, a conducting path may have formed between two or more of the electrodes or between one of the electrodes and some part of the distributor in contact with the cap. Evidence of a tracked cap is shown by the presence of a thin black line in the places indicated. A replacement distributor cap must be fitted in place of one that has become tracked.

Section B.13

TESTING THE LOW-TENSION CIRCUIT

Spring back the securing clips on the distributor and remove the moulded cap and rotor. If the rotor is a tight fit, it can be levered off carefully with a screwdriver.

Check that the contacts are clean and free from pits, burns, oil, or grease. Turn the engine and check that the contacts are opening and closing correctly and that the clearance is correct when the contacts are fully opened to between .014 and .016 in. (.36 and .40 mm.).

Correct the gap if necessary.

Disconnect the cable at the contact breaker terminal of the coil and at the low-tension terminal of the distributor, and connect a test lamp between these terminals. If the lamp lights when the contacts close and goes out when the contacts open, the low-tension circuit is in order. Should the lamp fail to light, the contacts are dirty or there is a broken or loose connection in the low-tension wiring.

Section B.14

LOCATING A LOW-TENSION CIRCUIT FAULT

Having determined, by testing as previously described, that the fault lies in the low-tension circuit, switch on the ignition, and turn the engine until the contact breaker points are fully opened.

Refer to the wiring diagram and check the circuit with a voltmeter (0-20 volts) as follows.

NOTE.–If the circuit is in order, the reading on the voltmeter should be approximately 12 volts.

1. **Battery to control box terminal 'B'.** Connect a voltmeter between control box terminal 'B' and earth. No reading indicates a damaged cable or loose connections.
2. **Control box terminal 'B' to ignition switch terminal (brown lead).** Connect a voltmeter between the ignition terminal and earth. No reading indicates a damaged cable or loose connections.
3. **Ignition switch (white lead).** Connect a voltmeter between the the ignition switch terminal and earth. Turn the ignition key to the ignition position. No reading indicates a fault in the ignition switch.
4. **Ignition switch (white with red lead).** Connect a voltmeter between the ignition switch terminal and earth. Turn the ignition key to the start position. No reading indicates a fault in the ignition switch.
5. **Ignition switch to fusebox terminal 'A3' (white lead).** Connect a voltmeter between the fuse unit terminal 'A' and earth. No reading indicates a damaged cable or loose connections.
6. **Fusebox terminal 'A3' to ignition coil terminal 'SW'.** Connect a voltmeter to the ignition coil terminal SW' and to earth. No reading indicates a fault in the primary winding of the coil and a new coil must be fitted.

Section B.15

SERVICING THE DISTRIBUTOR– Lucas type 45D4

Lubrication

1. Remove the distributor cover and rotor arm.
2. Lightly smear the cam and pivot post with grease.
3. Add a few drops of oil to the felt pad in the top of the cam spindle.
4. Add a few drops of oil through the gap between the cam spindle and base plate to lubricate the centrifugal weights.
5. Every 25,000 miles lubricate the contact breaker assembly centre bearing with a drop of oil in each of the two holes in the base plate.

   CAUTION: Do not oil the cam wiping pad.

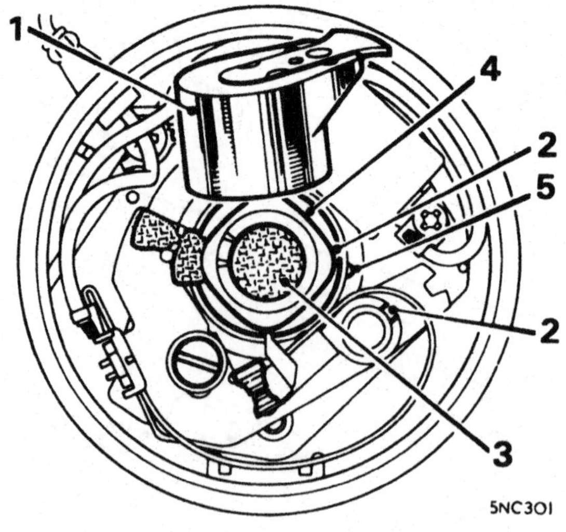

Fig. B.9

The rotor removed to show the lubrication points–Lucas 45D4.

1. Rotor.
2. Cam and pivot post.
3. Felt pad in the cam.
4. Gap between cam and base-plate (to lubricate centrifugal weights).
5. Centre bearing.

Renewing contact breaker points

6. Remove the securing screw with its spring and flat washer.
7. Lift the contact set.
8. Press the spring and release the terminal plate from the end of the spring.
9. Before fitting new contact points, wipe the points clean with fuel or methylated spirit.
10. Lightly grease the pivot post.
11. Re-connect the terminal plate to the end of the contact breaker spring.
12. Position the contact set on the distributor base plate and lightly tighten the securing screw. Ensure that the contact breaker spring is firmly in its register on the insulator and set the contact breaker gap.

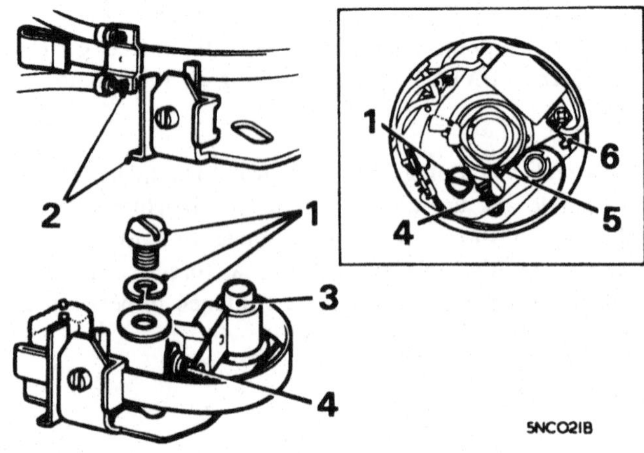

Fig. B.10

Removing a contact breaker set–Lucas 45D4.

1. Securing screw.
2. Terminal plate and contact breaker spring.
3. Pivot post.
4. Contact breaker points.
5. Heel of contact point on highest point of any one of the cam lobes.
6. Slot in contact breaker plate for adjusting gap with screwdriver.

Contact breaker gap–Checking–Adjusting

13. Turn the crankshaft until the heel of the contact point is on the highest point of any one of the cam lobes.
14. Check the contact gap; it should be 0.014 to 0.016 in. (0.35 to 0.40 mm.).
15. Adjust the gap; to adjust insert a screwdriver in the slot in the contact breaker plate and lever against the pip or cutout provided on the base plate.
16. Tighten the securing screw.
17. Turn the crankshaft until the heel of the contact is on the highest point of and alternative cam lobe.
18. Re-check the contact gap.
19. Repeat 17 and 18 for each remaining cam lobe.

Distributor cap–checking

20. Unclip and remove the distributor cap.
21. Remove the rotor arm.
22. Using a clean, nap-free cloth, wipe the rotor arm and the inside of the distributor cap.
23. Examine the cap and arm for cracks and signs of electrical tracking. Renew if necessary.
24. Check the condition and operation of the carbon brush. Refit the distributor cap.

Distributor dwell angle

25. Using suitable equipment, check the distributor dwell angle.
26. Readjust the contact breaker gap to obtain the correct dwell angle as follows:
    To increase the dwell angle, reduce the contact gap.
    To reduce the dwell angle, increase the contact breaker gap.
27. Re-check the ignition timing, and adjust if necessary.

Section B.16

DISTRIBUTOR–Lucas type 45D4 

Removing

1. Disconnect the battery.
2. Remove the distributor cap.
3. Rotate the crankshaft until the groove in the crankshaft pulley lines up with the static ignition point on the timing indicator (see 'ENGINE TUNING DATA') and at the same time the distributor rotor arm is in the firing position for No. 1 sparking plug.
4. Disconnect the low tension lead from the wiring harness.
5. Disconnect the vacuum pipe from the distributor vacuum advance unit.
6. Remove the two screws securing the distributor clamp plate to the cylinder block.
7. Withdraw the distributor from the engine.

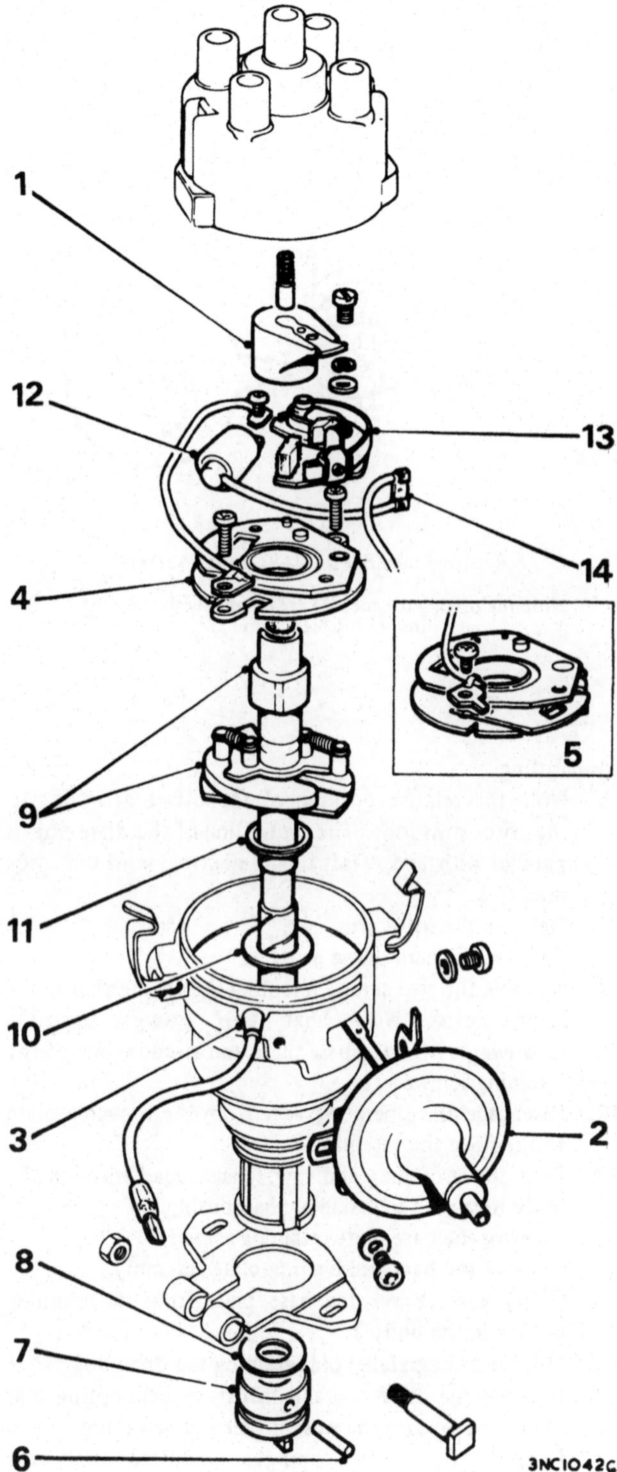

Fig. B.1

The distributor components (Lucas type 45D4)

1. Rotor arm.
2. Vacuum unit.
3. Low tension lead.
4. Base plate.
5. Base plate (early cars).
6. Retaining pin–drive dog
7. Drive dog.
8. Thrust washer.
9. Cam spindle and automatic advance weights assembly.
10. Steel washer.
11. Spacer.
12. Capacitor.
13. Contact set.
14. Low tension lead connector.

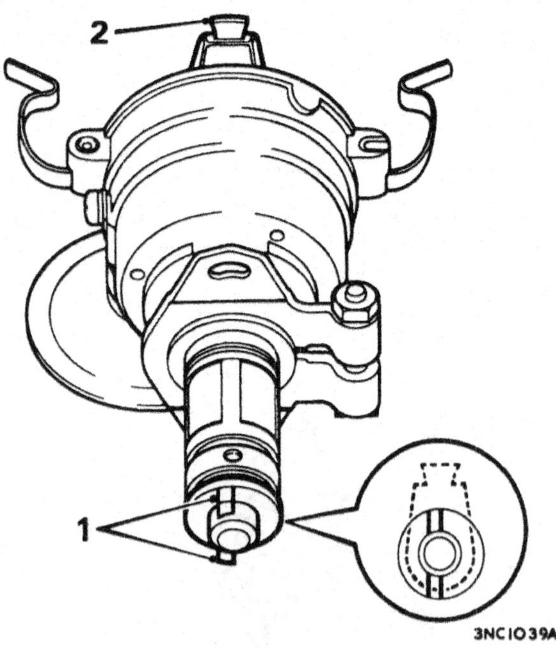

Fig. B.2

Refitting the drive dog (Lucas type 45D4)

Note the driving tongues (1) are parallel with the centre line of the rotor arm (2).

Dismantling

8. Note the relative position of the offset drive dog to the rotor arm lobe. The centre line of the drive dog is parallel with and offset to the centre line of the rotor arm.
9. Remove the rotor arm.
10. Remove the cam oiling pad.
11. Remove the two screws retaining the vacuum unit. (Early cars: Note that two prongs protrude downwards from the base plate and straddle one of the retaining screws.)
12. Disengage the operating arm from the movable plate and remove the assembly.
13. Push the grommet and low tension lead through the body towards the inside of the housing.
14. Remove the base plate retaining screws.
15. Remove the base and bearing plate assembly. (Early cars: Lever the base plate from its retaining groove in the body.)
16. Drive out the parallel pin retaining the drive dog.
17. Remove the drive dog and thrust washer, noting that the raised pips on the washer face the drive dog.
18. Remove the centre spindle complete with the automatic advance weights and springs.
19. Remove the steel washer and nylon spacer from the spindle.
20. Push the moving contact spring inwards and unclip the low tension lead.
21. Remove the screw retaining the earth lead tag and the capacitor.
22. Remove the screw, spring and plain washer retaining the fixed contact and remove the contact assembly.

Inspection

23. Examine the fit of the drive spindle in its bush, and the spindle cam for wear. The automatic advance mechanism should not be dismantled other than to remove the control springs. If any of the moving parts are excessively worn or damaged, the complete spindle assembly must be renewed. If the spindle bearing is worn allowing excessive side play, the complete distributor must be replaced.
24. Check the spring between the fixed and movable plates. Operate the plate and examine for freedom of movement and excessive wear. Renew as an assembly.
25. Examine the distributor and cap for cracks and signs of tracking. Examine the pick-up brush for wear and freedom of movement in its holder. Renew as necessary.
26. Check the rotor for damage, electrode security, and burning or tracking. Renew as necessary.

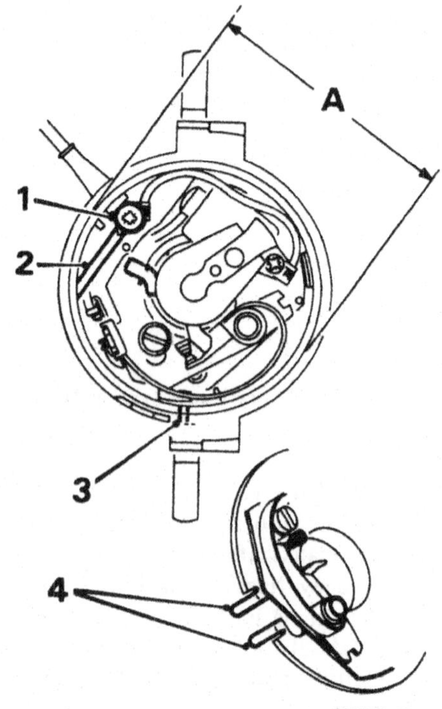

Fig. B.3

Refitting the base plate (early cars) (Lucas type 45D4)

1. Base plate.
2. Slot in base plate.
3. Screw hole.
4. Prongs.

'A': Diameter checking position.

Reassembling

27. During reassembly grease the pivots of the weights and springs and the spindle bearing area with Rocol MP (Molypad).
28. Grease the outside of the contact breaker hollow pivot post and lightly smear the spindle cam, using Retinax 'A' grease.
29. Apply one or two drops of clean engine oil to the oiling pad.
30. Reverse the procedure in 6 to 22, noting:
    a. Set the contact points gap to 0.014 to 0.016 in. (0.36 to 0.40 mm.).
    b. If a new drive spindle is fitted, tap the drive end of the distributor dog to flatten the pips on the thrust washer and ensure the correct amount of end-float.
    The new spindle should be drilled through the hole in the drive dog. Use a $\frac{3}{16}$ in. (4.76 mm.) drill. During drilling, push the spindle from the cam end, pressing the drive dog and washer against the body shank.

    EARLY CARS

    c. Ensure the base plate is pressed against the register in the body of the distributor so that the chamfered edge engages the undercut.
    d. Measure across the centre of the distributor at a right angle to the slot in the base plate.
    e. Tighten the securing screw and re-measure the distance across the body. Unless the measurement has increased by at least 0.006 in. (0.152 mm.) the contact breaker base plate must be renewed.

Refitting

31. Reverse the procedure in 4 to 7 but do not tighten the flange retaining screws.
32. With the crankshaft and distributor rotor set as in instruction 3, rotate the distributor within the limits of the slotted holes in the flange until the contact breaker points are just opening.
33. Tighten the flange retaining screws to 8 to 10 lbf. ft. (1.1 to 1.4 kgf. m.).
34. Refit the distributor cap.
35. Re-connect the battery.
36. Check the ignition timing.

SECTION C

THE COOLING SYSTEM

KEY TO THE RADIATOR, GRILLE, AND DIAPHRAGM COMPONENTS

(Illustrated on pages C.3 and C.4)

No.	Description
1.	Core assembly–radiator.
2.	Cap–filler.
3.	Tap–drain. } Early cars.
4.	Washer for tap } Early cars.
5.	Tube–drain.
6.	Clip–drain tube
7.	Packing.
8.	Diaphragm–radiator.
9.	Screw–long–radiator to diaphragm.
10.	Screw–short–radiator to diaphragm.
11.	Washer–spring–for screw.
12.	Screw–diaphragm to body.
13.	Washer–plain–for screw.
14.	Washer–spring–for screw.
15.	Rubber–radiator air seal.
16.	Tie–radiator–R.H.
17.	Tie–radiator–L.H.
18.	Washer–plain–radiator tie.
19.	Washer–spring–radiator tie.
20.	Nut–tie.
21.	Pipe–water pump connector.
22.	Plug–connector pipe.
23.	Washer–plug.
24.	Hose–connector.

No.	Description
25.	Clip–hose.
26.	Hose–top and bottom.
27.	Clip–hose.
28.	Case and grille assembly–radiator.
29.	Case assembly.
30.	Grille assembly.
31.	Bar–grille fixing–top.
32.	Bar–grille fixing–bottom.
33.	Slats–grille.
34.	Rivet–slat fixing.
35.	Bar and badge housing–centre.
36.	Badge.
37.	Fixing–blind badge.
38.	Screw–grille to case.
39.	Nut–spring.
40.	Fix–push-on–badge housing to case.
41.	Washer–spring.
42.	Washer–plain.
43.	Screw–grille to steady bracket.
44.	Bracket–steady grille centre assembly.
45.	Bracket–steady grille side assembly–R.H.
46.	Bracket–steady grille side assembly–L.H.
47.	Screw–steady bracket to bonnet lock platform.
48.	Washer–plain.

No.	Description
49.	Washer–spring.
50.	Nut.
51.	Buffer–grille top rail.
52.	Screw–grille to radiator duct panel.
Grille assembly (GHN5/GHD5 cars only)	
53.	Rubber–radiator air seal.
54.	Screw–radiator grille to bonnet lock platform.
55.	Plug–sealing.
56.	Grille assembly
57.	Washer.
58.	Washer–spring.
59.	Screw.
60.	Heater hose connection.
61.	Sealing washer.
62.	Self-tapping screw.
Grille assembly (GHN5/GHD5 cars)	
63.	Case assembly.
64.	Grille–R.H.
65.	Grille–L.H.
66.	Bracket–retaining grille to case.
67.	Screw.
68.	Motif.

THE RADIATOR, GRILLE, AND DIAPHRAGM COMPONENTS (GHN5/GHD5/CARS)

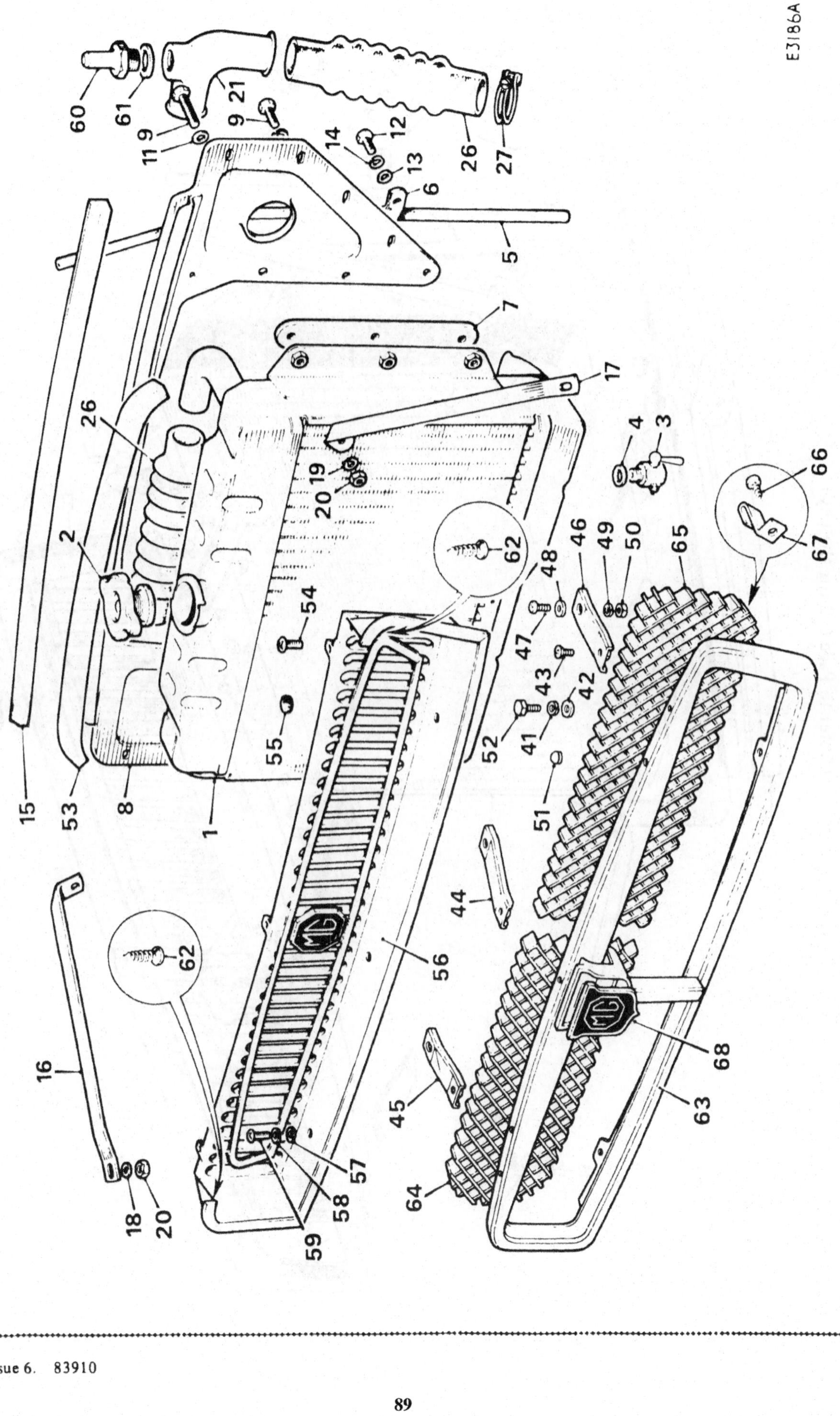

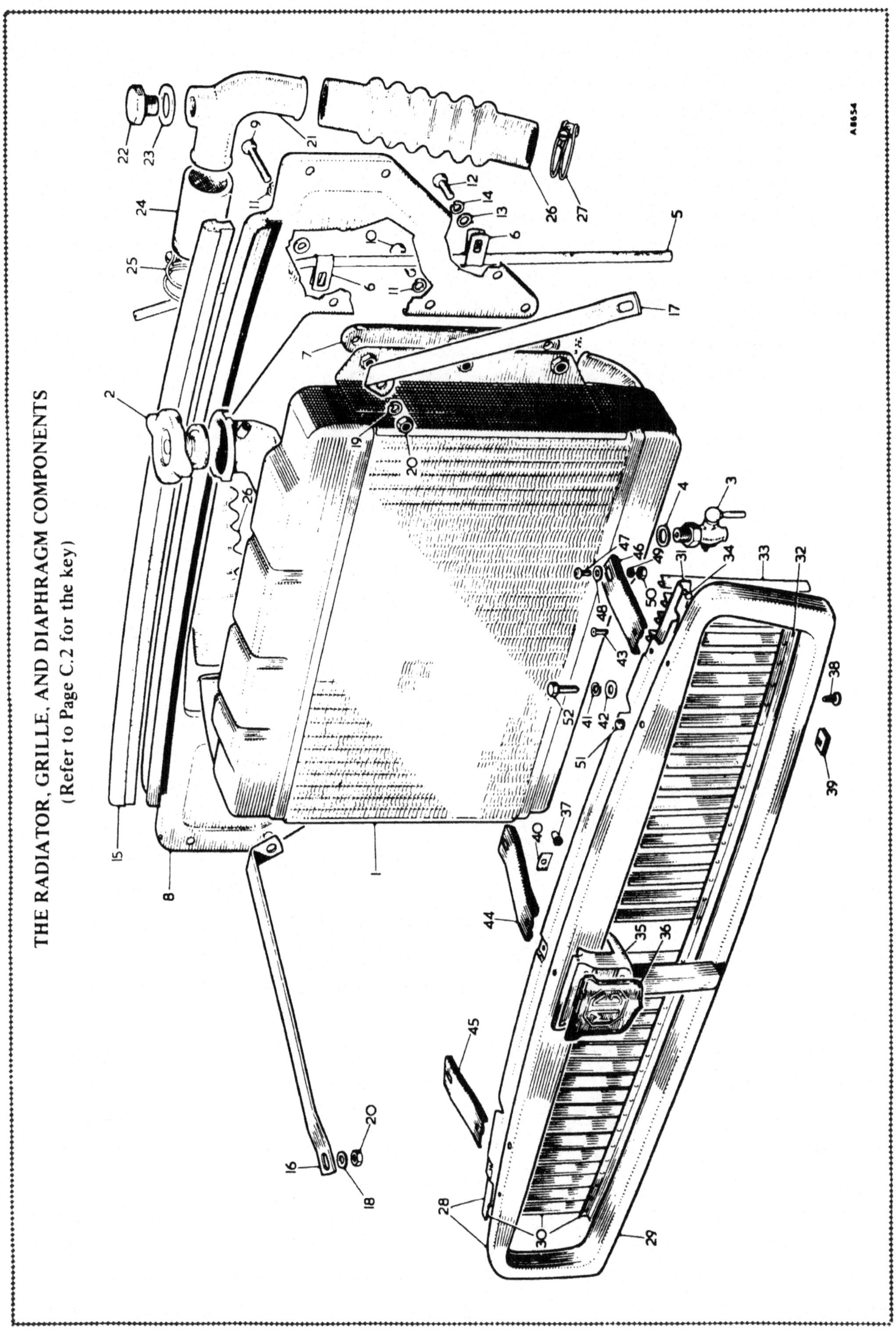

THE RADIATOR, GRILLE, AND DIAPHRAGM COMPONENTS
(Refer to Page C.2 for the key)

GENERAL DESCRIPTION

The cooling system is pressurized and the water circulation is assisted by a pump attached to the front of the engine and driven by a belt from the crankshaft pulley. A relief valve is incorporated into the radiator filler cap which controls the pressure.
The water circulates from the base of the radiator and passes round the cylinders and cylinder head, reaching the header tank of the radiator via the thermostat and top hose. From the header tank it passes down the radiator core to the base tank of the radiator. Air is drawn through the radiator by a fan attached to the water pump pulley.

Section C.1

LUBRICATION

Early cars
Remove the plug from the water pump body and add a small quantity of one of the recommended greases. Do not pressure-lubricate the water pump or the seal may be damaged.

Later cars
The greasing plug has been deleted from the water pump as no lubrication is necessary.

Section C.2

THERMOSTAT

IMPORTANT.–In hot climates where the thermostat is removed as a permanent measure, it is essential that a thermostat blanking sleeve is fitted. Failure to fit a sleeve will result in higher operating temperatures and possible damage.

Removing
1. Drain the cooling system–Section C.4.
2. Disconnect the radiator top hose from the water outlet elbow. Unscrew the three retaining nuts, detach the water outlet elbow and joint washer and withdraw the thermostat.

Inspection
3. Examine the thermostat for damage and check that the valve is in the closed position. Renew the thermostat if damaged or if the valve is open.
4. Immerse the thermostat in water heated to the temperature marked on the thermostat; the valve will start to open if it is functioning correctly. If the valve fails to open renew the thermostat.

Refitting
5. Reverse the removing procedure using a new joint washer, then refill the cooling system.

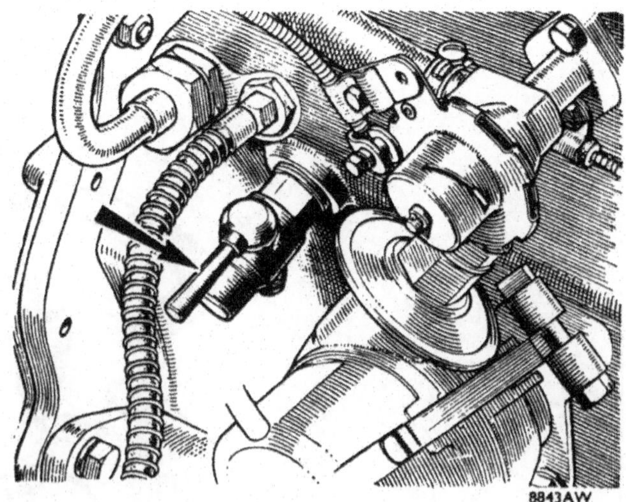

Fig. C.1
The engine drain tap on the right-hand side of the engine, later cars have a drain plug

Section C.3

TEMPERATURE GAUGE

A temperature gauge unit, consisting of a thermal transmitter and dial indicator, is fitted to the vehicle. The thermal transmitter is held in the cylinder head at the base of the thermostat housing by a gland nut. The dial indicator is situated in the instrument panel and is connected to the transmitter by a capillary tube.
If the unit fails to register the water temperature, check the thermal transmitter and dial indicator by substitution.
Cars built to certain specifications are fitted with electrical temperature gauges.

Section C.4

DRAINING, FLUSHING AND REFILLING THE COOLING SYSTEM

Removing the filler cap
The cooling system is under pressure while the engine is hot, and the radiator filler cap must be removed very carefully or left in position until the water has cooled.
If it is necessary to remove the filler cap when the engine is hot it is absolutely essential to release the cap gradually, and the filler spout is provided with a specially shaped cam to enable this to be done easily.
Unscrew the cap slowly until the retaining tongues are felt to engage the small lobes on the end of the filler spout cam, and wait until the pressure in the radiator is fully released before finally removing the cap.
It is advisable to protect the hand against escaping steam while removing the cap.

Draining the cooling system

EARLY CARS
Open the two drain taps, one at the rear of the engine cylinder block on the right-hand side, the other at the base

THE FAN AND WATER PUMP COMPONENTS

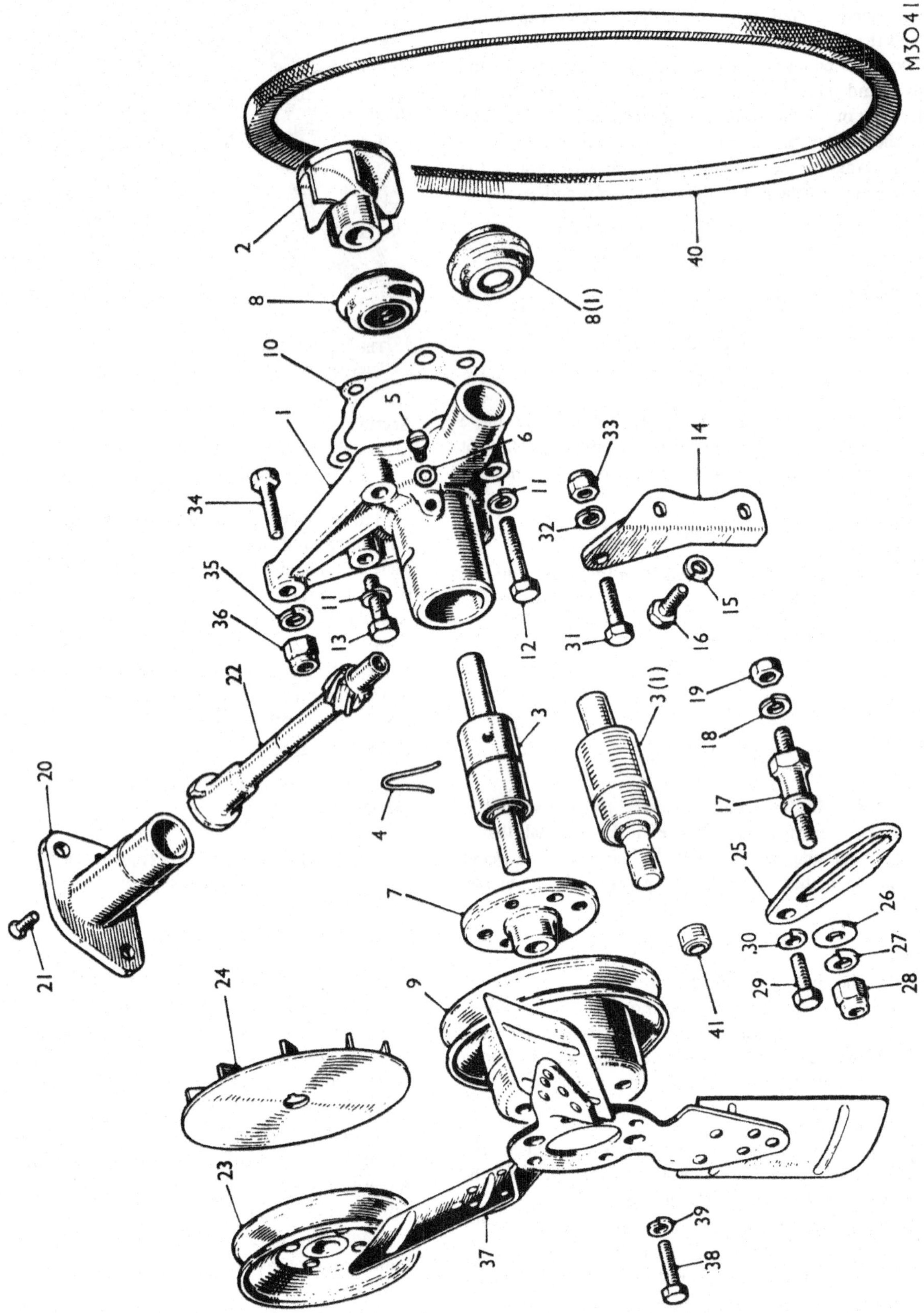

KEY TO THE FAN AND WATER PUMP COMPONENTS

No.	Description	No.	Description	No.	Description
1.	Pump assembly–water (with hub less pulley).	13.	Screw–short–water pump to crankcase.	27.	Washer–spring.
2.	Vane–water pump.	14.	Bracket–rear–dynamo.	28.	Nut–adjusting link to pillar.
3.	Bearing assembly complete with spindle.	15.	Washer–spring–screw.	29.	Screw–adjusting link to pillar.
3.	(1) Bearing assembly (later type).	16.	Screw–dynamo bracket to crankcase.	30.	Washer–spring–screw.
4.	Wire–bearing locating.	17.	Pillar–dynamo adjusting link.	31.	Bolt–dynamo to mounting bracket.
5.	Screw–lubricating point. } (early pumps only)	18.	Washer–spring–pillar.	32.	Washer–spring–bolt.
6.	Washer–fibre–screw. } (early pumps only)	19.	Nut–dynamo pillar.	33.	Nut–bolt.
7.	Hub–pulley.	20.	Housing–distributor.	34.	Bolt–dynamo to water pump body.
8.	Seal–water pump.	21.	Screw–housing to crankcase.	35.	Washer–spring–bolt.
8.	(1) Pressure balanced steel (later pumps).	22.	Spindle–distributor driving.	36.	Nut–bolt.
9.	Pulley–fan and water pump.	23.	Pulley–dynamo.	37.	Fan–water pump (six-bladed).
10.	Joint washer–pump to crankcase.	24.	Fan–dynamo.	38.	Screw–fan to pulley.
11.	Washer–spring–screw..	25.	Link–dynamo adjusting.	39.	Washer–spring–screw.
12.	Screw–long–water pump to crankcase.	26.	Washer–adjusting link to pillar.	40.	Belt–fan.

of the radiator. On 18GD and 18GG engines the engine cylinder block drain tap is replaced by a removable plug and sealing washer.

LATER CARS

Later cars have no provision for draining the radiator and the use of anti-freeze all-the-year round is recommended. To drain the coolant from the radiator, slacken the radiator bottom hose clip and remove the hose at its connection to the radiator.

When the system is completely drained and refilling is to be deferred until some later date a suitable notice should be fixed to the radiator filler cap, indicating that the coolant has been drained. As an alternative, place the radiator filler cap on the driver's seat or leave the filler cap access panel open as a reminder to fill the cooling system before the vehicle is used again

NOTE.--If a heater is fitted, under no circumstances should draining of the cooling system be resorted to as an alternative to the use of anti-freeze mixture, due to the fact that complete draining of the heater unit by means of the cooling system drain taps is not possible.

To ensure sufficient circulation of the coolant and to reduce the formation of scale and sediment in the radiator the system should be periodically flushed out with clear running water, preferably before putting in anti-freeze solution and again after taking it out.

The water should be allowed to run through until it comes out clear from the taps.

This method is adequate under normal conditions, but in extreme cases where excessive 'furring up' is experienced a more efficient method is to completely remove the radiator and flush in the reverse way to the flow, i.e. turn the radiator upside-down and let the water flow in through the bottom hose and out of the top connection.

Filling the cooling system

Close the radiator and cylinder block drain taps.

Fig. C.2
The location of the radiator drain tap (Early cars)

Ensure that all hose connections are tight.

Fill up the system through the filler in the radiator header tank until the level of water can just be seen. Run the engine until it is hot and then add sufficient water to raise the level to within 1 in. (25.4mm.) of the bottom of the filler neck.

When possible, soft water, such as clean rain-water, should be used to fill the system.

When using anti-freeze solution avoid overfilling to prevent loss from expansion.

Anti-freeze solutions having an alcohol base are unsuitable for use in the cooling system owing to the high temperatures attained in the top radiator tank. Only anti-freeze solutions of the ethylene glycol type incorporating the correct type of corrosion inhibitor should be employed. (See Section C.8).

Section C.5

FAN BELT

To fit a new fan belt slacken slightly the two bolts on which the dynamo pivots and release the bolt securing it to the slotted link and the nut securing the slotted link to the engine. Move the dynamo to the engine as far as possible. Slide the belt over the fan and onto the fan pulley; ease the belt onto the crankshaft pulley and dynamo pulley. It may be found helpful to turn the engine with the starting-handle whilst easing the belt over the dynamo pulley.

Adjustment is made by raising the dynamo upwards away from the engine. **A gentle hand pull only must be exerted on the dynamo, or the belt tension will be excessive and undue strain will be thrown onto the dynamo bearings.** Tighten up the bolts with the dynamo in this position. The belt should be sufficiently tight to prevent slip, yet it should be possible to move the belt laterally 1 in. (2.5 cm.) in the centre of its longest run.

On cars fitted with alternators the fan belt is renewed and adjusted in a similar manner.

Section C.6

RADIATOR AND DIAPHRAGM

The radiator block assembly is supported in a metal diaphragm which is secured to the body sides by screws and washers. The diaphragm has two holes in the right-hand side to permit the oil cooler pipes to pass from the cooler to the engine. A rubber air seal is fitted across the top channel of the diaphragm.

The radiator is supported in the diaphragm by three screws and washers each side and a tie-bar running forward from each top screw to the body sides.

The overflow pipe is secured by two clips that are retained by a radiator fixing screw and a diaphragm fixing screw respectively.

Removing

To remove the radiator drain the coolant–Section C.4, release the top and bottom hose clips, and detach the hoses from their connectors.

Where an oil cooler is not fitted the radiator and diaphragm may be removed as a complete assembly by removing the top radiator to diaphragm screws to release the stays and then removing the screws securing each side of the diaphragm to the body.

If an oil cooler is fitted the pipe connections must be disconnected from the cooler and the engine before removing the radiator and diaphragm assembly.

To remove the radiator without the diaphragm undo the radiator to diaphragm securing screws, slacken the diaphragm to body securing screws, remove the screw retaining the overflow pipe clip, and then lift the diaphragm sufficiently to allow the radiator to be pulled forward and lifted from the car.

Fig. C.4
The dynamo mounting bolts which must be slackened for fan belt tension adjustment

Replacing

Replacement is a reversal of the removal sequence, but ensure that the two packing pieces are correctly positioned either side of the radiator and that the overflow pipe is secured.

Close the drain taps, fill with coolant, and check for leaks.

Section C.7

WATER PUMP

Removing

1. Remove the radiator–Section C.6.
2. Remove the dynamo or alternator.
3. Unscrew the fan and pulley retaining screws and remove the fan and pulley.
4. Remove the water pump securing bolts and withdraw the pump.

Dismantling

5. Withdraw the pulley hub from the spindle.
6. Withdraw the bearing locating wire from the body aperture.
7. Tap the spindle rearwards and remove the spindle complete with the bearing. The bearing cannot be removed from the spindle.
8. Withdraw the impeller from the spindle and remove the seal.

Reassembling

9. If the interference fit of the fan hub was impaired when the hub was withdrawn from the spindle a new nut must be fitted. The hub must be fitted with its face flush with the end of the spindle (B, Fig. C.3).
10. Press the spindle bearing assembly into the pump body and take measurement E, Fig. C.5; adjust the

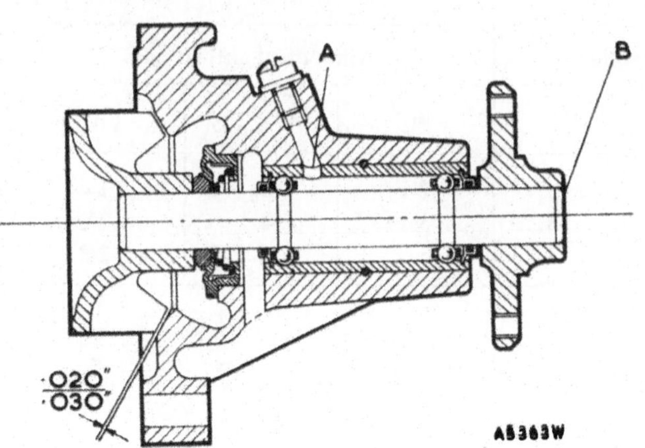

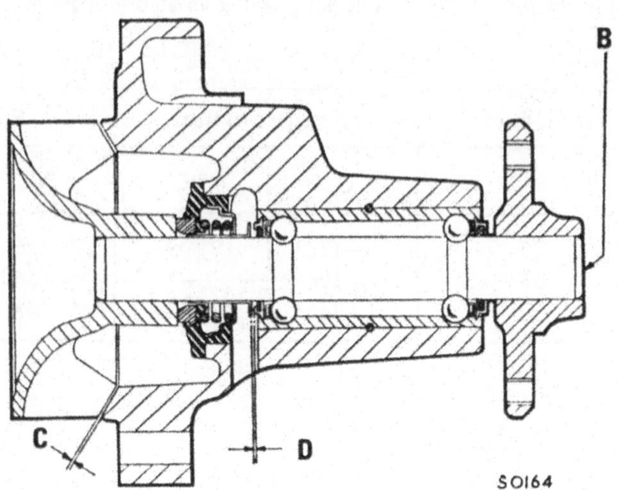

Fig. C.3
A section through the water pump showing: (left) early type with grease plug, and (right) later sealed type

A. Lubricating hole.
B. Hub face flush with spindle.
C. .020 to .030 in. (.51 to .76 mm.) clearance.
D. .042 to .062 in. (1.1 to 1.6 mm.) clearance.

position of the spindle bearing assembly to obtain the correct measurement.

(a) On pumps fitted with the early-type seal and thrower, check the bearing to thrower clearance before fitting the spindle (D, Fig. C.3).

(b) On pumps fitted with a greaser plug, align the holes in the bearing and body (A, Fig. C.3).

11. Fit a new seal. Smear the jointing face of the seal with a mineral base oil to ensure a watertight joint.
12. Press the impeller onto the spindle, ensuring that the correct running clearance (C, Fig. C.3) is maintained between the impeller vanes and the pump body.

Refitting

10. Reverse the removing procedure in 1 to 4.

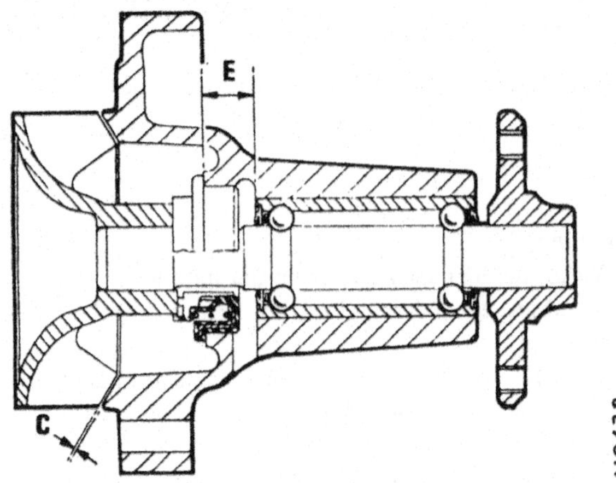

Fig. C.5
Pump with later-type seal, thrower deleted

E. Distance from rear face of spindle bearing (outer track) to seal housing shoulder should be .534 in.±.005 in. (13.56 mm.± 13 mm.) (pumps fitted with later-type seal only).

Section C.8

COLD WEATHER PRECAUTIONS

As the cooling system is pressurized, relatively high temperatures are developed in the radiator upper tank. For this reason anti-freeze solutions having an alcohol base are unsuitable owing to their high evaporation rate producing rapid loss of coolant and a consequent interruption of the circulation of coolant.

Only anti-freeze solution of the ethylene glycol type incorporating the correct type of corrosion inhibitor is suitable for use in the cooling system, and the recommended make is Bluecol, or any anti-freeze solution which conforms to Specification B.S. 3151 or B.S. 3152. The anti-freeze solution should be made up in the proportions given in the table below.

It is advisable for vehicles with an anti-freeze solution in the cooling system to have an identification mark on the header tank of the radiator.

The following precautions are necessary on vehicles so marked.

Make sure that the strength of the mixture is, in fact up to that instructed on the container of the particular anti-freeze solution used.

The strength of the mixture must be maintained by topping up with the anti-freeze solution as necessary when the system is hot. Topping up with water alone will reduce the degree of protection provided.

If the cooling system has to be emptied run the contents into clean containers, strain, and use again.

Anti-freeze can remain in the cooling system for two years provided that the specific gravity of the coolant is checked periodically and anti-freeze added as required. Specialized equipment, which can be obtained from the anti-freeze manufacturer, is necessary to check the specific gravity.

After the second winter, drain the system and flush out. Refill with fresh water or the recommended anti-freeze solution.

If for any reason the coolant is lost and the system is filled with water **remove the identification mark from the radiator header tank.**

Anti-freeze	Commences to freeze		Frozen solid		Amount of anti-freeze		
%	°C.	°F.	°C.	°F	Pts.	U.S. Pts.	Litres
25	−13	9	−26	−15	2½	3	1.4
33⅓	−19	−2	−36	−33	3½	4	2.0
50	−36	−33	−48	−53	5	6	2.8

Section C.9

DRAINING AND REFILLING THE COOLING SYSTEM
(GHN5 and GHD5 cars from Car No. 410002)

Draining

1. Stand the vehicle on level ground.
2. Remove the expansion tank cap and the filler plug from the coolant outlet pipe.
3. Slacken the hose clip and disconnect the bottom hose at the radiator.
4. Remove the cylinder block drain plug.

Filling

5. Refit the bottom hose and cylinder block drain plug.
6. Check that all hose connections are tight.
7. Turn the heater temperature control knob to 'HOT' to open the heater valve.
8. Top up the coolant in the expansion tank so that the tank is half-full and refit the cap.
9. Fill the system through the filler neck and bring the level up to the bottom of the threads.
10. Refit the filler plug.
11. Run the engine until the top radiator hose is warm and switch off the engine.
12. Turn the expansion tank cap to its safety stop to release the pressure and if necessary top up the expansion tank to half-full. Refit the cap.
13. Remove the filler plug and top up once more to the bottom of the threads. Refit the filler plug.

Section C.10

WATER PUMP
(GHN5 and GHD5 cars from Car No. 410002)

Removing

1. Drain the cooling system, see Section C.9.
2. Disconnect the alternator multi-connector plug.
3. Remove the alternator securing bolts.
4. Remove the alternator and drive belt.
5. Slacken the retaining clip and disconnect the radiator bottom hose from the water pump.
6. Remove the screws securing the water pump pulley.
7. Remove the spacer and water pump pulley.
8. Remove the bolts securing the water pump to the cylinder block.
9. Withdraw the water pump and joint washer.

Refitting

10. Reverse the procedure in 1 to 9, noting:
    a. Fit a new joint washer.
    b. Torque tighten the water pump securing bolts to the figure given in **'GENERAL DATA'**.
    c. Adjust the drive belt tension to the figure given in **'GENERAL DATA'**.

Section C.11

RADIATOR
(GHN5 and GHD5 cars from Car No. 410002)

Removing

1. Drain the cooling system, see Section C.9.
2. Slacken the hose clip and disconnect the top hose at the radiator.
3. Slacken the clip and disconnect the expansion tank hose from the radiator.
4. Disconnect the thermostatic switch wires connector.
5. Remove the screws securing the radiator to the mounting bracket.
6. Slacken the screws securing the radiator mounting bracket ties to the bonnet lock platform and swing the ties to one side.
7. Ease the radiator towards the front of the vehicle and withdraw the radiator from the engine compartment.

Refitting

8. Reverse the procedure in 1 to 7.

Section C.12

FAN MOTOR
(GHN5 and GHD5 cars from Car No. 410002)

Removing

1. Remove the radiator fan guard from the bonnet lock platform.
2. Disconnect the fan motor wires at the multi-connector plug.
3. Slacken the grub screw retaining the fan blades to the motor spindle.
4. Withdraw the fan blades off the spindle.
5. Slacken the two screws clamping the fan motor bracket.
6. Withdraw the fan motor from the bracket.

Dismantling

7. Remove the two through-bolts.
8. Withdraw the end cover complete with armature from the motor yoke, noting the assembly marks on the end cover and yoke.
9. Remove the circlip from the armature spindle and withdraw the two shims and the bowed washer.
10. Withdraw the armature assembly from the end cover.
11. Withdraw the thrust washer from the armature spindle.
12. Remove the circlip from the armature spindle.
13. Remove the three screws to release the brush carrier assembly from the end cover.

Inspection

14. Check the brush length, minimum length $\frac{3}{16}$ in (4.76 mm), renew the brush gear if necessary. If the brush leads are renewed, ensure that the black lead is connected to its correct brush and connector pin.

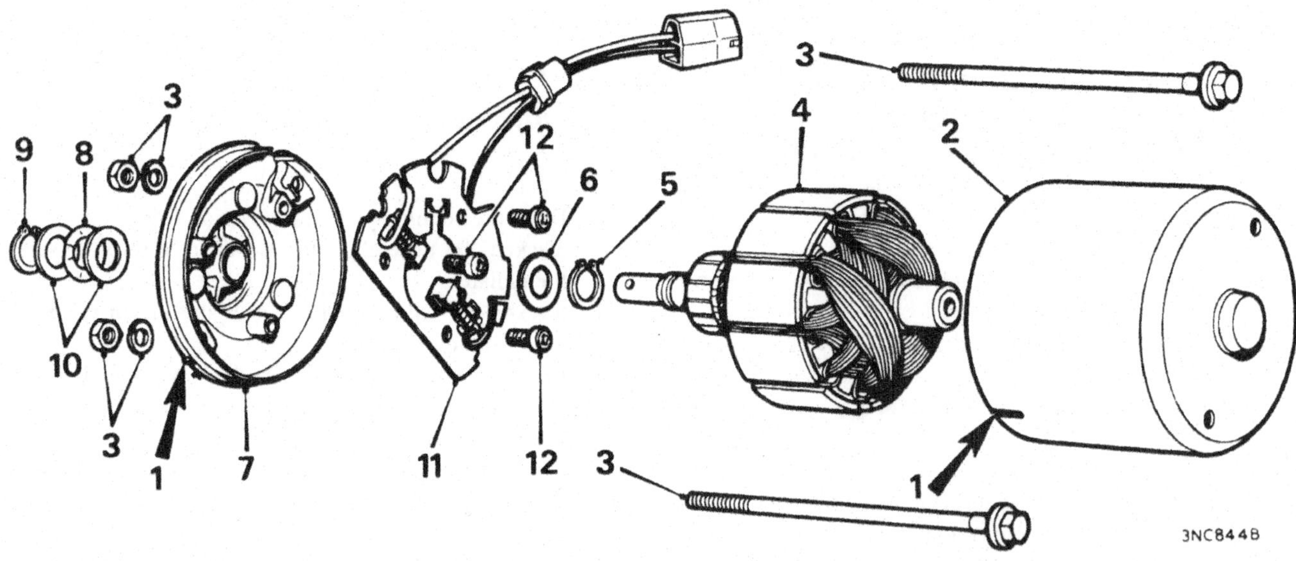

Fig. C.7

Radiator fan motor components

1. Assembley marks	5. Circlip	9. Circlip
2. Motor yoke	6. Thrust washer	10. Shims
3. Through-bolts	7. End cover	11. Brush carrier
4. Armature	8. Bower washer	12. Screws brush carrier

15. Connect a 110-volt a.c. supply with a 15-watt test lamp in circuit between the armature shaft and one of the commutator segments. If the test lamp lights, the armature insulation is faulty and the armature must be renewed.
16. Check the armature inter-winding for short circuits, using Growler test equipment.
17. Clean the commutator, using a petrol-moistened cloth; if necessary refinish the commutator, using very fine glass-paper. A badly burned or worn commutator should be skimmed lightly in a lathe. After skimming, clean the copper swarf from the inter-segment spacers. **CAUTION**: Do not undercut the commutator segments.

Reassembling

18. Reverse the procedure in 5 to 14, noting:
    a. Lubricate sparingly the bearing bushes and the armature shaft bearing surfaces with Shell Turbo 41 oil.
    b. Ensure that the assembly marks on the yoke and the end cover are in line.
    c. Fit the bowed washer between the two shim washers.
    d. Tighten the through-bolts to 14 lbf in (0.17 kgf m).
19. Test the fan motor, see Section C.13.

Refitting

20. Reverse the procedure in 1 to 4, ensuring to fit the motor to the mounting bracket so that the fan blades end of the motor body protrudes 2 in (50.8 mm) from the mounting bracket.

Section C.13

FAN MOTOR TEST

(GHN5 and GHD5 cars from Car No. 410002)

Test

1. Remove the fan motor, see Section C.12.
2. Slacken the grub screw and remove the fan blades.
3. Connect the motor to a 13.5-volt d.c. supply with a moving-coil ammeter in series and check that the motor light running current does not exceed 3 amps after 60 seconds from cold.
4. Check that the light running speed is between 3,500 and 4,000 rev/min at 13.5V after 60 seconds from cold.
5. If the motor current consumption and speed are low, a dirty commutator or faulty brush gear is indicated.
6. If the current consumption is high after the motor has been dismantled and reassembled, misalignment of the end cover bearing may be the cause, this can be corrected by applying a series of light blows to the side of the motor end cover only, using a hide or wooden mallet. If this does not correct high current consumption, a faulty armature is indicated.
7. Refit the fan blades.
8. Refit the fan motor.

Section C.14

THERMOSTAT

(GHN5 and GHD5 cars from Car No. 410002)

Removing

1. Remove the coolant filler plug and 'O' ring seal.
2. Remove the coolant drain plug from the cylinder block, partly drain, and refit the drain plug.
3. Remove the nuts, spring and plain washers and release the water outlet pipe.
4. Remove the joint washer.
5. Remove the thermostat from the cylinder head.

Testing

6. If the thermostat is stuck in the open position it is faulty and must be renewed.
7. Place the thermostat in a container of water and heat the water, noting the water temperature at which the thermostat opens. The nominal temperature in deg. C at which the thermostat opens is stamped on the base of the thermostat bulb. If it does not open at approximately the right temperature, renew the thermostat.

Refitting

8. Reverse the procedure in 1 to 5, noting:
   a. Use a new joint washer.
   b. Torque tighten the water outlet elbow nuts to the figure given in **'GENERAL DATA'**.

Insist on

UNIPART

British Leyland's comprehensive range of parts and accessories

Electrical components, filtration, cooling, transmission, braking and exhaust parts, are all covered by UNIPART, together with car care and maintenance items and an extensive range of other accessories.

Unipart means personalising your car with:

fog and spot lamps, wing mirrors, seat covers, a complete range of towing equipment, roof racks and ancillary instruments to name but a few products.

Unipart helps maintain that new car look with:

car polishes, chamois leathers, sponges, car vacuum cleaner, screen cleaners, touch up and aerosol paints.

Unipart means a range of Car Maintenance Products which includes:

tool kits, hydraulic jacks, foot pumps, inspection lamps, W.D. 40 and battery chargers.

You'll find Unipart stockists in the U.K., Eire and on the Continent—just look for the Unipart sign.

SECTION D

THE FUEL SYSTEM

† These operations must be followed by an exhaust emission check.

Section D.1

LUBRICATION

Carburetters

Unscrew the oil cap at the top of each suction chamber, top up with oil to within ½ in. (13 mm.) from the top of the hollow piston rod. Under no circumstances should a heavy-bodied lubricant be used.

Failure to lubricate the piston dampers will cause the pistons to flutter and reduce acceleration.

Section D.2

FUEL TANK

Removing

EARLY TOURER MODELS (10 gal. (12 U.S. gal., 45.4 litres))

Disconnect the battery and raise the car to a workable height.

Remove the hexagon drain plug and empty the tank.

Slacken the two clips on the filler neck hose, withdraw the filler extension and seal.

Disconnect the fuel pipe at the union and the fuel gauge cable from the tank unit, each on the right-hand side of the tank.

Support the tank and remove the two nuts from the bolts securing the straps at the rear of the tank to the anchorage brackets.

Swing away the straps and lower the tank.

LATER TOURER AND GT MODELS (12 gal. (14 U.S. gal., 54.5 litres)).

Disconnect the battery and raise the car to a workable height.

Remove the hexagon drain plug and empty the tank.

Slacken the two clips on the filler neck hose, withdraw the filler extension and seal. Disconnect the fuel pipe at the union and the fuel gauge cable from the tank unit, each on the right-hand side of the tank.

Support the tank and from inside the luggage compartment remove the set screws securing the tank to the luggage compartment floor.

Lower the tank.

Replacement is a reversal of the above instructions.

Fuel gauge tank unit

EARLY TOURER MODELS

Remove the six set screws securing the unit to the tank and withdraw the tank unit, taking care not to strain or bend the float lever. When replacing, a new joint washer must be fitted and a sealing compound used to make a fuel-tight joint.

LATER TOURER AND GT MODELS

Remove the tank gauge locking ring with Service tool 18G 1001 and lift out the gauge assembly and rubber sealing ring. When refitting the gauge unit a new rubber sealing ring should be fitted if necessary to ensure a fuel-tight joint.

Section D.3

FUEL PUMP

Removing and refitting

The fuel pump is mounted on a bracket secured to the heelboard adjacent to the front mounting right-hand rear spring, and is accessible from beneath the car.

Disconnect the earth lead from the batteries and the earth and supply leads from the terminals on the pump.

Disconnect the inlet and outlet pipe unions and the breather pipes (later cars).

Remove the two bolts securing the pump bracket to the heelboard.

When refitting, reverse the removing procedure ensuring that the breather pipes are connected to the pump and correctly retained by the 'T' pieces in the harness grommets in the boot floor.

Dismantling

CONTACT BREAKER

1. Remove the insulated sleeve or knob, terminal nut, and connector, together with its shakeproof washer. Remove the tape seal and take off the end cover.
2. Unscrew the 5 B.A. screw which holds the contact blade to the pedestal and remove the condenser from its clip. This will allow the washer, the long coil lead, and the contact blade to be removed.

COIL HOUSING AND DIAPHRAGM

3. Unscrew the coil housing securing screws, using a thick-bladed screwdriver to avoid damaging the screw heads.
4. Remove the earthing screw.
5. ROLLER TYPE. Hold the coil housing over a bench or receptacle to prevent the 11 brass rollers from being damaged or lost as they come free, unscrew the diaphragm assembly anti-clockwise until the armature spring pushes it free of the housing.
   GUIDE PLATE TYPE. Turn the back edge of the diaphragm and carefully lever the two end lobes of the armature guide plate from the recess in the coil housing, unscrew the diaphragm assembly anti-clockwise until the armature spring pushes it free of the housing. Remove the armature guide from the diaphragm assembly.

PEDESTAL AND ROCKER

6. Remove the end cover seal washer, unscrew the terminal nut, and remove the lead washer. This will have flattened on the terminal tag and thread and is best cut away with cutting pliers or a knife. Remove the terminal tag spring washer. Unscrew the two 2 B.A. screws holding the pedestal to the coil housing, remove the earth terminal tag together with the condenser clip. Tip the pedestal and withdraw the terminal stud from the terminal tag. The pedestal may now be removed with the rocker mechanism attached.

THE AUF 300 AND HP FUEL PUMP COMPONENTS

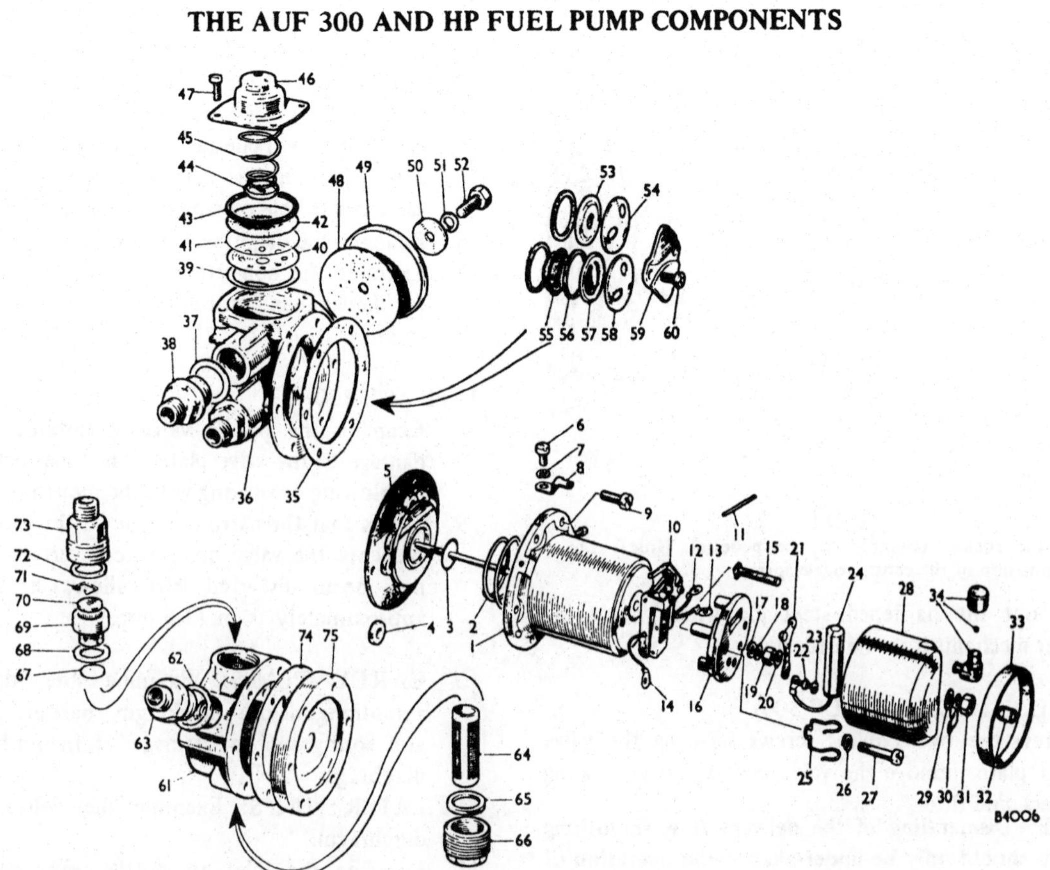

No.	Description	No.	Description		No.	Description	
1.	Coil housing.	26.	Spring washer.		51.	Spring washer.	
2.	Armature spring.	27.	Pedestal screw.		52.	Set screw.	
3.	Impact washer.	28.	End cover.		53.	Outlet valve.	
4.	Armature centralizing roller.	29.	Shakeproof washer.		54.	Valve cap.	
5.	Diaphragm and spindle assembly.	30.	Lucar connector.		55.	Filter.	AUF 300 Type.
6.	Set screw.	31.	Nut.		56.	Sealing washer.	
7.	Spring washer.	32.	Insulating sleeve.		57.	Inlet valve.	
8.	Earth connector.	33.	Sealing band.		58.	Valve cap.	
9.	Set screw.	34.	Vent valve.		59.	Clamp plate.	
10.	Rocker mechanism.	35.	Gasket.		60.	Set screw.	
11.	Rocker pivot pin.	36.	Pump body.		61.	Pump body.	
12.	Terminal tag.	37.	Fibre washer.		62.	Fibre washer.	
13.	Terminal tag.	38.	Outlet connection.		63.	Outlet connection.	
14.	Earth tag.	39.	Sealing washer.		64.	Filter.	
15.	Terminal stud.	*40.	Diaphragm plate.		65.	Washer.	
16.	Pedestal.	41.	Plastic diaphragm barrier.	AUF 300 Type.	66.	Plug.	
17.	Spring washer.	*42.	Rubber diaphragm.		67.	Inlet valve.	HP Type
18.	Lead washer.	43.	Rubber 'O' ring.		68.	Thin fibre washer.	
19.	Terminal nut.	*44.	Spring end cap.		69.	Outlet valve cage.	
20.	End cover seal washer.	*45.	Diaphragm spring.		70.	Outlet valve.	
21.	Contact blade.	†46.	Delivery flow smoothing device cover.		71.	Spring clip.	
22.	Washer.	47.	Set screw.		72.	Medium fibre washer.	
23.	Contact blade screw.	48.	Gasket.		73.	Outlet connection.	
24.	Condenser.	49.	Inlet air bottle cover.		74.	Gasket.	
25.	Condenser clip.	50.	Dished washer.		75.	Sandwich plate.	

* Early pumps. † Delivery air bottle (later pumps).

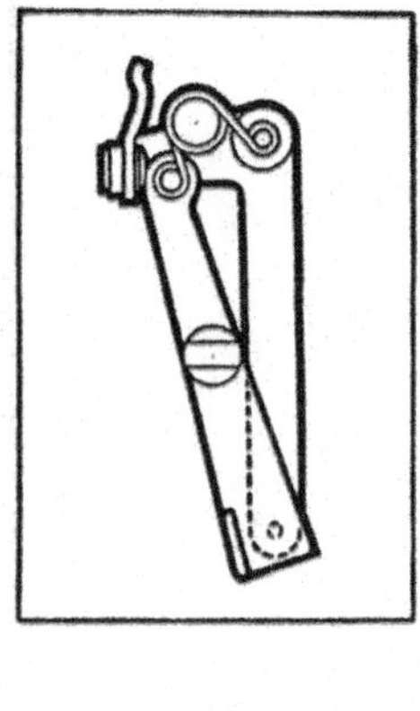

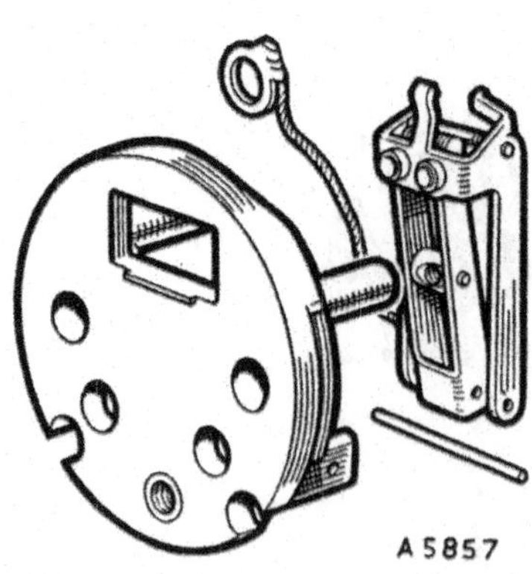

Fig. D.1
Fitting the rocker assembly to the pedestal. (Inset) the correct position of the centre toggle spring

7. Push out the hardened steel pin which holds the rocker mechanism to the pedestal.

BODY AND VALVES (type AUF 300)

8. Unscrew the two Phillips screws securing the valve clamp plate, remove the valve covers, valves, sealing washers, and filter.
   NOTE.–Dismantling of the delivery flow smoothing device should only be undertaken if the operation of it is faulty, and if the necessary equipment for pressure-testing after assembly is available. On this understanding proceed as follows:
9. Remove the four 4 B.A. screws securing the delivery flow smoothing device vent cover, remove the cover, the diaphragm spring, rubber 'O' rings, spring cap, diaphragm, barrier, diaphragm plate, and sealing washer.
10. Remove the single 2 B.A. screw securing the inlet air bottle cover, remove the cover and gasket.
11. Unscrew the inlet and outlet connections.

BODY AND VALVES (type HP)

12. Remove the inlet union, the outlet union, the outlet valve cage, and the inlet valve disc. Remove the base plug and filter.

Inspecting

GENERAL

If gum formation has occurred in the fuel used in the pump, the parts in contact with the fuel will have become coated with a substance similar to varnish. This has a strong, stale smell and will attack the neoprene diaphragm. Brass and steel parts so affected can be cleaned by being boiled in a 20 per cent. solution of caustic soda, dipped in a strong nitric acid solution, and finally washed in boiling water. Light alloy parts must be well soaked in methylated spirits and then cleaned.

1. Clean the pump and inspect for cracks, damaged joint faces, and threads.
2. Clean the filter with a brush and examine for fractures. Renew if necessary.
3. Examine the coil lead tags for security and the lead insulation for damage.
4. Examine the contact breaker points for signs of burning and pitting. If this is evident the rockers and spring blade must be renewed.
5. Examine the pedestal for cracks or other damage particularly to the narrow ridge on the edge of the rectangular hole on which the contact blade rests.
6. Examine the diaphragm for signs of deterioration.
7. Examine the non-return vent valve in the end cover for damage, and ensure that the small ball valve is free to move.

TYPE AUF 300

8. Examine the plastic valve assemblies for kinks or damage to the valve plates. They can best be checked by blowing or sucking with the mouth.
9. Check that the narrow tongue on the valve cage which prevents the valve being forced out of position, has not been distorted but allows a valve lift of approximately $\frac{1}{16}$ in. (1.6 mm.).
10. EARLY PUMPS: Examine the delivery flow smoothing device diaphragm, barrier, plate, spring, and spring cap for damage. If in doubt, renew the diaphragm.
    LATER PUMPS: Examine the delivery air bottle diaphragm.
11. Examine the inlet air bottle cover and gasket for damage.
12. Examine the valve recesses in the body for damage and corrosion. If it is impossible to remove the corrosion or if the recesses are badly pitted the body must be discarded.

TYPE HP

13. Remove the circlip in the outlet valve cage and examine the inlet and outlet valve discs for signs of wear. Scrap, if worn.
14. Examine the valve seat in the body and outlet valve cage for damage and corrosion. If it is impossible to remove the corrosion or if the seat is pitted the body or cage must be discarded.

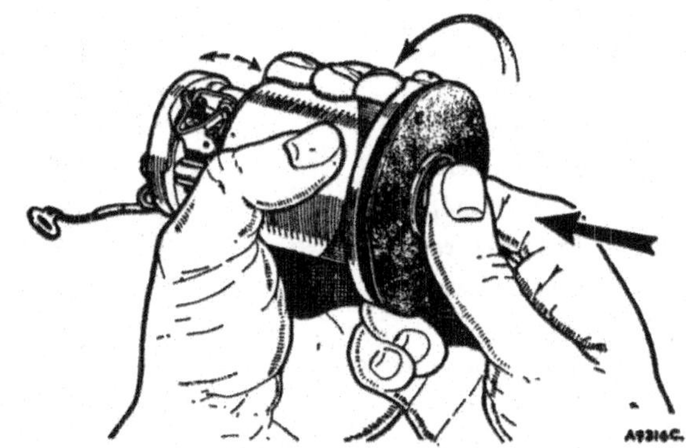

Fig. D.2
Setting the diaphragm. Unscrew until the rocker just 'throws over'

Reassembling

PEDESTAL AND ROCKER

NOTE.–The steel pin which secures the rocker mechanism to the pedestal is specially hardened and must not be replaced by other than a genuine S.U. part.

1. Invert the pedestal and fit the rocker assembly to it by pushing the steel pin through the small holes in the rockers and pedestal struts. Then position the centre toggle so that with the inner rocker spindle in tension against the rear of the contact point the centre toggle spring is above the spindle on which the white rollers run. This positioning is important to obtain the correct 'throw-over' action. It is also essential that the rockers are perfectly free to swing on the pivot pin and that the arms are not binding on the legs of the pedestal. If necessary, rockers can be squared up with a pair of thin-nosed pliers.
2. Assemble the square-headed 2 B.A. terminal stud to the pedestal, the back of which is recessed to take the square head.
3. Assemble the 2 B.A. spring washer and put the terminal stud through the 2 B.A. terminal tag then fit the lead washer, and the coned nut with its coned face to the lead washer (this makes better contact than an ordinary flat washer and nut). Tighten the 2 B.A. nut and finally add the end cover seal washer.
4. Assemble the pedestal to the coil housing by fitting the two B.A. pedestal screws, ensuring that the condenser wire clip on the left-hand screw (9 o'clock position) is between the pedestal and the earthing tag. The spring washer is not fitted when a condenser is used.
5. Tighten the screws, taking care to prevent the earthing tag from turning as this will strain or break the earthing flex. Do not overtighten the screws or the pedestal will crack. **Do not fit the contact blade at this stage.**

DIAPHRAGM ASSEMBLY

6. Place the armature spring into the coil housing with its large diameter towards the coil.

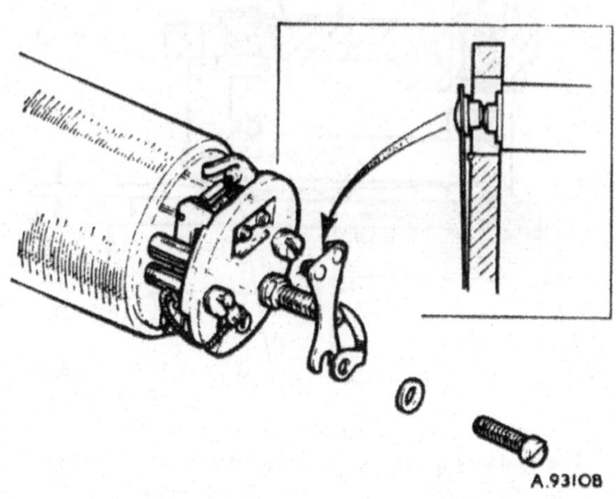

Fig. D.3
Setting the correct relative position of blade and rocker contact points

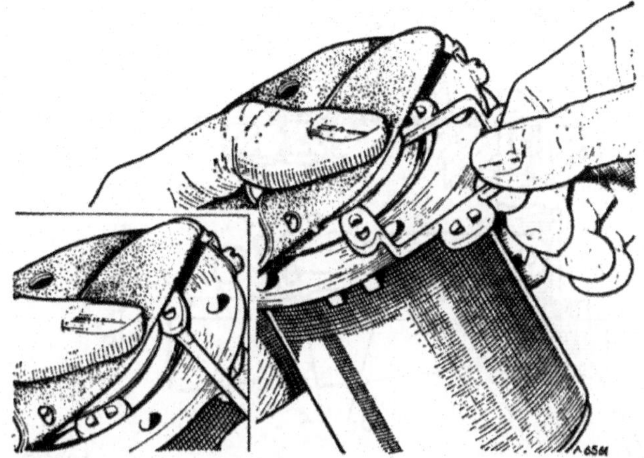

Fig. D.4
Fitting the armature guide plate. (Inset), levering one of the end lobes from the recess

7. Before fitting the diaphragm make sure that the impact washer (a small neoprene washer that fits in the armature recess) is fitted to the armature. Do not use jointing compound or dope on the diaphragm.
8. Fit the diaphragm by inserting the spindle in the coil and screwing it onto the threaded trunnion in the centre of the rocker assembly.
9. Screw in the diaphragm until the rocker will not 'throw over'. This must not be confued with jamming the armature on the coil housing internal steps.
10. ROLLER TYPE. With the pump held with the rocker end downwards, turn back the edge of the diaphragm and fit the 11 brass rollers into the recess in the coil housing.
    On later-type rocker mechanisms with adjustable fingers fit the contact blade and adjust the finger settings as described under those headings, then carefully remove the contact blade.
11. With the pump held horizontally, slowly unscrew the diaphragm while at the same time actuating it, until the rocker just throws over. Unscrew the diaphragm until the holes are aligned, then unscrew it a further quarter of a turn (four holes).
12. ROLLER TYPE. Press the centre of the armature and fit the retaining fork at the back of the rocker assembly.

BODY COMPONENTS (type AUF 300)

13. GUIDE PLATE TYPE. Turn back the edge of the diaphragm and insert one end lobe of the armature guide plate into the recess between the armature and the coil housing. Progressively position all four lobes, then commencing in the centre and finishing with the two end ones, press the lobes firmly into the recess.
14. Note that the inlet valve recess in the body is deeper than the outlet recess to allow for the filter and extra washer. Screw in the inlet and outlet connections with their sealing rings. Assemble the outlet valve

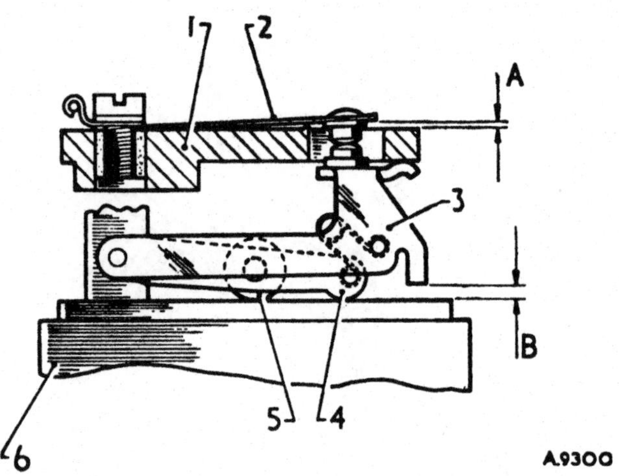

Fig. D.5
The rocker finger settings on modified rocker assemblies

1. Pedestal.
2. Contact blade.
3. Outer rocker.
4. Inner rocker.
5. Trunnion.
6. Coil housing.

A = .035 in. (.9 mm.) B = .070 in. (1.8 mm.).

components into the outlet recess in the following order: first a joint washer, then the valve (tongue side downwards), then the valve cover.

15. Assemble the inlet valve into the recess as follows: first a joint washer, then the filter (dome side downwards), then another joint washer, followed by the valve assembly (tongue side uppermost), then the valve cover.
16. Take care that both valve assemblies nest down into their respective recesses, place the clamp plate on top of the valve covers and tighten down firmly on to the body with the two screws. Replace the inlet air bottle cover with its joint washer and tighten down the central screw.
17. EARLY PUMPS: Place the sealing washer in the bottom of the delivery flow smoothing device recess, follow this with the perforated diaphragm plate (dome side downwards), then the plastic barrier followed by the rubber diaphragm. Insert the 'O' section sealing ring into the recess and ensure that it seats evenly. Place the diaphragm spring (large end towards the vented cover) into the cover, place the spring end cap on to the small end of the spring, pass the assembly tool through the cover, spring, and end cap, turn the tool through 90°, and tension the spring. Finally, fit the cap and spring assembly on to the diaphragm, tighten the four retaining screws and release the assembly tool.

    LATER PUMPS: Place the sealing washer in the bottom of the delivery air bottle recess, place the plastic diaphragm, dome side downwards, then add the 'O' section sealing ring and tighten down the cap with its four screws.

BODY COMPONENTS (type HP)

18. Assemble the brass outlet valve disc to the outlet valve cage, making sure that the smooth face of the disc faces the valve seat, retain it in position with the circlip, which must be located in its groove. The valve must rattle freely when the valve cage is shaken.
19. Drop the inlet valve disc, smooth face downwards, on to the inlet valve seat in the body of the pump, insert the thin fibre washer, drop the outlet valve cage in position and insert the medium fibre washer, then screw in the outlet union and tighten with a spanner. Fit the inlet union and filter.

BODY ATTACHMENT (type AUF 300)

20. Fit the joint washer to the body, aligning the screw holes, and offer up the coil housing to the body, ensuring correct seating between them.
21. Line up the six securing screw holes, making sure that the cast lugs on the coil housing are at the bottom, and insert the six 2 B.A. screws finger tight. Fit the earthing screw with its Lucar connector.
22. ROLLER TYPE. Carefully remove the retaining fork from the rocker assembly and check that the rollers are correctly positioned.
23. Tighten the securing screws in diagonal sequence.

BODY ATTACHMENT (type HP)

24. Place the sandwich plate joint gasket on the face of the body, lining up the holes in the body and washer, fit the sandwich plate (concave face to diaphragm) to the gasket on the body, again lining up the holes.
25. Offer up the coil housing to the body and sandwich plate and ensure correct seating between them, with the connections at the top and filter at the bottom.
26. Line up the six securing screw holes, making sure that the two cast lugs on the coil housing are at the bottom, and insert the six 2 B.A. screws finger tight. Fit the earthing screw with its Lucar connector.

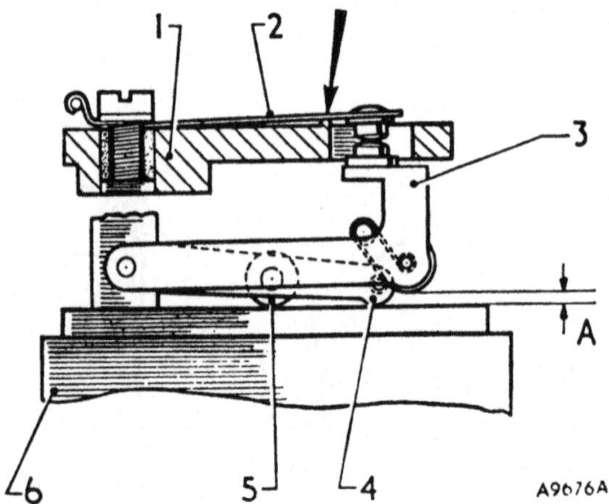

Fig. D.6
The contact gap setting on earlier-type rocker assemblies

1. Pedestal.
2. Contact blade.
3. Outer rocker.
4. Inner rocker.
5. Trunnion.
6. Coil housing.

A = .030 in. (.8 mm.).

27. **Remove the roller retaining fork carefully**, making sure that the rollers retain their position; a displaced roller will cut the diaphragm.
28. Tighten the securing screws in sequence as they appear diametrically opposite each other.

CONTACT BLADE

29. Fit the contact blade and coil lead to the pedestal with the 5 B.A. washer and screw. Place the condenser tag beneath the coil lead tag.
30. Adjust the contact blade so that the points on it are a little above the contact points on the rocker when the points are closed, also that when the contact points make or break one pair of points wipes over the centre line of the other in a symmetrical manner.
    The contact blade attachment screw slot allows a degree of adjustment.
31. Tighten the contact blade attachment screw when the correct setting is obtained.

CONTACT GAP SETTINGS

32. Check that when the outer rocker is pressed on to the coil housing the contact blade rests on the narrow rib which projects above the main face of the pedestal. If it does not, slacken the contact blade attachment screw, swing the blade clear of the pedestal, and bend it downwards a sufficient amount so that, when re-positioned, it rests against the rib.

(a) MODIFIED ROCKER ASSEMBLIES

33. Check the lift of the contact blade above the top of the pedestal (A) (Fig. D.5) with a feeler gauge, bending the stop finger beneath the pedestal, if necessary, to obtain a lift of .035±.005 in. (.9±.13 mm.).
34. Check the gap between the rocker finger and coil housing (B) (Fig. D.5) with a feeler gauge, bending the stop finger, if necessary, to obtain a gap of .070±.005 in. (1.8±.13 mm.).

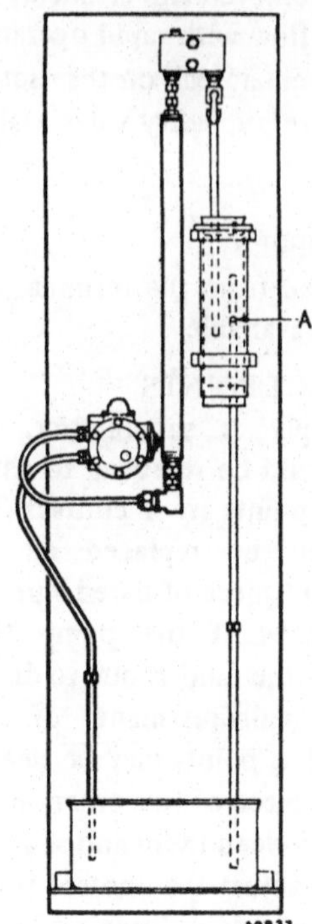

Fig. D.7

(1) The AUF 300 type pump mounted on the S.U. test stand
(A) Hole .187 to .192 in. (4.74 to 4.9 mm.) dia.

(2) The HP type pump mounted on the S.U. test stand.
(A) Hole .156 in. (4 mm.) dia.

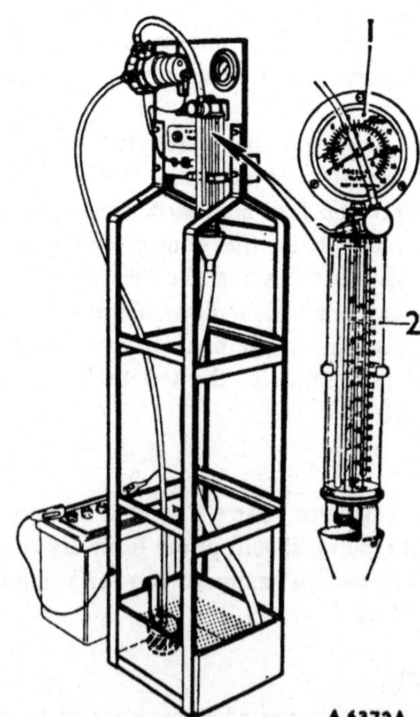

Fig. D.8

A checking rig for S.U. fuel pumps available from V.L. Churchill and Co. Ltd. The rig measures output in gallons of paraffin (kerosene) per hour, against required suction and delivery heads

1. Pressure gauge. 2. Flow glass.

(b) EARLIER-TYPE ROCKER ASSEMBLIES

35. Check the gap between the points indirectly by carefully holding the contact blade against the rib on the pedestal, without pressing against the tip (Fig. D.6), then check if a .030 in. (.8 mm.) feeler will pass between the fibre rollers and the face of the coil housing. If necessary, the tip of the blade can be set to correct the gap.

END COVER

36. Ensure that the end cover seal washer is in position on the terminal stud, fit the bakelite end cover and shakeproof washer, and secure with the brass nut. Fit the terminal tag or connector and the insulated sleeve. After test, replace the rubber sealing band over the end cover gap and seal with adhesive tape. This must be retained when the pump is not mounted internally in a moisture-free region.

Testing on a test stand

PREPARATION

1. Churchill test rig:
   Secure the pump in the clamping ring, with the outlet connection uppermost. Connect to a 12-volt battery,

and with the switch in the 'OFF' position, clip the connector to the pump. Connect the delivery and return of the correct bore to the pump.

S.U. test rig:

Mount the pump on the test stand, using the appropriate adaptor set according to the type of pump. Connect the feed and earth terminals to the test battery and check the contact gap setting as described under that heading. Replace the end cover with a cut-away one which allows observation of the rocker assembly while retaining the pivot pin.

Use paraffin (kerosene) in the test tank. Ensure an adequate supply.

PRIMING

2. Unscrew the regulator valve (Churchill rig only) and switch on: the pump should prime from dry in 10 to 15 seconds. Allow the pump to run for a minute to stabilize the flow.

AIR LEAK CHECK

3. When the pump is first started air bubbles will be mixed with the liquid discharged from the pipe projecting downwards into the flow meter; these bubbles should cease after a minute or so. If they do not, an air leak is indicated either in the pump or the connecting unions, and this must be rectified.

VALVE SEAT CHECK

4. Let the pump run for about 10 minutes and then test as follows:

   With the regulator valve (delivery tap) turned completely off the pump should stand without repeating for a minimum of 20 seconds at the correct delivery head. If it repeats, the inlet valve is not seating correctly. On AUF 300 type pumps malfunction of the inlet valve must be investigated. On HP-type pumps with metal valve discs this may be remedied by removing the discs and rubbing down the smooth face, using fine lapping paste on a smooth surface, or by dressing the valve seat.

DELIVERY CHECK

5. Churchill: Obtain a delivery head reading of 4 feet (1220 mm.) on the gauge by adjusting the regulator valve on top of the flow glass. When correct, the pump flow rate may be read directly from the appropriate colour scale on the flow glass.

   S.U. The paraffin (kerosene) should rise in the glass tube until it flows over the top of the pipe in which a side hole is drilled; if the output is not up to specification, the side hole will carry off all paraffin (kerosene) pumped and none will flow over the top. The maximum delivery should be timed as follows:

   AUF 300 type pump .. 1 pint in 30 sec.
   HP-type pump .. 1 pint in 1 min. 5 sec.

MINIMUM DELIVERY CHECK

6. Check with the tap turned on only slightly, and also by pressing gradually inwards on the tip of the contact blade, so as to reduce the effective stroke, that the pump continues to work with an increasing frequency until it eventually stops because there is no gap left between the points.

REDUCED VOLTAGE

7. Connect a resistance and voltmeter in circuit and test the pump at 9.5 volts with regulator valve open (tap full on); the pump should work satisfactorily although with reduced output.

SPARKING CHECK

8. Check for excessive sparking at the contact points. A moderate degree is permissible; excessive sparking would indicate that the special leak wire incorporated in the coil winding has fractured, necessitating a new coil unit, or that the condenser is faulty.

Fuel pump faults

1. SUSPECTED FUEL FEED FAILURE

Disconnect the fuel line at the carburetter and check for flow.

(a) If normal, examine for obstructed float-chamber needle seating or gummed needle.

(b) If normal initially, but diminishing rapidly and accompanied by slow pump operation, check for correct tank venting by removing the filler cap. Inadequate venting causes a slow power stroke with resultant excessive burning of contact points.

(c) If reduced flow is accompanied by slow operation of the pump, check for any restriction on the inlet side of the pump, such as a clogged filter, which should be removed and cleaned.

    In the case of reduced flow with rapid operation of the pump, check for an air leak on the suction side, dirt under the valve, or faulty valve sealing washers.

(d) If no flow, check for:

    (i) ELECTRICAL SUPPLY

    Disconnect the lead from the terminal and check if current is available.

    (ii) FAULTY CONTACT POINTS

    If electrical supply is satisfactory, the bakelite cover should be removed to check that the tungsten points are in contact. The lead should then be replaced on the terminal and a short piece of bared wire put across the contacts. If the pump then performs a stroke, the fault is due to dirt or corrosion, or maladjustment of the tungsten points. The points may be cleaned by folding a small piece of fine emery-paper and inserting it between them and sliding it to and fro. To re-adjust the contact points follow the procedure laid down under the appropriate heading.

    (iii) OBSTRUCTED PIPELINE BETWEEN FUEL TANK AND PUMP

    The inlet pipe should be disconnected. If the pump then operates, the trouble is due to a restriction in the pipeline between the pump and the tank. This may be cleared by the use of compressed air after removing the fuel tank filler cap. It should be noted, however, that compressed air should not be passed through the pump as this will cause serious damage to the valves.

(iv) FAULTY DIAPHRAGM ACTION
In the event of the previous operations failing to locate the trouble, it may be due to a stiffening of the diaphragm fabric or the presence of abnormal friction in the rocker 'throw-over' mechanism, or a combination of both. To remedy these faults the coil housing should be removed and the diaphragm flexed a few times, taking care not to lose any of the 11 rollers under the diaphragm. Prior to this resetting it is advisable to apply, very sparingly, a little thin oil to the throw-over spring spindles at the point where they pivot in the brass rockers. The diaphragm/armature assembly should then be reassembled in accordance with the instructions given under that heading.

2. NOISY PUMP
If the pump is noisy in operation, an air leak at the suction line may be the cause. Such a leak may be checked by disconnecting the fuel pipe from the carburetter and allowing the pump to discharge into a suitable container with the end of the pipe submerged. The emission of continuous bubbles at this point will confirm the existence of an air leak. The fault should be rectified by carrying out the following procedure:

(a) Check that all connections from the fuel tank to the pump are in good order.
(b) Check that the inlet union is tight and that the sealing 'O' ring is not damaged.
(c) Check that the coil housing securing screws are well and evenly tightened.

Air leaks on the suction side cause rapid operation of the pump and are the most frequent cause of permanent failure.

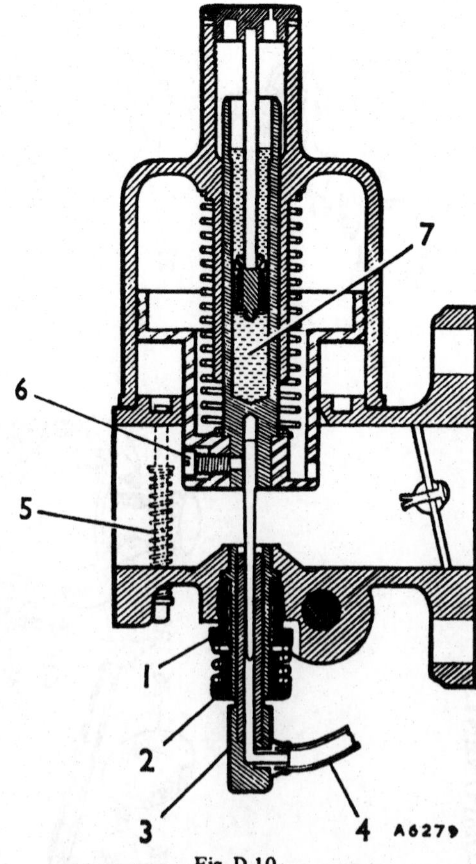

Fig. D.10
A sectional view of the HS4 carburetter

1. Jet locking nut.
2. Jet adjusting nut.
3. Jet head.
4. Feed tube from float-chamber.
5. Piston lifting pin.
6. Needle securing screw.
7. Oil damper reservoir.

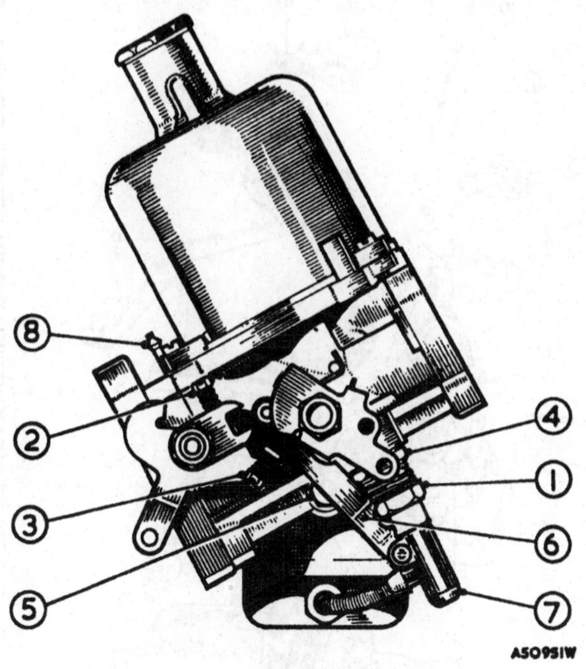

Fig. D.9
The HS4 carburetter

1. Jet adjusting nut.
2. Throttle stop screw.
3. Choke or fast-idle screw.
4. Jet locking nut.
5. Float-chamber securing nut.
6. Jet link.
7. Jet head.
8. Vacuum ignition take-off.

3. PUMP OPERATES WITHOUT DELIVERING FUEL
If the pump operates continuously without delivery of fuel the most likely causes are:

(a) A very serious air leak on the suction side or,
(b) Foreign matter lodged under one of the valves, particularly the inlet valve.

To remedy (a) see Section 2 (above).

In order to remove any foreign matter lodged under the valves, these should be removed for cleaning and great care taken that the plastic material of the valve disc is not scratched or damaged during this operation.

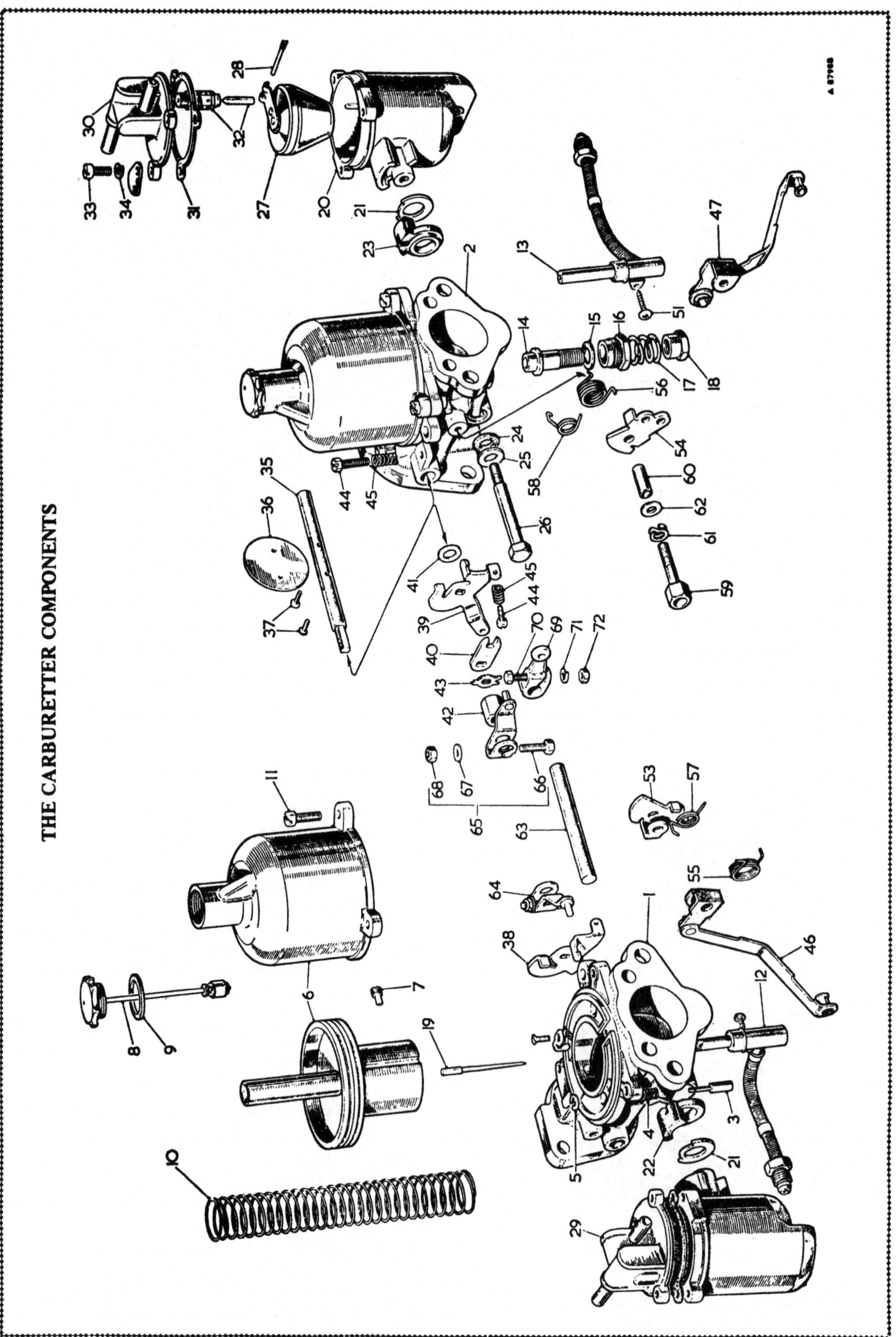

THE CARBURETTER COMPONENTS

KEY TO THE CARBURETTER COMPONENTS

No.	Description
1.	Body–front carburetter.
2.	Body–rear carburetter.
3.	Pin–piston lifting.
4.	Spring–pin.
5.	Circlip–pin.
6.	Chamber and piston assembly.
7.	Screw–needle locking.
8.	Cap and dampers assembly.
9.	Washer–cap (fibre).
10.	Spring–piston (red).
11.	Screw–chamber to body.
12.	Jet assembly–front carburetter.
13.	Jet assembly–rear carburetter.
14.	Bearing–jet.
15.	Washer–jet bearing (brass).
16.	Screw–jet locking.
17.	Spring–jet locking.
18.	Screw–jet adjusting.
19.	Needle.
20.	Chamber–float.
21.	Washer–support.
22.	Grommet–front carburetter (rubber).
23.	Grommet–rear carburetter (rubber).
24.	Washer (rubber).

No.	Description
25.	Washer–plain.
26.	Bolt–float-chamber fixing.
27.	Float assembly.
28.	Pin–hinged lever.
29.	Lid–float-chamber–front carburetter.
30.	Lid–float-chamber–rear carburetter.
31.	Washer–lid.
32.	Needle and seat assembly.
33.	Screw–lid.
34.	Washer–spring–screw.
35.	Spindle–throttle.
36.	Disc–throttle.
37.	Screw–disc.
38.	Lever–throttle return–front carburetter.
39.	Lever–throttle return–rear carburetter.
40.	Lever–lost motion.
41.	Washer–spacing.
42.	Nut–lever.
43.	Washer–tab–nut.
44.	Screw–throttle stop.
45.	Spring–throttle stop screw.
46.	Lever and link assembly–pick-up–front carburetter.

No.	Description
47.	Lever and link assembly–pick-up–rear carburetter.
51.	Screw–link to jet.
53.	Lever–cam–front carburetter.
54.	Lever–cam–rear carburetter.
55.	Spring–pick-up lever–front carburetter.
56.	Spring–pick-up lever–rear carburetter.
57.	Spring–cam lever–front carburetter.
58.	Spring–cam lever–rear carburetter.
59.	Bolt–pivot.
60.	Tube–pivot bolt.
61.	Washer–spring–pivot bolt.
62.	Washer–distance.
63.	Rod–jet connecting.
64.	Lever and pin assembly–front carburetter.
65.	Lever and pin assembly–rear carburetter.
66.	Bolt–lever.
67.	Washer–bolt.
68.	Nut–bolt.
69.	Lever–choke operating.
70.	Bolt–lever.
71.	Washer–spring.
72.	Nut.

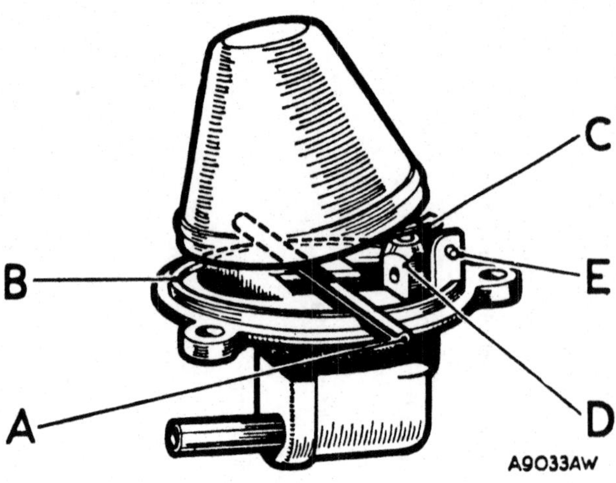

Fig. D.11
Checking the nylon float level

A ⅛ to $\frac{3}{16}$ in. (3.18 to 4.76 mm.) dia. bar.
B. Machined lip.
C. Float lever resetting point.
D. Needle valve assembly.
E. Hinge pin.

Section D.4

CARBURETTERS

(S.U. type HS4)

IMPORTANT.–The instructions given in **this section** for adjusting, dismantling and reassembling the carburetters applies only to **cars not fitted with exhaust emission control equipment**. Carburetters fitted to **cars with exhaust emission control equipment** must be tuned and serviced in accordance with the instructions given in **Workshop Manual Supplement AKD 4957.**

Removing and refitting

Release the spring clips and detach the breather hose between the air cleaner and rocker cover (early cars).

Disconnect the fuel supply pipe at the rear carburetter or at each carburetter float-chamber. Disconnect the overflow pipes.

Slacken off the bolt and nut securing the mixture and throttle cables respectively and withdraw the cables complete. Detach the throttle return springs. Pull off the rubber connection for the vacuum ignition control pipe from the top of the rear carburetter body.

Remove the four nuts securing the carburetter flanges and withdraw the carburetters and air cleaners as an assembly.

When refitting, the centre throttle return spring end eye is located between the flat washer and the throttle lever. The throttle linkage must be checked, and re-adjusted if necessary, after refitting.

Slow-running adjustments and synchronization

As the needle size is determined during engine development, tuning of the carburetters is confined to correct idling setting.

Run the engine until it attains its normal running temperature.

Slacken off the pinch-bolt of one of the coupling levers locating the carburetter interconnecting shaft to the carburetter throttle spindles so that each carburetter can be operated independently.

Disconnect the mixture control cable and slacken off the two pinch-bolts to free the choke actuating lever and unscrew the fast-idling screws.

Remove the pistons and suction chambers. Screw the jet adjusting nuts until each jet is flush with the bridge of its carburetter, or as near to this as possible (each jet being in the same relative position to the bridge of its respective carburetter). Replace the pistons and suction chamber assemblies, and check that the pistons fall freely onto the bridge of the carburetters (by use of the piston lifting pins).

Turn down the jet adjusting nut two complete turns (12 flats).

Restart the engine, and adjust the throttle adjusting screws to give the desired idling speed by moving each throttle adjusting screw an equal amount. By listening to the hiss in the intake, adjust the throttle adjusting screws until the intensity of the hiss is similar on each intake. This will synchronize the throttle setting.

When this is satisfactory the mixture should be adjusted by screwing each jet adjusting nut up or down by the same amount until the fastest idling speed is obtained consistent with even firing. During this adjusting it is necessary that the jets are pressed upwards to ensure that they are in contact with the adjusting nuts.

As the mixture is adjusted the mixture will probably run faster, and it may therefore be necessary to unscrew the throttle adjusting screws a little, each by the same amount, to reduce the speed.

Now check the mixture strength by lifting the piston of the rear carburetter by approximately $\frac{1}{32}$ in. (.75 mm.), when:

1. If the engine speed increases, the mixture strength of the rear carburetter is too rich.
2. If the engine speed immediately decreases, the mixture strength of the rear carburetter is too weak.

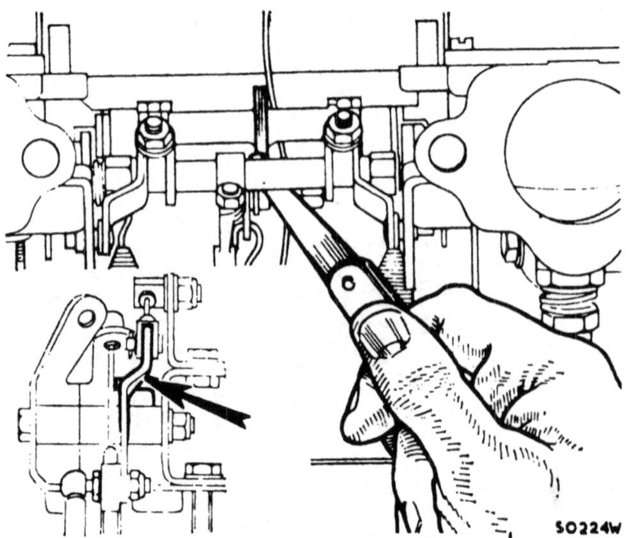

Fig. D.12
A feeler gauge between the throttle shaft stop and the choke interconnecting spindle. Inset shows the position for the feeler gauge on the cars fitted with automatic transmission

3. If the engine speed momentarily increases very slightly, the mixture strength of the rear carburetter is correct.

Repeat the operation at the front carburetter, and after adjustment re-check the rear carburetter, since the carburetters are interdependent.

When the mixture is correct the exhaust note should be regular and even. If it is irregular, with a splashy type of misfire and colourless exhaust, the mixture is too weak. If there is a regular or rhythmical type of misfire in the exhaust beat, together with a blackish exhaust, then the mixture is too rich.

The carburetter throttle on each carburetter is operated by a lever and pin, with the pin working in a forked lever attached to the throttle spindle. A clearance exists between the pin and the fork which must be maintained when the throttle is closed and the engine idling, to prevent any load from the accelerator linkage being transferred to the throttle butterfly and spindle.

To set the clearance on synchromesh cars, with the throttle shaft levers free on the throttle shaft, place a .12 in. (.3 mm.) feeler gauge between the throttle shaft stop and the choke interconnecting rod (see Fig. D.12). On cars fitted with automatic transmission place a .020 in (.5 mm.) feeler gauge between the throttle lever and the throttle lever stop (inset, Fig, 12). Move each throttle shaft lever downwards in turn until the lever pin rests lightly on the lower arm of the fork in the carburetter throttle lever. Tighten the clamp bolt of the throttle shaft lever at this position. When both carburetters have been dealt with, remove the feeler gauge. The pins on the throttle shafts should then have clearance in the forks.

Reconnect the choke cable, ensuring that the jet heads return against the lower face of the jet adjusting nuts and that the choke actuating levers are fully returned when the choke control is pushed fully in.

Pull out the mixture control knob on the dash panel until the linkage is about to move the carburetter jets (a minimum of ¼ in. or 6 mm.) and adjust the fast-idle adjusting screws to give an engine speed of about 1,000 r.p.m. when hot.

A small clearance must be maintained between the fast-idle cams and the abutment screws when the mixture control is pushed fully in.

Jet-centring

To check the jet for concentricity with the jet needle set the jet head and the jet adjusting nut in the uppermost position, lift the suction piston with the piston lifting pin, and allow the piston to fall. It should fall freely, and a definite soft, metallic click will be heard as the base of the piston strikes the jet bridge.

If this does not happen with the jet raised, but does occur when the jet is lowered, the jet bearing and jet must be recentred as follows.

Disconnect the lever between the interconnecting lever and the jet head.

Unscrew the union holding the nylon feed tube into the base of the float-chamber and withdraw the tube and jet together.

Unscrew the jet adjusting nut and remove the lock spring; screw up the nut to its fullest extent and refit the jet head and feed tube.

Slacken off the jet locking nut until the jet bearing is just free to rotate with finger pressure.

Remove the piston damper from the top of the suction chamber and gently press the piston down onto the jet bridge.

Tighten the jet locking nut, at the same time ensuring that the jet head is still in its correct angular position. Lift the piston and check that it falls freely and evenly, hitting the jet bridge with a soft, metallic click, with the jet in the raised and lowered position. If the result is not satisfactory and the piston is not sticking, the recentring operation must be repeated until the correct result is obtained.

When the operation is complete replace the adjusting nut lock spring and the jet operating lever.

The adjustment is best effected with the carburetters removed from the engine.

Float-chamber

The position of the hinged float lever must be such that the level of the float (and therefore the height of the fuel at the jet) is correct.

To check the float-level, hold the float-chamber lid and float assembly upside-down and place a ⅛ in. (3.18 mm.) diameter bar across the diameter of the machined lip of the float-chamber lid, parallel to the float lever hinge pin and under the float lever (see Fig. D.11). The face of the float lever should just rest on the bar when the float needle is held fully on its seating. If this is not so, carefully reset the angle made between the straight portion of the float lever and its hinge until the correct position is obtained

Float-chamber flooding

This is indicated by the fuel dripping from the drain pipe, and is generally caused by grit between the float-chamber needle and its guide. This is cured by removing the float-chamber, washing the valve and float-chamber components, and reassembling.

Float needle sticking

If the engine stops, apparently through lack of fuel, when there is plenty in the tank and the pump is working properly, the probable cause is a sticking float needle. An easy test for this is to disconnect the pipe from the electric pump to the carburetters and switch the ignition on and off quickly while the end of the pipe is directed onto a pad of cloth or into a container.

If fuel is delivered, starvation is almost certainly being caused by the float needle sticking to its seating, and the float-chamber lid should therefore be removed and the needle and seating cleaned and refitted. At the same time it will be advisable to clean out the entire fuel feed system as this trouble is caused by foreign matter in the fuel, and unless this is removed it is likely to recur. It is of no use whatever renewing any of the component parts of either carburetter, and the only cure is to make sure that the fuel tank and pipe lines are entirely free from any kind of foreign matter or sticky substance capable of causing this trouble.

Needles
Remove the piston and suction chamber assembly. Slacken the needle clamping screw, extract the needle and check its identifying mark (see **'GENERAL DATA'**). Refit the correct needle, ensuring that the shoulder on the shank is flush with the piston base.

Piston sticking
The piston assembly comprises the suction disc and the piston forming the choke, into which is inserted the hardened and ground piston rod which engages in a bearing in the centre of the suction chamber and in which is, in turn, inserted the jet needle. The piston rod running in the bearing is the only part which is in actual contact with any other part, the suction disc, piston and needle all having suitable clearances to prevent sticking. If sticking does occur the whole assembly should be cleaned carefully and the piston rod lubricated with a spot of thin oil. No oil must be applied to any other part except the piston rod. A sticking piston can be ascertained by removing the piston damper and lifting the piston by pressing the piston lifting pin; the piston should come up quite freely and fall back smartly onto its seating when released. On no account should the piston return spring be stretched or its tension altered in an attempt to improve its rate of return.

Section D.5

AIR CLEANERS

The air intake filters are of the dry paper element type requiring no attention between filter replacement.
The air filter casings should be removed and cleaned out periodically to remove any dust deposit.

Filter replacement
Disconnect the engine rocker cover breather pipe from the front filter (early cars). Unscrew the bolts securing each air filter to the choke bracket and fixing plate respectively and remove the filters from the vehicle complete.
Remove the base plate and throw away the old paper element. Clean the inside casing and intake tubes thoroughly and reassemble, using new paper elements.

Section D.6

CARBURETTERS
(S.U. Type HIF4)

IMPORTANT: The instructions given in **this section** for adjusting, dismantling and reassembling the carburetters apply only to **cars not fitted with exhaust emission control equipment**. Carburetters fitted to cars **with exhaust emission control equipment** must be tuned and serviced in accordance with the instructions given in **Workshop Manual Supplement AKD 4957.**

Tuning/adjust
Before tuning the carburetters in an endeavour to rectify poor engine performance, check the following items to ensure that the maladjustment or fault is not from another source.

a. Valve clearance
b. Spark plug condition
c. Contact breaker (dwell angle)
d. Ignition timing and advance
e. Presence of air leaks in the induction system
f. Operation of engine controls.
g. Compression pressures

Carburetter tuning is confined to setting the idle and fast idle speeds, and mixture at idle speed. To achieve the best results, a reliable tachometer, a balancing meter and an exhaust gas analyser (CO meter of the infra-red non-dispersive type or equivalent) are required. The instruments are essential when tuning vehicles equipped to conform with exhaust emission regulations.

1. Remove the air cleaners as detailed in Section D.5.
2. Check the throttle for correct operation and signs of sticking.
3. Unscrew each throttle adjusting screw until it is just clear of the throttle lever stop when the throttle is closed, then turn each screw one turn in a clockwise direction.
4. Raise the piston of each carburetter, using the lifting pin, and check that the piston falls freely onto the bridge in the carburetter body when the lifting pin is released. If the piston tends to stick, the carburetter must be serviced.
5. Remove the suction chamber assembly, and lift the piston clear of the bridge, so that the jet is visible.
6. Turn the jet adjusting screw of each carburetter until each jet is flush with the bridge in the carburetter body or as high as possible without exceeding the bridge height. Ensure that both jets are in the same relative position to the bridge of their respective carburetter.
7. Check that the shoulder of each needle is flush with the underside of its respective piston.
8. Turn the jet adjusting screw of each carburetter two turns clockwise.
9. Turn the fast idle adjusting screw of each carburetter in an anti-clockwise direction until it is well clear of its fast idle cam.
10. Refit the suction chamber assembly.
11. Unscrew and withdraw the piston dampers from the suction chambers. Top up with new engine oil (preferably S.A.E. 20) until the level is ½ in. (13 mm.) above the top of each hollow piston rod (see Fig. D.13). Refit the damper assemblies.

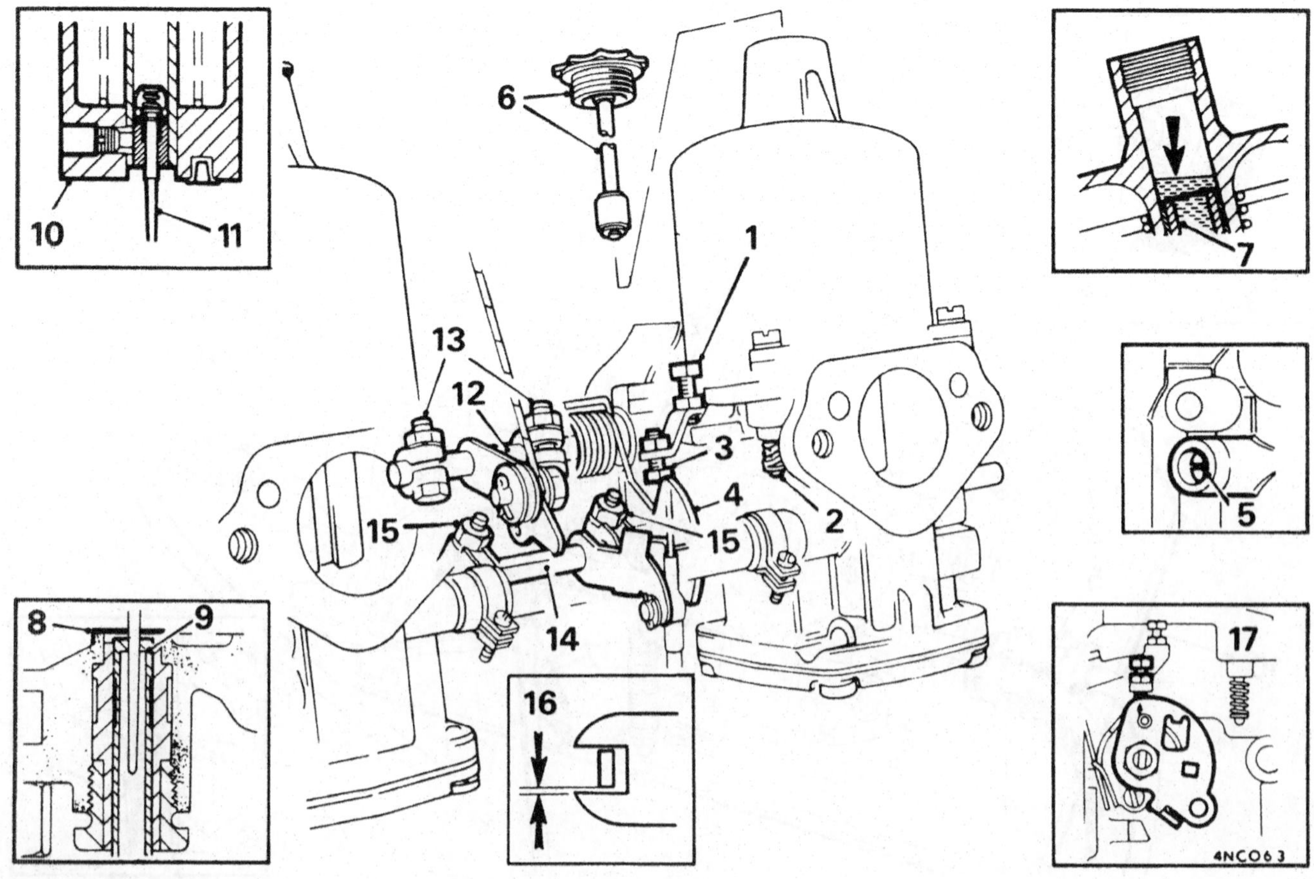

Fig. D.13

Carburetter tuning (S.U. HIF4)

1. Throttle adjusting screw
2. Piston lifting pin.
3. Fast idle adjusting screw.
4. Fast idle cam.
5. Jet adjusting screw.
6. Piston damper.
7. Piston rod.
8. Bridge.
9. Jet.
10. Piston
11. Jet needle.
12. Throttle inter-connection rod.
13. Throttle inter-connection rod lever clamp bolts.
14. Cold start inter-connection rod.
15. Cold start inter-connection rod lever clamp bolts.
16. Clearance of 0.012 in (0,31 mm) between throttle lever pin and lower arm of throttle fork.
17. Fast idle cam positioned for fast idle adjustment.

12. Connect the tachometer of tool 18G 677 Z to the engine.
13. Start the engine and run it at a fast idle until it attains normal running temperature, then run it for a further five minutes.
14. Increase the engine speed to 2,500 r.p.m. for 30 seconds.
15. Connect an exhaust gas analyser to the engine in accordance with the instrument manufacturers instructions.

Setting can now commence. If the correct setting cannot be obtained within three minutes, increase the engine speed to 2,500 r.p.m. for 30 seconds and then recommence tuning. Repeat this clearing operation at three minute intervals until tuning is completed.

16. Slacken both clamping bolts on the throttle spindle interconnections.
17. Slacken both clamping bolts on the cold start interconnection.
18. Using a balance meter in accordance with the manufacturer's instructions, balance the carburetters, altering the throttle adjusting screws until the correct idle speed (see **'ENGINE TUNING DATA'**) and balance is achieved. Alternatively, use a 'listening tube' to compare the intensity of the intake hiss from both carburetters and alter the throttle adjusting screws until the hiss from both carburetters is the same at idling speed.
19. Turn the jet adjusting screw of each carburetter by the same amount, clockwise to enrich or anti-clockwise to weaken, until the fastest engine speed is indicated on the tachometer; turn each adjusting screw anti-clockwise by the same amount until the engine speed just commences to fall. Turn each screw very slowly clockwise by the minimum but same amount until the maximum engine speed is regained.
20. Check the engine idling speed and re-adjust it as necessary, turning each throttle adjusting screw by the same amount.

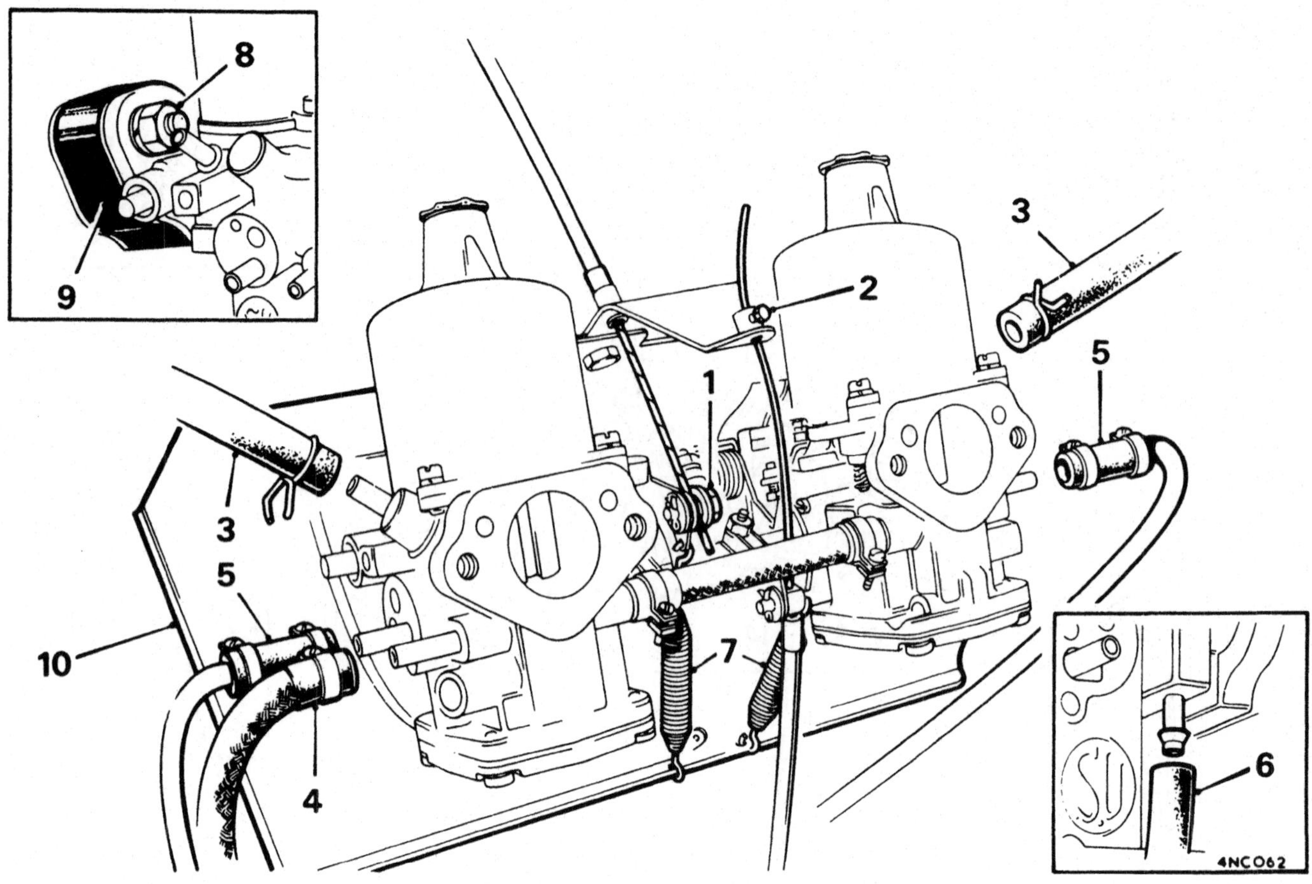

Fig. D.14
Carburetter installation (S.U. HIF4)

1. Throttle cable retaining nut.
2. Choke cable retaining screw.
3. Breather pipe.
4. Fuel feed hose.
5. Vent hose.
6. Distributor vacuum pipe.
7. Return springs.
8. Carburetter securing nuts.
9. Insulation block.
10. Heat shield.

21. Using the exhaust gas analyser, check that the carbon monoxide percentage is within the limits given in **'ENGINE TUNING DATA'**. If the reading falls outside the limits, reset both jet adjusting screws by the same but minimum amount necessary to bring the reading just within the limits. If an adjustment exceeding half a turn is required to achieve this, the carburetters must be removed and serviced.
22. Stop the engine and set the throttle interconnection rod levers so that a clearance of 0.012 in. (0,31 mm.) exists between each lever link pin and the lower arm of its respective throttle lever fork.
    a. Insert a 0.012 in. (0.31 mm.) feeler gauge lever between the throttle interconnection rod stop lever and the cold start interconnection rod.
    b. Move each throttle interconnection lever downwards until each lever link pin rests on the lower arm of its respective throttle lever fork. Tighten the throttle interconnection rod lever clamp bolts, ensuring that the throttle interconnection rod has an end-float of approximately 1/32 in. (0.8 mm.). Remove the feeler gauge.
23. Run the engine at 1,500 r.p.m. and re-check the carburetter balance to ensure that the throttle linkage is connected correctly.
24. Ensure that the fast idle cam lever of each carburetter is against its respective stop and tighten the cold start interconnection rod lever clamp bolts so that both cam levers begin to move simultaneously when the mixture control is operated.
25. Ensure that the fast idle cam lever of each carburetter is against its respective stop and check that the mixture control cable has 1/16 in. (1.5 mm.) free movement before it commences to operate the cam levers.
26. Pull out the mixture control (choke) until the arrow marked on the cam is positioned under the fast idle adjusting screw.
27. Run the engine and using the balance meter or 'listening tube' to ensure equal adjustment, turn the fast idle adjusting screws to set the engine fast idling to the speed given in **'ENGINE TUNING DATA'**.
28. Refit the air cleaners.

Removing

29. Remove the air cleaners as detailed in Section D.5.
30. Disconnect the throttle cable from the interconnection lever.
31. Disconnect the choke cable.
32. Disconnect the breather pipes from the carburetter adaptors.
33. Disconnect the fuel feed hose from the float chamber adaptor.
34. Disconnect the vent hoses from the carburetter adaptor.
35. Disconnect the distributor vacuum hose from the carburetter adaptor.
36. Disconnect the return springs from the heat shield.
37. Remove the four nuts securing the carburetters to the inlet manifold studs.
38. Lift the carburetter assembly off the inlet manifold studs.

Dismantling

39. Thoroughly clean the outside of the carburetter.
40. Remove the piston damper and its washer.
41. Mark the suction chamber to ensure it is refitted to the same body.
42. Unscrew the suction piston chamber retaining screws and remove the identity tag.
43. Lift the suction chamber vertically from the body without tilting the chamber.
44. Remove the piston spring, lift out the piston assembly and empty the oil from the piston rod.
45. Unscrew the needle guide locking screw.
46. Withdraw the needle, guide and spring.
47. Mark the bottom cover-plate and body to ensure correct reassembly, unscrew the retaining screws and remove the cover complete with sealing ring.
48. Remove the jet adjusting screw complete with 'O' ring.
49. Remove the jet adjusting lever retaining screw and spring.
50. Withdraw the jet complete with adjusting lever, and disengage the lever.
51. Remove the float pivot spindle and fibre washer. Withdraw the float.
52. Remove the needle valve and unscrew the valve seat.
53. Unscrew the jet bearing locking nut and withdraw the bearing complete with fibre washer.
54. Note the location of the ends of the fast idle cam lever return spring.
55. Unlock and remove the cam lever retaining nut and locking washer.
56. With the return spring held towards the carburetter body, prise off the cam lever and remove the return spring.
57. Unscrew the starter unit retaining screws and remove the cover-plate.
58. Withdraw the starter unit assembly and remove its gasket.
59. Withdraw the valve spindle and remove the 'O' ring, seals and dust cap.
60. Note the location and loading of the ends of the throttle lever return spring and remove the spring.
61. Unlock and remove the nut and tab washer retaining the throttle levers.
62. Remove the throttle lever and throttle actuating lever.
63. Remove the throttle disc retaining screws.
64. Close the throttle and mark the position of the throttle disc in relation to the carburetter flange. Do not mark the disc in the vicinity of the over-run valve. Open the throttle and carefully withdraw the disc from the throttle spindle taking care not to damage the over-run valve.
65. Withdraw the throttle spindle and remove its seals, noting the way it is fitted in relation to the carburetter body.

Inspection

66. Examine the throttle spindle and its bearings in the carburetter body; check for excessive play, and renew parts as necessary.
67. Examine the float needle and seating for damage and excessive wear; renew if necessary.
68. Examine all rubber seals and 'O' rings for damage and deterioration; renew as necessary. The cover-plate sealing ring must be renewed.
69. Check condition of all fibre washers and gaskets; renew as necessary.
70. Clean the inside of the suction chamber and piston rod guide with fuel or denatured alcohol (methylated spirit) and wipe dry. Abrasives must not be used.
71. Examine the carburetter body for cracks and damage and for security of the brass connections and the piston key.
72. Examine the suction chamber and piston for damage and signs of scoring.

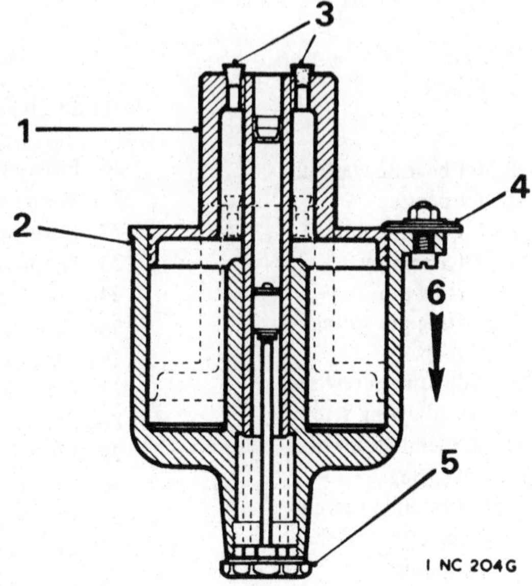

Fig. D.15
Suction chamber timing check (S.U. HIF)

1. Piston.
2. Suction chamber.
3. Plugs in piston transfer holes.
4. Nut and bolt with large washer overlapping suction chamber bore.
5. Damper.
6. Time for suction chamber to fall full extent of piston – 4 to 6 seconds.

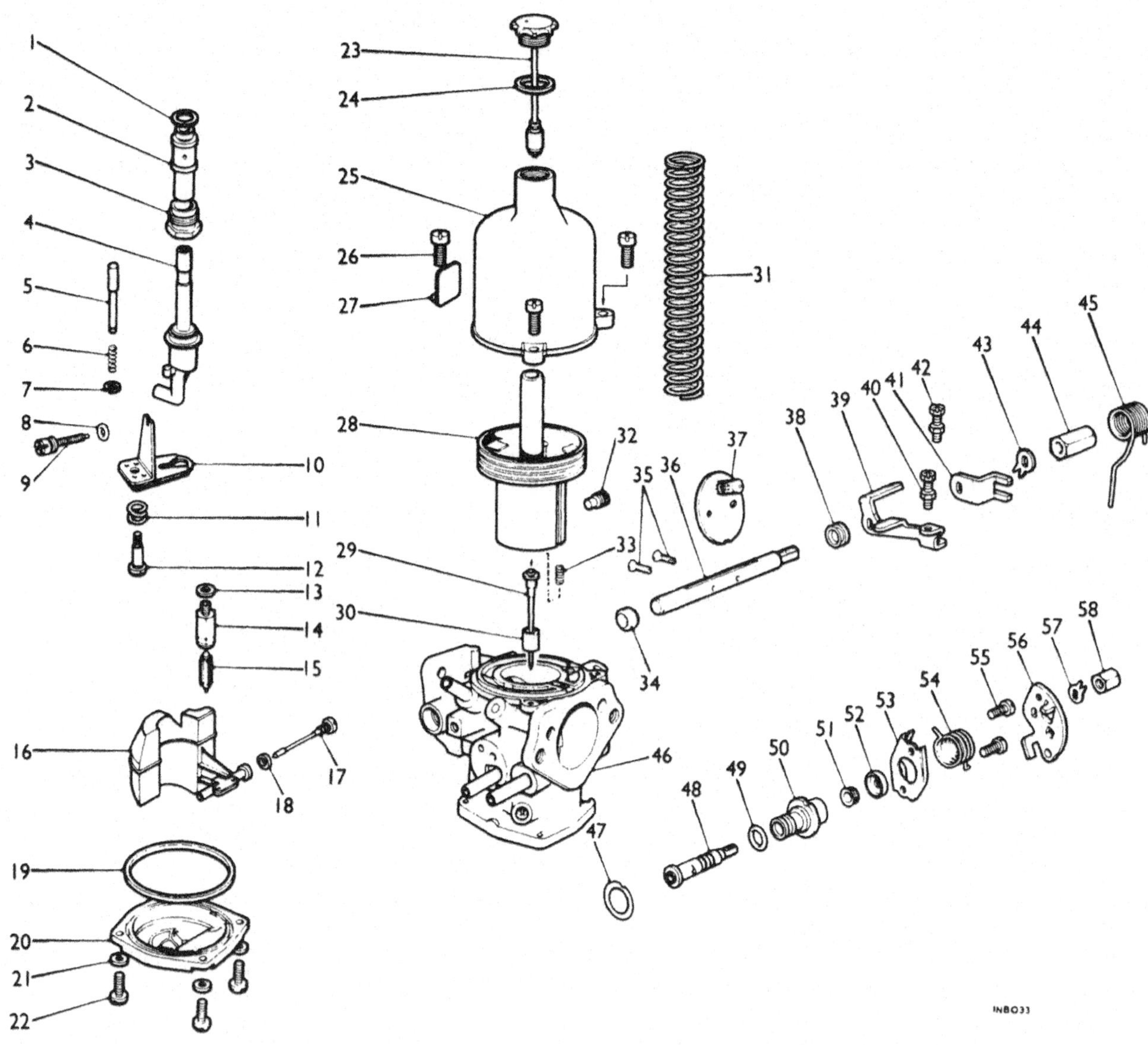

Fig. D.16
The S.U. type HIF carburetter components

1. Jet bearing washer.
2. Jet bearing.
3. Jet bearing nut.
4. Jet assembly.
5. Lifting pin.
6. Lifting pin spring.
7. Circlip.
8. Adjusting screw seal.
9. Jet adjusting screw.
10. Bi-metal jet lever.
11. Jet spring.
12. Jet retaining screw.
13. Needle seat washer (if required).
14. Float needle seat.
15. Float needle.
16. Float.
17. Float pivot.
18. Pivot seal.
19. Float-chamber cover seal.
20. Float-chamber cover.
21. Spring washer.
22. Cover screw.
23. Piston damper.
24. Damper washer.
25. Suction chamber.
26. Chamber screw.
27. Identity tag.
28. Piston.
29. Jet needle.
30. Needle guide.
31. Piston spring.
32. Needle retaining screw.
33. Needle spring.
34. Throttle spindle seal.
35. Throttle disc screws.
36. Throttle spindle.
37. Throttle disc.
38. Throttle spindle seal.
39. Throttle actuating lever.
40. Fast idle screw and nut.
41. Throttle lever.
42. Throttle adjusting screw and nut.
43. Tab washer.
44. Retaining nut.
45. Throttle spring.
46. Body.
47. Cold start seal.
48. Cold start spindle.
49. 'O' ring.
50. Cold start body.
51. Spindle seal.
52. End cover.
53. Retaining plate.
54. Cold start spring.
55. Retaining screw.
56. Fast idle cam.
57. Tab washer.
58. Retaining nut.

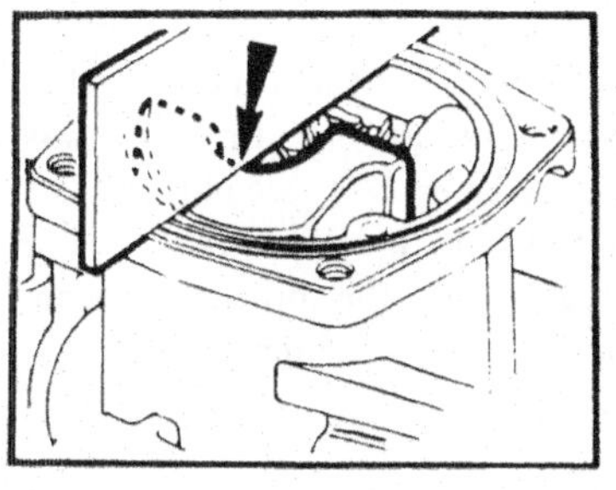

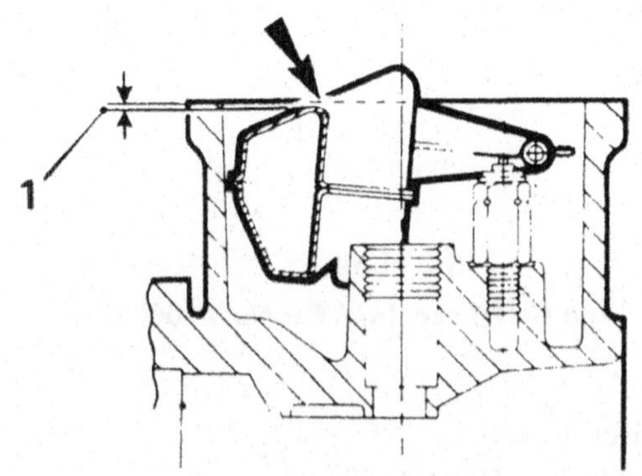

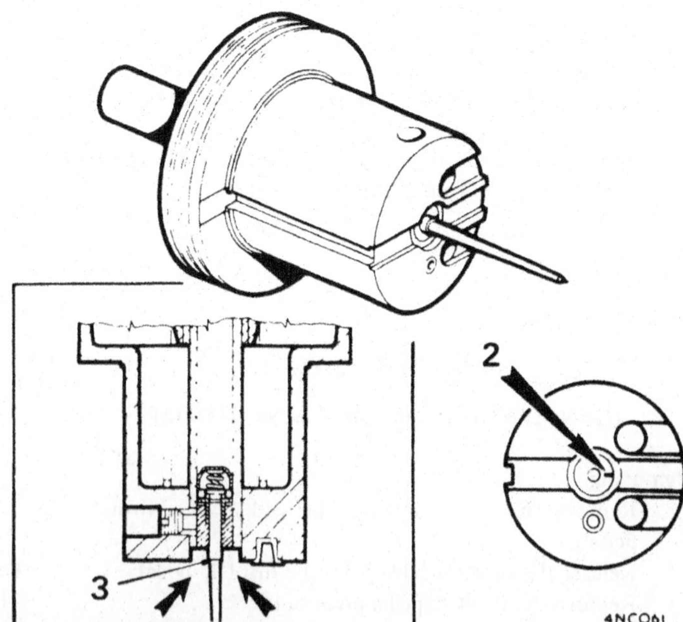

Fig. D.17
Carburetter reassembling (S.U. HIF) showing

1. Checking that the point of the float (arrowed) is 0.04 ± 0.02 in. (1.0 ± 0.5 mm.) below the level of the float chamber face.
2. Needle guide etch mark aligned correctly with piston transfer holes.
3. Shoulder of needle aligned with underside face of piston.

NOTE: It is only necessary to carry out the following timing check if the cause of the carburetter malfunction which necessitated the dismantling has not been located.

73. Temporarily plug the piston transfer holes.
74. Fit the piston into the suction chamber without its spring.
75. Fit a nut and screw, with a large flat washer under the screw head, into one of the suction chamber fixing holes, positioning the washer so that it overlaps the chamber bore.
76. Fit the damper and washer.
77. Check that the piston is fully home in the suction chamber, invert the assembly to allow the chamber to fall away until the piston contacts the washer.
78. Check the time taken for the chamber to fall the full extent of the piston travel; the time taken should be 4 to 6 seconds.
79. If the times are exceeded, check the piston and suction chamber for cleanliness and damage. If after rechecking the time is still not within these limits, renew the suction chamber and piston assembly.

Reassembling

80. Reverse the procedure in 39 to 79, noting the following:
    a. The throttle spindle must be fitted with the threaded end at the piston lifting pin side of the body.
    b. Ensure that the throttle disc is fitted in its original position; over-run valve at the top of the bore and its spring towards the inside of the carburetter when the throttle is closed.
    c. New throttle disc retaining screws must be used when refitting the disc. Ensure that the throttle disc is correctly positioned and closes correctly before tightening the retaining screws.
    d. Spread the split ends of the screws sufficiently to prevent turning.
    e. Position the throttle spindle end seals just below the spindle housing flange.
    f. The starter unit valve is fitted with the cut-out towards the top retaining screw hole and its retaining plate is positioned with the slotted flange towards the throttle spindle.
    g. When fitting the jet assembly to the adjusting lever ensure that the jet head moves freely in the bi-metal cut-out.
    h. After fitting the float and valve, invert the carburetter so that the needle valve is held in the shut position by the weight of the float only. Check that the point indicated on the float (see illustration) is 0.04 ± 0.02 in. (1.0 ± 0.5 mm.) below the level of the float-chamber face. Adjust the float position by carefully bending the brass pad. Check that the float pivots correctly about the spindle.
    j. Check that the small diameter of the jet adjusting screw engages the slot in the adjusting lever and set the jet flush with the bridge of the body.
    k. Use a new retaining screw when refitting the needle and ensure that the needle guide etch mark aligns correctly with the piston transfer holes (see illustration). After fitting the needle assembly, check that the shoulder of the needle aligns the under-side face of the piston.

Refitting

81. Reverse the procedure in 29 to 38, noting the following:
    a. Fit new joint washers on each side of the distance pieces and between the heat shield and the manifold.
    b. Check and adjust the carburetter settings as detailed in **'Tuning/adjust'**.

Section D.7

THROTTLE PEDAL

(GHN5 and GHD5 cars from Car No. 410002)

Removing

1. Remove the split pin from the end of the throttle pedal.
2. Release the throttle cable from the throttle pedal.
3. Remove the throttle pedal pivot bolt.
4. Withdraw the throttle pedal from the vehicle.

Refitting

5. Reverse the procedure in 1 to 4.

Section D.8

THROTTLE CABLE

(GHN5 and GHD5 cars from Car No. 410002)

Removing

1. Remove the securing clip and withdraw the clevis pin and washers to release the throttle cable from the throttle interconnection rod.
2. Unscrew the lower nut on the throttle cable adjuster.
3. Release the throttle cable from the abutment bracket.
4. Remove the screw to release the throttle cable retaining clip from the pedal bracket assembly.
5. Remove the split pin from the throttle pedal.
6. Release the throttle cable from the throttle pedal and withdraw the cable into the engine compartment.

Refitting

7. Reverse the procedure in 1 to 6.

Section D.9

FUEL PUMP

(GHN5 and GHD5 cars from Car No. 410002)

Removing

1. Disconnect the battery.
2. Open the luggage compartment lid.
3. Remove the fuel pump guard retaining screws.
4. Remove the fuel pump guard.
5. Slacken the clip retaining the pump in the support rubber.
6. Disconnect the lead from the terminal on the pump.
7. From beneath the car disconnect the inlet and outlet pipe unions.
8. Disconnect the breather pipe.
9. Disconnect the lead from the terminal on the pump.
10. Withdraw the pump from the support rubber.

Refitting

11. Reverse the procedure in 1 to 10, ensuring that the inlet and outlet pipe unions face upwards at an angle of 45° inclined to the centre line of the pump.

SECTION Da

THE FUEL SYSTEM (EVAPORATIVE LOSS)

The information given in this Section refers specifically to service operations on, or affected by, equipment fitted to the MGB (GHN5 and GHD5) in conformity with local and territorial requirements.

Section Da.1

FUEL TANK

Removing

1. Remove the spare wheel.
2. Disconnect the battery (negative earth) and drain the fuel tank.
3. Slacken the two hose clips securing the rubber hose to the tank fuel inlet pipe and filler tube.
4. Remove the screw, large plain washers and sealing washers securing the tank inside the boot.
5. Underneath the car, disconnect the petrol feed pipe and gauge unit electrical connections.
6. Remove the nuts and washer retaining the tank lip to the four studs. Release the two vapour pipe clips and move the pipe to one side.
7. Remove the tank.

Refitting

8. Reverse the removing procedure 1 to 7.

Section Da.2

VAPOUR SEPARATOR TANK

Removing

1. Disconnect the battery.
2. Remove the two flexible pipe connections from the tank. Remove the screw, nut and washer retaining the tank.
3. Remove the tank. **Caution.**--Under extreme operating conditions the tank may contain fuel.

Refitting

4. Reverse the removing procedure 1 to 3.

Section Da.3

LEAK TESTING

If a fault in the operation of the Evaporative Loss Control System is suspected or components of the system other than the filters or canister have been removed and refitted, the system must be pressure-tested in accordance with the test procedure given in **Workshop Manual Supplement AKD 4957.**

SECTION E

THE CLUTCH

SECTION

Description

THE CLUTCH COMPONENTS

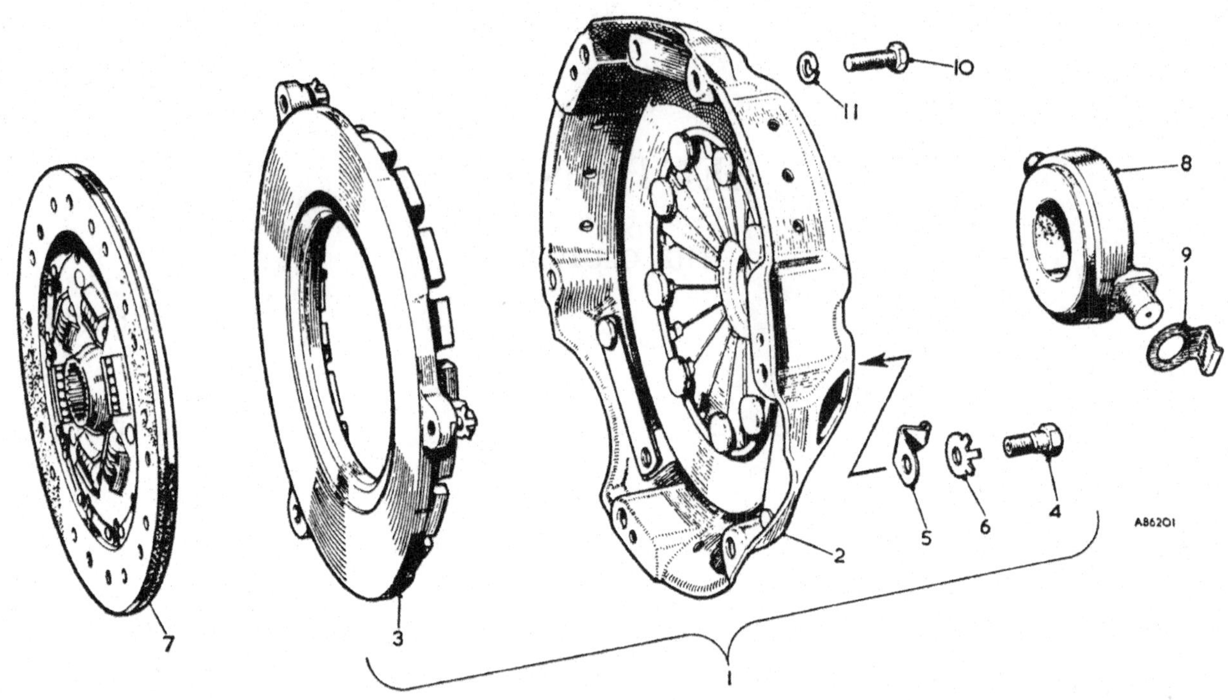

No.	Description
1.	Cover assembly.
2.	Cover with straps, diaphragm spring and release plate.
3.	Plate–pressure.
4.	Bolt–strap.
5.	Clip–pressure plate.
6.	Washer–tab.
7.	Plate assembly–driven.
8.	Bearing assembly–release.
9.	Retainer–bearing.
10.	Screw–clutch to flywheel.
11.	Washer for screw–spring.

GENERAL DESCRIPTION

The clutch mechanism is hydraulically operated and consists of a driven plate, a pressure plate, and a diaphragm spring and cover assembly. The cover is bolted to the flywheel and encloses the driven plate, pressure plate, and diaphragm spring.

The hydraulic system comprises a master cylinder coupled to a slave cylinder which operates the clutch release mechanism.

Section E.1

CLUTCH ASSEMBLY

The driven plate comprises a splined hub connected to a flexible steel plate by a spring mounting. The annular friction facings are riveted to the plate and damper springs are assembled around the hub to absorb power shocks and torsional vibration.

The diaphragm spring is interposed between two annular rings which provide fulcrum points for the diaphragm when it is flexed. The rings and the diaphragm are located and secured to the cover by nine equally spaced rivets. Three clips that engage the outer edge of the diaphragm are bolted to the pressure plate. The bolts pass through three straps which are riveted to the inside of the cover; the straps prevent the diaphragm and the pressure plate from rotating in relation to the cover.

The release plate is secured directly to the diaphragm and is an integral part of the clutch cover assembly. On early cars the release plate is retained with a circlip and can be removed when the circlip is released.

The release bearing is graphite and is mounted in a cup which fits into the fork of the clutch withdrawal lever. The cup is held in position by two spring retainers.

Removing

Remove the engine as described in Section A.21.

Loosen each of the bolts securing the clutch assembly to the flywheel by slackening them a turn at a time until spring pressure is released. The clutch cover can now be disengaged from the dowels on the flywheel and the assembly removed.

Dismantling

On earlier cars remove the circlip securing the release plate to the diaphragm and lift the plate from the diaphragm.

Unscrew the three screws securing the clips to the pressure plate, a turn at a time, until the diaphragm contacts the cover. Remove the screws, clips, and washers and the pressure plate.

Rotate the release bearing spring retainers through 90° and withdraw the bearing from the withdrawal lever fork.

Assembling

Assembly is a reversal of the dismantling sequence, but ensure that the release bearing retainers are correctly located.

Replacing

Position the driven plate assembly on the flywheel with the large end of the hub away from the flywheel.

Centralize the plate by using Service tool 18G 680, which fits the splined hub of the driven plate and the pivot bearing in the flywheel. As an alternative, a spare first motion shaft can be used.

Locate the cover assembly on the flywheel dowels and secure it with the bolts; tighten the bolts down a turn at a time by diametrical selection. Do not remove the centralizer until all bolts are securely tightened.

Remove the clutch centralizer and refit the engine. The weight of the gearbox must be supported during refitting in order to avoid strain on the first motion shaft and distortion or displacement of the release plate and straps, or driven plate assembly.

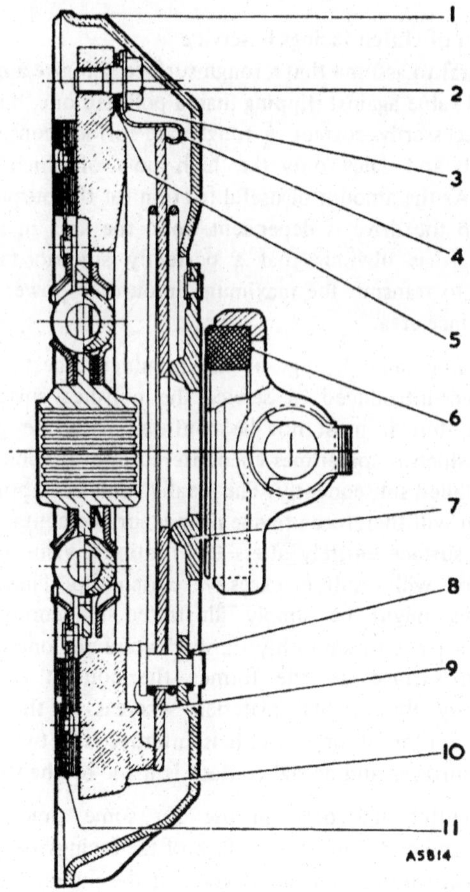

Fig. E.1
A section through the clutch

1. Cover.
2. Strap bolt.
3. Washer-tab.
4. Clip.
5. Strap-diaphragm cover.
6. Release bearing.
7. Release plate.
8. Strap-release plate/cover.
9. Diaphragm spring.
10. Pressure plate.
11. Driven plate.

Section E.2

SERVICING THE CLUTCH

Driven plates

It is important that neither oil nor grease should contact the clutch facings.

It is essential to install a complete driven plate assembly when the renewal of the friction surfaces is required. If the facings have worn to such an extent as to warrant renewal, then slight wear will have taken place on the splines, and also on the torque reaction springs and their seatings. The question of balance and concentricity is also involved. Under no circumstances is it satisfactory to repair or rectify faults in clutch driven plate centres.

Tolerances

Wear on the working faces of the driven plate is about .001 in. (.02 mm.) per 1,000 miles (1600 km.) under normal running conditions. The accuracy of the alignment of the face of the driven plate must be within .015 in. (.38 mm.).

Condition of clutch facings in service

It is natural to assume that a rough surface will give a higher frictional value against slipping than a polished one, but this is not necessarily correct. A roughened surface consists of small hills and dales, only the 'high-spots' of which make contact. As the amount of useful friction for the purpose of taking up the drive is dependent upon the area in actual contact, it is obvious that a perfectly smooth face is required to transmit the maximum amount of power for a given surface area.

Since non-metallic facings of the moulded asbestos type have been introduced in service the polished surface is common, but it must not be confused with the glazed surface which is sometimes encountered due to conditions to be detailed subsequently. The ideally smooth or polished condition will therefore provide proper surface contact, but a glazed surface entirely alters the frictional value of the facing and will result in excessive clutch slip. These two conditions might be simply illustrated by comparison between a piece of smoothly finished wood and one with a varnished surface; in the former the contact is made directly by the original material, whereas in the latter instance a film of dry varnish is interposed between the contact surfaces and actual contact is made by the varnish.

If the clutch has been in use for some time under satisfactory conditions, the surface of the facings assumes a high polish through which the grain of the material can be seen clearly. This polished facing is of light colour when in perfect condition.

Should oil in small quantities gain access to the clutch and find its way onto the facings, it will be burnt off as a result of the heat generated by the slipping occurring under normal starting conditions. The burning of this small quantity of lubricant has the effect of gradually darkening the facings, but provided the polish of the facing remains such that the grain of the material can be distinguished clearly, it has little effect on clutch performance.

Should increased quantities of oil obtain access to the facing, then one of two conditions, or a combination of these, may arise, depending upon the nature of the oil.

1. The oil may burn off and leave a carbon deposit on the surface of the facings, which assume a high glaze, producing further slip. This is a very definite, though very thin, deposit, and in general it hides the grain of the material.
2. The oil may partially burn and leave a resinous deposit on the facings. This has a tendency to produce a fierce clutch, and may also cause excessive 'spinning' due to the tendency of the face of the linings to adhere to the surface of the flywheel or pressure plate.
3. There may be a combination of conditions 1 and 2 which produces a tendency to 'judder' on such engagement.

Still greater quantities of oil produce a dark and soaked appearance of the facings, and the result will be further slip, accompanied by fierceness or 'juddering'.

If the conditions enumerated above are experienced, the clutch driven plate should be replaced by a new one. **The cause of the presence of the oil must be traced and removed.** It is, of course, necessary for the clutch and flywheel to be cleaned out thoroughly before assembly.

Where the graphite release bearing ring is badly worn in service a complete replacement assembly should be fitted, returning the old assembly for salvage of the metal cup. These graphite rings are inserted into their metal cup by heating the metal cup to a cherry red, then forcing the graphite ring into position. Immediately the ring is forced into position the whole should be quenched in oil. Alignment of the thrust pad in relation to its face and the trunnions should be within .005 in. (.12 mm.).

In almost every case of rapid wear on the splines of the clutch driven plate misalignment is responsible.

Looseness of the driven plate on the splined shaft results in noticeable backlash in the clutch. Misalignment also puts undue stress on the driven member, and may result in the hub breaking loose from the plate, with consequent total failure of the clutch.

It may also be responsible for a fierce chattering or dragging of the clutch, which makes gear-changing difficult. In cases of persistent difficulty it is advisable to check the flywheel for truth with a dial indicator. The dial reading should not vary more than .003 in. (.07 mm.) anywhere on the flywheel face.

Section E.3

MASTER CYLINDER

The master cylinder has an integral-type supply tank in which the barrel passes through the tank. A piston contained within the barrel has a rubber main cup and is spring-loaded against its inner end; between the piston and cup is a thin washer which prevents the cup being drawn into the feed holes drilled around the head of the piston. The outer end of the piston carries a secondary cup and is formed with a depression to receive the spherical end of the push-rod assembly. The push-rod has a piston stop that is retained in the body by a circlip. A rubber boot through which the push-rod passes is fitted to the end of the body. At the opposite end of the barrel to the push-rod an end plug screws down against a gasket. This plug forms the outlet connection for the pipe line to the slave cylinder.

Removing

Remove the screws securing the brake and clutch master cylinder cover and take off the cover.

Drain the fluid from the supply tank by attaching a rubber tube in the bleed screws in the clutch slave cylinder, opening the screw one full turn and then depressing the clutch pedal. Hold the pedal down and then tighten the screw and then let the pedal return unassisted. Repeat this operation until the tank is empty.

Remove the split pin, washer, and clevis pin from the push-rod and disengage the clutch pedal lever.

Clean the pipe connection, disconnect the pipe line, and fit a plug to the end of the cylinder to prevent the entry of dirt.

Unscrew the fixing bolts and detach the master cylinder from the box assembly.

Dimantling

Detach the rubber boot from the barrel.

Depress the piston to relieve the load on the circlip, then remove the circlip and the push-rod assembly.

Withdraw the piston, piston washer, main cup, spring retainer, and spring.

Remove the secondary cup by carefully stretching it over the end of the piston.

Examination

Place all metal parts in a tray of clean Clutch and Brake Fluid to soak. Dry them with a clean, non-fluffy cloth. Rubber components are to be examined for swollen or perished cups or other signs of deterioration. Any suspect parts must be renewed.

Swill the main castings in industrial methylated spirit and thoroughly dry out before assembly.

Ensure that the by-pass ports are free of obstruction. The port is drilled with a ⅛ in. (3.17 mm.) drill for half its length and then finished with a .028 in. (.711 mm.) drill.

Assembling

Dip all components in Clutch and Brake Fluid and assemble when wet.

Stretch the secondary cup over the piston with the lip of the cup facing the head of the piston. When the cup is in its groove work it round gently with the fingers to ensure that it is correctly seated.

Insert the return spring, largest diameter first, into the barrel and position the spring seat on the small-diameter end of the spring.

Assemble the main cup, piston washer, piston, and push-rod. When assembling the cups carefully enter the lip edge of the cups into the barrel first.

Depress the piston, position the piston stop, and retain it in the barrel with the circlip.

Place the rubber boot in position and fit the dust excluder.

Replacing

Refit the master cylinder to the master cylinder box and secure it with the bolts. The long bolt passes through the stiffener plate.

Remove the dust excluder and fit the pipe connection to the master cylinder.

Refit the clutch pedal lever to the push-rod and secure it with the clevis pin, washer, and a new split pin.

Refit the master cylinder cover.

Fill the master cylinder and then prime and bleed the system.

Section E.4

SLAVE CYLINDER

The slave cylinder incorporates two threaded connections for the feed hose and the bleed screw and accommodates in the body a piston, a cup, and a spring.

A rubber boot through which passes a push-rod is fitted to the body and is retained by two clips. The push-rod has an eye-end which connects with the clutch withdrawal fork.

Removing

Drain the system as described in Section E.3.

Release the feed pipe from the cylinder and remove the two screws securing the cylinder to the clutch housing. The cylinder may be withdrawn, leaving the push-rod attached to the clutch withdrawal fork, or the rod may be detached from the fork.

Dismantling

Remove the rubber dust cover and with an air line blow out the piston and seal. Extract the spring and cup filler.

Examine all components and renew any that are suspect.

Assembling

Place the spring in the cylinder, followed by the filler, cup, and piston. Depress the piston with the push-rod and refit the rubber boot. Secure the boot to the rod with the small clip and then fit the boot to the cylinder and secure it with the large circlip.

THE CLUTCH CONTROL COMPONENTS

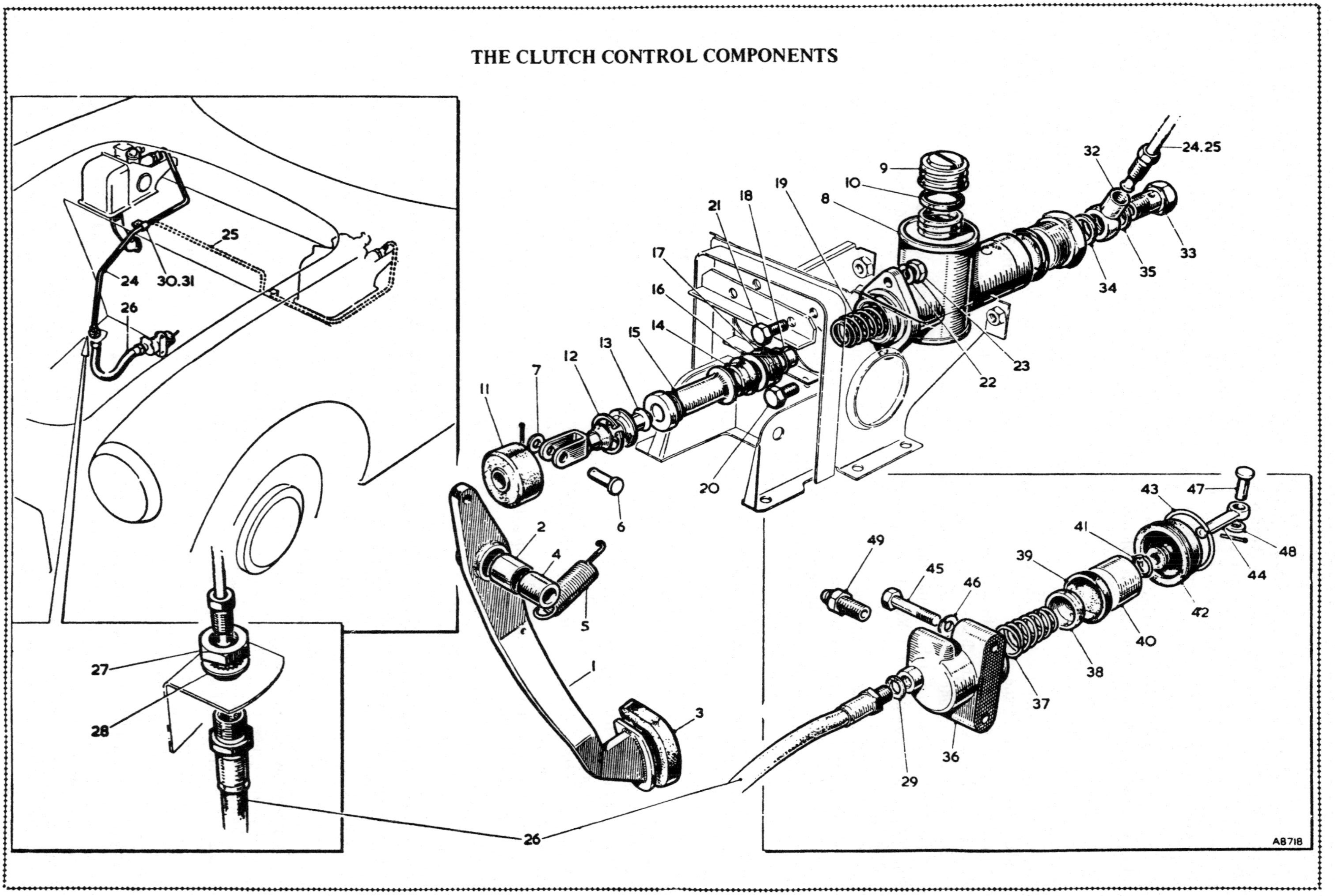

KEY TO THE CLUTCH CONTROL COMPONENTS

No.	Description	No.	Description	No.	Description
1.	Pedal–clutch.	18.	Retainer–spring.	34.	Gasket.
2.	Bush.	19.	Spring.	35.	Gasket.
3.	Pad–pedal (rubber).	20.	Screw–cylinder to box.	36.	Body.
4.	Tube–distance–clutch pedal.	21.	Screw–cylinder and stiffener to box.	37.	Spring–cup filler.
5.	Spring–pedal pull-off.	22.	Washer–spring–for screw.	38.	Filler–piston cup.
6.	Pin–clevis–fork end to pedal.	23.	Nut for screw.	39.	Cup piston.
7.	Washer–plain–for pin.	24.	Pipe–master cylinder to hose.	40.	Piston.
8.	Barrel and tank.	25.	Pipe–master cylinder to hose.	41.	Clip–boot (small).
9.	Cap–filler.	26.	Hose–clutch.	42.	Boot.
10.	Seal–cap.	27.	Locknut for hose.	43.	Clip–boot (large).
11.	Boot.	28.	Washer–shakeproot.	44.	Rod–push.
12.	Circlip.	29.	Gasket–hose to body.	45.	Bolt–cylinder to gearbox.
13.	Rod–push.	30.	Clip–clutch pipe to bulkhead.	46.	Washer–spring–for bolt.
14.	Cup–secondary.	31.	Clip–clutch pipe to bulkhead.	47.	Pin–clevis–cylinder to clutch fork.
15.	Piston.	32.	Connection–banjo.	48.	Washer–plain–for pin.
16.	Washer–piston.	33.	Bolt for banjo connection.	49.	Screw–bleeder.
17.	Cup–main.				

Replacing

Fit the cylinder to the clutch housing and secure it with the two screws. Assemble the push-rod to the clutch withdrawal fork. Connect the feed line and fill, prime, and bleed the system as described in Section E.5.

Section E.5

BLEEDING THE CLUTCH SYSTEM

Open the bleed screw on the slave cylinder three-quarters of a turn and attach a tube, immersing the open end in a clean receptacle containing a small quantity of the recommended hydraulic fluid. Fill the master cylinder reservoir with the recommended fluid (see **'GENERAL DATA'**). Using slow, full strokes, pump the clutch pedal until the fluid entering the container is completely free from air bubbles. On a down-stroke of the pedal tighten the bleed screw and remove the bleed tube.

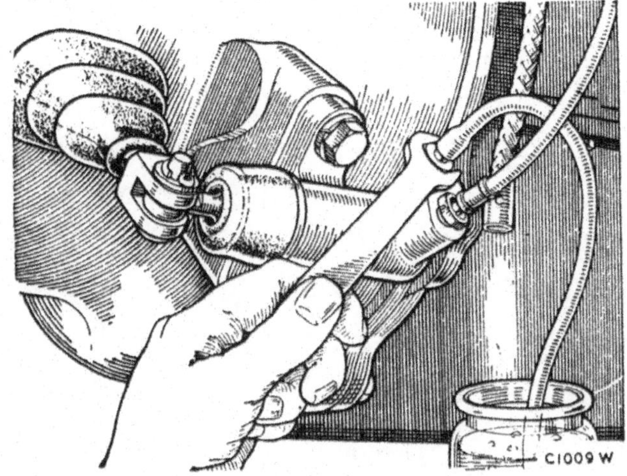

Fig. E.2
Bleeding the clutch hydraulic system at the slave cylinder

SECTION F

THE GEARBOX

THE GEARBOX COMPONENTS

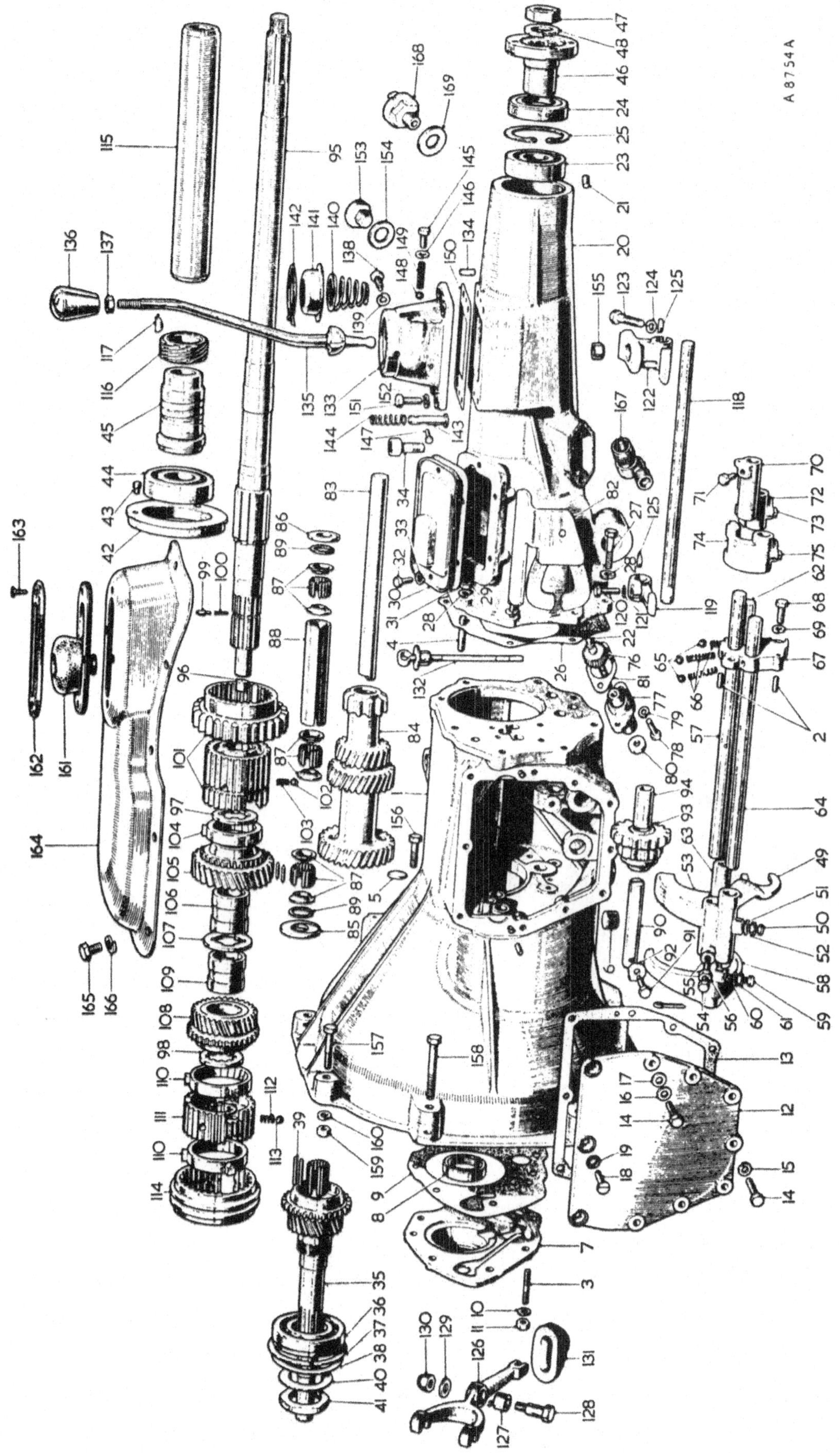

KEY TO THE GEARBOX COMPONENTS

No.	Description
1.	Casing assembly.
2.	Dowel–locating block to gearbox.
3.	Stud–front cover.
4.	Stud–rear extension.
5.	Plug–welch–casing.
6.	Plug–drain.
7.	Cover assembly–front.
8.	Seal–oil.
9.	Joint washer–front cover to casing.
10.	Washer–spring–stub–front cover to casing.
11.	Nut–stud.
12.	Cover–gearbox side.
13.	Joint washer–side cover to casing.
14.	Screw–gearbox side cover.
15.	Washer–spring–screw.
16.	Washer–plain–screw.
17.	Washer–fibre–screw.
18.	Screw–countersunk–gearbox side cover.
19.	Washer–shakeproof–screw.
20.	Extension–rear.
21.	Plug–taper–rear extension.
22.	Button–thrust–speedometer.
23.	Bearing–rear extension.
24.	Seal–oil–rear extension.
25.	Circlip–oil seal.
26.	Joint washer–extension to casing.
27.	Screw–extension to casing.
28.	Washer–spring–screw.
29.	Nut–stud–rear extension to casing.
30.	Cover–side–rear extension.
31.	Joint washer–side cover to extension.
32.	Screw–side cover to extension.
33.	Washer–spring–screw.
34.	Breather assembly.
35.	Shaft–first motion.
36.	Bearing.
37.	Ring–spring–bearing.
38.	Shim–first motion shaft–.002 in. (.051 mm.).
39.	Roller–needle–first motion shaft.
40.	Washer–locking–first motion shaft nut.
41.	Nut–first motion shaft.
42.	Housing–rear bearing.
43.	Peg–locating–rear bearing housing.
44.	Bearing–rear–third motion shaft.
45.	Distance piece assembly–speedometer gear to rear bearing.
46.	Flange–third motion shaft.
47.	Nut–third motion shaft flange.
48.	Washer–spring–nut.
49.	Fork–reverse.
50.	Screw–reverse fork locating.
51.	Washer–shakeproof–screw.
52.	Nut–screw–fork locating.
53.	Fork–first and second speed.
54.	Screw–fork locating.
55.	Washer–shakeproof–screw.
56.	Nut–screw–fork locating.
57.	Rod–first and second speed fork.
58.	Fork–third and fourth speed.
59.	Screw–fork locating.
60.	Washer–shakeproof–screw.
61.	Nut–screw–fork locating.
62.	Rod–third and fourth speed fork.
63.	Distance piece–third and fourth speed fork rod.
64.	Rod–reverse fork.
65.	Ball–fork locating.
66.	Spring–locating ball.
67.	Block–sliding shaft locating.
68.	Screw–locating block to gearbox.
69.	Washer–spring–screw.
70.	Selector–first and second gear.
71.	Screw–selector locating.
72.	Selector–third and fourth gear.
73.	Screw–selector locating.
74.	Selector–reverse gear.
75.	Screw–selector locating.
76.	Pinion–speedometer.
77.	Bush–speedometer pinion.
78.	Screw–speedometer pinion bush.
79.	Washer–lock–screw.
80.	Seal–oil–speedometer pinion.
81.	Joint washer–speedometer pinion bush.
82.	Arm assembly–interlocking.
83.	Layshaft.
84.	Gear unit–layshaft.
85.	Washer–thrust–front–laygear.
86.	Washer–thrust–rear–.154 to .156 in. (3.912 to 3.962 mm.).
87.	Roller–needle bearing–layshaft.
88.	Tube–distance–laygear bearing.
89.	Ring–spring–layshaft.
90.	Shaft–reverse.
91.	Screw–reverse shaft.
92.	Washer–locking screw.
93.	Gear assembly–reverse.
94.	Bush–reverse gear.
95.	Shaft–third motion.
96.	Restrictor–oil.
97.	Washer–thrust–rear–third motion shaft.
98.	Washer–thrust–front–.1565 to .1575 in. (3.962 to 3.9887 mm.).
99.	Peg–thrust washer.
100.	Spring–peg.
101.	First speed wheel and synchronizer assembly.
102.	Ball–synchronizer.
103.	Spring–synchronizer ball.
104.	Baulk ring–second speed gear.
105.	Gear–second speed.
106.	Bush–second speed mainshaft gear.
107.	Ring–interlocking–second and third gear bushes.
108.	Gear–third speed.
109.	Bush–third speed gear.
110.	Baulk ring–third and fourth speed gear.
111.	Synchronizer–third and fourth speed.
112.	Spring–synchronizer ball.
113.	Ball–synchronizer.
114.	Coupling–sliding–third and fourth speed.
115.	Distance piece–third motion shaft.
116.	Gear–speedometer.
117.	Key–speedometer gear.
118.	Shaft–remote-control (rear extension).
119.	Lever–selector–front.
120.	Screw–selector lever–front.
121.	Washer–shakeproof–screw.
122.	Lever–selector–rear.
123.	Screw–selector lever–rear.
124.	Washer–spring–screw.
125.	Key–selector lever.
126.	Lever–clutch withdrawal.
127.	Bush–withdrawal lever.
128.	Bolt–clutch withdrawal lever.
129.	Washer–bolt.
130.	Nut–stiff–bolt.
131.	Cover–dust–clutch withdrawal lever.
132.	Indicator–oil level–gearbox.
133.	Tower–remote-control.
134.	Dowel–remote-control tower.
135.	Lever–change speed.
136.	Knob–change speed lever.
137.	Locknut–change speed knob.
138.	Pin–locating–change speed lever.
139.	Washer–spring.
140.	Spring–change speed lever.
141.	Cover–ball spring.
142.	Circlip–ball spring cover.
143.	Plunger–reverse selector.
144.	Spring–reverse plunger.
145.	Screw–reverse plunger spring.
146.	Washer–spring–screw.
147.	Pin–locating–reverse plunger.
148.	Ball–reverse plunger.
149.	Spring–reverse plunger detent.
150.	Gasket–control tower.
151.	Screw–tower to extension.
152.	Washer–spring–screw.
153.	Plug–reverse light switch hole.
154.	Joint washer–plug.
155.	Bush–change speed lever.
156.	Bolt–gearbox to mounting plate.
157.	Bolt–gearbox to mounting plate.
158.	Bolt–gearbox to mounting plate.
159.	Nut–bolt.
160.	Washer–spring–bolt.
161.	Grommet–gear lever.
162.	Retainer–gear lever grommet.
163.	Screw–retainer to cover.
164.	Cover–gearbox remote-control.
165.	Screw–cover to tunnel.
166.	Washer–spring.
167.	Box–speedometer drive adaptor.
168.	Reverse light switch (later cars).
169.	Washer for switch (later cars).

GENERAL DESCRIPTION

The gearbox has four forward gears and a reverse gear. Top, third, and second gear engagement are effected by synchromesh hubs with direct drive for top gear and constant-mesh gears on the layshaft and mainshaft for third and second gears. First and reverse gears are sliding spur gears.
A combined dipstick and filler plug is housed in the top of the gearbox and a drain plug in the bottom.
The bell housing is integral with the gearbox and accommodates the clutch release mechanism and the starter motor driving pinion.
An extension bolted to the rear end of the gearbox contains the gear selector mechanism.
The gearbox is bolted at the front end to the engine mounting plate and is supported at the rear by two rubber mountings that locate on the rear cross-member mounting brackets. An engine stay-rod attached to the under side of the rear extension is anchored to the rear cross-member.

LUBRICATION

Oil level
When topping up the gearbox ensure that it is not filled above the 'HIGH' mark on the dipstick. If the level is too high, oil may get into the clutch case and cause clutch slip.
The combined filler plug and dipstick for the gearbox and overdrive is located beneath the rubber plug on the gearbox cover.

Draining
Remove the gearbox drain plug and drain off the oil.
When the gearbox has been drained, completely refill with fresh oil.

Section F.1

REMOVING THE GEARBOX

1. Prepare the engine for removal from the car as detailed in Section A and take the weight of the engine.
2. Drain the oil from the gearbox.
3. Disconnect and remove the propeller shaft as detailed in Section G and disconnect the speedometer pinion drive.
4. Disconnect the clutch slave cylinder push-rod from the clutch withdrawal lever and the slave cylinder from the clutch housing. Tie the cylinder clear of the gearbox.
5. Remove the screws securing the rear cross-member to the body and lower the engine and gearbox until the gearbox rests on the fixed body cross-member.
6. .Release the engine stay-rod bracket from the rear cross-member and remove tne four nuts and washers securing the gearbox rear rubber mountings to the cross-member. Withdraw the rear cross-member from the body.
7. Remove the gear lever knob and the rubber cover from the tunnel. Remove the remote-control tower complete with gear lever from the gearbox.
8. Ease the assembly forward until it is clear of the fixed body cross-member and then tilt the assembly and lift it from the car.
9. Remove the screws securing the gearbox to the engine rear mounting plate and separate the gearbox from the engine.

   NOTE.–Great care must be taken during this operation to ensure that no load is placed on the clutch release plate drive straps. Even slight damage to these may result in the clutch breaking up at high speeds.
10. Remove the stiffnut and washer from the clutch withdrawal lever bolt and take the dust cover and lever from the clutch housing.
11. Remove the nut, spring washer, and pin from the engine stay-rod and the stay-rod from the gearbox.
12. If the stay-rod and bracket are to be dismantled remove the rear nut and washer and slide off the plates, buffers, brackets, and distance tube. Separate the plates, buffers, and brackets from the distance tube.

Section F.2

DISMANTLING THE GEARBOX

1. Remove the dipstick, drain plug, and speedometer drive pinion.
2. Using Service tool 18G 2, remove the propeller shaft flange.
3. Remove the remote-control tower, the gearbox extension side cover, and the interlock plate and bracket.
4. Slacken the locating screw on the remote-control front selector lever, unscrew the screws and nuts securing the extension to the gearbox, and remove the extension.
5. Retain the remote-control selector lever, which will fall free as the extension is withdrawn. Withdraw the shaft and rear selector lever from the rear extension and remove the selector lever from the shaft; withdraw the split bush and circlip from the selector.
6. Remove the three countersunk screws and seven hexagon-headed screws from the gearbox side cover and lift off the cover and gasket.
7. Cut the locking wire, unscrew the three selector locating screws, and remove the selectors.
8. Unscrew the shift shaft locating block screws and remove the block from the rear face of the gearbox. Retain the three balls and springs which will be released when the block is withdrawn from the shafts. Two dowels on the block locate it on the rear face of the gearbox.
9. Release the locknuts and remove the fork locating screws and star washers from the change speed forks.

Slide out the shafts and remove the forks in the following order: reverse, fourth and third speed, second and first speed.

10. If difficulty is experienced in removing the shafts remove the front cover and use a soft drift to tap the shafts out from the front of the box.
11. Remove the nuts and washers securing the front cover and then remove the cover, gasket, and the first motion shaft bearing shims. Do not remove the oil seal from the cover unless it has to be renewed.
12. Unscrew the reverse shaft locating screw and remove the shaft and gear.
13. Using a soft drift, tap out the layshaft from the front of the box and allow the laygear to rest in the bottom of the box.
14. Ease the rear bearing housing from the rear of the gearbox and withdraw the third motion shaft assembly.
15. Withdraw the first motion shaft from the front of the gearbox. A soft drift may be used to tap the shaft from the inside of the box.
16. Reassemble the laygear on its shaft and check the end-float of the gear (see **'GENERAL DATA'**).
17. Remove the layshaft, laygear, and thrust washers.

Section F.3

DISMANTLING AND ASSEMBLING THE CONTROL TOWER

Do not dismantle the control tower unless worn or broken parts are to be renewed.

1. Remove the ball spring cover circlip to ease the tension on the spring and then remove the two change speed lever locating pins. Withdraw the lever, and from it, remove the knob, cover and spring.

Fig. F.1
Checking the laygear end-float

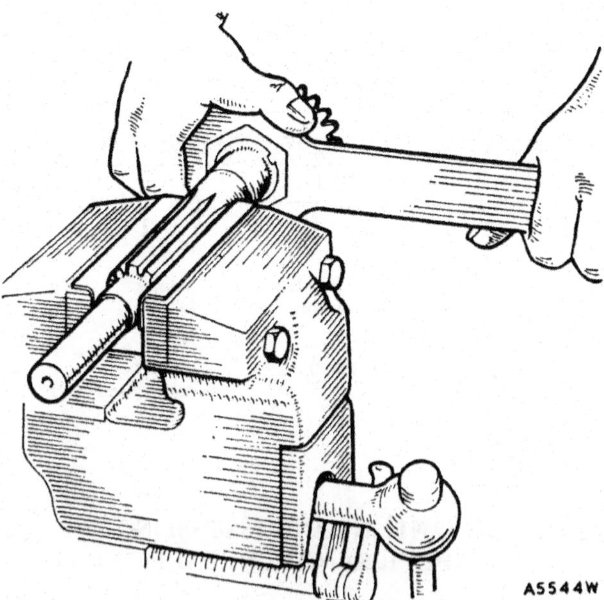

Fig. F.2
Using Service tool 18G 5 to unscrew a first motion shaft nut. This nut has a left-hand thread.

2. From the rear of the control tower unscrew the reverse plunger detent screw and remove the reverse plunger detent spring and ball.
3. From the side of the tower remove the reverse plunger locating pin and retain the plunger and spring that will be released from inside the tower.

Assembly is a reversal of the dismantling sequence, but care must be taken to ensure that the front and rear selectors are correctly lined up and that the clinch bolts pass across the flats on the remote-control shaft.

When fitting a new pin to retain the reverse selector plunger ensure that the plunger is depressed sufficiently enough to permit the pin to engage the flats on the plunger.

Section F.4

DISMANTLING AND ASSEMBLING THE REAR EXTENSION

1. Remove the rear selector lever clamp bolt, lever, and the Woodruff key and withdraw the shaft from the rear extension. Do not dismantle the rear extension any further unless the oil seal and/or bearing has to be renewed, in which case proceed as follows.
2. Using Service tool 18G 389 and 18G 389 C, remove the rear oil seal.
3. Remove the rear extension bearing circlip and press out the bearing.

Assembly is a reversal of the dismantling sequence. If the bearing and/or oil seal have/has been removed, press in the new bearing and secure it with the circlip, and, using Service tool 18G 134 and adaptor 18G 134 N, fit the new oil seal.

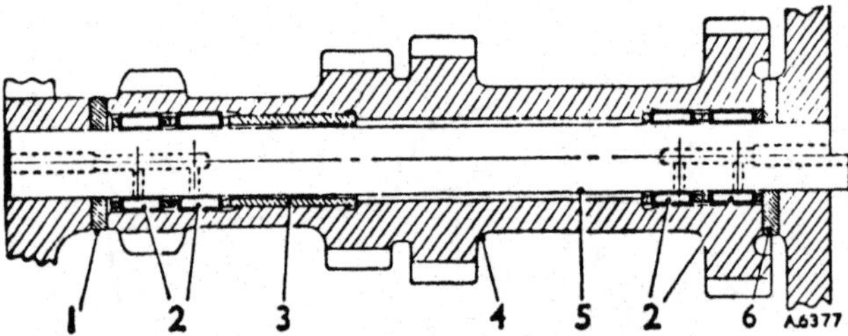

Fig. F.3
Laygear assembly - second type

1. Thrust washer - small.
2. Needle-roller bearing (pair).
3. Distance tube
4. Laygear.
5. Layshaft.
6. Thrust washer - large.

Section F.5

DISMANTLING AND ASSEMBLING THE FIRST MOTION SHAFT

1. Remove the spindle rollers from the spigot bearing housing.
2. Secure the shaft in a soft-jawed vice, release the lock washer, and, using Service tool 18G 5, unscrew the locknut.
   NOTE.–The locknut has a left-hand thread.
3. Press the bearing from the shaft and remove the spring ring from the bearing.

Assembly is a reversal of the dismantling sequence.

Section F.6

DISMANTLING AND ASSEMBLING THE LAYGEAR

FIRST TYPE

Remove the circlips from the ends of the laygear and withdraw the needle-roller bearing assemblies and the distance tube.

To assemble the laygear proceed as follows:

1. Hold the layshaft in a vice, stepped end downwards.
2. Smear the shaft with grease and assemble a bearing assembly, the distance tube, and the remaining two bearing assemblies to the shaft.
3. Fit a circlip to the front end of the laygear and place the laygear on the shaft.
4. Remove the laygear and shaft from the vice, fit the remaining circlip, and remove the shaft from the gear.

SECOND TYPE

The second-type laygear has a larger diameter shaft and a pair of caged needle-roller bearings at each end.

Extract the two pairs of needle-roller bearings from the ends of the laygear and the distance tube from the small end.

To assemble the laygear proceed as follows:

1. Dip the bearings in oil.
2. Hold the laygear in a vice and insert the distance tube and a pair of bearings at the small end.
3. Insert a pair of bearings at the large end.

Section F.7

DISMANTLING THE THIRD MOTION SHAFT

Before dismantling the third motion shaft check the end-float on the third speed mainshaft gear to ensure the fitting of the correct thrust washer during reassembly of the third motion shaft.

1. Remove the third and fourth speed gear front baulk ring, the synchromesh sleeve and hub, and the rear baulk ring. The synchromesh sleeve may be withdrawn from the hub, but care must be taken to retain the balls and springs that will be released when the sleeve is withdrawn from the hub.
2. Depress the front thrust washer retaining peg, rotate the washer to align its splines with those on the shaft, and remove the washer.
3. Withdraw the third speed gear and its bush and then remove the bush interlock ring to free the second speed gear. Remove the gear, baulk ring, bush, and thrust washer.
4. Withdraw the first and second speed synchromesh and gear. The first gear may be disengaged from the hub, but care must be taken to retain the balls and springs that will be released when the gear is withdrawn from the hub.
5. Remove the speedometer drive gear and its Woodruff key and then slide the distance piece from the shaft.
6. Press the bearing from the shaft and then from its housing.

Section F.8

EXAMINATION OF COMPONENTS

Thoroughly clean, dry, and examine all components for wear, distortion, deterioration, and thread damage, paying particular attention to the following:

1. Bushes fitted to the clutch withdrawal fork, third motion shaft, and reverse speed gear. Worn or damaged bushes should be renewed (Section F.11).

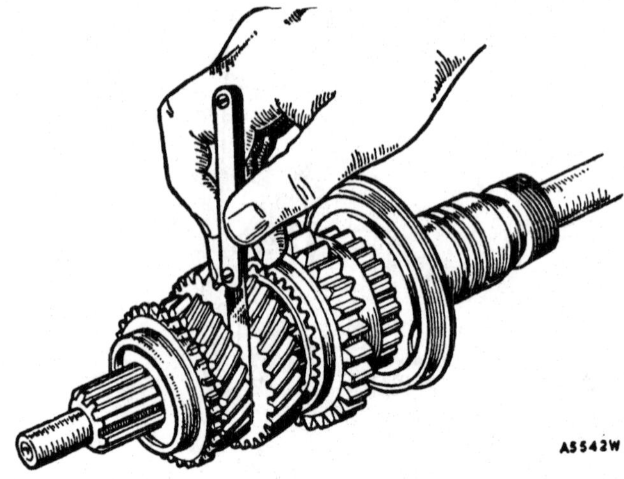

Fig. F.4
Checking the mainshaft second and third speed gear end-float

2. Bearings fitted to the first motion shaft, third motion shaft, and rear extension.
   Examine the bearings for looseness, pitting, security of cages, and fit in their housings and on their journals.

Examine also the needle rollers in the first motion shaft and the laygear.
Unserviceable bearings should be renewed.

3. Spring fitted to the synchromesh hubs, shaft locating block, reverse shaft, and reverse plunger detent.
   Comparisons may be made with new springs, but where facilities for test are available refer to the weights and lengths given under **'GENERAL DATA'**.
4. The rubber gaiters for the clutch withdrawal fork and gear lever for cracks or signs of deterioration.
5. Ensure that all oilways are clear of obstruction, including the oil restrictor in the front of the third motion shaft.
6. Examine the interlock arm for burrs and for security of the rivet.

Section F.9

ASSEMBLING THE THIRD MOTION SHAFT

Lubricate all contact surfaces with oil, and smear the bore of the gears with Duckham's Moly Disulphide Grease (max. size 5 microns).

1. Use Service tools 18G 222 and 18G 223 to assemble the second speed synchromesh hub and third and top gear synchromesh hub respectively.
2. Press the rear bearing into its housing and the bearing onto the shaft.

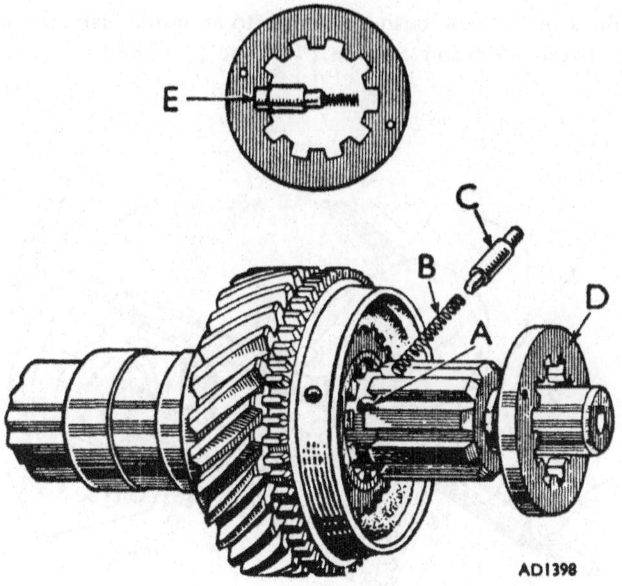

Fig. F.5
Securing the mainshaft gears
A. Hole for spring. C. Locating peg.
B. Spring. D. Locking washer.
E. Peg located in the washer.

Fig. F.6
Assembling a synchromesh hub, using Service tool 18G 222

3. Fit the speedometer gear drive to the shaft with its key.
4. Fit the first gear and second gear synchromesh to the shaft, followed by the baulk ring and rear thrust washer.
5. Fit the second speed gear bush to the shaft and ensure that the lugs face forward and that the oil hole in the bush is in alignment with the oil hole in the shaft.
6. Assemble the second speed gear and the interlock washer so that the washer engages the lugs on the bush.
7. Fit the third speed gear bush, lugs first, and ensure that the lugs engage the interlock washer and that the oil hole and cut-away in the bush are in alignment with the holes in the shaft.
8. Place the retaining pin spring and pin in the shaft and the third speed gear on the bush with the cone facing forward.
9. Position the gear so that the hole in the cone is in line with the retaining peg, depress the peg with a thin drift, fit the thrust washer to the shaft, then turn the washer to allow the peg to lock the washer in position.

Check the end-float of the second and third speed gear (see **'GENERAL DATA'** and Fig. F.4).

Thrust washers are available in four thicknesses as follows:

.1565 to .1575 in. (3.96 to 3.98 mm.).
.1585 to .1595 in. (4.01 to 4.03 mm.).
.1605 to .1615 in. (4.06 to 4.08 mm.).

10. Assemble the third and fourth speed gear rear baulk ring, synchromesh, and front baulk ring.

Section F.10

ASSEMBLING THE GEARBOX

Any gaskets or locking devices that are unserviceable or suspect should be renewed during assembly of the gearbox.

1. Place the laygear in the bottom of the gearbox together with the thrust washers (see Section F.2, paragraph 16) and thread a piece of stiff wire through the laygear to allow Service tool 18G 471 to

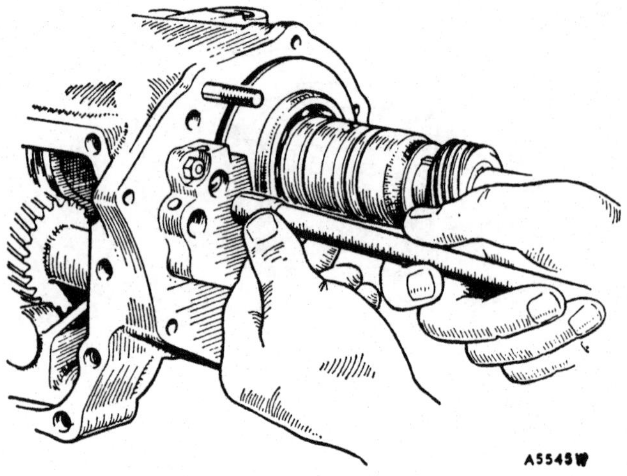

Fig. F.7
Assembling a selector shaft, using Service tool 18G 4

pick up the thrust washers and laygear. The washers are available in four thicknesses as follows:

.154 to .156 in. (3.81 to 3.96 mm.).
.157 to .159 in. (3.95 to 4.03 mm.).
.160 to .161 in. (4.06 to 4.08 mm.).
.163 to .164 in. (4.13 to 4.16 mm.).

2. Fit the first motion shaft assembly to the gearbox.
3. Insert the third motion shaft from the rear of the box, use the gearbox extension gasket to align the dowel in the bearing housing, enter the spigot in the first motion shaft, and push home the shaft and bearing housing.
4. Using Service tool 18G 471, fit the layshaft to the laygear and ensure that the cut-away end of the shaft faces forward.
5. Assemble the reverse gear and shaft and secure the shaft with the locating screw and a new tab washer. Lock the screw with the washer.
6. Refit the first motion shaft bearing shims, align the step on the end of the layshaft with the inside edge of the front cover, and, using Service tool 18G 598, fit the front cover as described in Section F.12.
7. Assemble the clutch withdrawal lever with its bolt and stiffnut.
8. Bolt the shaft locating block to the rear face of the gearbox and insert the three springs and balls into the block.
9. Assemble the selectors to the shafts and secure them with their locating screws. Lock the screw heads to the selectors with new locking wire.
10. Using Service tool 18G 41, depress the springs and balls in the locating block and pass the shafts through the block.
11. Position the gear change forks in the box in the following order: reverse, first and second speed, third and fourth speed.
12. Fit the distance piece to the third and fourth speed shaft, push the shafts through the forks, align the holes in the shafts and forks, and secure them with the fork locating screws. Tighten the locknut on each screw.
13. Replace the gearbox side cover and gasket.
14. Place the third motion shaft distance piece on the shaft and the extension gasket over the studs on the rear face of the gearbox.
15. Fit the rear extension to the gearbox and engage the rear extension remote-control shaft in the front selector and the dowel on the third motion shaft bearing housing with the hole in the extension.
16. Secure the selector with its Woodruff key and pinch-bolt and replace the extension side cover and gasket.
17. Refit the speedometer drive pinion, drain plug, dipstick, and rear joint flange.
18. After refitting the gearbox to the vehicle replace the control tower and its gasket and fill the box with clean oil.

Section F.11

FITTING REPLACEMENT BUSHES

When fitting replacement bushes to the reverse gear, the clutch withdrawal fork, and the third motion shaft remove the old bushes and fit the new ones as follows.

Reverse gear

Press the new bush into the gear from the small end of the gear until the end of the bush is flush with the face of the small end.

Finish to an internal diameter of between .6255 and .6265 in. (15.8 and 15.9 mm.) concentric with the gear teeth.

Clutch withdrawal fork

Press in the new bush and finish to an inside diameter of between .4996 and .5004 in. (12.6 and 12.7 mm.).

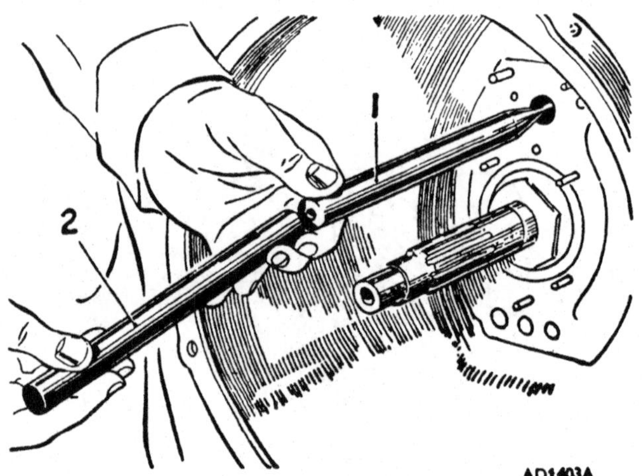

Fig. F.8
Using tool 18G 471 as a pilot when installing the layshaft
1. Pilot. 2. Layshaft.

Third motion shaft bushes

Heat the bushes to between 180 and 200° C. (356 and 392° F.), ensure that the locating tongues on the bushes are in line with the splines on the shaft and that the oil holes are in line, then assemble the second-speed bush, interlock washer, and third speed bush.

Section F.12

FITTING THE GEARBOX FRONT COVER

To prevent oil leaking past the gearbox front cover oil seal the cover must be correctly fitted to ensure that the seal is concentric with the first motion shaft. When refitting the cover proceed as follows.

Clean off the cover and examine it carefully for burrs and bruising, particularly around the bore, stud holes, and machined surfaces. Check the flat surfaces for twist and warp, and correct it if necessary. If the condition is too bad to correct, fit a new cover.

Remove and discard the front cover to gearbox gasket and clean off the flat surfaces around the base of all studs.

Offer the front cover (less oil seal) to the gearbox and push it fully home on the studs. The cover should be free to move in all directions, and points at which the holes may be binding on the studs must be relieved until the cover is free to 'float'.

Remove the cover and, using Service tool 18G 134 with adaptor 18G 134 N, fit the oil seal so that its lip faces inwards towards the gearbox. Lightly grease and fit a new gasket to the gearbox front face, then fit the centralizer (Service tool 18G 598) to the bore of the front cover and push it in until it is tight. Lightly oil the seal and pass the cover over the first motion shaft, taking particular care not to cut or damage the knife edge of the seal.

Keep the centralizer firmly in position, push the cover onto the studs, and fit the spring washers and nuts, tightening the nuts finger tight only. Use a suitable socket spanner and long extension to tighten the nuts a half-turn at a time by diametrical selection until all nuts are fully tightened.

Remove the centralizer and refit the clutch-operating components.

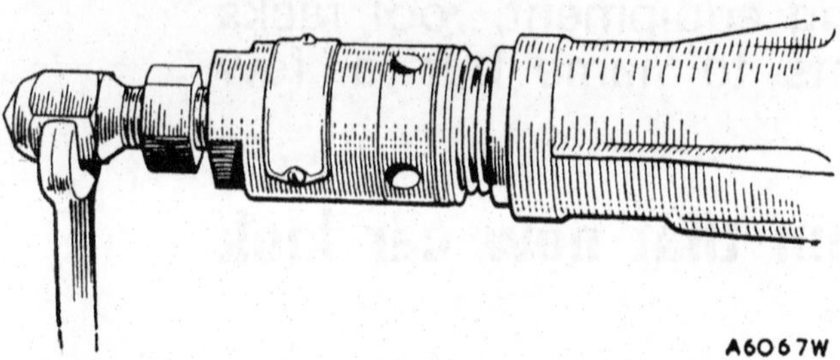

Fig. F.9
Removing a rear oil seal, using Service tools 18G 389 and 18G 389 B

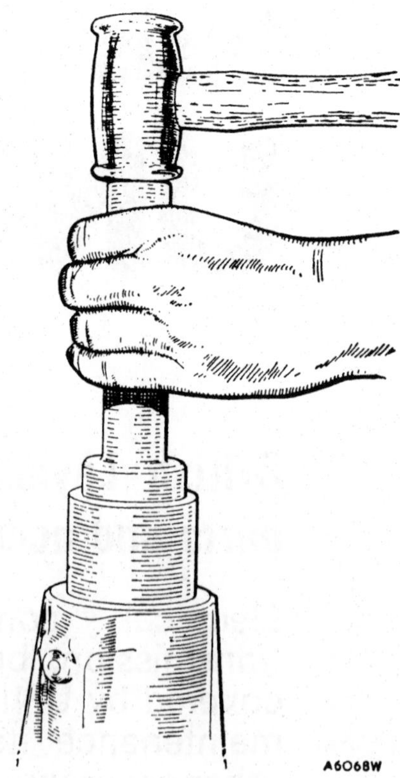

Fig. F.10
Installing a new rear oil seal, using Service tools 18G 134 and 18G 134 N

SECTION Fa

THE OVERDRIVE (TYPE 'D')

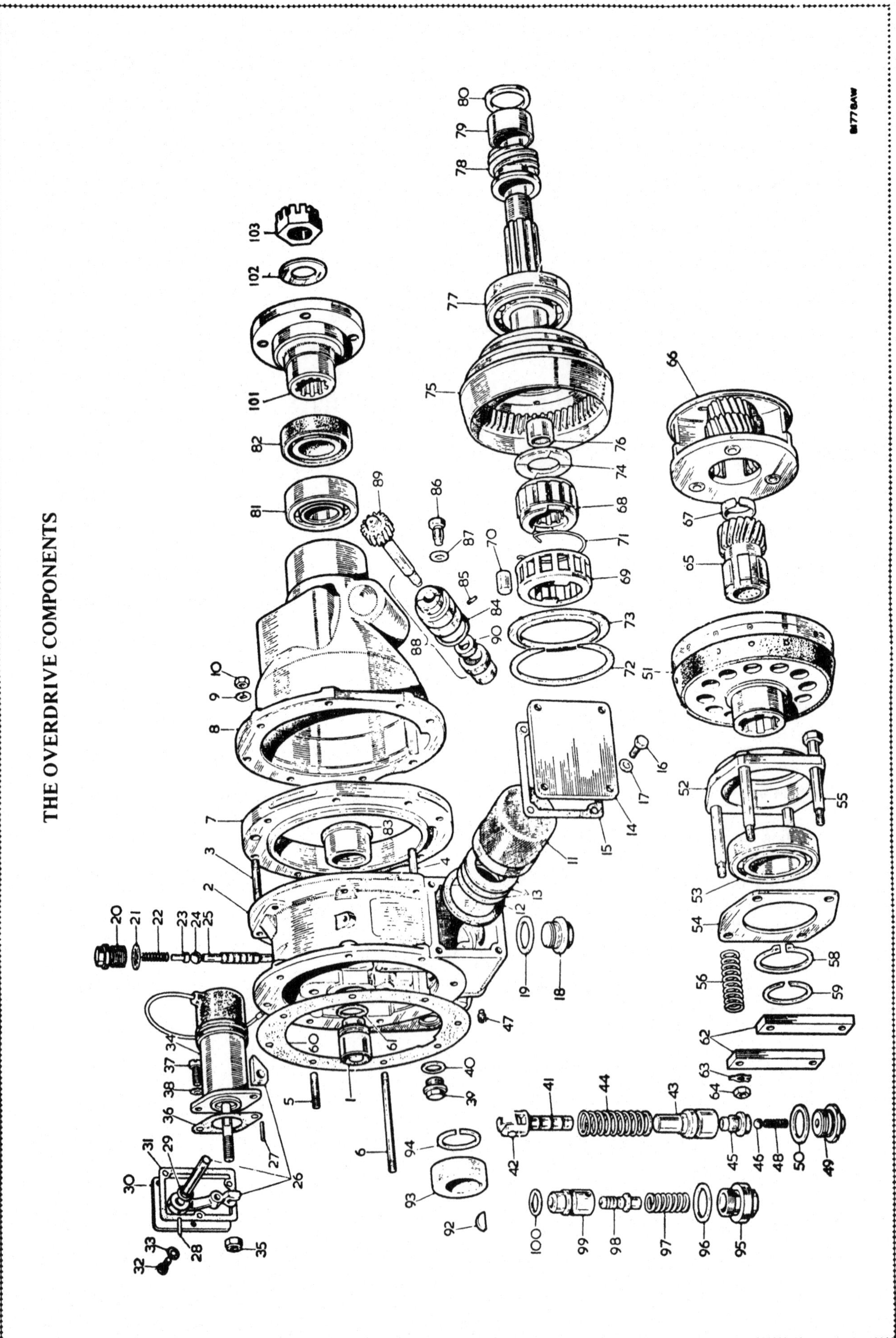

THE OVERDRIVE COMPONENTS

KEY TO THE OVERDRIVE COMPONENTS

No.	Description	No.	Description	No.	Description
1.	Operating piston.	35.	Self-locking nut.	70.	Roller–uni-directional clutch.
2.	Main casing assembly.	36.	Joint for solenoid.	71.	Spring for clutch.
3.	Stud–main casing to rear casing.	37.	Screw for solenoid.	72.	Snap ring.
4.	Stud–main casing to rear casing.	38.	Shakeproof washer.	73.	Oil thrower.
5.	Stud–main casing to gearbox adaptor.	39.	Plug for solenoid bracket.	74.	Thrust bearing.
6.	Stud–main casing to gearbox adaptor.	40.	Washer for plug.	75.	Annulus assembly.
7.	Brake ring.	41.	Pump plunger.	76.	Bearing–needle-roller.
8.	Intermediate casing.	42.	Pin.	77.	Bearing–inner.
9.	Spring washer.	43.	Pump body.	78.	Speedometer driving gear.
10.	Nut.	44.	Pump plunger spring.	79.	Bush.
11.	Filter.	45.	Non-return valve body.	80.	Thrust washer.
12.	Sealing plate.	46.	Steel ball.	81.	Bearing.
13.	Magnetic rings.	47.	Screw locating pump body.	82.	Oil seal.
14.	Side cover-plate.	48.	Spring–non-return valve.	83.	Steady bush–third motion shaft.
15.	Joint for cover-plate.	49.	Plug–non-return valve.	84.	'O' ring.
16.	Set screw.	50.	Washer for plug.	85.	Pin.
17.	Shakeproof washer.	51.	Clutch assembly.	86.	Locking screw–speedometer bearing.
18.	Drain plug.	52.	Bearing housing.	87.	Washer for locking screw.
19.	Washer for plug.	53.	Bearing–thrust.	88.	Speedometer drive bearing assembly.
20.	Plug for operating valve.	54.	Plate–retainer.	89.	Speedometer driven gear.
21.	Washer for plug.	55.	Bolt for bearing housing.	90.	Oil seal–speedometer bearing.
22.	Spring–operating valve.	56.	Spring–clutch return.	92.	Key–third motion shaft cam.
23.	Plunger–operating valve.	58.	Circlip–bearing retaining.	93.	Cam–third motion shaft.
24.	Steel ball.	59.	Snap ring–sun wheel retaining.	94.	Snap ring–third motion shaft.
25.	Operating valve.	60.	Joint for front cover.	95.	Plug–relief valve.
26.	Operating valve lever assembly.	61.	'O' ring.	96.	Washer for plug.
27.	Mills pin.	62.	Bridge piece.	97.	Spring–relief valve.
28.	Mills pin.	63.	Lock washer.	98.	Plunger–relief valve.
29.	'O' ring.	64.	Nut.	99.	Body–relief valve.
30.	Cover–solenoid.	65.	Sun wheel assembly.	100.	'O' ring–relief valve.
31.	Joint for cover-plate.	66.	Planet carrier.	101.	Flange–coupling.
32.	Set screw.	67.	Locating ring–third motion shaft.	102.	Washer–flange.
33.	Shakeproof washer.	68.	Inner member–uni-directional clutch.	103.	Nut–flange.
34.	Solenoid.	69.	Cage–uni-directional clutch.		

Section Fa.1

LUBRICATION

The overdrive shares a common oil supply with the gearbox; it is filled and topped up through the gearbox dipstick hole and the oil level is checked with the gearbox dipstick.

Draining

When an overdrive is fitted, remove the overdrive drain plug marked 'DRAIN' and the gearbox drain plug, and drain off the old oil.

Remove the overdrive filter cover-plate and gasket from the left-hand side of the unit and withdraw the filter gauze, together with the filter seal and magnetic rings. Wash the gauze in fuel and clean out the filter housing. Clean the filter seal and remove all deposits from the magnetic rings. Replace the filter seal (metal surface inwards) and place the magnetic rings in the filter location. Refit the filter, gasket, and cover-plate, replace the drain plugs, and refill with fresh oil. Check the filter cover-plate and drain plug for leaks.

Section Fa.2

DESCRIPTION

The overdrive unit comprises a hydraulically controlled epicyclic gear housed in a casing which is directly attached to an extension at the rear of the gearbox.

The gearbox third motion shaft is extended and carries at its end the inner member of a uni-directional clutch. The outer ring of the clutch is carried in the combined annulus and output shaft.

Also mounted on the third motion shaft are the planet carrier and a freely rotatable sun wheel, and sliding thereon is a cone clutch member the inner lining of which engages the outside of the annulus while the outer lining engages a cast-iron brake ring sandwiched between the main and tail casings.

The cone clutch is held in contact with the annulus by compression springs, thus locking the sun wheel to the annulus so that the entire gear train rotates as a solid unit, giving direct drive. In this condition the drive is taken through the uni-directional clutch. Reverse torque or overrun is taken by the planet wheels, which being locked by the sun wheel, transmit the drive via the planet carrier and third motion shaft.

Hydraulic pressure produced when overdrive is selected forces two pistons in the unit housing against the cone clutch and overcomes the spring pressure, causing the cone clutch to engage with the stationary brake ring and bring the sun wheel to rest, allowing the annulus to overrun the uni-directional clutch and give an increased speed to the output shaft, i.e. 'overdrive'.

When changing from overdrive to direct gear, if the accelerator pedal is released the vacuum switch holds 'overdrive' until the engine takes up the drive. If the accelerator pedal is not released, when contact between the cone clutch and brake is broken, the unit still operates momentarily in its overdrive ratio as engine speed and road speed remain unchanged. When the load on the engine is released it begins to accelerate, speeding up the sun wheel from rest until, just at the instant when its speed synchronizes with the speed of the annulus, the whole unit revolves solidly and the uni-directional clutch takes up the drive once more. The movement of the cone clutch is deliberately slowed down so that the uni-directional clutch is driving before the cone clutch contacts, ensuring a perfectly synchronized change.

Section Fa.3

CONSTRUCTION

The third motion shaft of the gearbox is extended to carry first a cam operating the oil pump and then a steady bearing with a plain phosphor-bronze bush carried in the main housing. Next is the sun wheel of the epicyclic gear carried on a Clevite bush, and behind this the shaft is splined to take the planet carrier and uni-directional clutch. The end of the shaft is reduced and is carried in a needle-roller bearing in the output shaft. The latter is supported in the rear housing by two roller bearings. The clutch member slides on the splines of the sun wheel

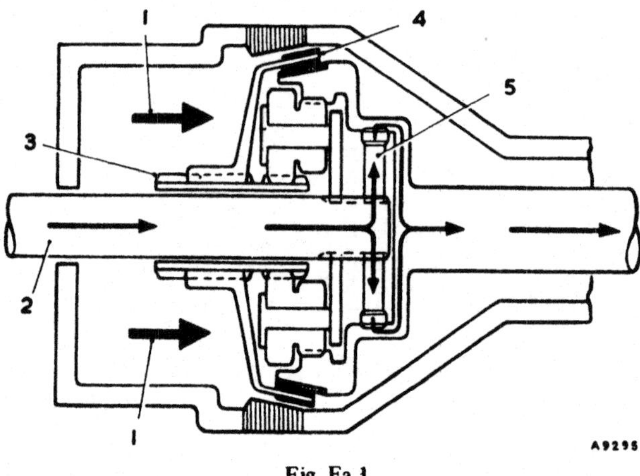

Fig. Fa.1
Direct drive

1. Spring pressure.
2. Third motion shaft.
3. Sun wheel.
4. Cone clutch.
5. Uni-directional clutch.

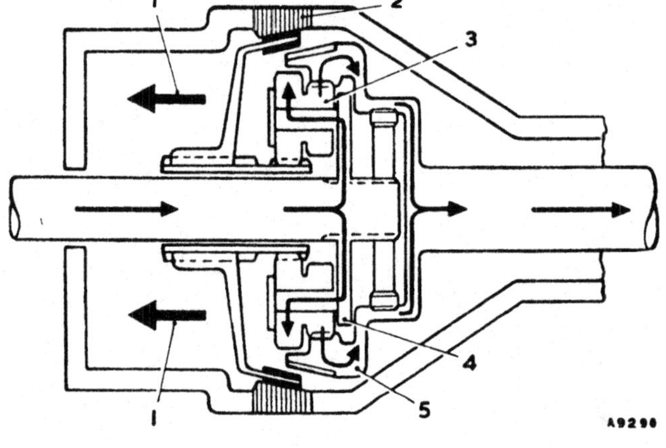

Fig. Fa.2
Overdrive engaged

1. Hydraulic pressure.
2. Brake ring.
3. Planet wheel.
4. Planet carrier.
5. Annulus.

extension to contact either the annulus or the cast-iron braking ring forming part of the unit housing.

A ball bearing housed in a flanged ring is secured to the cone clutch member. This carries four bolts which act as guides to compression springs by which the ring, and with it the clutch member, is held against the annulus. The action of the springs prevent free-wheeling on overrun and they are of sufficient strength to handle reverse torque. Also secured to the four bolts are two bridge pieces against which bear two pistons operating in cylinders formed in the unit housing. The cylinders are connected by ports in the hydraulic system to a relief valve which regulates the pressure developed by the oil pump. When the valve is open (overdrive selected), oil under pressure is admitted to the cylinders and pushes the pistons forward to engage the overdrive clutch. Closing the valve cuts off the supply of oil to the cylinders and allows it to escape. Under the influence of the springs the clutch member moves back to engage direct drive position. The escape of oil from the cylinders is deliberately restricted so that the clutch takes up slowly.

The sun wheel and pinions are case-hardened and the annulus heat-treated. Gear teeth are helical. The pinions have needle-roller bearings and run on case-hardened pins. The outer ring of the uni-directional clutch is pressed into the annulus member. The clutch itself is of the caged roller type, loaded by a lock-type spring made of round wire.

The hydraulic system is supplied with oil by a plunger-type pump operated by a cam on the gearbox third motion shaft. The pump body is pressed into the main housing and is located by a grub screw. The pump delivers oil through a non-return valve to a relief valve, in which a piston moves back against a compression spring until the required pressure is reached, at this point a hole in the relief valve is uncovered. The spill oil from the relief valve is led through drilled passages to an annular groove in the steady bush on the third motion shaft. Radial holes in the shaft collect oil and deliver it through an axial drilling to other radial holes in the shaft from which it is fed to the needle-roller bearing, thrust washer, and uni-directional clutch, and is led to the planet gear pins by a thrower attached to the planet carrier.

When 'Overdrive' is selected the valve is lifted, thus holding the ball off its seat against the spring pressure of the plunger spring. Oil passes to the operating cylinders, forcing the pistons forward to engage the overdrive clutch. With the selection of 'Normal' drive the spring plunger pushes the ball onto its seat and the valve falls away from the ball. Oil from the cylinders then returns through the centre of the valve to the sump. Near the bottom of the valve is a small jet which slows down the emptying of the cylinders, to provide smooth re-engagement of direct drive.

For direct drive the oil is returned to the sump via the operating valve and flows in open circuit (Fig. Fa.3).

Section Fa.4

GUIDE TO SERVICE DIAGNOSIS

Overdrive does not engage

1. Insufficient oil in the unit.
2. Solenoid not operating due to fault in electrical system.
3. Solenoid operating lever out of adjustment.
4. Insufficient hydraulic pressure due to pump non-return valve incorrectly seating (probably dirt on ball seat).

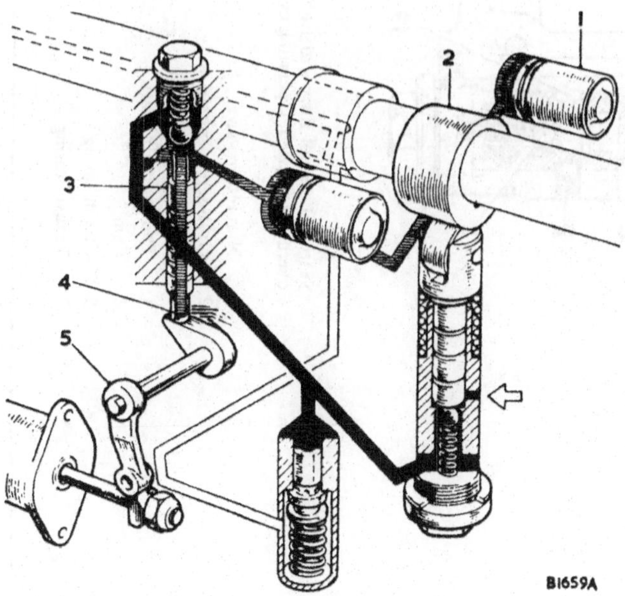

Fig. Fa.3
Hydraulic system–direct drive

1. Operating cylinders.
2. Cam.
3. Operating valve.
4. Jet.
5. Operating linkage.

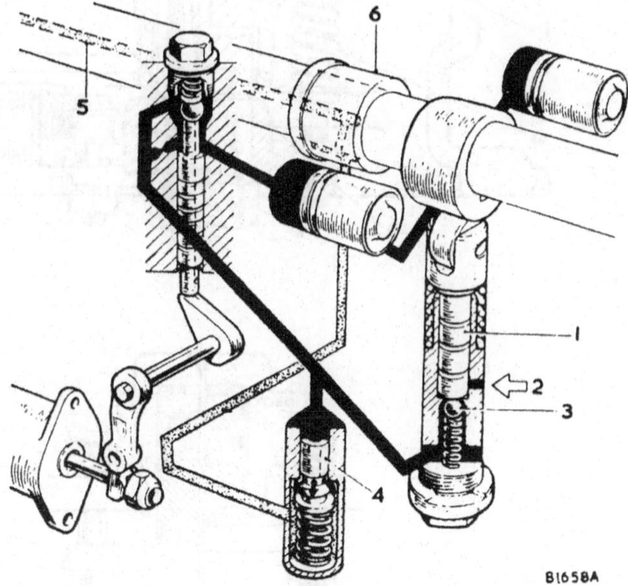

Fig. Fa.4
Hydraulic system–overdrive

1. Oil pump.
2. Oil inlet.
3. Non-return valve.
4. Oil relief valve.
5. Axial drilling–third motion shaft.
6. Third motion shaft steady bush.

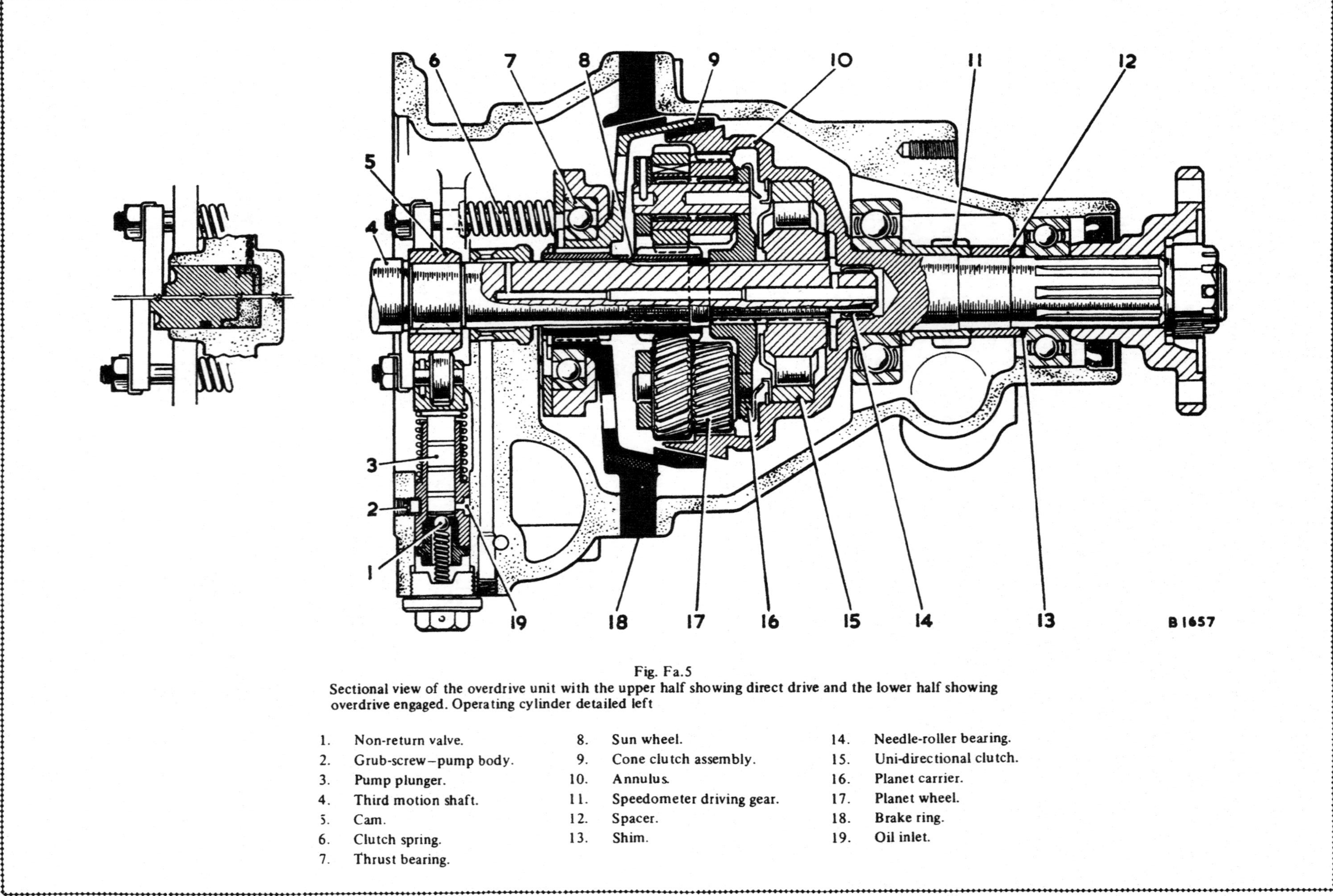

Fig. Fa.5
Sectional view of the overdrive unit with the upper half showing direct drive and the lower half showing overdrive engaged. Operating cylinder detailed left

1. Non-return valve.
2. Grub-screw–pump body.
3. Pump plunger.
4. Third motion shaft.
5. Cam.
6. Clutch spring.
7. Thrust bearing.
8. Sun wheel.
9. Cone clutch assembly.
10. Annulus.
11. Speedometer driving gear.
12. Spacer.
13. Shim.
14. Needle-roller bearing.
15. Uni-directional clutch.
16. Planet carrier.
17. Planet wheel.
18. Brake ring.
19. Oil inlet.

5. Insufficient hydraulic pressure due to sticking or worn relief valve.
6. Damaged gears, bearings, or moving parts within the unit requiring removal and inspection of the assembly.

Overdrive does not release
(NOTE.–Do not attempt to reverse the car or damage may be caused within the overdrive unit.)

1. Fault in electrical control system.
2. Blocked restrictor jet in operating valve.
3. Solenoid operating lever adjustment.
4. Sticking clutch.
5. Damaged parts within the unit necessitating removal and inspection of the assembly.

Clutch slip in overdrive
As 1, 3, 4, and 5 under **'Overdrive does not engage'**.

Clutch slip in reverse or free-wheel condition on overrun
1. Solenoid operating lever out of adjustment.
2. Partially blocked restrictor jet in operating valve.
3. Worn clutch linings.

Section Fa.5

PUMP NON-RETURN VALVE

Access to the pump non-return valve is gained through the centre cap in the bottom of the main casing (see [2], Fig. Fa.6).

Removing
1. Remove the engine stay rod from the gearbox adaptor and the stay rod bracket from the rear cross-member.
2. Remove the drain plugs and drain off the oil.
3. Unclip the locking wire. Unscrew the valve cap and take out the spring and ball and unscrew the non-return valve body from the pump body.

Clean the components and examine the seating for pits, etc. If the ball valve is not seating correctly the ball should be tapped sharply onto its seat in the non-return valve body, using a soft-metal drift.

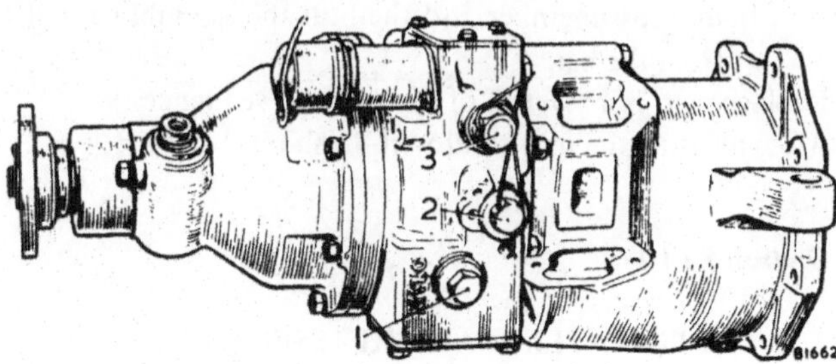

Fig. Fa.6
Bottom view of overdrive unit

1. Drain plug.
2. Non-return valve plug.
3. Relief valve plug.

Reassembly is the reverse of the above sequence. Position the ball on the spring with petroleum jelly. Ensure that the copper washer between the valve cap and main casing is fitted correctly over the step on the cap.
NOTE. The valve body must be removed from the pump body to reseat the ball valve, otherwise damage may be caused to the pump.

Section Fa.6

RELIEF VALVE

Access to the relief valve is gained through the right-hand cap in the bottom of the main casing (see [3], Fig. Fa.6).

Removing
1. Remove the engine stay rod from the gearbox adaptor and the stay rod bracket from the rear cross-member.
2. Remove the drain plugs and drain off the oil.
3. Unclip the locking wire. Unscrew the valve cap and remove the spring and piston.
4. Remove the relief valve body with circlip pliers, taking care not to damage the piston bore.

Reassembly is the reverse of the above sequence. Ensure that the copper washer between the cap and main casing is fitted correctly over the step on the cap.

Section Fa.7

HYDRAULIC LEVER SETTING

The setting of the operating lever can be checked by means of a hole in the lever accessible from under the car after removal of the cover-plate on the right-hand side of the unit.
The controls are set correctly when a $\frac{3}{16}$ in. (4.76 mm.) diameter rod can be passed through the hole in the lever into the hole in the casing with the solenoid energized, i.e. with the ignition switched on, top gear engaged, and the fascia switch in the 'Overdrive' position.
If the solenoid operates but does not move the setting lever far enough to allow the rod to be inserted, the solenoid plunger must be adjusted as follows.
Screw the self-locking nut on the plunger in or out, with the plunger pushed into the solenoid as far as it will go. The plunger must be held against rotation with a spanner on two flats on the spindle. The operating lever fork should just contact the nut with the $\frac{3}{16}$ in. (4.74 mm.) rod in position.
Operate the overdrive several times and check that the setting rod can be inserted and that the solenoid current does not exceed 2 amperes. If the current is maintained at 17 amperes (approx.), it indicates that the solenoid plunger is not moving far enough to switch from the operating to the holding coil; the plunger must therefore be readjusted.

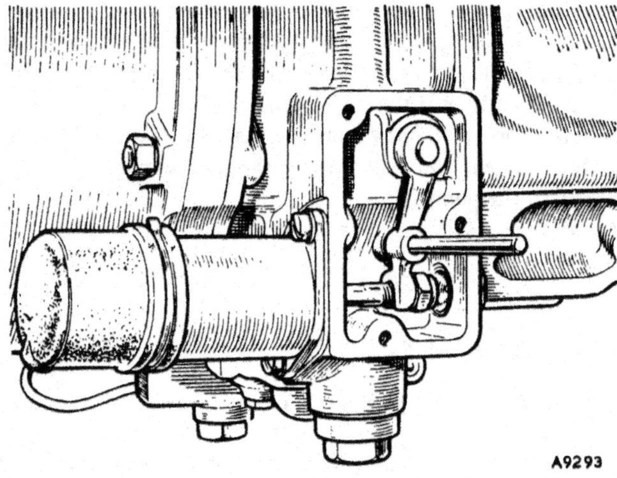

Fig. Fa.7
Align the operating lever to check the adjustment of the operating plunger

A new plunger must be fitted with a new solenoid. It will be necessary to check the setting for correct valve operation after fitment.

Section Fa.8

OPERATING VALVE

Access may be gained to the operating valve after removing the gear selector remote control assembly from inside the car (see Section Fa.9).
Having gained access, unscrew the plug and remove the spring and plunger. The ball valve will then be seen inside the valve chamber. The ball should be lifted $\frac{1}{32}$ in. (.8 mm.) off its seat when the solenoid is operated.
If the ball does not lift, the fault lies in the control mechanism (see Section Fa.7).
Remove the ball with a magnet and pull out the valve, using a piece of $\frac{1}{8}$ in. (3.175 mm.) dia. wire, taking care not to damage the seating at the top of the valve. Near the bottom of the valve will be seen a small hole breaking through the centre drilling; this is the jet for restricting the exhaust of oil from the operating cylinders. Check the bore of the operating valve with a $\frac{1}{8}$ in. (3.175 mm.) diameter drill and blow out the jet.
If the ball valve is not seated correctly the ball should be tapped sharply onto its seat in the casing, using a soft-metal drift.
If the unit fails to operate and the ball valve is seating and lifting correctly check that the pump is functioning, as follows.
Jack up the rear wheels, then with the engine idling and the valve plug removed engage top gear. Watch for oil being pumped into the valve chamber. If none appears, then the pump is not functioning.
Possible causes of trouble are: (1) Failure of the non-return valve due to foreign matter on the seat or to a broken valve spring, and (2) Breakage of the spring holding the pump plunger in contact with the cam.

Testing oil pressure
Remove the operating valve plug, fit an adaptor (Service tool 18G 251D) in its place, and connect up a pressure gauge. Jack up the rear wheels and then with the engine idling engage top gear. Operate the overdrive solenoid; a pressure of 540 to 560 lb./sq. in. (37.97 to 39.37 kg./cm.^{2}) should be recorded.

Section Fa.9

REMOVING AND REPLACING

To dismantle the unit further than already described necessitates the removal of the unit from the car.
It is not possible to lift out the overdrive alone from the car; the engine, gearbox, and overdrive must be removed complete.

Removing

1. Prepare the engine for removal from the car as detailed in Section A, and take the weight of the engine.
2. Remove the retainer and pull the gear lever grommet clear of the remote control cover. Release the circlip and withdraw the gear lever from its housing.
3. Withdraw the four screws securing the speaker panel and remove the panel. Pull back the tunnel carpet and remove the gearbox remote control cover.
4. Pull the solenoid wire from the snap connector and disconnect the gear switch wires.
5. Drain the oil from the gearbox and overdrive.
6. Disconnect and remove the propeller shaft as detailed in Section G, and disconnect the speedometer pinion drive.
7. Disconnect the clutch slave cylinder push-rod from the clutch withdrawal lever and the slave cylinder from the clutch housing. Tie the cylinder clear of the gearbox.
8. Remove the screws securing the rear cross-member to the body and lower the engine and gearbox until the gearbox rests on the fixed body cross-member.
9. Release the engine stay-rod bracket from the rear cross-member and remove the four nuts and washers securing the gearbox rear rubber mountings to the cross-member. Withdraw the rear cross-member from the body.
10. Ease the assembly forward until it is clear of the fixed body cross-member and then tilt the assembly and lift it from the car.

Replacement is a reversal of the removal sequence.
After refitting the unit refill with fresh oil.

Section Fa.10

DISMANTLING AND REASSEMBLING

Dismantling
Remove the remote control assembly after withdrawing the six bolts and spring washers securing the control to the

adaptor and the two screws from the rear support bracket. Take care not to damage the joint washer.

The unit is split at the gearbox adaptor, which is attached to the main casing by eight ¼ in. (6.35 mm.) diameter studs, one of which is extra long. After removing the eight nuts the unit can then be drawn off the third motion shaft.

Remove the operating valve plug (see Section Fa.8). This will allow air to enter the cylinders of the operating pistons and thus facilitate their removal. Release the lock washers securing the nuts on the two operating bridge pieces and remove the nuts, lock washers, and bridge pieces. Withdraw the operating pistons by gripping their spigots with pliers.

As the adaptor is separated from the unit the grub screw securing the pump body can be withdrawn and the body pulled from the casing after removing the non-return valve (see Section Fa.5).

The main and rear casings are secured by eight ¼ in. (6.35 mm.) diameter studs: unscrew the nuts a little at a time, gradually releasing the four clutch springs. Remove the main casing complete with brake ring. Take the four clutch springs off their guide bolts on the thrust plate and remove the clutch assembly complete with sun wheel.

The brake ring is spigoted into each casing and will come away with the main casing. A few light taps with a mallet around its flange will release the ring.

Remove the sun wheel from the cone clutch boss by withdrawing the snap ring in the forward end of the sun wheel hub. Remove the large circlip and withdraw the thrust bearing and housing complete.

Lift out the planet carrier assembly from the annulus. If it is necessary to remove the uni-directional roller clutch, first remove the circlip and brass retaining washer which are in front of the clutch.

Place Service tool 18G 178 centrally over the clutch and lift the inner member into it. This will ensure that the rollers do not fall out of the inner member. Remove the thrust washer. **DO NOT remove the outer bearing ring**, as it is expanded into the annulus.

A caged needle-roller bearing is fitted in the annulus centre spigot. If it is necessary to remove this use an extractor.

To remove the annulus from the rear casing withdraw the speedometer pinion and bush located by one dowel screw, take off the coupling flange at the rear of the unit, and drive out the annulus from the back. The front bearing will come away on the shaft, leaving the rear bearing in the casing.

Inspection

Each part should be thoroughly cleaned and inspected to determine which parts need renewing. It is important to appreciate the difference between parts which are worn sufficiently to affect operation of the unit and those which are merely 'worn in'.

1. Inspect the main casing for cracks, damage, etc. Examine the bores of the operating cylinders for scores or wear. Check for leaks at the plugged ends of the oil passages. Inspect the support bush in the centre bore for wear or damage.
2. Examine the clutch sliding member assembly. Ensure that the clutch linings are not burned or worn. Inspect the clutch spring locating bolts and bridge pieces and see that they are not distorted. Ensure that the ball bearing is in good condition and rotates freely. See that the sliding member slides easily on the splines of the sun wheel.
3. Check the springs for distortion and collapse (see **'GENERAL DATA'**).
4. Inspect the teeth of the gear train for damage. If the gears are damaged or the needle rollers worn, renew the planet carrier assembly. The sun wheel bush is bored to the pitch line of the teeth, and if worn, the gear will have to be renewed.
5. Examine the uni-directional clutch thrust washer.
6. See that the rollers of the uni-directional clutch are not chipped and that the outer ring is tight in the annulus. Ensure that the spring is free from distortion.
7. Inspect the output shaft ball bearings and see that there is no roughness when they are rotated slowly.
8. Ensure that there are no nicks or burrs on the third motion shaft splines and that the oil holes are open and clean.
9. Inspect the oil pump for wear on the pump plunger and roller pin. Ensure that the plunger spring is not distorted (see **'GENERAL DATA'**). Inspect the valve seat and ball and make sure that they are free from nicks and scratches.
10. Check the operating valve for distortion and damage and see that it slides easily in its bore. Inspect the relief valve body, 'O' ring, and ball, etc.

Reassembling the unit

Assemble the unit after all the parts have been thoroughly cleaned and checked to ensure that none is damaged or worn.

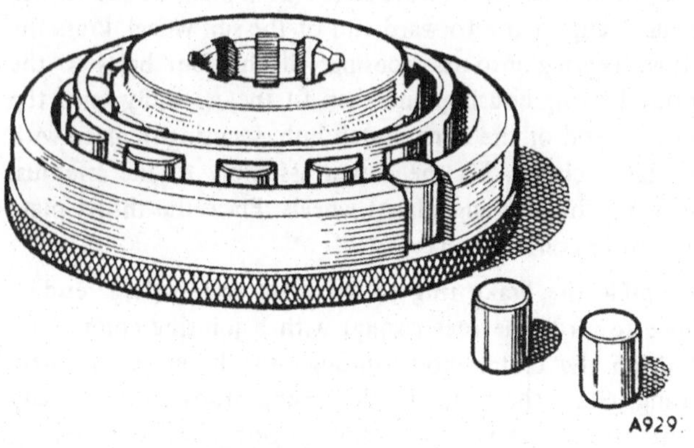

Fig. Fa.8
Use Service tool 18G 178 when removing or replacing the uni-directional clutch inner member.

Fit the annulus assembly with the speedometer drive gear, spacing tube, and shim which fit on the shaft between the front and rear ball bearings in the rear casing.

If a new bearing is fitted it becomes necessary to assess the thickness of shim required. To do this replace the annulus in the rear casing with the speedometer drive gear and distance tube in position, and with a depth gauge measure the distance between the rear ball bearing seating and the distance tube. To this figure add .005 to .010 in. (.13 to .25 mm.): this will give the actual shimming required.

The shims are available in the following thicknesses for selective assembly, which should allow an end-float of .005 to .010 in. (.13 to .25 mm.) on the output shaft and no preloading of the bearings:

.090 in.±.0005 in. (2.28 mm.±.01 mm.)
.095 in.±.0005 in. (2.41 mm.±.01 mm.)
.100 in.± 0005 in. (2.54 mm.±.01 mm.)
.105 in.±.0005 in. (2.67 mm.±.01 mm.)

Replace the coupling flange and tighten the nut to a torque reading of 100 to 130 lb. ft. (13.83 to 17.97 kg. m.), holding the flange against rotation with the aid of a wrench (Service tool 18G34A).

Fit the speedometer drive bush and pinion and lock in position with the dowel screw.

Replace the thrust washer and uni-directional clutch, using Service tool 18G178 to enter the rollers in the outer ring. Ensure that the spring is fitted correctly so that the cage urges the rollers up the ramp on the inner member.
Fit the brass retaining washer and locate it in position with the circlip.

To ensure that the second set of teeth on each planet wheel will mesh with the annulus teeth turn each planet wheel until its etched line coincides with an etched line on the carrier. Insert the sun wheel to hold the planet wheel in these relative positions. Fit the assembly to the annulus and withdraw the sun wheel.

As long as the planet carrier remains in the annulus the sun wheel can be removed and reinserted at any time. Should the planet carrier be removed from the annulus, the whole lining-up procedure must be repeated.

Pass the sun wheel into the cone clutch member and fit the small circlip at the forward end of the sun wheel. Press the thrust bearing into its housing, fit the four bolts to the thrust bearing housing, and then fit the assembly onto the forward end of the cone clutch hub, securing in place with the large circlip. Fit the clutch assembly to the annulus, engaging the sun and planet wheels. Place the thrust plate and springs on the bolts

Assemble the brake ring to the main casing (large end of taper towards the rear casing) with a jointing compound. Position the clutch bolts through the holes in the main casing. Start the nuts on the casing studs and gradually tighten to secure the two casings together. Ensure that the clutch spring bolts do not bind in their holes and that the casings go together easily.

Fit the two operating pistons, carefully easing their rubber sealing rings into the cylinder bores (the centre spigots of the pistons face towards the front of the unit). Fit the two bridge pieces, lock washers, and nuts.

If the pump body has been removed, insert its small end into the casing in the middle hole at the bottom of the casing, ensuring that the oil inlet faces to the rear. Gently tap into position until the groove lines up with the grub screw hole at the bottom of the casing front face. Fit the grub screw and tighten. Refit the non-return valve (see Section Fa.5). Insert the pump plunger and spring from inside the casing.

Replace the operating valve plug.

Support the unit upright and insert a dummy shaft or a spare third motion shaft so that the planet carrier and uni-directional clutch line up with each other; a long, thin screwdriver should be used to line by eye the splines (turn anti-clockwise only) in the planet carrier and the clutch before inserting the dummy shaft. Gently turn the dummy shaft to assist in feeling it into the splines, making sure that it goes fully home.

Make sure that the lowest part of the oil pump cam will contact the pump plunger and that the third motion shaft clip is seated in its groove; then with top gear engaged, carefully thread the third motion shaft into the centre bushing in the unit. Gently turn the first motion shaft to and fro to assist in engaging the splines of the planet carrier. As the adaptor and overdrive come together watch carefully to see that the oil pump engages the cam properly.

NOTE. The gearbox third motion shaft should enter the overdrive easily, provided that the lining-up procedure previously described is carried out and the unit is not disturbed. If any difficulty is experienced it is probable that one of the components has been misaligned, and the gearbox should be removed and the overdrive realigned with the dummy shaft.

Replace the remote control tower, ensuring that the change speed lever engages the selector.

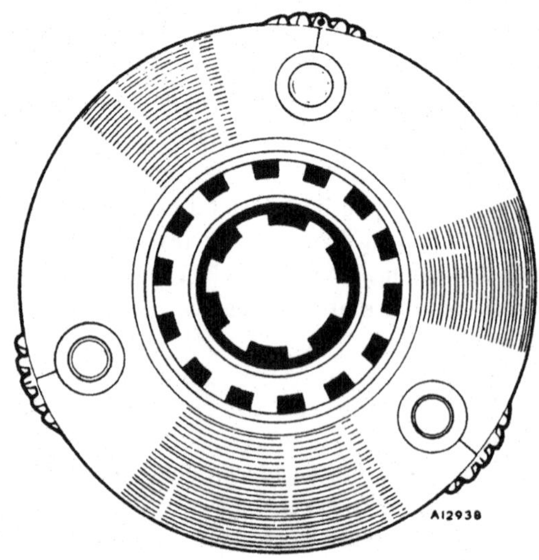

Fig. Fa.9
Before assembling the planet carrier to the sun wheel rotate the planet wheels until the etched line on the planet wheel lines up with the etched line on the planet carrier

Section Fa.11

DRIVE SHAFT BEARINGS AND SEAL

Removing

The drive shaft front bearing must be drawn from the shaft with a suitable puller.

The oil seal may be removed with the overdrive in position in the car after removing the propeller shaft and drive flange.

The rear bearing should be pressed from its seating with a suitable spigot.

Replacing

A press should be used when replacing the bearings. Fit a new oil seal.

Section Fa.12

OVERDRIVE RELAY SYSTEM

Description

Engagement of overdrive is controlled electrically through a manually operated toggle switch. The circuit is shown in Fig. Fa.10 and includes the following components:

1. RELAY. An electro-magnetic switch used with item 2 to enable an interlocking safeguard to be incorporated against changing out of overdrive with the throttle closed.
2. THROTTLE SWITCH. A vacuum-operated switch to over-ride the toggle switch under closed throttle conditions.
3. GEAR SWITCH. A small plunger-operated switch allowing overdrive to be engaged only in the two highest forward gear positions.
4. SOLENOID UNIT. An electro-magnetic actuator to engage the overdrive mechanism by opening the hydraulic control valve.

Operation

When the driver engages 'overdrive' by closing the contacts of the toggle switch, current is fed by way of the ignition switch and fuse unit supply terminal 'A3' to energize the relay operating coil. Closure of the relay contacts connects terminal 'A3' to the gear switch and, provided third or top gear is engaged, will energize the solenoid unit and effect a change from direct drive to overdrive.

Change from overdrive to direct drive is effected by selecting a low gear (when the gear switch contact will open) or by moving the toggle switch to 'NORMAL' with the throttle open (when the vacuum switch will open).

If effected with the throttle closed (high manifold depression) the vacuum switch will over-ride the toggle switch, delaying the change until the engine takes up the drive.

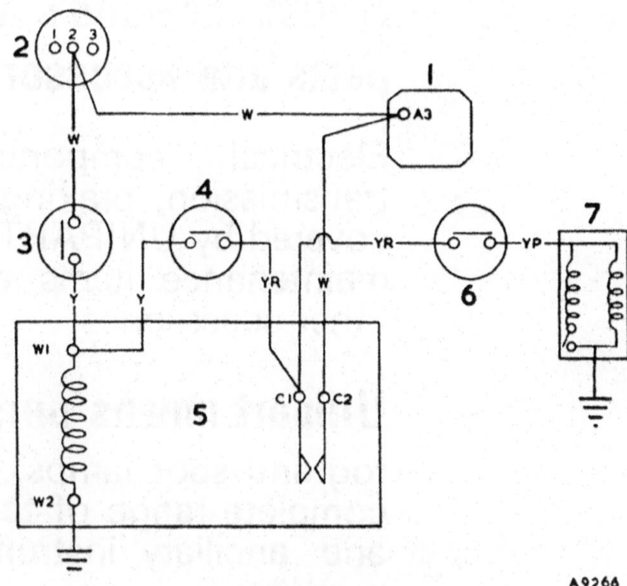

Fig. Fa. 10

Diagram of the overdrive electrical circuit

1. Fuse block.
2. Ignition switch.
3. Driver's switch.
4. Vacuum switch.
5. Relay.
6. Gearbox switch.
7. Solenoid.

CABLE COLOUR CODE

When a cable has two colour code letters the first denotes the main colour and the second denotes the tracer colour.

P. Purple. R. Red. W. White. Y. Yellow.

SECTION Fb

THE GEARBOX (ALL SYNCHROMESH)

Section Fb.1

GEARBOX ASSEMBLY

Removing

1. Remove the engine and gearbox from the car–Section A.21.
2. Remove the starter.
3. Unscrew the bolts securing the gearbox to the engine and withdraw the gearbox.

Refitting

4. Reverse the removing procedure in 1 to 3 and refill the gearbox with the correct quantity (see **'GENERAL DATA'**) of a recommended lubricant.

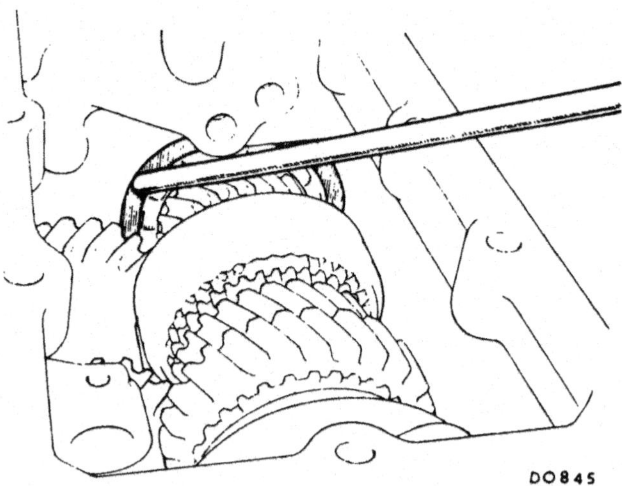

Fig. Fb.2
Drifting the first motion shaft from the casing

Section Fb.2

REAR EXTENSION

Removing

1. Drain the gearbox.
2. Using tool 18G 34 A to prevent rotation, unscrew the propeller shaft flange retaining nut and withdraw the flange.
3. Unscrew the bolts securing the remote-control housing to the gearbox and remove the remote control.
4. Withdraw the selector interlocking arm and plate assembly.

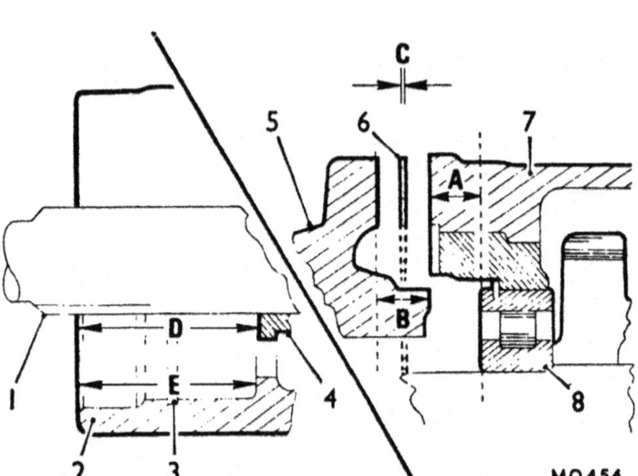

Fig. Fb.1
Rear extension setting up

1. Third motion shaft.
2. Rear extension.
3. Rear bearing circlip groove.
4. Distance tube.
5. Rear extension.
6. Gasket for rear extension.
7. Gearbox main casing.
8. Bearing.

A. Depth between bearing face and gearbox main casing face.
B. Depth between rear extension face and bearing flange.
C. Thickness of joint washer.
D. Depth from rear extension face to distance tube.
E. Depth from rear extension face to bearing register.

5. Unscrew the nuts securing the rear extension to the gearbox and withdraw the extension, ensuring that the shims fitted to the gearbox third motion shaft are not mislaid.

Dismantling

The following operations are only necessary if the bearing or oil seal are to be renewed.

6. Remove and discard the oil seal.
7. Remove the circlip retaining the bearing.
8. Press the bearing from the extension.

Reassembling

The following procedure must be carried out when fitting a new gearbox extension or if any of the third motion shaft components have been changed.

9. Calculate the thickness of shims required between the third motion shaft front bearing, and the gearbox rear extension case, as follows:
   a. Measure the depth A between the face of the front bearing and its housing, and add the thickness C of the joint washer.
   b. Measure the depth B from the joint face to the bearing register face of the rear extension.
   c. Fit shims between the extension and the face of the front bearing to bring the dimension measured in b .000 to .001 in. (.000 to .025 mm.) less than the dimension in a. Shims of .002 in. (.05 mm.) and .004 in. (.10 mm.) thickness are available.
   d. Fit the rear extension.

10. Calculate the thickness of shims required between the distance tube, and the third motion shaft rear bearing as follows:
    a. Measure the depth D between the rear face of the extension and the rear face of the distance tube.

b. Measure the depth E of the rear bearing register from the rear face of the extension.

c Fit shims between the distance tube and the bearing to bring the dimension measured in A from .000 to .001 in. (.000 to .025 mm) less than the dimension measured in B. Shims of .002 in. (.05 mm.), .005 in. (.13 mm.) and .010 in. (.25 mm.) thickness are available.

d. Press the bearing into the extension using tool 18G 186.

e. Select and fit the thickest circlip that will enter the rear bearing circlip groove from the following range:

.096 to .098 in. (2.43 to 2.49 mm.)
.098 to .100 in. (2.49 to 2.54 mm.)
.100 to .102 in. (2.54 to 2.59 mm.)

11. Using tool 18G 134 with adaptor 18G 134 BK, fit a new oil seal.

Refitting

- Check that the shims on the third motion shaft are correctly positioned against the distance tube shoulder, and fit the extension.

13. Fit and tighten the extension securing nuts.

14. Reverse the removing procedure 1 to 4.

Section Fb.3

FRONT COVER

Removing

1. Turn the clutch release bearing retaining clips and withdraw the bearing from the lever.
2. Remove the rubber boot from the clutch lever.
3. Unscrew the front cover retaining nuts and remove the cover, collecting the shims fitted in front of the first motion shaft bearing.

Dismantling

4. Remove the oil seal and gasket.
5. Unscrew the nut retaining the clutch lever pivot bolt, remove the bolt, and withdraw the lever.

Reassembling

The following procedure must be carried out when fitting a new front cover or if any of the first motion shaft components have been changed.

6. Calculate the thickness of shims required between the front cover and the bearing, as follows:

a. Measure the depth A from the face of the cover to the bearing register and add .012 in. (.31 mm.) for the compressed thickness C of the joint washer.

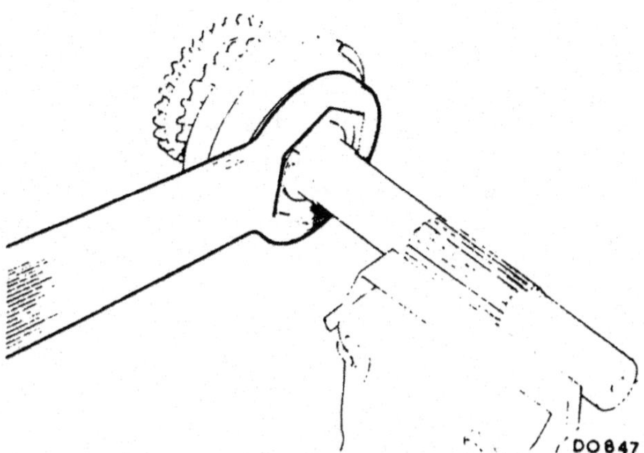

Fig. Fb.3
Removing the left-handed-threaded first motion shaft nut using tool 18G 48

b. Measure the distance B that the first motion shaft bearing protrudes from the casing.

c. Fit shims between the bearing and cover to bring the dimension measured in B from .000 to .001 in. (.000 to .025 mm.) greater than the dimension in A. Shims of .002 in. (.05 mm.) and .004 in. (.10 mm.) thickness are available.

7. Using tool 18G 134 with adaptor 18G 134 Q, fit a new oil seal to the cover.

8. Position the clutch lever, fit the pivot bolt, screw on and tighten the bolt retaining nut.

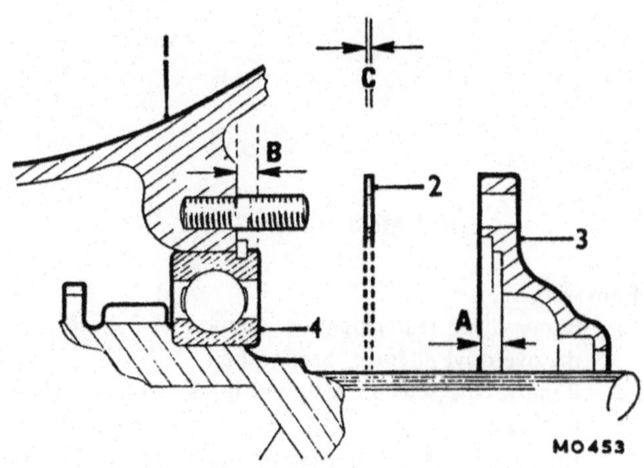

Fig. Fb.4
Front cover setting up

1. Gearbox main casing.
2. Gasket for front cover.
3. Front cover.
4. Bearing.

A. Depth of front cover to bearing register.
B. First motion shaft bearing protrusion.
C. Compressed thickness of joint washer.

Refitting

9. Reverse the removing procedure noting the following:
   a. Use a new gasket when refitting the cover; ensure that all traces of the old gasket are removed from the cover and gearbox jointing faces before fitting the new gasket.
   b. Check that the first motion shaft bearing shims are correctly positioned.

7. Inspect the gear bushes for signs of excessive wear; worn bushes may be removed and new bushes pressed in.

Refitting

8. Reverse the removing procedure in 1 to 4 using a new locking washer on the shaft retaining bolt.

Section Fb.4

SELECTOR RODS AND FORKS

Removing

1. Remove the rear extension–Section Fb.3, 1 to 3–or the overdrive adaptor–Section Fc.1.
2. Unscrew the side cover retaining bolts and remove the cover.
3. Remove the selector detent plunger plugs and springs.
4. Slacken the locknuts on each of the selector fork retaining bolts and remove the bolts.
5. Withdraw the selector rods and remove the selector forks.

Refitting

6. Reverse the removing procedure, noting the following points:
   a. Clean any burrs from the rods at the fork attachment points before refitting the rods.
   b. Check that the detent plungers are clear of the holes before fitting the rods.

Section Fb.5

REVERSE IDLER GEAR

Removing

1. Remove the rear extension–Section Fb.3, 1 to 3- or the overdrive adaptor Section Fc.1.
2. Remove the selector rods and forks--Section Fb.4, 2 to 5.
3. Knock back the locking tab on the shaft retaining bolt and remove the bolt.
4. Remove the shaft and withdraw the gear.

Inspection

5. Inspect the shaft for signs of excessive wear; renew the shaft if necessary.
6. Examine the gear teeth for wear and damage; renew the gear if necessary.

Section Fb.6

FIRST MOTION SHAFT

Removing

1. Remove the rear extension- Section Fb.2, 1 to 5.
2. Remove the front cover–Section Fb.3, 1 to 3.
3. Remove the selector rods and forks–Section Fb.4, 2 to 5.
4. Remove the reverse idler gear–Section Fb.5, 2 to 4.
5. Carefully drift the layshaft from the gearbox.
6. Check that the laygear teeth are clear of the first motion shaft gear teeth.
7. Using a soft metal drift registering against the bearing outer track, carefully drift the shaft assembly forward from the gearbox.

Dismantling

8. Withdraw the needle-roller bearing from inside the rear end of the shaft.
9. Tap back the locking tab on the bearing retaining nut.
10. Fit tool 18G 49 onto the nut and clamp the shaft in a soft-jawed vice.

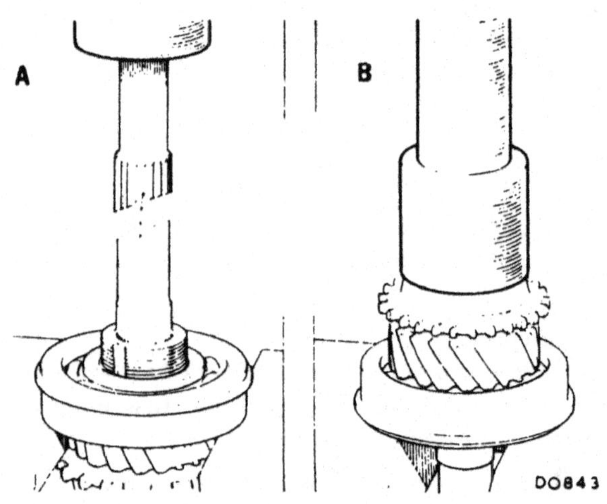

Fig. Fb.5
First motion shaft bearing

A. Removing the bearing from the shaft.
B. Refitting the bearing.

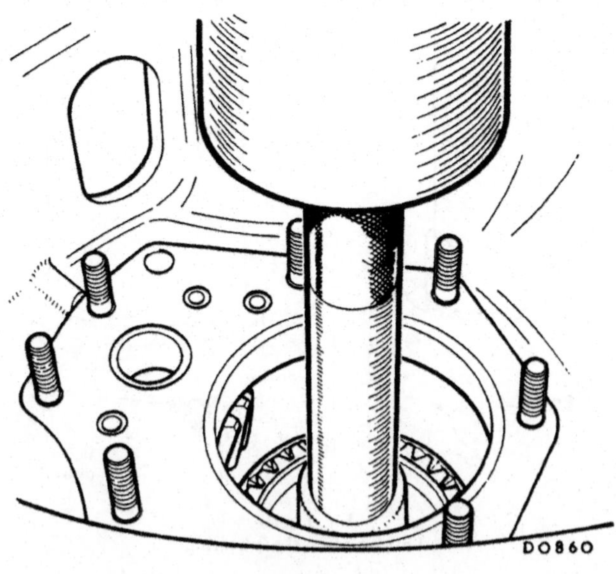

Fig. Fb.6
Pressing out the third motion shaft using tool 18G 1045

11. Unscrew the **left-hand-threaded** nut; remove the nut and lock washer.
12. Press the bearing from the shaft.

Inspection

13. Inspect the shaft for signs of wear and damage to the gear or splines.
14. Examine the bearings for wear and damage; renew the bearing as necessary.

Reassembling

15. Reverse the dismantling procedure in 8 to 12, using a new shaft nut locking washer.

Refitting

16. Carefully drift the assembled shaft into the casing ensuring that the laygear teeth do not foul the shaft gear teeth.
17. Reverse the removing procedure in 1 to 6.

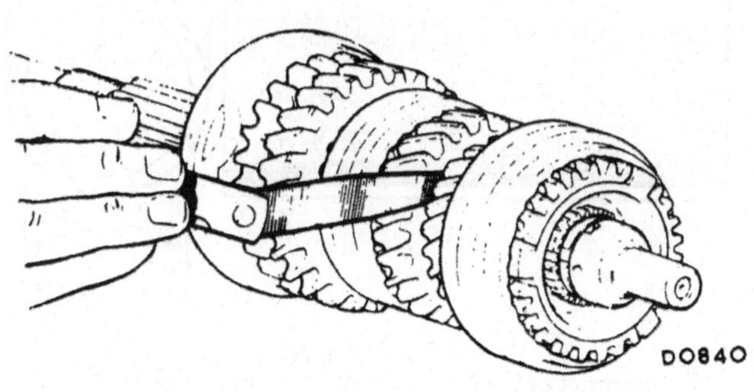

Fig. Fb.7
Checking the first and second speed gear end-float

Section Fb.7

THIRD MOTION SHAFT–NON-OVERDRIVE

Removing

1. Remove the rear extension–Section Fb.2. 1 to 5.
2. Remove the front cover–Section Fb.3, 1 to 3.
3. Remove the selector rods and forks–Section Fb.4, 2 to 5.
4. Remove the reverse idler gear–Section Fb.5, 2 to 4.
5. Remove the first motion shaft–Section Fb.6, 5 to 7.
6. Remove the shims and distance tube from the third motion shaft.
7. Unscrew the rear extension securing studs from the gearbox casing.
8. Check that the laygear teeth are clear of the gears and synchronizers.
9. Using tool 18G 1045, press the third motion shaft rearwards from the gearbox.

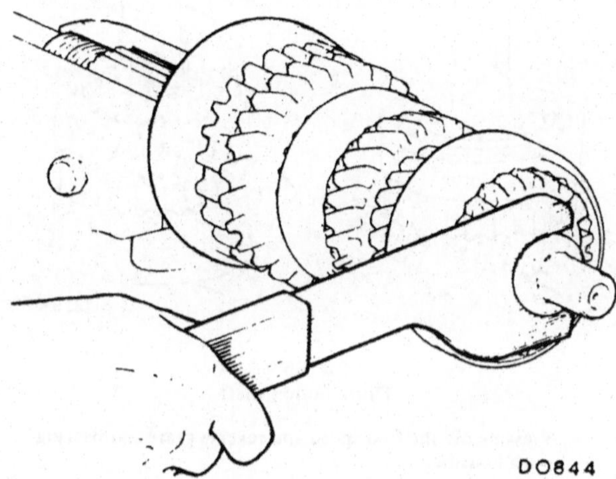

Fig. Fb.8
Using tool 18G 1024 to remove the front gear locking nut for the third motion shaft

Dismantling

SHAFT ASSEMBLY

10. Check the end-float on the first, second, and third speed gears against the figures given in **'GENERAL DATA'**.
11. Withdraw the third and fourth speed synchronizer assembly complete with baulk rings.
12. Tap back the locking tabs on front gear locking nut; unscrew the nut using tool 18G 1024 and remove the lock washer.
13. Withdraw the shaft sleeve, third speed gear, and interlocking thrust washer.
14. Withdraw the second speed gear and thrust washer.

15. Remove the first and second speed synchronizer assembly complete with baulk rings.
16. Withdraw the speedometer gear and remove the gear driving key.
17. Remove the shaft distance piece.
18. Press the first speed gear, reverse gear, and the bearing complete with housing from the shaft (see Fig. Fb.9).
19. Press the bearing from its housing (see Fig. Fb.10).

Synchronizers

20. Remove the baulk rings.
21. Wrap a cloth loosely around the assembly to retain the balls and springs and push the synchronizer hub from the sliding coupling.

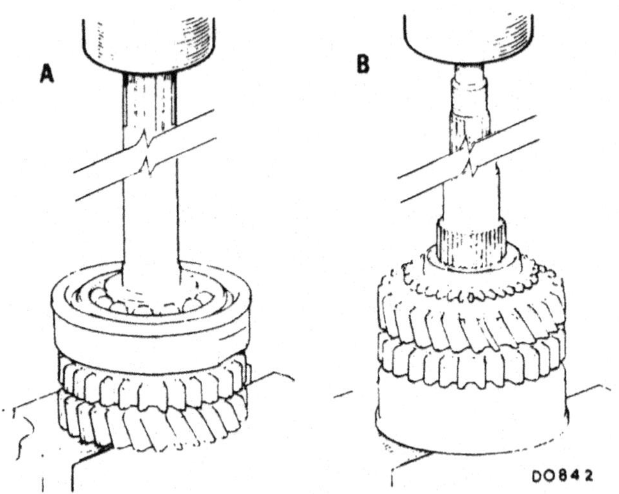

Fig. Fb.9
Third motion shaft

A. Pressing off the first speed and reverse gears and bearing with housing.
B. Refitting gears and bearing.

Inspection

22. If the end-float on the gears when checked in 10 exceeds the figures given, inspect the relevant gear and thrust washer bearing faces for wear. Renew worn gears and thrust washers as necessary.
23. Examine the gears, hubs, and couplings for wear and damaged or worn parts; replace as necessary.
24. Inspect the shaft for wear and damage to splines and bearing surfaces.
25. Examine the bearing for wear and damage.
26. Check the synchronizer springs against the dimension and pressure given in '**GENERAL DATA**'.

Reassembling

SYNCHRONIZERS

27. Fit tool 18G 1026 over the synchronizer hub.

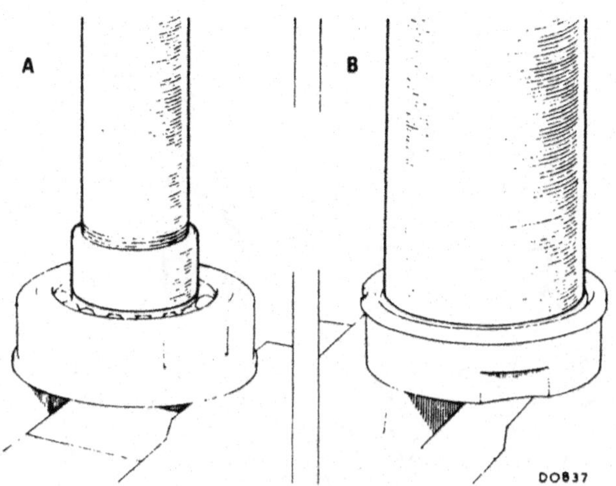

Fig. Fb.10
Third motion shaft bearing

A. Removing the bearing from its housing.
B. Refitting the bearing.

28. Turn the hub until one of the spring pockets is in line with the hole in the tool.
29. Fit the spring and ball into the pocket; depress the ball and turn the hub so that the ball is retained by the tool.
30. Repeat operations 28 and 29 for the remaining ball and springs.
31. Line up the cut-outs in the coupling with those in the hub and enter the hub into the coupling.
32. Press the hub from the tool into the coupling so that the springs and balls are retained by the coupling as the tool is removed.
33. Fit the baulk rings to the hub.

NOTE.–The baulk rings of the two synchronizer assemblies are not interchangeable. The first and second speed synchronizer baulk rings are identified (see Fig. Fb.14) by a drill point on one of the baulk ring lugs or by the fillets at the base of the lugs.

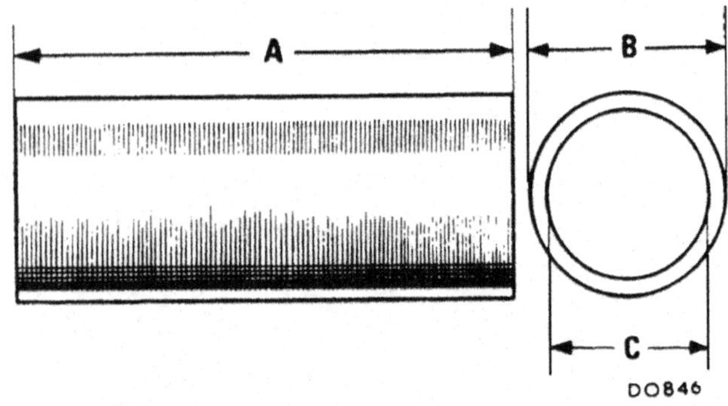

Fig. Fb.11
Dimensions of tool for refitting the third motion shaft

A = 19 in. (483 mm.) B = 3 in. (76 mm.)
C = 2.75 in. (69 mm.)

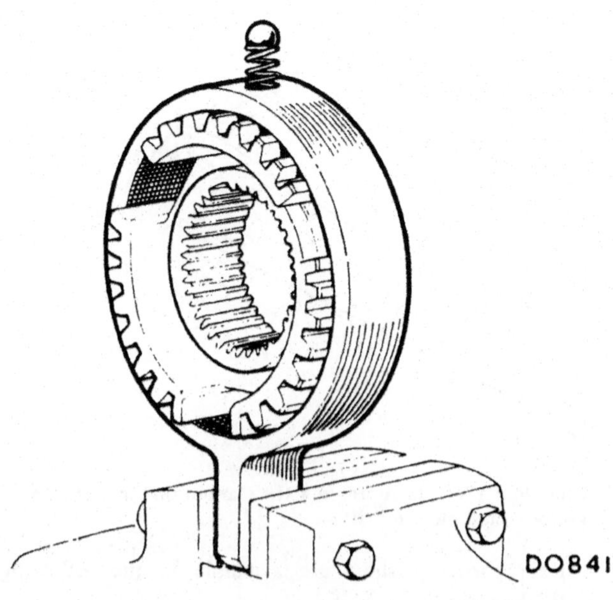

Fig. Fb.12
Reassembling the synchronizers using tool 18G 1026

SHAFT ASSEMBLY

34. Reverse the dismantling procedure in 10 to 19, noting the following points:
    a. Ensure that the lugs on the shaft sleeve are aligned with the cut-outs in the interlocking thrust washers.
    b. The synchronizer assemblies may be fitted either way round, but their baulk rings or the complete assemblies must not be interchanged with each other.

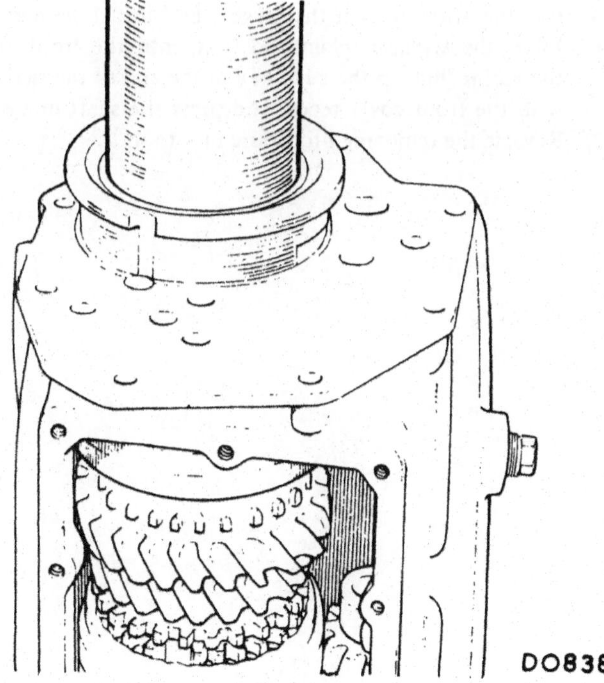

Fig. Fb.13
Refitting the assembled third motion shaft using the fabricated tool

    c. After reassembly re-check the end-float on the first, second, and third speed gears.

Refitting

35. Enter the assembled shaft into the gearbox from the rear; ensure that the third and fourth speed synchronizer assembly is fitted to the shaft.
36. Check that the laygear teeth are clear of the shaft gears.
37. Using a fabricated tool to the dimensions shown in Fig. Fb.11 registering on the outer track of the bearing, press the shaft assembly into the gearbox.
38. Reverse the removing procedure in 1 to 5.

Section Fb.8

THIRD MOTION SHAFT–WITH OVERDRIVE

Removing

1. Remove the overdrive unit and adaptor–Section Fc.1, 2 to 10.
2. Carry out the operation for removing the non-overdrive third motion shaft given in Section Fb.7, 2 to 9.

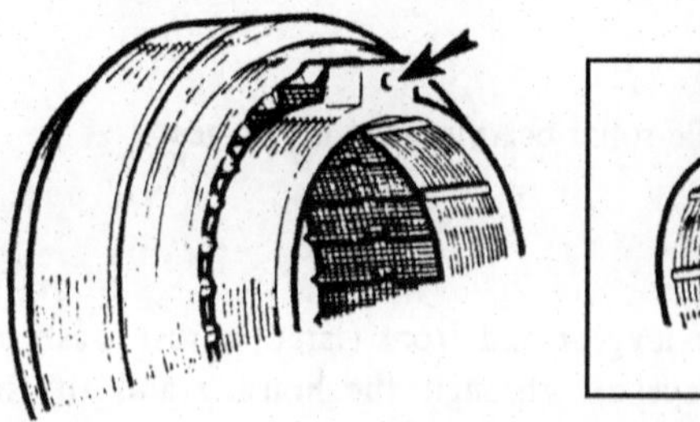
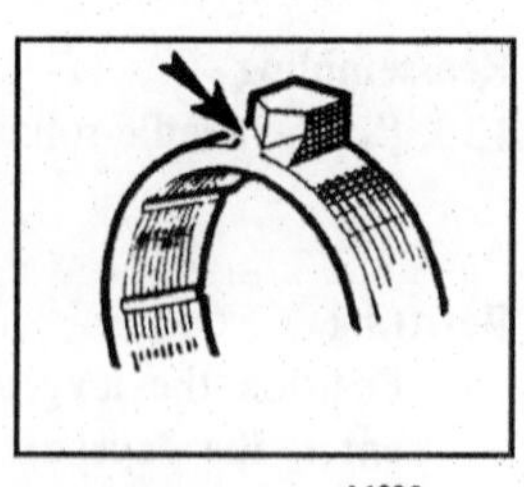

Fig. Fb.14
The identification drill point or fillets on the lugs of the first and second speed synchronizer baulk rings

Dismantling

3. Carry out operations in Section Fb.7, 10 to 15.
4. Tap back the locking tab on rear shaft nut.
5. Using tool 18G 391, unscrew the nut and remove the locking washer.
6. Withdraw the distance piece.
7. Carry out operations in Section Fb.7, 18 to 21.

Inspection

8. Carry out operations in Section Fb.7, 22 to 26.

Reassembling

9. Carry out operations in Section Fb.7, 27 to 33.
10. Reverse the dismantling procedure in 3 to 7.

Refitting

11. Reverse the removing procedure in Section Fb.7, 2 to 9.
12. Refit the overdrive unit and adaptor–Section Fc.9.

Section Fb.9

LAYGEAR

Removing

1. Remove the rear extension–Section Fb.2, 1 to 5.
2. Remove the front cover–Section Fb.3, 1 to 3.
3. Remove the selector rods and forks–Section Fb.4, 2 to 5.
4. Remove the reverse idler gear–Section Fb.5, 2 to 4.
5. Remove the first motion shaft–Section Fb.6, 5 to 7.
6. Remove the third motion shaft–Section Fb.7, 6 to 9.
7. Temporarily refit the layshaft and check the laygear end-float.
8. Withdraw the layshaft and remove the laygear and its thrust washers.

Dismantling

9. Withdraw the needle-roller bearings from inside the laygear.

Inspection

10. Inspect the layshaft for wear and damage to the bearing surfaces.
11. Examine the roller bearings for wear and damage.
12. Inspect the laygear teeth for damage and the bearing faces and bore for wear.

Reassembling

13. Fit the needle-roller bearings into the laygear.

Refitting

14. Position the laygear and front (large) thrust washer; enter the layshaft through the housing and thrust washer, and into the laygear.
15. If the laygear end-float measured in 7 is outside the limits given, select a rear thrust washer to give the correct end-float.

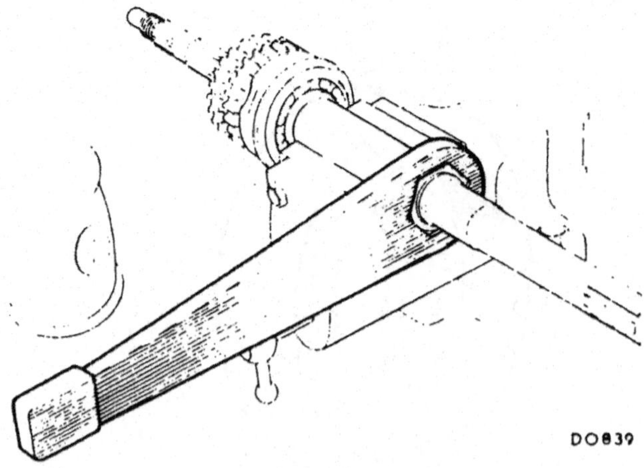

Fig. Fb.15
Using tool 18G 391 to unscrew the rear nut on the overdrive gearbox third motion shaft

Rear thrust washers are available in the following thicknesses:

.154 to .156 in. (3.91 to 3.96 mm.)
.157 to .158 in. (3.99 to 4.01 mm.)
.160 to .161 in. (4.06 to 4.08 mm.)
.163 to .164 in. (4.14 to 4.16 mm.)

16. Fit the rear thrust washer and thread a piece of soft wire through the housing, thrust washer, and into the laygear.
17. Withdraw the layshaft, at the same time thread the wire through the laygear and front thrust washer. This will enable the laygear and thrust washers to be retained ready for refitting the layshaft, and at the same time allow sufficient movement of the laygear to prevent the gear teeth obstructing the gears on the first and third motion shafts during refitting.
18. Refit the third motion shaft–Section Fb.7, 35 to 37.
19. Refit the first motion shaft–Section Fb.6, 16.
20. Use the wire to align the laygear and thrust washers.
21. Enter the layshaft, plain end first, into the front of the casing; line up the cut-away in the end of the shaft with the front cover recess and press the shaft home.
22. Reverse the removing procedure in 1 to 4.

SECTION Fc

THE OVERDRIVE (TYPE L.H.)

THE OVERDRIVE COMPONENTS (TYPE L.H.)

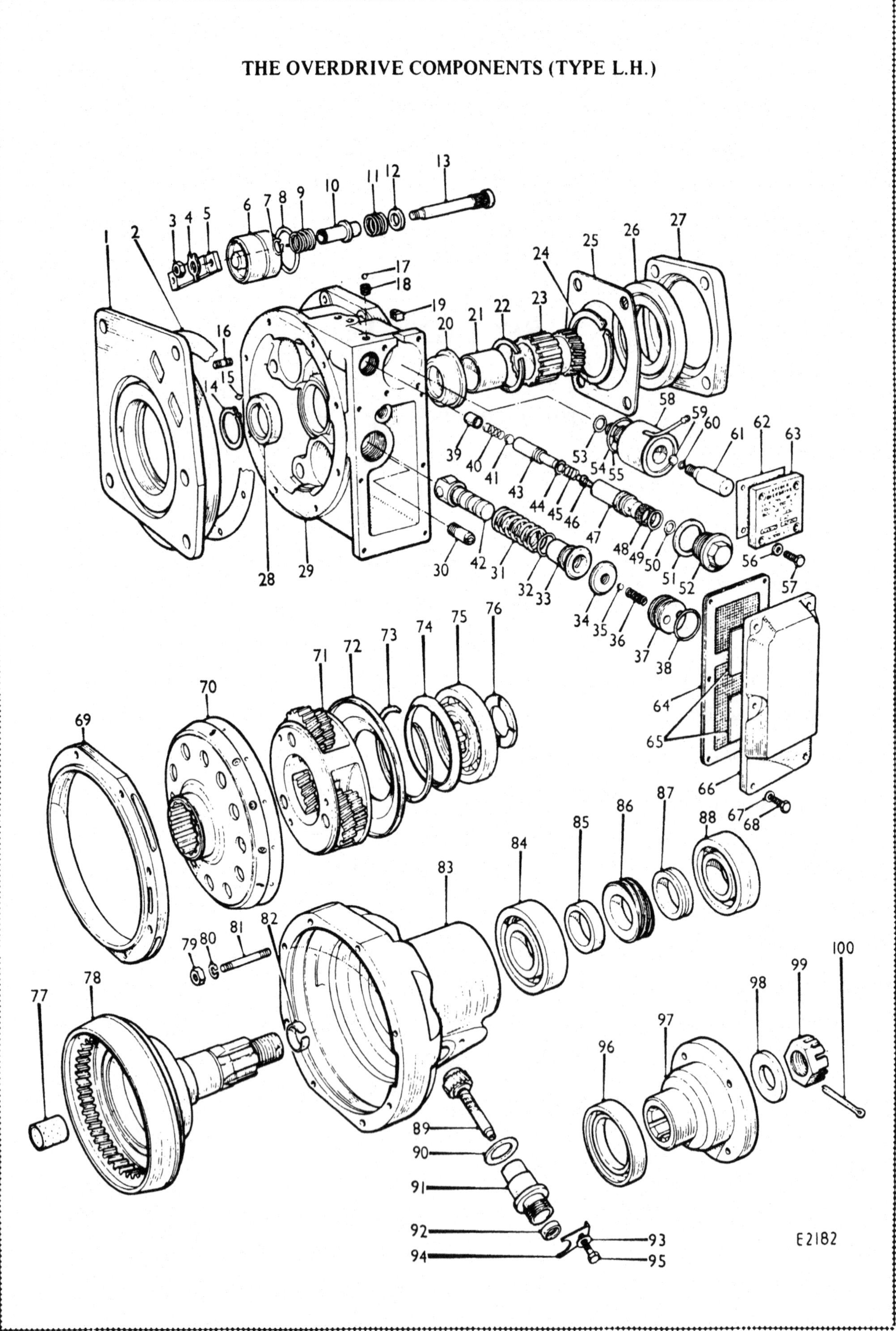

KEY TO THE OVERDRIVE COMPONENTS (TYPE L.H.)

No.	Description	No.	Description	No.	Description
1.	Adaptor plate.	34.	Non-return valve seat.	67.	Washer.
2.	Gasket.	35.	Valve ball.	68.	Screw.
3.	Nut.	36.	Valve spring.	69.	Brake-ring.
4.	Tab washer.	37.	Pump plug.	70.	Clutch sliding member.
5.	Bridge-piece.	38.	'O' ring.	71.	Planet carrier assembly.
6.	Operating piston.	39.	Low pressure valve plug.	72.	Oil catcher.
7.	Circlip.	40.	Valve spring.	73.	Circlip.
8.	'O' ring.	41.	Valve ball.	74.	Oil thrower.
9.	Spring.	42.	Pump plunger.	75.	Uni-directional clutch.
10.	Thrust rod.	43.	Low pressure valve body.	76.	Thrust washer.
11.	Spring.	44.	Washer.	77.	Bus.
12.	Washer.	45.	Relief valve spring.	78.	Annulus.
13.	Thrust housing pin.	46.	Valve plunger.	79.	Nut.
14.	Circlip.	47.	Valve body.	80.	.Washer.
15.	Key.	48.	Filter.	81.	Stud.
16.	Stud.	49.	'O' ring.	82.	Spring ring.
17.	Steel ball.	50.	'O' ring.	83.	Rear casing.
18.	Plug.	41.	Washer.	84.	Annulus front bearing.
19.	Grommet.	52.	Plug.	85.	Spacer.
20.	Sun wheel thrust bush.	53.	'O' ring.	86.	Speedometer drive gear.
21.	Sun wheel bush.	54.	Solenoid valve body.	87.	Selective spacer.
22.	Circlip.	55.	'O' ring.	88.	Annulus rear bearing.
23.	Sun wheel.	56.	Washer.	89.	Speedometer driven gear.
24.	Circlip.	57.	Screw.	90.	Sealing washer.
25.	Retainer plate.	58.	Solenoid coil.	91.	Speedometer bearing.
26.	Thrust ball-race.	59.	Valve ball.	92.	Oil seal.
27.	Thrust ring.	60.	'O' ring.	93.	Retaining clip.
28.	Pump cam.	61.	Solenoid plunger.	94.	Washer.
29.	Main casing.	62.	Gasket.	95.	Bolt.
30.	Pump suction tube.	63.	Solenoid cover.	96.	Oil seal.
31.	Spring.	64.	Sump filter and gasket.	97.	Drive flange.
32.	'O' ring.	65.	Filter magnets.	98.	Washer.
33.	Pump body.	66.	Sump.	99.	Nut.
				100.	Split pin.

Section Fc.1

GENERAL DESCRIPTION

The Laycock Type L.H. Overdrive fitted between the gearbox and propeller shaft is a self-contained gear unit which provides a higher overall gear ratio than that given by the final drive.

The overdrive gears consist of a central sun wheel and three planet gears which mesh with an internally toothed annulus. Fitted inside the annulus is a uni-directional clutch. A sliding clutch-member is secured to the sun wheel and is free to move forward and rearward on the sun wheel splines. Attached to a ball bearing, secured on the sliding clutch by a circlip, is a static thrust ring. The thrust ring is actuated by two hydraulic pistons and returned by primary and secondary return springs.

An electrically operated solenoid valve, mechanical pump, relief valve, and low pressure valve comprise the main components of the hydraulic system.

Overdrive engaged

With the overdrive switch selected the solenoid is energized and the ball valve is held in the closed position by the solenoid rod.

The input shaft to the overdrive unit carries a cam which operates the overdrive oil pump. The pump draws oil from

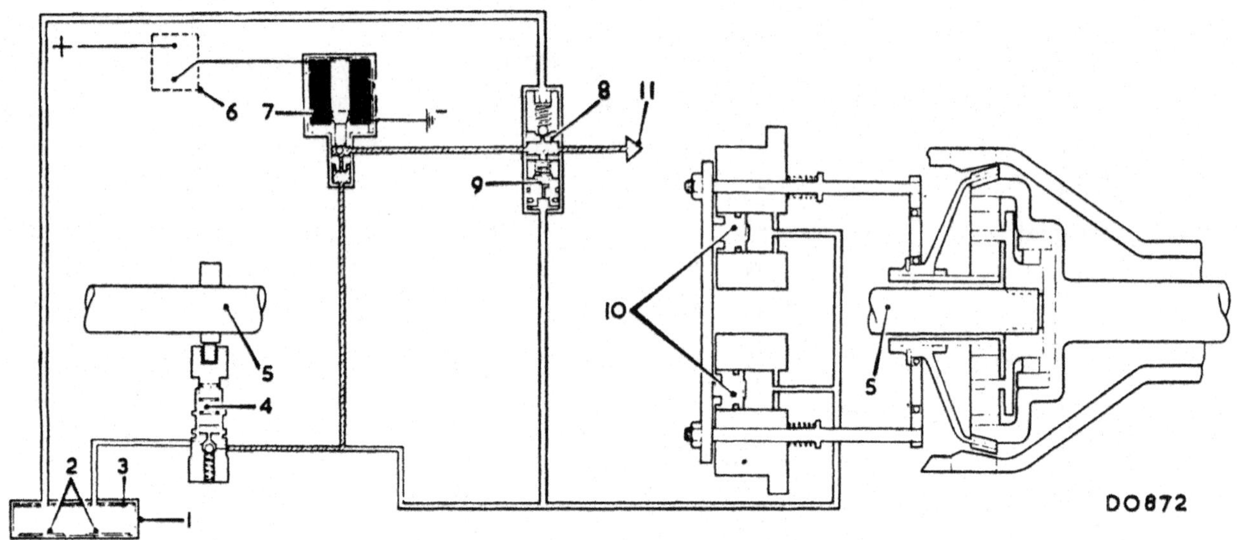

Fig. Fc.1
Direct drive

1. Sump.
2. Magnet filters.
3. Gauze filter.
4. Pump.
5. Third motion shaft (gearbox).
6. Control switch.
7. Solenoid operating valve.
8. Low pressure valve.
9. Relief valve.
10. Operating pistons.
11. Oil return to sump.

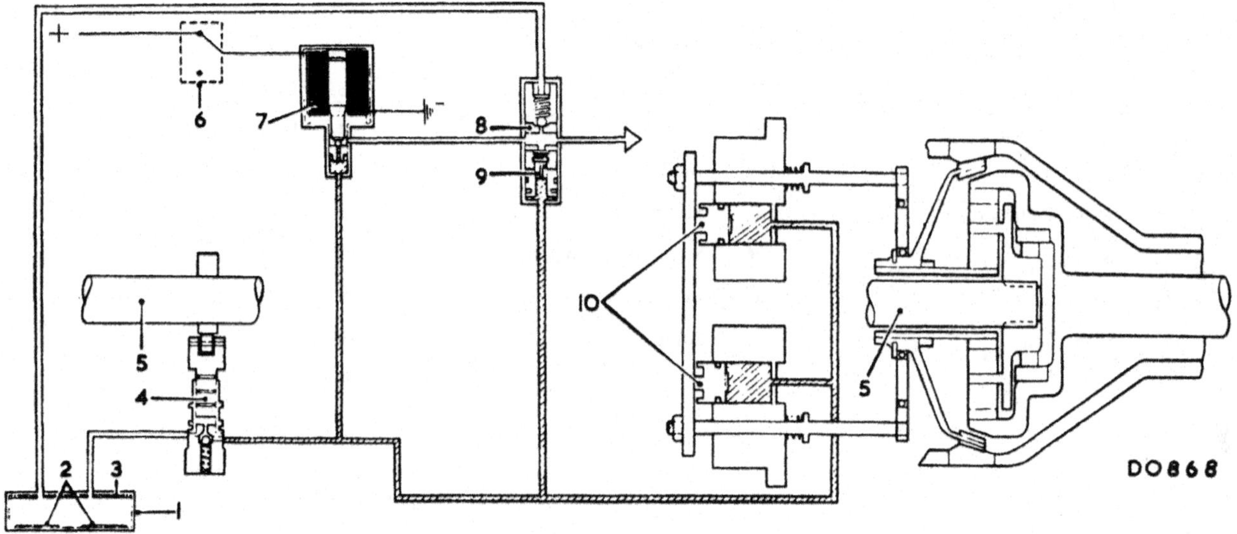

Fig. Fc.2
Overdrive engaged

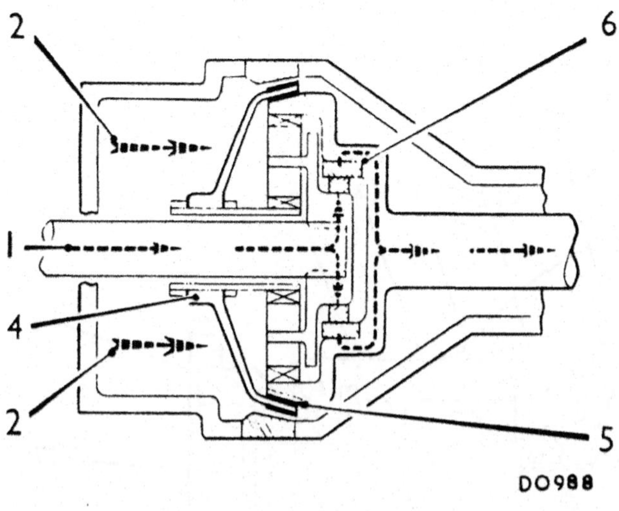

Fig. Fc.3
Direct drive

1. Third motion shaft.
2. Spring pressure.
4. Sun wheel.
5. Cone clutch.
6. Uni-directional clutch.

the sump and the oil from the pump discharge is ducted to the two operating pistons of the clutch sliding member. A build-up of oil pressure operates the two pistons and moves the sliding clutch-member, its outer brake surface contacts the stationary brake ring and the complete sliding member and sun wheel cease to rotate.

At a predetermined spring pressure the relief valve operates and relieves any pressure, in excess of the pressure required to keep the pistons operative, into the low pressure lubricating system. Build-up of pressure in the low pressure lubricating system is relieved by operation of the low pressure valve and the oil relieved returns to the sump.

The planet gear carrier is splined to, and rotates with, the input shaft. The planet gears, forced to turn about their own axis by movement of the carrier, while in mesh with the stationary sun wheel, impart driving force to turn the annulus. Because of the gearing arrangement the annulus turns faster than the input shaft. The propeller shaft, coupled to a flange rigidly secured to the shaft of the annulus, revolves at the same speed as the annulus.

In overdrive the outer bearing surface of the uni-directional clutch inside the annulus, over-rides the rollers, cage, and clutch, attached to the slower-moving input shaft. In this condition the uni-directional clutch is in the unlocked or free condition.

The solenoid valve acts as a safety valve. If the pressure becomes excessive the ball would be blown off its seat against the load of the solenoid.

Overdrive disengaged

CAUTION.–IF OVERDRIVE DOES NOT DISENGAGE, DO NOT REVERSE THE CAR OTHERWISE EXTENSIVE DAMAGE MAY RESULT.

With the overdrive switch in the 'off' position the operating solenoid is de-energized and the valve ball is free to move away from the valve seat. Oil from the pump discharge lifts the valve from its seat, flows to the low pressure valve, and is used for lubrication. This action relieves the oil pressure maintaining the pistons operative. The return springs act to close the pistons and the oil returning from the piston chambers is forced to mix with the pump flow, thus causing a restriction and damping the return movement of the sliding member. Action of the secondary return springs force the clutch sliding member rearward and its inner brake surface contacts the annulus brake ring. The sliding member and annulus commence to revolve in unison. As the sun wheel is splined to the sliding clutch member the complete gear train is locked.

Thrust from the input shaft locks the uni-directional clutch against the outer bearing surface, inside the annulus, and direct drive is applied to the propeller shaft through the annulus extension on which the propeller shaft coupling flange is mounted.

During over-run and reverse, additional load is imparted to the clutch sliding member by the helix thrust of the sun wheel, thus helping to retain direct drive.

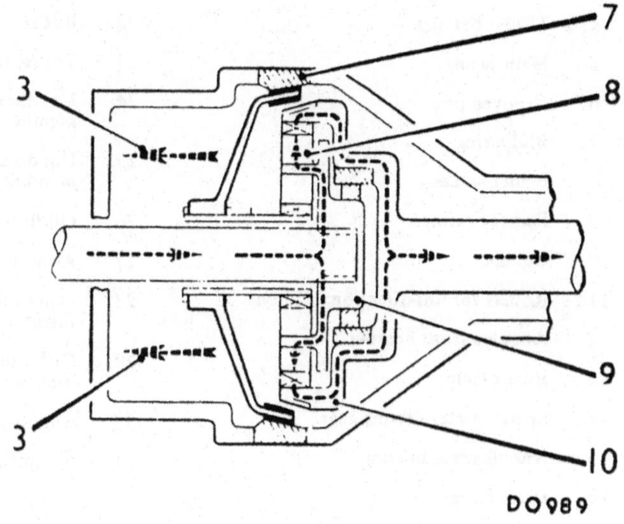

Fig. Fc.4
Overdrive engaged

3. Hydraulic pressure.
7. Brake ring.
8. Planet wheel.
9. Planet carrier.
10. Annulus.

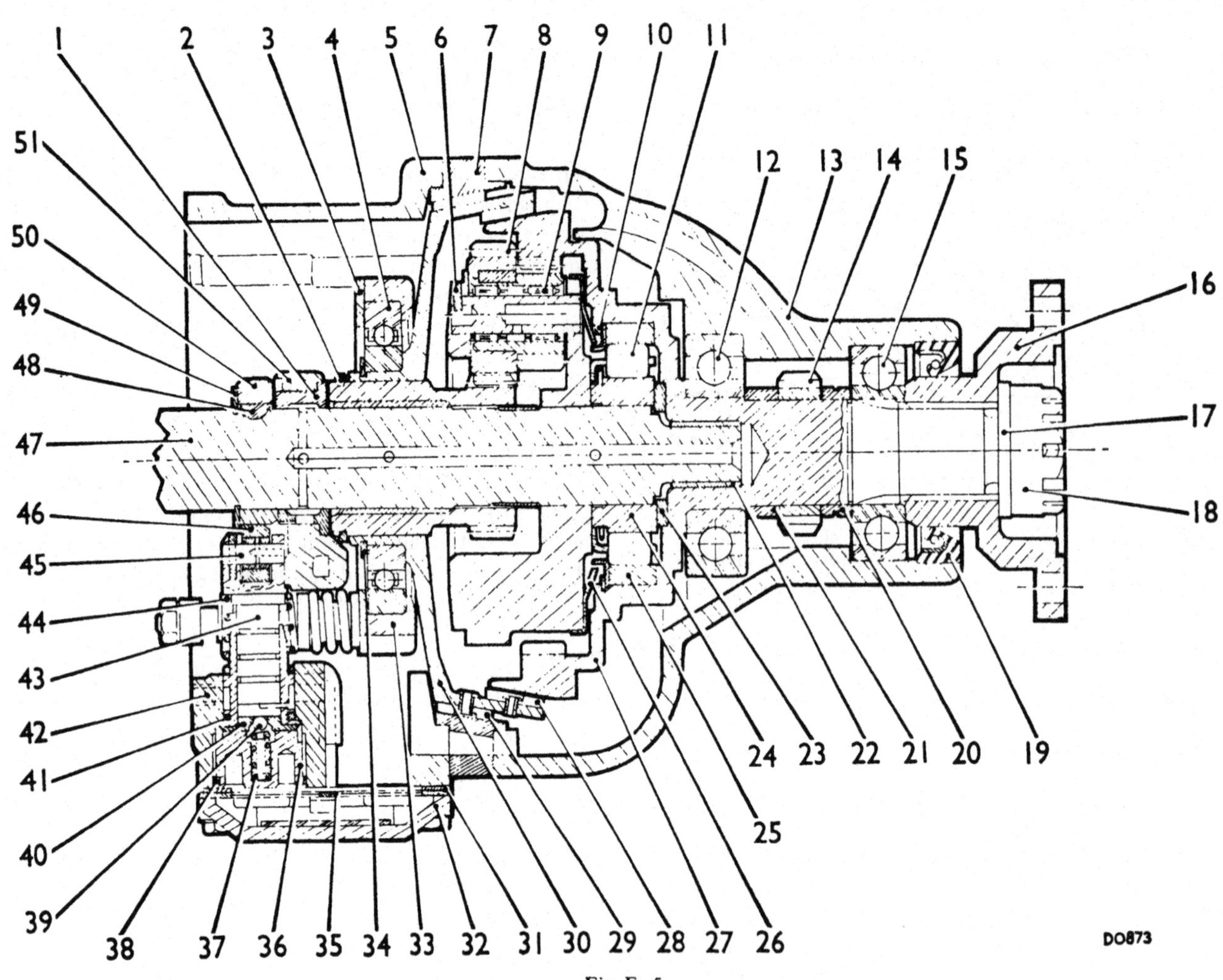

Fig. Fc.5
A section through the overdrive unit

1. Sun wheel thrust bush.
2. Snap ring for sun wheel.
3. Bearing retainer plate.
4. Thrust bearing.
5. Main casing.
6. Grooved pin.
7. Brake ring.
8. Planet wheel.
9. Planet bearing.
10. Circlip.
11. Rollers for uni-directional clutch.
12. Annulus front bearing.
13. Rear casing.
14. Speedometer driving gear.
15. Annulus rear bearing.
16. Drive flange.
17. Washer.
18. Nut.
19. Oil seal.
20. Selective spacer.
21. Spacer.
22. Bush.
23. Thrust washer.
24. Uni-directional clutch, inner member.
25. Uni-directional clutch, outer member.
26. Oil thrower.
27. Annulus.
28. Inner lining of clutch sliding member.
29. Outer lining of clutch sliding member.
30. Clutch sliding member.
31. Sump filter and gasket assembly.
32. Sump.
33. Thrust bearing housing.
34. Circlip.
35. Filter.
36. Pump plug.
37. Non-return valve spring.
38. 'O' ring.
39. Non-return valve ball.
40. Non-return valve seat.
41. Pump body.
42. Main case housing for pump.
43. Pump plunger.
44. Spring for pump plunger.
45. Pin for pump roller.
46. Pump roller.
47. Gearbox third motion shaft.
48. Key for pump cam.
59. Circlip.
50. Pump cam.
51. Main case housing for sun wheel and oil transfer bush.

Section Fc.2

FAULT DIAGNOSIS

OVERDRIVE DOES NOT ENGAGE

(1) Insufficient oil in gearbox	Top up to correct level.
(2) Electrical system fault	Check and rectify fault; check operation of solenoid.
(3) Low hydraulic pressure:	
(a) Pump non-return valve not seating	Remove and check the valve; clean or renew.
(b) Solenoid ball valve not seating	Remove and check the valve; clean or renew.
(c) Pump filter choked	Remove and clean filter.
(4) Damaged parts within unit	Remove, dismantle, and inspect unit.

OVERDRIVE DOES NOT DISENGAGE

NOTE.– If the overdrive does not disengage, do not reverse the car as extensive damage may result.

(5) Electrical control system fault	Check and rectify fault.
(6) Sticking clutch	On a new unit this may be due to insufficient bedding-in of the clutch. The clutch can usually be freed by giving the brake-ring, accessible from beneath the car, several sharp blows with a hide mallet.
(7) Damaged parts within unit	Remove, dismantle, and inspect unit.

OVERDRIVE SLIPS WHEN ENGAGED

(8) Insufficient oil in gearbox	Top up to correct level.
(9) Low hydraulic pressure:	
(a) Pump non-return valve not seating	Remove and check the valve; clean or renew.
(b) Relief valve not seating	Remove and check the valve; clean or renew.
(c) Solenoid valve not seating	Remove and check the valve; clean or renew.
(d) Partially blocked pump or relief valve filter	Remove and clean filters.
(10) Worn or glazed clutch lining	Remove, dismantle, and replace faulty parts.

SLIP IN REVERSE OR FREE WHEEL ON OVER-RUN

(11) Worn or glazed clutch lining	Remove, dismantle, and replace faulty parts.
(12) Broken circlip on sun wheel	Remove, dismantle, and replace faulty parts.

Section Fc.3

HYDRAULIC PRESSURE TEST

1. Check the gearbox oil level, and top up as necessary.
2. Raise and support the rear of the car so that the rear wheels are clear of the ground.
3. Securely chock the front wheels.
4. Remove the relief valve plug and its sealing washer.
5. Fit adaptor 18G 251 E, using the relief valve plug sealing washer, into the relief valve orifice.
6. Connect pressure gauge 18G 251.
7. Start the engine, engage top gear and select overdrive.
8. Set the speed to a speedometer reading of 30 m.p.h. (48 km.p.h.) and note the pressure gauge reading; the correct reading is 400 to 420 lb./sq. in. (28 to 29.5 kg./cm.^{2}).

   NOTE.–No pressure reading will be recorded with the overdrive disengaged.

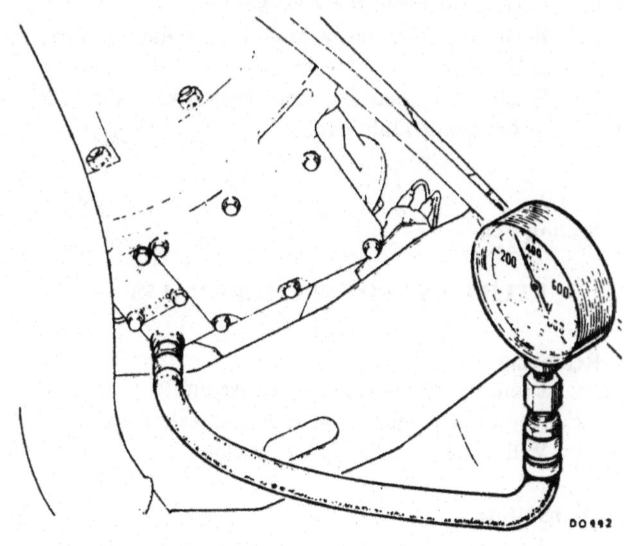

Fig. Fc.6
Pressure gauge 18G 251 and adaptor 18G 251 E connected to check the hydraulic pressure

Section Fc.4

LUBRICATION

IMPORTANT.–Anti-friction additives must not be used in the gearbox and overdrive.

Draining

1. Remove the gearbox drain plug to drain the oil from the gearbox and overdrive unit.

Filling

2. Remove the gearbox dipstick and add the correct quantity (see '**GENERAL DATA**') of one of the recommended lubricants.
3. Run the car for a short distance, allow to stand for a few minutes and check the level with the dipstick.

Section Fc.5

FILTERS

Sump

1. Drain the gearbox and overdrive unit.
2. Clean the sump cover and its surroundings.
3. Unscrew the sump cover securing screws and remove the cover and sump filter.
4. Clean all metallic particles from the two magnets fitted inside the cover; wash the cover and filter in petrol (gasoline).
5. Refit the filter and sump cover.
6. Refill the gearbox and overdrive unit with the correct quantity (see '**GENERAL DATA**') of one of the recommended lubricants.

Relief valve

7. Drain the gearbox and overdrive unit.
8. Remove the relief valve plug and sealing washer.
9. Withdraw the relief valve body and remove the filter.
10. Clean the filter in petrol (gasoline).
11. Refit the filter to the valve body.
12. Refit the valve body assembly, sealing washer, and plug.
13. Refill the gearbox and overdrive unit with a recommended lubricant.

Section Fc.6

RELIEF AND LOW PRESSURE VALVE

Removing

1. Drain the gearbox and overdrive unit.
2. Remove the relief valve plug and sealing washer.
3. Withdraw the relief valve assembly.

Dismantling

4. Remove the filter, spacer tube, low pressure valve assembly, and relief valve spring.
5. Remove the relief valve plunger.

Inspection

6. Examine the relief valve plunger and seat for pitting, scoring, and wear. Renew worn or damaged parts as necessary.
7. Inspect the relief valve body 'O' rings for signs of deterioration, and renew if necessary.
8. Check the relief valve spring for signs of collapse or weakness against the figures given in '**GENERAL DATA**'.
9. Test the low pressure valve for correct setting. The complete valve must be renewed if faulty.

Reassembling

10. Reverse the dismantling procedure in 4 and 5.

Refitting

11. Reverse the removing procedure in 2 and 3, noting that the spacer tube must be fitted with its slotted end farthest from the filter with the slots lining up respectively with the oil outlet hole and locating stud.

Section Fc.7

SOLENOID VALVE

Removing

1. Drain the gearbox and overdrive unit.
2. Unscrew the four screws securing the solenoid cover (name plate) and remove the cover and gasket.
3. Remove the solenoid and valve assembly by carefully pulling on the solenoid lead.

Dismantling

4. Withdraw the solenoid rod and operating valve assembly from the solenoid housing.

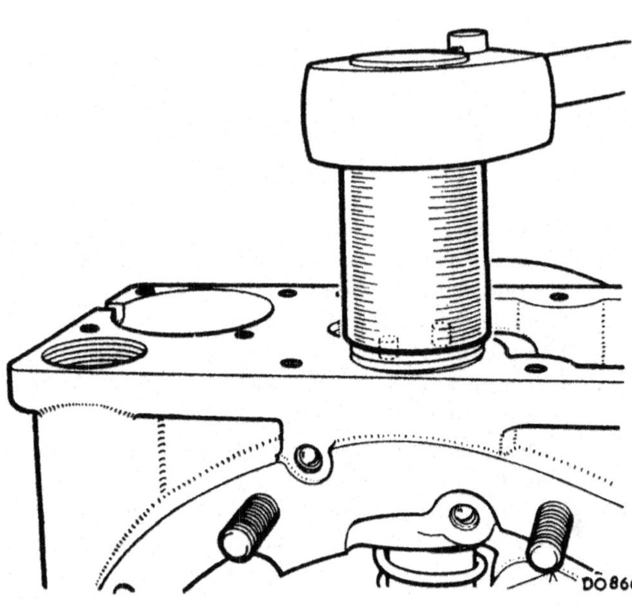

Fig. Fc.7
Removing the pump retaining plug using tool 18G 1118

5. Press the solenoid coil and base cap from the housing.
6. Remove the operating valve plunger and ball by shaking from the solenoid rod.

Inspection

7. Examine the valve ball and seat for pitting and scoring and renew damaged parts; the ball may be reseated by light tapping onto the seat using a suitable drift.
8. Inspect the 'O' ring seals for signs of deterioration, and renew as necessary.

Reassembling

9. Reverse the dismantling procedure 4 to 6.

Refitting

10. Reverse the removing procedure in 2 and 3, ensuring that the lead grommet is pressed fully into its slot, and using a new gasket under the solenoid cover.

Section Fc.8

PUMP AND NON-RETURN VALVE

Removing

1. Drain the gearbox and overdrive unit.
2. Remove the sump filter–Section Fc.5, 2 and 3.
3. Using tool 18G 1118, unscrew the pump retaining plug.
4. Remove the non-return valve spring and ball.
5. Remove the pump body, the pump plunger spring and plunger.

Dismantling

6. Using a suitable drift, separate the non-return valve seat from the pump body taking care not to damage the bore of the pump body.

Inspection

7. Examine the 'O' ring seals for signs of deterioration, and renew where necessary.
8. Examine the non-return valve ball and seat for scoring and pitting, and renew damaged parts; the ball may be reseated by lightly tapping onto its seat using a suitable drift.

Reassembling

9. Carefully refit the non-return valve seat to the pump body.

Refitting

10. Insert the pump plunger into the casing, ensuring that the flat side of the plunger is towards the rear of the overdrive unit and retain in position with tool 18G 1117.
11. Reverse the removing procedure in 2 to 5.

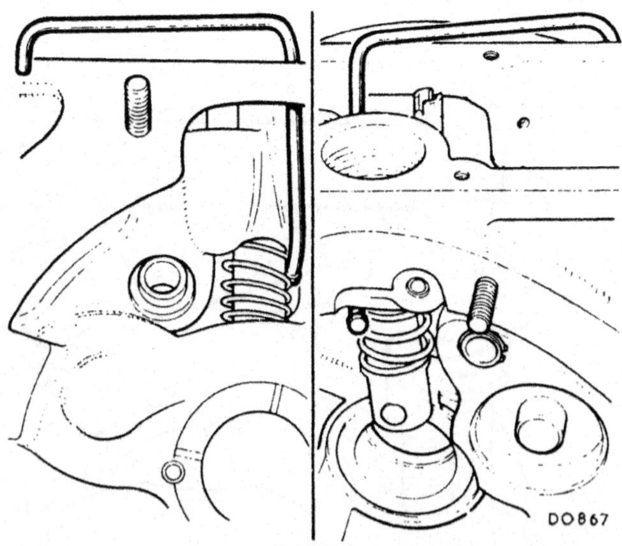

Fig. Fc.8
Using tool 18G 1117 to retain the pump components

Section Fc.9

OVERDRIVE ASSEMBLY

Removing

OVERDRIVE UNIT

1. Remove the engine and gearbox from the car as described in Section A.
2. Remove the gearbox drain plug and drain the oil from the gearbox and overdrive.
3. Unscrew the six bolts securing the remote control assembly to the gearbox and remove the remote control.
4. Remove the eight nuts from the studs securing the overdrive unit to the gearbox adaptor.
5. Withdraw the overdrive unit from the gearbox adaptor.

OVERDRIVE ADAPTOR

6. Remove the overdrive unit as in 1 to 5.
7. Slide the overdrive pump driving cam from the gearbox shaft and remove the cam locking ball from its pocket in the shaft.
8. Using tool 18G 1004, remove the pump cam circlip from the shaft.
9. Withdraw the selector interlocking arm and plate assembly.
10. Unscrew the eight nuts securing the adaptor to the gearbox and withdraw the adaptor.

Dismantling

11. Remove the solenoid cover and gasket.
12. Withdraw the solenoid and plunger.
13. Remove the relief valve assembly.
14. Remove the sump and filter.
15. Using tool 18G 1118, unscrew the pump retaining plug and remove the pump components.
16. Remove the speedometer drive retaining clip, drive gear, and sealing washer.

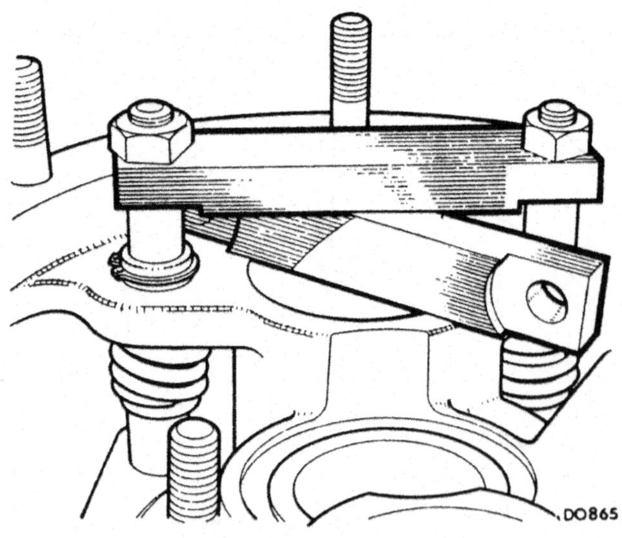

Fig. Fc.9
Using the bridge-pieces to remove the thrust rods

17. Unscrew the six rear retaining stud nuts and the two front nuts securing the rear casing to the main casing assembly.
18. Separate the rear casing from the main casing and remove the planet gear assembly.
19. Unlock and remove the nuts securing the bridge pieces and pistons in the main casing.
20. Remove the bridge piece, pistons, clutch sliding member, brake-ring and sun wheel.
21. Remove the four clutch springs and selective washers.
22. Lever the sun wheel split-ring from the retaining groove and push out the sun wheel.
23. Lift off the bearing retaining plate.
24. Using tool 18G 257, remove the bearing circlip.
25. Drift the clutch sliding member from the bearing.
26. Press the bearing from its housing.
27. Fit the four studs in the thrust ring and insert the studs into the thrust rods from the rear of the main casing.
28. Lay one bridge-piece on its side across one of the piston chambers and fit the remaining bridgepiece, inverted to its normal assembly position, on the two adjacent thrust ring studs and secure with two nuts.
29. Tighten both nuts evenly until the springs are compressed.
30. Remove the circlips securing the thrust rods and springs.
31. Slacken the two nuts evenly until the spring pressure is relieved and remove the nuts.
32. Repeat the operations in 28 to 31 for the remaining thrust rods.
33. Unlock the flange nut, using tool 18G 34A to prevent the shaft turning; remove the nut and washer and withdraw the flange.
34. Press the annulus forward out of the rear casing complete with the front bearing. If the bearing remains in the housing, carefully drift it out with a drift registering on the inner bearing track.
35. Remove the spacer, speedometer driving gear and selective spacer, noting the position of the selective spacer which is identified by a groove cut in its periphery.

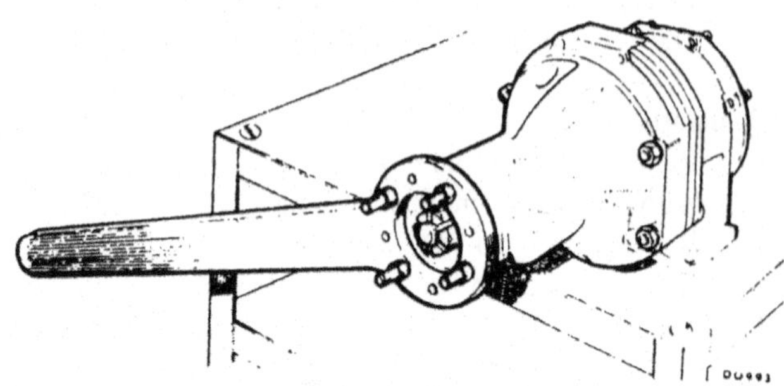

Fig. Fc.10
Using tool 18G 34A to prevent the drive flange from rotating

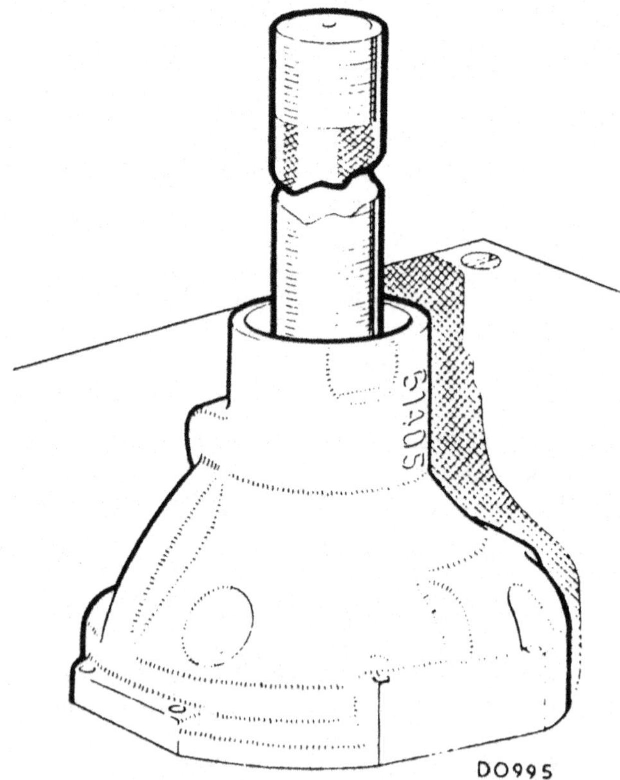

Fig. Fc.11
Fitting the rear bearing using tool 18G 186

36. Press out the rear bearing and oil seal.
37. Remove the front bearing from the annulus if it has been retaining to the shaft.
38. Remove the split ring, oil thrower ring, and uni-directional clutch, collecting the rollers as they come free.
39. Remove the thrust washer.

Inspection

40. Thoroughly clean the components in a cleaning solvent and dry them using lint-free or nylon material or compressed air.
41. Thoroughly examine each component for damage and excessive wear.
42. Examine the bearings for pitting or scoring of the tracks and balls.
43. Check the springs for weakness, collapse or distortion against the following:
44. Inspect the pistons and bores for signs of scoring.
45. Examine the rubber components for signs of deterioration.
46. Inspect the clutch for worn or charred linings and loose rivets. If the clutch is defective a complete new clutch sliding member must be fitted.
47. Examine the shaft splines for signs of wear and damage.
48. Check the condition of the sun wheel bush. If the bush is defective a complete new sun wheel assembly must be fitted.
49. Examine the selective washers for wear. If worn, a new set (four) of washers must be fitted.

Reassembling

50. Press the front bearing into its housing in the rear casing, ensuring that the outer track of the bearing is firmly against the shoulder of the casing.
51. Press the annulus into the front bearing.
52. Fit the spacer, speedometer driving gear, and selective washer.
53. If the rear casing, annulus, speedometer gear, or spacer have been renewed, proceed as follows:
    a. Using dial gauge 18G 191, take a reading from the rear face of the selective washer (Fig. Fc.12).
    b. Take another reading from the shoulder of the rear bearing housing.
    c. The dimension in a should be .010 in. (.254 mm.) $\pm^{0.000}_{0.005}$ in. (.127 mm.) greater than the dimension taken in b. If the correct reading is not obtained, check that the front bearing and annulus are firmly in contact with the shoulders of their respective housings.

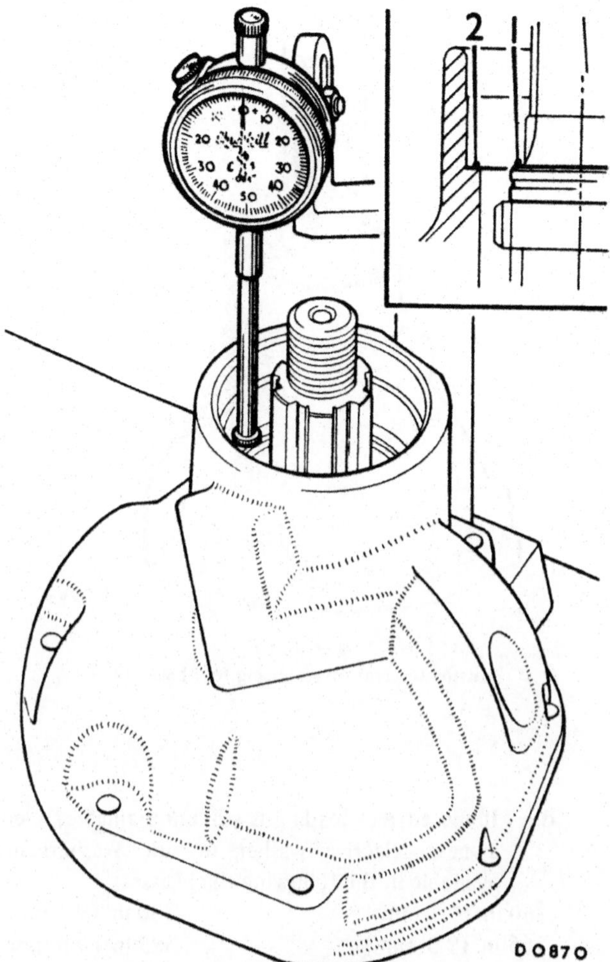

Fig. Fc.12
Using dial gauge 18G 191 to take measurements for the selective washer. Inset shows:

1. Rear face of the selective washer.
2. Shoulder of the bearing housing.

Spring	No. of coils	Wire diameter	Free length	Fitted length	Load at fitted length
Clutch engagement	3¾	.098 in. (2.5 mm.)	.78 in. (19.8 mm.)	.52 in. (13.2 mm.)	65 lb. (29.5 kg.)
Clutch release	4½	.128 in. (3.3 mm.)	.85 in. (21.6 mm.)	.625 in. (15.9 mm.)	150 lb. (68 kg.)
Relief valve	8	.092 in. (2.3 mm.)	1.182 in. (30 mm.)	.995 in. (25.3 mm)	38.35 lb. (17.5 kg.)
Pump	7	.064 in. (1.6 mm.)	1.75 in. (44.5 mm.)	.896 in. (22.8 mm.)	10.99 lb. (5 kg.)

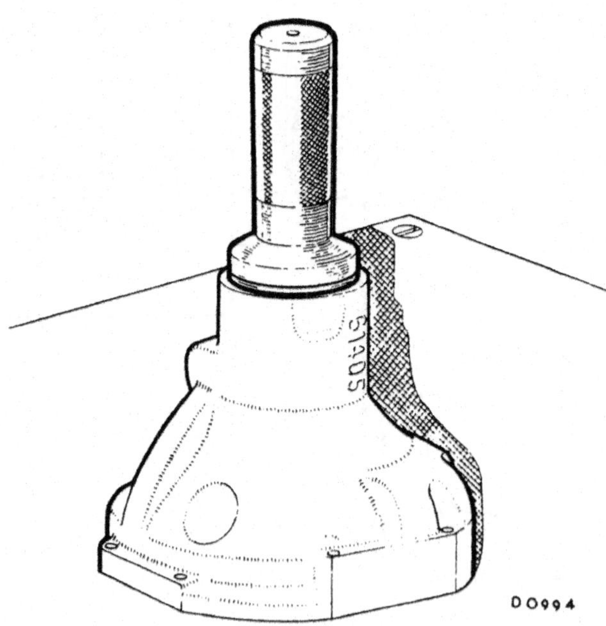

Fig. Fc.13
Fitting the rear oil seal using tool 18G 177

d. If the correct reading is still unobtainable, select a new selective washer to suit. Washers are available in the following thicknesses:

.360 in. (9.1 mm.)	.380 in. (9.7 mm.)
.365 in. (9.3 mm.)	.385 in. (9.8 mm.)
.370 in. (9.4 mm.)	.390 in. (9.9 mm.)
.375 in. (9.5 mm.)	

54. Using tool 18G 186, fit the rear bearing.
55. Smear the outer case of the new rear oil seal with grease, and fit the seal fully into its housing using tool 18G 177.
56. Fit the rear flange, tighten the nut to the torque figure given in '**GENERAL DATA**' and lock the nut using a new split pin.
57. Fit the thrust ring.

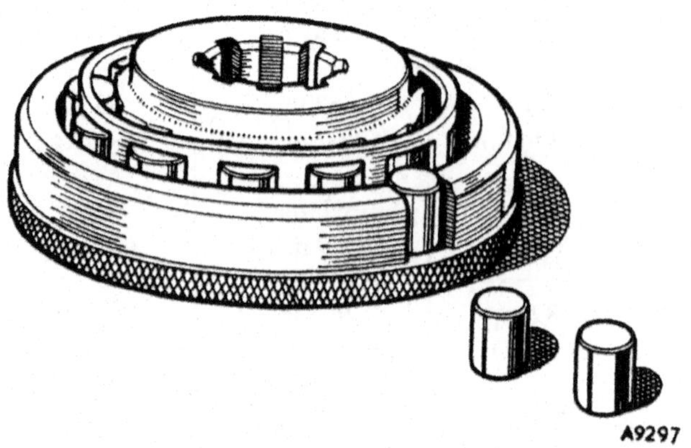

Fig. Fc.14
Assembling the uni-directional clutch using tool 18G 178

58. Fit the spring of the uni-directional clutch to the inner clutch member, and the inner member and spring into the clutch cage, then insert the assembly into tool 18G 178 and fit the clutch rollers.
59. Fit the uni-directional clutch assembly and remove tool 18G 178.
60. Fit the oil thrower and split ring and check that the clutch rotates in an anti-clockwise direction.
61. Rotate each planet wheel until the centre punch mark is radially outwards and in line with the wheel shaft locking pin.
62. Insert the sun wheel into the planet carrier and recheck the alignment of the planet wheel markings.
63. Install the assembled planet carried into the annulus.
64. Remove the sun wheel.
65. Using tool 18G 185, align the splines in the planet carrier and uni-directional clutch.

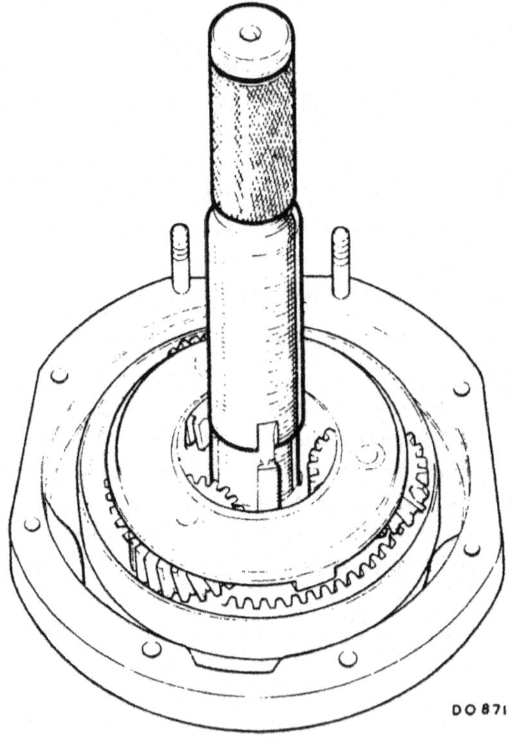

Fig. Fc.15
Using tool 18G 185 to align the splines

66. Refit the four clutch release thrust rods using the dismantling method in 27 to 32; fit new circlips if required.
67. Refit the pistons.
68. Reassemble the clutch sliding member and components by reversing the procedure in 21 to 26, ensuring that the four selective washers fitted are a complete set.

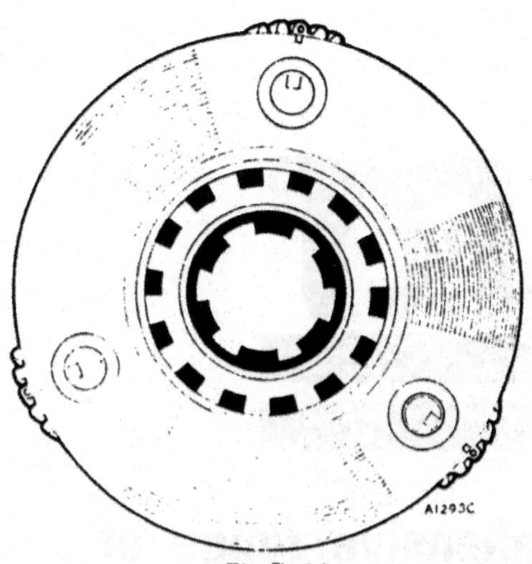

Fig. Fc.16
Place wheels correctly positioned for fitting the sun wheel and assembling in the annulus

69. Fit the sun wheel, brake ring and clutch sliding member reversing the procedure in 19 to 21 and noting that the jointing faces of the brake ring must be smeared with a liquid jointing compound and the nuts locked using new tab washers.
70. Smear the jointing faces of the two casings with liquid jointing compound and assemble the casings ensuring that the sun wheel meshes with the planet gears.
71. Fit and tighten the retaining nuts and spring washers.
72. Reverse the dismantling procedure in 11 to 16.

Refitting

OVERDRIVE ADAPTOR

73. Reverse the removing procedure in 6 to 10.

OVERDRIVE UNIT

74. Reverse the removing procedure in 1 to 5.

SECTION Fd

THE AUTOMATIC GEARBOX

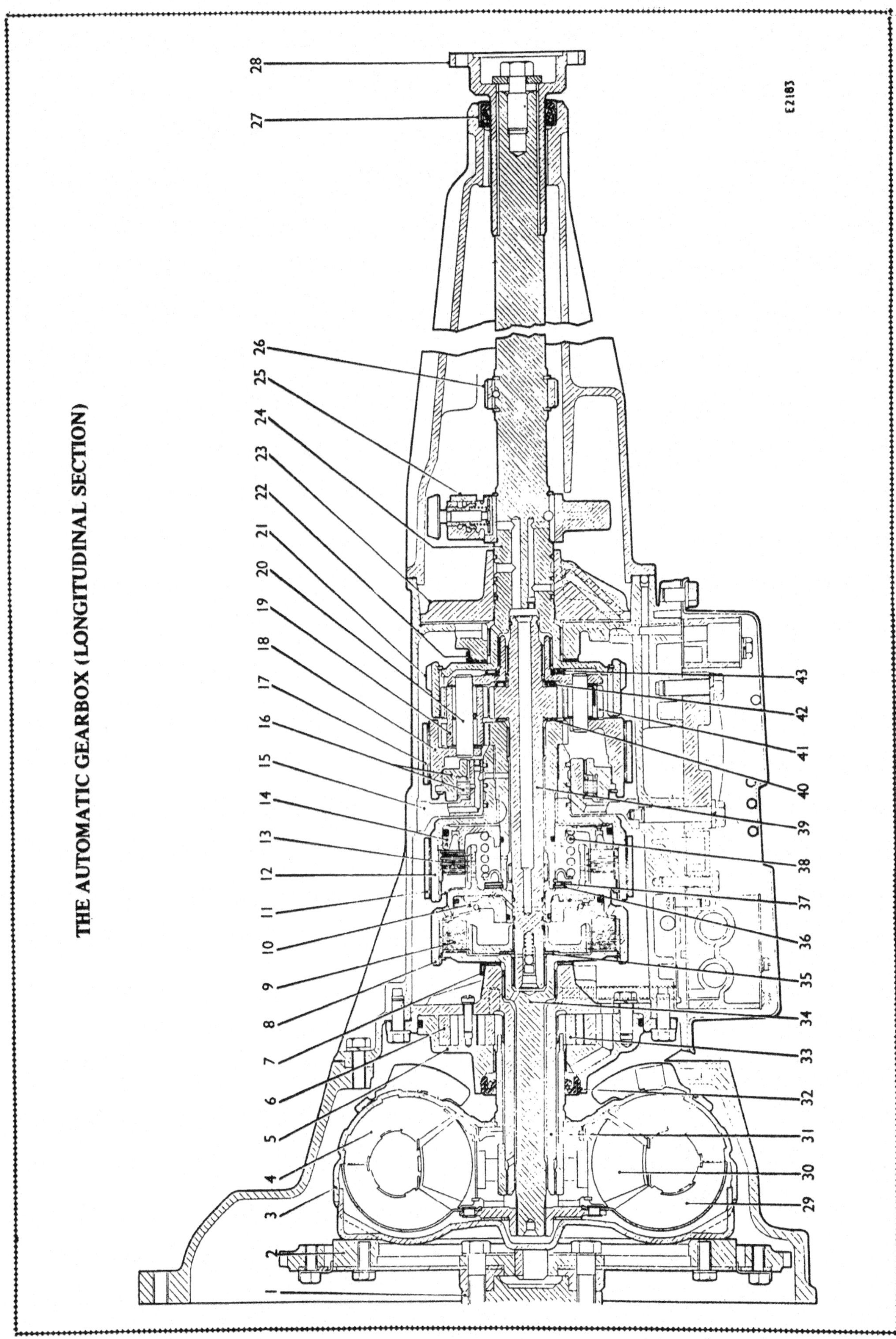

THE AUTOMATIC GEARBOX (LONGITUDINAL SECTION)

KEY TO THE AUTOMATIC GEARBOX

No.	Description	No.	Description	No.	Description
1.	Engine crankshaft.	16.	One-way clutch.	31.	Converter support.
2.	Converter drive plate.	17.	Rear brake band.	32.	Front oil seal.
3.	Converter.	18.	Planet carrier.	33.	Pump inner member.
4.	Impeller.	19.	Planet pinion–long.	34.	Input shaft.
5.	Pump housing.	20.	Pinion shaft.	35.	Thrust washer.
6.	Pump outer member.	21.	Ring gear.	36.	Thrust washer (bronze).
7.	Thrust washer.	22.	Thrust washer.	37.	Thrust washer (steel).
8.	Front clutch housing.	23.	Rear plate adaptor	38.	Rear clutch spring.
9.	Front clutch plates.	24.	Driven shaft.	39.	Forward sun gear.
10.	Front clutch piston.	25.	Governor assembly.	40.	Needle thrust washer.
11.	Front brake band.	26.	Speedometer drive gear.	41.	Planet pinion–short.
12.	Front drum assembly.	27.	Rear oil seal.	42.	Needle thrust washer.
13.	Rear clutch plates.	28.	Driving flange.	43.	Needle thrust washer.
14.	Rear clutch piston.	29.	Turbine.		
15.	Centre support.	30.	Stator.		

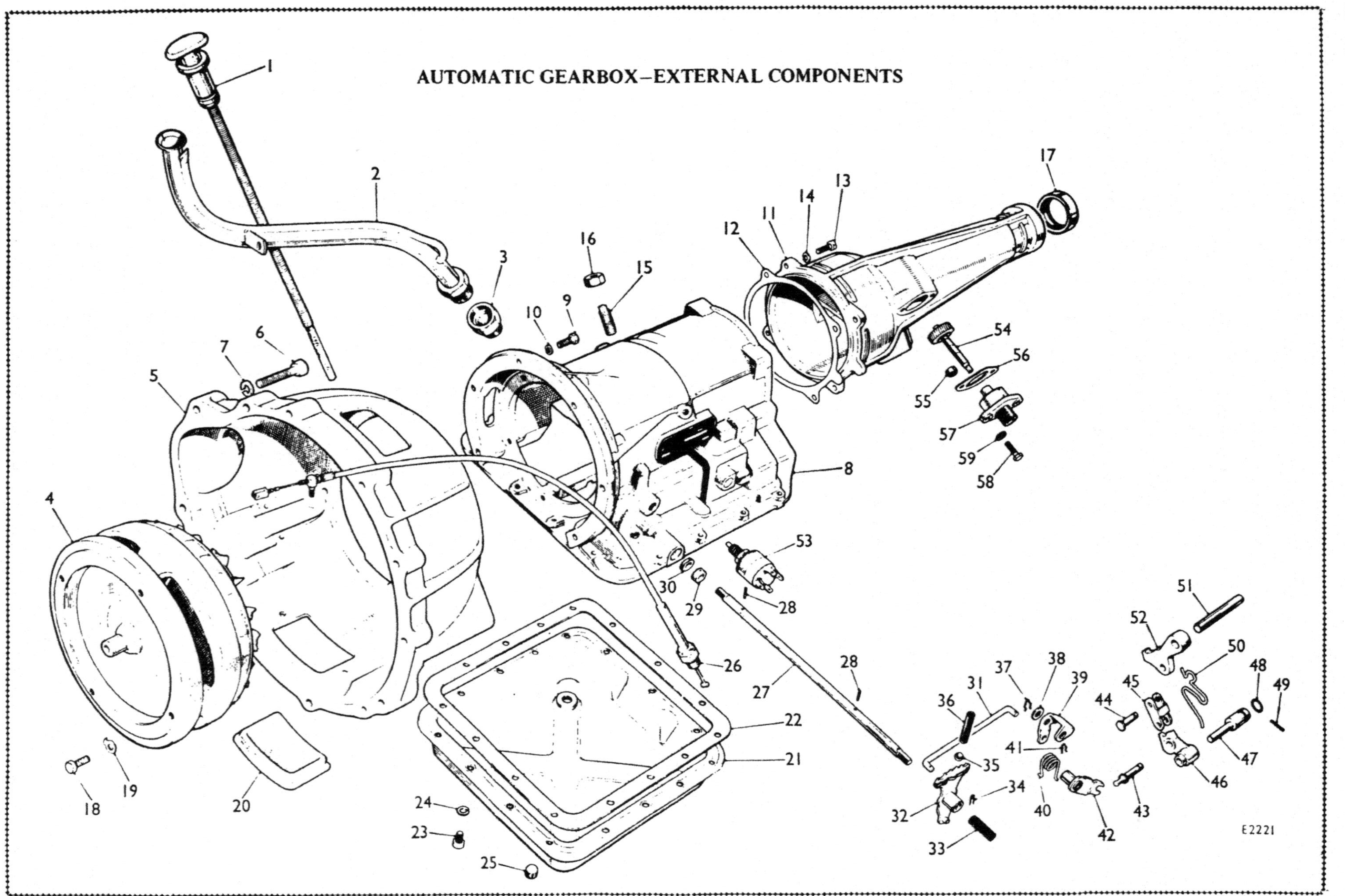

AUTOMATIC GEARBOX—EXTERNAL COMPONENTS

KEY TO EXTERNAL COMPONENTS

No.	Description	No.	Description	No.	Description
1.	Dipstick.	21.	Oil pan assembly.	41.	Clip.
2.	Oil filler tube and gearbox breather.	22.	Gasket for oil pan.	42.	Toggle arm assembly.
3.	Adaptor for filler tube.	23.	Bolt for oil pan.	43.	Toggle pin.
4.	Converter assembly.	24.	Washer for bolt.	44.	Toggle link pin.
5.	Converter housing.	25.	Drain plug.	45.	Toggle link.
6.	Bolt for housing.	26.	Down-shift cable assembly.	46.	Toggle lever.
7.	Spring washer for bolt.	27.	Manual control shaft.	47.	Toggle pin.
8.	Case assembly.	28.	Roll-pin.	48.	'O' ring for pin.
9.	Bolt for case.	29.	Collar.	49.	Slotted pin.
10.	Spring washer for bolt.	30.	Oil seal.	50.	Parking brake release spring.
11.	Rear extension housing.	31.	Manual linkage rod.	51.	Parking brake anchor pin.
12.	Gasket for extension housing.	32.	Manual detent lever.	52.	Parking brake pawl.
13.	Bolt for extension housing.	33.	Spring.	53.	Inhibitor switch.
14.	Spring washer for bolt.	34.	Clip.	54.	Speedometer pinion.
15.	Rear brake band adjusting screw.	35.	Ball.	55.	Oil seal for pinion.
16.	Locknut for adjusting screw.	36.	Spring.	56.	Gasket for pinion bush.
17.	Rear oil seal.	37.	Clip.	57.	Speedometer pinion bush.
18.	Bolt for converter.	38.	Washer.	58.	Bolt for pinion bush.
19.	Lock washer for bolt.	39.	Torsion lever.	59.	Washer for bolt.
20.	Stoneguard.	40.	Spring.		

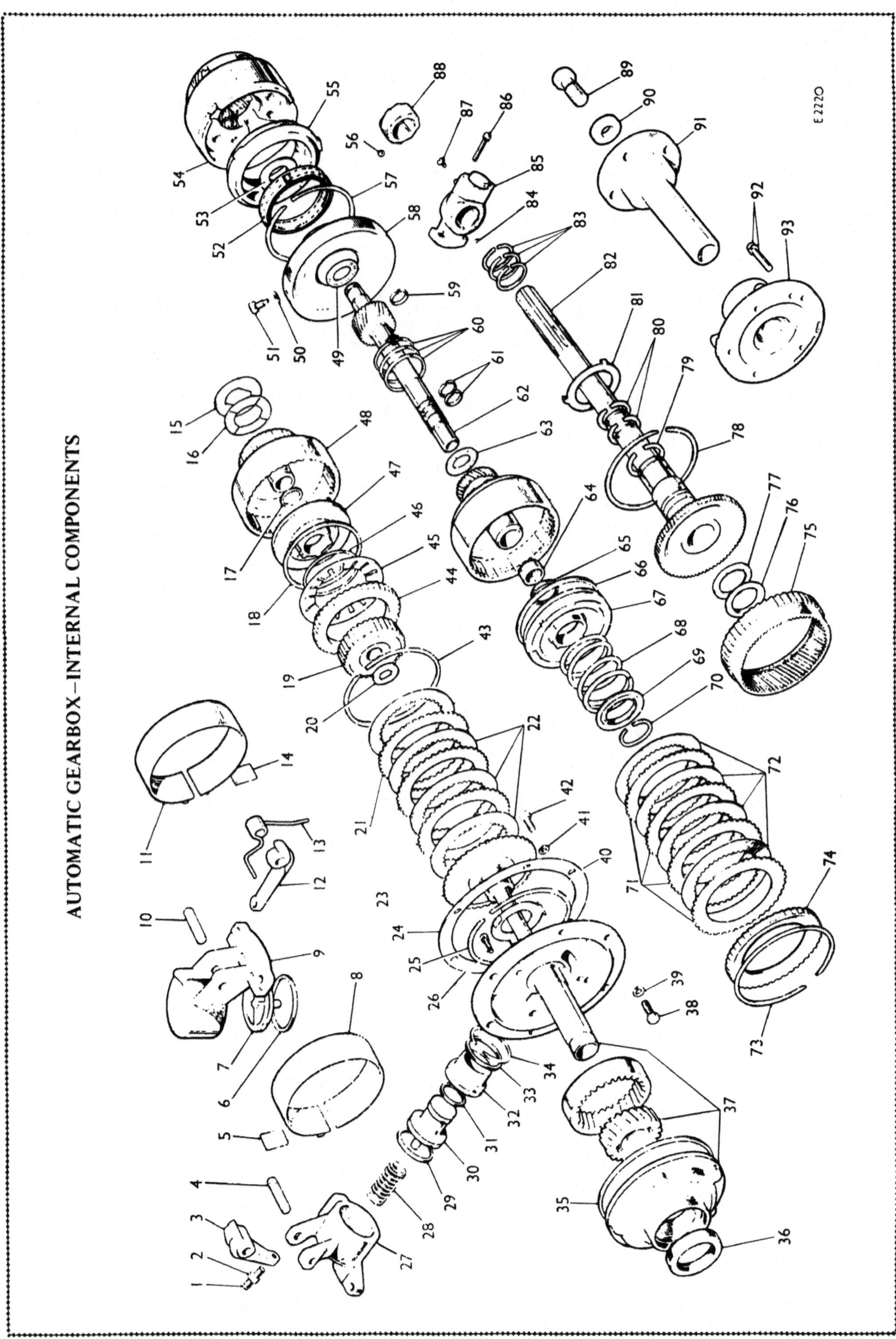

AUTOMATIC GEARBOX—INTERNAL COMPONENTS

KEY TO INTERNAL COMPONENTS

No.	Description
1.	Front servo adjuster.
2.	Locknut for adjuster.
3.	Front servo lever.
4.	Pivot pin for lever.
5.	Strut for front servo.
6.	'O' ring for rear servo piston.
7.	Rear servo piston.
8.	Front brake band.
9.	Rear servo body.
10.	Pivot pin for rear servo lever.
11.	Rear brake band.
12.	Rear servo lever.
13.	Rear servo spring.
14.	Strut for rear servo.
15.	Front clutch thrust washer.
16.	Front clutch thrust washer.
17.	'O' ring.
18.	Front clutch sealing ring.
19.	Front clutch hub.
20.	Thrust washer.
21.	Front clutch plates–outer.
22.	Front clutch plates–inner.
23.	Input shaft assembly.
24.	Gasket for converter support.
25.	Circlip.
26.	Screw.
27.	Front servo body.
28.	Spring.
29.	Piston seal.
30.	Front servo piston.
31.	Piston seal.
32.	Front servo sleeve.
33.	Oil sealing ring.
34.	Circlip.
35.	'O' ring.
36.	Front oil seal.
37.	Pump assembly.
38.	Bolt for pump.
39.	Washer for bolt.
40.	Input shaft thrust washer.
41.	Washer for bolt.
42.	Bolt for pump.
43.	Front clutch snap ring.
44.	Distance piece for front clutch.
45.	Spring for front clutch.
46.	Bearing ring for spring.
47.	Piston for front clutch.
48.	Front clutch housing.
49.	Needle thrust bearing.
50.	Lock washer for bolt.
51.	Centre support bolt.
52.	One-way clutch assembly.
53.	Needle thrust bearing plate.
54.	Planet gear and rear drum assembly.
55.	One-way clutch outer race.
56.	Speedometer gear drive ball.
57.	Snap-ring.
58.	Centre support.
59.	Output shaft oil sealing ring.
60.	Sealing rings–rear clutch.
61.	Oil sealing rings–sun gear.
62.	Forward sun gear.
63.	Needle thrust bearing.
64.	Front drum assembly.
65.	Rear clutch piston seal–inner.
66.	Rear clutch piston seal–outer.
67.	Rear clutch piston.
68.	Spring for rear clutch.
69.	Seat for spring.
70.	Snap ring.
71.	Rear clutch plates–outer.
72.	Rear clutch plates–inner.
73.	Snap-ring.
74.	Pressure plate for rear clutch.
75.	Ring gear.
76.	Needle thrust bearing plate.
77.	Needle thrust bearing.
78.	Snap ring.
79.	Oil sealing ring.
80.	Oil sealing rings.
81.	Driven shaft thrust washer.
82.	Driven shaft.
83.	Oil sealing rings.
84.	Governor drive ball.
85.	Governor assembly.
86.	Screw for governor valve.
87.	Screw for governor cover.
88.	Speedometer drive gear.
89.	Bolt for drive flange.
90.	Washer for bolt.
91.	Drive flange.
92.	Screw.
93.	Rear adaptor plate.

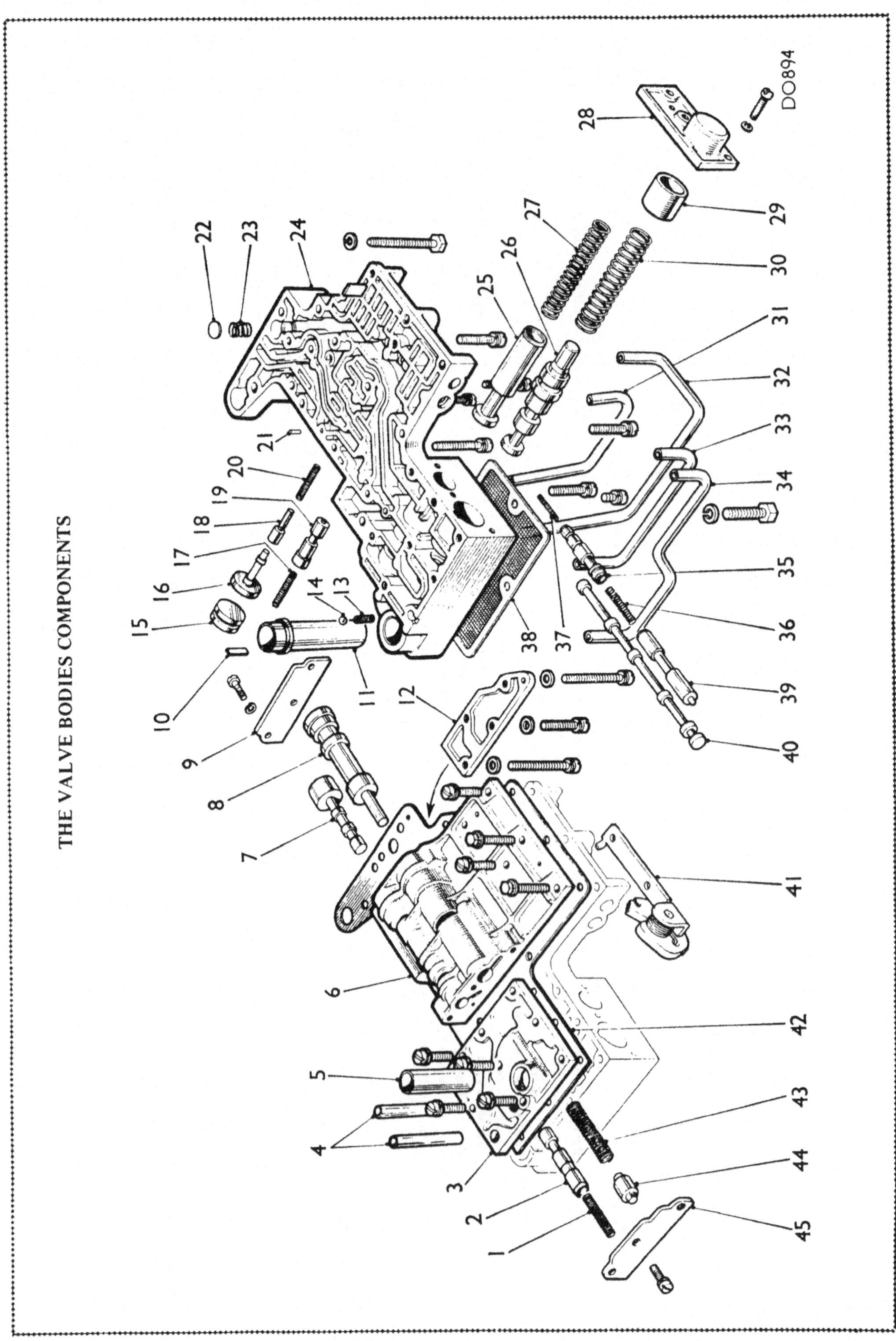

THE VALVE BODIES COMPONENTS

KEY TO THE VALVE BODIES COMPONENTS

No.	Description	No.	Description	No.	Description
1.	Spring–1-2 shift valve.	16.	Modulator valve.	31.	Rear servo tube.
2.	Plunger–1-2 shift valve.	17.	Spring–servo orifice control valve.	32.	Rear clutch tube.
3.	Oil tube collector.	18.	Modulator valve plug.	33.	Front servo apply tube.
4.	Converter oil tubes.	19.	Servo orifice control valve.	34.	Front servo release tube.
5.	Pump outlet tube.	20.	Spring–modulator valve.	35.	Throttle valve.
6.	Upper valve body.	21.	Modulator valve retainer dowel.	36.	Spring–throttle valve.
7.	Valve–1-2 shift.	22.	Pump check valve.	37.	Spring–throttle valve return.
8.	Valve–2-3 shift.	23.	Spring–pump check valve.	38.	Oil strainer.
9.	Rear end plate.	24.	Lower valve body.	39.	Down-shift valve.
10.	Servo orifice control valve stop.	25.	Secondary regulator valve.	40.	Manual control valve.
11.	Pump inlet tube.	26.	Primary regulator valve.	41.	Down-shift and throttle valve cam assembly.
12.	Governor line plate.	27.	Spring–secondary regulator valve.	42.	Separating plate.
13.	Check valve spring.	28.	Lower body end plate.	43.	Spring–2-3 shift valve.
14.	Check valve ball.	29.	Primary regulator valve sleeve.	44.	Plunger–2-3 shift valve.
15.	Modulator valve retainer.	30.	Spring–primary regulator valve.	45.	Front end plate.

THE AUTOMATIC GEARBOX

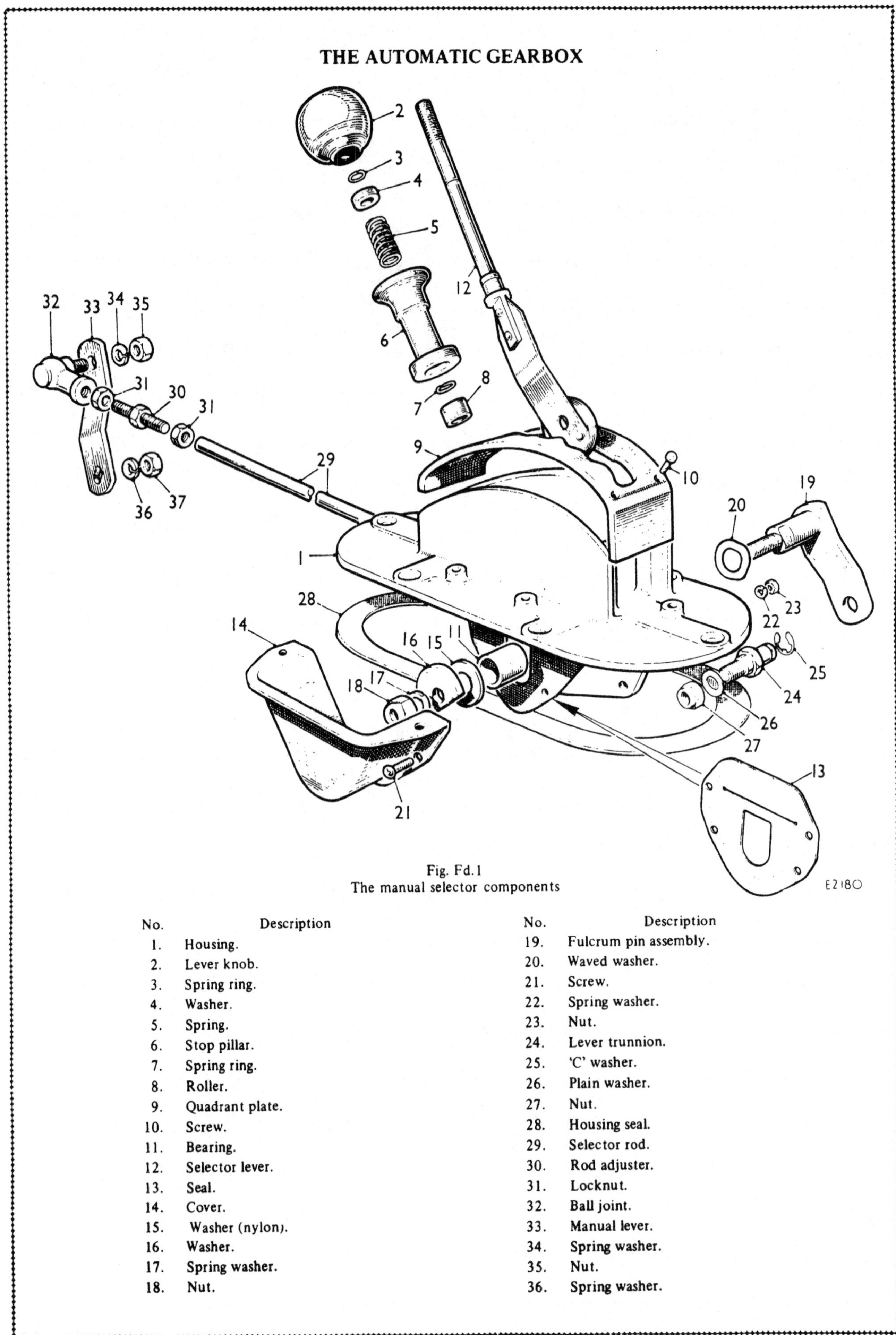

Fig. Fd.1
The manual selector components

No.	Description	No.	Description
1.	Housing.	19.	Fulcrum pin assembly.
2.	Lever knob.	20.	Waved washer.
3.	Spring ring.	21.	Screw.
4.	Washer.	22.	Spring washer.
5.	Spring.	23.	Nut.
6.	Stop pillar.	24.	Lever trunnion.
7.	Spring ring.	25.	'C' washer.
8.	Roller.	26.	Plain washer.
9.	Quadrant plate.	27.	Nut.
10.	Screw.	28.	Housing seal.
11.	Bearing.	29.	Selector rod.
12.	Selector lever.	30.	Rod adjuster.
13.	Seal.	31.	Locknut.
14.	Cover.	32.	Ball joint.
15.	Washer (nylon).	33.	Manual lever.
16.	Washer.	34.	Spring washer.
17.	Spring washer.	35.	Nut.
18.	Nut.	36.	Spring washer.

Section Fd.1

SELECTOR

Adjusting

1. Set the selector to the 'N' position on the selector quadrant.
2. Turn the gearbox shaft to the 'N' position, i.e. turn the shaft back (anti-clockwise) as far as it will go to the 'P' position, then turn it forward two clicks or detents.
3. Slacken the locknuts on the rod adjuster and turn the adjuster in the required direction until the lever fits easily onto the driving flats of the gearbox shaft.
4. Tighten the adjuster locknuts.
5. Fit and tighten the selector lever retaining nut and washer.

Removing

6. Set the selector to the 'N' position on the quadrant.
7. Remove the nut and washer securing the selector lever to the gearbox shaft and detach the lever from the shaft.
8. Unscrew the carpet retainer ring securing screws and remove the ring.
9. Ease back the carpet surrounding the selector assembly and remove the selector housing retaining screws.
10. Lift out selector assembly complete with rod and lever.

Dismantling

11. Remove the self-locking nut securing the rod to the selector and detach the rod.
12. Remove the trunnion circlip and withdraw the trunnion and anti-rattle washer from the rod.

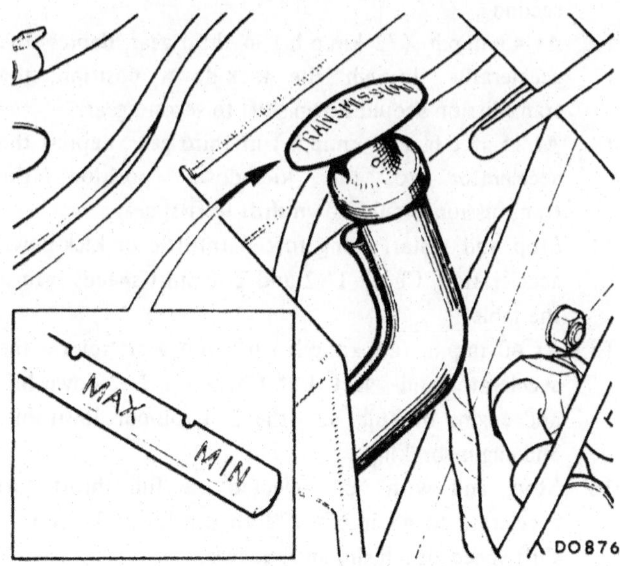

Fig. Fd.2
Dipstick and filler tube

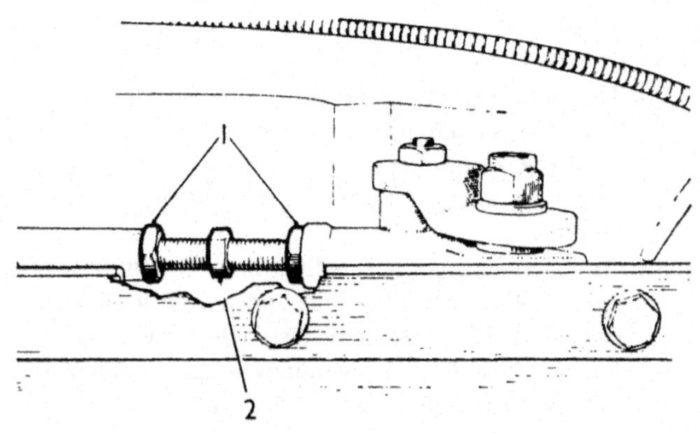

Fig. Fd.3
The selector rod adjuster

1. Locknuts. 2. Adjuster.

13. Unscrew the nuts and screws securing the selector cover and remove the cover.
14. Remove the self-locking nut securing the fulcrum pin.
15. Withdraw the fulcrum pin, collecting the spring washer, 'D' washer, nylon washer and anti-rattle washer.
16. Remove the selector cover gasket.
17. Withdraw the selector lever and unscrew the knob.
18. Press down the retainer ring in the upper end of the sliding pillar and remove the circlip.
19. Withdraw the retaining ring, spring, and sliding pillar.
20. The bronze fulcrum bush can be drifted from the selector housing for renewal if necessary.

Inspection

21. Examine the fulcrum pin and bush for wear, and renew if necessary.
22. Inspect the rod, levers and pivots for twisting, damage and wear; renew worn or damaged parts.

Reassembling

23. Reverse the dismantling procedure in 11 to 20, lubricating the trunnion liberally with Rocol MT265 Grease before assembling.

Refitting

24. Reverse the removing procedure in 6 to 10 noting that if new parts have been fitted or the lever does not fit easily to the gearbox shaft, the rod may require adjusting as described in 1 to 5.

Section Fd.2

MAINTENANCE

Checking fluid level

The markings on the dipstick are calibrated for the fluid level with the transmission at normal running temperature. If for any reason the level is checked when the transmission is cold, the correct level will be $\frac{5}{16}$ in. (8 mm.) below the 'MAX' mark.

The correct checking procedure is as follows.

1. With the car standing level apply the hand brake and move the selector lever to 'P'.
2. Start the engine and run it at idle speed for two minutes.
3. With the engine still idling in 'P', withdraw the dipstick from the filler tube and wipe it with a clean piece of paper, or nylon material. Do not use rag.
4. Reinsert the dipstick, withdraw it again immediately and check the fluid level indication.

Topping up fluid

5. Withdraw the dipstick and add the required quantity of a recommended Automatic Transmission Fluid through the combined dipstick/filler tube. Use only a recommended fluid; observe scrupulous cleanliness; **DO NOT OVERFILL.**
   The difference between the 'MAX' and 'MIN' marks on the dipstick is equivalent to 1 pint (1.2 U.S. pints: .57 litres).

Refilling after draining

6. The quantity of fluid required when refilling will depend on the amount still remaining in the torque converter, which can be up to 5 pints (6 U.S. pints; 2.8 litres).
   IMPORTANT.–Do not re-use fluid showing signs of contamination.

Towing for recovery

NOTE.–The car cannot be tow-started.

7. If the transmission is operating satisfactorily the car may be towed with the selector at 'N' after ensuring that the fluid is at the correct level, for distances up to 40 miles (64 km.) at a speed not exceeding 30 m.p.h. (48 km.p.h.). If the transmission is inoperative or if there is reason to suspect a fault or damage, or the towing distance or speeds exceeds the limits given, the propeller shaft must be disconnected, or alternatively, the car towed with the rear wheels clear of the ground.

Section Fd.3

ROAD TEST PROCEDURE

In order to ascertain the precise nature of a fault it is first essential to thoroughly investigate the effect. The following test procedure must be carried out in its entirety before referring to '**FAULT DIAGNOSIS**' (Section Fd.4).

Preliminary checks

1. Check the fluid level (Section Fd.2), and top up if necessary.
2. Check the adjustment of the down-shift and throttle cable as described in Section Fd.7.
3. Fully depress the accelerator pedal to the kick-down position and check that the carburetter is fully open.

Stationary tests

4. Check the operation of the starter inhibitor switch; the starter should only operate when the selector is in 'P' or 'N'.
5. Check that the reverse lights operate only when the selector is in 'R'.
6. With the engine idling and the brakes applied check that forward drive is obtained when 'D', 'L2', and 'L1' are selected and reverse drive is obtained when 'R' is selected.
7. With 'P' selected check that the selector lever is trapped by the gate.
8. Stall the transmission in 'L1' and 'R' as described in Section Fd.6 and check for slip and clutch squawk.
   NOTE.–Do not stall for longer than 10 seconds.

Driving tests

9. Select 'D', release the brakes and accelerate with minimum throttle opening. Check the 1–2 and 2–3 shift speeds against the table.
   NOTE. At minimum throttle openings the shifts may be difficult to detect.
10. Stop and restart, using full-throttle acceleration, i.e. pedal at detent. Check 1–2 and 2–3 shift speeds against the table.
11. At 35 m.p.h. (56 km.p.h.) in third gear, depress the accelerator to the full throttle position; the car should accelerate in third gear and should not down-shift to second.
12. At 45 m.p.h. (72 km.p.h.) in third gear, depress the accelerator through the kick-down position; the transmission should down-shift to second gear.
13. At 15 m.p.h. (24 km.p.h.) in third gear, depress the accelerator to the kick-down position; the transmission should down-shift to first gear.
14. Stop and restart using forced throttle or kick-down acceleration. Check 1–2 and 2–3 shift speeds against the table.
15. At 40 m.p.h. (64 km.p.h.) in third gear, release the accelerator and select 'L2'. Check for 3–2 downshift and engine braking, also the 2–1 roll-out down-shift and engine braking.
16. Stop, and with 'L2' selected use full throttle to accelerate to 45 m.p.h. (72 km.p.h.). Check for 1–2 shift speed clutch slip and squawk.
17. At 25 m.p.h. (40 km.p.h.) in 'L2', release the accelerator and select 'L1'. Check the 2–1 downshift speed and for full engine braking.

18. Stop, and with 'L1' selected use full throttle to accelerate up to 35 m.p.h. (56 km.p.h.). Check for no up-shift, clutch slip and squawk.
19. Stop, select 'R', reverse using full throttle if possible. Check for no slip or clutch squawk.
20. Stop facing downhill on a gradient and select 'P', release the brakes and check that the parking pawl holds the car; re-apply the brakes before dis-engaging the parking pawl. Repeat the test with the car facing uphill; check that in both cases the selector is trapped by the gate in the 'P' position.
21. Re-check the fluid level.
22. Check for transmission leaks.

Section Fd.4

CONVERTER FAULT DIAGNOSIS

Torque converter faults can only be correctly determined when road test findings, transmission performance, engine condition, and stall test results have all been considered.

Slipping stator (stator free-wheel slipping)
1. Inability to pull away on steep gradients.
2. Poor acceleration from rest.
3. Stall test reading LOW.

Seized stator (stator free-wheel seized–unusual fault)
1. Reduced maximum speed in all gears, pronounced in top ratio.
2. Severe overheating of converter and transmission.
3. Stall test reading NORMAL.

Transmission slip (selected gear components slipping)
1. If the fault is apparent in both 'L1' and 'R' it is usually due to low pressure.
2. If the fault is present in only one position a faulty component is the most likely cause.
3. Stall test reading HIGH.

Section Fd.5

STALL TEST

Stall speed is the maximum speed attainable at forced throttle (kick-down) with the converter turbine held stationary.

IMPORTANT.–Duration of stall must not exceed 10 seconds.
1. Apply the hand brake and chock the wheels.
2. Connect tool 18G 677 Z to the engine and position the instrument so that it can be read from the driving seat.
3. Run the engine until the normal operating temperature of the transmission is reached.
4. Select 'P' and check the transmission fluid level–Section Fd.2.
5. Apply the foot brake, select 'L1' or 'R' (as required for test elimination), depress the accelerator pedal to the kick-down position for not more than 10 seconds and note the highest r.p.m. reading on the instrument.
6. Check the reading obtained against the following chart, and refer to Section Fd.4 for '**FAULT DIAGNOSIS**'.

R.P.M.	CONDITION INDICATED
Under 1,250	Slipping stator
1,800 to 2,100	NORMAL
Over 2,700	Transmission slip

DRIVING CONDITIONS	UP-SHIFTS				DOWN-SHIFTS					
	1–2		2–3		3–2		3–1		2–1	
	m.p.h.	km.p.h.	m.p.h.	km.p.h.	m.p.h.	km.p.h.	m.p.h.	km.p.h.	m.p.h.	km.p.h.
'D' Selected										
Minimum throttle ..	8–12	13–19	13–17	21–27						
Full throttle	22–29	35–46	41–48	65–78						
Forced throttle (kick-down)	30–37	48–60	57–62	91–100	50–57	80–91	20–26	32–41	20–26	32–41
'L2' Selected										
Minimum throttle ..										
Full throttle									2–5	3–8
Forced throttle (kick-down)									20–26	32–41
'L1' Selected										
Minimum throttle ..									10–15	16–24

Section Fd.6

FAULT DIAGNOSIS

TEST NUMBER	FAULT	CHECK/RECTIFY
(4)	Starter will not operate in 'P' or 'N'	19
	Starter operates in all selector positions	20
(5)	Reverse light will not operate in 'R'	20
(6)	Excessive bump on engagement of 'D', 'L2', 'L1', or 'R'	4, 3
(8)	Stall speed high:	
	with slip and squawk in 'L2'	2, 3, 5, 6, 7, 11, 17
	with slip and squawk in 'L1'	2, 3, 8, 9, 10, 11, 17
	with slip and squawk in 'R'	2, 3, 12, 17
	Stall speed up to 600 r.p.m. low	23
	Stall speed more than 600 r.p.m. low	21
(9) (10) (14)	No drive in 'D'	1, 2, 3, 16
	No drive in 'D' 'L2' or 'L1'	1, 2, 3, 13, 11, 16
	No drive in 'D' 'L2', 'L1' or 'R'	1, 2, 3, 13, 11, 16, 17
	Delayed or no 1–2 shift	3, 14, 13, 5, 6
	Slip on 1–2 shift	2, 3, 5, 6, 7, 13
	Delayed or no 2–3 shift	3, 14, 13, 5, 6, 12
	Delayed or no 2–3 shift but normal in 'R'	3, 14, 13, 5, 6
	Slip or engine run-up on 2–3 shift	2, 3, 5, 13, 12
	Bumpy gear shift	3
	Drag in 'D2' and 'D3'	8
	Drag or binding on 2–3 shift	5, 6
(10) (14)	Slip, squawk or judder on full-throttle take-off in 'D'	1, 2, 3, 13, 11
	Loss of performance and overheating in 'D3'	21
(11)	Transmission down-shifts too easily	3
(12) (13)	Transmission will not down-shift	3, 13, 14
(15)	No 3–2 down-shift on engine braking	1, 5, 6, 7, 12
	No 2–1 down-shift or engine braking	8, 9, 10
(16)	Slip, squawk or judder on take-off in 'L2'	1, 2, 3, 13, 11
	Transmission up-shifts to top ratio	3
(17)	No 2–1 down-shift or engine braking	8, 9, 10
(18)	Slip, squawk or judder on take-off in 'L1'	1, 2, 3, 13, 11
	Transmission up-shifts	1
(19)	Slip, squawk or judder on take-off in 'R'	1, 2, 3, 13, 12
	Slip but no judder on take-off in 'R'	1, 2, 3,
	when engine braking is available in 'L1'	1, 2, 3, 8, 9, 10
	when no engine braking in 'L1'	5
	Drag in 'R'	
	No drive in 'R'	
	when engine braking is available in 'L1'	1, 2, 3, 13, 12
	when no engine braking in 'L1'	1, 2, 3, 8, 13, 9, 10, 12
(20)	No 'P'	1, 15
General	Screech or whine, increasing with engine speed	17
	Grinding or grating noise from gearbox	18
	Knocking noise from torque converter	22
	At high speeds, transmission down-shift to D2 and back	12

OPERATIONS KEY TO ACTION

1. Check manual linkage adjustment.
2. Check fluid level.
3. Check adjustment of down-shift and throttle valve cable, using line pressure gauge and tachometer.
4. Reduce engine idle speed.
5. Check adjustment of front band.
6. Check front servo seals and fit of tubes.
7. Check front band for wear.
8. Check adjustment of rear band.
9. Check rear servo seal and fit of tubes.
10. Check rear band for wear.
11. Examine front clutch and seals, also forward sun gear shaft sealing rings. Verify that cup plug in driven shaft is not leaking or dislodged.
12. Examine rear clutch, check valve, and seals. Check fit of tubes.
13. Strip and clean valve bodies.
14. Strip and clean governor valve.
15. Examine parking pawl, gear, and internal linkage.
16. Examine one-way clutch.
17. Strip and examine pump and drive tangs.
18. Strip and examine gear train.
19. Adjust starter inhibitor switch inwards.
20. Adjust starter inhibitor switch outwards.
21. Replace torque converter.
22. Examine torque converter drive plate for cracks or fracture.
23. Check engine performance.

Section Fd.7

PRESSURE TEST–DOWN-SHIFT VALVE CABLE

The following test is essential to determine the correct adjustment of the down-shift and throttle cable.

The effects of cable maladjustment are given in Section Fd.4, 'FAULT DIAGNOSIS'.

1. With the carburetters set at normal idle, check that the crimped stop on the down-shift valve inner cable just contacts the abutment on the outer cable
2. Remove the line pressure take-off blanking plug and fit adaptor.
3. Connect tool 18G 677 Z to the engine and adaptor; position the instrument so that it can be read from the driving seat.
4. Apply the hand brake and chock the wheels.
5. Select 'N' and run the engine until normal operating temperature is reached.
6. With the engine running at correct idle speed check that a line pressure of 55 to 65 lb./sq. in. is registered on the instrument.
7. Apply the foot brake, select 'D', increase the engine speed to 1,000 r.p.m. when a pressure reading of 90 to 100 lb./sq. in. should be registered.
8. If the pressure reading is less than the figure given, reset the cable adjuster so that the effective length of the outer cable is increased. If the reading is higher, readjust to decrease the effective length of the outer cable.

Section Fd.8

ADJUSTMENTS

Under normal operating conditions no periodic adjustments are required.

Starter inhibitor and reverse light switch

IMPORTANT.–Apply the brakes and chock the wheels before checking and adjusting the switch. The car may move off if the starter is operated with the selector in one of the drive positions.

CHECKING

1. Verify that the switch is at fault by disconnecting and shorting the leads of each circuit ('1' and '3' terminals are for the starter, '2' and '4' for the reverse lights). Check that each circuit functions regardless of the selector position.

ADJUSTING

2. Loosen the switch locknut, using tool 18G 679.

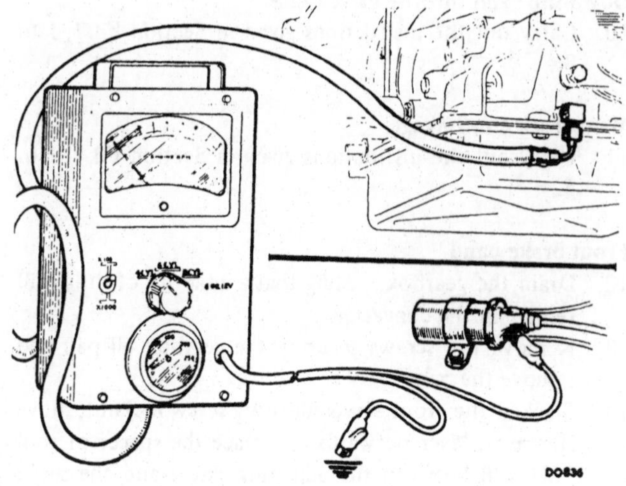

Fig. Fd.4
Service tool 18G 677 Z connected for pressure test, and (inset) electrical connections for stall test

1. **Pressure test connection.** 2. **Red lead to coil connection.** 3. **Black lead to earth.**

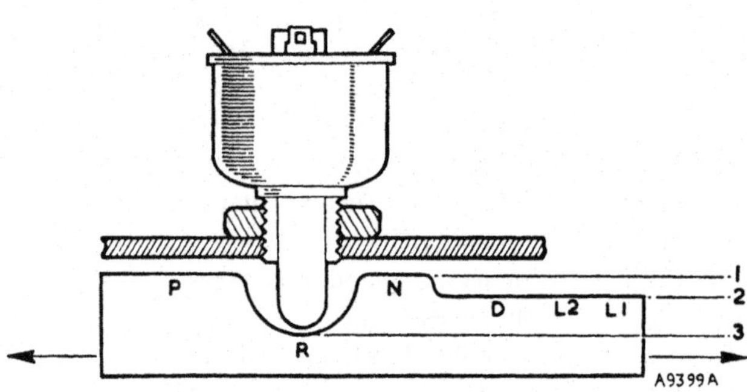

Fig. Fd.5
Starter inhibitor and reverse light switch
1. Starter operative. 2. Starter inoperative.
3. Starter inoperative, reverse light on.

3. Connect a test bulb and battery across the starter terminals and another across the reverse light terminals.
4. Select 'D', 'L1' or 'L2'.
5. Fully unscrew the switch from the casing, then screw it in until the reverse light contacts open. Mark the position of the switch relative to the casing.
6. Screw the switch in until the starter inhibitor contacts make, and mark the switch position.
7. Unscrew the switch to the midway point between the two markings.
8. Tighten the switch locknut and re-connect the wiring.
9. Check that the switch functions correctly; if the starter operates in any position other than 'P' or 'N', or if the reverse lights fail to operate only in 'R', renew the switch.

Down-shift and throttle valve cable

10. Carry out the instructions given in Section Fd.7, 1 to 8.

Manual selector linkage

11. Carry out the instructions given in Section Fd.1, 1 to 5.

Front brake band

12. Drain the gearbox, noting that a quantity of fluid will remain in the converter.
13. Remove the screws securing the gearbox oil pan and remove the pan.
14. Slacken the front servo adjusting screw locknut, move the servo lever outwards and place the spacer of tool 18G 678 between the adjusting screw and the servo piston pin.
15. Using tool 18G 678 with torque screwdriver 18G 681, tighten the adjusting screw to a torque of 10 lb. in. (.115 kg. m.).
16. Tighten the adjusting screw locknut to the torque figure given in **'GENERAL DATA'**.
17. Refit the oil pan and fill the gearbox with fluid to the correct level.

Rear brake band

18. Slacken the locknut on the external adjusting screw.
19. Using a torque wrench tighten the adjusting screw to a torque of 10 lb. ft. (1.4 kg. m.) then back off the screw one complete turn.
20. Tighten the locknut to the torque figure given in **'GENERAL DATA'**.

Section Fd.9

AIR PRESSURE TEST

Air pressure may be used to check that the clutch and brake bands are operating. These checks can be made with the gearbox installed in the car or on the bench.

1. Drain the transmission, noting that a quantity of fluid will remain in the torque converter.
2. Remove the valve bodies assembly–Section Fd.13, 1 to 6.

Front clutch and governor feed

3. Apply air pressure into passage 1 of the casing, noting a thump, indicating that the clutch is functioning; maintain air pressure for several seconds to check for leaks. If the transmission has been removed:
   a. Verify the clutch operation by turning the input shaft while applying the air pressure.
   b. Remove the extension housing, rotate the output shaft so that governor weight is at the bottom of the assembly, and check that the weight moves inwards when air pressure is applied.

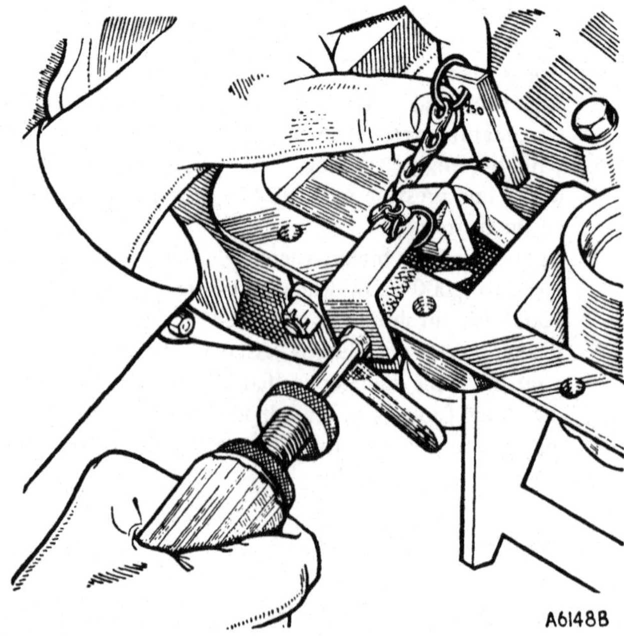

Fig. Fd.6
Adjusting the front brake band using tool 18G 678 and 18G 681

REAR CLUTCH

4. Apply air pressure into passage (2) in the casing web and check for thump, indicating that the clutch has applied. If the transmission has been removed turn the input shaft to verify clutch operation. Maintain air pressure for several seconds to check for leaks.

Front servo

5. Apply air pressure to the tube location (3) and observe the movement of the piston pin.

Rear servo

6. Apply air pressure to the tube location (4) and observe the movement of the servo lever.

Conclusions

7. If the clutch and bands operate satisfactorily with air pressure, faulty operation of the transmission indicates malfunction of the hydraulic control system which will necessitate removing and overhauling the valve bodies assembly.

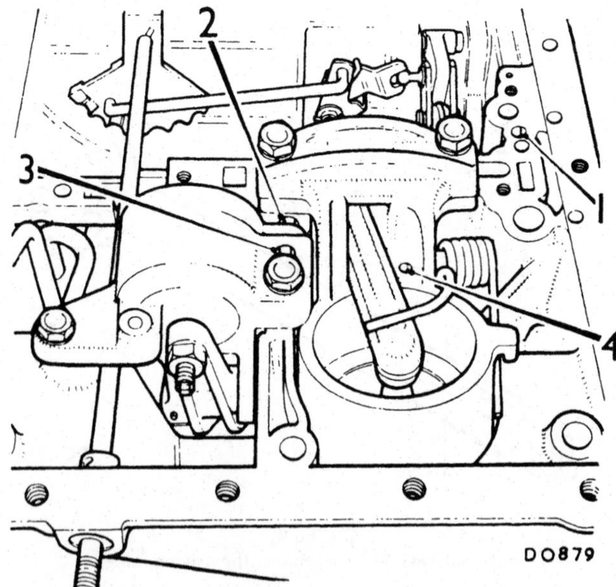

Fig. Fd.8
Air pressure check feed locations

1. Front clutch and governor.
2. Rear clutch.
3. Front servo.
4. Rear servo.

Section Fd.10

TRANSMISSION ASSEMBLY

Removing

1. Remove the engine and gearbox assembly – Section A.21.
2. Drain the gearbox.
3. Disconnect the down-shift and throttle valve cable from the carburetter linkage.
4. Unscrew the six bolts securing the gearbox to the converter housing and withdraw the gearbox.
5. If the gearbox has been removed for dismantling or component removal, the exterior of the gearbox should be thoroughly cleaned of all dirt before commencing dismantling operations.
   Use tool 18G 673 to support the gearbox during dismantling and assembling operations.

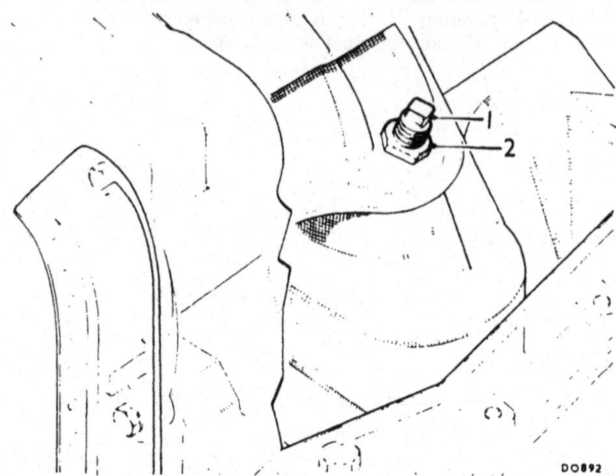

Fig. Fd.7
Rear brake band adjustment

1. Adjusting screw. 2. Locknut.

Refitting

6. Reverse the removing procedure in 1 to 5.

Section Fd.11

TORQUE CONVERTER

Removing

1. Remove the transmission assembly – Section Fd.9, 1 to 5.
2. Unscrew the bolts securing the converter housing to the engine and remove the housing.
3. Unscrew the four bolts securing the converter to the drive plate and remove the converter.

Refitting

4. Reverse the removing procedure in 1 to 3, leaving the converter bolts loose to allow the converter to centralize when the gearbox is fitted. Use new tab washers to lock the converter bolts when tightened after refitting the gearbox.

Section Fd.12

GOVERNOR ASSEMBLY AND SPEEDOMETER DRIVE

Removing

1. Remove the transmission assembly – Section Fd.9, 1 to 5.
2. Using tool 18G 34A to prevent the output shaft from turning, remove the drive flange securing bolt and withdraw the flange.
3. Unscrew the four bolts securing the rear extension housing and remove the housing.

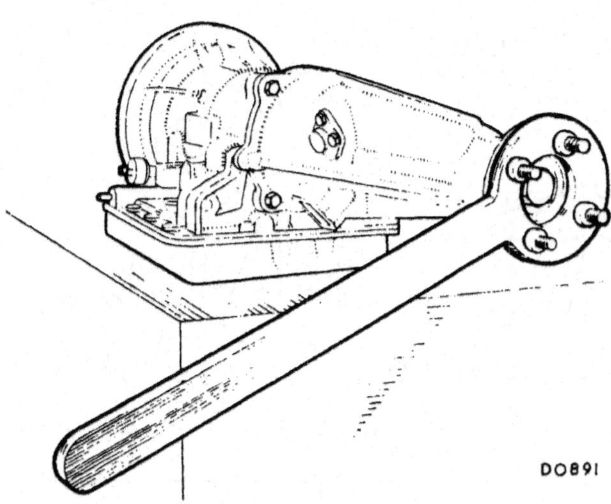

Fig. Fd.9
Using tool 18G 34 A to remove the driving flange

4. Using tool 18G 1004 with points 18G 1004 J, remove the circlip retaining the speedometer drive gear.
5. Withdraw the speedometer gear, and remove the gear driving ball.
6. Using tool 18G 1004 with points 18G 1004 J, remove the front speedometer gear circlip and the governor retaining circlip.
7. Withdraw the governor assembly and remove its drive ball.

Dismantling

8. Unscrew the cover-plate retaining screws and remove the plate.
9. Unscrew the two screws securing the valve body assembly to the counter-weight and remove the counter-weight. Check that the oilways of both components line up with each other.

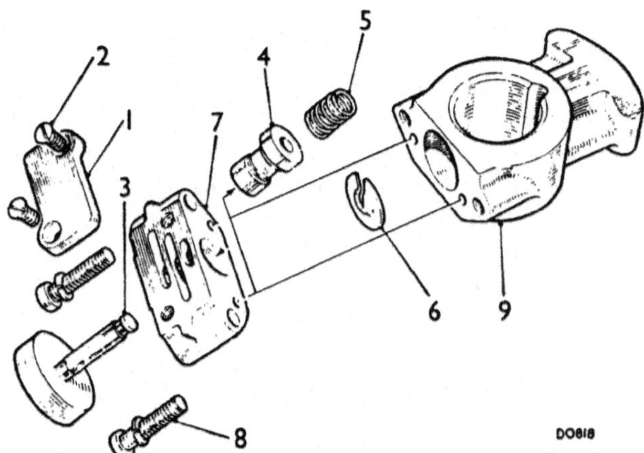

Fig. Fd.10
The governor components

1. Cover-plate.
2. Screws for cover-plate.
3. Valve.
4. Valve weight.
5. Valve spring.
6. Valve retainer.
7. Valve body.
8. Screws for valve body.
9. Counter-weight.

10. Remove the governor weight retainer and withdraw the weight, valve, and spring.

Inspection

11. Check the valve, weight and body bore for scores; renew scored components if the scores cannot be removed by polishing.
12. Clean out the oilways and passages.

Reassembling

13. Reverse the dismantling procedure in 7 to 9, ensuring that the valve and governor weight move freely.

Refitting

14. Reverse the removing procedure in 1 to 6, noting that the governor is fitted to the output shaft with the cover-plate facing away from the gearbox.

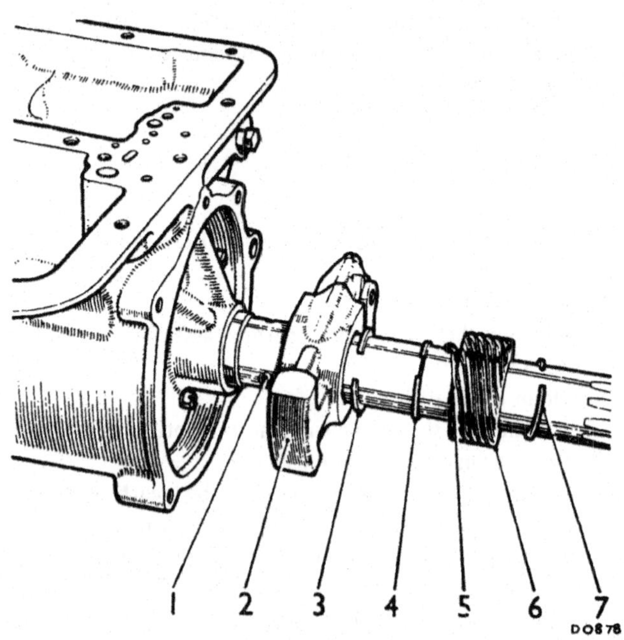

Fig. Fd.11
Governor and speedometer drive gear

1. Governor drive ball.
2. Governor assembly.
3. Circlip–governor.
4. Circlip–speedometer drive gear.
5. Speedometer drive ball.
6. Speedometer drive gear.
7. Circlip–speedometer drive gear.

Section Fd.13

VALVE BODIES ASSEMBLY

Removing

1. Drain the gearbox, unscrew the oil pan retaining screws and remove the pan.
2. Remove the magnet from the rear servo securing bolt.
3. Remove the rear servo, rear clutch, front servo apply and release tubes, by carefully levering them from their push-fit connections.

4. Detach the down-shift cable from the valve cam.
5. Remove the three valve bodies assembly retaining bolts.
6. Lift the valve bodies assembly, disengaging the manual control valve from the rod. Note that the pump tubes and the converter tubes may come away with the valve bodies assembly as it is removed, the tubes can be easily withdrawn from their connections.

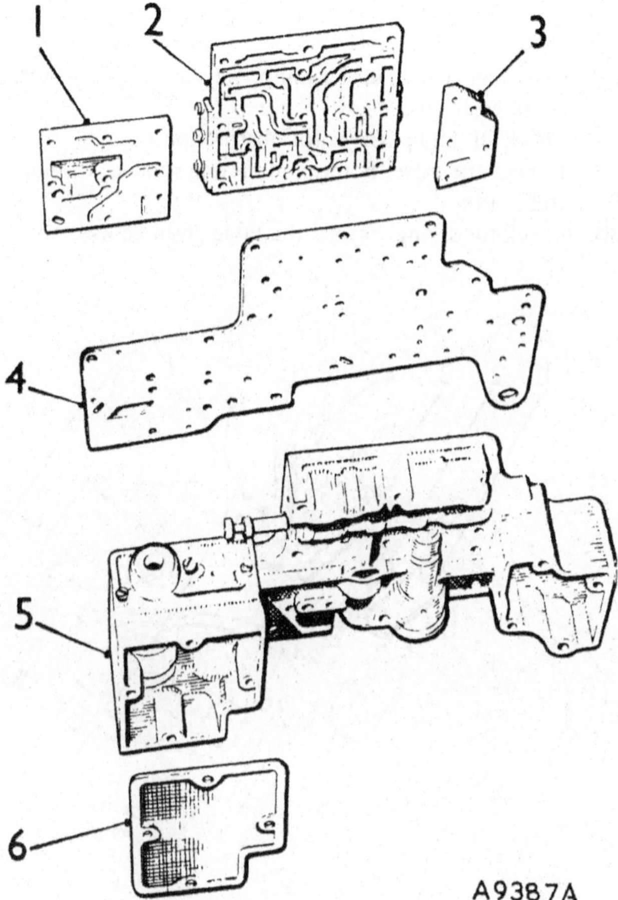

Fig. Fd.12
The valve bodies separated

1. Oil tube collector.
2. Upper valve body.
3. Governor line plate.
4. Separating plate.
5. Lower valve body.
6. Pump oil strainer.

Dismantling

7. Remove the four screws retaining the pump oil strainer and remove strainer.
8. Remove the two long and six short screws retaining the oil tube plate and remove the plate.
9. Unscrew the two screws securing the cam assembly to the valve bodies and remove the cam assembly.
10. Remove the two short screws, from the upper side of the valve bodies assembly.
11. Remove the six screws (five short, one long), from the under-side of the valve bodies assembly.

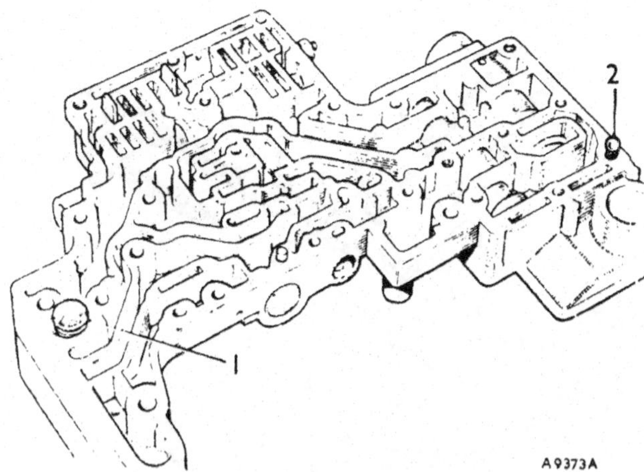

Fig. Fd.13
The check valves in the lower valve body

1 Pump check valve. 2. Converter outlet check valve.

12. Remove the upper valve body from the separator plate and lower body.
13. Unscrew the three screws securing the front end cover and remove the cover.
14. Unscrew the three screws securing the rear end cover and remove the cover.
15. Withdraw the 2 3 shift valve, valve spring, and plunger from the rear end orifice.
16. Withdraw the 1-2 shift valve from the rear end orifice.
17. Remove the 1-2 shift valve spring and valve plunger from the front end orifice.
18. Unscrew the four screws securing the governor line plate, remove the plate, taking care to hold the separating plate against the lower valve body to prevent the valve springs coming free and being misplaced.

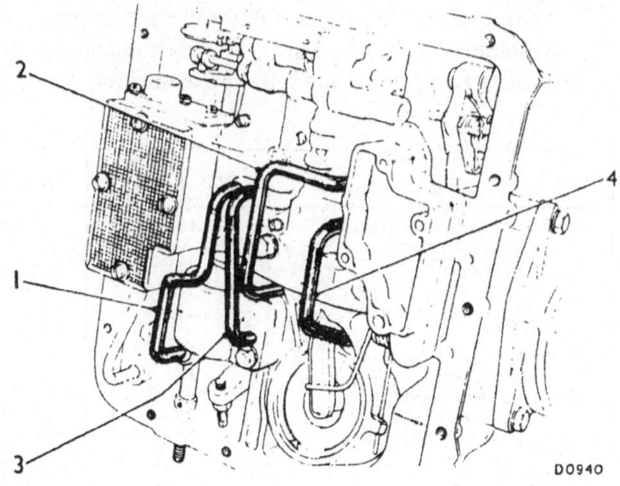

Fig. Fd.14
Location of the oil tubes

1. Front servo release.
2. Rear clutch.
3. Front servo apply.
4. Rear servo.

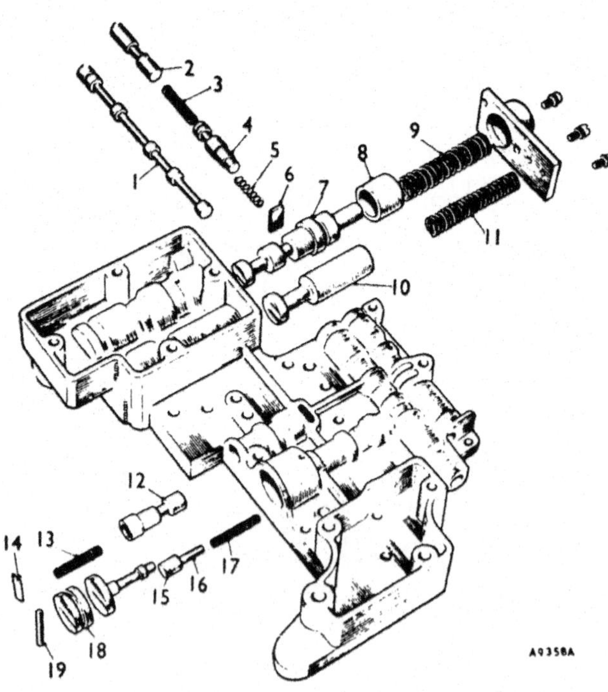

Fig. Fd.15
The lower valve body

1. Manual control valve.
2. Down-shift valve.
3. Spring-down-shift valve.
4. Throttle valve.
5. Spring-throttle valve.
6. Retainer.
7. Primary regulator valve.
8. Sleeve-primary regulator valve.
9. Spring-primary regulator valve.
10. Secondary regulator valve.
11. Spring-secondary regulator valve.
12. Servo orifice control valve.
13. Spring-servo orifice control valve.
14. Retainer.
15. Modulator valve.
16. Plug modulator valve.
17. Spring-modulator valve.
18. Retainer.
19. Dowel pin.

19. Carefully remove the separating plate from the lower valve body assembly.
20. Remove the pump check valve (disc) and spring, the converter check valve (ball) and spring, the manual control valve, and the down-shift valve and spring.
21. Withdraw the throttle valve stop plate and remove the throttle valve, spring and valve spring retainer.
22. Unscrew the three lower valve body end plate retaining screws and remove the end plate.
23. Remove the primary regulating valve spring, valve sleeve and valve.
24. Remove the secondary regulating valve spring and valve.
25. Remove the servo orifice control valve stop, valve spring and valve.
26. Remove the dowel retaining the modulator valve retainer, withdraw the retainer, modulator valve, valve plug and spring.

Inspection

27. Clean all parts in cleaning solvent and dry with compressed air.
28. Check all fluid passages for obstruction.
29. Inspect the valve, bores, and mating surfaces for burrs and scores.
30. Check the springs against the table given below.

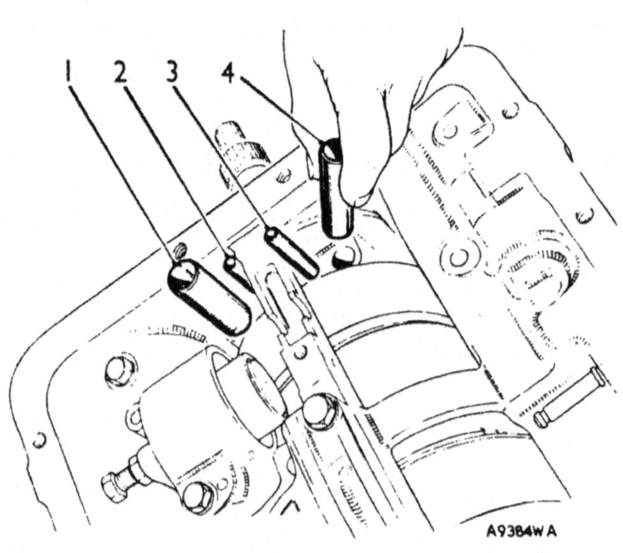

Fig. Fd.16
Location of the pump and converter oil tubes

1. Pump inlet.
2. Converter outlet.
3. Converter inlet.
4. Pump outlet.

Spring	No. of Coils	Wire diameter	Free length	Spring rate
Primary regulator valve	15	.056 in. (1.42 mm.)	2.850 in. (72.4 mm.)	9.3 to 8.4 lb. at 1.090 in. (4.2 to 3.8 kg. at 27.69 mm.)
(Alternative)	14½	.054 in. (1.37 mm.)	2.850 in. (72.4 mm.).	9.3 to 8.4 lb. at 1.090 in. (4.2 to 3.8 kg. at 27.69 mm.)
Secondary regulator valve	21½	.650 in. (16.51 mm.)	2.594 in. (65.9 mm.)	11.25 to 9.75 lb. at 1.937 in. (5.1 to 4.4 kg. at 48.2 mm.)
Throttle valve / (Alternative)	19½ / 18	.032 in. (.81 mm.)	1.175 to 1.185 in. (29.84 to 30.1 mm.)	4.04 to 3.66 lb. at .750 in. (1.8 to 1.6 kg. at 19.05 mm.)
Throttle valve return / (Alternative)	28 / 25	.018 in. (.45 mm.)	.807 in. (20.5 mm.)	.65 to .55 lb. at .593 in. (.29 to .25 kg. at 15.06 mm.)
Servo orifice control valve	25	.024 in. (.6 mm.)	1.213 in. (30.81 mm.)	1.27 to 1.39 lb. at .75 in. (.46 to .47 kg. at 19.05 mm.)
Modulator valve	17	.024 in. (.52 mm.)	1.005 in. (25.5 mm.)	1.01 to 1.13 lb. at .754 in. (.46 to .51 kg. at 19.15 mm.)
1 - 2 shift valve	13½	.024 in. (.52 mm.)	1.094 in. (27.8 mm.)	1.8 to 2.1 lb. at .5 in. (.82 to .95 kg. at 12.7 mm.)
2 - 3 shift valve	22½	.036 in. (.91 mm.)	1.59 in. (40.4 mm.)	1.47 to 1.33 lb. at 1.178 in. (.67 to .6 kg. at 29.92 mm.)

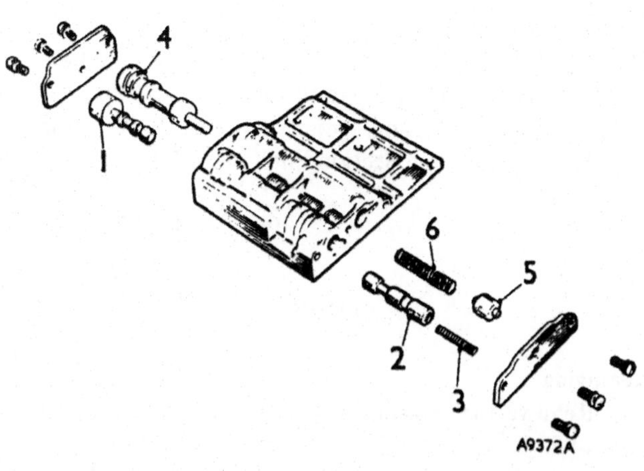

Fig. Fd.17
The upper valve body

1. 1–2 shift valve.
2. 1–2 valve plunger.
3. 1–2 valve spring.
4. 2–3 shift valve.
5. 2–3 valve plunger.
6. 2–3 valve spring.

Reassembling

31. Reverse the dismantling procedure in 7 to 26, noting the following points:
    a. Lubricate all the components with an approved automatic transmission fluid.
    b. Check that all the valves move freely in their bores.
    c. Ensure that the upper and lower valve bodies and the separating plate are correctly aligned before fitting and tightening all the screws.
    d. Tighten the screws evenly to the torque figures given in '**GENERAL DATA**'.

Refitting

32. Reverse the removing procedure in 1 to 6, noting the following points:
    a. Ensure that the pump pressure and converter tubes are correctly located.
    b. Refill the transmission with one of the recommended automatic transmission fluids.

Section Fd.14

FRONT SERVO

Removing

1. Drain the gearbox, unscrew the oil pan retaining screws and remove the pan.
2. Withdraw the tubes connecting the front servo to the valve bodies.
3. Unscrew the two servo securing bolts, lift out the servo and remove the strut from the operating lever.

Dismantling

4. Remove the snap-ring retaining the piston.
5. Withdraw the piston sleeve, piston and piston ring.
6. Remove the piston from its sleeve.
7. If necessary, the lever pivot can be pressed from the servo body and the lever removed.

Inspection

8. Examine the 'O' rings and oil sealing ring for signs of deterioration or damage; renew the rings as necessary.
9. Examine the piston, sleeve and body bore for cracks, scratches and wear.

Reassembling

10. Reverse the dismantling procedure in 4 to 7 ensuring that the piston and lever move freely.

Refitting

11. Reverse the removing procedure in 1 to 3, noting the following points:
    a. To assist refitting, petroleum jelly may be used to stick the strut to the lever.
    b. After refitting, adjust the front brake band as described in Section Fd.8, 12 to 17.

Section Fd.15

REAR SERVO

Removing

1. Drain the gearbox, unscrew the oil pan retaining screws and remove the pan.
2. Withdraw the rear servo, rear clutch and front servo apply tubes.
3. Remove the two rear servo securing bolts, noting that the front bolt is dowelled for the centre support location.
4. Lift out the servo assembly and remove the strut from the operating lever.

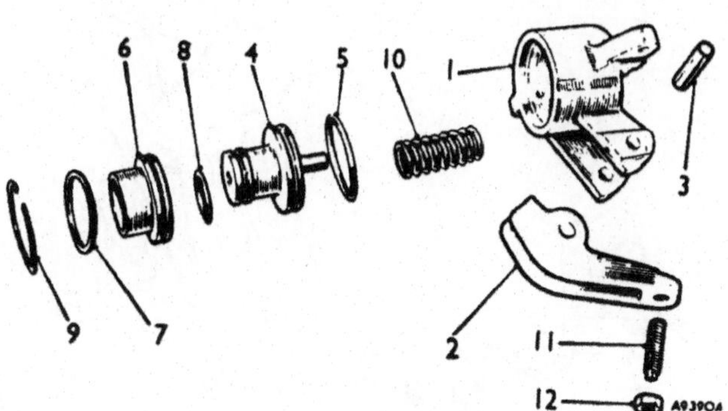

Fig. Fd.18
The front servo

1. Body.
2. Lever.
3. Lever pivot pin.
4. Piston.
5. 'O' ring.
6. Sleeve.
7. Oil sealing ring.
8. 'O' ring.
9. Snap-ring.
10. Spring.
11. Adjusting screw.
12. Locking nut.

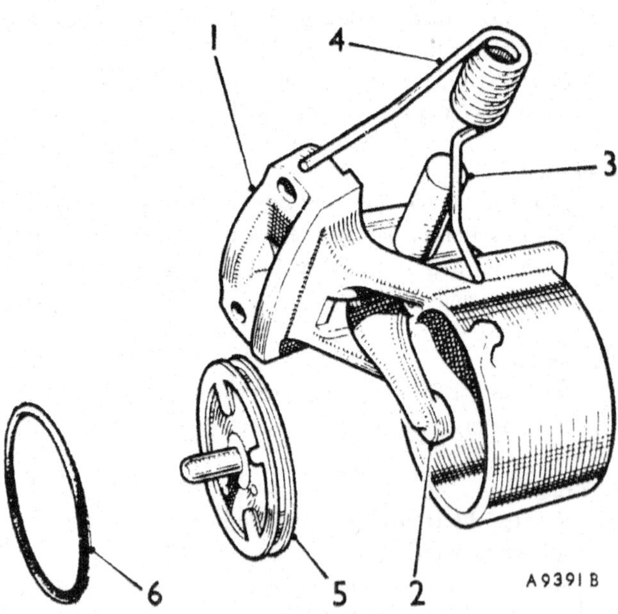

Fig. Fd.19
The rear servo

1. Body.
2. Lever.
3. Lever pivot pin.
4. Lever spring.
5. Piston.
6. Oil sealing ring.

Dismantling

5. Disengage and release the return spring.
6. Withdraw the piston assembly.
7. If necessary, the lever pivot pin can be pressed from the servo body and the lever removed.

Inspection

8. Examine the 'O' ring for signs of deterioration or damage; renew the ring if necessary.
9. Examine the piston and bore for cracks, scratches and wear.

Reassembling

10. Reverse the dismantling procedure in 5 to 7.

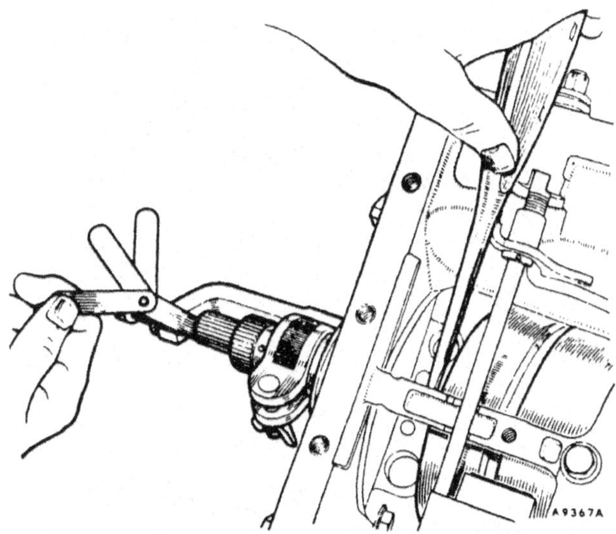

Fig. Fd.20
Using tool 18G 674 to check the gear train end-float

Refitting

11. Reverse the removing procedure in 1 to 4, noting the following points:
    a. To assist refitting, petroleum jelly may be used to stick the strut to the lever.
    b. After refitting, adjust the rear brake band as described in Section Fd.8, 18 to 20.

Section Fd.16

PUMP

Removing

1. Remove the transmission assembly – Section Fd.9, 1 to 5.
2. Invert the transmission assembly and support it in tool 18G 673.
3. Unscrew the oil pan retaining screws and remove the pan.
4. Remove the valve bodies assembly – Section Fd.13, 1 to 6.

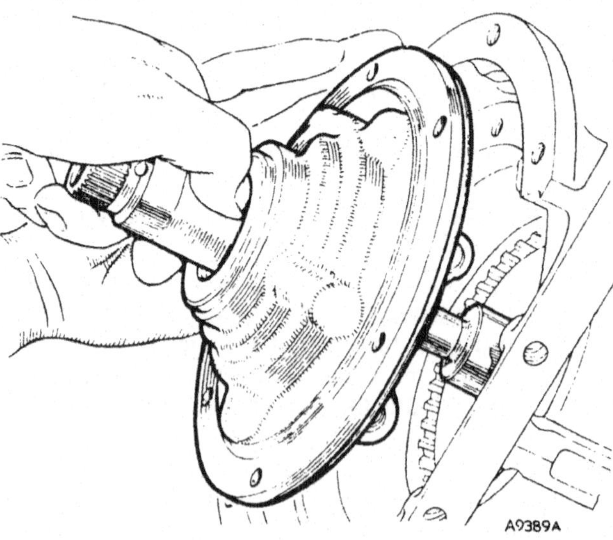

Fig. Fd.21
Withdrawing the pump assembly

5. Before dismantling the transmission any further and to enable any thrust washer wear to be compensated for on reassembly, the gear train end-float should be checked as follows:
    a. Clamp tool 18G 674 to the converter support shaft.
    b. Gently lever the gear train forward and adjust the screw of the tool until it just contacts the end of the input shaft.
    c. Using the minimum pressure, lever the front clutch back, and measure the gap between the tool screw and the end of the input shaft. The permissible end-float is .010 to .030 in. (.254 to .762 mm.).
6. Withdraw the pump inlet and outlet tubes and the converter tubes.
7. Unscrew the six pump retaining bolts and withdraw the pump assembly.
8. Remove the input shaft thrust washer.

Dismantling

9. Remove the five bolts securing the pump body to the converter support.
10. Remove the locating screw.
11. Withdraw the pump body from the converter support.
12. Mark the face of the drive and driven gears for correct reassembly and remove the gears.

Inspection

13. Examine the 'O' ring body seal for signs of deterioration; renew the seal if necessary.
14. Examine the converter support oil seal in the pump body for signs of wear of deterioration; renew the seal if necessary, ensuring that the new seal is fitted fully into the housing.
15. Examine the pump body and gear teeth for scores and excessive wear; light scores may be removed by polishing with a very fine abrasive cloth.

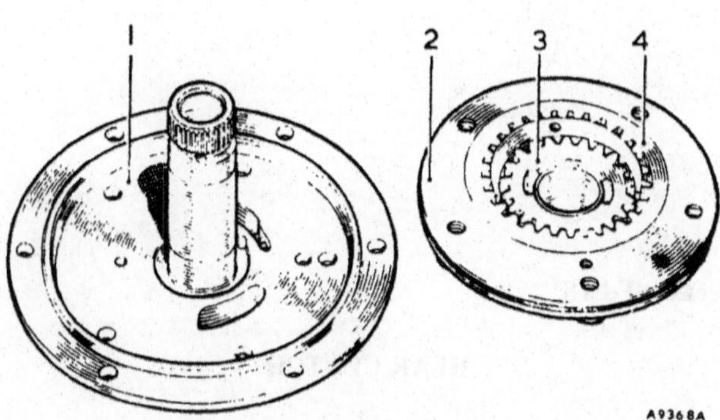

Fig. Fd.22
The pump components

1. Pump adaptor and converter support.
2. Body and bush assembly.
3. Driving gear.
4. Driven gear.

Reassembling

16. Reverse the dismantling procedure in 9 to 12, ensuring that the drive and driven gears are assembled correctly to their dismantling marks.

Refitting

17. Reverse the removing procedure in 1 to 8, noting the following points:
    a. If the end-float measured in 5 (c) exceeds the limit given, a new input shaft thrust washer must be fitted, or, if necessary, a complete new set of thrust washers.
    b. Use petroleum jelly to stick the input shaft thrust washer to the pump adaptor to assist refitting.
    c. Refit the pump assembly to the casing using a new gasket.
    d. Tighten the pump securing bolts to the torque figure given in **'GENERAL DATA'**.

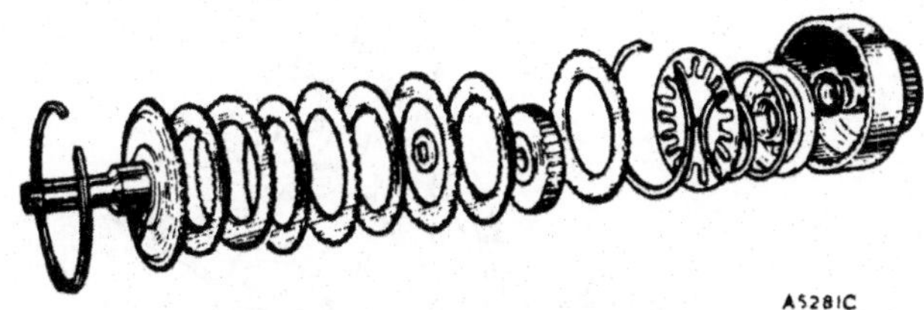

Fig. Fd.23
The front clutch components

Section Fd.17

FRONT CLUTCH

Removing

1. Remove the transmission assembly – Section Fd.9, 1 to 5.
2. Remove the pump assembly – Section Fd.16, 2 to 8.
3. Withdraw the input shaft and front clutch assembly.
4. Remove the bronze and steel thrust washer.

Dismantling

5. Carefully lever out the snap-ring and withdraw the input shaft assembly.
6. Remove the clutch hub thrust washer.
7. Withdraw the clutch hub.
8. Remove the four inner (fibre) and three outer clutch plates; retain the plates in their removal order for reassembly.

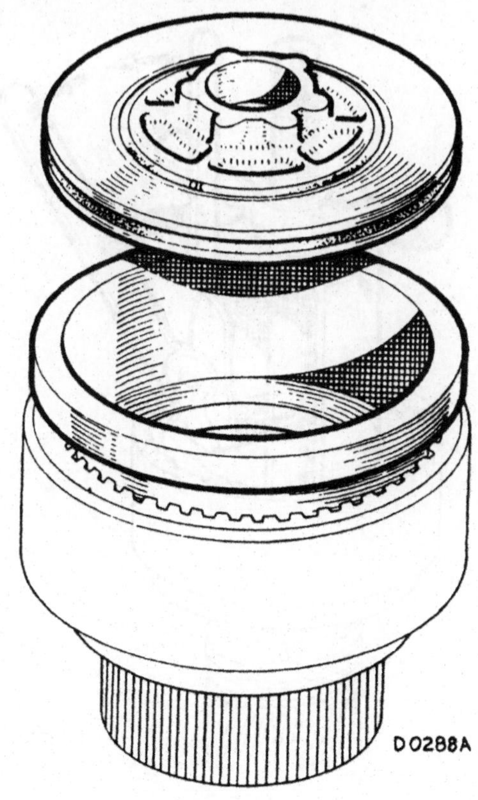

Fig. Fd.24
Using tool 18G 1107 to refit the front clutch piston

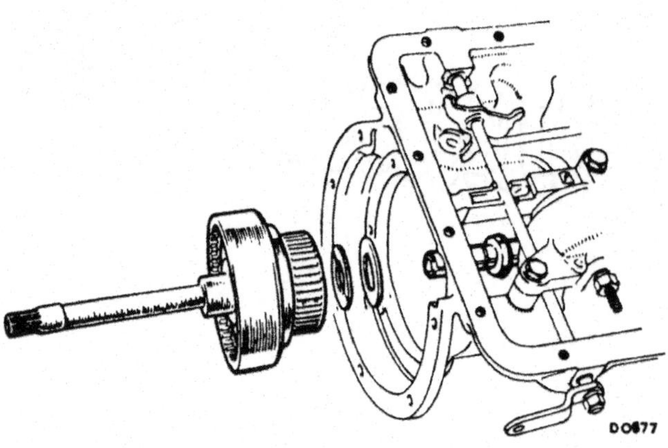

Fig. Fd.25
Fitting order for the thrust washers and front clutch

9. Remove the clutch distance piece.
10. Remove the dished piston spring retaining circlip and remove the spring.
11. Withdraw the piston; apply air pressure to the feed orifice to assist.
12. Remove the snap ring and sealing ring from the piston.
13. Remove the 'O' ring from the clutch housing boss.

Inspection

14. Examine the sealing ring and 'O' rings for signs of deterioration or wear; renew them as necessary.
15. Check the friction plates for wear and burning; burnt or worn plates must be replaced as a set, not individually.

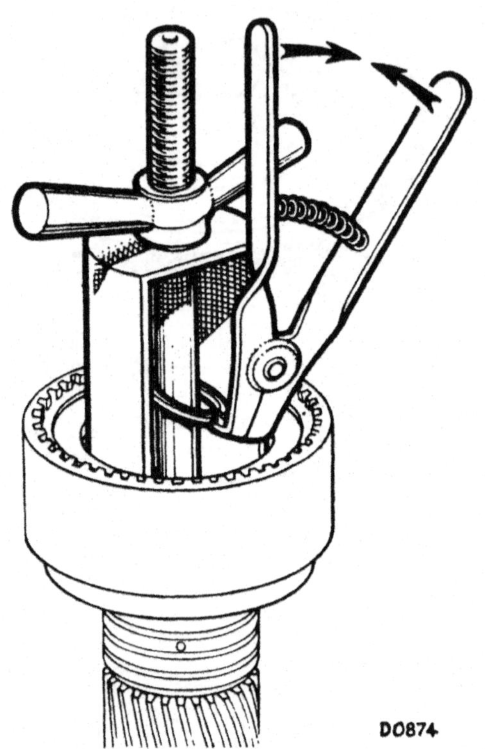

Fig. Fd.26
Using tool 18G 1016 and 18G 675 to remove the rear clutch piston

16. Check the steel plates for distortion. If the distortion exceeds .015 in. (.38 mm.) the plates must be renewed as a set.

Reassembling

17. Reverse the dismantling procedure in 5 to 13, noting that tool 18G 1107 should be used to refit the piston.

Refitting

18. Reverse the removing procedure in 1 to 4.

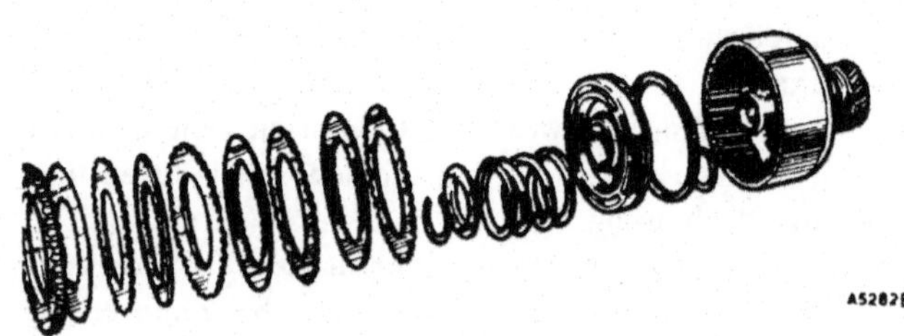

Fig. Fd.27
The rear clutch components

Section Fd.18

REAR CLUTCH

Removing

1. Remove the transmission assembly – Section Fd.10, 1 to 5.
2. Remove the pump assembly – Section Fd.16, 2 to 8.
3. Remove the front clutch – Section Fd.17, 3 to 4.
4. Remove the front servo – Section Fd.14, 1 to 3.
5. Remove the front brake band.
6. Withdraw the rear clutch assembly together with the forward sun gear.

Dismantling

7. Remove the two oil rings from the front of the sun gear shaft and withdraw the sun gear assembly rearwards from the clutch.
8. Remove the rear oil ring and the needle-roller thrust bearing from the forward sun gear.
9. Remove the three oil rings from the rear of the clutch assembly.
10. Lever the snap-ring from the front of the clutch drum and withdraw the pressure plate, the four inner (fibre) plates, and the four outer plates. Retain the plates in their removal order for reassembly.
11. Using tool 18G 1016, compress the piston spring.
12. Remove the retaining circlip using tool 18G 675 and withdraw the seat and spring.
13. Remove the piston by shocking the drum on a soft surface.
14. Remove the piston seal.

Inspection

15. Examine the piston and drum seals for signs of deterioration or wear; renew the seals if necessary.
16. Check the friction plates for wear and burning; burnt or worn plates must be replaced as a set, not individually.
17. Check the steel plates for wear. The plates are coned .010 to .020 in. (.03 to .05 mm.); renew the plates in sets only.
18. Examine the ring seals and internal bush for excessive wear or damage.
19. Examine the needle-roller thrust bearings for wear and damage.

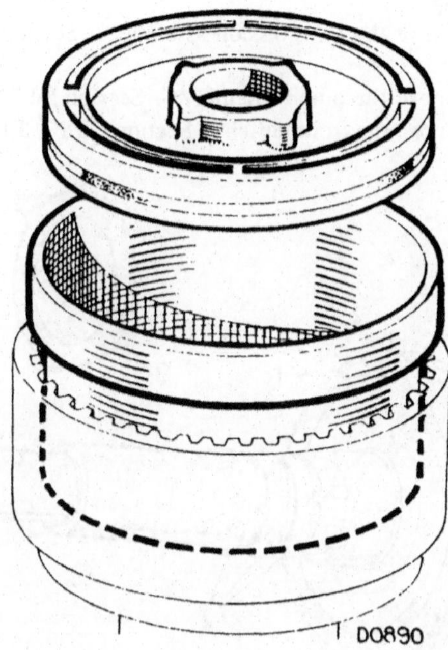

Fig. Fd.28
Using tool 18G 702 to refit the rear clutch piston

Reassembling

20. Reverse the dismantling procedure in 7 to 14, noting the following points:
    a. Refit the piston into the drum using tool 18G 702.
    b. Ensure that if the original clutch plates are being refitted they are in their dismantled positions, and that the coning on the steel plates is facing the same direction.

Refitting

21. Reverse the removing procedure in 1 to 6.

Section Fd.19

CENTRE SUPPORT AND PLANET GEARS

Removing

1. Remove the transmission assembly – Section Fd.10, 1 to 5.

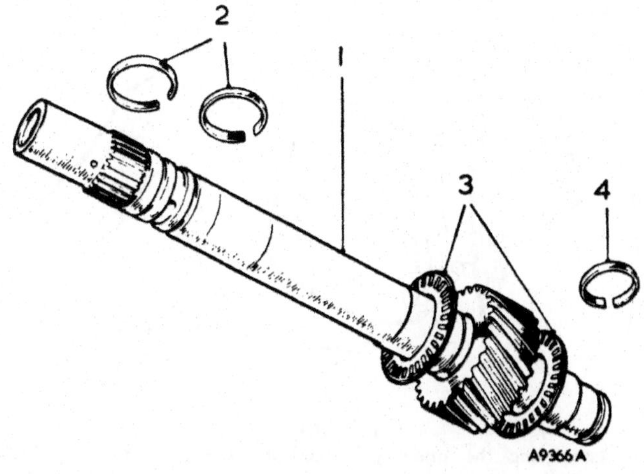

Fig Fd.29
Forward sun gear components

1. Forward sun gear assembly.
2. Front clutch sealing rings.
3. Needle thrust washer.
4. Governor feed sealing ring.

2. Remove the pump assembly – Section Fd.16, 2 to 8.
3. Remove the front clutch – Section Fd.17, 3 to 4.
4. Remove the front servo – Section Fd.14, 1 to 3.
5. Remove the rear clutch – Section Fd.18, 5 to 6.
6. Remove the rear servo – Section Fd.15, 2 to 4.
7. Unscrew the two remaining centre support locating bolts.
8. Drift the front servo stop from the casing.
9. Withdraw the centre support and planet gears from the casing.

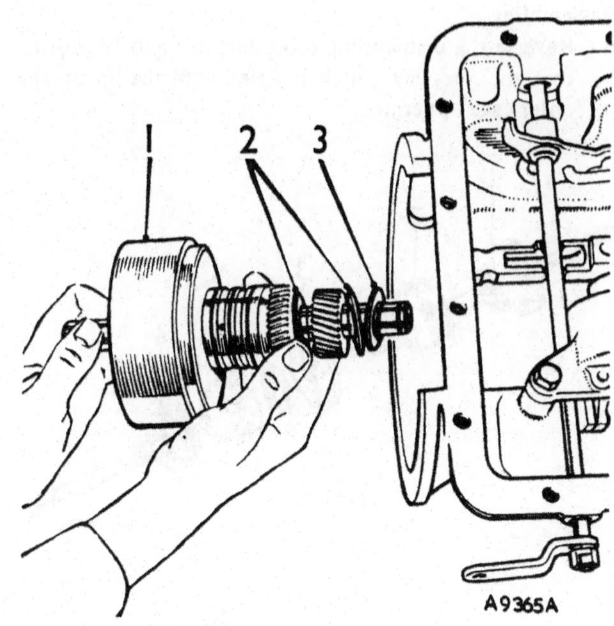

Fig. Fd.30
Fitting the rear clutch and forward sun gear

1. Rear clutch.
2. Needle thrust washers.
3. Needle thrust bearing plate.

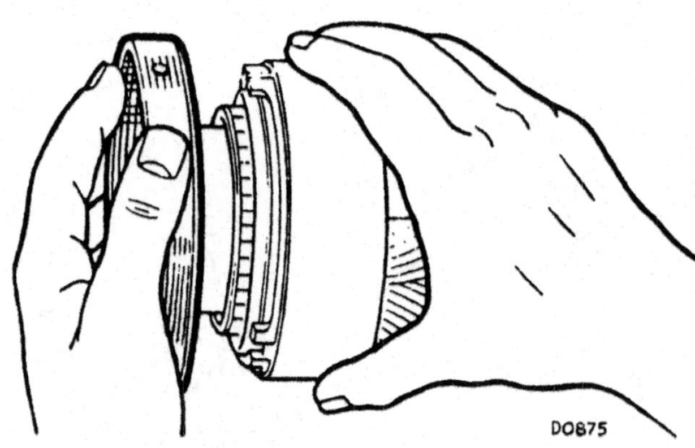

Fig. Fd.31
Assembling the one-way clutch, planet gears and centre support

10. Remove the bearing washer and needle-roller thrust bearing fitted between the gear carrier and the driven shaft.

Dismantling

11. Withdraw the centre support from the planet gear carrier, turning the support to relax the one-way clutch.
12. Ease the one-way clutch from the outer race.
13. Lever out the outer race retaining circlip and remove the outer race.

Inspection

14. Examine the gears for worn or damaged teeth. Check the fit of the gear carrier pins.
15. Inspect the bearing washer and needle-roller thrust bearing for wear and damage.

Reassembling

16. Reverse the dismantling procedure in 11 to 13, noting that the one-way clutch is fitted with the lip on the outer cage uppermost.

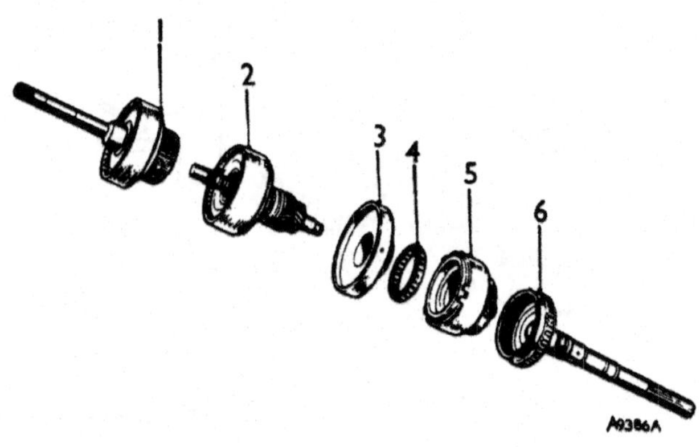

Fig. Fd.32
The gear train components

1. Input shaft and front clutch assembly.
2. Rear clutch and forward gear assembly.
3. Centre support.
4. One-way clutch.
5. Planet gears and rear drum assembly.
6. Driven shaft and ring gear assembly.

Refitting

17. Reverse the removing procedure in 1 to 10, noting that the thrust bearing washer is fitted with its lip towards the rear.

Section Fd.20

DRIVEN SHAFT AND RING GEAR

Removing

1. Remove the transmission assembly – Section Fd.10, 1 to 5.
2. Remove the pump assembly – Section Fd.16, 2 to 8.
3. Remove the front clutch – Section Fd.17, 3 to 4.

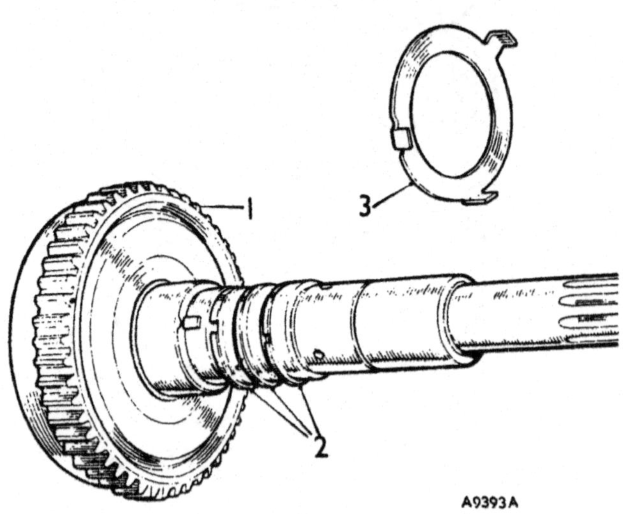

Fig. Fd.33
The drive shaft

1. Ring gear and driven shaft. 2. Oil sealing rings. 3. Thrust washer.

4. Remove the front servo – Section Fd.14, 1 to 3.
5. Remove the rear clutch – Section Fd.18, 5 to 6.
6. Remove the rear servo – Section Fd.15, 2 to 4.
7. Remove the governor assembly and speedometer drive – Section Fd.12, 2 to 7.
8. Remove the centre support and planet gears – Section Fd.19, 7 to 10.
9. Withdraw the rear brake band.
10. Withdraw the driven shaft and ring gear assembly.

Dismantling

11. Remove the thrust washer and the three oil sealing rings from the shaft.
12. Lever the snap-ring from the ring gear and withdraw the shaft from the gear.

Inspection

13. Examine the sealing rings for signs of deterioration or wear.

14. Check the ring gear and shaft splines for wear or damage.

Reassembling

15. Reverse the dismantling procedure in 11 and 12.

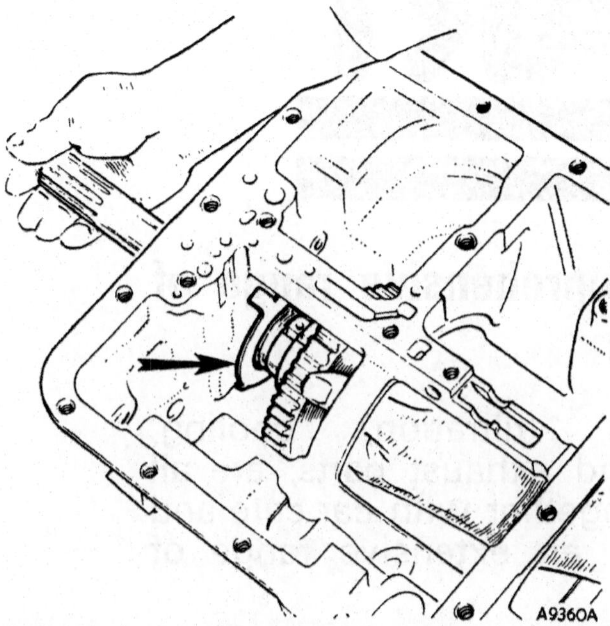

Fig. Fd.34
Fitting the driven shaft assembly. Note the position of the thrust washer (arrowed)

Refitting

16. Reverse the removing procedure in 1 to 10, noting that the tabs of the driven shaft washer fit into the recesses in the boss of the casing.

Section Fd.21

MANUAL VALVE SHAFT AND LEVER

Removing

1. Remove the valve bodies assembly – Section Fd.13, 1 to 6.
2. Withdraw the parking brake link retaining clip from the parking pawl end of the link and detach the link from the torsion lever.
3. Remove the roll pin retaining the locating collar to the shaft.
4. Slide the shaft away from the inhibitor switch and remove the detent ball and spring.
5. Slide the manual valve detent lever away from its retaining pin and remove the pin.
6. Withdraw the shaft and remove the collar, manual valve detent lever and lever spring.

Inspection

7. Examine the shaft and levers for excessive wear and damage.
8. Check the detent spring for loss of tension.

Refitting

9. Reverse the removing procedure in 1 to 6.

SECTION G

THE PROPELLER SHAFT

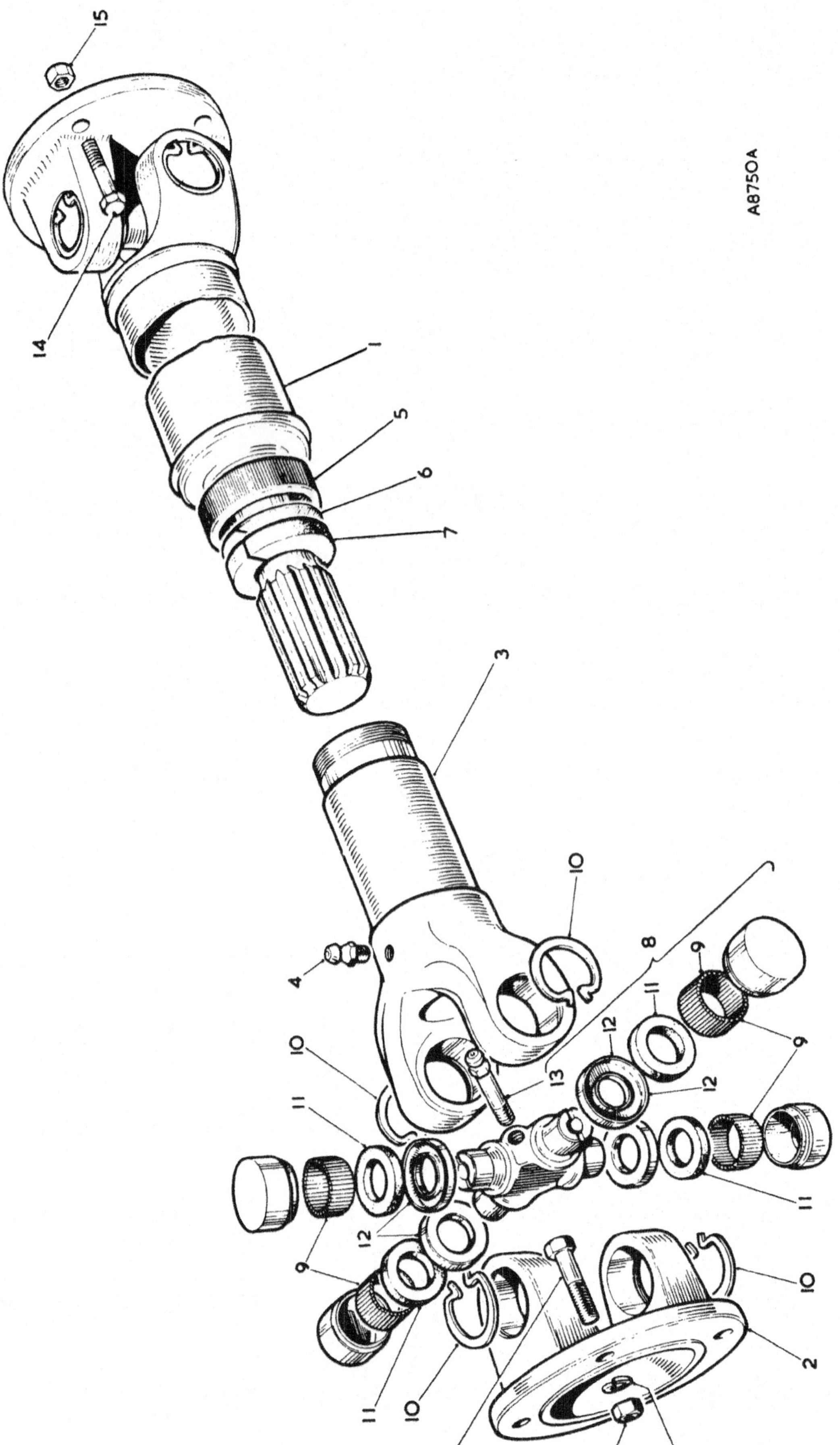

THE PROPELLER SHAFT COMPONENTS

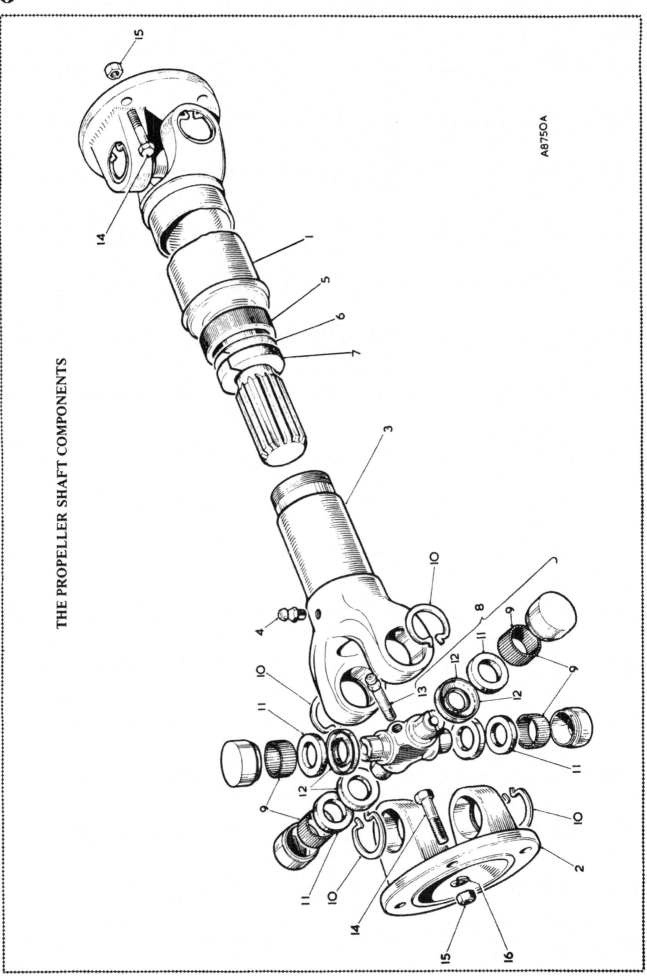

A8750A

KEY TO THE PROPELLER SHAFT COMPONENTS

No.	Description	No.	Description
1.	Shaft assembly–propeller.	9.	Bearing assembly–needle.
2.	Flange yoke.	10.	Circlip.
3.	Sleeve assembly–yoke.	11.	Gasket.
4.	Lubricator.	12.	Retainer–gasket.
5.	Cap–dust.	13.	Lubricator–journal.
6.	Washer–dust cap (steel).	14.	Bolt–shaft to pinion flange (front and rear).
7.	Washer–dust cap (cork).	15.	Nut for bolt.
8.	Journal assembly.	16.	Washer–spring–for front bolt.

GENERAL DESCRIPTION

The propeller shaft and universal joints are of the Hardy Spicer type with needle-roller bearings in the universal joints.

The rear end of the shaft is flanged and carries the rear universal joint flange yoke. The front end of the shaft is splined and engages a sleeve and yoke assembly. In the assembled condition a dust cap, steel washer, and cork washer seal the end of the sleeve and the sliding joint.

Each universal joint is made up of a spider and four gaskets, retainers, and needle bearing assemblies. Each needle bearing assembly is retained in its yoke by a circlip.

The yoke flanges are secured to the pinion and gearbox flanges respectively with eight bolts, spring washers, and Aerotight or Nyloc nuts.

Section G.1

LUBRICATION

A nipple is provided for lubricating the sliding yoke at the front end of the propeller shaft. On non-sealed type propeller shafts lubrication nipples are also provided on the front and rear universal joints. Three or four strokes of a grease gun are required when lubricating.

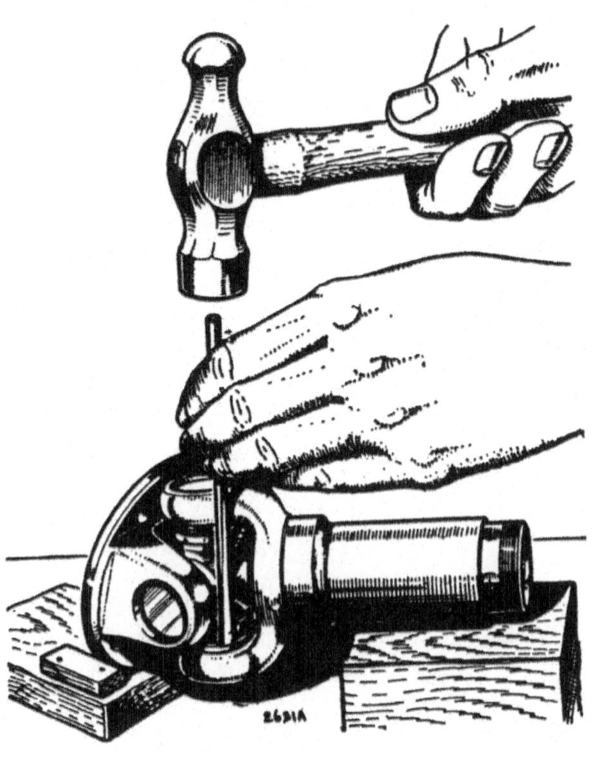

Fig. G.1
When dismantling a universal joint the bearings may be tapped out with a small diameter rod from the inside as shown. Take care not to damage the roller races

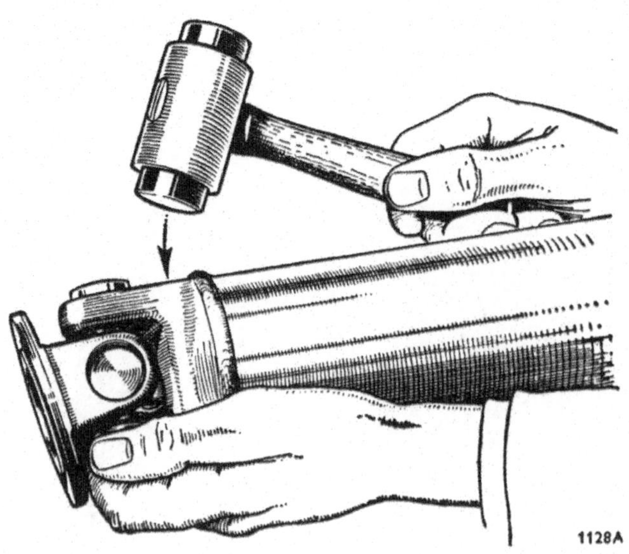

Fig. G.2
Where to apply light blows to the yoke after removing the retaining circlip

Section G.2

REMOVING AND REPLACING THE PROPELLER SHAFT

To remove the propeller shaft proceed as follows:

1. Mark the yoke flanges and the gearbox and rear axle flanges to assist in refitting them in their original positions. **This is most important.**
2. Remove the nuts, washers, and bolts securing the flanges and lower the propeller shaft.

Replacement is a reversal of the removal sequence, but ensure that the joint faces of the flanges are perfectly smooth and clean and that they are correctly aligned with the gearbox and rear axle flanges.

Section G.3

DISMANTLING THE PROPELLER SHAFT

1. Unscrew the dust cap from the sleeve and slide the sleeve off the shaft. Remove the steel washer and the cork washer.
2. Remove all circlips from the universal joints. If a circlip appears to be tight in its groove lightly tap the end of the bearing race to relieve the pressure against the ring.
3. Remove the lubricators from the journals and the sleeve.
4. Hold the shaft yoke in one hand and tap the radius of the yoke with a hammer. The bearing should begin to emerge. Turn the yoke over and remove the bearing with the fingers.
5. If necessary, tap the bearing race from inside with a small diameter bar taking care not to damage the bearing face.

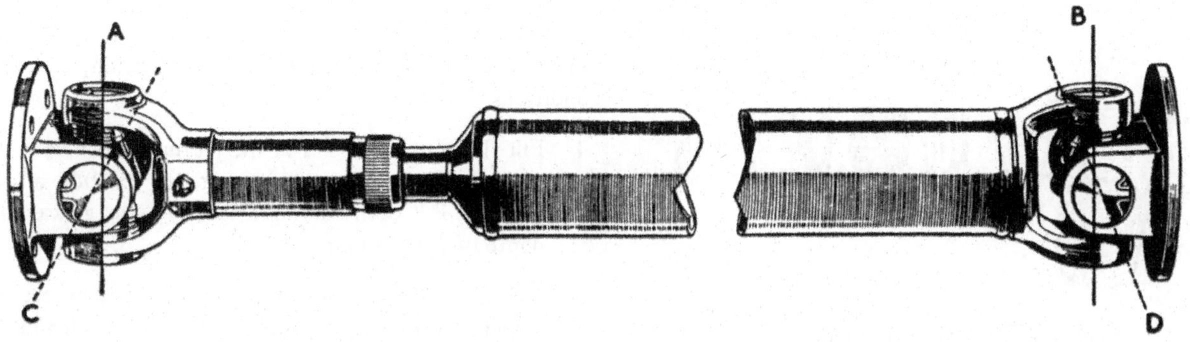

When the splined shaft is assembled to the drive shaft it is essential to see that the forked yokes on both shafts have their axes parallel to each other. In other words, the yoke (A) must be in alignment with the yoke (B), and the flange yoke (C) must be in alignment with the flange yoke (D)

6. Hold the bearing in a vertical position and remove the race from the bottom side to avoid dropping the needle rollers.
7. Repeat operations 4, 5, and 6 for the opposite bearing.
8. Rest the exposed trunnions on wood blocks and tap the top lug of the flange yoke to remove the bearing race. Turn the yoke over and repeat the operation to remove the remaining bearing.
9. Repeat operations 4 to 8 to remove the bearings from the sleeve and yoke assembly.
10. Remove the gaskets and their retainers from the spider journals.

Section G.4

EXAMINING THE PROPELLER SHAFT

Thoroughly clean, wash, and dry all components prior to examination, paying particular attention to the lubrication passages.

1. Check the splines on the sleeve and shaft for indentation.
2. Examine the bearing races and journals for wear.
3. Examine the holes in the yokes and flanges for ovality.
4. Ensure that the bearing races are a light driving fit in their yokes.
5. Check the flange yoke faces for burrs, cracks, or fractures.

All worn or unserviceable parts must be renewed.

Section G.5

ASSEMBLING THE PROPELLER SHAFT

1. To provide a good seal, apply a thin coat of shellac to the gasket retaining shoulders on the spiders.
2. Use a hollow drift to refit the retainers and then fit new gaskets.
3. Smear the walls of the races with grease (page P.2), fit the needle rollers to the races and then fill the races with grease.
4. Insert the spiders in the flange yokes and **ensure that the lubricating nipple bosses are facing away from the yoke flanges.**
5. Using a soft drift $\frac{1}{32}$ in. (.79 mm.) smaller than the diameter of the races fit the bearings to the spider journals and the holes in the yokes.
6. Place the dust cap, steel washer, and a new cork gasket over the spined portion of the shaft.
7. Grease the inside of the sleeve, line up the arrows on the sleeve and splined portion of the shaft, and fit the sleeve to the shaft. Fit the washers and screw the dust cap to the sleeve.
8. Wipe off any excess grease and fit the lubricators to the sleeve and spiders.

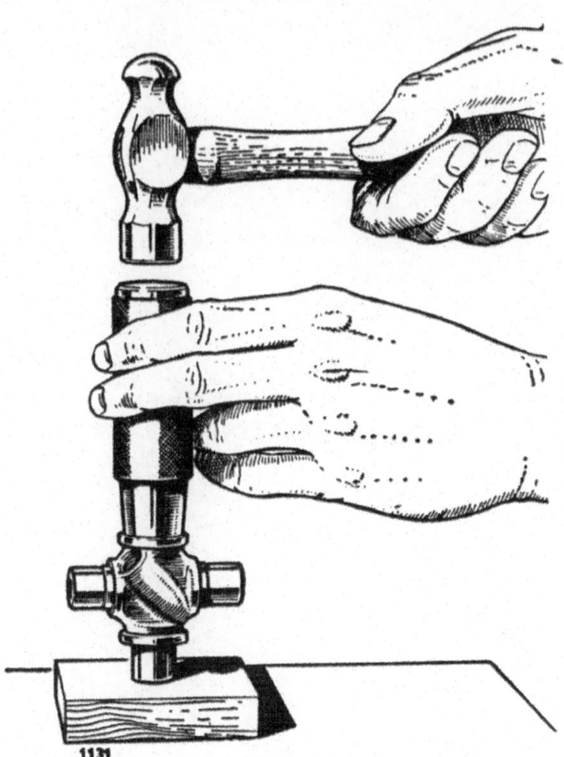

Fig. G.4
When replacing the gasket retainer use should be made of a hollow drift to tap it into place without damage

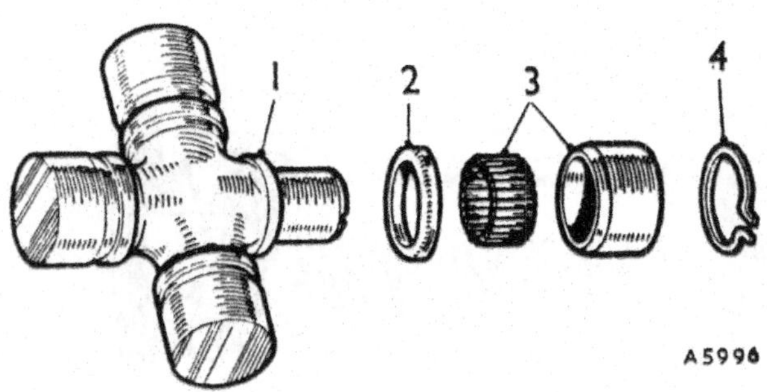

Fig. G.5
A universal joint bearing–sealed type

1. Journal spider.
2. Rubber seal.
3. Needle rollers and bearing.
4. Circlip.

Section G.6

PROPELLER SHAFT–SEALED TYPE

Dismantling

Carry out operations 1, 2, 4, 5, 6, 7, 8, and 9 of Section G.3.

Inspection

As detailed in Section G.4.

Reassembling

It is of extreme importance that the assembly of the journals be carried out under absolutely clean, dust-free conditions.

1. Fill the reservoir holes in the journal spider with the recommended grease taking care to exclude all air pockets. Fill each bearing assembly with grease to a depth of $\frac{1}{8}$ in. (3 mm.).
2. Fit new seals to the spider journals and insert the spider into the flange yoke, tilting it to engage in the yoke bores.
3. Fit a bearing assembly into the yoke bore in the bottom position, and using a soft-nosed drift slightly smaller in diameter than the hole in the yoke, tap it into the yoke bore until it is possible to fit the circlip. Repeat this operation for the other three bearings starting opposite the bearing first fitted.
4. After assembly, carefully remove all surplus grease with a soft cloth. If the bearing appears to bind, tap lightly with a wooden mallet; this will relieve any pressure of the bearing on the ends of the journals.

SECTION H

THE REAR AXLE AND SUSPENSION

THREE-QUARTER FLOATING

THE REAR AXLE COMPONENTS

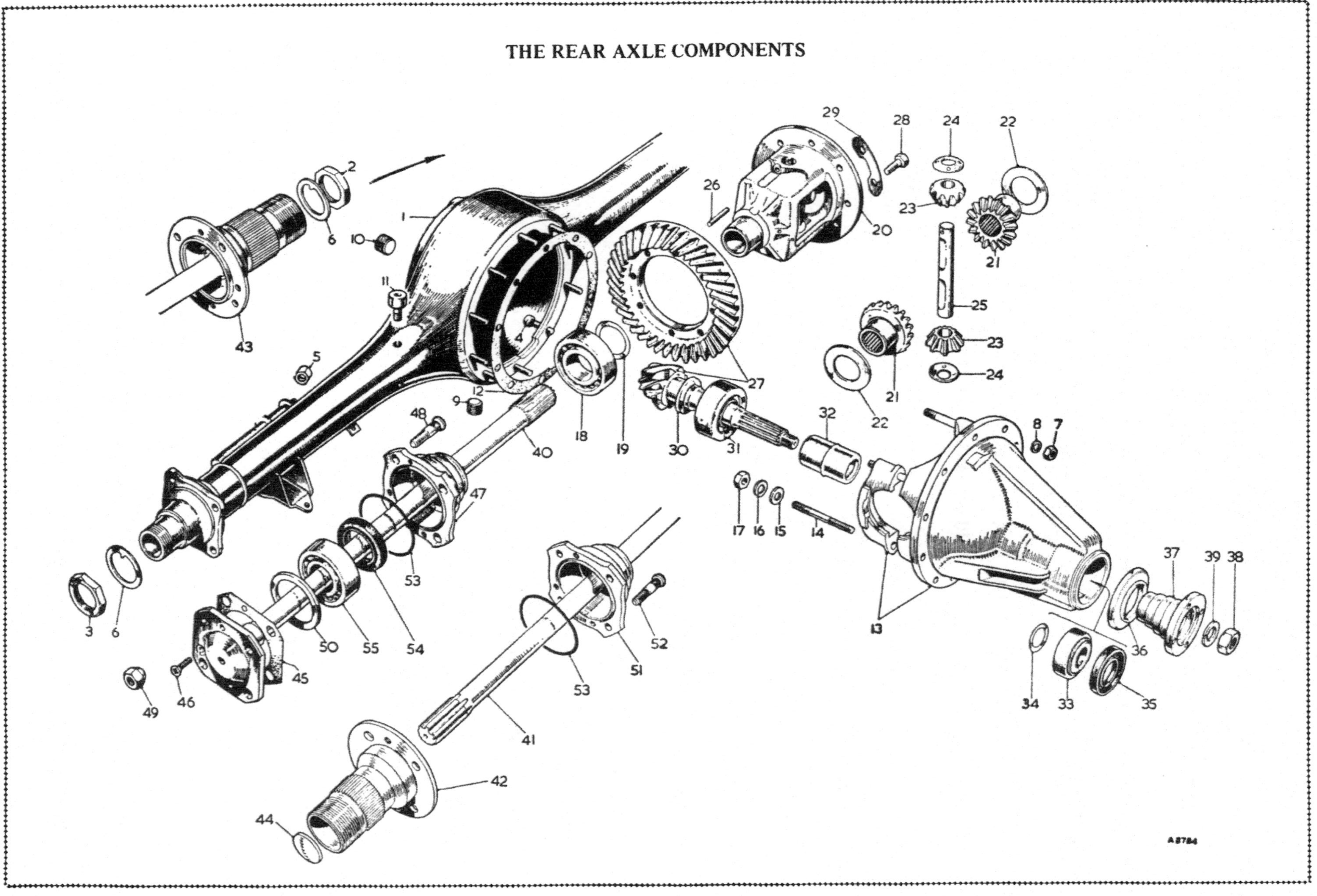

KEY TO THE REAR AXLE COMPONENTS

No.	Description	No.	Description	No.	Description	
1.	Case assembly.	20.	Cage–differential.	38.	Nut–pinion.	
2.	Nut–bearing retaining–R.H.T.	21.	Wheel–differential.	39.	Washer–spring–nut.	
3.	Nut–bearing retaining–L.H.T.	22.	Washer–thrust–differential wheel.	40.	Shaft–axle (disc wheels).	
4.	Stud–gear carrier.	23.	Pinion–differential.	41.	Shaft–axle	(wire wheels). (41–44)
5.	Nut–rebound spindle.	24.	Washer–thrust–differential pinion.	42.	Hub extension–R.H.	
6.	Washer–bearing retaining nut.	25.	Pin–pinion.	43.	Hub extension–L.H.	
7.	Nut–gear carrier to axle case.	26.	Peg–pinion pin.	44.	Plug–welch–hub extension	
8.	Washer–spring–nut.	27.	Crown wheel and pinion–11/43.	45.	Joint–shaft to hub.	
9.	Plug–drain.	28.	Bolt–crown wheel to differential cage.	46.	Screw–countersunk–shaft to hub.	
10.	Plug–filler.	29.	Lock washer–bolt.	47.	Hub assembly	(disc wheels). (47–50)
11.	Breather assembly.	30.	Washer–pinion–thrust–.112 to .126 in. (2.85 to 3.20 mm.).	48.	Stud–wheel	
12.	Joint–gear carrier to axle case.	31.	Bearing–pinion–inner.	49.	Nut–wheel stud	
13.	Carrier assembly.	32.	Spacer–bearing.	50.	Spacer–bearing	
14.	Stud–bearing cap.	33.	Bearing–pinion–outer.	51.	Hub assembly	(wire wheels). (51–52)
15.	Washer–plain–bearing cap.	34.	Shim–outer bearing–.004 to .030 in. (.102 to .762 mm.).	52.	Stud–wheel	
16.	Washer–spring–bearing cap.	35.	Seal–oil.	53.	Ring–oil seal.	
17.	Nut–stud.	36.	Cover–dust.	54.	Seal–hub.	
18.	Bearing–differential.	37.	Flange–universal joint.	55.	Bearing–hub.	
19.	Washer–bearing–packing–.002 to .010 in. (.051 to .254 mm.).					

GENERAL DESCRIPTION

The rear axle is of the three-quarter-floating type, incorporating hypoid final reduction gears. The axle shafts, pinion, and differential assemblies can be withdrawn without removing the axle from the vehicle. Wire wheels are available as optional equipment.

The rear axle wheel bearing outer races are located in the hubs; the inner races are mounted on the axle tube and secured by nuts and lock washers. Wheel studs in the hubs pass through the brake-drums and axle shaft driving flanges.

The differential and pinion shaft bearings are preloaded, the amount of preload being adjustable by shims. The position of the pinion in relation to the crown wheel is determined by a spacing washer. The backlash between the gears is adjustable by shims.

Suspension is by semi-elliptic leaf springs, rubber-mounted, and the shackles are fitted with rubber bushes of the flexing type.

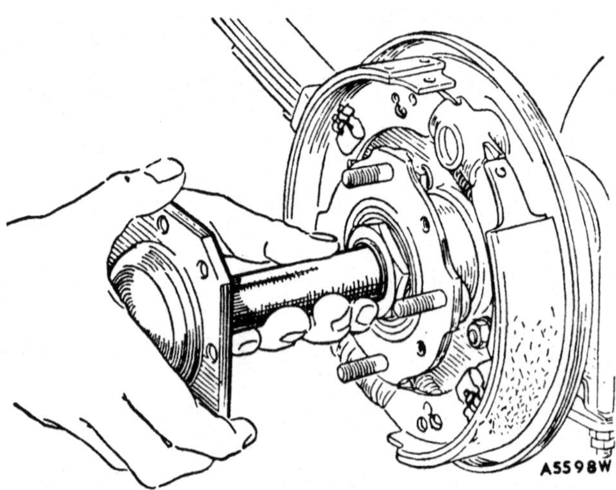

Fig. H.1
Remove the brake drum and drive shaft flange locating screws and then withdraw the axle shaft

LUBRICATION

Oil level
Check the level, and top up if necessary. The filler plug is located on the rear of the axle and also serves as an oil level indicator. After topping up allow time for any surplus oil to run out. This is most important; if the axle is overfilled, the oil may leak through to the brake linings and lessen their efficiency.
NOTE.–It is essential that only Hypoid oil be used in the rear axle.

Draining
The most suitable time for draining is after a long journey whilst the oil is still warm. Clean the drain plug before it is replaced and tightened.

Refill the axle with fresh oil.

Section H.1

REMOVING AND REPLACING A BRAKE-DRUM AND AXLE SHAFT

Jack up the car and place blocks under the spring as close as possible to the axle.

Remove the wheel.

Release the hand brake.

Disc wheels
Unscrew and remove the two countersunk Phillips screws locating the drum and tap it from the hub. It may be necessary to slacken off the brake adjustment slightly if the shoes hold the drum.

Unscrew the countersunk Phillips locating screw in the axle shaft driving flange.

Withdraw the axle shaft by gripping the flange or carefully prising it with a screwdriver. Note the gasket and bearing spacer between the axle flange and the hub.

Wire wheels
Unscrew the four nuts securing the drum to the hub and tap the drum from the hub. It may be necessary to slacken off the brake adjustment to free the drum.

Unscrew the countersunk Phillips screw securing the hub extension flange to the hub. Withdraw the hub extension and axle shaft. The extension flange has two threaded holes so that the shaft can be pulled out if it is tight. Note the rubber ring oil seal between the hub extension flange and the hub.

To replace the shaft and drum reverse the above sequence of operations.

Section H.2

REMOVING AND REPLACING A HUB

Remove the drum and axle shaft as detailed in Section H.1.

Fig. H.2
Use Service tool 18G 304 with adaptor 18G 304 A to withdraw the hub

Remove the bearing spacer.

Knock back the tab of the locking washer and unscrew the nut with a suitable spanner.

Tilt the lock washer to disengage the key from the slot in the threaded portion of the axle casing; remove the washer.

The hub can then be withdrawn with a suitable puller such as Service tools 18G 304 and 18G 304 A. The bearing and oil seal will be withdrawn with the hub.

Before assembly, repack the hub bearings with grease.

The bearing is not adjustable and is replaced in one straightforward operation.

When reassembling it is essential that the outer face of the bearing spacer should protrude from .001 in. (.025 mm.) to .004 in. (.102 mm.) beyond the outer face of the hub when the bearing is pressed into position. This ensures that the bearing is gripped between the abutment shoulder in the hub and the driving flange of the axle shaft.

Section H.3

RENEWING THE PINION OIL SEAL

Mark the propeller shaft and the pinion driving flanges so that they may be replaced in the same relative positions. Disconnect the propeller shaft.

Knock back the lock washer and unscrew the nut in the centre of the driving flange. Remove the nut and washer and withdraw the flange and pressed-on end cover from the pinion shaft.

Extract the oil seal from the casing.

Press a new oil seal into the casing with the edge of the sealing ring facing inwards.

Replace the driving flange end cover, taking care not to damage the edge of the oil seal. Tighten the nut with a torque wrench to a reading of 140 lb. ft. (19.34 kg. m.).

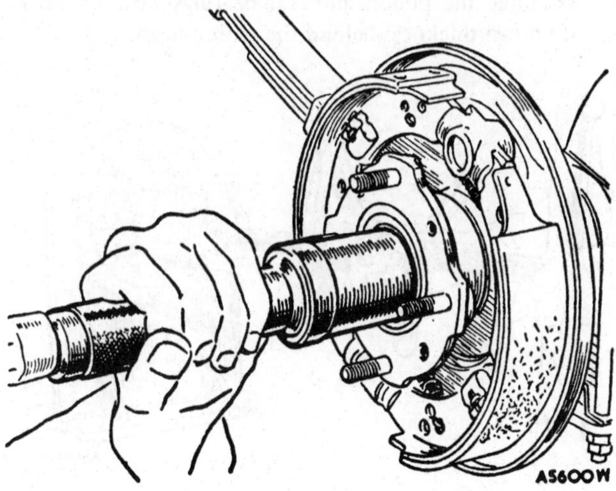

Fig. H.3
Use Service tools 18G 134 and 18G 134 P to drift the hub into position

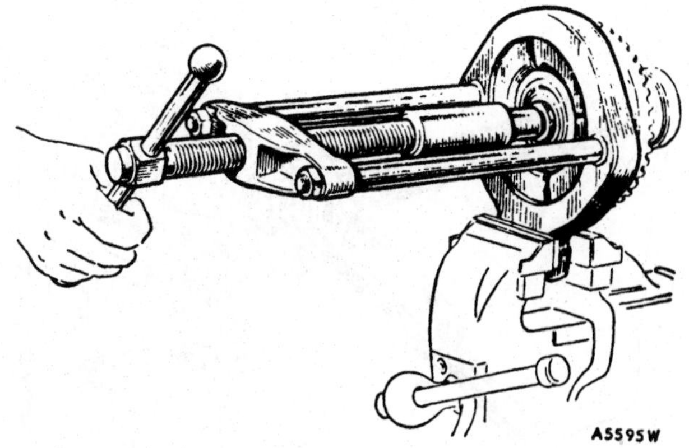

Fig. H.4
Use Service tool 18G 47 C and adaptor 18G 47 T to remove the differential bearings

Reconnect the propeller shaft, taking care to fit the two flanges with the locating marks in alignment.

Section H.4

REMOVING THE DIFFERENTIAL PINIONS

Drain the oil from the axle casing.

Remove the axle shafts as detailed in Section H.1.

Mark the propeller shaft and pinion shaft driving flanges so that they may be replaced in the same relative positions; unscrew the self-locking nuts and disconnect the joint.

Unscrew the 10 nuts securing the bevel pinion and gear carrier to the axle casing; withdraw the gear carrier complete with the pinion shaft and differential assembly.

Make sure that the differential bearing housing caps are marked so that they can be replaced in their original positions, then remove the four nuts and spring washers. Withdraw the bearing caps and differential assembly.

Tap out the dowel pin locating the differential pinion shaft. The diameter of the pin is $\frac{3}{16}$ in. (4.8 mm.) and it must be tapped out from the crown wheel side as the hole into which it fits has a slightly smaller diameter at the crown wheel end to prevent the pin from passing right through. It may be necessary to clean out the metal peened over the entry hole with a $\frac{3}{16}$ in. (4.8 mm.) drill in order to facilitate removal of the dowel pin. Drive out the differential pinion shaft. The pinions and thrust washers can then be removed from the cage.

Section H.5

REPLACING THE DIFFERENTIAL PINIONS

Examine the pinions and thrust washers and renew as required.

Replace the pinions, thrust washers, and pinion shaft in the differential cage and insert the dowel pin. Peen over the entry hole.

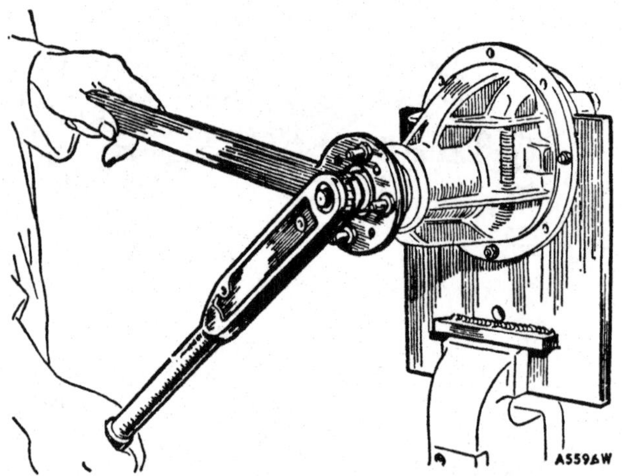

Fig. H.5
Use Service tool 18G 34 A to hold the bevel pinion flange while loosening or tightening the bevel pinion nut

Reassembly is now a reversal of the instructions given in Section H.4. Refill the axle with the recommended oil.

If it proves necessary to fit any new parts other than those detailed in Sections H.2, H.3, or H.5 the axle assembly must be set up as in Section H.7.

Section H.6

DISMANTLING THE CROWN WHEEL AND PINION

Remove the differential assembly as detailed in Section H.4.

Remove the differential bearings from the differential cage, using Service tool 18G 47 C with adaptors 18G 47 T. Note that the word 'THRUST' is stamped on the thrust face of each bearing and that shims are fitted between the inner ring of each bearing and the differential cage.

Knock back the tabs of the locking washers, unscrew the nuts from the bolts securing the crown wheel to the differential cage, and remove the crown wheel.

Knock back the tab of the locking washer and unscrew the pinion nut; remove the driving flange and the pressed end cover.

Drive the pinion shaft towards the rear; it will carry with it the inner race and the rollers of the rear bearing, leaving the outer race and the complete front bearing in position.

The inner race of the front bearing may be removed with the fingers and the outer races of both bearings withdrawn with Service tool 18G 264, using adaptors 18G 264 E and 18G 264 F.

Slide off the pinion sleeve and shims; withdraw the rear bearing inner race from the pinion shaft using Service tool 18G 47 C with adaptors 18G 47 AH (see Fig. H.8), noting the spacing washer against the pinion head.

Assembly and adjustment procedure are detailed in Section H.7.

Section H.7

ASSEMBLING AND SETTING THE CROWN WHEEL AND PINION

Apart from the fitting of components as detailed in Sections H.2, H.3, and H.5 it is not permissible to fit any new parts (e.g. crown wheel and pinion, pinion bearings, differential bearings, etc.) to the axle assembly without working through the procedure given in this Section. Furthermore, if a new crown wheel or a new pinion is needed, a **mated pair—crown wheel and pinion—must be fitted.**

Fitting a new crown wheel and pinion involves four distinct operations:

1. Setting the position of the pinion.
2. Adjusting the pinion bearing preload.
3. Setting the crown wheel position.
4. Adjusting the backlash between the gears.

The following Service tools are required to enable these operations to be carried out correctly:
Bevel pinion and differential setting gauge.
Bevel pinion inner race remover and replacer.
Bevel pinion outer race remover and replacer.
Bevel pinion preload gauge.

1. SETTING THE PINION POSITION

1. Fit the bearing outer races to the gear carrier, using the special pinion race replacing tool.
2. Smooth off the pinion head with an oil-stone, but do not erase any markings that may be etched on the pinion head.
3. Assemble the pinion and rear bearings with a washer of known thickness behind the pinion head.

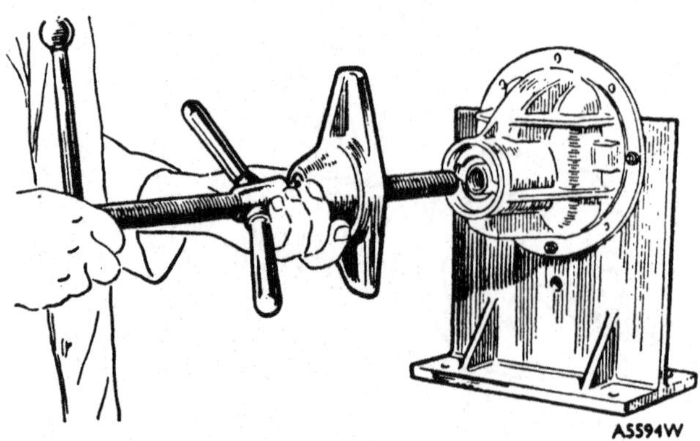

Fig. H.6
Use Service tool 18G 264 with adaptor 18G 264 E and 18G 264 F to remove the pinion front and rear bearing outer races

4. Position the pinion in the gear carrier without the shims, bearing spacer, and oil seal.

5. Fit the inner ring of the front bearing and the universal joint driving flange and tighten the nut gradually until a bearing preload of 10 to 12 lb. in. (.12 to .14 kg. m.) is obtained.

6. Remove the keep disc from the base of the magnet. Adjust the dial indicator to zero on the machined step 'B' of the setting block.

7. Clean the pinion head and place the magnet and dial indicator in position (Fig. H.9). Move the indicator arm until the foot of the gauge rests on the centre of the differential bearing bore at one side and tighten the knurled locking screw. Obtain the maximum depth reading and note any variation from the zero setting. Repeat the check in the opposite bearing bore. Add the two variations together and divide by two to obtain a mean reading.

8. Take into consideration any variation in pinion head thickness. This will be shown as an unbracketed figure etched on the pinion head and will always be minus (–). If no unbracketed figure is shown the pinion head is of nominal thickness. Using the mean clock gauge reading obtained and the unbracketed pinion head figure (if any), the following calculation can be made:

   a. **If the clock reading is minus** add the clock reading to the piston head marking, the resulting sum being minus. **Reduce** the washer thickness by this amount.

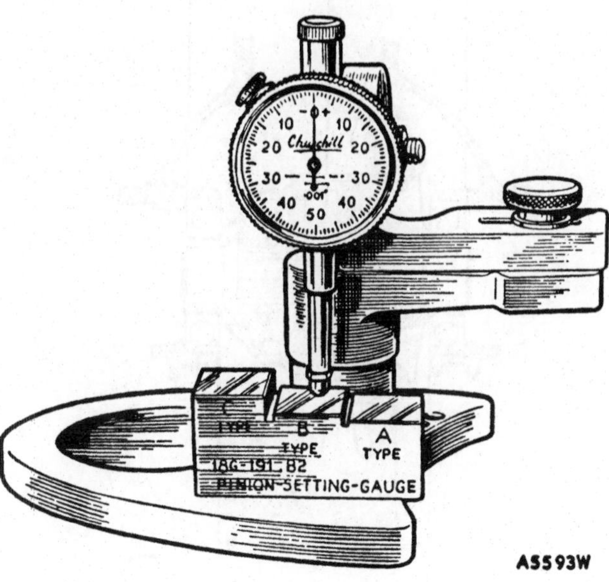

Fig. H.7
Setting the gauge to zero on the special block for determination of the pinion position

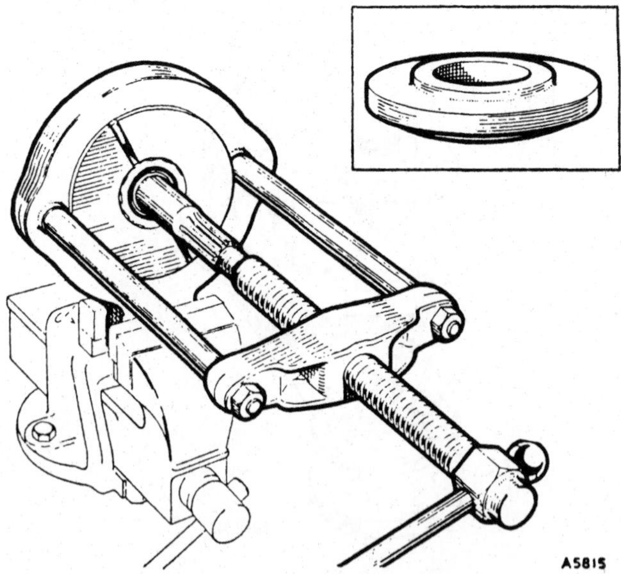

Fig. H.8
Use Service tool 18G 47 C and adaptors 18G 47 AH to remove the pinion bearing inner race. (Inset) Part of the adaptor set used to replace the bearing race

EXAMPLE:

Clock reading	–.002 in.
Pinion marking	–.005 in.
Variation from nominal	–.007 in.

Reduce the washer thickness by this amount.

   b. **If the clock reading is plus and numerically less** than the pinion marking **reduce** the washer thickness by the difference.

EXAMPLE:

Pinion marking	–.005 in.
Clock reading	+.003 in.
Variation from nominal	–.002 in.

Reduce the washer thickness by this amount.

   c. **If the clock reading is plus and numerically greater** than the pinion marking **increase** the washer thickness by the difference.

EXAMPLE:

Clock reading	+.008 in.
Pinion marking	–.003 in.
Variation from nominal	+.005 in.

Increase the washer thickness by this amount.

The only cases where no alterations are required to the washer thickness are when the clock reading is **plus** and **numerically equal** to the unbracketed pinion marking, or when the clock reading is zero and there is no unbracketed marking on the pinion head.

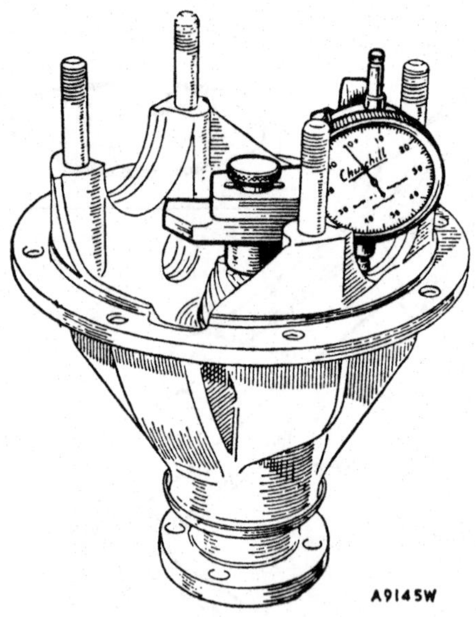

Fig. H.9
The gauge in position on the pinion with the dial indicating a variation from the standard setting

9. Allowance should then finally be made as follows for the mounting distance marked on the pinion head in a rectangular bracket:
   If the marking is a **plus** figure **reduce** the washer thickness by an equal amount.
   If the marking is a **minus** figure **increase** the washer thickness by an equal amount.
   A tolerance of .001 in. is allowed in the thickness of the washer finally fitted.

TABLE OF WASHER AND SHIM THICKNESSES	
Pinion head washer thickness	.112 to .126 in. in steps of .002 in.
Pinion bearing preload shims	.004 to .012 in. in steps of .002 in., plus .020 in. and .030 in.
Crown wheel bearing shims	.002 in., .004 in., and .006 in.
Pinion bearing preload	10 to 12 lb. in. without oil seal; 13 to 15 lb. in. with oil seal
Crown wheel bearing pinch	.002 in. each side

2. ADJUSTING PINION BEARING PRELOAD

Fit the appropriate washer to the pinion head.

Assemble the pinion shaft, bearings, distance tube, and shims to the gear carrier; fit the oil seal and driving flange. Shims to a thickness of .008 to .011 in. (.2 to .28 mm.) should be used as a starting-point for adjustment of the bearing preload.

Tighten the driving flange nut gradually with a torque wrench to 140 lb. ft. (19.34 kg. m.) and check the preload on the bearings during tightening to ensure that it does not exceed 13 to 15 lb. in. (.15 to .173 kg. m.), i.e. 3 lb. in. (.034 kg. m.) greater than the recommended figure since the oil seal is now fitted. If the preload is too great more shims must be added. If the preload is too small when the nut is tightened correctly the shim thickness must be reduced.

3. SETTING THE CROWN WHEEL POSITION

1. Before fitting the crown wheel and differential assembly to the gear carrier it is necessary to calculate the shim thickness required behind each bearing to give the required pinch. To facilitate the calculation, machining variations are indicated by stamped numbers on the carrier adjacent to the bearing bores. The dimensions to be considered are shown in Fig. H.10, (A) being the distance from the centre-line to the bearing register of the carrier on the left-hand side and (B) the distance from the centre-line to the bearing register of the carrier on the right-hand side. The (C) dimension is from the bearing register on one side of the cage to the register on the other side, while the (D) dimension is from the rear face of the crown wheel to the bearing register on the opposite side. Any variation from nominal on the (A) dimension will be found stamped on the carrier adjacent to the bearing bore, and similarly with the (B) dimension. The variations from nominal on (C) and (D) dimensions are stamped on the machined face of the differential cage.

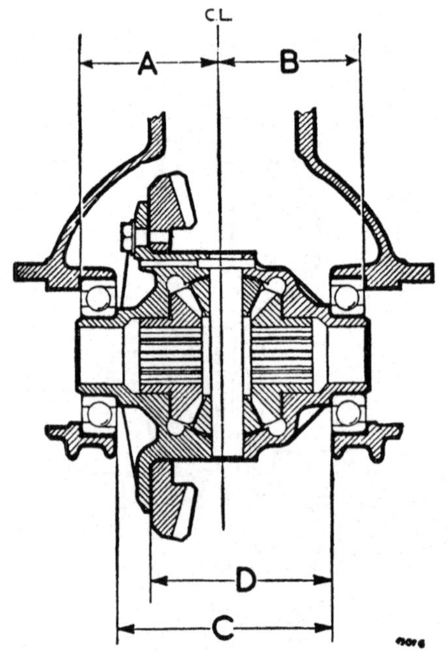

Fig. H.10
The dimensions referred to in the instructions for differential setting

It is possible to calculate the shim thickness required on the **left-hand side** by the use of the following formula:

A + D – C + .007 in.

Substituting the actual variations shown, this formula gives the shim thickness required to compensate for the variations in machining plus the extra .002 in. (.05 mm.) to give the necessary bearing pinch. In addition, allowance must be made for variations in bearing thickness in the following manner.

Rest the bearing, with the inner race over the recess and the outer ring thrust face downwards, on the small surface plate of tool 18G 191 A. Drop the magnet onto the surface plate and set the clock gauge to zero on the small gauge block on the step marked 'B'. (See Fig. H.11). This is the thickness of the standard bearing. Swing over the indicator until it rests on the plain surface of the inner race and, holding the inner race down against the balls, take a reading (Fig. H.12). Normally the bearing will be standard to –.003 in., though in some cases the tolerance may be from standard to –.005 in. A negative variation shown by this test indicates the additional thickness of shimming to be added to that side of the differential.

The formula for the **right-hand side** is:

B – D + .006 in.

and here again final allowance must be made for variation in bearing thickness.

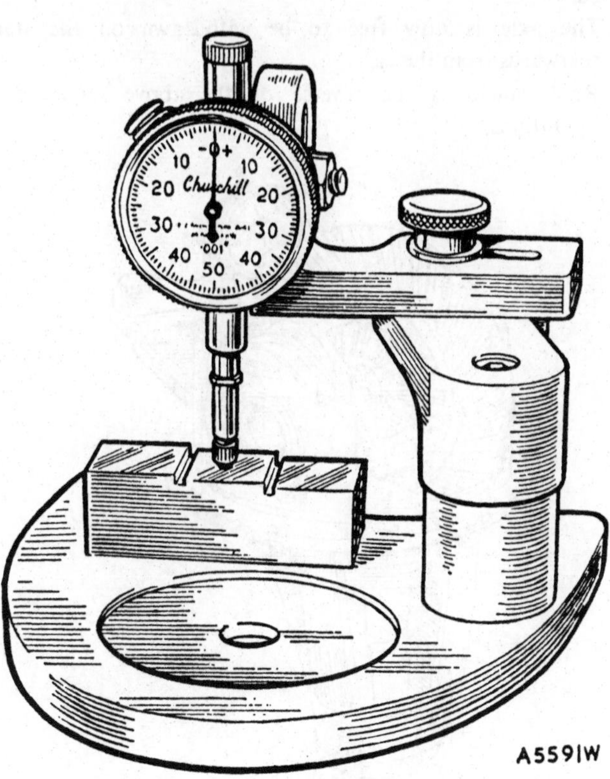

Fig. H.11
To measure variations in bearing thickness first zero the gauge on the appropriate portion of the gauge block

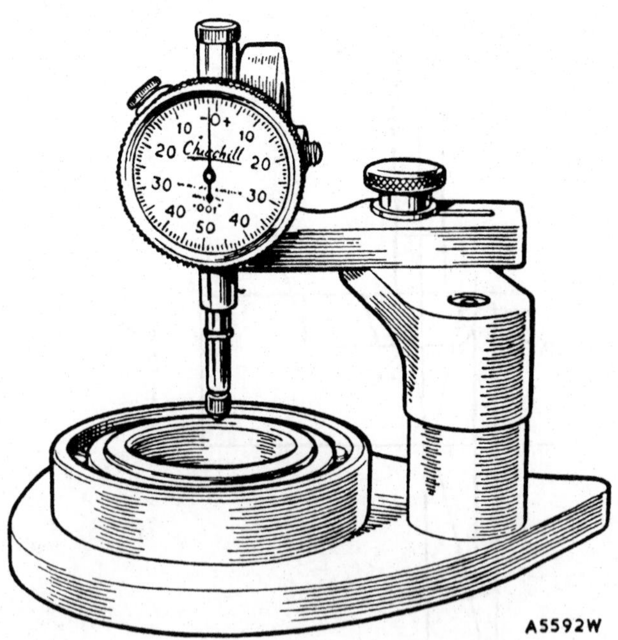

Fig. H.12
With the gauge set to zero, place the bearing on the surface plate with the outer ring thrust face down, and take a reading while the indicator foot contacts the inner ring

2. When a framed number is marked on the back of the crown wheel, e.g. –2, it must be taken into account before assembling the shims and bearings to the differential cage. This mark assists in relating the crown wheel with the pinion.

   If, for example, the mark is +2, then shims to the value of .002 in. (.05 mm.) must be transferred from the left-hand side (the crown wheel side) to the right-hand side. If the marking is –2, then shims to the value of .002 in. (.05 mm.) must be moved from the right-hand side to the left-hand side.

4. ADJUSTING THE BACKLASH

1. Assemble the bearings and shims as calculated to the differential cage.
2. Bolt the crown wheel to the differential case, but do not knock over the locking tabs. Tighten the nuts to a torque wrench reading of 60 lb. ft. (8.3 kg. m.).

   Fit the shims and differential bearings with the thrust faces outwards.

   Mount the assembly on two 'V' blocks and check the amount of run-out of the crown wheel, as it is rotated, by means of a suitably mounted dial indicator.

   The maximum permissible run-out is .002 in. (.05 mm.) and any greater irregularity must be corrected. Detach the crown wheel and examine the joint faces on the flange of the differential case and crown wheel for any particles of dirt.

   When the parts are thoroughly cleaned it is unlikely that the crown wheel will not run true.

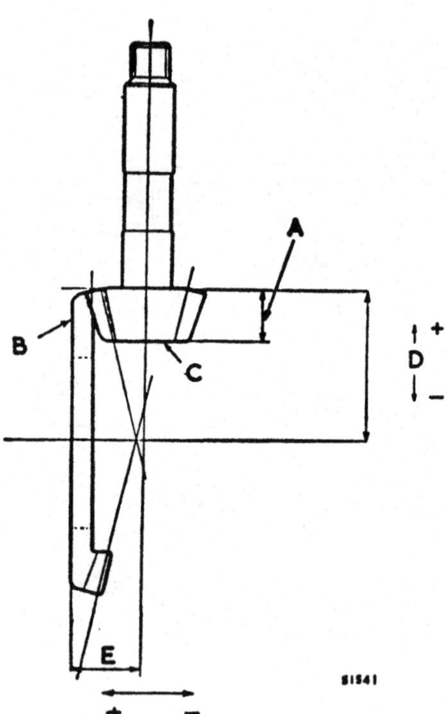

Fig. H.13
Crown wheel and pinion markings

A. Pinion head thickness.
B. Crown wheel marking.
C. Pinion marking.
D. Pinion mounting distance.
E. Crown wheel mounting distance.

Tighten the bolts to the correct torque wrench reading and knock over the locking tabs.

3. Fit the differential to the gear carrier. Replace the bearing caps and tighten the nuts to a torque wrench reading of 65 lb. ft. (8.99 kg. m.). Bolt the Service tool surface plate to the gear carrier flange and mount the clock gauge on the magnet bracket in such a way that an accurate backlash figure may be obtained. (See Fig. H.14.) The correct figure for the backlash to be used with any particular crown wheel and pinion is etched on the rear face of the crown wheel concerned and must be adhered to strictly.

A movement of .002 in. (.05 mm.) shim thickness from one side of the differential to the other will produce a variation in backlash of approximately .002 in. (.05 mm.). Thus it should be possible to set up the differential, even though the backlash is incorrect, by removing the bearings on one occasion only.

Great care must be taken to ensure absolute cleanliness during the above operations, as any discrepancies resulting from dirty assembly would affect the setting position of the crown wheel or pinion.

Section H.8

REMOVING AND REFITTING THE AXLE

Raise the rear of the car.

Mark the propeller shaft coupling flanges so that they may be replaced in the original relative positions. Remove the four bolts and self-locking nuts and release the rear end of the propeller shaft from the axle. Remove the nuts and spring and flat washers securing each end of each check strap to the anchor pins and remove the check straps.

Remove the split pin and clevis pin securing the brake cables to each brake operating lever. Remove the small nut and Phillips recessed-head screw securing the hand brake cable clip to the axle casing. Remove the self-locking nut and large flat washer securing the brake balance lever to the pivot on the axle casing.

Remove the nut and spring washer securing the lower end of each damper link to the rear spring clamp plate.

Unscrew the brake fluid supply pipe union and release the flexible pipe from the battery box support bracket.

Release the exhaust pipe from the exhaust manifold and the two supporting brackets and lower the exhaust pipe assembly.

Remove the nut and spring washer from the spring front anchor pin.

Support the axle casing and remove the rear shackle plates, brackets, and rubbers. Lower the axle support until the axle and spring assembly rests on the road wheels. Withdraw the front anchor pins and roll the assembly from beneath the car.

The axle is now free to be withdrawn on the stand rearwards from the car.

Replacement is the reverse of the above sequence of operations.

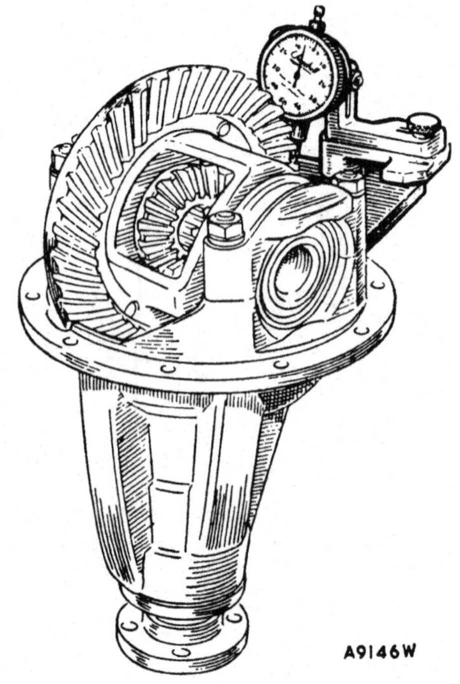

Fig. H.14
Measuring the crown wheel backlash

Section H.9

REAR ROAD SPRINGS

To remove a rear spring

1. Remove the road wheel adjacent to the spring to be removed.
2. Raise and support the body and support the axle with a hydraulic jack to enable the axle to be lowered to relieve the tension in the spring.
3. Disconnect the shock absorber link from its bracket and the rebound strap from the rebound spindle.
4. Remove the nuts and spring washers from the eyebolt and shackle plate pins and take off the outer shackle plate.
5. Using a suitable drift, tap each shackle plate pin alternately until the plate and pins are free of the spring and the mounting bracket.
6. Withdraw the eyebolt from the front of the spring.
7. From the two 'U' clips remove the locknuts and nuts. Retain the shock absorber bracket, locating plate, and pad which will fall from the under side of the spring.
8. Remove the spring and retain the upper locating plate, pad, pedestal, and 'U' clips.

To refit a rear spring

1. Offer the front of the spring to its bracket, and locate it with the front eyebolt.
2. Fit the shackle plate and pins to the rear eye and the body bracket.
3. Fit the upper locating plate and pad to the spring and locate the hole in the axle spring seat over the head of the centre-bolt.
4. Place the pedestal over the axle, fit the lower pad, locating plate, and shock absorber bracket, and pass the 'U' clips over the axle and through the locating plates. Secure the 'U' clips with the nuts and locknuts.
5. Refit the road wheel, remove the axle and body supports, and refit the washers and nuts to the front eyebolt and the shackle plate, nuts, and washers to the rear shackle plate pins.
6. Refit the shock absorber link and rebound strap.

Section H.10

DISMANTLING AND ASSEMBLING A REAR SPRING

Dismantling

1. Remove the rear spring as detailed in Section H.9.
2. Straighten the ends of the clips on the third and fourth spring leaves.
3. Support the spring in a vice with the top and bottom leaves against the vice jaws and the centre-bolt just clear of the jaws.
4. Remove the locknut and nut from the centre-bolt and withdraw the centre-bolt and distance piece from the spring.
5. Slowly open the vice to relieve the tension in the spring leaves and remove the leaves from the vice.
6. Remove the two rubber bushes from the rear eye of the main leaf and then press out the Silentbloc bush from the front eye.
7. Remove and discard the spring clip rivets and clips.

Clean and examine each leaf for signs of cracks or fractures, particularly around the centre-bolt holes.

Before assembly, cover each leaf with Shell Ensis 260 Fluid.

Assembling

1. Press a new Silentbloc bush into the main leaf front eye and ensure that the outer bush is perfectly central in the eye.
2. Rivet new spring clips to the third and fourth leaves.
3. Use a tapered mandrel having the same maximum diameter as the centre-bolt to align the holes in the spring leaves and assemble the leaves. The longest half of the spring faces the rear of the car.
4. Keep the leaves aligned and slowly compress them in a vice.
5. Remove the mandrel and assemble the distance piece and centre-bolt. Secure the centre-bolt with its nut and locknut.
6. Align the side of the spring and bend the spring clips over the main leaf.

After assembly, refit the spring to the car as detailed in Section H.9.

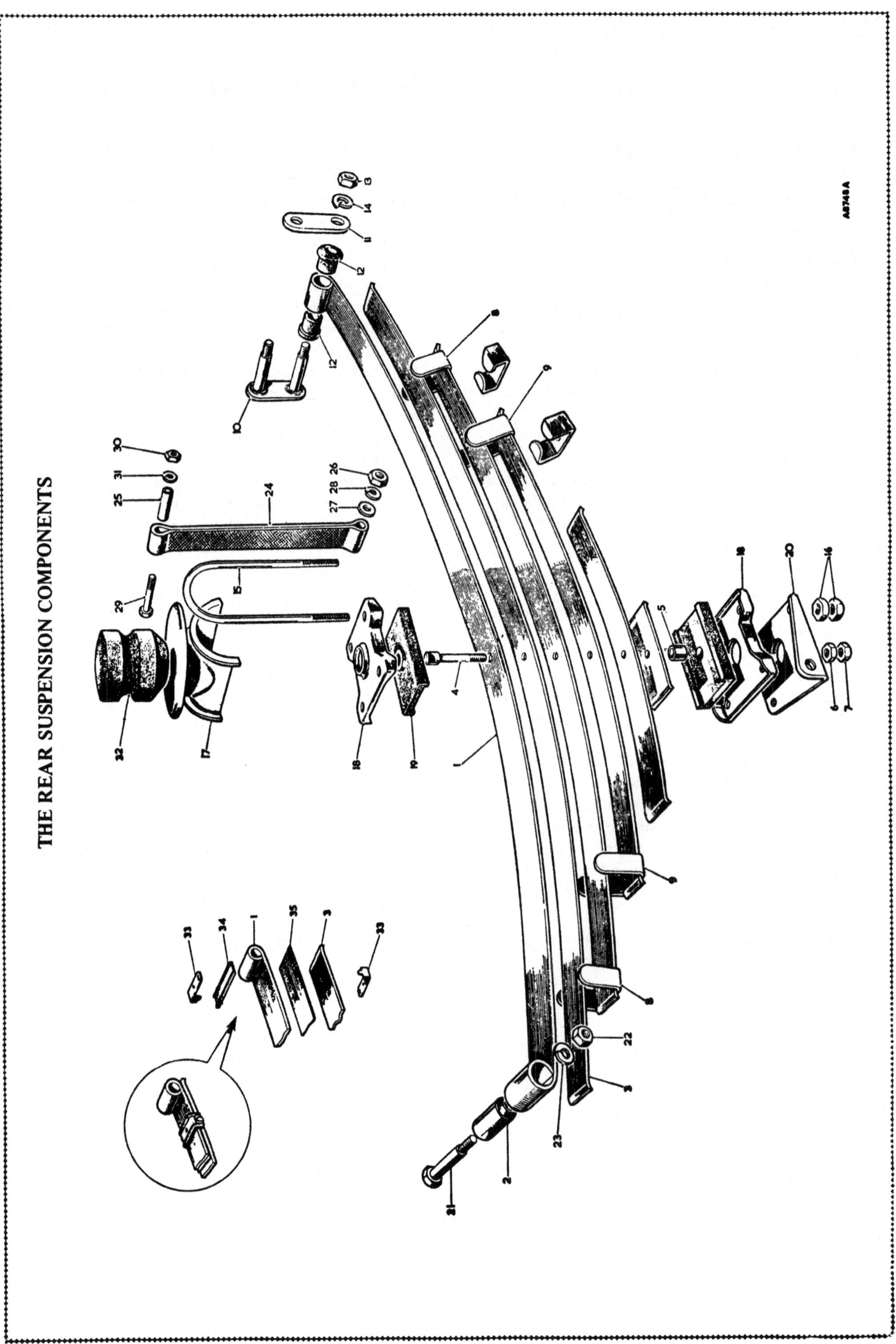

THE REAR SUSPENSION COMPONENTS

KEY TO THE REAR SUSPENSION COMPONENTS

No.	Description	No.	Description	No.	Description
1.	Leaf assembly–main.	13.	Nut–shackle plate pin.	25.	Distance tube–rebound strap.
2.	Bush.	14.	Washer–spring–nut.	26.	Nut–rebound strap to axle.
3.	Leaf–second.	15.	Clip–'U'–rear spring.	27.	Washer–plain–nut.
4.	Bolt–locating.	16.	Nut–'U' clip.	28.	Washer–spring–nut.
5.	Distance piece.	17.	Pedestal–bump rubber.	29.	Bolt–strap to bracket.
6.	Nut–bolt.	18.	Plate–spring locating.	30.	Nut–bolt.
7.	Locknut–bolt.	19.	Pad–spring seating.	31.	Washer–spring–nut.
8.	Clip–third leaf.	20.	Bracket–shock absorber to rear spring–R.H.	32.	Bump–rubber.
9.	Clip–fourth leaf.	21.	Bolt–spring–front end.	33.	Clip–second leaf } later type only.
10.	Plate–shackle and pins.	22.	Nut–bolt.	34.	Pad–second leaf clip } later type only.
11.	Plate–shackle.	23.	Washer–spring–nut.	35.	Strip–interleaf, 1 2, 2 3, 3 4 } later type only.
12.	Bush–shackle plate (rubber).	24.	Strap–rebound.		

SECTION Ha

THE REAR AXLE AND REAR SUSPENSION

(SEMI-FLOATING TYPE)

GENERAL DESCRIPTION

The rear axle assembly is of the semi-floating type. Adjustment to the bearing is by means of spacers, as also is the position of the pinion in relation to the crown wheel and the backlash between the gears.

Suspension is by semi-elliptic leaf springs, rubber-mounted, and the shackles are fitted with rubber bushes.

Section Ha.1

LUBRICATION

Oil level

Check the level, and top up if necessary. The filler plug is located on the rear of the axle and also serves as an oil level indicator. After topping up allow time for any surplus oil to run out. This is most important; if the axle is overfilled, the oil may leak through to the brake linings and lessen their efficiency.

NOTE.–It is essential that only Hypoid oil be used.

Draining

The most suitable time for draining is after a long journey while the oil is still warm. Clean the drain plug before it is replaced and tightened.

Refill the axle with fresh oil.

Section Ha.2

AXLE UNIT

Removing

Raise the rear of the car.

Mark the propeller shaft driving flanges so that they may be replaced in their original relative positions. Remove the four bolts and self-locking nuts and release the rear end of the propeller shaft from the axle. Remove the nuts and spring and flat washers securing each end of each check strap to the anchor pins on the axle and remove the check straps.

Remove the split pin and clevis pin securing the brake cable to each brake operating lever. Remove the set screw securing the hand brake cable clip to the axle casing. Remove the self-locking nut and large flat washer securing the brake balance lever to the pivot on the axle casing.

Remove the nut and spring washer securing the lower end of each damper link to the rear spring clamp plate.

Unscrew the brake fluid supply pipe union and release the flexible pipe from the battery box support bracket.

Release the exhaust pipe from the exhaust manifold and the supporting brackets and lower the exhaust pipe assembly.

Remove the nut and spring washer from each of the spring front anchor pins.

Support the axle casing and remove the rear shackle plates, brackets, and rubbers. Lower the axle support until the axle and spring assembly rests on the road wheels. Withdraw the front anchor pins and roll the assembly from beneath the car.

Refitting

Reverse the removal procedure when refitting.

Bleed and adjust the brakes (see Section M).

Section Ha.3

HUB AND AXLE SHAFT

Removing

Jack up the car and place blocks under the spring as close as possible to the axle. Remove the wheel. Release the hand brake.

Remove the two countersunk screws (disc wheels) or the four nuts (wire wheels) locating the brake-drum and tap it from the hub. It may be necessary to slacken off the brake adjusters slightly if the shoes hold the drum.

Remove the split pin, unscrew the slotted axle shaft nuts and withdraw the hub. Remove the clevis pin securing the brake cable to the operating lever, and disconnect the hydraulic pipe from the wheel cylinder. Remove the backplate. Remove the oil seal collar, bearing hub cap and oil seal from the axle shaft. Remove the axle shaft using impulse extractor 18G 284 with adaptor 18G 284 D and press the bearing from the shaft.

Refitting

Repack the bearings with grease before refitting.

Reverse the removal procedure, using tool 18G 1067 to drift the axle shaft into position. Lubricate and fit a new oil seal, lip facing inwards. Refit the oil seal collar and bearing hub cap. Tighten the axle shaft nut to the torque figure given in **'GENERAL DATA'**. Bleed and adjust the brakes as in Section M.

Section Ha.4

RENEWING THE PINION OIL SEAL

Removing

1. Raise and support the rear of the car.
2. Remove the rear road wheels and brake drums.
3. Drain the rear axle.
4. Mark the propeller shaft and pinion flanges to ensure correct reassembly and disconnect the propeller shaft.
5. Using 18G 207 (see Fig. Ha.5) measure and record the torque required to rotate the pinion.
6. Using 18G 34 A to prevent the pinion from rotating, remove the flange retaining nut and washer, and withdraw the pinion flange.
7. Extract and discard the oil seal.

Inspection

8. Examine the pinion flange for damage, paying particular attention to the oil seal track area.

Refitting

9. Grease the periphery and sealing lip of the new oil seal and fit the seal flush with the axle casing.

THE REAR AXLE COMPONENTS

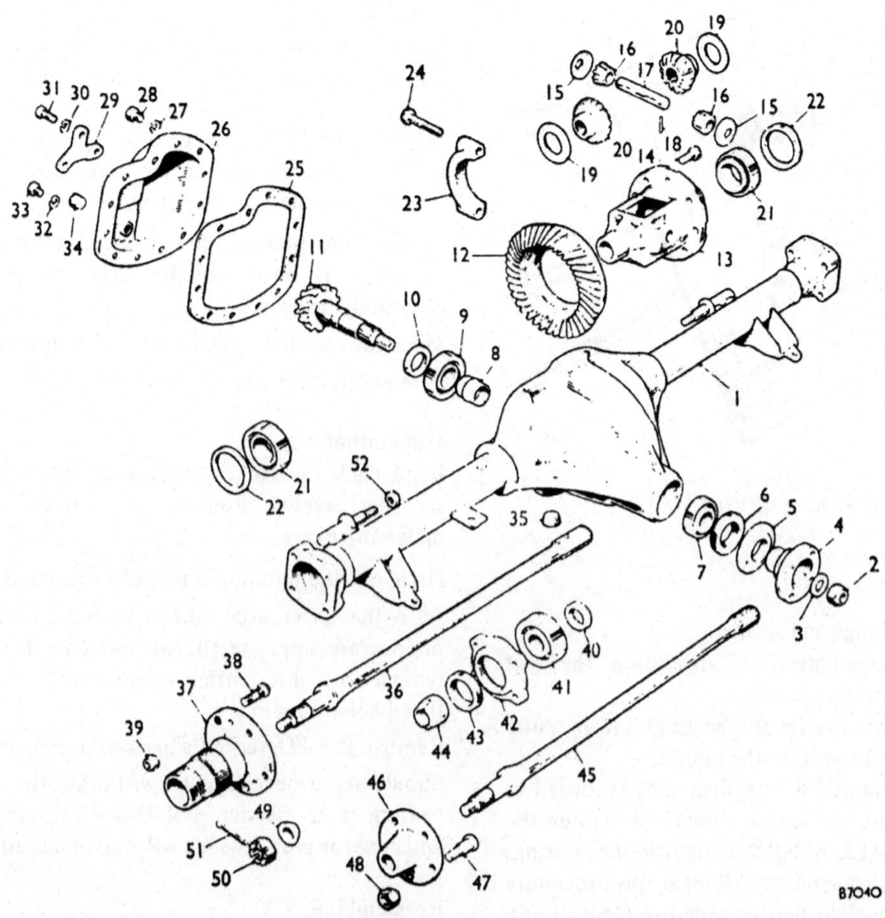

No.	Description	No.	Description	No.	Description	
1.	Case assembly.	18.	Roll-pin.	35.	Drain plug.	
2.	Nut.	19.	Thrust washer.	36.	Axle shaft.	Wire wheels only.
3.	Plain washer.	20.	Differential wheels.	37.	Driving flange.	Wire wheels only.
4.	Universal joint flange.	21.	Differential bearing.	38.	Stud.	Wire wheels only.
5.	Dust cover.	22.	Distance collars.	39.	Nut.	Wire wheels only.
6.	Oil seal.	23.	Bearing cap.	40.	Bearing spacer.	
7.	Outer pinion bearing.	24.	Bolt.	41.	Bearing.	
8.	Bearing spacer.	25.	Joint washer.	42.	Bearing hub cap.	
9.	Inner pinion bearing.	26.	Axle case cover.	43.	Oil seal.	
10.	Pinion thrust washer.	27.	Spring washer.	44.	Oil seal collar.	
11.	Pinion.	28.	Set screws.	45.	Axle shaft.	Disc wheels only.
12.	Crown wheel.	29.	Compensating lever bracket.	46.	Driving flange.	Disc wheels only.
13.	Differential cage.	30.	Spring washer.	47.	Wheel stud.	Disc wheels only.
14.	Bolt.	31.	Set screw.	48.	Wheel nut.	Disc wheels only.
15.	Thrust washer.	32.	Spring washer.	49.	Axle shaft collar.	
16.	Differential pinions.	33.	Set screw.	50.	Axle shaft nut.	
17.	Pinion pin.	34.	Filler and level plug.	51.	Split pin.	

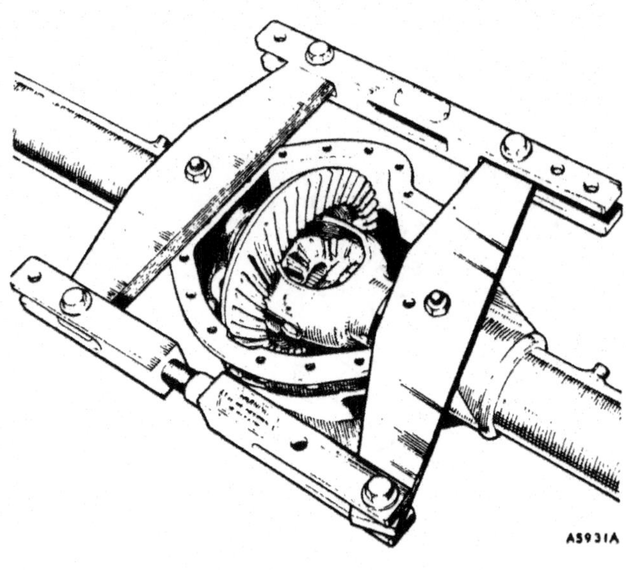

Fig. Ha.1
Axle stretcher 18G 131 C

10. Refit the pinion flange and washer.
11. Screw on the retaining nut, **tightening the nut gradually** until resistance is felt.
12. Rotate the pinion to settle the bearings and measure the torque required to rotate the pinion.
    If the reading obtained is less than that recorded in Operation 5, before the seal was removed; tighten the nut **A VERY SMALL AMOUNT**, resettle the bearings and recheck the torque reading. Repeat this procedure until a reading equal to that recorded in Operation 5 **BUT NOT LESS THAN 4 to 6 lb. in. (0.04 to 0.07 kg. m.)** is obtained.
    e.g. Reading in Operation 5 = 9 lb. in. (0.10 kg. m.).
    Adjust torque to this figure
    or
    Reading in Operation 5 = 0 lb. in.
    Adjust torque to 4 to 6 lb. in. (0.04 to 0.07 kg. m.).

CAUTION. Preload build up is rapid, tighten the nut with extreme care. IF AN ORIGINAL TORQUE READING, in excess of 6 lb. in. (0.7 kg. m.) is exceeded, THE AXLE MUST BE DISMANTLED AND A NEW COLLAPSIBLE SPACER FITTED.

Section Ha.5

DIFFERENTIAL AND PINION

Removing the differential

Drain and remove the axle from the car (see Section Ha.2).

Remove the axle shafts and wheel hubs (see Section Ha.3).

Remove the differential cover. Mark each differential bearing cap before removal to ensure correct replacement unscrew the two bolts and withdraw both caps.

Before the differential assembly can be withdrawn the axle case must be stretched with Service tool 18G 131 C. When using this tool tighten the turnbuckle one flat at a time until the differential unit can be prised out. Each flat on the turnbuckle is numbered to provide a check on the amount turned on the buckle. Prise the differential assembly out with two levers, one on each side of the differential case opening, using suitable packing between the levers and the gear carrier, and ensure that no leverage is placed upon the axle stretcher.

NOTE.–To prevent the axle case being permanently damaged, it must not be stretched any more than is absolutely necessary.

Maximum stretch is 0.012 in. (.31 mm.) 9 flats.

Release the stretcher.

Dismantling

Bend back the locking tabs and remove the crown wheel securing screws. Remove the crown wheel from the differential cage.

Drive out the pinion pin peg and remove the pin.

Turn the differential wheels by hand until the differential pinions are opposite the openings in the differential cage, remove the differential pinions and the thrust washers fitted behind them.

Remove the differential wheels and their thrust washers.

Should it be necessary to withdraw the differential inner bearing races, Service tool 18G 47 C, adaptor 18G 47 AK and adaptor plug 18G 47 AR must be used.

Reassembling

Use Service tool 18G 134 and adaptor 18G 134 CM to replace the differential bearings.

Fit the differential wheels with the thrust washers in position.

Insert the differential pinions through the opening in the differential cage and mesh them with the differential wheels. Hold the pinion thrust washers in position and install the pinion pin.

Line up the pinion pin with the hole in the differential cage and fit the pinion pin peg.

Bolt the crown wheel to the differential cage but do not knock over the locking tabs. Tighten the bolts to a torque wrench reading of 60 to 65 lb. ft. (8.3 to 8.9 kg. m.).

Mount the assembly on two 'V' blocks and check the amount of run-out of the crown wheel, as it is rotated, by means of a suitably mounted dial indicator. The maximum permissible run-out is .002 in. (.05 mm.) and any greater irregularity must be corrected. If there is excessive run-out, detach the crown wheel and examine the joint faces on the flange of the differential cage and on the crown wheel for any particles of dirt.

When the parts are thoroughly cleaned it is unlikely that the crown wheel will not run true.

Change the position of the crown wheel on the differential cage to correct any misalignment.

Tighten the bolts to the correct torque wrench reading and knock over the locking washers.

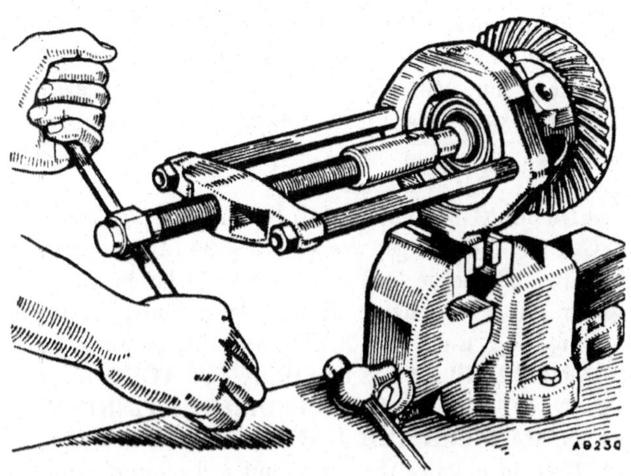

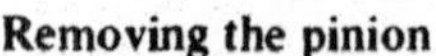

Fig. Ha.2
Use 18G 47 C, adaptor 18G 47 AK, and adaptor plug 18G 47 AR to remove the differential bearings

Removing the pinion

Before removing the pinion measure the preload: if this is zero, fit new pinion bearings.
Hold the flange with wrench 18G 34 A and remove the nut and washer.
Withdraw the flange by tapping it with a hide hammer.
Remove the bevel pinion. To prevent damaging the outer bearing the pinion must be pressed and not driven out.

Dismantling

To remove the bevel pinion front and rear outer races from within the gear carrier casing use Service tool 18G 264, with adaptors 18G 264 AA and 18G 264 AD for the front race, and adaptors 18G 264 AA and 18G 264 AB for the rear race. As the front outer race is withdrawn it will carry the pinion oil seal with it.

Use Service tool 18G 47 C and adaptor 18G 47 AS to remove the rear bearing inner race from the bevel pinion.

Reassembling

Refit the pinion front inner race using Service tool 18G 47C with adaptor 18G 47 AS. With the same tool assemble the rear bearing inner race to the bevel pinion, ensuring that the pressure is exerted on the inner race only.

Refitting the differential and pinion using original parts

Where it is only necessary to fit a new oil seal the differential can be refitted in the reverse order, assuming that the original shim thicknesses are retained, but ensure that the pinion preload figure noted before removing the pinion is achieved when tightening the flange nut.
If any new parts are fitted, i.e. crown wheel and pinion, pinion bearings, etc. the setting of the pinion (its position relative to the crown wheel) must be checked.
Examine the crown wheel teeth. If a new crown wheel is needed, a mated pair–crown wheel and pinion–must be fitted.
Fitting a new crown wheel and pinion involves four distinct operations.

1. Setting the pinion position.
2. Setting the pinion bearing preload.
3. Setting the crown wheel.
4. Setting the backlash.

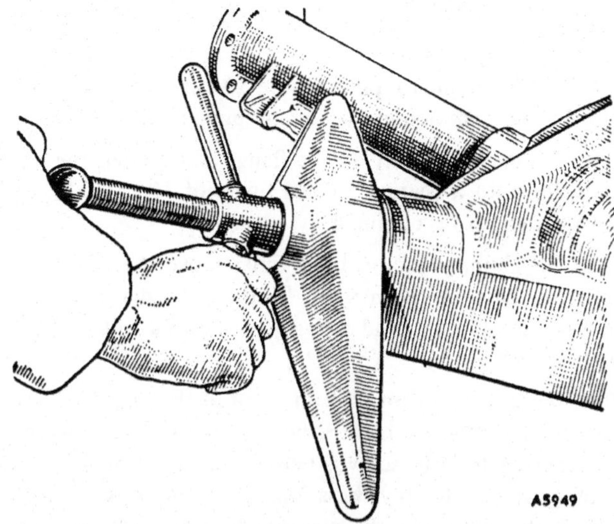

Fig. Ha.3
Use 18G 264 and adaptors 18G 264 AA, and 18G 264 AD, or 18G 264 AB to remove front and rear bevel pinion outer races

Refitting

1. SETTING THE PINION POSITION

Fit the bearing outer races to the axle casing using tool 18G 264 and 18G 264 AA with adaptors 18G 264 AD or 18G 264 AB.

The variation in the pinion head thickness is etched on the pinion head and is to be ignored for this setting.

Using the dummy pinion 18G 191 H, fit the inner race of the bearing to the pinion in the gear carrier without the

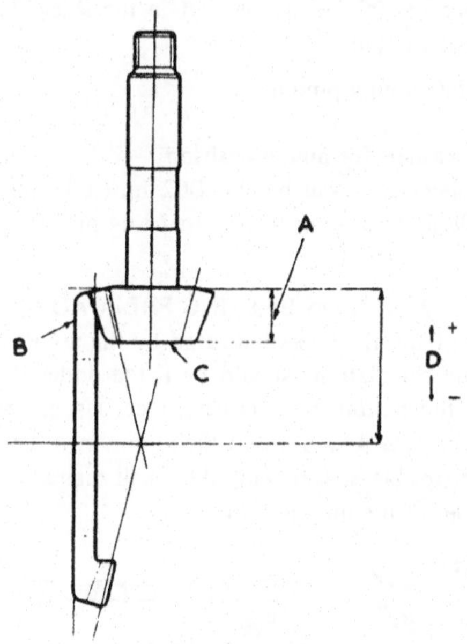

Fig. Ha.4
Crown wheel and pinion markings

A. Pinion head thickness. Max. –.007 in. (–.178 mm.).
B. Crown wheel marked here.
C. Pinion marked here.
D. Pinion mounting distance. Max. ±.004 in. (±.102 mm.).

collapsible spacer and oil seal. Fit the inner race of the front bearing.

NOTE.–The standard pinion head spacer (0.208 in. (5.3 mm.)) is incorporated in the dummy pinion.

Refit the universal joint driving flange and tighten the nut gradually until a bearing preload figure of 10 to 20 lb. in. (.11 to .2 kg. m.) is obtained.

Clean the dummy pinion head and remove the keep disc from the base of the magnet. Position the dial indicator foot on the pinion head and adjust the dial indicator to zero (see Fig. Ha.6).

Move the indicator arm until the foot of the gauge rests on the centre of the differential bore at one side and tighten the knurled locking screws. Obtain the maximum depth reading and note any variation from the zero setting. Repeat this check on the opposite bearing bore. Add the two variations together and divide by two to obtain a mean reading.

The reading shown on the clock will be the amount of correction necessary to the spacer which is 0.208 in. (5.3 mm.) thick.

(a) If the clock reading is **negative** (–) reduce the spacer thickness by this amount.

(b) If the clock reading is **positive** (+) increase the spacer thickness by this amount.

Allowance must finally be made for the mounting distance marked on the pinion head in a rectangular bracket. Proceed as follows:
If the marking is **positive** (+) reduce the washer thickness by an equal amount.
If the marking is **negative** (–) increase the washer thickness by an equal amount.

A tolerance of .001 in. is allowed in the thickness of the washer finally fitted.

Remove the dummy pinion.

Available washers for pinion position
Eight washers are available in .002 in. (.051 mm.) steps from 0.208 in. (5.3 mm.) to .222 in. (5.64 mm.).

2. PINION BEARING PRELOAD

A washer of the thickness indicated by the use of the tools and by the calculations should be fitted under the pinion head. Fit the pinion inner bearing race. Using 18G 47 C, and adaptor 18G 47 AS. Insert the pinion into the case and fit the collapsible spacer with the small diameter towards the shoulder of the pinion head.

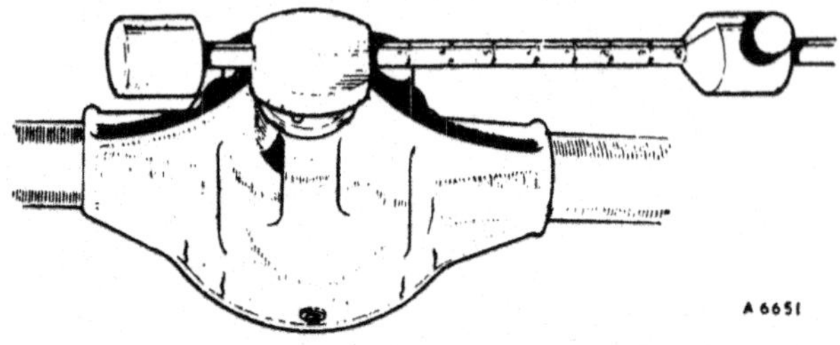

Fig. Ha.5
Checking the bevel pinion bearing preload (18G 207)

Support the head of the pinion and press the outer bearing onto the pinion; **do not compress the spacer.** Grease the periphery and sealing lip of the seal and fit the seal flush with the axle casing. Fit the universal joint flange, washer and nut.

Tighten the flange nut to 140 lb. ft. (20.7 kg. m.) using 18G 592 and flange wrench 18G 34 A, progressively increase the torque load by 10 lb. ft. (1 kg. m.) until the spacer starts to collapse. Rotate the pinion to settle the bearings and using 18G 207 B check the pinion pre-load. **BEARING PRELOAD IS RAPID. IF THE TORQUE OF 24 LB. IN. (0.3 KG. M.) IS EXCEEDED THE PINION MUST BE DISMANTLED AND A NEW COLLAPSIBLE SPACER FITTED**. In practice the pinion nut will require tightening **A VERY SMALL AMOUNT BETWEEN EACH PINION TORQUE CHECK**. When the nut is correctly tightened it should provide a pre-load of 14 to 18 lb. in. (0.10 to 0.16 kg. m.).

3. SETTING THE CROWN WHEEL POSITION

Assemble each inner and outer bearing race to the differential assembly.

Using crown wheel setting tools (18G 191, 18G 191 F, and 18G 191 J) place the differential assembly onto the jig and load the crown wheel assembly. Spin the unit to settle the bearings.

The standard measurement of the bearing bores is 7.243 in. (183.98 mm.). Any excess machined from the bores will be marked A and B on the axle casing. The A and B tolerances added to the standard measurement will determine the overall dimension (see **Example A**).

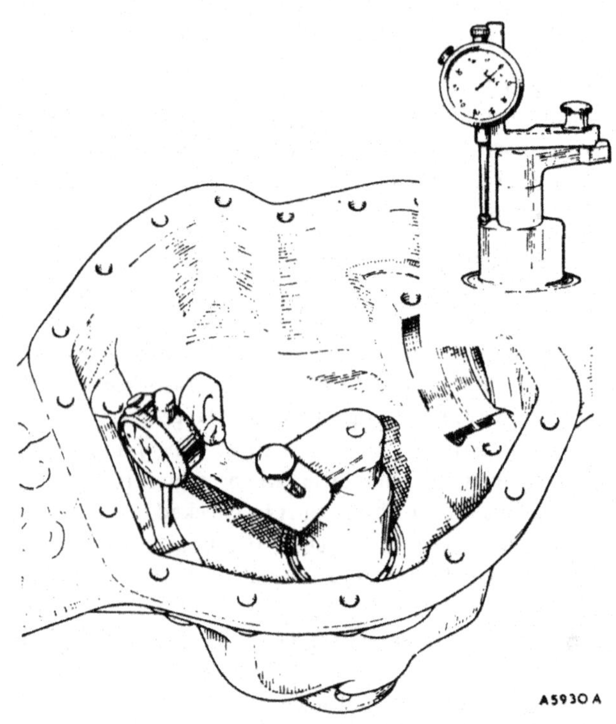

Fig. Ha.6
Taking a reading of the bearing bore and (inset) the dial gauge set at zero on the dummy pinion

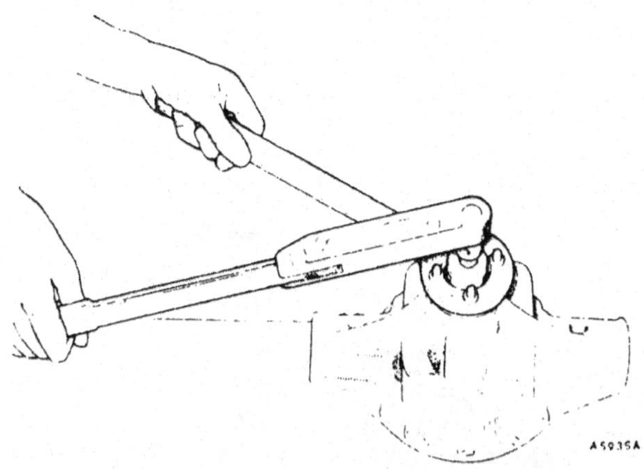

Fig. Ha.7
Use flange wrench 18G 34 A to hold the flange against rotation when tightening the pinion nut with torque wrench 18G 592

Clean the head of the jig pillar (18G 191 J) and remove the keep disc from the base of the magnet. Position the magnet on the pillar head and adjust the dial gauge to zero when the dial gauge foot is positioned on the pillar head (see Fig. Ha.9).

NOTE.–The pillar is the standard height of the differential assembly of 6.972 in. (177.10 mm.).

Spin the differential to settle the bearings, move the arm of the dial indicator to the machined face of the jig (see Fig. Ha.9), and take a reading. Add the variation to the standard height to obtain the total width of the differential assembly (see **Example B**).

Subtract the total width of the differential assembly, and the total distance collar thickness will be found. To this figure a further .004 in. (.102 mm.) must be added to give bearing 'pinch' (see **Example C**). Divide this total by two to obtain the distance collars of equal thickness (see **Example D**).

Example A

Differential case standard ..	7.243 in. (183.98 mm.)
Stamped on case 'A'	.001 in. (.025 mm.)
Stamped on case 'B'	.002 in. (.038 mm.)
Total distance between bores ..	7.246 in. (184.05 mm.)

Example B

Differential assembly standard	6.972 in. (177.10 mm.)
Clock reading (positive) ..	.008 in. (.203 mm.)
Total differential assembly ..	6.980 in. (177.30 mm.)

Example C

Total distance between bores ..	7.246 in. (184.05 mm.)
Minus total differential assembly	6.980 in. (177.30 mm.)
	.266 in. (6.75 mm.)
Plus bearing pre-load	.004 in. (.102 mm.)
	.270 in. (6.86 mm.)

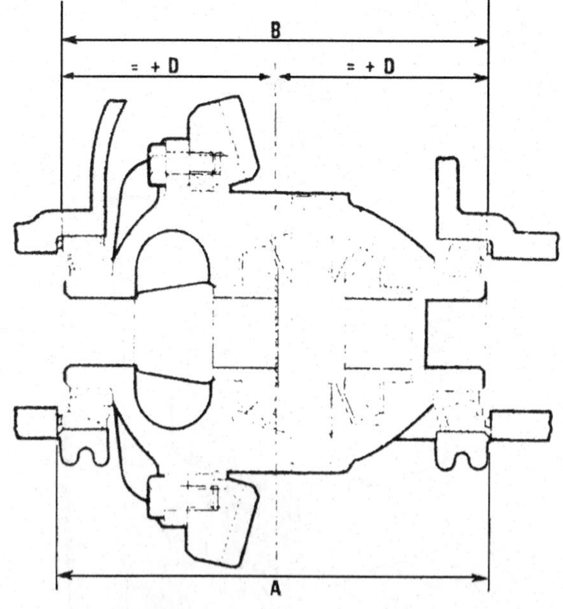

Fig. Ha.8
Illustrates the points from which the calculations must be made to determine the spacer thickness for the bearings on each side of the carrier

Example D

Spacers each side	.270 in.÷2 (6.86 mm.÷2)	.135 in. (3.43 mm.)

Available spacers for differential assembly

Eighteen spacers are available in .002 in. (.051 mm.) steps from 0.115 in. (2.92 mm.) to .149 in. (3.77 mm.).

Refitting

The correct figure for the backlash to be used with any particular crown wheel and pinion is etched on the rear face of the crown wheel concerned. Increase the spacer thickness on the opposite side of the crown wheel by this amount and decrease the spacer thickness on the crown wheel side by the same amount (see **Example E**).

Example E

Backlash .008

Spacer calculated	.135 in. (3.43 mm.)
Minus backlash	.008 in. (.203 mm.)
Crown wheel side spacer	.127 in. (3.23 mm.)
Spacer calculated	.135 in. (3.43 mm.)
Plus backlash	.008 in. (.203 mm.)
Opposite crown wheel side spacer ..	.143 in. (3.62 mm.)

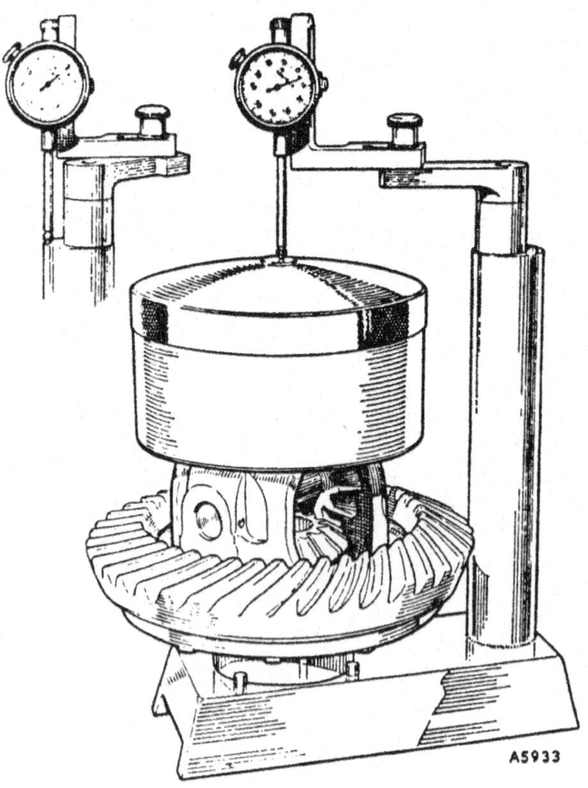

Fig. Ha.9
Taking a reading on the differential assembly and (inset) the dial gauge set at zero on the jig pillar

4. ADJUSTING THE BACKLASH

Fit the differential to the gear carrier. Replace the bearing caps and tighten the bolts to the correct torque wrench reading as given in (**'GENERAL DATA'**). Bolt the special tool surface plate to the gear carrier flange and mount the clock gauge in such a way that an accurate backlash figure may be obtained (see Fig. Ha.10).
A movement of .002 in. (.051 mm.) shim thickness from one side of the differential cage to the other will produce a variation in backlash of approximately .002 in. (.051 mm.).
Ensure absolute cleanliness during the above operations, as any discrepancies resulting from dirty assembly would affect the setting of the crown wheel or pinion.
Continue refitting by reversing the removing procedure. Finally, bend back the locating tabs around the bolt heads.

NOTE.–Ensure that the axle case jointing washer is coated with Hylomar Jointing Compound to obtain a perfect oil seal.

Fig. Ha.10
Checking crown wheel backlash

Section Ha.6

ROAD SPRINGS

For removal and dismantling see Section H.9 and H.10.

Section Ha.7

ANTI-ROLL BAR

(GHN5 and GHD5 cars from Car No. 410002)

Removing

1. Remove the battery.
2. Raise the rear of the vehicle and support the body just forward of the rear spring front shackle.
3. Disconnect the anti-roll bar from the body brackets.
4. Remove the bearing straps, bearing rubbers and anti-roll bar.
5. Remove the locators if fitting a new anti-roll bar.
6. Feed the anti-roll bar over the axle and down between the battery box and the front of the axle.
7. Check the bushes and anti-roll bar bearing rubbers; renew if worn.

Refitting

8. Reverse the procedure in 1 to 7, ensuring that the locators are fitted on the bar so that their inner faces are $9\frac{5}{16}$ in (237 mm) (A) from the centre line of the vehicle.

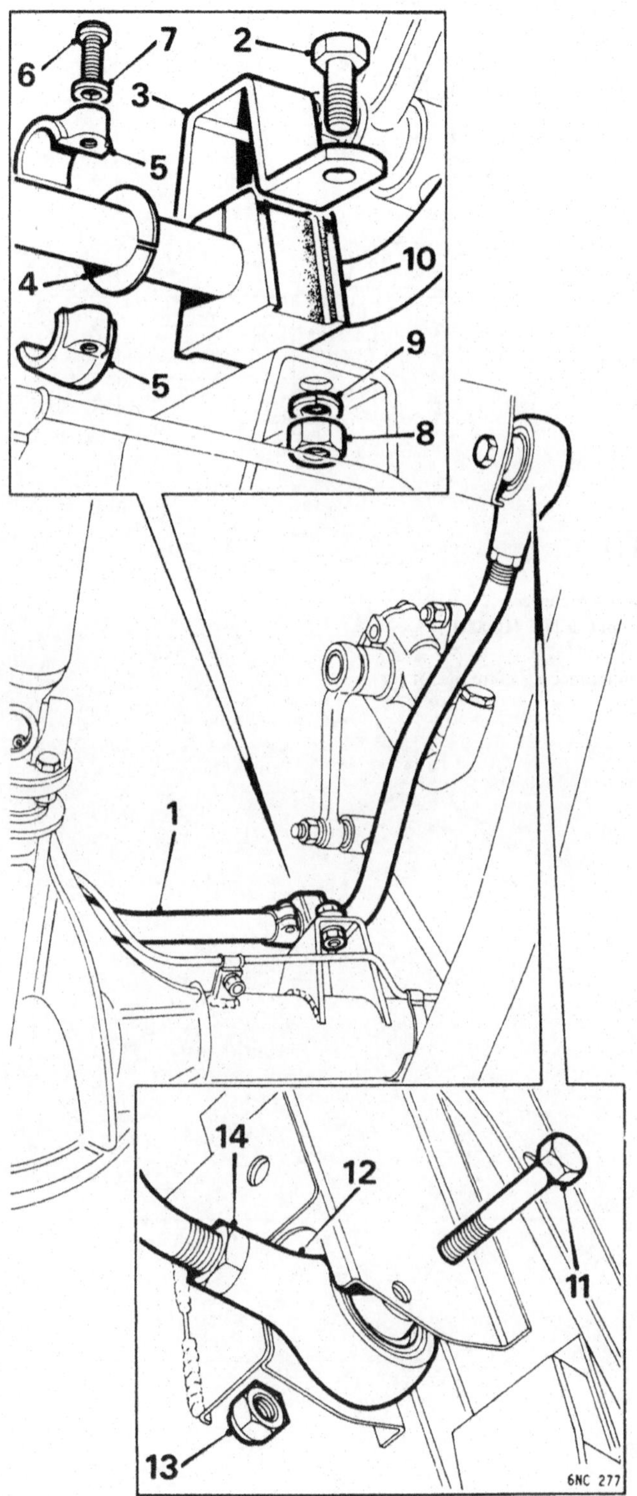

Fig. Ha.11

Rear anti-roll bar components
(GHN5 and GHD5 cars from Car No. 410002)

1. Anti-roll bar assembly
2. Screw
3. Bearing strap
4. Plastic washer
5. Locator
6. Screw
7. Spring washer
8. Nut
9. Spring washer
10. Bearing rubber
11. Bolt
12. End fitting
13. Nut
14. Locknut

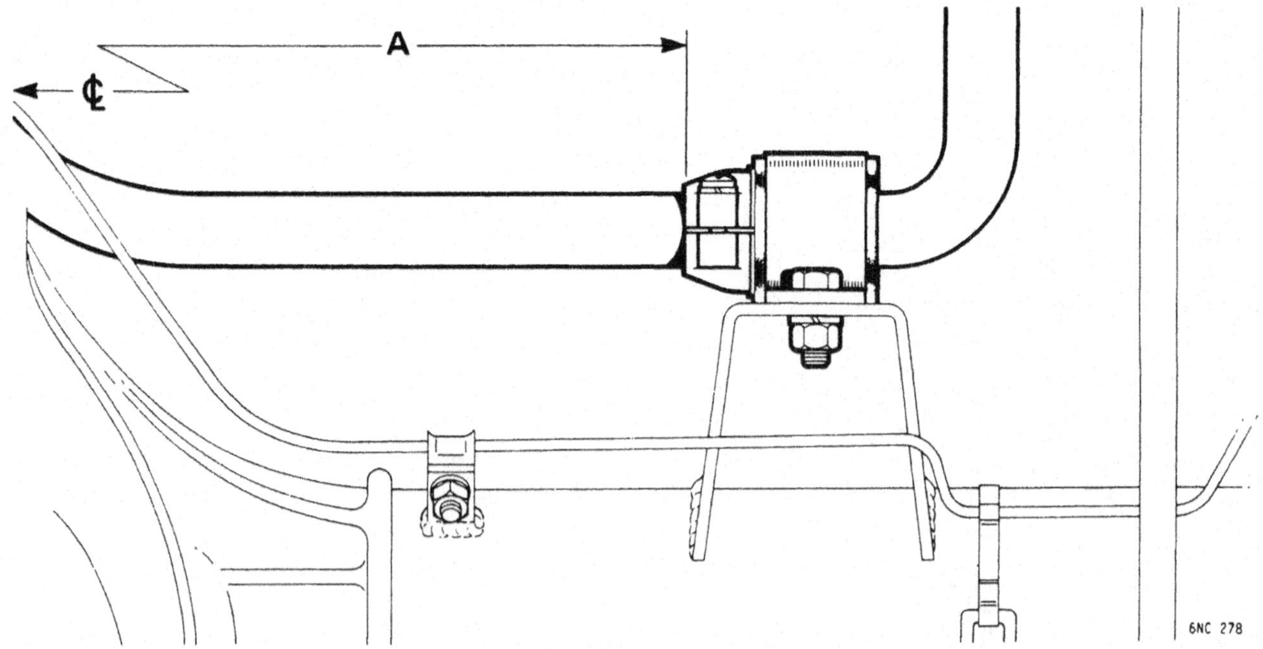

Fig. Ha.12

Rear anti-roll bar locator dimension
(GHN5 and GHD5 cars from Car No. 410002)

A = 11 in (279 mm) from locator inner face to centre line of car

SECTION J

THE STEERING GEAR

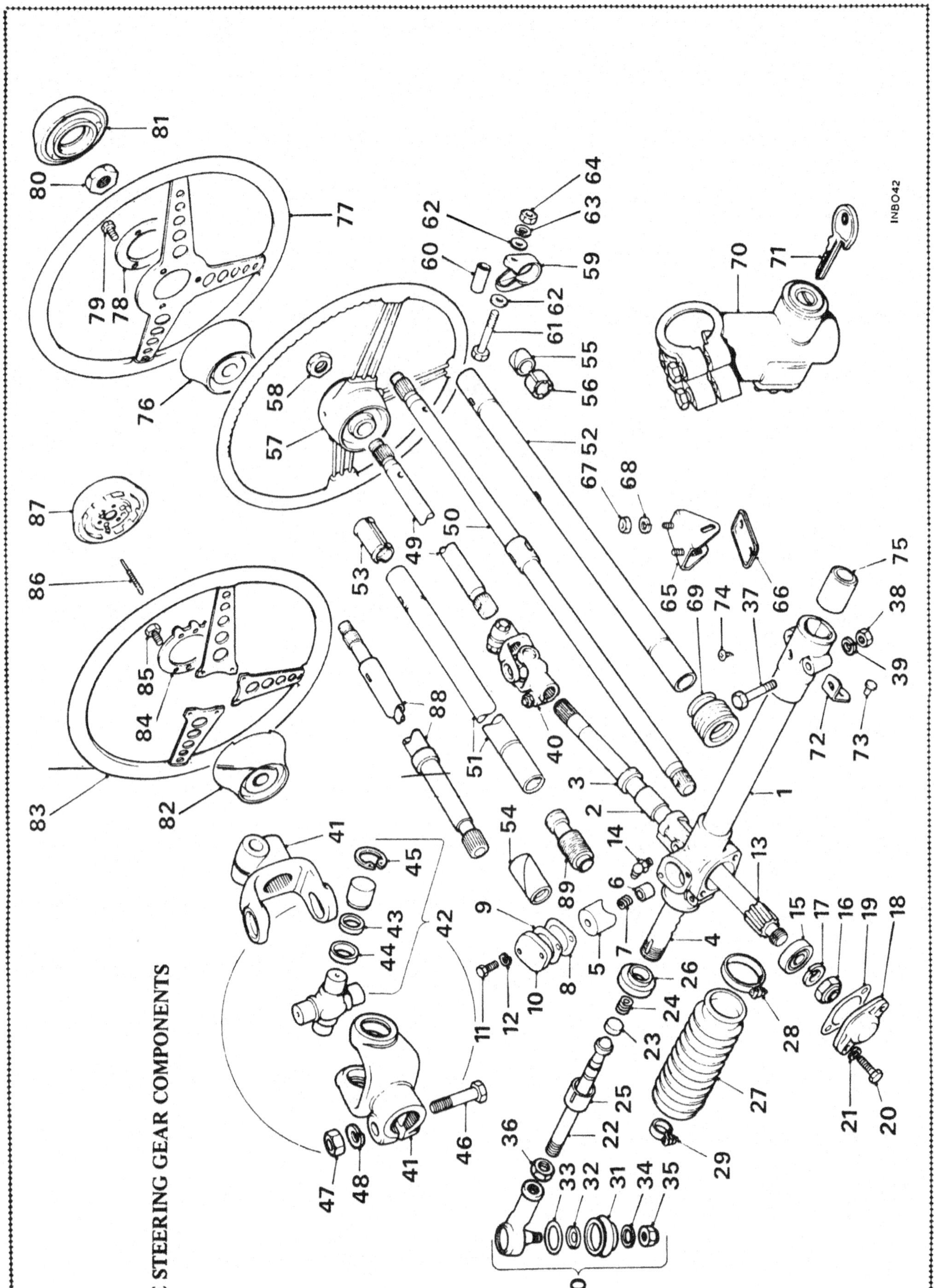

THE STEERING GEAR COMPONENTS

KEY TO THE STEERING GEAR COMPONENTS

No.	Description
1.	Housing assembly.
2.	Bush–pinion.
3.	Seal–oil.
4.	Rack.
5.	Yoke–rack support.
6.	Pad–damper.
7.	Spring–damper pad.
8.	Shim–cover-plate.
9.	Joint–cover-plate.
10.	Plate–cover–yoke.
11.	Bolt–cover-plate.
12.	Washer–spring–bolt.
13.	Pinion.
14.	Lubricator–pinion shaft.
15.	Bearing–ball–pinion.
16.	Nut–pinion bearing.
17.	Washer–spring–nut.
18.	Cover–end.
19.	Joint–end cover.
20.	Bolt–end cover.
21.	Washer–spring–bolt.
22.	Rod–tie.
23.	Seat–ball.
24.	Spring–thrust–ball seat.
25.	Housing–ball.
26.	Locknut–ball housing.
27.	Seal–rack.
28.	Clip–inner–seal.
29.	Clip–outer–seal.

No.	Description
30.	Socket assembly–ball.
31.	Boot.
32.	Retainer–boot.
33.	Spring–garter.
34.	Washer–boot.
35.	Nut–ball pin.
36.	Locknut.
37.	Bolt–track to bracket.
38.	Nut–bolt.
39.	Washer–spring.
40.	Joint–universal–steering-column.
41.	Yoke.
42.	Journal–assembly.
43.	Joint–journal.
44.	Retainer–joint.
45.	Circlip.
46.	Bolt–universal joint.
47.	Nut–bolt.
48.	Washer–spring–nut.
49.	Column assembly–inner.
50.	Column assembly–inner–R.H.D.
51.	Tube–column–outer.
52.	Tube–column–outer–R.H.D.
53.	Bearing–upper–column.
54.	Bearing–lower–column.
55.	Bush (felt) } When steering lock is fitted.
56.	Clip–retaining } When steering lock is fitted.
57.	Wheel–steering.
58.	Nut–steering-wheel.
59.	Clamp–steering-column.

No.	Description
60.	Distance piece.
61.	Bolt–clamp.
62.	Washer–plain–clamp bolt.
63.	Washer–spring–clamp bolt.
64.	Nut–bolt.
65.	Bracket–lower–steering-column.
66.	Plate–blanking–bracket.
67.	Nut–bracket to body.
68.	Washer–spring–nut.
69.	Excluder–draught–column to bulkhead.
70.	Lock assembly–steering and ignition.
71.	Key.
72.	Shim–cross-member bracket.
73.	Rivet.
74.	Screw–retaining bush.
75.	Bush–rack housing.
GHN5/GHD5 car only	
76.	Wheel hub.
77.	Steering-wheel.
78.	Lock ring.
79.	Screw.
80.	Nut.
81.	Motif and housing.
82.	Wheel hub.
83.	Steering wheel.
84.	Lock ring.
85.	Bolt.
86.	Horn push contact.
87.	Horn push.
88.	Steering column } From Car No. 258001.
89.	Sealing tube } From Car No. 258001.

GENERAL DESCRIPTION

The steering gear is of the direct-acting rack-and-pinion type, providing light and accurate control under all conditions.

It consists of a rack bar and toothed pinion mounted on the front suspension cross-member.

No adjustment for bearing wear in the box is provided, except by fitting of the necessary new parts.

The steering inner column is attached to the pinion by a universal coupling.

CAUTION.–If the vehicle is hoisted with its front wheels clear of the ground care should be taken to avoid forceful movement of the wheels from lock to lock, as damage may occur within the steering mechanism.

LUBRICATION

(Early cars)

Give the lubricating nipple on the steering-gear housing up to 10 strokes of the oil gun, but no more.

On R.H.D. cars the nipple is accessible from above the steering gearbox and on L.H.D. cars from below the car under the radiator.

Section J.1

FRONT WHEEL ALIGNMENT

The wheels should toe in $\frac{1}{16}$ to $\frac{3}{32}$ in. (1.6 to 2.4 mm.).

See that the tyres are inflated to the correct pressures. Set the wheels in the straight-ahead position.

Set the arms of a suitable trammel to the height of the hub centre on the outside of the wheels.

Place the trammel to the rear of the wheels and adjust the pointers to register with the wheel rims. Chalk the position of the pointers in each wheel rim and push the car forward one half-turn of the wheels. Take the front reading from the same marks on the rims.

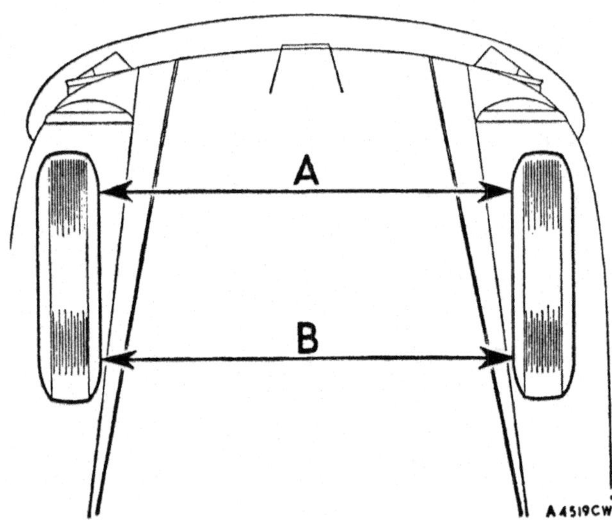

Fig. J.1
The front wheel alignment check must be taken with the front wheels in the straight-ahead position. Dimension (B) is $\frac{1}{16}$ to $\frac{3}{32}$ in. (1.6 to 2.4 mm.) greater than (A)

If adjustment is necessary, proceed as follows.

Slacken the locknuts at the ends of the short tie-rods and the clips securing the rubber gaiters to the tie-rods.

Use a wrench to rotate each of the tie-rods **equally** in the desired direction. These both have right-hand threads.

NOTE.–To ensure that the steering gearbox is in the central position and that the steering geometry is correct, it is important that the tie-rods are adjusted to exactly equal lengths. This can be ascertained by measuring the amount of thread visible behind each locknut, which should be equal.

After adjustment re-tighten the ball joint locknuts and rubber gaiter clips and ensure that the machined under sides of the ball joints are in the same plane.

Section J.2

STEERING–WHEEL

Release the three grub screws and remove the horn-push hub centre. Unscrew the steering-wheel nut and mark the wheel hub and column to ensure replacement in the original position. Pull off the wheel with a suitable tool. When replacing the wheel position it on the column splines in the original position to place the spokes equally about a horizontal datum line. Tighten the nut to the torque wrench setting given in **'GENERAL DATA'**.

GHN and GHD5 cars

1. Remove the steering-wheel motif assembly; it is a press-fit. Later type, remove the horn contact plunger.
2. Turn back the lock ring tabs and remove the bolts, lock ring, and steering-wheel.

NOTE: Early cars only, have lock tabs integral with the lock ring.

HUB

3. Slacken the steering-wheel nut and fit Service tool 18G 1181 to the hub using the special bolts.* Mark the hub and column to assist correct re-alignment and pull the hub until it is a loose fit on the steering-column. Remove 18G 1181, the steering-wheel nut and hub.
4. When refitting the hub, position it on the column splines in the original position. Fit the nut and tighten to the torque wrench setting given in **'GENERAL DATA'**.

*LATER TYPE STEERING WHEEL USE TWO $\frac{5}{16}$ UNF, $\frac{7}{8}$ in. threaded, $\frac{7}{8}$ in. plain shank, bolts to fit service tool 18G 1181.

Section J.3

STEERING-COLUMN

Removing and replacing

Withdraw the clamping bolt and nut securing the universal joint to the inner steering-column. Unscrew the four set screws from the direction indicator cowling and remove the indicator. Withdraw the clamping bolts, nuts, and spring and plain washers from the two brackets which support the column and remove the column complete.

NOTE.–Disconnect the wiring from the column lock when fitted and remove the ignition and auxiliary circuit fuses.

Bushes

Remove the steering-wheel and column and withdraw the inner column. Prise out the felt bush and pull out the polythene bush.

Soak a new felt bush in graphite oil before fitting.

Section J.4

STEERING-COLUMN UNIVERSAL JOINT

Removing

Bolts and nuts clamp the universal joint splines on the steering inner column and steering pinion, and the bolts must be withdrawn completely to release the universal joint assembly.

Slacken the bolts supporting the steering-column below the dash panel.

Withdraw the clamping bolts from the universal joint.

Move the steering-column assembly upwards to withdraw the steering inner column from the universal joint.

Withdraw the universal joint from the steering pinion.

Dismantling and reassembling

The Hardy Spicer joint has four needle-roller bearings retained on a centre spider by circlips. The joints are packed with grease on assembly and there is no further provision for lubrication.

Remove any enamel and dirt from the circlips and bearing races. Remove the circlips by pinching the ears together and prising them out with a screwdriver.

If a ring does not slide readily from its groove, tap the end of the bearing race lightly to relieve the pressure against the bearing.

Hold the joint in one hand with the side of a yoke at the top and tap the radius of the yoke lightly with a copper hammer. The bearing should begin to emerge; turn the joint over and remove the bearing and needle rollers with the fingers. If necessary, tap the bearing race from the inside with a small-diameter bar, taking care not to damage the bearing face, or grip the needle bearing race in a vice and tap the yoke clear.

Repeat this operation for the opposite bearing.

One yoke can now be removed. Rest the two exposed trunnions on wood or lead blocks to protect their ground faces, and tap the top lug of the flange yoke to remove the bearing race.

Turn the yoke over and repeat the operation.

When reassembling, replace the cork gaskets and gasket retainers on the spider journals, using a tubular drift. The spider journal shoulders should be shellacked prior to fitting the retainers to ensure a good oil seal.

Smear the walls of the races with grease and assemble the needle rollers to the bearing races and pack with grease.

Insert the spider in one yoke and, using a soft-nosed drift slightly smaller in diameter than the hole in the yoke, tap the bearings into position. It is essential that the bearing races are a light drive fit in the yoke trunnions.

Repeat this operation for the other bearings and replace the circlips, making sure that they are firmly located in their grooves. If the joint appears to bind, tap lightly with a wooden mallet to relieve any pressure by the bearings on the ends of the journals.

Section J.5

STEERING GEAR

Removing

The procedure detailed here will remove the steering rack and pinion from a completely assembled car.

Support the front end of the car by placing jacks beneath the lower suspension arm springs pans and remove the road wheels.

Remove the locknuts and drive the tie-rod ball pins from the steering-arms. Turn the steering onto the left lock (R.H.D. cars) or right lock (L.H.D. cars). Withdraw the clamping nut and bolt from the universal joint on the pinion shaft. Remove the nuts and bolts securing the steering rack to the front suspension cross-member, noting that the front bolts are fitted with self-locking nuts, and packing shims may be found between the rack and the frame brackets.

The steering assembly can now be withdrawn downwards.

Replacing

The steering gear is assembled to the car by reversing the above procedure although special attention should be given to the instructions in Section J.7.

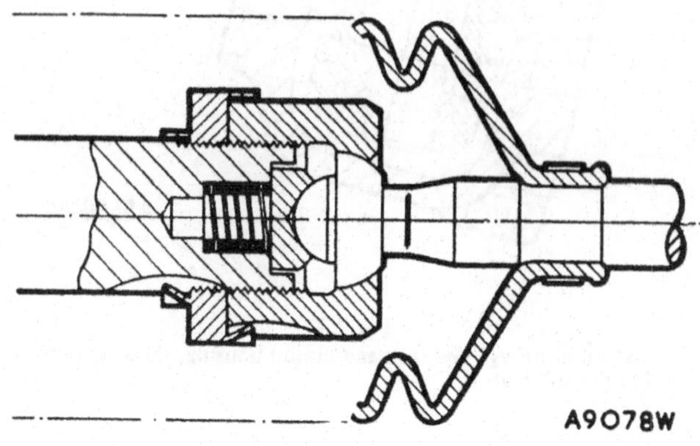

Fig. J.2
The assembly of a tie-rod ball joint

Section J.6

RACK AND PINION

Dismantling

Hold the rack housing between suitable clamps in a vice. Remove the pinion end cover and joint washer, placing a container to catch the oil that may drain from the housing. Remove the damper cover and shims, exposing the yoke, damper pad, and spring. After removal of these the pinion, complete with ball race and locknut may be withdrawn.

Unlock the tie-rod ball end locknuts and disconnect the ball end assemblies. Release the rubber gaiter seal clips and withdraw the seals.

Prise up the indentations in the locking rings clear of the slots in the rack and ball housing. Slacken back the locking ring and unscrew the housing to release the tie-rod, ball seat, and seat tension spring.

Withdraw the rack from the pinion end of the housing; if removed from the other end the teeth may damage the rack housing bush.

To remove the rack housing bush unscrew the self-tapping screw retaining it and carefully drive the bush out.

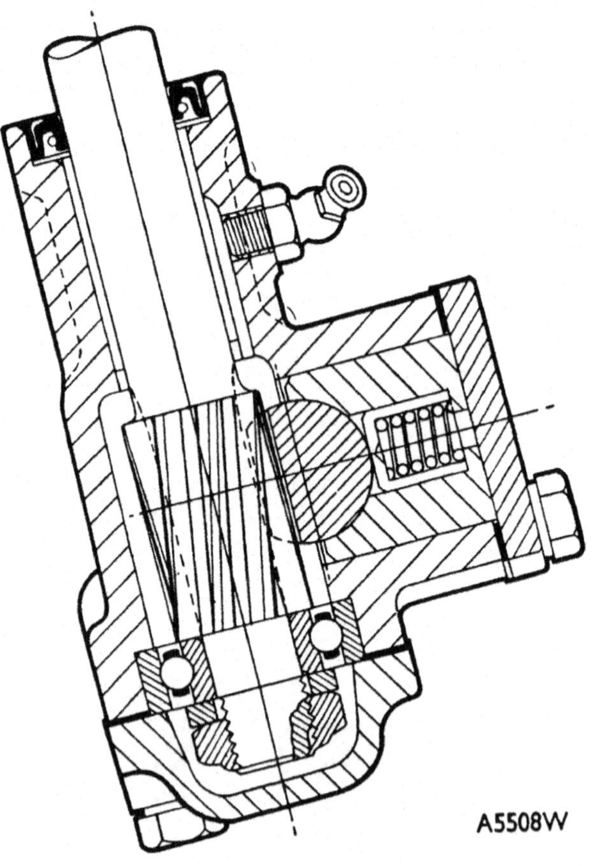

Fig. J.3
A section through the rack and pinion housing, showing the damper and seals

Examining for wear

Thoroughly clean and examine all parts of the assembly; components showing signs of wear must be replaced with new parts. Fractures, hollows, or roughness in the surfaces of the rack or pinion teeth will render them unserviceable. Take particular note of the rubber gaiters; should they be damaged or show the slightest sign of deterioration, they must be replaced with new ones. The tie-rod ball housing and ball seat should also be subjected to a careful check and new parts fitted if excessive wear is evident.

The outer ball socket assembly cannot be dismantled, and must therefore be renewed complete if it is worn or damaged.

Examine the bush fitted in the end of the rack housing and fit a new one if it shows signs of damage or wear.

Reassembling

Insert the rack housing bush and carefully drive or press it in until the bush is flush with the housing end. Enter a $\frac{7}{64}$ in. (2.78 mm.) diameter drill through the retaining screw hole and drill the outer shell of the bush to receive the retaining screw. A depth of .24 in. (6.3 mm.) will achieve this.

NOTE.–Bushes of sintered iron with an outer shell of pressed steel and rubber injected between the two have superseded the lead-bronze type in earlier use.

Smear the head of the screw with jointing compound before tightening so as to ensure an oil-tight joint.

Replace the rack from the pinion end. Refit the seat spring, seat, tie-rod, and ball housings, smearing the ball seats liberally with S.A.E. 90 oil. Tighten the ball housings until the tie-rod is held firm and without free play. When correctly adjusted a torque of 32 to 52 lb. in. (.359 to .594 kg. m.) must be required on the rod to produce articulation. Relock the housing by tightening up the locking ring to a torque of 33 to 37 lb. ft. (4.60 to 5.63 kg. m.) and secure in the locked position by punching the lips of the locking ring into the slots in the ball housing and rack. It is recommended that new locking rings are fitted whenever these have been disturbed.

Insert the pinion complete with ball race and locking nut into its housing. Replace the pinion end cover and seal, using a sealing compound to make an oil-tight joint. The outer edge of the ball race locknut must be peened into the slot in the pinion shaft if removed and refitted.

To adjust the rack damper replace the plunger in the housing and tighten the cover down without the spring or shims until it is just possible to rotate the pinion shaft by drawing the rack through its housing. With a feeler gauge measure the clearance between the cover and its seating on the rack housing. To this dimension must be added an additional clearance of .0005 to .003 in. (.013 to .076 mm.) to arrive at the correct thickness of shims which must be placed beneath the damper cover-plate.

Remove the damper cover-plate and plunger and replace the assembly, using a sealing compound to make an oil-tight joint.

Refit the rubber gaiters to the housing and the tie-rods. Before securing the gaiter clip on the tie-rod at the pinion end, stand the assembly upright, and pour in $\frac{1}{3}$ pint (.4 U.S.

pint, .2 litre) of Extreme Pressure S.A.E. 90 oil through the end of the gaiter, or pump the oil into the rack housing through the nipple provided.
Refit and tighten the gaiter clip.
Refit the ball ends and locknuts.

Section J.7

STEERING-COLUMN ALIGNMENT

Set the steering in the straight-ahead position and check that the trafficator cancellation stud at the top of the column is in the correct angular position when the serrations on the coupling and column are aligned.
When assembling the steering-column or steering gearbox assembly to the car care must be taken to ensure a free condition at the universal joint before the column or gearbox securing bolts are tightened. For the universal joint to be completely unloaded the centre-line of the steering-column and the centre-line of the steering rack pinion must pass through the centre of the universal joint spider when the assembly is viewed from above and from the side. Failure to ensure complete freedom at the universal joint will load the steering pinion upper bearing and cause extreme wear and steering stiffness.
To enable the assembly to be secured in the correct position the steering-column support bracket and plate may be moved up and down and sideways, and packing shims may be fitted between the steering rack mounting bosses and the brackets on the front suspension member.
Tighten the universal joint clamp bolts.
With all column and rack securing bolts slack, position the universal joint and tighten the support bracket clamp bolts at the lower end of the column.
Should there be a gap between the gearbox bosses and mounting brackets, remove the bolts, pack with shims as required, and replace and tighten the securing bolts.
To ensure complete alignment again slacken and re-tighten the steering-column lower support bolt.
Tighten the upper support bracket bolt.

Section J.8

NYLON-SEATED BALL JOINTS

Nylon-seated ball joints, which are sealed in manufacture and require no lubrication, are fitted at the steering-arm tie-rod ball joints.
It is essential that no dirt or abrasive matter should enter the nylon ball joint; in the event of a rubber boot being torn or damaged in service it is probable that the ball joint has been left exposed, and it is therefore important to renew both the ball joint and the boot.
If damage to the boot occurs whilst the steering side- or cross-rod is being removed in the workshop, only a new rubber boot need be fitted, provided the ball joints is clean. Smear the area adjacent to the joint with a little Dextragrease Super G.P. prior to assembling the boot.
Early production cars are fitted with a plain washer under the steering ball joint nut.
Later production cars are fitted with steering levers having a reduced diameter taper hole. These levers have a longer ball joint pin, are fitted with a thicker nut and have no plain washer.
When early production cars with a plain washer under the steering ball joint nut are fitted with service steering levers the plain washer must not be replaced.

Section J.9

STEERING LOCK IGNITION SWITCH

Cars exported to certain markets are fitted with a combined ignition/starter switch and steering-column lock mounted on the steering-column.
On cars fitted with the lock a sleeve integral with the inner column is slotted to permit engagement of the lock tongue; the outer column is also slotted to allow the lock tongue to pass through. A hole drilled in the upper surface of the outer column locates the steering-lock bracket. The bracket is secured by two bolts each waisted below the head to permit removal of the heads by shear action during assembly.
To remove the lock, disconnect the battery and the ignition/starter switch connections and turn the lock setting to 'GARAGE' to unlock the steering. Free the steering-column assembly as described in Section J.3 and remove the lock securing bolts with an easy-out.

Section J.10

STEERING-COLUMN
(GHN5 and HGD5 cars from Car No. 258001)

Removing

1. Disconnect the battery.
2. Turn the steering to the straight-ahead position.
3. Mark the inner steering-column and the universal joint to ensure correct alignment when refitting.
4. Remove the pinch bolt and nut securing the universal joint to the steering-column.
5. Disconnect the multi connector block.
6. Disconnect the wiring from the ignition switch.
7. Remove the bolts retaining the steering-column upper and lower support clamp brackets.
8. Remove the steering-column complete with the sealing tube, steering wheel, direction indicator and ignition/steering lock switch.

Refitting

9. Check that the steering rack is in the straight ahead position.
10. Check that the steering-column is in the straight ahead position.
11. Reverse the removing procedure in 1 and 4 to 8 noting:
    a. That the sealing tube is fitted to the steering-column with the gaitered end towards the toe-board.
    b. Ensure that the marks made in 3 align when fitting the inner column to the universal joint.

Section J.11

STEERING LOCK AND IGNITION STARTER SWITCH (GHN5 and GHD5 cars from Car No. 258001)

Removing

1. Remove the steering-column–Section J.10.
2. Remove the steering-wheel and hub–Section J.2.
3. Remove the direction indicator/headlight flasher/low-high beam switch–Section N.30.
4. Remove the direction indicator switch trip from the inner steering-column.
5. Slide the top clamp bracket off the steering-column.
6. Turn the ignition key to position '1' to ensure that the steering lock is disengaged.
7. Drill out or remove with a suitable proprietary tool, the retaining shear bolts.
8. Unscrew the steering lock locating grub screw.
9. Remove the steering lock and ignition starter switch.

Refitting

10. Reverse the removing procedure in 1 to 9, using new shear bolts and ensuring that the shear bolts are tightened until the bolt heads shear at the waisted point giving a torque tightness of 12 lbf. ft. (1.66 kgf. m.).

SECTION Ja

THE STEERING GEAR (ENERGY ABSORBING COLUMN)

The information given in this Section refers specifically to service operations on, or affected by, equipment fitted to the MGB (GHN5/GHN4 and GHD5/GHD4) in conformity with local and territorial requirements, and must be used in conjunction with Section J.

Section Ja.1

STEERING-COLUMN

Removing

1. Disconnect the batteries.
2. Remove the carburetter air cleaners.
3. Remove the upper pinch-bolt from the steering-column universal joint.
4. Remove lower panel from under the left-hand side of the fascia panel.
5. Disconnect the steering-column switch wiring at the snap connectors below the fascia.
6. Unscrew the three bolts securing the steering-column to the toe-plate.
7. Note the location, quantity, and thickness of the packing washers between the column upper fixing flanges and the body brackets, remove the securing bolts and collect the packing washers. **If the packing washers are mislaid or their fitting positions are not recorded, the steering must be aligned as described in Section Ja.3 when refitted.**
8. Withdraw the steering-column complete with steering-wheel and switches.

Dismantling

9. Withdraw the motif disc from the centre of the steering-wheel; unscrew the steering-wheel retaining nut and, using a suitable puller-type extractor, remove the wheel.
10. Remove the three left-hand switch cowl retaining screws.
11. Unscrew the panel light switch retaining screws and remove the left-hand switch cowl.
12. Remove the screw retaining the right-hand switch cowl.
13. Unscrew the two screws securing the combined overdrive and windshield wiper/washer switch and remove the switch complete with wiring.
14. Unscrew the two screws securing the combined headlamp flasher, horn and direction indicator switch, and remove the switch complete with wiring.
15. Unscrew the four ignition switch retaining screws and remove the switch complete with wiring.

Reassembling

16. Reverse the dismantling procedure in 9 to 15.

Refitting

NOTE.–If a new steering-column is being fitted it must be aligned as described in Section Ja.3.

17. Fit the column assembly into the car and enter the inner column into the universal joint.
18. Fit the packing washers in their original positions between the column fixing flanges and the body brackets; fit the three securing bolts, tightening them by hand until the packing washers are just pinched.
19. Fit and tighten the three column to toe-plate fixing bolts.
20. Tighten the three upper fixing bolts to the torque figure given in '**GENERAL DATA**'.
21. Fit and tighten the universal joint pinch-bolt to the torque figure given in '**GENERAL DATA**'.

Section Ja.2

RACK ASSEMBLY

Removing

1. Raise and support the front of the car and remove both front road wheels.
2. Remove the tie-rod ball pin locknuts.
3. Using tool 18G 1063, detach the tie-rod ball pins from the steering arms.
4. Turn the steering onto the right lock and remove the universal joint lower pinch-bolt.
5. Remove the nuts and bolts securing the rack assembly to the front cross-member, noting that the front bolts are fitted with self-locking nuts.
6. Withdraw the rack assembly downwards from the car.

Dismantling

7. Carry out the operations detailed in Section J.6.

Refitting

NOTE.–If a new rack assembly is being fitted it must be aligned as described in Section Ja.3.

8. Reverse the removing procedure in 1 to 6 ensuring that when entering the pinion shaft into the universal joint both the steering-column and rack are in the straight-ahead position.

Section Ja.3

ALIGNMENT

1. Fit the toe-plate seal to the steering-column and position the column in the car.
2. Fit one packing washer between each of the two top column fixing flanges and the body brackets.
3. Screw in the two top fixing bolts by hand until the packing washers are just pinched.
4. Check that the column is free to move forwards, backwards and sideways.
5. Screw in the three toe-plate fixing bolts, tightening them by hand only.
6. Check that the lower end of the column is free to move and position it centrally in the aperture.
7. Fit one of the two larger point gauges of tool 18G 1140 on the lower end of the column, positioning it so that the retaining screw tightens onto the flat machined in the splines.
8. Fit the remaining large points gauge of 18G 1140 to the pinion shaft so that the retaining screw tightens onto the radial groove machined in the splines.
9. Fit the rack assembly and tighten the rack fixing bolts.
10. Slacken the screw on the column point gauge and slide the gauge down until the points of both gauges are on the same plane but not overlapping.

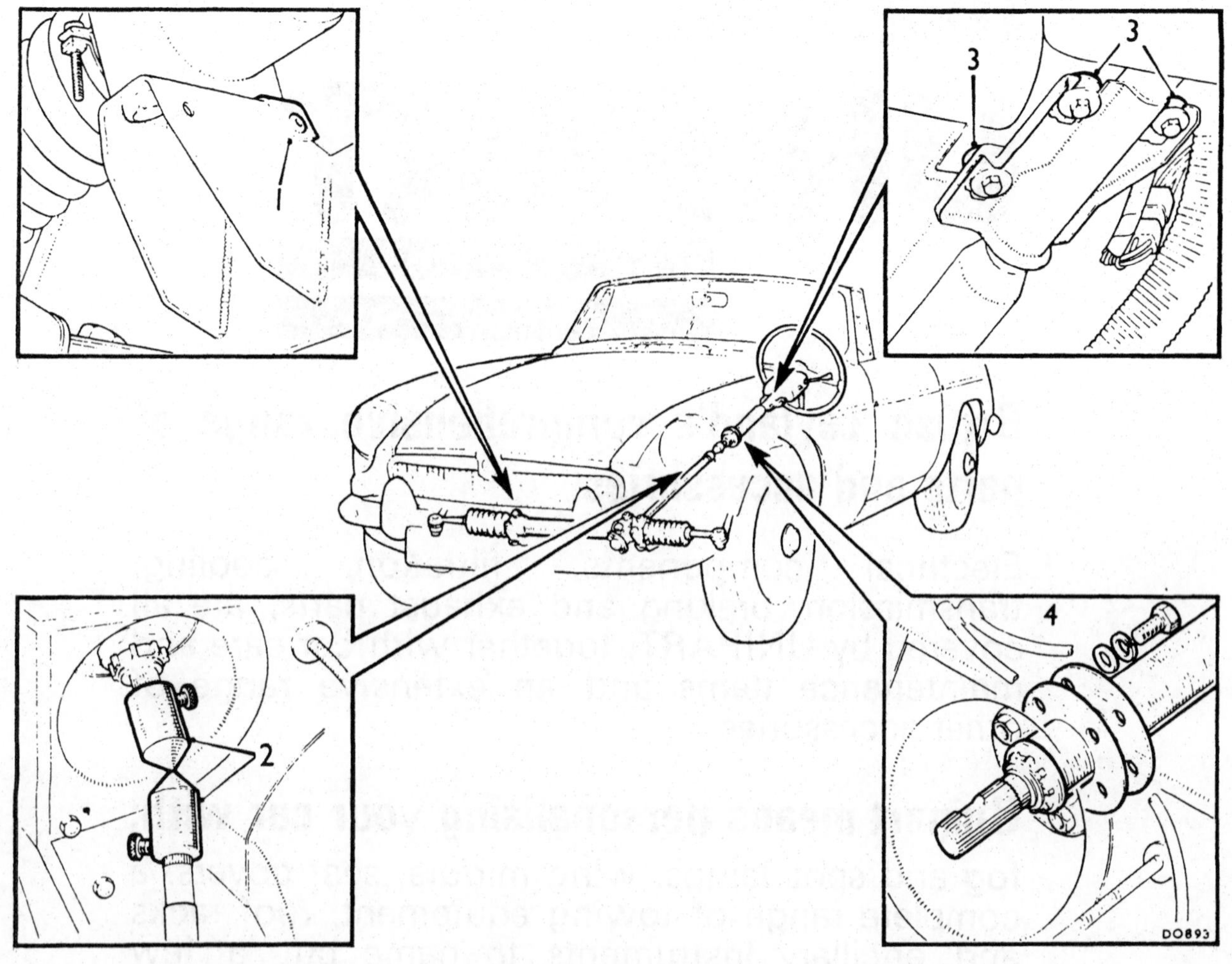

Fig. Ja.1
Steering alignment

1. Rack shims.
2. Alignment gauge, 18G 1140.
3. Packing washers fitted between column top fixing brackets.
4. Toe-plate fixings.

11. The steering-column and rack assembly are correctly aligned when the gauges meet exactly at their points (see Fig. Ja.1).
12. Correct any horizontal misalignment by moving the end of the steering-column.
13. If any vertical misalignment exists between the gauge points, proceed as follows:
    a. Remove the rack fixing bolts.
    b. Add sufficient shims (shim thickness .020 in. (.508 mm.)) to correct the misalignment, between the left-hand and right-hand mounting brackets and the cross-member mounting bosses. Do not rivet the shims to the bosses at this stage.
    c. Refit and tighten the rack mounting bolts.
    d. Recheck the alignment of the gauge points.
    e. If the alignment is still unsatisfactory, adjust the shim thickness.
    f. When correct alignment of the gauge points has been achieved, rivet the shims to the mounting bosses through the holes provided.
14. Remove the rack assembly.
15. Remove the gauges from the pinion and steering-column.
16. Check that the steering-column is in the straight-ahead position, and fit the universal joint on to its splines with the pinch-bolt hole aligned with the machined flat.
17. Check that the rack is in the straight-ahead position.
18. Fit the rack assembly and fully tighten the rack mounting bolts.
19. Tighten the three toe-plate to steering-column securing bolts.
20. Tighten the two steering-column upper fixing bolts to the torque figure given in **'GENERAL DATA'**.
21. Measure the gap between the column upper mounting flange and the body bracket at the third bolt position. Fit packing washers to the thickness of the gap, then fit and tighten the bolt to the torque figure given in **'GENERAL DATA'**.
22. Fit the two universal joint pinch-bolts and tighten them to the torque figure given in **'GENERAL DATA'**.

SECTION K

THE FRONT SUSPENSION

GENERAL DESCRIPTION

The independent front suspension is of the wishbone and coil type in which the suspension units are mounted one on each end of the cross-member assembly. The cross-member is rubber-mounted and bolted to the body side-members.

This design allows the front suspension to be removed as a complete unit.

The cross-member embodies two mounting brackets for the steering rack, a bracket at each end for the bump rubbers, a towing-eye plate, two front brake hose brackets, and two brake pipe clips.

Each suspension unit comprises a coil spring, a swivel axle unit, a lower wishbone assembly, and an upper assembly formed by the arms of the double-acting dampers mounted on top of the cross-member.

The lower arms are rubber-mounted on a pivot that is bolted to the cross-member; the outer ends of the arms are bolted to the lower end of the swivel pin. The outer ends of the shock absorber arms are secured to the swivel pin upper trunnion link by a fulcrum pin and tapered rubber bushes.

A spring pan secured between the lower wishbone arms supports the coil spring; the upper end of the spring is located by a spigot bolted to the under side of the cross-member.

Both suspension units may be interconnected by a rubber-mounted anti-roil bar.

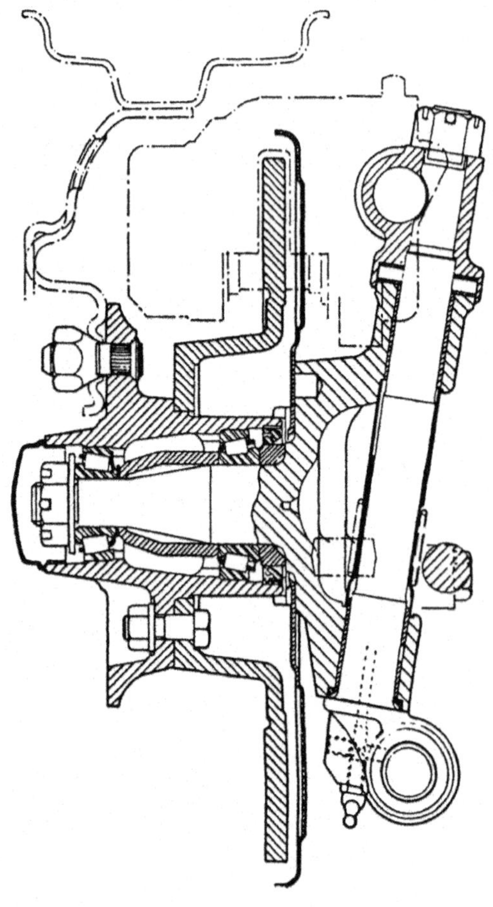

Fig. K.1
Cross-section of a swivel axle and hub

Section K.1

LUBRICATION

Lubrication nipples are provided on the top and bottom swivel pin bushes and in the base of the swivel pin. Each nipple should be charged with grease.

Section K.2

FRONT HUBS

Disc wheels

The front hubs are supported on taper-roller bearings that are mounted on the swivel axles. Four wheel disc studs are pressed into the hub, and the brake disc is secured to the hub by nuts and bolts.

An oil seal is fitted to the inner end of the hub and a spacer and shims are interposed between the inner and outer bearing. The assembly is retained on the swivel axle by a washer, nut, and split pin, and the outer end of the hub is closed by a grease-retaining cap.

Wire wheels

The construction of the wire wheel hubs is similar to that of the disc wheel hubs. Externally the outer end of the hub takes the form of splines, and the grease retainer is fitted inside the hub to close an access hole to the split pin. The outer edge of the hub is threaded externally to permit the fitting of a hub cap.

NOTE.--The right-hand hub is threaded right-hand and the left-hand hub is threaded left-hand.

Removing a hub

To remove a hub apply the hand brake, lift and support the front of the car, and remove the road wheel.

Remove the two studs securing the brake calliper to the swivel axle and support the calliper clear of the hub assembly.

Withdraw the grease retainer and remove the split pin from the stub axle nut. Unscrew the nut.

Using Service tool 18G 363 (wire wheels) or 18G 304 with adaptors 18G 304 B and 18G 304 J (disc wheels), withdraw the hub and disc assembly.

From the hub withdraw the bearing retaining washer, outer bearing, shims, spacer, inner bearing, oil seal collar, and oil seal.

The outer bearing races should be left in the hub unless they are to be renewed.

Inspection of bearings

Wash the bearings in paraffin and thoroughly dry them in an air blast or with a non-fluffy cloth.

Examine the rollers for chips, pitting, or other damage and for security in their cages. Examine also the inner and outer races.

Bearings damaged or suspect must be renewed.

After examination immerse the bearings in mineral oil.

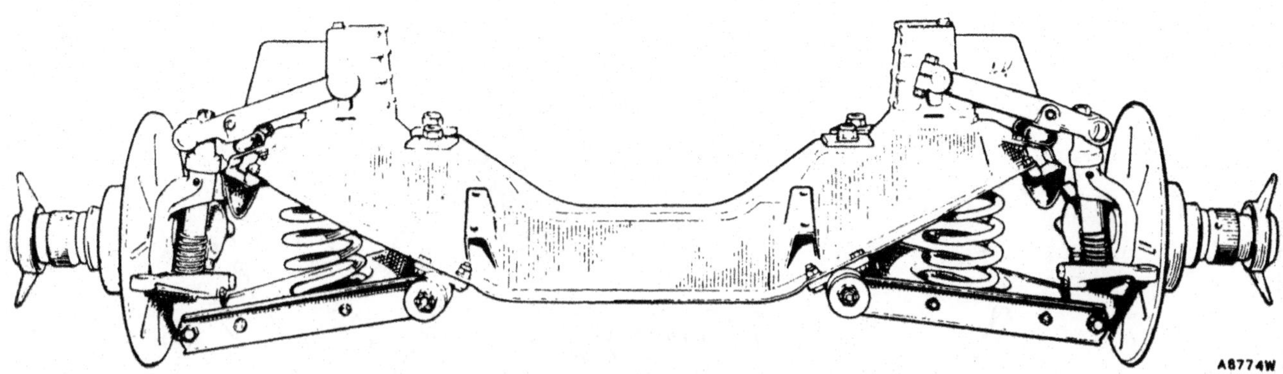

Fig. K.2
The front suspension cross-member and the suspension units

Refitting a hub
If the bearing outer races have been removed refit the new ones by pressing them into the hub.
Fill each bearing with grease ensuring a small protrusion either side of the bearing. Fill the cavity between the bearing and the oil seal and lightly smear the spacer with grease. Do not fill the cavity between the bearings or the grease-retaining cap with grease.
Fit the inner bearing to its race and the collar and seal to the hub, position the spacer and outer bearing, and assemble the hub to the axle.
Adjust the hub bearings as follows to obtain the correct end-float of between .002 and .004 in. (.05 and .10 mm.).

1. Assemble the hub without the shims and mount the assembly on the axle. Fit the retaining washer and nut and tighten the nut until the bearings bind. This will pull the outer races fully against their locating flanges inside the hub.
2. Remove the nut and washer and pull out the roller race of the outer bearing. Insert sufficient shims to produce an excessive end-float and note the thickness of shims used. Refit the bearing, washer, and nut and tighten the nut.
3. Using a clock gauge, measure accurately the end-float in the bearings. Remove the nut, washer, and outer bearing and reduce the number of shims to produce the required end-float.
   The shims are available in thicknesses of .003 in. (.076 mm.), .005 in. (.127 mm.), and .010 in. (.254 mm.).
4. Replace the bearing, washer, and nut and tighten the nut to a torque loading of between 40 and 70 lb. ft. (5.3 and 9.6 kg. m.). Latitude for the torque wrench reading is given so that the nut can be tightened sufficiently to align a slot in the nut with the hole in the axle. Fit a new split pin.
5. Refit the hub caps.

Section K.3

COIL SPRINGS

Each coil spring is located between a spring pan bolted to the lower wishbone arms and a spigot bolted to the under side of the cross-member assembly.
To remove a spring fit a spring compressor (Service tool 18G 693) to the lower wishbone arms and take the weight of the spring.
Remove the anti-roll bar link, if fitted, and the bolts securing the spring pan to the wishbone arms.
Unscrew the spring compressor to release the tension in the spring and then remove the spring pan and spring.
Replacement is a reversal of the removal sequence.

Section K.4

SWIVEL AXLES

The swivel axles work on the swivel pins, which are supported at their upper ends by the trunnion links, which are bolted to the shock absorber arms, and at their lower ends by the fulcrum pins, which connect with the lower wishbone arms.
The centre portion of the pins are protected by upper and lower spring-loaded dust shields.
The steering levers and the disc brake dust plates are bolted to the inside of the swivel axles.

Removing and dismantling
To remove the swivel axles jack up and support the car and, dealing with each axle in turn, proceed as follows:

1. Remove the front road wheel.
2. Detach the brake calliper and support it clear of the hub.
3. Remove the hub and brake disc assembly as described in Section K.2.
4. Remove the steering lever bolts and detach the lever and then the disc cover bolts and the cover.
5. Remove the coil spring as described in Section K.3.
6. Extract the split pins from the upper trunnion pin and fulcrum pin and remove the nuts.
7. Unscrew the clamp bolt and centre-bolt of the shock absorber arm, ease the arm outwards, and remove the swivel axle.

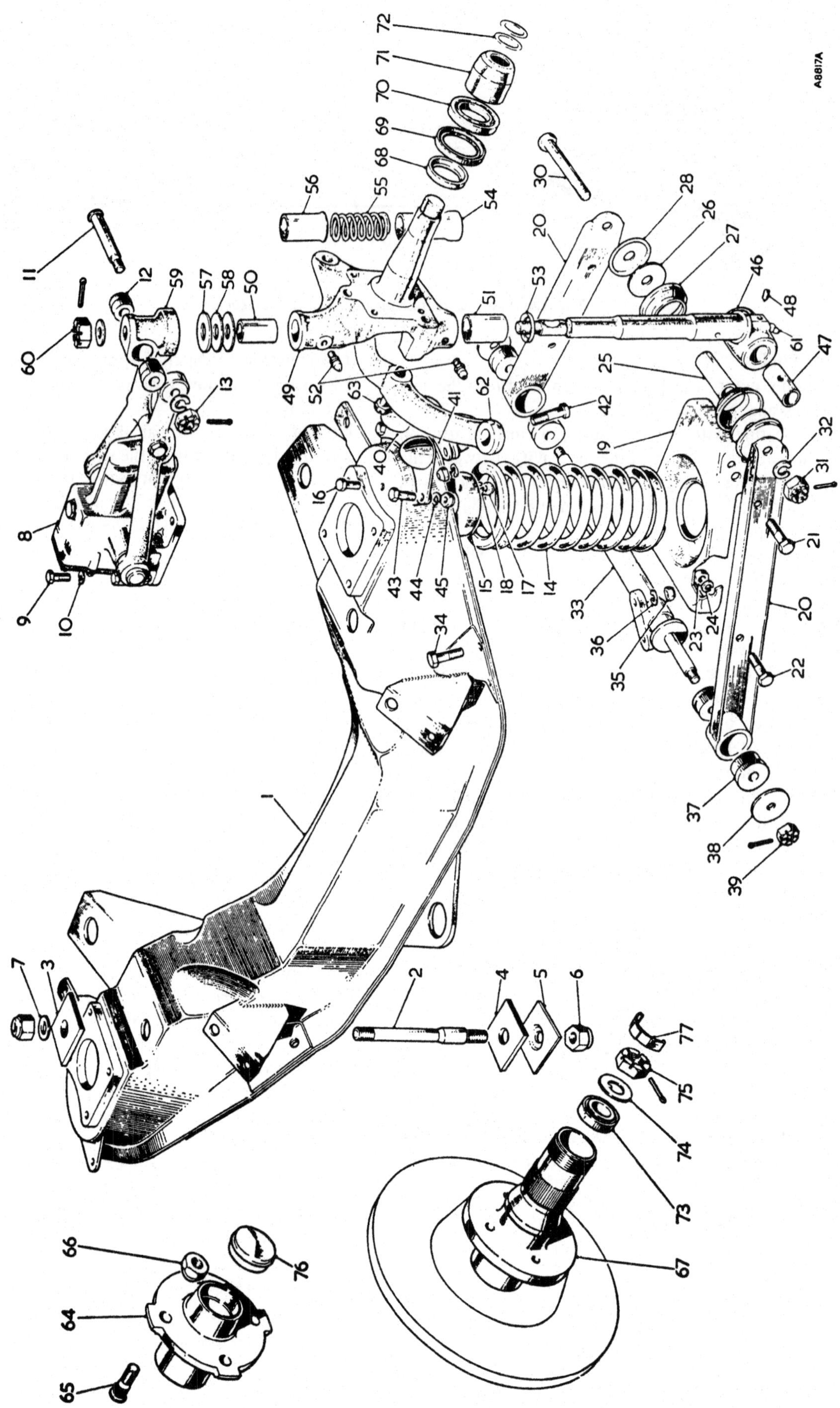

THE FRONT SUSPENSION COMPONENTS

A8817A

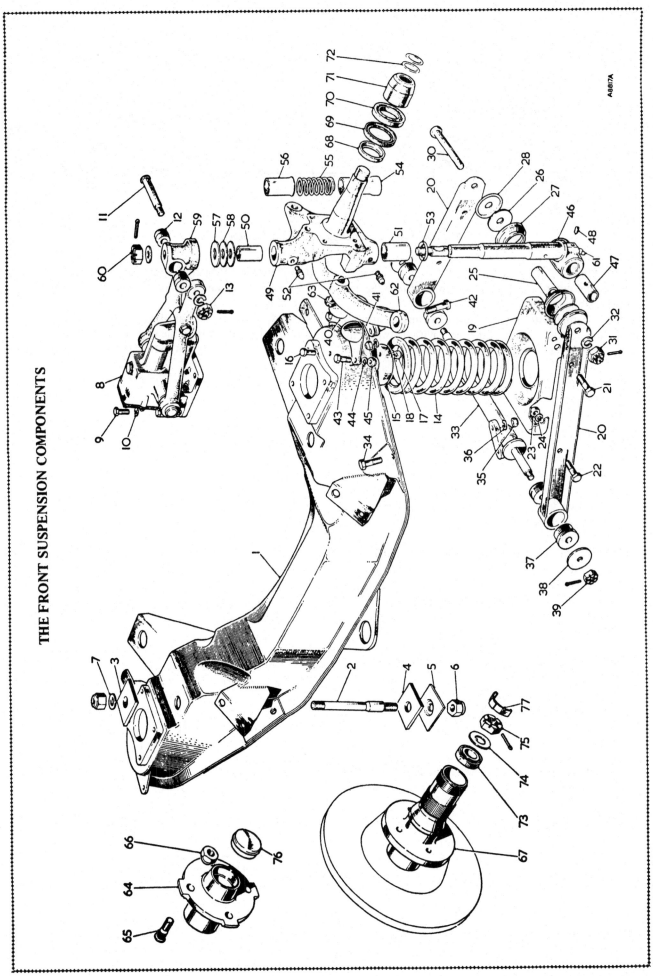

KEY TO THE FRONT SUSPENSION COMPONENTS

No.	Description	No.	Description.	No.	Description
1.	Cross-member.	27.	Seal–link.	53.	Ring–swivel axle pin (cork).
2.	Bolt–cross-member to body.	28.	Support–link seal.	54.	Tube–dust excluder–bottom.
3.	Pad–mounting–upper (rubber).	29.	Nut–wishbone pivot.	55.	Spring–dust excluder.
4.	Pad–mounting–lower (rubber).	30.	Bolt–wishbone to link.	56.	Tube–dust excluder–top.
5.	Plate–clamp.	31.	Nut–bolt.	57.	Washer–thrust.
6.	Nut–mounting bolt.	32.	Washer–spring–nut.	58.	Washer–floating thrust–.052 to .057 in. (1.32 to 1.44 mm.).
7.	Washer–plain–nut.	33.	Pivot–wishbone.	59.	Trunnion–suspension link.
8.	Absorber–shock.	34.	Bolt–pivot to member.	60.	Nut–swivel axle pin.
9.	Screw–shock absorber to cross-member.	35.	Nut–bolt.	61.	Lubricator–swivel pin.
10.	Washer–screw–spring.	36.	Washer–spring–nut.	62.	Lever–steering–R.H.
11.	Pin–fulcrum–top link to shock absorber arm.	37.	Bush–wishbone.	63.	Bolt–steering lever to swivel axle.
12.	Bearing–link.	38.	Washer–wishbone pivot.	64.	Hub assembly.
13.	Nut–fulcrum pin.	39.	Nut–wishbone pivot.	65.	Stud–wheel.
14.	Spring–coil.	40.	Buffer–rebound.	66.	Nut–wheel stud.
15.	Spigot–spring.	41.	Distance piece.	67.	Hub assembly–R.H.
16.	Screw–spigot to cross-member.	42.	Bolt–rebound buffer to cross-member.	68.	Collar–oil seal.
17.	Nut–screw.	43.	Screw–rebound buffer to cross-member.	69.	Seal–oil.
18.	Washer–spring–nut.	44.	Washer–spring.	70.	Bearing for hub–inner.
19.	Pan assembly–spring.	45.	Nut.	71.	Spacer–bearing.
20.	Wishbone assembly–bottom.	46.	Pin–swivel.	72.	Shim–.003 in. (.76 mm.).
21.	Screw–spring pan to wishbone.	47.	Bush–swivel pin.	73.	Bearing–hub–outer.
22.	Screw–spring pan to wishbone.	48.	Screw–grub–swivel pin.	74.	Washer–bearing retaining.
23.	Nut–screw.	49.	Axle assembly–swivel–R.H.	75.	Nut–bearing retaining.
24.	Washer–spring–nut.	50.	Bush–swivel–top.	76.	Cup–grease-retaining.
25.	Tube–distance–link.	51.	Bush–swivel–bottom.	77.	Cup–grease-retaining.
26.	Washer–thrust–link.	52.	Lubricator–swivel bush.		

8. Extract the split pin from the swivel axle and remove the nut, upper trunnion suspension link, steel and bronze thrust washers, swivel pin, and dust covers and spring. From the swivel pin remove the cork washer.

Examination

Wash all parts and thoroughly dry them with a non-fluffy cloth. Examine all parts for wear or damage, paying particular attention to the swivel pins, lower fulcrum pins, and all bushes. Check the pins for ovality. Worn or suspect pins or bushes must be renewed.

Assembling and replacing

Reverse the dismantling sequence to reassemble the axles, and, if necessary, renew the thrust washers by selective assembly to produce a condition that will permit the swivel axle to rotate freely on the pin with a minimum amount of end-play. The maximum permissible end-play is .002 in. (.05 mm.).

The thrust washers are available in the following sizes: .052 to .057 in. (1.32 to 1.44 mm.), .058 to .063 in. (1.47 to 1.60 mm.), .064 to .069 in. (1.62 to 1.75 mm.).

After assembly reverse the removal sequence to refit the assembly to the hub.

Section K.5

REMOVING AND REFITTING BUSHES

Swivel pin bush

1. Press out the old bush and ensure that the lubrication channels are clean and free from obstruction.
2. Position the new bush with the split in the bush adjacent to the outer face of the base. This will ensure that the grease channel in the bush is in line with the channel in the pin.

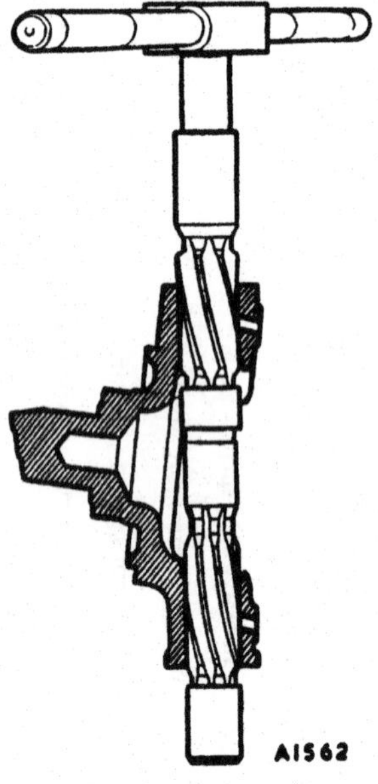

Fig. K.3
Line-reaming a swivel axle

3. Press the bush into the pin squarely and evenly and ream to between .7495 and .7505 in. (19.02 and 19.05 mm.).

Swivel axle bushes

1. Press out the old bushes from the bottom of the axle.
2. Press in the new upper bushes from the bottom of the axle and ensure that the open end of the oil groove enters the axle first and that the hole in the bush is in line with the lubrication channel in the axle. Press the bush in until its top face is flush with the top face of the axle.
3. Assemble the bottom bush in a similar manner but press it in until the lower face of the bush is flush with the counterbore in the under side of the axle.
4. Line-bore the bushes to the following dimensions:
   Top bush .. .. .7815 to .7820 in. (19.83 to 19.86 mm.).
   Bottom bush .. .9075 to .9080 in. (23.03 to 23.06 mm.).

Section K.6

FRONT SUSPENSION UNIT

Removing

1. Jack up and support the front of the car and remove the road wheels.
2. Disconnect the anti-roll bar links from the spring pans.
3. Remove the steering-rack as described in Section J.5.
4. Drain the hydraulic fluid from the braking system.
5. Disconnect the brake pipes from the flexible hoses and from the clips on the front suspension cross-member.
6. Support the cross-member with a trolley jack positioned under its centre point.
7. Remove the nuts and washers from the tops of the support bolts, lower the cross-member, and remove it from the under side of the car.
8. From the under side of the cross-member remove the bolts, mounting plates, and the upper and lower rubber mounting pads.

Dismantling

1. Remove the coil springs as described in Section K.3, the hubs as described in Section K.2, and the swivel axles as described in Section K.4.
2. Retain the rubber bushes from the upper trunnion link and the distance tube, thrust washers, seals, and supports from the lower end of the swivel pin.
3. Unscrew the shock absorber bolts and remove the shock absorbers.
4. Unscrew the pivot to cross-member securing bolts and remove the pivot and wishbone arms.
5. Unscrew the pivot nuts and from each end of the pivot remove the washer, bush, arm, and inner bush.

6. Remove the two bolts and two screws securing the rebound buffer brackets to the cross-member and remove the brackets.

Examination of components

Thoroughly clean and dry all components and inspect them for cracks, fractures, deterioration, and thread damage. Additionally, carry out the following examinations:

1. Check the hub bearings as described in Section K.2 and the swivel axles and pins as described in Section K.4.
2. Renew rubber bushes or seals that are perished, split, eccentric, or oil-soaked.
3. Examine the holes in the wishbone arms and spring pans for elongation.
4. Examine the coil spring for correct length and weight as given under **'GENERAL DATA'**.
5. Check the fulcrum pin distance tubes for scoring or wear. The tubes are 2.337 in. (59.36 mm.) long by .748 in. (19.0 mm.) diameter.
6. Examine the fulcrum pin thrust washers for wear or ridging. The faces should be flat and parallel to within .0005 in. (.01 mm.). The washers are between .065 and .068 in. (1.68 and 1.73 mm.) thick.

Assembling and replacing

Assembly and replacement is a reversal of the dismantling and removal sequence, but attention must be given to the following:

1. The swivel axles must be free to rotate on the pins as described in Section K.4.
2. The fulcrum pin distance tubes, thrust washers, seal supports, and seals should be temporarily assembled and the swivel pin end-float checked. This should be between .008 and .013 in. (.20 and .32 mm.).
3. When assembling the lower wishbone arms the inner pivot must be fully tightened before the coil spring is fitted. This may be done in either the static or rebound position.

Section K.7

ADDITIONAL SWIVEL PIN GREASE NIPPLE

On later production cars an additional grease nipple is provided on the swivel pin lower bush.

Earlier cars can be modified as follows

1. Remove the swivel axles as described previously.
2. Using a No. 3 (.213 in. (.541 mm.)) drill, carefully drill each swivel axle in the position shown at 'X' in Fig. K.4.
   NOTE.–Drilling is in the same position for both hands, i.e. facing forward on L.H. side, rearward on R.H. side.
3. Tap the ¼in. UNF. drilled holes ¼in. (6.35 mm.) deep.

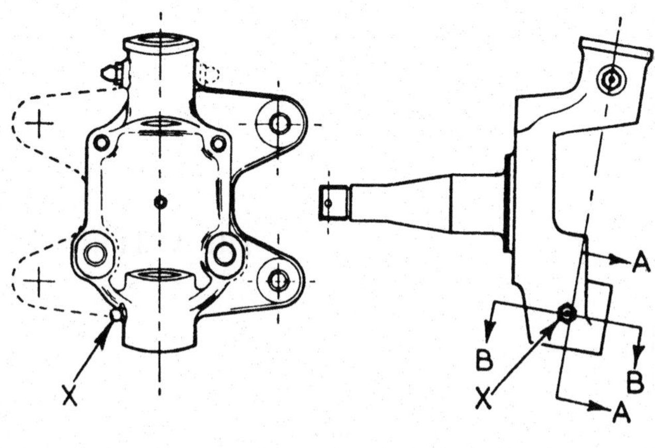

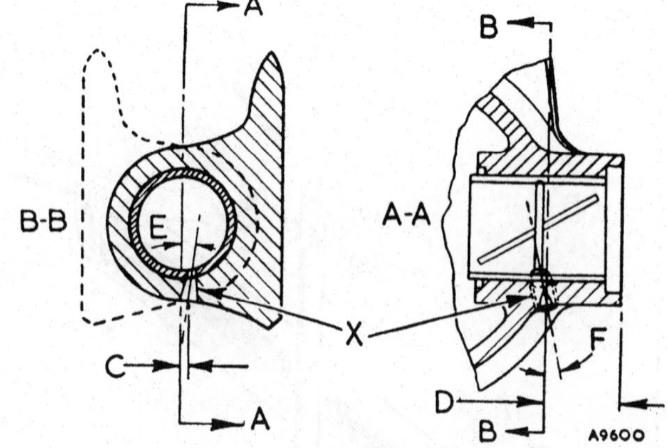

Fig. K.4

Fitting additional grease nipple to swivel pin lower bush (earlier cars)

C. $\frac{1}{16}$ in. (1.6 mm.). E. 6°.
D. ¾ in. (19 mm.). F. 12°.

4. Remove drilling swarf and any fraze from inside bush bore.
5. Fit grease nipple (UHN 400) to both swivel axles.
6. Coat swivel pins with grease before assembly.

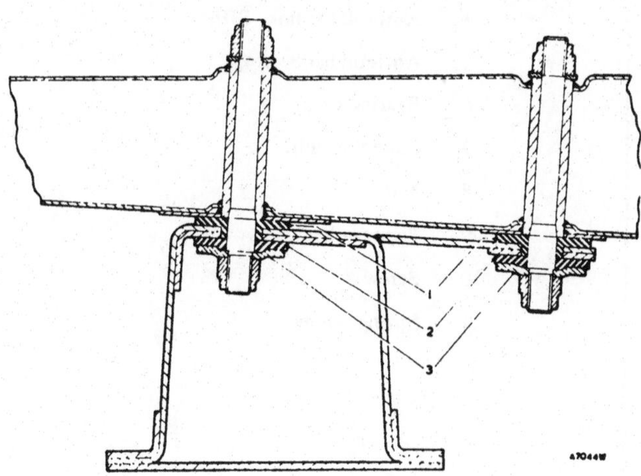

Fig. K.5

Assembly of front suspension cross-member to body side-member showing:

1. Upper mounting pad. 2. Lower mounting pad. 3. Clamp plate.

THE ANTI-ROLL BAR COMPONENTS

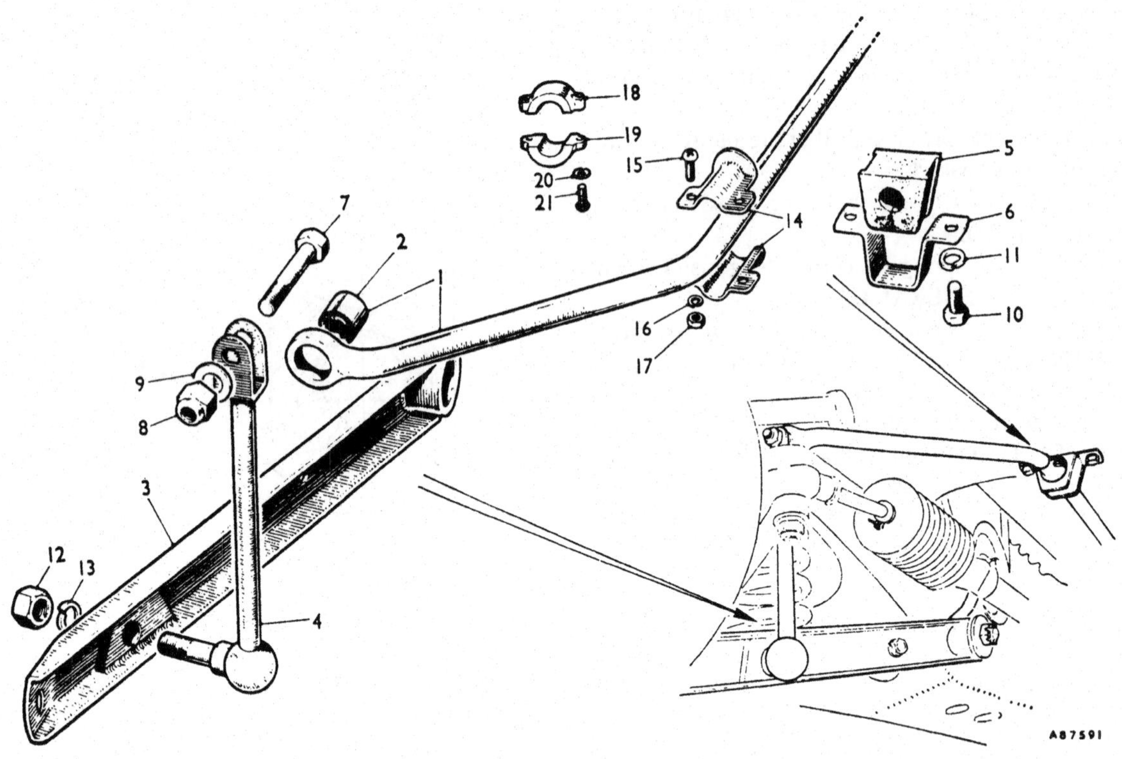

No.	Description
1.	Anti-roll bar assembly.
2.	Bush.
3.	Bottom wishbone assembly–R.H.
4.	Anti-roll bar link–R.H.
5.	Anti-roll bar bearing.
6.	Bearing strap.
7.	Clamping bolt.
8.	Nut.
9.	Plain washer.
10.	Screw.
11.	Spring washer.

No.	Description	
12.	Nut.	
13.	Spring washer.	
14.	Location stop end.	
15.	Screw.	
16.	Spring washer.	
17.	Nut.	
18.	Upper locator	GT only.
19.	Lower locator	GT only.
20.	Spring washer	GT only.
21.	Set screws	GT only.

Section K.8

ANTI-ROLL BAR

Removing

TOURER

The front suspension units on later cars are inter-connected by a rubber mounted anti-roll bar: this can also be fitted to early cars.

To fit the anti-roll bar proceed as follows:

1. Remove the coil springs as described in Section K.3 and the front lower wishbone arms as described in Section K.6.
2. Assemble the new right-hand and left-hand wishbone arms to the pivot and swivel pins.
3. Refit the coil spring and then fit the lower ends of the anti-roll bar links to the wishbone and spring pan.
4. Fit the two rubber bearings to the bar and loosely assemble the end location stops outboard of the bearings.
5. Fit the straps to the bearings and then secure the straps to the right-hand and left-hand body side-members respectively with the spring washers and screws.
6. Position the location stops so that their inner faces are $11\frac{1}{16}$ in. (28.1 cm.) from the centre-line of the bar. Tighten the screw and nuts to secure the stops.
7. Place the ends of the bar into the fork ends of the links and secure them with the clamping bolts, washers, and stiff nuts. The Metalastik bushes are pressed into the ends of the anti-roll bar.

GT

Raise the car to a workable height. Remove the nuts and washers securing the anti-roll bar link to the bottom wishbones. Remove the set screws securing the bearing straps to the front longitudinal members and lift away the anti-roll bar assembly.

Refitting

Reverse the removal procedure.

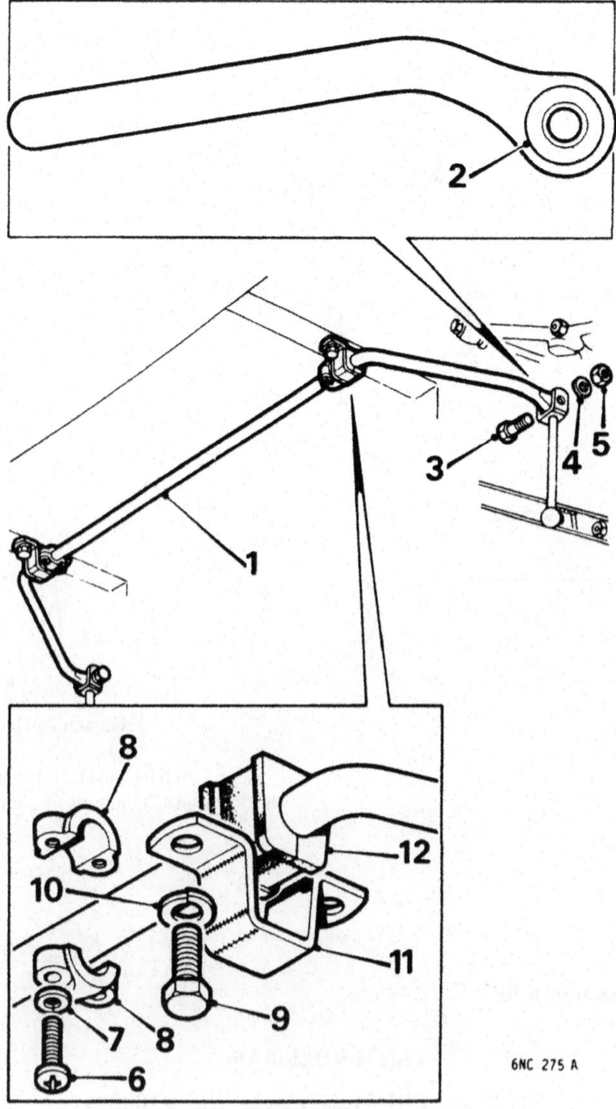

Fig. K.6

Front anti-roll bar compontents
(GHN5 and GHD5 cars from Car No. 410002)

1. Anti-roll bar assembly
2. Bush
3. Clamping bolt
4. Spring washer
5. Spring washer
6. Set screw
7. Spring washer
8. Locator
9. Screw
10. Spring washer
11. Bearing strap
12. Bearing

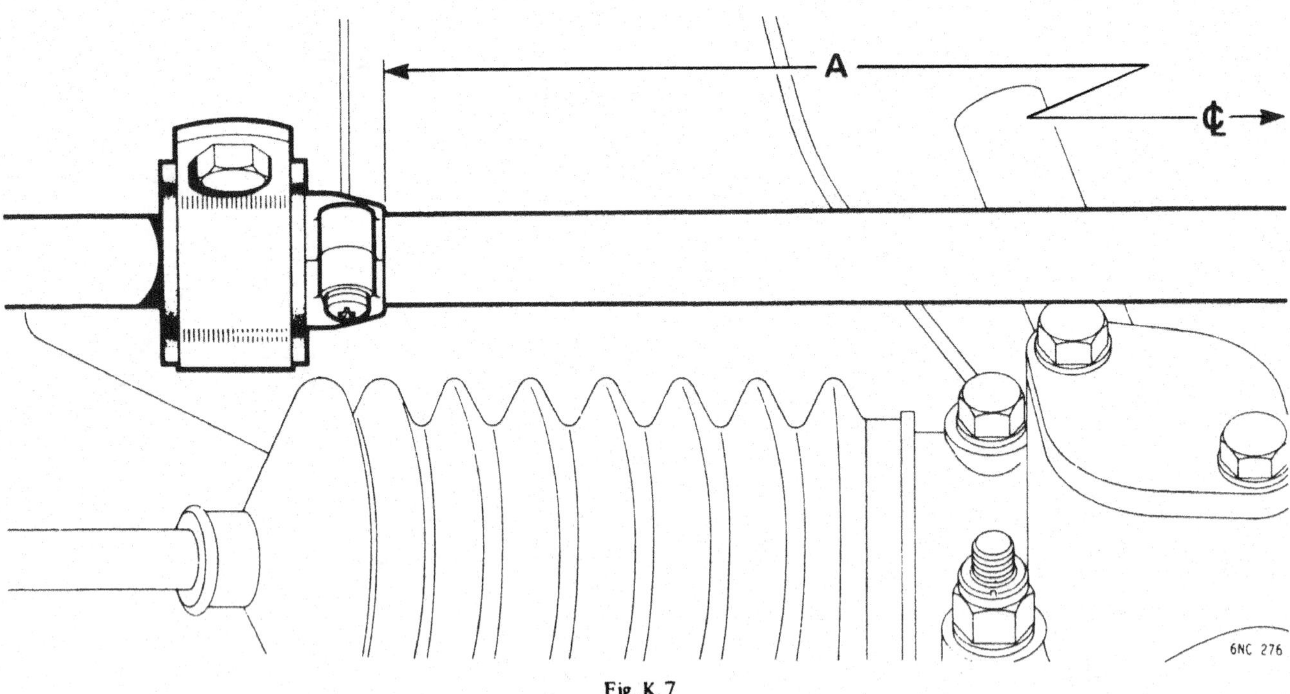

Fig. K.7

Front anti-roll bar locator dimension

(GHN5 and GHD5 cars from Car No. 410002)
A = 9 $\frac{5}{16}$ in (237 mm) from locator inner face to centre line of car

Section K.9

ANTI-ROLL BAR

(GHN5 and GHD5 cars from Car No. 410002)

Removing

1. Raise the vehicle and support the chassis member.
2. Disconnect the anti-roll bar from the support link on each side.
3. Swing the anti-roll bar down.
4. Remove the bearing straps, bearing rubbers and anti-roll bar.
5. Remove the locators if fitting a new anti-roll bar.
6. Check the bushes and anti-roll bar bearing rubbers: renew if worn.

Refitting

7. Fit the bushes and bearing rubbers to the anti-roll bar.
8. Fit the locators, ensuring their inner faces are approximately 9 $\frac{5}{16}$ in (237 mm) (A) from the centre of the roll bar.
9. Fit the anti-roll bar to the longitudinal members. **WARNING**: The anti-roll bar must be fitted with the crank (bolt eye for support link) facing downwards.
10. Connect the anti-roll bar to the support link on each side.
11. Lower the vehicle.

SECTION L

THE HYDRAULIC DAMPERS

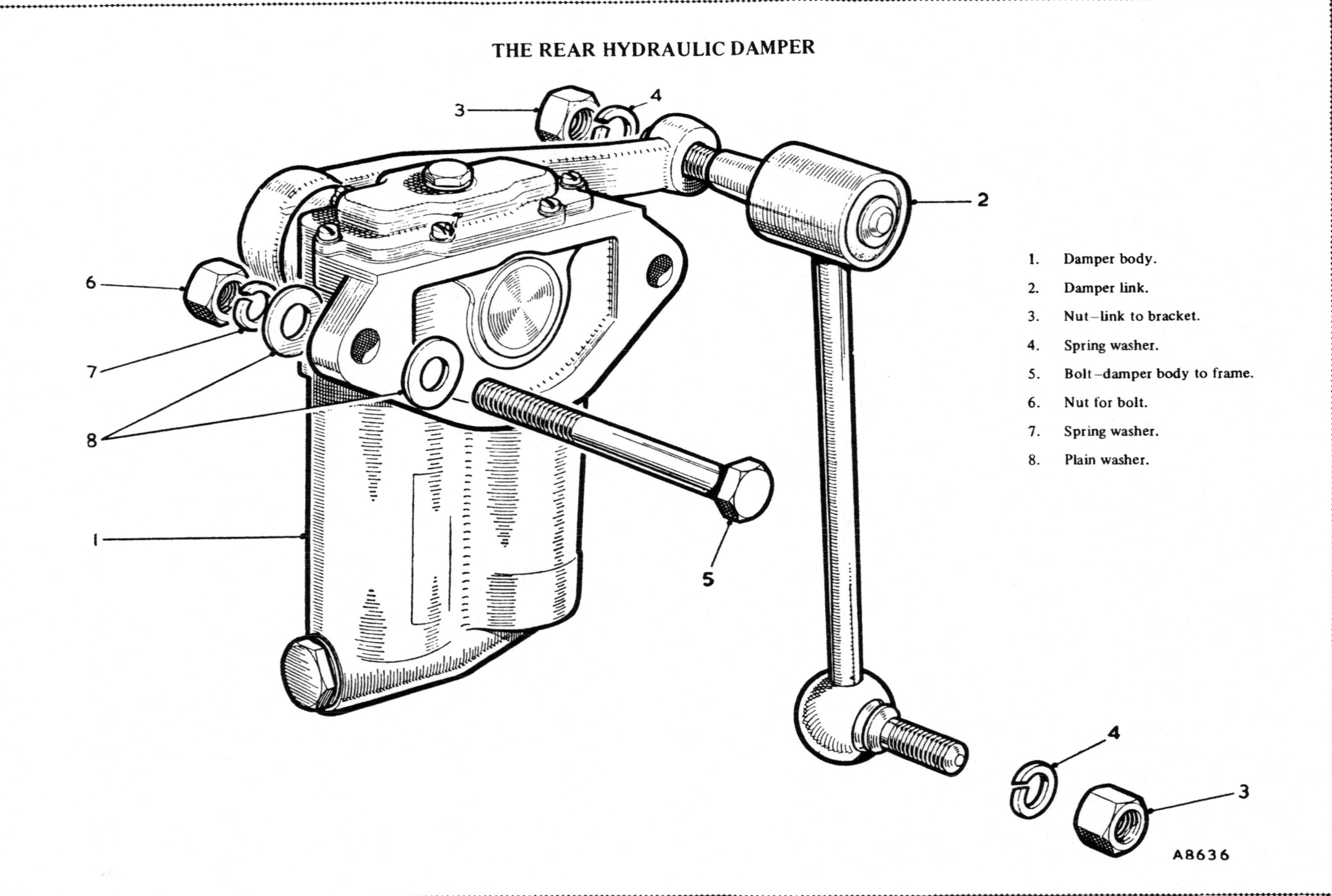
THE REAR HYDRAULIC DAMPER
1. Damper body.
2. Damper link.
3. Nut—link to bracket.
4. Spring washer.
5. Bolt—damper body to frame.
6. Nut for bolt.
7. Spring washer.
8. Plain washer.
A8636

GENERAL DESCRIPTION

The hydraulic dampers are Armstrong double-acting-type in which resistance is offered to the compression and to the recoil of the front suspension coil and rear leaf springs.

The front dampers are bolted to the front suspension cross-member above the coil spring seats. The damper arms are connected to the upper swivel pin link.

The rear dampers are bolted to the body rear side-members and are connected by a link to the rear axle.

Section L.1

MAINTENANCE

The maintenance of the hydraulic dampers, when in position on the vehicle, is confined to examination for leakage and examination of the anchorage to the chassis to ensure that the fixing bolts are tight. No adjustment of the hydraulic dampers is required or provided. They are accurately set before leaving the manufacturer to give the amount of damping most suitable for the car. **Any attempt to dismantle the assembly will seriously affect the operation and performance.**

The dampers are topped up by removing the filler plug and filling up to the bottom of the filler plug hole. **Use Armstrong Super (Thin) Shock Absorber Fluid No. 624.** (If this fluid is not available, any good-quality mineral oil to specification S.A.E. 20W should be used, but this alternative is not suitable for low-temperature operation).

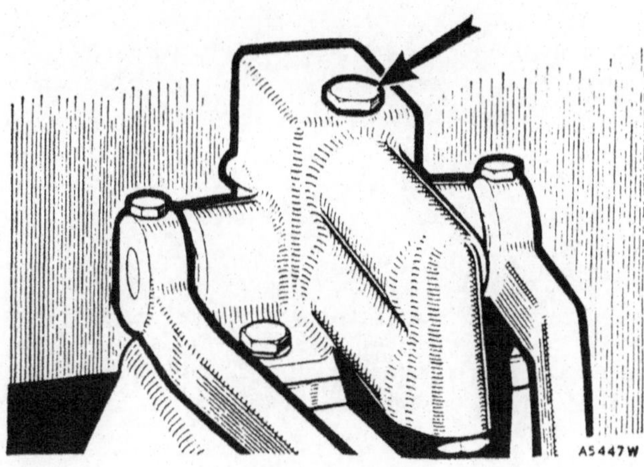

Fig. L.1
The front hydraulic damper filler plug

Before removing the filler cap, which is located on the top of the damper, carefully wipe the exterior, as it is of utmost importance that no dirt whatever enters through the filler hole.

On no account neglect the operation of topping up the damper fluid because if the low-pressure chamber of the unit is allowed to become empty, air will enter the pressure cylinders and the action of the damper will be impaired.

Access to the rear dampers is obtained by removing the rubber plugs in the rear floor panel adjacent to the battery cover.

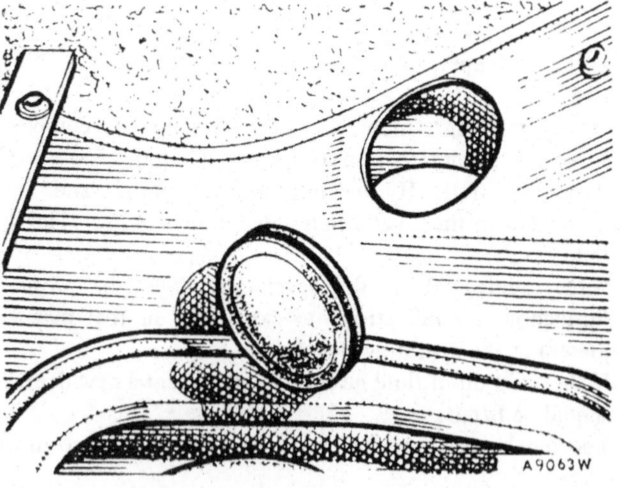

Fig. L.2
A rubber plug removed from the rear floor panel to give access to the rear hydraulic damper filler plug.

Section L.2

REMOVING AND REPLACING THE DAMPERS

Front

Jack up the car under the lower wishbone spring pan until the wheel is clear of the ground.

Remove the wheel and take out the swivel pin top pivot bolt. Swing out the hub unit clear of the upper wishbone and support it on a suitable stand to prevent straining the brake hose. Unscrew the four nuts holding the damper to the cross-member.

Rear

Jack up the rear of the car below the axle or rear springs and remove the rear wheel.

Remove the nut and spring washers securing the damper arm to the bracket on the rear spring.

Remove the nuts, spring and flat washers from the two bolts securing the damper to the side-member, and withdraw the damper.

NOTE.–When handling hydraulic dampers that have been removed for any purpose, it is important to keep the assemblies upright as far as possible, otherwise air may enter the operating chamber and result in free movement.

Replacement is a reversal of the above procedure; ensure that the servicing bolts are tightened to the torque figure given in **'GENERAL DATA'**.

Section L.3

TESTING THE DAMPERS

If the hydraulic dampers do not appear to function satisfactorily, the resistance may be roughly checked by bouncing each corner of the car up and down. A uniform movement indicates that no attention is required, but if the resistance is erratic or free movement of the car is felt the damper should be removed for checking and topping up.

Indication of their resistance can be obtained by carrying out the following check:
Bolt the damper, in an upright position, to a plate held in a vice.
Move the lever arm up and down through its complete stroke. A moderate resistance throughout the full stroke should be felt. If the resistance is erratic, and free movement in the lever arm is noted, it may indicate lack of fluid.
While adding fluid the lever arm must be worked throughout its full stroke to expel any air that may be present in the operating chamber.
If the addition of fluid gives no improvement a new damper should be fitted.
Too much resistance, i.e. when it is not possible to move the lever arm by hand, indicates a broken internal part or a seized piston.
The arms should not be removed from the dampers at any time as it is essential that they should be assembled to the damper shaft in the right relation to the damper cam lever so that there is the full range of movement on either side of the centre-line.
It must be clearly understood that there is no provision for adjusting the setting of the dampers, and if they are in any way defective they must be returned to the manufacturers for attention.
Leakage from the damper lid may be rectified by fitting a new lid gasket and fully tightening the screws.
A weep from the valve screw may be stopped by gently tightening the screw.

SECTION M

THE BRAKING SYSTEM

GENERAL DESCRIPTION

The Lockheed hydraulic brake system comprises a master cylinder and fluid supply reservoir, automatically adjusted disc brake assemblies at the front of the vehicle, and manually adjusted drum-type brakes at the rear.

The master cylinder and fluid supply reservoir assembly is mounted on the engine side of the bulkhead above the brake pedal.

The front brake units are of the rotating disc and rigidly mounted calliper type, each calliper carrying two friction pad assemblies between which the disc revolves. The rear brake units are of the internal-expanding shoe and drum type, each unit being operated by a single wheel cylinder which is actuated hydraulically by the foot pedal and mechanically by the hand brake.

Section M.1

MAINTENANCE

Periodically examine the quantity of brake fluid in the master cylinder. The fluid level should never be higher than ¼ in (6.35 mm.) below the bottom of the filler neck, and the cylinder must never be less than half-full.

A considerable drop in the level of the fluid in the reservoir is an indication of a leak in the system which should at once be traced and rectified.

The grease nipple on the hand brake cable should be charged with grease.

Brake adjustment

FRONT

Wear on the front pads is automatically compensated during braking, and manual adjustment therefore is not provided. In order to maintain peak braking efficiency and to obtain the maximum life from the friction pads they should be examined at the recommended periods, and if the wear on one pad is greater than that on the other their operating positions must be changed over.

Fig. M.1
The square head of the adjuster spindle

REAR

As the brake-shoe linings wear, the movement of the brake pedal will increase, indicating that adjustment is necessary. Block the front wheels and jack up each rear wheel in turn. Fully release the hand brake. Turn the expander in a clockwise direction until the wheel is locked, then turn back one notch only. The wheel should be free to rotate without the shoe rubbing. Adjust the other rear brake in a similar way. Adjustment of the brake-shoes automatically adjusts the hand brake mechanism.

Preventive maintenance

To safeguard against the possible effects of wear, or deterioration, it is recommended that:

1. Disc brake pads, drum brake linings, hoses, and pipes should be examined at intervals no greater than those laid down in the Passport to Service.
2. Brake fluid should be changed completely every 18 months or 24,000 miles (40000 km.) whichever is the sooner.
3. All fluid seals in the hydraulic system and all flexible hoses should be examined and renewed if necessary every 3 years or 40,000 miles (65000 km.) whichever is the sooner. At the same time the working surface of the pistons and of the bores of the master cylinder, wheel cylinders, and other slave cylinders should be examined and new parts fitted where necessary.

Care must be taken always to observe the following points:

a. At all times use the recommended brake fluid.

b. Never leave fluid in unsealed containers. It absorbs moisture quickly and this can be dangerous.

c. Fluid drained from the system or used for bleeding is best discarded.

d. The necessity for absolute cleanliness throughout cannot be over-emphasized.

Section M.2

BRAKE PEDAL

The brake and clutch pedals are mounted at a common fulcrum point inside the master cylinder cover.

Removing

Remove the screws securing the brake and clutch master cylinder cover and take off the cover.

Extract the split pin and withdraw the clevis pin to release the master cylinder push-rod from the brake pedal. Detach the brake pedal return spring and remove the nut and spring washer from the pedal fulcrum bolt .The fulcrum bolt may now be withdrawn together with the brake pedal and internal distance sleeve. The clutch pedal will remain in position held by its return spring and master cylinder push-rod.

Reverse the above procedure to replace the brake pedal, noting that the head of the fulcrum bolt is at the clutch pedal side of the assembly.

Section M.3

HAND BRAKE

The hand brake, which is of the lever type, incorporating a thumb-operated ratchet release in the handle, is located on the right-hand side of the floor tunnel between the seats.

Pulling the handle operates the rear shoes only by means of cable-operated levers. The action of the inner and outer cables is employed through the action of a balance lever mounted on the rear axle to ensure even braking on the rear wheels.

Adjustment of the rear brake-shoes automatically adjusts the hand brake, but excessive movement of the hand brake lever due to cable stretch should be taken up as follows.

Adjust the inner cable length by turning the brass adjusting nut at the lower end of the hand brake lever below the car floor. The adjustment is correct if the hand brake is applied fully when the lever is pulled up three or four notches.

The rear brake-shoes should be adjusted as described in Section M.1 before taking up the hand brake cable stretch.

To remove (lever and cable assembly)

Unscrew and remove the adjusting nut, withdraw the end of the cable from the lower end of the lever, and remove the spring and flat washers.

Remove the nut securing the brake lever to the hand brake spindle and withdraw the spring washer, forked lever, and plain washer. The hand lever may now be withdrawn from inside the car.

Remove the right-hand seat (see Section R). Unscrew the three screws securing the ratchet plate to the floor tunnel. Lift the carpet and remove the nut and spring washer securing the outer cable front abutment. Disconnect the clips securing the cable assembly to the body and rear axle. Remove the bolt, nut, and spring washer connecting the two halves of the brake compensating lever to each other, slacken fully the self-locking nut securing the lever to the axle bracket, and release the cable abutment trunnion from the lever. Extract the split pins and withdraw the clevis pins to release the cable yokes from the levers on the brake backplates.

On replacement, check the hand brake lever operation as detailed above.

Section M.4

BLEEDING THE BRAKE SYSTEM

The following procedure should be adopted either for initial priming of the system or to bleed in service if air has been permitted to enter the system. Air may enter the system if pipe connections become loose or if the level of fluid in the reservoir is allowed to fall below the recommended level. During the bleeding operation it is important to keep the reservoir at least half-full to avoid drawing air into the system.

Check that all connections are tightened and all bleed screws closed. Fill the fluid reservoir with the recommended fluid (see **'GENERAL DATA'**). Keep it at least half-full throughout the bleeding operation, otherwise air will be drawn into the system, necessitating a fresh start.

Attach the bleeder tube to the bleed screw on the near-side rear brake and immerse the open end of the tube in a small quantity of brake fluid contained in a clean glass jar. Slacken the bleed screw and depress the brake pedal slowly through its full stroke and allow it to return without assistance. Repeat this pumping action with a slight pause before each depression of the pedal. When fluid entering the jar is completely free of air bubbles hold the pedal firmly against the floorboards and tighten the bleeder screw.

This process must be repeated at each of the three remaining brake assemblies.

Top up the fluid reservoir to its correct level, $\frac{1}{4}$ in. (6.35 mm.) below the filler neck.

If the disc brake callipers have been disturbed it will be necessary to pump the brake pedal several times to restore the automatic adjustment of the friction pads.

Apply a normal working load on the brake pedal for a period of two or three minutes and examine the entire system for leaks.

Section M.5

MASTER CYLINDER

Description

The master cylinder piston is backed by a rubber cup normally held in the 'off' position by a piston return spring. Immediately in front of the cup, when it is in the 'off' position, is a compensating orifice connecting the cylinder with the fluid supply. Pressure is applied to the piston by means of the push-rod attached to the brake pedal.

The reduced skirt of the piston forms an annular space

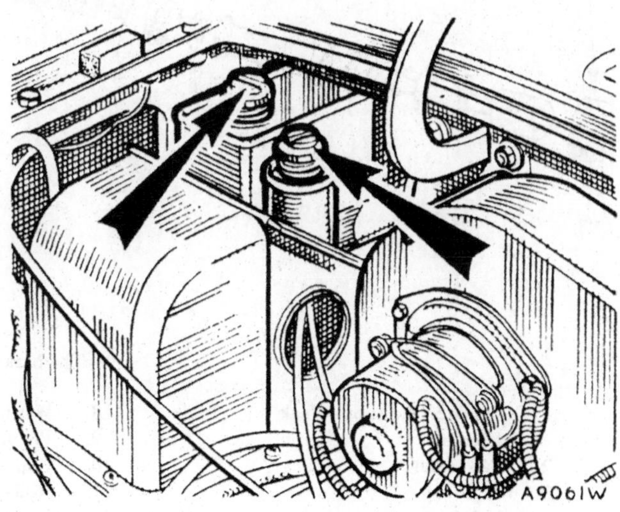

Fig. M.2
The upper arrow shows the brake master cylinder filler cap

which is filled with fluid from the supply tank. On releasing the brake pedal after application the piston is returned quickly to its stop by the return spring. A small bleed hole is drilled in the side of the check valve body to prevent any fluid pressure being retained in the system.

Removing

Remove the screws securing the brake and clutch master cylinder cover and take off the cover.

Drain the fluid from the supply tank reservoir by attaching a rubber tube to a brake calliper bleed screw, open the screw one full turn, and then depress the brake pedal. Hold the pedal down, tighten the bleed screw, and then let the pedal return unassisted. Repeat this operation until the tank is empty.

Remove the split pin, washer, and clevis pin from the push-rod and disengage the brake pedal lever.

Clean the pipe connection, disconnect the pipe line, and fit a plug to the end of the cylinder to prevent the entry of dirt.

Unscrew the fixing bolts and detach the master cylinder from the box assembly.

Dismantling

Detach the rubber dust cover from the cylinder barrel and move it along the push-rod.

Depress the push-rod to relieve the load on the circlip, then remove the circlip and the push-rod assembly.

Withdraw the piston, piston washer, main cup, spring retainer, and valve assembly.

Remove the secondary cup by carefully stretching it over the end of the piston.

Assembling

Clean all parts thoroughly, using brake fluid or methylated spirit. If spirit is used the rubber should not be allowed to soak but should be dried and dipped in clean brake fluid. The main casing, if cleaned with spirit, must be dried out before assembly. Ensure that the compensating port in the cylinder barrel is clear by probing with a piece of fine wire.

Examine all the rubber parts for damage or distortion. It is usually advisable to renew the rubbers when rebuilding the cylinder. Dip all the internal parts in brake fluid and assemble when wet.

Stretch the secondary cup over the piston with the lip of the cup facing the head of the piston. When the cup is in its groove work it round gently with the fingers to ensure that it is correctly seated.

Fit the check valve assembly onto the large end and the spring retainer onto the small end of the return spring and insert the spring, check valve first, into the cylinder.

Insert the main cup, lip first, and press it down onto the spring retainer, taking care not to damage or turn back the lip.

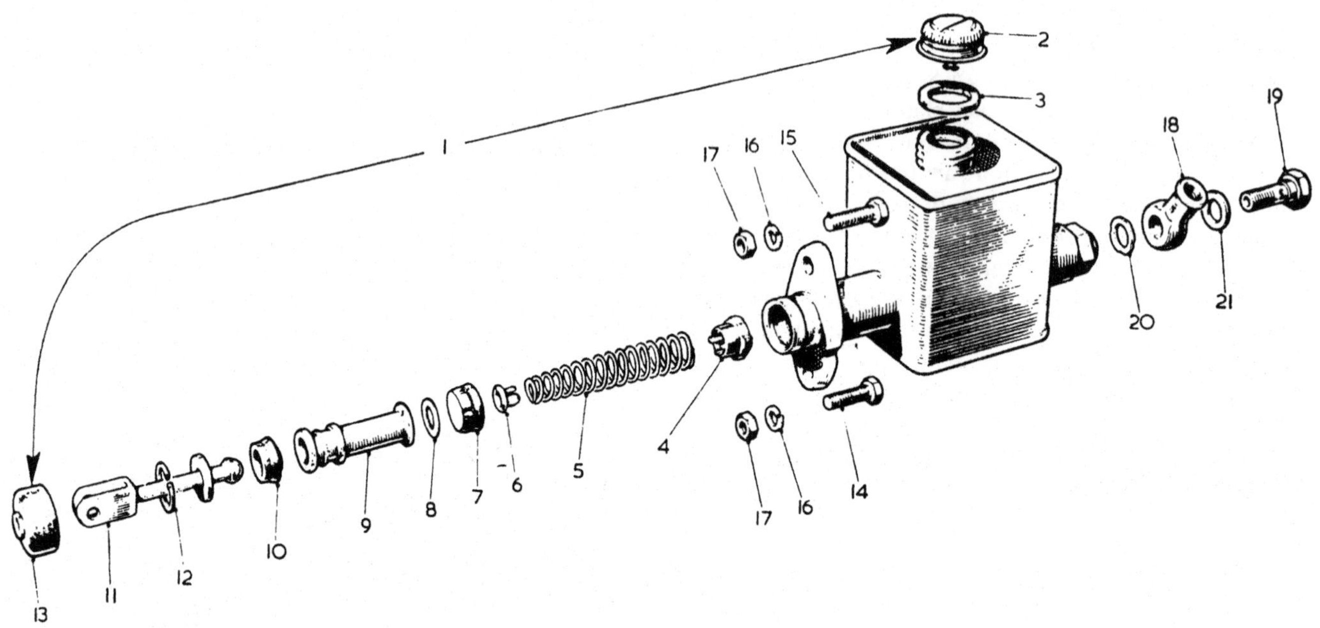

Fig. M.3
The brake master cylinder

1. Cylinder and supply tank assembly.
2. Cap–filler.
3. Seal–cap.
4. Valve assembly.
5. Spring–piston return.
6. Retainer–return spring.
7. Cup–main.
8. Washer–piston.
9. Piston.
10. Cup–secondary.
11. Rod–push.
12. Circlip.
13. Boot.
14. Screw–cylinder to box.
15. Screw–cylinder and stiffener to box.
16. Washer–spring–screw.
17. Nut–screw.
18. Banjo–master cylinder.
19. Bolt–banjo.
20. Gasket–banjo connection.
21. Gasket–banjo connection.

Place the main cup washer in position with its concave face next to the main cup and insert the piston, taking care not to damage or turn back the lip of the secondary cup.
Place the push-rod in position, push the piston down the bore, and with the piston stop washer in the bore refit the retaining circlip. Refit the dust cover.

Replacing

Refit the master cylinder to the master cylinder box and secure it with bolts. The long bolt passes through the stiffener plate.
Remove the dust excluder and fit the pipe connection to the master cylinder.
Refit the clutch pedal lever to the push-rod and secure it with the clevis pin, washer, and a new split pin.
Refit the master cylinder cover.
Fill the master cylinder and then prime and bleed the system.

Section M.6

DISC BRAKE UNITS

Description

Each front wheel brake unit comprises a hub-mounted disc rotating with the wheel and a braking unit rigidly attached to the swivel axle. The brake unit consists of a calliper manufactured in two halves—the mounting half and the rim half—which are held together by three bolts. A cylinder in each calliper half houses a self-adjusting hydraulic piston, a fluid seal, a dust seal, and a seal retainer. The pistons are interchangeable side for side.
The friction pad assemblies are fitted adjacent to the pistons and are retained in position by a retainer spring and pin.
Fluid pressure generated in the master cylinder enters the mounting half of each calliper and passes through the internal fluid ports into the rim half. An even pressure is therefore exerted on both hydraulic pistons, moving them along the cylinder bores until the friction pad assemblies contact the disc. In order to compensate for wear of the pads the pistons move progressively along each cylinder. The movement of the piston deflects the fluid seal in the cylinder bore, and on releasing the pressure the piston moves back into its original position thus providing the required clearance for the friction pads.

Removing the disc friction pads

Apply the hand brake, jack up the car, and remove the road wheel.
Depress the pad retaining springs and remove the split pins and the retaining springs; lift the pads out of the calliper.
Before the lining material has worn down to a minimum permissible thickness of in. (1.59 mm) the friction pads must be renewed.
Thoroughly clean the exposed end of each piston and ensure that the recesses which are provided in the calliper to receive the friction pads are free from rust and grit.
Before fitting new friction pads the calliper pistons which will be at their maximum adjustment, must be returned to the base of the bores, using a suitable clamp.

NOTE.—The level of the fluid in the master cylinder supply tank will rise during this operation and it may be necessary to siphon off any surplus fluid to prevent it from overflowing.

Check that the portion that has been machined away from the face of each piston is correctly positioned at the inner end of the calliper (see Fig. M.6). Insert the friction pads (which are interchangeable side for side), replace the retaining springs, and fit the split pins. Ensure that the pad assemblies are free to move easily in the calliper recesses. Remove any high-spots from the pad pressure plate by filing carefully.
Pump the brake pedal several times to readjust the pistons and top up the fluid supply reservoir.

Removing a calliper unit

Apply the hand brake, jack up the car, and remove the road wheel. Withdraw the brake friction pads.
Attach a bleeder tube to the bleed screw and drain the fluid by pumping the brake pedal. Disconnect the flexible hose on the mounting half of the calliper (see Section M.4) and plug the end of the hose to prevent the entry of foreign matter.
Press back the ears of the locking washer, unscrew the two bolts securing the calliper to the swivel axle and withdraw the calliper complete.

Replacing

Reverse the above instructions. Tighten the calliper securing bolts to the torque spanner reading of 40 to 45 lb. ft. (5.6 to 6.2 kg. m.). Finally bleed the system as described in Section M.4.

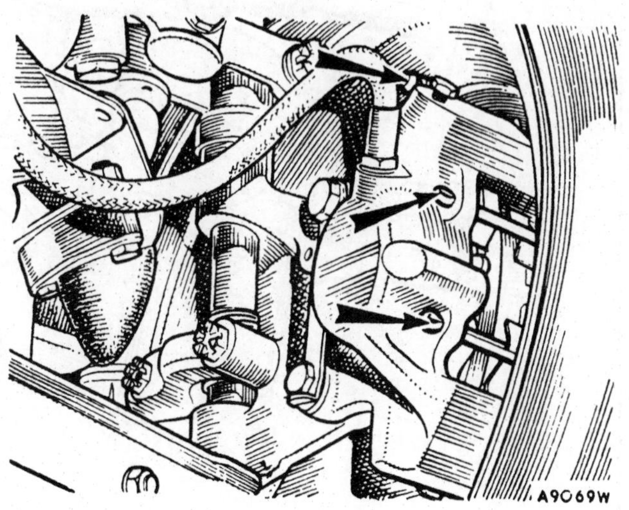

Fig. M.4
Friction pad retaining pins and bleed screw location

THE DISC BRAKE COMPONENTS

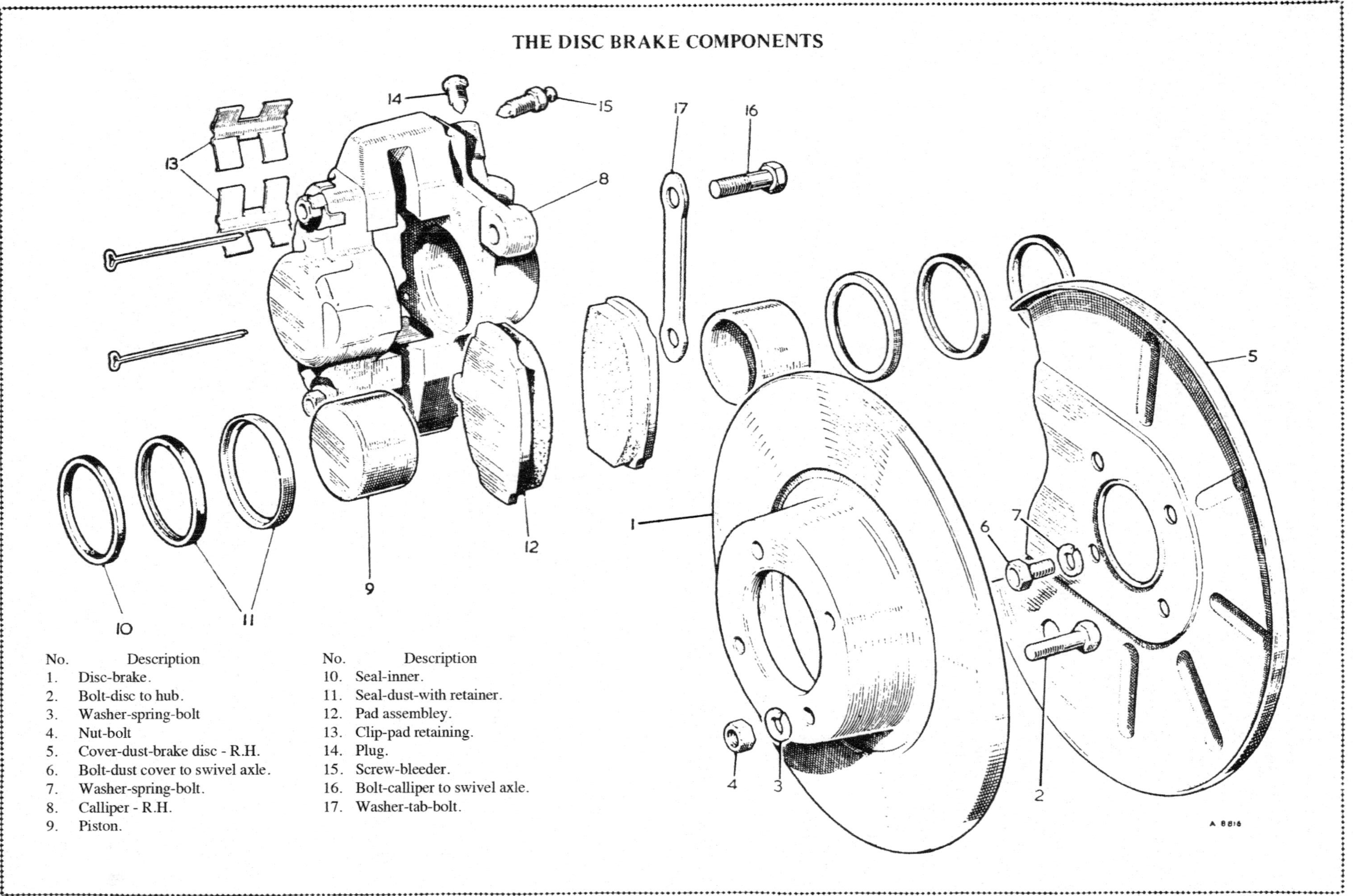

No.	Description
1.	Disc-brake.
2.	Bolt-disc to hub.
3.	Washer-spring-bolt
4.	Nut-bolt
5.	Cover-dust-brake disc - R.H.
6.	Bolt-dust cover to swivel axle.
7.	Washer-spring-bolt.
8.	Calliper - R.H.
9.	Piston.
10.	Seal-inner.
11.	Seal-dust-with retainer.
12.	Pad assembley.
13.	Clip-pad retaining.
14.	Plug.
15.	Screw-bleeder.
16.	Bolt-calliper to swivel axle.
17.	Washer-tab-bolt.

Removing the calliper pistons

Unscrew and remove the two bolts securing the calliper to the front hub and withdraw the calliper from the disc and hub. Do not remove the rubber hose, and support the calliper to avoid straining the hose. Remove the friction pads and clean the outside of the calliper, making sure that all dirt and traces of cleaning fluid are completely removed. Clamp the piston in the mounting half of the calliper and gently apply the foot brake. This operation will force the piston in the rim half of the calliper to move outwards. Continue with gentle pressure on the foot pedal until the piston has emerged sufficiently for it to be removed by hand. Have a clean receptacle ready to catch the fluid as the piston is removed.

With a suitable blunt-nosed tool remove the fluid seal from its groove in the bore of the calliper, taking great care not to damage the bore of the calliper or the seal retaining groove.

The dust seal retainer can be removed by inserting a screwdriver between the retainer and the seal and gently prising the retainer from the mouth of the calliper bore. The rubber seal can then be detached.

Remove the clamp from the mounting-half piston. To remove the mounting-half piston from the calliper it is necessary first to refit the rim-half piston, and thereafter the procedure is as previously detailed.

When cleaning out the calliper it is essential that only methylated spirit or Lockheed Brake Fluid be used as a cleaning medium. Other types of cleaning fluid may damage the internal rubber seal between the two halves of the calliper.

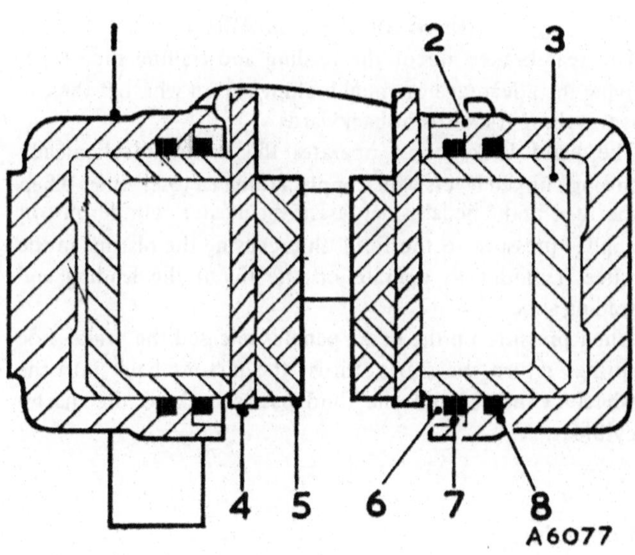

Fig. M.5

A disc brake in section

1. Calliper–mounting half.
2. Calliper–rim half.
3. Hydraulic piston.
4. Pad backing plate.
5. Friction pad.
6. Dust seal retainer.
7. Dust seal.
8. Fluid seal.

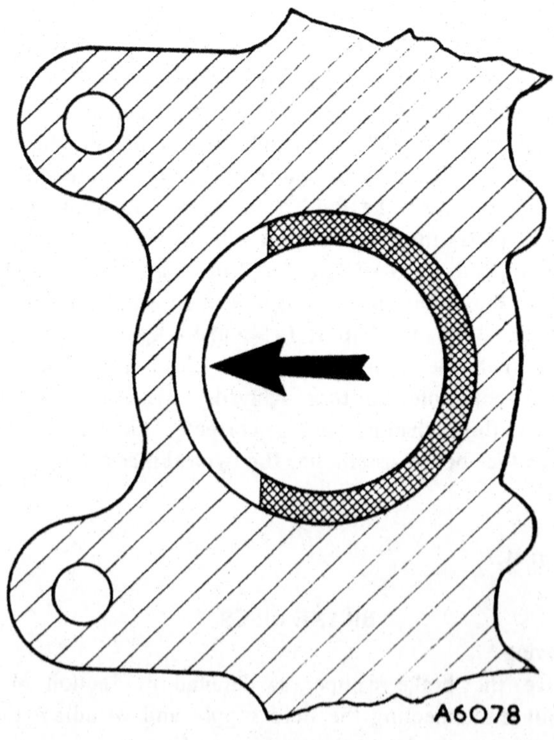

Fig. M.6

The cut-away porttion of the piston (arrowed) must be located at the inner edge of the calliper, i.e. towards the hub

Reassembling

Coat a new fluid seal with Lockheed Disc Brake Lubricant, making sure that the seal is absolutely dry before so doing, and ease the seal into its groove with the fingers until it is seating correctly in the groove.

Slacken the bleeder screw in the rim half of the calliper one complete turn. Coat the piston with Lockheed Disc Brake Lubricant and locate the piston squarely in the mouth of the bore with the cutaway portion of the piston face correctly positioned (see Fig. M.6).

Press in the piston until approximately $\frac{5}{16}$ in. (7.94 mm.) of the piston is protruding from the bore. Take great care to prevent the piston tilting during this operation. If the dust seal and retainer have been previously removed, take a new, perfectly dry dust seal, coat it with Lockheed Disc Brake Lubricant, and fit the seal into its retainer. Position the seal assembly on the protruding portion of the piston with the seal innermost, ensuring that the assembly is square with the piston. Press home the piston and seal assembly with clamp. Retighten the bleeder screw.

The mounting-half piston is dealt with in the same manner as described for the rim-half piston. The rubber hose must be disconnected to allow the clamp to be used and the bleeder screw must be slackened.

Reconnect the hose and bolt the calliper to the hub. Do not depress the brake pedal. Fit the friction pad assemblies, together with the retaining springs and split pins, and bleed the system.

After bleeding operate the brake pedal several times to adjust the brake.

Dismantling the calliper

Further servicing of the calliper should be confined to removing the bleeder screw and the fluid pipe line and blowing the fluid passages clear with compressed air.

Unless it is absolutely unavoidable the calliper should not be separated into two halves. In the event of separation becoming essential, the fluid channel seal, clamping bolts, and lock plates must be renewed when reassembling. Only bolts supplied by BMC Service Ltd. may be used. On assembly these must be tightened with a torque wrench set at between 35.5 and 37 lb. ft. (4.9 and 5.1 kg. m.).

Ensure that the calliper faces are clean and that the threaded bolt holes are thoroughly dry. Make certain that the new fluid channel seal is correctly located in the recessed face before assembling the two calliper halves.

Section M.7

BRAKE DISCS

Removing

Remove the brake calliper as detailed in Section M.6 without disconnecting the fluid supply and withdraw the hub by the method described in Section K.

Separate the disc from the hub by removing the four securing nuts and washers.

Replacing

Assemble the brake disc to the hub and refit the assembly to the swivel hub.

Check the disc for true rotation by clamping a dial indicator to a suitable fixed point on the vehicle with the needle pad bearing on the face of the hub. Run-out must not exceed .003 in. (.076 mm.) and in the event of this dimension being exceeded the components should be examined for damage and, if necessary, renewed. Damaged disc faces may be rectified by grinding (see below).

Replace the brake calliper as detailed in Section M.6.

A certain amount of concentric and even scoring of the disc faces is not detrimental to the satisfactory operation of the brakes.

If it is found necessary to regrind the disc faces they can be ground up to a maximum of only .040 in. (1.016 mm.) off the original thickness of .350 to .340 in. (8.89 to 8.63 mm.). This may be ground off equally each side, or more on one side than the other, provided that the total reduction does not exceed the maximum limit of .040 in. (1.016 mm.). The reground surface must not exceed 63 micro-in.

After grinding, the faces must run true to within a total clock reading of .002 in. (.05 mm.) and the thickness must be parallel to within .001 in. (.0254 mm.) clock reading.

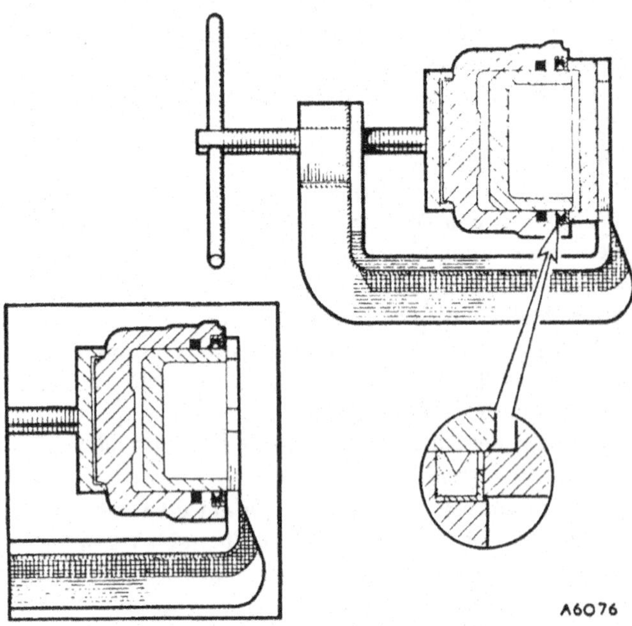

Fig. M.7

Using Service tool 18G590 to install the dust seal and retainer in the recessed mouth of the calliper cylinder. Shown inset is the tool, less the adaptor, being used to reset a piston

Section M.8

FLEXIBLE HOSES

Do not attempt to release a flexible hose by turning either end with a spanner. It should be removed as follows:

Unscrew the metal pipe line union nut from its connection to the hose.

Remove the locknut securing the flexible hose union to the bracket and unscrew the hose from the wheel cylinder.

Section M.9

REAR BRAKE ASSEMBLY

The rear brakes are of the leading and trailing shoe type, giving the advantage of equal braking action whether the car is travelling forwards or backwards.

The hand brake lever operates the brakes mechanically through linked levers which apply a force to each shoe. When the foot brake pedal is depressed the master cylinder piston applies pressure to the fluid, thus causing the pistons in the wheel cylinder to operate on the tip of the leading and trailing shoes.

When pressure on the brake pedal is released the brake-shoe springs return the shoes, thrust the pistons back into the wheel cylinders, and the fluid passes back to the master cylinder.

Dismantling

Jack up the car and remove the road wheel.

Remove the brake-drum as described in Section H.1.

Slacken fully the brake-shoe adjuster.

Depress each shoe steady spring retaining washer and turn to release them from the anchor brackets on the backplate.

Pull the trailing shoe against the load of the springs and disengage at each end; on releasing the tension on the springs the other shoe will fall away.

THE REAR BRAKE COMPONENTS

No.	Description	No.	Description
1.	Backplate.	15.	Spring washer.
2.	Backplate to axle case bolt.	16.	Wheel cylinder assembly.
3.	Nut.	17.	Piston.
4.	Spring washer.	18.	Piston seal.
5.	Shoe assembly.	19.	Piston boot.
6.	Pull-off spring–cylinder end.	20.	Wheel cylinder retaining clip.
7.	Pull-off spring–adjustment end.	21.	Bleeder screw.
8.	Brake-shoe steady pin.	22.	Hand brake lever.
9.	Brake-shoe steady spring.	23.	Hand brake lever boot.
10.	Retainer washer.	24.	Brake-drum.
11.	Adjuster assembly.	25.	Drum to hub screw.
12.	Tappet.	26.	Drum retaining nut (wire wheels).
13.	Wedge spindle.		
14.	Adjuster to backplate nut.		

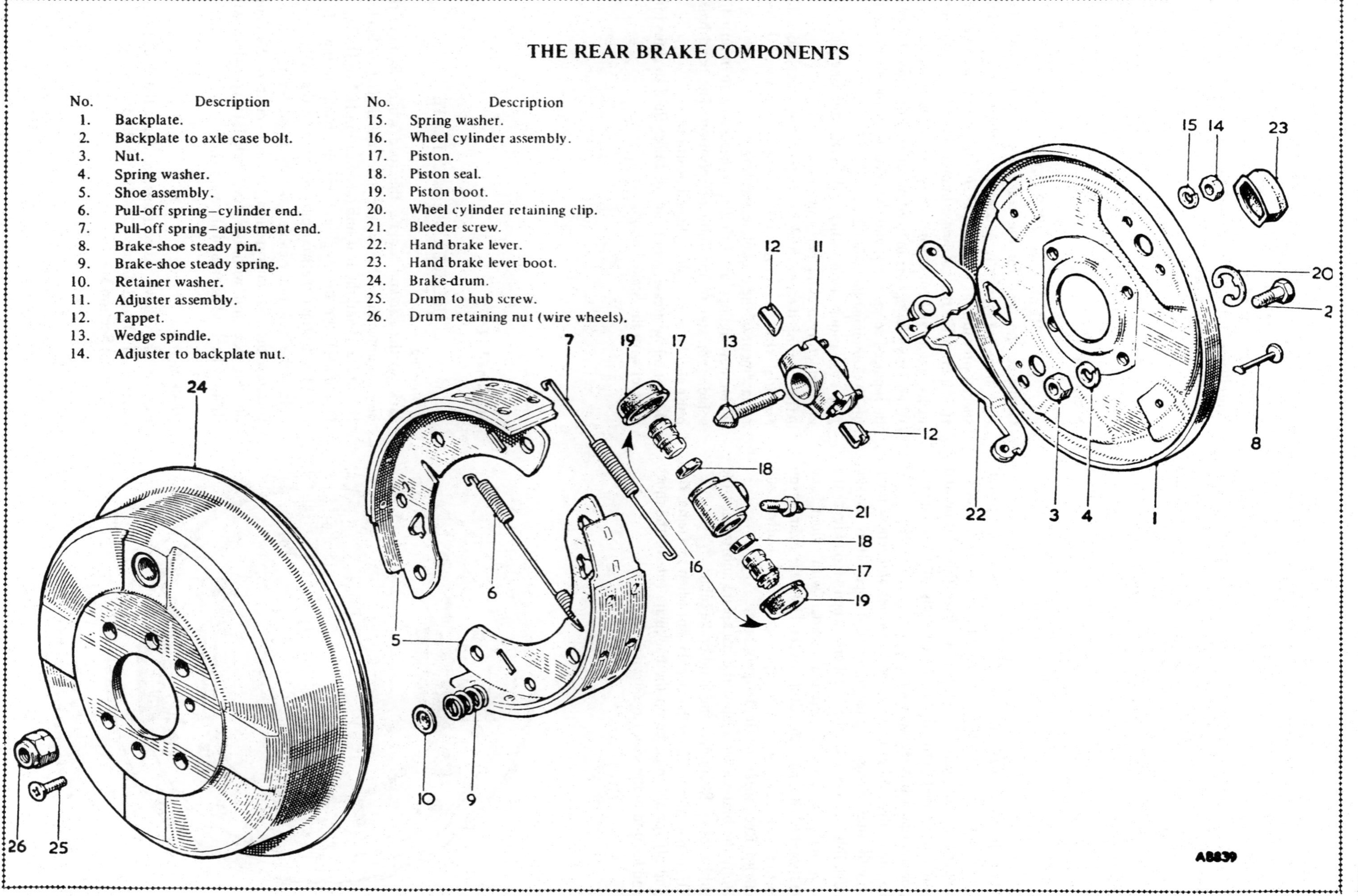

To remove the wheel cylinder disconnect the brake fluid supply pipe, placing a container to catch the fluid. Withdraw the circlip and retaining washer and remove the cylinder.

Extract the split pin and withdraw the clevis pin to release the hand brake cable from the lever. Detach the rubber dust cover from the brake lever at the rear of the backplate and withdraw the lever.

Withdraw the tappets from the spindle adjuster and screw the adjusting spindle inwards until clear of the threads. Remove the two nuts and spring washers from the rear of the backplate to release the adjuster body.

Assembling

Thoroughly clean the adjuster body, tappets, and adjuster. Smear the adjuster threads and tappets with Lockheed Expander Lubricant. Screw the adjuster fully home and slide the tappets into the body, ensuring that the tapered portion on each is facing inwards.

Examine the rubber seals on both pistons and renew them should they appear damaged or distorted. It is usually advisable to renew the rubbers when rebuilding the cylinders. Smear all internal parts with fluid and reassemble. Replace the dust covers. Hold the cylinder up against the backplate and replace the flat washer and circlip. Reconnect the fluid supply pipe.

Hold the brake lever against the backplate and replace the rubber boot. Reconnect the hand brake cable.

The brake shoes are interchangeable, but when replacing, the pull-off springs must be on the backplate side of the shoes and located in the shoes as shown in Fig. M.8.

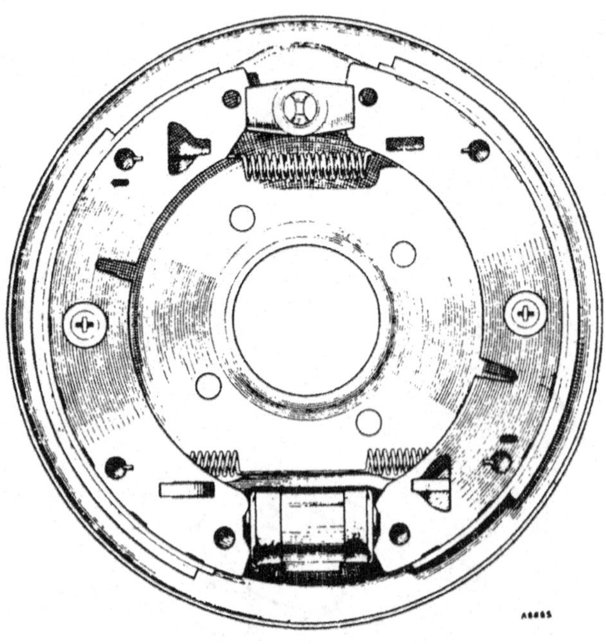

Fig. M.8
The rear brake assembly

Replace the steady springs on the shoe web and locate them with the brackets on the backplate by depressing and turning the retaining washer.

Ensure that all adjustments are off and that the shoes are centralized. Fit the drum and the road wheel, bleed the system, and adjust the brakes.

Section M.10

RELINING THE BRAKE-SHOES

Owing to the need for the brake linings to be finished so that they are perfectly concentric with the brake-drums, special precautions must be taken when relining the shoes.

It is imperative that all brake linings should be of the same make, grade, and condition to ensure even braking.

When brake linings are in need of renewal they must always be replaced in axle sets, and the relining of the shoes in one brake-drum must be avoided.

Any variations from this will give an unequal and unsatisfactory braking performance.

After riveting the new brake linings to the brake-shoes it is essential that any high-spots should be removed before replacement of the backplate assembly.

When new linings are fitted it is necessary to return the spindle adjuster to the fully off position. The hand brake must also be in the fully released position.

Do not allow grease, paint, oil, or brake fluid to come into contact with the brake linings.

Section M.11

REAR BRAKE BACKPLATE

Removing

Jack up the car and remove the road wheel. Remove the brake-drum and withdraw the axle half-shaft (see Section H.1 or Ha.3) and the rear hub (see Section H.2 or Ha.3).

Disconnect the brake pipe from the back of the wheel cylinder. Extract the split pin and remove the clevis pin to detach the hand brake cable from the brake lever.

Unscrew the four nuts securing the backplate to the flange on the axle and withdraw the backplate complete with shoes, wheel cylinder, and shoe adjuster.

Replacing

Reverse the above instructions; readjust the brakes (see Section M.1) and finally, bleed the hydraulic system as detailed in Section M.4.

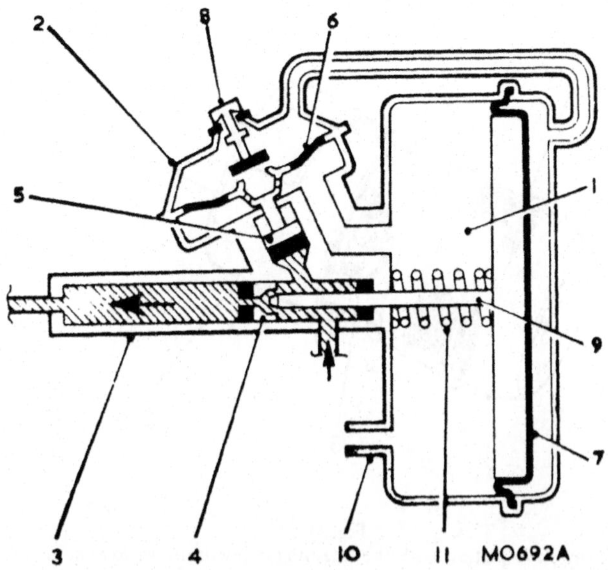

Fig. M.9
A schematic diagram showing the principle of operations and the main components of the vacuum servo unit. The shaded area represents brake fluid

Section M.12

SERVO UNIT
(Lockheed Type 6)

Operation

Refer to Fig. M.9. The vacuum-operated servo unit consists of three main components, namely the vacuum cylinder (1), the air valve assembly (2), and the slave cylinder (3) which is connected in the hydraulic circuit between the main master cylinder and the wheel cylinders. Under light braking fluid is allowed to pass directly to the wheel cylinders via the hollow centre of the slave piston (4) and no braking assistance is obtained; fluid pressure acting on the air valve piston (5) closes the diaphragm (6), thus separating the chamber behind the main servo diaphragm (7) from the one in front. Under heavier braking, further movement of the air valve piston opens the air valve and allows air to enter the chamber behind the main diaphragm, destroying the vacuum. The central rod (9) is thus pushed to the left, sealing the hollow centre of the slave piston and pushing it down its bore, so increasing the fluid pressure at the wheel cylinders. When the brake pedal is released, the pressure beneath the air valve piston is destroyed, the diaphragm (6) re-opens and the air valve closes. Via the non-return valve (10), a suspended vacuum is recreated around the main diaphragm. Under the action of the spring (11), the diaphragm and push-rod, and thus the slave piston, are returned to their original positions, and the pressure in the wheel cylinders is lost.

Removing

1. Disconnect the battery.
2. Remove the two captive screws securing the base of the servo cylinder bracket (LHD cars), one screw (RHD cars).
3. Remove the bolt securing the vacuum hose clip to the servo cylinder bracket.
4. Disconnect the master cylinder feed outlet hydraulic connections at the servo. Ensure the feed pipe from the master cylinder is blanked to prevent fluid loss.
   R.H.D. CARS. Remove the three nuts and spring washers retaining the servo to the rear bracket. Remove the servo unit and extract the vacuum hose connection from the servo.
   L.H.D. CARS. From inside the car, remove the bulkhead grommet and remove the three nuts and spring washers retaining the servo to the rear bracket. Remove the servo unit and extract the vacuum hose connection from the servo.

Dismantling

AIR VALVE ASSEMBLY (FIG. M.10)

5. Grip the slave cylinder in a soft jawed vice with the air valve uppermost and disconnect the rubber pipe from the connection on the end cover.
6. Remove the screws securing the plastic air valve cover to the valve housing, lift off the cover complete with the air valve sub-assembly. Suspect functioning of the air valve must be remedied by fitting a replacement air valve cover assembly comprising cover, filter, and air valve as an assembled part of the relevant repair kit.
7. Remove the rubber diaphragm and its plastic support to obtain access to valve housing securing screws. Remove the three screws and take off the housing and joint washer.
8. Seal one of the slave cylinder fluid ports with a finger, apply a low-pressure air-line to the remaining port and blow the air control valve piston from its bore. Remove the rubber cup from the valve piston.

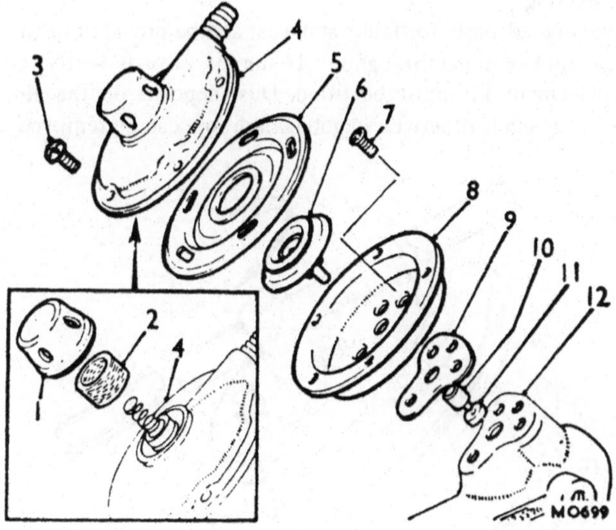

Fig. M.10.
The air valve assembly components and piston

1. Domed cover for filter
2. Air filter.
3. Air valve cover securing screws.
4. Air valve cover.
5. Diaphragm.
6. Diaphragm support.
7. Valve housing securing screws.
8. Valve housing.
9. Joint washer.
10. Piston.
11. Piston cup.
12. Slave cylinder.

SERVO CYLINDER ASSEMBLY

9. Use thumb pressure to prise the non-return valve from the servo shell and extract the rubber valve mounting.
10. To remove the end cover from the servo shell, locate Service tool C2030* over the three studs and secure tightly with suitable nuts (see Fig. M.11). Turn the removal tool anti-clockwise with a ½ in. (13 mm.) square drive socket 'T' bar as far as the stops on the cover will allow and lift off the cover.
11. Turn the diaphragm support so that the push-rod retaining key faces downwards. Apply light fluctuating hand pressure on the support into the shell; this will allow the retaining key to drop out, releasing the support from the push-rod under pressure of the main return spring. Extract the spring from the servo shell.
12. Bend back the locking tabs of the servo shell to slave cylinder securing bolts; remove the bolts, together with the locking and abutment plates. Lift off the servo shell and retrieve the joint washer from the mounting face of the slave cylinder.

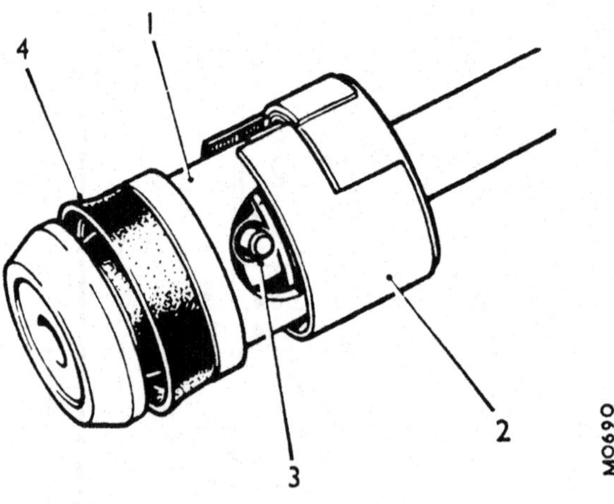

Fig. M.12
The slave piston, with the retaining clip withdrawn to expose the connecting pin

1. Piston body.
2. Retaining clip.
3. Connecting pin.
4. Piston seal.

SLAVE CYLINDER ASSEMBLY

13. Pull the servo push-rod and the piston assembly attached to it from the slave cylinder bore. Slide off the plastic bearing, rubber cup and plastic spacer, noting their relative positions for refitting.
14. Prise off the rubber seal from the head of the slave piston. Open the retaining clip with a small screwdriver to expose the connecting pin, which may then be driven out to separate the piston from the rod (see Fig. M.12).

Inspecting

Examine all parts for faults and wear and be prepared to fit new rubber parts throughout. If the air valve is faulty, a replacement kit must be fitted. Dust deposits on the air filter, which is otherwise in good condition, can be removed by blowing through with a low-pressure air-line. Do not use a cleaning fluid or lubricant of any description on the filter. Wash all original components of the slave cylinder assembly and remove light deposits from the cylinder bore with clean brake fluid. If the slave cylinder bore is scored, a replacement unit will be required.

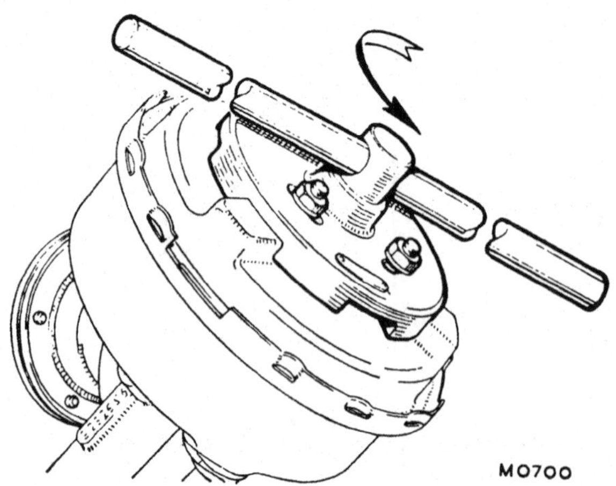

Fig. M.11
Using Service tool C 2030* to remove and refit the end cover

*Obtainable from: V. L. Churchill & Co. Ltd.

Reassembling

Scrupulous cleanliness of all parts of the servo unit is essential. Lay out all parts to be assembled on a clean sheet of paper. Use clean brake fluid as a lubricant when reassembling the hydraulic components of the servo unit.

SLAVE CYLINDER ASSEMBLY

15. If the piston and push-rod were separated in item 10, a new retaining clip and connecting pin will be required. Insert the chamfered end of the push-rod into the rear of the piston and depress the spring inside it to uncover the hole in the end of the rod. Fit the pin, followed by its retaining clip; see that this is a snug fit, and does not protrude beyond its groove, otherwise the bore will become scored.
    Using only the fingers, bed the rubber seal evenly into the groove on the head of the piston, with the lips of the seal pointing away from the push-rod.
16. Insert the piston into the lubricated bore of the slave cylinder, then, one by one, slide the spacer, the rubber cup, and the bearing over the push-rod into the mouth of the bore. Take care not to bend back the lips of either the seal or the cup, and bed in each part individually.

THE VACUUM SERVO COMPONENTS
(Lockheed Type 6)

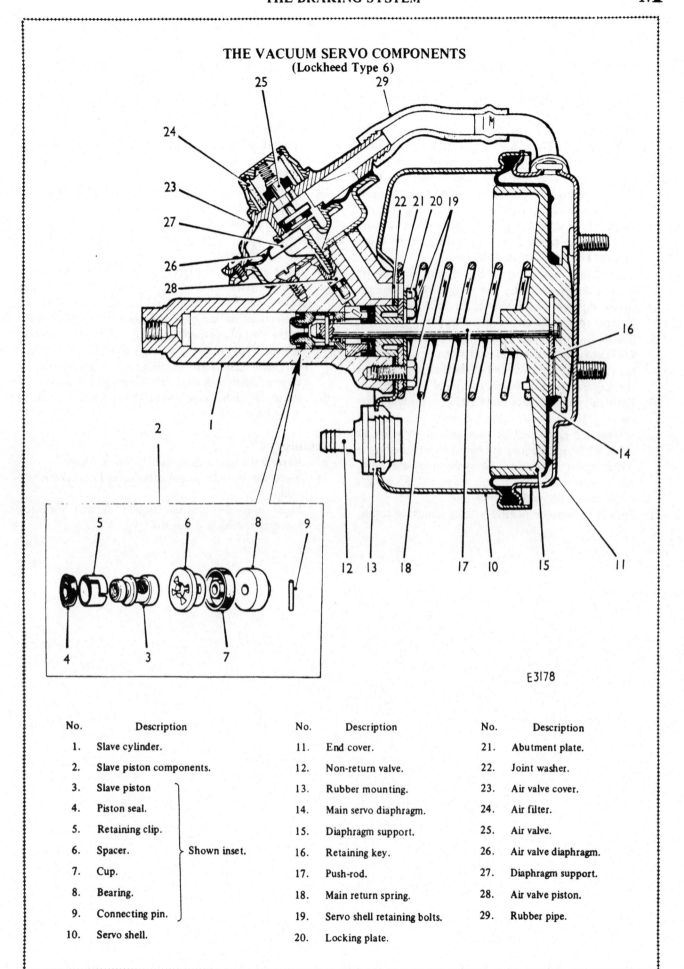

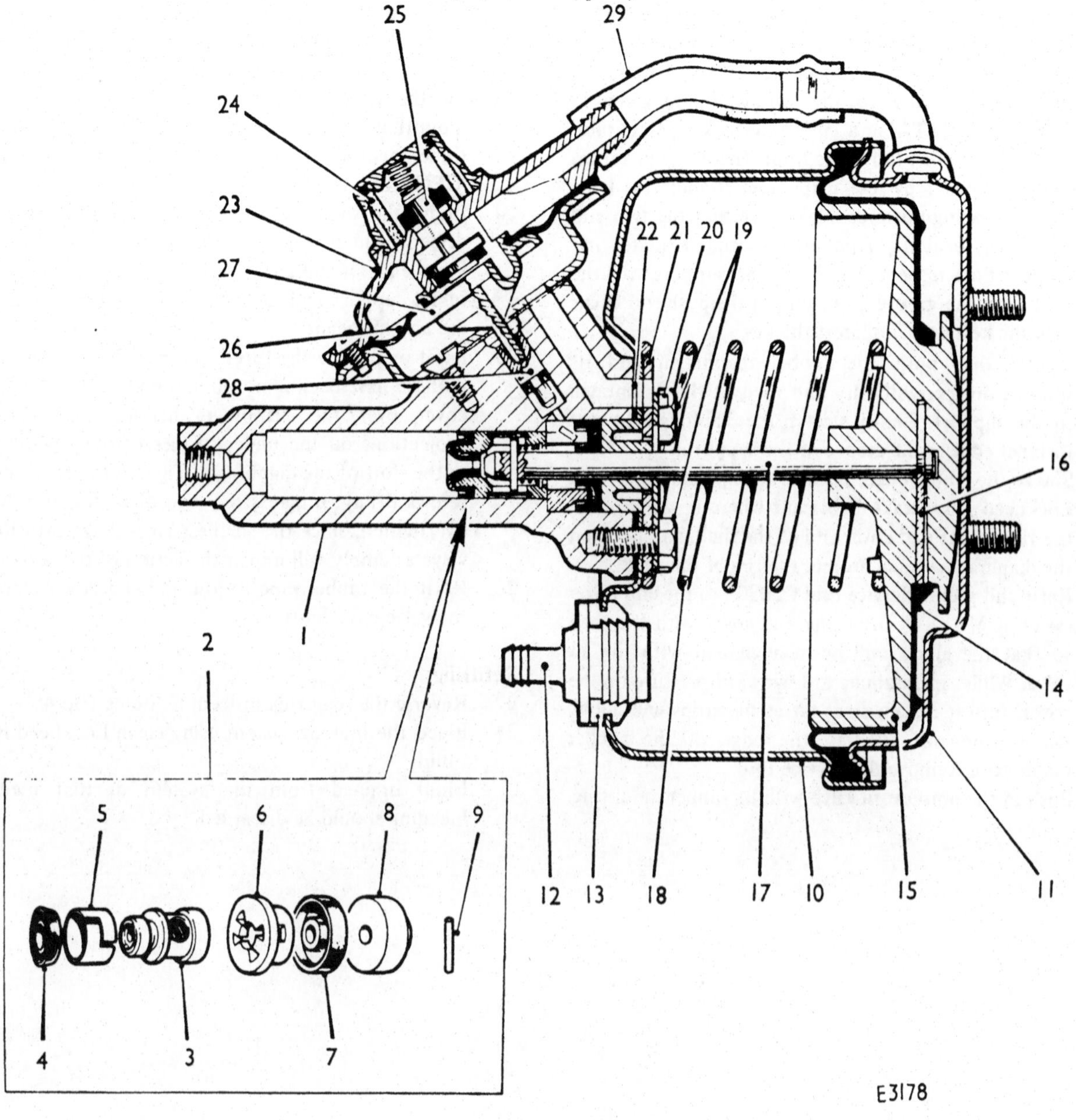

No.	Description	No.	Description	No.	Description
1.	Slave cylinder.	11.	End cover.	21.	Abutment plate.
2.	Slave piston components.	12.	Non-return valve.	22.	Joint washer.
3.	Slave piston (Shown inset)	13.	Rubber mounting.	23.	Air valve cover.
4.	Piston seal. (Shown inset)	14.	Main servo diaphragm.	24.	Air filter.
5.	Retaining clip. (Shown inset)	15.	Diaphragm support.	25.	Air valve.
6.	Spacer. (Shown inset)	16.	Retaining key.	26.	Air valve diaphragm.
7.	Cup. (Shown inset)	17.	Push-rod.	27.	Diaphragm support.
8.	Bearing. (Shown inset)	18.	Main return spring.	28.	Air valve piston.
9.	Connecting pin. (Shown inset)	19.	Servo shell retaining bolts.	29.	Rubber pipe.
10.	Servo shell.	20.	Locking plate.		

SERVO CYLINDER ASSEMBLY

17. Grip the slave cylinder in a soft-jawed vice, position the mounting face joint washer and refit the servo shell. After correctly positioning the abutment plate and locking plate, which must be renewed if it has been used more than once previously, tighten the three bolts evenly to the torque figure given in **'GENERAL DATA'** and tap up the locking plate tabs.
18. Pull out the push-rod to its limit, fit the main return spring followed by the diaphragm support, with its key slot facing upwards. Make sure that the two end coils are located round the abutment plate and support boss respectively. Press the support into the shell until the groove in the end of the push-rod aligns with the key slot, and insert the key.

    Ensure that both the rubber diaphragm and its support are perfectly dry and then fit the diaphragm to the support. Gently stretch the diaphragm to seat its inner edge in the groove of the support.
19. Smear the outer edge of the rubber diaphragm with Lockheed Disc Brake Lubricant where it will contact the rim of the end cover and of the shell, and position the diaphragm evenly around the rim of the shell.
20. Refit and secure Service tool C2030* to the end cover (see Fig. M.11). Position the end cover with the shell so that the elbow will be in alignment with the air valve. Whilst maintaining a downward pressure on the cover, turn it clockwise as far as the stops will allow, taking care not to trap the edge of the rubber diaphragm. Remove the Service tool.
21. Push in the non-return valve with its rubber mounting.

AIR VALVE ASSEMBLY (Fig. M.10)

22. Using only the fingers, fit the rubber cup to the spigot of the air valve piston, with the lips pointing away from the drilled head, and insert the piston into its bore, spigot end first. Do not bend over the lips of the cup.
23. Fit the valve housing, with its joint washer, to the mounting face of the slave cylinder and tighten the three securing screws to the torque figure given in **'GENERAL DATA'**.
24. Insert the spigot of the diaphragm support into the drilled head of the air valve piston, and then fit the inner edge of the air valve diaphragm into the groove of its support and align the screw hole slots. Do not use any lubricant.
25. Refit or replace the filter and snap-fit the dome cover if these have been removed in item (6). Place the valve cover over the diaphragm making sure that the projections on the under surface of the cover engage in the slots of the diaphragm. Tighten the five securing screws firmly, progressively and diametrically; do not overtighten, since the smallest air leakage into the air valve assembly will impair the action of the servo.
26. Refit the rubber pipe to join the end cover elbow to the valve cover port.

Refitting

27. Reverse the removing procedure, items 1 to 4.
28. Bleed the braking system using clean Lockheed Brake Fluid.

    Fluid drained from the system or that used for bleeding should be discarded.

WARNING: It is imperative that the correct brake fittings are used. The threads of components must be compatible.

UNIFIED	METRIC	COMMENTS
		The illustrations show metric and the equivalent Unified (U.N.F.) parts for comparison.
		Metric pipe nuts, hose ends, unions and bleed screws are coloured **GOLD** or **BLACK** and most are also identified with the letter **'M'**.
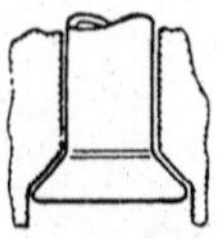	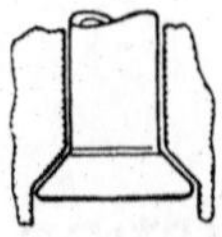	The correct metric or Unified pipe flares must be used.
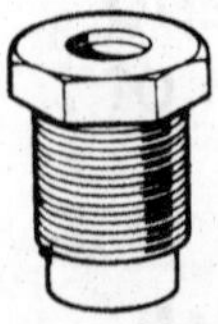	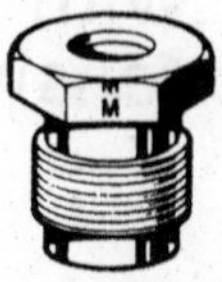	

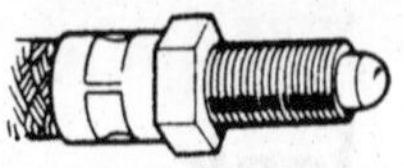 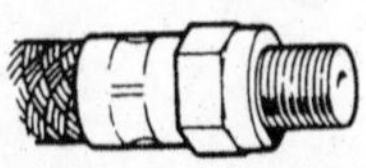	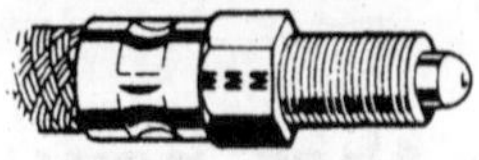 	End of a metric hose is also coloured **GOLD** or **BLACK**.
	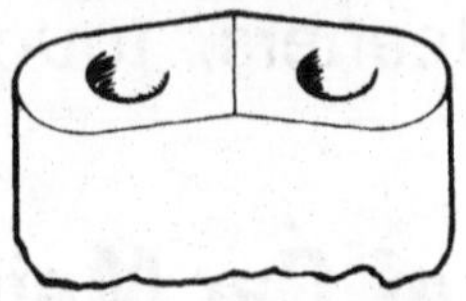	Metric parts are not counterbored; some U.N.F. threaded parts also had no counterbore; always check.
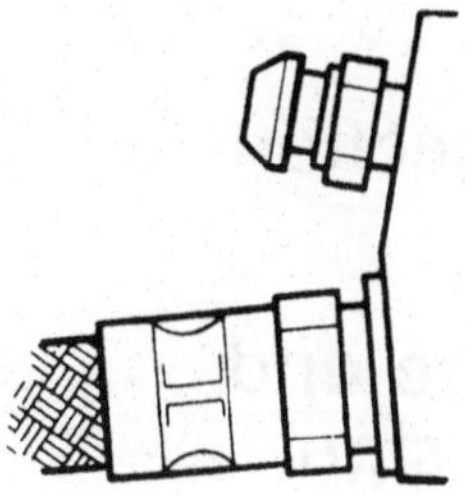	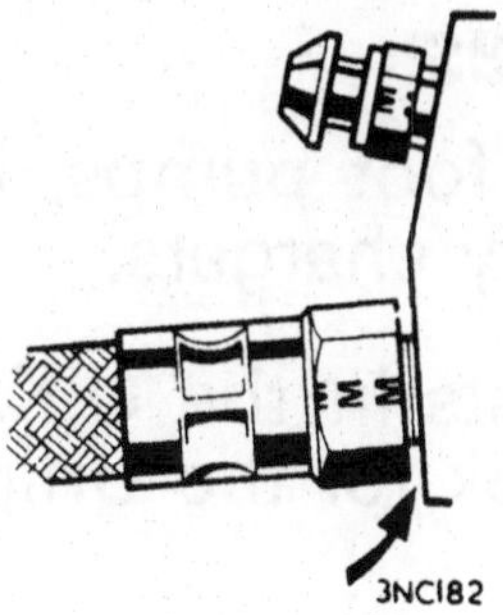 3NC182	If the thread of a component is in doubt, screw the hydraulic connections and bleed screw fully in with the fingers. If they cannot be screwed right in or if they are unduly slack, the threads may not be compatible. Metric hose seals against the bottom of the port, gap between hose hexagon and face of cylinder or calliper.

SECTION Ma

THE BRAKING SYSTEM (TANDEM MASTER CYLINDER)

The information given in this Section refers specifically to service operations on, or affected by, equipment fitted to the MGB (GHD5/GHD4 and GHN5/GHN4) in conformity with local and territorial requirements, and must be used in conjunction with Section M.

Section Ma.1

PEDAL FREE MOVEMENT

A free movement of ⅛ in. (3.2 mm.) measured at pedal pad must be maintained on the brake pedal.
To adjust the free movement, slacken the stop light switch locknut and turn the switch clockwise to decrease or anti-clockwise to increase the clearance. Tighten the stop light switch locknut.

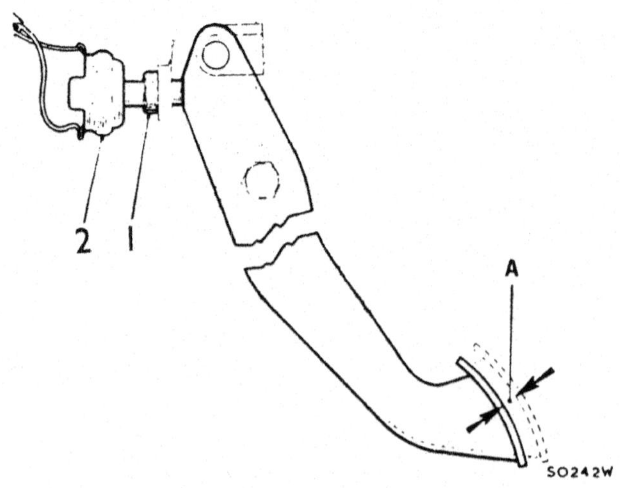

Fig. Ma.1
Brake pedal adjustment

1 Switch locknut. 2. Stop light switch.
A = ⅛ in. (3.2 mm.).

Section Ma.2

TANDEM MASTER CYLINDER

Removing

1. Remove the four screws securing the master cylinder cover and remove the cover.
2. Drain the fluid from the reservoir as follows:
   a. Attach a rubber tube to one of the front brake calliper bleed screws.
   b. Attach a rubber tube to one of the rear wheel brake cylinder bleed screws.
   c. Slacken both bleed screws one complete turn.
   d. Depress the brake pedal, hold it in the down position and tighten the bleed screws.
   e. Repeat the operations in (d.) until the reservoir is empty.
3. Drain the clutch master cylinder reservoir by the same method on the brakes from the slave cylinder bleed screw.
4. Disconnect the pipes from the brake master cylinder and plug the pipe ends.
5. Disconnect the pipe from the clutch master cylinder and plug the pipe and connection.
6. Remove the split pin and clevis pin from the push-rod and disconnect the pedal lever.
7. Disengage the clutch and brake pedal return springs.
8. Remove the left-hand lower fascia panel.
9. Unscrew the two bolts securing the pedal box to the toe-plate.
10. Unscrew the nut retaining the pedal pivot bolt, withdraw the bolt, remove the centre spacer and temporarily refit the bolt.
11. Unscrew the six bolts securing the pedal box to the bulkhead and remove the pedal box complete with master cylinders and pedals.
12. Unscrew the two bolts securing the brake master cylinder and remove the master cylinder.

Dismantling

13. Ensure that the pipe connections are securely plugged and the reservoir cap is fitted and thoroughly clean the exterior of the assembly.
14. Detach the rubber boot and withdraw the push-rod.
15. Grip the cylinder body in a soft-jawed vice with the mouth of the bore uppermost.
16. Compress the return spring and remove the Spirolox ring from its groove in the primary piston, taking care not to distort the coils of the ring or score the bore of the cylinder.
17. Using tool 18G 1112, remove the piston retaining circlip.
18. Move the piston up and down in the bore to free the nylon guide bearing and cap seal; remove the guide bearing and seal.
19. Remove the plain washer.
20. Using tool 18G 1112, remove the inner circlip.
21. Withdraw the primary and secondary piston assembly complete with stop washer.
22. Remove the stop washer.
23. Compress the spring separating the two pistons and drive out the roll-pin retaining the piston link.
24. Note the positions of the rubber cups by their moulded identations and remove the cups and washers from the pistons.
25. Unscrew the four bolts securing the plastic reservoir to the body and remove the reservoir.
26. Remove the two reservoir sealing rings.
27. Unscrew the front brake pipe connection adaptor and discard the copper gasket.
28. Withdraw the springs and trap valves from the connection ports.

Inspection

29. Clean all the parts thoroughly using the recommended brake fluid and dry them with clean lint-free cloth.
30. Examine the metal parts for wear and damage; inspect the rubber components for swelling, perishing, distortion or any other signs of deterioration. Renew all worn, damaged, or suspect parts.

Reassembling

31. Dip all the internal components in the recommended brake fluid and assemble them while wet.

32. Locate the piston washer on the head of the secondary piston, convex surface first.
33. Carefully ease the secondary main cap, lip last, over the end of the piston, using the fingers, and seat it correctly in the groove adjacent to the washer.
34. Carry out operations 32 and 33 with the washer and main cup of the primary piston.
35. Reverse the dismantling procedure in 13 to 23 and 25 to 28.

Refitting

36. Reverse the removing procedure in 1 and 4 to 12.
37. Fill the brake and clutch master cylinders with the recommended fluid (see '**GENERAL DATA**').
38. Bleed the brake system (see Section M.4) commencing with the rear brakes.
39. Bleed the clutch system–Section E.5.
40. Check and, if necessary, adjust the brake pedal free movement–Section Ma.1.

Section Ma.3

PRESSURE FAILURE SWITCH ASSEMBLY

Removing

1. Disconnect the wiring from the switch.
2. Clean the switch assembly and its surroundings, particularly the pipe connections.
3. Disconnect and plug the hydraulic pipes.
4. Unscrew the retaining bolt and remove the assembly.

Dismantling

5. Remove the end plug and discard the copper washer.
6. Unscrew the nylon switch.
7. Withdraw the shuttle valve piston assembly from the bore; use a low pressure air-line to free the piston if necessary.
8. Remove and discard the two piston seals.

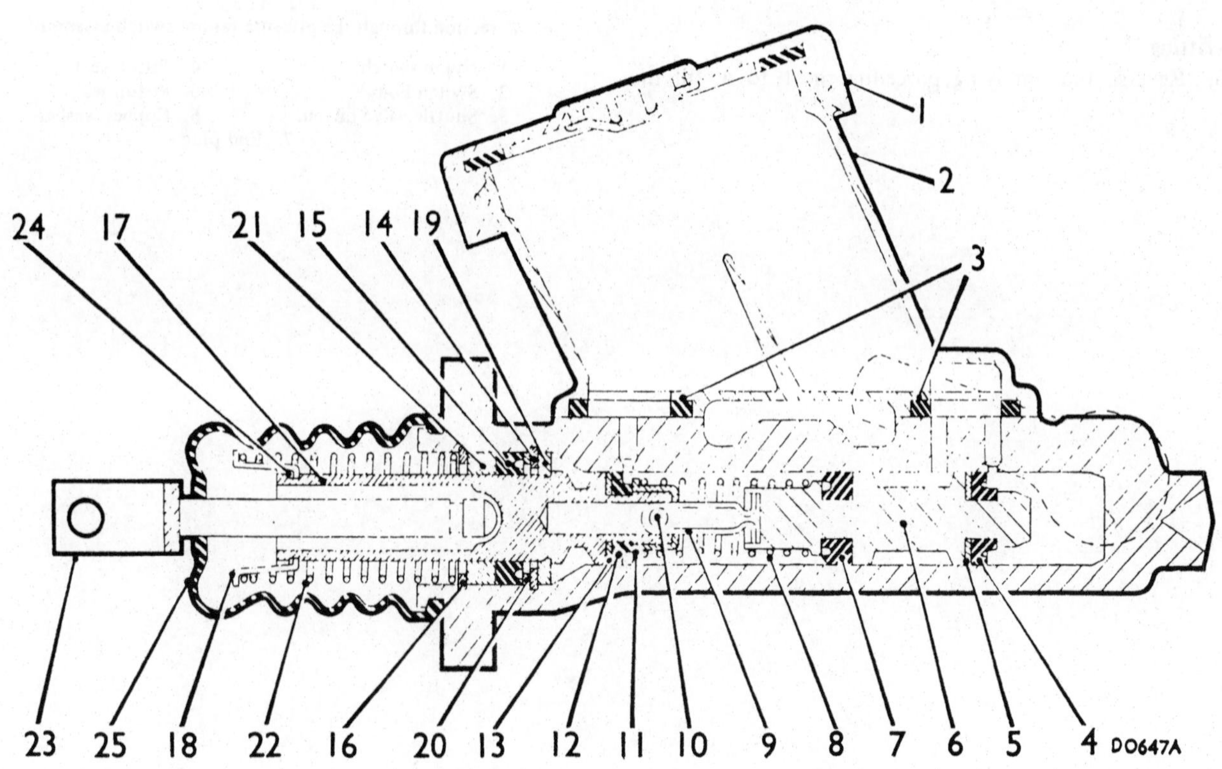

Fig. Ma.2
A section through the master cylinder

1. Filler cap.
2. Plastic reservoir.
3. Reservoir seals.
4. Main cup.
5. Piston washer.
6. Piston.
7. Main cup.
8. Spring.
9. Piston link.
10. Pin.
11. Pin retainer.
12. Main cup.
13. Piston washer.
14. Circlip.
15. Cup.
16. Circlip.
17. Piston.
18. Spring retainer.
19. Stop washer.
20. Washer.
21. Bearing.
22. Spring.
23. Push-rod.
24. Spirolox ring.
25. Rubber boot.

Inspection

9. Thoroughly clean all the components using methylated spirit (denatured alcohol) or the recommended brake fluid, and dry with lint-free cloth.
10. Inspect the bore of the casing for scoring and damage; the complete assembly must be renewed if the bore is not in a perfect condition.
11. Reconnect the wiring to the switch and actuate the switch plunger, with the ignition switched on, to test the switch operation and warning light circuit.

Reassembling

12. Fit two new seals, lip facing outwards, to the piston.
13. Lubricate the piston assembly with Lockheed Disc Brake Lubricant and fit the piston into the bore, taking care that the lip of the leading seal is not turned back.
14. Fit a new copper washer to the end plug, screw in and tighten the plug to the torque figure given in **'GENERAL DATA'**.
15. Screw in the switch and carefully tighten it to the torque figure given in **'GENERAL DATA'**.

Refitting

16. Reverse the removing procedure in 1 to 4, fill the master cylinder with the recommended fluid (see **'GENERAL DATA'**) and bleed the system (see Section M.4) commencing with the rear brakes.

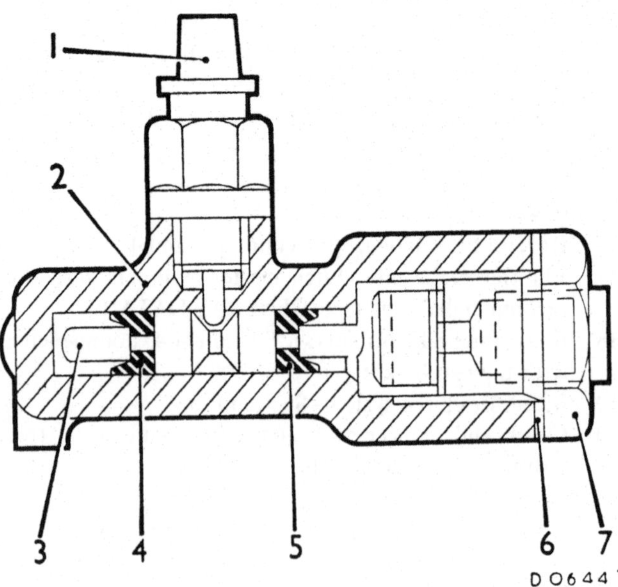

Fig. Ma.3
A section through the pressure failure switch assembly

1. Nylon switch.
2. Switch body.
3. Shuttle valve piston.
4. Piston seal.
5. Piston seal.
6. Copper washer.
7. End plug.

SECTION N

THE ELECTRICAL SYSTEM

GENERAL DESCRIPTION

The electrical system is 12-volt NEGATIVE earth return. The electrical system on early cars is 12-volt POSITIVE earth.

Two 6-volt batteries wired in series are carried in trays mounted beneath the rear cockpit floor; each battery is retained by a clamp plate and two fixing bolts. A battery access panel is provided in the rear cockpit floor and is secured to the floor by five quick-release fasteners.

Section N.1

BATTERY

The batteries are 6-volt lead-acid type, having six cells in each consisting of a group of positive and negative plates immersed in a solution of sulphuric acid (electrolyte).

The Type CA batteries fitted to later cars have a special filling device which automatically ensures the correct electrolyte level when topping-up.

Remove the battery vent cover; use the grip at the centre of the cover, this will ensure that the filling valves are operated correctly. If no electrolyte is visible inside the battery, pour distilled water into the filling trough until the three tubes and the connecting trough are filled. Refit the vent cover. Check the second battery.

Except when topping-up or taking hydrometer readings the vent cover must be kept fitted. The electrolyte will flood if the cover is removed for a long period during or within 30 minutes of the battery being normal (5 amp.) or fast charged (30–40 amps.).

Caution.—Single-cell discharge testers cannot be used on the Type CA battery. Operation of the filling device will be destroyed if the battery case is drilled or punctured.

Fast charging

During fast charging the vent cover may be removed, providing all filling tubes are pressed downwards to break the air lock.

The battery is 'fast charged' at 30–40 amps., when the on-charge voltage across the battery terminals is less than 15·5 volts. Above 15·5 volts, charge the battery at normal rate until the specific gravity readings indicate that the battery is fully-charged.

The battery has three functions; to supply current for starting, ignition, and lighting; to provide a constant supply of current to the electrical equipment under normal operating conditions and when the consumption of the electrical equipment exceeds the output of the dynamo; and to control the voltage of the electrical supply system.

Adjustments in the vehicle

The purpose of the following operations is to maintain the performance of the battery at its maximum.

The battery and its surrounding parts should be kept dry and clean, particularly the tops of the cells, as any dampness could cause a leakage between the securing strap and the battery negative terminal and result in a partially discharged battery. Clean off any corrosion from the battery bolts, clamps, and trays with diluted ammonia, afterwards painting the affected parts with anti-sulphuric paint.

The electrolyte levels should be maintained just level with the tops of the separator guards by adding distilled water. Never add acid.

Check the terminal posts. If they are corroded remove the cables and clean with diluted ammonia. Smear the posts with petroleum jelly before remaking the connections and ensure that the cable terminal screws are secure.

Check the condition of the battery cells using a hydrometer. If the level of the electrolyte is too low for hydrometer readings to be taken, top up with distilled water and recharge the battery for at least 30 minutes before taking readings. The hydrometer readings and their indications are as follows:

For climates below 27° C. (80° F.)	
Cell fully charged	1·270 to 1·290
Cell about half-charged	1·190 to 1·210
Cell completely discharged	1·110 to 1·130

For climates above 27° C. (80° F.)	
Cell fully charged	1·210 to 1·230
Cell about half-charged	1·130 to 1·150
Cell completely discharged	1·050 to 1·070

The figures given in the table are corrected to an electrolyte temperature of 16° C. (60° F.) and the hydrometer readings obtained must also be corrected to suit the temperature of the electrolyte.

For every 3° C. (5° F.) above 16° C. (60° F.) add ·002.

For every 3° C. (5° F.) below 16° C. (60° F.) subtract ·002.

The readings of all the cells should be approximately the same. If one cell gives a reading which differs from the remainder by 40 points (·040 S.G.) or more, an internal fault in that cell is indicated. Should the battery be in a low state of charge, it should be recharged by taking the car for a long daytime run or by charging from an external source of D.C. supply at a current rate of 5·0 amps. until the cells are gassing freely.

Removing

Remove the moulded carpet and release the five quick-release screws in the panel. Take off the panel, disconnect the electrical leads to the batteries, remove the four fixing bolts and two clamp plates, and lift out the batteries.

Viewing

Place the battery on a lead-covered bench or on a wooden bench treated with anti-sulphuric paint.

Check the electrolyte levels.

Inspect the container for cracks, which may be indicated by external corrosion or extreme variation in the electrolyte levels.

Recharging from an external source

The length of time for a used battery to remain on charge before it can be accepted as fully charged depends entirely on the specific gravity before charging commences and the charging rate. The charging should continue at 5 amps. until all cells are gassing freely and evenly and the specific gravity in each of the six cells has reached a maximum, i.e. has shown no further rise in four hours. The specific gravity at the end of charging should be within the limits given and should not vary .005 from the values given.

Do not allow the temperature of the electrolyte to exceed the maximum permissible temperature, i.e.:

For climates below 27°C. (80°F.) .. 38°C. (100°F.).
For climates above 27°C. (80°F.) .. 49°C. (120°F.).

If this temperature is reached the charge should be suspended to allow the temperature to fall at least 6° C. (10° F.), otherwise the life of the battery will tend to be shortened.

Refitting

The installation of the battery is a reversal of the procedure **'Removing'**. Smear the terminal posts and cable connections with petroleum jelly and tighten the retaining screws sufficiently to prevent the cables from moving on the terminal posts when tested by hand, but do not overtighten.

NOTE.–Whenever booster charging of the battery or electric welding of the body is carried out, the battery earth lead must be disconnected to prevent damage to the electrical system.

Section N.2

PREPARING DRY-CHARGED BATTERIES FOR SERVICE

Dry-charged batteries are supplied without electrolyte but with the plates in a charged condition. When they are required for service it is only necessary to fill each cell with sulphuric acid of the correct specific gravity. No initial charging is required.

Preparing electrolyte

The electrolyte is prepared by mixing together distilled water and concentrated sulphuric acid, taking the precautions given in Section N.3. The specific gravity of the filling electrolyte depends on the climate in which the battery is to be used.

Filling the battery

Carefully break the seals in the cell filling holes and fill each cell with electrolyte to the top of the separator guards **in one operation.** The temperature of the filling room, battery, and electrolyte should be maintained between 16 and 38° C. (60 and 100°F.). If the battery has been stored in a cool place it should be allowed to warm up to room temperature before filling.

Putting into use

Measure the temperature and specific gravity of the electrolyte in each of the cells. Allow to stand for 20 minutes and then re-check. The battery is ready for service unless the electrolyte temperature has risen by more than 5.5°C. (10°F.), or the specific gravity has fallen by more than 10 points (.010 S.G.). In this event, re-charge the battery at the normal re-charge rate until the specific gravity remains constant for three successive hourly readings and all cells are gassing freely. During the charge the electrolyte must be kept level with the top of the separator guards by the addition of distilled water.

Section N.3

PREPARING NEW, UNFILLED, UNCHARGED BATTERIES FOR SERVICE

Preparing electrolyte

Batteries should not be filled with acid until required for initial charging. Electrolyte is prepared by mixing distilled water and concentrated sulphuric acid, usually of 1.840 S.G. The mixing must be carried out either in a lead-lined tank or in suitable glass or earthenware vessels. Slowly add the acid to the water, stirring with a glass rod. **Never add the water to the acid,** as the resulting chemical reaction causes violent and dangerous spurting of the concentrated acid. The approximate proportions of acid and water are indicated in the following table:

For climates	To obtain specific gravity (corrected to 16°C. (60°F.)) of	Add 1 vol. of 1.840 S.G. acid to distilled water as below
Below 27°C. (80°F.)	1.260	3.2 volumes of water
Above 27°C. (80°F.)	1.210	4.3 volumes of water

Heat is produced by mixing acid and water, and the electrolyte should be allowed to cool before taking hydrometer readings–unless a thermometer is used to measure the actual temperature and a correction applied to the readings before pouring the electrolyte into the battery.

Filling the battery

The temperature of the electrolyte, battery, and filling room should be maintained between 16° and 38° C. (60° and 100°F.).

Carefully break the seals in the filling holes and **half-fill** each cell with electrolyte of the appropriate specific gravity. Allow the battery to stand for at least 12 hours in order to dissipate the heat generated by the chemical action of the acid on the plates and separators, and then add sufficient electrolyte to fill each cell to the top of the separators. Allow to stand for a further two hours and then proceed with the initial charge.

Initial charge

The initial charging rate is 3.5 amps. Charge at this rate until the voltage and specific gravity readings show no increase over five successive hourly readings. This will take from 48 to 80 hours, depending on the length of time the battery has been stored before charging.

Keep the current constant by varying the series resistance of the circuit or the generator output. **This charge should not be broken by long rest periods.** If, however, the temperature of any cell rises above the permissible maximum, i.e.

For climates below 27°C. (80°F.)	..	38°C. (100°F.)
For climates above 27°C. (80°F.)	..	49°C. (120°F.)

the charge must be interrupted until the temperature has fallen at least 5.5°C. (10°F.) below that figure. Throughout the charge the electrolyte must be kept level with the top of the separators by the addition of acid solution of the same specific gravity as the original filling-in acid until specific gravity and charge readings have remained constant for five successive hourly readings. If the charge is continued beyond that point, top up with distilled water. At the end of the charge carefully check the specific gravity in each cell to ensure that, when corrected to 16° C. (60° F.) it lies between the specified limits. If any cell requires adjustment some of the electrolyte must be siphoned off and replaced either by distilled water or by acid of strength originally used for filling in, depending on whether the specific gravity is too high or too low. Continue the charge for an hour or so to ensure adequate mixing of the electrolyte and again check the specific gravity readings. If necessary, repeat the adjustment process until the desired reading is obtained in each cell. Finally, allow the battery to cool, and siphon off any electrolyte over the top of the separators.

Section N.4

DYNAMO

Testing on vehicle when dynamo is not charging

Make sure that belt slip is not the cause of the trouble. It should be possible to deflect the belt approximately ½ in. (13 mm.) with moderate hand pressure at the centre of its longest run between two pulleys. If the belt is too slack, tightening is effected by slackening the two dynamo suspension bolts and then the bolt of the slotted adjustment link. A gentle pull on the dynamo outwards will enable the correct tension to be applied to the belt and all three bolts should then be tightened firmly.

Check that the dynamo and control box are connected correctly. The dynamo terminal 'D' should be connected to the control box terminal 'D' and the dynamo terminal 'F' connected to the control box terminal 'F'.

After switching off all lights and accessories disconnect the cables from the dynamo terminals marked 'D' and 'F' respectively.

Connect the two terminals with a short length of wire.

Start the engine and set to run at normal idling speed.

Clip the negative lead of a moving-coil-type voltmeter calibrated 0–20 volts to one dynamo terminal and the other lead to a good earthing point on the dynamo yoke.

Gradually increase the engine speed: the voltmeter reading should rise rapidly and without fluctuation. Do not allow the voltmeter reading to reach 20 volts. Do not race the engine in an attempt to increase the voltage. It is sufficient to run the dynamo up to a speed of 1,000 r.p.m.

If there is no reading check the brush gear.

If the reading is low (approximately ½ to 1 volt) the field winding may be faulty.

If the reading is approximately 4 to 5 volts the armature winding may be faulty.

If the dynamo is in good order leave the temporary link in position between the terminals and restore the original connections, taking care to connect the dynamo terminal 'D' to the control box terminal 'D' and the dynamo terminal 'F' to the control box terminal 'F'. Remove the lead from the 'D' terminal on the control box and connect the voltmeter between this cable and a good earthing point on the vehicle. Run the engine as before. The reading should be the same as that measured directly on the dynamo. No reading on the voltmeter indicates a break in the cable to the dynamo. Carry out the same procedure for the 'F' terminal, connecting the voltmeter between cable and earth. Finally, remove the link from the dynamo. If the reading is correct test the control box.

Removing

To remove the dynamo disconnect the dynamo leads from the dynamo terminals.

Slacken all the attachment bolts and pivot the dynamo towards the cylinder block to enable the fan belt to be removed from the dynamo pulley. The dynamo can then be removed by withdrawing the two upper and one lower attachment bolts.

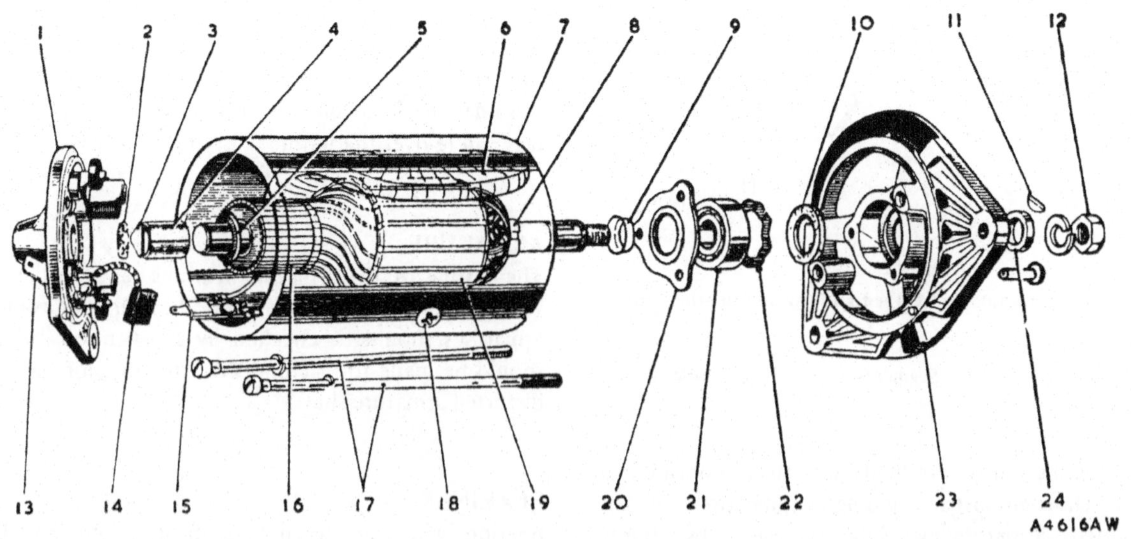

Fig. N.1
The C40/1 type dynamo

1. Commutator end bracket.
2. Felt ring.
3. Felt ring retainer.
4. Bronze bush.
5. Thrust washer.
6. Field coils.
7. Yoke.
8. Shaft collar.
9. Shaft collar retaining cup.
10. Felt ring.
11. Shaft key.
12. Shaft nut.
13. Output terminal 'D'.
14. Brushes.
15. Field terminal 'F'.
16. Commutator.
17. Through-bolts.
18. Pole-shoe securing screws.
19. Armature.
20. Bearing retaining plate.
21. Ball bearing.
22. Corrugated washer.
23. Driving end bracket.
24. Pulley spacer.

Dismantling

Remove the securing nut and take off the drive pulley.

Remove the Woodruff key from the commutator shaft.

Unscrew and remove the two through-bolts and take off the commutator end bracket. The driving end bracket, together with the armature and its ball bearing, can now be lifted out of the yoke. Unless the ball bearing is damaged or requires attention it need not be removed from the armature. Should it be necessary to remove the bearing, the armature must be separated from the end bracket by means of a hand press.

Servicing

BRUSHES

Lift the brushes up in the brush boxes and secure them in that position by positioning each brush spring at the side of the brush. Fit the commutator end bracket over the commutator and release the brushes. Hold back each of the brush springs and move the brush by pulling gently on its flexible connector. If the movement is sluggish, remove the brush from its holder and ease the sides by lightly polishing it on a smooth file. Always refit the brushes in their original positions. If the brushes are badly worn, new brushes must be fitted and bedded to the commutator. The minimum permissible length of brush is $\frac{9}{32}$ in. (7.14 mm.).

Test the brush spring tension, using a spring scale. The tension of the springs when new is 18 to 24 oz. (510.7 to 681 gm.). In service it is permissible for this value to fall to 15 oz. (425 gm.) before performance may be affected. Fit new springs if the tension is low.

COMMUTATOR

A commutator in good condition will be smooth and free from pits or burned spots. Clean the commutator with a cloth moistened with fuel. If this is ineffective carefully polish with a strip of fine glass-paper while rotating the armature. To remedy a badly worn commutator mount the armature (with or without the drive end bracket) in a lathe, rotate at high speed, and take a light cut with a very sharp tool. Do not remove more metal than is necessary. Polish the commutator with very fine glass-paper. Undercut the mica insulation between the segments to a depth of $\frac{1}{32}$ in. (.8 mm.) with a hacksaw blade ground down to the thickness of the mica.

Some commutators are of the moulded type and may be skimmed to a minimum diameter of 1.45 in. (36.8 mm.). The undercut must conform to the following dimensions

Width .. .. .040 in. (1.02 mm.).

Depth .. .. .020 in. (.51 mm.).

It is important that the sides of the undercut clear the moulding material by a minimum of .015 in. (.38 mm.).

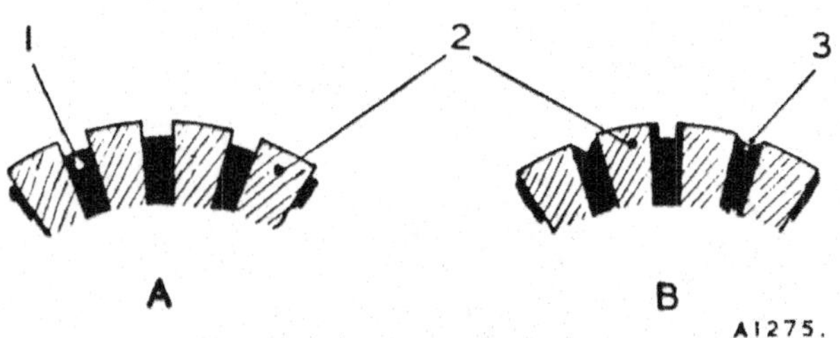

Fig. N.2
Undercutting the commutator (A) the right way and (B) the wrong way

1. Insulator 2. Segments. 3. Insulator

The most common armature faults are usually confined to open- or short-circuited windings. Indication of an open-circuited armature winding is given by burnt commutator segments. A short-circuited armature winding is easily identified by discoloration of the overheated windings and badly burnt commutator segments.

FIELD COILS

Test the field coils with an ohmmeter without removing them from the dynamo yoke. The reading on the ohmmeter should be between 6.0 and 6.3 ohms. If this is not available connect a 12-volt D.C. supply with an ammeter in series between the field terminal and the dynamo yoke. The ammeter reading should be approximately 2 amps. If no reading is indicated the field coils are open-circuited and must be renewed.

If the current reading is much more than 2 amps. or the ohmmeter reading much below 6 ohms, it is an indication that the insulation of one of the field coils has broken down.

In either case, unless a substitute dynamo is available, the field coils must be renewed. To do this carry out the procedure outlined below.

Drill out the rivet securing the field coil terminal assembly to the yoke and unsolder the field coil connections.

Remove the insulation piece which is provided to prevent the junction of the field coils from contacting the yoke.

Mark the yoke and pole-shoes in order that they can be refitted in their original positions.

Unscrew the two pole-shoe retaining screws by means of a wheel-operated screwdriver.

Draw the pole-shoes and coils out of the yoke and lift off the coils.

Fit the new field coils over the pole-shoes and place them in position inside the yoke. Take care that the taping of the field coils is not trapped between the pole-shoes and the yoke.

Locate the pole-shoes and field coils by lightly tightening the fixing screw.

Fully tighten the screws by means of a wheel-operated screwdriver and lock them by caulking.

Replace the insulation piece between the field coil connections and the yoke.

Resolder the field coil connections to the field coil terminal tags and re-rivet the terminal assembly to the yoke.

ARMATURE

The testing of the armature winding requires the use of a voltage drop-test and growler. If these are not available the armatures should be checked by substitution. No attempt should be made to machine the armature core or to true a distorted armature shaft.

BEARINGS

Bearings which are worn to such an extent that they will allow side-movement of the armature shaft must be renewed.

To renew the bearing bush in a commutator end bracket proceed as follows.

Remove the old bearing bush from the end bracket. The bearing can be withdrawn with a suitable extractor or by screwing a ⅝ in. tap into the bush for a few turns and pulling out the bush with the tap. Screw the tap squarely into the bush to avoid damaging the bracket.

Press the new bearing bush into the end bracket, using a shouldered, highly polished mandrel of the same diameter as the shaft which is to be fitted in the bearing, until the visible end of the bearing is flush with the inner face of the bracket. Porous bronze bushes should not be opened out after fitting or the porosity of the bush may be impaired.

NOTE.–Before fitting the new bearing bush it should be allowed to stand for 24 hours completely immersed in thin (S.A.E. 20) engine oil; this will allow the pores of the bush to be filled with lubricant. In cases of extreme urgency this period may be shortened by heating the oil to 100° C.

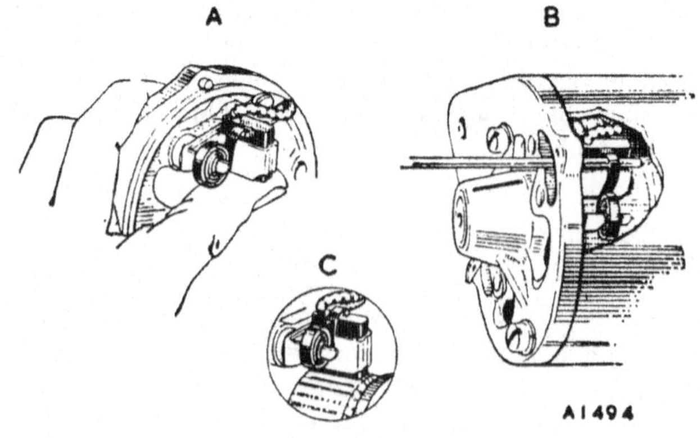

Fig. N.3
Fitting the commutator end bracket

A. Brush trapped by spring in raised position.
B. Releasing the brush onto the commutator.
C. Normal position of brush.

(212° F.) for two hours, then allowing it to cool before removing the bearing bush.

The ball bearing is renewed as follows.

Drill out the rivets which secure the bearing retaining plate to the end bracket and remove the plate. Press the bearing out of the end bracket and remove the corrugated washer, felt washer, and oil-retaining washer.

Before fitting the replacement bearing see that it is clean and pack it with high-melting-point grease.

Place the oil-retaining washer, felt washer, and corrugated washer in the bearing housing in the end bracket.

Press the bearing into the housing. The outer bearing journal is a light push-fit in the bearing housing.

Refit the bearing retaining plate, using rivets having the same dimensions as those originally fitted.

NOTE.–When fitting a drive end bracket to the armature shaft the inner journal of the bearing MUST be supported by a mild-steel tube–do not use the drive end bracket.

Reassembling

The reassembly of the dynamo is a reversal of the dismantling sequence.

If the end bracket has been removed from the armature in dismantling, press the bearing end bracket onto the armature shaft, taking care to avoid damaging the end plate and armature winding. When assembling the commutator end bracket the brushes must first be held clear of the commutator by partially withdrawing them from their boxes until each brush is trapped in position by the side pressure of its spring. The brushes can be released onto the commutator by a small screwdriver or similar tool when the end bracket is assembled to within about ½ in. (13 mm.) of the yoke. Before closing the gap between the end bracket and the yoke see that the springs are in correct contact with the brushes.

Add a few drops of oil through the hole in the armature end cover.

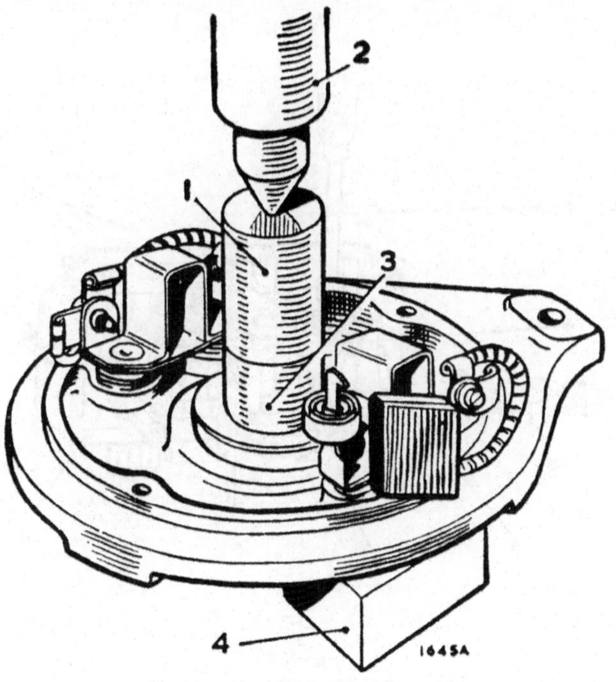

Fig. N.4
The method of pressing in the commutator end bracket bush is shown in this illustration

1. Shouldered mandrel.
2. Hand press.
3. Bearing bush.
4. Support block.

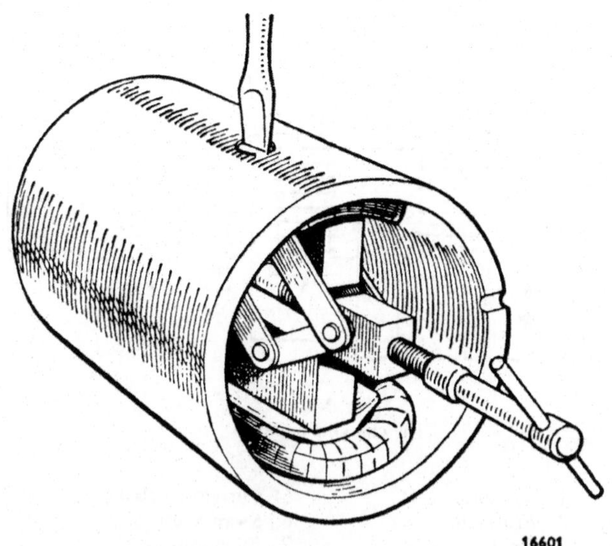

Fig. N.5
Expanding the pole-shoes in the yoke

Refitting

Reverse the removal procedure, noting that on later models plain washers are fitted under the heads of the two upper fixing bolts.

Section N.5

CONTROL BOX MODEL RB340

General description

The RB340 control box operates on the current-voltage system of dynamo output regulation. Three units are housed in the control box: two separate vibrating armature-type single-contact regulators and a cut-out relay. One regulator is responsive to changes in current and the other to changes in voltage.

The voltage regulator and cut-out relay are temperature-compensated to allow for operating changes in the circuit resistance and for climatic variations in battery voltage. The effect of temperature fluctuation on control box settings is further minimized by the use of a swamp resistor connected in series with the shunt coils of the voltage regulator and cut-out relay.

For adjustment purposes toothed cams are carried on the front limb of each magnet frame to enable voltage and current settings to be made with a special tool (see Fig. N.7).

The control box settings are accurately adjusted during manufacture and the cover should not be removed unnecessarily.

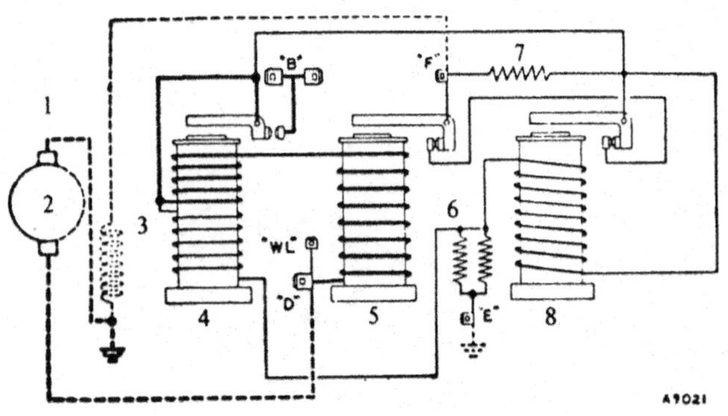

Fig. N.6
The charging circuit

1. Dynamo.
2. Armature.
3. Field.
4. Cut-out relay.
5. Current regulator.
6. Swamp resistor.
7. Field resistor.
8. Voltage regulator.

Preliminary checking of charging circuit

Before disturbing any electrical adjustments examine the items mentioned below to ensure that the fault does not lie outside the control box.

Check the battery by substitution or with a hydrometer and a heavy-discharge tester. Inspect the dynamo driving belt. This should be just taut enough to drive without slipping. Check the dynamo by substitution, or by disconnecting the cables from the dynamo terminals and linking the large terminal 'D' to the small terminal 'F', connecting a voltmeter between this link and earth, and running the dynamo up to about 1,000 r.p.m., when a rising voltage should be shown.

Inspect the wiring of the charging circuit and carry out continuity tests between the dynamo, control box, and battery.

Check the earth connections, particularly that of the control box.

In the event of reported undercharging, ascertain that this is not due to low mileage.

Voltage regulator (open circuit)

METHOD OF ADJUSTMENT

Checking and adjusting should be completed as rapidly as possible to avoid errors due to heating of the operating coil. Withdraw the cables from the control box terminal blades 'B'. To enable the engine to be started it will be necessary to join the ignition and battery feeds together with a suitable lead. Connect a first-grade 0–20 moving-coil voltmeter between control box terminal 'D' and a good earthing point. A convenient method of making this connection is to withdraw the ignition warning light feed from the control box terminal 'WL' and to clip the voltmeter lead of appropriate polarity to the small terminal blade thus exposed, this terminal being electrically common with terminal 'D'. Start the engine and run the dynamo at 3,000 r.p.m. The voltmeter reading should be steady and lie between the appropriate limits according to the temperature (see **'GENERAL DATA'**).

An unsteady reading may be due to dirty contacts. If the reading is steady but occurs outside the appropriate limits an adjustment must be made. Proceed as follows.

Stop the engine and remove the control box cover. Restart the engine and run the dynamo at 3,000 r.p.m. Using a suitable tool (see Fig. N.7), turn the voltage adjustment cam until the correct setting is obtained. Turn the tool clockwise to raise the setting or anti-clockwise to lower it. Check the setting by stopping the engine and then again raising the generator speed to 3,000 r.p.m. Restore the original connections and refit the cover.

Cut-out relay

CUT-IN ADJUSTMENT

Checking and adjusting should be completed as rapidly as possible to avoid errors due to heating of the operating coil. Connect a first grade 0–20 moving-coil voltmeter between control box terminal 'D' and a good earthing point. A convenient method of making this connection is to withdraw the ignition warning light feed from control box terminal 'WL' and to clip the voltmeter lead of appropriate polarity to the small terminal blade thus exposed, this terminal being electrically common with terminal 'D'. Switch on an electrical load such as the headlamps, start the engine, and gradually increase the engine speed. Observe the voltmeter pointer. The voltage should rise steadily and then drop slightly at the instant of contact closure. The cut-in voltage is that which is indicated immediately before the pointer drops back and should be within the limits 12.7 to

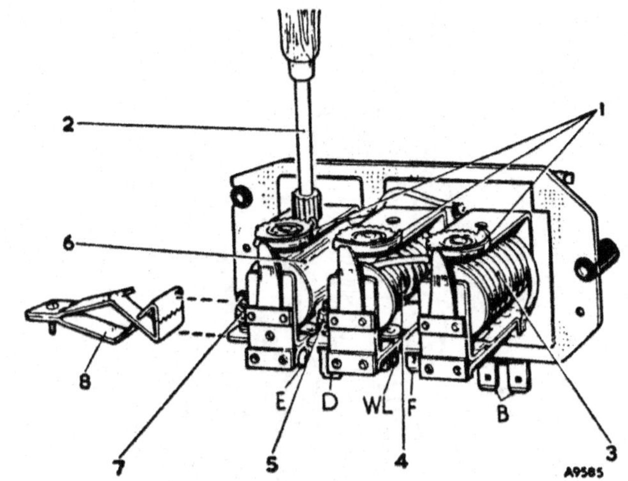

Fig. N.7
The control box with cover removed

1. Adjustment cams.
2. Setting tool.
3. Cut-out relay.
4. Current regulator.
5. Current regulator contacts.
6. Voltage regulator.
7. Voltage regulator contacts.
8. Clip.

13.3 volts. If the cut-in occurs outside these limits an adjustment must be made. In this event proceed as follows. Remove the control box cover. Using a suitable tool (see Fig. N 7), turn the cut-out relay adjustment cam until the correct setting is obtained. Turn the tool clockwise to raise the setting or anti-clockwise to lower it. Stop the engine, restore the original connections, and refit the cover.

DROP-OFF ADJUSTMENT

Withdraw the cables from control box terminal blades 'B'. To enable the engine to be started it will be necessary to join the ignition and battery feeds together with a suitable lead. Connect a first-grade 0–20 moving-coil voltmeter between control box terminal 'B' and a good earthing point. Start the engine and run up to approximately 3,000 r.p.m.

Slowly decelerate and observe the voltmeter pointer. Opening of the contacts, indicated by the voltmeter pointer dropping to zero, should occur between 9.5 and 11 volts. If the drop-off occurs outside these limits an adjustment must be made. Proceed as follows.

Stop the engine and remove the control box cover. Adjust the drop-off voltage by carefully bending the fixed contact bracket. Reducing the contact gap will raise the drop-off voltage and increasing the gap will lower it. Retest, and if necessary readjust until the correct drop-off setting is obtained. This should result in a contact 'follow through' or blade deflection of .010 to .020 in. (.254 to .508 mm.). Restore the original connections and refit the cover.

Current regulator

ON-LOAD SETTING

The current regulator on-load setting is equal to the maximum rated output of the dynamo, which is 22 amps.

METHOD OF ADJUSTMENT

The dynamo must be made to develop its maximum rated output whatever the state of charge of the battery might be at the time of setting. The voltage regulator must therefore be rendered inoperative, and to do this the bulldog clip shown in Fig. N.7 is used to keep the voltage regulator contacts together.

Remove the control box cover and, using a bulldog clip, short out the contacts of the voltage regulator.

Withdraw the cables from the control box terminal blades 'B' and connect a first-grade 0–40 moving-coil ammeter between these cables and one of the terminal blades 'B'. It is important that terminal 'B' should carry only this one connection. All other load connections, including the ignition coil feed, must be made to the battery. Switch on all lights and accessories, start the engine, and run the dynamo at 3,000 r.p.m. The ammeter pointer should be steady and indicate a current of 19–22 amps. An unsteady reading may be due to dirty contacts. If the reading is too high or too low an adjustment must be made. Proceed as follows.

Using a suitable tool (see Fig. N.7), turn the current adjustment cam until the correct setting is obtained. Turn the tool clockwise to raise the setting or anti-clockwise to lower it. Stop the engine, restore the original connections, and refit the control box cover.

Adjustment of air gap settings

Air gap settings are accurately adjusted during manufacture and should require no further attention. If the original settings have been disturbed, it will be necessary to make adjustments in the manner described below.

ARMATURE-TO-BOBBIN CORE GAPS OF VOLTAGE AND CURRENT REGULATORS

Disconnect the battery. Using a suitable tool (see Fig. N.7), turn the adjustment cam of the regulator being adjusted to the point giving minimum lift to the armature tensioning spring (by turning the tool to the fullest extent anti-clockwise). Slacken the appropriate contact locking nut and unscrew the contact. Insert a feeler gauge of .056 in. (1.42 mm.) thickness between the armature and the regulator head as far back as the two rivet heads on the underside of the armature. With the gauge in position, press squarely down on the armature, and screw in the contact until it just touches the armature contact. Tighten the locknut and withdraw the gauge. Repeat this procedure on the remaining regulator.

NOTE.—On earlier type regulators having a copper shim on the regulator head the air gap setting is .045 in. (1.15 mm.) and care must be taken not to damage the copper shim.

Carry out the electrical setting procedure.

CONTACT 'FOLLOW THROUGH' AND ARMATURE-TO-BOBBIN CORE GAP OF CUT-OUT RELAY

Press the armature squarely down against the copper separation on the core face. Adjust the fixed contact bracket to give a 'follow through' or blade deflection of the moving contact of .010 to .020 in. (.254 to .508 mm.).

Adjust the armature back stop to give a core gap of .035 to .045 in. (.889 to 1.147 mm.).

Check the cut-in and drop-off voltage settings.

Cleaning contacts

REGULATOR CONTACTS

To clean the voltage or current regulator contacts use fine carborundum stone or silicon-carbide paper, followed by methylated spirit (denatured alcohol).

CUT-OUT RELAY CONTACTS

To clean the cut-out relay contacts use a strip of fine glass-paper—never carborundum stone or emery-cloth.

Section N.6

STARTER

Testing on vehicle when starter is not operating

In the following test it is assumed that the battery is in a charged condition.

Switch on the lamps and operate the starter control. If the lights go dim but the starter is not heard to operate, an indication is given that the current is flowing through the starter motor windings, but that for some reason the armature is not rotating; possibly the starter pinion is

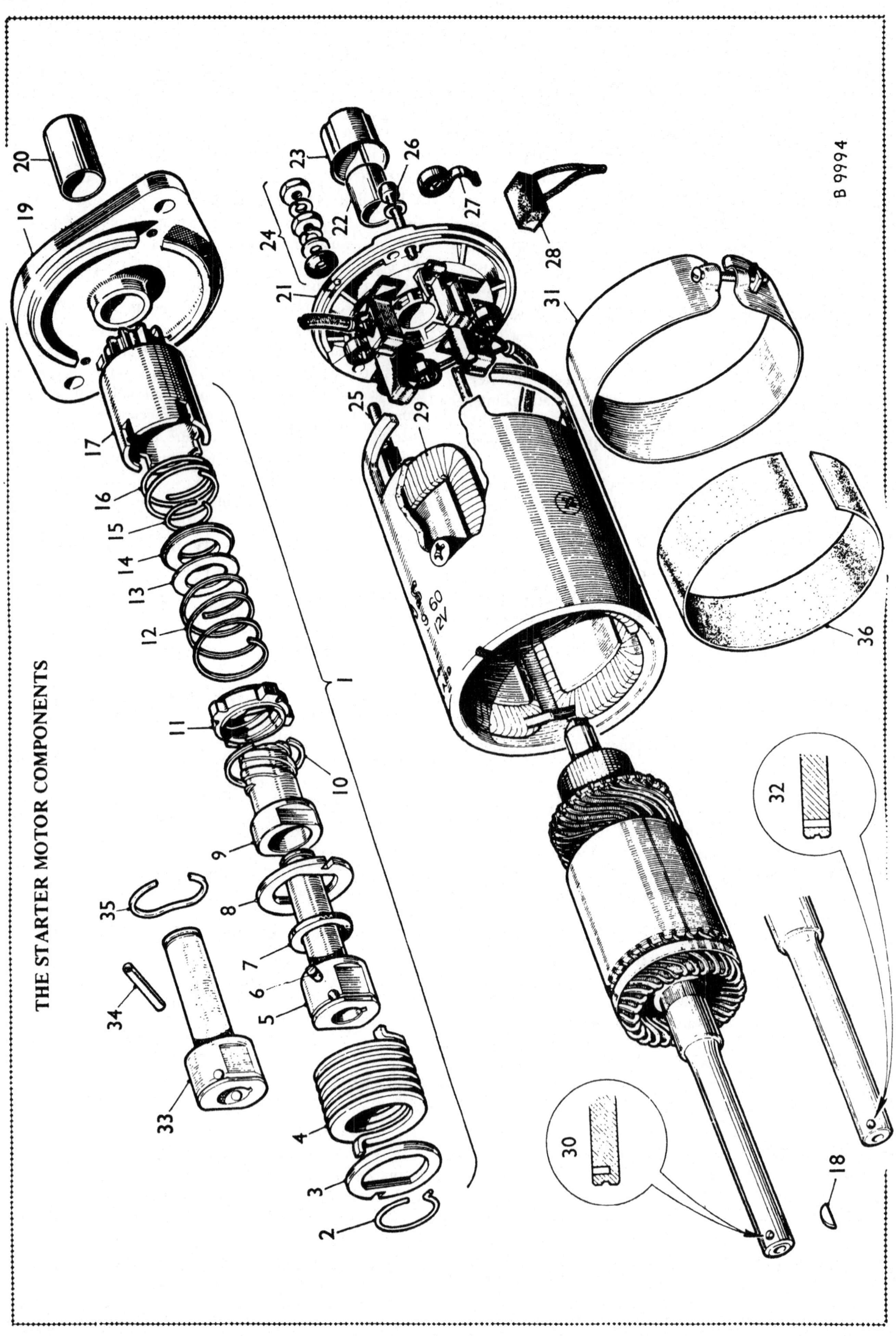

THE STARTER MOTOR COMPONENTS

KEY TO THE STARTER MOTOR COMPONENTS

No.	Description	No.	Description	No.	Description
1.	Drive assembly.	13.	Thrust washer–control nut.	25.	Terminal post.
2.	Retaining ring.	14.	Locating collar.	26.	Through-bolt.
3.	Anchor plate–front.	15.	Retaining ring.	27.	Brush tension spring.
4.	Main spring.	16.	Spring.	28.	Brush.
5.	Centre sleeve.*	17.	Pinion and barrel.	29.	Field coils.
6.	Retaining pin.*	18.	Woodruff key.*	30.	Armature.*
7.	Thrust washer (fibre).	19.	Drive end bracket.	31.	Cover band.
8.	Anchor plate–rear.	20.	Bush–driving end.	32.	Armature.†
9.	Screwed sleeve.	21.	Commutator end bracket.	33.	Centre sleeve.†
10.	Retaining ring.*	22.	Bush–commutator end.	34.	Spiral pin.†
11.	Control nut.	23.	Shaft cap.	35.	Waved circlip.†
12.	Restraining spring.	24.	Terminal nuts and washers.	36.	Cover band seal.†

* For starter motors Serial No. 25555.

† For starter motors Serial No. 25598.

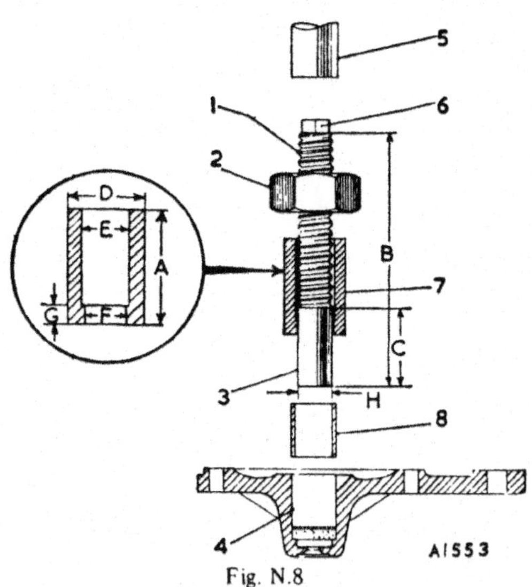

Fig. N.8
Using a self-extracting-type tool to fit an end bracket bush

1. $\frac{5}{8}$ in. B.S.F. truncated thread.	A. 1½ in. (38 mm.).
2. Extracting nut.	B. 4 in. (10.2 cm.).
3. Fitting pin.	C. 1¼ in. (31.8 mm.).
4. Bearing housing.	D. $1\frac{5}{16}$ in. (33.3 mm.).
5. Hand press.	E. .625 in. (15.87 mm.).
6. Squared end.	F. .605 in. (15.37 mm.).
7. Sleeve.	G. ¼ in. (6.35 mm.).
8. Bush.	H. .5924 in. (15.05 mm.).

meshed permanently with the geared ring on the flywheel. This could be caused by the starter being operated while the engine is still moving. In this case the starter motor must be removed from the engine for examination.

Should the lamps retain their full brilliance when the starter switch is operated, check that the switch is functioning. Next, if the switch is in order examine the connections at the battery and starter switch, and also examine the wiring joining these units. Continued failure of the starter to operate indicates an internal fault in the starter, which must be removed for examination.

Sluggish action of the starter is usually caused by a poor connection in the wiring which causes a high resistance in the starter circuit. Check the wiring as described above.

Removing

Disconnect the cable from the earth terminal on the battery and the cable from the terminal on the starter. Remove the external oil filter, the ignition coil and bracket, and the distributor. Unscrew the two bolts securing the starter to the flywheel housing and engine rear plate and withdraw the starter upwards from the engine compartment.

Servicing

EXAMINATION OF COMMUTATOR AND BRUSH GEAR

Remove the starter cover band and examine the brushes and the commutator. Hold back each of the brush springs and move the brush by pulling gently on its flexible connector. If the movement is sluggish remove the brush from its holder and ease the sides by lightly polishing on a smooth file. Always replace brushes in their original positions. If the brushes are worn so that they no longer bear on the commutator or if the brush flexible lead has become exposed on the running face, they must be renewed.

If the commutator is blackened or dirty clean it by holding a cloth moistened with fuel against it while the armature is rotated.

Secure the body of the starter in a vice and test by connecting it with heavy-gauge cables to a 12-volt battery. One cable must be connected to the starter terminal and the other held against the starter body or end bracket. Under these light load conditions the starter should run at a very high speed.

If the operation of the starter is still unsatisfactory it should be dismantled for detailed inspection and testing.

DISMANTLING

Take off the cover band at the commutator end, hold back the brush springs, and take out the brushes.

Remove the circlip from the outer end of the drive head sleeve and take off the front spring anchor plate, the main spring and the rear spring anchor plate.

Withdraw the pin securing the drive head sleeve to the armature shaft, push the sleeve assembly down the shaft and remove the Woodruff key. Slide the complete drive assembly from the armature shaft.

Remove the barrel retaining ring from the inside of the barrel and pinion assembly and withdraw the barrel and anti-drift spring from the screwed sleeve.

From the inner end of the drive head sleeve remove the circlip, locating collar, control nut thrust washer, cushioning spring, control nut, screwed sleeve and the drive head thrust washer.

Remove the terminal nuts and washers from the terminal post and screw out the two through-bolts.

Remove the commutator end bracket, the drive end bracket, and the armature.

BRUSHES

1. Test the brush springs with a spring balance. The correct tension is 30 to 40 oz. (850 to 1134 gm.). Fit a new spring if the tension is low.
2. If the brushes are worn so that they no longer bear on the commutator, or if the flexible connector has become exposed on the running face, they must be renewed. Two of the brushes are connected to terminal eyelets attached to the brush boxes on the commutator end bracket. The other two brushes (Fig. N.9) are connected to tappings on the field coils.

The flexible connectors must be removed by unsoldering and the connectors of the new brushes secured in their place by soldering. The brushes are preformed so that bedding of the working face to the commutator is unnecessary.

DRIVE

1. If the pinion is tight on the screwed sleeve wash away any dirt with paraffin (kerosene).

2. If any parts are worn or damaged they must be renewed.

COMMUTATOR

A commutator in good condition will be smooth and free from pits and burned spots. Clean the commutator with a cloth moistened with petrol (gasoline). If this is ineffective carefully polish with a strip of fine glass-paper while rotating the armature. To remedy a badly worn commutator dismantle the starter drive as described above and remove the armature from the end bracket. Now mount the armature in a lathe, rotate it at a high speed, and take a light cut with a very sharp tool. Do not remove any more metal than is absolutely necessary, and finally polish with very fine glass-paper.

The mica on the starter commutator **must not be undercut.**

FIELD COILS

The field coils can be tested for an open circuit by connecting a 12-volt battery, having a 12-volt bulb in one of the leads, to the tapping-point of the field coils to which the brushes are connected and the field terminal post. If the lamp does not light there is an open circuit in the wiring of the field coils.

Lighting of the lamp does not necessarily mean that the field coils are in order as it is possible that one of them may be earthed to a pole-shoe or to the yoke. This may be checked by disconnecting the battery lead from the tapping-point of the field coils and holding it on a clean part of the starter yoke. Should the bulb now light, it indicates that the field coils are earthed.

NOTE.–When carrying out this test the brushes connected to the field coils must not be in contact with the starter yoke.

Should the above tests indicate that the fault lies in the field coils, they must be renewed. When renewing field coils carry out the procedure detailed in Section N.4.

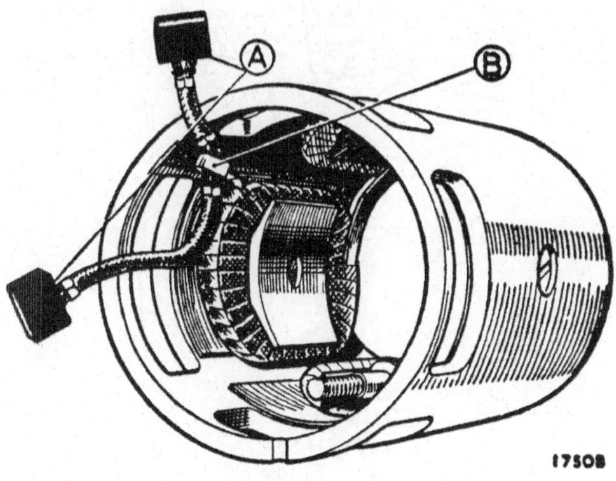

Fig. N.9
The starter brush connections.

A. Brushes. B. Tapping on field coils.

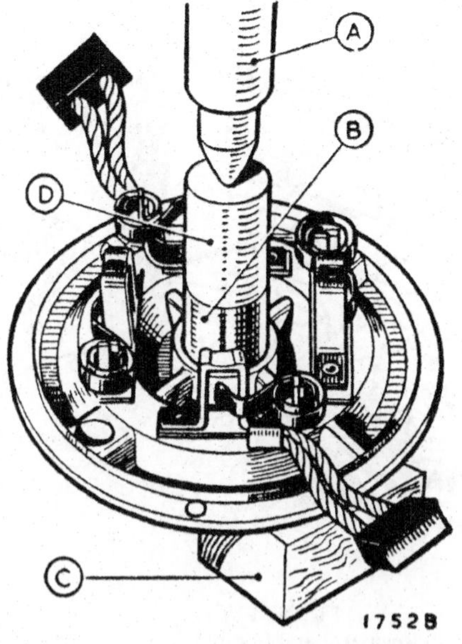

Fig. N.10
Fitting a new bush, using a shouldered mandrel

A. Hand press. C. Supporting block.
B. Bearing bush. D. Shouldered mandrel.

ARMATURE

Examination of the armature will in many cases reveal the cause of failure, e.g. conductors lifted from the commutator due to the starter being engaged while the engine is running and causing the armature to be rotated at an excessive speed. A damaged armature must in all cases be renewed–no attempt should be made to machine the armature core or to true a distorted armature shaft.

BEARINGS (COMMUTATOR END)

Bearings which are worn to such an extent that they will allow excessive side-play of the armature shaft must be renewed. To renew the bearing bush proceed as follows.

Press the new bearing bush into the end bracket, using a shouldered mandrel of the same diameter as the shaft which is to fit in the bearing.

NOTE.–The bearing bush is of the porous phosphor-bronze type, and before fitting, new bushes should be allowed to stand completely immersed for 24 hours in thin engine oil in order to fill the pores of the bush with lubricant.

REASSEMBLING

The reassembly of the starter is a reversal of the operations described in this Section.

Section N.7

FUSES

The fuses are mounted in a separate holder located under a large plastic cover on the right-hand wing valance.

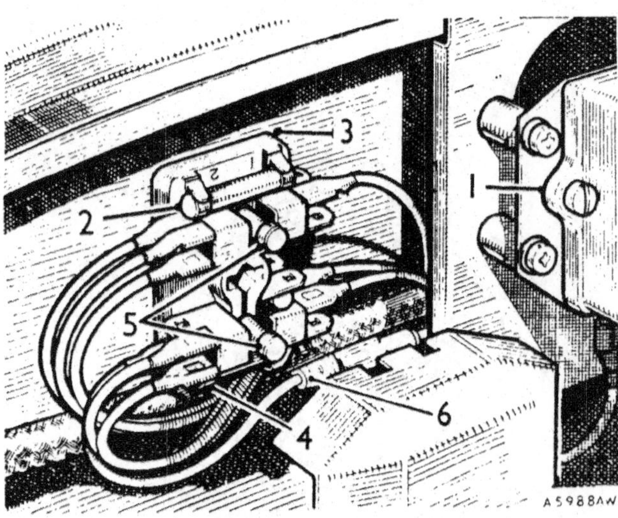

Fig. N.11
Regulator and fuse block

1. Regulator.
2. AUX. IGN. fuse (35-amp.).
3. Fuse block.
4. AUX. fuse (35-amp.).
5. Spare fuses.
6. Line fuse–heated back-light light (GT)'

The fuse between terminals '1' and '2' protects the accessories which operate irrespective of whether the ignition is on or off and the fuse between terminals '3' and '4' protects the accessories which operate only when the ignition is switched on.

Two spare fuses are provided, and it is important that only fuses of the correct value, marked inside the fuse tube, should be used.

Blown fuses

The units which are protected by each fuse can readily be identified by referring to the wiring diagram.

A blown fuse is indicated by the failure of all the units protected by it and is confirmed by examination of the fuse, which can easily be withdrawn from the spring clips. If it has blown the fused state of the wire will be visible inside the glass tube. Before renewing a blown fuse inspect the wiring of the units that have failed for evidence of a short circuit or other faults which may have caused the fuse to blow, and remedy the cause of the trouble.

Section N.8

WINDSHIELD WIPER

Apart from the renewal of perished wiper blades, the windshield wiper requires no periodic maintenance.

Inspect the rubber wiping elements, which after long service become worn and should be renewed.

The gearbox and cable rack are packed with grease during manufacture and need no further lubrication.

Resetting the limit switch

If the wiper fails to park or parks unsatisfactorily, the limit switch in the gearbox cover should be checked. Unless the limit switch is correctly set, it is possible for the wiper motor to overrun the open-circuit position and continue to draw current.

Slacken the four screws securing the gearbox cover and observe the projection near the rim of the limit switch. Position the projection in line with the groove in the gearbox cover. Turn the limit switch 25° in an anti-clockwise direction and tighten the four securing screws. If the wiper blades are required to park on the opposite side of the windshield, the limit switch should be turned back 180° in a clockwise direction.

Testing on a vehicle

If the wiper fails to operate, or operates unsatisfactorily, connect a 0–15 moving-coil ammeter in the wiper circuit, switch on the wiper, and note the current being supplied to the motor. The normal running current should be 2.7 to 3.4 amps.

WIPER TAKES NO CURRENT

Examine the fuse protecting the wiper circuit. If the fuse has blown examine the wiring of the motor circuit and of all other circuits protected by that fuse. Renew, if necessary, any cables which are badly worn or chafed, fitting protective sleeving over the cables to prevent a recurrence of the fault.

If the external wiring is found to be in order, replace the fuse with one of the recommended rating. Then proceed as for the wiper taking an abnormally high current.

If the fuse is intact, examine the wiring of the motor circuit for breaks and ensure that the wiper control switch is operating correctly.

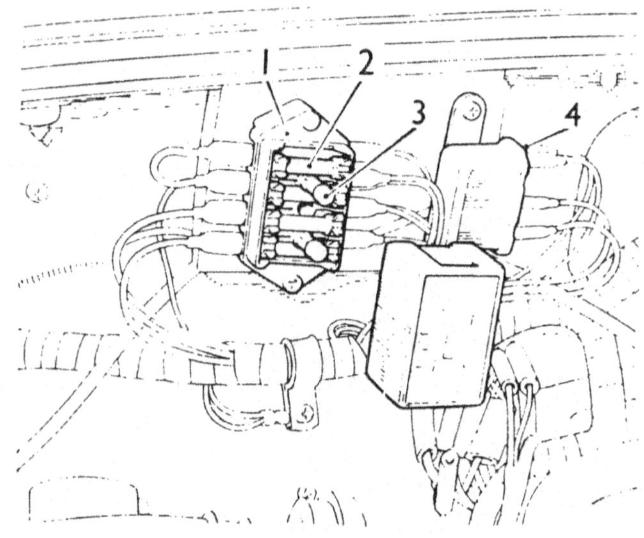

Fig. N.12
Lucas type 7FJ fuse block
(GHN5 and GHD5 cars)

1. Four-way fuse block.
2. Current rated 17-amp. 35-amp. blow rated) fuses.
3. Spare fuses.
4. Starter solenoid.

WIPER TAKES ABNORMALLY LOW CURRENT

Check that the battery is fully charged. The performance of the motor is dependent on the condition of the battery.

Remove the commutator end bracket and examine the brush gear, ensuring that it bears firmly on the commutator. The tension spring must be renewed if the brushes do not bear firmly on the commutator. Brush levers must move freely on the pivots. If these levers are stiff they should be freed by working them backwards and forwards by hand.

Examine the commutator and, if necessary, clean with a fuel-moistened cloth. A suspected armature should be checked by substitution.

WIPER TAKES ABNORMALLY HIGH CURRENT

If an abnormally high current is shown on the ammeter, this may be due to excessive load on the driving shaft. The stall current of the motor when cold is 14 amps. and when hot is 8 amps.

If there is no obvious reason for this, such as a sticking wiper blade, a check should be made at the gearbox.

Remove the gearbox cover and examine the gear assembly, checking that a blow on the gearbox end bracket has not reduced the armature end-float. The armature end-float adjusting screw must be set to give an armature end-play of .008 to .012 (.20 to .30 mm.).

Sluggish operation with excessive current consumption may be caused through frictional losses in badly positioned or defective connecting tubes. The connecting tubes can be checked, using a cable gauge. (Details of this gauge can be obtained from any Lucas Agent.) The gauge cable is similar in appearance to the driving rack but is .010 in. (.25 mm.) larger in diameter and is less flexible. The gauge will not easily pass through connecting tubes having less than the minimum permissible curvature.

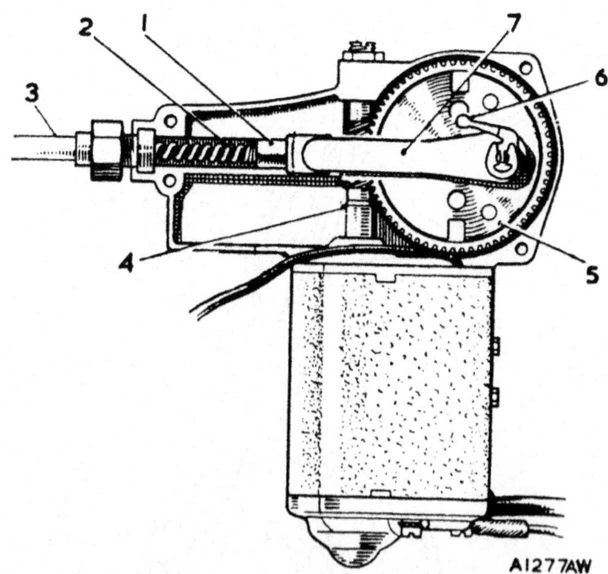

Fig. N.13
Windshield wiper drive components

1. Cross-head
2. Cable rack.
3. Outer casing.
4. Armature.
5. Final gear.
6. Park switch.
7. Connecting rod.

To check the tubing remove the motor and inner rack. Insert the gauge into the connecting tube as far as the first wheelbox and then withdraw it. Remove the tubing connecting the wheelboxes. Insert and withdraw the gauge. If the gauge moves freely the tubing is correctly installed. If the gauge does not move freely the tubing must be checked for sharp bends and obstructions. Check the wheelboxes for alignment and then reassemble.

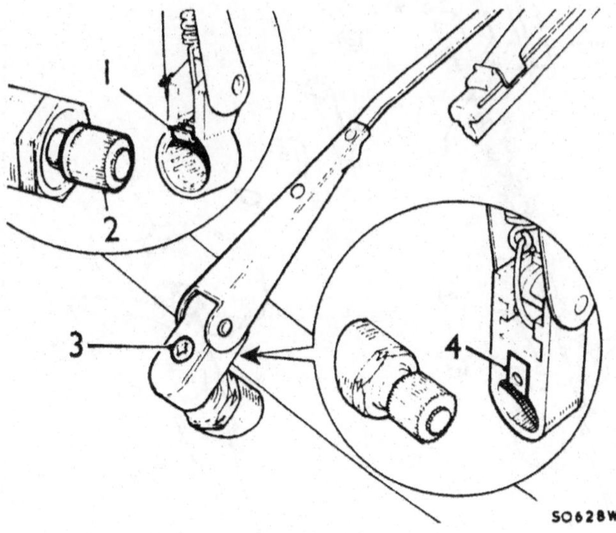

Fig. N.12
Wiper arm fixing details

1. Retaining clip.
2. Splined drive.
3. Locking screw.
4. Locking wedge.

Removing the motor, gearbox, and wheelboxes

The motor and gearbox is located beneath the passenger's side of the fascia panel and is mounted on a bracket secured to the bulkhead panel by three screws.

The cable rack connected to the cross-head in the gearbox passes through outer casings which connect the gearbox to the first wheelbox and the first wheelbox to the second wheelbox.

Disconnect the wiper arms, the electrical connections from the motor, and the outer cable from the gearbox housing. Remove the three screws securing the bracket to the bulkhead panel and withdraw the motor, bracket, and cable rack from beneath the fascia panel.

Slacken the cover screws in each wheelbox and remove the cable rack outer casings.

Remove the nut, front bush, and washer from the front of each wheelbox and remove the wheelbox together with the rear bush and spindle tube from beneath the fascia panel.

Replacement is a reversal of the removal sequence, but care must be taken to ensure that the wheelboxes are correctly lined up and that the cable rack engages the gear and spindle assemblies.

THE WINDSHIELD WIPER COMPONENTS

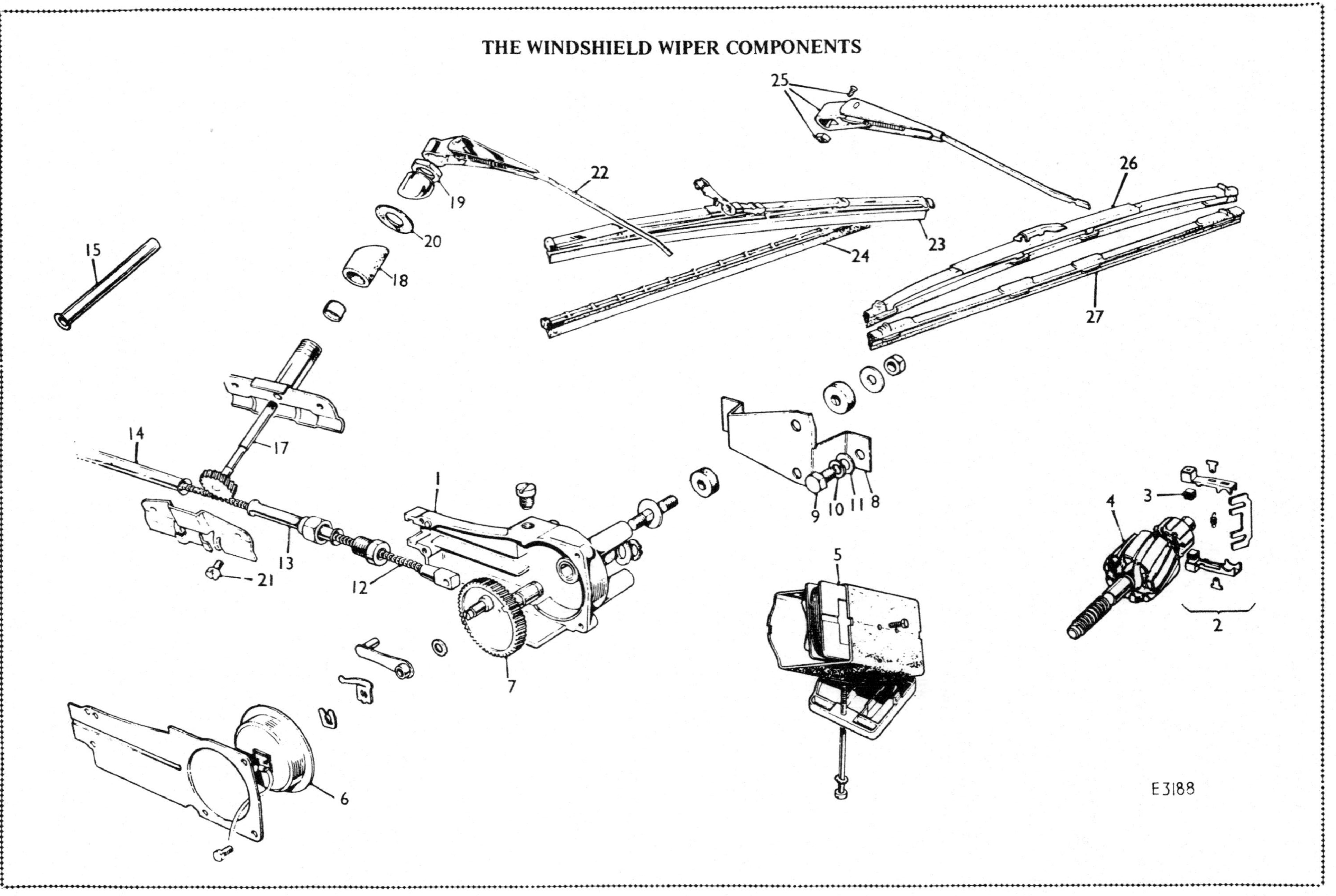

KEY TO THE WINDSHIELD WIPER COMPONENTS

No.	Description	No.	Description	No.	Description
1.	Motor–windshield wiper.	9.	Screw–bracket to bulkhead.	17.	Spindle and gear.
2.	Brush gear.	10.	Washer–spring.	18.	Tube–spindle–rubber.
3.	Brush.	11.	Washer–plain.	19.	Nut–wheelbox.
4.	Armature.	12.	Crosshead and rack.	20.	Washer (rubber).
5.	Coil–field.	13.	Casing–motor to wheelbox.	21.	Screw–cover.
6.	Switch–parking.	14.	Casing–wheelbox to wheelbox.	22.	Arm–wiper.
7.	Shaft and gear.	15.	Casing–wheelbox to extension.	23.	Blade–wiper.
8.	Bracket–wiper motor.	16.	Wheelbox.	24.	Rubber.

Later-type wiper arms (item 22), are retained to the wheelbox spindle by a screw and locking wedge. The end of the wiper arm and blade connector are also slightly modified (page N.16).

Dismantling the motor

Withdraw the four screws securing the gearbox cover and remove the cover.

Withdraw the connectors and through-bolts at the commutator end bracket.

Remove the commutator end bracket clear of the yoke.

The brush gear can be removed by lifting it clear of the commutator and withdrawing it as a unit. Care should be taken at this point to note the particular side occupied by each brush so that each may be replaced in its original setting on the commutator.

Access to the armature and field coils can be gained by withdrawing the yoke.

If it is necessary to remove the field coil, unscrew the two screws securing the pole-piece to the yoke. These screws should be marked so that they can be returned to their original holes.

Press out the pole-piece complete with field coil, marking the pole-piece so that it can be replaced in its correct position inside the yoke. The pole-piece can now be pressed out of the field coil.

Pieces of carbon short-circuiting adjacent segments of the commutator will also cause excessive current consumption. The resistance between adjacent commutator segments should be .34 to .41 ohm. Cleaning the commutator and brush gear removes this fault. When dismantling, check the internal wiring of the motor for evidence of short-circuiting due to chafed or charred insulation. Slip a new piece of sleeving over any charred connections, and arrange them so that they do not rub against sharp edges.

While the motor is dismantled check the value of the field resistance. If it is found to be lower than 12.8 to 14 ohms a short circuit in the windings is indicated and a new field coil must be fitted. Other evidence of a short circuit will be given by charred leads from the field coil.

Dismantling the gearbox unit

Remove the circlip and washer from the cross-head connecting link pin and lift off the cross-head and cable rack assembly. Then remove the circlip and washer from the final gear shaft located underneath the gearbox unit. Remove any burr from the circlip groove before lifting out the final gear. The armature and worm drive can now be withdrawn from the gearbox. All gear teeth should be examined for signs of damage or wear and, if necessary, new gears fitted.

Reassembling

Reassembly is a reversal of the above procedures. When reassembling, the following components should be lubricated, using the lubricants recommended.

ARMATURE BEARINGS

These should be lubricated with S.A.E. 20 engine oil, the self-aligning bearing being immersed in this for 24 hours before assembly.

ARMATURE SHAFT (COMMUTATOR END)

Apply S.A.E. 20 engine oil.

FELT LUBRICATOR IN GEARBOX

Apply S.A.E. 20 engine oil.

WORM WHEEL BEARINGS, CROSS-HEAD, GUIDE CHANNEL, CONNECTING ROD, CRANKPIN, WORM, AND FINAL GEAR SHAFT

Grease liberally.

CABLE RACK AND WHEELBOXES

Grease liberally.

Testing

Switch on the ignition and the wiper control. The two wiper areas should be approximately symmetrical on the windshield.

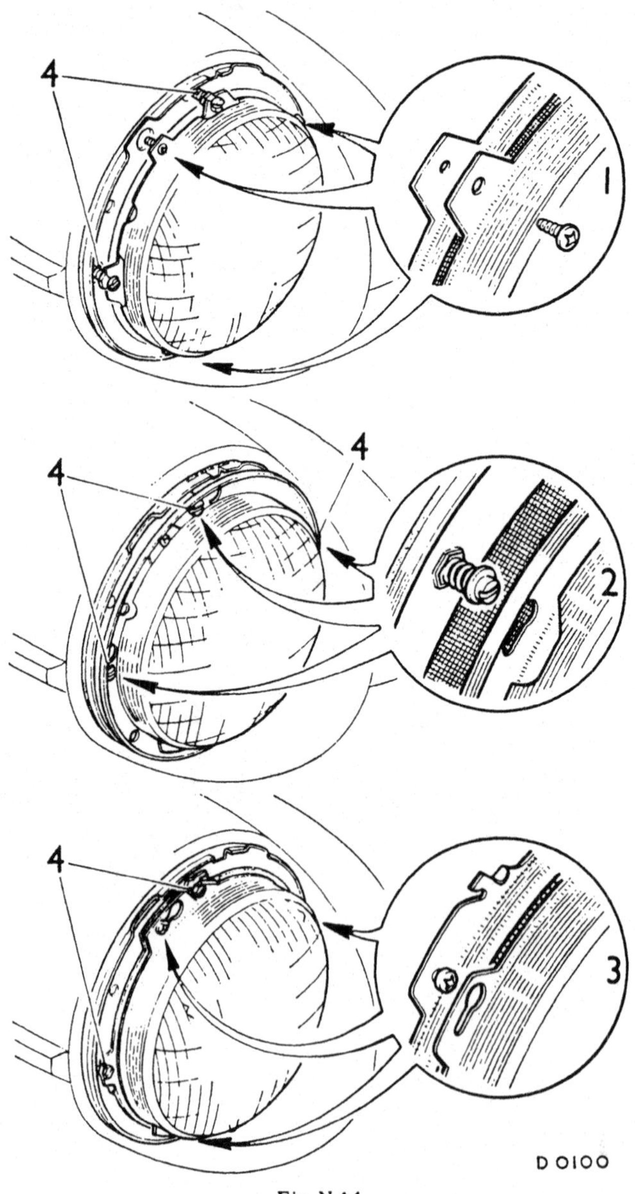

Fig. N.14
Light unit retaining screws

1. Removable screw.
2. Combined adjusting/ retaining screw.
3. Captive retaining screw.
4. Beam-setting adjusting screws.

Section N.9

HEADLAMPS

The two types of headlamp fitted have sealed-beam units or, alternatively, replaceable bulb light units.
Variations within the two basic types cater for the local lighting regulations existing in the country for which the car was produced. The method of retaining and adjusting the light unit together with the type of lens and bulb used are subject to territorial variation. Fig. N.14 shows the alternative methods of retaining and adjusting the light unit and Fig. N.15 the different types of bulb fittings used.

Removing a light unit

REMOVABLE-TYPE RETAINING SCREW (1) Fig. N.14

1. Ease the bottom of the outer rim forward away from the lamp, and lift it off the retaining lugs at the top of the lamp.
2. Remove the rubber dust excluder (if fitted).
3. Remove the three screws securing the light unit retaining plate and withdraw the light unit from the lamp body.

COMBINED ADJUSTING/RETAINING SCREW (2) Fig. N.14

4. Carry out the operations detailed in 1 and 2.
5. Press the light unit inwards against the tension of the springs and turn it in an anti-clockwise direction until the heads of the screws can pass through the enlarged ends of the slots in the retaining plate, then withdraw the light unit.

CAPTIVE-TYPE RETAINING SCREW (3) Fig. N.14

6. Carry out the operations detailed in 1 and 2.
7. Slacken the three retaining screws and turn the light unit retaining plate in an anti-clockwise direction until the heads of the screws can pass through the enlarged ends of the slots in the retaining plate, then withdraw the retaining plate and light unit.

Bulb replacement

CAP-TYPE HOLDER (1) Fig. N.15

8. Press and turn the cap anti-clockwise, lift off the cap and withdraw the bulb.
9. Fit the bulb into the reflector ensuring that the notch in the bulb flange locates on the ridge in the reflector.
10. Engage the cap lugs in the reflector slots, press and turn the cap clockwise.

SPRING CLIP TYPE (2) Fig. N.15

11. Withdraw the three-pin socket.
12. Disengage the spring clip from the reflector lugs, swing the clip up and withdraw the bulb.
13. Fit the bulb into the reflector ensuring that the pip on the bulb flange engages the slot in the reflector.
14. Swing the spring clip back, ensure that the coils in the clip are resting on the base of the bulb, and engage the legs of the spring clip under the reflector lugs.

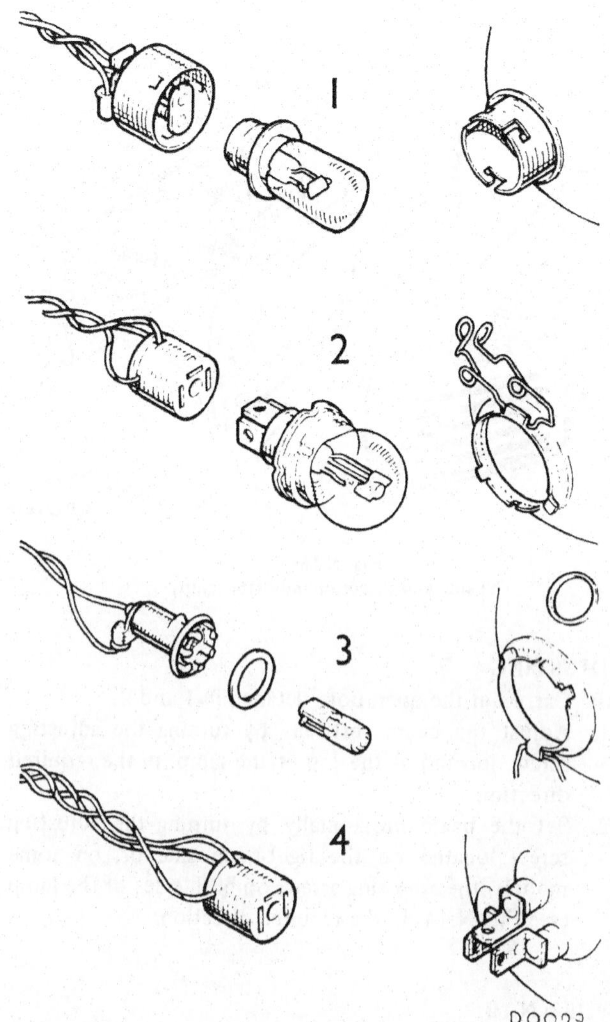

Fig. N.15
Bulb holders and fixings

1. Cap-type holder
2. Spring clip type.
3. Headlamp pilot lamp.
4. Sealed-beam unit.

HEADLAMP PILOT LAMP (3) Fig. N.15

15. Withdraw the holder from the reflector.
16. Press and turn the bulb anti-clockwise and withdraw the bulb.
17. Locate the pins of the bulb in the grooves in the holder, press and turn the bulb clockwise.
18. Press the holder into its hole in the reflector.

Refitting a light unit

19. Reverse the removing procedure, noting that the outer rim is refitted as follows:
    a. Position the rim on the retaining lugs with the cut-away portion of the rim at the bottom of the lamp.
    b. Press the rim downwards and inwards.

Beam setting

The headlamps must be set so that the main driving beams are parallel with the road surface or in accordance with local regulations.

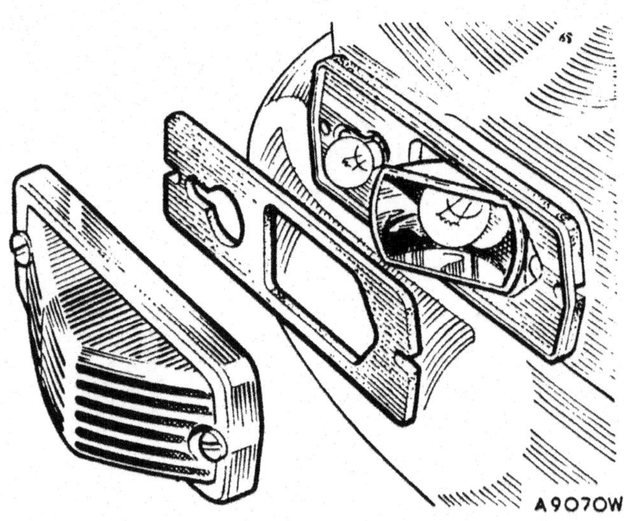

Fig. N.16
The side and direction indicator lamps

ADJUSTING

20. Carry out the operations detailed in 1 and 2.
21. Adjust the beam vertically by turning the adjusting screw, located at the top of the lamp, in the required direction.
22. Set the beam horizontally by turning the adjusting screw located on the right-hand side or, on some models, the adjusting screws on both sides of the lamp (see Fig. N.14) in the required direction.

Section N.10

SIDE AND DIRECTION INDICATOR LAMPS

To gain access to the side and direction lamps remove the two screws securing the lamp lens and take off the lens. Both bulbs are of the bayonet-fixing type and may be fitted either way round.
The lamp bodies are secured to the front of each wing by two studs and nuts.

Section N.11

TAIL AND STOP AND DIRECTION INDICATOR LAMPS

The tail lamp bulbs are of the double-filament type, the second filament giving a marked increase in brilliance when the brakes are applied.
Access to the bulbs is gained by extracting the securing screws from the outer face of the lamp lens to release the lens.
The tail and stop lamp bulbs must be fitted one way only; offset retaining peg ensure that they are replaced correctly.
The lamp body can be removed when the lens is taken off as indicated in Fig. N.17 and the three screws located in the lamp body withdrawn. When refitting the glass to the body make certain that it is seating correctly over the sealingrubber.

Section N.12

NUMBER-PLATE LAMPS

The rear number-plate lamps are fitted one to each inside face of the rear bumper over-riders.
To dismantle a lamp remove the two securing screws and retain the nuts and distance pieces from the inside of the over-rider. Take off the lamp hood and remove the lens, washer, and plinth.
When refitting the screws and nuts ensure that the thick edge of the wedge-shaped distance piece is fitted so that it faces the front of the car.

Section N.13

PANEL, MAP, AND WARNING LIGHTS

The location of the panel and warning lights are shown in the accompanying illustration.
The panel and warning light bulb holders are a push fit in their housings and are accessible from below the fascia panel.
To change a map lamp bulb remove the lamp cover screws and the cover.

Section N.14

RELAYS

Relays are electromagnetically operated switches that enable large currents to be controlled by smaller pilot currents. They are adjusted and sealed and the only maintenance required is an occasional check of the terminal connections for looseness.

Fog lamp relay (Early cars only)
The relay is attached by two screws and washers to the engine side of the bulkhead. When the switch is closed the

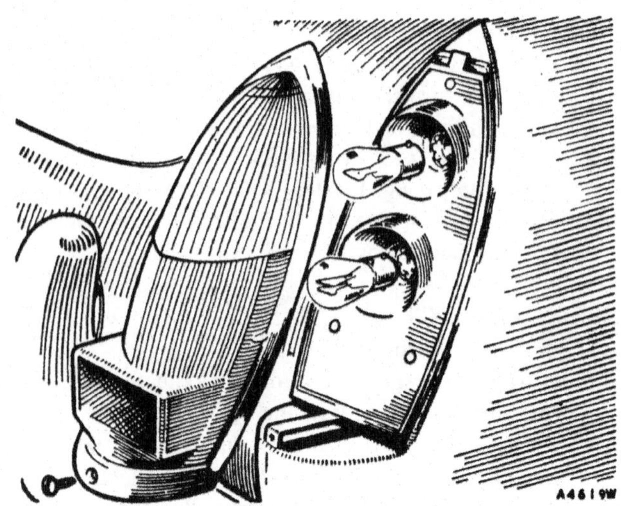

Fig N.17
The tail, stop, and direction indicator lamps

relay contacts close and permit current to flow to the lamps. When the switch is opened the relay contacts open and interrupt the circuit.

Starter motor relay (Car Number prefix GHN5 and GHD5 cars)
The non-adjustable relay is mounted next to the four-way fuse block.

Removing
Disconnect the battery. Remove the electrical connections and securing screws. Remove the relay.

Fig. N.19
A rear number-plate lamp (early cars)

Section N.15

HORN

Removing the horn
Disconnect the electrical connections, remove the screws and washers securing the horn to the bonnet lock platform or from the wing valance and withdraw the horn.

Maintenance
If the horn fails to operate, or operates unsatisfactorily, first carry out the following external checks.
Check the current consumption, which should be 3 to 3½ amps. when the horn is operating correctly.
After making a thorough external check remove the horn cover and examine the cable connections inside the horn. Examine the contact breaker contacts. If they are burnt or blackened clean them with a fine file, then wipe with a petrol-moistened cloth.

Adjusting
Withdraw the cover securing screw and remove the cover and its retaining strap.
Slacken the locking nut on the fixed contact stem and rotate the adjusting nut clockwise until the contacts just separate (indicated by the horn failing to sound when the horn-push is operated). Rotate the adjusting nut one half-turn in the opposite direction and secure it in this position with the locknut. Refit the cover and strap.

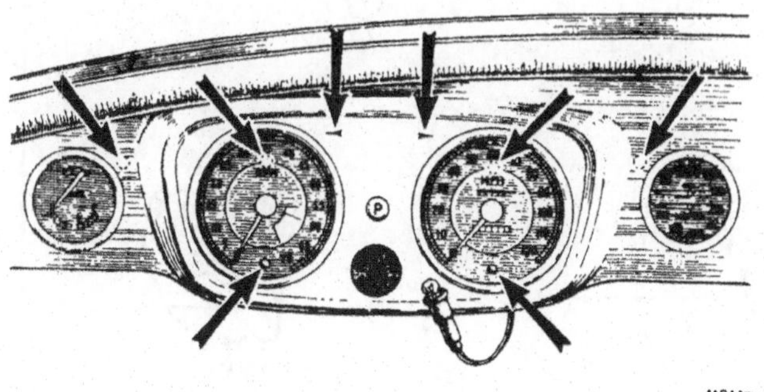

Fig. N.18
The location of the panel and warning lights

Section N.16

FLASHER UNIT

Description
The unit is contained in a small cylindrical metal container, one end of which is rolled over onto an insulated plate carrying the mechanism and three terminals. The unit depends for its operation on the linear expansion of a length of wire which becomes heated by an electric current flowing through it. This actuating wire controls the movement of a spring-loaded armature attached to a central steel core and carrying a moving contact—the sequence of operation being as follows.
When the direction indicator switch is turned either to the left or right, current flows through the actuating wire, ballast resistor, and coil wound on the central core and hence to earth via the flasher lamp filaments. This current is limited by the ballast resistor to a value which will ensure that the flasher lamp filaments do not light at this stage. The actuating wire increases in length under the heating influence of the current and allows the armature to move inwards to its alternative position, thereby closing a pair of contacts in the supply circuit to the flasher lamps and at the same time short-circuiting the actuating wire. The increased electromagnetic attraction of the armature to the core, due to the full lamp current now flowing through the coils, serves to hold the closed contacts firmly together. At the same time a secondary spring-loaded armature is attracted to the core and closes a pilot warning lamp circuit so that now both flasher lamps and warning lamp are illuminated.
Since, however, heating current no longer flows through the short-circuited actuating wire, the latter cools and consequently contracts in length. The main armature is therefore pulled away from the core, the contacts opened,

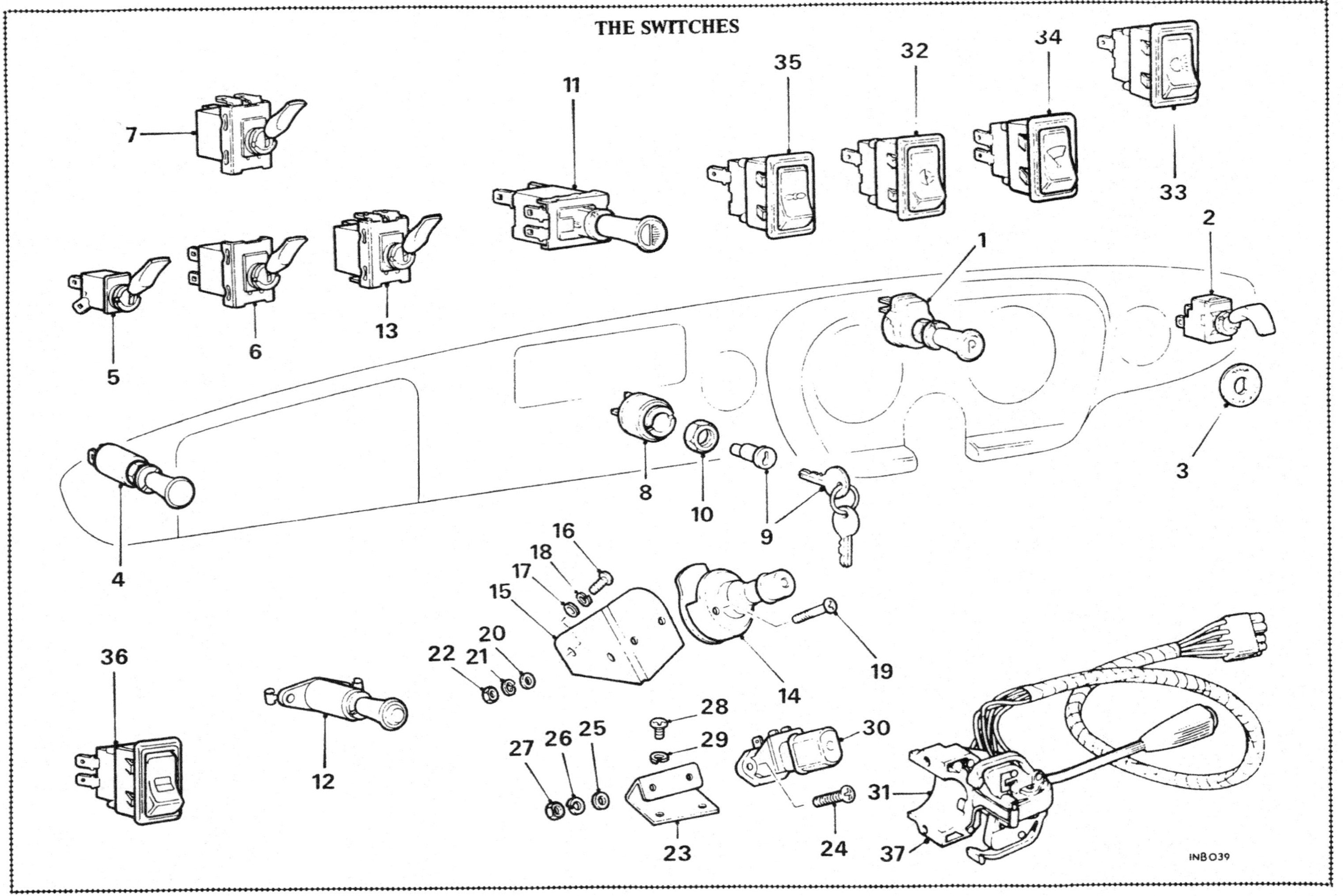
THE SWITCHES
INBO39

KEY TO THE SWITCHES

No.	Description
1.	Panel light switch.
2.	Overdrive switch.
3.	Bezel for overdrive switch.
	Up to and including early GHN5 and GHD5 cars
4.	Map light switch.
5.	Heater blower switch.
6.	Windscreen wiper switch (GT).
7.	Windscreen wiper switch (Tourer).
8.	Ignition/starter switch.
9.	Ignition switch lock and key.
10.	Locknut for ignition/starter switch.
11.	Light switch (later cars).
12.	Electrically heated back-light switch (GT).
	GHN3 and GHD3 cars
13.	Light switch.
14.	Headlight dip switch.

No.	Description
	Up to and including GHN4 and GHD4 cars–R.H.D.
15.	Bracket for dip switch (R.H.D.).
16.	Screw–bracket to pedal box.
17.	Plain washer.
18.	Spring washer.
19.	Screw–dip switch to bracket.
20.	Plain washer.
21.	Spring washer.
22.	Nut.
	Up to and including GHN4 and GHD4 cars–L.H.D.
23.	Bracket for dip switch (L.H.D.).
24.	Screw–dip switch to bracket.
25.	Plain washer.
26.	Spring washer.
27.	Nut.
28.	Screw–bracket to pedal box.
29.	Spring washer.

No.	Description
	GHN4 and GHD4 cars
30.	Headlight dip switch.
	Early GHN5 and GHD5 cars
31.	Combined direction indicator, headlamp, high-low beam, headlamp flasher, horn-push switch.
	GHN5 and GHD5 cars from Car No. 258001
32.	Fog and spot light switch.
33.	Light switch.
34.	Windscreen wiper switch.
35.	Heater blower switch.
36.	Electrically heated back-light switch (GT).
37.	Combined direction indicator, headlamp high-low beam, headlamp flasher switch.

and the light signals extinguished. The consequent reduction of electromagnetism in the core allows the secondary armature to return to its original position and so extinguish the pilot warning light. The above sequence of operations continues to be repeated until the indicator switch is returned to the 'off' position.

Functions of warning lamp

The warning lamp not only serves to indicate that the flasher unit is functioning correctly, but also gives a warning of any bulb failure occurring in the external direction indicator lamps—since a reduction in bulb current flowing through the coil reduces the electromagnetic effect acting on the secondary armature and so prevents closure of the pilot light contacts.

Checking faulty operation

In the event of trouble occurring with a flashing light direction indicator system the following procedure should be followed.

Check with a voltmeter between the flasher unit terminal 'B' (or '+') and earth that battery voltage is present.

Check the bulbs for broken filaments.

Refer to the vehicle wiring diagram and check all flasher circuit connections.

Check the appropriate fuse.

Switch on the ignition.

Connect together flasher unit terminals 'B' (or '+') and 'L' and operate the direction indicator switch. If the flasher lamps now light, the flasher unit is defective and must be renewed.

Maintenance

Flasher units cannot be dismantled for subsequent reassembly. A defective unit must therefore be renewed.

When renewing a flasher unit or installing a flashing light system it is advisable to test the circuits before connections to flasher terminals are made. When testing join the cables normally connected to those terminals (green, green with brown, and light green) together and operate the direction indicator switch. In the event of a wrong connection having been made, the ignition auxiliaries fuse will blow but no damage will be done to the flasher unit.

Section N.17

SWITCHES

Always disconnect the batteries before removing any switches and refer to the wiring diagram and switch contact numbers when refitting switches.

Ignition/starter switch

Disconnect the Lucar connectors and, using Service tool 18G 671, remove the bezel lock ring. Withdraw the switch assembly from the rear of the fascia.

To remove the locking barrel from the switch body insert the ignition key and turn the switch to 'ON' to align the barrel retaining plunger with the small hole in the switch body. Using an awl, depress the plunger and withdraw the barrel and key.

Reverse the removal and dismantling procedure to assemble and refit the switch.

Lighting, wiper, and blower switches

Disconnect the Lucar connectors and, using Service tool 18G 671, unscrew the bezel lock rings. Remove the switches from the rear of the fascia.

To refit the switches reverse the removal sequence.

Panel and map-reading lamp switches

The panel light switch is controlled by a rheostat-type rotary switch and the map-reading light by a push-pull-type switch.

To remove the switches depress the spring-loaded plunger in the switch knobs and withdraw the knobs. Use Service tool 18G 671 to remove the bezel lock rings and remove the switches from the rear of the fascia panel.

Reverse this sequence to refit the switches.

Direction indicator and headlight flasher switch (GHN4 and GHD4 cars).

Unscrew the four screws securing the two halves of the cowling and remove the cowling. Disconnect the switch lead connectors and remove the two switch bracket fixing screws.

Reverse this sequence to refit the switch and cowling but ensure that the locating pin on the switch and the locating peg on the cowling are correctly aligned.

NOTE.—**When replacing an early type switch with one using spring-loaded metal paws and spring leaves, a square-headed trip stud must be used. Set the height of the stud to between 1.177 and 1.187 in. (29.9 and 30.45 mm.) from the underside of the column.**

Dip switch (GHN4 and GHD4 cars)

The dip switch is mounted on a bracket secured to the front pedal box by two screws. Remove the screws to free the switch and bracket, disconnect the electrical connections, and remove the switch.

To refit the switch reverse the removal sequence.

Direction indicator/headlamp flasher/high-low beam/horn switch (GHN5 and GHD5 cars)

Refer to the instructions given for removing and refitting the direction indicator and headlamp flasher switch (GHN4 and GHD4 cars).

Section N.18

LOCATION AND REMEDY OF FAULTS

Although every precaution is taken to eliminate possible causes of trouble, failure may occasionally develop through lack of attention to the equipment or damage to the wiring. The following set-out is the recommended procedure for a systematic examination to locate and remedy the causes of some of the more usual faults encountered.

The sources of trouble are by no means always obvious, and in some cases a considerable amount of deduction from the symptoms is needed before the cause is disclosed.

For instance, the engine might not respond to the starter switch; a hasty inference would be that the starter motor is at fault. However, as the motor is dependent on the battery it may be that the battery is exhausted.

This in turn may be due to the dynamo failing to charge the battery, and the final cause of the trouble may be, perhaps, a loose connection in some part of the charging circuit.
If, after carrying out an examination the cause of the trouble is not found, the equipment should be checked.

CHARGING CIRCUIT

1. **Battery in low state of charge**
   a. This state will be shown by lack of power when starting, poor light from the lamps, and the hydrometer readings below 1.200. It may be due to the dynamo not charging or giving low or intermittent output. The ignition warning light will not go out if the dynamo fails to charge, or will flicker on and off in the event of intermittent output.
   b. Examine the charging and field circuit wiring. Tighten any loose connections, or renew any broken cables. Pay particular attention to the battery connections.
   c. Examine the dynamo driving belt: take up any undue slackness by swinging the dynamo outwards on its mounting after slackening the attachment bolts.
   d. Check the regulator setting, and adjust if necessary.
   e. If, after carrying out the above, the trouble is still not cured, have the equipment examined.

2. **Battery overcharged**
This will be indicated by burnt-out bulbs, very frequent need for topping up the battery, and high hydrometer readings. Check the charge reading with an ammeter when the car is running. It should be of the order of only 3 to 4 amps.
If the ammeter reading is in excess of this value it is advisable to check the regulator setting, and adjust if necessary.

STARTER MOTOR

1. **Starter motor lacks power or fails to turn engine**
   a. See if the engine can be turned over by hand. If not, the cause of the stiffness in the engine must be located and remedied.
   b. If the engine can be turned by hand first check that the trouble is not due to a discharged battery.
   c. Examine the connections to the battery, starter, and starter switch, making sure that they are tight and that the cables connecting these units are not damaged.
   d. It is also possible that the starter pinion may have jammed in mesh with the flywheel. To disengage the pinion rotate the squared end of the starter shaft by means of a spanner.

2. **Starter operates but does not crank the engine**
This fault will occur if the pinion of the starter drive is not allowed to move along the screwed sleeve into engagement with the flywheel, due to dirt having collected on the screwed sleeve. Remove the starter and clean the sleeve carefully with paraffin (kerosene).

3. **Starter pinion will not disengage from flywheel when engine is running**
Stop the engine and see if the starter pinion is jammed in mesh with the flywheel, releasing it if necessary by rotation of the squared end of the starter shaft. If the pinion persists in sticking in mesh have the equipment examined. Serious damage may result to the starter if it is driven by the flywheel.

LIGHTING CIRCUITS

1. **Lamps give insufficient illumination**
   a. Test the state of charge of the battery, recharging it if necessary from an independent electrical supply.
   b. Check the setting of the lamps.
   c. If the bulbs are discoloured as the result of long service they should be renewed.
2. **Lamps light when switched on but gradually fade out**
   As paragraph 1 (a).
3. **Brilliance varies with speed of car**
   a. As paragraph 1 (a).
   b. Examine the battery connections, making sure that they are tight, and renew any faulty cables.

Section N.19

BI-METAL RESISTANCE INSTRUMENTATION

General description
The bi-metal resistance equipment for fuel and temperature gauges consists of an indicator head and transmitter unit connected to a common voltage stabilizer. The system by which the equipment functions is voltage-sensitive and the voltage stabilizer is necessary to ensure a constant supply of a predetermined voltage to the equipment.

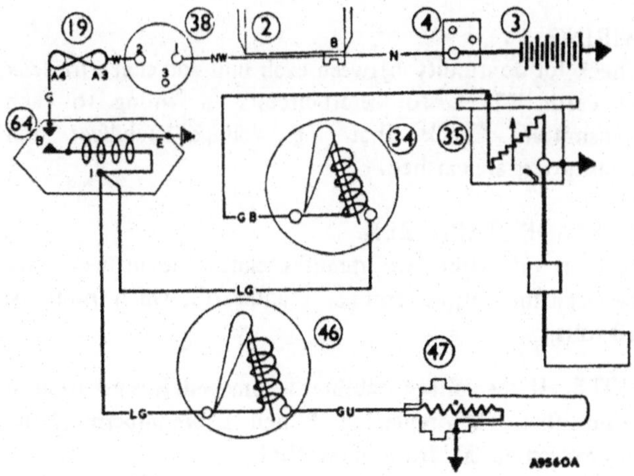

Fig. N.20
The bi-metal resistance instrumentation circuit

2. Control box.
3. Batteries (12-volt).
4. Starter solenoid.
19. Fuse (A3–A4).
34. Fuel gauge.
35. Fuel tank unit.
38. Ignition switch.
46. Coolant temperature gauge.
47. Coolant temperature transmitter.
64. Voltage stabilizer.

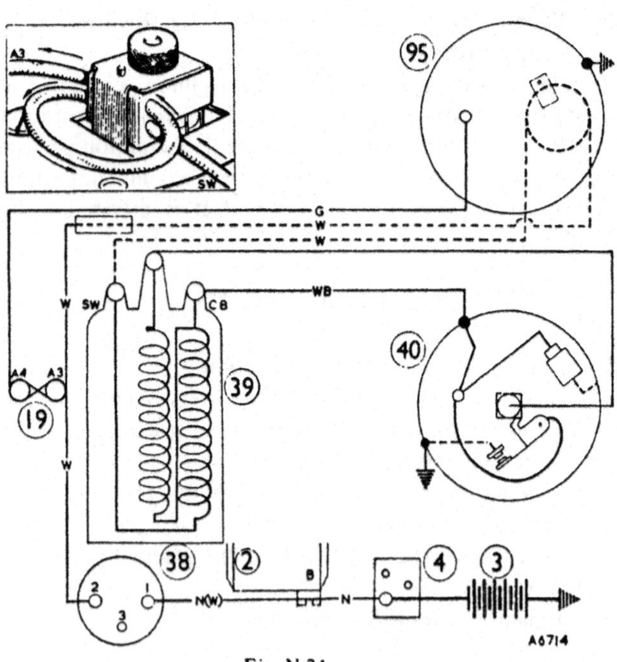

Fig. N.21
Impulse tachometer circuit

2.	Control box.	38.	Ignition switch.
3.	Batteries (12-volt).	39.	Ignition coil.
4.	Starter solenoid.	40.	Distributor.
19.	Fuse–A3–A4.	95.	Tachometer.

Inset: symmetrical loop of pulse lead

Fault analysis

For rapid diagnosis of a faulty unit use Smiths Automotive Instrument Tester (which incorporates a thermal sensitive voltmeter).

BATTERY VOLTAGE

Connect voltmeter to control box terminal 'B' and earth:

a. Engine stationary: 12 volts, approx.
b. Engine running at 1,000 r.p.m. and ignition warning light out, 12-13 volts approx.

WIRING

Check for continuity between each unit and check for leak to earth. Check for short-circuits in wiring to each transmitter. Check that the voltage stabilizer and transmitters are earthed.

VOLTAGE STABILIZER

Ignition on; after two minutes check the main voltage between the output terminal 'I' and earth, which should be 10 volts.

NOTE.--If the voltage stabilizer is removed, it is essential to ensure that, when replacing, 'B' and 'E' are uppermost and not exceeding 20° from the vertical.

Substitute voltage stabilizer is faulty.

GAUGES

Check for continuity between terminals with wiring disconnected.

The gauges must not be checked by short-circuiting to earth.

Substitute gauge if faulty.

TRANSMITTER

Check for continuity between terminal and case with leads disconnected.

Substitute transmitter if faulty.

Section N.20

TACHOMETER–IMPULSE TYPE

The equipment consists of an indicator head and pulse lead. The pulse lead is connected in series between the ignition switch and the ignition coil, and transmits voltage pulses to the indicator head.

Faulty operation

Check wiring connections to the indicator head and continuity of the circuit. Poor connections may result in faulty readings.

The pulse lead should form a symmetrical loop and not tight across the plastic forms (inset Fig. N.21).

Section N.21

REVERSE LAMPS

Bulb replacement

1. Remove the screws securing the reverse lamp to the rear panel.
2. Withdraw the lens.
3. Press the bulb down towards the lower contact and withdraw it from the lamp.
4. Fit one end of the bulb into the hole in the lower contact, then press the top of the bulb until the point on the bulb cap engages in the hole in the upper contact.
5. Refit the lens and securing screws.

Fig. N.22
The reverse lamp

Section N.22

ELECTRICALLY HEATED BACK-LIGHT (GT)

Removing and refitting

For removing and refitting procedure refer to Section R.27.

Fuse

A line fuse to protect the heated back-light is located below the main fuse block (see Fig. N.11).

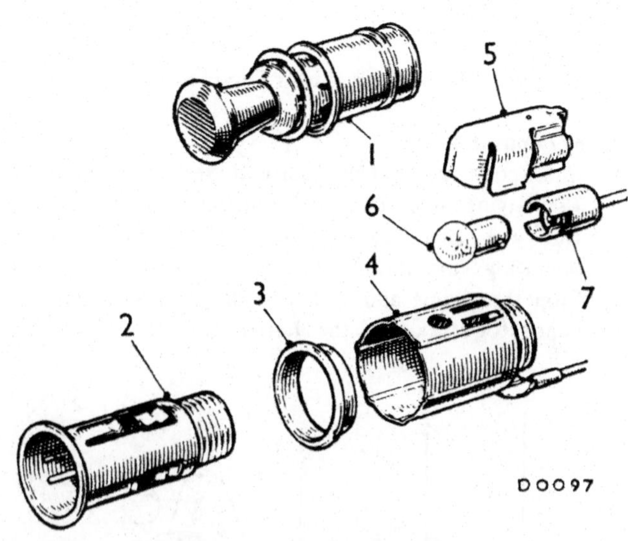

Fig. N.23
The cigar lighter components

1. Pop-out heater unit.
2. Switch base.
3. Glow ring.
4. Shell.
5. Lamp cover.
6. Bulb.
7. Bulb holder.

Section N.23

CIGAR LIGHTER

Removing

1. Disconnect the cigar-lighter feed wire from the ignition switch terminal.
2. Disconnect the earth wire from the cigar-lighter.
3. Press in the sides of the illumination lamp cover and withdraw the lamp unit from the lighter shell.
4. Unscrew the lighter shell from the switch base.
5. Withdraw the switch base and glow ring from the front of the fascia panel.

Refitting

6. Reverse the removing procedure in 1 to 5.

Section N.24

CHARGING SYSTEM (GHN4 and GHD4 Cars)

Description

The 12-volt NEGATIVE-earth charging system consists of an alternator and a voltage regulator supplying current to two 6-volt batteries connected in series.

Diodes contained within the alternator provide rectification of its output current for battery charging and also prevent reverse current flow. These and other design features overcome the necessity of a cut-out and current regulator.

Precautions

To prevent inadvertent damage to the charging system equipment the following points must be observed.

1. Do not run the engine with the battery or any of the charging circuit cables disconnected.
2. Ensure that all electrical connections in the generating and charging circuits are maintained tight at all times.
3. Ensure that the correct battery polarity (**NEGATIVE EARTH**) is maintained at all times.
4. If electric arc-welding is to be used on the car, all electric cables must be disconnected from the alternator and control box terminals.

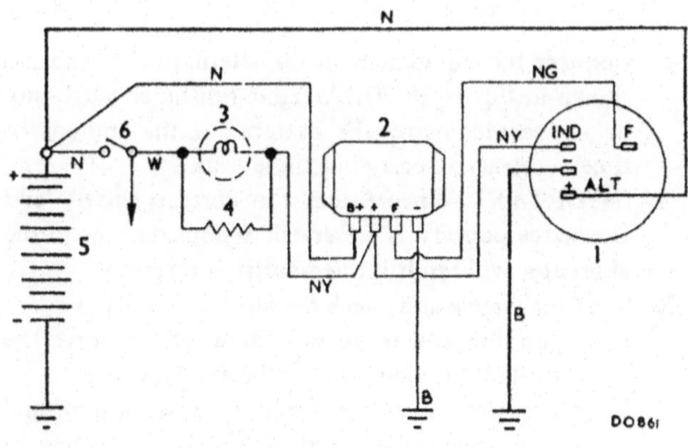

Fig. N.24
16AC alternator charging circuit

1. Alternator.
2. Control box.
3. Warning light.
4. Resistance.
5. Battery.
6. Ignition switch.

Section N.25

ALTERNATOR (Lucas Type 16AC)

Testing in position

1. Check that the fan belt is correctly tensioned and that all charging circuit electrical connections are tight.
2. Run the engine at fast idle speed until normal operating temperature is reached.
3. Stop the engine and withdraw the moulded terminal connector block from the alternator.

Fig. N.25
The 16AC alternator components

1. Cover.
2. Rectifier pack.
3. Through-bolt.
4. Slip-ring end bracket.
5. Stator.
6. Slip-rings.
7. Slip-ring end bearing.
8. Rotor.
9. Field windings.
10. Drive end bearing.
11. Circlip.
12. Oil sealing ring.
13. Drive end bracket.
14. Shaft nut.
15. Brush box moulding.
16. Brush assembly.

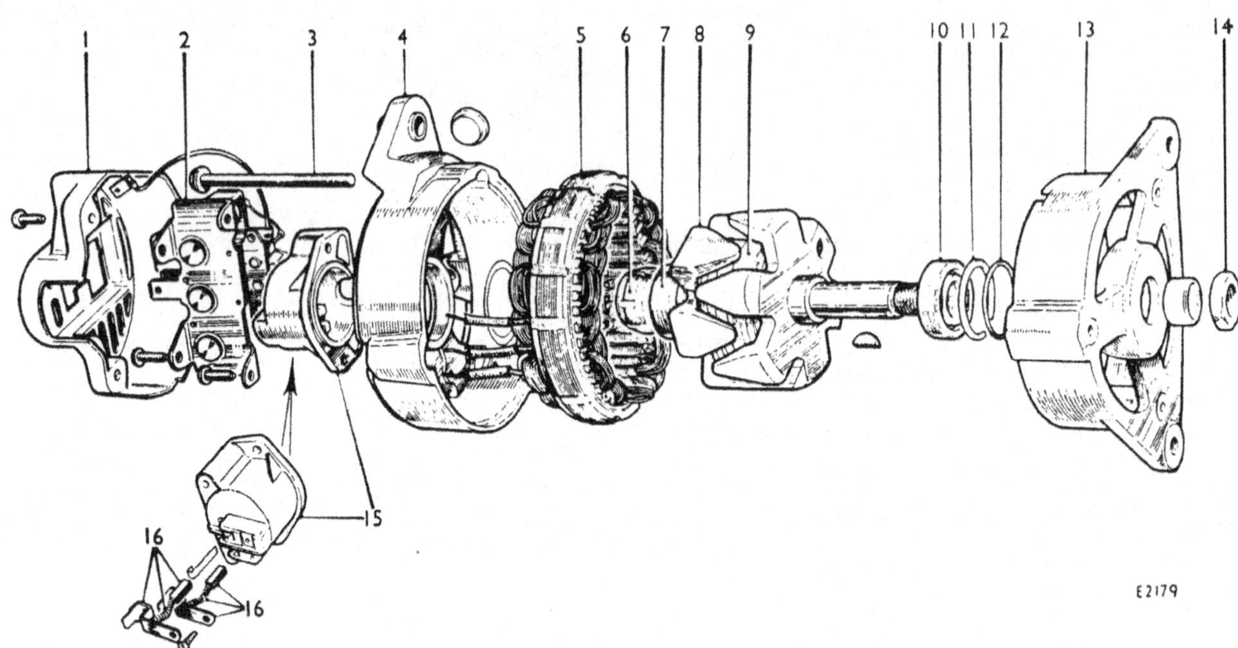

4. Connect test equipment to the alternator terminals as shown in Fig. N.26. The variable resistance must only be connected across the battery for the amount of time necessary to carry out these tests.
   IMPORTANT.–Ensure that the correct battery and alternator polarity is preserved. Serious damage to the alternator will result if the polarity is reversed.
5. Start the engine and check the alternator output.
   a. Run the engine at 850 r.p.m. and observe the test bulb; the bulb should be extinguished.
   b. Increase the engine speed to 3,300 r.p.m. and adjust the variable resistance until a reading of 14 volts is registered on the voltmeter; at these settings the ammeter should register a reading of approximately 34 amps.

   If the test bulb does not extinguish or its brilliance fluctuates, or if the ammeter reading varies considerably from the correct reading, a fault on the alternator is indicated and the alternator must be removed for further tests.

   Failure of one or more of the diodes will affect the alternator output and in some instances raise the alternator temperature and noise level. The following table indicates the effects that diode failure may have on test results.

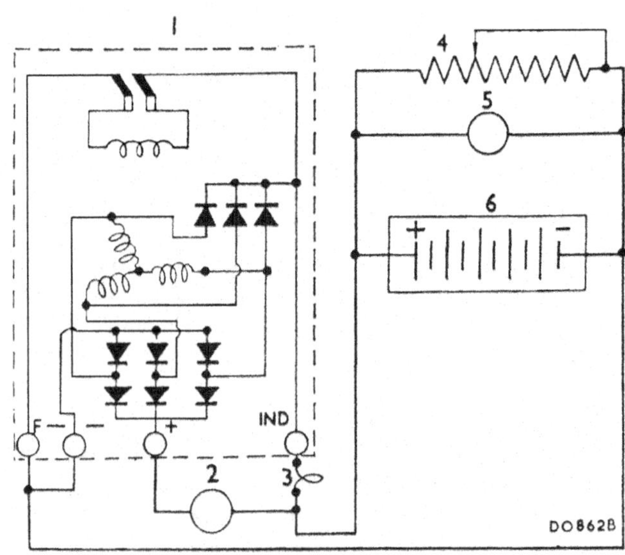

Fig. N.26
16AC alternator output test circuit

1. Alternator.
2. 0–40 amp. ammeter.
3. 12-volt, 2.2-watt bulb.
4. 0–15 ohm, 35-amp. variable resistance.
5. 0–20 volt voltmeter.
6. 12-volt battery.

6. If the tests in 5 show the alternator to be operating satisfactorily, disconnect the test circuit and reconnect the alternator terminal connector.
7. Connect a low-range voltmeter between the positive terminals of the alternator and battery.
8. Switch on the headlamps, start the engine and check the volt drop in the charging circuit as follows:
   a. Run the engine at 3,300r.p.m. and note the voltmeter reading.
   b. Transfer the voltmeter connections to the negative terminals of the alternator and battery, and repeat the test in a.

   If the voltmeter reading in either of the tests exceeds .2 volts a high resistance exists which must be traced and remedied.

Removing

9. The following operations, a to d, are necessary on engines fitted with exhaust emission control air pumps.
   a. Disconnect the hoses from the air pump discharge connections.
   b. Slacken the air pump mounting bolt.
   c. Remove the air pump adjusting link bolt from the air pump.
   d. Slip the belt from the air pump pulley and raise the air pump.
10. Withdraw the terminal block from the alternator.
11. Remove the adjusting link bolt from the alternator.
12. Slacken the alternator mounting bolts, lower the alternator and slip the fan belt from the alternator pulley.
13. Unscrew the alternator mounting bolts and remove the alternator.

Testing–alternator removed

14. Unscrew the cover retaining screws and remove the cover.
15. Unsolder the three stator connections from the rectifier pack, noting the connection positions.

    IMPORTANT.–When soldering or unsoldering connections to the diodes great care must be taken not to overheat the diodes or bend the pins. During the soldering operations the diode pins should be gripped lightly with a pair of long-nosed pliers which will then act as a thermal shunt.

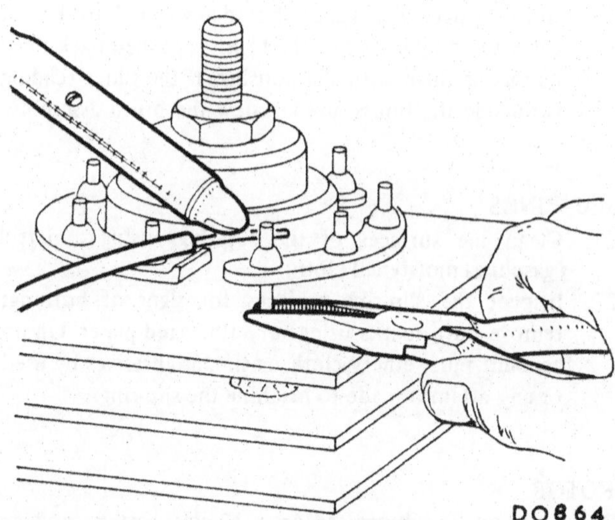

Fig. N.27
Using pliers as a thermal shunt when soldering the alternator diodes

Test bulb	Alternator			Probable fault and associated damage
	Temperature	Noise	Output	
Glows at stand-still, goes out at 850 r.p.m., then glows progressively brighter as the speed is increased.	High	Normal	Higher than normal–40 amps. approximately at 3,300 r.p.m.	Live side output diode open-circuit (May damage rotor windings and regulator output stage, overheat brush boxes, and blow warning light).
Light out under all conditions.	High	Excessive	Very low–10 amps. approximately at 3,300 r.p.m.	Live side output diode short-circuit. (May cause failure of associated field diode).
Glows at stand-still, dims appreciably at 850 r.p.m. and gets progressively dimmer as speed is increased.	Normal	Excessive	Poor at low speed, slightly below normal at 3,300 r.p.m.–32 amps. approximately.	Earth side output diode open-circuit.
Glows at a stand-still, dims slightly at 850 r.p.m. and remains so throughout speed range.	Normal	Excessive	Very low at all speeds above 850 r.p.m.–7 amps. approximately.	Earth side output diode short-circuit or one phase winding shorted to earth.
Glows at stand-still, dims slightly at 850 r.p.m. and remains so throughout speed range.	Normal	Normal	Lower than normal–29 amps. approximately at 3,300 r.p.m.	Field diode open-circuit.
Glows at stand-still, dims appreciably at 850 r.p.m. and remains so as speed is increased.	Normal	Excessive	Very low–7 amps. approximately at 3,300 r.p.m.	Field diode short-circuit.

16. Unscrew the two brush moulding securing screws.
17. Slacken the rectifier pack retaining nuts and withdraw the brush moulding and rectifier pack.

BRUSHES

18. Check the brushes for wear by measuring the length of brush protruding beyond the brushbox moulding. If the length protruding is .2 in. (5 mm.) or less the brush must be renewed.
19. Check that the brushes move freely in their holders. If a brush shows a tendency to stick, clean it with a petrol (gasoline) moistened cloth or, if necessary polish the sides of the brush with a fine file.
20. Check the brush spring pressure using a push-type spring gauge. The gauge should register 7 to 10 oz. (198 to 283 gm.) when the brush is pushed back until its face is flush with the housing. If the gauge reading is outside the limits given, renew the brush assembly.

SLIP-RINGS

21. Clean the surfaces of the slip-rings using a petrol (gasoline) moistened cloth.
22. Inspect the slip-ring surfaces for signs of burning; remove burn marks using very fine sand-paper. On no account must emery-cloth or similar abrasives be used or any attempt made to machine the slip-rings.

ROTOR

23. Connect an ohmmeter or a 12-volt battery and an ammeter to the slip-rings. An ohmmeter reading of 4.3 ohms or an ammeter reading of 3 amps. should be recorded.
24. Using a 110-volt A.C' supply and a 15-watt test lamp, test for insulation between one of the slip-rings and one of the rotor poles. If the test lamp lights the rotor must be renewed.

STATOR

25. Connnect a 12-volt battery and a 36-watt test lamp to two of the stator connections. Repeat the test replacing one of the two stator connections with the third. If the test lamp fails to light in either of the tests the stator must be renewed.
26. Using a 110-volt A.C. supply and a 15-watt test lamp, test for insulation between any one of the three stator connections and the stator laminations. If the test lamp lights, the stator must be renewed.

DIODES

27. Connect a 12-volt battery and 1.5-watt test lamp in turn to each of the nine diode pins and its corresponding heat sink on the rectifier pack, then reverse the connections. The lamp should light with the current flowing in one direction only. If the lamp lights in both directions or fails to light in either, the rectifier pack must be renewed.

IMPORTANT.–See notes on soldering the diodes given in 2.

DISMANTLING

28. Carry out the operations detailed in 14 to 17.
29. Remove the three through-bolts.
30. Fit a tube of the dimensions given in Fig. N.28 over the slip-ring moulding so that it registers against the outer track of the slip-ring end bearing and carefully drive the bearing from its housing.

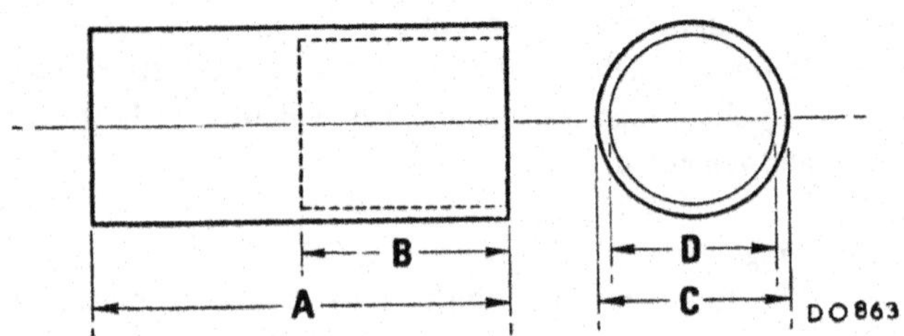

Fig. N.28
Dimensions of the rotor removing tool

A = 3 in. (76 mm.) B = 1.5 in. (38 mm.)
C.= 1.32 in. (33.5 mm.) D = 1.24 in. (31.5 mm.)

31. Remove the shaft nut, washer, pulley, fan, and shaft key.
32. Press the rotor from the drive end bracket.
33. Remove the circlip retaining the drive end bearing and remove the bearing.
34. Unsolder the field connections from the slip-ring assembly and withdraw the assembly from the rotor shaft.
35. Remove the slip-ring end bearing.

Reassembling

36. Reverse the dismantling procedure in 29 to 35 and 14 to 17, noting the following points.
    a. Use Shell Alvania 'RA' to lubricate the bearings where necessary.
    b. When refitting the slip-ring end bearing, ensure that it is fitted with its open side facing towards the rotor and is pressed onto the rotor shaft as far as it will go.
    c. Re-solder the field connections to the slip-rings using Fry's H.T.3 solder.
    d. When refitting the rotor to the drive end bracket, support the inner track of the bearing with a suitable piece of tube. Do not use the drive end bracket as the only support for the bearing when fitting the rotor.
    e. Tighten the through-bolts evenly.
    f. Check that the brushes are entered in their housings before fitting the brush moulding.
    g. Tighten the shaft nut to the torque figure given in 'GENERAL DATA'.

Section N. 26

ALTERNATOR (Lucas Type 16ACR)

The construction of the model 16ACR alternator is similar to the 16AC as illustrated in Fig. N.25, except that a voltage regulator of micro-circuit construction is incorporated on the slip-ring end casing (see Fig. N.29). The procedure given for removing, testing, and dismantling the 16AC alternator in Section N.25, operations 9 to 36, should be followed. For regulator removal see operations 17 to 18 of this Section.

Testing in position

OUTPUT TEST

1. Check that the fan belt is correctly tensioned and that all charging circuit electrical connections are secure.
2. Run the engine at fast idle speed until normal operating temperature is reached.
3. Ensure that the battery is fully charged; if not, fit a slave battery.
4. Disconnect both connector blocks from the alternator.
5. Switch on the ignition and connect a voltmeter, negative to earth positive lead to each cable connector tag of the two connector blocks in turn. If battery voltage is not registered at any cable, locate and remedy the fault.
6. Remove the alternator end cover.
7. Bridge the regulator green connector 'F' to earth (see Fig. N.29).
8. Refit the three-way connector block to the alternator. Connect an ammeter in series with the positive lead of the two-way connector block and the positive output tag of the alternator.
9. Start the engine and run at 3,300 r.p.m. The ammeter should read 34 amps. If the correct alternator output cannot be obtained, replace or service the alternator.

REGULATOR TEST

10. Disconnect the bridge from the regulator green connector 'F' and earth.
11. Connect a voltmeter across the battery terminals. Start the engine and run at 3,300 r.p.m. If the ammeter reads zero, the regulator pack must be replaced.
12. Adjust the engine speed until the ammeter reading falls below 10 amps. The voltmeter should read 14.0 to 14.4 volts. If the voltmeter reading is not within the limits stated, a faulty regulator or high resistance in the charging circuit cables is indicated. Re-connect the cables.

CHARGING CIRCUIT RESISTANCE TEST

13. Connect a voltmeter between the positive terminal of the alternator and the positive terminal of the battery.
14. Start the engine, switch on the headlamps, and run the engine at 3,300 r.p.m. The voltmeter reading should not exceed .5 volts.
15. Transfer the voltmeter connections to the negative terminals of the alternator and battery. Run the engine at 3,300 r.p.m. The voltmeter reading should not exceed .25 volt.
    If the readings in 14 and 15 are in excess of that stated, the charging circuit has developed a high-resistance fault which must be traced and remedied.
16. If the charging circuit resistance test is satisfactory, the failure is due to the regulator pack and the alternator must be replaced or removed for overhaul.

Removing the regulator

17. Remove the alternator.
18. Remove the moulded end cover, and identify the type of regulator pack fitted; the 8TR-type has two short mounting screws at each end, while the 11TR type has a single longer one, with a spacer, screwed into the top lug of the brush box moulding only. Both type have two legs which locate in the brush box moulding.
    Disconnect the coloured tag lead connectors from the bruch box, (1, 2 and 3) and detach the black (earth) lead (4), after removing the lower mounting screw (8TR) or one of the brush box retaining screws (6) (11TR). Remove the remaining screw (5) securing the regulator pack. Collect the spacer (7), (11TR only).

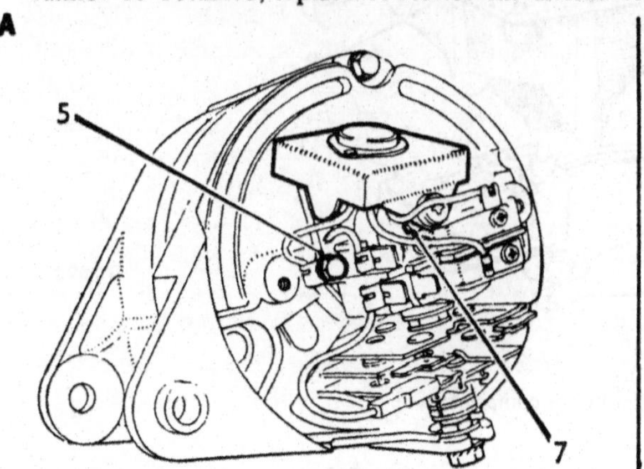

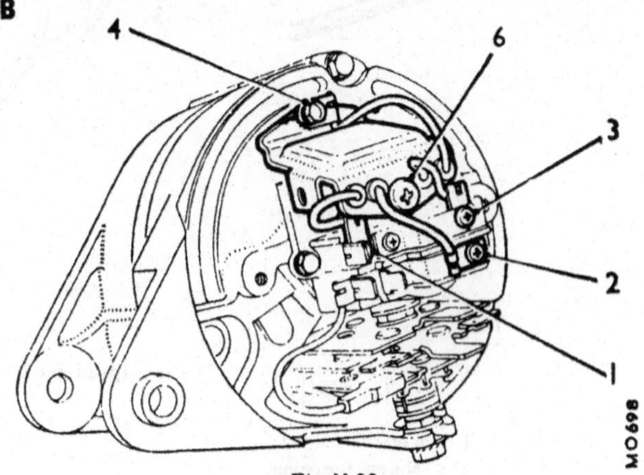

Fig. N.29
The in-built regulator connections, showing 8TR (B) and (A) 11TR type of regulator units

1. Battery + (B+).
2. Positive (+).
3. Field (F).
4. Negative earth (–).
5. Brush box retaining screw.
6. Upper mounting screw.
7. Spacer (11TR only).

Section N.27

WINDSHIELD WIPERS–TWO SPEED

Removing

MOTOR AND GEARBOX ASSEMBLY

1. Disconnect the battery.
2. Remove the wiper arms.
3. Remove the right-hand fascia under-panel if fitted.
4. Disconnect the wiring from the motor terminals.
5. Unscrew the outer cable retaining nut from the motor housing.
6. Remove the two motor securing bolts.
7. Withdraw the motor and gearbox assembly complete with the inner drive cable. The inner cable will rotate the wiper spindles as it is withdrawn.

WHEELBOXES

8. Remove the motor and gearbox as in 1 to 7.
9. Slacken the cover screws on each wheelbox and detach the cable outer casings.
10. Unscrew the spindle housing retaining nut and remove the front bush and washer from each wheelbox.
11. Remove the wheelboxes complete with rear bushes from beneath the fascia.

Dismantling

MOTOR AND GEARBOX ASSEMBLY

12. Unscrew the four gearbox cover retaining screws and remove the cover.
13. Remove the circlip and flat washer securing the connecting rod to the crankpin.
14. Withdraw the connecting rod taking care not to lose the flat washer fitted under it.
15. Remove the circlip and washer securing the shaft and gear.

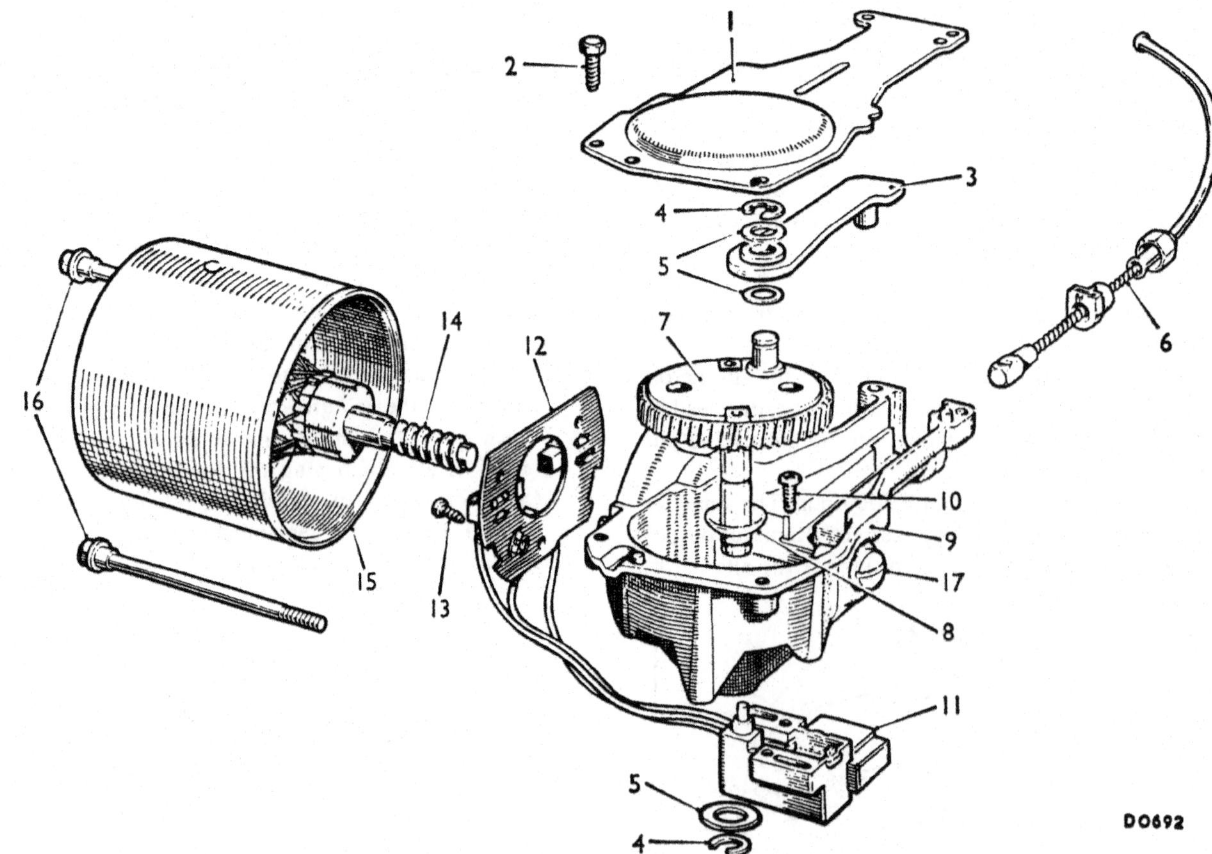

Fig. N.30
The two-speed windshield wiper motor components

1. Gearbox cover.
2. Screw for cover.
3. Connecting rod.
4. Circlip.
5. Plain washer.
6. Cable assembly.
7. Shaft and gear.
8. Dished washer.
9. Gearbox.
10. Screw for limit switch.
11. Limit switch assembly.
12. Brush gear.
13. Screw for brush gear.
14. Armature.
15. Yoke assembly.
16. Armature adjusting screw.

16. Clean any burrs from the gear shaft and withdraw the gear, taking care not to lose the dished washer fitted under it.
17. Mark the yoke and gearbox for reassembly.
18. Unscrew the two fixing bolts from the yoke and remove the yoke assembly and armature. The yoke must be kept clear of metallic particles which will be attracted to the pole-piece.
19. Remove the screws securing the brush gear and the terminal end switch assembly, and remove both assemblies.

Inspection

MOTOR AND GEARBOX ASSEMBLY

20. Examine the brushes for excessive wear. If the main bushes (diametrically opposite) are worn to $\frac{3}{16}$ in (4.8 mm.) or if the narrow section of the third brush is worn to the full width of the brush the brush gear assembly must be renewed.
21. Check the brush spring pressure with a push-type gauge. The gauge reading should be 5 to 7 oz. (140 to 200 gm.) when the bottom of the brush is level with the bottom of the slot in the brush box. The brush gear assembly must be renewed if the springs are not satisfactory.
22. Test the armature for insulation and open- or short-circuits. Renew the armature if faulty.
23. Examine the gear wheel for damage or excessive wear. Renew if necessary.

Reassembling

MOTOR AND GEARBOX ASSEMBLY

24. Reverse the dismantling procedure in 12 to 19, noting the following points:
    a. Use Ragosine Histate Grease to lubricate the gear wheel teeth and cam armature shaft worm gear, connecting rod and pin, cross-head slide, cable rack, and wheelbase gear wheels.
    b. Use Shell Turbo 41 oil to lubricate the bearing bushes, armature shaft bearing journals (sparingly), gear wheel shaft and crankpin, felt washer in the yoke bearing (thoroughly soak), and the wheelbox spindles.
    c. Tighten the yoke fixing bolts to a torque figure of 20 lb. in. (.23 kg. m.).
    d. If a replacement armature is being fitted, slacken the thrust screw to provide end-float for fitting the yoke.
    e Fit the thrust disc inside the yoke bearing with its concave side towards the end face of the bearing.
    f Fit the dished washer beneath the gear wheel with its concave side towards the gear wheel.
    g. When fitting the connecting rod to the crankpin ensure that the larger of the two flat washers is fitted under the connecting rod with the smaller one on top beneath the circlip.
    h. With the thrust screw fully tightened against the gearbox casing, an end-float of .004 to .008 in. (.1 to .21 mm.) should exist on the armature. Adjustment of the armature end-float can be achieved by adjustment of the thrust screw.

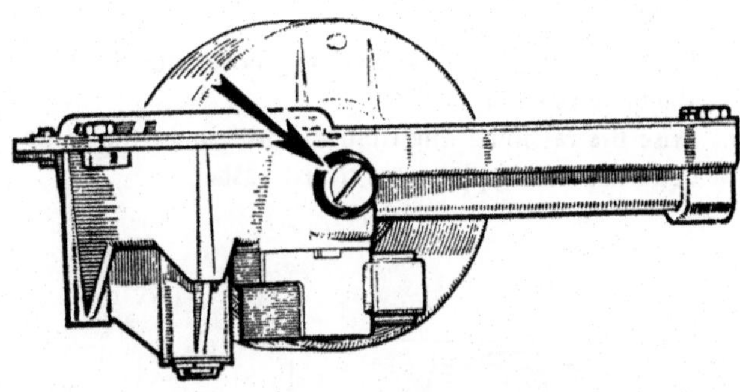

Fig. N.31
The armature end-float adjusting screw

Refitting

WHEELBOXES

25. Reverse the removing procedure in 8 to 11.

MOTOR AND GEARBOX ASSEMBLY

26. Reverse the removing procedure in 1 to 7 ensuring that the inner cable engages correctly with the wheelbox gear teeth.

Section N.28

STARTER (Lucas Type M418G Pre-engaged)

Removing

1. Disconnect the battery.
2. Remove the distributor Section B.5.
3. Remove the starter top securing bolt.
4. Disconnect the wiring from the starter terminals.
5. Remove the starter lower securing bolt and remove the starter.

Dismantling

6. Disconnect the lower solenoid terminal marked 'STA'.
7. Remove the solenoid unit securing nuts.
8. Withdraw the solenoid from the drive end bracket, carefully disengaging the solenoid plunger from the drive engagement lever.
9. Remove the cover band and lift the brushes from their holders.
10. Unscrew the two through-bolts from the commutator end bracket.
11. Slacken the drive engagement lever pivot pin securing nut; unscrew and withdraw the pin.

12. Position the starter with the solenoid housing uppermost; separate the drive end bracket from the yoke and remove the drive engagement lever.
13. Withdraw the armature and separate the commutator end bracket from the yoke.
14. Remove the thrust washer from the armature shaft and the thrust collar from the end of the shaft extension.
15. Prise the retaining ring from its groove and withdraw the drive assembly.
16. Prise the retaining ring from the drive and remove the collar, operating plate, and thrust washer.

Inspection

BRUSH GEAR

17. Check the length of the brushes. When they have worn to (or are approaching) $\frac{5}{16}$ in. (8 mm.) renew them by unsoldering their flexible connectors, two from the uninsulated brush holders and two from the field coils, then solder the new brush connectors in place. New brushes are pre-formed and bedding to the commutator is unnecessary.
18. Check the brushes for freedom of movement in their holders and, if necessary, clean them with a petrol-moistened cloth.

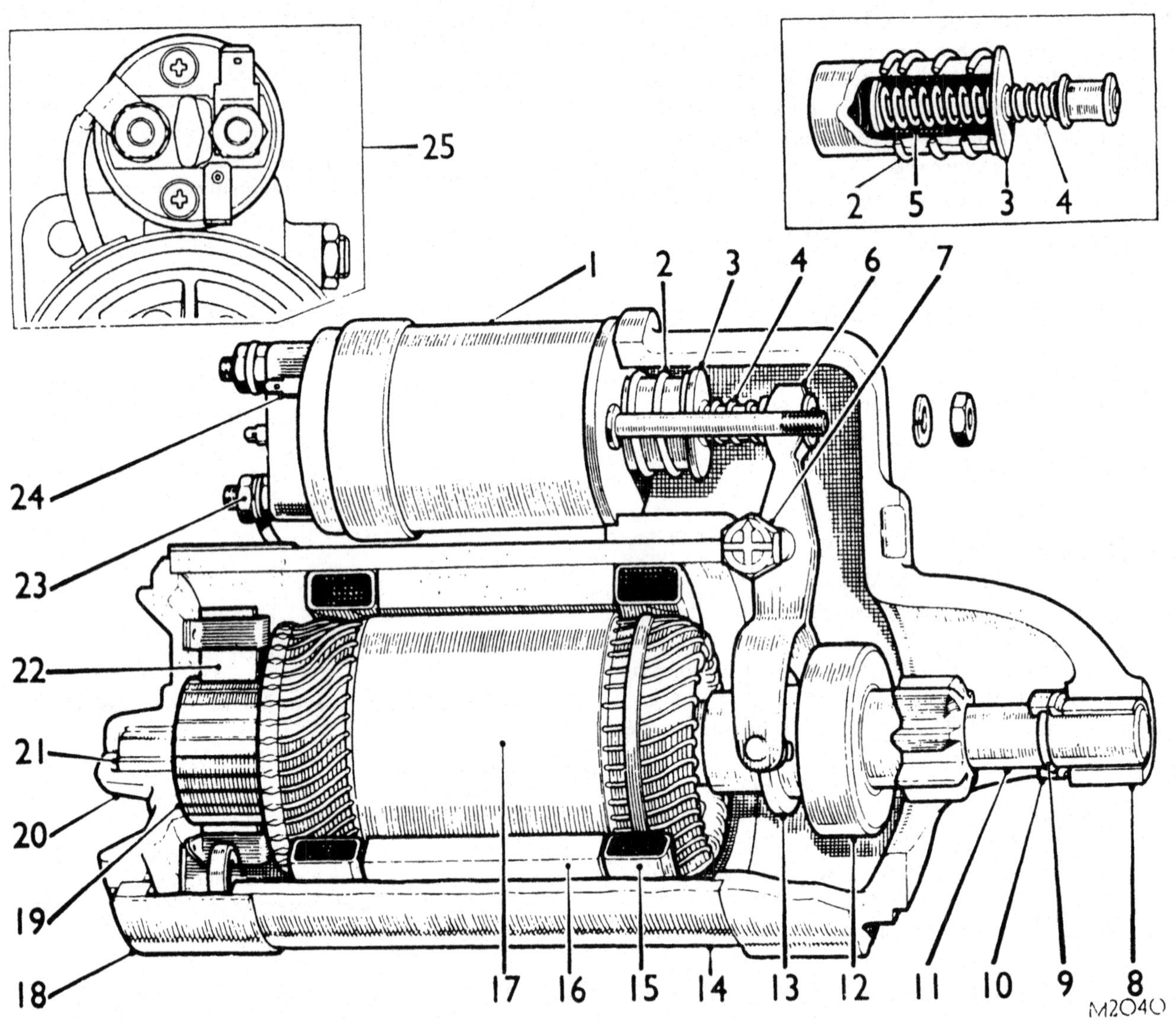

Fig. N.32
The starter motor – Lucas type M418 pre–engaged

1. Solenoid.
2. Plunger return spring.
3. Plunger.
4. Lost motion spring.
5. Drive engagement spring.
6. Engaging lever.
7. Pivot pin.
8. Fixing bracket.
9. Retaining ring.
10. Thrust collar.
11. Armature shaft extension.
12. Clutch.
13. Drive operating plate.
14. Yoke.
15. Field coils.
16. Pole shoes.
17. Armature.
18. Cover band.
19. Commutator.
20. End bracket.
21. Bush bearing.
22. Brushes.
23. Solenoid 'STA' terminal.
24. Solenoid operating terminal.
25. Repositioned solenoid (later cars).

19. Check the brush spring pressure. Each spring should exert a minimum of 36 oz. (1.02 kg.) with a new (full-length) brush in position.

COMMUTATOR

20. The commutator should be burnished, free of pits or burned spots, and can be cleaned with a petrol-moistened cloth. If this cleaning is ineffective, spin the armature and polish the commutator with fine glass-paper, removing all abrasive dust with a dry air blast.
21. In the case of a badly worn commutator, mount the armature between centres in a lathe and rotate it at high speed. Take a light cut with a very sharp tool and do not remove more metal than is necessary to clean the commutator. Finally, polish with very fine glass-paper. The insulators between the commutator segments **must not be undercut**.

ARMATURE

22. Examine the armature for conductors which have lifted from the commutator risers. This would indicate overspeeding and the drive clutch should be checked (see 28).
23. Check for signs of the armature fouling the pole shoes indicating a distorted armature shaft or worn bearings (see 29 and 30). Do not attempt to machine the armature core or to true a distorted shaft; a damaged armature must be renewed.
24. To make a thorough check on the condition of the armature it should be tested on a 'growler'. The armature insulation can be checked by means of a 110-volt A.C. test lamp connected between each commutator segment in turn and the armature shaft. The test lamp should not light.

FIELD COILS

25. Test the field coils for continuity. Ensure that both brushes and their flexible connectors are clear of the yoke and connect a 12-volt test lamp and battery between the cable connection to 'STA' and each of the field coil brushes in turn. If the lamp does not light, an open circuit in the field coil is indicated and they should be renewed as follows:
    a. Using a wheel-operated screwdriver, unscrew the four pole-shoe retaining screws.
    b. Withdraw the inter-coil connector insulating piece and remove the pole shoes and coils from the yoke.
    c. Fit new coils to the pole shoes and position them inside the yoke. Make sure that the coil taping is not trapped between the pole shoes and the yoke, then lightly tighten the pole-shoe retaining screws.
    d. Fit the insulator to the field coil terminal and position the inter-coil connection insulator inside the yoke. Hold the pole shoes in position with a pole-shoe expander and tighten the retaining screws with a wheel-operated screwdriver.
26. Test the field coils for insulation from the yoke. Ensure that both brushes and their flexible connectors are clear of the yoke and connect a 110-volt A C. test-lamp between the terminal post and the yoke. If the lamp lights, earthing of the field coils is indicated and they should be renewed as described in 25 a to d.

COMMUTATOR END BRACKET

27. Clean all traces of brush deposit from the commutator end bracket and connect a 110-volt A.C. test lamp between the end bracket and each insulated brush box in turn. If the lamp lights, faulty insulation is indicated and the commutator end bracket should be renewed.

DRIVE CLUTCH

28. Check the operation of the drive clutch. It should provide instantaneous take-up of the drive in one direction, yet rotate easily and smoothly in the opposite direction. It should also move freely on the armature shaft splines without any roughness or tendency to bind.

BEARINGS

29. Renew the bearings which are worn to such an extent that they allow excessive side-play of the armature shaft. Remove the bearing from the commutator end bracket by screwing a tap squarely into the bearing and withdrawing the bearing with the tap. The drive end bracket bearing can be pressed out.
30. Press the new bearings into position using a shouldered highly polished mandrel .0005 in. (0.13 mm.) larger in diameter than the shaft which will run in the bearing.
    NOTE.– The commutator and drive end bracket bearings are porous bronze and should be immersed in clean engine oil for 24 hours before fitting. In an emergency this period may be reduced by maintaining the oil at a temperature of 100°C. (212°F.) for two hours and allowing the oil to cool before removing the bearing. Porous bronze bushes should not be reamed, as the porosity of the bush would be impaired.

Reassembling

31. During reassembly lubricate all moving parts with Shell Retinax A grease, or an equivalent.
32. Reassemble the starter motor by reversing the procedure in 6 to 16.
33. Set the pinion travel as follows:
    a. Connect a 6-volt supply, with a switch in circuit, between the small unmarked solenoid terminal and earth. The period of energization should be kept as brief as possible to avoid overheating the series winding.

   b. Close the switch (this throws the drive assembly into the engaged position) and measure the distance between the pinion and the thrust collar on the armature shaft extension. When making the measurement, take up the slack in the engagement linkage by lightly pressing the pinion towards the armature. The measurement should be .005 to .015 in. (.13 to .4 mm.). To adjust this setting, slacken the locknut on the engagement lever pivot pin and rotate the pin until the measurement is correct. The arc of adjustment is 180 degrees and the head of the arrow marked on the pivot pin should be set only between the arrows on the arc marked on the drive end bracket.
   c. Tighten the locknut to secure the pivot pin.

34. After setting the pinion travel, check the opening and closing of the starter switch contacts as follows:
   a. Connect 10-volt supply, with a switch in circuit, between the small unmarked solenoid terminal and earth.
   b. Connect a separately energized test lamp circuit across the solenoid main terminals.
   c. Insert a stop in the drive end bracket to restrict the pinion travel to that of the normal out-of-mesh clearance.
   d. Close the switch (the period of energization should be as brief as possible to avoid over-heating the series winding). The test lamp should now give a steady light indicating that the solenoid contact is remaining fully closed.
   e. Switch off and remove the stop.
   f. Switch on, hold the pinion assembly in the fully engaged position and switch off. The test lamp should now go out indicating that the solenoid contacts have opened.

Bench testing

LIGHT RUNNING TEST

35. Using heavy-gauge cables, connect the starter to a fully charged 12-volt 120-amp.-hour battery with a switch and ammeter in circuit. The starter motor should run freely at 5,800 to 6,500 r.p.m. with a current consumption of 70 amps.

TORQUE TEST

36. Check the lock torque and running torque, against the figures given in **'GENERAL DATA'**.

Refitting

37. Reverse the procedure in 1 and 5.

Section N.29

CONTROL UNIT (Lucas Type 4TR)

Testing

1. Check that the alternator is functioning correctly as described in Section N.25 1 to 8.
2. Check that the batteries are in a fully charged state; if not, temporarily connect fully charged replacements.
3. Connect an accurate voltmeter across the battery terminals.
4. Connect a 0–40 amp. ammeter in series with the alternator main output cable.
5. Start the engine and run it at 2,750 r.p.m. until a steady ammeter reading of not more than 5 amps. is obtained. At this setting the voltmeter should give a steady reading of 14.3 to 14.7 volts. If the voltmeter reading is unsteady or is outside the limits given, the control unit must be renewed.

Removing

6. Disconnect the positive connection from the battery terminal.
7. Withdraw the terminal connector block from the control unit.
8. Remove the control unit securing screws and remove the unit.

Refitting

9. Reverse the removing procedure in 6 to 8.

Section N.30

SWITCHES
(GHN5 and GHD5 cars from Car No. 258001)

Removing

IMPORTANT.– Disconnect the batteries before attempting to remove any of the switches and refer to the wiring diagram and switch contact numbers when refitting the switches.

HEATER, WIPER, AND LIGHTING SWITCHES

1. Remove the face level vents–Section R.35.
2. Disconnect the wiring from the back of the switches.
3. Using tool 18G 1202 press in the four retaining lugs and withdraw the heater and wiper switches.
4. To remove the lighting switch, depress the retaining lugs on one side of the switch, ease one side of the switch through the aperture, depress the retaining lugs on the other side and withdraw the switch.

CONSOLE SWITCHES

5. Remove the console–Section R.34.
6. Using tool 18G 1202 press in the four retaining lugs and withdraw the switches.

IGNITION SWITCH

7. Turn the key to position 'O'.
8. Disconnect the wiring from the switch.
9. Remove the two screws retaining the switch to the steering lock.
10. Withdraw the switch.

DIRECTION INDICATOR/HEADLIGHT FLASHER/LOW-HIGH BEAM SWITCH

11. Unscrew the four switch cowl retaining screws and remove the cowl.
12. Disconnect the switch wiring from the multi connector block and unclip it from the steering-column.
13. Remove the two screws retaining the direction indicator/headlight flasher/low-high beam switch and remove the switch and retaining clip.

Refitting

HEATER, WIPER AND LIGHTING SWITCHES

14. Reverse the removing procedure in 1 to 4.

CONSOLE SWITCHES

15. Reverse the removing procedure in 5 to 6.

IGNITION SWITCH

16. Reverse the removing procedure in 7 to 10.

DIRECTION INDICATOR/HEADLIGHT FLASHER/LOW-HIGH BEAM SWITCH

17. Reverse the removing procedure in 11 to 13 ensuring that the small tongue on the switch engages in the cut-away of the steering outer column.

Section N.31

STARTER (Lucas Type 2M100 Pre-engaged)

Removing

1. Disconnect the battery.
2. SYNCHROMESH GEARBOX ONLY: Detach the clutch slave cylinder from the gearbox and move the cylinder clear of the starter.
3. Remove the starter top securing bolt.
4. Disconnect the wiring from the solenoid terminals.
5. Remove the starter motor lower securing bolt and withdraw the starter.

Dismantling

6. Remove the nut securing the (solenoid-to-starter) connecting link to the solenoid 'STA' terminal.
7. Pull back the connecting link from the solenoid terminal.
8. Remove the nuts securing the solenoid to the drive end bracket. Refit torque 4.5 lb.ft. (0.63 kg.m.).
9. Remove the solenoid unit from the drive-end bracket.
10. Lift the solenoid plunger and return spring from the engagement lever.
11. Remove the block-shaped grommet.

CAUTION—Before carrying out instructions 7 to 15 ensure that new retaining rings are available for the armature shaft and engagement lever pivot pin are available for reassembly of the starter.

12. Remove the end cap seal.
13. Remove the armature shaft retaining ring (Spire nut).
14. Remove the through-bolts. Refit torque 8 lb.ft. (1.11 kg.m.).
15. Detach the commutator end cover from the yoke, disengaging the field brushes from the brush box moulding, and remove the end-cover.
16. Remove the thrust washer from the armature shaft.
17. Withdraw the yoke from the armature and drive-end assembly.
18. Remove the retaining ring (Spire nuts) from the engagement lever pivot pin.
19. Remove the pivot pin from the engagement lever and drive-end bracket.
20. Move the thrust collar clear of the jump ring, and remove the jump ring from the armature shaft.
21. Remove the thrust collar.
22. Remove the roller clutch drive and engagement lever assembly from the armature shaft.

Inspection

BRUSH GEAR, COMMUTATOR AND ARMATURE

23. Refer to Section N.28.

FIELD WINDINGS

24. Connect a 12-volt battery-operated test lamp between each of the field brushes and a clean part of the yoke; the lamp will light if continuity is satisfactory between the brushes, windings, and yoke connection.
25. Disconnect the field windings from their riveted connection with the yoke. Using a 110-volt A.C., 15-watt test lamp connected between each of the brushes in turn and the yoke, check the insulation of the field windings, if the lamp lights the windings must be renewed.
26. The field windings may be renewed as follows:
    a. Disconnect the end of the field winding where it is riveted to the yoke.
    b. Remove the four pole-shoe retaining screws using a wheel-operated screwdriver.
    c. Withdraw the field coil assembly from the yoke.
    d. Clean the inside of the yoke and insulating pieces which the through-bolts locate.
    e. Loosely fit the new field coil assembly with the pole-shoes into the yoke.
    f. Fit the pole-shoe retaining screws but do not tighten.
    g. Slide the insulating pieces between the field coils and the yoke, positioned 90° each side of the field coil brush connection point.
    h. Tighten the pole-shoe screws evenly using a wheel-operated screwdriver. Torque 30 lb.ft. (4.15 kg.m.).
    j. Reconnect the end of the winding to the yoke.

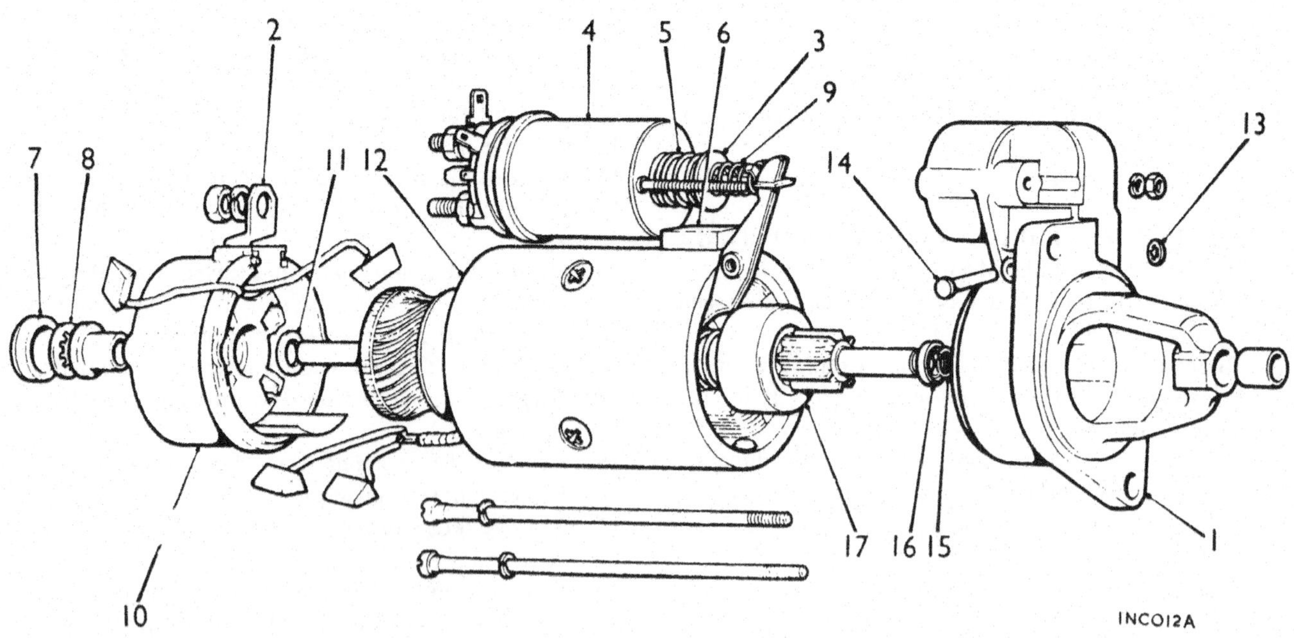

Fig. N.33
The starter motor–Lucas type 2M100 pre-engaged

1. Fixing bracket.
2. Solenoid 'STA' terminal.
3. Plunger.
4. Solenoid.
5. Plunder return spring.
6. Block shaped grommet.
7. End cap seal.
8. Armature shaft retaining ring.
9. Lost motion spring.
10. Commutator end cover.
11. Thrust washer.
12. Yoke.
13. Pivot pin retaining ring.
14. Pivot pin.
15. Jump ring.
16. Thrust collar.
17. Roller clutch.

COMMUTATOR END BRACKET

27. Check the insulation of the brush springs by connecting a 110-volt A.C., 15-watt test lamp between a clean part of the commutator and cover each of the springs in turn; the lamp will light if the insulation is not satisfactory.

BEARINGS

28. If the bearings in the commutator end cover and the drive-end bracket are worn sufficiently to allow excessive side-play of the armature shaft, the bearing bush must be renewed as follows:
    a. Support the bracket and drive out the bush using a suitable sized mandrel.
    b. Using a polished, shouldered mandrel, the same diameter as the shaft bearing journal, press the new bushes into the brackets.

    NOTE.–New bushes must be immersed in S.A.E. 30/40 engine oil for 24 hours or in oil heated to 100° C. (212° F.) for two hours prior to fitting. The bushes must not be reamed after fitting.

ROLLER CLUTCH DRIVE

29. Check the operation of the drive clutch, it should provide instantaneous take-up of the drive in one direction and rotate easily and smoothly in the other direction.
30. Check that the drive moves freely on the armature splines without binding or sticking.

Reassembling

31. Reverse 1 to 17, noting the following:
    a. When assembling the drive-end bracket use a new retaining ring (Spire nut) to secure the engagement lever pivot pin.
    b. Ensure that the internal thrust washer is fitted to the commutator end of the armature shaft before the armature end cover is fitted.
    c. Fit a new retaining ring (Spire nut) onto the armature shaft to a maximum clearance of 0.010 in. (0.25 mm.) between the retaining ring and the bearing bush shoulder (Armature end-float).

Bench testing

LOCK TORQUE AND CURRENT

32. Clamp the starter firmly in a vice.
33. Connect a starter switch, a 0–600 amp. ammeter and a 12-volt battery in series to the starter.
34. Connect a voltmeter between the solenoid two main terminals.
35. Secure an arm to the driving pinion.
36. Connect a spring balance to the free end of the arm.
37. Operate the switch and note the ammeter, voltmeter, and spring balance readings. Calculate the lock torque by multiplying the reading of the spring balance in pounds by the length of the arm in feet.

38. Check the readings obtained in 37 against the figures given in '**GENERAL DATA**' for lock torque current and voltage.

NOTE: If a constant-voltage supply is used for this test, a higher voltage may be registered on the voltmeter than the figure given. If this should occur, a variable resistance must be added to the circuit and adjusted to give the required reading and the test repeated.

Solenoid–coil

39. Check the continuity of the coil windings between the terminal 'STA' and a good earth point on the solenoid body, using an ammeter (in series); a reading of 11.2 to 11.8 amps should be obtained. If no reading, renew the solenoid.
40. Using an ohmmeter connected between the small unmarked Lucar terminal and terminal 'STA'; check the resistance of the closing (series) winding; if the reading differs considerably from the limits given the solenoid must be renewed.
41. Using an ohmmeter connected between the small unmarked Lucar terminal and a good earth on the solenoid body, check the resistance of the hold-on (shunt) winding; if the reading differs considerably from the limits given, the solenoid must be renewed.

Solenoid contacts

42. Check the contacts for correct opening and closing by carrying out the instructions 27 to 31 plus the following:
    a. Operate the switch and note the voltmeter reading; it should register practically zero if the solenoid is satisfactory. Alternatively the solenoid should be checked by substitution.
43. The contacts must only be renewed as a set, e.g. moving and fixed contacts. The fixed contacts are an integral part of the moulded cover. Renew a set of contacts as follows:
    a. Remove the screws securing the terminal and base assembly to the solenoid.
    b. Undersolder the coil connections from the cover terminals.
    c. Clamp the solenoid in a vice.
    d. Remove the terminal and base assembly.
    e. Assemble the new terminal and base assembly.
    f. Resolder the connections to the terminal and base assembly.
    g. Refit the securing screws. Torque 1.8 lbf ft (0.25 kgf m).

Refitting

44. Reverse the removing procedure in 1 to 5.

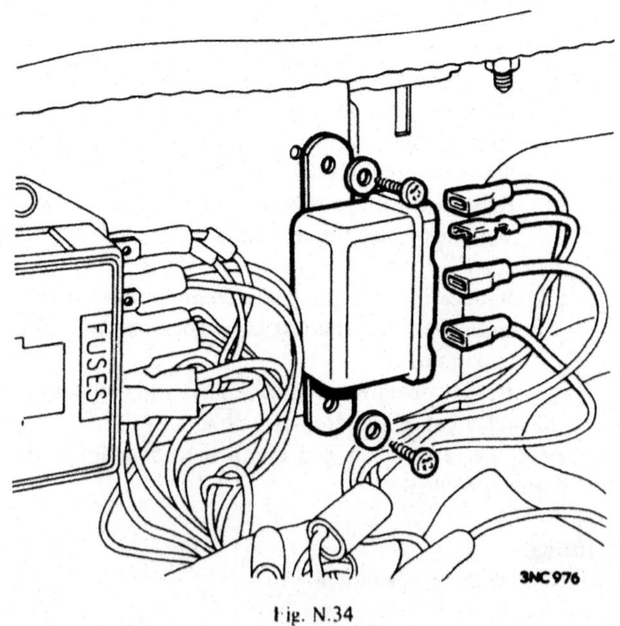

Fig. N.34
Starter motor relay

Section N.32

STARTER MOTOR RELAY

Removing

1. Disconnect the batteries.
2. Disconnect the wiring harness from the terminal blades on the starter motor relay.
3. Remove the two screws to release the starter motor relay from the right-hand wing valance.

Testing

4. Connect a 12-volt direct-current supply between the relay terminals 'W1' and 'W2', and a 12-volt, 2.2-watt test lamp in circuit with a 12-volt direct-current supply between terminals 'C1' and 'C2'.
    a. If the test lamp fails to light check the relay winding resistance, using an ohmmeter connected between terminals 'W1' and 'W2'. Renew the relay if a reading of 76 ohms is not obtained.
    b. If the winding resistance is correct, faulty contact adjustment is indicated which may be corrected as follows:
        i. Uncrimp and remove the cover from the relay.
        ii. Check the air gap between the relay bobbin core and the underside of the armature. The air gap should be 0.030 ± 0.005 in (0.76 ± 0.13 mm) when the contact points are open, and 0.010 ± 0.003 in (0.25 ± 0.08 mm) when the points are closed. Bend the fixed contact post as necessary.

5. After any adjustment to the air gap, check the relay cut-in and drop-off voltages as follows:
   a. Connect a variable direct current supply between the relay terminals 'W1' and 'W2' and a 12-volt direct-current supply in circuit with a test lamp between terminals 'C1' and 'C2'.
   b. Raise the voltage slowly from zero to 15 volts and check that the test lamp lights at 4.0.to 7.5 volts.
   c. Reduce the voltage slowly from 15 to zero volts and check that the test lamp goes out at 5 volts maximum.
   d. Repeat operation 4 as necessary, and recheck the relay cut-in and drop-off voltages.
6. Refit the relay cover and crimp the cover lip at the points provided.

Refitting

7. Reverse the procedure in 1 to 3.

Section N.33

BRAKE WARNING SWITCH

(GHN5 and GHD5 cars from Car No. 410002)

Removing

1. Remove the driver's seat assembly, see Section R.14.
2. Fold back the carpets and disconnect the switch wires at the multi-connector plug.
3. Remove the locknut and withdraw the switch from the bracket on the hand brake lever assembly.

Refitting

4. Reverse the procedure in 1 to 3, noting that the switch should be adjusted so that the warning light flashes when the hand brake lever is pulled up onto the first ratchet tooth.

Section N.34

SWITCHES

(GHN5 and GHD5 cars from Car No. 410002)

Removing

IMPORTANT: Disconnect the battery before attempting to remove any of the switches.

Light switch

1. Remove the three bolts securing the steering-column to the fascia support rail and lower the column.
2. Remove the three screws securing the right-hand half of the steering-column cowl.
3. Withdraw the right-hand cowl over the column switch.
4. Disconnect the wires from the light switch, noting their connected positions.
5. Depress the switch retaining clips and withdraw the switch from the cowl.

Ignition starter switch and steering lock

6. Remove the three bolts securing the steering-column to the fascia support rail and lower the column.
7. Remove the four screws securing the two halves of the steering-column cowl.
8. Withdraw the cowl halves over the column switches.
9. Disconnect the ignition switch wires at the multi-connector plug.
10. Remove the small retaining screw and withdraw the ignition starter switch assembly out of the steering lock housing.
11. Drill out the shear bolt heads from the clamp plate. Alternatively; use an extractor to remove the bolts.
12. Free the lock assembly from the clamp plate.

Fascia switches

13. Remove the fascia assembly, see Section R.39.
14. Disconnect the multi-connector plugs from the switch terminals.
15. Depress the switch retaining clips and withdraw the switch from the fascia.

Panel lamp rheostat switch

16. Remove the fascia, see Section R.39.
17. Disconnect the wires from the switch terminals.
18. Depress the pin in the switch knob and withdraw the knob from the switch.
19. Unscrew the switch retainer and remove the switch from the fascia.

Direction indicator/main beam/horn control switch

20. Remove the steering-wheel pad.
21. Remove the steering-wheel.
22. Remove the steering-column cowls, as in 6 to 8.
23. Disconnect the switch multi-connector plugs.
24. Slacken the switch clamp screw.
25. Withdraw the switch assembly from the steering-column.
26. Remove the insulating tape to separate the electrical leads of the two switches.
27. Drill out the two rivets securing the wiper/washer switch to the mounting plate.
28. Remove the screw and detach the wiper/washer switch from the direction indicator switch mounting plate.

Wiper/washer switch

29. Remove the switch as in 20 to 28.

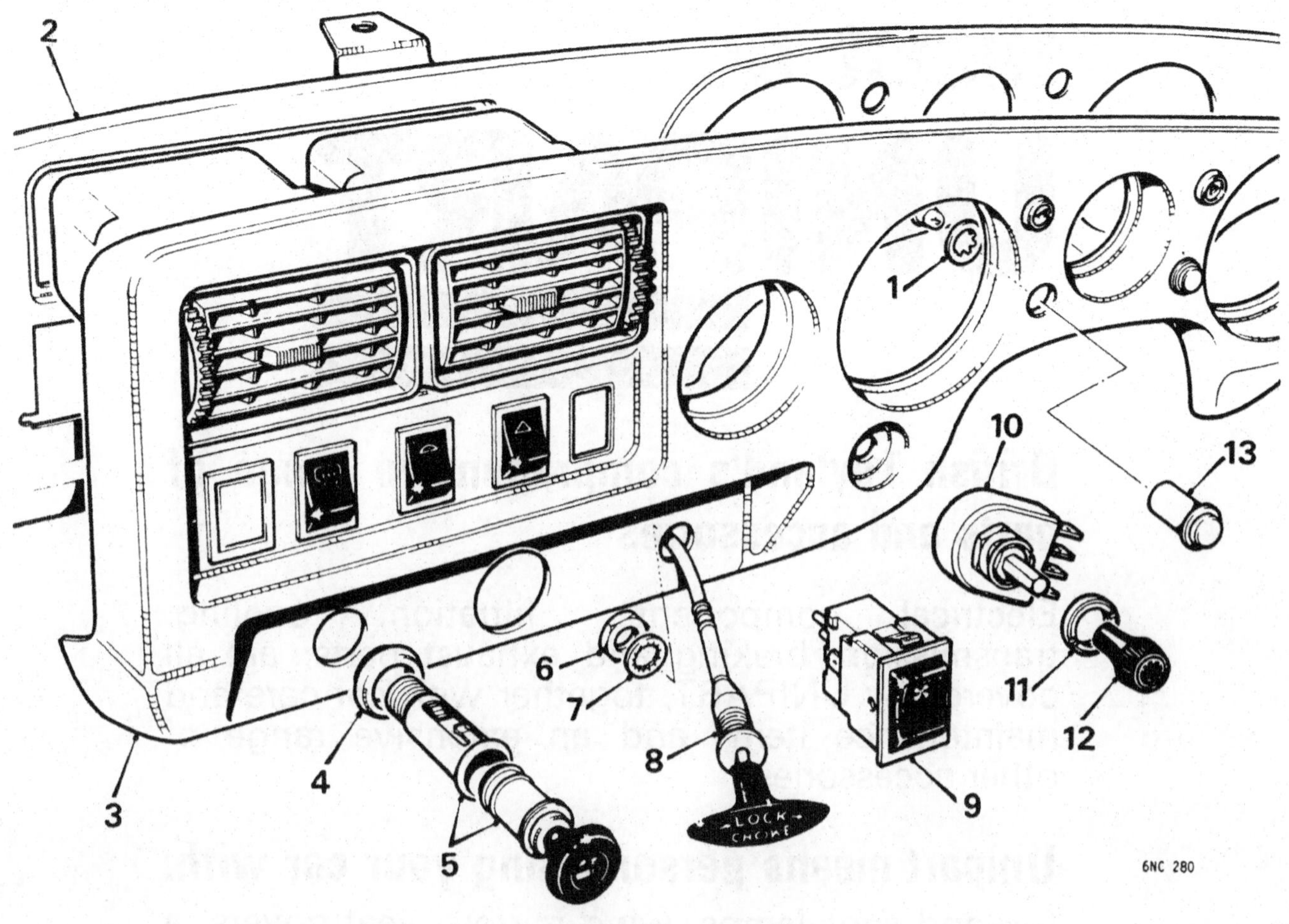

Fig. N.35
Switches
(GHN5 and GHD5 cars from Car No. 410002)

1. Clip
2. Fascia
3. Instrument housing
4. Illumination ring
5. Cigar lighter
6. Nut
7. Washer
8. Mixture control (choke) cable
9. Fascia switch
10. Panel lamp rheostat
11. Retaining ring
12. Knob
13. Warning lamp

Refitting

Light switch

30. Reverse the procedure in 1 to 5.

Ignition starter switch and steering lock

31. Centralize the lock body over the slot in the outer column and fit the clamp plate, but do not shear the bolt heads.
32. Refit the ignition starter switch and reconnect the multi-connector plug. **Check that the steering lock and switch operate correctly.**
33. Tighten the new shear bolts until the heads break off.
34. Reverse the procedure in 6 to 8.

Fascia switches

35. Reverse the procedure in 13 to 15.

Panel lamp rheostat switch

36. Reverse the procedure in 16 to 19.

Direction indicator/main beam/horn control switch

37. Reverse the procedure in 20 to 28 as applicable, noting the following:
    a. Ensure that the cancelling ring is free to rotate in the switch assembly.
    b. Locate the lug on the inner diameter of the switch in the slot of the outer steering-column.
    c. Ensure that the striker dog on the nylon switch centre is in line with and adjacent to the direction indicator switch stalk.
    d. Ensure that the cancelling ring is free to rotate after the switch is fitted.
    NOTE: Slacken the screws and reposition the top plate if the ring is tight.
    e. Ensure that the lugs of the steering-wheel engage easily with the cancelling ring.

Wiper/washer switch

38. Refit the switch as in 37.

Insist on

UNIPART

British Leyland's comprehensive range of parts and accessories

Electrical components, filtration, cooling, transmission, braking and exhaust parts, are all covered by UNIPART, together with car care and maintenance items and an extensive range of other accessories.

Unipart means personalising your car with:

fog and spot lamps, wing mirrors, seat covers, a complete range of towing equipment, roof racks and ancillary instruments to name but a few products.

Unipart helps maintain that new car look with:

car polishes, chamois leathers, sponges, car vacuum cleaner, screen cleaners, touch up and aerosol paints.

Unipart means a range of Car Maintenance Products which includes:

tool kits, hydraulic jacks, foot pumps, inspection lamps, W.D. 40 and battery chargers.

You'll find Unipart stockists in the U.K., Eire and on the Continent—just look for the Unipart sign.

Section Na

THE ELECTRICAL SYSTEM

The information given in this Section refers specifically to service operations on, or affected by, equipment fitted to the MGB (GHN5/GHN4 and GHD5/GHD4) in conformity with local and territorial requirements, and must be used in conjunction with Section N.

THE SWITCHES

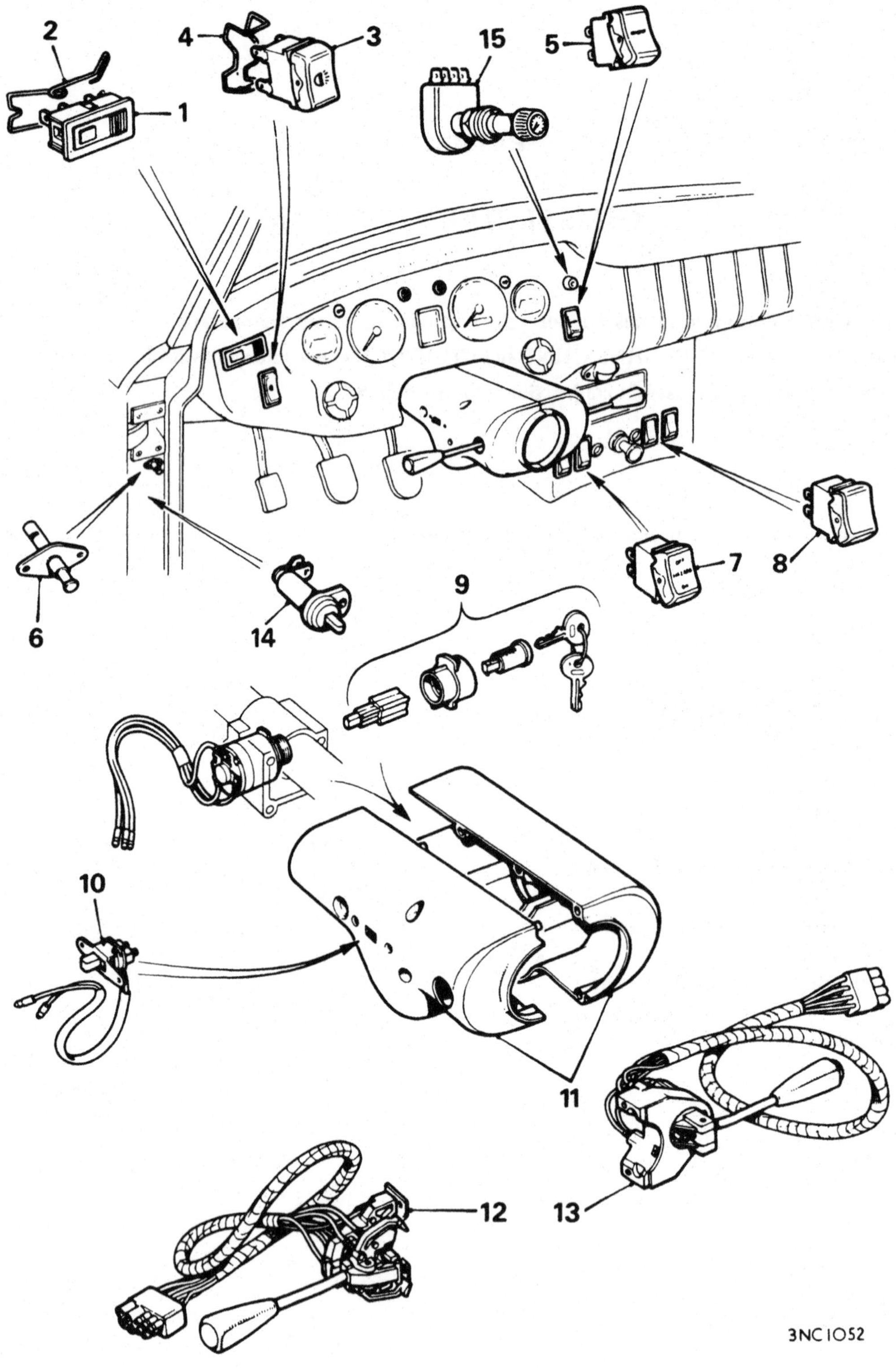

No.	Description	No.	Description	No.	Description
1.	Brake pressure—warning light/test push.	6.	Door switch—interior light.	12.	Direction indicator/headlight flasher—low/high beam/horn switch.
2.	Retaining clip.	7.	Hazard warning switch.	13.	Windshield wiper/washer and overdrive switch.
3.	Lighting switch.	8.	Map light switch.	14.	Audible warning door switch.
4.	Retaining clip.	9.	Ignition switch.	15.	Panel lamp rheostat switch.
5.	Heater blower switch.	10.	Panel light switch.		
		11.	Steering-column switch cowl.		

Section Na.1

INSTRUMENTS AND SWITCHES

Removing

IMPORTANT.–Disconnect the battery before attempting to remove any of the switches or instruments.

TACHOMETER

1. Remove the left-hand lower fascia panel cover.
2. Unscrew the two knurled retaining nuts, disconnect the earth cable and remove the retaining brackets.
3. Withdraw the instrument from the fascia and disconnect the wiring.

OIL PRESSURE GAUGE

4. Remove the tachometer as in 1 to 3.
5. Remove the ignition warning lamp and holder.
6. Unscrew the two retaining nuts, withdraw the instrument from the fascia and disconnect the wiring.

SPEEDOMETER

7. Remove the heater air control knob, unscrew the control retaining nut, and disengage the control from its mounting bracket.
8. Unscrew the trip recorder reset knob retaining nut and disengage the reset from its bracket.
9. Unscrew the two knurled retaining nuts remove the retaining brackets and withdraw the instrument from the fascia.
10. Disconnect the drive cable from the back of the speedometer.

TEMPERATURE GAUGE

11. Remove the heater air control as described in 7.
12. Unscrew the knurled retaining nut and withdraw the instrument from the fascia.
13. Disconnect the wiring from the back of the instrument.

MIXTURE CONTROL (CHOKE)

14. Remove the speedometer as in 7 to 10.
15. Remove the temperature gauge as in 12 and 13.
16. Disconnect the inner cable from the carburetter linkage.
17. Release the cable from its clip on the left-hand side of the gearbox cover.
18. Unscrew the control retaining nut from behind the fascia and withdraw the control.

HEATER BLOWER SWITCH

19. Remove the heater air control as described in 7.
20. Disconnect the wiring from the back of the switch.
21. Using service tool 18G 1145, depress the switch interior retaining lugs and withdraw the switch interior.

LIGHTING SWITCH

22. Disconnect the wiring from the back of the switch.
23. Using service tool 18G 1145, depress the switch interior retaining lugs and withdraw the switch interior.

FUEL GAUGE

24. Unscrew the knurled retaining nut from the back of the instrument.
25. Withdraw the instrument from the fascia, disconnect the wiring and remove.

BRAKE FAILURE WARNING LAMP ASSEMBLY

26. Remove the speedometer as in 7 to 10.
27. Remove the fuel gauge as in 24 to 25.
28. Disconnect the wiring from the back of the lamp assembly.
29. Disengage the spring retaining clip and withdraw the lamp assembly.

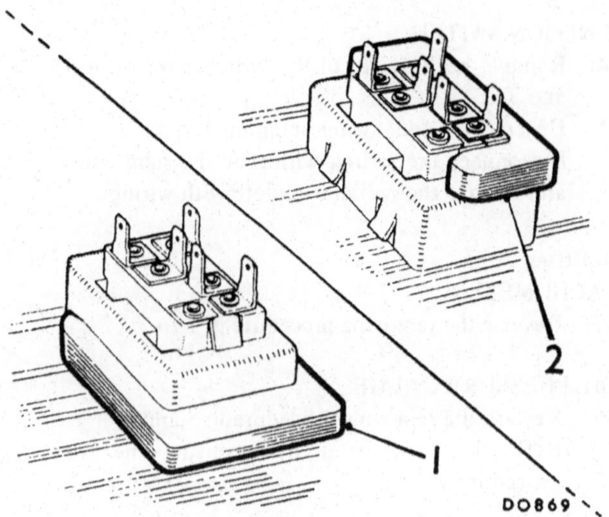

Fig. Na.1
Using tool 18G 1145 to remove the switches
1. Switch complete with bezel. 2. Switch interior only.

HAZARD WARNING SWITCH

30. Remove the control console–Section Ra.1.
31. Disconnect the wiring from the switch.
32. Using tool 18G 1145 press in the four retaining lugs and withdraw the switch.

MAP LIGHT SWITCH

33. Carry out operations 30 to 32 as for the hazard warning switch.

PANEL LIGHT SWITCH

34. Withdraw the centre motif from the steering-wheel, unscrew the retaining nut and remove the steering-wheel using a pull-type extractor.
35. Remove the three retaining screws from the left-hand switch cowl and remove the cowl half.

36. Unscrew the two switch retaining screws, disconnect the switch wiring and remove the switch.

WINDSHIELD WIPER/WASHER AND OVERDRIVE SWITCH

37. Remove the left-hand switch cowl half as in 34 and 35.
38. Remove the screw retaining the right-hand cowl half and remove the cowl.
39. Remove the two switch retaining screws
40. Disconnect the switch wiring at the snap connectors and remove the switch complete with wiring.

DIRECTION INDICATOR; HORN AND HEADLAMP FLASHER SWITCH

41. Detach the windshield wiper/washer and overdrive switch as in 37 to 39.
42. Remove the two switch retaining screws.
43. Disconnect the switch wiring at the snap connectors and remove the switch complete with wiring.

IGNITION SWITCH

44. Remove both halves of the switch cowl as in 34, 35, and 38.
45. Unscrew the four switch retaining screws.
46. Disconnect the switch wiring at the snap connectors and remove the switch complete with wiring.

Refitting

TACHOMETER

47. Reverse the removing procedure in 1 to 3.

OIL PRESSURE GAUGE

48. Reverse the removing procedure in 5 and 6.
49. Refit the tachometer by reversing the removing procedure in 1 to 3.

SPEEDOMETER

50. Reverse the removing procedure in 7 to 10.

TEMPERATURE GAUGE

51. Reverse the removing procedure in 11 to 13.

MIXED CONTROL (CHOKE)

52. Reverse the removing procedure in 16 to 18.
53. Refit the temperature gauge by reversing the removing procedure in 12 and 13.
54. Refit the speedometer by reversing the removing procedure in 7 to 10.

HEATER BLOWER SWITCH

55. Press the switch firmly and evenly into the aperture until it is held by the retaining lugs.
56. Re-connect the wiring to the switch.
57. Refit the heater air control.

LIGHTING SWITCH

58. Press the switch firmly and evenly into the aperture until it is held by the retaining lugs.
59. Re-connect the wiring to the switch.

FUEL GAUGE

60. Reverse the removing procedure in 24 and 25.

BRAKE FAILURE WARNING LAMP ASSEMBLY

61. Fit the lamp assembly into the aperture and retain it with the spring clip.
62. Reconnect the wiring.
63. Refit the fuel gauge by reversing the removing procedure in 24 and 25.
64. Refit the speedometer by reversing the removing procedure in 7 to 10.

HAZARD WARNING SWITCH

65. Press the switch firmly and evenly into the aperture until it is held by the retaining lugs.
66. Reconnect the wiring to the switch.
67. Refit the control console--Section Ra.1.

MAP LIGHT SWITCH

68. Carry out operations 65 to 67 as for the hazard warning switch.

PANEL LIGHT SWITCH

69 Reverse the removing procedure in 34 to 36, tightening the steering-wheel nut to the torque figure given in **'GENERAL DATA'**.

WINDSHIELD WIPER/WASHER AND OVERDRIVE SWITCH

70. Reverse the removing procedure in 37 to 40, tightening the steering-wheel nut to the torque figure given in **'GENERAL DATA'**.

DIRECTION INDICATOR, HORN AND HEADLAMP FLASHER SWITCH

71. Reverse the removing procedure in 41 to 43, tightening the steering-wheel nut to the torque figure given in **'GENERAL DATA'**.

IGNITION SWITCH

72. Reverse the removing procedure in 44 to 46, tightening the steering-wheel to the torque figure given in **'GENERAL DATA'**.

GHN5 and GHD5 cars only

AUDIBLE WARNING BUZZER

73. Disconnect the electrical leads and remove the screw retaining the buzzer unit. No adjustment is possible and in the event of malfunction the buzzer unit must be replaced.

AUDIBLE WARNING DOOR SWITCH

74. Remove the one self tapping screw, extract the switch unit and disconnect the leads from the rear of the switch.

Section Na.2

WINDSHIELD WASHER MOTOR

Removing

(1) Disconnect the battery.
(2) Disconnect the wiring from the motor terminals.
(3) Disconnect the water tubes.
(4) Unscrew the two pump mounting screws and remove the pump assembly.

Refitting

(5) Reverse the removing procedure in (1) to (4).

Section Na.3

LAMPS

Front and rear side-marker lamps

(1) Disconnect the battery.
(2) Remove the two nuts and four washers securing the lamp.
(3) Partially remove the lamp and disconnect the electrical leads at the harness connectors.

Number-plate lamp

(1) Disconnect the battery.
(2) Remove the two nuts and washers retaining the lamps to the lamp bracket; alternatively, remove the lamp complete with the bracket.
(3) Disconnect the electrical leads at the harness connections, and remove the lamp.

Section Na.4

HAZARD WARNING FLASHER UNIT AND AUDIBLE WARNING BUZZER

Removing

Hazard warning flasher unit

(1) Disconnect the battery.
(2) Remove the centre console—Section R.34.
(3) Withdraw the flasher unit from its retaining clip.
(4) Disconnect the wiring plug from the flasher unit.

Audible warning buzzer

(5) Disconnect the battery.
(6) Remove the centre console—Section R.34.
(7) Remove the screw or nut retaining the buzzer.
(8) Disconnect the wiring from the buzzer.

Refitting

Hazard warning flasher unit

(9) Reverse the removing procedure in (1) to (4).

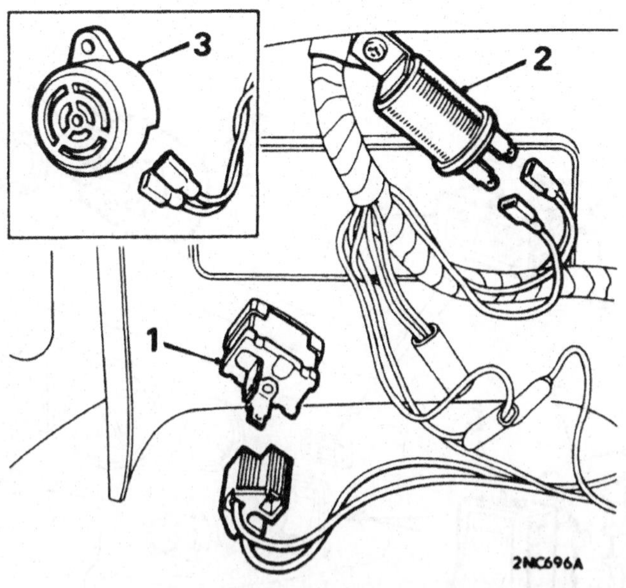

Fig. Na.2

The centre console removed showing:

1. The hazard warning flasher unit
2. Early type warning buzzer.
3. Later type warning buzzer.

Audible warning buzzer

(10) Reverse the removing procedure in (5) to (8).

Section Na.5

SWITCHES, WARNING LAMPS AND CONTROLS
(GHN5 and GHD5 cars from Car No. 294251)

NOTE: Refer to Section Na.1 for the removal and refitting of the instruments, steering-column switches, door courtesy switch, audible warning switch and buzzer.

Removing

IMPORTANT: Disconnect the battery before attempting to remove any of the switches, warning lamps or controls.

Hazard warning switch

(1) Remove the centre console—Section R.34.
(2) Withdraw the bulb holder from the switch retainer.
(3) Disconnect the wiring plug from the switch.
(4) Remove the retainer from the switch and withdraw the switch from the console.

Lighting switch

(5) Unscrew the three screws securing the fascia L.H. lower trim board and pull the board forward to release it from its retaining clips at the back of the fascia.
(6) Remove the bulb holder from the switch retainer.
(7) Disconnect the wiring from the switch.
(8) Remove the retainer from the switch and withdraw the switch from the fascia.

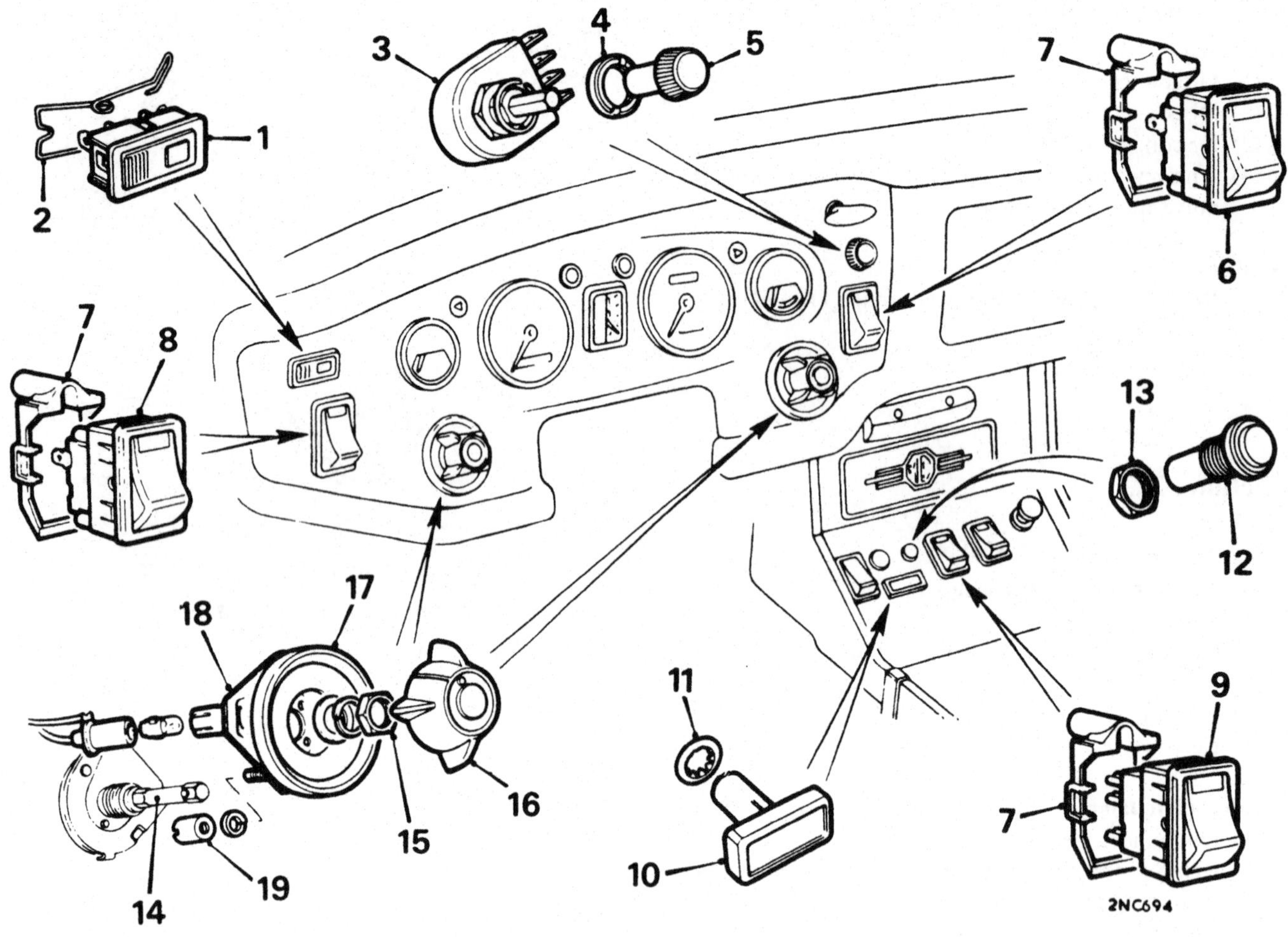

Fig. Na.3

The switches, lamps, and controls (GHN5/GHD5 cars from Car No. 294251)

1. Brake pressure warning light test-push.
2. Retaining clip.
3. Panel lamp rheostat switch.
4. Retainer.
5. Knob for rheostat switch.
6. Heater blower switch.
7. Retainer for rocker switch.
8. Lighting switch.
9. Hazard warning switch.
10. Seat belt warning lamp.
11. Retainer for seat belt warning lamp.
12. Hazard warning lamp.
13. Retainer for hazard warning lamp.
14. Rotary control.
15. Retaining nut.
16. Rotary control knob.
17. Dial assembly.
18. Light box.
19. Retaining nut.

Heater blower switch

(9) Remove the glovebox—Section Ra.3.
(10) Remove the face-level vents—Section Ra.4.
(11) Disconnect the bulb holder from the switch retainer.
(12) Disconnect the wiring from the switch.
(13) Remove the retainer from the switch and withdraw the switch from the fascia.

Panel lamp rheostat switch

(14) Remove the glovebox—Section Ra.3.
(15) Remove the face-level vents—Section Ra.4.
(16) Disconnect the wiring from the switch.
(17) Depress the pin in the switch knob and withdraw the knob from the switch.
(18) Unscrew the switch retainer and remove the switch from the fascia.

Seat belt warning lamp

(19) Remove the centre console—Section R.34.
(20) Remove the bulb holder from the warning lamp.
(21) Remove the warning lamp clip retainer and push the warning lamp out of the centre console.

Hazard warning lamp

(22) Remove the centre console—Section R.34.
(23) Remove the bulb holder from the warning lamp.
(24) Unscrew the warning lamp retainer and remove the warning lamp from the centre console.

Temperature rotary control

(25) Unscrew the three screws securing the fascia L.H. lower trim board and pull the board forward to release it from its retaining clips at the back of the fascia.

(26) Remove the screw retaining the fascia to the cross-tube L.H. bracket.
(27) Depress the pin in the switch knob and withdraw the knob from the spindle.
(28) Remove the bulb holder from the rotary control light box.
(29) Unscrew the nut retaining the rotary control to the fascia and remove the spring and plain washer.
(30) Remove the rotary control from the fascia.
(31) Unscrew the three nuts and remove the three spring and plain washers to release the light box from the dial assembly.
(32) Remove the dial assembly from the fascia.

Air flow rotary control
(33) Unscrew the three screws securing the fascia L.H. lower trim board and pull the board forward to release it from its retaining clips at the back of the fascia.
(34) Depress the pin in the switch knob and withdraw the knob from the spindle.
(35) Remove the bulb holder from the rotary control light box.
(36) Unscrew the nut retaining the rotary control to the fascia and remove the spring and plain washer.
(37) Remove the rotary control from the fascia.
(38) Unscrew the three nuts and remove the three spring and plain washers to release the light box from the dial assembly.
(39) Remove the dial assembly from the fascia.

Refitting

Hazard warning switch
(40) Reverse the removing procedure in (2) to (4).
(41) Refit the centre console—Section R.34.

Lighting switch
(42) Reverse the removing procedure in (5) to (8).

Heater blower switch
(43) Reverse the removing procedure in (11) to (13).
(44) Refit the face-level vents—Section Ra.4.
(45) Refit the glovebox—Section Ra.3.

Panel lamp rheostat switch
(46) Reverse the removing procedure in (16) to (18).
(47) Refit the face level vents—Section Ra.4.
(48) Refit the glovebox—Section Ra.3.

Seat belt warning lamp
(49) Reverse the removing procedure in (20) to (21).
(50) Refit the centre console—Section R.34.

Hazard warning lamp
(51) Reverse the removing procedure in (23) to (24).
(52) Refit the centre console—Section R.34.

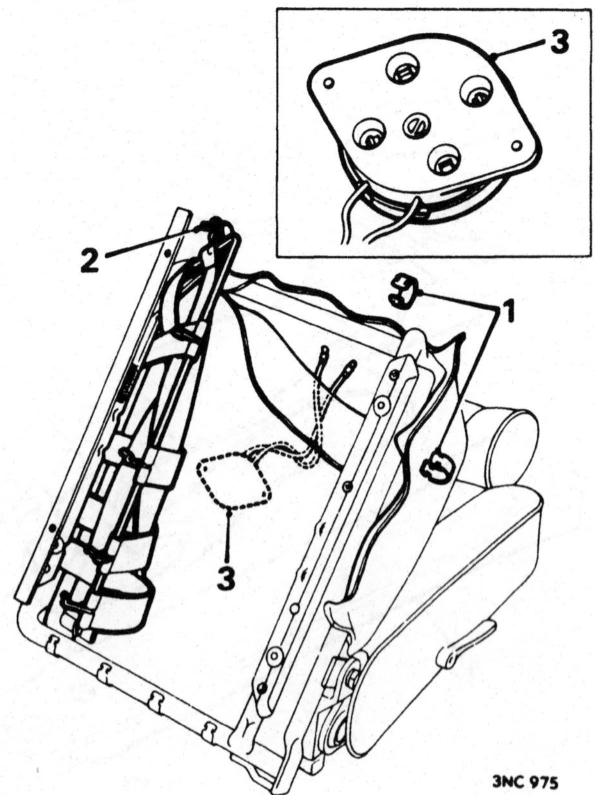

Fig. Na.4

Seat belt warning lamp and buzzer—seat switch

1. Seat cover clip. 2. Seat strapping and frame. 3. Switch.

Temperature rotary control
(53) Reverse the removing procedure in (25) to (32).

Air flow rotary control
(54) Reverse the removing procedure in (33) to (39).

Section Na.6

SEAT BELT WARNING LAMP AND BUZZER—SEAT SWITCH

Removing
(1) Disconnect the batteries.
(2) Remove the four bolts to release the seat from the floor of the car.
(3) Disconnect the wiring harness from the seat switch at the snap connectors beneath the seat and withdraw the seat from the car.
(4) Remove the clips to release the seat cover from the rear and one side of the seat frame.
(5) Detach the seat strapping and frame from the front, rear and one side of the seat frame.
(6) Detach the hessian cover from the underside of the seat cushion and withdraw the seat switch.

Refitting
(7) Reverse the procedure in (1) to (6).

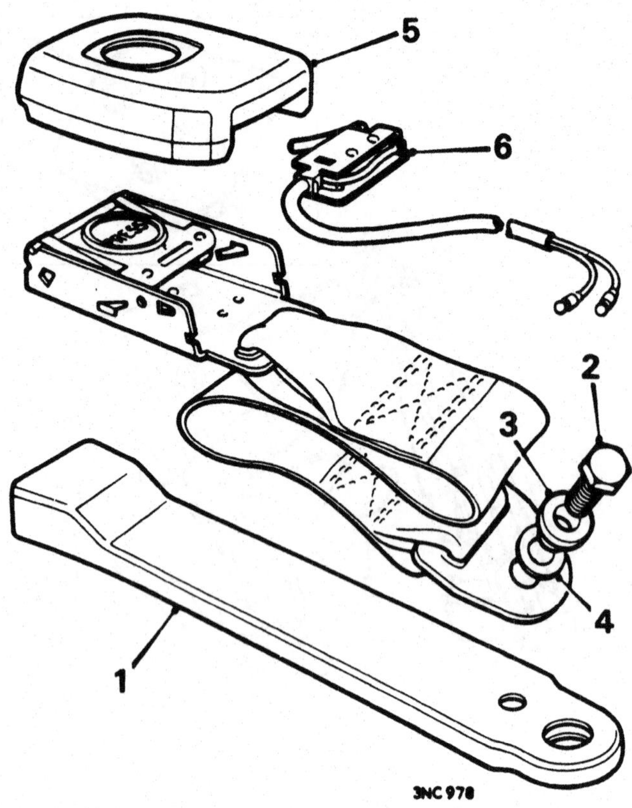

Fig. Na.5

Seat belt warning lamp and buzzer—seat belt switch

1. Sleeve.
2. Retaining bolt.
3. Spacer.
4. Bowed spring washer.
5. Switch and buckle cover.
6. Switch.

Section Na.7

SEAT BELT WARNING LAMP AND BUZZER—SEAT BELT SWITCH

Removing

(1) Disconnect the batteries.
(2) Remove the bolt to release the seat belt buckle assembly from the floor tunnel.
(3) Disconnect the belt switch cables from the wiring harness at the snap connectors under the tunnel carpet.
(4) Withdraw the sleeve from the buckle until the sleeve is clear of the switch and the buckle cover.
(5) Prise the sides off the belt switch cover at its lower end away from the buckle and withdraw the switch cover.
(6) Remove the rivetted ends of the switch retaining rivets, using a drill, to release the switch from the seat buckle.
(7) Unsolder the cables from the switch.

Refitting

(8) Reverse the procedure in 1 to 7.

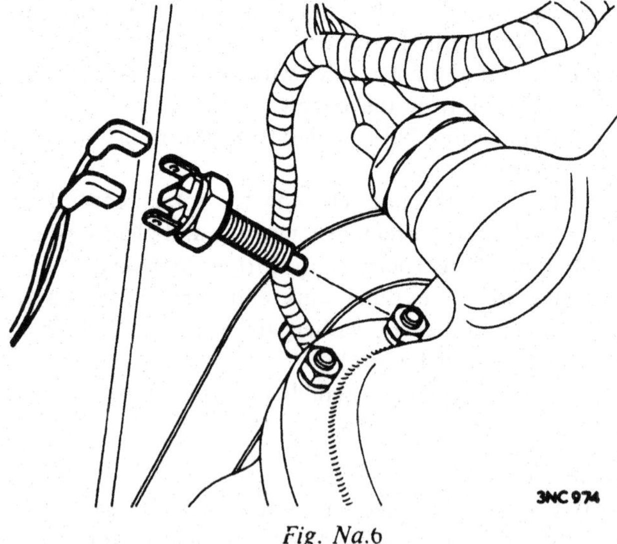

Fig. Na.6

Seat belt warning lamp and buzzer—gearbox switch

Section Na.8

SEAT BELT WARNING LAMP AND BUZZER—GEARBOX SWITCH

Removing

(1) Disconnect the battery.
(2) Disconnect the wiring harness from the terminal blades on the gearbox switch.
(3) Unscrew the switch from the gearbox remote control housing.

Refitting

(4) Reverse the procedure in 1 to 3.

Section Na.9

SEQUENTIAL SEAT BELT SYSTEM CONTROL UNIT

Removing

(1) Disconnect the battery.
(2) Detach the centre console from the floor tunnel as described in Section R.34. It is not necessary to disconnect the wiring harness from the back of the console.
(3) Remove the nut to release the warning buzzer from the fascia rail support.
(4) Remove the two screws and nuts to release the sequential seat belt system control unit from the fascia rail support.
(5) Compress the two retaining tags and withdraw the wiring harness plug from the control unit.

Refitting

(6) Reverse the procedure in 1 to 5.

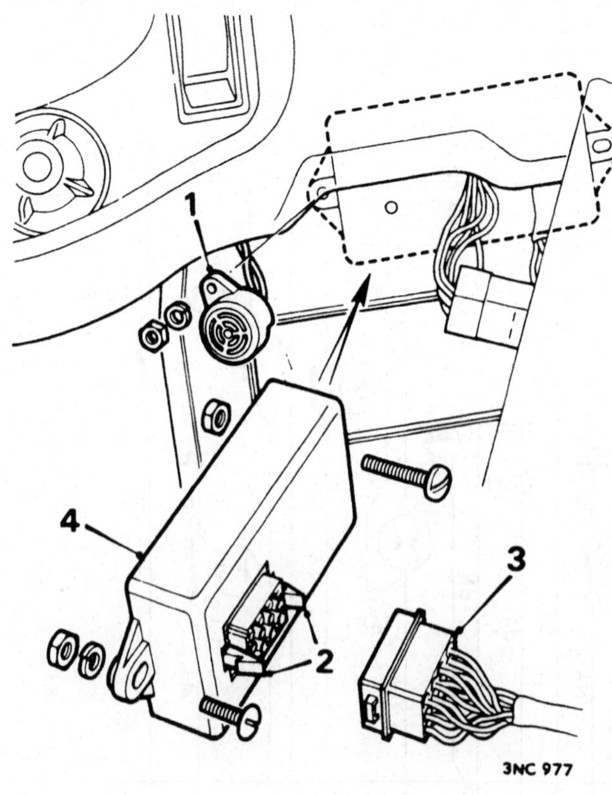

Fig. Na.7

Sequential seat belt system control unit

1. Warning buzzer.
2. Retaining tags.
3. Wiring harness plug.
4. Control unit.

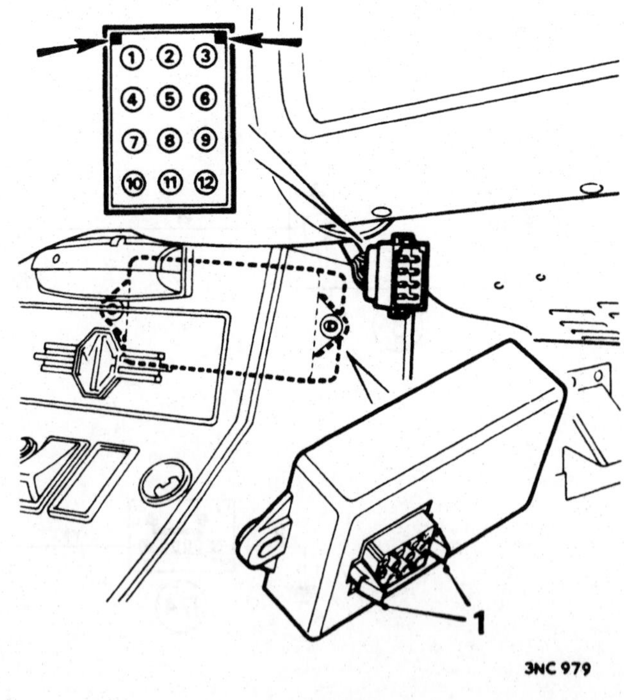

Fig. Na.8

Sequential seat belt system control unit wiring harness plug pin identification numbers. The arrows indicate the plug polarizing keys. Compress the two retaining tags (1) to withdraw the plug from the control unit.

Section Na.10

TESTING THE SEQUENTIAL SEAT BELT SYSTEM

Test conditions

(1) Batteries in good condition.
(2) 500 milliamp. line fuse and the 35-amp. fuse connecting fusebox terminals 5 and 6 in good condition.
(3) Gear lever in neutral position.
(4) Hand brake applied.
(5) Compress the two retaining tags (see Fig. Na.8) on the front of the seat belt system control unit and disconnect the wiring harness plug from the control unit.

Control unit

The control unit is proven by substitution.

Switches and circuit wiring

Referring to Figs. Na.8 and Na.9 for circuit diagram and wiring harness plug pin identification numbers, carry out the following test procedure, using a 12-volt 2·2-watt test lamp and a length of insulated cable.

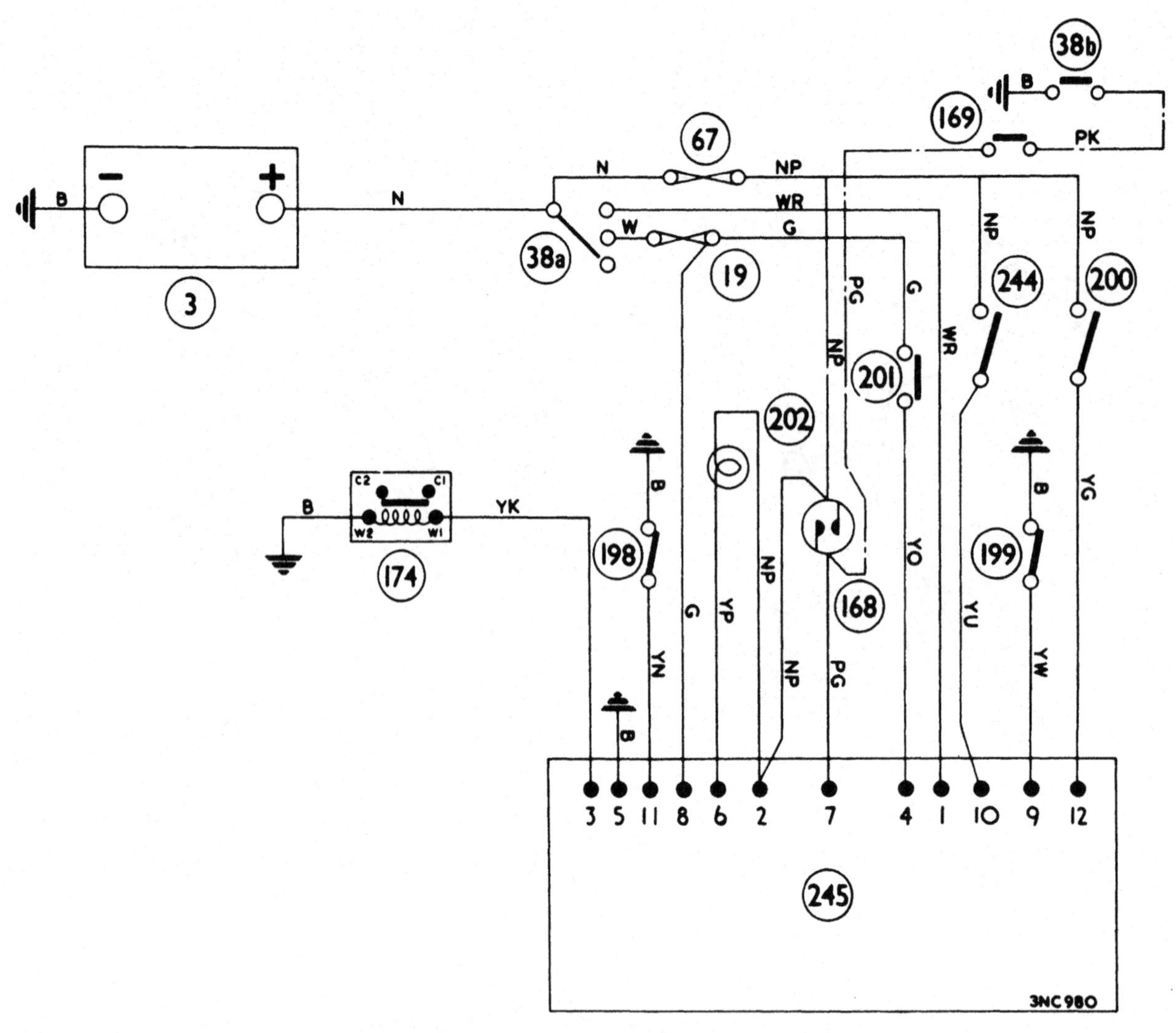

Fig. Na.9

Sequential seat belt system circuit wiring diagram

3. Battery.
19. Fuse—35 amp. (connecting fusebox terminals 5 and 6).
38a. Ignition/starter switch.
38b. Ignition key switch.
67. Line fuse—500 milliamp.
168. Warning buzzer.
169. Warning buzzer door switch.
174. Starter motor relay.
198. Driver's seat belt switch (normally closed).
199. Passenger's seat belt switch (normally closed).
200. Passenger's seat switch (normally open).
201. Gearbox switch (closed in gear).
202. 'Fasten belts' warning lamp.
244. Driver's seat switch (normally open).
245. System control unit.

CABLE COLOUR CODE

B. Black.	N. Brown.	U. Blue.
G. Green.	O. Orange.	W. White.
K. Pink.	P. Purple.	Y. Yellow.
	R. Red.	

When a cable has two colour code letters, the first denotes the main colour and the second denotes the tracer colour.

Test	Procedure		Circuit	Requirements	Remarks
	Using test lamp to bridge plug pins	Using cable only to bridge plug pins			
1. Supply from battery	2 and 5	—	Positive battery feed to earth	Test lamp ON	If the test lamp does not operate, the circuit is faulty.
2. Driver's seat belt switch	2 and 11	—	Positive battery feed via belt switch to earth	(*a*) Test lamp ON—seat belt unfastened (*b*) Test lamp OFF—seat belt fastened	If the test lamp does not operate in (*a*) or lights in (*b*) either the seat belt switch or the circuit wiring is faulty.
3. Driver's seat switch	5 and 10	—	Positive battery feed via driver's seat switch to earth	(*c*) Test lamp ON—driver seated (*d*) Test lamp OFF—driver unseated	If the test lamp does not operate in (*c*) or lights in (*d*), either the seat switch or the circuit wiring is faulty.
4. Passenger's seat belt switch	2 and 9	—	Positive battery feed via belt switch to earth	(*e*) Test lamp ON—seat belt unfastened (*f*) Test lamp OFF—seat belt fastened	If the test lamp does not operate in (*e*) or lights in (*f*), either the seat belt switch or the circuit wiring is faulty.
5. Passenger's seat switch	5 and 12	—	Positive battery feed via passenger's seat switch to earth	(*g*) Test lamp ON—passenger seated (*h*) Test lamp OFF—passenger unseated	If the test lamp does not operate in (*g*) or lights in (*h*), either the seat switch or the circuit wiring is faulty.
6. Gearbox switch	4 and 5 (ignition on)	—	Positive battery feed via ignition and gearbox switches to earth	Test lamp ON—gear engaged	If the test lamp does not operate when a gear is engaged, either the ignition or the gearbox switch, or the circuit wiring is faulty. If the test lamp lights when the gear lever is in neutral, the gearbox switch is faulty.

Test	Procedure		Circuit	Requirements	Remarks
	Using test lamp to bridge plug pins	Using cable only to bridge plug pins			
7. Steering-column lock, ignition/starter switch	1 and 5	—	Positive battery feed via starter switch to earth	(*j*) Test lamp ON—switch in position 'III' (*k*) Test lamp OFF—switch in position 'O' or 'I' or 'II'	If the test lamp does not operate in (*j*), either the steering column lock, ignition/starter switch or the circuit wiring is faulty. If the test lamp lights in (*k*), the steering-column lock, ignition/starter switch is faulty.
8. Starter relay	—	2 and 3	Positive battery feed via starter relay to earth	Starter motor operates	If the starter motor does not operate, either the starter relay or its circuit wiring or the starter or its circuit wiring is faulty.
9. Seat belt warning lamp	—	5 and 6	Positive battery feed via warning lamp to earth	Warning lamp ON	If the warning lamp does not operate, either the warning lamp bulb or the circuit wiring is faulty.
10. Warning buzzer	—	5 and 7	Positive battery feed via warning buzzer to earth	(*l*) Warning buzzer operates—ignition key removed (*m*) Warning buzzer does not operate—ignition key in switch, driver's door closed, and bridging cable disconnected from pins 5 and 7.	If the warning buzzer does not operate in (*l*), either the warning buzzer or the circuit wiring is faulty. If the warning buzzer operates in (*m*), either the driver's door switch or the circuit wiring between the warning buzzer and the door switch is faulty.

Key to the wiring diagrams: **Nos. 1 to 13 on page Nb.2**
No. 14 onwards on page Nb.16

MGB, positive earth
Car Nos. GHN3-101 to 48756–Tourer only (1962-64) .. .. **Diagram 1**

MGB, positive earth
Car Nos. GHN3-48766 to 138800–Tourer
GHD3-71933 to 139823–GT } (1964-67) .. .. **Diagram 2**

MGB, negative earth
Car Nos. GHN4-138801 to 158370–Tourer
GHD4-139824 to 158230–GT } (1967-68) .. .. **Diagram 3**

MGB, negative earth
Car Nos. GHN4-158371 to 187169–Tourer
GHD4-158231 to 187840–GT } (1968-69) .. .. **Diagram 4**

MGB, negative earth
Car Nos. GHN5-187170 to 219000–Tourer
GHD5-187841 to 219000–GT } (1969-70) .. .. **Diagram 5**

Car Nos. GHN5-219001 to 258000–Tourer
GHD5-219002 to 258003–GT } (1970-71) .. .. **Diagram 6**

Car Nos. GHN5-258001 to 294250–Tourer
GHD5-258004 to 296000–GT } (1971-72) .. .. **Diagram 11**

Car Nos. GHN5-294251 to 328100–Tourer
GHD5-296001 to 328800–GT } (1972-73) .. .. **Diagram 14**

Car Nos. GHN5-328101 to 360300–Tourer
GHD5-328801 to 361000–GT } (1973-74) .. .. **Diagram 16**

Car Nos. GHN5-36030i-onwards–Tourer
GHD5-361001-onwards–GT } (1975-76) .. .. **Diagram 18**

Car Nos. GHN5 410002 onwards–Tourer
GHD5 410351 onwards–GT } (1977) .. .. **Diagram 19**

The following wiring diagrams are for MGB cars fitted with electrical equipment in conformity with various local and territorial motor vehicle regulations

MGB North America, negative earth
Car Nos. GHN4-138401 to 158232–Tourer
GHD4-139472 to 158370–GT } (1967-68) .. .. **Diagram 7**

Car Nos. GHN4-158233 to 187169–Tourer
GHD4-158371 to 187840–GT } (1968-69) .. .. **Diagram 8**

MGB North America, negative earth
Car Nos. GHN5-187170 to 219000–Tourer
GHD5-187841 to 219000–GT } (1969-70) .. .. **Diagram 9**

Car Nos. GHN5-219001 to 258000–Tourer
GHD5-219002 to 258003–GT } (1970-71) .. .. **Diagram 10**

Car Nos. GHN5-258001 to 267579–Tourer
GHD5-258004 to 268280–GT } (1971-72) .. .. **Diagram 12**

Car Nos. GHN5-267580 to 294240–Tourer
GHD5-268281 to 296000–GT } (1971-72 with seat belt warning) .. .. **Diagram 13**

Car Nos. GHN5-294241 to 328100–Tourer
GHD5-296001 to 328800–GT } (1972-73) .. .. **Diagram 15**

Car Nos. GHN5-328101 onwards–Tourer
GHD5-328801 onwards–GT } (1973-74) .. .. **Diagram 17**

KEY TO THE WIRING DIAGRAMS – Nos. 1 to 13

(Refer to page Nb.16 for the key to diagrams No. 14 onwards)

Use this one key to identify components on the wiring diagrams Nos. 1 to 13. Refer to the appropriate wiring diagram, and disregard any additional numbered items appearing in the key and not on a particular diagram.

No.	Description
1.	Alternator or dynamo.
2.	Control box.
3.	Batteries–6-volt.
4.	Starter solenoid.
5.	Starter motor.
6.	Lighting switch.
7.	Headlamp dip switch.
8.	R.H. headlamp.
9.	L.H. headlamp.
10.	High-beam warning lamp.
11.	R.H. parking lamp.
12.	L.H. parking lamp.
13.	Panel lamp switch or rheostat switch.
14.	Panel lamps.
15.	Number-plate illumination lamp.
16.	R.H. stop and tail lamp.
17.	L.H. stop and tail lamp.
18.	Stop lamp switch.
19.	Fuse unit.
20.	Interior courtesy lamp or map light (early cars).
21.	R.H. door switch.
22.	L.H. door switch.
23.	Horns.
24.	Horn-push.
25.	Flasher unit.
26.	Direction indicator switch.
	or
26.	Direction indicator/headlamp flasher.
	or
26.	Combined direction indicator/headlamp flasher/headlamp high-low beam/horn-push switch.
	or
26.	Combined direction indicator/headlamp flasher/headlamp high-low beam switch.
27.	Direction indicator warning lamps.
28.	R.H. front flasher lamp.
29.	L.H. front flasher lamp.

No.	Description
30.	R.H. rear flasher lamp.
31.	L,H. rear flasher lamp.
32.	Heater booster motor switch.
33.	Heater booster motor, or fresh-air motor.
34.	Fuel gauge.
35.	Fuel gauge tank unit.
36.	Windshield wiper switch.
37.	Windscreen wiper motor.
38.	Ignition/starter switch.
39.	Ignition coil.
40.	Distributor.
41.	Fuel pump.
43.	Oil pressure gauge.
44.	Ignition warning lamp.
45.	Speedometer.
46.	Coolant temperature gauge.
47.	Coolant temperature transmitter.
49.	Reverse lamp switch.
50.	Reverse lamp.
53.	Fog and driving lamp switch.
54.	Driving lamp.
55.	Fog lamp.
57.	Cigar-lighter illuminated.
59.	Map light switch (early cars).
60.	Radio.
64.	Bi-metal instrument voltage stabilizer.
65.	Luggage compartment lamp switch.
66.	Luggage compartment lamp.
67.	Line fuse.
68.	Overdrive relay unit.
71.	Overdrive solenoid.
72.	Overdrive manual control switch.
73.	Overdrive gear switch.
74.	Overdrive throttle switch.

No.	Description
76.	Automatic gearbox gear selector illumination lamp.
77.	Windscreen washer pump.
82.	Switch illumination lamp.
95.	Tachometer.
101.	Courtesy or map light switch.
102.	Courtesy or map light.
115.	Heated back-light switch. } GT only
116.	Heated back-light } GT only
118.	Combined windshield washer and wiper switch.
131.	Combined reverse lamp switch and automatic transmission safety switch.
147.	Oil pressure transmitter.
150.	Heated back-light warning lamp (GT only).
152.	Hazard warning lamp.
153.	Hazard warning switch.
154.	Hazard warning flasher unit.
159.	Brake pressure warning lamp and lamp test push.
160.	Brake pressure failure switch.
168.	Ignition key audible warning buzzer.
169.	Ignition key audible warning door switch.
170.	R.H. front side-marker lamp.
171.	L,H. front side-marker lamp.
172.	R.H. rear side-marker lamp.
173.	L.H. rear side-marker lamp.
174.	Starter solenoid relay.
198.	Driver's seat belt buckle switch.
199.	Passenger's seat belt buckle switch.
200.	Passenger's seat switch.
201.	Gearbox switch seat belt warning.
202.	Warning light–fasten belts.
203.	Line diode.

CABLE COLOUR CODE

N. Brown.	P. Purple.	W. White.
U. Blue.	G. Green.	Y. Yellow.
R. Red.	LG. Light Green.	B. Black.
	O. Orange.	

When a cable has two colour code letters the first denotes the main colour and the second denotes the tracer colour.

DIAGRAM 1

(Refer to page Nb.2 for the key)

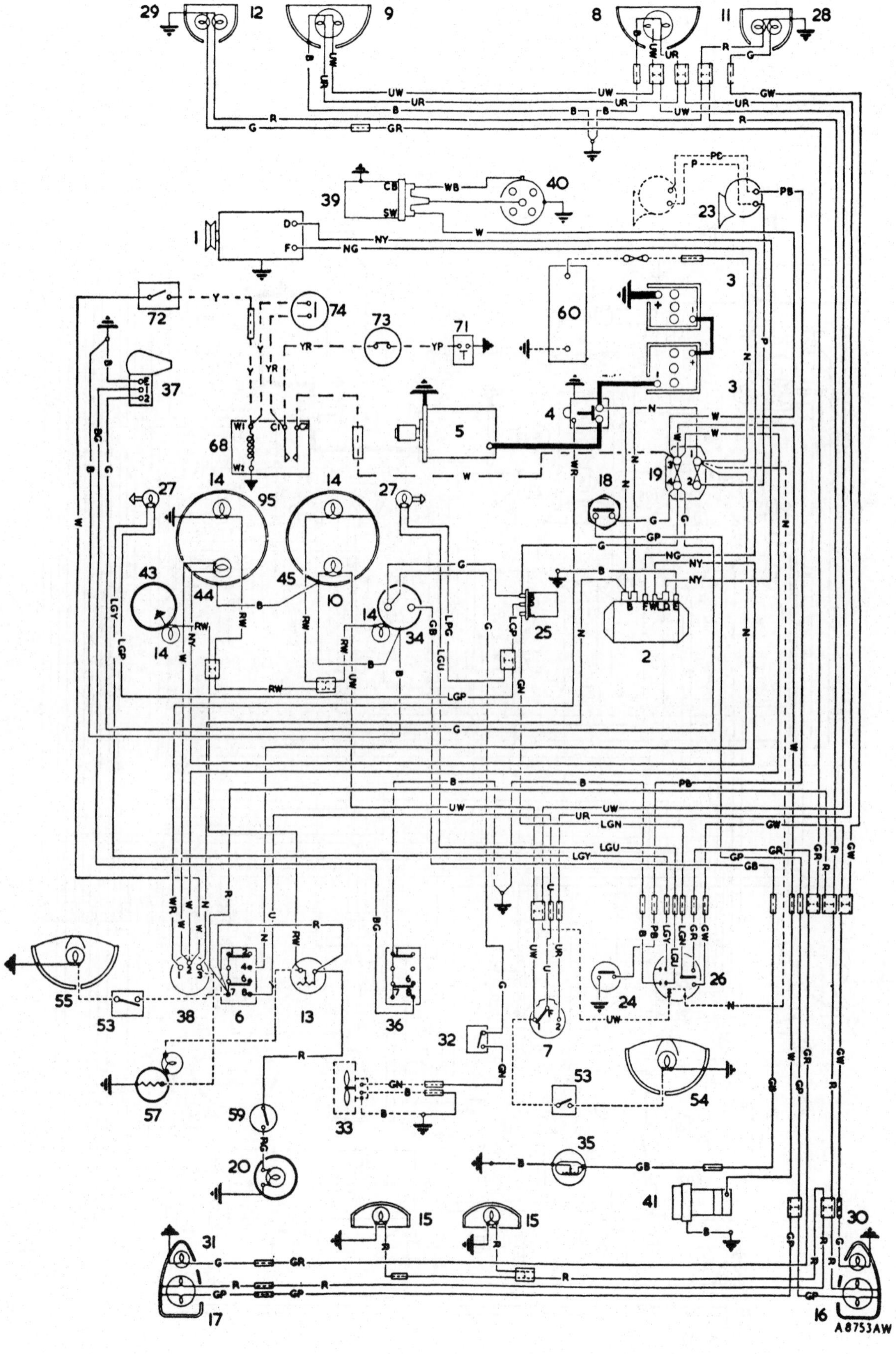

A8753AW

DIAGRAM 2

(Refer to page Nb.2 for the key)

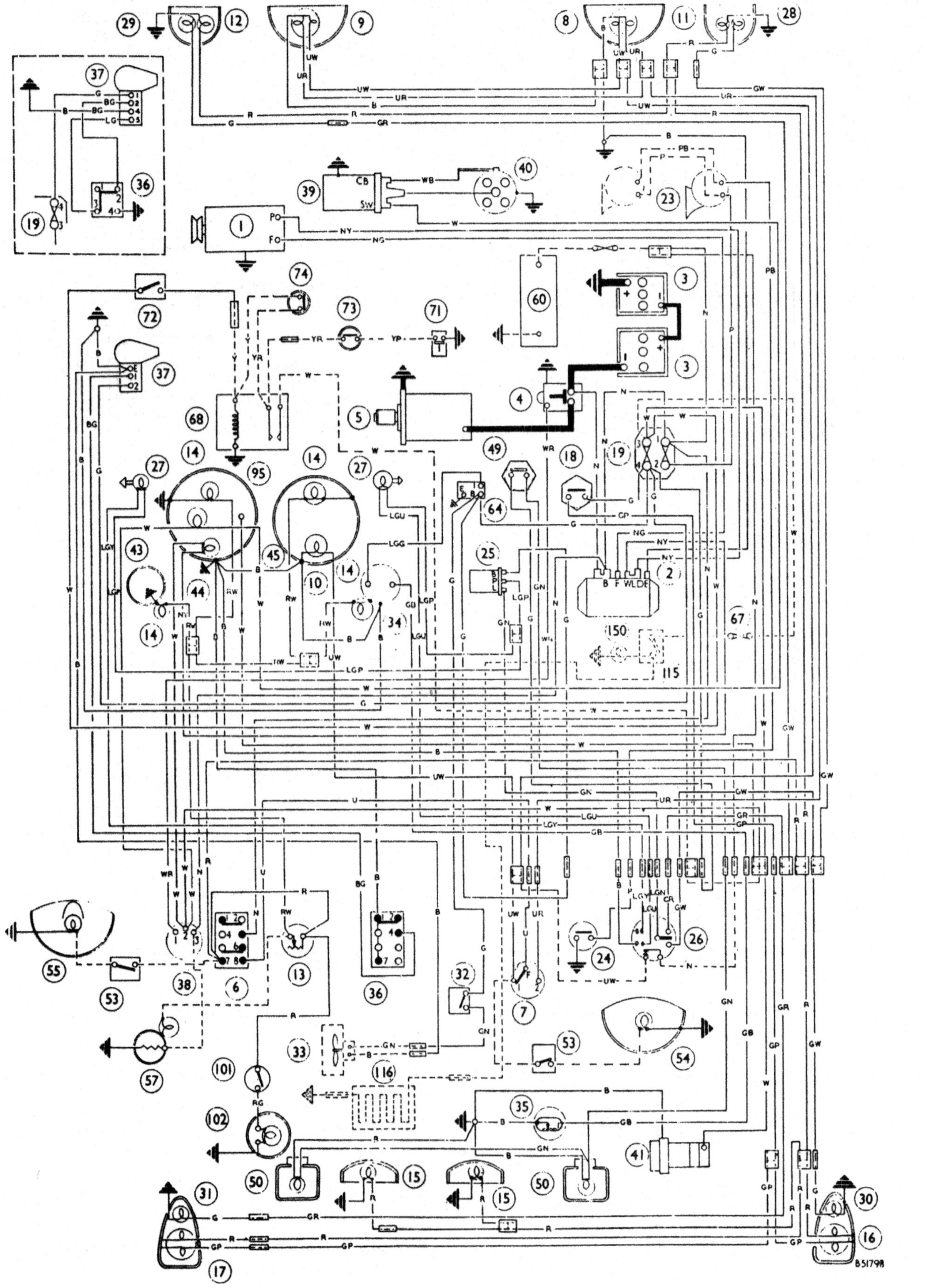

DIAGRAM 3

(Refer to page Nb.2 for the key)

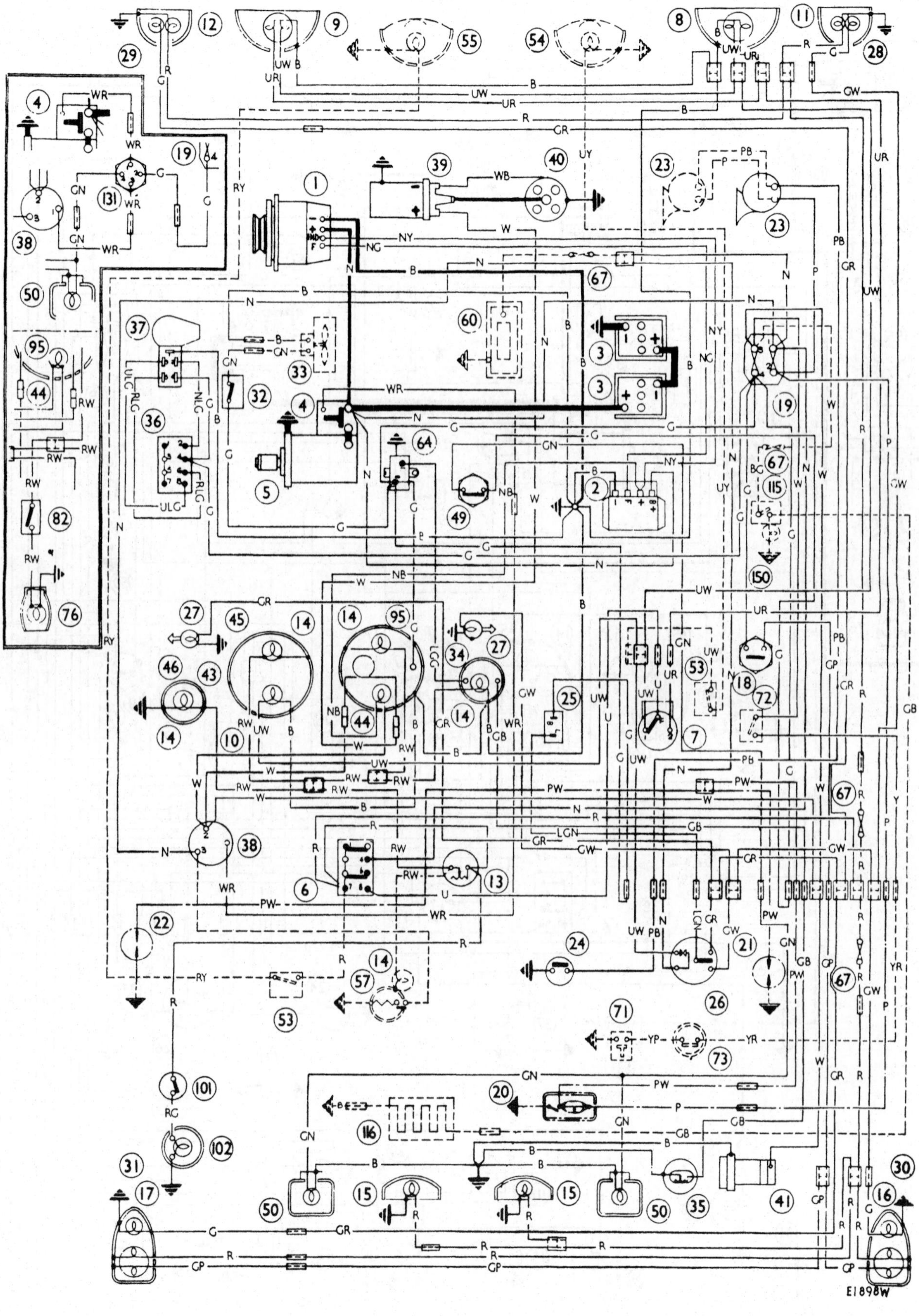

E1898W

DIAGRAM 4
(Refer to page Nb.2 for the key)

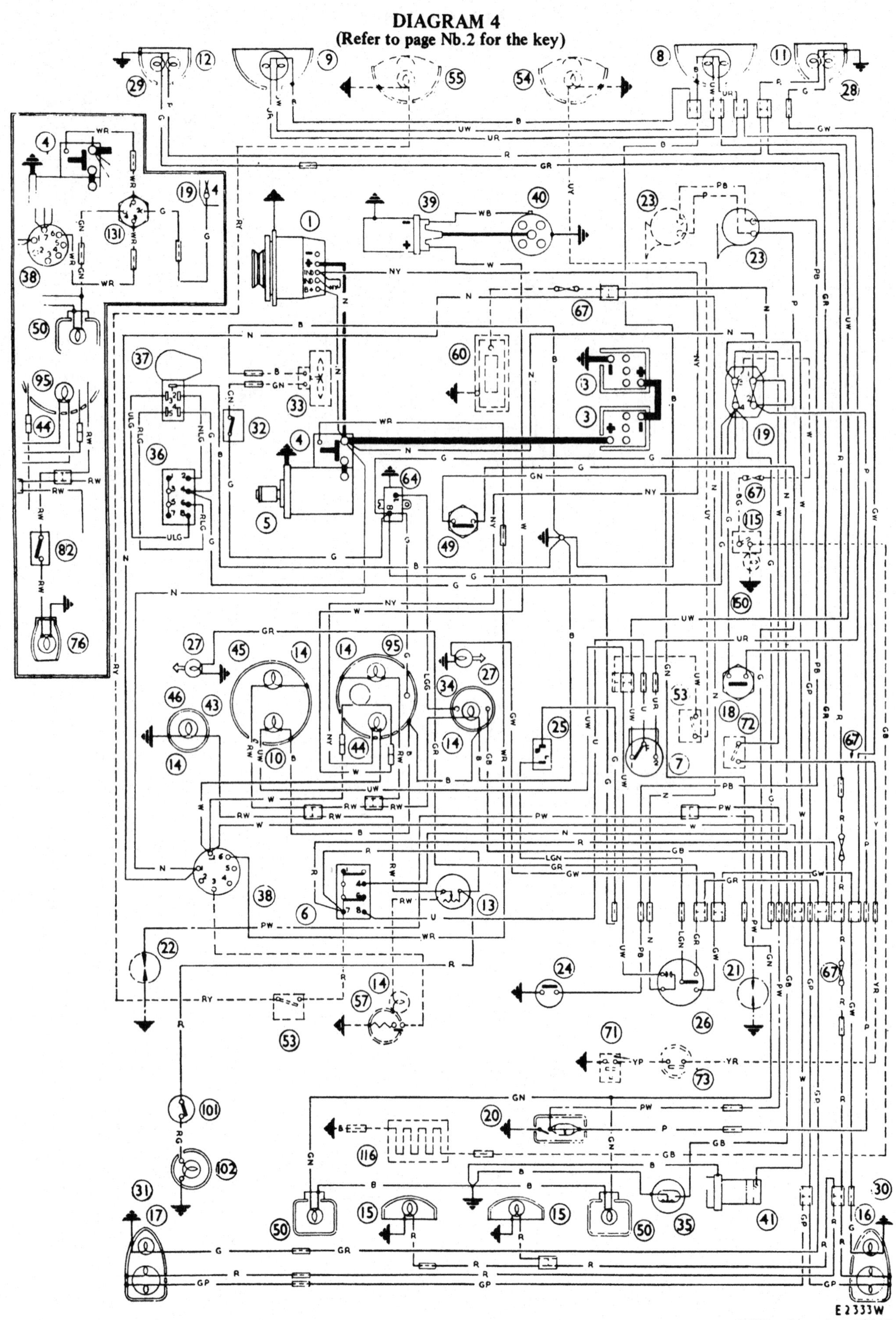

E2333W

MGB. Issue 1. 86842

DIAGRAM 5
(Refer to page Nb.2 for the key)

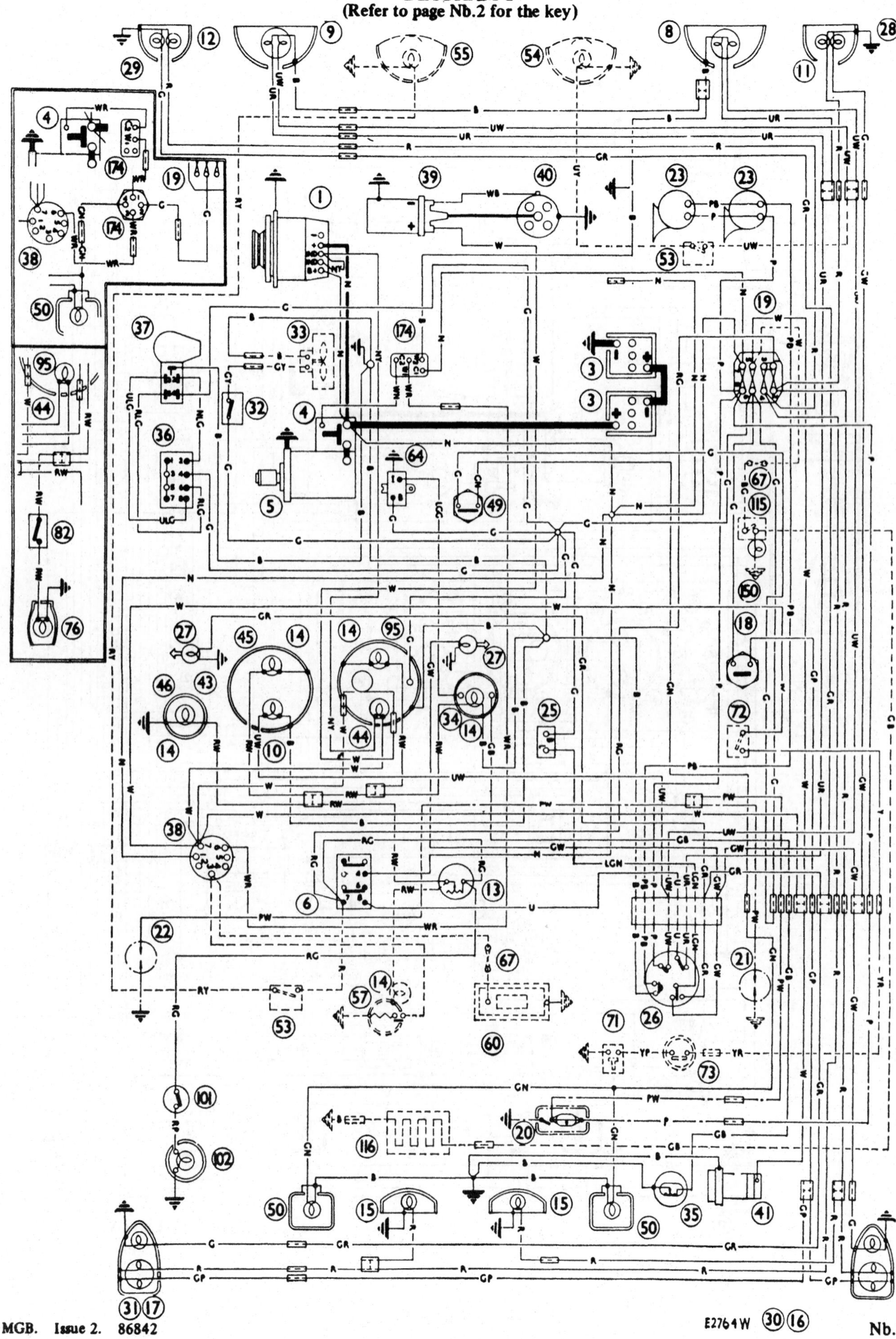

E2764W

DIAGRAM 6

(Refer to page Nb.2 for the key)

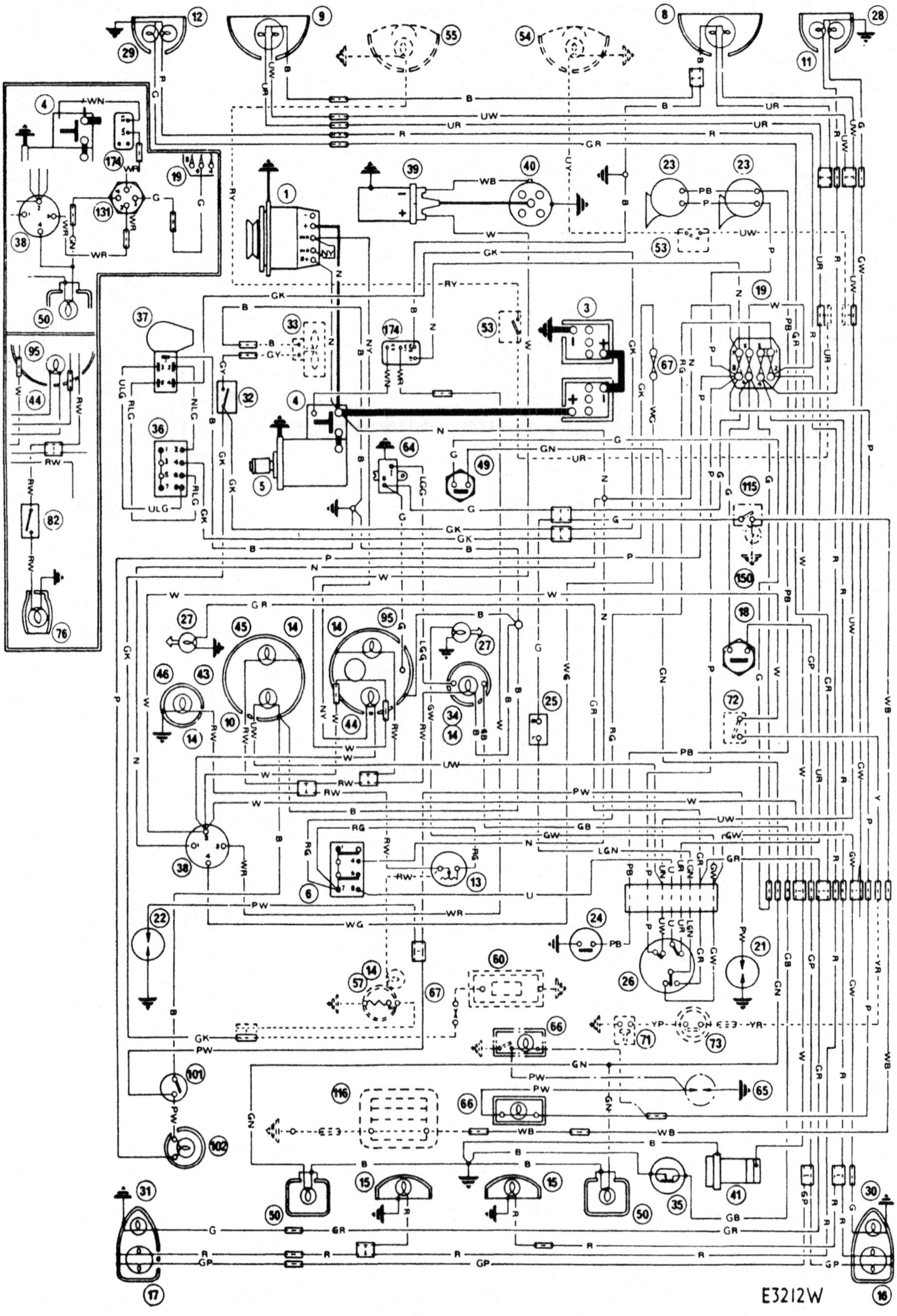

E3212W

DIAGRAM 7

(Refer to page Nb.2 for the key)

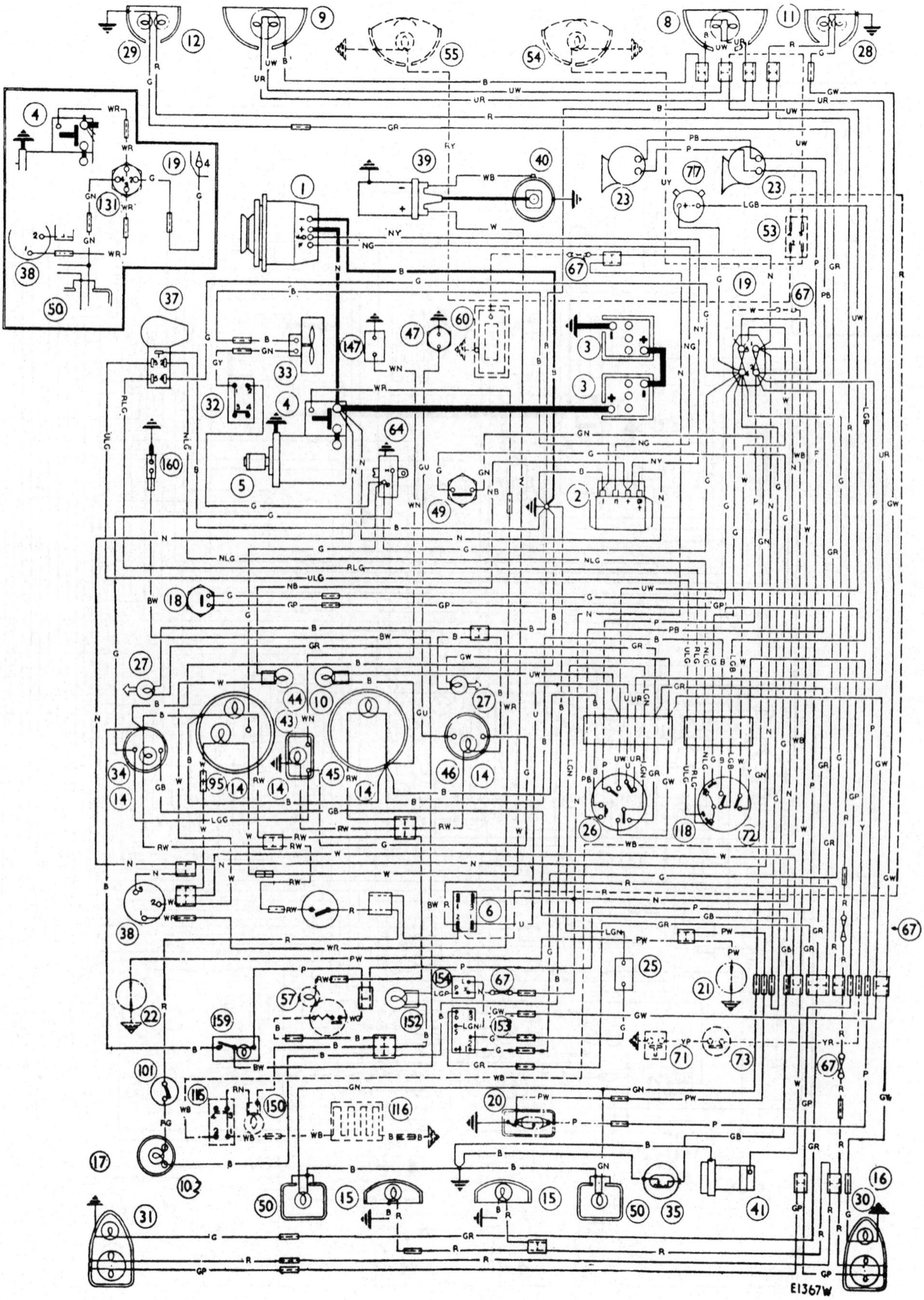

E1367W

DIAGRAM 8

(Refer to page Nb.2 for the key)

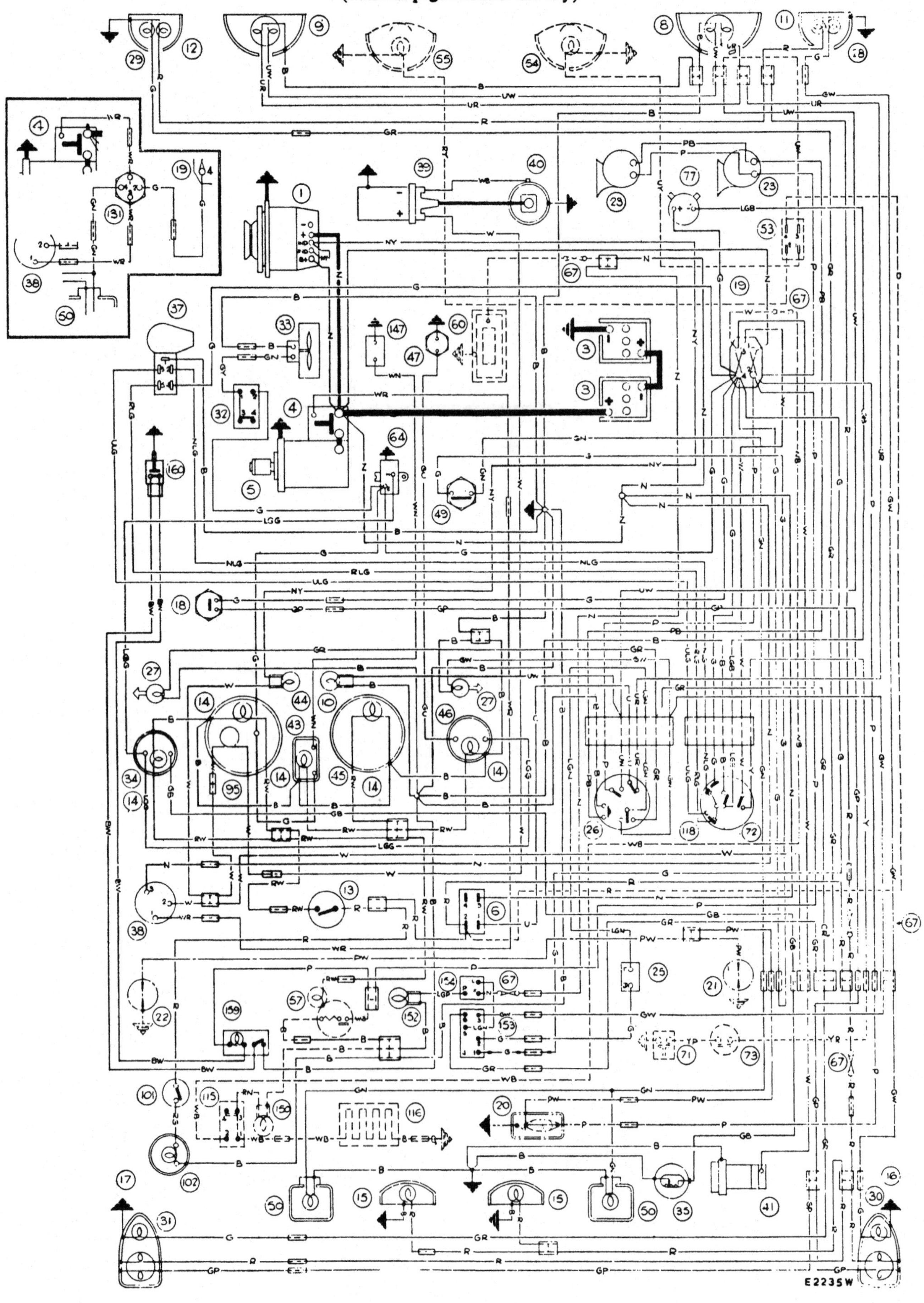

DIAGRAM 9

(Refer to page Nb.2 for the key)

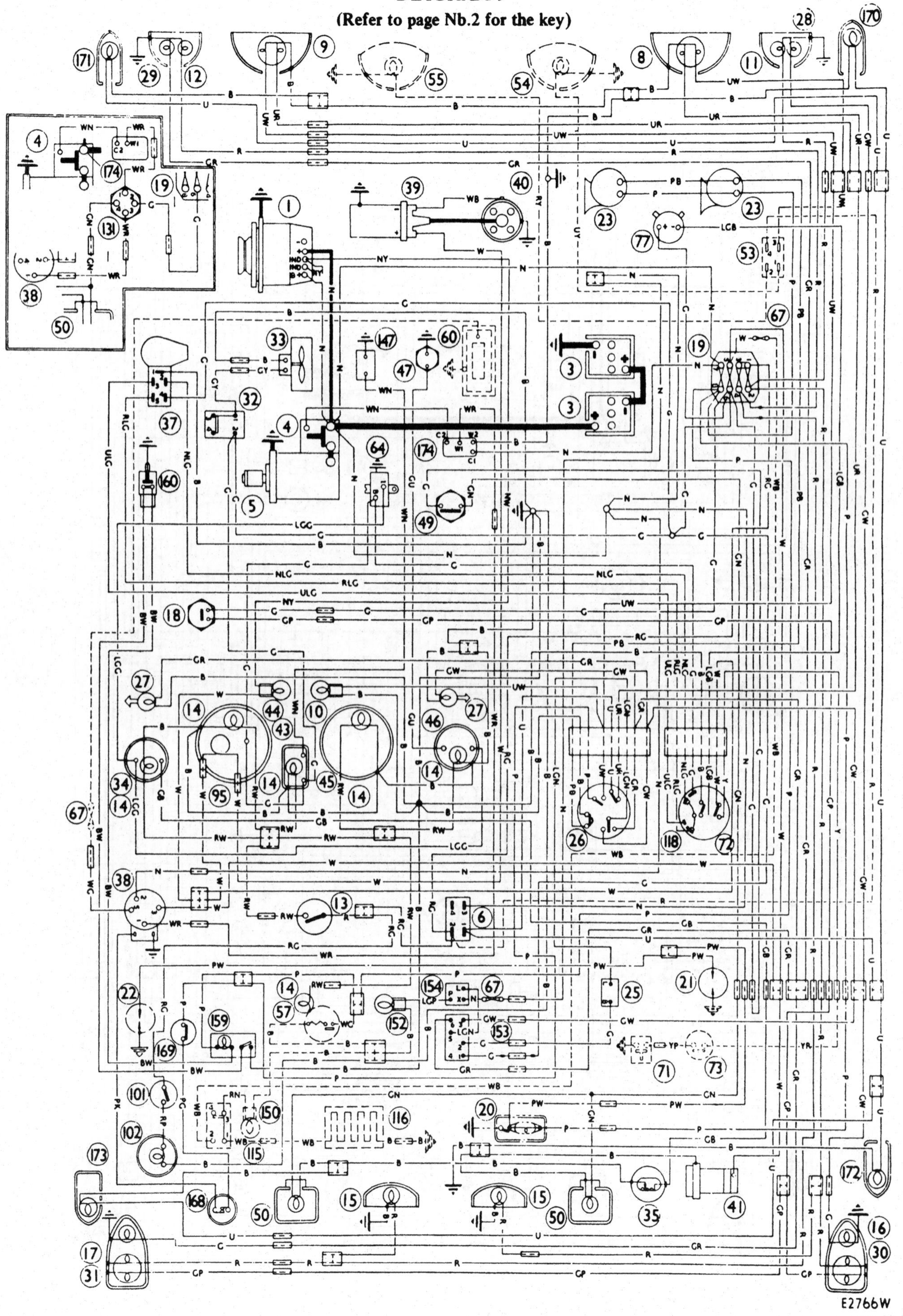

E2766W

DIAGRAM 10

(Refer to page Nb.2 for the key)

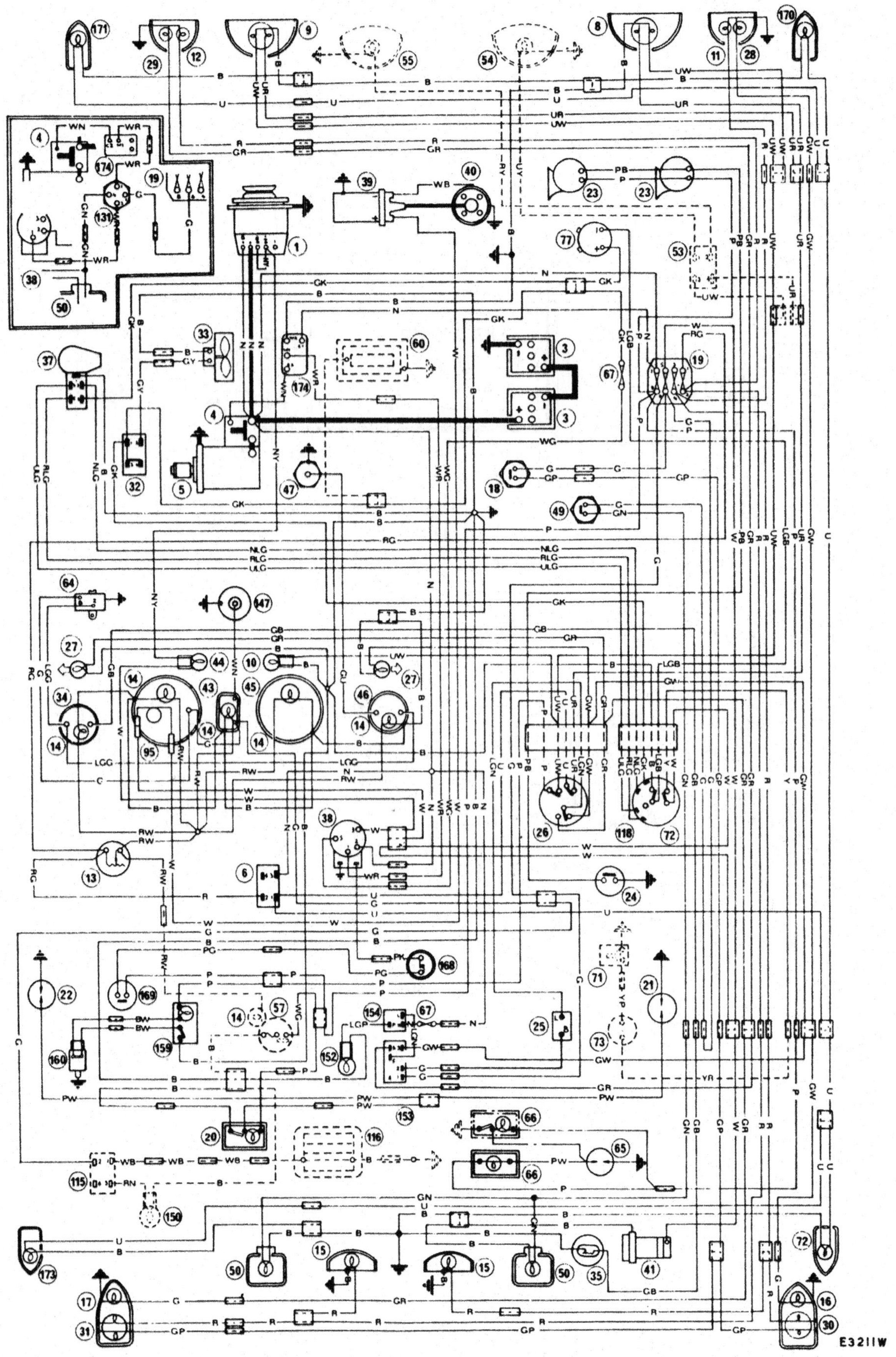

DIAGRAM 11

(Refer to page Nb.2 for the key)

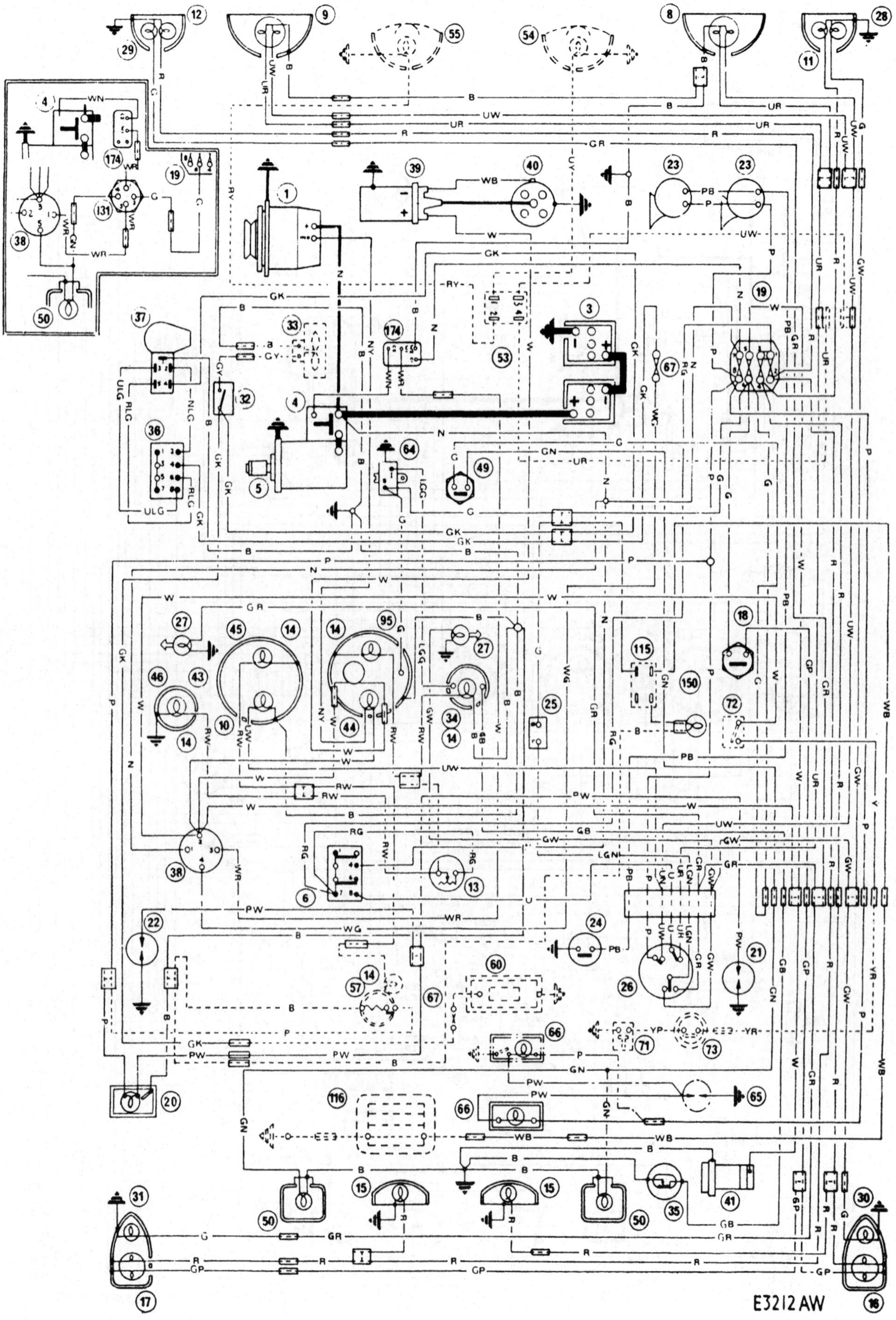

E3212 AW

DIAGRAM 12

(Refer to page Nb.2 for the key)

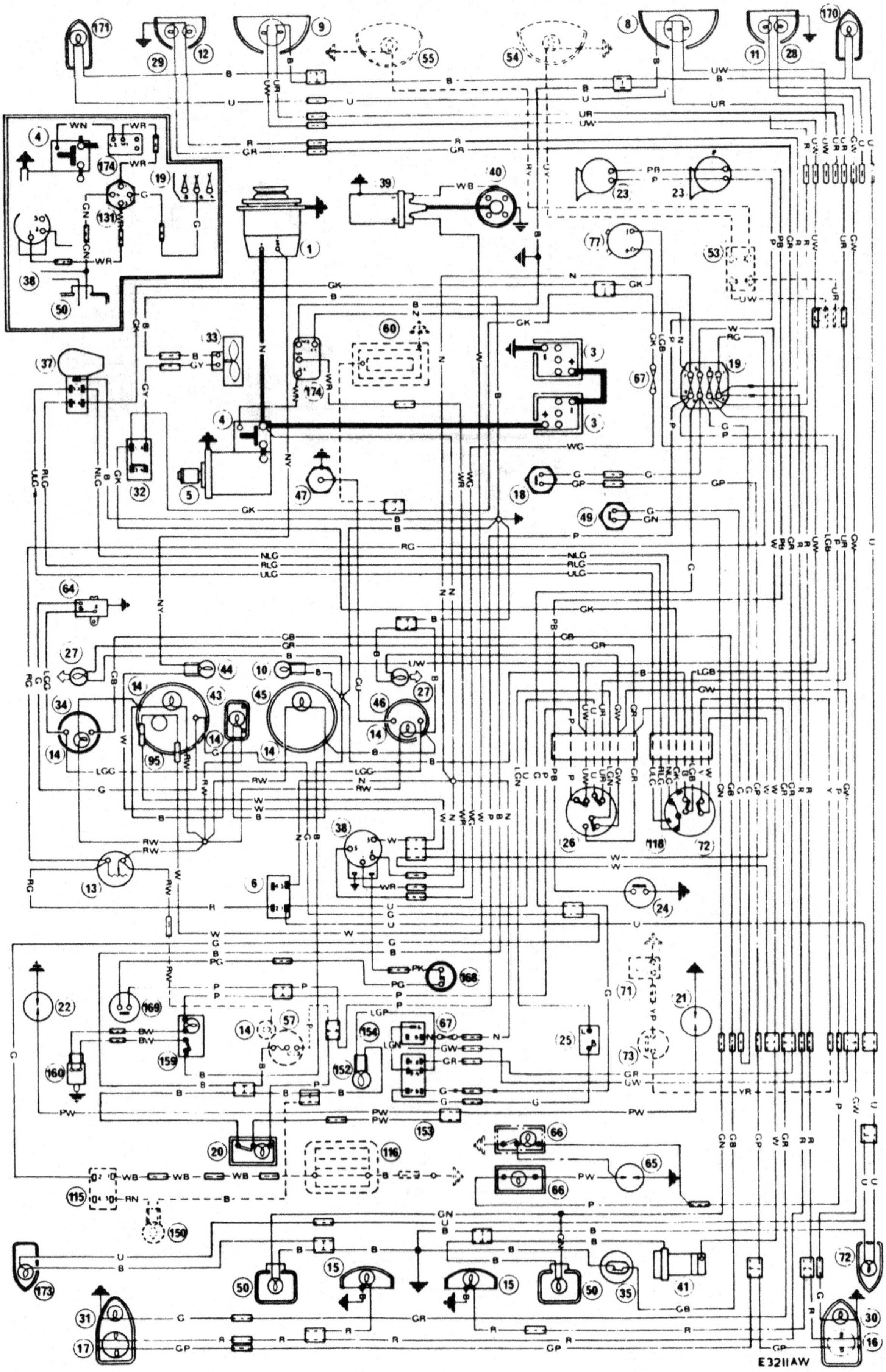

E3211AW

DIAGRAM 13

(Refer to page Nb.2 for the key)

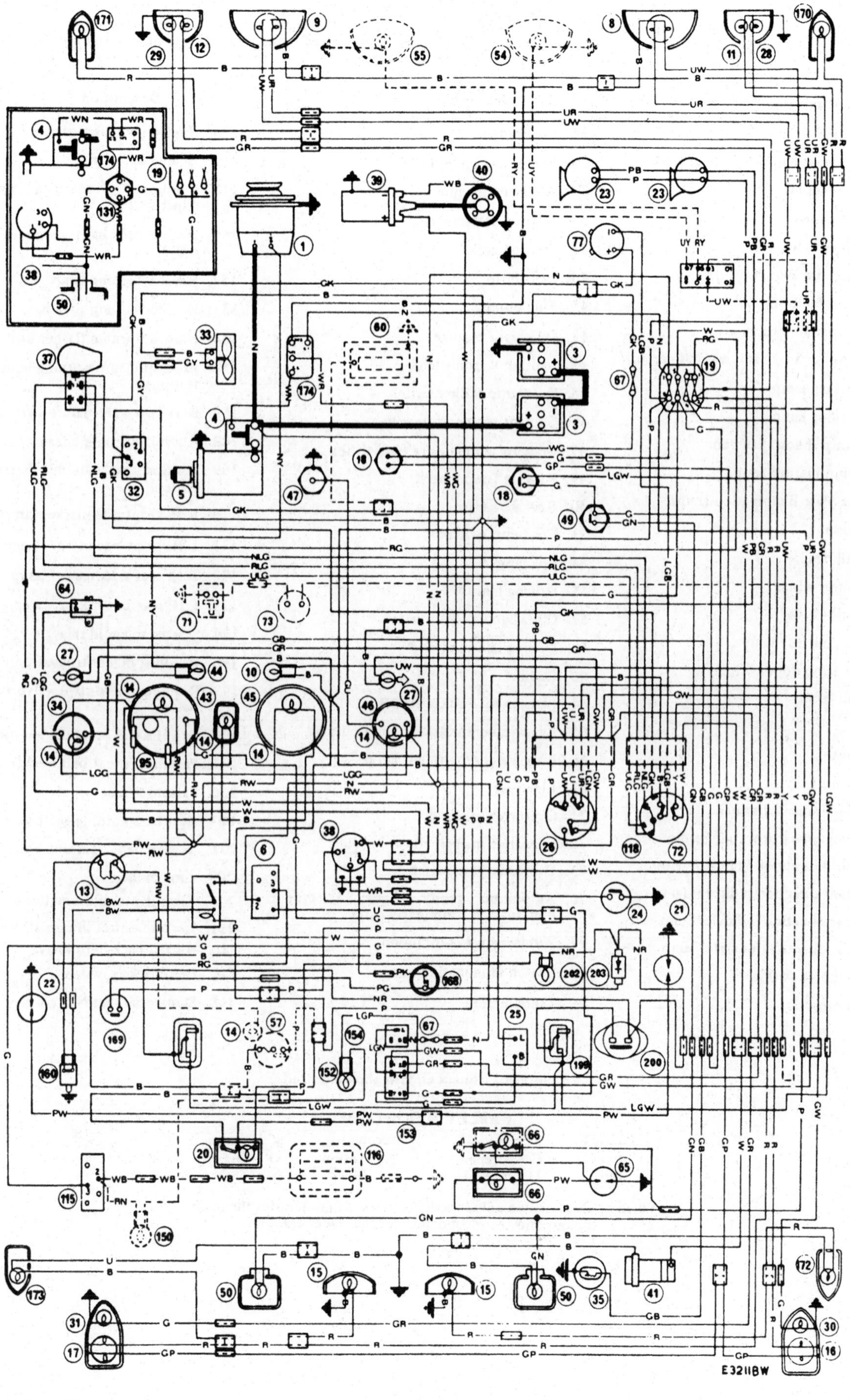

E3211BW

KEY TO THE WIRING DIAGRAMS – Nos. 14 onwards

(Refer to page Nb.2 for the key to diagrams Nos. 1 to 13)

Use this one key to identify components on the wiring diagrams from No. 14 onwards. Refer to the appropriate wiring diagram, and disregard any additional numbered items appearing in the key and not on a particular diagram.

No.	Description
1.	Alternator.
3.	Batteries (6-volt)/battery (12-volt).
4.	Starter solenoid.
5.	Starter motor.
6.	Lighting switch.
7.	Headlamp dip switch.
8.	Headlamp dip beam.
9.	Headlamp main beam.
10.	Headlamp main beam warning lamp
11.	R.H. parking lamp.
12.	L.H. parking lamp.
13.	Panel lamp rheostat switch.
14.	Panel illumination lamp.
15.	Number-plate illumination lamps.
16.	Stop lamp.
17.	R.H. tail lamp.
18.	Stop lamp switch.
19.	Fuse unit (4-way).
20.	Interior courtesy lamp.
21.	Interior lamp door switch.
22.	L.H. tail lamp.
23.	Horn.
24.	Horn-push.
25.	Flasher unit.
26.	Direction indicator switch.
27.	Direction indicator warning lamp.
28.	R.H. front direction indicator lamp.
29.	L.H. front direction indicator lamp.
30.	R.H. rear direction indicator lamp.
31.	L.H. rear direction indicator lamp.
32.	Heater motor switch.
33.	Heater motor.

No.	Description
34.	Fuel gauge.
35.	Fuel gauge tank unit.
37.	Windscreen wiper motor.
38.	Ignition/starter switch.
39.	Ignition coil.
40.	Distributor.
41.	Fuel pump.
43.	Oil pressure gauge.
44.	Ignition warning lamp.
45.	Headlamp flasher switch.
46.	Coolant temperature gauge.
47.	Coolant temperature transmitter.
49.	Reverse lamp switch.
50.	Reverse lamp.
53.	Fog lamp switch.*
54.	Fog lamp.*
55.	Driving lamp.*
57.	Cigar lighter–illuminated.*
58.	Driving lamp switch.*
60.	Radio.*
64.	Instrument voltage stabilizer.
65.	Luggage compartment lamp switch.
66.	Luggage compartment lamp.
67.	Line fuse.
71.	Overdrive solenoid.*
72.	Overdrive manual control switch.*
73.	Overdrive gear switch.*
76.	Automatic gearbox gear selector illumination lamp (early cars).
77.	Windscreen washer pump.
82.	Switch illumination lamp.
95.	Tachometer.

No.	Description
115.	Heated back-light switch* } GT only
116.	Heated back-light* } GT only
118.	Combined windscreen washer and wiper switch.
150.	Heated back-light warning lamp * (GT only).
152.	Hazard warning lamp.
153.	Hazard warning switch.
154.	Hazard warning flasher unit.
159.	Brake pressure warning lamp and lamp test-push.
160.	Brake pressure failure switch.
168.	Audible warning buzzer.
169.	Ignition key audible warning door switch.
170.	R.H. front side-marker lamp.
171.	L.H. front side-marker lamp.
172.	R.H. rear side-marker lamp.
173.	L.H. rear side-marker lamp.
174.	Starter solenoid relay.
196.	Running-on control valve.
197.	Running-on control valve oil pressure switch.
198.	Driver's seat belt buckle switch.
199.	Passenger's seat belt buckle switch.
200.	Passenger seat switch.
201.	Seat belt warning gearbox switch.
202.	'Fasten belts' warning light.
203.	Line diode.
208.	Cigar lighter illumination.
211.	Heater control illumination lamp.
240.	Heated back-light relay.
244.	Driver's seat switch.
245.	Sequential seat belt control unit.

* Optional fitment circuits shown dotted.

CABLE COLOUR CODE

N.	Brown.	P.	Purple.	W.	White	K.	Pink.
U.	Blue.	G.	Green.	Y.	Yellow	O.	Orange.
R.	Red.	LG.	Light Green.	B.	Black.	S.	Slate.

When a cable has two colour code letters the first denotes the main colour and the second denotes the tracer colour.

DIAGRAM 14

(Refer to page Nb.16 for the key)

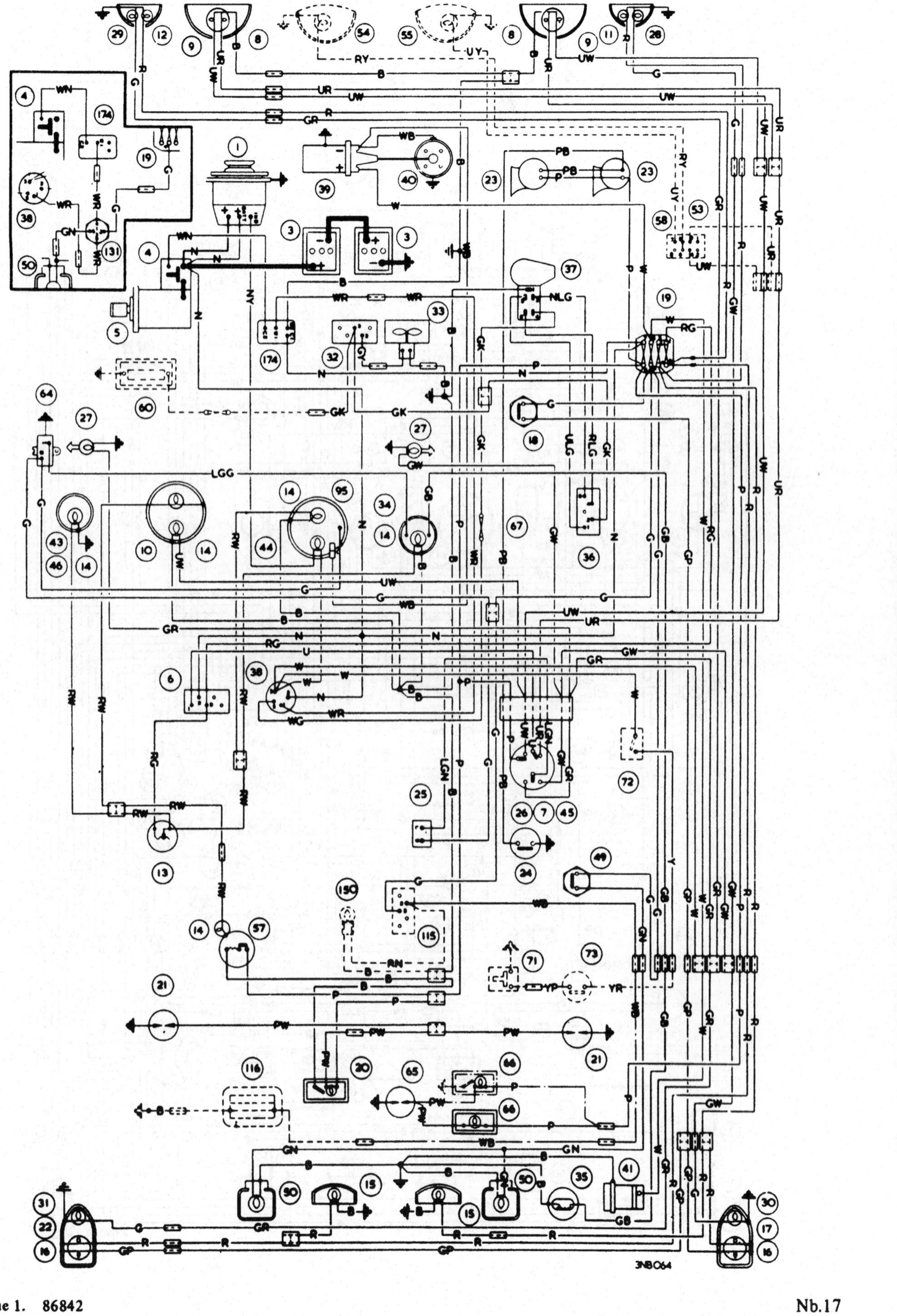

3NB064

DIAGRAM 15

(Refer to page Nb.16 for the key)

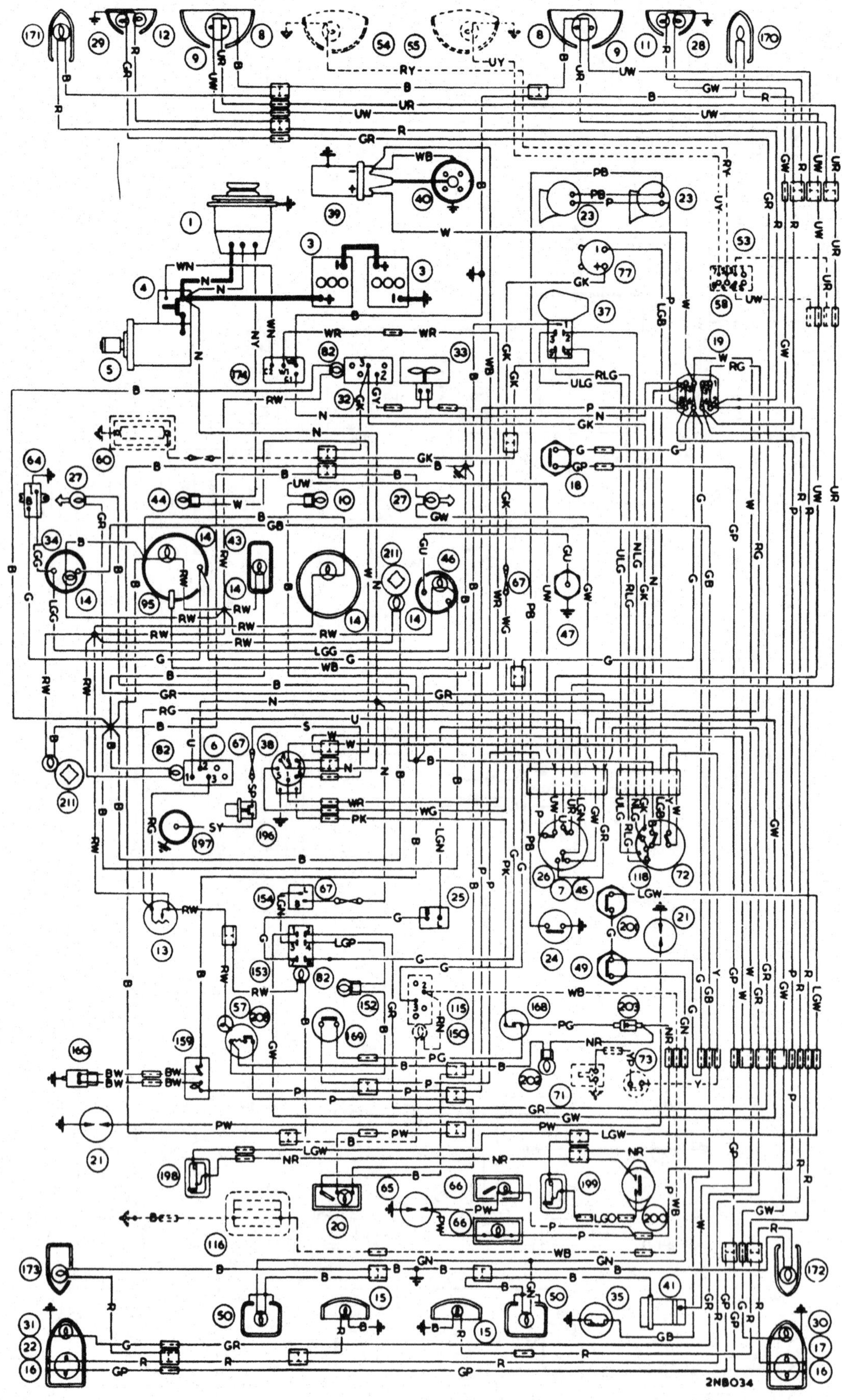

DIAGRAM 16

(Refer to page Nb.16 for the key)

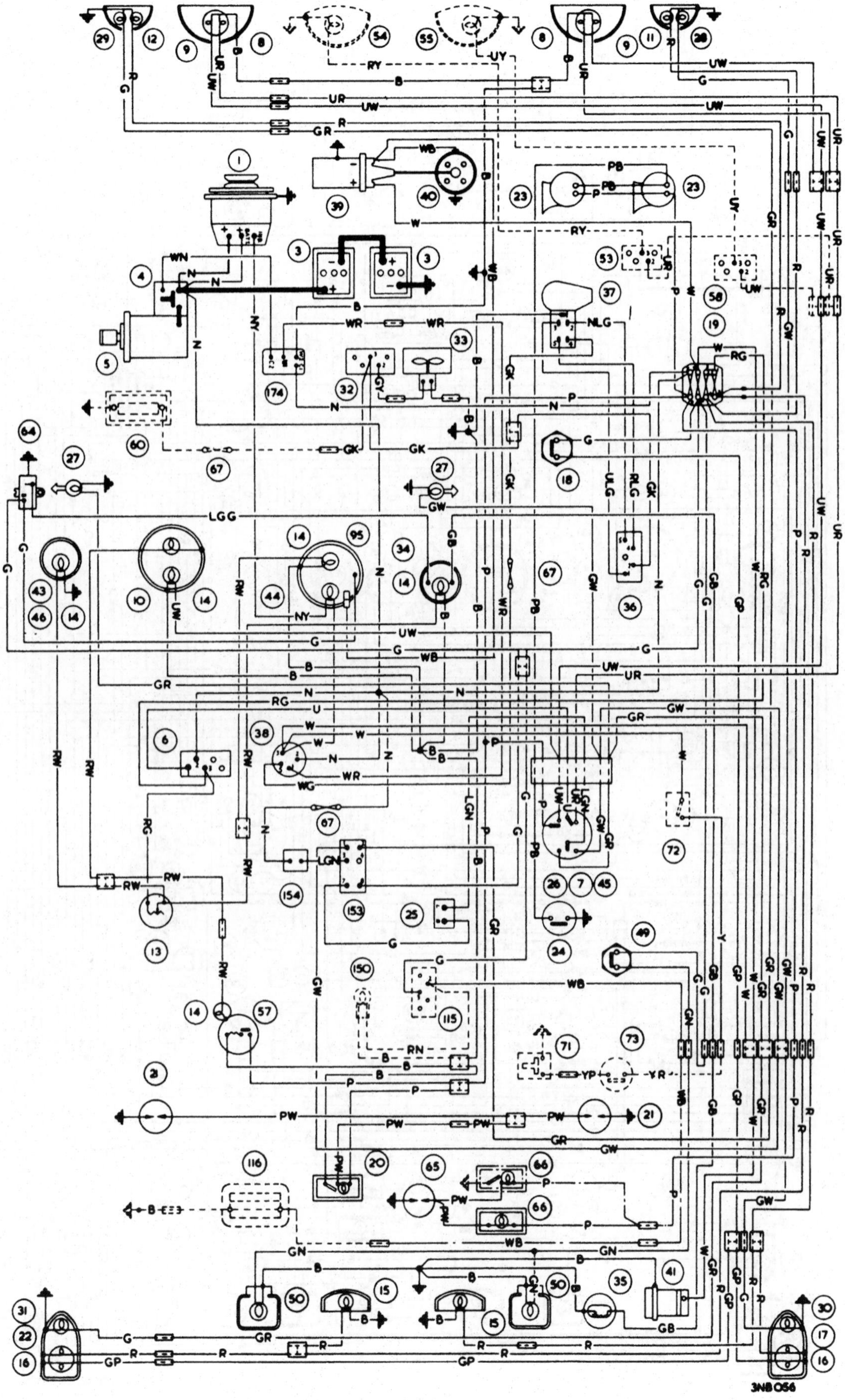

3NB056

DIAGRAM 17

(Refer to page Nb.16 for the key)

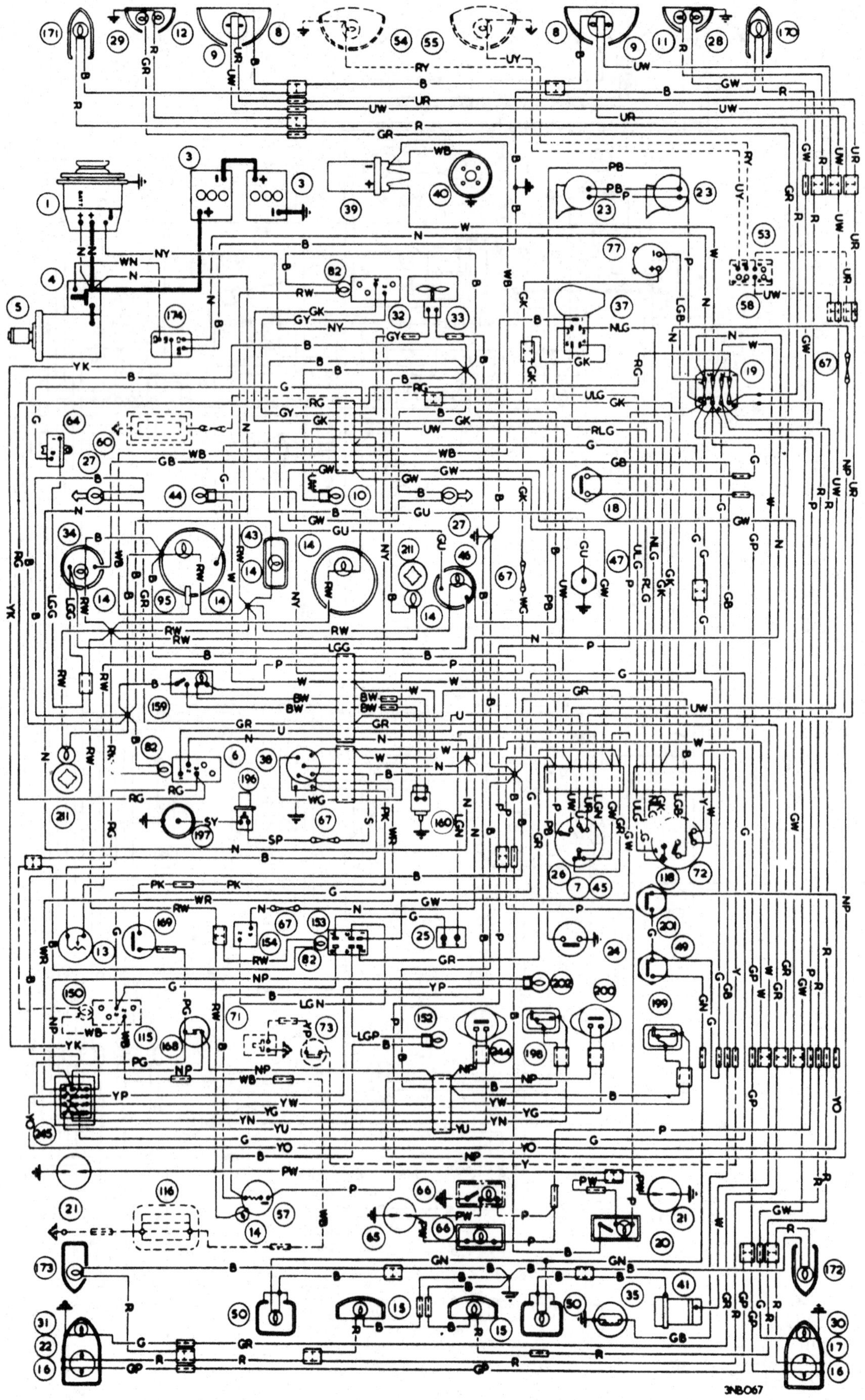

3NB067

DIAGRAM 18

(Refer to page Nb.16 for the key)

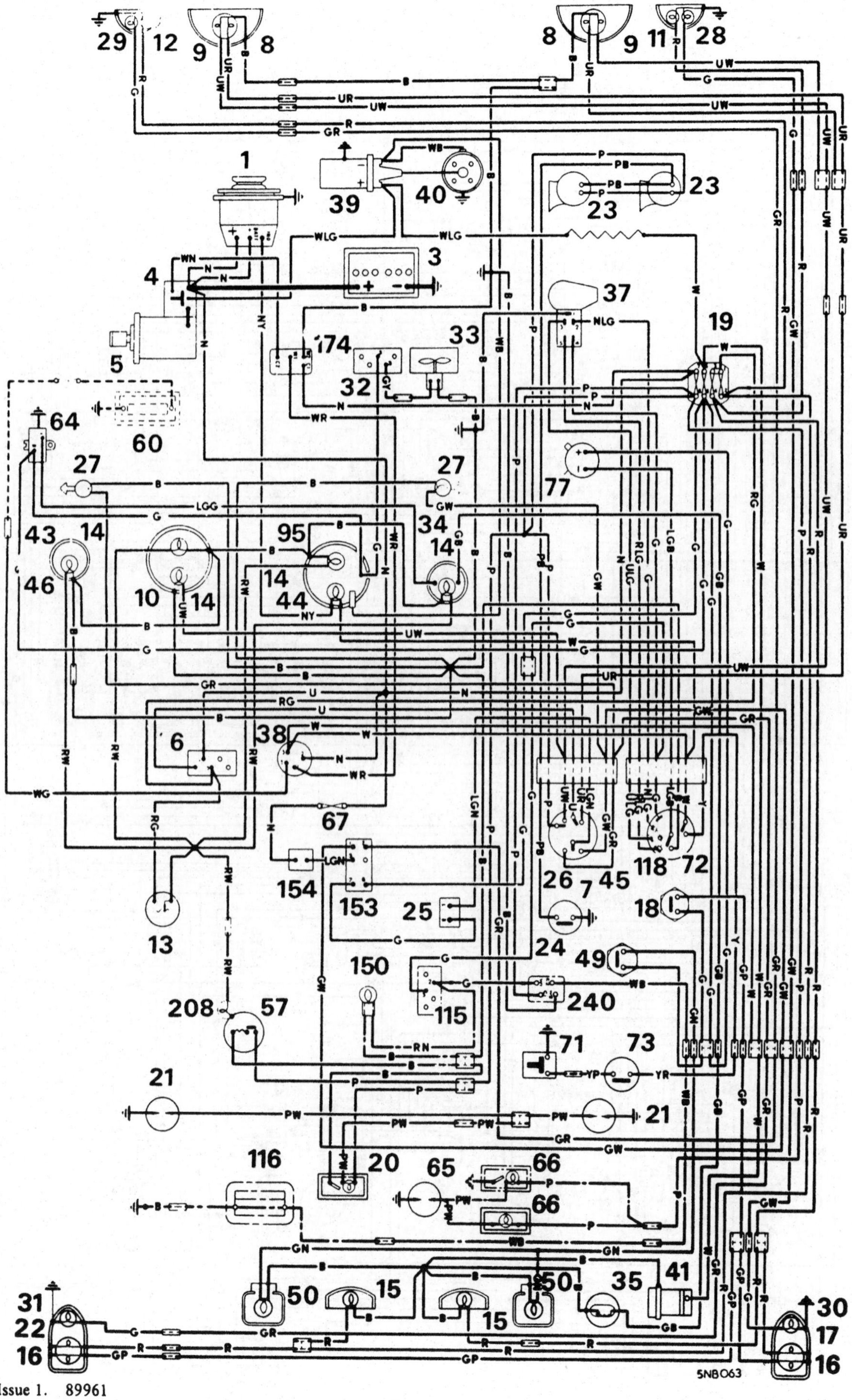

5NBO63

DIAGRAM 19

(Refer to the page opposite for the key)

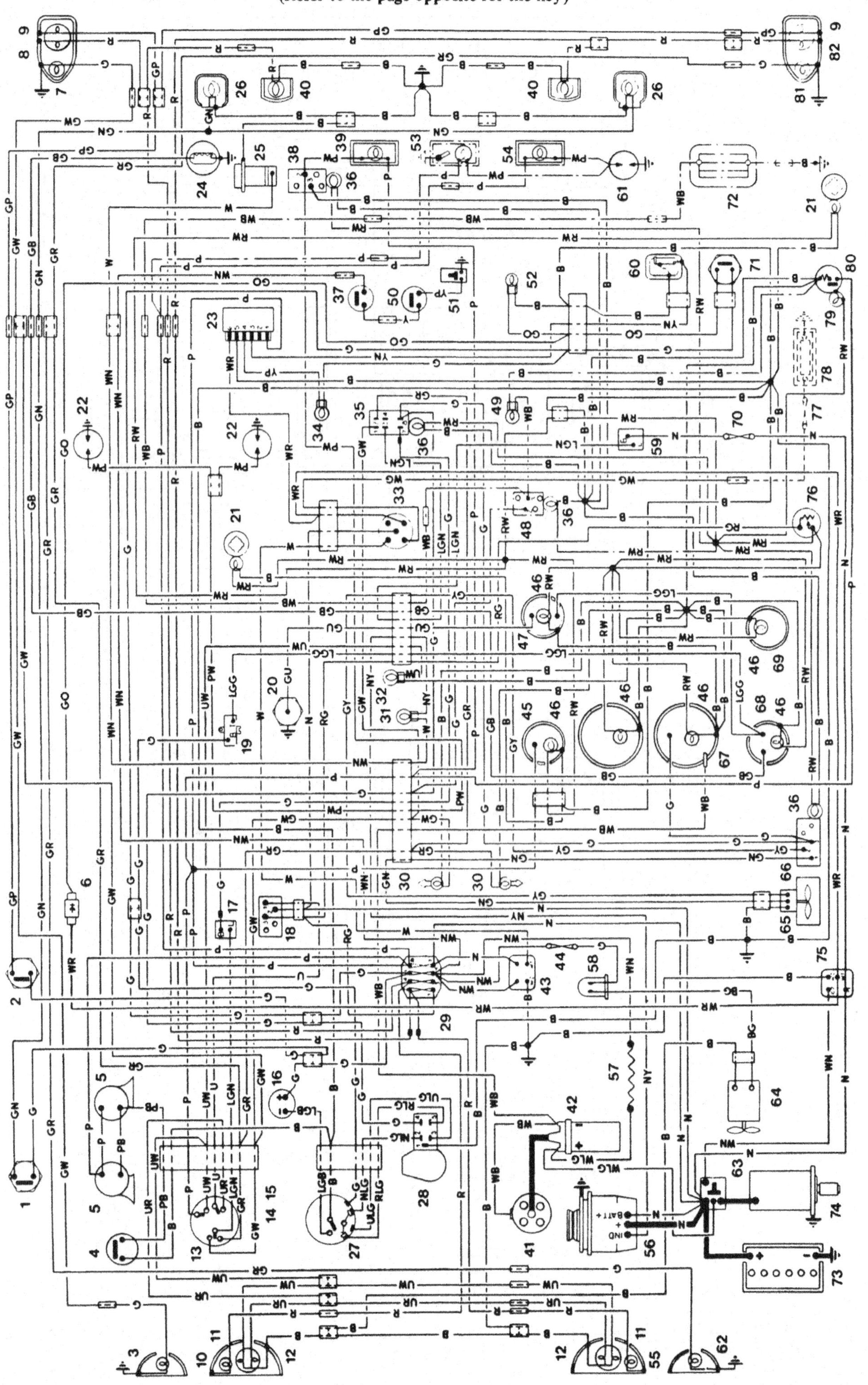

KEY TO THE WIRING DIAGRAM – 1977

Several of the components listed in this key may not be included in the specification of all models

1. Reverse lamp switch
2. Stop lamp switch
3. R.H. front direction indicator lamp
4. Horn-push
5. Horn
6. Diode for brake warning
7. R.H. rear direction indicator lamp
8. R.H. tail lamp
9. Stop lamp
10. R.H. parking lamp
11. Headlamp main beam
12. Headlamp low beam
13. Direction indicator switch
14. Headlamp dip switch
15. Headlamp flasher switch
16. Windscreen washer pump
17. Flasher unit
18. Lighting switch
19. Instrument voltage stabilizer
20. Coolant temperature gauge
21. Heater control illumination
22. Interior courtesy lamp door switch
23. Time delay unit
24. Fuel gauge tank unit
25. Fuel pump
26. Reverse lamp
27. Combined windscreen washer and wiper switch
28. Windscreen wiper motor
29. Fuse unit
30. Direction indicator warning lamp
31. Ignition warning lamp
32. Headlamp main beam warning lamp
33. Ignition starter switch
34. Seat belt warning lamp
35. Hazard warning switch
36. Switch illumination lamp
37. Overdrive manual control switch (if fitted)
38. Interior courtesy light switch
39. Interior courtesy light
40. Number-plate illumination lamp
41. Distributor
42. Ignition coil
43. Ignition switch relay
44. Line fuse for radiator cooling fan thermostat
45. Clock
46. Panel illumination lamp
47. Coolant temperature gauge
48. Heated rear window (GT)
49. Heated rear window warning light (GT)
50. Overdrive gear switch (if fitted)
51. Overdrive solenoid (if fitted)
52. Handbrake warning lamp
53. Luggage compartment lamp (GT)
54. Luggage compartment lamp (Tourer)
55. L.H. parking lamp
56. Alternator
57. Resistive cable
58. Radiator cooling fan thermostat
59. Hazard warning flasher unit
60. Driver's seat belt buckle switch
61. Luggage compartment lamp switch
62. L.H. front direction indicator lamp
63. Starter solenoid
64. Radiator cooling fan motor
65. Heater motor
66. Heater motor switch
67. Tachometer
68. Fuel gauge
69. Oil pressure gauge
70. Line fuse for hazard warning
71. Handbrake switch
72. Heated rear window (GT)
73. Battery
74. Starter motor
75. Starter solenoid relay
76. Panel lamp switch
77. Line fuse for radio*
78. Radio*
79. Cigar lighter illumination
80. Cigar lighter
81. L.H. rear flasher lamp
82. L.H. tail lamp

* Optional fitment circuits shown dotted

CABLE COLOUR CODE

N.	Brown	P.	Purple	W.	White	K.	Pink
U.	Blue	G.	Green	Y.	Yellow	O.	Orange
R.	Red	LG.	Light Green	B.	Black	S.	Slate

When a cable has two colour code letters the first denotes the main colour and the second denotes the tracer colour.

SECTION O

THE WHEELS AND TYPES

GENERAL DESCRIPTION

The wheels fitted as standard equipment are of the pressed-steel ventilated disc type having four-stud fixing holes.

A spare wheel complete is housed in the luggage compartment and is retained by a clamp plate and bolt.

The jack is a standard side-lift type and is also stowed in the luggage compartment when not in use.

Section O.1

MAINTENANCE

Attention should be paid to the following points with a view to obtaining the maximum mileage from the road wheels and tyres.

1. Change the positions of the tyres on the car at regular intervals.
2. Test the pressures of the tyres with an accurate pressure gauge. Restore any air lost. Inflate the spare wheel to the rear wheel pressure. It is not sufficient to make a visual examination of the tyres for correct inflation.
3. Keep the treads free of grit, flint, stones, or other foreign matter, and repair cuts as soon as they are found.
4. Clean the wheel rims and keep them free of rust. Repaint them when necessary.
5. Keep the brakes and clutch correctly adjusted as fierceness or uneven action from either of these units has a detrimental effect on tyre wear.
6. Suspect misalignment if rapid wear of the front tyres is noticed and correct the fault at once. See Section J for details of front wheel alignment.

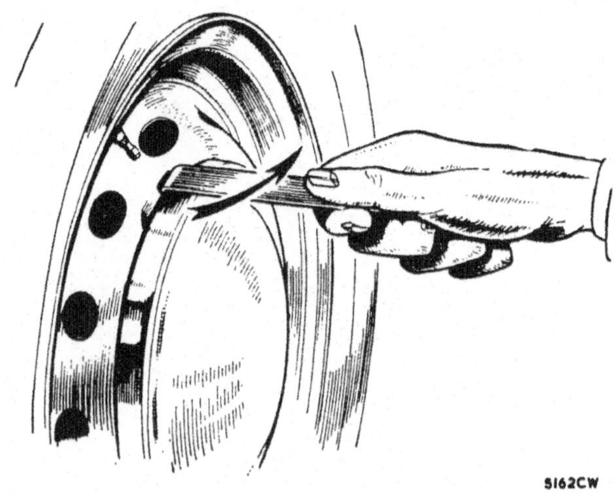

Fig. O.2
Removing the hub cap (disc wheels)

7. Remove oil or grease with petrol sparingly applied and wipe off immediately.
8. Avoid over- and under-inflation, kerbing, and other causes of severe impact.
9. Repair any damage immediately it is discovered and remove tyres before they have worn too far for remoulding.

Tyre replacement

Radial-ply tyres should only be fitted in sets of four, although in certain circumstances it is permissible to fit a pair on the rear wheels; tyres of different construction must not be used on the same axle. A pair must never be fitted to the front wheels with conventional tyres at the rear. The positional changing of wheels must not be undertaken if radial-ply tyres have been to fitted the rear wheels only.

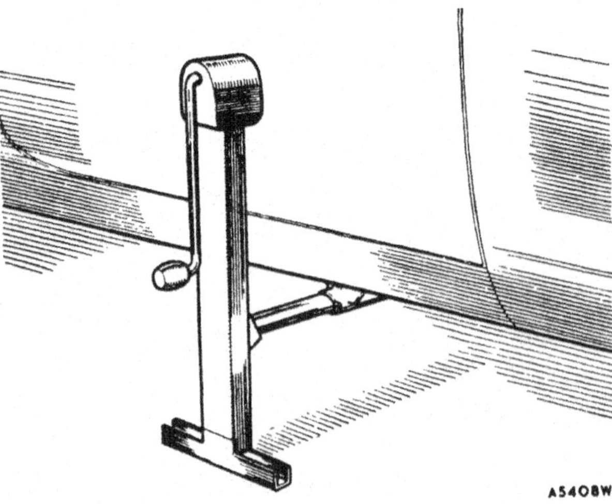

Fig. O.1
The side-lift jack

Section O.2

JACKING UP THE CAR

A jacking tube is fitted to each side ot the car under the floor panel approximately midway along the body. The jack will lift one side of the car and thus enable a front or rear wheel to be changed.

Before jacking up the car apply the hand brake and if the car is standing on an incline chock the wheels. Place the jack in the appropriate jacking tube so that the top of the jack leans slightly outwards to allow for radial movement of the body when the car is lifted.

Remove the hub cover and slacken the wheel nuts a turn or two before commencing to lift the car.

Operate the jack until the road wheels are clear of the ground.

After changing the wheel lower the car and remove and stow the jack.

Do not use the jack as a support for the car when carrying out servicing operations underneath the car.

Fig. O.3
Removing a road wheel (disc type)

Section O.3

REMOVING AND REPLACING ROAD WHEELS

Disc wheels

1. Insert the hub cover lever in the recess adjacent to the hub cover retaining studs and give it a sideways twist.
2. Remove the four nuts securing the road wheels to the hub. The wheel nuts have right-hand threads.
3. Lift the road wheel from the studs.

Reverse this procedure when replacing the road wheel and ensure that the nuts are refitted with their tapered side towards the wheel.

Tighten the nuts to a torque figure of between 60 and 62.5 lb. ft. (8.3 and 8.65 kg. m.). Do not overtighten.

To refit the hub disc place the rim of the disc over two of the buttons on the wheel centre and give the disc a sharp blow with the fist over the third button.

Wire wheels

Use a copper mallet to slacken the winged hub nut securing the wheel to the splines on the hub extension. The hub nuts on the left-hand side of the car have right-hand threads (unscrew anti-clockwise) and the nuts on the right-hand side of the car have left-hand threads (unscrew clockwise).

Section O.4

VALVES

Valve caps, in addition to preventing dirt from entering the valve, form a secondary air seal and should always be fitted. The valves may be tested for airtightness by rotating the wheel until the valve is at the top and inserting its end in an eggcup full of water. If bubbles appear the seating is faulty and should be removed and a new one fitted. It is advisable to change the valve interiors every 12 months.

Section O.5

TYRE REMOVAL

Remove all valve parts to deflate the tyre completely, and push both edges into the base of the rim at a point diametrically opposite the valve. Lever the cover edge, near the valve, over the rim of the wheel, using two levers at intervals of 6 in. (15 cm.) apart.

NOTE.–**Do not attempt to stretch the edges of the tyre cover over the rim edge.**

Force is entirely unnecessary and is detrimental, as it tends to damage the wired edges. Fitting or removing is quite easy if the tyre edges are carefully adjusted into the rim base; if found difficult, the operation is not being performed correctly.

Remove the tube carefully; do not pull on the valve. Stand the tyre and wheel upright, keeping the bead on the base of the rim. Lever the bead over the rim flange and at the same time push the wheel away from the cover with the other hand.

Section O.6

INSPECTION OF WHEELS AND TYRES

In addition to a visual examination a detailed inspection of wheels and tyres may be carried out where a specialist and the necessary specialist equipment is available for this purpose.

Disc wheels

1. Clean the wheel rim with a wire brush and remove all traces of corrosion.
2. Examine the rim and the welds or rivets securing the rim to the wheel centre. Damage to the rim may be repaired provided it is slight and is confined to the flange tip area.

Fig. O.4
Removing a road wheel (wire type)

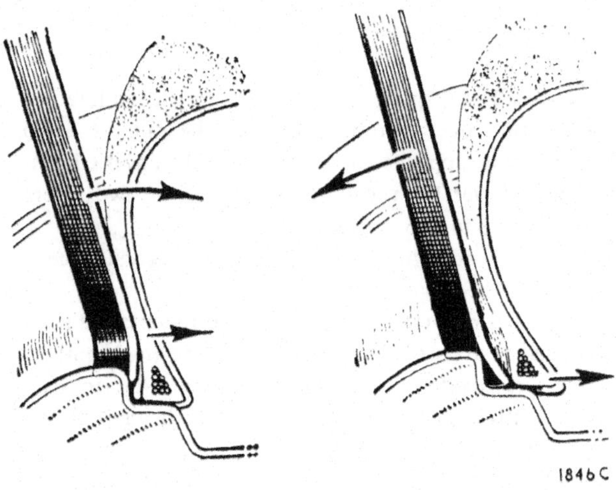

Fig. O.5
The tyres have wired edges and no attempt must be made to stretch them. If the cover fits tightly on the rim seating it should be freed by using the tyre levers as indicated

3. Inspect the wheel centre for flaws, cracks, or fractures.
4. Check the wheel wobble. This is the lateral variation measured on the inside vertical face of the flange and should not exceed 0.55 in. (1.4 mm.). An additional .015 in (.38 mm.) is permissible at the welded joint.
5. Check the wheel lift. This is the difference in height between the high and low points measured at any location on either tyre seat on a truly mounted and revolving wheel. The difference should not exceed .055 in. (1.4 mm.). An additional .015 in. (.38 mm.) is permissible at the welded joint.

Wire wheels

1. Examine the wheel as in 1 and 2 above.
2. Check the spokes and nipples for security and damage. Any unserviceable parts must be renewed.
3. Examine the splines in the wheel centre for wear. If the splines are worn renew the hub centre.

Tyres

Examine all tyres internally and externally for:

1. The degree and regularity of tread wear.
2. Cuts, penetrations, and impact bruises.
3. Kerb damage to walls and shoulders.
4. Oil and grease contamination.
5. Bead damage and chafing.

Section O.7

REPAIR OF TYRES AND TUBES

Minor injuries confined to the tread rubber, such as from small pieces of glass or road dressing material, require no attention other than the removal of the objects. Cold filling compound of 'stopping' is unnecessary in such cases.

More severe tread cuts and wall damage, particularly if they penetrate to the outer ply of the fabric casing, require vulcanized repairs. The Dunlop Spot Vulcanizing Unit is available for this purpose and it is also suitable for all types of tube repairs.

Injuries which extend into or through the casing, except clean nail holes, seriously weaken the tyre. Satisfactory repair necessitates new fabric being built in and vulcanized. This requires expensive plant and should be undertaken by a tyre repair specialist.

Loose gaiters and 'stick-in' fabric repair patches are not satisfactory substitutes for vulcanized repairs and should be used only as a temporary 'get-you-home' measure if the tyre has any appreciable tread remaining. They can often be used successfully in tyres which are nearly worn out and which are not worth the cost of vulcanized repairs.

Clean nail holes do not necessitate cover repairs. If a nail has penetrated the cover the hole should be sealed by a tube patch attached to the inside of the casing. This will protect the tube from possible chafing at that point.

If nail holes are not clean, and particularly if frayed or fractured cords are visible inside the tyre, expert advice should be sought.

Repairing tubes

Punctures or injuries must be vulcanized. Ordinary patches should only be used for emergencies and cannot be relied upon.

Section O.8

FITTING TYRES AND TUBES

Inspect the inside of the cover carefully and remove all dirt. The wheel rim must be clean, free from dust and undamaged.

In order to obtain good steering it is of importance to ensure that the wheels, with tyres fitted, are in good balance. To assist this, the tyre manufacturers are now

Fig. O.6
Push the cover bead into the well-base of the wheel as indicated by the arrow

marking their tyres with a white spot in the neighbourhood of the bead at the lightest point of the cover; similarly, they are marking the inner tubes with spots to indicate their heaviest point. When tyres are assembled care must therefore be taken to see that they are assembled with the spots on the cover coinciding with the spots on the tube.

It must be noted, in addition, that special balancing discs are fitted to the inside of the cover casing in some cases that these should on no account be removed as the tyre balance will be upset if this is done. These balance discs are not repair patches and do not indicate any fault in the tyre.

Dust the inside of the cover with french chalk. Inflate the tube until it begins to round out, then insert it in the cover. Apply a frothy solution of soap and water generously around the centre base of the **tube**, extending upwards between the tyre beads and the tube itself for at least 2 in. (50 mm.) on both sides. Also apply the sclution to the bottom and outside of the tyre beads. Do not allow the solution to run into the crown of the tyre. The solution must be strong enough to feel slippery when the fingers are wetted with the solution and rubbed together.

Mount the tyre on the rim immediately, whilst the soap solution is still wet.

Push one edge of the cover over the edge of the rim. It will go quite easily if the part first put on is fitted on the opposite side of the valve and is pushed right down into the rim base. Move it round so that its balance spots coincide with those of the inner tube when it is inserted with the valve passing through the hole in the rim. (Take care that the valve, fitted in the side of the tube, is on the correct side of the rim.).

Before inflating, be sure that the tyre beads are clear of the well of the rim all the way round and **push the valve into the tyre as far as possible in order to ensure the tube is not trapped between the bead and the rim, then pull it out again into its correct position.**

Inflate slowly until the beads are fully seated.

Fig. O.7
Lever the cover edge over the rim all round the wheel

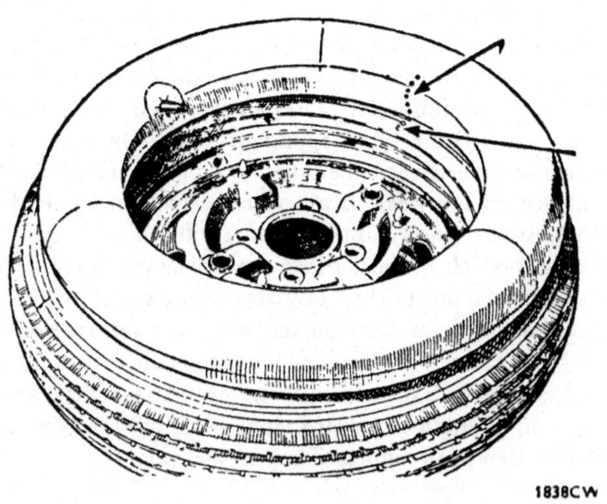

Fig. O.8
Balance marks on tyre and tube

Remove the valve core to **deflate the tube completely** to permit any stretched portions of the tube to readjust themselves in the cover and relieve any local strains in the tube.

Reinflate to the correct working pressure (see **'GENERAL DATA'**). This procedure must be followed whenever a tube is fitted.

Section O.9

WHEEL AND TYRE BALANCE

Unbalance in wheel and tyre assemblies may be responsible for various effects such as wheel wobble, abnormal wear of tyres and suspension parts, vibration in the steering or, in extreme cases, in the whole car. If any of these faults develop, for which no other cause can be found, wheel and tyre balance should be checked and corrected according to instructions supplied by the manufacturer of the balancing machine.

When wheels are to be re-balanced it is essential that the weight of the car be removed from the tyres as soon as possible after a run so that temporary flat spots do not form on the tyres. Nylon tyres are particularly prone to this and re-balancing with the tyres in this condition is pointless.

Section O.10

FACTORS AFFECTING TYRE LIFE

Inflation pressures

All other conditions being favourable there is an average loss of 13 per cent. tread mileage for every 10 per cent. reduction in inflation pressure below the recommended figure.

A tyre is designed so that there is a minimum pattern shuffle on the road surface and a suitable distribution of load over the tyre's contact area when deflection is correct. Moderate underinflation causes an increased rate of tread wear although the tyre's appearance may remain normal. Severe and persistent underinflation produces unmistakable evidence on the tread. It also causes structural failure due to excessive friction and temperature within the casing.
Pressures which are higher than those recommended for the car reduce comfort. They may also reduce tread life due to a concentration of the load and wear on a smaller area of tread, aggravated by increased wheel bounce on uneven road surfaces. Excessive pressures overstrain the casing cords, in addition to causing rapid wear, and the tyres are more susceptible to impact fractures and cuts.

Effect of temperature

Air expands with heating and tyre pressures increase as the tyres warm up. Pressures increase more in hot weather than in cold weather and as a result of high speed. These factors are taken into account when designing the tyre and in preparing Load Pressure schedules.
Pressures in warm tyres should not be reduced to standard pressure for cold tyres. 'Bleeding' the tyres increases their deflections and causes their temperatures to climb still higher. Their tyres will also be underinflated when they have cooled.

Climatic conditions

The rate of tread wear during a reasonably dry and warm summer can be twice as great as during an average winter. Water is a rubber lubricant and tread abrasion is much less on wet roads than on dry roads. In addition resistance of the tread to abrasion decreases with increase in temperature.
When a tyre is new its thickness and pattern depth are at their greatest. It follows that heat generation and pattern distortion due to flexing, cornering, driving, and braking are greater than when the tyre is part worn.
Higher tread mileages will usually be obtained if new tyres are fitted in the autumn or winter rather than in the spring or summer. This practice also tends to reduce the risk of road delays because tyres are more easily cut and penetrated when they are wet than when they are dry. It is, therefore, advantageous to have maximum tread thickness during wet seasons of the year.

Road surface

Present day roads generally have better non-skid surfaces than formerly. This factor, combined with improved car performance, has tended to cause faster tyre wear, although developments in tread compounds and patterns have done much to offset the full effects.
Road surfaces vary widely between one part of the country and another, often due to surfacing with local material. In some areas the surface dressing is coarser than others; the material may be comparatively harmless rounded gravel, or more abrasive crushed granite, or knife-edged flint. Examples of surfaces producing very slow tyre wear are smooth stone setts and wood blocks, but their non-skid properties are poor.
Bends and corners are severe on tyres because a car can be steered only by misaligning its wheels relative to the direction of the car. This condition applies to the rear tyres as well as the front tyres. The resulting tyre slip and distortion increase the rate of wear according to speed, load, road camber, and other factors.
The effect of hills, causing increased driving and braking torques with which the tyres must cope, needs no elaboration.

Impact fractures

In order to provide adequate strength, resistance to wear, stability, road grip, and other necessary qualities, a tyre has a certain thickness and stiffness. Excessive and sudden local distortion, such as may result from striking a kerb, a large stone or brick, an upstanding manhole cover, or a deep pothole, may fracture the casing cords.
Impact fractures often puzzle the car owner because the tyre and road spring may have absorbed the impact without his being aware of anything unusual. Only one or two casing cords may be fractured by the blow and the weakened tyre fails some time later. Generally, there is no clear evidence on the outside of the tyre unless the object has been sufficiently sharp to cut it.

Wheel alignment and road camber

It is very important that correct wheel alignment should be maintained. Misalignment causes a tyre tread to be scrubbed off laterally because the natural direction of the wheel differs from that of the car.
An upstanding fin on the edge of each pattern rib is a sure sign of misalignment and it is possible to determine from the position of the 'fins' whether the wheels are toed in or toed out. Fins on the inside edges of the pattern ribs--nearest to the car--and particularly on the off-side tyre, indicate toe-out.
With minor misalignment the evidence is less noticeable and sharp pattern edges may be caused by road camber even when wheel alignment is correct. In such cases it is better to make sure by checking with an alignment gauge.
Road camber affects the direction of the car by imposing a side thrust and if left to follow its natural course the car will drift to the near side. This is instinctively corrected by steering towards the road centre. As a result the car runs crab-wise.
The near front tyre sometimes persists in wearing faster and more unevenly than the other tyres even when the mechanical condition of the car and tyre maintenance are satisfactory. The more severe the average road camber the more marked will this tendancy be. This is an additional reason for the regular interchange of tyres.

Camber angle

This angle normally requires no attention unless disturbed

by a severe impact; however, it is always advisable to check this angle if steering irregularities develop.

Wheel camber usually combined with road camber, causes a wheel to try to turn in the direction of lean, due to one side of the tread attempting to make more revolutions per mile than the other side. The resulting increased tread shuffle on the road and the off-centre tyre loading tend to cause rapid and one-sided wear. If wheel camber is excessive for any reason the rapid and one-sided tyre wear will be correspondingly greater. Unequal cambers introduce unbalanced forces which try to steer the car one way or the other. This must be countered by steering in the opposite direction which results in faster tread wear.

Section O.11

HIGH-SPEED TYRE PRESSURE CONDITIONS

During high-speed driving and in competition work, the tyres are subjected to greater stresses than those produced during ordinary driving.

Many factors, some probably as important as the physical characteristics of the tyre itself, affect the speed at which it should be driven: road surface, air temperature, and in particular the duration of high-speed driving. However, a normal tyre in good condition and at the correct pressure can be relied upon to perform satisfactorily at speeds up to 80 m.p.h. (144 km.p.h.) and intermittently in excess of this by 10 m.p.h. (18 km.p.h.). If the car is to be driven consistently at speeds near the maximum of which it is capable special tyres should be fitted on the advice of the tyre manufacturers.

When it is intended to indulge in high speeds or competition work we advise the use of first tread tyres.

SECTION R

THE BODY

Section R.1

FRONT GRILLE

Removing

Unscrew the three screws securing the steady brackets. Remove the three hexagon-headed screws securing the bottom of the grille. Remove the motif, steady brackets, and the rubber buffers.

GHN5 and GHD5 cars

1. Remove the three screws in the bonnet lock platform, and the two self-tapping screws securing the grille outer surround to the body.
2. Prise out the three rubber body plugs and remove the three screws securing the bottom of the grille to the radiator duct panel.

Section R.2

BONNET AND BONNET LOCK

Removing

The bonnet is of light-alloy material. Mark the hinges, support it in the open position and remove the two nuts, washers, and screws that secure each hinge to the bonnet. Disengage the stay and lift the bonnet from the car.

Slacken the nut from the bonnet lock pin and withdraw the pin, thimble, and spring. Remove the three screws securing the safety catch to the bonnet and detach the safety catch. From the bonnet lock platform remove the two screws securing the safety catch bracket and take off the bracket. Release the bonnet lock control cable clamp screw and pull the cable from the bonnet lock plate. Unscrew the three screws securing the locating cup and bonnet lock to the platform and remove the cup and lock.

Refitting

Refitting is a reversal of the removal sequence, but ensure that the bonnet lock, safety catch, and the bonnet are correctly aligned before finally tightening the securing screws. After assembly adjust the latch pin to obtain ease of closing, lubricate the lock, catch, hinges and check them for correct operation.

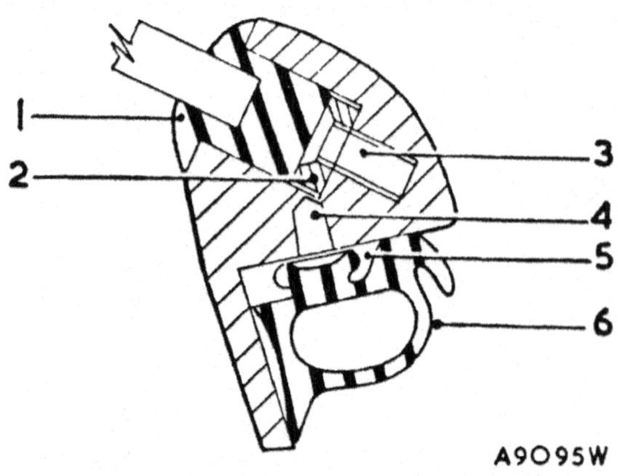

Fig. R.1
A section through a windscreen pillar, showing:

1. Glazing rubber.
2. Bottom reinforcement.
3. Screw–reinforcement to pillar.
4. Rivet–seal retainer.
5. Seal retainer.
6. Seal.

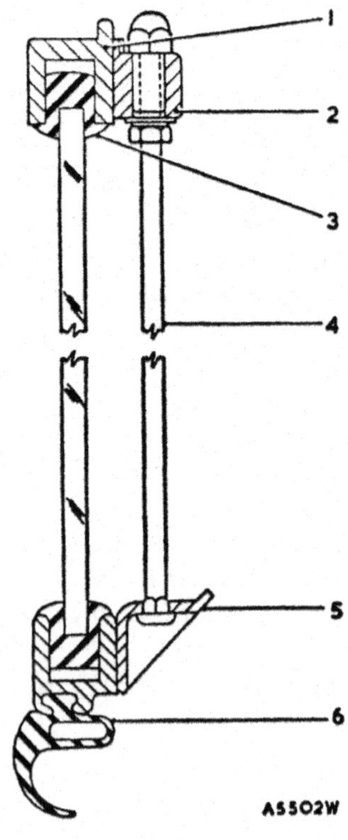

Fig. R.2
A section through the windscreen showing:

1. Top rail.
2. Centre rod upper bracket.
3. Glazing rubber.
4. Centre rod.
5. Bottom bracket.
6. Seal.

Section R.3

WINDSCREEN (Tourer)

Removing

Unscrew the two screws securing the lower centre rod bracket to the body. Remove the fascia panel (Section R.20) to gain the access to the windscreen securing bolts, and then remove the bolts. Lift the windscreen from the car.

Dismantling

Remove the dome nut from the centre rod, draw the rod through the upper bracket, remove the plain washer, spring washer, and nut, and then withdraw the rod from the bottom bracket.

Remove the bottom rail sealing rubber and the two screws securing each corner of the bottom rail to the lower reinforcement pieces. Remove the three screws securing each end of the top rail to the pillars. Gently ease the two side pillars from the top and bottom rails and the rails from the windscreen glass.

Reassembling

Fit the glazing rubber to the screen and then mark the centre of the glass with a wax crayon to align it with the centre of the top and bottom rails. Fit the top and bottom rails and ensure that the centres of the brackets are accurately aligned with the centre-line of the glass screen. Retain the rails in this position by means of a clamp lightly applied or by temporarily assembling the centre rod.

Starting at the bottom of the pillar, carefully tap it into place with the palm of the hand, working alternately from bottom to top. When both pillars have been correctly located refit the securing screws and the lower sealing rubber.
Assemble the centre rod and ensure that the dome nut is not overtightened.

Refitting
The foot of each pillar is supported in the body by a metal and a fibre packing piece. The packing pieces are screwed to the side of the body and should not normally be removed. If a new windscreen is being fitted or extensive body repairs carried out, check the fit of the windscreen by fitting it to the car and checking the clearance between the body and the foot of each pillar. Adjust the fit by inserting or removing the $\frac{3}{32}$ in. (2.38 mm.) fibre packing pieces.
Place the bottom bracket packing piece on the body and the sealing grommets on the windscreen pillars. Fit the windscreen to the body and align the holes in the pillar feet with the packing pieces. Place a special washer on each of the four bolts and screw the bolts through the packing pieces and into the pillars. Spread the bottom rail sealing rubber, secure the centre rod bottom bracket to the body, and finally tighten the windscreen pillar securing bolts. Close the doors and check the fit of the ventilator window against the pillar sealing rubbers.

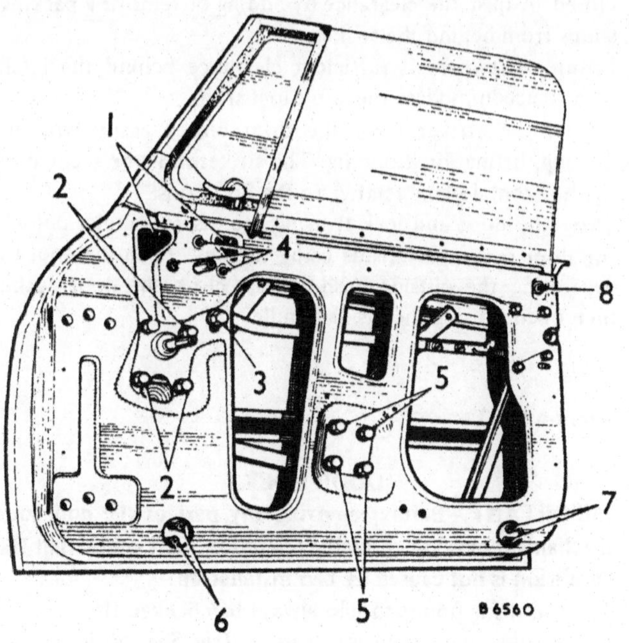

Fig. R.3
The door assembly (early tourer models)

1. Ventilator securing nuts.
2. Regulator securing set screws.
3. Regulator arm stop.
4. Door lock remote control securing screws.
5. Regulator extension securing set screws.
6. Front door glass mounting bracket securing screws.
7. Rear door glass mounting bracket securing screws.
8. Door glass channel securing screws.

Section R.4

DOOR TRIM PAD

Removing
Remove the inner door handle, door pull, and window regulator handle (Section R.8). Remove the waist rail securing screws and the screws securing the trim pad to the door panel. Lift off the waist rail and trim pad. If necessary, remove the inside trim liner which is secured to the door panel with an adhesive.

TOURER (EARLY MODELS)
Remove the inner door handle door pull and window regulator handle (Section R.8). Remove the locking knob from the passenger door. Remove the drive screws securing the trim pad and the ends of the waist rail to the door panel. Lift off the trim pad to expose the centre screw of the waist rail which may now be removed together with the rail. If necessary remove the inside trim liner which is secured to the door panel with an adhesive.

Refitting
Reverse the removal sequence.

Section R.5

VENTILATORS

Removing
Remove the inner door handle, door pull, and window regulator handle (Section R.8). Remove the door trim pad and door glass assembly (Sections R.4 and R.6). Remove the set screws and nuts securing the ventilator top to the door. Remove the ventilator steady set screws and the set screws securing the front door glass channel to the bottom of the door. Lift out the ventilator assembly.

TOURER (EARLY MODELS)
Remove the inner door handle, door pull and window regulator handle (Section R.8). Remove the door trim pad assembly (Section R.4.). Release the lower end of the door glass front channel from its fixing bracket on the door. Remove the screws adjacent to the ventilator sleeve nuts and remove the sleeve nuts. Wind the door glass to its lowest position and remove the ventilator from the door.

Refitting
Reverse the removing procedure.

Section R.6

DOOR GLASS

Removing
Remove the inner door handle, door pull, and window regulator handle (Section R.8). Remove the door trim pad (Section R.4). Remove the regulator securing screws and the regulator extension securing screws. Release the window regulator arc from the bottom of the door glass, lift the door glass up to clear the regulator and remove the regulator and extension assembly through the door panel aperture. Remove the nut securing the door glass rear guide channel to the door. Lift out the door glass.

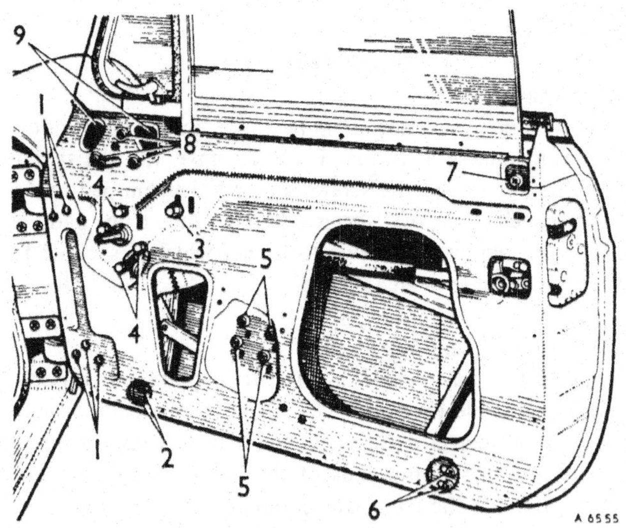

Fig. R.4
The door assembly (later models)

1. Door hinge securing set screws.
2. Front door glass mounting bracket securing screws.
3. Regulator arm stop.
4. Regulator securing set screws.
5. Regulator extension securing set screws.
6. Rear door glass mounting bracket securing screw.
7. Door glass channel securing screws.
8. Door lock remote control securing screws.
9. Ventilator securing nuts.

TOURER (EARLY MODELS)
Remove the inner door handle, door pull, and window regulator handle (Section R.8). Remove the door trim pad (Section R.4). Remove the door glass rear channel top and bottom fixings with the glass in the upper position. Release the regulator and the regulator extension and slide the arms forward to disengage the studs from the door glass bottom channel, lift the glass from the door.

Refitting
Reverse the removing procedure.

Section R.7

DOOR GLASS REGULATORS

Removing
Remove the inner door handle, door pull, and window regulator handle (Section R.8). Remove the door trim pad (Section R.4). Remove the regulator securing screws and the regulator extension securing screws. Release the window regulator arc from the bottom of the door glass, lift the door glass up to clear the regulator and remove the regulator and extension assembly through the door panel aperture.

Refitting
Reverse the removal procedure.

Section R.8

WINDOW REGULATORS AND INTERIOR DOOR HANDLES

Removing
Remove the centre screw, spring and washer and pull off the handle and finisher.
Remove the two screws securing the door pull to the door assemblies and lift off the door pull.
Remove the centre screw securing the locking knob on the passenger door (early touring models).

Refitting
Reverse the removal procedure.

Section R.9

STRIKERS

Removing
Mark the position of the striker on the door pillar to assist when refitting. Remove the set screws securing the striker to the door pillar and lift away the assembly together with the packing pieces.

Refitting
Reverse the removal procedure, and adjust as necessary.

Checking and adjusting
Check that a clearance of $\frac{1}{32}$ in. (1 mm.) to $\frac{1}{16}$ in. (1.6 mm.) exists between the striker and lock face when the door is closed. Adjust the clearance by adding or removing packing shims from behind the striker.
Ensure that there is sufficient clearance behind the latch cam to accommodate the anti-burst strap.
Adjust the striker until the door closes easily without rattling, lifting, or dropping. The striker must be secured in the horizontal plane relative to the door axis.
Close the door and lock it using the inside handle, unlock the door from the outside using the key, open the door by depressing the outside push-button, close the door again, then open it using the inside handle.

Section R.10

DOOR LOCKS

IMPORTANT.–Before removing any part of the door lock mechanism because of faulty operation, first check that the condition is not caused by bad installation.
The following points should always be checked first.

a. Striker and latch cam clearance (see Section R.9).
b. Remote-control adjustment (see Section R.11).
c. Outer door handle plunger clearance (see Section R.12).

Removing
Remove the inner door handle, door pull, and window regulator handle (Section R.8). Remove the door trim pad (Section R.4).

Remove the 'C' clip retaining the remote control link to the door lock and detach the link. Remove the screws securing the lock to the door and withdraw the lock assembly.

TOURER (EARLY MODELS)
Remove the inner door handle, door pull, and window regulator handle (Section R.8). Remove the door trim pad and door glass assembly (Sections R.4 and R.6).
Disconnect the remote-control link by unscrewing the two screws, remove the three screws securing the remote-control mechanism to the door, and withdraw the mechanism from the rear access panel.
Remove the two screws securing the outer door handle, disengage the handle from the lock, and remove it from the door. From inside the door panel slide the retaining clip from the barrel of the private lock and withdraw the lock barrel and the coupling link from the outside of the door. Remove the four screws securing the lock to the door and withdraw the lock.

Refitting
Reverse the removing operations, noting that the latch must be in the open position when refitting the lock to the door, and that the locking lever must be engaged with the private lock operating fork. Check for correct functioning (Secttion R.9).

Tourer (early models)
Reverse the removal sequence. Elongated holes in the door panel will allow the remote-control mechanism to be correctly adjusted. After refitting lubricate the lock assembly and check it for correct functioning.

Section R.11

DOOR LOCK REMOTE CONTROL UNIT
(Later Models and GT)

Removing
Remove the inner door handle, door pull, and window regulator handle (Section R.8). Remove the trim pad (Section R.4). Detach the remote control link from the door lock by removing the 'C' retaining clip.
Remove the screws securing the remote control unit to the door.
Remove the moulded rubber hood covering the upper end of the window run channel, from the top of the front quarter-light.
Remove the nut securing the window regulator upper limit stop and remove the stop. Wind the window up until the lifting studs can be disengaged from the lifting channel.
Remove the screws securing the lower end of the front window run channel. Retain the glass in the up position with wedges or remove it from the door.
Remove the window regulator securing screws. Press the window regulator and front window run channel away from the inner door panel and withdraw the remote control unit

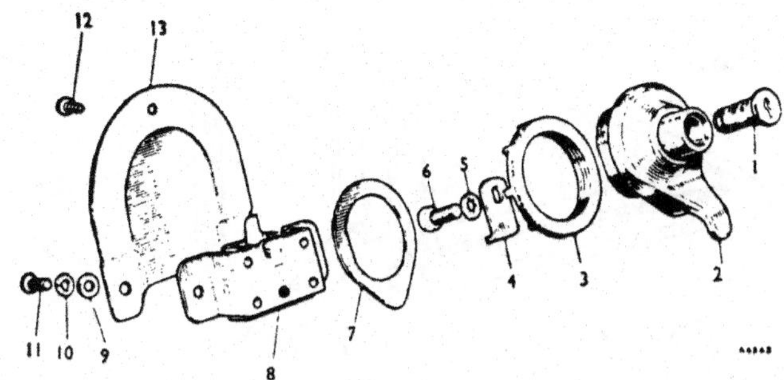

Fig. R.5
The luggage compartment lock

1. Lock barrel.
2. Push-button assembly.
3. Nut.
4. Operating lever.
5. Washer.
6. Set screw.
7. Seating washer.
8. Latch lock.
9. Plain washer.
10. Spring washer.
11. Set screw.
12. Screw. } GT only.
13. Latch cover. } GT only.

down between the window regulator and inner door panel, and the out of the door through the large aperture in the inner door panel.

Refitting
Reverse the removing sequence, noting that elongated holes in the inner door panel allow the remote control unit to be correctly adjusted with the spring loaded lever of the remote control link just contacting the spring.

Section R.12

OUTER DOOR HANDLES

Removing
Remove the inner door handle, door pull, and window regulator handle (Section R.8). Remove the trim pad (Section R.4). With the door glass in the fully up position remove the nuts and washers securing the door handle to the door and lift off the handle.

TOURER (EARLY MODELS)
Remove the door panel-to door handle securing set screws and lift away the outer handle.

Refitting
Reverse the removing procedure, noting the following. A minimum clearance of $\frac{1}{32}$ in. (1 mm.) must be maintained between the push-button plunger bolt and the lock contactor. Adjust the clearance by turning the plunger bolt in the required direction, after slackening the locknut. Retighten the locknut when the correct clearance has been obtained.

Section R.13

PRIVATE LOCK (Later Models and GT)

Removing
Close the window and remove the inner door handle, door pull, and window regulator handle (Section R.8). Remove the trim pad (Section R.4).

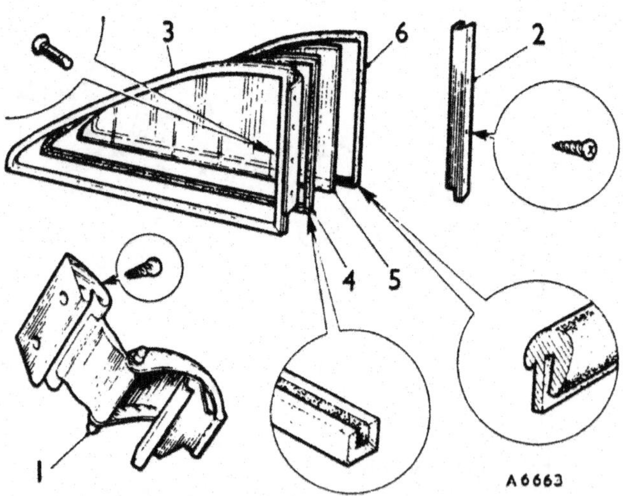

Fig. R.6
The rear quarter-light (GT only)

1. Toggle catch.
2. Hinge.
3. Frame.
4. Glazing rubber.
5. Glass.
6. Sealing rubber.

From inside the door, compress the legs of the retainer spring collar and withdraw the lock barrel from the outside of the door.

Refitting
Ensure that the spring collar is in place on the lock barrel, enter the lock barrel into the door aperture with its operating fork inclined away from the door shut face, and press the lock barrel firmly into position.

Section R.14

SEATS

Removing (front)
Release the seat catch and push the seat fully back to gain access to the front screws. Remove the screws and push the seat fully forward; remove the rear screws and lift the seat and seat runners from the car. Slide the seat from its runners. Retain the wooden strips and spacers.

Rear (GT)
Unlock the seat squab and move it forward to a horizontal position. Lift the luggage compartment floor carpet and remove the screws securing the hinges to the luggage compartment floor. Lift away the seat assembly.

Refitting
Refitting is a reversal of the removal sequence. Before finally tightening the front seat runners check the seats for ease of movement and correct alignment.

Section R.15

LUGGAGE COMPARTMENT LOCK

Do not in any circumstances close the luggage compartment lid when the lock mechanism is in the process of being removed or refitted.

Removing
Remove the lock cover (GT only). Remove the set screw securing the lock assembly to the luggage compartment lid. Remove the notched locking ring and withdraw the push-button and lock assembly.

Refitting
Reverse the removal procedure.

Section R.16

LUGGAGE COMPARTMENT LID

Removing
TOURER
Retain the lid in the open position with the stay and mark the hinges to assist when refitting. Remove the lid to hinge securing screws, detach the stay and lift the lid from the body.

GT
Retain the lid in the open position and mark the hinges to assist when refitting. Take the weight of the lid and remove the hinge securing screws. Remove the set screws securing the lift assisting springs to the body and lift away the lid.

Refitting
Refitting is a reversal of the removal procedure. Check the lid for fit to the body and check the operation of the latch before finally tightening the hinge to lid securing screws.

Section R.17

REAR QUARTER-LIGHT (GT)

Removing
Remove the finisher securing screws. Remove the screws securing the toggle catch to the body. Remove the hinge securing screw and lift away the assembly.

Refitting
Reverse the removal procedure.

Section R.18

DOORS AND HINGES

Removing
Remove the inner door handle, door pull, and window regulator handle (Section R.8). Remove the door trim pad (Section R.4).
Remove the set screws securing the hinge to the door and lift away the door.
To remove the hinge; from the underside of the front wing remove the six screws securing the splash panel to the body and remove the panel to gain access to the hinge bracket nuts; remove the nuts.

Unscrew the four screws securing the hinge bracket to the body and remove the hinge and bracket assembly.

Refitting
Refitting is a reversal of the removal sequence, but before finally tightening the hinge leaf screws ensure that the door lock engages correctly and that the door is correctly positioned with the body.

Section R.19

WINDSCREEN AND BACK-LIGHT GLASSES (GT)

Removing
Lift the windscreen wiper arms clear of the glass.
Remove the finisher strip.
Prise up the end of the locking filler and carefully pull it from the channel in the surround rubber.
Press the glass from inside the car, commencing at a corner, and ease the surround rubber from the metal edge of the body aperture.

Refitting
If the glass has been broken, remove any pieces which remain in the channel. Examine the rubber, and use a new rubber should there be any signs of damage or deterioration.
Fit the surround rubber to the body aperture and lubricate the 'glass' channel with a soap-and-water solution.
Place the glass into the lower channel of the rubber surround and commence at the corner to lift the lip of the rubber over the glass, using Service tool 18G 468. Use the short peg on the handle of the installation tool for this purpose.
Apply a soap-and-water solution to the locking filler strip channel to assist in fitting the strip.
Using Service tool 18G 468 with adaptor 18G 468 A, thread the end of the filler strip through the eye of the adaptor and under the roller. Lay the filler strip in position

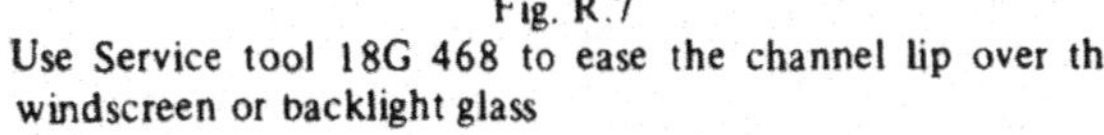

Fig. R.7
Use Service tool 18G 468 to ease the channel lip over the windscreen or backlight glass

Fig. R.8
The use of the glazing tool and eye to thread the locking filler strip into the rubber channel

over the groove in the surround rubber. Insert the eye of the tool in the filler strip groove, hold the filler strip in position, and commence to push the tool along the groove, rolling the strip into position. A slight side-to-side action will assist when rounding the corners.
After completing the circuit cut off any surplus strip to make a neat butt joint at the centre-line of the glass. Ensure that the filler strip is fitted with its thicker section facing towards the glass of the windscreen.
NOTE.–In the event of windscreen breakage, minute particles of glass fall into the windscreen demister ducts and tubes. When the blower motor is switched on these particles are discharged into the driver's or passenger's face. The demister ducts and tubing must be disconnected from the heater box and blown out before the new windscreen glass is fitted.

Section R.20

FASCIA PANEL, INSTRUMENTS, AND CONTROLS

Removing
Disconnect the battery, drain the cooling system, and remove the temperature gauge capillary capsule from the cylinder head.
Remove the speaker panel surround.
Release the steering-column upper fixing bracket and lower the steering-column.
Disconnect the choke cable from the air cleaner bracket, unscrew the outer cable fixing nut behind the fascia, and withdraw the choke cable complete.
Depress the plunger in each heater control knob and withdraw the knobs. Unscrew the heater control securing nuts and detach the controls from the rear of the fascia panel.
Unscrew the bezel nut securing the windscreen washer plunger and withdraw the plunger from the rear of the fascia.
Disconnect the oil pressure gauge pipe union.

Remove the nuts and washers securing the top of the fascia to the body, the screw and nut securing the steady bracket to the glovebox attachment, and the two screws securing the bottom centre of the panel to the speaker panel. Retain the weld nut assembly.

Pull the fascia forward and disconnect the speedometer and revolution indicator drives.

Pull the panel and warning lamps from their housings and disconnect the electrical connections from the switches and the fuel gauge.

Thread the temperature gauge capillary through the bulkhead and lift the fascia panel from the car.

Release the fixing straps on the oil pressure and temperature gauge, speedometer, revolution indicator, and fuel gauge and remove the instruments from the panel.

Using Service tool 18G 670 and 18G 671, unscrew the bezel nuts from the ignition and the toggle switches and withdraw the switches from the panel.

Unscrew the two screws securing the map-reading lamp and remove the lamp.

Depress the plunger in the panel lamp and map-reading lamp switches and remove the knobs, locknuts, and switches.

Refitting

Refitting of the panel is a reversal of the removal sequence, but refer to the wiring diagrams before making the electrical connections.

After refitting the panel reconnect the batteries and refill the cooling system. Test all switches and controls.

Section R.21

BODY ALIGNMENT

To check the body alignment of a car which has been damaged when the correct jig is not available, a system of diagonal and measurement checks from points projected from the underframe onto a level floor is used (see pages R.12 and R.13).

To ensure that the alignment check is carried out accurately, the vehicle must be raised so that it is parallel with the floor, both from side-to-side and from front-to-rear. Use the comparative measurements given on page R.12 to do this. Lift the vehicle to a convenient working height and adjust the front or rear of the vehicle until the points given on page R.12 for the front and rear on both sides of the car are in correct vertical position relative to each other; for example, if the rear points (J) are 36 in. (91.4 cm.) from the floor, as the rear points are $\frac{49}{64}$ in. (19.45 mm.) higher in relation to the front points (A), the front points must be set at a height of $35\frac{15}{64}$ in. (89.5 cm.) above the floor.

At the same time, it will be helpful to check the **relative** heights of all the intermediate points given on page R.12 so that any distortion of the car in the vertical plane will be ascertained.

Chalk over the area of the floor directly below the points shown on page R.13. Using a plumb-line, project the points from the car onto the floor, marking the positions with a pencilled cross. The centre between each pair of points can be established by means of a large pair of compasses, and the central points marked on the floor. In addition, diagonals can be determined between any two pairs of points and the points of intersection marked on the floor. At this stage a length of thin cord, covered with chalk, can be held by two operators in such a position that it passes through as many of the central points and intersections marked as possible. While the cord is held taut a third operator raises the centre of it and then allows it to spring back smartly to the floor. If the resulting white line passes through all the points the body alignment is satisfactory. Any points through which the white line does not pass will be in a position where the underframe is out of alignment.

Considerable deviations in the transverse and longitudinal measurements, given on pages R.12 and R.13, confirm body misalignment. It must be understood that allowance be made for normal manufacturing tolerances and that a reasonable departure from nominal dimensions can be permitted without detriment to road performance.

Section R.22

PAINT REFINISHING INSTRUCTIONS

Section R.22

PAINT REFINISHING INSTRUCTIONS

Operation	Material	Thinning	Drying times	Application	Instructions
Stripping original paint	Water-soluble paint remover, e.g. Sunbeam Anti-corrosives Stripolene 799	—	—	Brush	Remove the original finish with a scraper after allowing paint-strip 10 minutes to react (repeat if necessary). Wash off thoroughly with cold water, rubbing with wire wool. Dry. Blow out crevices with compressed air. Strip a small area at a time to enable correct neutralizing of the stripper
Metal abrading	Emery-cloth, e.g. Howarth Blue Twill, grade 1½ M	—	—	Hand or disc	Paper thoroughly to ensure satisfactory key. Wipe with cleaner solvent or white spirits
Acid etching	Apply Deoxidine 125 (I.C.I.)	1 part Deoxidine, 1 part water	—	Brush	Apply solution generously and rub in with wire wool. Do not allow Deoxidine solution to dry off before the wash-off operation. Allow approximately five minutes to complete reaction. Wash thoroughly with cold water to remove all traces of Deoxidine solution, followed by a hot rinse. Thoroughly dry surfaces with a clean cloth and blow out crevices with compressed air
Priming	Synthetic primer G.I.P. No. S3178	6 to 1 with Z1048	½-hour to 4 hours	Spray	Apply one thin coat of synthetic primer (recommended for superior adhesion) or one thin coat of cellulose primer (recommended for good adhesion). The use of a primer coat enhances adhesion and gives the system a much greater safety factor.
	or Grey cellulose primer G.I.P. C3971 MOD	50/50 with 2045M	¼-hour	Spray	
Applying stopper	Stopper Grey G.I.P. 824D or Stopper Brown G.I.P. 1543	—	6-8 hours, or overnight if possible	Glazing knife	Apply stopper in thin layers, allowing 15–20 minutes' drying between applications. Heavy layers result in insufficient drying, with subsequent risk of cracking
Filling	Primer Filler Grey G.I.P. C3663M	50/50 with 2045M	3-4 hours	Spray	Apply two or three full coats, allowing 15–25 minutes' drying time between coats.

Wet-sanding	Abrasive paper 280 grade	—	—	—	Rub down wet until smooth; a guide coat (a weak contrasting colour) may be used to ensure that the whole surface is rubbed level. Wash off thoroughly with water, sponge all sludge, wash off, dry with clean sponge. Dry off. Minimum of paint should be removed consistant with a satisfactory surface. Film thickness after rubbing should be .0025 in. (.06 mm.) min.
Applying sealer or undercoat	Sealer Grey or Sealer White or Red undercoat (see BMC Paint Scheme schedule)	50/50 with 2045M	15-20 minutes	Spray	Apply one coat, flash off
Dry-sanding or de-nibbing as required	320 grade paper	—	—	—	De-nib or dry-sand with 320 paper. Clean with white spirit. The grade of paper quoted is from the 3M Company (Minnesota Mining and Mfg. Co. Ltd.); the grade of paper may vary according to manufacture
Applying colour coats	BMC body finishes (see BMC Paint Schemes schedule)	50/50 with 2045M	5-10 minutes' flash between coats. Overnight dry	Spray	Apply two double coats with a 5–10-minute flash between coats. Overnight dry
Flatting colour coat	320 or 400 paper (dependent on conditions)	—	—	Hand	Flat with 320 or 400 paper, dependent on conditions
Applying final colour coat	BMC body finishes (see BMC Paint Scheme schedule)	50/50 with 2045M	Overnight dry	Spray	Spray final double colour coat
Polishing	Cut and polish (see BMC Paint Scheme schedule)	—	—	Hand or machine	The colour coat must be thoroughly dry before polishing. After cutting, burnish to a high gloss with a clean mop, and finally clean with a liquid polish, e.g. BMC car polish

NOTE.—(1) For faster drying of undercoats or local repairs G.I.P. thinners 1523 may be used.
(2) Under extreme circumstances of heat and /or humidity retarder G.I.P. Z1694 can be used added to the 2045M thinners.

Section R.23

VERTICAL ALIGNMENT CHECK

(early cars)

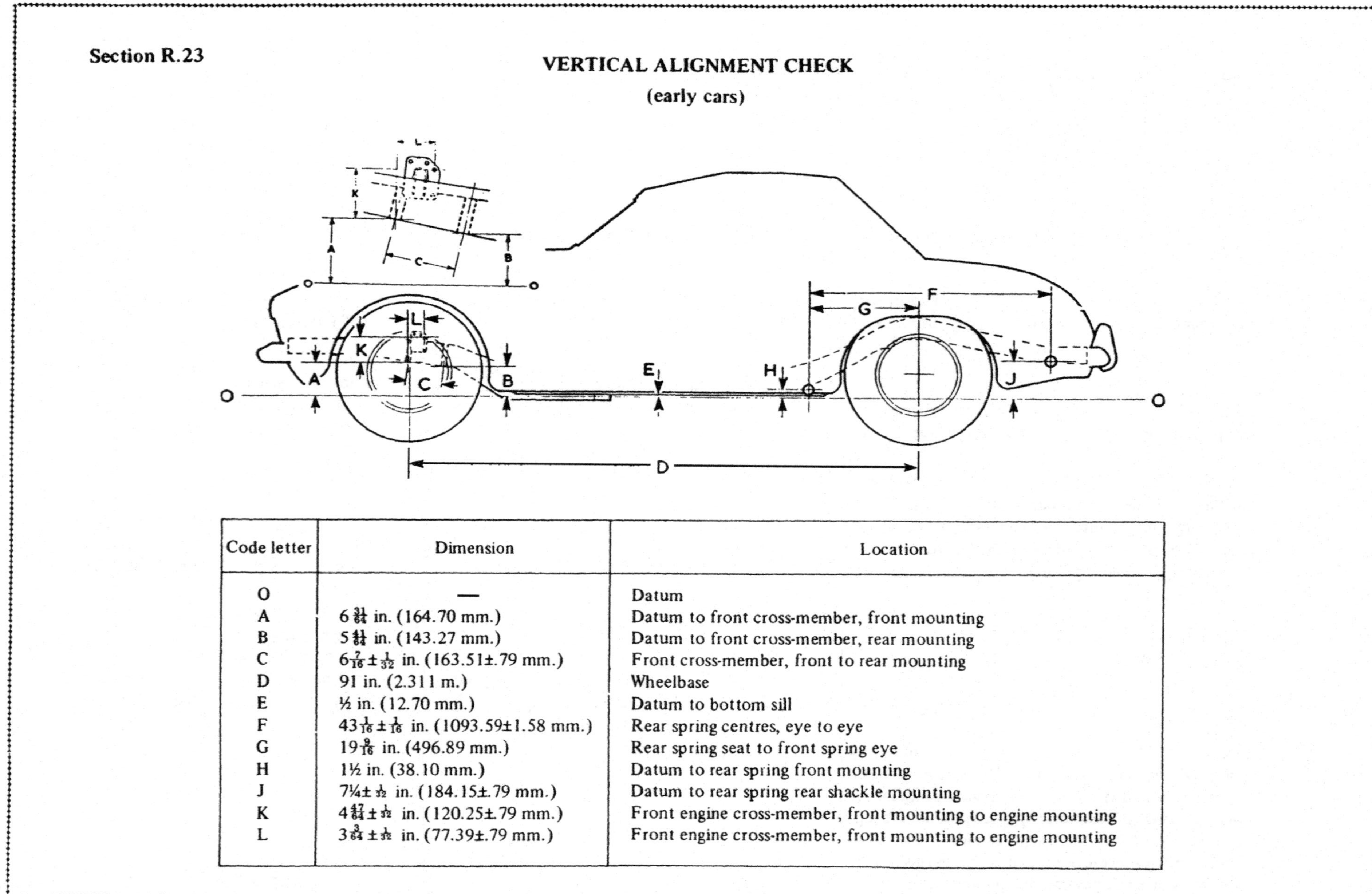

Code letter	Dimension	Location
O	—	Datum
A	$6\frac{31}{64}$ in. (164.70 mm.)	Datum to front cross-member, front mounting
B	$5\frac{41}{64}$ in. (143.27 mm.)	Datum to front cross-member, rear mounting
C	$6\frac{7}{16} \pm \frac{1}{32}$ in. (163.51±.79 mm.)	Front cross-member, front to rear mounting
D	91 in. (2.311 m.)	Wheelbase
E	½ in. (12.70 mm.)	Datum to bottom sill
F	$43\frac{1}{16} \pm \frac{1}{16}$ in. (1093.59±1.58 mm.)	Rear spring centres, eye to eye
G	$19\frac{9}{16}$ in. (496.89 mm.)	Rear spring seat to front spring eye
H	1½ in. (38.10 mm.)	Datum to rear spring front mounting
J	$7\frac{1}{4} \pm \frac{1}{32}$ in. (184.15±.79 mm.)	Datum to rear spring rear shackle mounting
K	$4\frac{47}{64} \pm \frac{1}{32}$ in. (120.25±.79 mm.)	Front engine cross-member, front mounting to engine mounting
L	$3\frac{3}{64} \pm \frac{1}{32}$ in. (77.39±.79 mm.)	Front engine cross-member, front mounting to engine mounting

Section R.24

HORIZONTAL ALIGNMENT CHECK
(early cars)

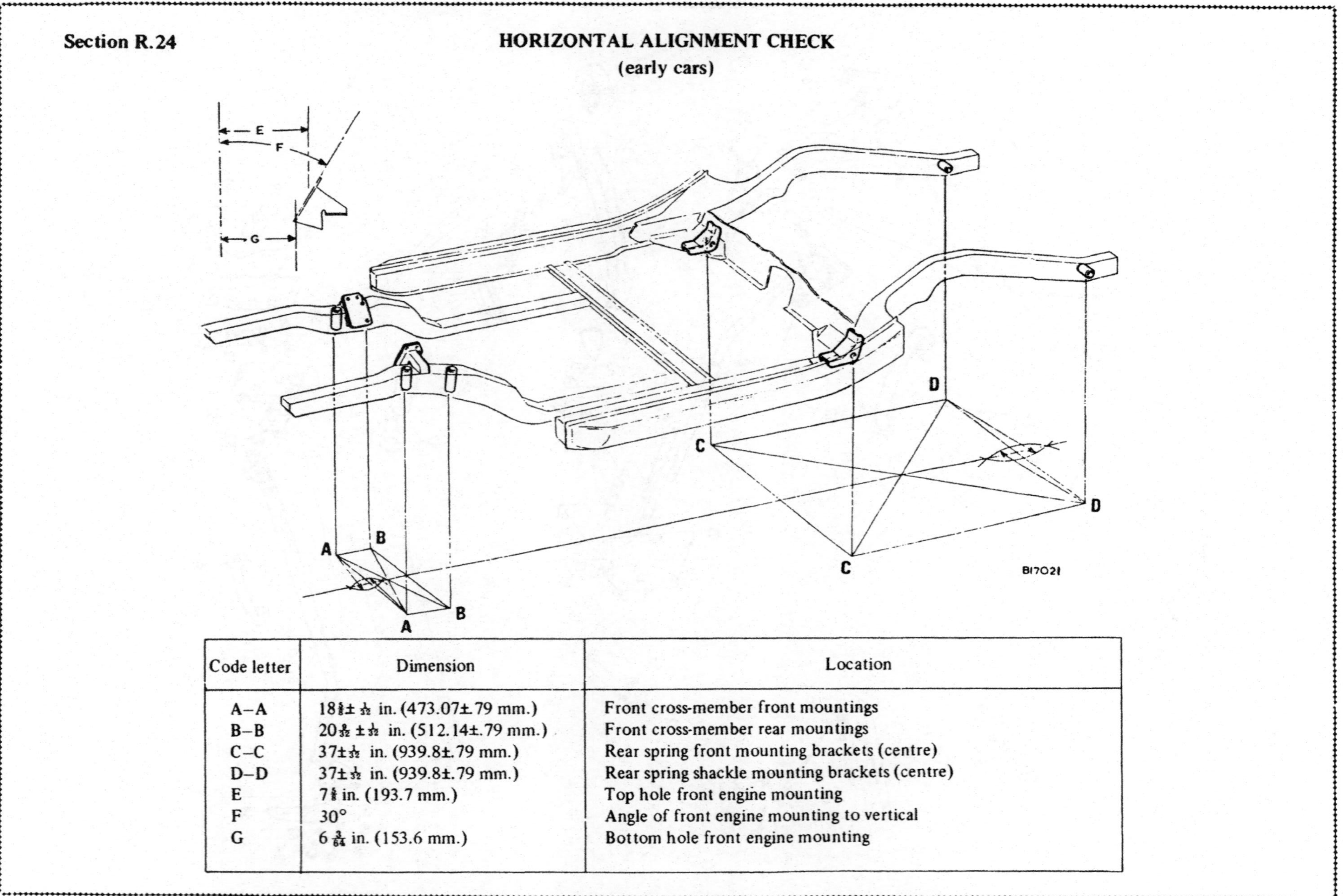

Code letter	Dimension	Location
A–A	$18\frac{5}{8} \pm \frac{1}{32}$ in. (473.07±.79 mm.)	Front cross-member front mountings
B–B	$20\frac{5}{32} \pm \frac{1}{32}$ in. (512.14±.79 mm.)	Front cross-member rear mountings
C–C	$37 \pm \frac{1}{32}$ in. (939.8±.79 mm.)	Rear spring front mounting brackets (centre)
D–D	$37 \pm \frac{1}{32}$ in. (939.8±.79 mm.)	Rear spring shackle mounting brackets (centre)
E	$7\frac{5}{8}$ in. (193.7 mm.)	Top hole front engine mounting
F	30°	Angle of front engine mounting to vertical
G	$6\frac{3}{64}$ in. (153.6 mm.)	Bottom hole front engine mounting

THE DOOR COMPONENTS

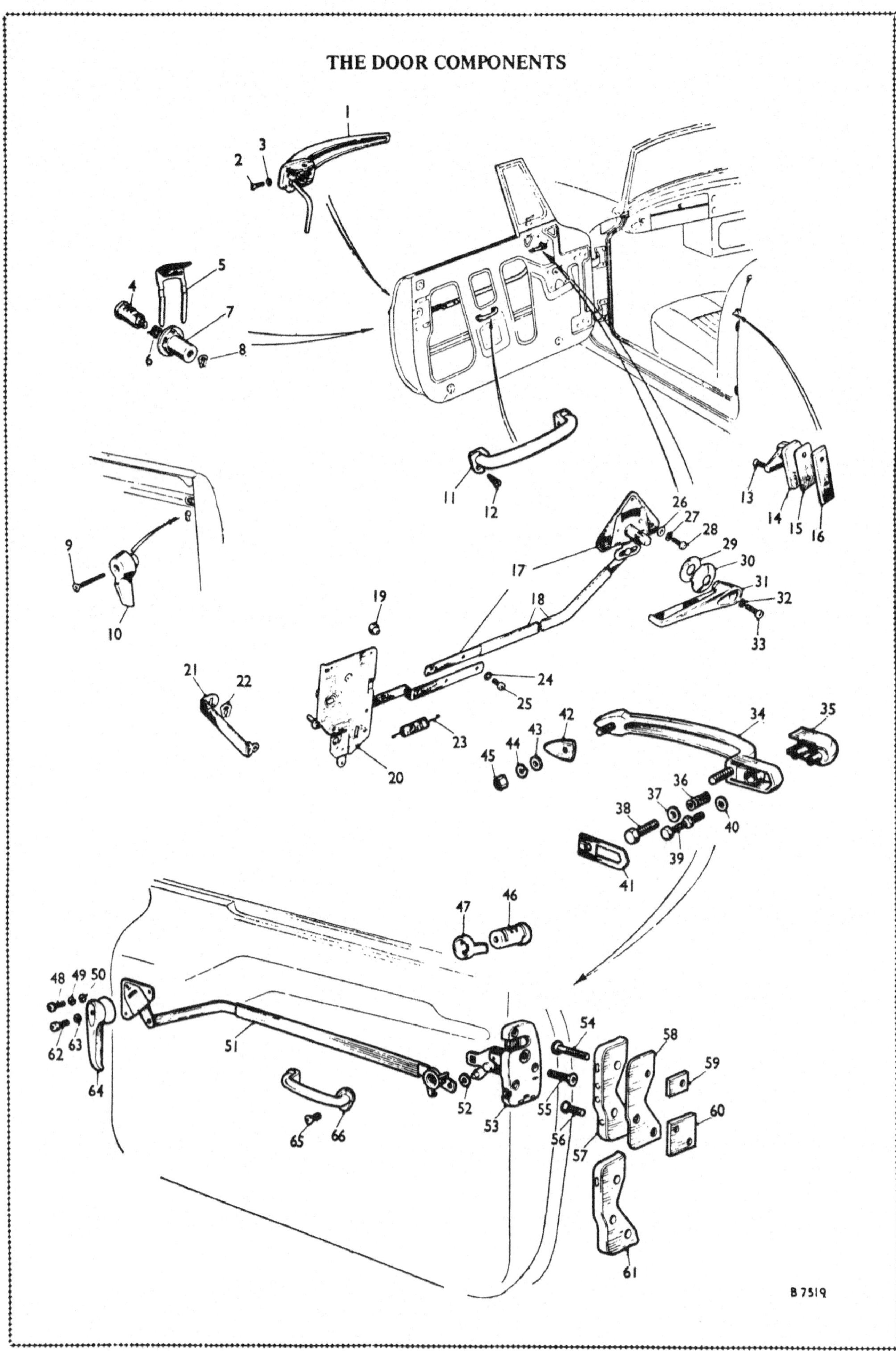

KEY TO THE DOOR COMPONENTS

No.	Description
1.	Outer door handle.
2.	Screw.
3.	Washer.
4.	Lock barrel.
5.	Lock retaining clip.
6.	Self-centring spring.
7.	Lock housing.
8.	Anderton clip.
9.	Screw.
10.	Inner locking knob.
11.	Door pull.
12.	Screw.
13.	Screw.
14.	Striker.
15.	Packing.
16.	Tapping plate.
17.	Remote control lock.
18.	Anti-rattle sleeve.
19.	Outside door handle buffer.
20.	Lock.
21.	Operating link.
22.	Anderton clip.
23.	Tension spring.
24.	Shakeproof washer.
25.	Screw.
26.	Plain washer.
27.	Spring washer.
28.	Screw.
29.	Fibre washer.
30.	Finisher.
31.	Inner door handle.
32.	Spring washer.
33.	Screw.

Items 1–33: Early Tourer Models

No.	Description
34.	Outer door handle.
35.	Push-button.
36.	Spring.
37.	Shakeproof washer.
38.	Set screw.
39.	Set screw with locknut.
40.	Shakeproof washer.
41.	Fibre washer.
42.	Fibre washer.
43.	Plain washer.
44.	Spring washer.
45.	Nut.
46.	Lock barrel.
47.	Retaining clip.
48.	Screw.
49.	Spring washer.
50.	Plain washer.
51.	Remote-control lock.
52.	Anti-rattle washer.
53.	Lock.
54.	Screw.
55.	Screw.
56.	Screw.
57.	Striker.
58.	Shim–.003 in. or .006 in. (.8 mm. or 1.6 mm.).
59.	Tapping plate (upper).
60.	Tapping plate (lower).
61.	Striker lock.
62.	Screw.
63.	Spring washer.
64.	Inner door handle.
65.	Screw.
66.	Door pull.

THE WINDOW COMPONENTS

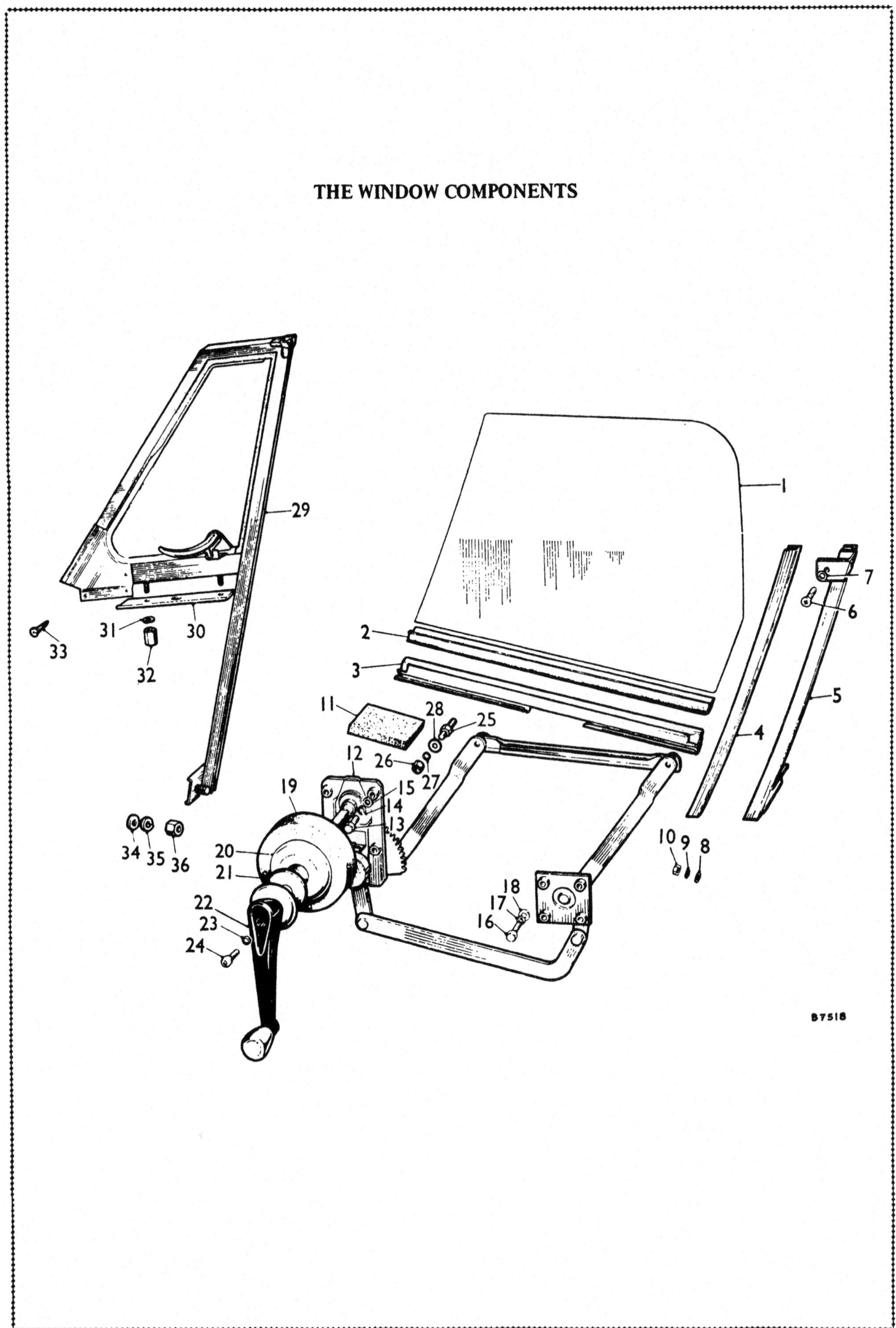

KEY TO THE WINDOW COMPONENTS

No.	Description	No.	Description
1.	Door glass.	19.	Pad.
2.	Glazing channel.	20.	Escutcheon.
3.	Lower channel.	21.	Fibre washer.
4.	Flexible channel.	22.	Handle and finisher.
5.	Channel.	23.	Spring washer.
6.	Screw.	24.	Screw.
7.	Cup washer.	25.	Stop.
8.	Plain washer.	26.	Nut.
9.	Spring washer.	27.	Spring washer.
10.	Nut.	28.	Plain washer.
11.	Buffer.	29.	Ventilator.
12.	Regulator.	30.	Seating washer.
13.	Set screw.	31.	Spring washer.
14.	Spring washer.	32.	Nut.
15.	Plain washer.	33.	Screw.
16.	Set screw.	34.	Plain washer.
17.	Spring washer.	35.	Spring washer.
18.	Plain washer.	36.	Nut.

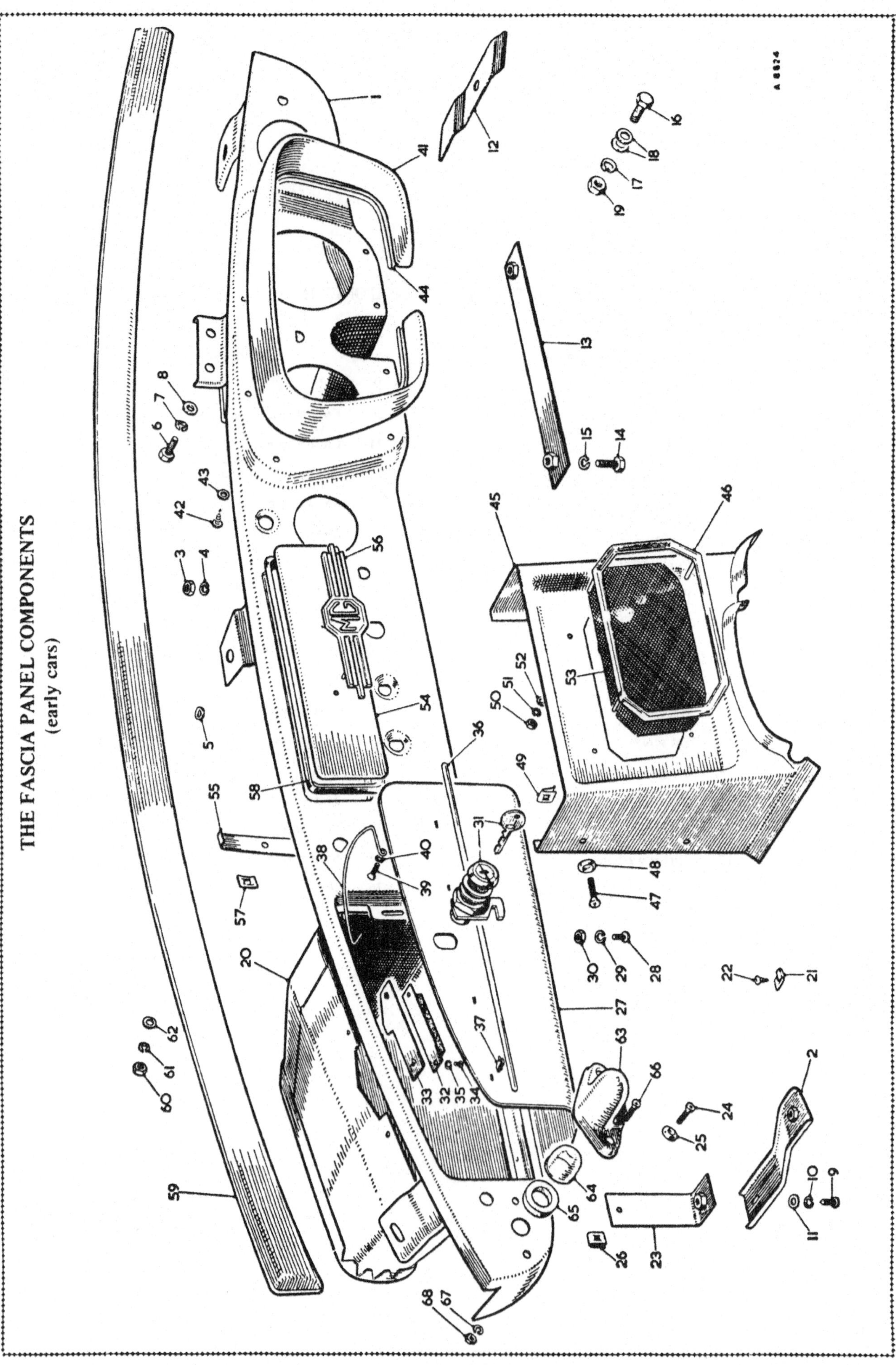
THE FASCIA PANEL COMPONENTS
(early cars)
A 8824

KEY TO THE FASCIA PANEL COMPONENTS

No.	Description
1.	Panel assembly–fascia.
2.	Bracket–steady.
3.	Nut–fascia to body.
4.	Washer–spring.
5.	Washer–plain.
6.	Screw–fascia to body.
7.	Washer–spring.
8.	Washer–plain.
9.	Screw–attachment bracket to steady bracket.
10.	Washer–spring.
11.	Washer–plain–attachment bracket to steady bracket.
12.	Plate–washer–fascia fixing.
13.	Plate assembly–fascia fixing.
14.	Screw–fascia to centre reinforcement.
15.	Washer–spring.
16.	Screw–steering-column support bracket to cross-tube.
17.	Washer–spring.
18.	Washer–plain.
19.	Nut–screw.
20.	Box–glove.
21.	Nut–spring.
22.	Screw–glovebox to fascia.
23.	Bracket–attachment–glovebox.
24.	Screw–attachment bracket to glovebox.
25.	Washer–cup.
26.	Nut–spring.
27.	Lid assembly–glovebox.
28.	Screw–glovebox lid to fascia.
29.	Washer–spring.
30.	Nut–screw.
31.	Lock assembly–glovebox lid.
32.	Buffer–glovebox lid.
33.	Catch–glovebox lock.
34.	Screw–catch and buffer to glovebox.
35.	Washer–spring.
36.	Finisher–glovebox lid.
37.	Clip–finisher to glovebox.
38.	Arm–check–glovebox.
39.	Screw–check arm to glovebox lid.
40.	Washer–spring.
41.	Hood–instrument.
42.	Screw–hood to fascia panel.
43.	Washer–plain.
44.	Finisher–instrument hood.
45.	Panel–radio speaker.
46.	Bezel–radio speaker panel.
47.	Screw–speaker panel fixing.
48.	Washer–cup.
49.	Nut–spring.
50.	Nut–bezel to speaker panel.
51.	Washer–spring.
52.	Washer–plain.
53.	Grille–radio speaker.
54.	Plate–blanking–radio aperture.
55.	Clip–blanking plate to fascia panel.
56.	Motif–'MG'.
57.	Nut–clip (spire).
58.	Bezel–radio aperture.
59.	Roll assembly–crash–Black with Black piping.
60.	Nut–crash roll fixing.
61.	Washer–spring.
62.	Washer–plain.
63.	Cover–map light.
64.	Glass–map light.
65.	Gasket–seating.
66.	Screw–map light to fascia panel.
67.	Washer–spring.
68.	Nut–screw.

THE HEATER COMPONENTS
(early cars)

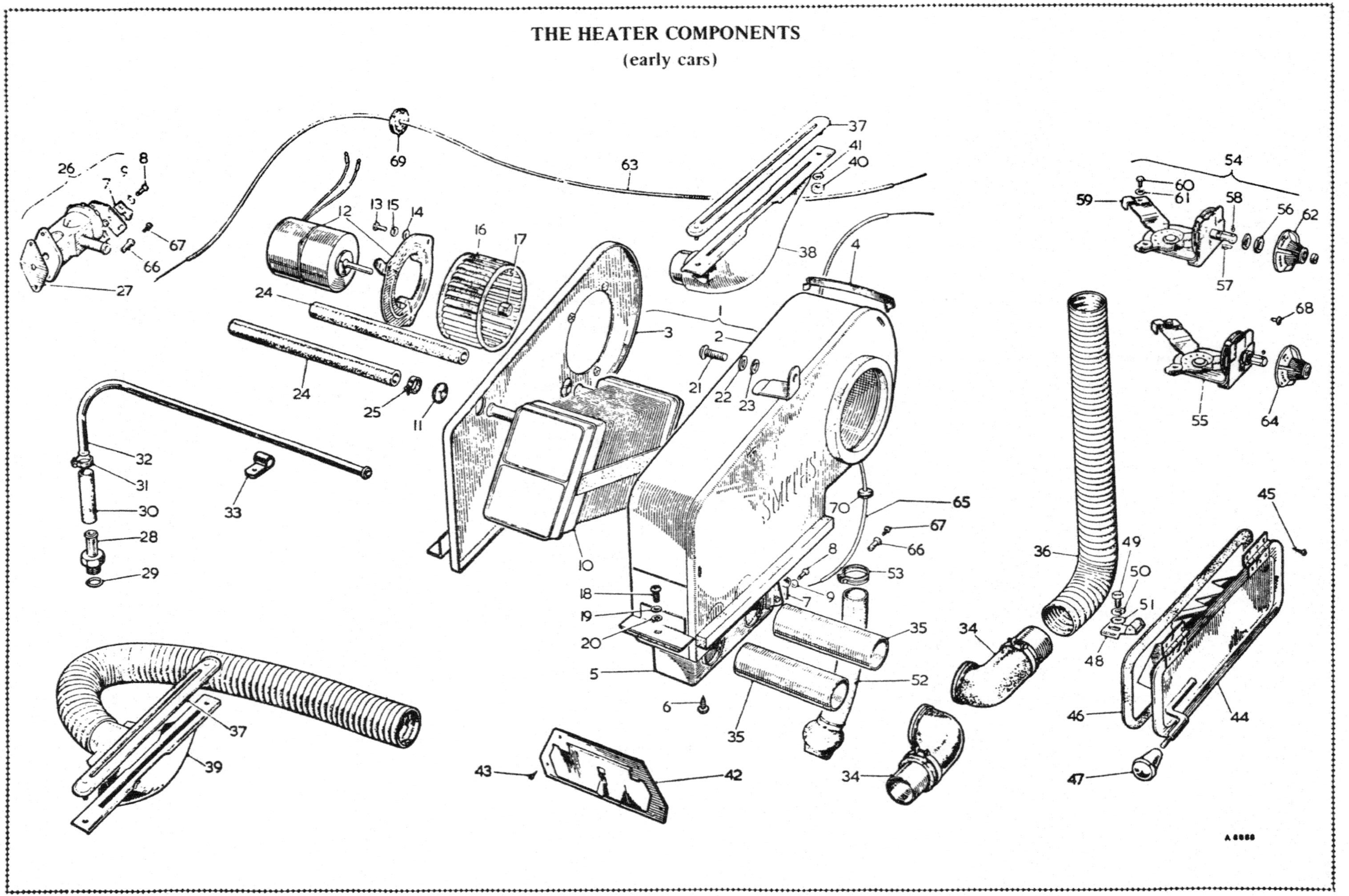

KEY TO THE HEATER COMPONENTS

No.	Description	No.	Description	No.	Description
1.	Heater assembly.	25.	Clip–hose.	48.	Spring assembly–fresh-air vent door.
2.	Cover.	26.	Valve–assembly–water.	49.	Screw–spring to body bracket.
3.	Cover–motor side.	27.	Gasket–water valve.	50.	Washer–spring.
4.	Clip–cover.	28.	Union–water.	51.	Washer–plain.
5.	Duct–outlet.	29.	Washer–union.	52.	Tube–drain and dust valve assembly.
6.	Screw–outlet duct.	30.	Hose–water–2" x ½".	53	Clip–tube assembly to air box.
7.	Clamp–cable.	31.	Clip–hose.	54.	Control–rotary–heat.
8.	Screw–cable clamp.	32.	Pipe–water return.	55.	Control–rotary–air.
9.	Washer–shakeproof–screw.	33.	Clip to inlet manifold.	56.	Nut–locking.
10.	Radiator.	34.	Elbow–demister.	57.	Clip–knob.
11.	Washer–radiator pipe.	35.	Tube–connector.	58.	Pin–knob.
12.	Motor and mounting plate assembly.	36.	Hose–air–demister.	59.	Clamp–cable.
13.	Screw–motor fixing.	37.	Escutcheon assembly–demister.	60.	Screw–clamp.
14.	Washer–plain–screw.	38.	Noozle assembly–demister R.H.	61.	Washer–spring.
15.	Washer–spring–screw.	39.	Nozzle assembly–demister L.H.	62.	Knob–heat.
16.	Runner.	40.	Nut–escutcheon and demister nozzle to scuttle.	63.	Cable–heat control.
17.	Nut–collet.	41.	Washer–spring.	64.	Knob–air.
18.	Screw–heater unit to bulkhead.	42.	Door–heater outlet.	65.	Cable–air control.
19.	Washer–plain.	43.	Screw–outlet door to air box.	66.	Trunnion.
20.	Washer–spring.	44.	Door assembly–fresh-air vent.	67.	Screw–trunnion.
21.	Screw–heater unit to bulkhead.	45.	Screw–door to bulkhead.	68.	Rivet–heater control.
22.	Washer–plain.	46.	Seal–door.	69.	Grommet–heater control cable.
23.	Washer–spring.	47.	Knob–door.	70.	Grommet–air control cable.
24.	Hose–water–8½" x ½".				

Section R.25

BODYWORK

Coachwork

Regular care of the body finish is necessary if the new appearance of the car exterior is to be maintained against the effects of air pollution, rain, and mud.

Wash the bodywork frequently, using a soft sponge and plenty of water containing a mild detergent. Large deposits of mud must be softened with water before using the sponge. Smears should be removed by a second wash in clean water, and with the sponge if necessary. When dry, clean the surface of the car with a damp chamois-leather. In addition to the regular maintenance, special attention is required if the car is driven in extreme conditions such as sea spray, or on salted roads. In these conditions and with other forms of severe contamination an additional washing operation is necessary, which should include underbody hosing. Any damaged areas should be immediately covered with paint and a complete repair effected as soon as possible. Before touching-in light scratches and abrasions with paint thoroughly clean the surface. Use petrol/white spirit (gasoline/hydrocarbon solvent) to remove spots of tar or grease.

The application of BMC Car Polish is all that is required to remove traffic film and to ensure the retention of the new appearance.

Bright trim

Never use an abrasive on stainless, chromium, aluminium, or plastic bright parts and on no account clean them with metal polish. Remove spots of grease or tar with petrol/white spirit (gasoline/hydrocarbon solvent) and wash frequently with water containing a mild detergent. When the dirt has been removed polish with a clean dry cloth or chamois-leather until bright. Any slight tarnish found on stainless or plated parts which have not received regular washing may be removed with BMC Chrome Cleaner. An occasional application of mineral light oil or grease will help to preserve the finish, particularly during winter, when salt may be used on the roads, but these protectives must not be applied to plastic finishes.

Windscreen

If windscreen smearing has occurred it can be removed with BMC Screen Cleane'

Interior

Decosol Interior Cleaner is recommended for cleaning the interior of your car, and may be safely applied to carpets, upholstery and roof linings. Decosol must not be used on painted surfaces.

CARPETS

Remove surface dirt with a semi-stiff brush or a vacuum cleaner. Apply Decosol, diluted with an equal quantity of water, brush vigorously with a semi-stiff brush, then clean off using a moistened sponge or cloth.

UPHOLSTERY AND ROOF LININGS

Apply neat Decosol with a soft brush or cloth, leave for five minutes, then wipe clean using a moistened sponge or cloth. A razor blade will remove transfers from the window glass.

Cleaning the hood (Tourer)

To clean the hood it is only necessary to use soap and water with a soft brush to remove any ingrained dirt. Frequent washing with soap and water considerably improves the appearance and wearing qualities of the hood, and it should be washed at least as often as the rest of the car.

Do not use caustic soaps, detergents, or spirit cleaners to clean the hood or the hood back-light.

Preservative on export cars

Certain cars leaving the factory are sprayed with a wax preservative to safeguard their body finish. The wax can be removed by the following procedure. Wash the waxed surfaces liberally with water to remove dirt. To soften the wax apply white spirit, either by using a spray and wiping off with mutton-cloth, or by using the cloth dipped in white spirit.

Polish the body with clean dry mutton cloth.

Coachwork repairs

The specially designed body jack 18G 308 B is an essential item when rectifying any misalignment of the body construction.

With the addition of a suitable oxy-acetylene outfit any type of mono-construction repair can be effected.

Section R.26

BUMPERS

Removing (Front)

Unscrew the two steady bracket to bumper securing screws and the nuts and bolts securing the spring blades to the body. Pull the bumper bar forward and lower it to the ground.

If over-riders are fitted, unscrew the nuts and remove the washers, over-riders, and distance pieces.

Removing (Rear)

Disconnect the electrical leads from the number-plate lamps, remove the nuts and washers that secure the bumper bar spring to the mounting brackets, and withdraw the assembly from the car.

Remove the nuts and washers securing the bar to the mounting bracket.

Reassembling and refitting

Reassembly and refitting of the front and rear bumpers is a reversal of the removal and dismantling sequence. After refitting check the bars for alignment and the number-plate lamps for correct functioning.

Section R.27

ELECTRICALLY HEATED BACK-LIGHT (GT)

Removing

1. Remove both rear upper quarter trim panels.
2. Disconnect the heated back-light wires from the snap connectors inside the right-hand and left-hand body quarters.
3. Remove the back-light glass as detailed in Section R.19.
4. Withdraw the wires through the holes in the body and surround rubber.

Refitting

5. Thread the wires through the holes in the body and rubber surround.
6. Refit the back-light glass as detailed in Section R.19.
7. Reverse the procedure in 1 and 2.

Section R.28

SEAT BELTS

The following instructions refer to fitting the approved 'Kangol Magnet' seat belts to the fixing points incorporated in the body structure.

Rear wheel arch

EARLY CARS

1. Remove the two domed nuts and plain washers from the fixing studs.
2. Fit the bracket on the studs and secure it, using plain washers, spring washers and domed nuts.

LATER CARS

3. Remove the plastic cap from the fixing boss.

FIRST-TYPE SEAT BELT

4. Fit a spring washer to the short 7/16 in. bolt, pass the bolt through the centre of the three holes in the belt bracket and secure the bracket to the fixing boss.

SECOND-TYPE SEAT BELT

5. Fit the belt bracket on the short 7/16 in. bolt, followed by a waved washer and a distance piece, with the small diameter end of the distance piece towards the bolt head.
6. Secure the assembled bracket to the fixing boss.

Sill

7. Locate the fixing point (its position can be felt through the trim) and cut the trim to expose the fixing hole.

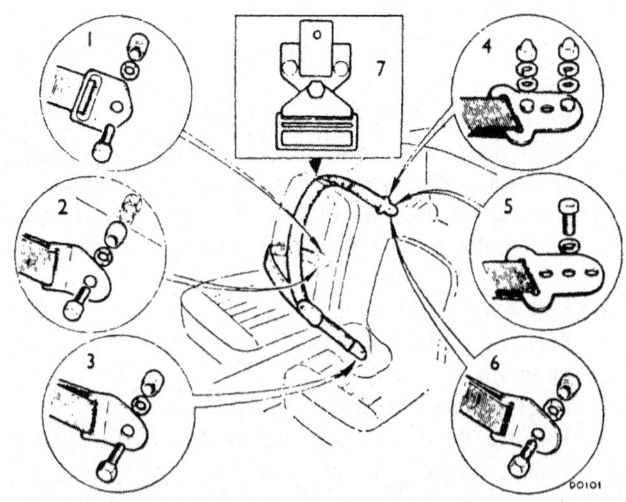

Fig. R.9
Seat belt fixings

1. Sill.
2. Drive shaft tunnel (early cars).
3. Drive shaft tunnel (later cars).
4. Wheel arch (early cars).
5. Wheel arch, first-type belt (later cars).
6. Wheel arch, second-type belt (later cars).
7. Stowage clip.

8. Fit the belt bracket to one of the 7/16 in. bolts, followed by a waved washer and a distance piece (small diameter end towards the bolt head).
9. Screw the assembled bracket to the sill.

Drive shaft tunnel

EARLY CARS

10. Remove the plug from the fixing point on the opposite side of the tunnel to the seat for which the belt is being fitted.
11. Fit the bracket of the short belt to the remaining 7/16 in. bolt followed by a waved washer and a distance piece (small diameter end towards the bolt head).
12. Secure the assembled bracket with the spring washer and nut fitted from inside the tunnel.

LATER CARS

13. Fit the belt bracket of the short belt to the remaining 7/16 in. bolt followed by a waved washer and a distance piece (smaller diameter end towards the head of the bolt).
14. Secure the assembled bracket to the exposed fixing boss on the opposite side of the tunnel to the seat for which the belt is being fitted.

Stowage clip

15. Fit the stowage clip under the head of the centre hood socket securing screw.

Section R.29

HEATER

Removing

BLOWER MOTOR ONLY

1. Disconnect the batteries.
2. Disconnect the motor wiring at the snap connectors.
3. Remove the three screws securing the motor mounting plate and withdraw the motor complete with plate.

HEATER ASSEMBLY

5. Carry out operations 1 and 2.
6. Drain the cooling system.
7. Disconnect the hoses from the heater unit.
8. Remove the screws securing the heater unit to the engine compartment bulkhead.
9. Remove the speaker panel or control console.
10. Unscrew the demister tube retaining clip screws.
11. Withdraw one of the demister tube elbows and remove the tube plate.
12. Withdraw the fibre demister tubes.
13. Remove the overdrive vacuum switch (early cars).
14. Detach the heater air control from the fascia panel and disconnect the control cable.
15. Slacken the clip securing the air control cable to the heater unit and slide the outer cable free of the clip.
16. Lift the heater assembly from the car.

Dismantling

17. Remove the securing clips and withdraw the front panel complete with the blower motor and heater matrix.
18. Withdraw the matrix from the plate.
19. Unscrew the blower motor securing screws and remove the motor.
20. Disconnect and remove the air control cable.

Reassembling

21. Reverse the dismantling procedure in 17 to 20.

Refitting

HEATER ASSEMBLY

22. Reverse the removing procedure in 5 to 16 ensuring that the air control cable is correctly routed through the body panel, and the control functions correctly before refitting the demister tubes and speaker panel.

BLOWER MOTOR

23. Reverse the removing procedure in 1 to 3.

Section R.30

DOOR LOCK ADJUSTMENT (GHN4/5 AND GHD4/5 CARS)

Checking

1. Wind the window down and close the door.
2. Move the locking latch rearwards to the locked position.
3. Unlock the door by turning the key through 90 degrees towards the rear of the car.
4. Open the door by depressing the outside push-button.
5. Close the door, then open it again using the inside handle.

Adjustments

OUTSIDE PUSH-BUTTON

6. See Section R.32.

REMOTE CONTROL AND CONNECTING RODS

7. See Section R.33.

STRIKER

8. Check that with the door closed a clearance of $\frac{1}{32}$ to $\frac{1}{16}$ in. (1 to 1.6 mm.) exists between the striker and latch faces. Adjust the clearance by adding or removing shims behind the striker.
9. Slacken the striker securing screws sufficiently to permit the striker to move but tight enough to allow the door to be closed to the fully-latched position.
10. Press the door inwards or pull it outwards until it lines up correctly with the body. **Never slam the door while making adjustments.**
11. Open the door and draw a pencil line round the striker to establish its horizontal position.
12. Set the striker at right angles to the hinge axis and tighten the striker securing screws.
13. Open and close the door to check for drop or lift; slacken the securing screws to adjust the striker in the vertical plane until the door can be closed easily without rattling, lifting, or dropping. When correctly adjusted, with the door closed in the fully latched position, a fractional movement should be possible when the door is pressed in against its seals.

Section R.31

INTERIOR DOOR HANDLES AND TRIM PAD (GHN4/5 AND GHD4/5 CARS)

Removing

1. Close the window, remove the screw and spring washer retaining the window regulator handle and remove the handle and its fibre washer.
2. Withdraw the two-piece plastic bezel from the remote control unit (the top half upwards, bottom half downwards).
3. Unscrew the pull handle/arm-rest securing screws and remove the pull handle/arm-rest.
4. Unscrew the waist rail securing screws and remove the waist rail.
5. Unscrew the screws securing the trim pad and remove the pad.
6. Peel the plastic waterproof cover from the door as required.

Refitting

7. Reverse the removing procedure in 1 to 6 ensuring that the lock and window mechanism is adequately greased and that the door cut-outs and waterproof cover are securely taped.

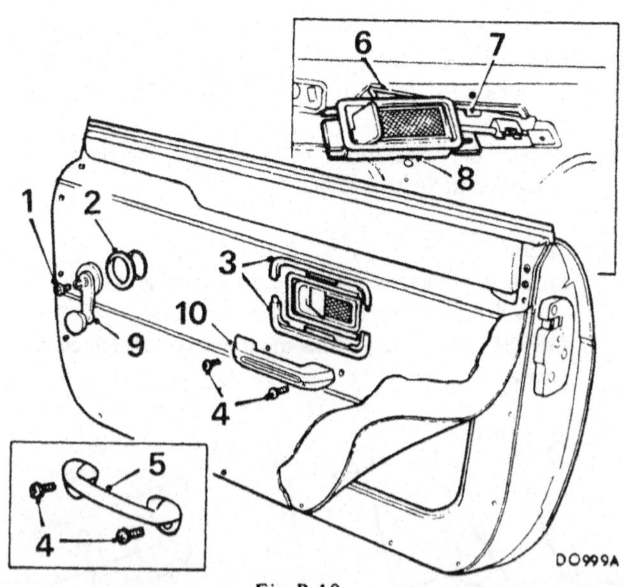

Fig. R.10
Interior door fittings–insert shows remote control being removed

1. Window regulator handle screw.
2. Fibre washer.
3. Remote control unit bezel.
4. Pull handle screw.
5. Pull handle.
6. Lock control rod.
7. Anti-rattle clip.
8. Remote control unit.
9. Window regulator handle.
10. Arm-rest GHN5 and GHD5 cars from Car No. 294251.

Section R.32

OUTSIDE DOOR HANDLES (GHN4/5 and GHD4/5 Cars)

Removing

1. Remove the interior door handles and trim pad–Section R.31.
2. Wind the window fully up, remove the two nuts, spring and plain washers securing the door handle to the door and remove the handle complete with its seating washers.

Refitting

3. Set the latch to the closed position and temporarily fit the handle and seating washers.
4. With access through one of the inner door panel apertures, check the clearance between the push-button plunger bolt and the latch contactor; do not depress the push-button while checking the clearance. The clearance must not be less than $\frac{1}{32}$ in. (1 mm.). Adjust the clearance by slackening the locknut and screwing the plunger bolt in or out as required. Tighten the locknut.
5. Fit the spring and flat washers and screw on and tighten the securing nuts.

Section R.33

DOOR LOCKS (GHN4/5 and GHD4/5 Cars)

IMPORTANT.–Before removing any part of the door lock mechanism because of unsatisfactory operation, first check that the condition is not caused by incorrect adjustment. See Section R.30.

Removing

1. Remove the interior door handles and trim pad–Section R.31.

REMOTE CONTROL UNIT

2. Detach the latch release rod and lock control rod from their retaining clips and bushes on the latch levers.
3. Remove the three remote control retaining screws and washers, and self-tapping screw (later cars).
4. Withdraw the lock control rod from its bush in the top of the locking latch.
5. Remove the remote control unit complete with the latch release rod. If necessary, the lock control rod can be removed after withdrawing it downwards from its anti-rattle clip.

LATCH UNIT

6. Remove the three screws securing the latch to the door and remove the latch.

KEY-OPERATED LOCK

7. From inside the door, compress the legs of the retaining collar and withdraw the lock barrel from outside the door.

Refitting

KEY-OPERATED LOCK

8. Check that the retaining collar is correctly positioned; enter the lock barrel into the door aperture with its operating fork inclined away from the door shut face and press the lock barrel firmly into position.

LATCH UNIT

9. Check that the plastic bushes and spring clips are correctly assembled in their respective holes in the release lever and the locking slide. Each bush must be fitted with its head away from the centre of the latch with the spring clip fitted under the head (see inset A, Fig. R.11).
10. Locate the latch on the door face with the levers entered through the slots provided.
11. Engage the locking lever with the key-operated lock fork.
12. Fit and tighten the latch securing screws.

REMOTE-CONTROL UNIT

13. Check that the latch release rod is fully engaged in its plastic clip attached to the remote-control unit.
14. Check that the lock control rod is fully pressed up into the anti-rattle clip inside the door.
15. Position the remote-control unit in the door and press the end of the lock control rod into the bush in the locking latch.
16. Fit the remote control securing screws and washers but do not tighten.
17. Press the end of the latch release rod into its bush and clip in the latch release lever.
18. Press the lock control rod pivot end into the bush in the locking slide.

Adjusting the remote control

19. With the remote-control unit securing screws slackened, move the control unit towards the latch,

without compressing the rod spring, until the latch release lever just contacts its stop, then tighten the control unit screws. If the control unit adjustment is restricted by the securing screw slots, enlarge the slots by filing.

20. With the latch in the closed position, check the operation of the latch release handle. The striker should be released before the handle has reached the full extent of its movement. Fit self-tapping screw.
21. With the latch in the closed position set the locking latch rearwards to the locked position.
22. Adjust the position of the screwed pivot on the lock control rod so that the locking latch overlaps the latch release handle, the pivot pin fits freely into its bush in the locking slide, before being pressed into the spring clip.
23. Check the operation of the lock mechanism as described in Section R.30.

Lubrication

24. Smear the linkages inside the door with grease and add a few drops of thin oil into the key slots.
IMPORTANT.–Key locks must not be lubricated with grease.

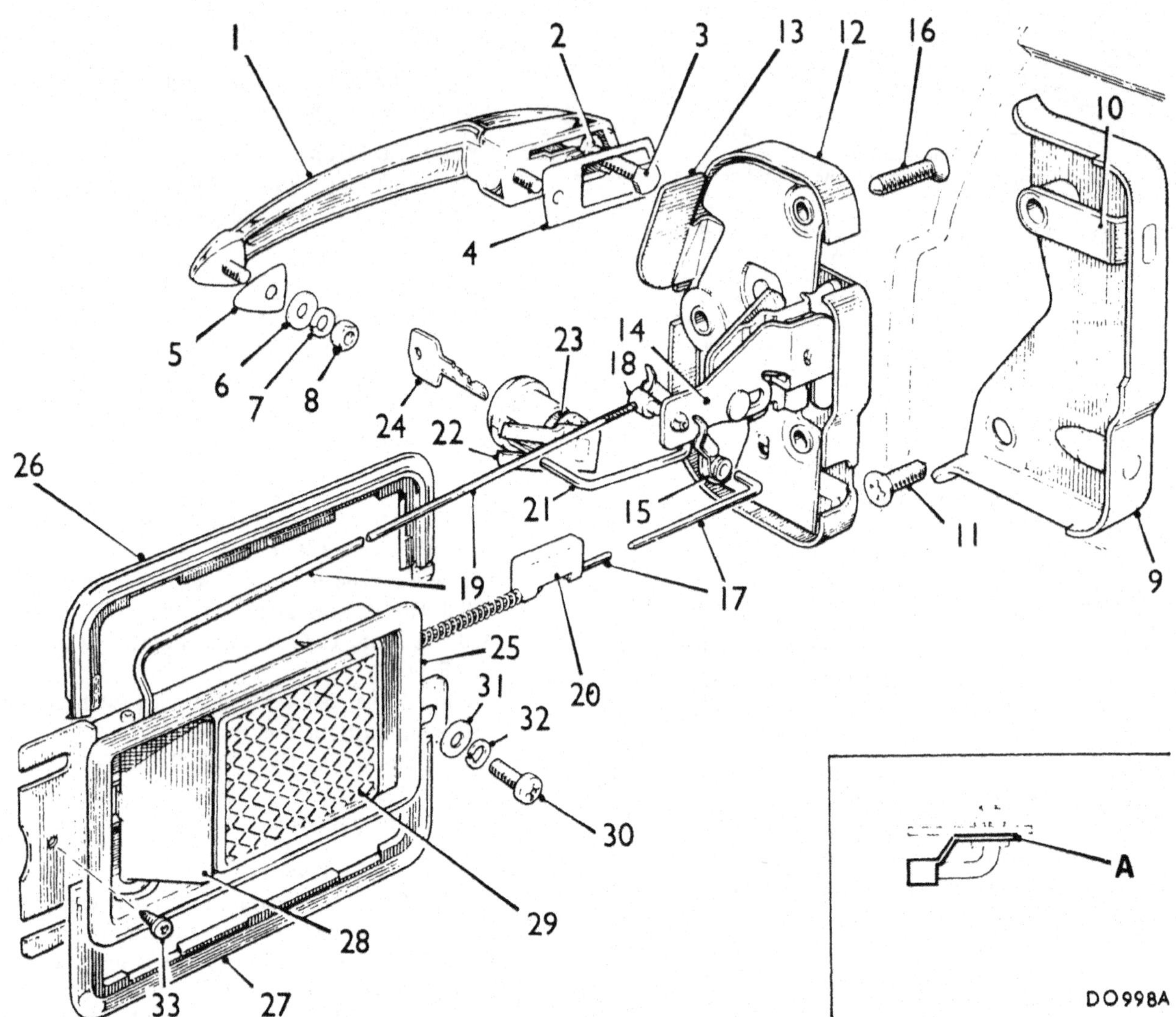

Fig. R.11
Exploded view of door lock mechanism

1. Push-button.
2. Locknut.
3. Push-button plunger bolt.
4. Sealing washer.
5. Sealing washer.
6. Plain washer.
7. Spring washer.
8. Nut.
9. Striker.
10. Anti-burst strap.
11. Striker screw.
12. Latch unit.
13. Latch contactor.
14. Locking slide.
15. Latch release lever.
16. Latch unit screw.
17. Latch release rod.
18. Screwed pivot.
19. Lock control rod.
20. Plastic clip.
21. Locking lever.
22. Lock operating fork.
23. Key operated lock.
24. Key.
25. Remote control unit.
26. Remote control bezel–upper.
27. Remote control bezel–lower.
28. Locking latch.
29. Inside door handle.
30. Remote control unit screw.
31. Plain washer.
32. Spring washer.
33. Self-tapping screw.

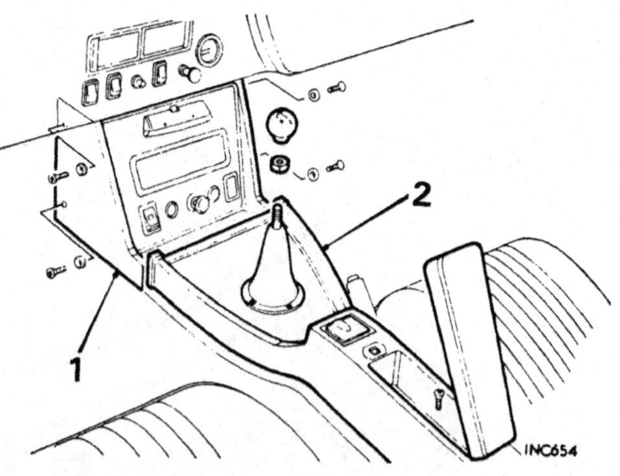

Fig. R.12
Removing the console with hinged arm rest

1. Console 2. Arm rest.

Section R.34

CONSOLE
(With hinged arm-rest)

Removing

1. Disconnect the battery.
2. Remove the change speed lever knob and locknut.
3. Unscrew the four screws securing the retaining ring.
4. Raise the hinged arm-rest, remove the retaining screw and withdraw the arm-rest assembly complete with the change speed lever gaiter and retaining ring.
5. Remove the four screws retaining the console.
6. Partially withdraw the console, disconnect the wiring from the back and then remove the console.

Refitting

7. Reverse the removing procedure in 1 to 6.

Section R.35

FACE-LEVEL VENTS

Removing

1. Disconnect the air duct hoses from the back of the face level vents.
2. Ease up the bottom locating tag of one vent and slightly withdraw the vent until the locating tag rests on the lip of the fascia aperture.
3. Ease down the top locating tag and remove the vent and the anti-rattle packing.
4. Repeat 2 and 3 for the remaining face-level vent.

Refitting

5. Reverse the removing procedure in 1 to 4 noting the following:
   a. Ensure that the rounded corners of the face level vent, adjacent to the serrated wheel, register with the rounded corners of the fascia recess.
   b. The vent assemblies are marked L.H. (left-hand) and R.H. (right-hand) on their flaps for correct assembly when viewing the fascia from inside the car.
   c. Ensure the anti-rattle packing is wedged between the ends of each vent to prevent the vents from butting against each other.

Section R.36

FRONT GRILLE
(GHN5 and GHD5 cars from Car No. 294251)

Removing

GRILLE ASSEMBLY

1. Remove three screws securing the front grille support brackets to the bonnet locking platform.
2. Remove the three hexagon headed screws securing the bottom of the front grille to the radiator duct panel.
3. Remove the radiator grille.

GRILLE PANEL

4. Carry out operations 1 to 3.
5. Remove the 12 screws and clips to release the R.H. and L.H. grille panels from the grille panel.

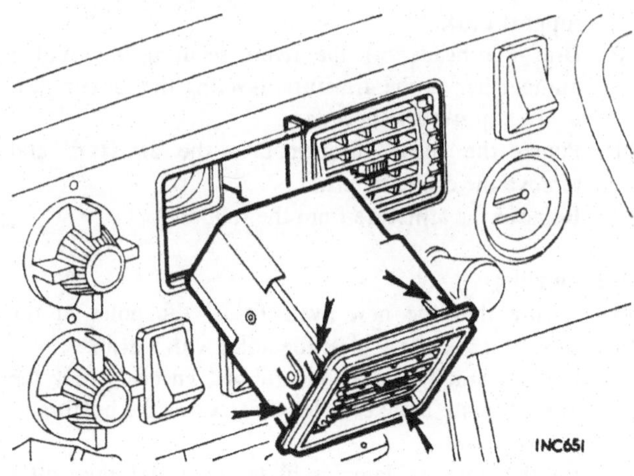

Fig. R.13
Removing the face level vents showing the locating tags arrowed

Refitting

GRILLE PANEL

6. Position the grille panels on the finisher, ensuring that the grille panel thin slats are in a vee formation when viewed from the front of the grille (see illustration on page C.4).
7. Fit the 12 screws and clips to secure the grille panels to the grille finisher.
8. Reverse the removing procedure in 1 to 3.

GRILLE ASSEMBLY

9. Reverse the removing procedure in 1 to 3.

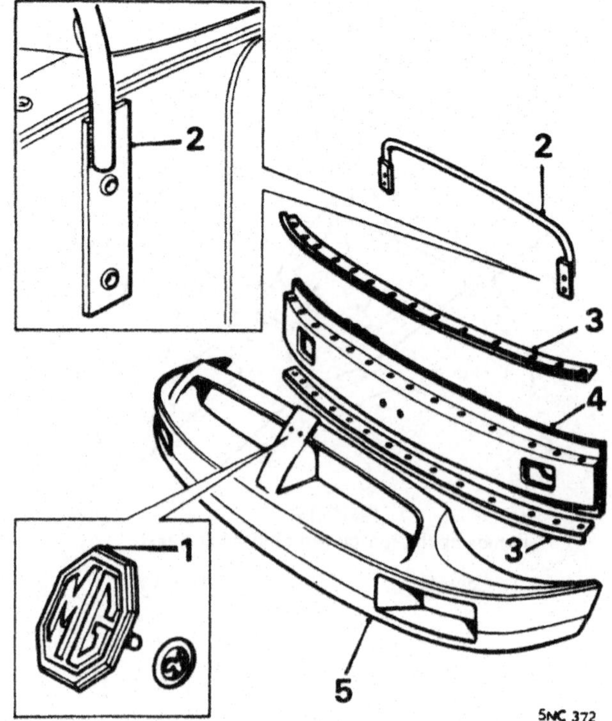

Fig. R.14

The front bumper components

1. 'MG' motif.
2. Support tube.
3. Clamping plate.
4. Armature.
5. Rubber bumper bar.

Section R.37

FRONT BUMPER ASSEMBLY

Removing

1. Disconnect the battery.
2. Disconnect the parking flasher lamp wiring at the connectors under the bonnet and pull the leads through the rubber grommet so they hang under the front wings.
3. Remove the four nuts and eight washers securing the bumper inner mountings to the longitudinal chassis members.
4. Remove the four bolts and eight washers securing the bumper to the outer springs.
5. Remove the bumper assembly and collect the two towing eyes from the outer springs, and the spacer plates (if fitted) from the inner mountings, noting the quantity of spacer plates on each side.

Dismantling

6. Remove the two bolts and washers to release the number-plate assembly.
7. Remove the lamp lens and lamp assemblies.
8. Remove the 'MG' motif.
9. Drill the heads of the four rivets and remove the support tube.
10. Drill the heads off the rivets securing the rubber bumper bar to the armature, levering the rubber clear of the top rivets as necessary.
11. Punch the rivets through into the armature and remove the clamping plates.
12. Remove the armature from the rubber.

Reassembling

13. Ensure that the new rivets fit all the holes in the rubber; if necessary clear the holes with a drill.
14. Fit the armature into the rubber, ensuring that the number-plate bracket holes are towards the bottom of the assembly.
15. Fit the bottom clamping plate and insert the centre rivet and both end rivets.
16. Secure the three fitted rivets.
17. Fit and secure the remainder of the bottom rivets.
18. Fit the top clamping plate and insert the centre rivet and both end rivets.
19. Clamp the rubber to the armature with 'G' clamps.
20. Lever back the rubber as necessary and secure the three fitted rivets.
21. Lever back the rubber as necessary and fit and secure the remainder of the top rivets.
    NOTE: It may be necessary to move the clamps so that they are close to the area being levered.
22. Rivet on the support tube.
23. Fit the 'MG' motif, the number-plate assembly and the lamp assemblies and lenses, noting that the drain slots in the lenses fit downwards.

Refitting

24. Reverse the procedure in 1 to 5.

Section R.38

REAR BUMPER ASSEMBLY

Removing

1. Remove the nut, washer and spacer securing the bumper to each rear wing.
2. Bend back the rubber from the rear wing and detach the side fixing bracket and spacer from each side of the bumper.

3. Remove from inside the boot, the three nuts and six washers securing the bumper assembly to the L.H., R.H. and centre of the rear body panel.
4. Remove, from under the rear body panel, the two nuts and four washers securing the bumper assembly to the body.
5. Remove the bumper assembly.

Dismantling and reassembling

6. Follow as necessary the procedure for dismantling and reassembling the front bumper, see Section R.37, noting that the rear bumper is fitted with lashing brackets which should be refitted towards the bottom of the assembly.

Refitting

7. Reverse the procedure in 1 to 5, ensuring that the bumper assembly is central about the body before tightening the five nuts securing the assembly to the rear body panel.

Section R.39

FASCIA

(GHN5 and GHD5 cars from Car No. 410002)

Removing

1. Disconnect the battery.
2. Withdraw the centre console and place to one side to give access to the fascia centre fixing screws, see Section R.40.
3. Withdraw the face-level vents from the fascia.
4. Remove the three fascia upper retaining nuts, washers and brackets.
5. Remove the four lower fixing screws.
6. Remove the bolts securing the steering-column to the fascia support rail and lower the column.
7. Remove the screw, nut and bracket securing the rear of the glovebox to the fascia support rail.
8. Ease the fascia assembly downwards to clear the upper fixing studs and then pull the assembly forward.
9. Disconnect the speedometer cable.
10. Disconnect the oil pressure gauge pipe.
11. Disconnect the fascia wiring harness from the front harness at the wiring multi-connector plugs.
12. Disconnect the mixture control (choke) cable at the carburetters and feed the cable through the bulkhead.
13. Remove the fascia assembly from the vehicle.

Refitting

14. Reverse the procedure in 1 to 13.

Section R.40

CONSOLE

(GHN5 and GHD5 cars from Car No. 410002)

Removing

1. Remove the gaiter retaining ring securing screws, noting that the front screw is the shortest.
2. Remove the gaiter retaining ring.
3. Raise the hinged arm-rest and remove the retaining screw.
4. Remove the arm-rest, easing it up over the gaiter and gear lever.
5. Remove the four screws retaining the centre console and move the console rearwards.
6. Remove the heater control knobs, press in the retainer clips using a small pin through the holes in the knobs.
7. Remove the nuts securing the heater controls to the centre console and withdraw the controls.
8. Remove the bulb holders from the heater controls, clock and warning lights.
9. Disconnect the wires from the clock.
10. Remove the two knurled nuts and retaining bracket and withdraw the clock from the console.
11. Remove the warning lights from the console.
12. Remove the securing nuts and remove the light boxes and illumination dial.
13. Remove the centre console.

Refitting

14. Reverse the procedure in 1 to 13.

Section R.41

HORIZONTAL ALIGNMENT CHECK

(GHN5 and GHD5 cars with impact absorbing bumpers)

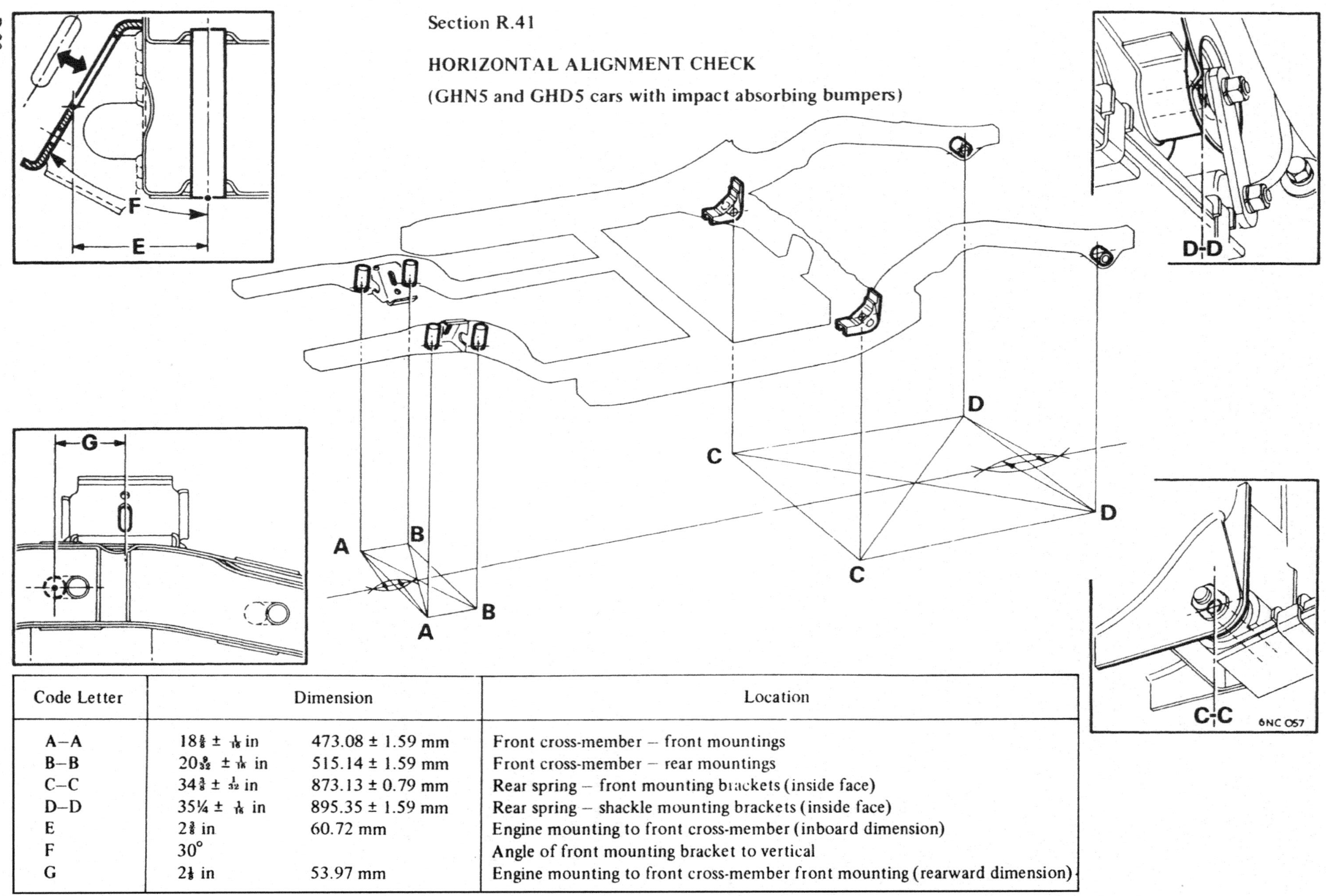

Code Letter	Dimension		Location
A–A	$18\frac{5}{8} \pm \frac{1}{16}$ in	473.08 ± 1.59 mm	Front cross-member – front mountings
B–B	$20\frac{9}{32} \pm \frac{1}{16}$ in	515.14 ± 1.59 mm	Front cross-member – rear mountings
C–C	$34\frac{3}{8} \pm \frac{1}{32}$ in	873.13 ± 0.79 mm	Rear spring – front mounting brackets (inside face)
D–D	$35\frac{1}{4} \pm \frac{1}{16}$ in	895.35 ± 1.59 mm	Rear spring – shackle mounting brackets (inside face)
E	$2\frac{3}{8}$ in	60.72 mm	Engine mounting to front cross-member (inboard dimension)
F	30°		Angle of front mounting bracket to vertical
G	$2\frac{1}{8}$ in	53.97 mm	Engine mounting to front cross-member front mounting (rearward dimension)

Section R.42

VERTICAL ALIGNMENT CHECK

(GHN5 and GHD5 cars with impact absorbing bumpers)

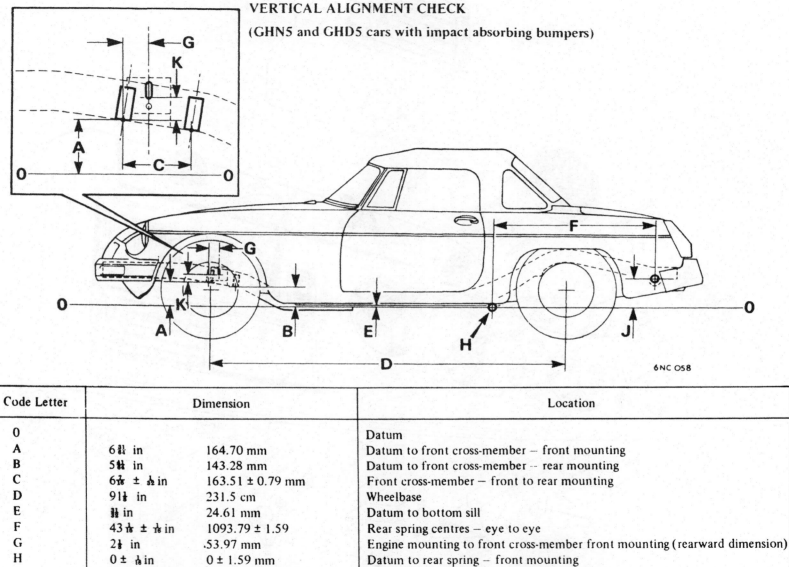

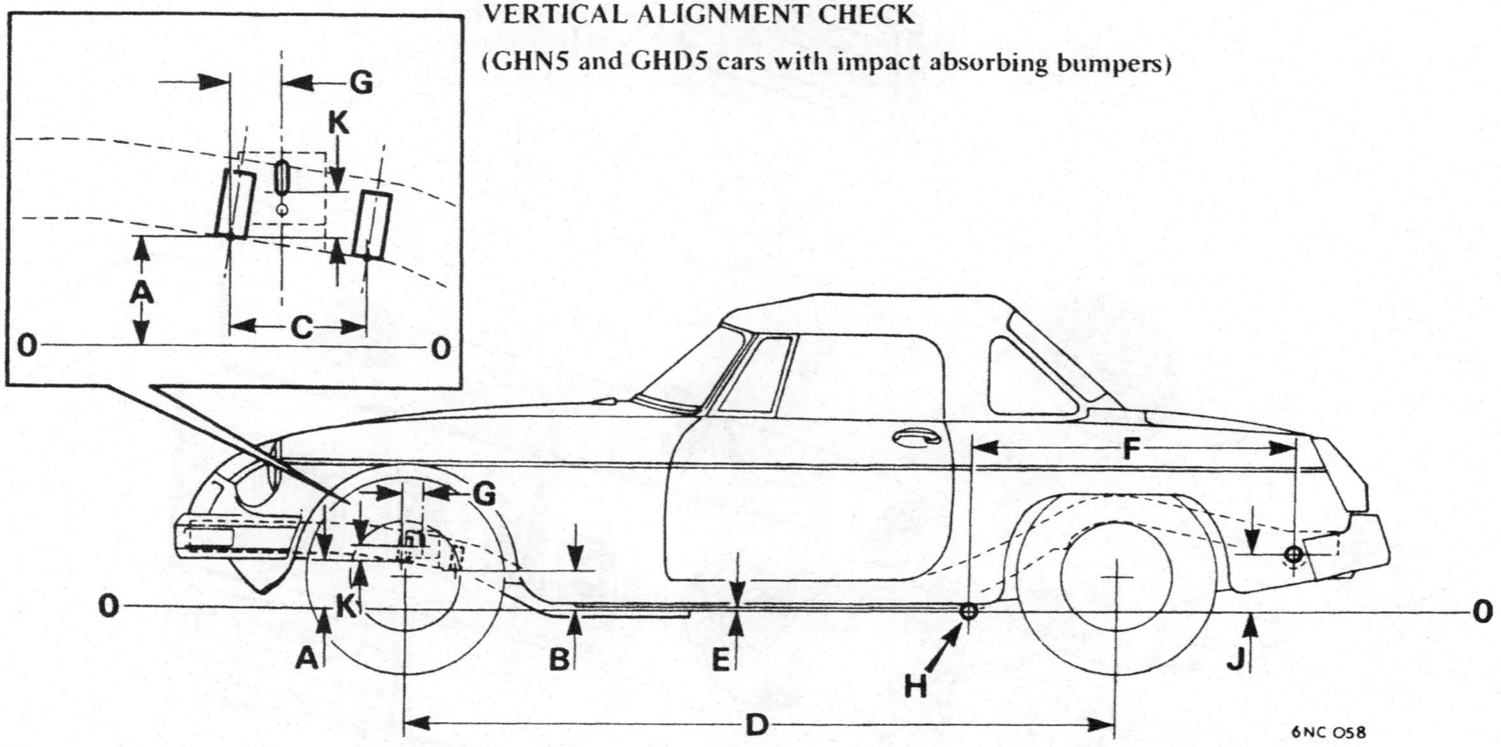

Code Letter	Dimension		Location
0			Datum
A	6 31/64 in	164.70 mm	Datum to front cross-member – front mounting
B	5 41/64 in	143.28 mm	Datum to front cross-member – rear mounting
C	6 7/16 ± 1/32 in	163.51 ± 0.79 mm	Front cross-member – front to rear mounting
D	91 1/8 in	231.5 cm	Wheelbase
E	31/32 in	24.61 mm	Datum to bottom sill
F	43 1/16 ± 1/16 in	1093.79 ± 1.59	Rear spring centres – eye to eye
G	2 1/8 in	53.97 mm	Engine mounting to front cross-member front mounting (rearward dimension)
H	0 ± 1/16 in	0 ± 1.59 mm	Datum to rear spring – front mounting
J	5 5/8 ± 1/32 in	142.87 ± 0.79 mm	Datum to rear spring – rear shackle mounting
K	1 13/32 ± 1/32 in	35.72 ± 0.79 mm	Engine mounting to front cross-member front mounting (height)

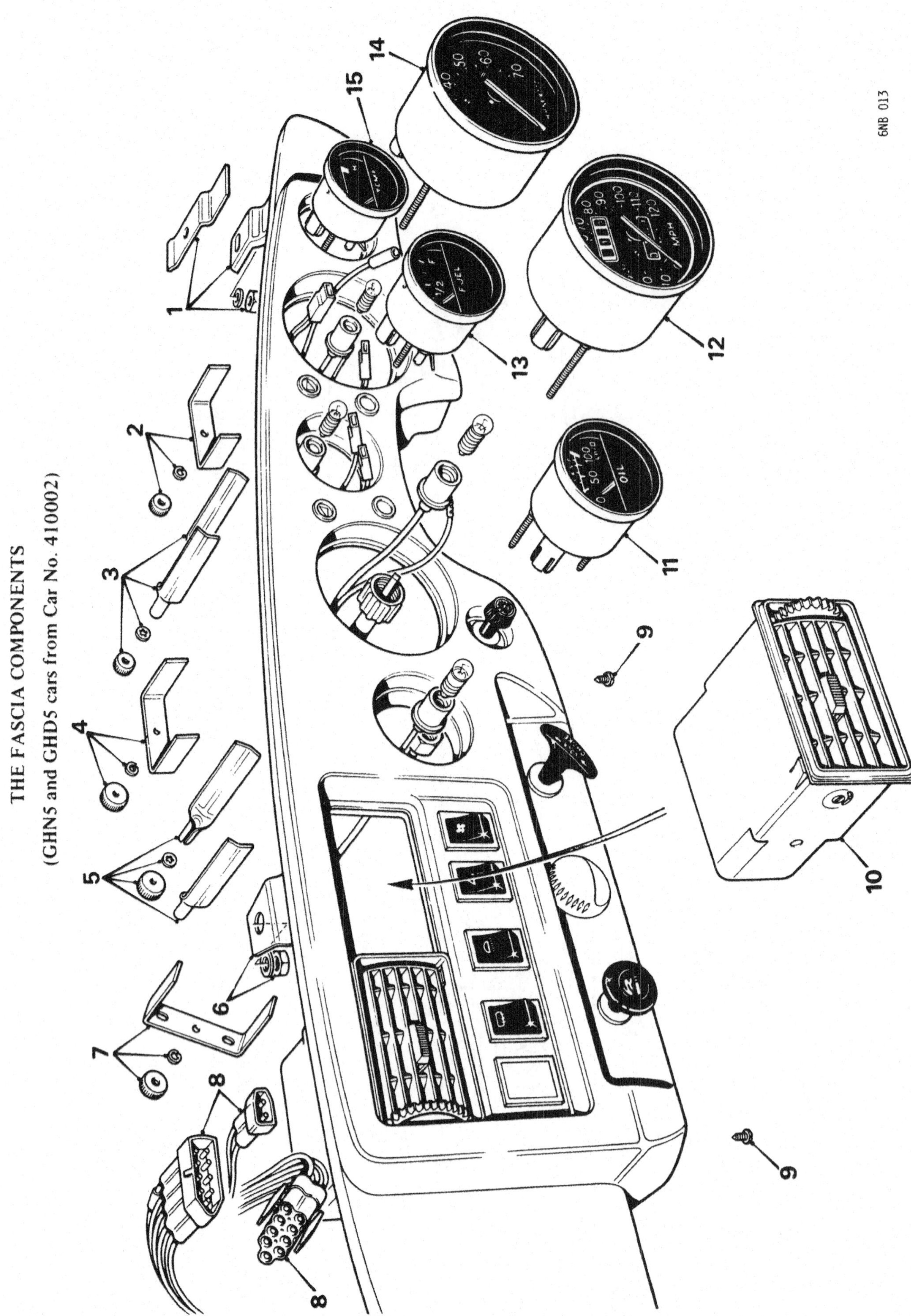

THE FASCIA COMPONENTS
(GHN5 and GHD5 cars from Car No. 410002)

KEY TO THE FASCIA COMPONENTS

No.	Description	No.	Description	No.	Description
1.	Fascia right-hand fixings	6.	Fascia centre fixings	11.	Oil pressure gauge
2.	Temperature gauge fixings	7.	Oil pressure gauge fixings	12.	Speedometer
3.	Tachometer fixings	8.	Wiring multi-connector plugs	13.	Fuel gauge
4.	Fuel gauge fixings	9.	Fascia lower fixing screw	14.	Tachometer
5.	Speedometer fixings	10.	Face level vent	15.	Temperature gauge

THE CONSOLE COMPONENTS

(GHN5 and GHD5 cars from Car No. 410002)

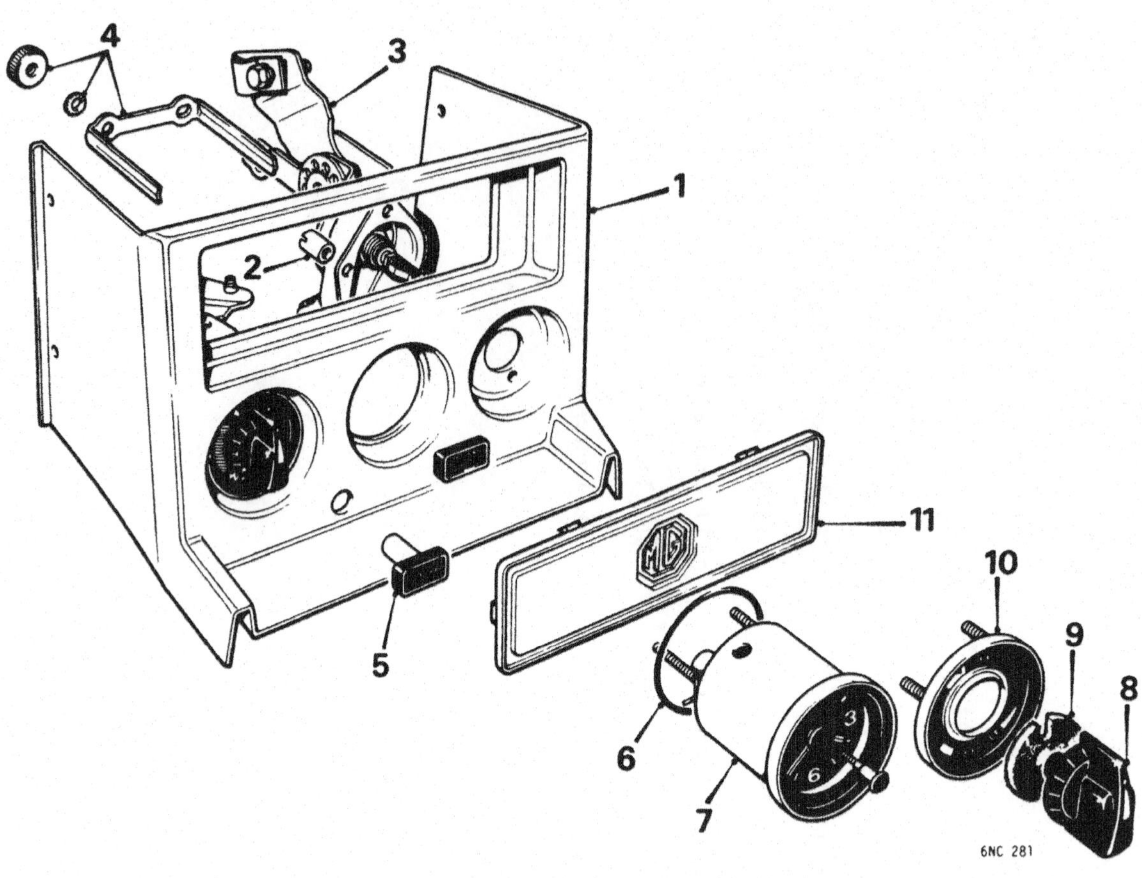

KEY TO THE CONSOLE COMPONENTS

No.	Description	No.	Description	No.	Description
1.	Console	5.	Warning lamp	9.	Felt washer
2.	Nut–light boxes	6.	Sealing ring	10.	Illumination dial
3.	Heater control	7.	Clock	11.	Blanking plate
4.	Clock fixings	8.	Heater control knob		

Section R.43

HEATER
(GHN5 and GHD5 cars from Car No. 410002)

Removing
1. Disconnect the battery.
2. Drain the cooling system, see Section C.9.
3. Disconnect the heater wires at the wiring multi-connector plug.
4. Slacken the clips and disconnect the heater hoses.
5. Remove the screws securing the heater unit to the body.
6. Release the washer motor wires from the clip on the heater unit casing.
7. Withdraw the centre console to give access to the heat control mechanism, see Section R.40.
8. Disconnect the heater temperature control cable.
9. Disconnect the demister tubes from the heater unit.
10. Withdraw the heater unit from the body aperture.

Refitting
11. Reverse the procedure in 1 to 10, feeding the heater temperature control cable through the slot in the bulkhead before fitting the heater unit.

Section R.44

HEATER WATER VALVE
(GHN5 and GHD5 cars from Car No. 410002)

Removing
1. Drain the cooling system, see Section C.9.
2. Slacken the clip and disconnect the heater hose from the valve.
3. Slacken the heater temperature control inner cable securing trunnion.
4. Slacken the outer cable retaining bracket securing screw.
5. Withdraw the heater control cable from the valve.
6. Remove the two securing bolts.
7. Withdraw the valve and joint washer from the cylinder head.

Refitting
8. Reverse the procedure in 1 to 7, using a new joint washer if necessary.

Section R.45

HEATER FAN MOTOR
(GHN5 and GHD5 cars from Car No. 410002)

Removing
1. Disconnect the battery.
2. Disconnect the wires at the terminals on the fan motor.
3. Remove the three screws securing the fan motor to the heater casing.
4. Withdraw the fan motor from the casing.
5. Remove the clip retaining the fan to the fan motor spindle.
6. Remove the fan from the spindle.

Refitting
7. Reverse the procedure in 1 to 6.

Section R.46

HEATER MATRIX
(GHN5 and GHD5 cars from Car No. 410002)

Removing
1. Remove the heater unit, see Section R.41.
2. Empty any remaining coolant from the heater matrix.
3. Remove the heater casing retaining clips.
4. Lift the side of the heater casing over the heater matrix outlets and place to one side, noting that the heater fan motor wires are connected to the heater fan motor resistor inside the main casing.
5. Withdraw the heater matrix from the main casing.
6. Remove the packing foam from around the heater matrix.

Refitting
7. Reverse the procedure in 1 to 6.

Section R.47

HEATER AIR FLOW CONTROL CABLE
(GHN5 and GHD5 cars from Car No, 410002)

Removing
1. Remove the heater unit, see Section R.41.
2. Slacken the outer cable retaining bracket screw.
3. Slacken the inner cable trunnion screw.
4. Withdraw the cable from the heater flap bracket.

Refitting
5. Reverse the procedure in 1 to 4.

Section R.48

HEATER CONTROLS
(GHN5 and GHD5 cars from Car No. 410002)

Removing

1. Withdraw the centre console to give access to the heater controls, see Section R.40.
2. Remove the heater control knob, press in the retainer clip using a small pin through the hole in the knob.
3. Remove the heater control securing nut.
4. Withdraw the control from the centre console.
5. Slacken the outer cable retaining bracket screw.
6. Slacken the inner cable trunnion screw.
7. Withdraw the heater control from the cable assembly.

Refitting

8. Reverse the procedure in 1 to 7.

Section R.49

HEATER TEMPERATURE CONTROL CABLE
(GHN5 and GHD5 cars from Car No. 410002)

Removing

1. Slacken the outer cable retaining bracket screw on the water heater valve.
2. Slacken the inner cable trunnion screw.
3. Disconnect the cable assembly from the water heater valve.
4. Withdraw the centre console to give access to the heater temperature control, see Section R.40.
5. Slacken the outer cable retaining bracket screw.
6. Slacken the inner cable trunnion screw.
7. Withdraw the cable assembly from the heater temperature control.
8. Feed the cable through the bulkhead and remove from the vehicle.

Refitting

9. Reverse the procedure in 1 to 8.

SECTION Ra

THE BODY

The information given in this Section refers specifically to service operations on, or affected by equipment fitted to the MGB (GHN5/GHN4 and GHD5/GHD4) in conformity with local and territorial requirements, and must be used in conjunction with Section R.

Section Ra.1

CONSOLE

Removing

1. Disconnect the battery.
2. Remove the four retaining screws.
3. Remove the ashtray (if fitted).
4. Turn back the carpet and withdraw the console.
5. Disconnect the wiring from the back of the console and remove the console assembly.

Refitting

6. Reverse the removing procedure in 1 to 5.

Section Ra.2

Fascia

Removing

1. Disconnect the battery.
2. Unscrew the three retaining screws from the lower fascia cover panels and remove the panels.
3. Disconnect the mixture control (choke) cable from the carburetters.
4. Remove the heater air control knob, unscrew the control securing nut and disengage the control from its fixing bracket.
5. Remove the heater temperature control knob, unscrew the control securing nut and disengage the control from its fixing bracket.
6. Remove the two fixing screws from the lower edge of the fascia.
7. Unscrew the two knurled nuts retaining the tachometer, disconnect the earth wire, and remove the retaining brackets.
8. Disconnect the wiring from the tachometer and remove the instrument.
9. Remove the six nuts from the fascia upper edge fixing studs.
10. Remove the screws securing each end of the fascia trim piping from behind the fascia.
11. Unscrew the trip recorder reset knob retaining nut and disengage the reset from its bracket.
12. Disconnect the speedometer drive cable from the back of the instrument.
13. Ease the fascia assembly rearwards to disengage the top fixing studs from the body panel, then lift the assembly clear of the steering-column switch cowl.
14. Disconnect the wiring from the instruments and switches, withdraw the mixture control cable and remove the fascia complete with instruments and switches.

Refitting

15. Reverse the removing procedure in 1 to 14.

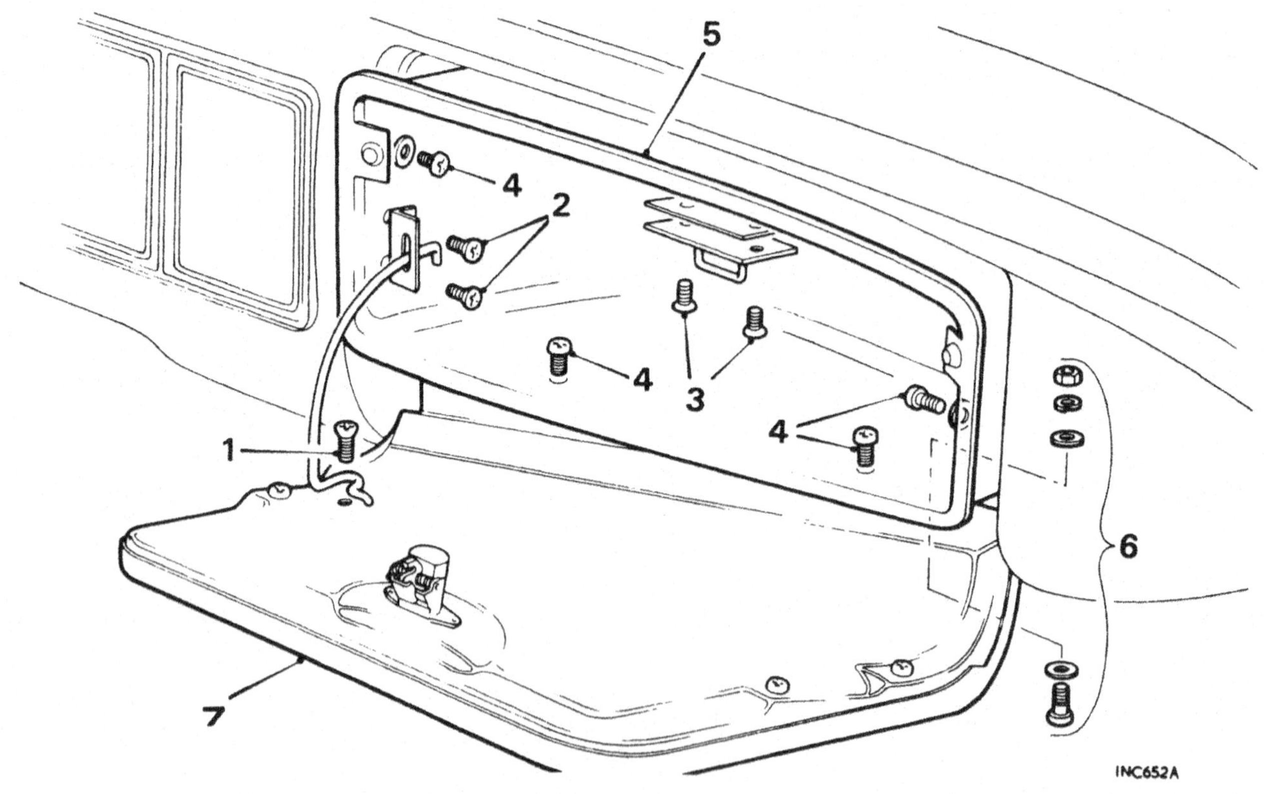

Fig. Ra.1
The glovebox and lid

1. Screw for glovebox lid stay.
2. Screws for glovebox lid stay.
3. Screws for catch.
4. Screws for glovebox.
5. Glovebox.
6. Screws for glovebox lid hinge.
7. Glovebox lid.

Section Ra.3

GLOVEBOX AND LID
(GHN5 and GHD5 cars from Car No. 258001)

Removing
GLOVEBOX ONLY

1. Remove the screw retaining the stay to the glovebox lid.
2. Remove the screws retaining the glovebox lid stay to the glovebox.
3. Remove the screws securing the glovebox lid catch.
4. Remove the screws retaining the glovebox.
5. Withdraw the glovebox.

GLOVEBOX LID

6. Carry out operations 1 to 5.
7. Remove the screws and nuts securing the glovebox lid and withdraw the lid.

Refitting
GLOVEBOX LID

8. Reverse the removing procedure in 6 to 7.

GLOVEBOX

9. Reverse the removing procedure in 1 to 5.

Section Ra.4

FACE-LEVEL VENTS
(GHN5 and GHD5 cars from Car No. 258001)

Removing
FACE-LEVEL VENTS AND ESCUTCHEON ASSEMBLY

1. Remove the glovebox--Section Ra.3.
2. Disconnect the air duct hoses from the back of the face-level vents.
3. Remove the two screws and retaining strap securing the escutcheon assembly to the fascia.
4. Withdraw the face-level vents and escutcheon assembly from the fascia.

FACE-LEVEL VENTS

5. Carry out operations 1 to 4.
6. In turn, ease each bottom locating tag of one vent inwards and slightly withdraw the vent until the tag rests on the lip of the escutcheon.

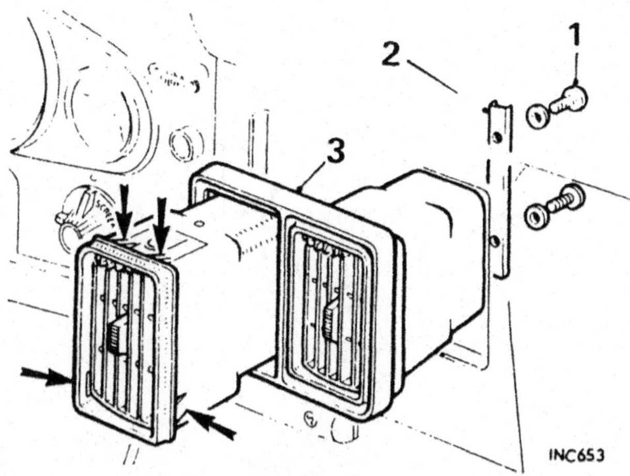

Fig. Ra.2
Removing the face-level vent showing the locating tags arrowed

1. Screw for retaining strap 2. Retaining strap. 3. Escutcheon.

7. With the aid of a narrow blade tool, inserted from the back between the escutcheon and the vent, depress the two top locating tags.
8. Withdraw the vent from the escutcheon.
9. Repeat 6 to 8 for the remaining face-level vent.

Refitting
FACE-LEVEL VENTS

10. Push one only of the face-level vents into the escutcheon noting:
    a. Ensure that the rounded corners of the face-level vent adjacent to the serrated wheel registers in the recess of the escutcheon with the rounded corners.
    b. The vent assemblies are marked L.H. (left-hand) and R.H. (right-hand) on their flaps for correct assembly when viewing the fascia from inside the car.
11. Reverse the removing procedure in 3 to 4 ensuring that the escutcheon assembly is fitted with the serrated wheels uppermost.
12. Push in the remaining face-level vent into the escutcheon noting operation 10 a.
13. Reverse the removing procedure in 1 to 2.

FACE-LEVEL VENT AND ESCUTCHEON ASSEMBLY

14. Reverse the operations 6 to 8 to refit one of the face-level vents.
15. Carry out operations 11 to 13.

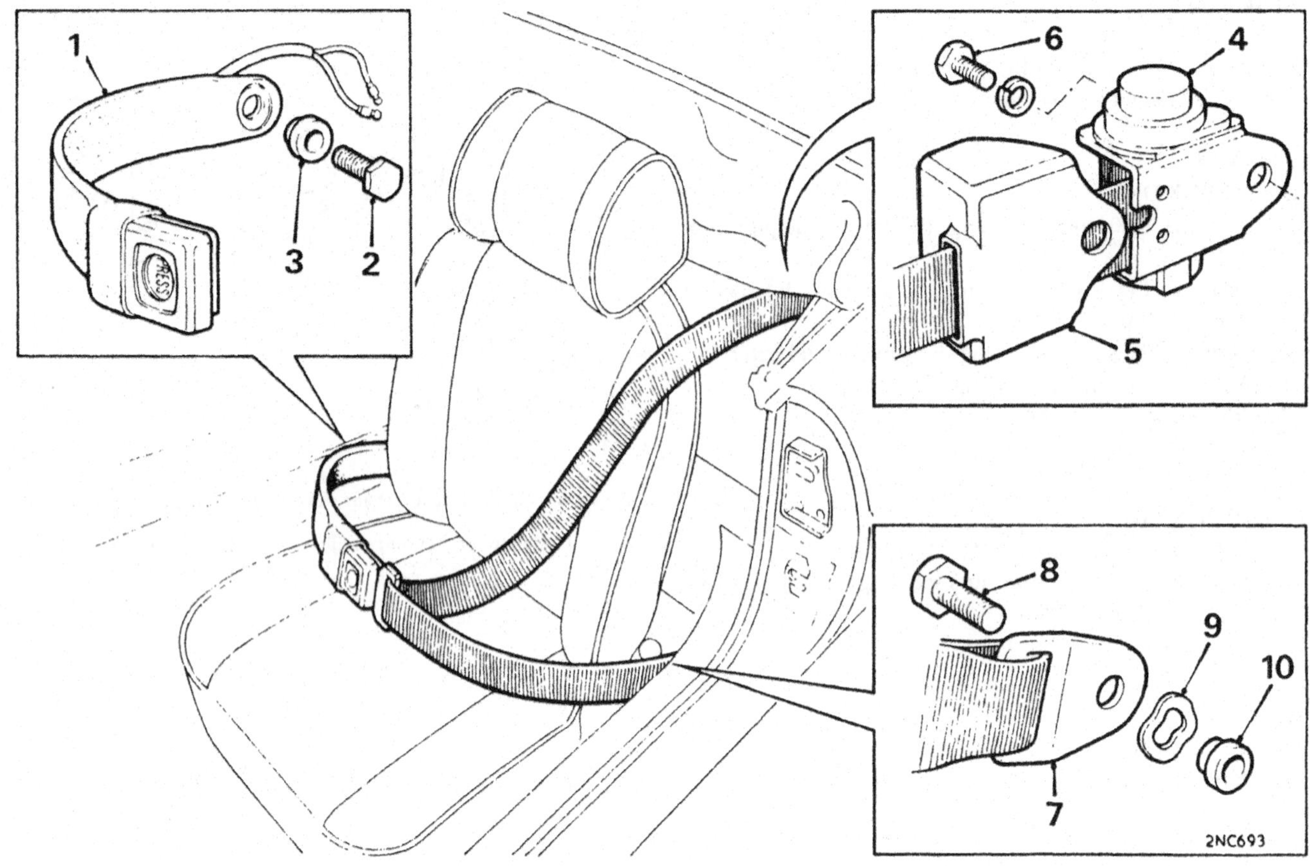

Fig. Ra.3
Seat belt fixings

1. Short belt.
2. Retaining bolt.
3. Spacer.
4. Seat belt reel.
5. Cover for reel.
6. Retaining bolt.
7. Seat belt sill mounting.
8. Retaining bolt.
9. Anti-rattle washer.
10. Spacer.

Section Ra.5

SEAT BELTS

Removing

SHORT BELT

1. Lift the carpet adjacent to the tunnel and disconnect the wiring from the seat belt.
2. Remove the bolt and spacer to release the belt.

LONG BELT AND REEL

3. Remove the bolt, waved washer and spacer to release the belt from the sill.
4. Remove the bolt and spring washer to release the reel from the rear wheel arch.

Refitting

LONG BELT AND REEL

5. Reverse the removing procedure in 3 to 4.

SHORT BELT

6. Reverse the removing procedure in 1 to 2.

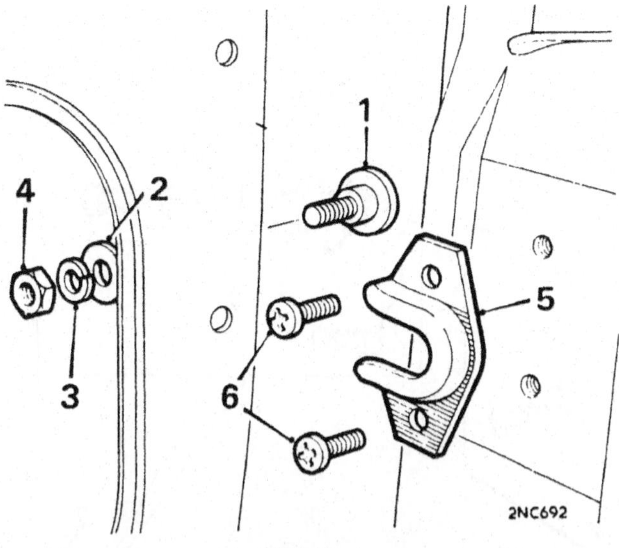

Fig. Ra.4
Anti-burst door unit

1. Door pin.
2. Plain washer.
3. Spring washer.
4. Retaining nut for pin.
5. Plate.
6. Retaining screws.

Section Ra.6

ANTI-BURST DOOR UNITS (GHN5 and GHD5 cars from Car No. 294251)

Removing

ANTI-BURST PLATE UNIT

1. Remove the two screws to release the plate from 'B' post.

ANTI-BURST PIN UNIT

2. Remove the door trim pad–Section R.31.
3. Unscrew the nut and remove the spring washer to release the pin unit from the door.

Refitting

ANTI-BURST PIN UNIT

4. Reverse the removing procedure in 2 to 3.

ANTI-BURST PLATE UNIT

5. Refit the plate unit to the 'B' post and retain in position with the two screws.

Section Ra.7

THE FRONT BUMPER AND OVER-RIDERS

(GHN5 and GHD5 cars from Car No. 339095)

Removing

1. Remove the bolts securing each end of the bumper bar to the body, noting the rubber pad fitted between the steady bracket and the body.
2. Remove the nuts and bolts securing each bumper spring to the longitudinal member and remove the bumper assembly.
3. Unscrew the nuts and remove the dome headed bolts, noting:
   a. The small distance piece fitted between the steady bracket and the bumper bar.
   b. The medium size distance piece fitted between the bumper spring and the bumper bar.
4. Remove each over-rider assembly retaining bolt to separate the over-rider assembly and its support casting from the bumper and main spring, noting the large distance piece fitted between the bumper spring and the bumper bar.
5. Remove the nut and bolt to release the lashing bracket from the bumper spring.
6. If it is necessary to dismantle the over-rider assembly proceed as follows:
   a. Mark the over-rider clamping bracket and the mounting bracket at the top to assist reassembling.
   b. Remove the clamping bracket securing screws and remove the clamping bracket.
   c. Slide the mounting bracket from the over-rider.

Refitting

7. Reverse the procedure in 1 to 6, referring to Fig. Ra.6 and noting the following:
   a. Ensure that the clamping bracket is correctly fitted to the over-rider.
   b. Ensure that each over-rider assembly and support casting is fitted to the correct side of the bumper as the over-rider assemblies are handed.
   c. The fitted position of the over-rider assembly retaining bolt is at an angle; ensure when fitting not to damage the thread.

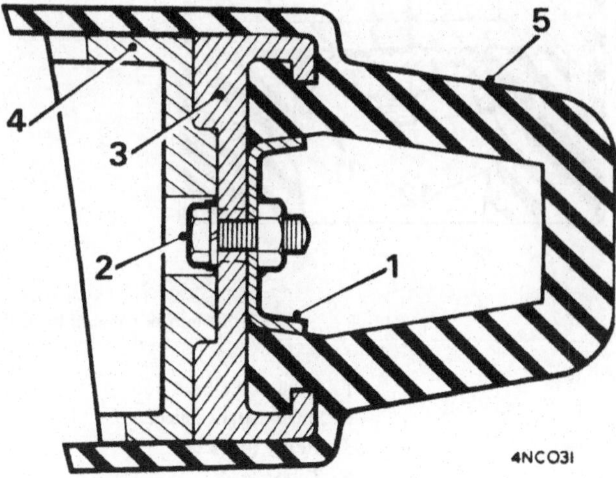

Fig. Ra.5
The over-rider assembly and support casting

1. Clamping bracket.
2. Clamping bracket securing bolt.
3. Mounting bracket.
4. Support casting.
5. Over-rider.

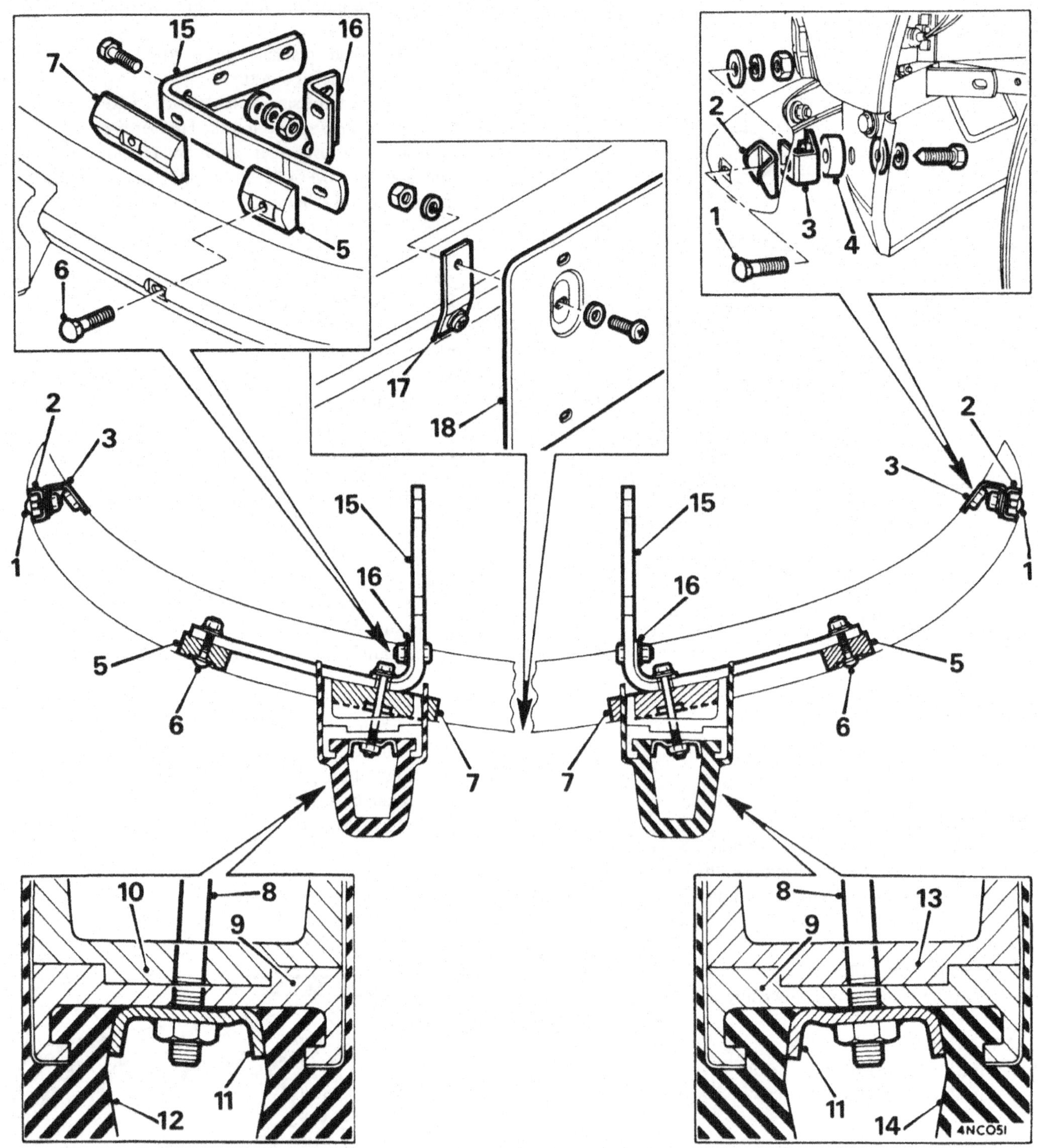

Fig. Ra.6
The front bumper assembly (GHN5 and GHD5 cars from Car No. 339095)

1. Small dome head bolt.
2. Small distance piece.
3. Steady bracket.
4. Rubber pad.
5. Medium distance piece.
6. Long dome head bolt.
7. Large distance piece.
8. Over-rider assembly securing bolt.
9. Over-rider mounting bracket.
10. Right-hand over-rider support casting.
11. Over-rider clamping bracket.
12. Right-hand over-rider.
13. Left-hand over-rider support casting.
14. Left-hand over-rider.
15. Bumper spring.
16. Lashing bracket.
17. Number-plate support bracket.
18. Number-plate.

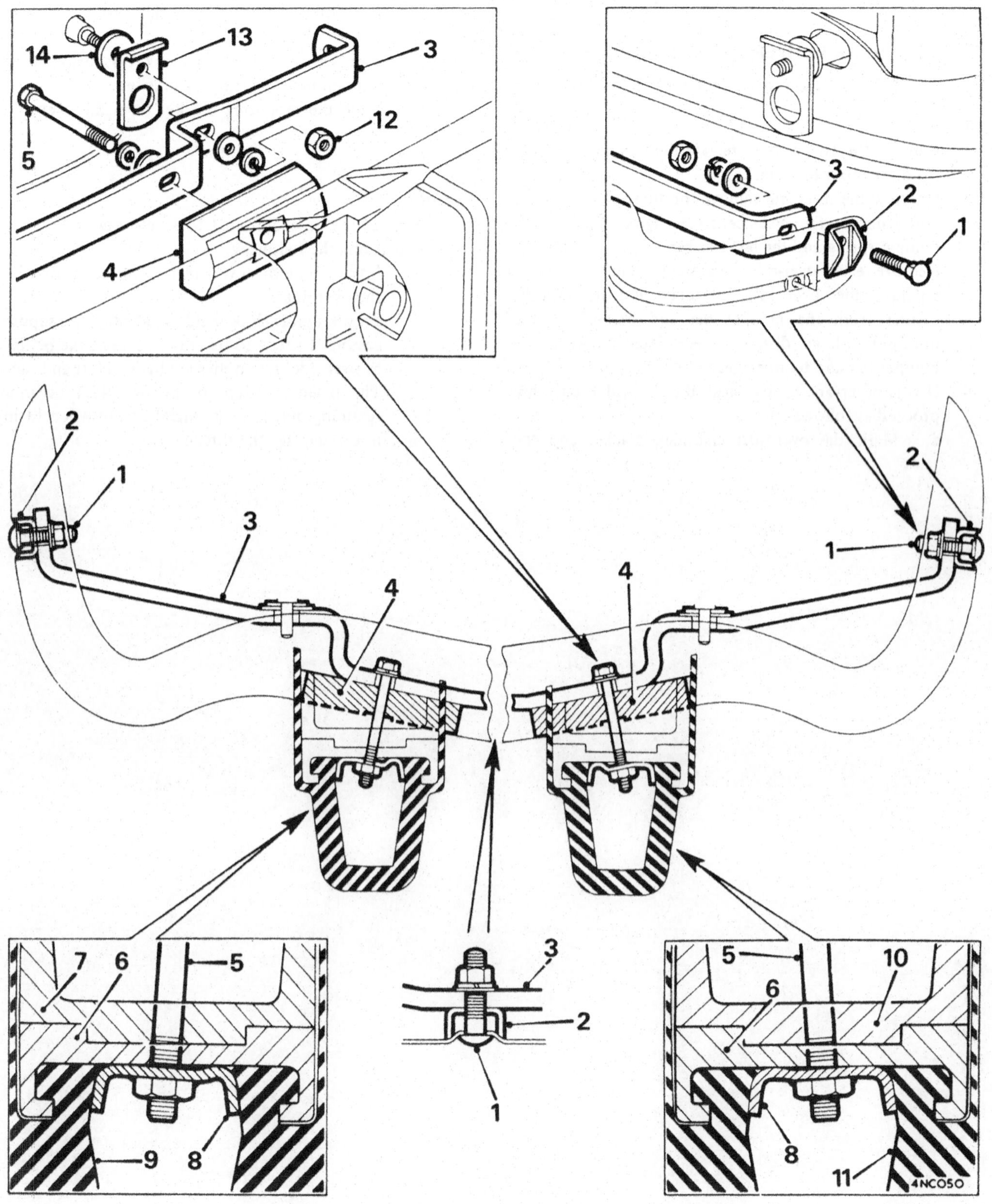

Fig. Ra.7
The rear bumper assembly (GHN5 and GHD5 cars from Car No. 339095)

1. Dome head bolt.
2. Small distance piece.
3. Bumper spring.
4. Large distance piece.
5. Over-rider assembly securing bolt.
6. Over-rider mounting bracket.
7. Left-hand over-rider support casting.
8. Over-rider clamping bracket.
9. Left-hand over-rider.
10. Right-hand over-rider support casting.
11. Right-hand over-rider.
12. Bumper assembly securing nut.
13. Lashing bracket.
14. Large flat washer.

Section Ra.8

THE REAR BUMPER AND OVER-RIDERS
(GHN5 and GHD5 cars from Car No. 339095)

Removing

1. Remove the two nuts to release the bumper assembly from the mounting brackets.
2. Unscrew the nuts and remove the three dome headed bolts, noting the distance pieces fitted between the bumper spring and the bumper bar.
3. Remove each over-rider assembly retaining bolt to separate the over-rider assembly and its support casting from the bumper bar and bumper spring, noting the large distance piece fitted between the bumper bar and bumper spring.
4. If it is necessary to dismantle the over-rider assembly proceed as follows:
   a. Mark the over-rider clamping bracket and the mounting bracket at the top to assist reassembling.
   b. Remove the clamping bracket securing screws and remove the clamping bracket.
   c. Slide the mounting bracket from the over-rider.

Refitting

5. Reverse the procedure in 1 to 4, referring to Fig. Ra.7 and noting the following:
   a. Ensure that the over-rider is correctly fitted to the over-rider.
   b. Ensure that each over-rider assembly and support casting is fitted to its correct side of the bumper as over-rider assemblies are handed left and right.
   c. The fitted position of the over-rider assembly retaining bolt is at an angle; ensure when fitting not to damage the thread.

SECTION S

SERVICE TOOLS

All Service tools mentioned in this Manual are only obtainable from the tool manufacturer:

Messrs. V. L. Churchill & Co. Ltd.
P.O. Box No. 3,
London Road, Daventry,
Northants, England.

OPERATION	TOOL No.	PAGE No.
ENGINE		
Camshaft liner reaming	18G 123 A	S.9
	18G 123 B	S.9
	18G 123 E	S.9
	18G 123 F	S.9
	18G 123 L	S.9
	18G 123 T	S.10
	18G 123 AB	S.10
	18G 123 AC	S.10
	18G 123 AD	S.10
Camshaft liner removing and replacing	18G 124 A	S.10
	18G 124 B	S.10
	18G 124 C	S.10
	18G 124 F	S.10
	18G 124 H	S.10
Crankshaft gear and pulley removing	18G 2	S.6
Crankshaft oil seal replacing	18G 134 CQ	S.11
	18G 1108	S.22
Crankshaft pulley nut removing	18G 98 A	S.9
Crankshaft spigot bush removing and replacing	18G 284 H	S.15
	18G 284 L	S.15
	18G 1037	S.21
Gudgeon pin, removing and replacing	18G 1150	S.23
	18G 1150 D	S.23
Main bearing cap removing	18G 284	S.15
	18G 284 A	S.15
	18G 284 AC	S.15
Oil pump relief valve seat grinding	18G 69	S.9
Piston refitting	18G 55 A	S.9
Timing cover locating and oil seal replacing	18G 134	S.11
	18G 134 BD	S.11
Cover locating — Early models	18G 3	S.6
Cover locating — Later models	18G 1046	S.21
Torque spanners	18G 372	S.16
	18G 536	S.17
	18G 537	S.17
Valve removing and refitting	18G 45	S.8

OPERATION		TOOL No.	PAGE No.
Valve seat cutting		18G 25	S.6
		18G 25 A	S.6
		18G 25 C	S.6
		18G 27	S.6
		18G 28	S.7
		18G 28 A	S.7
		18G 28 B	S.7
		18G 28 C	S.7
		18G 174 B	S.12
		18G 174 D	S.12
Valve seat grinding		18G 29	S.7
		18G 29 A	S.7
CLUTCH			
Refitting		18G 1027	S.20
(Involute spine clutch plates)		18G 680	S.19
GEARBOX			
Bevel pinion flange retaining		18G 34 A	S.7
First motion shaft assembling and replacing		18G 4	S.6
		18G 5	S.6
Layshaft replacing	.646 in. dia. shaft	18G 471	S.17
	.670 in. dia. shaft	18G 1138	S.22
Propeller shaft flange removing		18G 2	S.6
Rear oil seal removing and replacing		18G 389	S.16
		18G 389 B	S.16
		18G 134	S.11
		18G 134 BK	S.11
Selector fork and rod guiding		18G 41	S.7
Third motion shaft, synchromesh assembly: Early models		18G 222	S.13
		18G 223	S.13
Later models		18G 262	S.14
		18G 1026	S.20
Laycock Overdrive Type 'D'			
Annulus spigot bearing replacing		18G 1042	S.21
Clip removing		18G 1004	S.20
Hydraulic pressure testing		18G 251	S.14
		18G 251 D	S.14
Mainshaft bearing removing and replacing		18G 47 C	S.8
		18G 47 CZ	S.8
		18G 47 AP	S.8
		18G 134	S.11
		18G 1039	S.21
Oil pump body removing		18G 183	S.12
		18G 183 A	S.12
		18G 1040	S.21
Rear oil seal removing and replacing		18G 134 BK	S.11
		18G 389 B	S.16
Roller clutch assembling		18G 178	S.12

OPERATION		TOOL No.	PAGE No.
Laycock Overdrive, Type 'LH'			
Hydraulic pressure testing		18G 251	S.14
		18G 251 E	S.14
Mainshaft bearing removing and replacing		18G 185	S.12
		18G 186	S.12
		18G 391	S.17
		18G 1045	S.21
		18G 1024	S.20
Oil pump removing and replacing		18G 1117	S.22
		18G 1118	S.22
Rear oil seal removing and replacing		18G 389	S.16
		18G 389 D	S.16
		18G 177	S.12
Roller clutch assembling		18G 178	S.12
AUTOMATIC GEARBOX			
Clutch compressing and seal replacing		18G 702	S.19
		18G 1107	S.22
		18G 1016	S.20
Circlip removing and replacing		18G 1004	S.20
Spare points		18G 1004 J	S.20
	Alternative	18G 675	S.19
Front servo spanner and gauge		18G 678	S.19
Input shaft end-float checking		18G 674	S.18
Inhibitor switch locknut		18G 679	S.19
Pressure testing		18G 677 Z	S.19
	Alternative	18G 502 A	S.17
	Alternative	18G 502 K	S.17
Torque spanners		18G 536	S.17
		18G 536 A	S.17
		18G 536 B	S.17
		18G 537	S.17
		18G 681	S.19
		18G 681 A	S.19
		18G 681 B	S.19
		18G 537 A	S.17
		18G 537 B	S.17
REAR SUSPENSION AND FINAL DRIVE			
Three-quarter-floating Rear Axle			
Bevel pinion bearing removing and replacing		18G 47 C	S.8
		18G 47 AH	S.8
		18G 207	S.13
		18G 191	S.13
Bevel pinion flange wrench		18G 34 A	S.7
Bevel pinion outer race removing		18G 264	S.14
		18G 264 E	S.15
		18G 264 F	S.15

OPERATION	TOOL No.	PAGE No.
Differential bearing removing and replacing	18G 47 C	S.8
	18G 47 T	S.8
	18G 134	S.11
	18G 134 P	S.11
	18G 191 A	S.13
Propeller shaft flange removing	18G 2	S.6
Semi-floating Rear Axle		
Axle shaft assembly replacing	18G 1067	S.21
Bevel pinion bearing removing and replacing	18G 47 C	S.8
	18G 47 AS	S.8
	18G 191	S.13
	18G 264	S.14
Bevel pinion flange wrench	18G 34 A	S.7
Bevel pinion outer race removing	18G 264	S.14
	18G 264 AA	S.15
	18G 264 AB	S.15
	18G 264 AD	S.15
Differential bearing removing and replacing	18G 47 C	S.8
	18G 47 AK	S.8
	18G 134	S.11
	18G 134 CM	S.11
Differential reassembling	18G 191	S.13
	18G 191 F	S.13
	18G 191 H	S.13
	18G 191 J	S.13
Final drive and rear axle shaft nut	18G 586	S.18
Impulse extractor	18G 284	S.15
Propeller shaft flange removing	18G 2	S.6
Rear axle casing stretching	18G 131 C	S.10
Torque setting spanner	18G 592	S.18
FRONT SUSPENSION AND STEERING		
Spring compressing	18G 693	S.19
Steering-arm ball pin removing	18G 1063	S.21
Steering-wheel hub removing	18G 1181	S.23
Steering rack ball joint spanners	18G 706	S.20
Swivel axle bush removing, replacing, and reaming	18G 68	S.9
	18G 596	S.18
	18G 597	S.18
	18G 1063	S.21

OPERATION		TOOL No.	PAGE No.
FRONT AND REAR HUBS			
Hub removing and replacing		18G 304	S.16
	Disc wheels	18G 304 A	S.16
		18G 304 J	S.16
	Wire wheels	18G 1032	S.20
		18G 363	S.16
Front hub bearing cup replacing		18G 1122	S.22
		18G 1122 A	S.22
Front hub oil seal replacing		18G 134	S.11
		18G 134 BH	S.11
Rear hub bearing removing		18G 134	S.11
		18G 134 P	S.11
Rear hub nut spanner		18G 152	S.11
BRAKING SYSTEM			
Brake adjusting (rear only)		18G 619 A	S.18
Disc brake piston re-setting		18G 590	S.18
MISCELLANEOUS			
Light switch bezel, removing and replacing		18G 671	S.18
Petrol gauge tank attachment lock ring spanner		18G 1001	S.20
Remover; hydraulic version of 18G 304		18G 304 Z	S.16
Rocker type switch and bezel, removing		18G 1145	S.22
Rocker type switch (slim type) removing		18G 1202	S.23

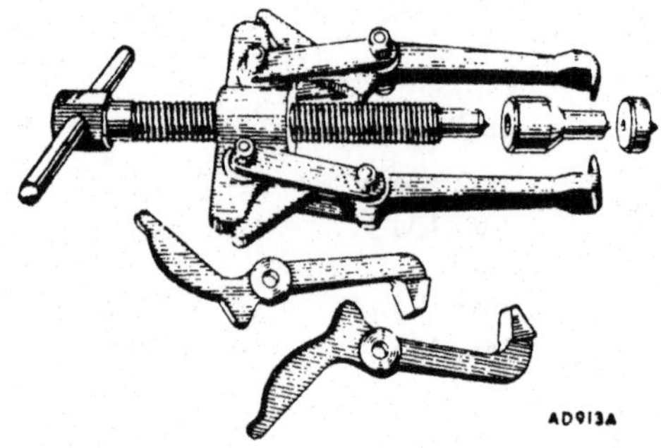

18G 2. Crankshaft Gear, Pulley, and Propeller shaft Flange Remover.

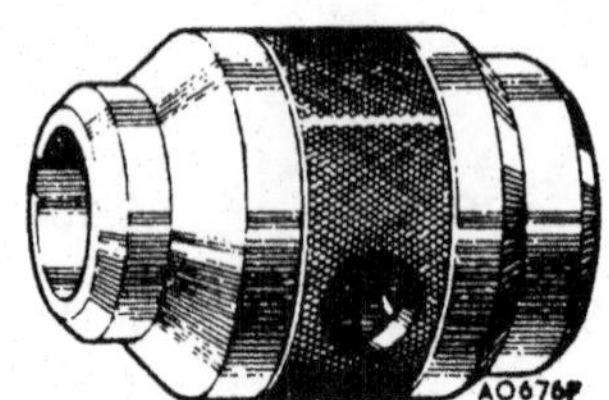

18G 3. Engine Front Cover Locating Bush.

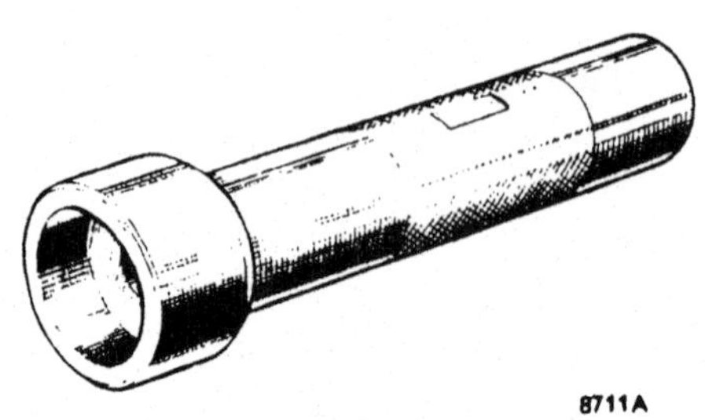

18G 4. First Motion Shaft Assembly Replacer.

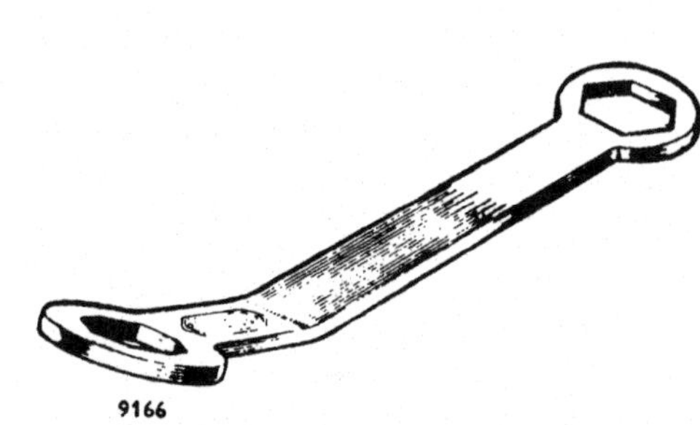

18G 5. First Motion Shaft Nut Spanner.

18G 25. Valve Seat Finishing Cutter (exhaust).

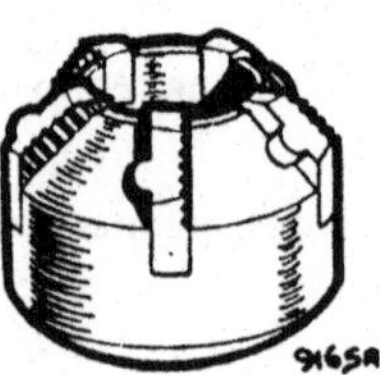

18G 25 A. Valve Seat Glaze Breaker (exhaust)

18G 25 C. Valve Seat Narrowing Cutter—Bottom (exhaust).

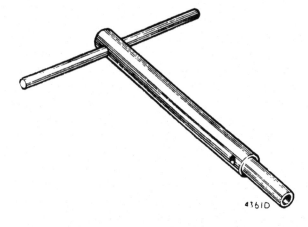

18G 27. Valve Seat Cutter and Pilot Handle.

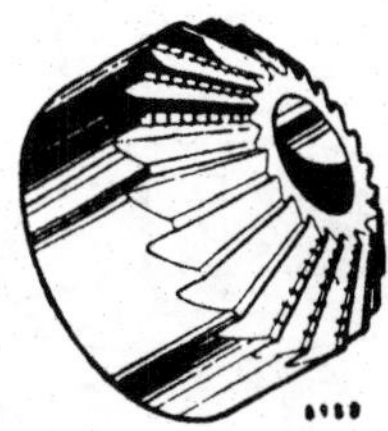

18G 28. Valve Seat Finishing Cutter (inlet).

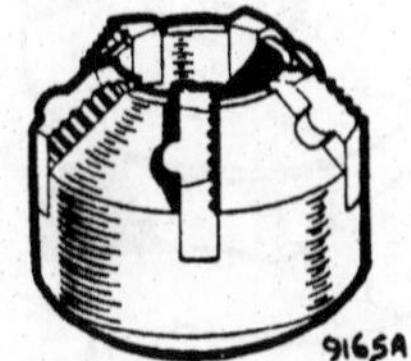

18G 28 A. Valve Seat Glaze Breaker (inlet).

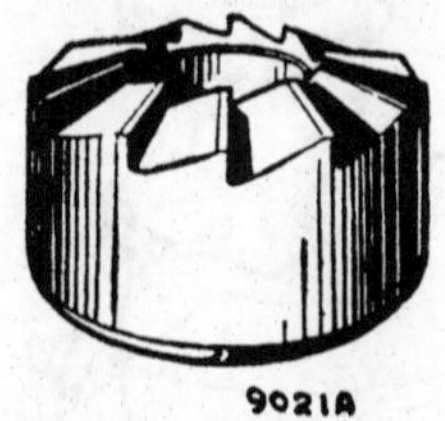

18G 28 B. Valve Seat Narrowing Cutter–Top (inlet).

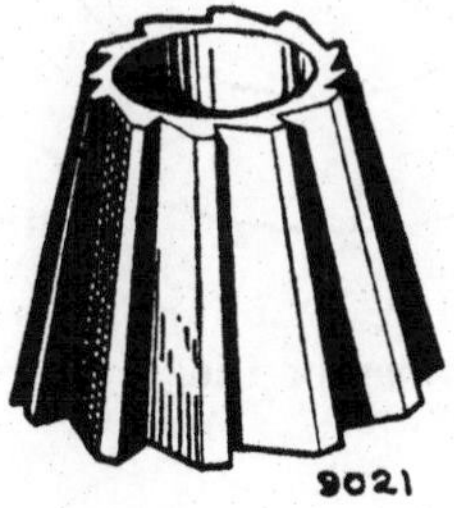

18G 28 C. Valve Seat Narrowing Cutter–Bottom (inlet).

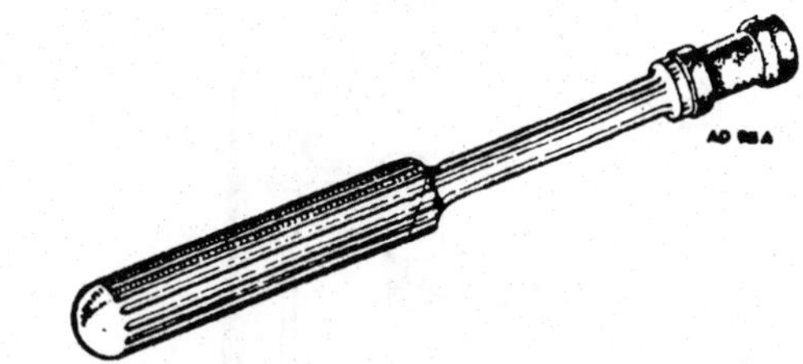

18G 29. Valve Grinding-in Tool.

18G 29 A. Valve Grinding-in Tool Suction Pad.

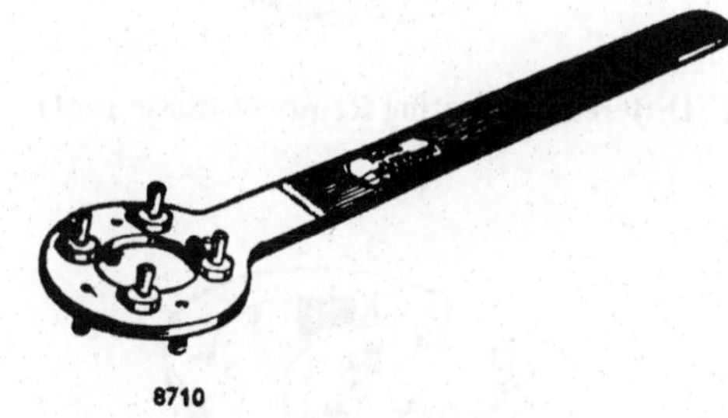

18G 34 A. Bevel Pinion Flange Wrench.

18G 41. Selector Fork and Rod Guide.

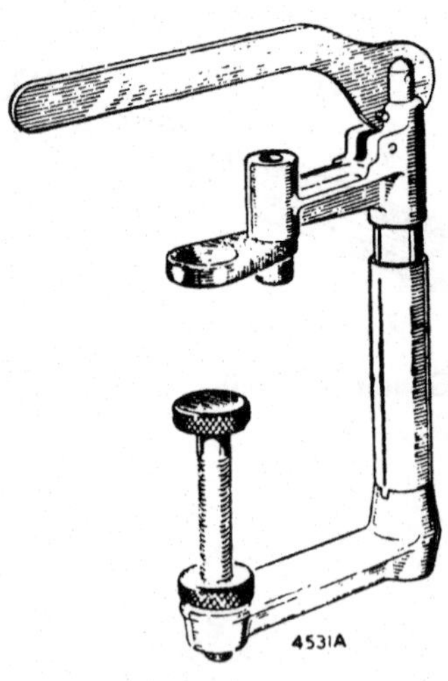

18G 45. Valve Spring Compressor.

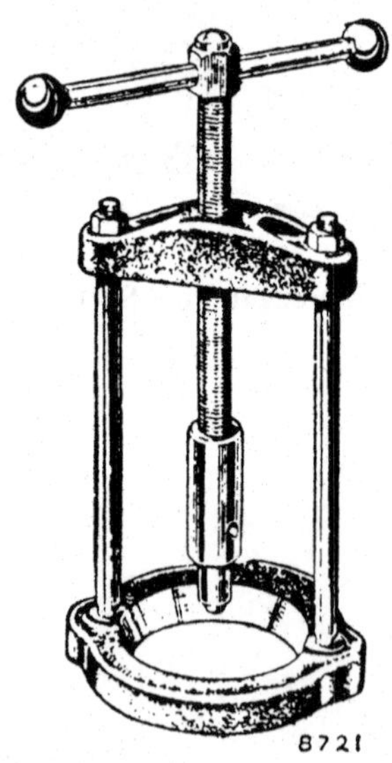

18G 47 C. Differential Bearing Remover (basic tool).

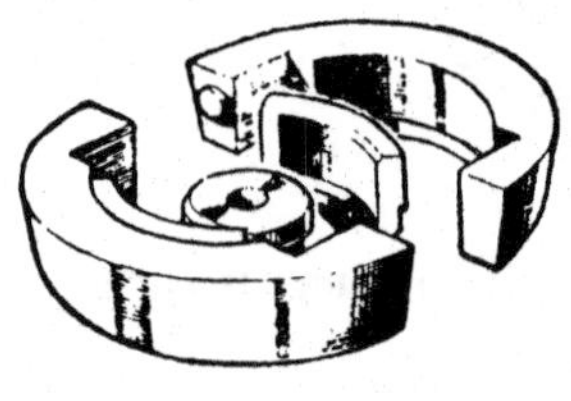

18G 47 T. Differential Bearing Remover Adaptor.

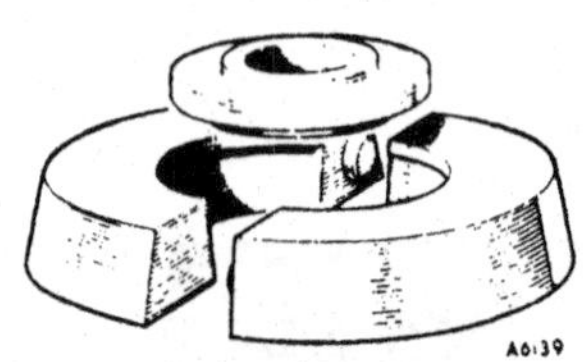

18G 47 AH. Bevel Pinion Inner Race Remover and Replacer Adaptor.

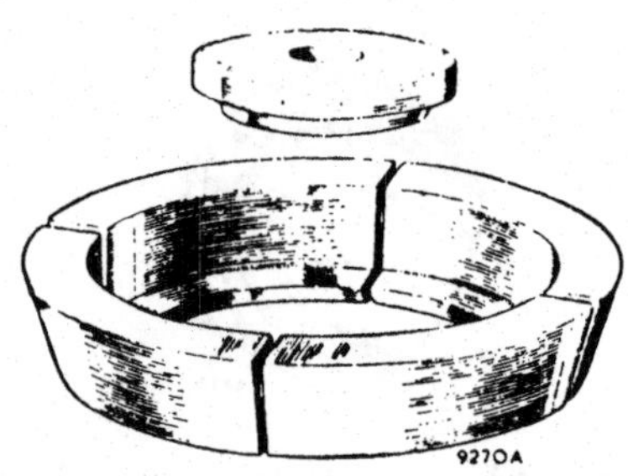

18G 47 AK. Differential Bearing Remover Adaptor.

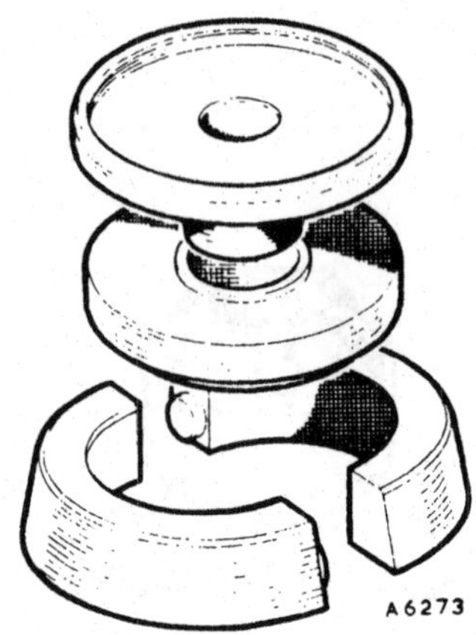

18G 47 AP. Annulus Tail Shaft Bearing Remover and Replacer Adaptor.

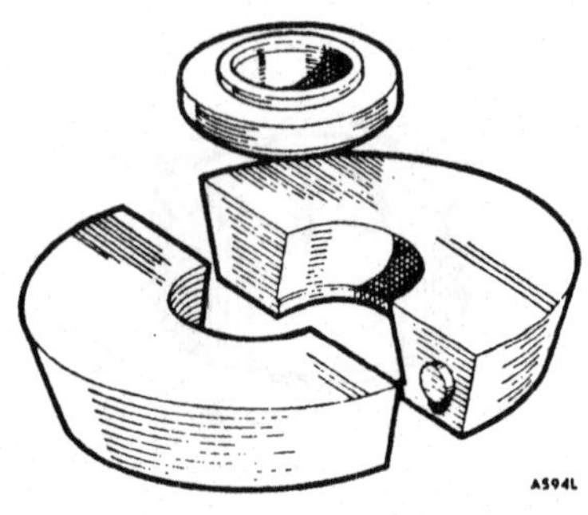

18G 47 AS. Bevel Pinion Bearing Remover and Replacer Adaptor.

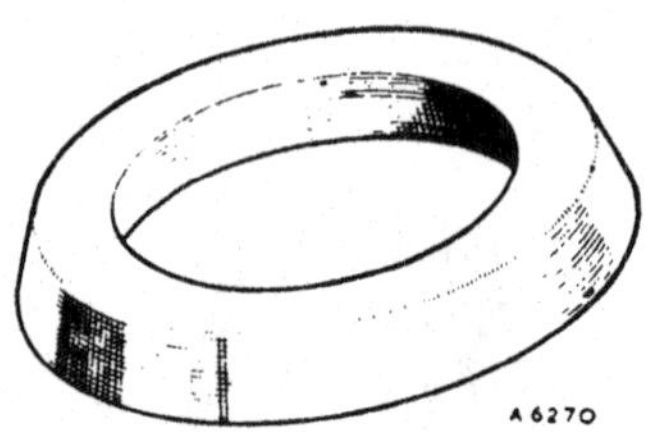

18G 47 CZ. Basic Adaptor Ring.

NOTE.–If 18G 12 A is held, this may be used with 18G 47 AP in lieu of 18G 47 CZ.

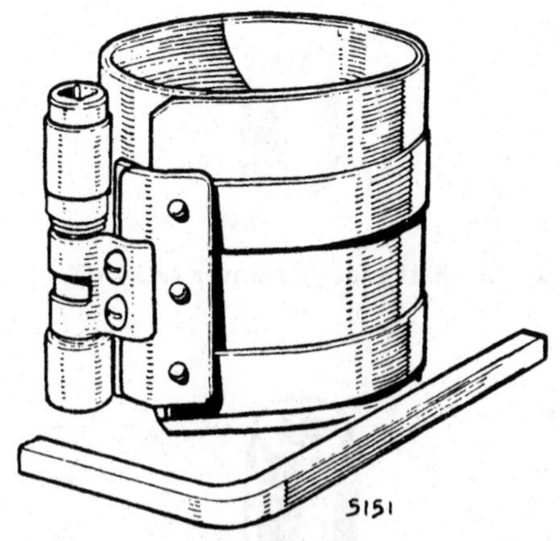

18G 55 A. Piston Ring Clamp.

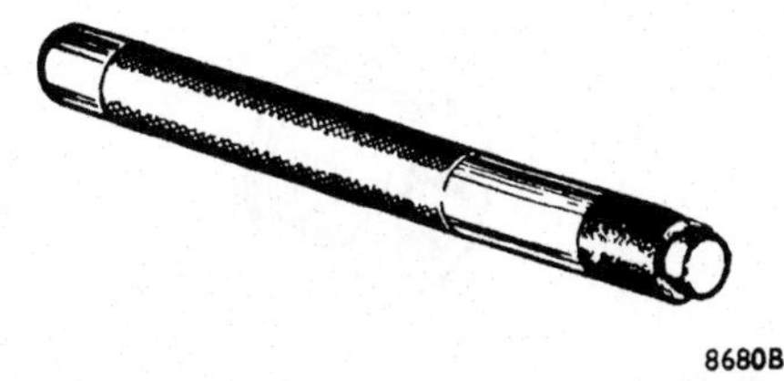

18G 69. Oil Pump Relief Valve Grinding-in Tool.

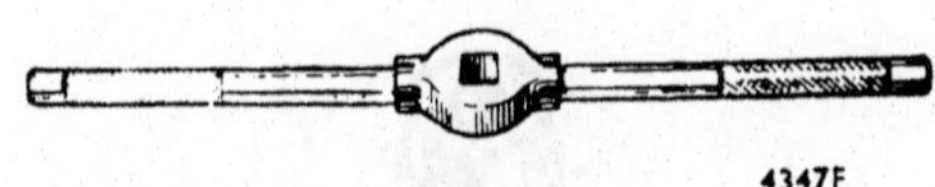

18G 68. Swivel Axle Bush Reamer Wrench.

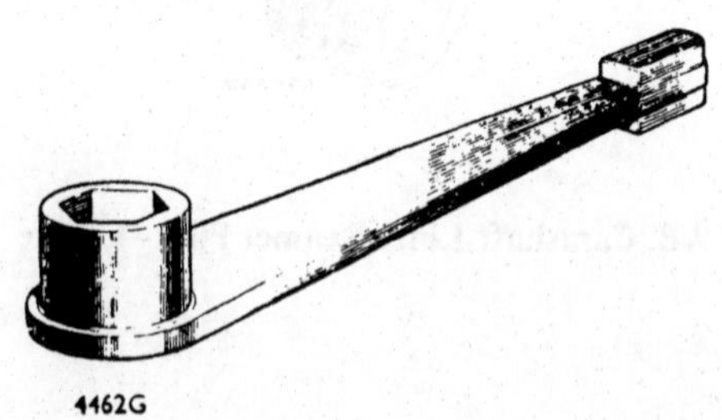

18G 98 A. Starting Nut Spanner.

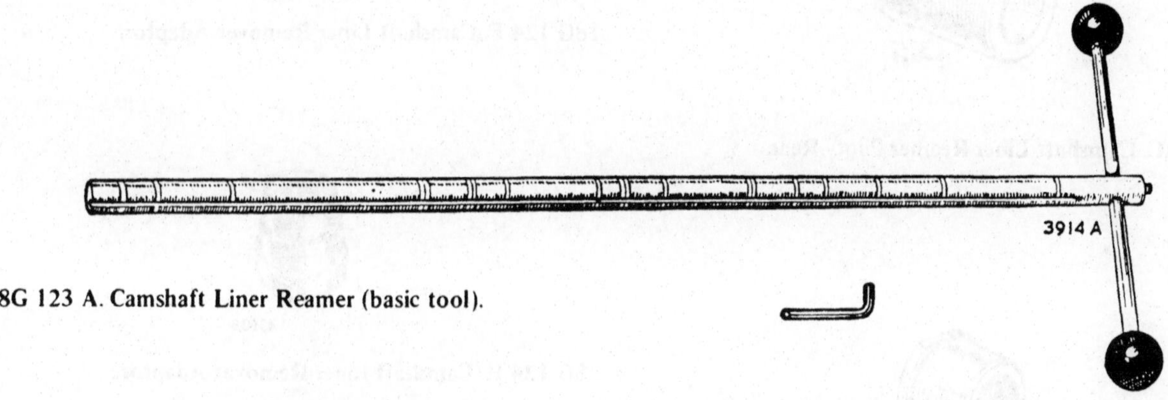

18G 123 A. Camshaft Liner Reamer (basic tool).

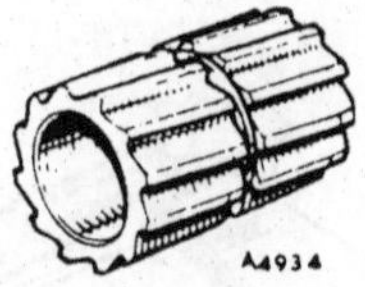

18G 123 B. Camshaft Liner Reamer Cutter–Rear.

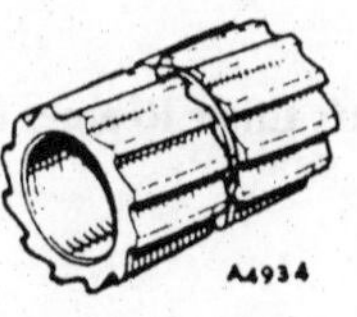

18G 123 F. Camshaft Liner Reamer Cutter–Centre.

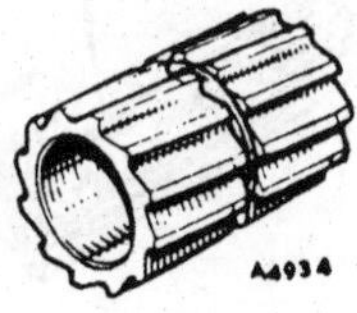

18G 123 E. Camshaft Liner Reamer Cutter–Front.

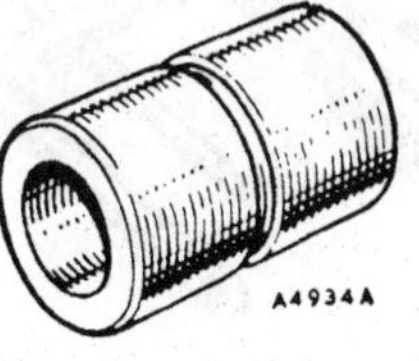

18G 123 L. Camshaft Liner Reamer Pilot–Front.

18G 123 T. Camshaft Liner Reamer Pilot–Front.

18G 124 B. Camshaft Liner Remover Adaptor.

18G 123 AB. Camshaft Liner Reamer Pilot–Centre.

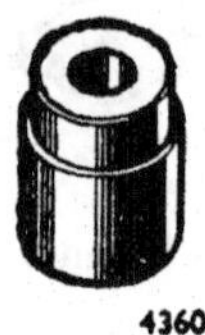

18G 124 C. Camshaft Liner Remover Adaptor.

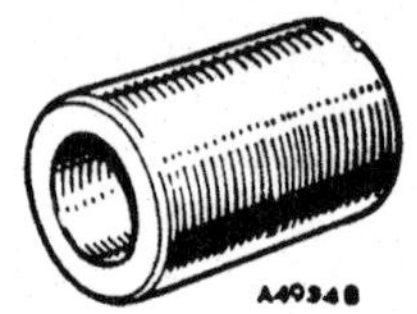

18G 123 AC. Camshaft Liner Reamer Pilot–Rear.

18G 124 F. Camshaft Liner Remover Adaptor.

4360B

18G 124 H. Camshaft Liner Remover Adaptor.

18G 123 AD. Camshaft Liner Reamer Pilot–Rear.

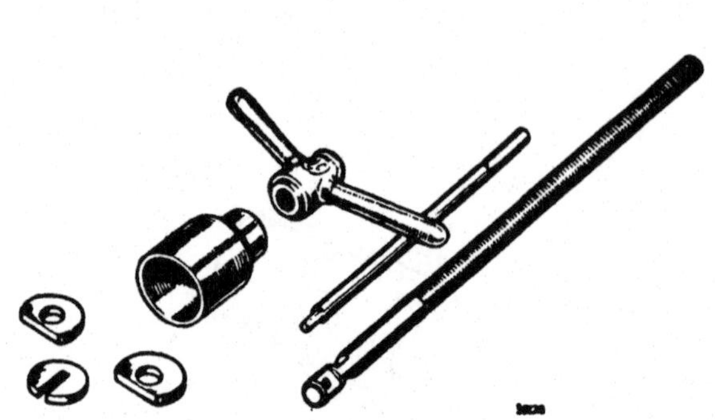

18G 124 A. Camshaft Liner Remover and Replacer (basic tool).

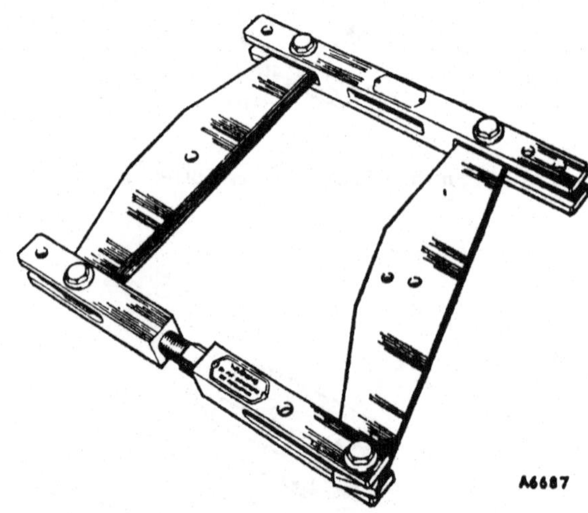

18G 131 C. Rear Axle Casing Stretcher.

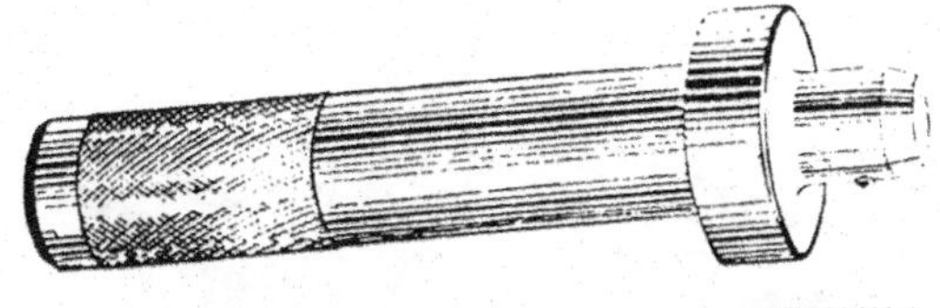

18G 134. Bearing and Oil Seal Replacer (basic tool).

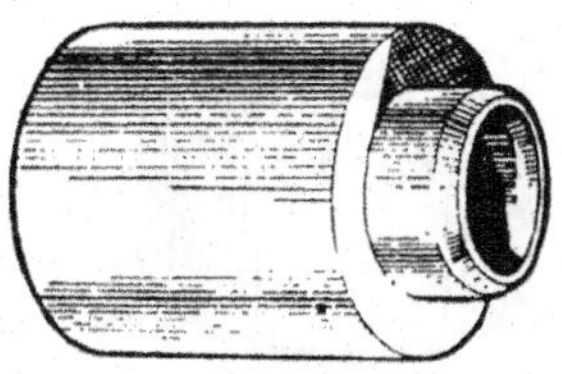

18G 134 BK. Gearbox Rear Oil Seal Replacer Adaptor.

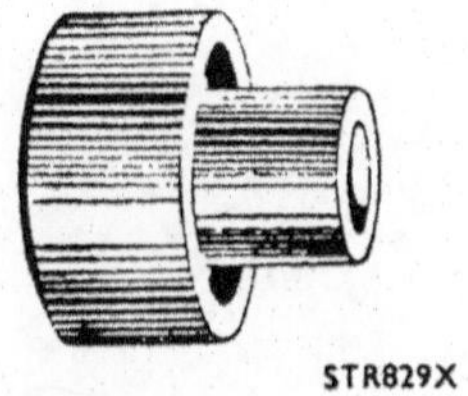

18G 134 P. Rear Hub Replacer Adaptor.

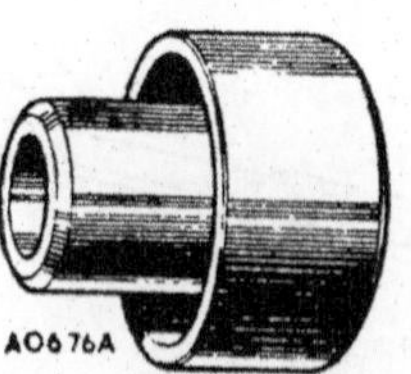

18G 134 CM. Differential Bearing Replacer Adaptor.

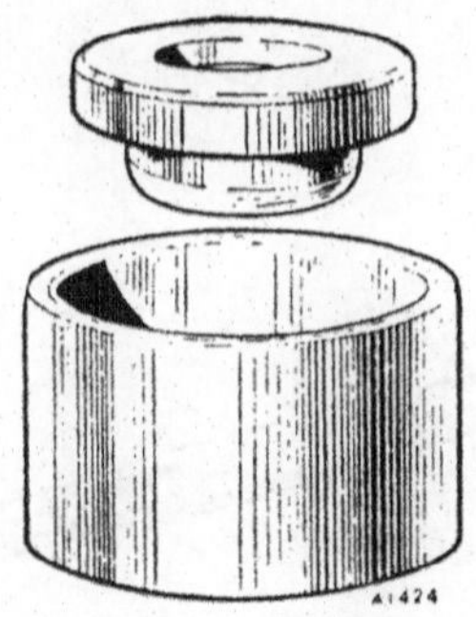

18G 134 BD. Timing Case Oil Seal Replacer Adaptor.

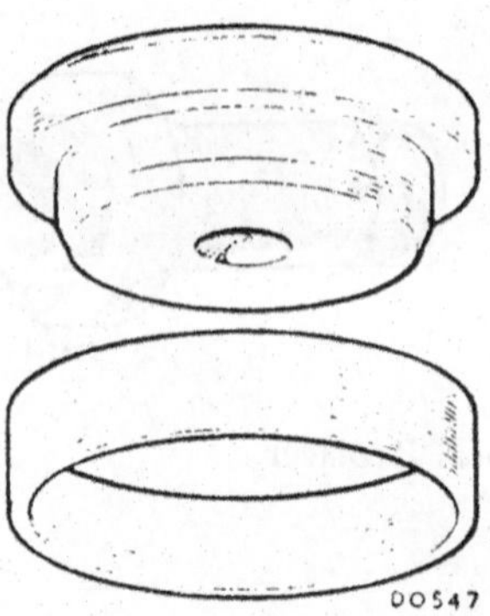

18G 134 CQ. Crankshaft Oil Seal Replacer Adaptor.

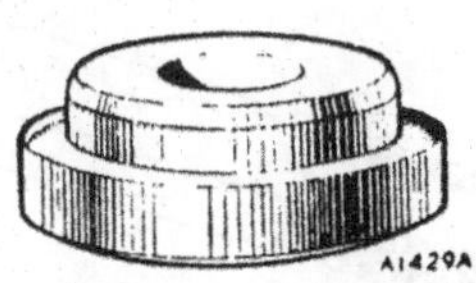

18G 134 BH. Flywheel and Front Hub Oil Seal Replacer Adaptor.

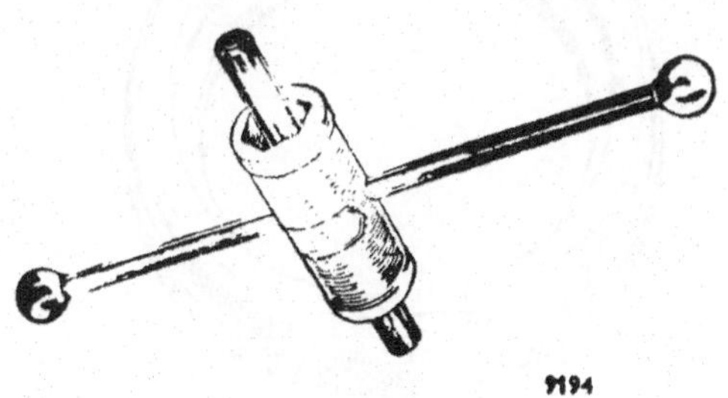

18G 152. Rear Hub Nut Spanner.

18G 174 B. Valve Seat Narrowing Cutter–Top (exhaust).

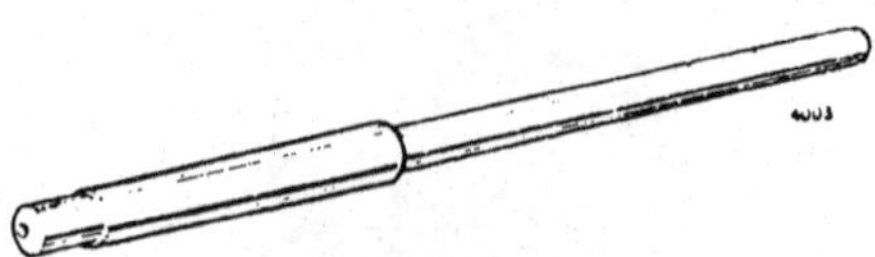

18G 174 D. Valve Seat Cutter Pilot.

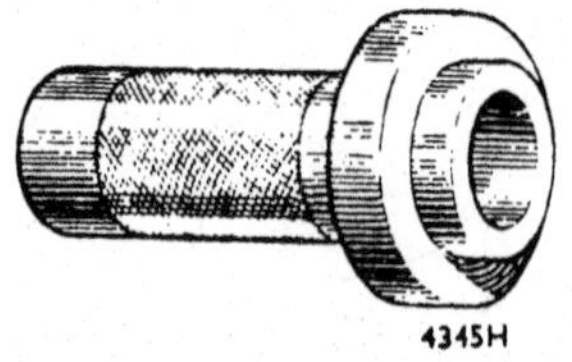

18G 177. Oil Seal Replacer.

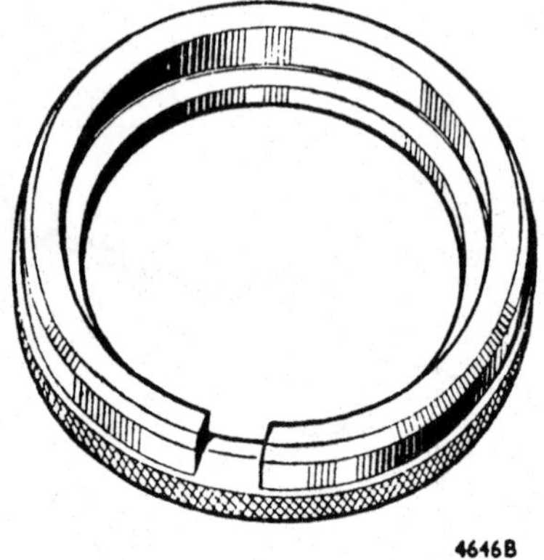

18G 178. Roller Clutch Assembly Ring.

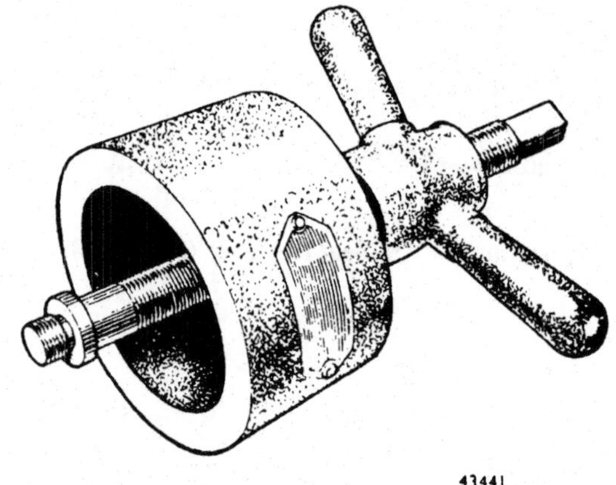

18G 183. Oil Pump Body Replacer.

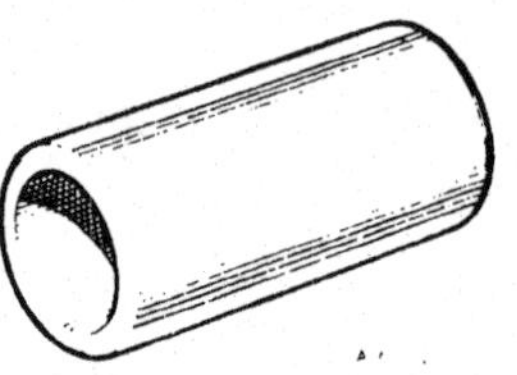

18G 183 A. Oil Pump Barrel Remover Adaptor.

18G 185. Dummy Layshaft.

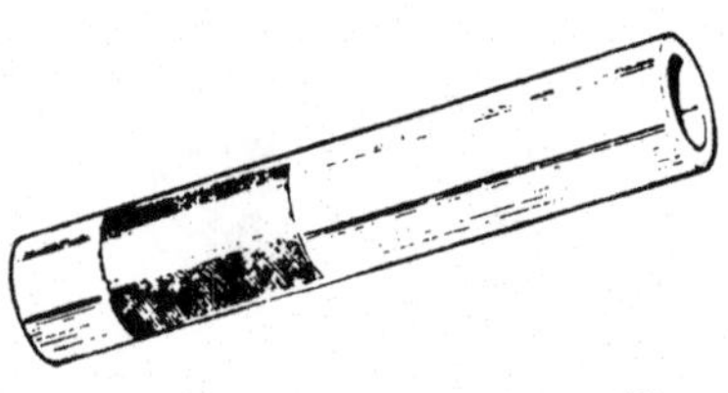

18G 186. Mainshaft Bearing Replacer.

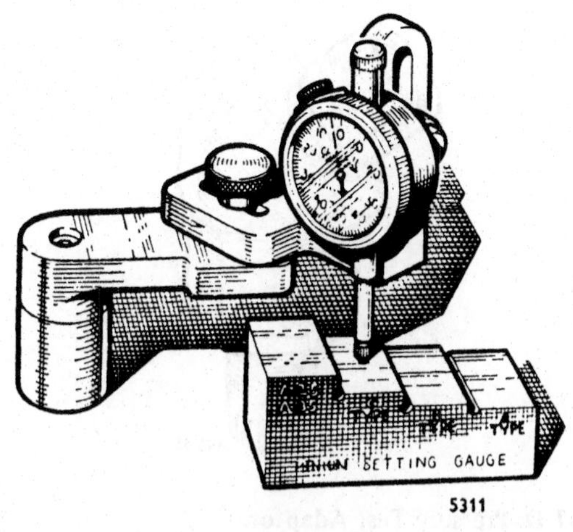

18G 191. Bevel Pinion Setting Gauge.

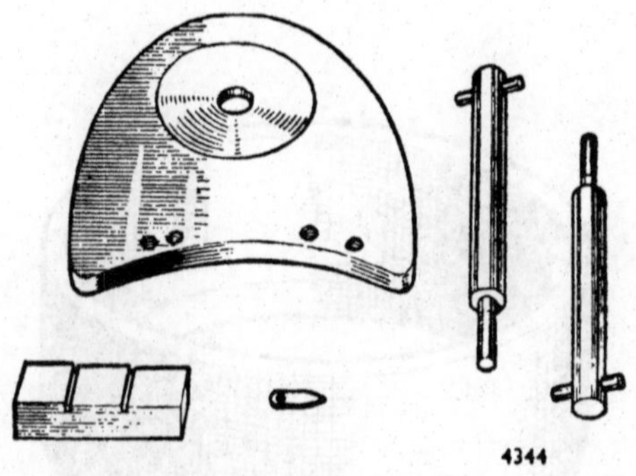

18G 191 A. Differential Bearing Gauge.

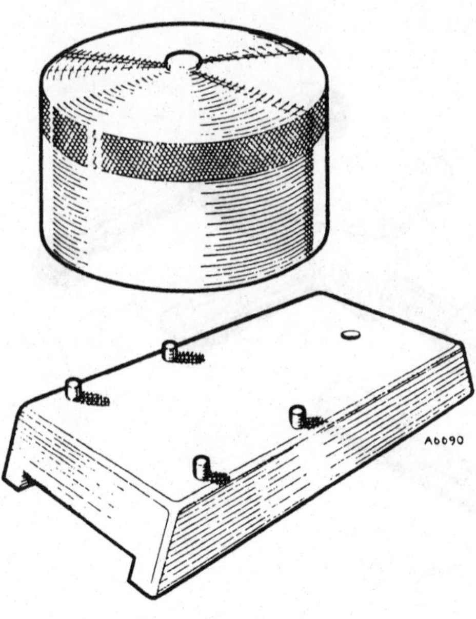

18G 191 F. Differential Case Assembly Gauge.

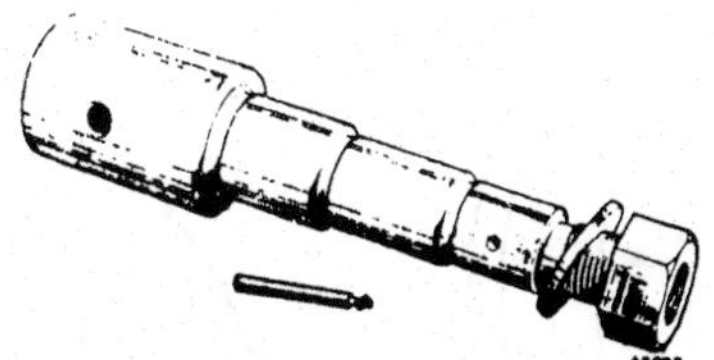

18G 191 H. Dummy Pinion.

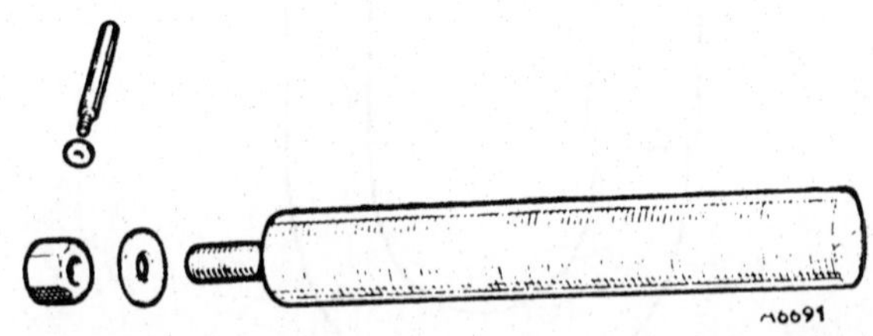

18G 191 J. Differential Case Assembly Gauge Pillar Adaptor.

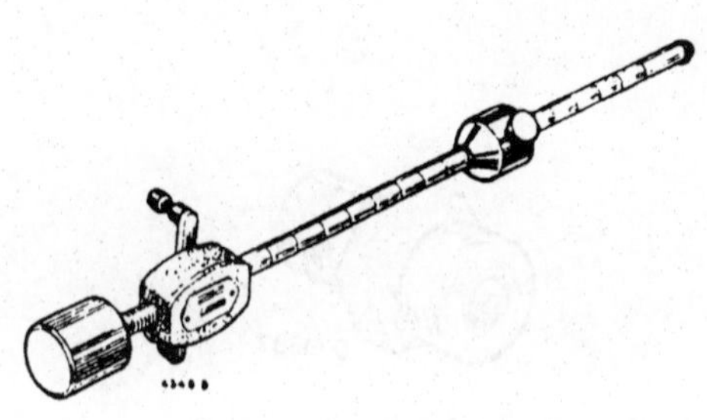

18G 207. Bevel Pinion Preload Gauge.

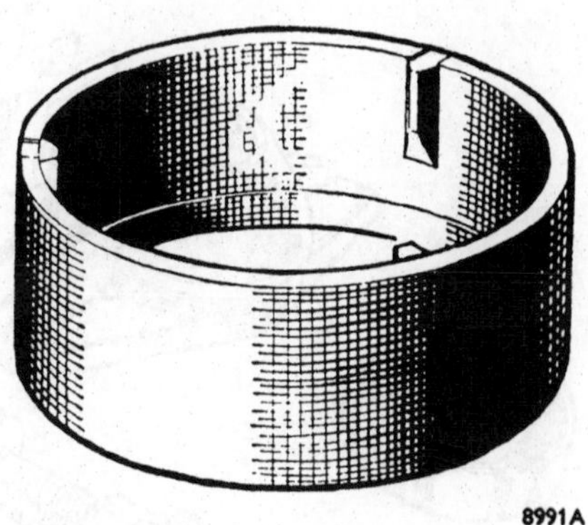

18G 222. Synchromesh Unit Assembly Ring–Second Speed.

18G 223. Synchromesh Unit Assembly Ring–Third and Top.

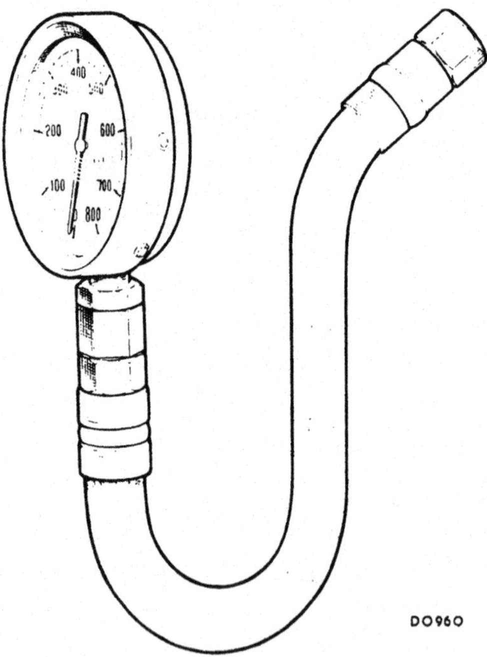

18G 251. Hydraulic Pressure Gauge.

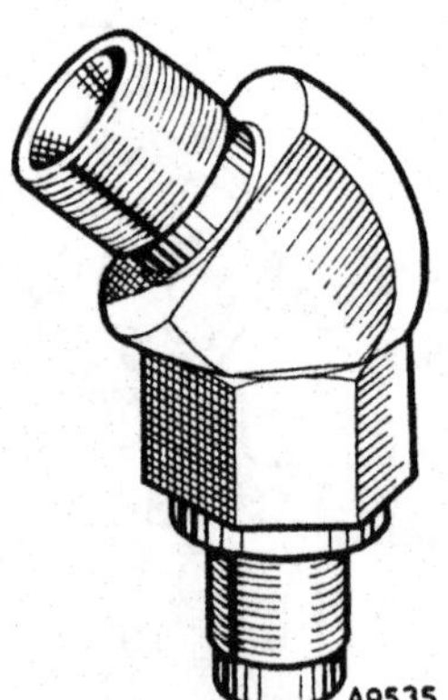

18G 251 D. Pressure Test Adaptor.

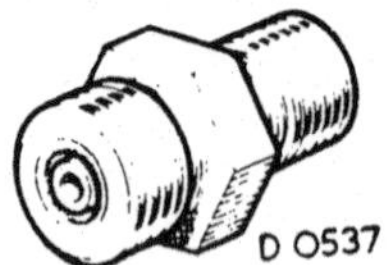

18G 251 E. Pressure Test Adaptor.

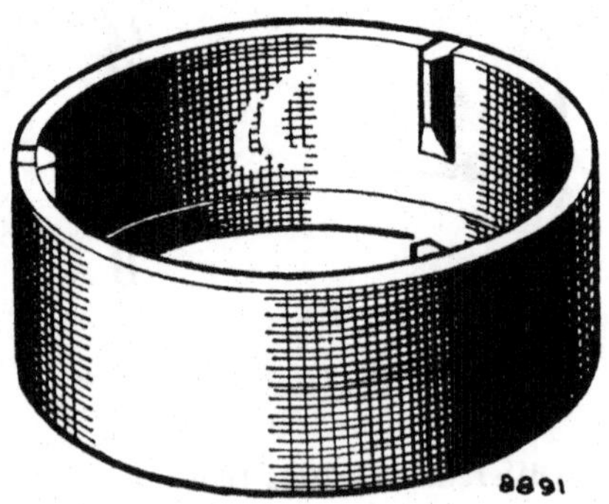

18G 262. Synchromesh Unit Assembly Ring (First and Second Speed).

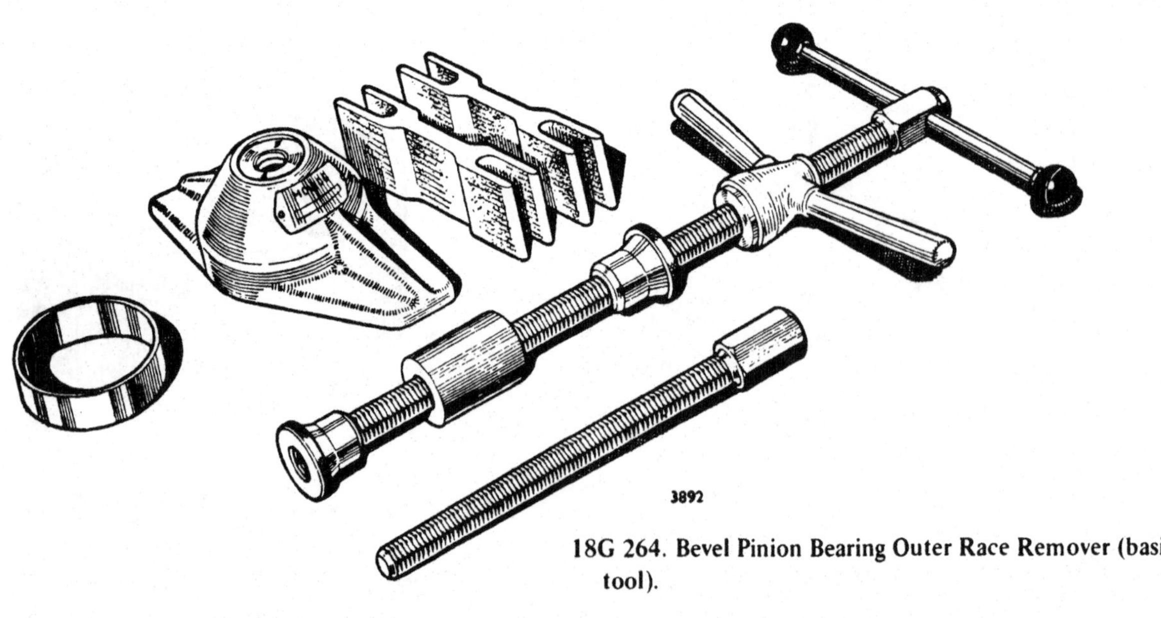

18G 264. Bevel Pinion Bearing Outer Race Remover (basic tool).

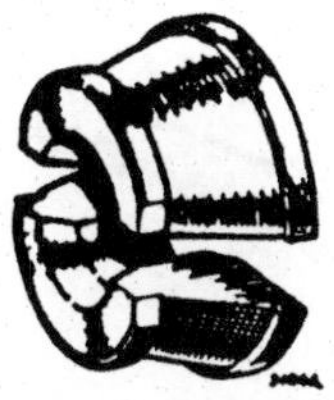

18G 264 E and 18G 264 F. Bevel Pinion Bearing Outer Race Remover Adaptors–Rear.

18G 284 A. Main Bearing Cap Remover Adaptor.

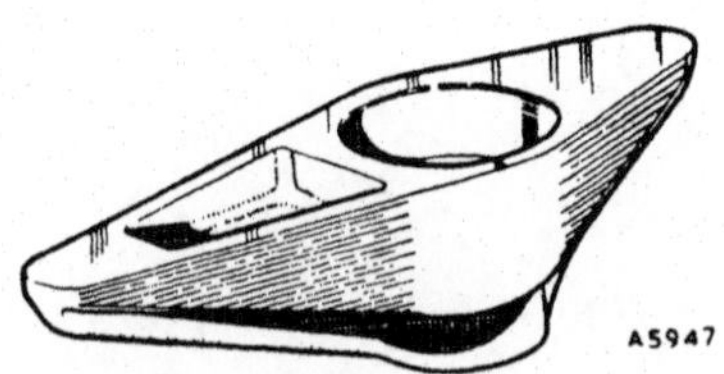

18G 264 AA. Bridge Piece Adaptor–Large.

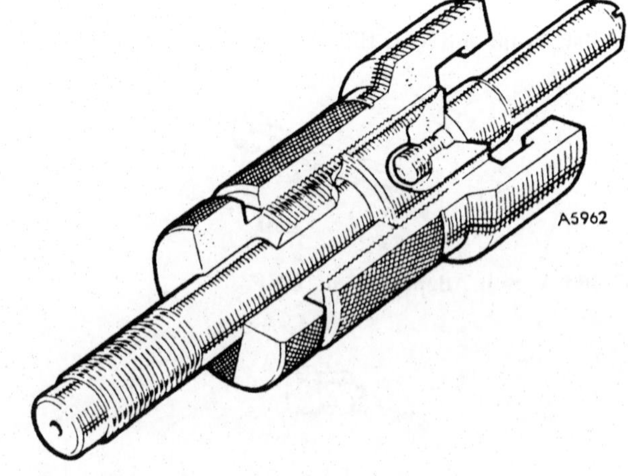

18G 284 H. Basic Bearing Remover Adaptor.

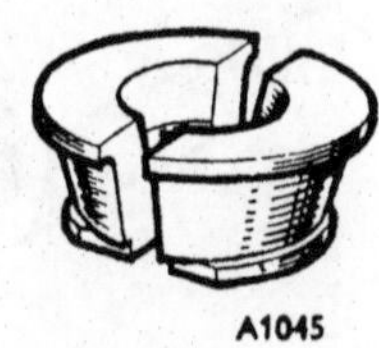

18G 264 AB. Bevel Pinion Outer Race Remover and Replacer Adaptor (Rear).

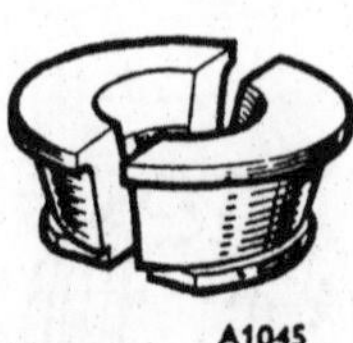

18G 264 AD. Bevel Pinion Outer Race Remover and Replacer Adaptor (Front).

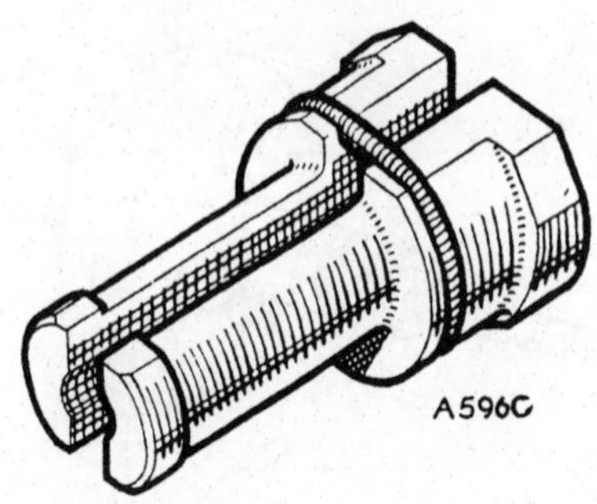

18G 284 L. Crankshaft Spigot Bush Remover Adaptor.

Used in conjunction with basic tool adaptors 18G 284 H.

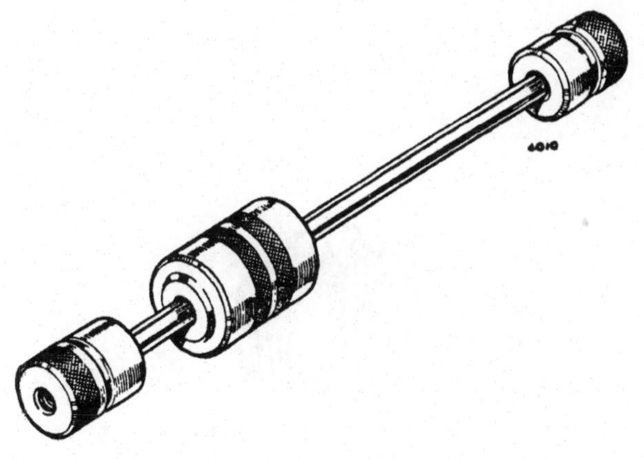

18G 284. Impulse Extractor–UNF. (basic tool).

18G 284 AC. Main Bearing Cap Remover Adaptor.

For removing the intermediate main bearing caps commencing at the following engine numbers:

18GB/U/H68055	18GB/RU/H68315
18GB/U/L60571	18GB/RU/L58224

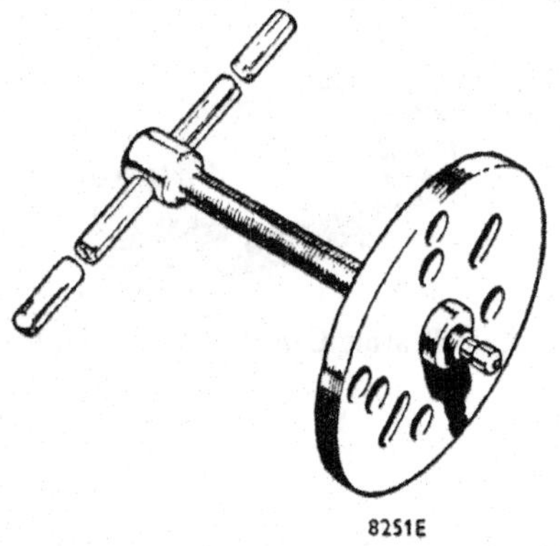

18G 304. Front and Rear Hub Remover (basic tool).

18G 304 A. Bolt Adaptor–½ in. UNF.

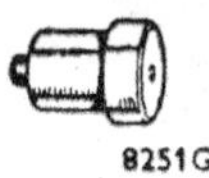

18G 304 J. Hub Remover Thrust Pad.

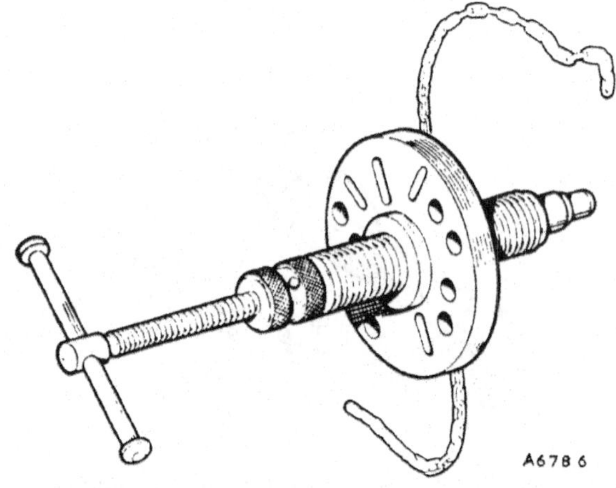

18G 304 Z. Hydraulic Hub Remover (basic tool).

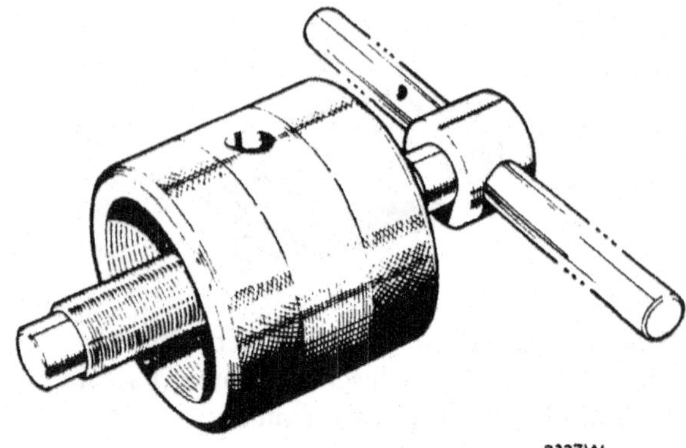

18G 363. Hub Remover Wire Wheels (12 T.P.I.).

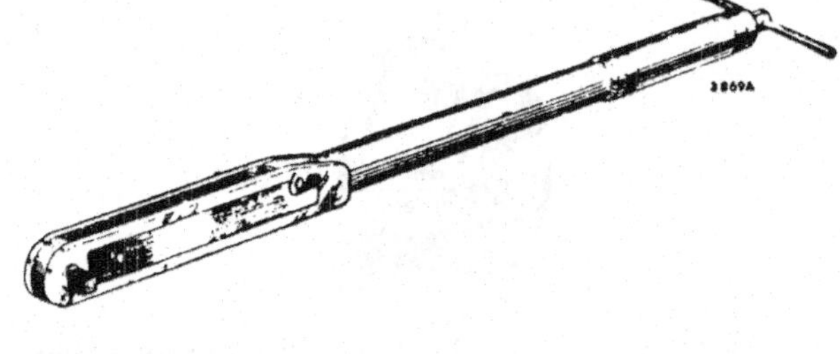

18G 372. Torque Wrench–30 to 140 lb. ft. (4.15 to 19.4 kg. m.).

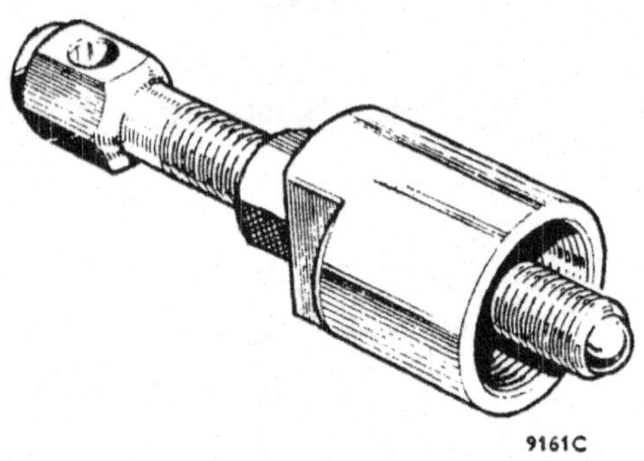

18G 389. Gearbox Rear Oil Seal Remover (basic tool).

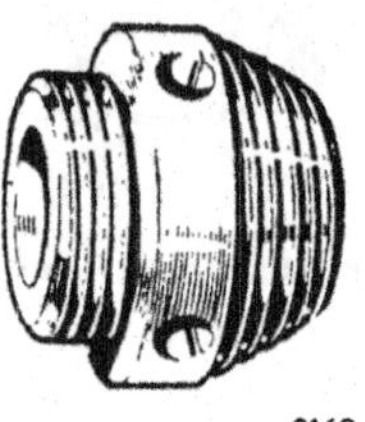

18G 389 B. Gearbox Rear Oil Seal Remover Adaptor.

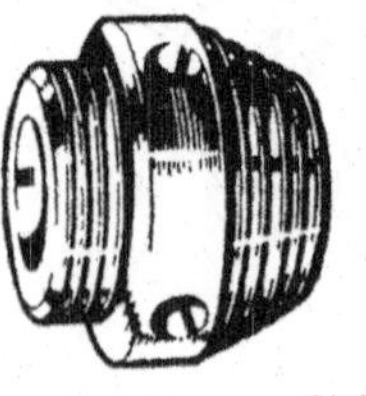

18G 389 D. Gearbox Rear Oil Seal Remover Adaptor.

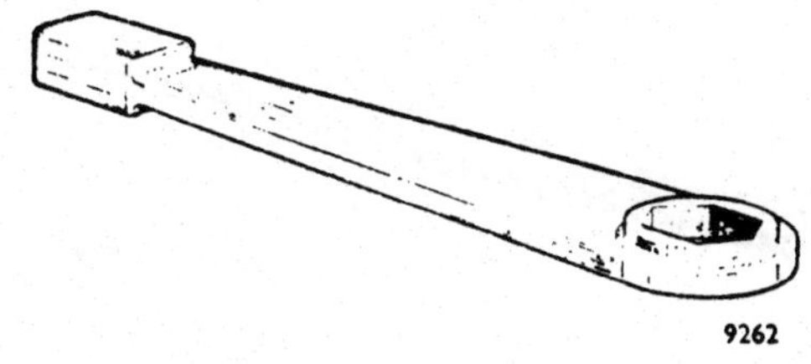

18G 391. Starting Dog Nut Spanner.

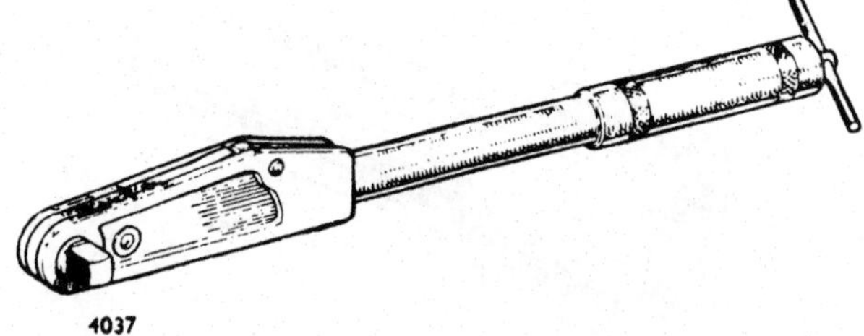

18G 536. Torque Wrench–20 to 100 lb. in.–2 to 8 lb. ft. (300 to 1200 gm. m.).

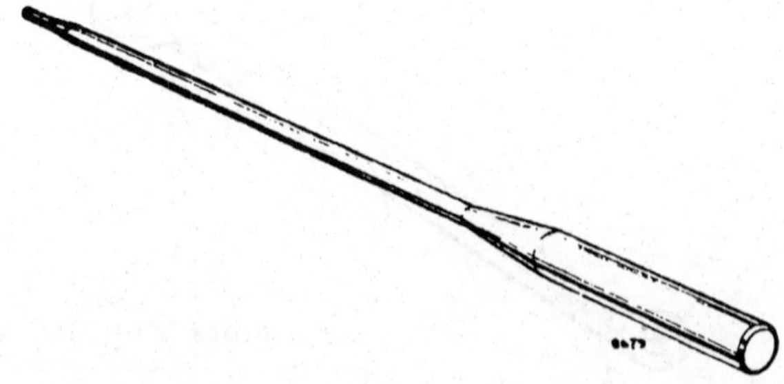

18G 471. Dummy Layshaft.

18G 536 A. Torque Wrench Adaptor–$\frac{3}{8}$ to ½ in.

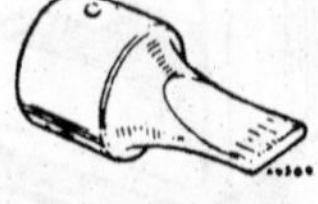

18G 536 B. Torque Wrench to Screwdrive Blade Adaptor.

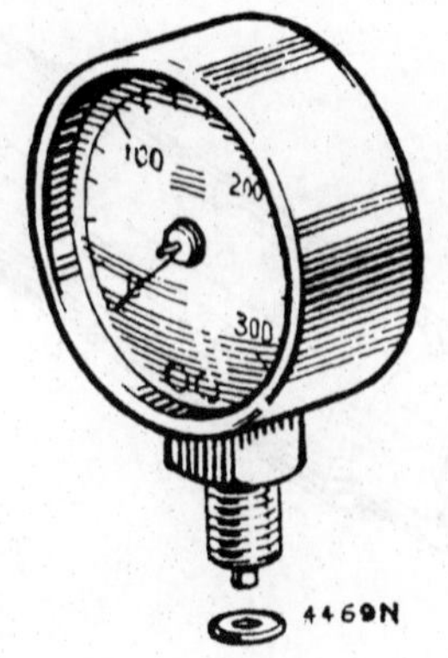

18G 502 A. Hydraulic Pressure Gauge.

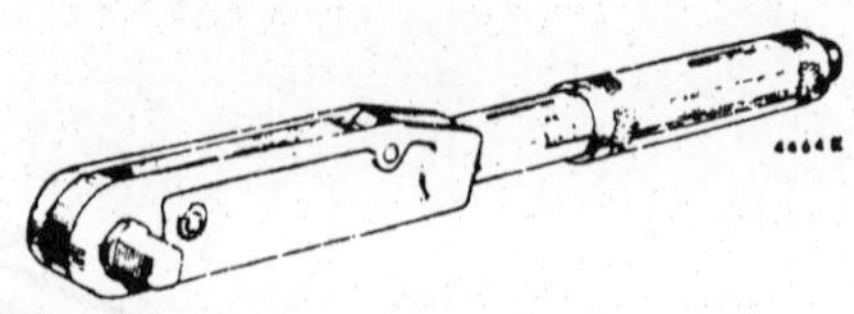

18G 537. Torque Wrench–10 to 50 lb. ft. (2 to 7 kg. m.).

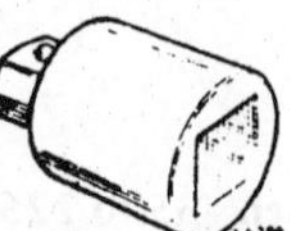

18G 537 A. Torque Wrench Adaptor–½ to $\frac{3}{8}$ in. square drive.

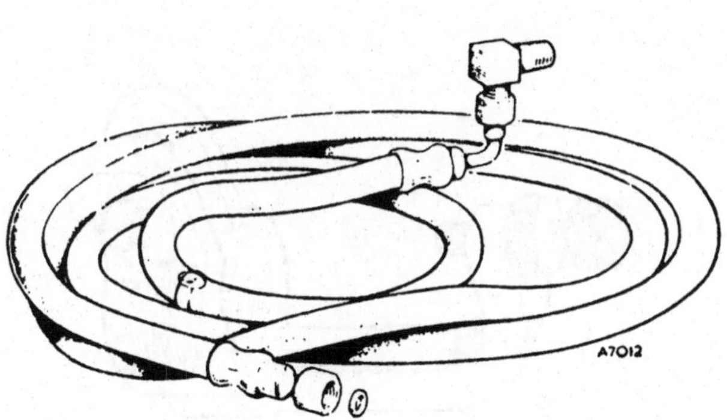

18G 502 K. Pressure Hose with Adaptor.

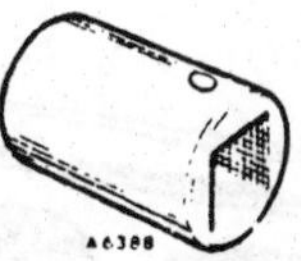

18G 537 B. Torque Wrench Adaptor–$\frac{3}{8}$ to $\frac{5}{16}$ in. (9.5 to 8 mm.) internal.
Use with 18G 537 and 18G 537 A

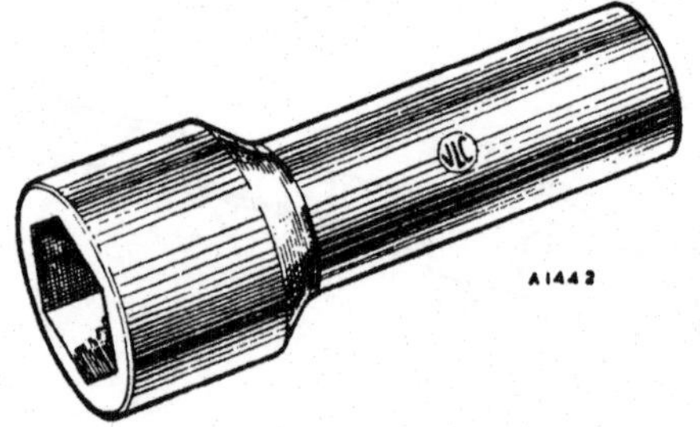

18G 586. Rear Axle Shaft Nut Spanner (Wire Wheel).

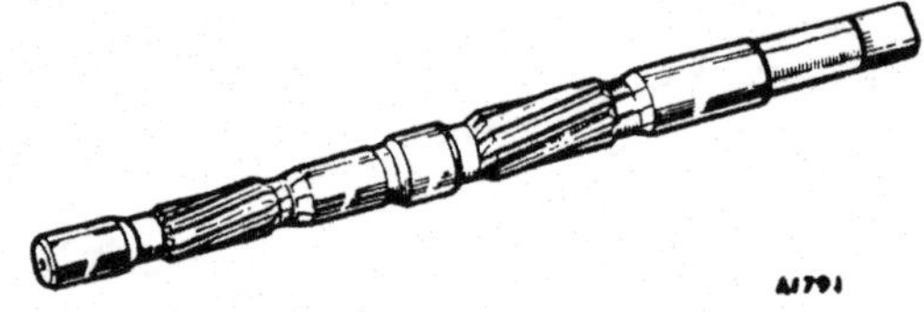

18G 597. Swivel Axle Bush Reamer.

18G 590. Disc Brake Piston Resetting Tool.

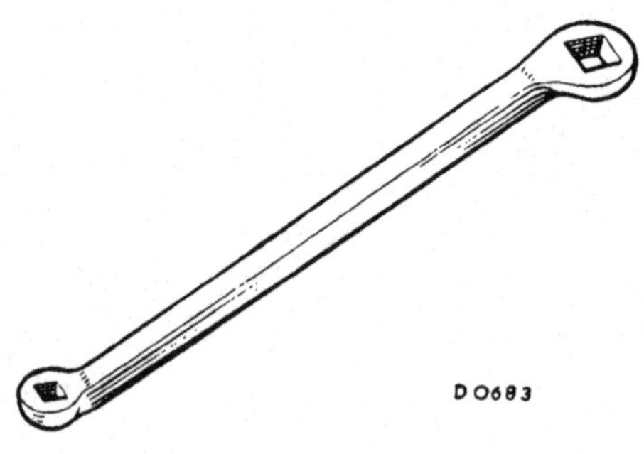

18G 619 A. Brake Adjusting Spanner.

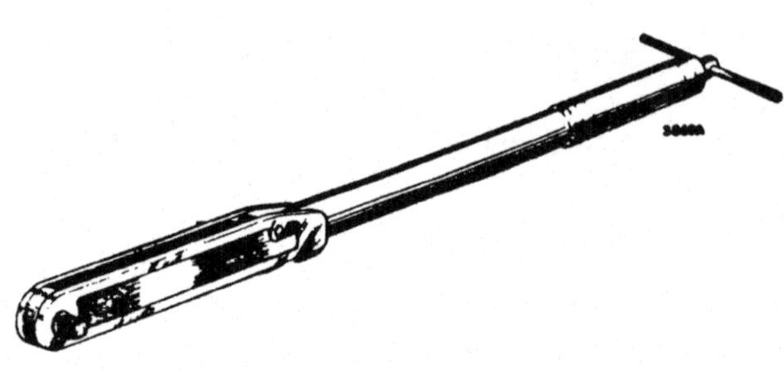

18G 592. Torque Wrench–35 to 225 lb. ft. (4.84 to 31.144 kg. m.).

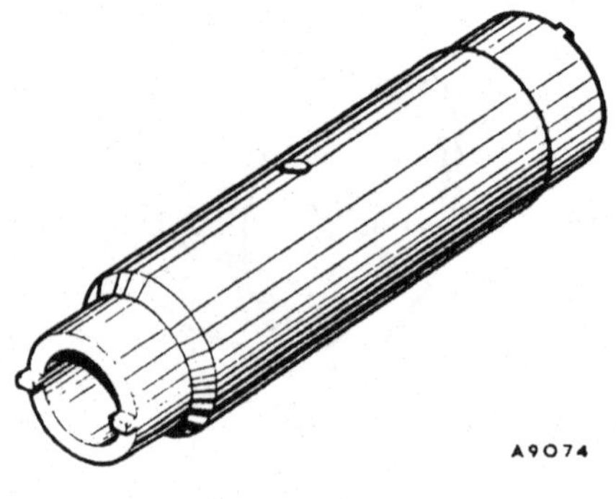

18G 671. Switch Bezel Light Spanner.

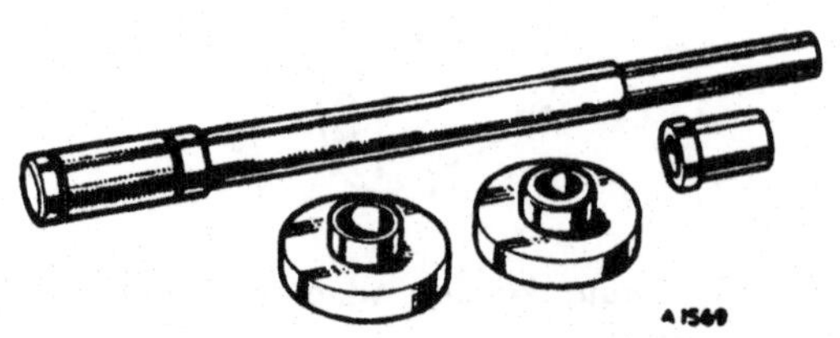

18G 596. Swivel Axle Bush Remover and Replacer.

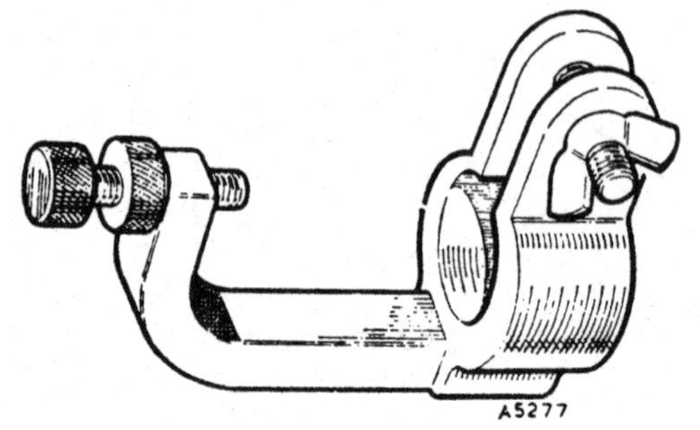

18G 674. Gear Train End-float Checking Tool.

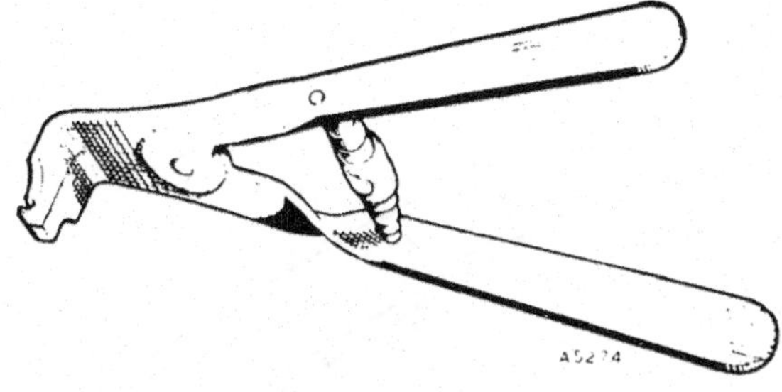

18G 675. Snap-ring Pliers.

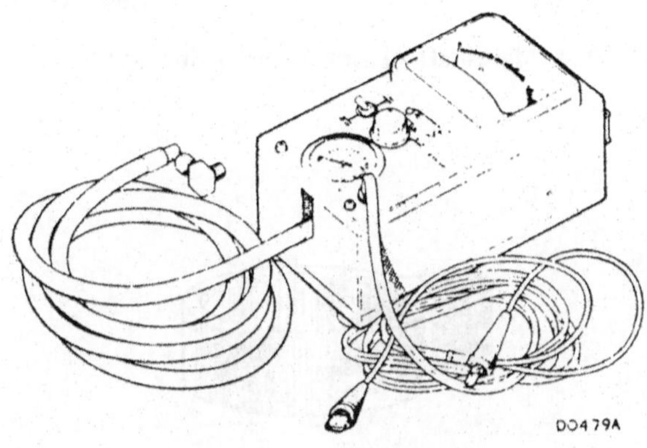

18G 677 Z. Pressure Test Equipment.

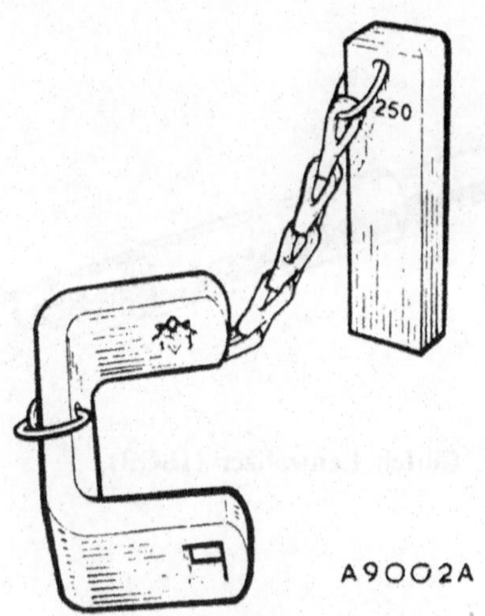

18G 678. Front Servo Spanner and Gauge.

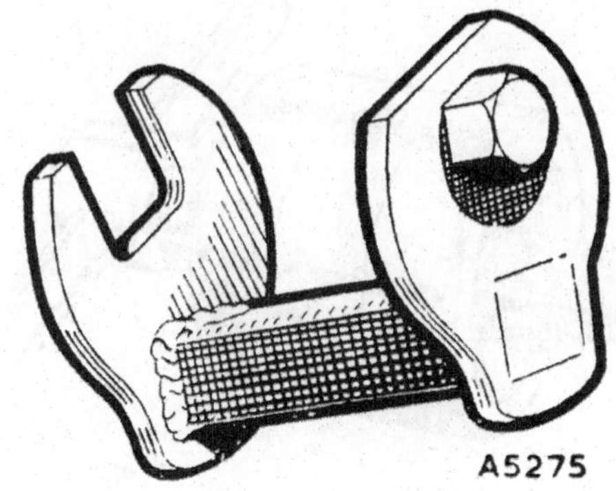

18G 679. Inhibitor Switch Locknut Spanner.

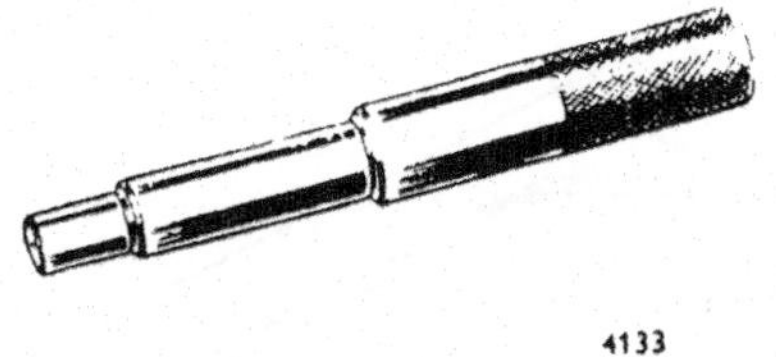

18G 680. Clutch Plate Centralizer.

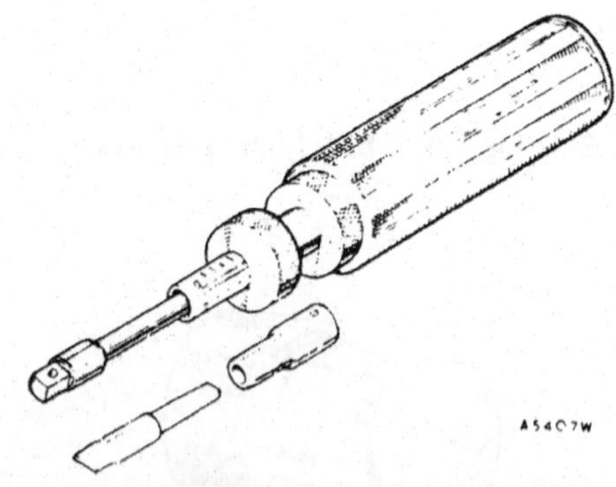

18G 681. Torque Screwdriver Set–0 to 40 lb. in. (0 to 400 gm. m.).

18G 681 A. Torque Screwdriver Bit.

18G 681 B. Torque Screwdriver Bit Holder.

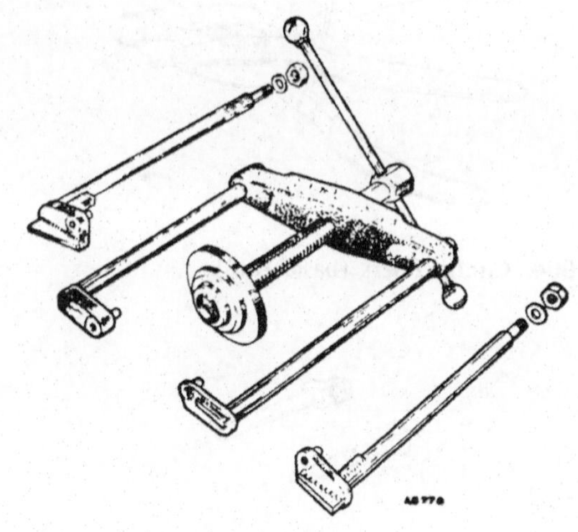

18G 693. Coil Spring Compressor.

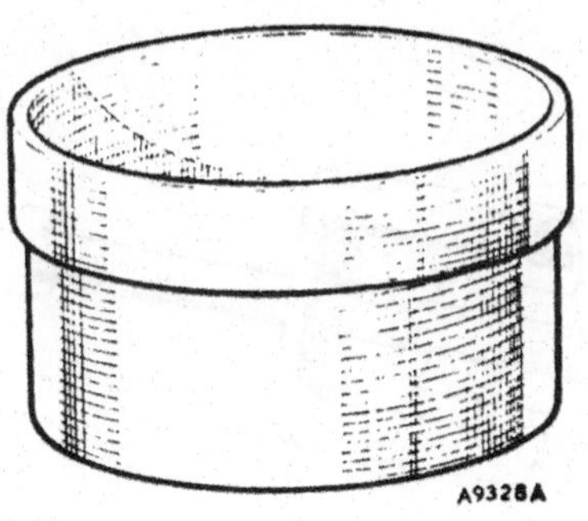

18G 702. Pistons Rear Clutch and Seal Replacer.

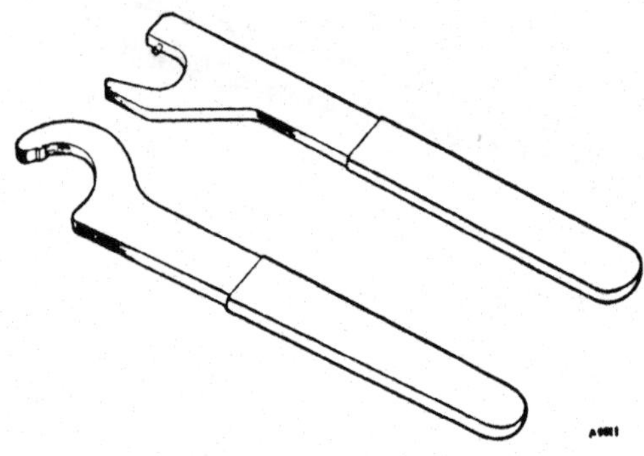

18G 706. Steering Rack Ball Joint Spanners.

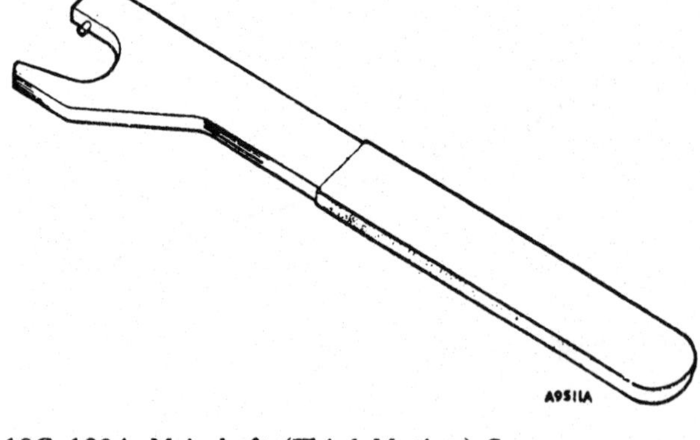

18G 1024. Mainshaft (Third Motion) Spanner.

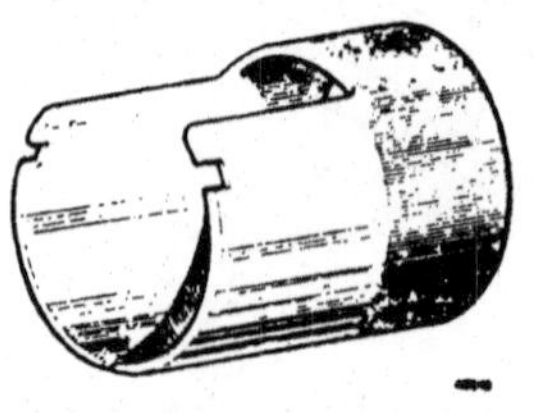

18G 1001. Gauge Locking Ring.

18G 1026. Synchromesh Assembly Ring.

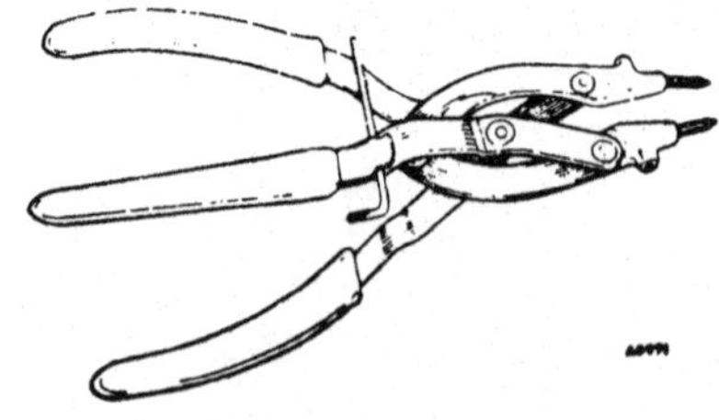

18G 1004. Circlip Pliers (basic tool).

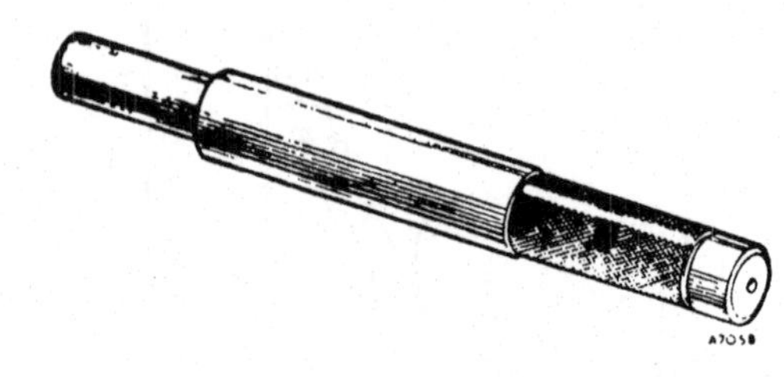

18G 1027. Clutch Centralizer (18GB).

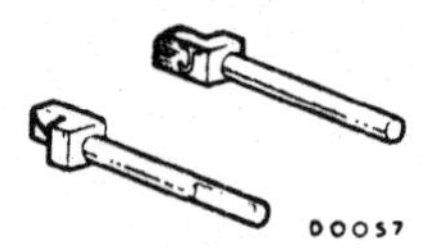

18G 1004 J. Circlip Plier Points.

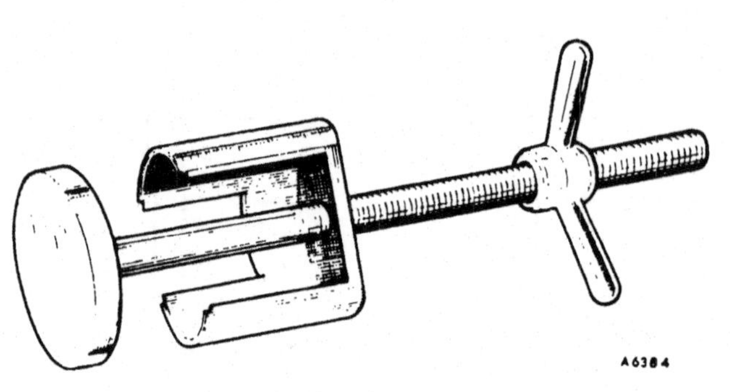

18G 1016. Clutch Spring Compressor–Rear.

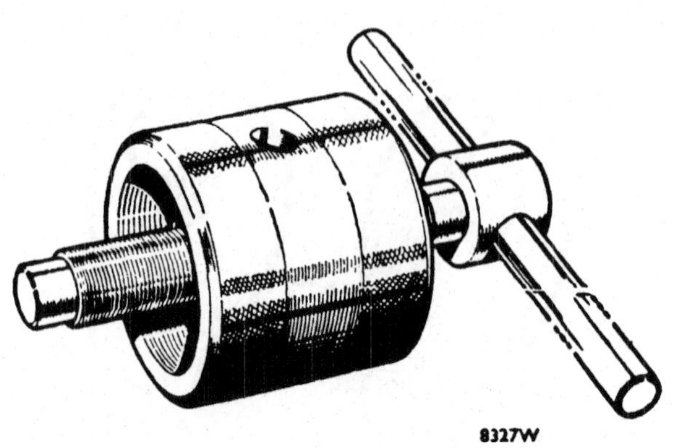

18G 1032. Wire Wheel Hub Remover (8 T.P.I.).

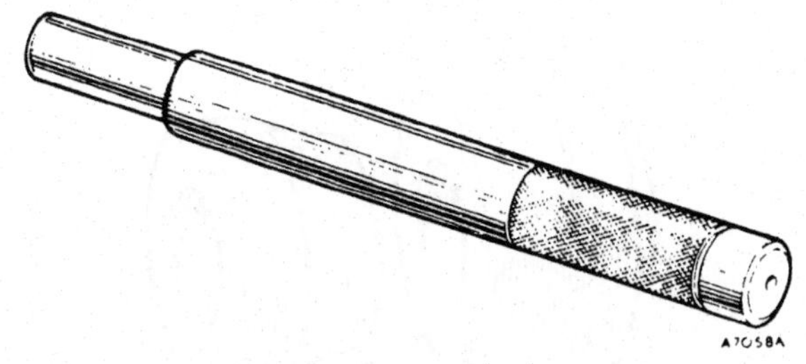
18G 1037. Crankshaft Spigot Bush Replacer.

18G 1039. Dummy Mainshaft.

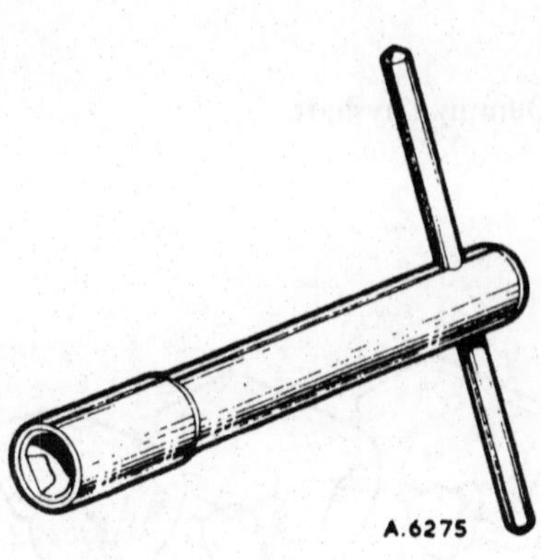

18G 1040. Oil Pump Body Key.

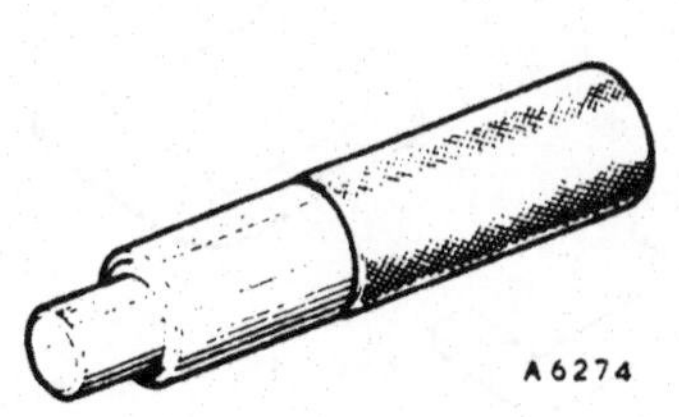

18G 1042. Annulus Spigot Bearing Replacer.

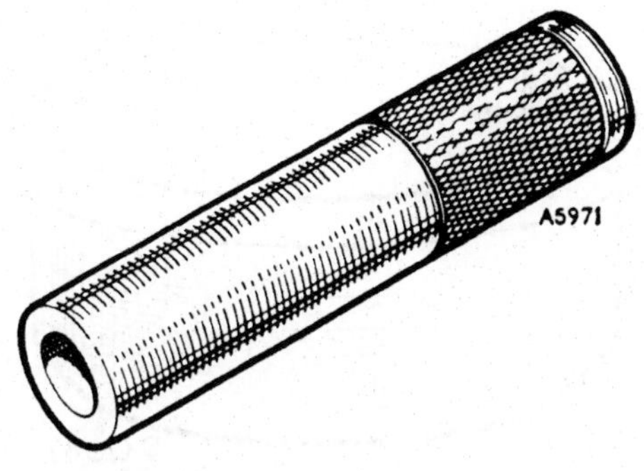

18G 1045. Mainshaft (Third Motion) Drift.

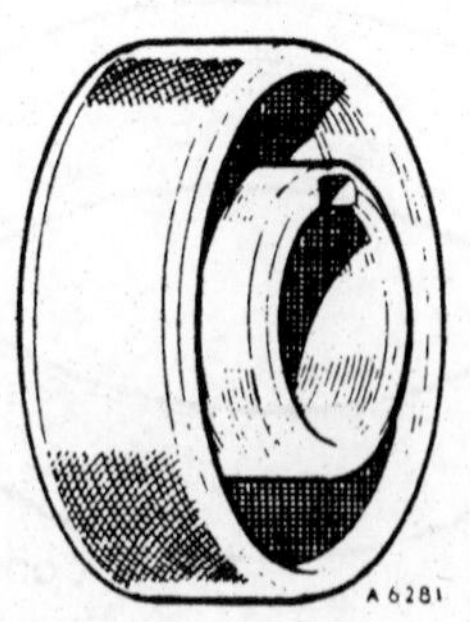
18G 1046. Engine Front Cover Centralizer.

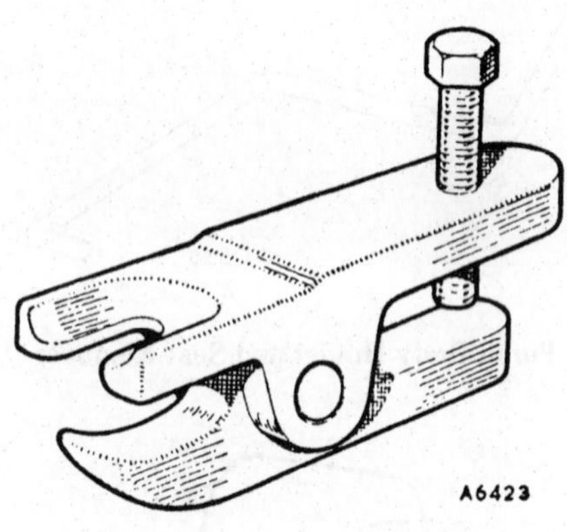

18G 1063. Steering Arm and Swivel Hub Ball Pin Remover.

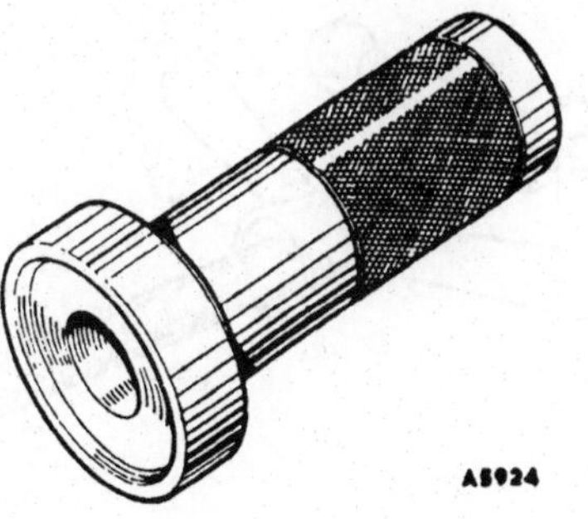
18G 1067. Rear Axle Shaft Assembly Replacer.

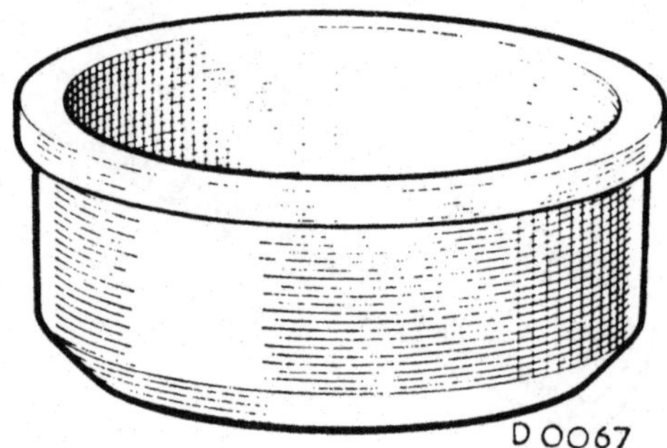

18G 1107. Front Clutch Piston and Seal Replacer.

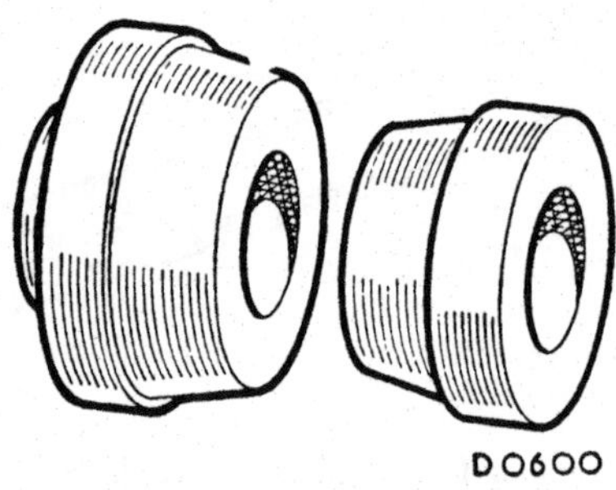

18G 1122 A. Front Hub Bearing Cups Replacing Adaptor.

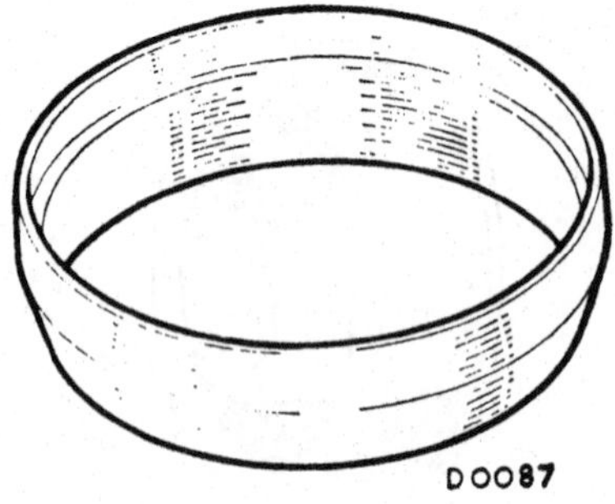

18G 1108. Crankshaft Oil Seal Protection Sleeve.

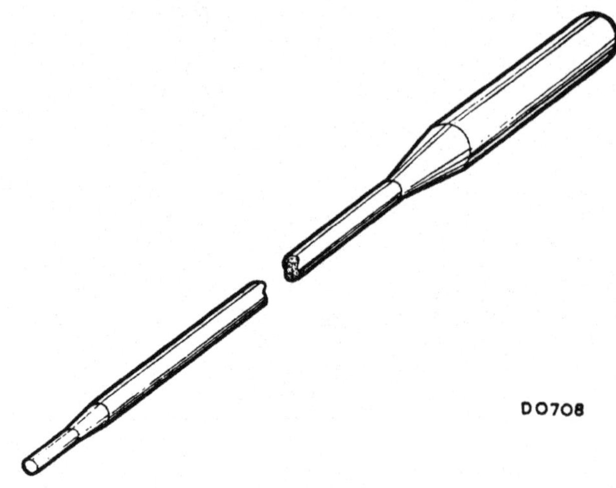

18G 1138. Dummy Layshaft.

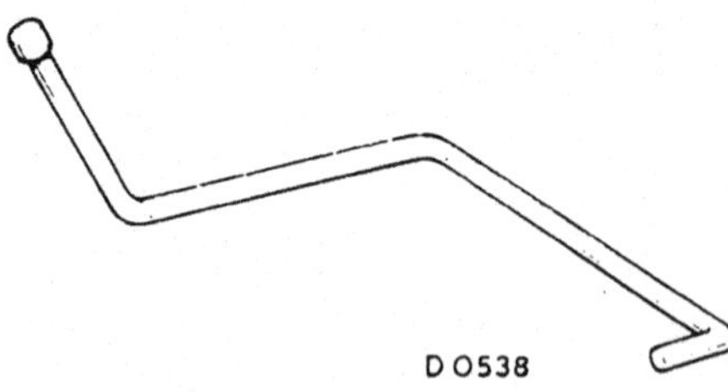

18G 1117. Pump Body Holder and Seat Remover.

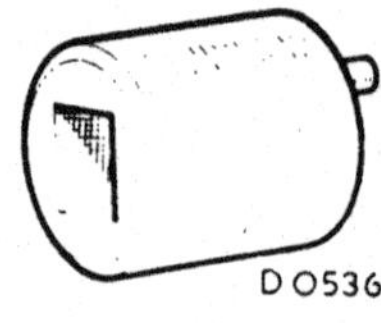

18G 1118. Oil Pump Body Socket.

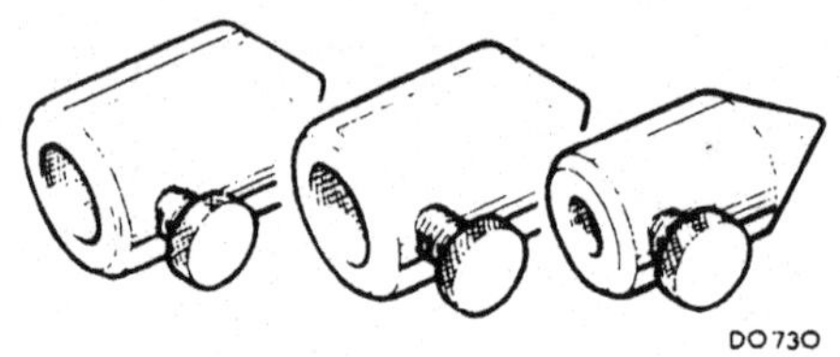

18G 1140. Steering-column Alignment Gauge.

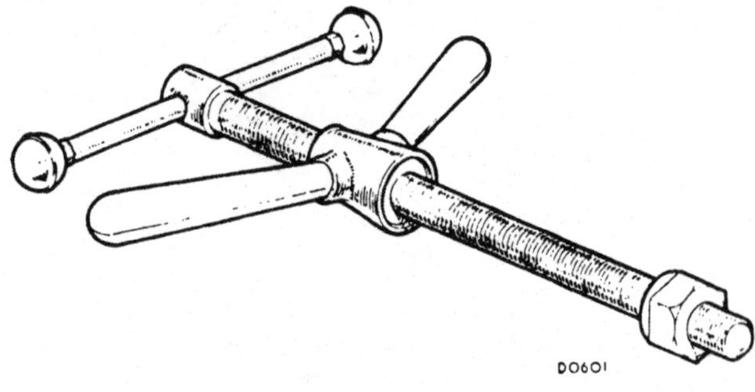

18G 1122. Bearing Cup Replacer (basic tool).

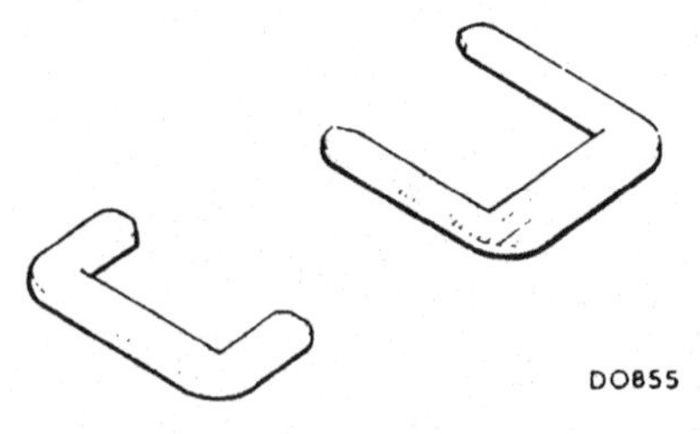

18G 1145. Rocker Type Switch and Bezel Remover.

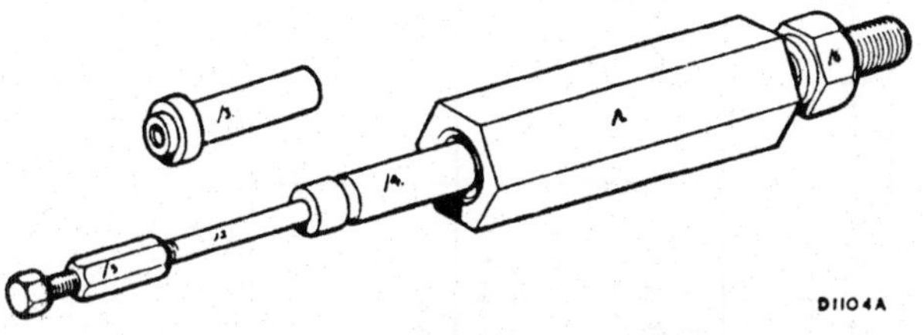

18G 1150. Basic Tool–Remover and Replacer–Gudgeon Pin.

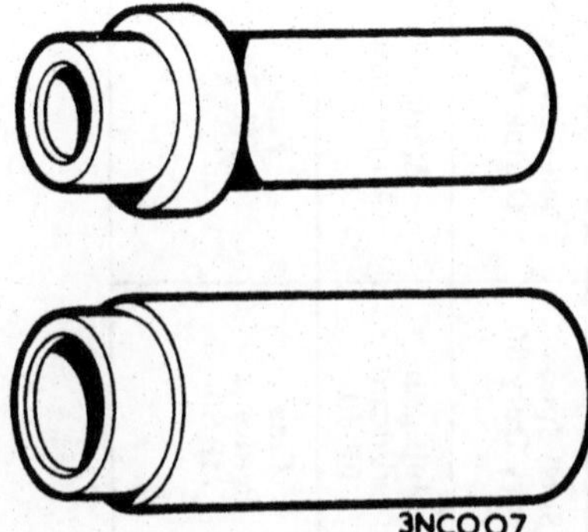

18G 1150 D. Adaptor Set–Remover and Replacer–Gudgeon Pin.

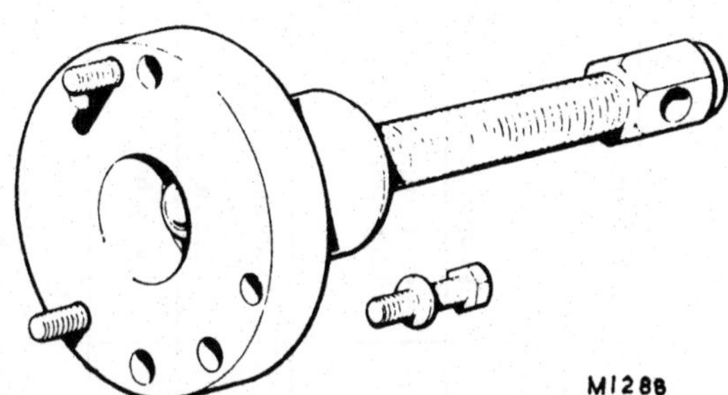

18G 1181. Steering Wheel Hub Remover.

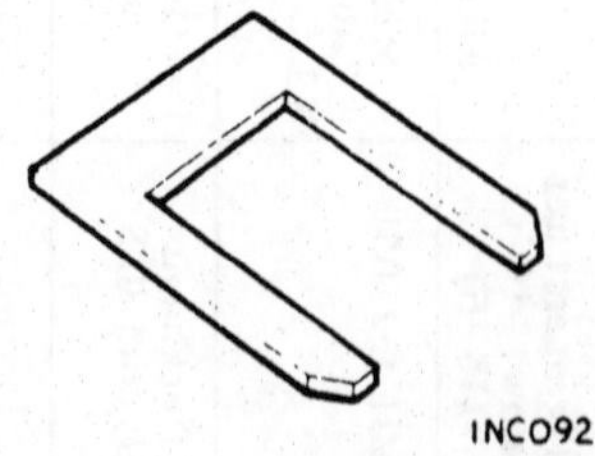

18G 1201. Rocker Type Switch (Slim Type) Remover.

SERVICE LUBRICANTS

Component	Engine, Synchromesh, Gearbox and Carburetter			Rear Axle and Steering Gear		Grease Points	Upper Cylinder Lubrication	Automatic Transmsission
Climatic Conditions	**All temperatures above −10°C (15°F)**	**All temperatures 10°C to 20°C (50°F to −5°F)**	**All temperatures below −10°C (15°F)**	**All temperatures above −10°C (15°F)**	**All temperatures below −10°C (15°F)**	**All conditions**	**All conditions**	**All conditions**
Minimum performance level	British Leyland Service Fill Lubricating Oil Specification for Passenger Car and Light Commercial Petrol Engines BLS 0L.02			MIL-L-2105B	MIL-L-2105B	Multi-purpose Litbium Grease N.L.G.1 Consistency No. 2	Upper Cylinder Lubricant	Automatic Transmission Fluid Type F
DUCKHAMS	Duckhams Q. 20-50	Duckhams Q. 5500	Duckhams Q. 5-30	Duckhams Hypoid 90 S	Duckhams Hypoid 80 S	Duckhams L.B. 10 Grease	Duckhams Adcoid Liquid	Duckhams Q-matic
CASTROL	Castrol GTX	Castrolite	Castrol GTZ	Castrol Hypoy B 90	Castrol Hypoy B 80	Castrol L.M. Grease	Castrollo	Castrol TQF
ESSO	Esso Uniflo 10W/50	Esso Uniflo 10W/50	Esso Extra Motor Oil 5W/20	Gear Oil GX 90/140	Esso Gear Oil GX 80	Esso Multi-purpose Grease H	Esso Upper Cylinder Lubricant	Esso Glide
MOBIL	Mobiloil Special 20W/50 or Super 10W/50	Mobiloil Super 10W/50	Mobiloil 5W/20	Mobilube HD 90	Mobilube HD 80	Mobilgrease M.P.	Mobil Upperlube	Mobil ATF 210
BP	BP Super Visco-Static 20/50 or 10W/40	BP Super Visco-Static 10W/30 or 10W/40	BP Super Visco-Static BP Super Visco-Static 5W/20	BP Hypogear 90 EP	BP Hypogear 80 EP	BP Energrease MP* BP Energrease L2	BP Powerlube* BP Upper Cylinder Lubricant	BP Autran B
SHELL	Shell Super 20W/50	Shell Super 10W/50	Shell Super 5W/30	Shell Spirax Heavy Duty 90	Shell Spirax Heavy Duty 80	Shell Retinax A Darina AX*	Shell Upper Cylinder Lubricant	Shell Donax T7
TEXACO	Havoline 20W/50 or 10W/40	Havoline 10W/40	Havoline 5W/30	Multigear Lubricant EP 90	Multigear Lubricant EP 80	Marfak All purpose	Special Upper Cylinder Lubricant	Texamatic Type F
PETROFINA	Fina Supergrade 20W/50 or 10W/50 or 10W/40	Fina Supergrade 10W/50 or 10W/40	Fina Supergrade 5W/20	Fina Pentonic XP 90-140	Fina Pentonic MP 80	Fina HTL 2	Fina Cyltonic	Fina Purfimatic

* America only

ENGINE EMISSION CONTROL SUPPLEMENT

Publication Part No. AKD 4957 (5th Edition)

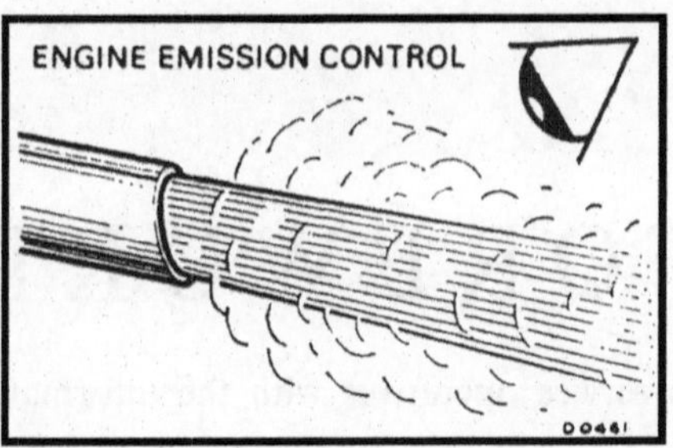

ENGINE EMISSION CONTROL SUPPLEMENT

CONTENTS

FOREWORD

This supplement provides service operatives with the information necessary to carry out the maintenance, servicing, and testing of engine emission and fuel evaporative loss control systems fitted to vehicles manufactured by BRITISH LEYLAND (AUSTIN-MORRIS) LTD. for which a certificate has been issued in accordance with the UNITED STATES CLEAN AIR ACTS and any applicable State Legislation.

Distributors and Dealers are advised to familiarize themselves with the legal requirements, in particular those concerning minimum standards of facilities, personnel, and servicing equipment.

Service operations in Workshop Manuals, where applicable, which may affect the efficiency of the emission or evaporative loss control equipment carry the following symbol, denoting that the control system must be checked on completion of the operation

SECTION 1

EQUIPMENT AND SERVICING

Section 1-A

EQUIPMENT

The recommended equipment for servicing should include at least the following:

- Ignition Analyser Oscilloscope
- Ohmmeter
- Voltmeter
- Tachometer
- Vacuum Gauge
- Pressure Gauge (0–10 lb./sq. in.)
- Carburetter Balance Meter
- Cam Angle Dwell Meter
- Ignition Timing Light
- Engine Exhaust Combustion Analyser
- Cylinder Leak Tester
- Distributor Advance Tester
- Carburetter Piston Loading Tool

The following equipment covers most of the requirements for engine testing and tuning vehicles fitted with exhaust emission control devices.

Equipment	*Type/Model*	*Manufacturer*
Oscilloscope Engine Tuning Set and Exhaust Gas Analyser	1020 or 720	Sun Electric Corp.
Engine Analyser	40–162	Marquette
Exhaust Gas Analyser	42–141	Marquette

Equipment made by other suppliers may also be adequate.

It is important that your test equipment has regular maintenance and calibration.

Section 1-B

SERVICING

General

The efficient operation of the exhaust emission control system is dependent on the engine being in good mechanical condition and correctly tuned to the settings given in **'TUNING DATA'**.

Tuning and test procedure for the carburetters, ignition system, and engine are given at the end of the manual. These procedures are the quickest and surest way of locating engine faults or maladjustments and are the only methods that should be used for engine tuning.

Fault diagnosis

After tuning the engine to the correct settings, check for indications of the following symptoms:

Symptons	Causes	Cure
Backfire in exhaust system	1. Leak in exhaust system	Locate and rectify leak
	● 2. Leaks in hoses or connections to gulp valve, vacuum sensing pipe or other inlet manifold joint ●	Locate and rectify leak
	3. Faulty gulp valve	Test gulp valve, and renew if faulty
	4. Leak in intake system	Locate and rectify leak
	5. High inlet manifold depression on over-run—faulty carburetter limit valve	Fit new throttle disc and limit valve assembly

Symptons	Causes	Cure
●Hesitation to accelerate after sudden throttle closure	1. Low carburetter damper oil	Top up to correct level
	2. Leaks in hoses or connections to gulp valve, vacuum sensing pipe or other inlet manifold joint	Locate and rectify leak
	3. Faulty gulp valve	Test gulp valve, and renew if faulty
	4. Leak in intake system	Locate and rectify leak
Engine surges (erratic operation at varying throttle openings)	1. Leaks in hoses or connections to gulp valve, vacuum sensing pipe or other inlet manifold joint	Locate and rectify leak
	2. Faulty gulp valve	Test gulp valve, and renew if faulty
	3. Air supply to adsorption canister restricted	Check air filter pad, vent pipe, and canister for obstruction
Erratic idling or stalling	1. Carburetter damper oil low	Top up to correct level.
	2. Leaks in hoses or connections to gulp valve or vacuum sensing pipe or other inlet manifold joint	Locate and rectify leak
	3. Faulty gulp valve	Test gulp valve, and renew if faulty
	4. Incorrect carburetter settings	Reset to **TUNING DATA**
	5. Carburetter limit valve not seating	Fit new throttle disc and limit valve assembly
	6. Carburetter suction chamber damaged	Replace carburetter or components
Burned or baked hose between air pump and check valve	1. Faulty check valve	Test check valve, and renew if faulty
	2. Air pump not pumping	Test air pump; service or renew if faulty
Noisy air pump	1. Incorrect belt tension	Adjust belt tension
	2. Pulleys damaged, loose or misaligned	Tighten loose pulleys, renew damaged pulleys
	3. Air pump failing or seizing	Test air pump; service or renew if faulty
Excessive exhaust system temperature	1. Incorrect ignition timing	Recheck timing against **'TUNING DATA'**
	2. Choke control system not fully returned	Check choke mechanism for correct operation; instruct driver on correct usage
	3. Fast idle speed too high	Reset fast idle speed—see **'TUNING DATA'**
	4. Air injector missing	Remove air manifold and check injectors
	5. Air pump relief valve inoperative	Test relief valve, and renew if faulty●

Symptons	Causes	Cure
Mixture requires excessive enriching to obtain correct exhaust emission readings	1. Air leak into crankcase	Locate and rectify leak
	2. Early cars—Diaphragm of crankcase control valve perforated or not correctly seated	Locate and rectify leak or control valve
	Later cars—Crankcase breather hose or connections to carburetter leaking	Locate and rectify leak
Fuel leakage	1. Fracture in fuel pipe or fuel vapour ventilation system	Locate and rectify leak
	2. Fuel filler cap not sealing	Check condition of cap and filler seal
	3. Leak on fuel filler tube or tank unit	Locate and rectify leak
Engine stops after short running periods (i.e. fuel starvation)	1. Obstructed vapour line between fuel tank and adsorption canister	Locate and clear obstruction
	2. Air supply to adsorption canister restricted	Check air filter pad, vent pipe and canister for obstruction
	3. Faulty fuel pump	Check operation and rectify fault
Engine runs after ignition is switched off	1. Fuel grade too low	Refill with correct grade fuel
	2. Ignition retarded	Reset timing to **'TUNING DATA'**
	3. Idle speed too high	Reset to **'TUNING DATA'**
	4. Fuel mixture too weak	Tune carburetter(s)

SECTION 2

CRANKCASE EMISSION CONTROL

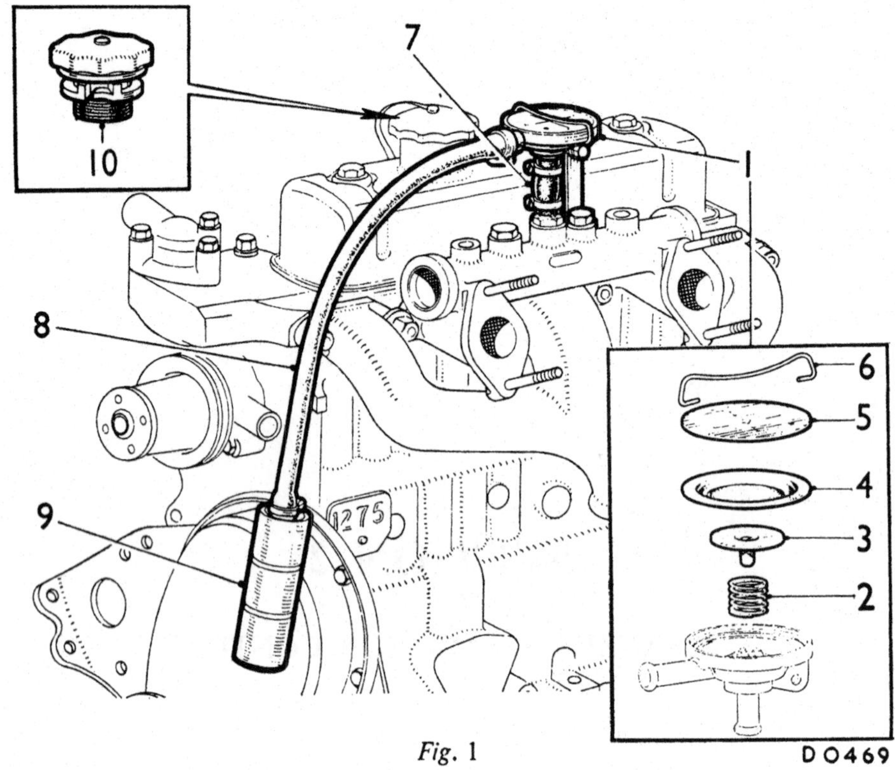

Fig. 1

A typical crankcase emission valve control system

1. Emission control valve.
2. Valve spring.
3. Metering valve.
4. Diaphragm.
5. Cover plate.
6. Spring clip.
7. Manifold connection.
8. Breather hose.
9. Oil separator.
10. Filtered filler cap.

Section 2-A

VALVE CONTROL SYSTEM—General description

The system consists of a diaphragm control valve connected by hoses between the inlet manifold and the engine crankcase. The crankcase outlet connection incorporates an oil separator to prevent oil being pulled over with the vapours leaving the crankcase. On four-cylinder engines a filtered, restricted orifice ($\frac{9}{64}$ in. diameter) in the oil filler cap provides a supply of fresh air into the crankcase as vapours are withdrawn by inlet manifold depression. Six-cylinder engines are fitted with a standard oil filler cap and a tube connected between the rocker cover oil filler tube and the air intake filter provides the supply of fresh air to the engine. The control valve diaphragm varies the opening to the inlet manifold according to the depression or pressure acting on it. With a decrease in manifold depression or when the crankcase obtains a positive pressure the diaphragm opens the valve allowing the crankcase vapours to be drawn into the inlet manifold. During conditions of high manifold depression, e.g. low engine speeds or loads, the diaphragm closes the valve and restricts the flow into the inlet manifold, thus preventing a leaning-off of the air/fuel mixture to the cylinders.

Section 2-B

VALVE CONTROL SYSTEM—Testing

(1) Warm up the engine to normal operating temperature.

(2) With the engine running at idling speed remove the oil filler cap.
  - (*a*) A rise in engine speed, the change being audibly noticeable, indicates that the control valve is functioning correctly.
  - (*b*) No rise in speed, service the control valve.

Section 2-C

VALVE CONTROL SYSTEM—Servicing

Oil filler cap (*four-cylinder engines only*)

(1) Renew every 12,000 miles or 12 months.

Control valve

(2) Disconnect the hoses and renew the valve assembly, or clean as follows:
  - (*a*) Remove the spring clip and withdraw the cover plate, diaphragm, metering valve and spring.
  - (*b*) Clean all metal parts with a solvent (trichlorethylene, fuel, etc.). **Do not use an abrasive.** If deposits are difficult to remove, immerse in boiling water before applying the solvent.
  - (*c*) Clean the diaphragm with a detergent or methylated spirit (denatured alcohol).
  - (*d*) Examine the parts thoroughly for wear or damage, and renew where necessary.
  - (*e*) Reassemble the valve ensuring that the metering valve fits correctly in its guides and the diaphragm is correctly seated.
  - (*f*) Refit the valve and check its operation.

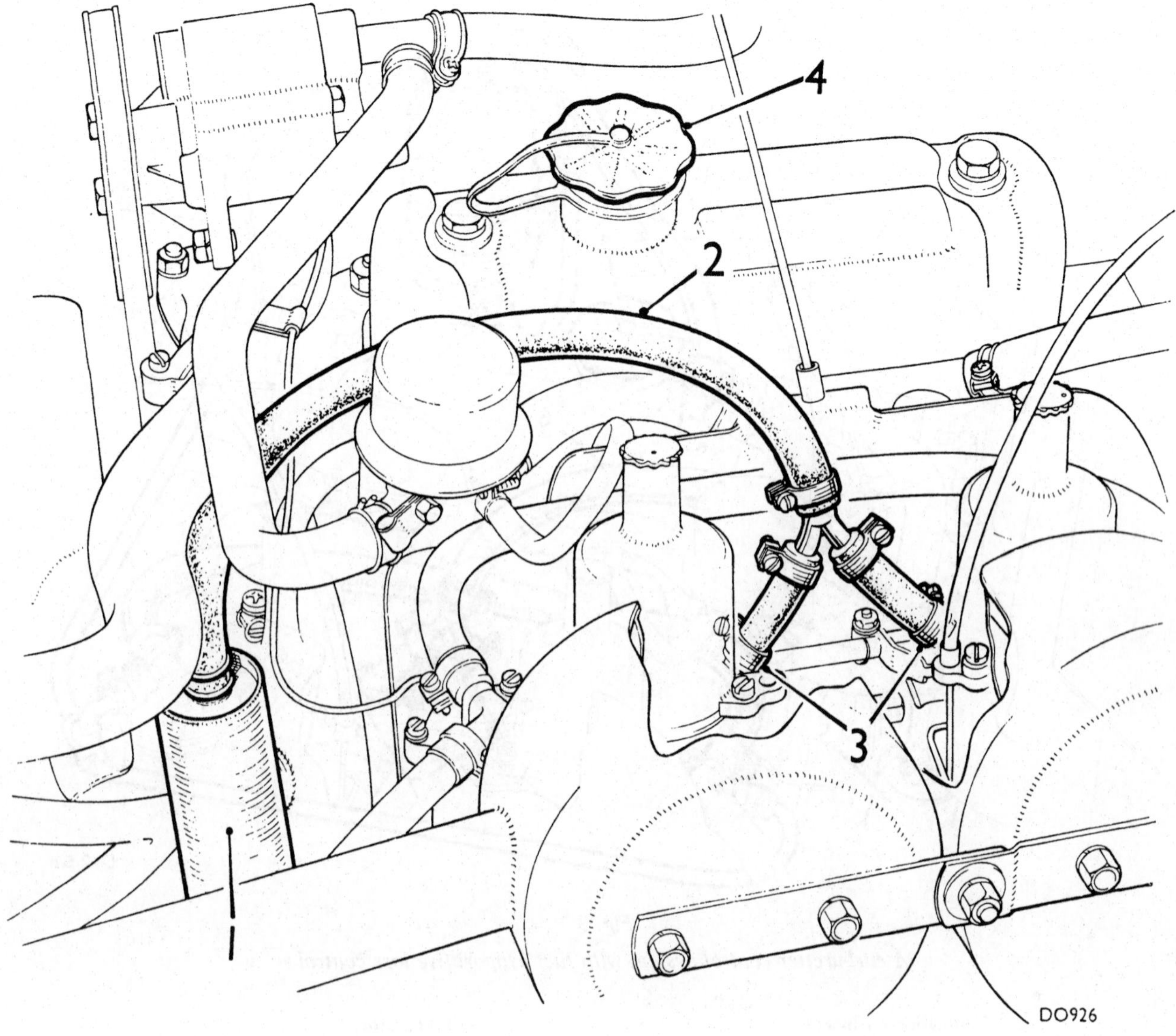

Fig. 2
Carburetter control system

1. Oil separator.
2. Breather hose.
3. Carburetter chamber connection.
4. Filtered filler cap.

Section 2-D

CARBURETTER CONTROL SYSTEM

Description

With this system the engine breather outlet is connected by hoses to the controlled depression chamber; the chamber between the piston and the throttle disc valve, of the carburetter(s). Engine fumes and blow-by gases are drawn from the crankcase by the depression in this chamber, through an oil separator incorporated in the engine outlet connection, and from there to the inlet manifold. Fresh air is supplied to the engine through the combined oil filler cap and filter (four-cylinder engines) or through the air intake filter (six-cylinder engines).

Servicing

The oil filler cap (four-cylinder engines only) must be renewed every 12,000 miles (20000 km.) or 12 months; no other service is required.

If a failure of the system is suspected, check the hoses and connections for leaks and obstructions. An indication of a failure is loss of crankcase depression.

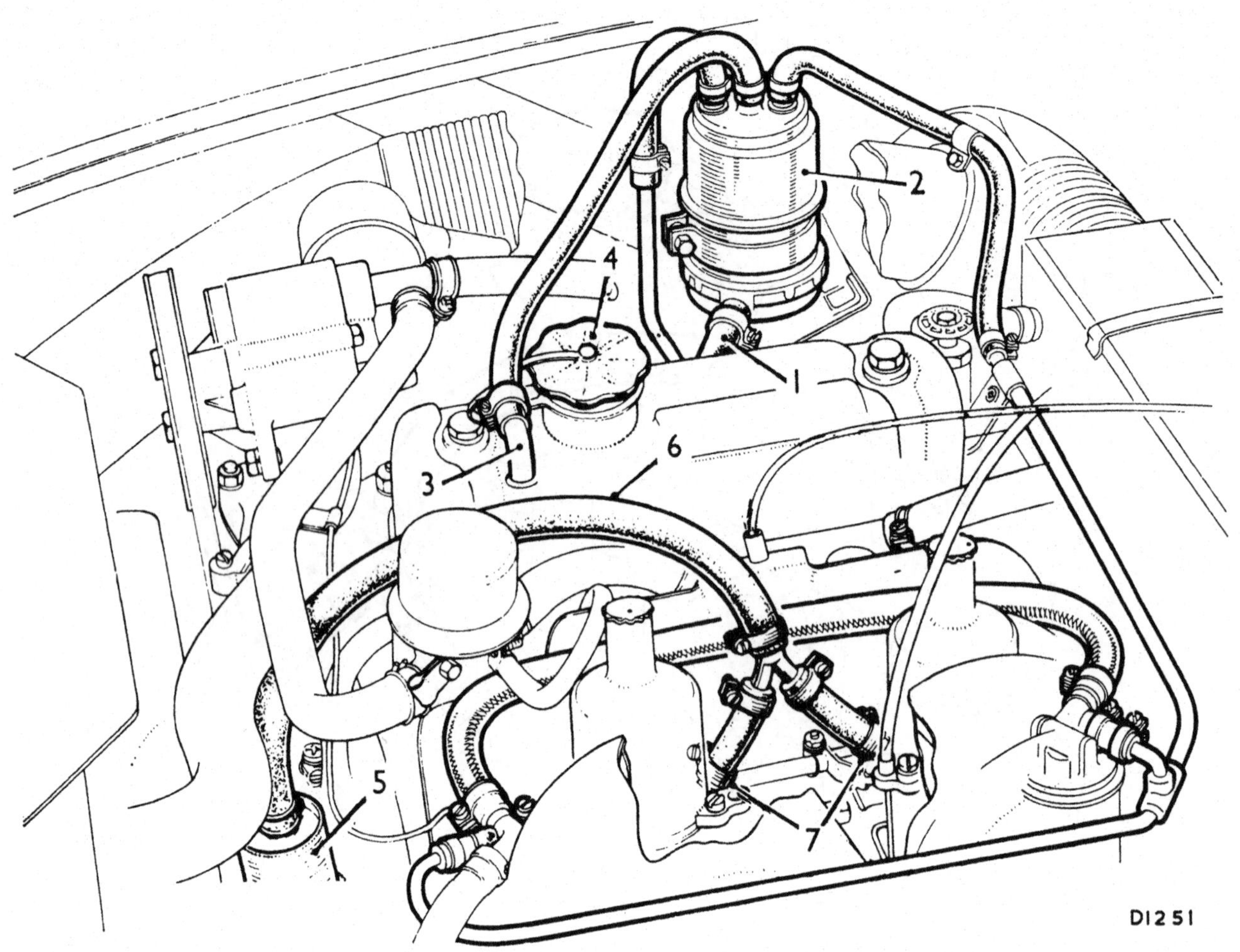

Fig. 3

A carburetter control system with fuel evaporative loss control

1. Ventilation air intake.
2. Absorption canister.
3. Restricted connection to rocker cover.
4. Sealed oil filler cap.
5. Oil separator.
6. Breather hose.
7. Carburetter chamber connections.

Section 2-E

CARBURETTER CONTROL SYSTEM—with evaporative loss control

This system incorporates most of the components of the carburetter control system, with the exception of the combined oil filler cap and filtered air intake. Its operation differs in that air for engine breathing is drawn through the filtered adsorption canister of the evaporative loss control system into the engine valve rocker cover. A restrictor in the rocker cover connection reduces the air flow to ensure crankcase depression under all conditions.

Engine fumes and blow-by gases are drawn from the crankcase, through an oil separator, into the inlet manifold by the controlled depression chamber of the carburetter.

Servicing

No direct servicing of the system is required. The air intake filter pad in the absorption canister is renewed at the intervals required by the fuel evaporative loss control.

If a failure of the system is suspected, check the hoses and connections for leaks and obstruction. An indication of a failure is loss of crankcase depression.

SECTION 3

EXHAUST EMISSION CONTROL
(Exhaust Port Air Injection)

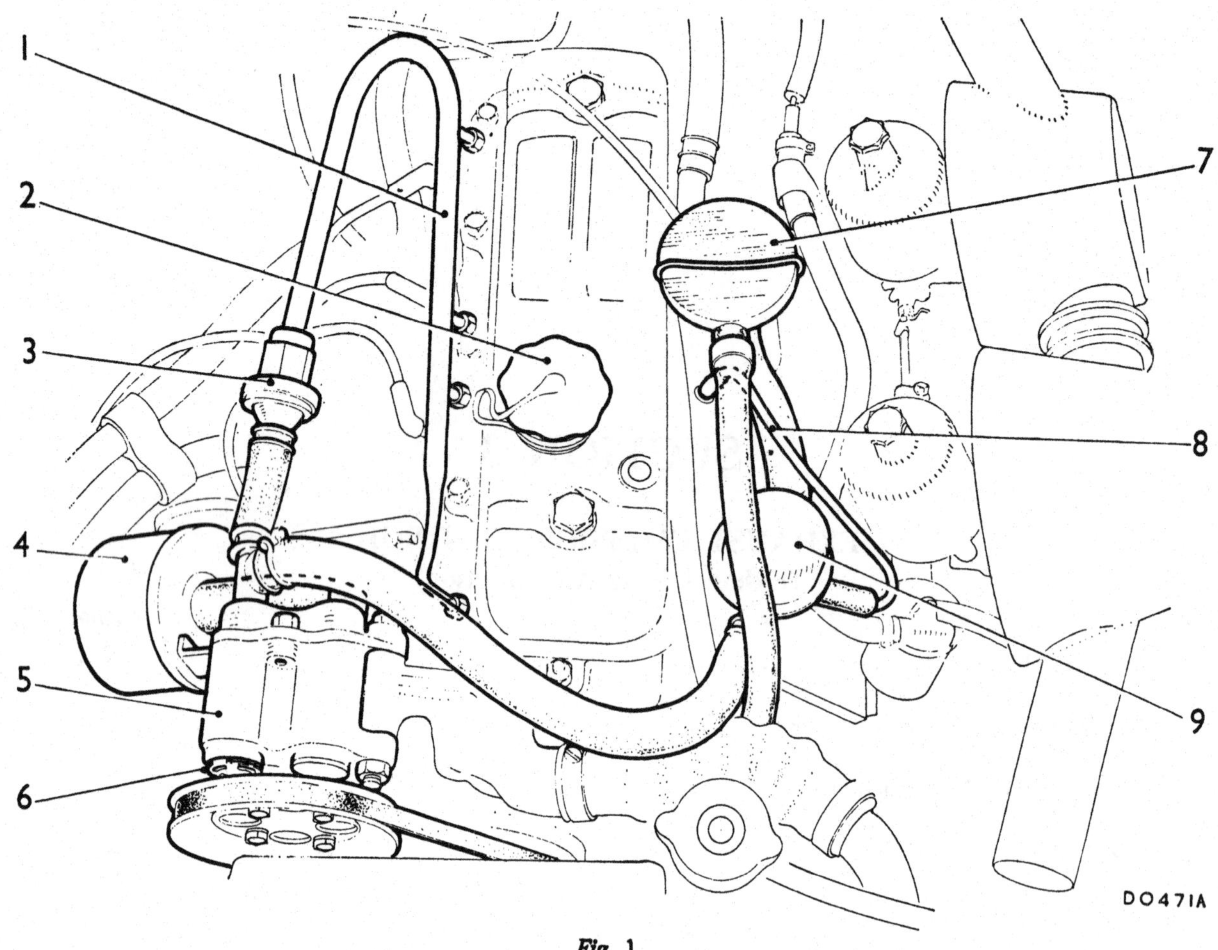

Fig. 1

A typical engine emission control system layout

1. Air manifold.
2. Filtered oil filler cap.
3. Check valve.
4. Emission air cleaner.
5. Air pump.
6. Relief valve.
7. Crankcase emission valve.
8. Vacuum sensing tube.
9. Gulp valve.

Section 3-A

GENERAL DESCRIPTION

Air is pressure-fed from an air pump via an injection manifold to the cylinder head exhaust port of each cylinder. A check valve in the air delivery pipe prevents blow-back from high pressure exhaust gases. The pump also supplies air through a gulp valve to the inlet manifold to provide air during conditions of deceleration and engine over-run.

IMPORTANT. The efficient operation of the system is dependent on the engine being correctly tuned. The ignition and spark plug settings, valve clearances, and carburetter adjustments given for a particular engine (see **'TUNING DATA'**) must be strictly adhered to at all times.

Air pump

The rotary vane type air pump is mounted on the front of the cylinder head and is belt driven from the water pump pulley. Provision is made for tensioning the belt.

Air is drawn into the pump through a dry-type renewable element filter. A relief valve in the pump discharge port allows excessive air pressure at high engine speeds to discharge to the atmosphere.

Check valve

The check valve, fitted in the pump discharge line to the injection manifold, protects the pump from the back-flow of exhaust gases.

The valve shuts if the air pressure ceases while the engine is running; for example, if the pump drive belt should break.

Gulp valve

The gulp valve, fitted in the pump discharge line to the inlet manifold, controls the flow of air for leaning-off the rich air/fuel mixture present in the inlet manifold immediately following throttle closure after running at full throttle opening (i.e. engine over-run).

A sensing pipe connected between the inlet manifold and the gulp valve maintains manifold depression directly to the underside of the diaphragm and through a bleed hole to the upper side. Sudden increases in manifold depression which occur immediately following throttle closure act on the underside of the diaphragm which opens the valve and admits air to the inlet manifold. The bleed hole allows the differences in depression acting on the diaphragm to equalize and the valve closes.

On some engines a restrictor is fitted in the air pump discharge connection to the gulp valve, to prevent surging when the gulp valve is operating.

Carburetter

The carburetters are manufactured to a special exhaust emission control specification and are tuned to give optimum engine performance with maximum emission control.

A limit valve is incorporated in the carburetter throttle disc which limits the inlet manifold depression ensuring that under conditions of high inlet-manifold depression the mixture entering the cylinders is at a combustible ratio.

Section 3-B

AIR PUMP (four-cylinder engines)

Drive belt tension

When correctly tensioned, a total deflection of ½ in., under moderate hand pressure, should be possible at the midway point of the longest belt run between the pulleys.

To tension the belt:

(1) Slacken the air pump mounting bolt and adjusting link bolts (see Fig. 3).

(2) Using hand pressure only, move the pump in the required direction until the correct tension is obtained.

(3) Tighten the mounting and adjusting bolts to a torque figure of 10 lb. ft.

Testing

(1) Check the drive belt for correct tensioning.

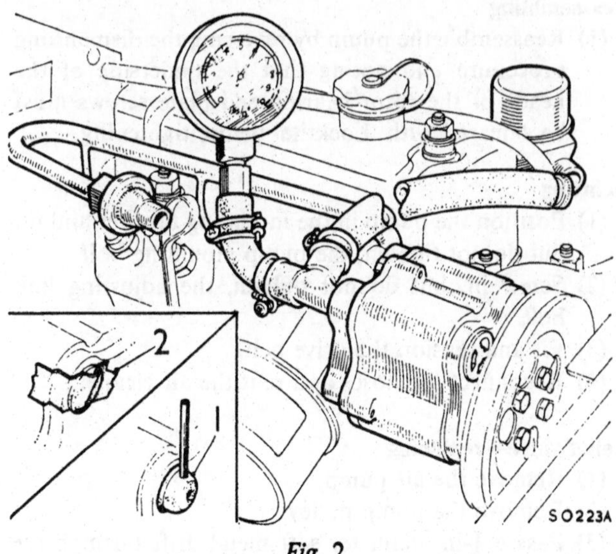

Fig. 2

The pressure gauge connected (four-cylinder engines)

1. Relief valve test tool. 2. Tape used to duct air.

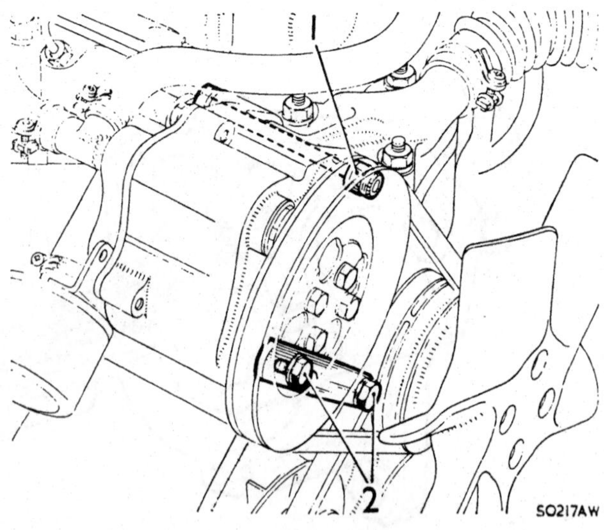

Fig. 3

Air pump (four-cylinder engines)

1. Pump mounting bolt. 2. Adjusting link bolts.

(2) Connect a tachometer to the engine in accordance with the instrument-maker's instructions.

(3) Disconnect the gulp valve air supply hose at the gulp valve and securely plug the hose.

(4) Disconnect the air manifold supply hose at the check valve, and connect a pressure gauge to the hose (see Fig. 2).

(5) Run the engine at the air pump test speed given in **'TUNING DATA'**: a gauge reading of not less than 2·75 lb./sq. in. should be registered.

(*a*) If a lower reading is obtained, remove, dismantle and clean the pump air cleaner. Reassemble using a new element, refit the air cleaner and repeat the test.

(*b*) If the reading is still unsatisfactory, temporarily blank off the relief valve and repeat the test; if the reading is now correct, renew the relief valve.

(*c*) If a satisfactory reading is still unobtainable, remove and service the air pump.

(6) Stop the engine and fit a temporary air duct over the face of the relief valve. Two methods of doing this are shown in Fig. 2. The tool (1) may be fabricated from grommet (Part No. 1B 1735) and a short length of metal brake tube, or (2) by using a piece of adhesive tape to form the duct.

DO NOT ATTEMPT TO CHECK AIR FLOW FROM THE RELIEF VALVE BY PLACING A FINGER BETWEEN THE VALVE AND THE DRIVING PULLEY.

(*a*) Start the engine and slowly increase the speed until air flow from the relief valve duct is detected, when a gauge reading of 4·5 to 6·5 lb./sq. in. should be registered.

(*b*) If the relief valve fails to operate correctly, remove the pump and renew the valve.

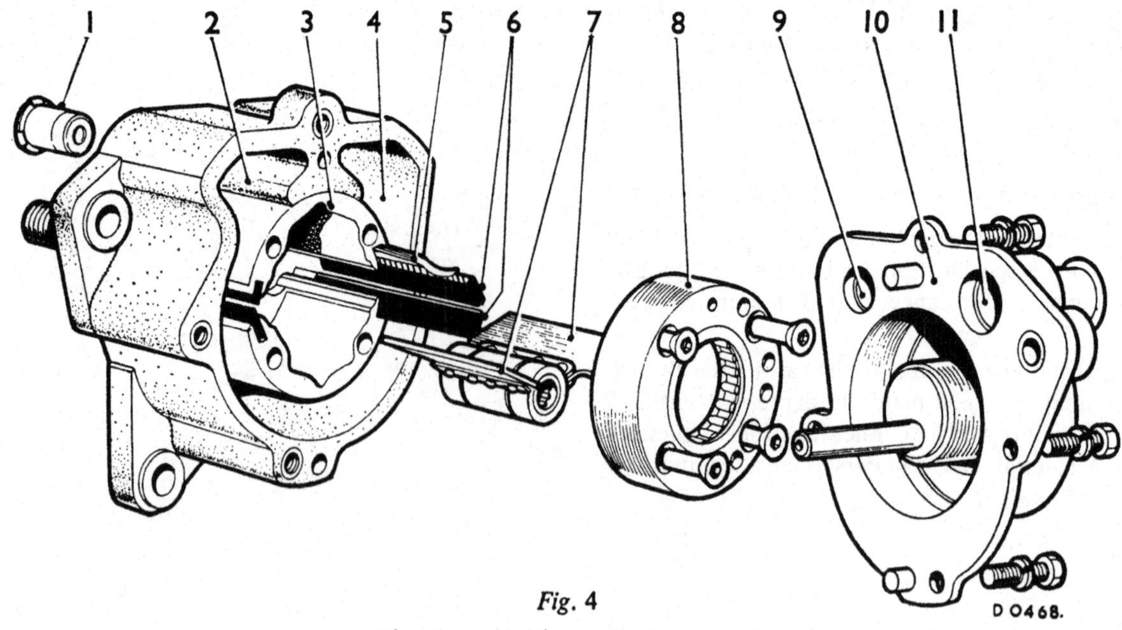

Fig. 4

The air pump (four-cylinder engines)

1. Relief valve.
2. Inlet chamber.
3. Rotor.
4. Outlet chamber.
5. Spring.
6. Carbons.
7. Vane assemblies.
8. Rotor bearing end plate.
9. Outlet port.
10. Port-end cover.
11. Inlet port.

Removing

(1) Disconnect the air hoses from the pump connections and remove the air cleaner.
(2) Slacken the mounting and adjusting link bolts and slip the drive belt from the pump pulley.
(3) Remove the top adjusting link bolt and the nut securing the pump mounting bolt.
(4) Support the pump, withdraw the mounting bolt and lift the pump from the engine.

Dismantling

(1) Remove the four port-end cover retaining bolts and withdraw the cover.
(2) Remove the four screws securing the rotor bearing end plate to the rotor and remove the end plate.
(3) Lift out the vane assemblies.
(4) Remove the carbon and spring assemblies from the rotor.

Servicing

(1) Wipe the interior and components of the pump clean, using a lint-free cloth.

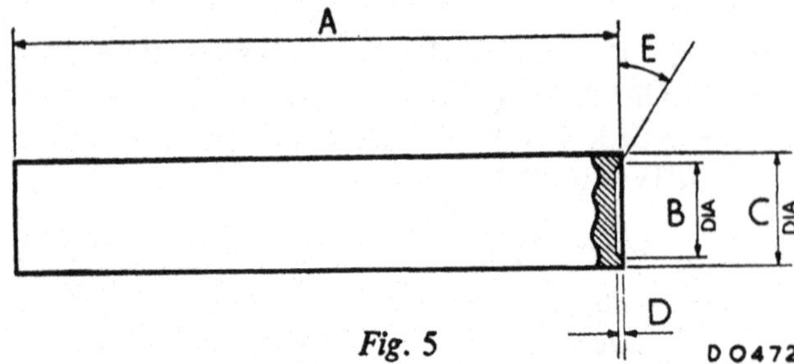

Fig. 5

The dimensions of the relief valve replacing tool

A = 5 in. B = ·986 in. C = 1·062 in.
D = ·05 in. E = 30°.

(2) Clean the vane carrier roller bearings and the rotor end plate bearing and repack the bearings with Esso 'Andok' 260 lubricant.
(3) Inspect the vane assemblies for signs of having fouled the pump wall, and for grooving in area of contact with the carbons. Renew worn or damaged vanes.
(4) Fit new carbons (the original springs may be re-used if serviceable). Note that the slots which carry the carbon and springs are the deeper ones, and the carbons are all fitted with the chamfered edge to the inside.

Reassembling

(1) Reassemble the pump by reversing the dismantling procedure and noting that the underside of the heads of the rotor bearing end plate screws must be smeared with 'Locktite' before tightening.

Refitting

(1) Position the pump in the mounting bracket and fit, but do not tighten, the pump mounting bolt.
(2) Screw in, but do not tighten, the adjusting link bolt.
(3) Fit and tension the drive belt.
(4) Reconnect the hoses and refit the air cleaner.

Relief valve—replacing

(1) Remove the air pump.
(2) Remove the pump pulley.
(3) Pass a ½-in. diameter soft metal drift through the pump discharge connection so that it registers against the relief valve, and drive the valve from the pump.

(4) Fit a new copper seating washer to the new relief valve and enter the valve into the pump body.

(5) Using a tool made to the dimensions shown in Fig. 5, drive the valve into the pump until the copper seating washer is held firmly, but not compressed, between the valve and the pump.

(6) Refit the pulley and refit the air pump.

Section 3-C

AIR PUMP (six-cylinder engines)

Drive belt tension

When correctly tensioned, a total deflection of ½ in., under moderate hand pressure should be possible at the midway point of the longest belt run between the pulleys.

To tension the belt:

(1) Slacken the air pump mounting bolt and adjusting link bolts (see Fig. 6).

(2) Using hand pressure only, move the pump in the required direction until the correct tension is obtained.

(3) Tighten the mounting and adjusting link bolts to a torque figure of 10 lb. ft.

Testing

Faulty operation of the air pump is indicated by excessive pump noise. If excessive noise is present and the air pump is suspected, remove the air pump drive belt and run the engine to check that the noise is not from another source. If this check shows that the air pump is excessively noisy renew the air pump assembly or proceed as follows:

(1) Check the drive belt for correct tensioning.

(2) Run the engine at idle speed and check the air supply hoses and connections for leaks and for intermittent contact with other parts of the vehicle.

(3) Connect a tachometer to the engine in accordance with the instrument maker's instructions.

(4) Disconnect the air supply hose tee connection from its connection with the air pump discharge hose.

(5) Connect a pressure gauge to the air pump discharge hose (see Fig. 7).

(6) Run the engine at the air pump test speed given in **'TUNING DATA'**. A gauge reading of not less than 2·75 lb./sq. in. should be registered.

   (*a*) If a lower reading is obtained, remove, dismantle, and clean the pump air cleaner. Reassemble using a new element, refit the air cleaner, and repeat the test.

   (*b*) If the reading is still unsatisfactory, temporarily blank off the relief valve and repeat the test; if the reading is now correct, renew the relief valve.

   (*c*) If a satisfactory reading is still unobtainable the air pump assembly must be replaced.

   (*d*) From idling speed, slowly increase the engine speed until air flow from the relief valve is detected, this should occur before the gauge reading exceeds 10 lb./sq. in.

   (*e*) If the relief valve fails to operate correctly, remove the pump and renew the valve.

(7) If the foregoing tests fail to remedy or locate the cause of the air pump noise renew the air pump assembly.

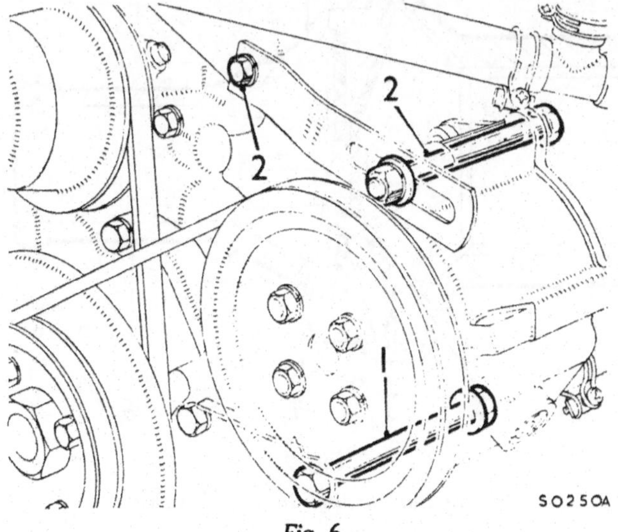

Fig. 6

Air pump (six-cylinder engines)

1. Pump mounting bolt. 2. Adjusting link bolts.

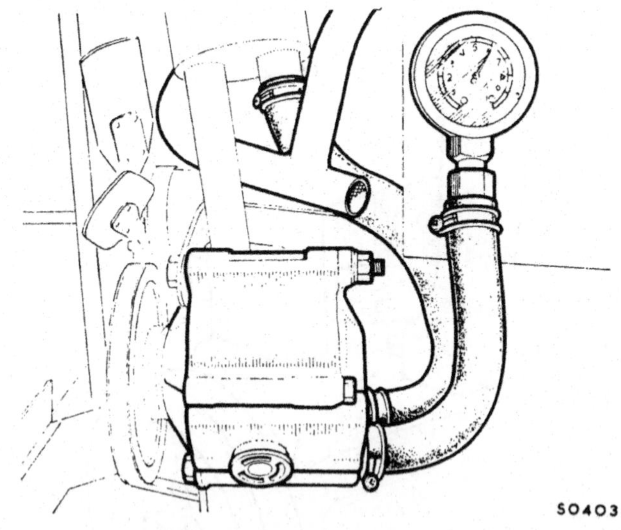

Fig. 7

The pressure gauge connected (six-cylinder engines)

Removing

(1) Disconnect the hoses from the pump connections and remove the air cleaner.

(2) Slacken the mounting and adjusting link bolts and slip the drive belt from the pump pulley.

(3) Remove the nut from the adjusting link bolt, support the pump and withdraw the bolt.

(4) Unscrew the mounting bolt and remove the pump.

Fig. 8

Removing the relief valve (six-cylinder engines)

Relief valve—replacing

(1) Remove the air pump.

(2) Using a gear puller and a fabricated bridge as shown in Fig. 8, withdraw the relief valve from the pump body.
DO NOT HOLD THE PUMP BY CLAMPING IT IN A VICE.

(3) Enter the new relief valve into the pump body.

(4) With a protective plate over the valve, carefully drive the valve into the pump until its flange registers lightly on the pump body.

(5) Insert the pressure setting plug into the relief valve, using a suitable tool, apply pressure to the centre of the plug until the legs of the plug lock under the relief valve cage.

Section 3-D

CHECK VALVE

Removing

(1) Disconnect the air supply hose from the check valve connection.

(2) Hold the air manifold connection to prevent it twisting and unscrew the check valve.

Testing

(1) Blow through the valve, orally, in turn from each connection. Air should only pass through the valve when blown from the air supply hose connection. If air passes through when blown from the air manifold connection, renew the check valve.

On no account may an air blast be used for this test.

Refitting

(1) Hold the air manifold connection to prevent it twisting, screw in and tighten the check valve.

(2) Reconnect the air supply hose to the check valve.

Section 3-E

AIR MANIFOLD AND INJECTORS

Testing

(1) Disconnect the air manifold from the cylinder head connections.

(2) Slacken the air supply hose clip at the check valve connection.

(3) Rotate the manifold about its connection axis until the injector connections are accessible.

(4) Tighten the air supply hose clip.

(5) Run the engine at idle speed and observe the flow of air from each of the manifold connection tubes. Should the flow of air from any of the connections be restricted, remove the manifold and clear the obstruction using an air blast.

(6) With the engine running at idle speed, check that exhaust gases blow from each of the cylinder head injectors.

IMPORTANT.—The injectors may be free in the cylinder head and care must be taken to ensure that they are not displaced during this test.

To clear a restricted injector:

(*a*) Crank engine until the exhaust valve below the injector is closed.

(*b*) Using a hand drill (not power-driven), pass a ⅛-in. drill through the injector bore, taking care that the drill does not contact the exhaust valve stem after passing through the injector. Damage may result if a power-driven drill is used.

(*c*) Insert an air-blast nozzle into the injector connection to clear carbon dust from the exhaust port.

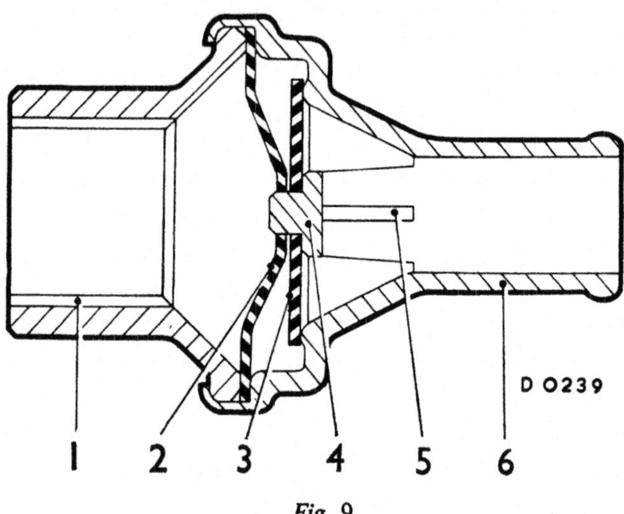

Fig. 9

A section through the check valve

1. Air manifold connection.
2. Diaphragm.
3. Valve.
4. Valve pilot.
5. Guides.
6. Air supply connection.

Section 3-F

GULP VALVE

Testing

(1) Disconnect the gulp valve air supply hose from the air pump connection.

(2) Connect a vacuum gauge, with a tee connection to the disconnected end of the gulp valve air hose.

(3) Start the engine and run it at idle speed.

(4) Temporarily seal the open connection on the gauge tee and check that a zero gauge reading is maintained for approximately 15 seconds; if a vacuum is registered, renew the gulp valve. It is most important that the engine speed is not increased above idling during this test.

(5) With the gauge tee connection temporarily sealed, operate the throttle rapidly from closed to open; the gauge should then register a vacuum. Repeat the test several times, temporarily unsealing the tee piece connection to destroy the vacuum before each operation of the throttle. If the gauge fails to register a vacuum, renew the gulp valve.

Removing

(1) Disconnect the air hoses.

(2) Unscrew the mounting screw and remove the gulp valve.

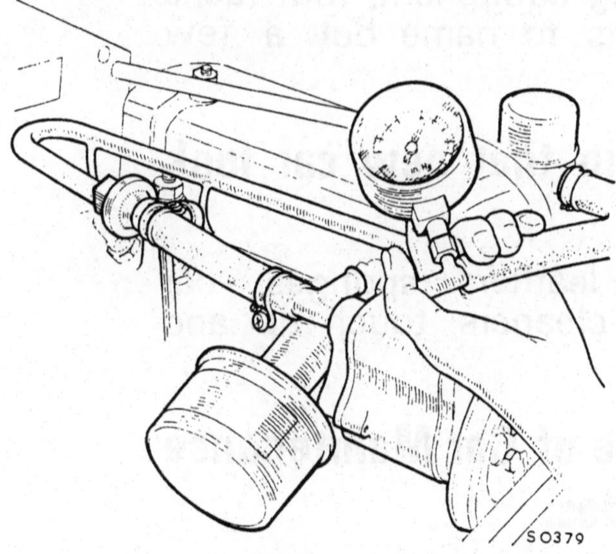

Fig. 10

The vacuum gauge connected for testing the gulp valve

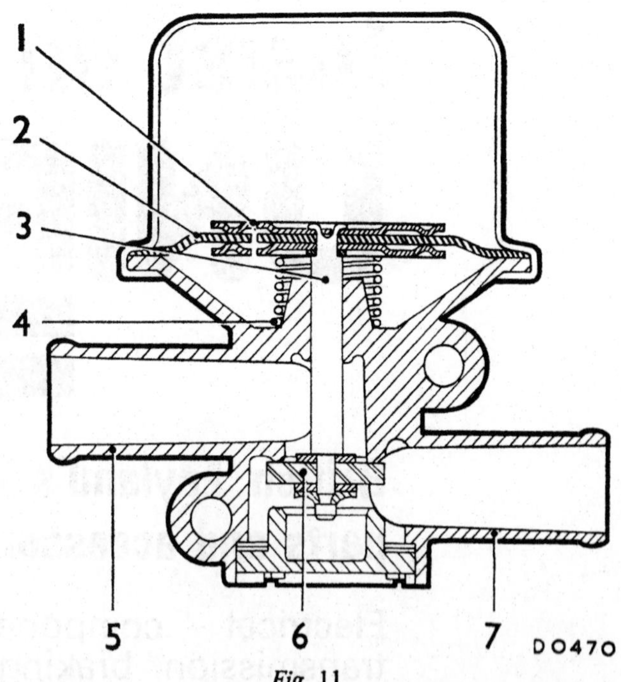

Fig. 11

A section through the gulp valve

1. Metering balance orifice.
2. Diaphragm.
3. Valve spindle.
4. Return spring.
5. Inlet manifold hose connection.
6. Valve.
7. Air pump hose connection.

Refitting

(1) Reverse the removing procedure.

Section 3-G

LIMIT VALVE (INLET MANIFOLD DEPRESSION)

Testing

(1) Disconnect the gulp valve sensing pipe from the inlet manifold.

(2) Connect a vacuum gauge to the sensing pipe connection on the inlet manifold.

(3) Connect a tachometer in accordance with the instrument maker's instructions.

(4) Warm the engine at fast idle speed until normal operating temperature is reached.

(5) Increase the engine speed to 3,000 r.p.m. then release the throttle quickly; the vacuum gauge reading should immediately rise to between 20·5 and 22 in. Hg. If the gauge reading falls outside these limits the carburetter must be removed and the throttle disc and limit valve assembly renewed. After refitting, the carburetter must be tuned as described in Section 4-A.

SECTION 3A

EXHAUST EMISSION CONTROL
(Engine Modifications System)

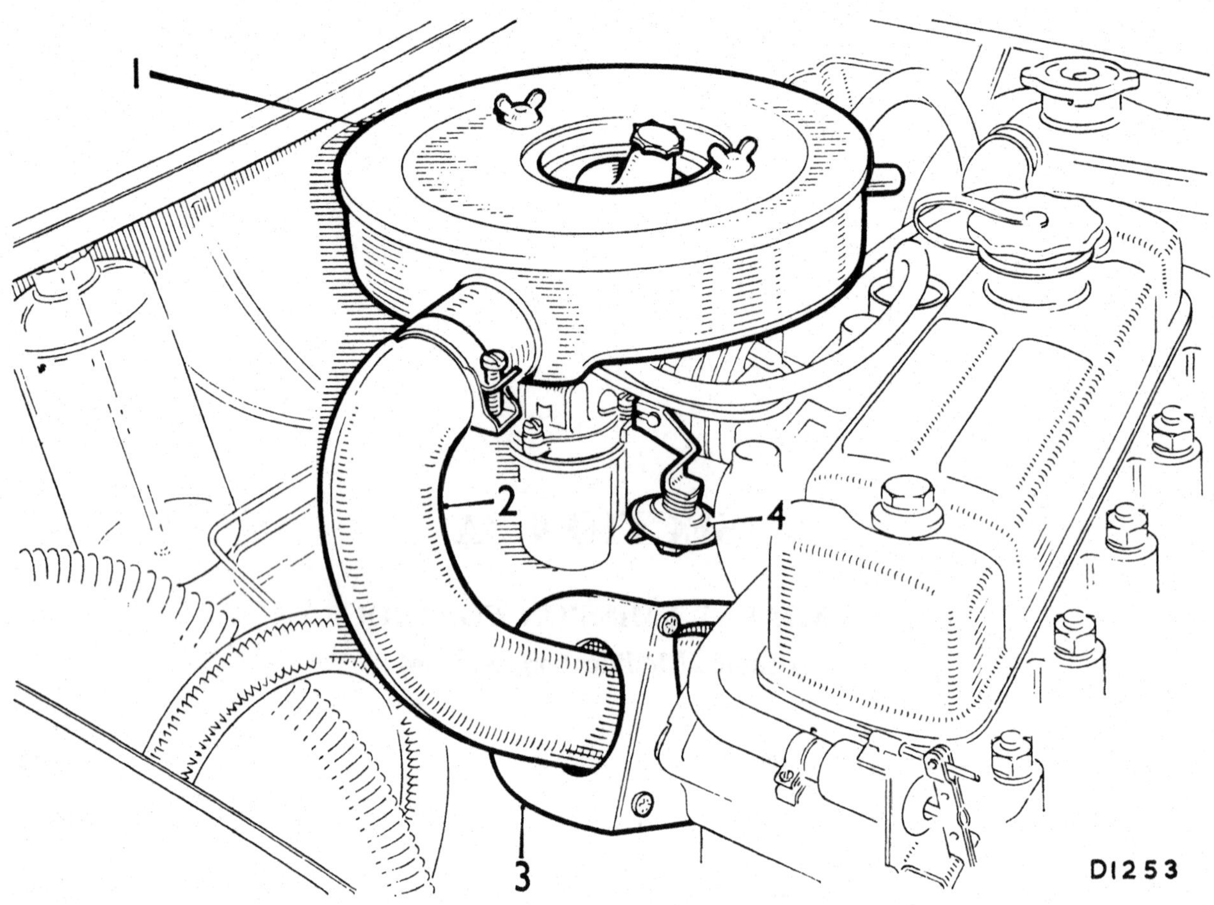

Fig. 1
An engine modification exhaust emission control system showing the air intake tube in the low ambient temperature operating position

1. Air cleaner.
2. Air intake tube.
3. Manifold shroud.
4. Throttle damper.

Section 3A-A

GENERAL DESCRIPTION

This system incorporates modifications to a high compression ratio engine and using a carburetter manufactured to a special exhaust emission control specification.

IMPORTANT. The efficient operation of the system is dependent on the engine being correctly tuned. The settings given for a particular engine (see **'TUNING DATA'**) must be strictly adhered to at all times.

Carburetter

The carburetter is tuned to give optimum engine performance with maximum exhaust emission control.

A limit valve is incorporated in the carburetter throttle disc which limits the inlet manifold depression ensuring that under conditions of high inlet-manifold depression the air/fuel mixture entering the cylinders is at a combustible ratio.

Throttle damper

A damper is fitted to act on the throttle lever as it returns to the closed position ensuring a gradual closing of the throttle valve giving smooth deceleration. Provision is made for adjusting the damping effect; the correct setting is given in **'TUNING DATA'.**

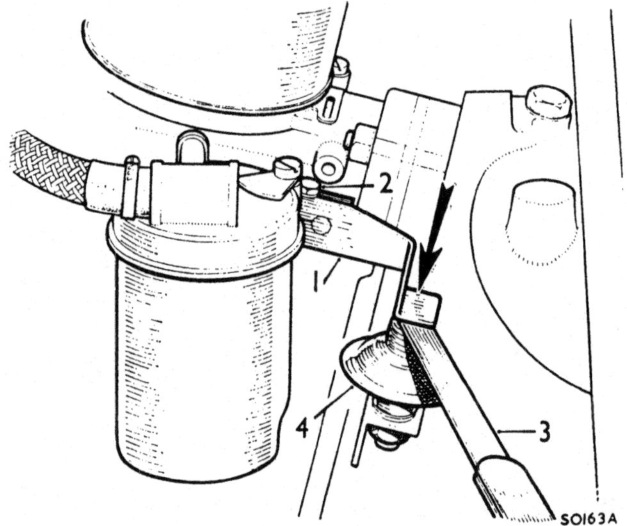

Fig. 2
Adjusting the throttle damper setting

1. Throttle lever.
2. Clamp screw
3. Feeler gauge.
4. Throttle damper.

Air intake

In low ambient temperature conditions the intake tube of the air cleaner is positioned in a shroud formed over a section of the exhaust manifold. Air drawn through the cleaner to the carburetter is warmed by heat given off by the manifold.

In high ambient temperature conditions the air intake tube is positioned away from the manifold and air entering the carburetter is drawn into the air cleaner from the engine compartment at ambient temperature.

Section 3A-B

THROTTLE DAMPER

Adjusting

(1) Slacken the clamp nut on the damper operating lever.

(2) Insert a feeler gauge (see **'TUNING DATA'**) between the damper plunger and the operating arm.

(3) With the carburetter throttle disc valve in the fully closed position, press the operating lever down until the plunger is fully depressed.

(4) Hold the lever in this position and tighten the clamp nut.

(5) Remove the feeler gauge.

Section 3A-C

AIR INTAKE

Repositioning

(1) Slacken the intake tube securing clip.

(2) Slacken the air cleaner wing nuts.

(3) Withdraw the intake tube from the air cleaner and manifold shroud.

(4) Refit the intake tube with its entry positioned adjacent to the end of the rocker cover.

(5) Tighten the wing nuts and securing clip.

●

Section 3A-D

AIR BLEED COMPENSATOR

Description

An air bleed temperature compensator is fitted to some engines equipped with twin type HS carburetters required to conform with European E.C.E. or E.E.C. exhaust emission control regulations.

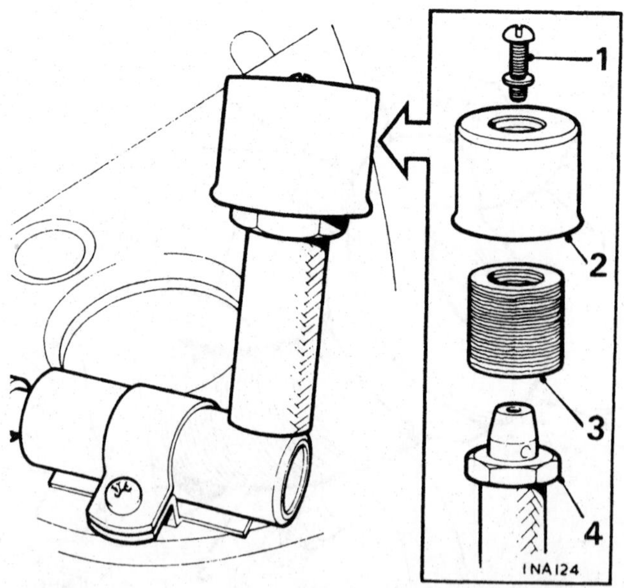

Fig. 3

The air bleed temperature compensator (showing the cap type air filter components)

1. Cap retaining screw.
2. Filter cap.
3. Filter element.
4. Filter base.

The air bleed temperature compensator is fixed to the underside of the carburetter air cleaner and consists of a bi-metal air control valve and an air filter. It is connected by hoses to the constant depression chambers, between the piston and the throttle disc valve, of the carburetters.

With an increase in engine or engine compartment air temperature, the valve will open and allow air at ambient temperature to be drawn through the air filter and into the carburetter constant depression chambers.

The controlled admission of air into the carburetter chambers reduces the velocity and volume of air passing the needles of the carburetters, causing the pistons to fall and subsequently reduce the amount of fuel supplied, thus giving a constant air/fuel mixture ratio.

Servicing

The air bleed temperature compensator air filter must be renewed every 12,000 miles (20000 km.) or 12 months.

(1) Disconnect the air cleaner to carburetter hoses.

(2) Remove the air cleaner.

(3) *Push-on type filters:* withdraw and discard the filter. *Cap type filters:* unscrew the filter cover retaining screw, remove the cover, and discard the filter element. Clean the base and cover of the filter, fit a new element, refit the cover and retaining screw.

(4) Refit the air cleaner and reconnect the hoses.

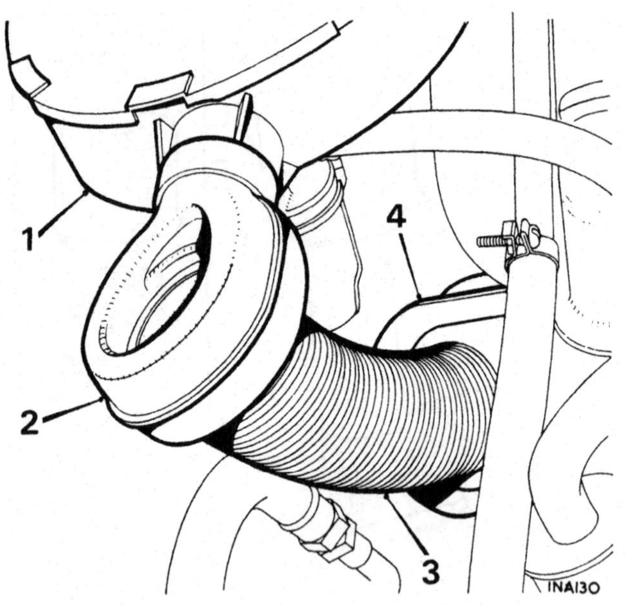

Fig. 4
The air intake temperature control

1. Air cleaner.
2. Air intake temperature control.
3. Air intake tube.
4. Exhaust manifold shroud.

Section 3A-E

AIR INTAKE TEMPERATURE CONTROL

An air intake temperature control is fitted to some engines equipped with single Type H.S. carburetters required to conform with European E.C.E. or E.C.C. exhaust emission control regulations.

The control consists of a bi-metal operated valve, fitted in the air intake of the carburetter air cleaner, and is designed to maintain the temperature of the ingoing air within predetermined limits.

When the engine is cold, air is drawn into the air cleaner from the shrouded area adjacent to the exhaust manifold. As the temperature of the air entering the air cleaner rises, the valve opens and admits cooler air at ambient temperature to mix with the hot air and maintain a constant temperature.

SECTION 4

CARBURETTERS

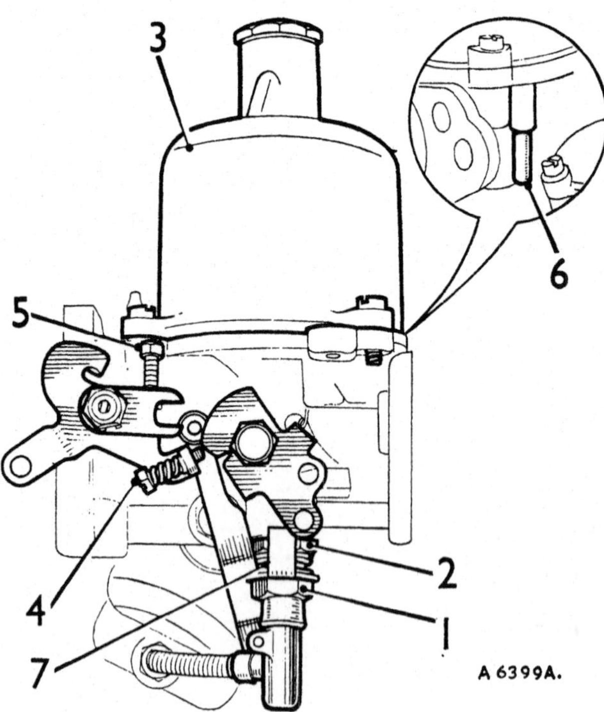

The type HS carburetter

1. Jet adjusting nut.
2. Jet locking nut.
3. Piston suction chamber.
4. Fast-idle adjusting screw.
5. Throttle adjusting screw.
6. Piston lifting pin.
7. Jet adjustment restrictor.

Section 4-A

CARBURETTER TUNING—BASIC

GENERAL

The carburetters fitted to cars equipped with engine emission control systems are balanced to provide maximum performance with maximum pollution control. Under no circumstances may they be interchanged, or parts substituted.

Tuning must be carried out with the engine emission control equipment connected and operating, and is confined to the following procedure. If the required settings cannot be obtained, the service procedure detailed under **'CARBURETTER SERVICING'** must be carried out and then the carburetter tuned in accordance with the procedure given in **'CARBURETTER TUNING—COMPLETE'.**

Tuning conditions

To ensure that the engine temperature and mixture requirements are stabilized, tuning must be carried out in accordance with the following setting cycle.

(1) Connect a tachometer in accordance with the instrument-maker's instructions.

(2) Warm the engine at a fast idle to normal operating temperature, preferably with the car standing in an ambient temperature of between 16 and 27° C. (60 to 80° F.). Run the engine for at least five minutes after the thermostat has opened; the thermostat opening point can be detected by the sudden rise in temperature of the radiator header tank.

(3) Set the engine speed at 2,500 r.p.m., at no load, and run for one minute.

(4) Tuning operations may now be commenced and must be carried out in the shortest possible time. If the time for settings exceeds a three-minute period, open the throttle and run the engine at 2,500 r.p.m. for one minute then resume tuning. Repeat this clearing operation if further periods of three minutes are exceeded.

SINGLE CARBURETTERS

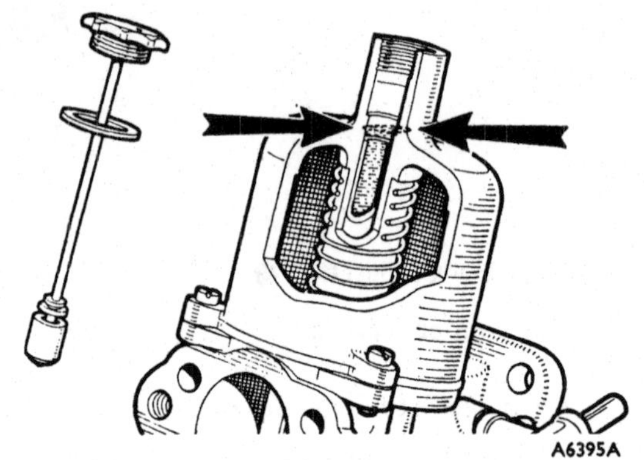

NOTE.—In no case should the jet adjustment restrictor be removed or repositioned. Only mixture adjustments within the limits of the restrictor are available for tuning. If satisfactory adjustment is not obtainable within the limits of the jet adjustment restrictor refer to **'CARBURETTER SERVICING'.**

(1) Top up the piston damper with the recommended engine oil until the level is ½-in. above the top of the hollow piston rod.

NOTE.—On dust-proofed carburetters, identified by a transverse hole drilled in the neck of the suction chambers and no vent hole in the damper cap, the oil level must be ½-in. below the top of the hollow piston rod.

(2) Check throttle control action for signs of sticking.

(3) Check the idling speed (Tachometer) against the figure given in **'TUNING DATA'.**

(*a*) If the reading is correct and the engine runs smoothly, proceed to operations (7) and (8).

(*b*) If the reading is not correct, adjust the speed by turning the throttle adjusting screw in the required direction until the correct speed consistent with smooth running is obtained, then proceed to operations (7) and (8).

(*c*) If a smooth idle at the correct speed is not obtainable by turning the throttle adjusting screw, carry out operations (4) to (8).

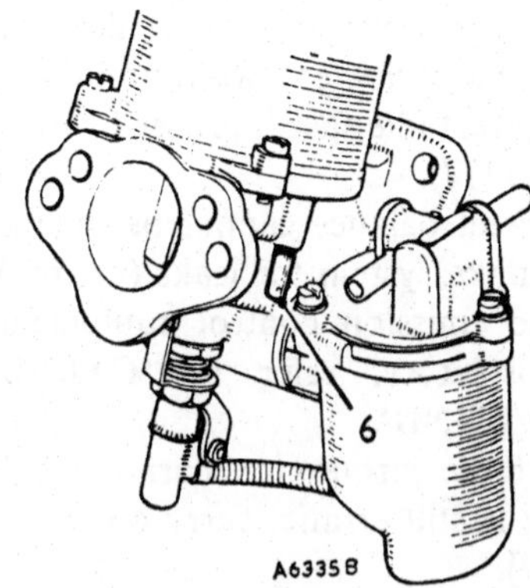

(4) With the engine stopped, check that the piston falls freely onto the bridge, indicated by a distinct metallic click, when the lifting pin (6) is released. If not refer to **'CARBURETTER SERVICING'**.

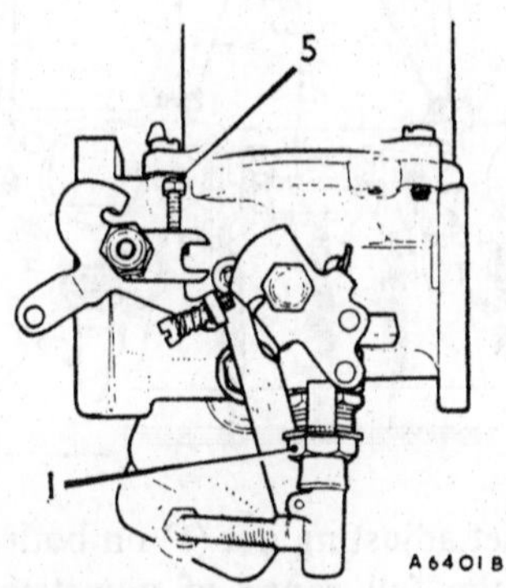

(5) Turn the jet adjusting nut (1) to cover the full range of adjustment available within the limits of the restrictor, selecting the setting where maximum speed is recorded on the tachometer consistent with smooth running.

(6) Readjust the throttle adjusting screw (5) to give the correct idling speed if necessary.

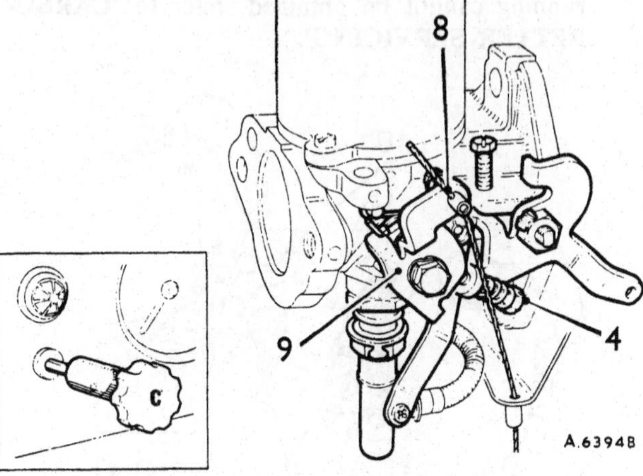

(7) Check, and if necessary adjust, the mixture control wire (8) to give a free movement of approximately $\frac{1}{16}$-in. before it starts to pull on the jet lever (9).

(8) Pull the mixture control knob until the linkage is about to move the carburetter jet and adjust the fast-idle screw (4) to give the engine fast-idle speed (Tachometer) given in **'TUNING DATA'**.

TWIN CARBURETTERS

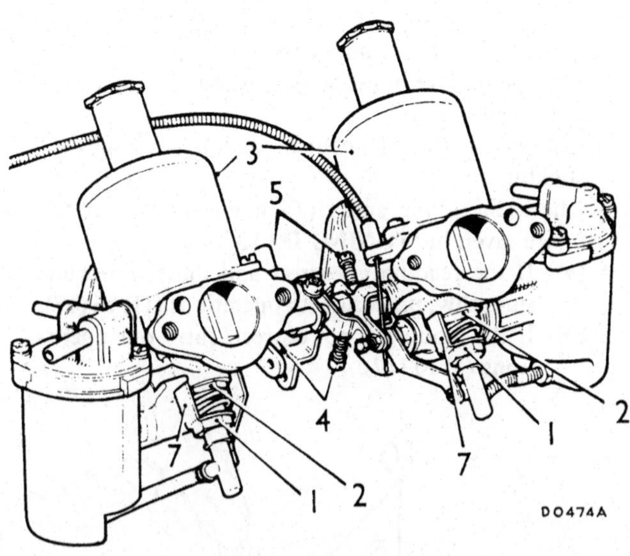

A twin-carburetter installation

1. Jet adjusting nuts.
2. Jet locking nuts.
3. Piston/suction chambers.
4. Fast-idle adjusting screws.
5. Throttle adjusting screws.
7. Jet adjustment restrictors.

NOTE.—In no case should the jet adjustment restrictor be removed or repositioned. Only mixture adjustments within the limits of the restrictor are available for tuning. Balancing of twin carburetters must only be carried out with the use of an approved balancing meter. If satisfactory adjustment or balancing is not obtainable within the limits of the jet adjustment restrictor, refer to **'CARBURETTER SERVICING'**.

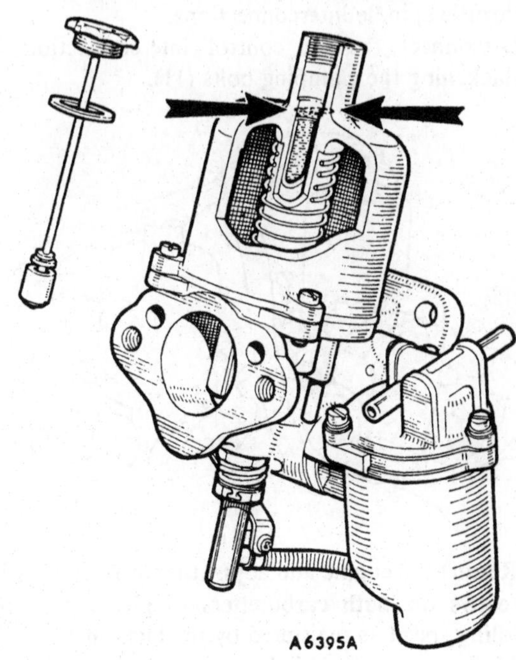

(1) Top up the piston damper with the recommended engine oil until the level is $\frac{1}{2}$-in. above the top of the hollow piston rod.

NOTE.—On dust-proofed carburetters, identified by a transverse hole drilled in the neck of the suction chambers and no vent hole in the damper cap, the oil level must be ½-in. below the top of the hollow piston rod.

(2) Check the throttle control action for signs of sticking.

(3) Check the idling speed (Tachometer) against the figure given in **'TUNING DATA'**.

(*a*) If the reading is correct and the engine runs smoothly, proceed with operations (11) to (17).

(*b*) If the reading is not correct, carry out operations (4) to (17).

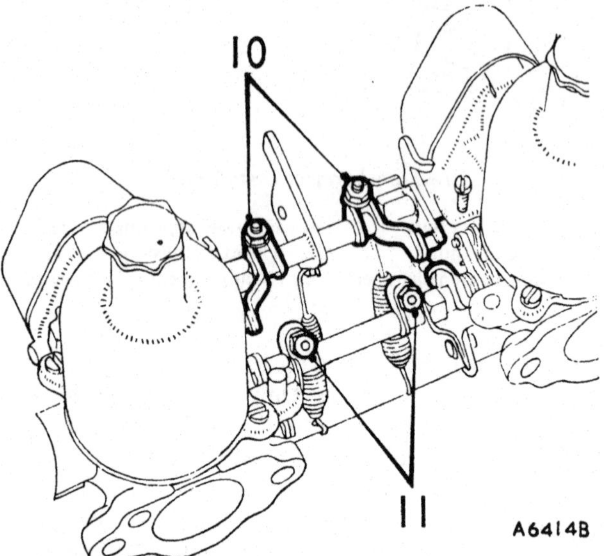

(4) Stop the engine and remove the air cleaners.

(5) Slacken both of the clamping bolts (10) on the throttle spindle interconnections.

(6) Disconnect the jet control interconnection by slackening the clamping bolts (11).

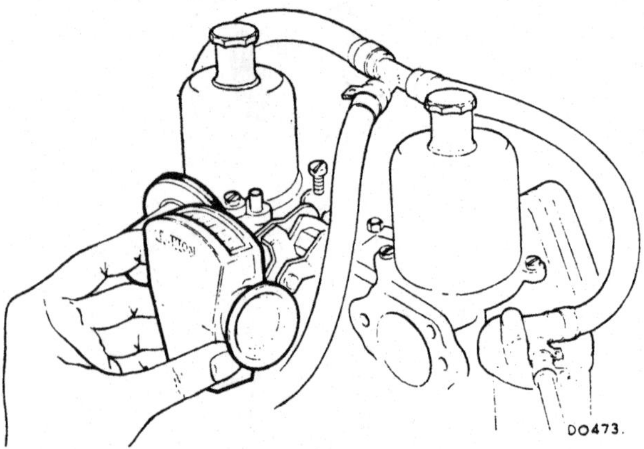

(7) Restart the engine and adjust the throttle adjusting screws on **both** carburetters to give the correct idling speed as registered by the tachometer.

(8) Using an approved balancing meter in accordance with the maker's instructions, balance the carburetters by altering the throttle adjusting screws; the idling speed obtained during this operation must be as given in **'TUNING DATA'**.

(*a*) If after this operation the balance is satisfactory and consistent with smooth running at the correct idle speed, proceed with operations (14) to (17).

(*b*) If correct balance cannot be obtained, check the intake system for leaks (i.e. brake servos, engine emission control equipment); if still unsatisfactory, refer to **'CARBURETTER SERVICING'**.

(*c*) If with the carburetters correctly balanced the idling is still erratic, carry out operations (9) to (17).

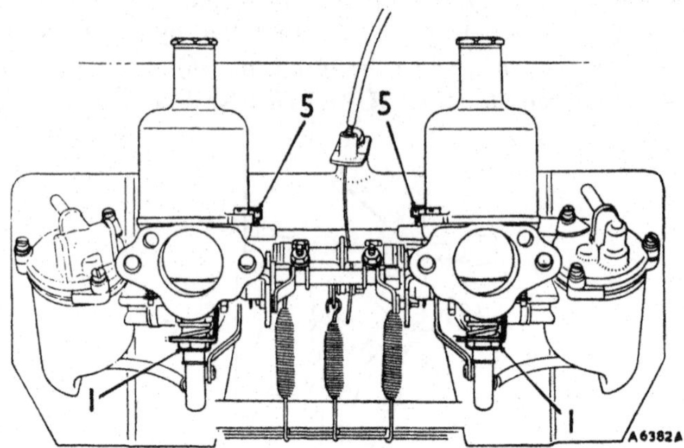

(9) Turn the jet adjusting nut (1) on both carburetters to cover the full range of adjustment available within the limits of the restrictor, selecting the setting where maximum speed is recorded on the tachometer consistent with smooth running.

(10) Readjust the throttle adjusting screws (5) to give the correct idling speed (see **'TUNING DATA'**) if necessary, ensuring that both carburetters are adjusted by an equal amount.

If the correct idling speed consistent with smooth running cannot be obtained, refer to **'CARBURETTER SERVICING'**.

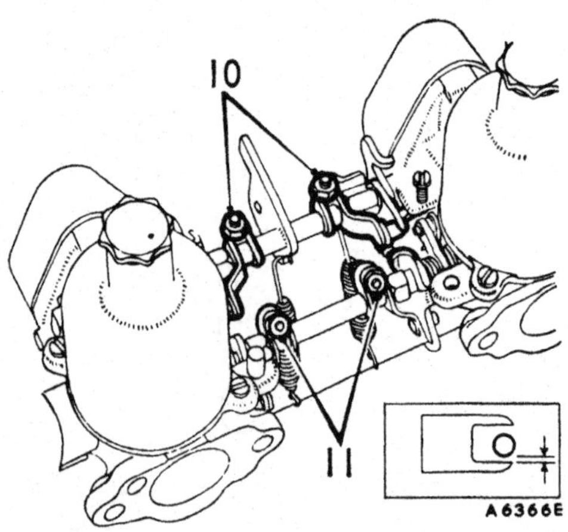

(11) Set the throttle interconnection clamping levers (10) so that the link pin is ·012 in. away from the lower edge of the fork (see inset). Tighten the clamp bolts ensuring that there is approximately $\frac{1}{32}$ in. end-float on the interconnection rod.

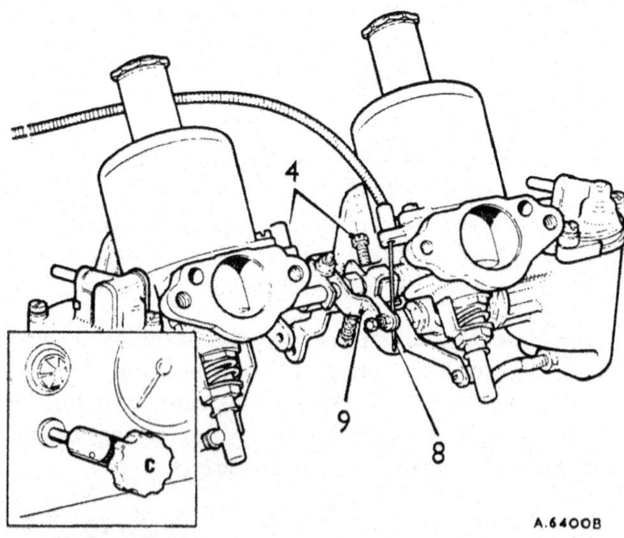

(12) With both jet levers at their lowest position, set the jet interconnection lever clamp bolts (11) so that both jets commence to move simultaneously.

(13) Run the engine at 1,500 r.p.m. and, using the balance meter, check that the carburetters are balanced. If they are not balanced, reset the levers, rebalance at idle speed, then recheck at 1,500 r.p.m.

(14) Check, and if necessary adjust, the mixture control wire (1) to give approximately $\frac{1}{16}$ in. free movement before it starts to pull on the jet levers (9).

(15) Pull the mixture control knob until the linkage is about to move the carburetter jets.

(16) Using the carburetter balancing meter to ensure equal adjustment, turn the fast idle adjusting screws (4) to give the correct fast idling speed (see 'TUNING DATA').

(17) Refit the air cleaners.

Section 4-B

CARBURETTER SERVICING

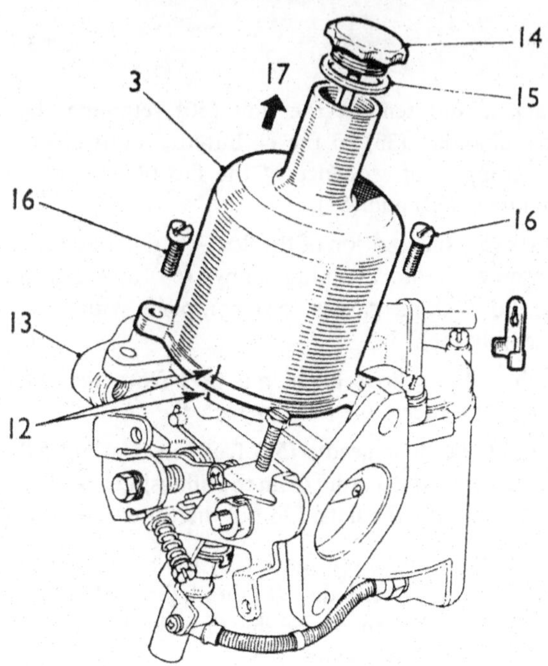

Dismantling

Carburetters—all types

(1) Thoroughly clean the outside of the carburetter.

(2) Mark the relative position (12) of the suction chamber (3) and the carburetter body (13).

(3) Remove the damper (14) and its washer (15). Unscrew the chamber retaining screws (16).

(4) Lift off the chamber in the direction of arrow (17) without tilting.

(5) Remove the piston spring (18).

(6) Carefully lift out the piston assembly (19) and empty the damper oil from the piston rod (20).

Carburetters—fixed needle type

(7) Remove the needle locking screw (21) and withdraw the needle (22). If it cannot easily be removed, tap the needle inwards first and then pull outwards. Do not bend the needle.

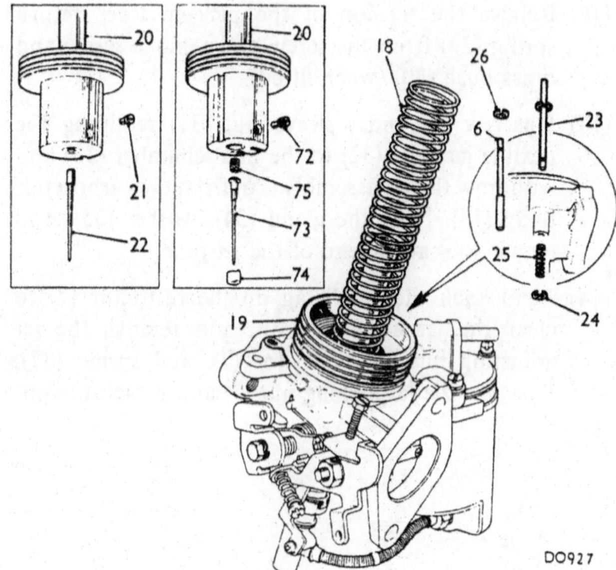

Carburetters—spring-loaded needle type

(8) Remove the guide locking screw (72), withdraw the needle assembly (73), needle support guide (74) and spring (75), taking care not to bend the needle.

(9) Withdraw the needle from the guide and remove the spring from the needle assembly.

Carburetters—all types

(10) If a piston lifting pin (23) with an external spring is fitted, remove the spring retaining circlip (24) and spring (25), then push the lifting pin upwards to remove it from its guide. With the concealed spring type (6) press the pin upwards, detach the circlip (26) from its upper end, and withdraw the pin and spring downwards.

(11) Support the moulded base of the jet (26) and slacken the screw (27) retaining the jet pick-up link (28).

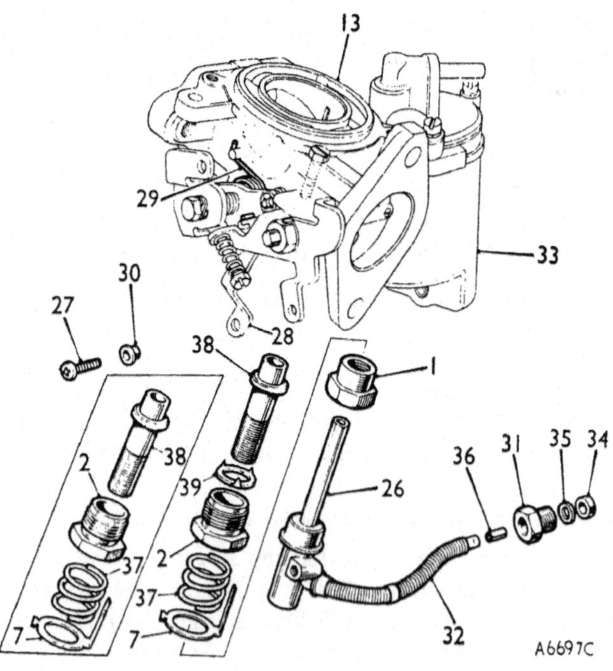

(12) Relieve the tension of the pick-up lever return spring (29) from the screw and remove screw and brass bush (30) (when fitted).

(13) Unscrew the brass sleeve nut (31) retaining the flexible jet tube (32) to the float-chamber (33) and withdraw the jet assembly (26) from the carburetter body (13). Note the gland (34), washer (35), and ferrule (36) at the end of the jet tube.

(14) Bend back the small tag on the restrictor (7) to clear the jet adjusting nut, and remove the jet adjusting nut (1), restrictor (7), and spring (37). Unscrew the jet locking nut (2) and detach the nut and jet bearing (38). Withdraw the bearing from the nut, noting, on fixed needle carburetters only, the locking washer (39) under the shoulder of the bearing.

(15) Note the location points (see inset, 40) of the two ends of the pick-up lever return spring (41). Unscrew the lever pivot bolt (42) together with its double-coil spring washer (43), or spacer (44). Detach the lever assembly (9) and return spring.

(16) Note the location (see inset, 45) of the two ends of the cam lever spring (46) and push out the pivot bolt tube (47) (or tubes), taking care not to lose the spring. Lift off the cam lever (48), noting the skid washer (49) between the two levers.

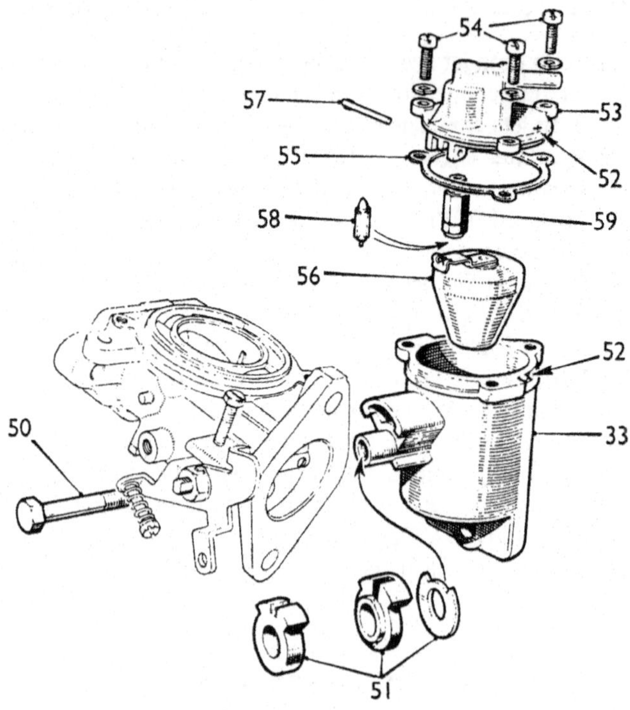

(17) Slacken and remove the bolt (50) retaining the float-chamber (33) to the carburetter body. Note the component sequence of the flexibly mounted chambers (33) and (51).

(18) Mark (52) the location of the float-chamber lid (53). Unscrew the lid retaining screws (54) and detach the lid and its gasket (55) complete with float assembly (56).

(19) Push out the float hinge pin (57) from the end opposite its serrations and detach the float.

(20) Extract the float needle (58) from its seating (59) and unscrew the seating from the lid, using a wrench ·338 in. across the flats. Do not distort the seating.

(21) Close the throttle and mark (60) the relative positions of the throttle disc (61) and the carburetter flange (62). **Do not mark the throttle disc in the vicinity of the limit valve** (63).

(22) Unscrew the two disc retaining screws (64). Open the throttle and ease out the disc from its slot in the throttle spindle (65). The disc is oval and will jam if care is not taken; store the disc in a safe place until required for reassembly.

(23) Tap back the tabs of the tab washer (66) securing the spindle nut (67). Note the location of the lever arm (68) in relation to the spindle and carburetter body; remove the nut and detach the arm.

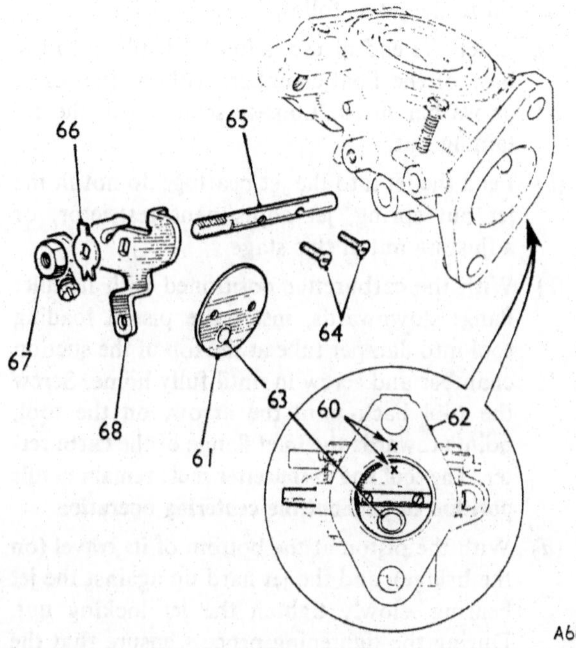

Reassembling

Carburetters—all types

NOTE.—Before reassembling, examine all components for wear and damage. Renew unserviceable components, ensuring that only parts to the correct specification (see **'TUNING DATA'**) are used.

(1) Examine the throttle spindle and its bearings in the carburetter body. Check for excessive play. Renew parts as necessary.

(2) Refit the spindle to the body. Assemble the operating lever with tab washer and spindle nut, to the spindle. Ensure that when the stop on the lever is against the abutment on the carburetter body (i.e. throttle closed position) the countersunk ends of the holes in the spindle face outwards. Tighten the spindle nut and lock with the tab washer.

(3) Insert the throttle disc in the slot in the spindle in its original position as marked. Manœuvre the disc in its slot until the throttle can be closed, snap the throttle open and shut to centralize it in the bore of the carburetter, taking care not to damage the throttle limit valve. When assembled, the valve must be positioned at the bottom of the disc with the head of the valve towards the engine. Fit two new disc retaining screws but do not fully tighten. Check visually that the disc closes fully, and adjust its position as necessary. With the throttle closed there must be clearance between the throttle lever and the carburetter body. Tighten the screws fully and spread their split ends just enough to prevent turning.

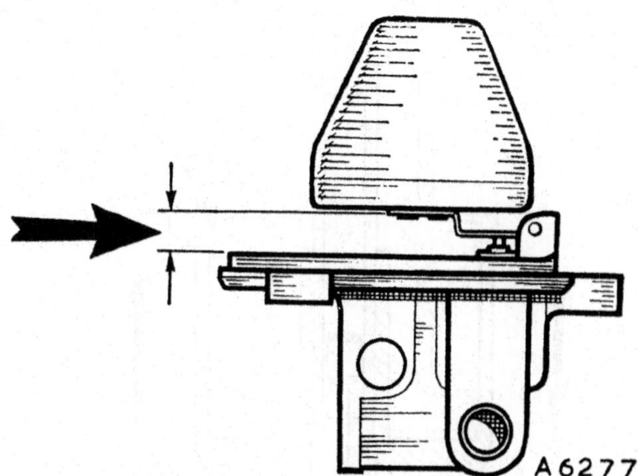

(4) Examine the float needle and seating for damage. Check that the spring-loaded plunger in the end of the plastic-bodied needle operates freely.

(5) Screw the seating into the float-chamber carefully. Do not overtighten. Replace the needle in the seating, coned end first. Test the assembly for leakage with air pressure.

(6) Refit the float and lever to the lid and insert the hinge pin and invert the float-chamber lid. With the needle valve held in the shut-off position by the weight of the float only, there should be a $\frac{1}{8}$ to $\frac{3}{16}$ in. gap (arrowed) between the float lever and the rim of the float-chamber lid.

(7) Examine the lid gasket for re-use. Assemble the gasket on the lid and refit the lid to the float-chamber in the position marked on dismantling. Tighten the securing screws evenly.

(8) Refit the float-chamber assembly to the carburetter body and tighten the retaining bolt fully, making sure that the registers on the body and the chamber engage correctly.

(9) Refit the piston lifting pin, spring and circlip.

(10) Examine the piston assembly for damage on the piston rod and the outside surface of the piston. The piston assembly must be scrupulously clean. Use gasoline or methylated spirit (denatured alcohol) as a cleaning agent. **Do not use abrasives.** Wipe dry, using a clean dry cloth.

(11) Clean inside the suction chamber and piston rod guide using gasoline or methylated spirit (denatured alcohol) and wipe dry. Refit the damper and washer. Temporarily plug the piston transfer holes (69) and fit the piston into the suction chamber. Fit a nut and screw, with a large flat washer under the head of the screw into one of the suction

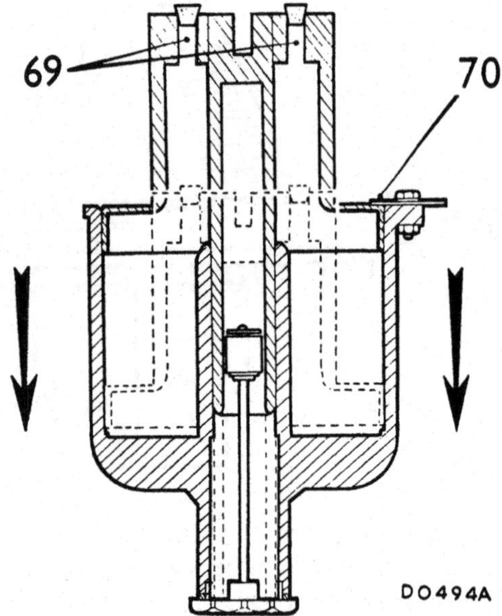

chamber fixing holes, positioning the washer (70) so that it overlaps the suction chamber bore (see illustration). Check that the piston is fully home in the suction chamber and invert the assembly to allow the chamber to fall away from the piston until the piston contacts the flat washer. Check the time taken for the suction chamber to fall the full extent of the piston travel. For HS2-type carburetters of 1¼ in. bore the time taken should be 3 to 5 seconds, and for larger carburetters 5 to 7 seconds. If these times are exceeded check the piston and suction chamber for cleanliness and mechanical damage. If after rechecking the time taken is still not within these limits, renew the suction chamber and piston assembly.

Carburetters—fixed needle type

(12) Refit the needle to the piston assembly (19). The lower edge of the needle shoulder (22) must be level with the bottom face of the piston rod (20).

(13) Fit a new needle locking screw (21) and tighten. Invert the suction chamber and spin the piston assembly inside it to check for concentricity of the needle.

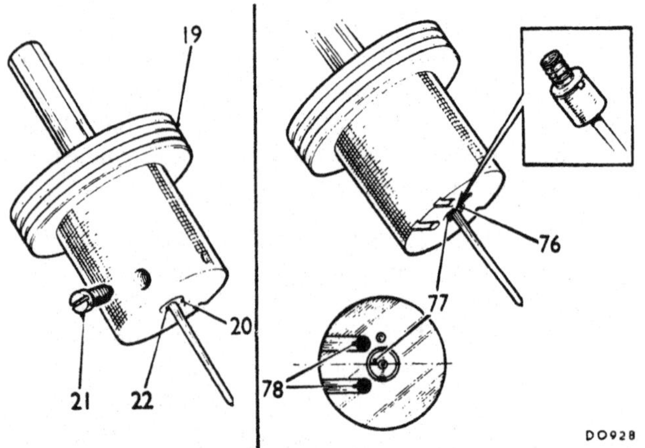

(14) Check the piston key for security in the carburetter body. Refit the piston assembly to the body and replace the piston spring over the piston rod.

(15) Fit the suction chamber and retaining screws, taking care not to wind up the spring; tighten the securing screws evenly.

(16) Refit the jet bearing, a new locking washer, and the locking nut; do not tighten the nut.

(17) Centralize the jet as follows:

(*a*) Enter the end of the nylon feed tube into the base of the float-chamber, without the gland or washer fitted. Loosely secure with the retaining nut.

(*b*) Feed the jet into the jet bearing; do not fit the jet nut spring, jet adjustment restrictor, or adjusting nut at this stage.

(*c*) With the carburetter positioned with its inlet flange downwards, insert the piston loading tool into damper tube at the top of the suction chamber and screw in until fully home. Screw the tool back until the arrow, on the tool, points towards the inlet flange of the carburetter. **The tool and carburetter must remain in this position throughout the centering operation.**

(*d*) With the piston at the bottom of its travel (on the bridge), and the jet hard up against the jet bearing, slowly tighten the jet locking nut. During the tightening process ensure that the jet is not binding in its bearing when drawn in and out. If any tightness between the jet and bearing is detected, the jet locking nut must be slackened and the process repeated.

(*e*) Remove the jet loading tool.

(18) Withdraw the jet and tube; refit the spring, restrictor and jet adjusting nut. Fit the gland and washer to the flexible tube. The end of the tube should project a minimum of $\frac{3}{16}$ in. beyond the gland. Refit the jet and tube. Tighten the sleeve nut until the neoprene gland is compressed. Overtightening can cause leakage.

Carburetters—spring-loaded needle type

(19) Refit the jet bearing, fit and tighten the jet locking nut. No jet centering is required with the spring-loaded type jet needle.

(20) Fit the jet nut spring and adjustment restrictor. Fit the jet adjusting nut and screw it up as far as possible.

(21) Feed the jet into the jet bearing. Fit the sleeve nut, washer and gland to the end of the flexible tube. The tube must project a minimum of $\frac{3}{16}$ in. (4·8 mm.) beyond the gland. Tighten the sleeve nut until the gland is compressed. Overtightening can cause leakage.

(22) Refit the spring to the jet needle assembly, ensuring that it locates completely in the groove of the needle support.

(23) **IMPORTANT.** Spring-loaded needles are supplied complete with shouldered spring seats; no attempt should be made to alter the position of the spring seat or convert a fixed-type needle to spring-loaded application. The raised 'pip' formed in the needle guide ensures that the needle is correctly centralized. Under no circumstances must the 'pip' be removed or repositioned.

Fit the needle assembly into its guide and fit the assembly into the piston. The lower edge of the guide (76) must be flush with the face of the piston and the guide positioned so that the etched locating mark (77) on its lower face is adjacent to and in line with the midway point between the two piston transfer holes as illustrated.

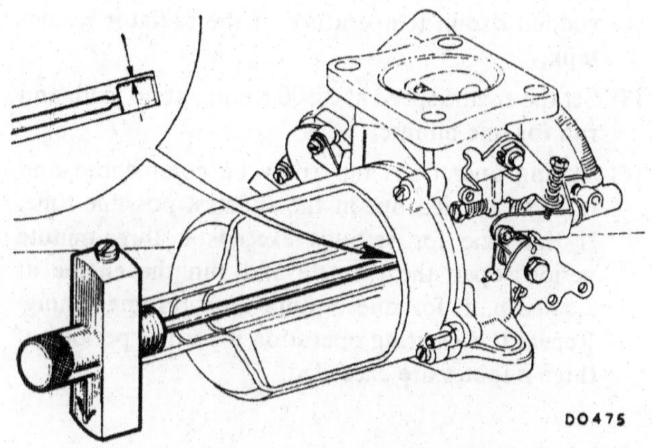

Alternative needle guides have a flat machined on the guide which must be positioned so that the guide locking screw tightens down onto the flat. If the guide is incorrectly positioned so that the locking screw has not tightened down on the flat, the head of the screw will protrude from the piston.

(24) Fit a new guide locking screw. **NOTE.**—Guide locking screws for spring-loaded needles are shorter than the needle locking screws used with fixed needles.

(25) Check the piston key for security in the carburetter body. Refit the piston assembly to the body and place the piston spring over the piston rod.

(26) Fit the suction chamber and retaining screws, taking care not to wind up the spring; tighten the securing screws evenly.

Carburetters—all types

(27) Refit the damper and washer.

(28) Reassemble the pick-up lever, cam lever, cam lever spring, skid washer, and pivot bolt tube or tubes in the positions noted on dismantling.

(29) Place the pick-up lever return spring in position over its boss and secure the lever assembly to the carburetter body with the pivot bolt. Ensure that the double-coil spring washer or spacer fits over the projecting end of the pivot bolt tube.

(30) Register the angled end of the return spring in the groove in the pick-up lever, and hook the other end of the spring around the moulded peg on the carburetter body.

(31) Fit the brass ferrule to the hole in the end of the pick-up link. Relieve the tension of the return spring and fit the link to the jet with its retaining screw. When finally tightening the screw, support the moulded end of the jet.

(32) Without removing the suction chamber, screw the jet adjusting nut until the top face of the jet is flush with the bridge of the carburetter.

(33) Turn down the jet adjusting nut to the initial jet setting given in **'TUNING DATA'**.

(34) Refit the carburetter(s) to the engine, following the instructions given in the relevant vehicle Workshop Manual.

Tune the carburetters in accordance with the instructions given in **'CARBURETTER TUNING —COMPLETE'**.

Section 4-C

CARBURETTER TUNING—COMPLETE

The following instructions apply only to new carburetters or carburetters which have been serviced as described in **'CARBURETTER SERVICING'.**

The tuning must be carried out with the engine emission control equipment connected and operating.

SINGLE CARBURETTERS

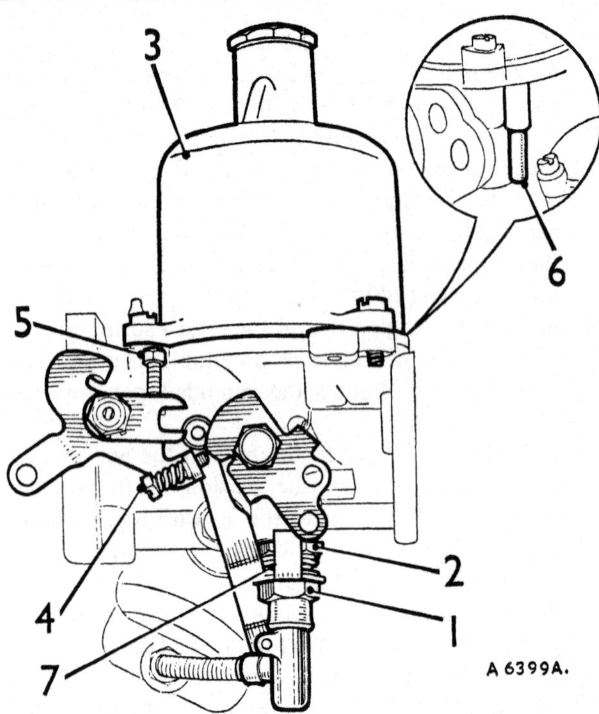

The type HS carburetter

1. Jet adjusting nut.
2. Jet locking nut.
3. Piston suction chamber.
4. Fast-idle adjusting screw.
5. Throttle adjusting screw.
6. Piston lifting pin.
7. Jet adjustment restrictor.

Initial setting

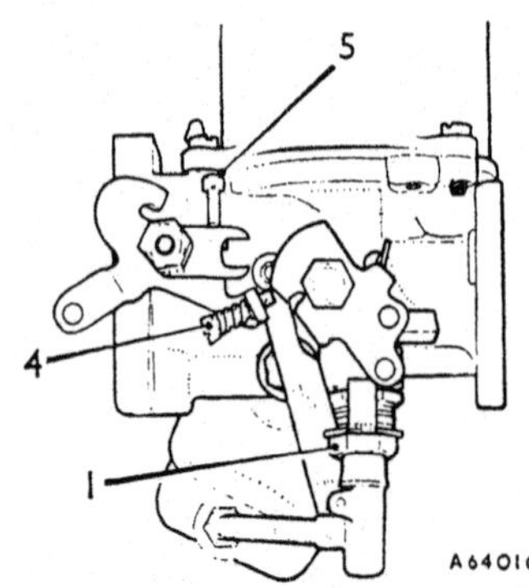

(1) Disconnect the mixture control (choke) wire if fitted.

(2) Unscrew the fast-idle screw (4) until it is well clear of the cam.

(3) Unscrew the throttle adjusting screw (5) until it is just clear of its stop and the throttle is closed.

(4) Set the throttle adjusting screw one full turn open.

(5) The jet adjusting nut must not be altered at this stage as it will be initially set to a datum setting at the factory or during the carburetter servicing procedure.

Tuning conditions

To ensure that the engine temperature and mixture requirements are stabilized, tuning must be carried out in accordance with the following setting cycle.

(1) Connect a tachometer and an approved exhaust gas analyser in accordance with the instrument-maker's instructions.

(2) Warm the engine at a fast idle to normal operating temperature preferably with the car standing in an ambient temperature of between 16 and 27° C. (60 to 80° F.). Run the engine for at least five minutes after the thermostat has opened; the thermostat opening point can be detected by the sudden rise in temperature of the radiator header tank.

(3) Set the engine speed at 2,500 r.p.m., at no load, and run for one minute.

(4) Tuning operations may now be commenced and must be carried out in the shortest possible time. If the time for settings exceeds a three-minute period, open the throttle and run the engine at 2,500 r.p.m. for one minute then resume tuning. Repeat this clearing operation if further periods of three minutes are exceeded.

Tuning procedure

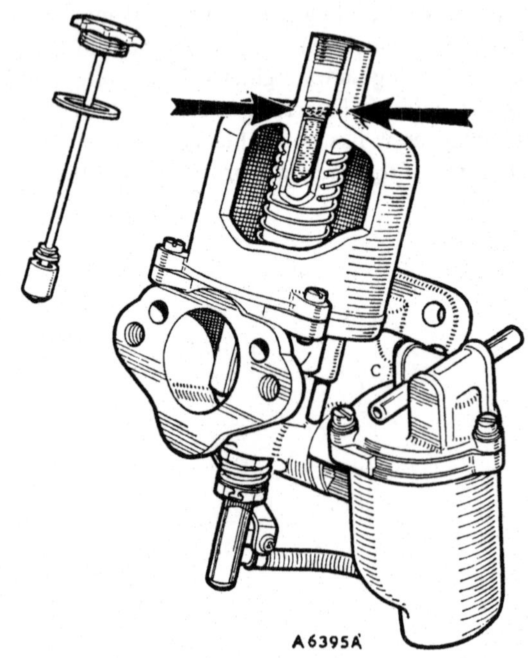

(1) Top up the piston damper with the recommended engine oil until the level is ½ in. above the top of the hollow piston rod.

NOTE.—On dust-proofed carburetters, identified by a transverse hole drilled in the neck of the suction chambers and no vent hole in the damper cap, the oil level must be $\frac{1}{2}$ in. below the top of the hollow piston rod.

(2) Warm up the engine as described in **'Tuning conditions'.**

Turn the throttle adjusting screw until the idling speed given in **'TUNING DATA'** is obtained.

(3) During the following procedure, just before the readings of the tachometer and exhaust gas analyser are taken gently tap the neck of the suction chamber with a light non-metallic instrument (e.g. a screwdriver handle).

Turn the jet adjusting nut up to weaken, down to richen, until the fastest speed is recorded on the tachometer. Turn the jet adjusting nut very slowly up (weaken) until the engine speed just commences to fall, then turn the nut one flat down (rich). Check the idling speed against the figure given in **'TUNING DATA'**, and adjust if necessary using the throttle adjusting screw.

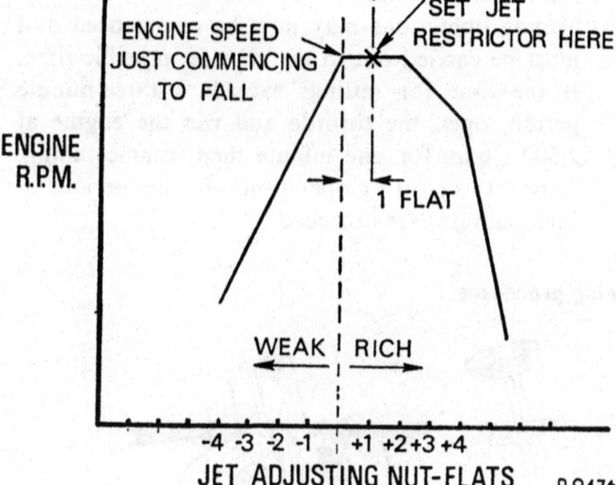

(4) Using the exhaust gas analyser, check that the percentage CO reading is within the limits given in **'TUNING DATA'.**

If the reading falls outside the limits given, reset the jet adjusting nut by the minimum amount necessary to bring the reading just within the limits. If an adjustment exceeding two flats is required to achieve this the test equipment should be checked for correct calibration.

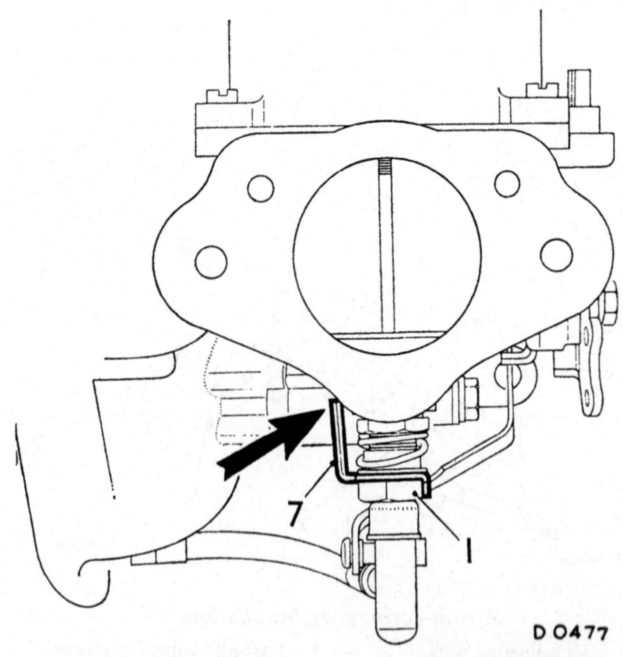

(5) Hold the jet adjusting nut (1) to prevent it turning, and rotate the adjustment restrictor (7) round the nut until the vertical tag contacts the carburetter body on the left-hand side when viewed from the air cleaner flange (see illustration). In this position, bend the small tag on the adjustment restrictor down so that the restrictor locks to the nut and will follow its movements.

(6) Paint the small tag of the jet adjusting nut restrictor and the adjacent flat of the jet nut to identify the locking position.

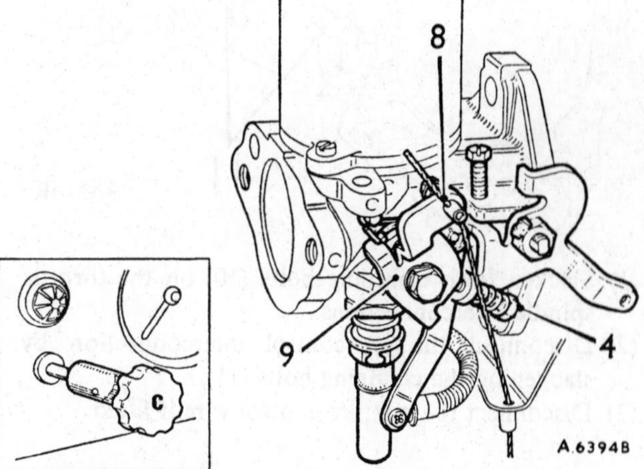

(7) Reconnect the mixture control wire (8) with approximately $\frac{1}{16}$ in. free movement before it starts to pull on the jet lever (9).

(8) Pull the mixture control knob until the linkage is about to move the carburetter jet and adjust the fast-idle screw (4) to give the engine fast-idle speed.

(9) Check and if necessary adjust the throttle damper setting—if fitted (see **'TUNING DATA'**).

TWIN CARBURETTERS

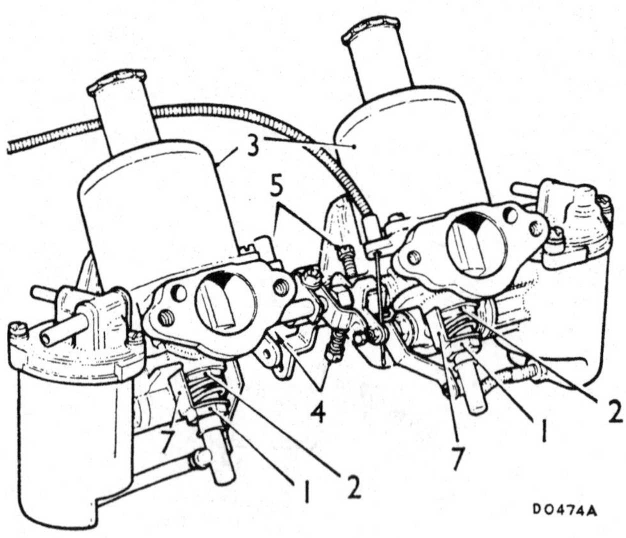

A twin-carburetter installation

1. Jet adjusting nuts.
2. Jet locking nuts.
3. Piston/suction chambers.
4. Fast-idle adjusting screws.
5. Throttle adjusting screws.
7. Jet adjustment restrictors.

Initial settings

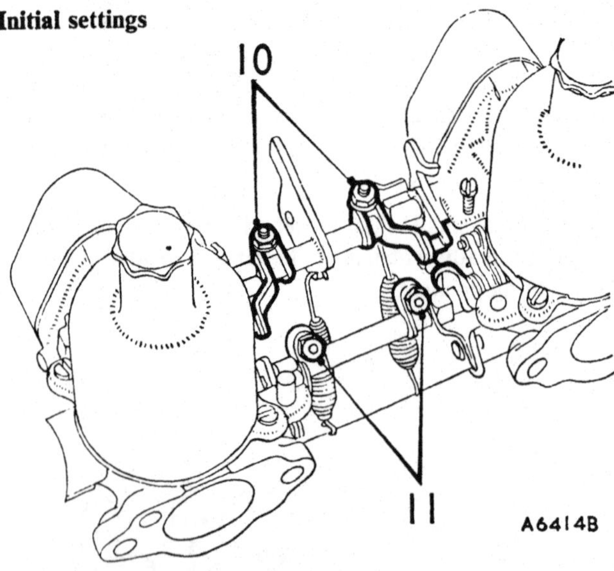

(1) Slacken both clamping bolts (10) on the throttle spindle interconnections.
(2) Disconnect the jet control interconnection by slackening the clamping bolts (11).
(3) Disconnect the mixture control wire if fitted.

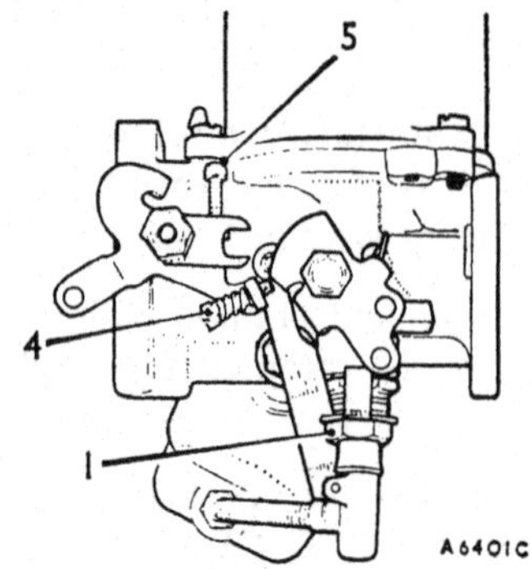

(4) Unscrew the fast-idle screw (4) on both carburetters until they are well clear of the cams.
(5) Unscrew the throttle adjusting screw (5) on both carburetters until they are just clear of their stops and the throttles are closed.
(6) Set the throttle adjustment screws on both carburetters half a turn open.
(7) The jet adjusting nuts must not be altered at this stage as they will be initially set to a datum setting either at the factory or during the carburetter servicing procedure.

Tuning conditions

To ensure that the engine temperature and mixture requirements are stabilized, tuning must be carried out in accordance with the following setting cycle.

(1) Connect a tachometer and an approved exhaust gas analyser in accordance with the instrument-maker's instructions.
(2) Warm the engine at a fast idle to normal operating temperature preferably with the car standing in an ambient temperature of between 16 and 27° C. (60 to 80° F.). Run the engine for at least five minutes after the thermostat has opened; the thermostat opening point can be detected by the sudden rise in temperature of the radiator header tank.
(3) Set the engine speed at 2,500 r.p.m., at no load, and run for one minute.
(4) Tuning operations may now be commenced and must be carried out in the shortest possible time. If the time for settings exceeds a three-minute period, open the throttle and run the engine at 2,500 r.p.m. for one minute then resume tuning. Repeat this clearing operation if further periods of three minutes are exceeded.

Tuning procedure

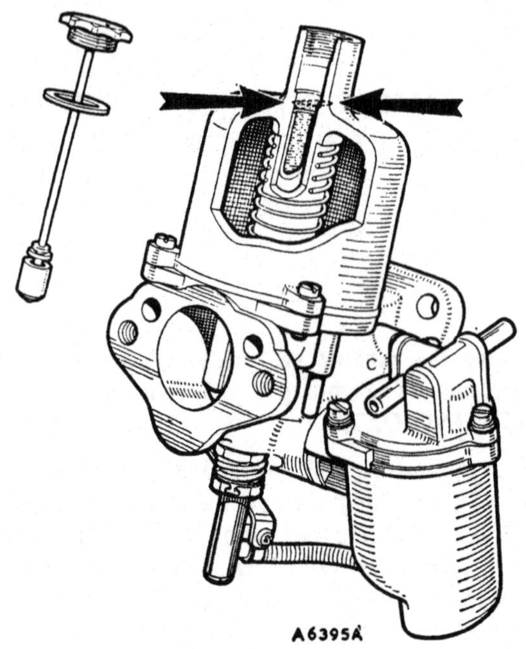

(1) Top up the piston damper with the recommended engine oil until the level is ½ in. above the top of the hollow piston rod.

NOTE.—On dust-proofed carburetters, identified by a transverse hole drilled in the neck of the suction chambers and no vent hole in the damper cap, the oil level must be ½ in. below the top of the hollow piston rod.

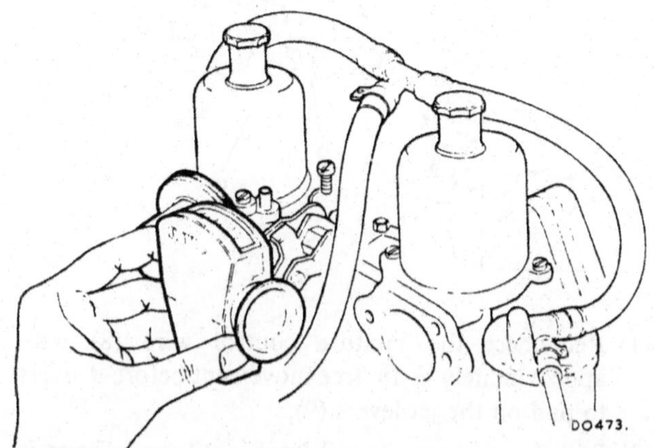

(2) Warm up the engine as described in **'TUNING CONDITIONS.'**

(3) Turn the throttle adjusting screw on both carburetters until the idling speed given in **'TUNING DATA'** is obtained.

(4) Using an approved balancing meter in accordance with the maker's instructions, balance the carburetters by altering the throttle adjusting screws; the idling speed obtained during this operation must be as given in **'TUNING DATA'.**

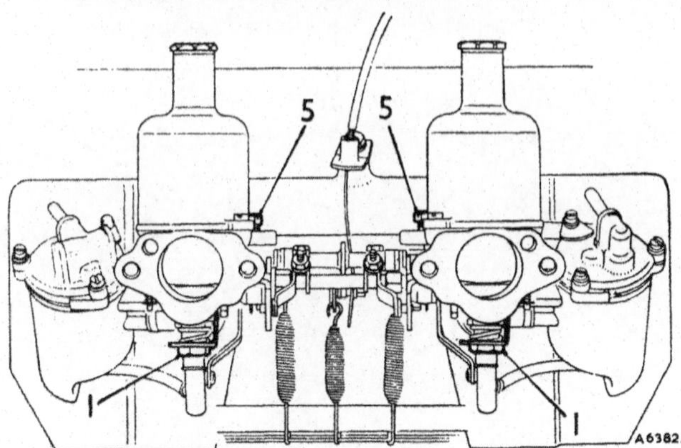

(5) During the following procedure, just before the readings of the tachometer and exhaust gas analyser are taken, gently tap the neck of each suction chamber with a light non-metallic instrument (e.g. a screwdriver handle).

Turn the jet adjusting nut (1) on both carburetters up to weaken, down to richen, the same amount until the fastest speed is recorded on the tachometer.

Turn both adjusting nuts very slowly up (weaken) until the engine speed just commences to fall, then turn both adjusting nuts one flat down (rich).

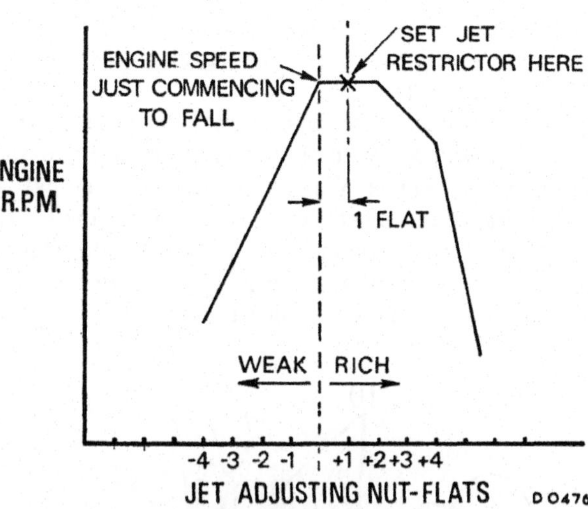

Check the idling speed against the figure given in **'TUNING DATA'**, and adjust if necessary by altering both throttle adjusting screws, each by the same amount. Using the balancing meter, check that the carburetters are balanced.

(6) Using the exhaust gas analyser, check that the percentage CO reading is within the limits given in **'TUNING DATA'.**

If the reading falls outside the limits given, reset both jet adjusting nuts by the minimum amount necessary to bring the reading just within the limits. If an adjustment exceeding two flats is required to achieve this the test equipment should be checked for correct calibration.

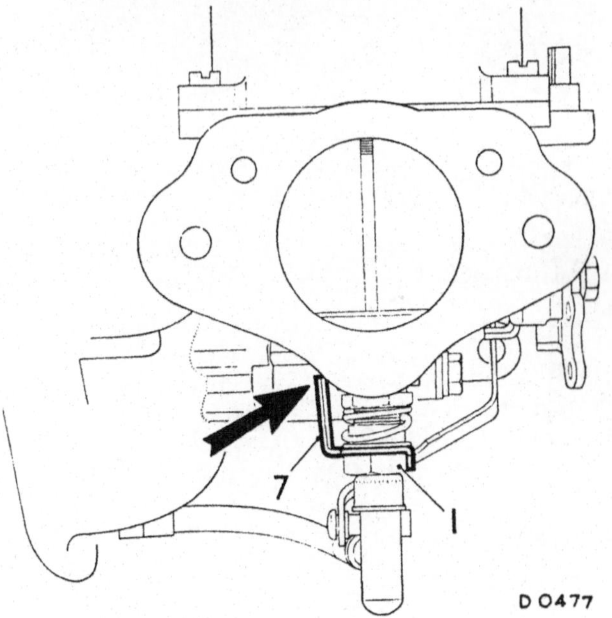

(7) Hold the jet adjusting nut (1) on each carburetter, to prevent it turning, and rotate the adjustment restrictor (7) round the nut until the vertical tag contacts the carburetter body on the left-hand side when viewed from the air cleaner flange (see illustration). In this position, bend the small tag on the adjustment restrictor down so that the restrictor locks to the nut and will follow its movements.

(8) Paint the small tag of the jet adjusting nut restrictor and the adjacent flat of the jet nut to identify the locking position.

(9) Set the throttle interconnection clamping levers (10) in accordance with the instructions given in the relevant vehicle Workshop Manual, so that a clearance exists between the link pin and the lower edge of the fork (see inset). Tighten the clamp bolts ensuring that there is approximately $\frac{1}{32}$ in. end float on the interconnection rod.

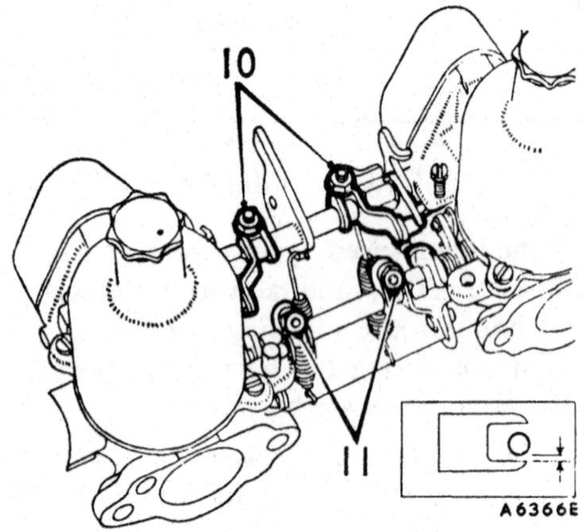

(10) With both jet levers at their lowest position, set the jet interconnection lever clamp bolts (11) so that both jets commence to move simultaneously.

Run the engine at 1,500 r.p.m. and, using the balance meter, check that the carburetters are balanced.

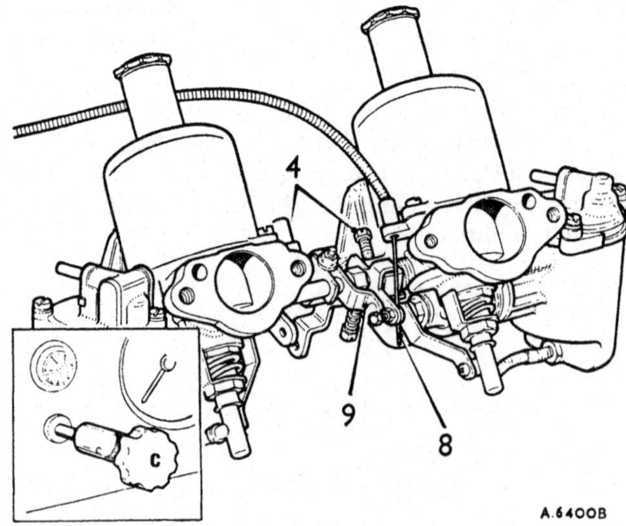

(11) Reconnect the mixture control wire (8) with approximately $\frac{1}{16}$ in. free movement before it starts to pull on the jet levers (9).

(12) Pull the mixture control knob until the linkage is about to move the carburetter jets.

(13) Using the carburetter balancing meter to ensure equal adjustment, turn the fast-idle adjusting screws (4) to give the correct fast idling speed (see **'TUNING DATA'**).

(14) Refit the air cleaners.

Section 4-D

TYPE HIF CARBURETTERS—TUNING
(Fitted to MGB from 1972 Model Year)

General

The carburetters fitted to cars equipped with engine emission control systems are balanced to provide engine performance with pollution control. Under no circumstances may they or their components be interchanged or substituted with normal carburetters.

Tuning must be carried out with the engine emission control equipment connected and operating.

IMPORTANT.—Before servicing or tuning a carburetter in an endeavour to rectify poor engine performance, make sure that the maladjustment or fault is not from another source by checking the following:

Valve clearance
Spark plug condition
Contact breaker (dwell angle)
Ignition timing and advance
Presence of air leaks into the induction system

Single and twin carburetters

(1) Remove the air cleaner(s).
(2) Check the throttle for correct operation and signs of sticking.
(3) Unscrew the throttle adjusting screw (both screws on twin carburetters) until it is just clear of the throttle lever, with the throttle closed, then turn the screw clockwise two full turns.
(4) Raise the piston of each carburetter with the lifting pin and check that it falls freely onto the bridge when the pin is released. If the piston shows any tendency to stick, the carburetter must be serviced.
(5) Lift and support the piston clear of the bridge so that the jet is visible; if this is not possible due to the installed position of the carburetter, remove the suction piston chamber.
(6) Turn the jet adjusting screw anti-clockwise until the jet is flush with the bridge or as high as possible without exceeding the bridge height. Ensure that both jets on twin carburetters are in the same relative position to the bridge of their respective carburetters.
(7) Check that the needle guide(s) is flush with the bottom of the piston groove.
(8) Turn the jet adjusting screw two turns clockwise (both screws on twin carburetters).
(9) Turn the fast idle adjusting screw anti-clockwise (both screws on twin carburetters) until it is well clear of the cam.
(10) Refit the suction piston chamber if it has been removed and, using the lifting pin, check that the piston falls freely onto the bridge.
(11) Top up the piston damper reservoir(s) with a recommended oil until the level is ½ in. (13 mm.) above the top of the hollow piston rod.

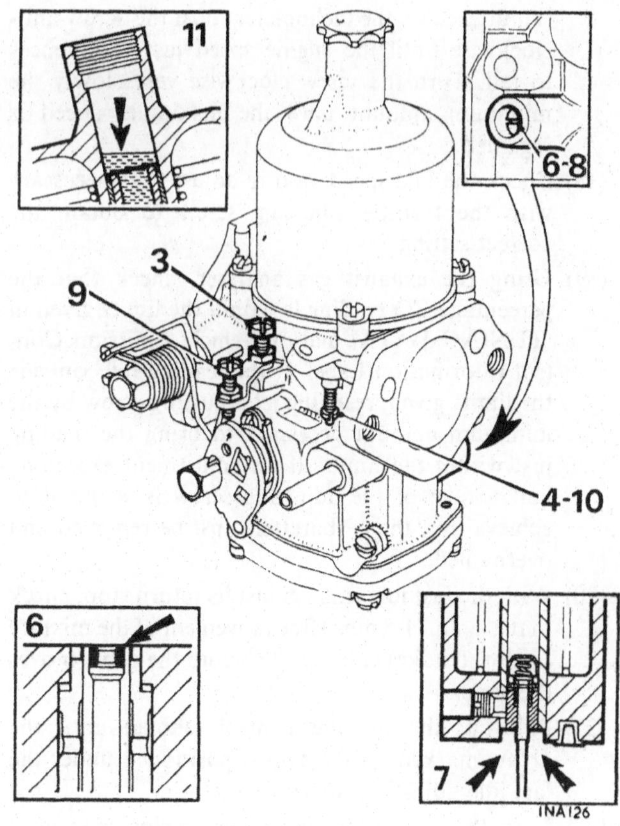

(12) Connect a reliable tachometer to the engine in accordance with the instrument manufacturer's instructions.

(13) Start the engine and run it at a fast idle speed until it attains normal running temperature, then run it for a further five minutes.

(14) Increase the engine speed to 2,500 r.p.m. for thirty seconds.

(15) Connect an approved exhaust gas analyser to the engine in accordance with the instrument manufacturer's instructions.

NOTE.—Tuning can now commence. If the correct setting cannot be obtained within three minutes, increase the engine speed to 2,500 r.p.m. for thirty seconds and then recommence tuning. Repeat this clearing operation at three-minute intervals until tuning is completed.

Single carburetters

(16) Adjust the throttle adjusting screw until the correct idle speed (see **'TUNING DATA'** and/or Vehicle Emission Control Information Label) is obtained.

NOTE.—During the following procedure, just before the readings of the tachometer and exhaust gas analyser are taken, gently tap the neck of the suction chamber with a light-metallic instrument (e.g. a screwdriver handle).

(17) Turn the jet adjusting screw, clockwise to enrich or anti-clockwise to weaken, until the fastest speed is indicated on the tachometer; turn the screw anti-clockwise until the engine speed just commences to fall. Turn the screw clockwise very slowly the minimum amount until the maximum speed is regained.

(18) Check the idle speed, and re-adjust it as necessary with the throttle adjusting screw to obtain the correct setting.

(19) Using the exhaust gas analyser, check that the percentage CO reading is within the limits given in **'TUNING DATA'** and/or Vehicle Emission Control Information Label. If the reading falls outside the limits given, reset the jet adjusting screw by the minimum amount necessary to bring the reading just within the limits. If an adjustment exceeding half a turn of the adjusting screw is required to achieve this, the carburetter must be removed and overhauled.

(20) With the fast idle cam against its return stop, check that a $\frac{1}{16}$ in. (1·5 mm.) free movement of the mixture control (choke) cable exists before the cable moves the cam.

(21) Pull out the mixture control (choke) until the arrow marked on the cam is positioned under the fast idle adjusting screw.

(22) Turn the fast idle adjusting screw clockwise until the correct fast idle speed (see **'TUNING DATA'** and/or Vehicle Emission Control Information Label) is obtained.

(23) Refit the air cleaner.

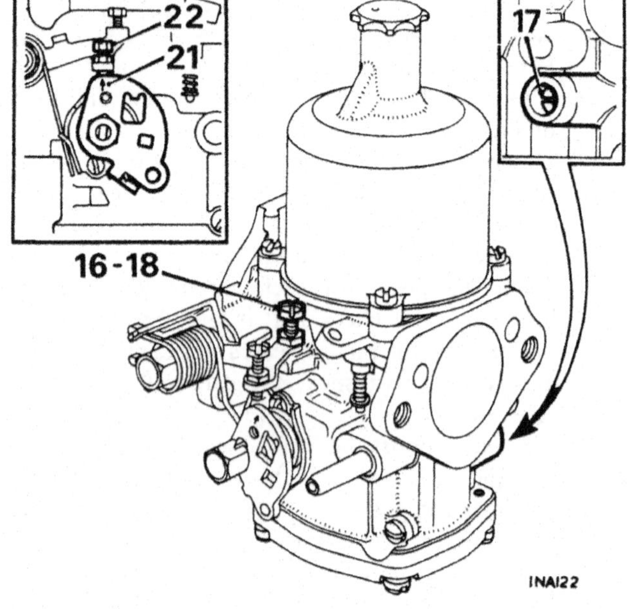

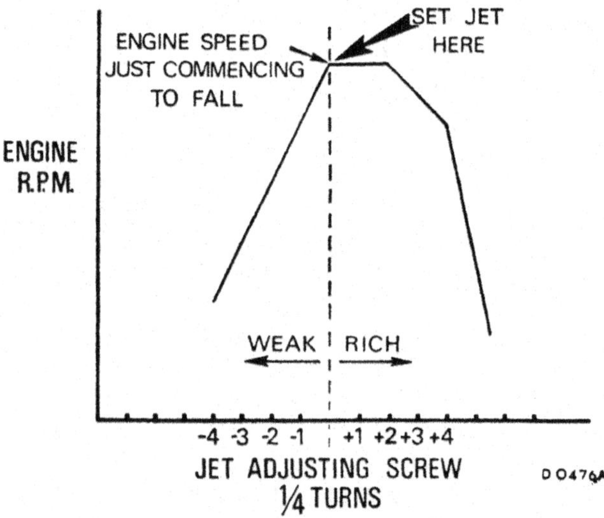

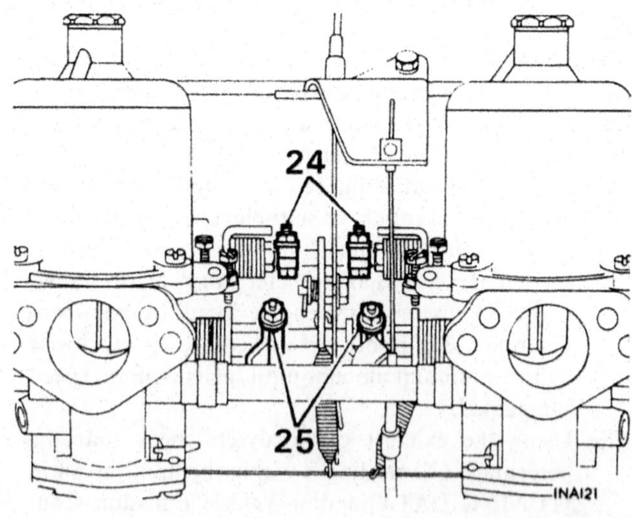

Twin carburetters

(24) Slacken both clamping bolts on the throttle spindle interconnections.

(25) Slacken both clamping bolts on the cold start interconnections.

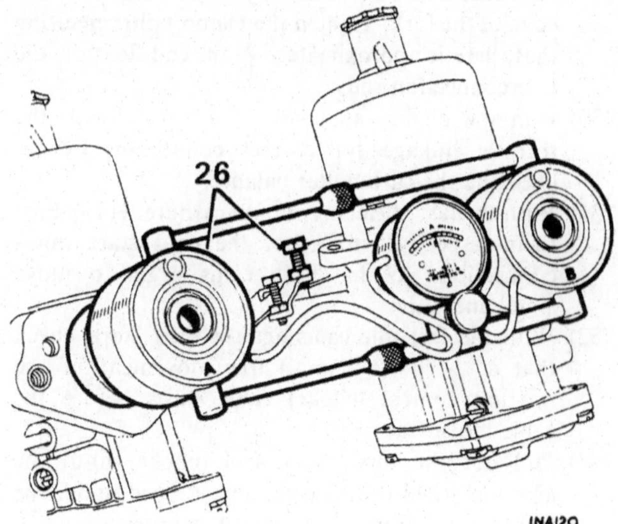

(26) Using an approved balancing meter in accordance with the maker's instructions, balance the carburetters by altering the throttle adjusting screws until the correct idle speed and balance is achieved.

NOTE.—During the following procedure, just before reading the tachometer and exhaust gas analyser, gently tap the neck of each suction chamber with a non-metallic instrument (e.g. a screwdriver handle).

(27) Turn the jet adjusting screw on both carburetters clockwise to enrich or anti-clockwise to weaken, by the same amount until the fastest speed is registered on the tachometer; turn both screws anti-clockwise until the engine speed just commences to fall. Turn both screws very slowly clockwise by the minimum amount until the maximum speed is regained.

(28) Using the exhaust gas analyser, check that the percentage CO reading is within the limits given in **'TUNING DATA'** and/or Vehicle Emission Control Information Label. If the reading falls outside the limits given, reset both jet adjusting screws by the minimum amount necessary to bring the readings just within the limits. If an adjustment exceeding half a turn is required to achieve this the carburetters must be removed and overhauled.

(29) Set the throttle interconnection clamping levers, in accordance with the instructions given in the relevant vehicle Workshop Manual, so that a clearance exists between the link pin and the lower edge of the fork. Tighten the clamp bolts, ensuring that there is approximately $\frac{1}{32}$ in. end-float on the interconnection rod.

(30) Run the engine at 1,500 r.p.m. and check the throttle linkage for correct connection by re-checking the carburetter balance.

(31) With the fast idle cams of both carburetters against their respective stops, set the cold start interconnections so that both cams begin to move simultaneously.

(32) With the fast idle cams against their stops check that a $\frac{1}{16}$ in. (1·5 mm.) free movement of the mixture control (choke) cable exists before the cable moves the cams.

(33) Pull out the mixture control (choke) until the arrow marked on the cam is positioned under the fast idle adjusting screw of each carburetter.

(34) Using the balancing meter to ensure equal adjustment, turn the fast idle adjusting screws to give the correct fast idle speed (see **'TUNING DATA'** and/or Vehicle Emission Control Information Label).

(35) Refit the air cleaners.

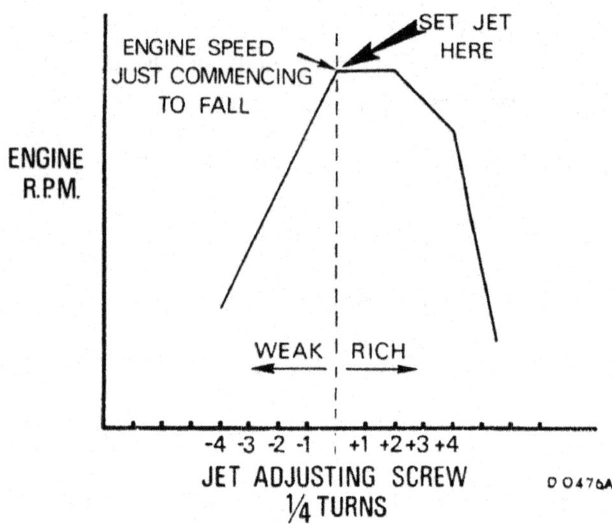

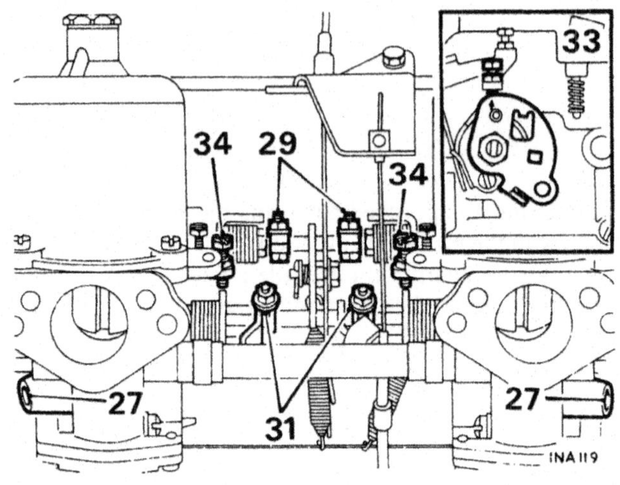

Section 4-E

TYPE HIF CARBURETTERS—OVERHAULING (Fitted to MGB from 1972 Model Year)

Dismantling

(1) Thoroughly clean the outside of the carburetter.
(2) Remove the piston damper and its washer.
(3) Unscrew the suction piston chamber retaining screws and remove the identity tag.
(4) Lift the chamber vertically from the body without tilting it.
(5) Remove the piston spring, lift out the piston assembly and empty the oil from the piston rod.
(6) Unscrew the needle guide locking screw.
(7) Withdraw the needle, guide and spring.

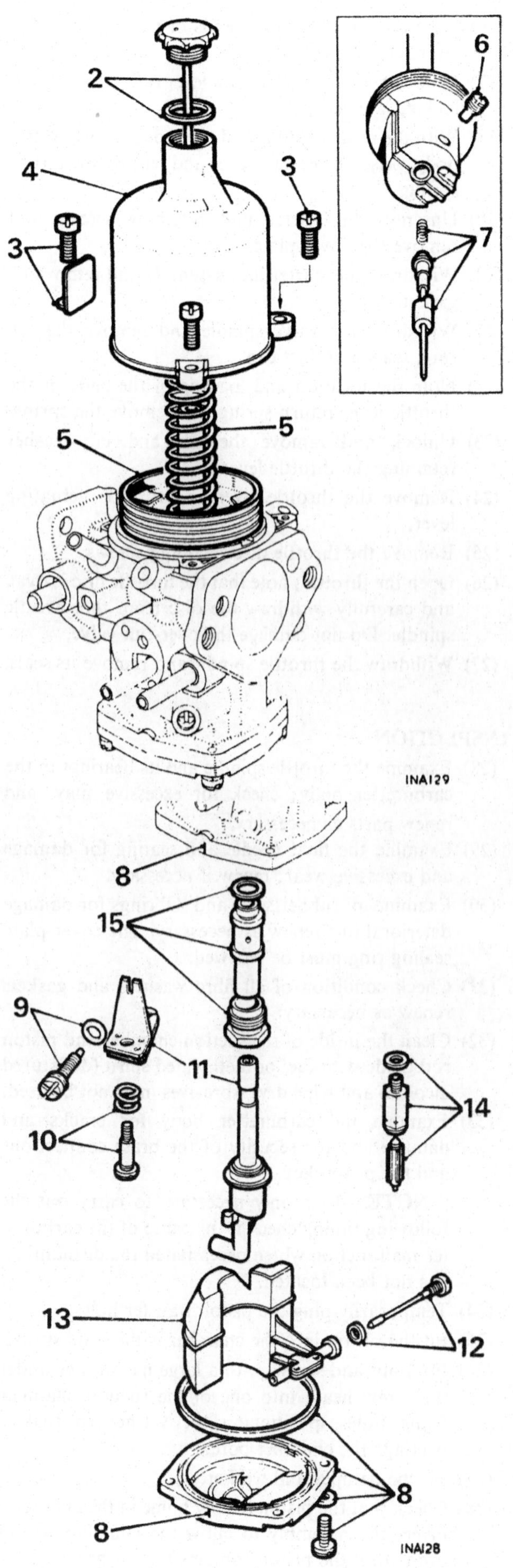

(8) Mark the bottom cover-plate and body to ensure correct reassembly, unscrew the retaining screws and remove the cover complete with sealing ring.
(9) Remove the jet adjusting screw complete with 'O' ring.
(10) Remove the jet adjusting lever retaining screw and spring.
(11) Withdraw the jet complete with adjusting lever and disengage the lever.
(12) Remove the float pivot spindle and fibre washer.
(13) Withdraw the float.
(14) Remove the needle valve and unscrew the valve seat.
(15) Unscrew the jet bearing locking nut and withdraw the bearing complete with fibre washer.

(16) Note the location of the ends of the fast idle cam lever return spring.
(17) Unlock and remove the cam lever retaining nut and locking washer.
(18) With the return spring held towards the carburetter body, prise off the cam lever and remove the return spring.
(19) Unscrew the starter unit retaining screws and remove the cover-plate.
(20) Withdraw the starter unit assembly and remove its gasket.
(21) Withdraw the valve spindle and remove the 'O' ring, seals and dust cap.
(22) Note the location and loading of the ends of the throttle lever return spring and remove the spring.
(23) Unlock and remove the nut and tab washer retaining the throttle levers.
(24) Remove the throttle lever and throttle actuating lever.
(25) Remove the throttle disc retaining screws.
(26) Open the throttle; note that the throttle disc is oval, and carefully withdraw the disc from the throttle spindle. Do not damage the over-run valve.
(27) Withdraw the throttle spindle and remove its seals.

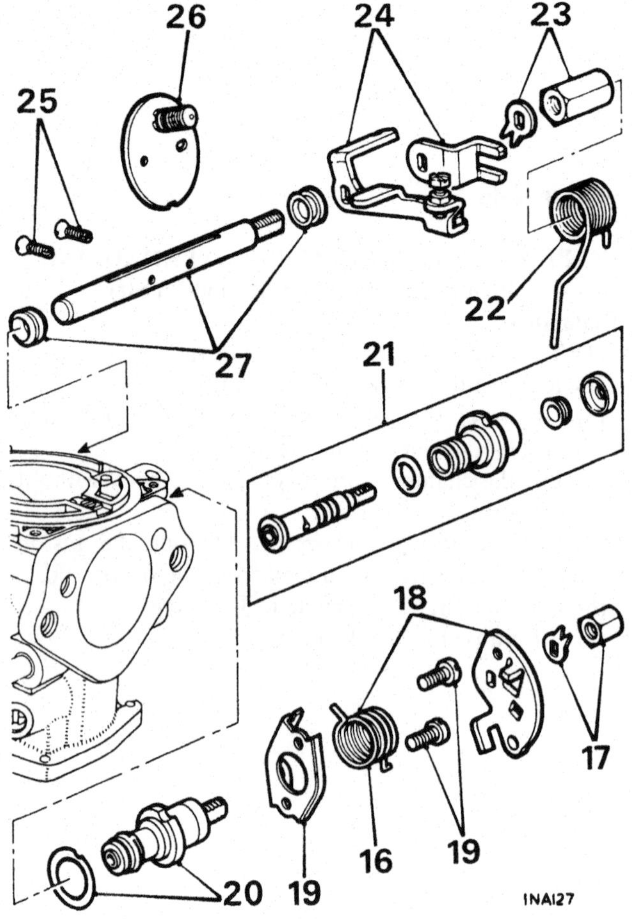

INSPECTION

(28) Examine the throttle spindle and its bearings in the carburetter body; check for excessive play, and renew parts as necessary.
(29) Examine the float needle and seating for damage and excessive wear; renew if necessary.
(30) Examine all rubber seals and 'O' rings for damage deterioration; renew as necessary. The cover-plate sealing ring must be renewed.
(31) Check condition of all fibre washers and gaskets renew as necessary.
(32) Clean the inside of the suction chamber and piston rod guide with fuel or methylated spirit (denatured alcohol) and wipe dry. Abrasives must not be used.
(33) Examine the carburetter body for cracks and damage and for security of the brass connections and the piston key.

NOTE.—It is only necessary to carry out the following timing check if the cause of the carburetter malfunction which necessitated the dismantling has not been located.

(34) Temporarily plug the piston transfer holes.
(35) Fit the piston into the chamber without its spring.
(36) Fit a nut and screw, with a large flat washer under the screw head, into one of the suction chamber fixing holes, positioning the washer so that it overlaps the chamber bore.
(37) Fit the damper and washer.
(38) Check that the piston is fully home in the chamber, invert the assembly to allow the chamber to fall away until the piston contacts the washer.

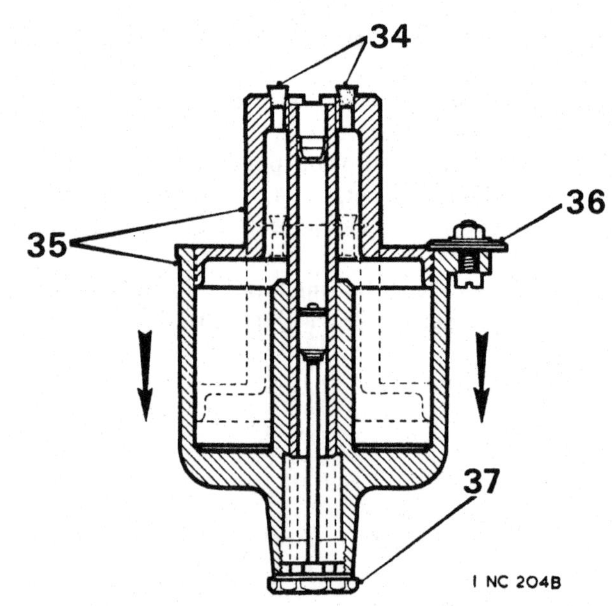

(39) Check the time taken for the chamber to fall the full extent of the piston travel. For HIF carburetters 1½ in. (38 mm.) bore the time taken should be 4 to 6 seconds; for HIF6 1¾ in. (44·5 mm.) bore the time taken should be 5 to 7 seconds.

(40) If the times are exceeded, check the piston and chamber for cleanliness and damage. If after re-checking the time is still not within these limits, renew the chamber and piston assembly.

Reassembling

(41) Reverse the procedure in 1 to 28, noting the following:

(*a*) The throttle spindle must be fitted with the threaded end at the piston lifting pin side of the body.

(*b*) Fit the throttle disc so that the over-run valve is at the top of the bore and its spring towards the inside when the throttle is closed.

(*c*) New throttle disc retaining screws must be used when refitting the disc. Ensure that the throttle disc is correctly positioned and closes correctly before tightening and locking the retaining screw.

(*d*) Position the throttle spindle end seals just below the spindle housing flange.

(*e*) The starter unit valve is fitted with the cut-out towards the top retaining screw hole, and its retaining plate is positioned with the slotted flange towards the throttle spindle.

(*f*) After fitting the float and valve, invert the carburetter so that the needle valve is held in the shut position by the weight of the float only. Check that the point indicated on the float (see illustration) is 0·04±0·02 in. (1·0 ±·5 mm.) below the level of the float chamber face. Adjust the float position by carefully bending the arm.

(*g*) Check that the small diameter of the jet adjusting screw engages the slot in the adjusting lever and set the jet flush with the bridge of the body.

(*h*) Use a new retaining screw when refitting the needle and ensure that the needle guide etch mark aligns correctly with the piston transfer holes (see illustration). After fitting the needle assembly, check that the shoulder of the needle aligns the full face of the piston.

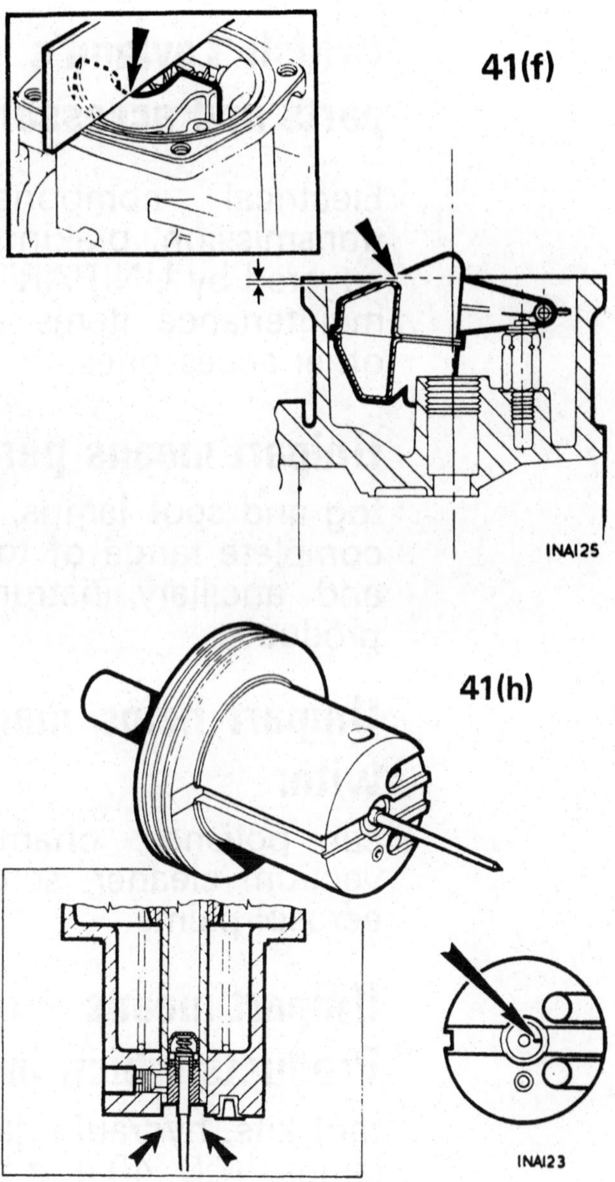

SECTION 5

EVAPORATIVE LOSS CONTROL

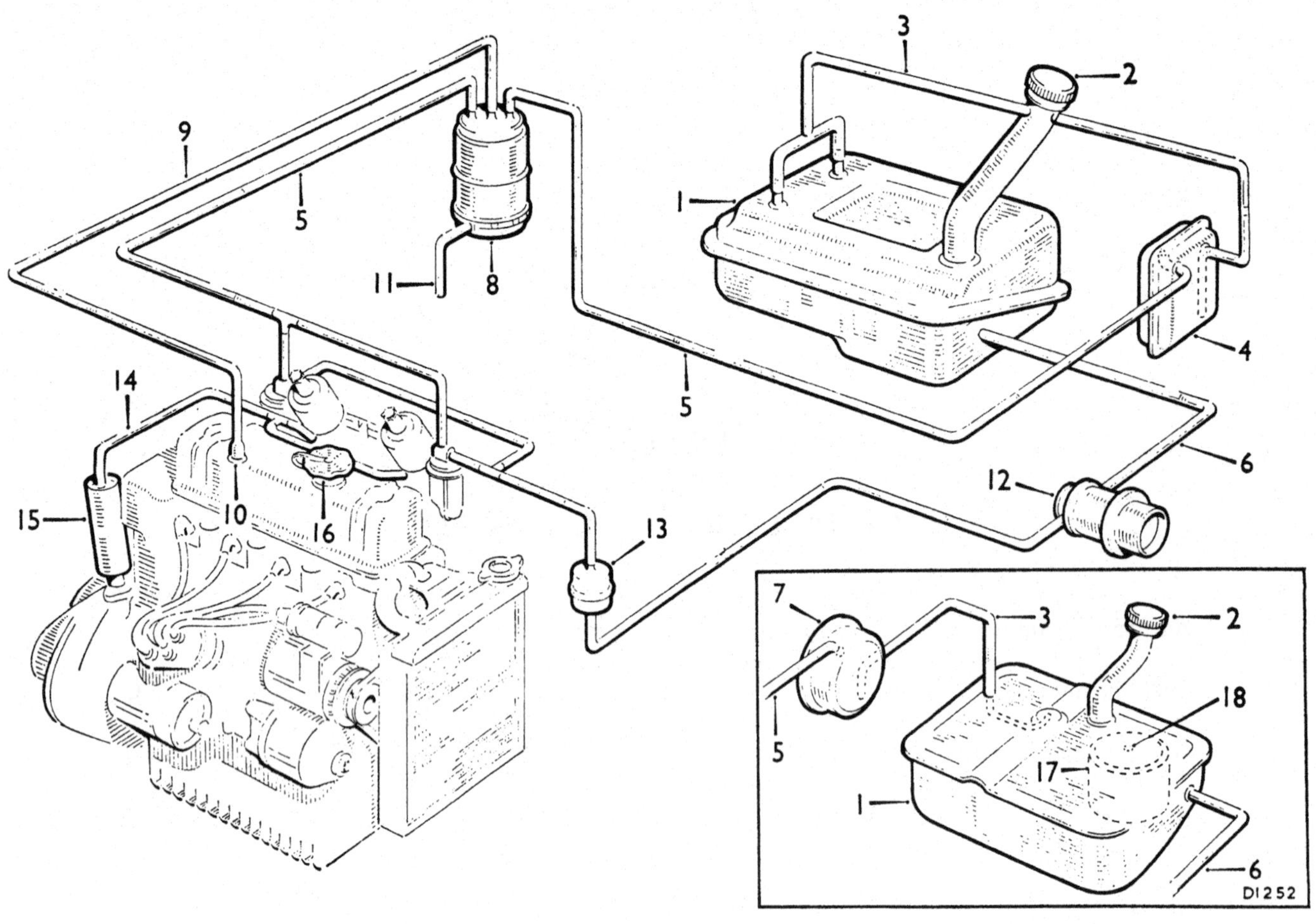

Fig. 1

A typical evaporative loss control system, with inset showing the arrangement of a separation tank and capacity-limiting fuel tank

1. Fuel tank.
2. Sealed fuel filler cap.
3. Expansion/vapour line.
4. Expansion tank.
5. Vapour pipe.
6. Fuel pipe.
7. Separation tank.
8. Adsorption canister.
9. Purge line.
10. Restricted connection.
11. Air vent.
12. Fuel pump.
13. Fuel line filter.
14. Breather pipe.
15. Oil separator.
16. Sealed oil filler cap.
17. Capacity limiting tank.
18. Air lock bleed.

Section 5-A

GENERAL DESCRIPTION

The system is designed to collect fuel vapour evaporated from the fuel in the fuel tank, and on some twin carburetter cars from the fuel in the carburetter float-chambers. The vapour is stored in an adsorption canister while the engine is stopped, and then after the engine is restarted, passed through the crankcase emission control system to the combustion chambers. While the car is being driven the vapours are drawn directly to the crankcase emission control system.

Ventilation tubes on the fuel tank ensure that vapours are vented through the control system when the car is parked on other than a level surface.

To prevent spillage of fuel by displacement due to expansion, sufficient capacity is provided in the expansion tank to accommodate the amount of fuel from a full tank which would be displaced by a high temperature rise.

By the positioning of the expansion tank connections, or by the inclusion of a small separation tank in the vapour line, liquid fuel is prevented from being carried with the vapour to the storage canister.

IMPORTANT. The fuel and oil filler caps seal the system, and it is essential for its efficient function that they are correctly refitted after removal.

Adsorption canister

The adsorption or vapour storage canister mounted in the engine compartment contains activated charcoal (carbon) granules. Filter pads are fitted at both sides of the charcoal to filter incoming ventilating air and to prevent the granules from leaving the canister through the purge line. Provision is made for renewing the ventilation air filter pad. Vapour tubes from the fuel tank and carburetter float-chambers and the purge line from the engine breather system are connected to the ports on the top of the canister. The port on the bottom section provides a connection for the ventilating air tube.

Fuel vapour entering the canister through the vapour tubes is adsorbed and held by the charcoal. When the engine is started, air is drawn by the crankcase emission control system, through the ventilation tube and into the canister. As the air passes over the charcoal granules the vapours are given up and are carried with the air through the crankcase emission system to the combustion chambers.

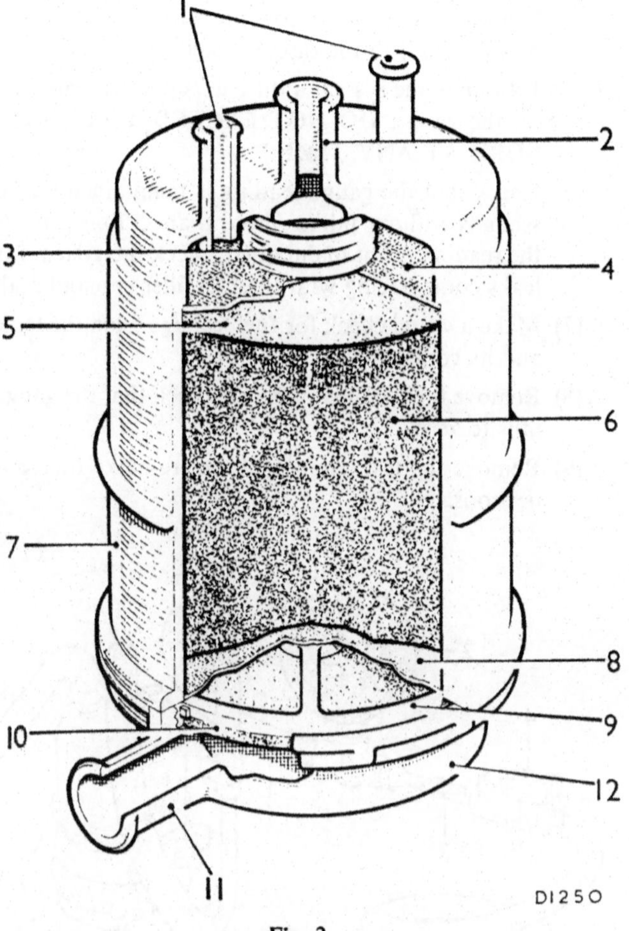

Fig. 3

The adsorption canister

1.	Vapour pipe connections.	7.	Canister.
2.	Purge pipe connection.	8.	Gauze.
3.	Spring.	9.	Retainer.
4.	Gauze.	10.	Filter pad.
5.	Filter pad.	11.	Air vent connection.
6.	Charcoal granules.	12.	End cap.

Fuel expansion

Two methods are used to ensure that sufficient space is available to accommodate fuel displaced by expansion due to high ambient temperatures. The method used on the Austin America is by fitting an additional tank into which the displaced fuel flows when the volume of the fuel exceeds that of the fuel tank. The MGB and MG Midget use an air lock chamber in the fuel tank which prevents the tank being completely filled with fuel, thereby ensuring that sufficient space is always available for expansion.

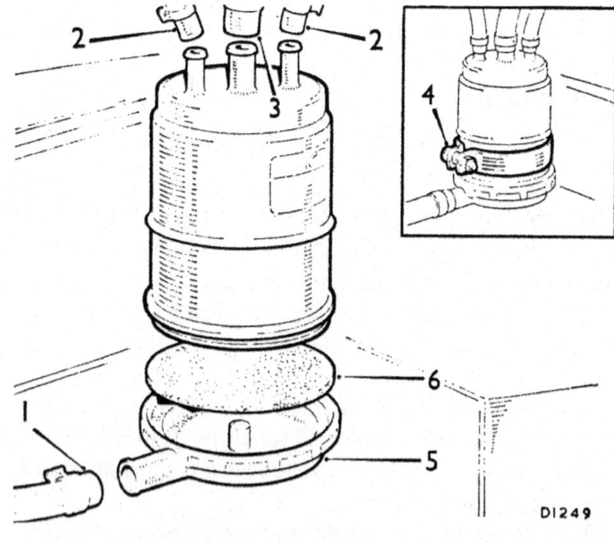

Fig. 2

The adsorption canister air filter pad

1.	Air vent tube.	4.	Canister securing clip.
2.	Vapour pipes.	5.	End cap.
3.	Purge pipe.	6.	Air filter pad.

Fuel line filter

On some models an additional renewable filter is fitted in the main fuel line as an added safeguard against foreign matter causing the setting of the carburetter float-chamber level to be exceeded.

Mixture temperature compensator

On some applications a small temperature-sensitive valve is fitted adjacent to the carburetter. The valve is connected between the air cleaner and the controlled depression chamber of the carburetter.

Under conditions where fuel is entering the carburetter at high temperature, i.e. prolonged idling in high ambient temperatures, the valve opens and allows a small quantity of air to pass into the carburetter, bypassing the jet. The air leans off the mixture which has been enriched by vapours from the evaporative loss control system and by

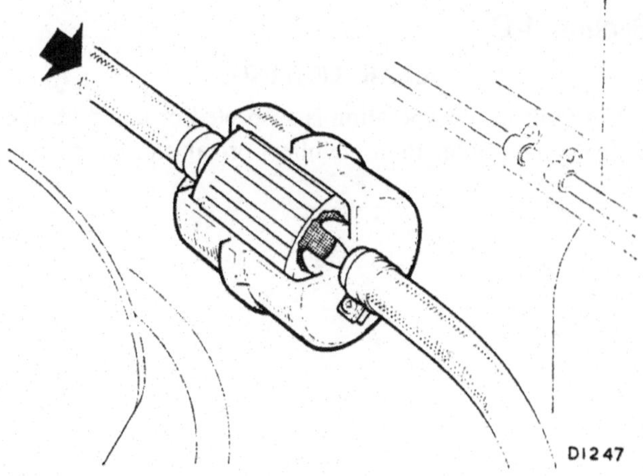

Fig. 4

The fuel line filter

the increase in fuel flow through the carburetter due to the high fuel temperature.

Section 5-B

ADSORPTION CANISTER

Renewing

The air filter fitted in the bottom section of the canister must be renewed every 12,000 miles (20000 km.) or more frequently in dusty operating conditions. The complete canister must be renewed every 50,000 miles (80000 km.) or if at any time it should inadvertently become saturated with liquid fuel.

WARNING. Do not attempt to recover a saturated canister by passing compressed air through the charcoal.

(1) Disconnect the air vent tube from the bottom of the canister.
(2) Disconnect the vapour and purge pipes from the top of the canister.
(3) Unscrew the securing clip screw and lift out the canister.
(4) If the air filter pad only is being renewed:
  (*a*) Unscrew the lower end cap of the canister.
  (*b*) Remove and discard the filter pad.
  (*c*) Clean any dirt from the cap.
  (*d*) Fit the new filter pad and refit the cap.
(5) Fit the canister ensuring that the purge pipe (from the engine rocker cover) is connected to the large centre connection on the top of the canister.

Section 5-C

FUEL LINE FILTER

Renewing

The fuel line filter must be renewed every 12,000 miles (20000 km.).

(1) Check that the ignition is switched off.
(2) Disconnect and discard the filter.
(3) Connect the new filter.
(4) Switch on the ignition and check the filter connections for fuel leakage.
(5) Start the engine and recheck for fuel leakage.

Section 5-D

LEAK TESTING

If a fault in the operation is suspected or components of the system other than the filters or canister have been removed and refitted, the evaporative loss control system must be pressure-tested for leaks as follows:

(1) Check that there is at least one gallon of fuel in the fuel tank.
(2) Switch on the ignition for one minute to prime the fuel system.
(3) Switch off the ignition and disconnect the fuel tank ventilation pipe from its connection on the adsorption canister.
(4) Connect a 0 to 10 lb./sq. in. pressure gauge, a Schrader valve, and a low-pressure air supply (i.e. a tyre pump) to the disconnected pipe.
(5) Pressurize the system until 1 lb./sq. in. is registered on the gauge. **DO NOT EXCEED THIS PRESSURE AT ANY TIME.**
(6) Check that the gauge reading is maintained for 10 seconds without falling more than ·5 lb./sq. in. If the reading is not maintained, check the system for leaks commencing with the fuel filler cap and seal.
(7) Make a visual check for fuel leakage from the tank and its connections.
(8) Remove the fuel filler cap and check that the gauge falls to zero.
(9) Remove the test equipment and re-make the connections.

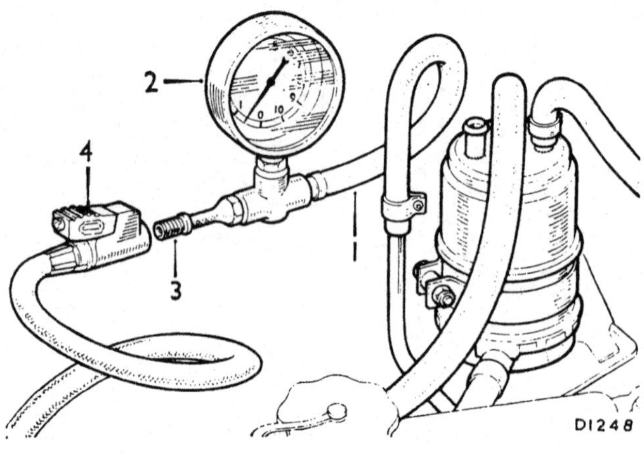

Fig. 5

Leak-testing the control system

1. Fuel tank ventilation pipe.
2. Pressure gauge.
3. Schrader valve.
4. Low-pressure air supply.

SECTION 6

TUNING DATA

MODEL: MGB

	To 1971	1971
ENGINE		
Type	18GF, 18GH, or 18GJ	18GK
Firing order	1, 3, 4, 2,	1, 3, 4, 2
Capacity	1798 c.c. (109·8 cu. in.)	1798 c.c. (109·8 cu. in.)
Compression ratio	8·8 : 1	8·8 : 1
Compression pressure	160 lb./sq. in. (11·25 kg./cm.^{2})	160 lb./sq. in. (11·25 kg./cm.^{2})
Idle speed	900 r.p.m.	900 r.p.m.
Fast idle speed	1,300 to 1,400 r,p.m.	1,300 to 1,400 r.p.m.
Valve rocker clearance	·015 in. (·38 mm.) set cold	·015 in. (·38 mm.) set cold
Stroboscopic ignition timing*	20° B.T.D.C. at 1,000 r.p.m.	15° B.T.D.C. at 1,500 r.p.m.
Static ignition timing	10° B.T.D.C.	10° B.T.D.C.
Timing mark location	Pointer on timing case, notch on crankshaft pulley	Pointer on timing case, notch on crankshaft pulley
DISTRIBUTOR		
Make	Lucas	Lucas
Type	25D4	25D4
Serial number	40897 or 41155	41339
Contact breaker gap	014 to ·016 in. (·35 to ·40 mm.)	·014 to ·016 in. (·35 to ·40 mm.)
Rotation of rotor	Anti-clockwise	Anti-clockwise
Dwell angle	57° to 63°	57° to 63°
Condenser capacity	·18 to ·24 mF	·18 to ·24 mF
Centrifugal advance		
Crankshaft degrees*	10° at 400 to 600 r.p.m. 24° at 1,500 to 1,750 r.p.m. 30°±2° at 3,000 r.p.m.	10° at 900 to 1,100 r.p.m. 24° at 2,700 to 2,900 r.p.m. 30°±2° at 4,600 r.p.m.
Vacuum advance		
Starts	5 in. Hg	7 in. Hg
Finishes	13 in. Hg	13 in. Hg
Total crankshaft degrees	20°±2°	10°±2°
SPARKING PLUGS		
Make	Champion	Champion
Type	N–9Y	N–9Y
Gap	·024 to ·026 in. (·625 to ·660 mm.)	·024 to ·026 in. (·625 to ·660 mm.)
IGNITION COIL		
Make	Lucas	Lucas
Type	HA12	HA12
Resistance—primary	3·1 to 3·5 ohms at 20° C. (68° F.)	3·1 to 3·5 ohms at 20° C. (68° F.)
Consumption		
Ignition on—standing	3·9 amps.	3·9 amps.
at 2,000 r.p.m.	1·4 amps.	1·4 amps.
CARBURETTER(S)		
Make	S.U.	S.U.
Type	Twin HS4	Twin HS4
Specification—fixed needle type	AUD 265	—
—spring-loaded needle type	AUD 326	AUD 465
Choke diameter	1½ in. (38·1 mm.)	1½ in. (38·1 mm.)
Jet size	·090 in. (2·2 mm.)	·090 in. (2·2 mm.)
Needle—fixed type	FX	—
spring-loaded type	AAE	AAL
Piston spring	Red	Red
Initial jet adjustment	14 flats from bridge	12 flats from bridge
EXHAUST EMISSION		
Exhaust gas analyser reading:		
At engine idle speed	4·5% CO (maximum)	4·5% CO (maximum)
Air pump test speed	1,000 r.p.m. (engine)	1,000 r.p.m. (engine)

* Vacuum pipe disconnected.

MODEL: MGB from 1972 on

ENGINE		
Type	18V	
Firing order	1, 3, 4, 2,	
Capacity	1798 c.c. (109·8 cu. in.)	
Compression ratio	8·0 : 1	
Compression pressure	160 lb./sq. in. (11·25 kg./cm.²)	
Idle speed	850 r.p.m.	
Fast idle speed	1,300 to 1,400 r.p.m.	
Valve rocker clearance	·015 in. (·38 mm.) set cold	
Stroboscopic ignition timing*	1972—16° B.T.D.C. at 1,500 r.p.m.; from 1973—11° B.T.D.C. at 1,500 r.p.m.	
Static ignition timing	1972—10° B.T.D.C.; from 1973—6° B.T.D.C.	
Timing mark location	Pointer on timing case, notch on crankshaft pulley	
DISTRIBUTOR		
Make	Lucas	
Type	25D4	
Serial number	1972—41370; from 1973—41491	
Contact breaker gap	·014 to ·016 in. (·35 to ·40 mm.)	
Rotation of rotor	Anti-clockwise	
Dwell angle	57° to 63°	
Condenser capacity	·18 to ·24 mF	
Centrifugal advance	*Serial No.* 41370 (1972)	*Serial No.* 41491 (1973)
Crankshaft degrees*	20° at 1,700 to 2,000 r.p.m.	16° at 1,800 to 2,250 r.p.m.
	35° at 3,300 to 3,900 r.p.m.	32° at 3,600 to 4,050 r.p.m.
	41°±2° at 4,800 r.p.m.	39°±2° at 4,800 r.p.m.
Vacuum advance		
Starts	7 in. Hg	10 in. Hg
Finishes	13 in. Hg	15 in. Hg
Total crankshaft degrees	6°±2°	10°±2°
SPARKING PLUGS		
Make	Champion	
Type	N-9Y	
Gap	·024 to ·026 in. (·625 to ·660 mm.)	
IGNITION COIL		
Make	Lucas	
Type	HA12	
Resistance—primary	3·1 to 3·5 ohms at 20° C. (68° F.)	
Consumption		
Ignition on—standing	3·9 amps.	
at 2,000 r.p.m.	1·4 amps.	
CARBURETTER(S)		
Make	S.U.	
Type	Twin HIF4	
Specification	1972—AUD 493; from 1973—AUD 550	
Choke diameter	1½ in. (38·1 mm.)	
Jet size	·090 in. (2·2 mm.)	
Needle	1972—AAU; from 1973—ABD	
Piston spring	Red	
Initial jet adjustment	2 turns down from bridge	
EXHAUST EMISSION		
Exhaust gas analyser reading:		
At engine idle speed	1972—3·5% CO (maximum); 1973—2·5% CO (maximum)	
Air pump test speed	1,000 r.p.m. (engine)	

* Vacuum pipe disconnected.

SPEED ENGINE	TEST	COMPONENT CONDITION	READ/OBSERVE
START (cranking)	Cranking voltage	Battery; starting system	Voltmeter
	Cranking coil output	Coil and ignition circuit	Scope trace
	Positive crankcase ventilation/ cranking vacuum	Crankcase emission equipment	Vacuum gauge
IDLING (see 'TUNING DATA')	Idle speed	Carburetter idle setting	Tachometer
	Dwell	Distributor/drive; points	Dwell meter; scope
	Initial timing	Spark timing setting	Timing light
	Fuel mixture	Carburetter setting	Exhaust gas analyser
	Manifold vacuum	Engine idle efficiency	Vacuum gauge
FAST IDLE (see 'TUNING DATA')	Dwell variation	Distributor mechanical	Dwell meter
	Coil polarity	Ignition circuit polarity	Scope trace
	Cam lobe accuracy	Distributor cam	Scope trace
	Secondary circuit	Plugs; leads; cap; rotor	Scope trace
	Coil and condenser condition	Coil windings; condenser	Scope trace
	Breaker point condition	Points closing/opening/bounce	Scope trace
	Spark plug firing voltage	Fuel mixture; compression; plug/ rotor gaps	Scope trace
ACCELERATE— DECELERATE	Spark plugs under load	Spark plugs	Scope trace
	Carburetter open/close action	Carburetter	Exhaust gas analyser and vacuum gauge
TURNPIKE (Maximum ignition advance speed see 'TUNING DATA')	Timing advance	Distributor mech./vacuum advance	Timing light/advance meter
	Maximum coil output	Coil; condenser; ignition primary	Scope trace
	Secondary circuit insulation	H.T. cables, cap, rotor	Scope trace
	Charging voltage	Regulator; cut-out	Voltmeter
	Fuel mixture	Air cleaner, carburetter	Exhaust gas analyser
	Exhaust restriction	Exhaust system	Vacuum gauge

READINGS	CHECK SEQUENCE—FAULT LOCATION
9·6 volts minimum at the battery	Battery—connections/cables—starter motor—dynamo/alternator—regulator
17 KV. minimum	Ignition coil
6—10 in. Hg (crankcase ventilation operating) 8—15 in. Hg (crankcase ventilation blanked)	Hoses and connections—Oil filler cap—Valve rocker clearance—Emission valve—Gulp valve—Oil separator—Servo (if fitted)—Inlet manifold leaks—Valves or seats—Piston rings—Any air leak to crankcase
See 'TUNING DATA'	Carburetter adjustment—Hoses and connections—Gulp valve—Servo (if fitted)—Carburetter limit valve or mechanical condition
4-cyl. : 57 to 63°; 6-cyl. : 34 to 37°. See Pattern 1 (see inset A)	Breaker points—Distributor and drive mechanical condition
See 'TUNING DATA'	Distributor adjustment
See 'TUNING DATA'	Carburetter adjustment—Hoses and connections—Gulp valve—Crankcase emission valve—Servo (if fitted)—Carburetter limit valve or mechanical condition—Air pump—Check valve—Spark plugs
12 in. Hg minimum (engine fully run in)	Hoses and connections—Gulp valve—Inlet manifold leaks—carburetter limit valve—Valves or seats—Piston rings
Variation of 2° maximum	Distributor and drive mechanical condition
See Pattern 2 (Trace inverted)	Ignition circuit connections—Ignition coil
3° max. variation. See Pattern 3 (inset A correct; inset B—overlap indicates cam error)	Distributor mechanical condition (cam)
Standard pattern	Spark plugs and leads—Breaker points—Carburetter adjustment—Hoses and connections—Gulp valve—Servo (if fitted)
See Pattern 4 (lack of oscillations indicate fault)	Ignition coil—Condenser
See Pattern 1 (inset B)	Breaker points—Condenser
See Pattern 5; voltage 6—9 kV	Spark plugs and leads—Distributor cap and rotor—Carburetter adjustment (multi-carburetters)
See Pattern 6; acceptable voltage rise 6 to 10 kV	Spark plugs and leads
Initial rich, lean off at throttle closure	Carburetter limit valve and mechanical condition—Hoses and connections—Gulp valve—Air pump
See 'TUNING DATA'	Distributor mechanical condition, vacuum unit, centrifugal weights and springs
Standard pattern; minimum reserve ⅗ more than requirement	Ignition coil—H.T. circuit insulation
Standard pattern	H.T. leads—Distributor cap and rotor
14·5 volts; steady reading	Cut-out—Voltage regulator—Dynamo/Alternator
Leaning off following peak when test speed is reached	Hoses and connections—Carburetter adjustment—Air cleaners—Gulp valve—Air pump—Check valve—Injectors
No variation in reading at constant speed for 10 sec.	Exhaust system

A
B
POINTS CLOSED
POINTS OPEN
60°
(4 CYL)

Pattern 1

Pattern 2

A
B

Pattern 3

FAULT

Pattern 4

10
KV
5
WIDE GAP

Pattern 5

10
KV
5
ACCEPTABLE VOLTAGE RISE
DO478B

Pattern 6

OFFICIAL TECHNICAL BOOKS

Brooklands Technical Books has been formed to supply owners, restorers and professional repairers with official factory literature.

Workshop Manuals

Title	Code	ISBN
Midget Instruction Manual		9781855200739
Midget TD & TF	AKD580A	9781870642552
MGA 1500 1600 & 1600 Mk. 2	AKD600D	9781869826307
MGA Twin Cam	AKD926B	9781855208179
Austin-Healey Sprite Mk. 2, Mk. 3 & Mk. 4 and MG Midget Mk. 1, Mk. 2 & Mk. 3	AKD4021	9781855202818
Midget 1500	AKM4071B	9781855201699
MGB & MGB GT	AKD3259 & AKD4957	9781855201743
MGB GT V8 Supplement		9781855201859
MGB, MGB GT and MGB GT V8		9781783180578
MGC	AKD 7133	9781855201828
Rover 25 & MG ZR 1999-2005	RCL0534ENGBB	9781855208834
Rover 75 & MG ZT 1999-2005	RCL0536ENGBB	9781855208841
MGF - 1.6 MPi, 1.8 MPi, 1.8VVC	RCL 0051ENG, RCL0057ENG & RCL0124	9781855207165
MGF Electrical Manual 1996-2000 MY	RCL0341	9781855209077
MG TF	RCL0493	9781855207493
MGB Tourer & GT (Pub 1969)	AKD3900J	9781855200609
MGB Tourer & GT (Pub 1974)	AKD7598	9781869826727
MGB Tourer & GT (Pub 1976)	AKM3661	9781869826703
MGB GT V8	AKD8423	9781869826710
MGB Tourer & GT (US 1968)	AKD7059B	9781870642514
MGB Tourer & GT (US 1971)	AKD7881	9781870642521
MGB Tourer & GT (US 1973)	AKD8155	9781870642538
MGB Tourer (US 1975)	AKD3286	9781870642545
MGB (US 1979)	AKM8098	9781855200722
MGB Tourer & GT Tuning	CAKD4034L	9780948207051
MGB Special Tuning 1800cc	AKD4034	9780948207006
MGC	AKD4887B	9781869826734
MGF (Modern shape)	RCL0332ENG	9781855208339

Parts Catalogues

Title	Code	ISBN
MGA 1500	AKD1055	9781870642569
MGA 1600 Mk. 1 & Mk. 2	AKD1215	9781870642613
Austin-Healey Sprite Mk. 1 & Mk. 2 and MG Midget Mk. 1 (Mechanical & Body Edition)	AKD3566 & AKD3567	9781783180509
Austin-Healey Sprite Mk. 3 & Mk. 4 and MG Midget Mk. 2 & Mk. 3 (Mechanical & Body Edition 1969)	AKD3513 & AKD35149781783180554	
Austin-Healey Sprite Mk. 3 & Mk. 4 and MG Midget Mk. 2 & Mk. 3 (Feb 1977 Edition)	AKM0036	9780948207419
MGB up to Sept 1976	AKM0039	9780948207068
MGB Sept 1976 on	AKM0037	9780948207440

Owners Handbooks

Title	Code	ISBN
Midget Series TD		9781870642910
Midget TF and TF 1500 Operation Manual	AKD658A	9781870642934
MGA 1500	AKD598G	9781855202924
MGA 1600	AKD1172C	9781855201668
MGA 1600 Mk. 2	AKD1958A	9781855201675
MGA Twin Cam (Operation)	AKD879	9781855207929
MGA Twin Cam (Operation)	AKD879B	9781855207936
MGA 1500 Special Tuning	AKD819A	9781783181728
MGA 1500 and 1600 Mk. 1 Special Tuning	AKD819B	9781783181735
Midget TF and TF 1500	AKD210A	9781855202979
Midget Mk. 3 (GB 1967-74)	AKD7596	9781855201477
Midget (Pub 1978)	AKM3229	9781855200906
Midget Mk. 3 (US 1967-74)	AKD7883	9781855206311
Midget Mk. 3 (US 1976)	AKM3436	9781855201767
Midget Mk. 3 (US 1979)	AKM4386	9781855201774
MGB Tourer (Pub 1965)	AKD3900C	9781869826741

Owners Workshop Manuals - Autobooks

MGA & MGB & GT 1955-1968 (Glove Box Autobooks Manual)	9781855200937
MGA & MGB & GT 1955-1968 (Autobooks Manual)	9781783180356
Austin-Healey Sprite Mk. 1, 2, 3 & 4 and MG Midget Mk. 1, 2, 3 & 1500 1958-1980 (Glove Box Autobooks Manual)	9781855201255
Austin-Healey Sprite Mk. 1, 2, 3 & 4 and MG Midget Mk. 1, 2, 3 & 1500 1958-1980 (Autobooks Manual)	9781783180332
MGB & MGB GT 1968-1981 (Glove Box Autobooks Manual)	9781855200944
MGB & MGB GT 1968-1981 (Autobooks Manual)	9781783180325

Carburetters

SU Carburetters Tuning Tips & Techniques	9781855202559
Solex Carburetters Tuning Tips & Techniques	9781855209770
Weber Carburettors Tuning Tips and Techniques	9781855207592

Restoration Guide

MG T Series Restoration Guide	9781855202115
MGA Restoration Guide	9781855203020
Restoring Sprites & Midgets	9781855205987
Practical Classics On MGB Restoration	9780946489428

MG - Road Test Books

MG Gold Portfolio 1929-1939	9781855201941
MG TA & TC GOLD PORT 1936-1949	9781855203150
MG TD & TF Gold Portfolio 1949-1955	9781855203167
MG Y-Type & Magnette Road Test Portfolio	9781855208629
MGB & MGC GT V8 GP 1962-1980	9781855200715
MGA & Twin Cam Gold Portfolio 1955-1962	9781855200784
MGB Roadsters 1962-1980	9781869826109
MGC & MGB GT V8 LEX	9781855203631
MG Midget Road Test Portfolio 1961-1979	9781855208957
MGF & TF Performance Portfolio 1995-2005	9781855207073
Road & Track On MG Cars 1949-1961	9780946489398
Road & Track On MG Cars 1962-1980	9780946489817

From MG specialists, Amazon and all good motoring bookshops.

Brooklands Books Ltd., P.O. Box 146, Cobham, Surrey, KT11 1LG, England, UK

www.brooklandsbooks.com

Printed and bound in Great Britain by
Marston Book Services Ltd, Oxfordshire